Dalí

Dawn Ades

Dalí
The Centenary Retrospective

With 640 illustrations, 370 in colour

Thames & Hudson

Exhibition realized by Palazzo Grassi with the Fundació Gala-Salvador Dalí on the occasion of the Salvador Dalí Centennial

In collaboration with The Philadelphia Museum of Art, and the support of The Salvador Dalí Museum, St. Petersburg, and of the Museo Nacional Centro de Arte Reina Sofía, Madrid

Venice, Palazzo Grassi
12 September 2004–16 January 2005

Philadelphia, The Philadelphia Museum of Art
16 February–15 May 2005

jacket
Salvador Dalí, *The Architectonic Angelus of Millet*, 1933
Madrid, Museo Nacional
Centro de Arte Reina Sofía

back jacket
Man Ray, *Salvador Dalí*, 1936

page 5
Salvador Dalí, *Figure at a Window* (detail), 1925
Madrid, Museo Nacional
Centro de Arte Reina Sofía

page 6
Salvador Dalí, *Impressions of Africa* (detail), 1938
Rotterdam, Museum Boijmans
Van Beuningen

pages 10-11
Salvador Dalí, *The Weaning of Furniture Nutrition* (detail), 1934
St. Petersburg (FL), The Salvador Dalí Museum

page 12
Salvador Dalí, *Premature Ossification of a Railway Station* (detail), 1930
Chicago (IL), Alan Koppel Gallery

DALÍ 2004

First published in the United Kingdom in 2004 by Thames & Hudson Ltd,
181A High Holborn,
London WC1V 7QX

www.thamesandhudson.com

All the works by Salvador Dalí:
© Fundació Gala-Salvador Dalí, Figueres, 2004

Under the patronage of
His Majesty the King of Spain
and the President of the Italian Republic

Barcelona, Generalitat de Catalunya Departament de la Presidència

Barcelona, Museu de Montserrat

Barcelona, Museu Nacional d'Art de Catalunya

Barcelona, Ricard Mas

Barcelona, Solans

Berlin, The Ulla and Heiner Pietzsch Collection

Berlin, Galerie Brusberg Berlin

Berlin, Staatliche Museen zu Berlin, Nationalgalerie

Berlin, Staatliche Museen zu Berlin, Kupferstichkabinett

Bern, Kunstmuseum Bern

Beverly Hills, J. Nicholson

Birmingham, Birmingham Museum of Art

Bruxelles, Musées Royaux des Beaux-Arts de Belgique

Buffalo, Albright-Knox Art Gallery

Cadaqués, Pere Vehí

Cambridge, Fogg Art Museum, Harvard University Art Museum

Chichester, Edward James Foundation

Città del Vaticano, Musei Vaticani

Cleveland, The Cleveland Museum of Art

Dallas, William B. Jordan

East Lansing, Kresge Art Museum, Michigan State University

Edinburgh, Scottish National Gallery of Modern Art

Figueres, Fundació Gala-Salvador Dalí

Fukuoka City, Fukuoka Art Museum

Hamburg, Kunsthalle Hamburg

Hannover, Sprengel Museum Hannover

Hiroshima City, Hiroshima Prefectural Art Museum

Köln, Museum Ludwig

London, Freud Museum

London, Helly Nahmad Gallery

London, Tate

London, The Mayor Gallery

Madrid, Arango Collection

Madrid, Juan Abelló Collection

Madrid, Fundación Federico García Lorca

Madrid, Galeria Guillermo de Osma

Madrid, Museo Nacional Centro de Arte Reina Sofía

Madrid, Museo Thyssen-Bornemisza

Mexico, Collezione JAPS

Mie-ken, Mie Prefectural Art Museum

Milano, Fondazione Antonio Mazzotta

Milwaukee, Patrick and Beatrice Haggerty Museum of Art, Marquette University

Minneapolis, The Minneapolis Institute of Arts

Montréal, Musée des Beaux-Arts de Montréal

München, Bayerische Staatsgemäldesammlungen, Pinakothek der Moderne

München, Staatliche Graphische Sammlung

New Haven, Yale University Art Gallery

New York, Timothy Baum Collection

New York, The Howard Greenberg Gallery

New York, The Metropolitan Museum of Art

New York, The Solomon R. Guggenheim Museum

Ottawa, National Gallery of Canada

Paris, Centre Georges Pompidou, Musée national d'Art moderne

Paris, Horacio Amigorena Collection

Paris, Jacques Herold Collection

Paris, Galerie Natalie Seroussi

Paris, Musée Picasso

Philadelphia, The Philadelphia Museum of Art

Rio de Janeiro, Musei Castro Maya

Roma, Fondazione Isabella Scelsi

Rotterdam, Museum Boijmans Van Beuningen

San Francisco, San Francisco Museum of Modern Art

St. Petersburg, The Salvador Dalí Museum

Shizuoka-Ken, Ikeda Museum of 20th Century Art

Stuttgart, Staatsgalerie Stuttgart

Tel Aviv, Tel Aviv Museum of Art

Utica, Munson Williams Proctor Arts Institute, Museum of Art

Valladolid, Museo Patio Herreriano

Venezia, Collezione Peggy Guggenheim

Washington, Hirshhorn Museum and Sculpture Garden, Smithsonian Institution

Wuppertal, Von der Heydt-Museum Wuppertal

Yokohama, Yokohama Museum of Art

Zürich, Kunsthaus Zürich

And all those people who wanted to remain anonymous.

The exhibition at Palazzo Grassi, held on the centenary of the artist's birth, and for which this volume was published, is the result of a collaboration with the Fundació Gala-Salvador Dalí in Figueres.

For this reason and for their willing cooperation, special thanks are due to the Fundació, in particular its president Ramon Boixadós Malé, as well as its other members, and all those – starting with the editor of this catalogue, Dawn Ades, and the architect Oscar Tusquets Blanca, the designer of the exhibition installations – who have helped to get this project off the ground.

Finally, the contribution of the lenders has been of vital importance, and I would like to express our gratitude to them for their willingness to help and the interest they have shown in the exhibition.

Cesare Annibaldi, President, Board of Trustees, Palazzo Grassi

Catalog

Director
Mario Andreose

Coordinating editor
Giovanna Vitali

Editing
Martine Buysschaert &
Francesca Malerba
with Anne Ellis, Suna Erdem

Graphic design
Sabina Brucoli

Iconographic research
Silvia Borghesi

Translations
Elisabetta Hicks Da Pra
David Stanton

Technical staff
Sergio Daniotti
Valerio Gatti

Exhibition

Curator
Dawn Ades
in collaboration with
Tomas Sharman

Associate curator
Montse Aguer i Teixidor
(director of the Centro de
Estudios Dalinianos)

Curator for Philadelphia
Michael R. Taylor

Exhibition secretariat
Silvia Roman

Installation
Òscar Tusquets i Blanca
with Silvia Farriol

Graphic design
Dario Zannier
with Fabio Zannier

Lighting consultant
Piero Castiglioni

Film consultant
Gian Piero Brunetta
Josep Rovira

Press office
Lucia Pigozzo

Displays in the lobby
Guerrino Lovato

Transport
Tratto s.r.l.

The curators would like to thank
the following for the generous
help, support or advice they
have given us the course of
preparing this exhibition:

Daniel Abadie
Branko Aleksic
Vicenç Altaió i Morral
Eulalia Bas Dalí
Agnès de la Beaumelle
Perrine Le Blan
Ursula Bode
Ina Conzen
Victoria Combalia
Manuel Barbié-Nogaret
Timothy Baum
Anita Beloubek-Hammer
Neil Benezra
Maria Teresa Bermejo
de Santos Torroella
Richard Calvocoressi
Anna Capella
James Cuno
Chris Dercon
Polissena Di Bagno
Emmanuel Di-Donna
John Elderfield
Patrick Elliott
Manuel Fernández-Montesinos
García
Hartwig Fischer
Ulrike Gauss
Jaap Guldemond
Christian von Holst
Charles Henry Hine
William Jeffett
Elliott H. King
Werner Klein
Hélène Klein-Seckel
Kasper König
Gerhard Kolberg
Joan Kropf
Brigitte Léal
Frederik Leen
Tomas Llorens
Josep Lloveras
Ulrich Luckhardt
Laurence Madeline
Daniel Malingue
Maja Majer-Wallat
Ricard Mas Peinado

Ariadna Mas Vall
Giorgio Mastinu
Jacqueline Matisse-Monnier
Karin von Maur
Claire Maupas
Kynaston McShine
Isabelle Monod-Fontaine
Jennifer Mundy
Helly Nahmad
Didier Oettinger
Guillermo de Osma
Alfred Pacquement
Pilar Parcerisas
Carlo Perrone
François-Xavier Petit
Heiner Pietzsch
Eleonor Reynolds Morse
Larry Saphire
Carla Schulz-Hoffmann
Hein-Th. Schulze
Altcappenberg
Natalie Seroussi
Marshall T. Rousseau
Michael Semff
Àlex Susanna
Miguel del Valle-Inclán
Pere Vehí
Darrell Wilkins
Eric Zafran
Jaka Žuraj

Library and Archives
of the Salvador Dalí Museum,
St. Petersburg
Bibliothèque Kandinsky,
Centre de Documentation
et de Recherche
du MNAM CCI, Paris
Biblioteca Museo Nacional
Centro de Arte Reina Sofía,
Madrid
Archives du Musée Picasso,
Paris

Acknowledgments

Palazzo Grassi would like to thank the
Fundació Gala-Salvador Dalí in Figueres,
in particular its president Ramon Boixadós
i Malé, the director Antonio Pitxot i Soler,
Joan Manuel Sevillano i Campalans, and
Montse Aguer i Teixidor, as well as all the
other members of its staff. We are also
indebted to The Salvador Dalí Museum of
St. Petersburg in Florida and its president
Thomas A. James, as well as to Eleanor
Morse, co-founder of the Museum, the
present director Charles Henry Hine III,
the curator William Jeffett and the previous
director, Marshall T. Rousseau, with whom
the first important contacts were made,
leading to the present close collaboration.
In addition, we would like to express our
gratitude to The Philadelphia Museum of
Art, its director Anne d'Harnoncourt, the
curator Michael R. Taylor and the
individuals on its staff who have worked
on this exhibition, which will be hosted
by the museum in 2005.

We also wish to extend our deep thanks to
the Spanish cultural institutions, especially
the Centro de Arte Reina Sofía and the
Museo Thyssen Bornemisza, and the many
private museums and other lenders of
fourteen nations who have generously made
their works available for this exhibition
devoted to the great Catalan artist on the
occasion of the centenary of his birth.

We are also most grateful, for their assistance,
to the Istituto Luce in Rome, the Halsman
Estate, New York, the Filmoteca Española,
and the Alliance Française, Venice.

Thanks to the Assicurazioni Generali SpA
for the support in the publication of the
proceedings of the Conference devoted
to Dalí organized in St.Petersburg in
March 2004.

Finally, very special thanks are due to Sharp
Italia for the audiovisual displays.

Contents

Introduction

Dalí is one of the best-known and most instantly recognizable artists in the world. He is also one of the most controversial. No other major 20th-century artist combines such widespread popular appeal with so much critical disdain from official institutions and historians of modern art. This exhibition, which celebrates the centenary of his birth, is an occasion to re-assess his contested reputation, explore the myths that he constructed round himself and his lifelong companion Gala and, most vitally, look closely at his work in all its variety and depth.

The introduction to the last great retrospective exhibition in Dalí's lifetime, at the Centre Pompidou, Paris, in 1979, drew attention to the ways in which Dalí's exhibitionist tactics and public masks diverted attention from his more serious purposes: "Dalí, behind the spectacular windshield of his personality, maintained the invisibility of his deep project. Who, having laughed, would give time to any serious reflection?"[1] The Pompidou exhibition explored the ideas behind the entertainment and the dazzle, and demonstrated that serious reflection was rewarded with a deeper understanding of a very complex artist. The current exhibition intends to take this process further, to respond to the fruits of new research on Dalí's production, projects and their sources. It also intends to ask in what sense there is a "real" Dalí behind the "public masks" of the showman and the mythical identities he created for himself. One of our aims is to dispel generalizations and assumptions about Dalí's post-1939 work, long viewed as kitsch by artists, critics and curators and all too often lumped under the single term "late."

Dalí was not only a painter but also writer, poet, theorist, print-maker, designer, photographer, editor, sculptor, filmmaker, inventor of objects, theater designer and installer of exhibitions. The exhibition covers as much as possible of his multifarious production, though the greatest emphasis is on his paintings. In the last twenty years there have been several carefully focused exhibitions on particular aspects of Dalí's work, and these have informed and enriched our selection.[2] Literature on Dalí has expanded recently as critical approaches to his work have become more sophisticated and the exhibition and catalogue have drawn deeply on the insights and research of many scholars to whom we are greatly indebted.[3] With a view to making this catalogue as informative and accessible as possible, we have focused on detailed commentaries on most works in the exhibition, an "Encyclopedia" and an illustrated chronology. The works are arranged in a broadly chronological order; catalogue entries address a single work or on occasion a small group linked by a common theme. These groupings sometimes cross strict chronological bounds, but on the whole themes are temporally defined. In the Encyclopedia, people, objects, and ideas crucial to an understanding of Dalí's work are given succinct descriptions and definitions. Dalí himself planned to rewrite the Larousse: "Everything in the present Larousse is totally wrong. I've checked off all the definitions and I've been writing an average of five pages a day. In a few years I'll have my very own personal and private Larousse, and the world will learn what I think about everything."[4] This would have been a formidable addition to the tradition, much amplified by the surrealists, of the "critical dictionary," like that instigated by Georges Bataille in *Documents*. We have no pretensions to replicate such a dictionary, but the mobility of Dalí's ideas, the shifting meanings of his motifs and objects and the variety of their sources (acknowledged and unacknowledged) make this Encyclopedia an essential tool.

Dalí was both an international celebrity and an intensely local artist, rooted in the Catalan culture and landscape. Trilingual in Catalan, French and Spanish, he made French his operational language, allowing him to play a central role in international Surrealism. This is one of the many paradoxes of his life and work. He knew he wanted to be a painter from childhood, but was to live through an age that increasingly despised painting. Photography, objects, conceptual art, installations, happenings, all challenged pictorial representation; Dalí both vigorously contributed to these alternative modes of artistic practice and continued to maintain the validity of painting.

Already as an adolescent Dalí acknowledged that paintings had as much reality for him as lived experience. So intense was the emotional identification with the paintings he saw as a child that these scenes and the events of real life became inextricably entangled. "From a very early age I remember the [Gowans's] collection in our home and I use to look at the reproductions with positive delight...Today I sometimes have to make an effort to separate out a real lived incident from one of these reproductions. Many times, lived events and pictures fuse in my memory. When I leaf through these pages again, I feel that I've really seen all this and that I've known these people for ages and very intimately. I feel sure that I picnicked once in that shady Watteau glade, or that, when I was small, my nurse was that giggling cuddly girl by Teniers; I've walked at twilight by a fountain in a garden with a Renaissance building, through one of those landscapes used by Titian as backdrops for his Venuses of golden flesh..."[5] The reality of the imagination for Dalí was often as real as empirical experience; this made Surrealism a natural home for him, but also stored up problems as he championed the total discrediting of "reality" while the Surrealists sought to maintain the dialectical relationship between the imagination and the real, dream and waking states.

Virtually from the moment Dalí started to exhibit in the mid-1920s, spectacular success was accompanied by controversy. The causes of controversy were to multiply dramatically in later years but some of the early criticisms—that he was inauthentic, cold, obscure and immoral—already alert us to unusual features of his formation as an artist and to an early tension with modernism.

Critics of his first solo exhibitions in the 1920s were both dazzled and suspicious at his ability to paint apparently simultaneously in radically opposed styles. He was, effectively, auditioning the styles of the avant-garde: Cubism, *Neuesaclichkeit* (New Objectivity), Neo-Classicism, the metaphysical mode of de Chirico and Carrà, and the biomorphic abstraction of Arp. Some critics thus saw him as inauthentic, lacking a voice of his own. He seemed deliberately to ignore the twin impulses of modernism: to express an individual self, on the one hand, or to pursue the medium for its own sake (which leads to abstraction) on the other. He went through a crisis in ca. 1928, with a group of aggressive, stark "anti-paintings" (*Sun, Four Fisherwomen of Cadaqués,* cat. 62).[6] For a time, he abandoned painting in favor of photography and film, collaborating on *Un Chien andalou* with Buñuel. When he returned to painting, it was in a style of maximum objectivity—a blend of academic precision and photographic realism, in which he absorbs traces of the avant-garde, such as the collage fragments in *First Days of Spring* or the biomorphic shapes in *The Great Masturbator.* He was to continue to plan films for the rest of his life; although most remained unrealized or partially shot, the potential of the medium to create an alternative reality through motion and narrative was a constant lure.

Dalí was inexorably drawn towards Surrealism, as he recognized that it offered not just stylistic solutions within the narrow field of the visual arts but an intellectual environment where philosophical and psychological enquiry underpinned poetic and artistic practices. *Un Chien andalou* and the 1929 paintings like *First Days of Spring* announced his allegiance to the movement, and he was to become one of its most energetic, if unorthodox, proponents. His unprecedented manner of painting, visually precise and dedicated to what he called "the conquest of the irrational," his paranoiac-critical method, the elaboration of the Surrealist object and major theoretical and poetic texts such as *La Femme visible* and *Le mythe tragique de l'Angelus de Millet* gave new impetus to the movement. His "exceptional interior 'boiling' was," Breton said, "an invaluable ferment for Surrealism."[7] Dalí fully shared the Surrealist interest in Freud, whose ideas dominated André Breton's first *Surrealist Manifesto.* But whereas Freud's proof of the importance of the unconscious had led Breton to celebrate the liberation of the imagination, Dalí was to seize more directly on Freud's ideas about the centrality of sexuality to the human psyche.

His voice was one of the most original of the 20th-century, but it was forged less through a desire to express "himself" or to liberate the unconscious than to give visible form to mental processes, psychical drives and other invisible forces that govern life. He absorbed the ideas, the language and the methods not only of psychoanalysis, but also of natural history, optics, biology, physics and mathematics. He gave visible, concrete form to, for example, the sensations of disgust and repulsion described by Kolnai as well as to Freud's central notion of the Oedipal complex. He created a series of mythical figures who symbolize familial and sexual relationships. The paternal imago is figured through legendary and mythical characters such as William Tell, Lenin and God the Father, while Millet's famous painting *The Angelus* is interpreted in terms of a vengeful mother. In *Le mythe tragique de l'Angelus de Millet*, in which he analyzes his obsession with the painting, Dalí follows the model of a Freudian case history and is clearly familiar with Freud's essays on Leonardo, Michelangelo and Narcissism. Through his use of psychoanalytical theory, dreams, and myths, Dalí constructs, as much as he reveals, identity and his work is peculiarly treacherous if it is approached as a key to his own personality. "Psychopathology" is universal, not personal, as J.G. Ballard recognized:

"The art of Salvador Dalí, an extreme metaphor at a time when only the extreme will do, constitutes a body of prophecy about ourselves unequalled in accuracy since Freud's *Civilization and its Discontents*. Voyeurism, self-disgust, the infantile basis of our fears and longings, and our need to pursue our own psychopathologies as a game—these diseases of the psyche Dalí has diagnosed with dismaying accuracy. His paintings not only anticipate the psychic crisis that produced our glaucous paradise, but they also document the uncertain pleasures of living within it. The great twin leitmotifs of the 20th-century—sex and paranoia—preside over his life, as over ours."[8]

A similar point was made in one of the best early studies of Dalí, by James Thrall Soby, who asked, in 1941: "Is he an isolated phenomenon projected into fame by an unusual technique, a weird imagination and a flair for publicity? Or does he reflect, in exaggerated form, the psychology of his epoch? Is he pure eccentric or part prophet?"[9] Although cautious about drawing parallels between a contemporary artist and his times, Soby points to the changing perception of Surrealism, once seen as a childish retreat from reality but now open to be "re-read as a passionate espousal of a counter-reality to which all France, all civilized Europe, had been clinging for assurance."[10] Dalí's double images, the product of his "paranoiac-critical method" (see *Invisible Sleeper, Lion, Horse*, cat. 74), no longer appear as a purely personal obsession in a "world where statesmen as well as painters have portrayed objectives with such cunning that they have become 'without the slightest physical or anatomical change, the representation of another entirely different object.'"[11] While the Surrealists had dismissed double image paintings such as *The Endless Enigma* (1938; cat. 183) as no more than puzzle pictures, Soby's perception of them as a critique of the double dealing and smokescreens of international politics (no less relevant to the present day than to the Second World War to which Soby refers) puts Dalí's play with the "real" and the authentic in a new light.

Dalí's early and "Surrealist" periods are today relatively exempt from critical disapproval. The critic Robert Hughes recently went so far as to assert that Dalí's *Soft Construction with Boiled Beans—Premonition of Civil War* (1936; cat. 159) was not only his greatest painting, but that "this, not Picasso's *Guernica*, is modern art's strongest testimony on the [Spanish] Civil War, and on war in general. Not even the failures of Dalí's later work can blur that fact." However, for Hughes "you would have to be a pictorial illiterate to prefer the later to the earlier Dalí."[12] Controversial as Hughes' first claim may be, the second should be regarded as even more so. The assumptions made here about the "later" Dalí are ripe for revision. Two decades ago, "Late Picasso" came under similar scrutiny, but whereas this had some coherence as a historical and visual category, "late Dalí" has no such rationale.[13] Over forty years of diverse activity, including some of his most powerful works, cannot be accounted for under this single rubric.

The division between the Surrealist and the so-called "late work" was, to be true, to an extent self-imposed, with Dalí's announcement of his decision to "become classic" that followed his final exclusion from the Surrealist movement in 1939. He also all too neatly divided his psychoanalytically inspired works from those driven by his fascination with physics: "In the Surrealist period I wanted to create the iconography of the interior world—the world of the marvelous, of my father Freud. I succeeded in doing it. Today, the exterior world—that of physics—has transcended the one of psychology. My father today is Dr Heisenberg."[14]

The explosion of the atomic bomb shook Dalí "seismically," and there is no denying that physics was a defining factor in the postwar period. But there are also clear continuities: psychoanalytical references still flow into postwar works by Dalí while scientific ones are present earlier. The *Angelus* theme, (see cats. 116, 117, 119, 120), for instance—the core subject of his work of the 1930s—, has a magnificent reprise much later in *The Railway Station at Perpignan* of 1965 (cat. 241) and in *The Portrait of My Dead Brother* (cat. 240). One of his greatest paranoiac-critical works is the *Hallucinogenic Toreador* of 1968. *The Persistence of Memory* (1931; cat. 89) invokes Einstein and the Theory of Relativity just as *The Disintegration of the Persistence of Memory* (cat. 224) or *Raphaelesque Head Exploding* (cat. 220) respond to Heisenberg.

The tendency to merge the man with his art, undeniably fostered by Dalí's own exhibitionist tactics and by his eloquence, colors reactions to his later persona. The break with Surrealism unleashed vocal opposition to his pursuit of fame and publicity-seeking self-promotion. The publication of his autobiography, *The Secret Life of Salvador Dal,í* in 1942, during his long war-time exile in the United States, prompted violent reactions partly because the often outrageous imaginary incidents recounted were taken literally. George Orwell, reviewing *The Secret Life of Salvador Dalí,* which profoundly shocked him ("Dalí is as antisocial as a flea"), tried to turn the knife in the wound by comparing Dalí with the Edwardian children's book illustrator Arthur Rackham, eliding esthetic kitsch with ethical transgression.[15] Equally as damaging in the postwar period were the commercial exploitation of his talent and his ambiguous politics (See Encyclopedia "Politics"). The fallout from his return to Franco's Spain, while Picasso's public resistance to any compromise with the dictatorship stood as a permanent reminder of Dalí's compromise, was long-lasting. The very thorough, indispensable biography of Dalí by Ian Gibson is entitled *The Shameful Life of Salvador Dalí,* and, as with Orwell, the prejudice against Dalí the man, is combined with a cut and dried reading of his politics while little attempt is made to explore the complexities of his later work. It is assumed that the break is both ideological and aesthetic, and that his work has become as "retrogressive" as his politics.[16]
But already in the early years of his affiliation with Surrealism Dalí had dismissed "modern art" as detestable "bullshit." In a letter to Breton published as the preface to his 1933 exhibition he eulogizes the 19th-century academic painter Meissonier "who, all of a sudden, has just recovered in my life, in my thoughts, in my preferences, the most obvious and parched relevance."[17] *The Conquest of the Irrational*, meanwhile, lavishes its verbal extravagance on "The illusionism of the most despicably go-getting and irresistible imitative art, the skilful tricks of paralyzing *trompe-l'œil*, the most analytically narrative and discredited academicism."[18] Indeed his ambition to "become classic" marks a change of degree rather than kind; the old masters were never far from his thought even in his Surrealist period. His admiration for Vermeer is well attested and *The Lacemaker* makes a fleeting appearance in *Un Chien andalou*, but there are also pictorial references throughout the 1930s to numerous old masters: to Titian, Tintoretto, Caravaggio—the list can go on.

There is no doubt that the divorce from the Surrealists had a far-reaching effect and he was, from that moment—and for the first time since his earliest career—alone. Never again was he part of a community of artists. Gala became his sole companion and collaborator. But even if Dalí was no longer a member of a group and liked to present himself as unique, he was, in reality, not as isolated from postwar visual practices as he, as well as the historians, claim. Was his own practice totally severed from the painterly convulsions of Abstract Expressionism, from the cocky adoptions of popular culture and the media by Pop artists, from the happenings of the 1960s and the re-discovery of the readymade? In the *Sistine Madonna*, the confident but subtle use of benday dots anticipates the Pop experiments of the 1960s. Were his epic history paintings so regressive? Their size after all is not unlike that of the mural-scale paintings by Jackson Pollock or Morris Louis. Among the many paradoxes of his long career is the fact that despite his eloquent attachment to tradition and ancient techniques he was ever eager to explore new technologies. He was among the first artists to experiment with holograms, for example, which gave a new dimension to his lifelong interest in the relationship between reality and illusion, and would have been enchanted at the possibilities of computer animation.

The most startling aspect of Dalí's later work for Surrealists and Modernists alike was his adoption of religious subject matter and adaptations of Christian iconography. In the *Madonna of Port Lligat* (cat. 214) he makes explicit reference to Piero della Francesca's Brera *Virgin*, for instance, while Raphael's *Madonna and Child* is embedded in the Pope's ear in the *Sistine Madonna* (cat. 233). But there is an ambiguous undertone: the *Madonna of Port Lligat* is more a portrait of Gala than a devotional image, and the objects floating in space refer to the dematerialization of the theory of the atom— "today's counterpart of divine gravitation." Rather than take Christianity as the alternative to science, incompatible with its rationalist description of space, time and matter, he brings them together as potential partners. So the Virgin in his *Assumption* "ascends to heaven by the very strength of her antiprotons,"[19] while Christ's Cross in *Corpus Hypercubicus* (cat. 225) is a form of "hypercube" that by switching optically back and forth from convex to concave fuses notions of a fourth dimension with a mystical reverie of heaven. His Christ, he explains in his *Mystical Manifesto* of 1951, will be the "absolute contrary in every respect to the materialist and savagely anti-mystical Christ of Grünewald." Dalí's notions of mysticism—in which his "Paranoiac-Critical Activity" still plays a part—refer back to both Spanish mystics such as Saint John of the Cross and Saint Teresa of Avila as well as to the medieval Catalan writer and alchemist Ramon Llull.

Dalí made the two last great mysteries of life his subject: the human mind and the structure of the physical universe. Just as he had followed with passionate interest the successive attempts of psychologists and psychoanalysts to describe and explain the hidden world of the mind: not just Freud, but Kraepelin, Serieux and Capgras, Ferenzci, Kolnai and the one closest to him, Jacques Lacan, so he followed the discoveries in physics, from the relativity theory to quantum mechanics. His postwar paintings may embrace atomic theory, but they constantly bear in mind the philosophical and psychological uncertainties that drive metaphysical and scientific investigation.
For Dalí, making hidden structures and invisible forces visible demanded a visual language that distended and questioned day-to-day reality. So he played with perspective and space, and also developed a dense metaphorical iconography. Any description of the meaning of process whether in science, philosophy or psychology relies upon analogy. Physicists talk about attraction and repulsion. Freud had to describe mental functioning in terms of "topographical, dynamic, economic and therefore purely physical processes."[20] Wittgenstein described both his own and Freud's real achievements as "inventing similes."[21] The Hungarian psychoanalyst Ferenczi argued that this analogical method "should be drawn from fields as remote as possible. Analogies derived from related fields would tend to be, indeed, mere tautologies, and as such could hardly serve the function of proof."[22] At about the same time Breton was formulating his idea of the Surrealist poetic image: the more remote the terms of the image, the stronger the poetic spark would be. And Breton uses the language of physics: "The value of the image depends on the beauty of the spark obtained; it is consequently a function of the difference of potential between the two conductors. When the difference is slight, as in a comparison, the spark is lacking."[23] The same prin-

ciple holds for the visual as for the poetic or scientific, and no one possessed a more abundant imagination than Dalí to invent visual analogies for the mysteries of the mind, of desire, of death, of space and time. The artist Georges Matthieu wrote: "Endowed with the most prodigious imagination, with a taste for splendor, for theater, for the grandiose, but also for games and for the sacred, Dalí disconcerts shallow minds because he uses the dialectic of analogy rather than that of identity."[24]

In *Diary of a Genius* Dalí wrote, "I am grateful to modern science for corroborating by its researches that 'space is finite'. My emotion has the perfect shape of a four-buttock continuum, the tenderness of the very flesh of the universe."[25] The humorous and sensuous metaphor of the notion of curvature as a 'four-buttock continuum' or indeed the famous soft watches, and 'paranoiac-critical camembert of time and space' are not as distant from the speculative languages of scientific and philosophical methodologies as one might think. The degree of Dalí's technical understanding of the discoveries of physics and the theories of mathematics and psychoanalysis remains a fascinating question addressed in this catalogue; that his use of his own and Gala's readings therein was prophetic as well as imaginative is becoming clearer every day. Artists are happily not constrained by demands for accuracy in relation to their sources; what they make of them has its own value that often outlasts their origin.

[1] Daniel Abadie "Les obsessions déguisées de Salvador Dalí," in *Salvador Dalí* (Paris: Centre Pompidou, 1979), p. 11.

[2] The retrospective exhibitions in Paris (Daniel Abadie, see note 1) and Stuttgart (Karin von Maur, 1989) have been invaluable general sources. The more specialized exhibitions include *Salvador Dalí: The Early Years* (Ades & Beristain, London: Hayward Gallery, 1994); *Dalí: Arquitectura* (Lahuerta, Barcelona: La Pedrera, 1996); *Salvador Dalí: A Mythology* 1998 (Ades & Bradley, Liverpool: Tate,); *Salvador Dalí: Dream of Venus* (Aguer & Fanes, Barcelona: 1999); Dawn Ades, *Dalí's Optical Illusions* (Connecticut: Wadsworth Atheneum, 2000); Fèlix Fanés, *Dalí: Cultura de Masas* (Barcelona: Caixa Forum, 2004); Pilar Parcerisas, *Dalí: Elective Affinities* (Barcelona: 2004). Robert Lubar's catalogue of the collection of the Salvador Dalí Museum in St. Petersburg, and Robert Descharnes' *Catalogue Raisonné* of the paintings have been constant points of reference.

[3] Pioneering studies by James Thrall Soby and Rafael Santos Toroella have been followed by numerous monographs and critical studies including: Fèlix Fanés, *La Construccion de la imagen 1925-1930* (1999); Juan Antonio Ramirez, *Dalí: Lo crudo i lo podrido* (2002); Ricard Mas, *Salvador Dalí* (2004). David Lomas, *The Haunted Self* (New Haven: Yale, 2000) and Robert Radford (2001) have brought out the depth of his debt to psychoanalytical ideas. Paul Hammond's BFI Film Classics study of *L'Age d'or* (1997) is the best account of this cinematic Surrealist collaboration. Biographical studies include Agustin Sanchez Vidal, *Dalí, Lorca and Buñuel* and Ian Gibson *The Shameful Life of Salvador Dalí*, by far the most complete survey of his life. Haim Finkelstein's critical edition of Dalí's writings translated into English was published in 1998; the Fundació Gala-Salvador Dalí is producing translations of Dalí's writings in Spanish.

[4] Alain Bosquet, *Conversations with Dalí* (New York: Dutton, 1969), p. 82.

[5] Ana María Dalí, *Noves imatges de Salvador Dalí*, pp. 74-75. Quoted in Ian Gibson, *The Shameful Life of Salvador Dalí* (London: Faber & Faber, 1997), p. 42.

[6] See Dawn Ades, "Dalí's Anti-paintings," *Companion to Spanish Surrealism* (forthcoming)

[7] André Breton "What is Surrealism?" (1934), in *What is Surrealism*, ed. F. Rosemont (London: Pluto Press, 1978), p. 136.

[8] J.G. Ballard, "The Art of Salvador Dalí," introduction to *Diary of a Genius* (London: Creation Books 1998), p. 5.

[9] James Thrall Soby, *Salvador Dalí* (New York: Museum of Modern Art, 1946), p. 26.

[10] *Ibid.*, p. 27.

[11] *Ibid.,* p. 27.

[12] Robert Hughes, "Homage to Catalonia," *The Guardian* London, March 13, 2004.

[13] David Sylvester defined "late Picasso" for his 1988 exhibition as the period from 1953 to Picasso's death in 1972; *Late Picasso* (Musée national d'art moderne, Paris and Tate Gallery, London 1988).

[14] *Anti-matter manifesto*, exhibition catalogue (New York: Carstairs Gallery, December 1958-January 1959).

[15] George Orwell, "Benefit of Clergy" (1944), in *Collected Essays* (London: Mercury Books, 1961), p. 213.

[16] See Robin Greeley, "Dalí's Fascism; Lacan's Paranoia," *Art History*, vol. 24, no. 4 (September 2001) for a nuanced and careful assessment of Dalí's politics.

[17] Salvador Dalí "cher Breton" preface to exhibition catalogue Pierre Colle Gallery 1933; trans. Haim Finkelstein, in *The Collected Writings of Salvador Dalí* (Cambridge: Cambridge University Press, 1998), p. 249.

[18] Dalí, *Conquest of the Irrational* (Paris: Éditions surréalistes, 1935).

[19] Dalí, *Diary of a Genius* (London: Creation Books 1998), p. 51.

[20] Sandor Ferenczi *Thalassa, a theory of genitalia* (1938) (London: Karnac Books, 1938), p. 3.

[21] GE. Moore, "Wittgenstein's Lectures 1930-33," *Philosophical Papers*, pp. 252-354.

[22] Ferenczi, *op. cit.,* p. 3.

[23] André Breton *Manifeste du Surréalisme* (1924) (Paris: NRF, 1967), p. 51.

[24] Dalí, *Diary of a Genius,* cit., p. 168.

Catalog of Works

Portraits: The Early Years

The great majority of Dalí's earliest paintings are of the buildings and landscapes around Figueres and Cadaqués, and of his friends and his family, including a number of self-portraits. An exception is the imaginary portrait of *El Sanyó Pancraci*, who was, according to Ian Gibson a local eccentric. A group of young radicals in Figueres, including Dalí and Jaume Miravitlles named a satirical journal after him, but it had only three issues. Dalí painted this "mock-Goya" portrait, together with some folkloric murals, as decoration for a studio he rented at 4, Carrer Muralla.[1]

Given the distinctive and complex role his own image played in his later work, it is interesting to see the way he treats it in these early canvases. Already, he tends to dramatize his presence rather than submit his appearance to close scrutiny in the manner of, say, Rembrandt, Chardin or Cézanne. However, his primary concern in these canvases painted between the ages of fifteen and seventeen is with color, light and the direct handling of paint. Only in the summers spent by the family at Cadaqués was Dalí able to give himself up totally to painting; because there was no room in the holiday house a separate studio was rented for him, which had previously been used by Ramon Pichot. Another member of this talented family, the cellist Ricard, sat for Dalí. In June 1920, Dalí notes in his diary that he can think of nothing but the coming months in Cadaqués. There is then a long pause in the diary until October when he writes, "Everything is over, the summer, happiness, art too!"[2] In the *Self-portrait in the studio* Dalí depicts himself in the act of painting with the results of the productive summer hanging on the high walls around him. Dalí later commented that this was the first time he had painted a self-portrait in profile, with the aid of three mirrors.[3] The whole scene glows with heightened color dominated by red, orange and pink, which transform even the painter's hands and his black hair.

Although Dalí refers in his letters and diary to Impressionism, it is really the brilliant color and excited handling of paint of the Post-Impressionist generation that is evident in his work between 1918 and 1920. Dalí may also be aware of the culmination of Post-Impressionism in the Fauve works of Matisse and Derain. The *Self-portrait in the Studio* recalls Matisse's luminous interiors with window and balcony opening onto the Mediterranean sea; however, the color contrasts Dalí favors here still strongly reflect the influence of Ramon Pichot whose recent paintings he vividly recalled seeing while staying at Ramon's brother Pepito Pichot's country home in June 1916: "The paintings that filled me with the greatest wonder were the most recent ones, in which deliquescent Impressionism ended in certain canvases by frankly adopting in an almost uniform manner the *pointilliste* formula. The systematic juxtaposition of orange and violet produced in me a kind of illusion and sentimental joy like that which I had always experienced in looking at objects through a prism, which edged them with the colors of the rainbow."[4] In *Self-portrait in the studio* the apparent spontaneity in the handling of paint is underpinned by the considered color scheme of red, orange and violet, following the example of Ramon Pichot. The cooler and darker gray-blue in the studio walls gives a tonal effect, however, and hints at the young painter's not entirely successful struggle to free himself from the more traditional use of light and shade and to reach the pure color contrasts sought by the Fauve painters. "I'm growing more and more aware all the time," he wrote to his Uncle Anselm Domènech, "of the difficulty of art."[5] The thick slabs and smears of paint are far from the ordered manner of the neo-Impressionists, (or Pointillists), and come closer to the Fauves.

Dalí's description of the studio breathes his joy in this private space: "It was a large, whitewashed room on the upper floor of a miserable fisherman's house. The first time I entered it was full of … ants, jars of anchovies, stored chairs, barrels of wine, and bundles of dirty, heaped up clothes. The roof was in danger of caving in. Patches of blue sky could be seen through the thatching. It was very picturesque but very dirty and a bit dangerous. The debris was cleared away and once inside I studied the room more closely. At the front end was a balcony from which the sea—a very blue and serene sea—and the sky could be seen. Boats passed by with their sails open, golden from the sun, and the swallows and birds flew around, gaily chirping. On the other side was a window from which one could see Mount Pani, and an almond tree orchard in the foreground. A baroque, whitewashed altar was on one wall, where I placed a jug full of rosemary… I organized some books in a worm-eaten cupboard—something by Baroja, Rubén Darío, Erça de Queiróc and I think a volume by Kant—that I didn't open the entire summer. There were also some books with reproductions, and the complete Gowans collection. On a table there was a jug with brushes, a paint box, paper, an inkwell, a pencil, a hammer to straighten out the chairs and frames, rolls of Ingres paper and canvas. A large easel was in the middle of the room and a small one hung from a nail. I rubbed my hands with satisfaction and I began to look tenderly upon that studio which, almost without my realizing it, I had already begun to love."[6]

If *Self-portrait in the Studio* shows the working artist, with a canvas in progress reflecting the painting itself with its orange and violet pigments (but no identifiable subject) the other two portraits position his head against the bay of

1. Self-portrait in the Studio, ca. 1919

1. Oil on canvas
27 × 21 cm
$10^{5/8} \times 8^{1/4}$ in.
St. Petersburg (FL),
The Salvador Dalí Museum

Cadaqués, thus bringing together his two favorite subjects. The *Self-Portrait with the Neck of Raphael* is a homage to one of his favorite painters, in particular to Raphael's *Self-Portrait* reproduced as frontispiece in the little book about the artist in the Gowans series that Dalí had in his studio.

The other *Self-portrait* is a more romantic image, showing the painter with long hair and sideburns with tilted head and a yearning expression. Above his head a bunch of grapes lures the viewer in parallel with the handsome young Bacchus himself, whose white flowing necktie and cape hint at the artist's persona.

Though Dalí's youthful self-portraits inevitably reflect the vigorous stylistic experiments of these early years, they are also the medium through which he already enacts different personae. Although his undoubted fascination with his own image points to a certain Narcissism, it is not, as in the classical myth to which he later turned in *Metamorphosis of Narcissus* (cat. 167), a question of indifference to the admiration or attention of others, but to the contrary, a desire to attract it on his own terms. Dalí frankly admits to his exhibitionism, and his self-images show him variously in the guise of delicate aesthete, romantic outcast, great artist. D.A.

[1] Ian Gibson, *The Shameful Life of Salvador Dalí* (London: Faber and Faber, 1997), pp. 67-68.

[2] Salvador Dalí, *Un diari: 1919-1920. Les meves impressions I records intims*, ed. Fèlix Fanés (Barcelona: Fundació Gala-Salvador Dalí, Edicions 62, 1994), p. 129.

[3] Robert Descharnes, *Dalí de Gala* (Lausanne: Éditions Denöel, 1962), p. 14.

[4] Salvador Dalí, *The Secret Life of Salvador Dalí* (London: Vision Press, 1968), p. 81.

[5] Salvador Dalí, *Un Diari, cit.,* p. 57.

[6] *Ibid.* p. 134. English translation by Robert Lubar Dalí in *The Salvador Dalí Museum Collection* (St. Petersburg [FL]: Salvador Dalí Museum, 2000), p. 11.

2. Portrait of El Sanyó Pancraci, ca. 1919   3. Portrait of the Cellist Ricard Pichot, 1920

2. Oil on canvas
74 × 42.5 cm
29 1/8 × 16 3/4 in.
Private collection, courtesy
Galeria d'art Dolors Junyent,
Barcelona

3. Oil on canvas
61.5 × 49 cm
24 1/4 × 19 1/4 in.
Private collection

4. Self-portrait with the Neck of Raphael, 1920-21

4. Oil on canvas
41.5 × 53 cm
$16^{1/4} \times 20^{7/8}$ in.
Figueres, Fundació
Gala-Salvador Dalí,
gift of Dalí to the Spanish State

5. Self-portrait, ca. 1921

5. Oil on canvas
52 × 45 cm
20³/8 × 17³/4 in.
Private collection

6. Study for "Self-portrait," 1920
7. Family Portrait, 1920

6. Pencil on paper
16.5 × 22 cm
8⁵/8 × 6¹/2 in.
Figueres, Fundació
Gala-Salvador Dalí, gift
of Dalí to the Spanish State

7. Pencil on paper
22 × 16.5 cm
8⁵/8 × 6¹/2 in.
Private collection

8. Untitled (Portrait of the Artist's Mother, Doña Felipa
Domènech de Dalí), 1920

8. Oil on canvas
40 × 40 cm
15³/4 × 15³/4 in.
Private collection

9. Portrait of Grandmother Ana Sewing, 1921

9. Oil on canvas
53 × 41 cm
20$^{7/8}$ × 16$^{1/8}$ in.
Private collection

Dalí's maternal grandmother Ana, (Maria Anna Ferrés Sadurní), together with her daughter Catalina, ("la tieta"), came to live with Dalí's family in Figueres in 1910. Both Salvador and his sister Ana María recall in their memoirs the serene and reassuring atmosphere of the extended and largely female family circle. During Dalí's frequent childhood illnesses "Llucia, my old nurse, would come and keep me company every afternoon and my grandmother would come and settle down to her knitting near the window of my room."[1] Llucia and Grandmother Ana were "two of the neatest old women, with the whitest hair and the most delicate and wrinkled skin I have ever seen. The first was immense in stature and looked like a pope. The second was tiny and resembled a small spool of white thread."[2]

Ana María delightfully contrasts the quiet old woman in black with the bright life and sounds of the balcony of their apartment: "Our maternal grandmother sewed in silence, overflowing with serenity. And her figure was like an evocation of Flemish painting, in contrast with the shadows, birds and flowers of the gallery, so purely impressionist."[3] This memory is clearly filtered through the youthful paintings of her brother, which shifted between the quiet tones of genre scenes like this to the vivid colors and dramatic contrasts of light and shade in landscapes and other portraits of this time. *Portrait of Grandmother Ana Sewing* was, in fact, painted at Cadaqués, the bay visible through the window of the house where the family spent their summers. (The separate studio found for Dalí in Cadaqués had a floor-length window and balcony). Dalí's enthusiastic experiments with heightened color during these longed-for summers devoted to painting are nonetheless visible, if muted, in the red-orange strip of coast beyond the water and the glowing basket on the chair, which create skilful complementary tones to the overall silvery-blue. Ana María described such evening calm after a day of wind: "The white-calm covered the sea that the *tramontana* had painted throughout the day with a lively and opaque blue. The transparent air is covered with streaks of gold and winged ants that fly at dusk."[4]

Genre scenes of domestic interiors by Spanish artists like Urgell and Manuel Benedito often pay homage to Dutch and Flemish 17th-century painting. Dalí made a copy of Manuel Benedito's *Dutch Interior* in about 1915. But he was also familiar from a very early age with reproductions of the Old Masters in the Gowans Art Books, a series of pocket-sized monographs that Dalí's father started collecting soon after it began in 1905. They were a very important part of his childhood: "I adored Rubens's sensual nudes and the Flemish domestic scenes."[5]

Dalí's mother and grandmother, quite as much as his father, encouraged his artistic bent. Grandmother Ana herself came from a family of craftsmen and after her father died had taken over the work-shop in Barcelona, which specialized in tortoise shell *objets d'art*. She had an artistic sensibility and entertained Salvador and Ana María with paper cut-outs. Felipa, Dalí's mother, who before her marriage had helped in the workshop, inherited her talents; she was "deft with her fingers and drew well. The delicate wax figurines she enjoyed fashioning out of candles would delight the future painter as a child."[6] D.A.

[1] Salvador Dalí, *The Secret Life of Salvador Dalí*, trans. Haakon Chevalier (London: Vision Press, 1968), p. 67.
[2] *Ibid.*, p. 67.
[3] Ana María Dalí, *Salvador Dalí visto por su hermana* (Barcelona: Ediciones del Cotal, S.A., 1983), p. 12.
[4] *Ibid.*, p. 24.
[5] Ian Gibson, *The Shameful Life of Salvador Dalí* (London: Faber & Faber, 1997), p. 42.
[6] *Ibid.*, p. 17.

10. Portrait of my Father, 1920-21

10. Oil on canvas
91 × 66.5 cm
35⁷/₈ × 26¹/₈ in.
Figueres, Fundació
Gala-Salvador Dalí, gift
of Dalí to the Spanish State

Dalí here depicts the imposing figure of his father with the Bay of Cadaqués as backdrop. This cannot be a "realistic" setting, given the father's position, although it may have been painted during the summer months while the family were at Cadaqués. As in so many of his landscapes of this period, it is an evening light. "His portrait had to be painted by the reddish light of the setting sun. He came to pose each evening, enflamed by the last rays of the sunset."[1] This, together with dark, formal clothes, gold watch chain, the ribbon of an order and spotted bow tie suggest that Don Salvador came to pose after work each day, which would point to the picture being painted in Figueres. There is also a possibility that the black clothes indicate mourning: Dalí's mother died in February 1921.

Dalí has positioned his father so high against the bay that he appears to be standing on a high hill—Mount Pani, perhaps. Dalí later read into the thickness of the paint a curious motive, linking this portrait to his later theme of the dominating Father, round which he constructs some of his favorite myths: "Idea that my father was Moses, William Tell, Jupiter. His portrait having to weigh more than all the others, I voluntarily added heavy layers of paint."[2]

Irrational though this idea is, it is not unlike the association that is made between emotional or ritual value and material value in the case of icons and devotional objects and images.

The most curious element in this painting is the running figure wearing a short red gown and clasping a bowl, emerging from the rear of the father. It is hard to identify this and even its gender is indeterminate, though it would seem to be female and is vaguely classical in appearance. Although it has some remote similarities with the dancing figures in the paintings Dalí made of local Festivals, this does not seem the right context. It may not be too fanciful to connect it with a widespread revival of interest in classical myths, which in literature often evoked the uncanny presence of the spirit of a place. D.A.

[1] Robert Descharnes, *Dalí de Gala* (Lausanne: Éditions Denöel, 1962), p. 134.
[2] *Ibid.*

Fig. 1. Salvador Dalí, *Study for "Portrait of my Father"* Figueres, Fundació Gala-Salvador Dalí, gift of Dalí to the Spanish State

11. The Voyeur, ca. 1921

11. Gouache on cardboard
32 × 50 cm
$12^{5/8} \times 19^{5/8}$ in.
Figueres, Fundació
Gala-Salvador Dalí

12. Romería – Pilgrimage, ca. 1921

12. Gouache on cardboard
52 × 52 cm
$20^{1/2}$ × $20^{1/2}$ in.
Figueres, Fundació
Gala-Salvador Dalí

Landscapes: The Early Years

Between summers, as a teenager, Dalí used to dream of Cadaqués, where he spent the holidays with his family and was free all day to paint. "Cadaqués is above all very picturesque, very bright and very calm."[1] The light, the boats, the white houses along the quay, the steep alleys leading up to the church on the hill, the terraced olive groves, the monastery high on Mount Pani with the mountains beyond and above all the series of beautiful bays made it an ideal place for the young artist. Back in Figueres in October 1920, he wrote in his dairy:

"And there, in that town of white houses and tranquil days I consecrated all my skills to art, to painting, and I lived like a nut, painting and learning, going into raptures in front of the nature that is also art, watching the sun set on the damp sand of the beach, inebriating myself with poetry in the long, blue twilight, half-asleep in the sweet world of of greenish waves, and then the stars that reflect in the calm waters, the pale, moonlit nights, beautiful women's eyes, with a sparkle of love, and the azure mornings, full of sun, that bathed in the green waters of a bay… what pleasure and what life!"[2]

Dalí and his family regularly spent their summers there, in a white house on the beach at the bay of Es Llane, rented from and eventually bought from their close friends the Pichots, a local dynasty of artists and musicians (see Encyclopedia, "Music"). The journey over the tortuous mountain road separating Cadaqués from the Ampurdàn plain where Figueres lies was by cart and used to take all day. The holiday house being too small, a studio was found for him, which had formerly been used by Ramon Pichot. Dalí had been transfixed as a boy by Pichot's paintings, which hung in the dining room at the Pichot's house near Figueres, El Molí de la Torre: "These breakfasts were my discovery of French Impressionism, the school of painting which has in fact made the deepest impression on me in my life because it represented my first contact with an anti-academic and revolutionary esthetic theory. I did not have eyes enough to see all that I wanted to see in those thick and formless daubs of paint, which seemed to splash the canvas as if by chance…Yet as one looked at them from a certain distance and squinting one's eyes, suddenly there occurred that miracle of vision by virtue of which this musically colored medley became organized, transformed into pure reality."[3]

In these early landscapes and sea scenes Dalí experiments with the changing light effects favored by Impressionism, although often using a heavy impasto and reaching an intensity of color closer to the post-impressionists. Canvases like *Landscape near Cadaqués* and *View of Cadaqués from Mount Pani* clearly show the influence of Ramon Pichot in their free brushstrokes and luminous colors. Dalí emphasizes the complementary colors, blue/orange and red/green, although he rarely adopts the Neo-Impressionist style of separate, even, dabs of paint visible in Pichot's *Cala Nans* (fig. 1). In *Port of Cadaqués (Night)* he marks the reflections of the white buildings along the front with thick squiggles of paint, and the black prow of the large ship seems

Fig. 1. Ramon Pichot, *Cala Nans*
Barcelona, Private collection

13. View of Cadaqués from Mount Pani, ca. 1921
14. Cadaqués, ca. 1922

13. Oil on canvas
39.5 × 48.3 cm
15¹/² × 19¹/⁸ in.
St. Petersburg (FL),
The Salvador Dalí Museum

14. Oil on canvas
31 × 34 cm
12¹/⁸ × 13³/⁸ in.
Bern, Kunstmuseum

to pierce the church on the hill. In a number of the views he painted at this time, such as *Olive Trees. Landscape at Cadaqués* (fig. 2) he chooses an evening light, with the glow of sunset illuminating the houses and their reflections in the distance, with the foreground earth red against the green trees.

A quieter and more muted canvas, *The Lane to Port Lligat with View of Cap Creus,* depicts the path across the hill dividing Cadaqués form the tiny fishing hamlet of Port Lligat, with its gray stone walls and silvery olives. At the top of the hill is the cemetery where most of Dalí's family including his father and sister are buried. Cap Creus, a rocky promontory beyond Port Lligat, is just visible in the distance. This is indeed the place where the great mountain range of the Pyrenees meets the sea, and the dramatic geography of the region was a constant source of inspiration for Dalí (see *The Railway Station at Perpignan,* cat. 241). The remarkably jagged shapes and viciously sharp surfaces of the rocks were to provide the setting for the opening scenes of *L'Âge d'or* and are a source

for famous images such as *The Great Masturbator.* Port Lligat, where Dalí bought a fishermen's shack from his friend Lídia Noguer after being banished from the family home in 1930, was to be his and Gala's home and is the setting for many of his most famous works. The bay with its island and the terraced hill topped with a tower are familiar from paintings like the *Madonna of Port Lligat.* Despite his international success and his lengthy stays in Paris, New York and California, these scenes remained potent for the rest of his life. D.A.

[1] Salvador Dalí, *Un diari: 1919-1920. Les meves impressions I records intims*, ed. Félix Fanés (Barcelona: Fundació Gala-Salvador Dalí, Edicions 62, 1994), p. 132.
[2] *Ibid.*, p. 130.
[3] Salvador Dalí, *The Secret Life of Salvador Dalí*, trans. Haakon Chevalier (London: Vision Press, 1968). In 1910 Picasso, a friend of Pichot, spent the summer in a house on the sea front. There seems no trace of picturesque Cadaqués in the cubist works of the time, which are among his most uncompromisingly abstracted.

15. The Lane to Port Lligat with View of Cap Creus, ca. 1921
16. Port of Cadaqués (Night), ca. 1918

15. Oil on canvas
55.2 × 67.9 cm
21³/4 × 26³/4 in.
St. Petersburg (FL),
The Salvador Dalí Museum

16. Oil on canvas
18.7 × 24.2 cm
7³/8 × 9¹/2 in.
St. Petersburg (FL),
The Salvador Dalí Museum

17. El Molí – Landscape of Cadaqués, ca. 1923

17. Oil and gouache
on cardboard
75 × 98 cm
$29^{1/2} \times 38^{5/8}$ in.
Private collection

18. Untitled (Landscape of Madrid), ca. 1922
19. Madrid, Architecture and Poplars, ca. 1922

18. Oil on cardboard
30.1 × 35.8 cm
11⁷/₈ × 14 in.
Madrid, Galeria
Guillermo De Osma

19. Oil on cardboard
47 × 62.9 cm
15¹/₂ × 24³/₄ in.
Private collection

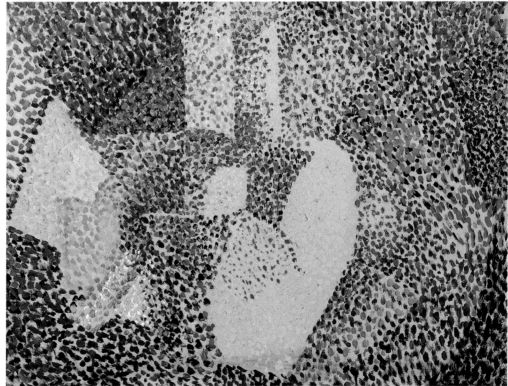

20. Self-portrait with "L'Humanité," 1923
21. Untitled – Self-portrait, 1923

20. Oil, gouache and collage
on cardboard
105 × 74 cm
41³/₈ × 29¹/₈ in.
Figueres, Fundació
Gala-Salvador Dalí,
gift of Dalí to the Spanish State

21. India ink and pencil
on paper
31.5 × 23.5 cm
12¹/₂ × 9¹/₈ in.
Figueres, Fundació
Gala-Salvador Dalí

The severity of these self-portraits is in striking contrast with the picturesque images of his earlier Cadaqués period. Only part of the difference can be ascribed to the adoption of Cubism. In *Self-portrait with "L'Humanité"* the painter shows himself square to the canvas wearing what appear to be workman's overalls. In 1921, Dalí had taken out a subscription to the French Communist newspaper *L'Humanité*, and in the autumn of 1922, anticipating his forthcoming move to the art school in Madrid, wrote to his uncle asking him to transfer the subscription there. This was the period of an intense involvement in radical politics; in autumn 1921 Dalí, together with Figueres comrades including Jaume Miravittles, launched a Marxist group called Social Renovation (*Renovacio Social*) together with a short-lived journal of the same name. His response to the colonial war in Morocco has interesting parallels with the later attitude of the Surrealists to the French colonial struggles in North Africa; "I consider myself," he wrote, "completely Moorish."[1]

That his political ideas survived the first year of his studies at the Special School of Painting, Sculpture and Engraving, the teaching department of the San Fernando Royal Academy of Fine Arts in Madrid, is evident in the *Self-portrait with "L'Humanité."* In depicting himself in worker's clothes together with the fragment of the Communist newspaper, he is clearly still far from adopting the attitudes and the dandy dress of the group of students from La Residencia with whom he was shortly to become closely involved. Al-

though in the following passage from the *Secret Life* he dwells rather on the picturesque "artistic" aspect of his appearance, the difference is still marked: "My serious, studious air, totally lacking in humour, made me appear to their sarcastic eyes a lamentable being, stigmatized with mental deficiency and at best picturesque. Nothing indeed

Fig. 1. Salvador Dalí,
Cubist Self-portrait, 1923
Madrid, Museo Nacional
Centro de Arte Reina Sofía

Fig. 2. Dalí with schoolfriends
from the Academia de Bellas Artes
in a photo by Manuel Belio Madrid
ca. 1922-23

could contrast more violently with their British-style tailored suits and golf jackets than my velvet jackets and my flowing neck-ties; nothing could be more diametrically opposed to them than my long tangled hair, falling to my shoulders, and their smartly trimmed hair, regularly worked over by the barbers of the Ritz or the Palace Hotel."[2] Photographs of the young student among his fellow art students do indeed show him with the locks, necktie and jacket described above (fig. 2). Dalí's rapid passage through the dramatic and fast-changing field of avant-garde painting through the next few years is breath-taking. When and how he first encountered Cubism is unclear, but it may have been through the Galeries Dalmau exhibition of recent, largely French art, whose illustrated catalogue—if not the show itself—he must have seen. He also regularly received avant-garde periodicals such as L'*Esprit nouveau*. He therefore probably encountered si-

multaneously Braque and Picasso's hermetic Cubism of ca. 1911 and 1912 and the next development, cubist collage. While the *Cubist Self-Portrait* (fig. 1) of 1923 has a splintered surface of cascading vertical and quasi-abstract shapes, with his own highly simplified face standing out towards the center, in *Self-portrait with "L'Humanité"* he adopts the larger flat forms of collage. However, the rectangular shapes in the background can be read as picture frames. A real fragment of the communist newspaper is pasted onto the surface. The ink and wash *Self-portrait*, while closely related, interestingly shows the young artist with flowing neck-tie rather than overalls. As in *Self-portrait with "L'Humanité,"* the rectangles represent canvases, framing the painter's double outline. A table and bottle seen from a steep perspective jut beside him. This drawing is linked to the series of watercolors and wash drawings of Madrid nightlife (cats. 22-25), of which the masterpiece is *Late-night Dreams,* where his own familiar outline and simplified features—long hair, narrow oval face and sharply caricatured eyebrows—are repeated in different scenes. (fig. 3) D.A.

Fig. 3. Salvador Dalí,
Late-night Dreams, 1923
Figueres, Fundació
Gala-Salvador Dalí

[1] Unpublished notebook, *Les cançons del dotze anys* (Figueres: Fundació Gala-Salvador Dalí, 1922), quoted in Ian Gibson, *The Shameful Life of Salvador Dalí* (London: Faber and Faber, 1997), p. 83.
[2] Salvador Dalí, *The Secret Life of Salvador Dalí*, trans. Haakon Chevalier (London: Vision Press, 1968), p. 175.

21

22. Christmas Scene, 1922

23. Summer Night, 1922

22. China ink and gouache
on paper
21.1 × 15.3 cm
8 1/4 × 6 in.
Figueres, Fundació
Gala-Salvador Dalí,
gift of Dalí to the Spanish State

23. China ink and gouache
on paper
20.8 × 15 cm
8 1/8 × 5 7/8 in.
Figueres, Fundació
Gala-Salvador Dalí

24. Madrid, Drunk Man, 1922

25. The First Days of Spring, 1922-23

24. China ink and gouache
on paper
21 × 15 cm
8 1/4 × 5 7/8 in.
Figueres, Fundació
Gala-Salvador Dalí

25. China ink and gouache
on paper
20.8 × 15 cm
8 1/8 × 5 7/8 in.
Figueres, Fundació
Gala-Salvador Dalí

26. Portrait of Luis Buñuel, 1924

26. Oil on canvas
70 × 60 cm
27⁵/8 × 23⁵/8 in.
Madrid, Museo Nacional
Centro de Arte Reina Sofía,
formerly in the collection
of Luis Buñuel

It was the portrait of Luis Buñuel that marked Dalí's breakthrough outside of Catalunya when it was first exhibited (together with *Bather*, fig. 3, and cats. 27-28) at the "Primera Exposición de la Sociedad de Artistas Ibéricos" held in the Palacio de Exposiciones del Retiro of Madrid in May and June 1925.
In September 1924, Dalí returned to the Real Academia de Bellas Artes de San Fernando after a year of suspension for insubordination and his ensuing imprisonment in Figueres and Gerona. In October, at the Residencia de Estudiantes, Luis Buñuel directed an adaptation of *Don Juan Tenorio de Zorrilla*, entitled *La profanacion de Don Juan*. Dalí acted in the production, playing Don Luis Mejia, Don Juan's antagonist. Buñuel himself played the title role.
Dalí painted his visionary portrait of the future film director during this period. It shows an astonishing assimilation of different fronts of European Modernism—from Picasso to *Neue Sachlichkeit*, from works published in 1920 in *Esprit nouveau* and *Valori Plastici*—to portraits of the Italian Renaissance painters like Bronzino.
In *Mi ultimo suspiro* (1982) Buñuel recalls the making of his portrait at the Residencia: "In 1979, on the occasion of the important Dalí exhibition at Paris's Beaubourg Museum, I decided to lend the portrait Dalí had made of me in another epoch, when we were both students in Madrid: a minutious portrait that he made by dividing the canvas up into small squares and measuring the exact dimensions of my nose, lips and to which he added, upon my request, long thin clouds like the ones I liked so much in a painting by Mantegna."
The clouds in the portrait, a quotation from Mantegna's *Death of the Virgin* (fig. 2) at the Prado, reappear in the 1929 film *Un Chien andalou*, on which Dalí collaborated with Buñuel. Mantegna's clouds pass over the moon, just before the famous sequence of the razor cutting the eye.
The Spanish critic Eugenio D'Ors reviewed the "Artistas Ibéricos" exhibition in Madrid singing high praises to Dalí:
"It looks as though he was drawn to the articulation, the architecture, the construction. The only thing is that at first, in the hour—or, better, quarter of an hour—of Cubism, he figured he had to make it according to a watchmaker's precision and now he has learned to make things the way mothers do. I like the portrait labeled number 81 [*Portrait of Luis Buñuel*] most of all. It is not his supreme effort, but it is the most serious and calm. For the good student, for the able apprentice, it represents the highest grade *cum laude*. From here we move on—Cubism was the first year at the school, the current production may constitute the second—to the subject that should be called 'training in eternal values.'"[1] T.S.

[1] Eugenio D'Ors, in *ABC*, June 3, 1925

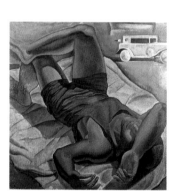

Fig. 3. Salvador Dalí, *Bather*, 1924
Private collection

Fig. 1. Man Ray, *Portrait of Luis Buñuel*

Fig. 2. Andrea Mantegna,
The Death of the Virgin, ca. 1460
Madrid, Museo Nacional del Prado

27. Still Life (fragment), 1924

27. Oil on panel
52 × 40 cm
20¹/² × 15³/⁴ in.
Montreal, Musée des Beaux Arts

Fig. 1. Salvador Dalí,
Still Life, ca. 1925
Figueres, Fundació
Gala-Salvador Dalí

Fig. 2. Salvador Dalí and Ana María
Figueres, Museu del Joguet
de Catalunya

All that remains of this still life, which is just previous to cat. 28 and was exhibited with it at the "Primera Exposición de la Sociedad de Artistas Ibéricos" in Madrid, is the fragment preserved in Montreal. In 1925, Dalí divided the panel into four parts and painted *The Portrait of María Carbona* (cat. 42) on the reverse of the present fragment.[1]
From 1923 to 1925, Dalí produced not only portraits but also a series of still lifes that were the result of a short experimental period devoted to this genre. After a number of Cubist still lifes inspired, in particular, by Juan Gris (*Still Life*, 1923, Museo Nacional, Centro de Arte Reina Sofía, Madrid; *Still Life*, 1922, The Salvador Dalí Museum, St. Petersburg, FL), Dalí switched to Purism (*Purist Still Life*, 1924, Fundació Gala-Salvador Dalí, Figueres) and Metaphysical Painting.
The stylistic influences of the journals *L'Esprit nouveau* (Paris, 1920-25) and *Valori Plastici* (Rome, 1918-21) on the artist from 1923 onward, during the years he spent in Madrid, are clearly evident in the still lifes of 1924 displayed at the Sociedad de Artistas Ibéricos exhibition, where they formed the most significant nucleus of Dalí's works. His works of this period reflect the theories of one or other of these periodicals and sometimes those of both of them. The *Still Life* of 1925 (fig. 1) is probably the apotheosis of this experimentation, combining Cubism, Purism, and Metaphysical Painting in the same picture.
As was pointed out by James Thrall Soby in the catalogue of the retrospective held at the Museum of Modern Art in New York in 1941, and subsequently by Rafael Santos Torroella,[2] the Metaphysical Painting of Giorgio de Chirico, Carlo Carrà, and Giorgio Morandi was discussed in Spanish artistic circles with just as much fervor as were the most outstanding figures of the École de Paris.[3] And while de Chirico played an important role, especially in the 1930s, this still life—like the contemporary still life *Siphon and Small Bottle of Rum*, 1924, Fundació Gala-Salvador Dalí, Figueres—has a particular affinity with Carrà's and Morandi's painting. T.S.

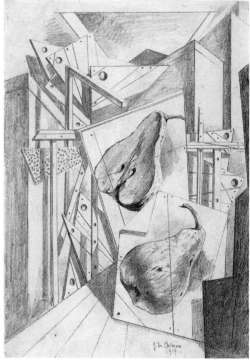

Fig. 3. Carlo Carrà, *Still Life with Square*, 1917
Milan, Civiche Raccolte

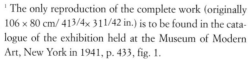

Fig. 4. Giorgio de Chirico, *Still Life with Two Pears*
Berlin, Stiftung Sammlung Dieter Scharf

[1] The only reproduction of the complete work (originally 106 × 80 cm/ 41³/⁴× 31¹/⁴2 in.) is to be found in the catalogue of the exhibition held at the Museum of Modern Art, New York in 1941, p. 433, fig. 1.
[2] Rafael Santos Torroella, *Dalí. Epoca de Madrid* (Madrid: Residencia de Estudiantes, 1994), p. 34.
[3] "Dalí's exposure to the art of the *scuola metafisica* was of paramount importance in his early career. The school's doctrine was eventually to swerve him from the abstract approach of the Cubist-Futurist tradition toward the Surrealist movement's concern with man's psychology. For the *scuola metafisica* had directly prefigured the reaction

against purely abstract art which Surrealism in general and Dalí in particular were to exemplify so forcefully.... It emphasized the artist's salvation through philosophical speculation, his comfort in the enigma, his retreat to dream. However important the differences between its program and that of Surrealism, there can be no question that Dalí was prepared for his career as a Surrealist by his eager adoption of the tenets of *pittura metafisica*." James Thrall Soby, *Salvador Dalí*, exhibition catalogue, Museum of Modern Art (New York: 1941), pp. 4-5.

28. Still Life, 1924

28. Oil on canvas
125 × 99 cm
49¹/4 × 38⁷/8 in.
Madrid, Museo Nacional,
Centro de Arte Reina Sofía

Painted by Dalí when he was only twenty, this is perhaps the most notable of the six still lifes that the artist displayed at the "Primera Exposición de la Sociedad de Artistas Ibéricos"[1] in 1925 in Madrid. The picture was subsequently exhibited with the title *Sifón e botellita de ron* at the artist's first solo show at the Galeries Dalmau, Barcelona, in the same year.[2] While the second title is an intentional reference to Juan Gris (*Le bouteille de rhum*, 1912), an important source of inspiration for Dalí in his Madrid period, the present work attests to the special attention the artist paid to Giorgio Morandi's still lifes published in *Valori Plastici* (III, no. 4, Rome1921). The artist gave the work to his friend Federico García Lorca who published the oneiric poem "Ode to Salvador Dalí" in April 1926 in the *Revista de Occidente*. In this poem there are references to the still lifes displayed in the Sociedad de Artistas Ibéricos exhibition.
In his *Historia de mi vida*,[3] Joaquin Torres-García, who had an opportunity to see this still life during a visit to García Lorca's house in 1933, recalls it with admiration.

"Ode to Salvador Dalí"
…
A desire for forms and limits overwhelms us.
Here comes the man who sees with a yellow ruler.
Venus is a white still life
and the butterfly collectors run away.
…
You love a matter definite and exact,
where the toadstool cannot pitch its camp.

You love the architecture that builds on the absent
and admit the flag simply as a joke.

The steel compass tells its short, elastic verse.
Unknown islands rise to deny the sphere exists.
The straight line tells of its upward struggle
and the learned crystals sing their geometries.

(Federico García Lorca)

"It is one of the most explicit pictures in the exhibition. It depicts the remains of a meal. The pears have been left because they are still green—see the picture—and the bottle is half empty because they have drunk the rest of its contents." (Manuel Abril, Madrid, June 21, 1925). T.S.

[1] Catalogue of the exhibition "Primera Exposición de la Sociedad de Artistas Ibéricos," Palacio de Esposiciones del Retito, May-June 1925, Madrid, p. 3.
[2] Catalogue of the exhibition at the Galerie Dalmau, 1925; cat. no. 17, *Sifon ui ampolelta de rhum (Pintura cubista)*
[3] Joaquin Torres-García, *Historia de mi vida* (Montevideo, 1939) p. 298

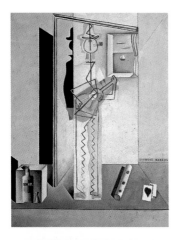

Fig. 1. Salvador Dalí,
Pierrot and Guitar, 1925
Madrid, Museo Nacional
Centro de Arte Reina Sofía

Fig. 2. Federico García Lorca
photographed in front of Dalí's
Still Life (1924)
Madrid, Fundación Federico
García Lorca

Fig. 3. Giorgio Morandi, *Still Life,* 1919
Milan, Pinacoteca di Brera

Fig. 4. Giorgio Morandi, *Still Life,* 1919
Milan, Pinacoteca di Brera

29. Pierrot and Guitar, 1924

29. Oil and collage
on cardboard
55 × 52 cm
21$^{5/8}$ × 20$^{1/2}$ in.
Madrid, Museo
Thyssen-Bornemisza

Unlike most of his fellow students and indeed teachers at the Academy in Madrid, Dalí was eagerly absorbing the dramatic developments of European avant-garde art, largely through magazines and books. One of the most important of these was the Italian journal *Valori Plastici*, which contained an eclectic range of modern paintings including cubist works by both Picasso and Braque as well as the metaphysical paintings of Carrà, de Chirico and Morandi.

This bold cubist collage shows Dalí's inventive response to the fragmentation and abstract planes of Cubism as well as to the idea of incorporating extraneous materials on to the picture's surface. A *Still Life* by Picasso, reproduced in *Valori Plastici* no. 2 (1919), offers a particularly close parallel to *Pierrot and Guitar.* Picasso has added sand to parts of the painting, clearly visible in the photograph in *Valori Plastici*, and there are also heavy black outlines to the shapes in *Still Life* similar to those in Dalí's collage. He is also evidently interested in the rhythmic repetition of forms: so the two tiny tin toy plates echo the sound hole of the guitar while the spoons resemble the guitar pegs. Pierrots and Harlequins had become part of Picasso's repertoire after ca. 1914, and musical instruments, especially the guitar, were commonplace in cubist works. Like Picasso, Dalí here merges instrument and figure. The face of Pierrot appears as a highly abstracted geometric wedge, outlined in white, towards the top center of the picture. Just to its right there is another fragment of a head with "eye" and "moustache," a doubling of Pierrot's presence. Dalí has not fully understood the intricate interplay of representation and reality in cubist works, however. Where in Picasso there is a subtle relationship between the flat planes of collage and the representation of objects, with indications of shadow and depth, Dalí leaves some areas quite abstract and undefined. Nonetheless, the arrangement of the planes which fan out from the center of the picture have an unusual dynamism, and remind us that Dalí was also interested in Futurism at this time. D.A.

30. Venus and Sailor (Homage to Salvat-Papasseit), 1925
31. Venus and Sailor, ca. 1925
32. Sailor and His Family, ca. 1925
33. Departure (Homage to the Noticiario Fox), 1926

30. Oil on canvas
216 × 147 cm
85 × 57⁷/8 in.
Shizuoka (Japan), Ikeda
Museum of 20th Century Art

31. Oil on canvas
198 × 149 cm
77¹/8 × 58⁵/8 in.
Figueres, Foundation
Gala-Salvador Dalí

32. China ink on paper
27.1 × 21.1 cm
10⁵/8 × 8¹/4 in.
Figueres, Fundació
Gala-Salvador Dalí

33. Oil on panel
43 × 31.5 cm
16⁷/8 × 12¹/2 in.
Madrid, Private collection

Dalí returned several times to the theme of the Classical goddess of love and the modern sailor in the mid 1920s. Not only does he encapsulate within this encounter a many-layered relationship between tradition and modernity, Neo-Classicism and the avant-garde, but also the life of the Mediterranean port.
The Neo-Classical figure of Venus looks to Picasso's classicism of the early 1920s; the massive, slightly flattened curves of her body and the simple white drapery recall Picasso's *Three Women at the Spring*, while the vigorous dance of the unfinished *Venus and Sailor* of 1926 is closer to a work like *The Race (Two Women running on the Beach*; fig.1) What is often called "the return to order" was for Picasso a deeply pondered dialogue with the art of the past, and Picasso's comments about the great masters were to echo in Dalí's own writings: "It's only the Masters who count."[1] Just before his premature death in 1918 Apollinaire had written to Picasso urging him to do some "grand paintings like Poussin's," and described his own attempt "to renew the accent of poetry while retaining a classical rhythm."[2] Dalí's paintings, however, mix the flatter, abstract planes of late Cubism and Purism with the Neo-Classical more impudently than Picasso ever did. The sailor in *Venus and Sailor* is like a ghostly, flat cut-out, while in *Depart* the shifts in scale, the doubled figure of the sailor and the over-lapping profiles of the two heads introduce a dimension of time and memory reminiscent of Futurism.
Dalí's connections with contemporary Catalan literature and culture in the mid 1920s are often overlooked in favor of his striking experiments with avant-garde European art. The juxtaposition of classical and cubist modes in these three paintings reflects the uneasy but often fruitful tension between *Noucentisme* and the avant-garde in Catalonia. *Noucentisme* is "a term which means "20th-century" but was probably intended to convey cultural overtones by analogy with Italian *cinquecento*."[3] The differences between *Noucentisme* and its predecessor *Modernisme* (see Encyclopedia) stem from differing interpretations of *catalanitat*: the question of Catalan identity, of what being Catalan means, was a pressing issue "in a society which is undergoing a crisis of national consciousness."[4] *Noucentisme* challenged the Romanticism and subjectivity of the earlier generation and espoused Classicism, the Mediterranean, the urban and "objectivity." Eugenio D'Ors, one of its chief proponents, promoted the idea of Barcelona as a new Athens. The poet who most successfully bridges the gap between *Noucentisme* and the avant-garde was Dalí's friend Josep Vincenç Foix; both were closely involved with the review *L'Amic de les Arts* (1926-29), whose illustrations range from classicizing woodcuts to Surrealism. Foix accepted the basis tenets of *Noucentisme* and especially the need to "restore the broken tradition of Catalan human-

ism." He was one of the first Catalan writers to look back to Ramon Llull, but also shows a definite Surrealist sensibility. Foix wrote, "The new excites me and I love the old," which could as well be Dalí's motto at this time. In these paintings, the new Athens and the industrial port, with its transient population, ships, and brothels, come together to create a modern mythology.
Venus and Sailor contained for Josep Maria Junoy "the breath of adventure, the song of the unknown and the passion for the voyage."[5] It was dedicated to Joan Salvat-Papasseit, who had died in 1924, at the age of thirty. He was the only major Catalan working-class poet of the period, and Dalí shared his anarchist sympathies as well as his interest in the avant-garde. Salvat-Papasseit's experimental work uses typographical devices drawn from Apollinaire and the Futurist Marinetti. The theme itself of Venus and the sailor could have been inspired by Salvat-Papasseit's collection of love poems, *La rosa als llavis* (The Rose at the lips, 1923). The protagonist of these wistful and eroic poems is a sailor:

"Wayfarer, don't speak, no,
'cause the breeze is bringing it nearer, and watch,
it will carry off your love, sir
- so the sailor sighed."[6]

Drawings by Dalí from this period of sailors, prostitutes and brothels, based on nighttime excursions to the harbor area of Barcelona, make the nature of the sexual encounters of these paintings more explicit. He even inscribed lines from one of the calligrams that intersperses *The Rose at the Lips* on a female body in a drawing of sailors in a brothel. Venus thus stands not just for the antique myth but for the fleeting eroticism of the brothel. The sailor is the figure of a transient, impersonal sexuality. But perhaps there is also a memory of the child Dalí dressed in his sailor suit, who was to appear in later works like *The Spectre of Sex Appeal* (cat. 135).

In *Venus and Sailor (Homage to Salvat-Papasseit)*, Dalí's modern sailor embracing the statuesque figure of Venus by night on a balcony over-looking the sea and the flag-decked ships draws new and old together in a remarkable balance; the black walls frame the couple and the scene through the window in an almost abstract fashion as though they were strips of *papier collé*. The sailor's face is a sharp but ghostly profile against the heavily modeled red-lipped beauty of Venus. She holds a mirror whose silver edge is also a crescent moon; the moonlight on the water and flooding past the black railings reflects on their white clothes. The sailor holds a pipe whose shape resembles the funnels of the ships; visible through the window is a bare fork-branched tree, a motif that carries on into some of Dalí's most famous paintings like *Persistence of Memory*. That

Fig. 1. Pablo Picasso, *Two Women Running on a Beach*, 1922 Paris, Musée Picasso

loss of restraint of the more barbaric Dionysus. A drawing is more explicitly erotic than the painting, in which drapery has been pulled down to cover the pubic hair. The painting's composition is strongly marked by diagonal lines which radiate from the genital areas of the two figures.

In *Depart "Homage to Fox News"* the modern world enters abruptly into the domain of a more naked Venus. Fox News was the newsreel bulletin screened in the popular cinemas. This painting also contains for the first time a strange geometric apparatus, which was to figure in *Honey Is Sweeter than Blood* (see p. 88, fig. 3) and to take center stage in *Apparatus and Hand* (see p. 90, fig. 1) as well as the curious stick clutched in the "toy" sailor's hand. Possibly a thermometer with which the temperature of passion was to be measured, it appears in *Neo-cubist Academy* in the hand of the Saint Sebastian-sailor. (cat. 48)

Venus and Sailor (Homage to Salvat-Papasseit) was exhibited at Dalí's first solo exhibition at the Galeries Dalmau in 1925, and *Departure (Homage to the Noticiario Fox)* (cat. 33) at his second the following year. D.A.

Venus was born of the sea is casually alluded to where the horizon of the blue sea is carried on over Venus's arm, making it appear to be under water. Dalí is also here playing with the surface/depth effects of cubist painting.

The dynamic, dancing figures in the unfinished *Venus and Sailor* recall Picasso's energetic beach scenes with bathers running and playing, such as *The Race*, although the geometry of the construction could be seen in the light of the order and objectivity encouraged by *Noucentisme*. Dalí, who by his own account had read Nietzsche, might here be alluding to the notion of the Dionysian from *The Birth of Tragedy*: to the idea that the work of art should contain not just the order and reason of the Apollonian but also the intoxication, excess and

[1] M. Georges-Michel *From Renoir to Picasso: Artists I have Known* (Boston: Houghton Mifflin, 1957), p. 82. Quoted in Elizabeth Cowling, *Picasso: Style and Meaning* (London: Phaidon, 2003), p. 393.

[2] Cowling, *op. cit.*, p. 409.

[3] Arthur Terry, *A Companion to Catalan Literature* (Woodbridge: Tamesis Books, 2003), p. 84.

[4] *Ibid.* p. 87.

[5] Joseph Maria Junio, "Les Exposicions," *Bellaterra* (Barcelona), 1925-26, pp. 116-117. Quoted in Felix Fanés, *La Construcción de la Imagen 1925-1930* (Milan: Electa, 1999) p. 42.

[6] Joan Salvat-Papasseit, "Quina grua el meu estel," *El Poema de la Rosa als Llavis* (1923), *Poesies Completes* (Barcelona: Editorial Ariel, 1962), p. 130.

32

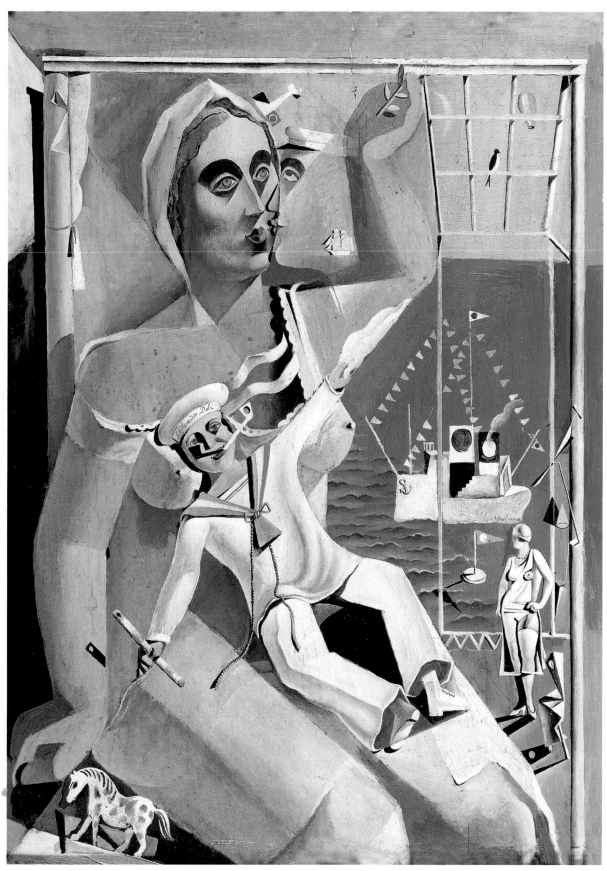

34. Portrait of My Father, 1925

34. Oil on canvas
104.5 × 104.5 cm
41$^{1/8}$ × 41$^{1/8}$ in.
Barcelona, Museu Nacional
d'Art de Catalunya

Fig. 1. Salvador Dalí, *Don Salvador and Ana María Dalí*, 1925
Barcelona, Museu Nacional
d'Art de Catalunya

To judge from photographs, Dalí's father was quite as imposing and majestic a figure as he appears here. The town notary in Figueres, a position of social as well as legal authority, he was at this period a free-thinker and Catalan federalist and the most powerful early influence on the young Salvador. The pose is similar to that in the large drawing of Dalí's father and sister, but there are some interesting differences. Whereas in the drawing he is in formal clothes, with tie, three-piece suit with buttonhole and pocket watch, smoking a cigar, here he is dressed more informally and holds a pipe. Both the painting and drawing were in Dalí's first solo exhibition at the Galeries Dalmau (Barcelona, November 14-27, 1925) and were reproduced in the catalogue, indicating that Dalí felt they were among his best works to date (cat. 37). The exhibition was, Dalí wrote to Lorca, "a complete success, both critically and in terms of sales." He sent Lorca "the harshest criticism"—the only one of any interest. Rafael Benet regarded his approach as "too cerebral: too philosophical and not sufficiently artistic." Looking more closely, however, Benet found a lyricism in his painting closer to the Valori Plastici painters than to the Cubists, and mentions the Neo-Classical style of Casorati and Oppi. This is a perceptive comment, and Dalí was certainly familiar with the Italians' work. However, Dalí chose to point the viewer to an older Neo-Classical source when he included no less than three quotations from Ingres in the catalogue. Commenting later on the drawing, Dalí said that he wished it to prove Ingres' famous saying "Drawing is the probity of art," one of the chosen quotations. However, the drawing as reproduced in the catalogue also reveals Dalí's close attention to Picasso, whose Post-Cubist drawings, in his new "Classical Realist" manner sometimes combined an extreme linearity with a heavily tonal treatment of the head.

The other two Ingres quotations throw light on Dalí's current attitude to his work. One concerns the age-old debate between originality and imitation. "He who is not willing to include in his contribution any mind other than his own will find himself reduced to the most miserable type of imitation, that is of himself." Neo-Classicism held to the idea that it was essential to learn from and indeed quote the great examples of the past. For Dalí, bringing this up to date, the examples to be mined for ideas included contemporary artists some of whom, such as Picasso and the Italians, recently had invented new forms of Classicism themselves. With an insatiable appetite, Dalí was working his way through the plethora of modern developments in painting. The final quotation from Ingres concerns style. "Beautiful forms consist in straight planes with curves. Beautiful forms are those with firmness and fullness in which details do not compromise the appearance of large masses." The large, simplified forms in *Portrait of my Father*, with slightly flattened planes curved at the side, especially noticeable in the hands and the head, recall the work of Morandi as well as Picasso. But it is also interesting to compare the painting with Ingres himself,

one of whose greatest early portraits, *Monsieur Bertin*, similarly eliminates decorative detail and is almost monochrome, painted predominantly in grays and browns. Both sitters are evidently powerful characters, but whereas Monsieur Bertin faces the viewer full-on, Dalí depicts his father from a three-quarter view. It would be more natural for him therefore to be looking away from the artist (and us), but his glance is sharply angled towards us, giving him an anxious and somewhat apprehensive expression, as though he wants to keep an eye on his brilliant, wayward son. The father was becoming aware that success for a painter was no longer assured by following a safe academic path; modern art was taking new and puzzling routes and Dalí had demonstrated a rebellious streak, having been suspended the previous year from the Academy for indiscipline. He was to be expelled in June 1926, for declaring his examiners in Fine Art Theory incompetent to examine him. In *The Secret Life* Dalí places this drawing, "one of my most successful of this period," at the time of his return to Figueres following his final expulsion, probably confusing this with his earlier suspension. But his cool recognition of his father's state of mind holds good: "In the expression of my father's face can be seen the mark of the pathetic bitterness which my expulsion form the Academy had produced on him."[1]

Nonetheless, the father had already seen his gifts acknowledged in group shows in Figueres and in Madrid, and was impressed by his dazzling friends such as the poet Federico García Lorca. He kept a meticulous scrapbook containing all the press cuttings and other records of young Salvador's achievements, which was scrupulously maintained until the rupture in 1929. And this portrait for which he is sitting is destined for the first real test of his son's career: the Dalmau exhibition. In December 1925, following the exhibition, he wrote a preface to the scrapbook, in which pride struggles with parental anxiety: "I should not be telling the truth if I were to deny that my son's present success pleases me, for if it should happen that my son would not be able to win an appointment to a professorship, I am told that the artistic orientation he is following is not entirely erroneous, and that however badly all this should turn out, whatever else he might take up would definitely be an even greater disaster, since my son has a gift for painting and only for painting."[2] It would not, therefore, be just already to inscribe this portrait among the images of the threatening father, from de Chirico's *The Child's Brain* (see p. 138, fig. 2) to Ernst's *Pietà* (see p. 124, see fig. 1), to which Dalí was from 1929 to refer frequently in his portrayals of the familial drama. Nonetheless, the intensity of the relationship and the manifest force of the father undoubtedly set the scene for Dalí's later insistence on the vengeful paternal imago. D.A.

[1] Salvador Dalí, *The Secret Life of Salvador Dalí* (London: Vision Press, 1968), p. 204
[2] *Ibid.*, p. 156

35. Study for "Portrait of Manuel de Falla," 1924-25
36. Study for "Portrait of my Father," 1925
37.–38. Galeries Dalmau catalogue, 1925

35. Pencil on paper
30 × 28 cm
11⁷/₈ × 16¹/₈ in.
St. Petersburg (FL),
The Salvador Dalí Museum

36. Engraving
29 × 21.5 cm
41¹/₂ × 8¹/₂ in.
Madrid, Museo Nacional
Centro de Arte Reina Sofía

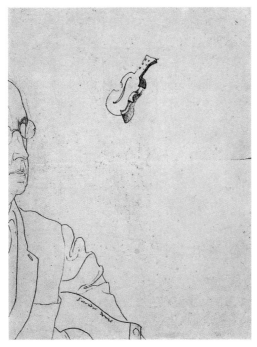

37.-38. Catalogue of the solo
exhibition held at the Galeries
Dalmau, Barcelona, November
14-27, 1925
Private collection

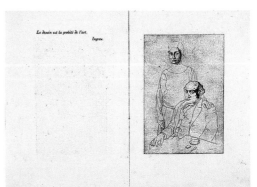

39. Don Salvador and Ana María Dalí
(Portrait of the Artist's Father and Sister), 1925

39. Pencil on Paper
50 × 33 cm
19⁵/8 × 13 in.
Madrid, Juan Abelló Collection

40. Figure at a Window, 1925

40. Oil on panel wood
103 × 75 cm
40$^{1/2}$ × 29$^{1/2}$ in.
Madrid, Museo Nacional
Centro de Arte Reina Sofía

Dalí's younger sister Ana María was a willing and favorite sitter in the 1920s, especially in the months leading up to his first solo exhibition, at the Galeries Dalmau in Barcelona (14 to 27 November 1925). It is thus not surprising that his paintings of her reflect his experiments with various figurative styles. Dalí paid special homage to Ingres in the catalogue for the exhibition and the drawing of his father and sister (cat. 39) is a superb essay in academic draftsmanship. At the same time, in the contrast between the delicately modeled faces and the simple linearity of the bodies he is looking towards Picasso's post-cubist return to the figure. In several of his paintings he explores a simplified representational technique, with smooth slightly geometrical rounded forms and flattened planes, as in *Girl resting on her elbow – Ana María Dalí, the artist's sister (Thought)*. Indeed in most of his figure paintings at this time, despite the obvious contrast with the Cubist and Purist works, there is an interest in surface pattern and abstract rhythm which derives from his avantgarde experiments. He is also exploring a wide range of earlier and contemporary figurative painting, including the Italian *novecento* artists. The critic Rafael Benet, noting the echoes of *Valori Plastici*, wrote: "Because of this Italian connection, the young man from Ampurdàn looks to us more like a decorator than a painter. In his less abstract tendency, Neo-Classicism in the manner of Casorati is apparent as well as the more "academic" tendency in the manner of Ubaldo Oppi."[1]

Among the most striking images of Ana María are those depicting her from the back. Dalí never had any difficulty in getting a likeness in his portraits, so this position was not chosen to avoid that problem. Unlike sitters who wanted a portrait, Ana María was happy to pose as one object among others, and paintings like *Figure at a Window* and *Seated Girl from the Back* give as much weight and meaning to the surroundings as to the figure. While in *Seated Girl from the Back* the rhyme of the shoulder and the building just beyond it instigates an intricate harmony of body and architecture, *Figure at a window* draws the viewer into the figure's own absorption in the sea and sky. The pose was congenial to Ana María . Every morning, during the summer holidays at Cadaqués, she posed for him: "During the hours I served him as model, I never tired of looking at the landscape which already, and forever, formed part of me. He always painted me near a window. And my eyes had time to take in all the smallest details."[2] The open window, symbol of aspiration and spiritual hope, was a familiar subject among 19th-century German romantic painters. Caspar David Friedrich depicted a very similar scene of a woman standing with her back to the painter before an open casement.

In *Figure at a window* Dalí is particularly fascinated by the curls of the hair and the folds in the dress, curtains and cloth draped over the windowsill. The movements of body and wind create the random shapes which, painted, become as fixed as the regular patterns of the waves in the bay.

Dalí took his forthcoming exhibition at the Galeries Dalmau very seriously. "The studio was filled with canvases which Salvador selected with care. The portrait of my father, my portraits, the landscapes of Cadaqués those of two of his girl friends, blonde, pretty with fair complexions."[3] The *Portrait of María Carbona* is doubtless one of those described by Ana María, and was included in the Dalmau exhibition. Dalí has confidently chosen to frame the white-clad, red-haired girl with a stark black ground against which the gleaming, black wood of the chair is a painterly tour de force. D.A.

[1] Rafael Benet, *La Veu de Catalunya*, November 27, 1925.
[2] Ana María Dalí, *Salvador Dalí visto por su hermana,* Ediciones del Cotal (Barcelona: Ediciones del Cotal, 1983), p. 111.
[3] *Ibid.*, p. 116.

41. Study for "Portrait of María Carbona"
(Dedicated to Puig Pujades), 1925

41. Leadpoint on paper
49 × 32 cm
19$^{1/4}$ × 12$^{5/8}$ in.
Montserrat, Museu
de Montserrat

42. Portrait of María Carbona, 1925

42. Oil on cardboard
52.6 × 39.2 cm
20³/4 × 15¹/2 in.
Montreal, Montreal Museum
of Fine Arts

43. Figure from the Back, 1925

43. Gouache and oil
on cardboard
74.5 × 53 cm
29 3/8 × 20 7/8 in.
Private collection

44. Figure at a Table (Portrait of my Sister), 1925

44. Oil on cardboard
46 × 48 cm
18 1/8 × 18 7/8 in.
Private collection

45. Woman Sewing (Study for "Ana María"), 1926

45. Pencil on paper
53 × 32.5 cm
$20^7/8 \times 12^3/4$
Figueres, Fundació
Gala-Salvador Dalí

46. Woman at the Window at Figueres, 1926

46. Oil on canvas
21 × 21.5 cm
8^1/4 × 8^3/8 in.
Figueres, Fundació
Gala-Salvador Dalí

47. Homage to Fra Angelico (The Birth of Christ), ca. 1926

47. Collage and ink on paper
45.5 × 36.5 cm
17⁷/₈ × 14³/₈ in.
Madrid, Fundación
Federico García Lorca

This homage to Fra Angelico is part of a fascinating series of collages that Salvador Dalí dedicated to his friend Federico García Lorca in 1925 and 1926. The folds that have remained on many of the sheets suggest that the collages were sent by post. The subjects are very specific and refer to the themes that the two young men often dealt with in a sort of complex code that reveals the depth of the relationship between them. *Buster Keaton's Wedding* (1925), for example, alludes not only to the passion for the silent cinema shared by Lorca and Dalí—especially for Keaton's film *Seven Chances*—but also to the distance separating Granada from Cadaqués, and the poetry of Joan Salvat-Papasseit, an exponent of the Catalan avant-garde movement. The *Collage of the Shoes* (1926) brings frivolity and objectivity into play, while the *Book of Varicose Veins* (1926) is concerned with the eternal dichotomy between love and death represented by varicose veins, which become a metaphor for sexual intercourse that may cause infection with syphilis.

Homage to Fra Angelico (*The Birth of Christ*), the most abstract collage of the whole series, is inspired by the visits that Dalí paid almost very day to the Museo Nacional del Prado, and also to the aesthetic of putrefaction linked to the excesses of sentimentalism. The traces of glue present on the collage

indicate that a number of elements of the upper part of the work have been lost: they are probably those representing a Madonna with a halo in pink cloth. The Virgin is receiving the three Magi, represented symbolically by three moustaches made of blue wool. In the lower part of the sheet a silver moon has remained next to a trace of glue: it is probably the last fragment of the figure of the Christ Child, at whose feet some humble straw from the stable may be noted. Dalí admired Raphael and the Netherlandish painters more than he did Fra Angelico, four of whose works are in the Prado. Nevertheless, in his eyes, the artist's naïve and highly detailed style made him a Renaissance Rousseau. It is likely, moreover, that Dalí was attracted by the blue of the draperies that appear in many of Fra Angelico's works: this is an element that has fascinated many painters and poets. For example, Rafael Alberti, a poet belonging to Dalí's and Lorca's generation, dedicated the poem "Azul" (Blue) to Fra Angelico:

"He descended to his palette. He brought with him the most secret blue of the skies.
He painted his blues while kneeling.
The angles baptized him with blue.
They called him: Blessed Blue Angelico…".
R.M.P.

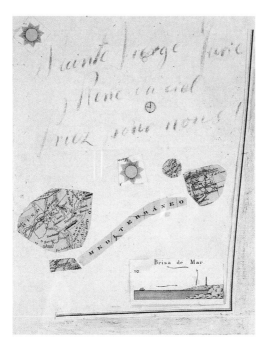

Fig. 1. Salvador Dalí,
Buster Keaton's Wedding
Madrid, Fundación
Federico García Lorca

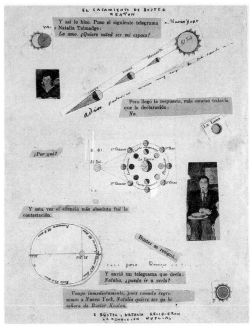

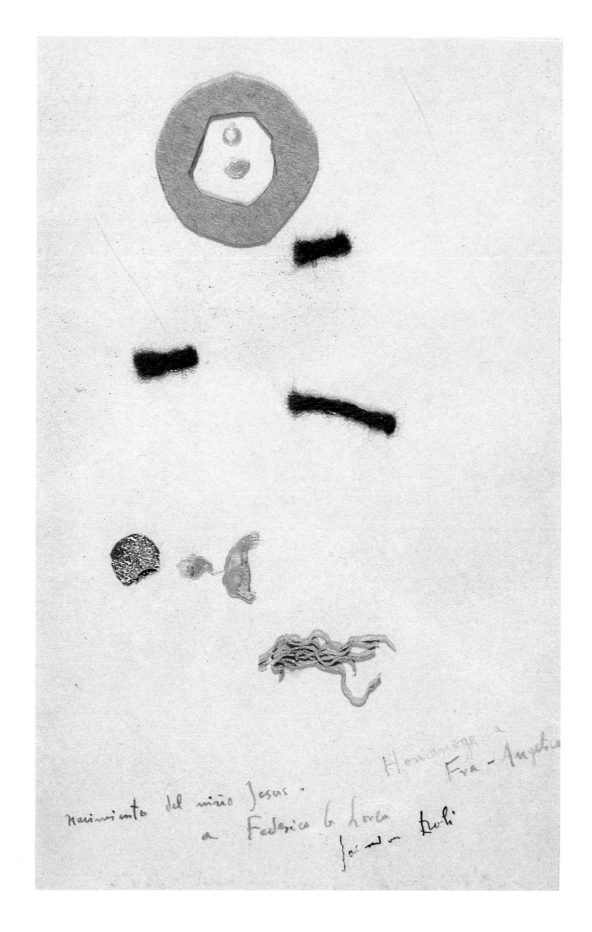

nacimiento del niño Jesus.

a Federico G Lorca

Homenage a Fra-Angelico

48. Neo-Cubist Academy (Composition with Three Figures), 1926

48. Oil on canvas
190 × 200 cm
74⁷/8 × 78³/4 in.
Montserrat, Museu
de Montserrat

Fig. 1. Bronzino, *Andrea Doria as Neptune*, ca. 1532-33
Milan, Pinacoteca di Brera

This was the largest of Dalí's early works and it dominated his second one-man show at the Galeries Dalmau in Barcelona (December 31, 1926-January 14, 1927). It was listed no. 1 in the catalogue as *Composicio amb tres figures: "Academia neocubista."* In the title, as Rafael Santos Toroella has suggested, Dalí takes revenge on the Academy of San Fernando in Madrid, from which he had finally been expelled that summer, "by bringing its name ironically up to date."[1]. However, the 'Neo-Cubist' manner of which this was the summation was only one aspect of Dalí's work at the time; he took the unusual step of dividing the paintings in the Dalmau exhibition into two separate spaces. One contained the 'cubist and neo-cubist works,' the other the 'miniaturist' ones. The latter included *Basket of Bread* (cat. 51) and *Woman at the Window at Figueres* (cat. 46), the former, *Figure on the Rocks*, as well as *Neo-Cubist Academy*.

The brief catalogue, which had no preface, contained carefully chosen quotations: from Braque: "The painter thinks in forms and colors," and from Ingres: "Consulting experience one discovers that it is by making the inventions of others familiar that one learns, in Art, to invent oneself, just as one learns to think in reading the ideas of others." Thus Dalí frankly acknowledges the influences he has been absorbing from a remarkably wide range of avant-garde and other sources.

Dalí neatly conflates the double debt both to Picasso's Cubism and his neo-classical manner in the term 'Neo-cubist.' His new Cubism is a hard-edged re-working of the voluptuous draped bathers of Picasso's apparently regressive post-war classical period. Dalí had frequently depicted Venus as a modern goddess and linked her to sailors, as in *Venus and Sailor* (cat. 31), a theme he reworks here. His Neo-Cubism, however, differs strikingly from late Cubism and Purism in his emphatic and idiosyncratic perspective: here he uses it, not to construct a fully illusionistic space, but to direct our gaze and subject the female nudes to geometric order. There are two perspectival triangles; one, formed by the left-hand nude's thigh, forms a pyramid ending in the male's sailor hat, while the other, most clearly marked rising from the lower right corner of the painting, peaks at his genitals. Dalí is clearly manipulating the resources of academic painting for ends of his own, to bring out the sexual undertones.

Santos Toroella suggests that the left-hand female nude represents Venus, or perhaps Lust, while the more modest right-hand one represents Virtue or Reflection. He interprets the painting overall as an "emblematic and metaphorical representation of the Christian Martyr Saint Sebastian, with whose drama Dalí felt himself darkly and pathetically identified."[2]. There is no doubt that Saint Sebastian played a key role in the shared fantasies of Dalí and Lorca at this time (see *Honey Is Sweeter than Blood,* p. 90, fig. 3). The sailor's hat doubles as a halo and as in many representations of Saint Sebastian, Dalí's youth has one arm held behind his back, but his unpierced body, with the other arm outstretched, recalls Apollo or Hermes. As far as visual antecedents are concerned, in fact, Dalí has drawn broadly from the rich tradition of the male nude in antique sculpture and Renaissance painting. The fact that the sailor/saint is rising from the sea even hints at a male version of Venus Anadyomene. Bronzino's portrait of *Andrea Doria as Neptune* (fig. 1) displays the male torso in a manner similar to Dalí's youth, although he is of course a much older man. Dalí is the process of inventing his own modern myth and many elements in the image carry a personal meaning.

Fig. 2. Pablo Picasso,
Studio with Plaster Head , 1925
New York, The Museum
of Modern Art
© 2004, Digital image,
The Museum of Modern Art,
New York / Scala, Firenze

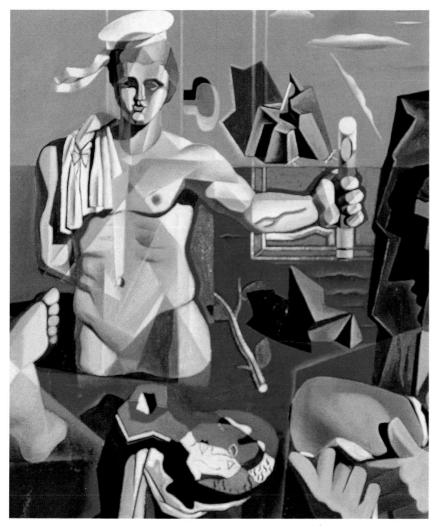

Fig. 3. Salvador Dalí
Neo-Cubist Academy (Composition with Three Figures) (detail), 1926
Montserrat, Museu
de Montserrat

duced in *L'Amic de les Arts*. Santos Toroella has suggested that it might even be one of the first instances of the 'double portrait' in which Dalí merges his own head with that of Lorca. The curious staff in the sailor's hand may represent one of the instruments or gadgets Dalí described in his text "Saint Sebastià," which measure passion or agony.

The device of the "picture within a picture" contributes to the spatial intricacy in the painting; there is a tension between the limitless vista of the sea, with the familiar elements of the rocky cliffs of Cap Creus and the beach of Es Llane, and the enclosed interior, whose moulded panellings visible in the sky are also an echo of Picasso's *Studio with Plaster Head.*

The Dalmau exhibition received considerable critical attention. Dalí's friend the poet J.F. Foix evoked the strange atmosphere of the 'phantasms' in the canvases and reported a conversation with the painter: "'Superrealism?'—'No, no.'—'Cubism?' 'No, not that either: painting, painting if you please.'"[3] Already the question of Dalí's relationship to Surrealism had arisen, and perhaps prompted Sebastià Gasch's firm insistence on a very different quality: composition, which is, he says, "at the base of all Dalí's works."[4]

Neo-Cubist Academy was reproduced on the front page of the January 1927 issue of *L'Amic de les Arts;* however, it was bought by a family acquaintance and was not shown again in public until it entered the collection of the Monastery at Montserrat in 2000. This is the first time it has been exhibited outside Spain. D.A.

The disembodied head suspended between the three figures, familiar from several works of the period such as *Still Life by Moonlight,* derives from Picasso's *Studio with Plaster Head* (1925), which Dalí saw when he visited Picasso in Paris in April 1926. It closely resembles the self-portrait drawing repro-

[1] Rafael Santos Toroella, "The Madrid Years," in Ian Gibson, *Salvador Dalí: The Early Years* (London: South Bank Centre, 1994), p. 87.

[2] *Ibid.*, p. 88.

[3] J.V. Foix, "Presentació de Salvador Dalí," *L'Amic de les Arts*, no. 10, (Sitges: January 31, 1927), p. 3.

[4] Sebastià Gasch, "Salvador Dalí," *L'Amic de les Arts*, no. 11, (Sitges: February 28, 1927, p. 16.

49. Penya-Segats (Woman by the Cliffs), 1926

49. Oil on wood
26 × 40 cm
$10^{1/4} \times 15^{3/4}$ in.
Private collection

50. Figures Lying on the Sand, 1926

50. Oil on wood
20.7 × 27.3 cm
8 1/8 × 10 3/4 in.
Figueres, Fundació
Gala-Salvador Dalí

51. The Basket of Bread, 1926

51. Oil on panel
31.5 × 31.5 cm
12¹/2 × 12¹/2 in.
St. Petersburg (FL),
The Salvador Dalí Museum

This jewel-like still life painting was made when the artist was just twenty-two years old, but already points to his lifelong interest in *trompe-l'œil* illusionism and his fascination with Old Master painting. Painted on a wood panel, whose raised surface enhances the textural effect of the lined wicker basket and its four pieces of bread, this virtuoso painting was first shown in the artist's second exhibition at the Galeries Dalmau in Barcelona in 1926-27.[1] However, the international fame of the painting was secured when it was included, along with two other works by Dalí, in the "27th International Exhibition of Paintings" at the Carnegie Institute in Pittsburgh in 1928.[2] This was the first time that the artist had shown his work in the United States and the critical and commercial success of this exhibition may have persuaded Dalí to move to America in the following decade. Although the first prize for painting went to André Derain, Dalí's meticulously rendered *The Basket of Bread* caused a stir among visitors and critics to the 1928 Carnegie exhibition, where it was favorably compared to the work of earlier masters of the still life genre such as Michelangelo Merisi da Caravaggio and Francisco de Zurbarán. The reference to Zurbarán was particularly convincing, since the Spanish artist often included a remarkably similar motif combining a woven basket and a crumpled white cloth in paintings such as *The Annunciation*, of 1638-39 (fig. 1).

The use of strong chiaroscuro and heightened realism in *The Basket of Bread* is a clear reference to the 17th-century Spanish tradition of *bodegones* (eating houses), in which artists such as Zurbarán and Sánchez Cotán depicted commonplace things like food, drink, and kitchen utensils with such clarity and emotional force that they became transformed and transfigured into objects of mystery and contemplation. This type of painting had originated in Northern Europe around the middle of the 16th-century, and toward 1600 it was widely practiced in Italy, where the genre was enriched by the unmitigated realism of Caravaggio and his followers. Spanish artists such as Velázquez and Zurbarán drew on the pictorial techniques of Italian and Netherlandish art in their own still life paintings, which typically used dark and austere background settings to dramatically focus attention on the inanimate objects being depicted. These items of food or drink were also bathed in a strong light that imbued them with an aura of mystery and religious intensity. Dalí's extensive academic training would have brought him into contact with this *bodegon* tradition of Spanish Golden Age painting, which he replicates in the technical brilliance of his work, but also updates, and even violates, through the imposition of his own secular obsessions and neuroses.

As Dalí explained in a catalogue note for his 1945 exhibition at the Bignou Gallery in New York, "bread has always been one of the oldest fetishistic and obsessive subjects in my work, the one to which I have remained the most faithful."[3] A symbol of nutrition with fetishistic and sacred overtones for the artist, bread would become a recurring motif in his work after this time, appearing in paintings such as *Anthropomorphic Bread*, of 1932, and *Two Pieces of Bread Expressing the Sentiment of Love*, of 1940 (cat. 188), as well as in the object assemblage *Retrospective Bust of a Woman*, of 1933, which famously featured a loaf of French bread balanced precariously on the head of the porcelain figure. But as the artist explained in his statement for the Bignou Gallery exhibition, "this typically realistic picture [*The Basket of Bread*] is the one which has satisfied my imagination the most. Here is a painting about which there is nothing to explain. The total enigma!"[4] M.R.T.

[1] The painting was shown under the title of *Panera del pa* in the "Exposicio S. Dalí," held at the Galeries Dalmau, Barcelona, December 31, 1926-January 14, 1927, catalogue number 5.
[2] The catalogue of the "Twenty-Seventh International Exhibition of Paintings," held at the Carnegie Institute, Pittsburgh, from October 18-December 9, 1928, lists three paintings by Salvador Dalí Y Doménech: 361 *Basket of Bread*; 362 *Ana María* ; 363 *Seated Girl* (lent by Pedro Corominas). These works were shown in the Spanish section in Gallery 7. The portrait of Ana María was the only work by Dalí to be illustrated in the exhibition catalogue, which gives Dalí's address as Calle de Monturiol 24, Figueres, Spain.
[3] Salvador Dalí, artist's statement in *Recent Paintings by Salvador Dalí*, exh. cat., The Bignou Gallery, New York, November 20-December 29, 1945, n.p.
[4] *Ibid.*

Fig. 1. Francisco de Zurbarán,
The Annunciation, 1638-39
Grenoble, Musée de Grenoble

52. Mannequin (Barcelona Mannequin), 1926-27

52. Oil on canvas
198 × 148 cm
77⁷/₈ × 58¹/₄
Figueres, Fundació
Gala-Salvador Dalí, gift
of Dalí to the Spanish State

Fig. 1. Picasso, *Harlequin*, 1923
Paris, Musée national d'Art moderne
Centre Georges Pompidou

Fig. 2. Salvador Dalí, *Self-portrait*,
(*L'Amic de les Arts*, January 1927,
p. 3)

This large canvas was reproduced, together with *Figures Lying on the Sand* (cat. 50) in *L'Amic de les Arts* in February 1927, under the title "La Maniquí." Unlike *Figures Lying on the Sand*, however, it had not been included in Dalí's two week exhibition at the Galeries Dalmau (December 31–January 14), which suggests that it had not been completed in time for the exhibition that included closely related works such as *Still Life (Naturaleza muerta "Invitacion al sueño")* 1926.

It was probably one of the last paintings Dalí completed before beginning his military service in February 1927, although this did not interrupt too severely his creative activities, as he did the designs for two theater productions: Adrià Gual's *The Family of Harlequin* and Lorca's *Mariana Pineda*, in March and June, and in July published in *L'Amic de les Arts* his text "Saint Sebastià." In October, at the Autumn Salon in Barcelona, he showed *Gadget and Hand* and *Honey Is Sweeter than Blood*, paintings that mark a dramatic shift away from the influence of Picasso and *Valori Plastici*. It is interesting that the 1926 *Still Life*, which was reproduced in the catalogue for the Dalmau exhibition, already includes the strange construction, like a three-dimensional set square propped on a staff, which was to become the central figure in *Apparatus and Hand*. He had thus already begun to develop his idea of the 'gadgets' that measure Saint Sebastian's pain and pleasure (see p. 90, fig. 1). Their origin in de Chirico's Mannequins is suggested in the clearly anthropomorphic character of the geometrical figure in *Still Life*. The staff on which it leans may also be the first appearance of what was to become the famous supporting crutch of so many of his later paintings.

The Mannequin here, however, is a strange creature, heavily sexualized though ambiguous as to gender. The painting hums with references to both Dada and to Picasso's later Cubism. While the sources can be tracked, the real interest is in what Dalí makes of them. Although this is a painting, the influence of Max Ernst's collages, such as *Sacred Conversation*, or those for the book of collages and poems Ernst made with Paul Eluard, *Répétitions* (1921), is evident. In *Sacred Conversation*, the nude figure is constructed partially of human and partially of objects and other creatures. A bird covers or replaces the genitals, just as a fish does in *Mannequin*, and its sexual symbolism is equally evident, if carrying differ-

ent personal associations. The multiple outlines of the figure in *Mannequin* resemble Picasso's late cubist works such as the 1923 *Harlequin* where the face of Harlequin is repeated in both linear curves and flat planes (fig. 1). But the strong black shadow that creates an additional silhouette also harks back to Francis Picabia's work of ca. 1922-23, especially the covers for the 1923 series of the dada review *Littérature* (see p. 110, fig. 4). Picabia had an exhibition at the Galeries Dalmau in 1922, and although it is unknown if Dalí actually visited this exhibition, he would certainly have been aware of him and have seen reproductions of his work. Whether Dalí was aware of the full drama of Picabia's scornful reaction to Picasso's return to Neo-Realist figuration following the abstractions of early Cubism, and the way he mocks it in his parody of classical drawing, yoked to flat posterlike outlines, as in the cover for *Littérature* (15 October 1923), is unclear.

What is striking in Dalí's painting is a vigorous and unashamed eclecticism that he turns to wholly individual ends. Although the gestures of the Mannequin, the breasts and the high heeled shoe all point to a female figure, the head is divided between a female profile to the left, and a profile with prominent ear to the right which resembles Dalí's numerous self-portrait drawings of the period, of which several were reproduced in Spanish periodicals (fig. 2). The 'shadow' outlines of the head derive from 1925 drawings by Picasso. Dalí is, therefore, turning the formal ambiguities of Picasso's Cubism into an image of explicit sexuality but ambiguous gender. The doubling effects in both Picabia's and Picasso's work, the overlappings and repetitions of shapes for largely formal ends, are taken literally by Dalí as he juxtaposes his own head with the mannequin.

De Chirico was hailed by Breton as the creator, with Apollinaire, of a 'modern mythology': the pioneer in the exploration of the objects of a new poetry to be found in fashion and in the street, juxtaposed in startling ways. His mannequins, modern versions of the classical statue, inhabit mysterious and sometimes theatrical settings. Dalí pushes the 'uncanny' quality of the mannequin even further in his mingling of 'real' and dummy figures. His/her gestures also evoke not only the typical pose of a model but also the dance crazes that swept Europe in the 1920s, adding an additional hint of animation. D.A.

53. Study for "Honey Is Sweeter than Blood," 1927

53. Oil on panel
36 × 45.4 cm
15 1/8 × 17 7/8 in.
Paris, Private collection

Fig. 1. Salvador Dalí,
Apparatus and Hand, 1927
St. Petersburg (FL), The Salvador
Dalí Museum

Fig. 2. Bruegel the Elder,
Triumph of Death (detail), ca. 1562
Madrid, Museo Nacional del Prado

The arresting title and the unprecedented imagery of the painting for which this is a study already announce the unique voice Dalí was to bring to Surrealism. However, although Dalí was aware at this period of the Surrealists' interest in the unconscious and experiments with automatism, and had tried his hand at automatic drawing, he still asserted his independence. In the summer of 1927, he excitedly announced the inauguration of "a new orbit, equidistant between Cubism and Surrealism on the one hand and a primitive art such as the Breughels' on the other."[1] Dalí's reference to Breughel as a primitive already signals his difference from both Cubists and Surrealists, whose embrace of 'primitive art' implied non-Western: in the case of Cubism, African sculpture, and in the case of the Surrealists, Pacific and North West Coast carvings. The fantastic imagery of Breughel or of Bosch, familiar to Dalí from the Prado, was a significant model if not a direct source for the original blend of the local, the personal and the avant-garde in *Honey Is Sweeter than Blood*. Perhaps under Dalí's influence, Breughel the Elder's *Triumph of Death* (fig. 2) was reproduced in the same issue of *L'Amic de les Arts* (October 1927) as *Honey Is Sweeter than Blood*. Although this key picture was never exhibited in Paris, it achieved international fame when it appeared in the journal *Documents* in 1929 (fig. 3).[2]

The Study shares much of the strange iconography of *Honey Is Sweeter than Blood*: the abstract constructions or 'gadgets,' headless, bleeding female torso, rotting donkey and fragments of anatomical and plantlike shapes. Especially prominent in the Study is the head of the poet Federico García Lorca, Dalí's closest friend and collaborator, who spent July with him in Cadaqués and gave *Honey Is Sweeter than Blood* its original title, *The Wood of Gadgets*. On leaving Cadaqués he wrote to Dalí nostalgically: "From where I am I can hear (how sad it makes me, dearest chap!) the soft trickle of blood from the Sleeping Beauty of the Wood of Gadgets…"[3] Behind Lorca's allusions lie an extensive private set of references which focus on the figure of Saint Sebastian, a long-standing shared obsession. In July Dalí published the extraordinary text he had been working on since the Spring, 'Sant Sebastià,' in which he talks of: "precise instruments belonging to an unknown physics… *Distilled Gadgets.*"[4] Dalí identifies the Saint both with Lorca and with himself, signing a letter to him "your SAINT SEBASTIAN." But the Saint's pain, for Dalí, is "a mere pretext for an aesthetics of objectivity." In accord with his espousal of a hygienic modernity, bolstered by a horror of sentimentality and emotional entanglement, Dalí propounds his notion of objectivity, symbolized in the gadgets that ironically measure "Pure aesthetic values" and "Pure sensual values."

Fig. 3. Salvador Dalí, *Honey Is Sweeter than Blood*, 1927
location unknown

Honey Is Sweeter than Blood seems to have been a catch phrase that haunted Dalí; he adds it as subtitle to his text "Le meva amiga i la platja" (November 1927) and recalls chanting this 'marvellous cry' (inverted) while running through the streets of Madrid: "Blood is sweeter than HONEY." He also ascribed it to Lídia Noguer (see Encyclopedia) the widow of a fisherman of Cadaqués, who according to Dalí had "a marvellously paranoiac brain" and "was capable of establishing completely coherent relations between any subject whatsoever and her obsession of the moment."[5] In *The Secret Life* he describes an incident when Lídia eviscerates a still bleeding chicken on a table where he has placed an expensive book of Bellini drawings. When Dalí anxiously intervenes, Lídia comments "Blood does not spot," and then "Blood is sweeter than honey. I am blood, and honey is all the other women!"[6] Dalí places this memory after his encounter with Gala, but the phrase evidently has its origins earlier. Again in the *Secret Life* Dalí described the solitary pleasures of masturbation as "sweeter than honey…" while Lorca regarded sexual intercourse as a fearful "jungle of blood."[7] The accumulation of motifs around this double anxiety of the threat posed by the female sex and the guilt of masturbation was to reach a climax in the paintings of 1929 such as *Lugubrious Game*.

In the Study, the poet's head, bisected by the horizon, its veins visible and eyes closed, lies opposite a headless female torso. Absent from the Study, however, is Dalí's own head, which appears in the final painting as a simplified angular form to the right of the central 'gadget.' Advancing to the foreground is an irregular line of 'eye-tacks' or nails, invoking the Saint Sebastian theme, which form geometrical rows in the final painting. The slanting horizon bristles with white stakes, veins like corals and the uncanny constructions (or 'gadgets') which have precedents in the work of de Chirico, Max Ernst and Yves Tanguy. Dalí's fa-

Fig. 4. José Bello,
Putrefacts, 1927-28
Madrid, Fundación Federico
García Lorca

Fig. 5. Federico García Lorca,
Putrefact, 1927
Madrid, Fundación Federico
García Lorca

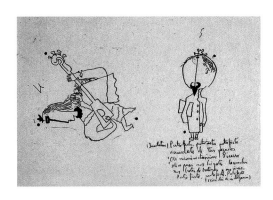

miliarity with Yves Tanguy is also evident in the hovering shapes and the ambiguity of a landscape that might also be a sea-bed.

The rotting donkey invokes the notion of the *putrefact*, a rich seam of satire mined in numerous drawings by the group in the Residencia de Estudiantes in Madrid which included Dalí, Lorca and Pepin Bello who was credited with inventing the term. Under the guise of the *putrefact* Dalí and his friends mocked the values of the bourgeois and traditional society they despised. The origin of the 'putrefying' donkey itself lies in a sentimental tale by the 'arch putrefact' as Dalí called him, the poet Juan Ramon Jimenez: *Platero y Yo* recounts the life and death of a beloved donkey, which Dalí mercilessly depicts here covered in flies. The rotting donkey became an icon of horror and repulsion in

Dalí and Buñuel's film *Un Chien andalou.*
Honey Is Sweeter than Blood and a closely related picture, *Gadget and Hand,* provoked a scandal when they were exhibited at the 1927 Autumn Salon at the Sala Pares in Barcelona. The critics found these paintings mystifying, obscure and probably Surrealist. Dalí counter-attacked in a text inserted in the Catalan avant-garde review *L'Amic de les Arts*, contrasting the 'naturalness' of his pictures with 'artistic' painting. His own paintings, 'anti-artistic and direct,' are "marvellously and totally understood by the children and fishermen of Cadaqués."[8] D.A.

[1] Letter to José Maria Junoy, quoted in Ian Gibson, *The Shameful Life of Salvador Dalí* (London: Faber & Faber, 1997), p. 162.
[2] The whereabouts of *Honey Is Sweeter than Blood* are unknown; it is now thought to have been destroyed. It was bought by the Duchess of Lerma from a group exhibition in the Botanical Gardens in Madrid in 1929.
[3] Federico García Lorca, Letter to Dalí, quoted in Ian Gibson, *The Shameful Life*, p. 164.
[4] "Sant Sebastià," *L'Amic de les Arts* (Sitges), July 1927.
[5] Salvador Dalí, *The Secret Life of Salvador Dalí*, trans. Haakon Chevalier (London: Vision Press, 1968), p. 265.
[6] *Ibid.*, p. 298.
[7] Ian Gibson, *The Shameful Life,* p. 165.
[8] "Els meus Quadros del Saló de Tardor," *L'Amic de les Arts* (Sitges: October 1927).

54. Untitled (Study for "Honey Is Sweeter than Blood"), 1926
55. Untitled, 1926
56. Untitled, 1926

54. Ink on paper
36.5 × 45 cm
14$^{3/8}$ × 17$^{5/8}$ in.
New York (NY), The Museum
of Modern Art
© 2004, Digital image,
The Museum of Modern Art,
New York / Scala, Firenze

55. Ink on paper
17 × 20 cm
6$^{3/4}$ × 7$^{7/8}$ in.
Private collection

56. Ink on paper
6 × 19 cm
2$^{3/8}$ × 7$^{1/2}$ in.
Private collection

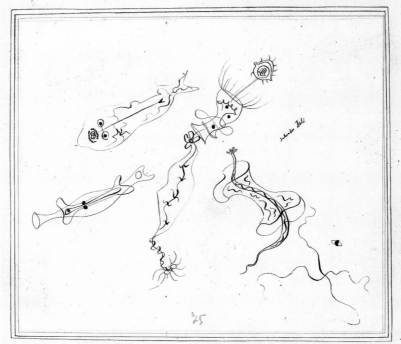

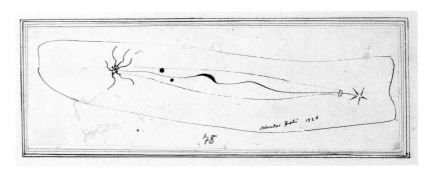

57. Unsatisfied Desires, 1928

57. Oil, seashells,
and sand on cardboard
76 × 62 cm
29 7/8 × 24 1/2 in.
San Francisco (CA), San
Francisco Museum of Modern
Art; fractional, gift of Jan
and Mitsuko Shrem, Clos Pegase
Winery Collection

The bather was a favorite subject for Dalí through the 1920s, and as with Picasso and Miró was often the opportunity to introduce eroticism. The visualization of desire is especially interesting in the context of the continuing dialogue between Abstraction and Realism in the avant-garde of the 1920s. The embrace of automatism in Miró's hands had led in the direction of a biomorphic abstraction in which the human body could be manipulated at will, often with enlarged, swelling feet and other organs. In paintings such as *Unsatisfied desires* or the closely related *Bather* (1928, see p. 52, fig. 3). Dalí turns his fragmented and distorted bodies into anatomies of desire. In *Unsatisfied Desires*, rather than depicting a passively voluptuous nude, he presents active, if abstracted, bodies, engaged in a sexual encounter but at a distance. Two pink anatomical forms, disturbing lumps of erect flesh, confront each other on an empty beach, which is literally represented with sand, little pebbles and shells. Towering into the sky, like a ghostly rock, is the rough outline of an enormous and unmistakably phallic big toe. Dalí was to discuss the disturbing character of the 'isolated finger' in an important text in *L'Amic de les Arts* in March 1929 (see p. 102, fig. 1). However, despite the explicitly sexualized forms they are not straightforwardly identifiable as male and female; the contracted form on the left, both hand and genitals, frames ruby lips, while the bulbous shape on the right, which prefigures the scene in *Un Chien andalou* when breasts suddenly mutate into buttocks, spurts red. It could be that Dalí is already experimenting with the idea of sex without physical contact which he later baptized 'Cledalism' (see Encyclopedia).

Dalí's bodies, unlike the biomorphic forms of Miró and Arp, cast shadows and thus introduce a spatial ambiguity into the painting, which is partially flat and partially illusionistic. Similarly the sand both adds materiality and texture to the surface as it had in Picasso's later Cubism but also clearly stands for itself, anchoring the scene to Cadaqués, whose beaches were its source. Dalí may also have been aware of André Masson's sand paintings of the mid 1920s (see. p. 104, fig. 1). Masson, inspired by the sand patterns left by retreating tides, covered areas of his paintings randomly with glue and then sprinkled on them layers of sand, which he subsequently developed into complete images.

In the autumn of 1928, Dalí sent *Unsatisfied Desires,* then entitled *Two Figures on a Beach,* to the "Autumn Salon" at the Sala Peres in Barcelona. This picture was rejected by the director Maragall, because, apparently, of its unacceptably explicit representation of sexual organs. The gallery owner Dalmau, who had given Dalí his first one-man exhibition in 1925, agreed to hang it in his annual

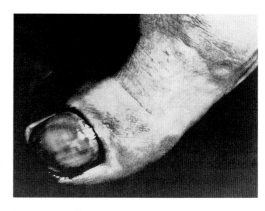

Fig. 1. J.A. Boiffard, *Big Toe*, 1929

"Inaugural Exhibition" in October, together with *Female Figure and Masculine Figure on a Beach* and the collage-object, *Female Nude* (cat. 58). However, he too got cold feet and, taking a cue from Dalí's *Female Nude*, a curvilinear lump of cork, suspended a piece of cork over the male figure in *Unsatisfied Desires*. "Nothing so logical," as Gasch commented to Miró about the incident, "as hanging a piece of cork over the PYRAMIDAL member."[1] (see cat. 58). D.A.

[1] Fèlix Fanés, *Salvador Dalí. La construcción de la imagen, 1925-1930* (Madrid: Electa, 1999), p. 125.

58. Female Nude (1928)

58. The artist's name
is printed on paper and
affixed to the canvas
Oil, cork and rope on canvas
70.5 × 60 cm / 27³/4 × 23⁵/8 in.
Collection William B. Jordan
and Robert Dean Brownlee

Fig. 1. Salvador Dalí,
Anthropomorphic Beach, 1928
St. Petersburg (FL), The Salvador
Dalí Museum

Fig. 2. Joan Miró,
Relief Construction, 1930
New York, The Museum
of Modern Art
© 2004, Digital image,
The Museum of Modern Art,
New York / Scala, Firenze

Salvador Dalí's *Female Nude* (1928), or *Nu feminí* in Catalan, is one of a small group of works, like *Anthropomorphic Beach* (1928; fig. 1), that employ a cork relief on canvas to represent the female body. It is a painting that anticipates the Surrealist objects of symbolic function destined to become such a focus of interest in 1931 on the part of Alberto Giacometti, Dalí and Joan Miró. In Dalí's *Female Nude* the cork relief stands in for the nude woman's body: it is soft and tactile, inviting us to touch it, and replaces the pictorial representation of the woman's flesh. This is a more literal than metaphoric substitution, for beneath the piece of cork is a conventional representation of a nude by the sea. In this way, the cork blocks our visual perception of this scene and replaces it with a tactile equivalent. The cork is bound with cords to the surface of the canvas, and additionally fixed from behind by two wood screws. There is a slit in the center of the cork relief suggesting the possibility of seeing a glimpse of the hidden scene through the cork. At the same time, the slit may be read as referring to the sex of the female body represented by the piece of cork. If we compare *Female Nude* with the *Anthropomorphic Beach*, the full extent of Dalí's literal treatment of the female body as tactile and fetishistic object of desire is apparent so that the cork becomes both the sex of woman and her voluptuous body. *Female Nude* may be compared with Joan Miró's *Relief Construction* (1930; fig. 2), which it anticipates and with which it shares a similar subject, though Miró arguably is more in dialogue with Jean Arp's reliefs than with Dalí's cork paintings.[1]

Female Nude figured prominently in the controversial events surrounding Dalí's exhibitions in the autumn of 1928. Dalí planned to exhibit another painting, *Diàleg a la platja* (later known as *Les désirs inassouvis / Unsatisfied Desires*), at the "Autumn Salon" scheduled to take place in October at Joan Maragall's Sala Parés in Barcelona. Maragall, however, tactfully refused the painting because of its erect phallic finger, that is on the grounds of its obscenity. Dalí then protested in a letter dated October 4, 1928. The final agreement was that Dalí withdrew the painting, but, as a compromise, Maragall bought and exhibited another painting, *Big Thumb, Beach, Moon and Decaying Bird* (1928; fig. 3), and Dalí agreed to give his lecture scheduled for October 16: "Contemporary Catalan Art Related to the Most Recent and Young Intelligence," which alone guaranteed to generate controversy.[2]

Also on the October 4, 1928, Dalí wrote to Josep Dalmau proposing the exhibition of the rejected painting. Dalmau, responding on October 6 and again on October 10, agreed to exhibit the work only following the closing of Maragall's exhibition, and accordingly delayed the opening of the exhibition until October 28.[3] Dalí's father, however, intervened with a letter (October 21, 1928) to Dalmau

urging him not to exhibit the painting.[4] Dalmau's plan was to exhibit *Unsatisfied Desires* along with another sand painting, *Feminine and Masculine Figures on a Beach* [*Dues figures en una platja*], and the cork painting *Female Nude* in the forthcoming Inaugural exhibition opening the new, 1928-29 season of exhibitions. After receiving the letter from Dalí's father, Dalmau had second thoughts; then he wrote to Dalí (October 26, 1928) explaining how he had applied a similar piece of cork as the one in *Female Nude* to hide the offending bits of *Unsatisfied Desires*.[5] Dalí immediately protested. Writing back the same day (October 26, 1928), he argued that any alteration of the work would destroy it and that clearly, from now on, he could no longer exhibit in Barcelona.[6]

Dalmau's catalogue listed all three works, with *Nu feminí* as exh. cat. 20; the offending painting was indicated as *Dues figures en una platja* and listed as exh. cat. 21.[7] The press response to the exhibition is revealing. Rafael Benet's review in *Gaseta de les Arts* (Barcelona) reproduced *Figura masculina i figura feminina en una platja* (Dalmau, exh. cat. 19), and praised Dalí for his intensity even if this was perhaps a quality which undermined a total work of art.[8] Sebastià Gasch made specific mention of the presence of the materials cork (indirectly referring to *Female Nude*) and sand in his *L'Amic de les Arts* (Sitges) review, where he wrote of the anti-pictorial nature of Dalí's materials: "One must mention, besides, in the Ampurdànese painter's recent works, the constant use of extra-pictorial materials: sand and cork." He immediately went on to link these materials with anti-painting, that is Miró and Dalí's discourse on the assassination of painting. "Procedure totally driven out, nearly to the antipodes, away from the ends now used by painters. Procedure neatly ANTI-PICTORIAL. Here we are already in front of the famous assassination of art."[9]

In the days preceding the opening of the Inaugural exhibition, Dalí wrote to Dalmau (October 19, 1928), specifically referring to *Female Nude*, "The cork [painting] is the *Nu féminin*: one of the things that I most esteem for the purity of expression that I belive it contains. Watch out that no one badly treats it."[10] It is clear from this passage that Dalí highly valued this work, though he perhaps missed the irony of insisting on the care and protection of a work of anti-art made up of non-artistic materials.

Female Nude was again exhibited in March 1929 in a group exhibition of avant-garde Spanish artists resident in Paris presented at the Jardín Botánico in Madrid. Though Dalí had yet to move to Paris, he was represented by two works from the Dalmau show, *Desnudo de Mujer* [*Female Nude*] (exh. cat. 57) and *Figura masculina y figura feminina en una playa* [*Feminine and Masculine Figures on a Beach*] (exh. cat. 59), as well as three other new works: *Aparato y mano* [*Apparatus and Hand*] (exh. cat. 55;

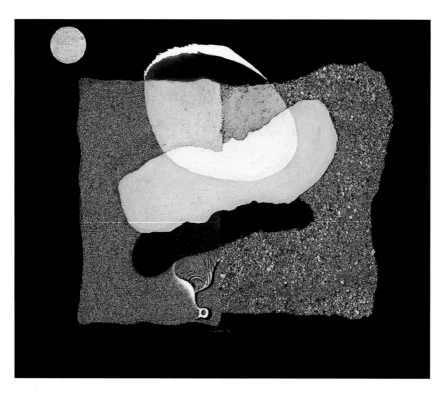

Fig. 3. Salvador Dalí, *Big Thumb,*
Beach, Moon and Decaying Bird, 1928
St. Petersburg (FL), The Salvador
Dalí Museum

Salvador Dalí Museum), *Los esfuerzos estériles*
[*Sterile Efforts*] (exh. cat. 56) and *La Miel es más*
dulce que la sangre [*Honey is Sweeter then Blood*]
(exh. cat. 58).[11] This selection must have made a
shocking impact in conservative Madrid. And *Fe-*
male Nude was one of the works, which prompted
the ire of the conservative critic Juan Farragut. His
article in *Nuevo Mundo* (Madrid) reproduced the
painting, and the text made specific reference to the
material cork as a means of dismissing it: "…that a
piece of cork nailed to a canvas would be a female
nude—'your cork grandmother,' as the gypsies
say—;…" *Female Nude*, like the rest of the exhibition, was rejected as either neurotic humor or as
avant-garde fashion: "Holy vanguard art, that will
make humanity joyous and optimistic, and with the
tonic of laughter will cure a legion of melancholics
and neurotics, that today nourish the practices of
the psychiatrists."[12] This reviewer missed the obvious poetic substitution of a curvilinear piece of cork
for the body of a woman, and, presumably, had he
understood the reference he would have found the
work all the more objectionable.

The more sympathetic Gasch again turned his attention to *Female Nude* in his April 1930 article devoted to Dalí in *Cahiers de Belgique* (Brussels),
where the painting was again reproduced. Though
Gasch made neither specific reference to this work
nor to its materials, he frames Dalí's recent works
and writings as anti-art; at precisely the point where
it is reproduced, he writes, "His works, as we have
seen, were therefore an exact dosage of form and
poetry. Meanwhile, the increasing desire for lyrical

liberty has totally seized him, [and] this painter has
finished by escaping from all formal preoccupations. In the struggle between form and poetry, the
latter finally has triumphed. And Salvador Dalí's
present works are born." That *Female Nude* was the
most recent work reproduced, and given its erroneous dating in the caption as 1929, confirms the
likelihood that the above comments refer specifically to this work. Gasch continued, drawing attention
to Dalí's writings, "This painter, and talented writer,
has issued alongside his recent works, violent pamphlets against painting, pamphlets which aroused in
our country vehement protests against an attitude
considered contradictory."[13]

The 1930 reproduction of this painting in *Cahiers*
de Belgique introduces a problem into its history as
it has been understood to date, and provides new
evidence that the conceptual intention of the work
remained constant despite later minor restora-
tions. Sotheby's (London) 1997 sale catalogue reported the following history, "Executed in 1928
(first state), modified by Dalí in 1970 (final state).
The central element in the first state of *Female*
Nude was composed of some type of cork and
plastic float, which over the years was lost or possibly deteriorated. André-François Petit, who acquired this work from Paul Éluard's daughter Cécile, took *Female Nude* to Dalí in 1970 who recti-
fied it using the present piece of cork and added
the printed artist's name. Not knowing that he
would later rectify the present work, Dalí made a
variant of *Female Nude* in 1964 (see: Descharnes &
Néret, no. 1224)."[14] There are two problems with
this account. First, the current state of the cork appears the same as the reproductions of the work in
1929 and 1930. Further the reproductions indicate
that the relief was cork and not partially plastic as
suggested in the entry. Second, in the 1930 reproduction the paper printed with the artist's name is
already present. Robert Descharnes reproduces
the painting with no cork, revealing the under-
painting, and with a signature in the lower right,
there being no printed name.[15] As early as 1930,
when it was reproduced in *Cahiers de Belgique*,
this signature must have disappeared in favor of
the printed paper. Given these two points, we
must speculate that by 1970 the cork had detached
from the canvas and perhaps also the paper had
deteriorated. Dalí then probably re-affixed the
cork to the canvas and perhaps also replaced the
printed piece of paper with his name. This means
that there was no conceptual modification of the
work in 1970, even if minor restoration took place.
Dalí may have made the variant version in 1964
(Descharnes & Néret exh. cat. 1224), because of
the detached cork, though, beyond this, his moti-
vation for making this replica is not clear.

We know the full provenance for *Female Nude*. Following Éluard, his daughter Cécile and Petit, it was

Fig. 4. Salvador Dalí in front of his house in Port Lligat, 1930s

sold at Sotheby's (1997) to Guillermo de Osma (Madrid), who then presented it in ARCO in 1998.[16] Subsequent to the Sotheby's sale, the cork became detached in transit. In 1999 it was re-affixed by Philip Young Paintings Conservation (London). The conservation report noted that the painting was lined (it is not clear when) and the cork had been fixed by two wood screws fixed through the canvas from behind. Young concluded, "Whether or not this is the original method [of fixing] or a subsequent adaptation is unclear at this stage." He further noted, "the general slackness and undulation in the canvas which may partly be a result of the lining and canvas tension but also of the stresses and strains on the canvas with a relatively heavy piece of solid cork attached directly to it." Based on the art historical and material evidence, we might speculate that the lining, and perhaps the wood screws, was likely added in 1970 at the time that Dalí re-affixed the original cork. In 1999, or shortly thereafter, it was acquired by the current owner. W.J.

[1] See my *Dalí and Miró, circa 1928* (St. Petersburg, Florida: Salvador Dalí Museum, 2003), p. 23 and "La conscience malheureuse de Miró: sculptures et objets, 1930-32" in *Joan Miró* (Paris: Musée National d'Art Moderne Centre Georges Pompidou, 2004).

[2] Rafael Santos i Torroella, *Salvador Dalí i el Saló de Tardor: Un episodi de la vida artística barcelonina el 1928* (Barcelona: Reial Acadèmia Catalana de Belles Arts de Sant Jordi, 1985), pp. 13-16.

[3] *Ibid.*, pp. 17-21.

[4] *Ibid.*, pp. 17-18, 25-26.

[5] *Ibid.*, pp. 27-29.

[6] *Ibid.*, pp. 29-31. It appears the painting was exhibited, but Fèlix Fanés and Joan Minguet suggest Dalí may have withdrawn the painting some days following the opening.

[7] Galeries Dalmau, *Exposició Inaugural, Temporada* 1928-29 (Barcelona), October 22-November 6, 1928.

[8] "Perhaps Dalí's delicate and provocative sensibility made it impossible for intensity to take the form of a more *total* concept of the art of painting." Rafael Benet, "A l'entorn de la inaugural de can Dalmau," *Gaseta de les Arts*, vol. I, no. 3, (Barcelona: November 1928), p. 12.

[9] Sebastià Gasch, "Inaugural de les Galeries Dalmau," *L'Amic de les Arts*, vol. III, no. 30 (Sitges: December 1928), p. 237.

[10] Rafael Santos Torroella, 1985, *op. cit.*, p. 24.

[11] "Exposición de pintura y esculturas de Españoles residentes en Paris" (Madrid: Jardín Botánico, March 20-25, 1928).

[12] Juan Farragut, "La Exposición del Botánico y la triste farsa del vanguardismo español," *Nuevo Mundo* (Madrid: March 29, 1929).

[13] Sebastià Gasch, "Salvador Dalí," *Cahiers de Belgique*, vol. III, no. 4, (Brussels: April 1930), pp. 128-129.

[14] Impressionist and Modern Art Part II, including Property from the collection of André-François Petit, Paris (London: Sotheby's, Wednesday, June 25, 1997), Lot 219, pp. 144-145.

[15] Robert Descharnes and Gilles Néret, Dalí: *The Paintings* (Cologne: Taschen, [1993], 2001), exh. cat. 288, p. 131.

[16] ARCO '98, "Feria internacional de Arte Contempoáneo" (Madrid: IFEMA, Feria de Madrid, 1998), p. 241. For a more complete listing of the exhibition history see *Sothebys*, 1997, *op. cit.*

59. Cenicitas (Little Ashes), 1928

59. Oil on panel
68 × 48 cm
26³/4 × 18⁷/8 in.
Madrid, Museo Nacional,
Centro de Arte Reina Sofía

Cenicitas is one of the most striking of the paintings in Dalí's new manner that dated from the summer of 1927. This was a highly individual experimental period when a private dialogue with his close friend Federico García Lorca intersected with Dalí's well-informed exploration of the avant-garde. Later that year, Dalí wrote to Lorca that he was painting pictures that "make me die of happiness; I'm inventing in a way which is purely natural, without a trace of artistic consideration… now I'm painting a beautiful woman, smiling, convulsed with multi-colored feathers…and there are donkeys in the sky with heads of tiny parrots…"[1] The stylistic clashes—a meticulously painted, academic nude torso contrasting with the rudimentary, even caricature-like birds and donkey, and the Purist-style guitars—confirm Dalí's claim to be melding Cubism, Surrealism and "a Breughel-like Primitivism."

Cenicitas was originally known as *The Birth of Venus*, but was exhibited under the title *Sterile Efforts* in a collective exhibition of painting and sculpture by Spanish artists resident in Paris at the Botanical Gardens in Madrid in March 1929. Under the same title, *Les efforts stériles*, Dalí included it in his first one-man exhibition at the Goemans Gallery in Paris in November 1929, where it is dated 1926, and again at his 1931 exhibition in the Pierre Colle Gallery, where it is dated 1927. However, it seems likely that Dalí worked on it over the winter 1927-28. It is signed and dated 1928. The picture was in Dalí's own collection at his death in 1989.

As in *Honey Is Sweeter than Blood* and *Apparatus and Hand,* a swarm of objects and fragments of figures proliferate in a minimal landscape, dominated by a large pink torso swinging across the horizon between two heads identifiable as Dalí, to the right, and Lorca on the far left, his eyes closed, in sleep or in imitation of death. The female torso spouts blood that forms a geometric shape on the ground. Lorca wrote to Dalí shortly after leaving him: "The decap-itated woman is the finest imaginable poem on the theme of blood."[2]

The horizon line and intense blue sky recall Miró's blue-ground automatic paintings of the mid-1920s and Dalí is evidently also familiar with the floating elements and abstract constructions of Tanguy's recent work. The strangest figure is the lumpen torso, perhaps once a Venus rising from the sea but now winging across the sky like Mercury, its gender ambiguous. The shape seems in the process of transformation, slipping from one identity to another. In a contemporary prose text, "My girlfriend and the beach," Dalí describes a hallucinatory chain of images: a newborn infant painted with Ripolin, which he realizes is "the pink breast of my girlfriend being frenetically eaten by the bright metallic thickness of phonograph needles. It wasn't her breast either but the little pieces of cigarette paper nervously clumped round the magnetic topaz of my fiancée's ring."[3] Such shifts can more easily be realized in film than in the static medium of oil paint. One sequence in *Un Chien andalou*, the film he and Buñuel made early in 1929, dissolves from a hand full of crawling ants into a close up of a woman's armpit, to a sea-urchin's spines, and finally a head seen from above. The idea that such transformative sequences occur as a form of delirious interpretation on the part of the subject anticipates Dalí's 'critical paranoia.' D.A.

[1] Dalí, letter to Lorca, early December 1927, in *Poesía* no. 33 (Madrid: Ministerio de Cultura, 14 April 1987).
[2] Federico García Lorca, letter to Dalí, quoted in Ian Gibson, *The Shameful Life of Salvador Dalí* (London: Faber & Faber, 1997), p. 164.
[3] Salvador Dalí, "Dues proses. La meva amiga i la platja. Nadal a Brusselles (conte antic)" in *L'Amic de les Arts* no. 20 (Sitges: November, 30 1927). Trans. in Robert Descharnes, *Oui 1: The Paranoid-critical revolution, writings 1927-33* (Boston: Exact Change, 1998), p. 20.

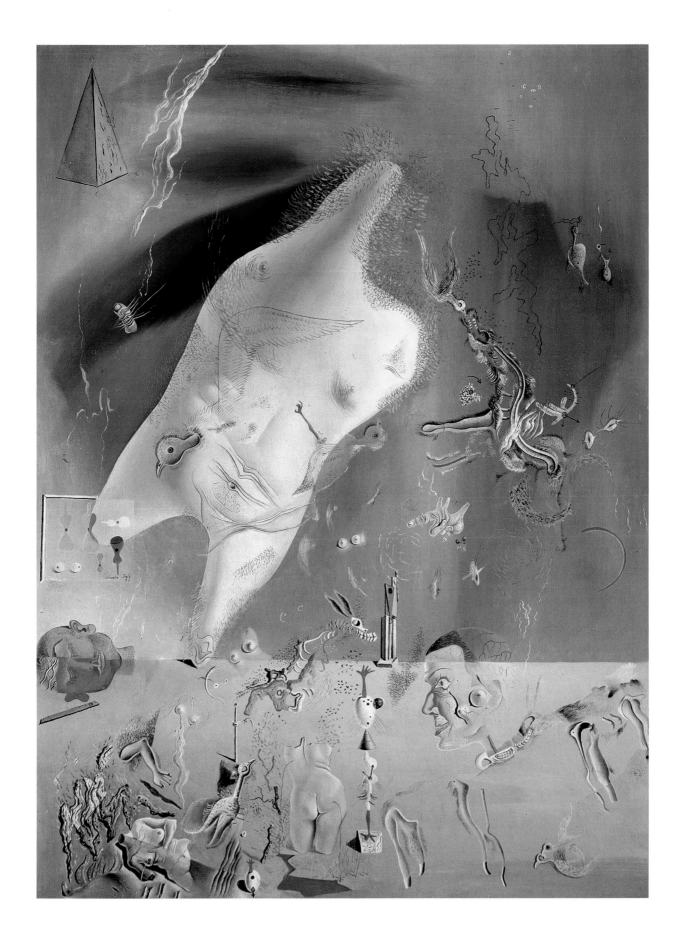

60. The Wounded Bird, 1928

60. Oil, sand and coarse sand
on cardboard
55 × 65.5 cm
21 5/8 × 25 3/4 in.
Tel Aviv (Israel) Tel Aviv
Museum of Art,
The Mizne-Blumental Collection

The subject matter of this important early painting can be discerned from the title of a variant work in the Salvador Dalí Museum in St. Petersburg, Florida, which is known as *Big Thumb, Beach, Moon, and Decaying Bird* of 1928 (see p. 98, fig. 3). Images of decay and putrefaction abound in Dalí's work of the late 1920s, which include numerous depictions of severed body parts and skeletal birds (referenced here in Dalí's slightly puzzling title), while the unorthodox use of sand to signify a beach setting reflects the impact of the recent work of the Surrealist artist André Masson, whose innovative use of sand in his paintings of 1926-27 was widely admired by the European Avant-Garde. Like Masson, Dalí is interested in the coarse texture and reflective light effects of sand, which he has embedded in the paint to function as both the ground of the painting and as the material setting for the smoothly painted tumescent thumb that floats on its rough surface. That the disembodied thumb can be read as an erect member, and by extension a symbol of castration, is confirmed by an essay published by the artist in the following year, entitled "The Liberation of the Fingers," in which he explored the phallic associations of fingers and toes.[1] This text discussed his obsession with the disturbing image of an isolated, floating finger, which Dalí suggests might have originated in 'a hypnagogic image of pre-sleep,' but which he also related to the sudden terror he experienced on seeing his own thumb poking through the hole of his palette.

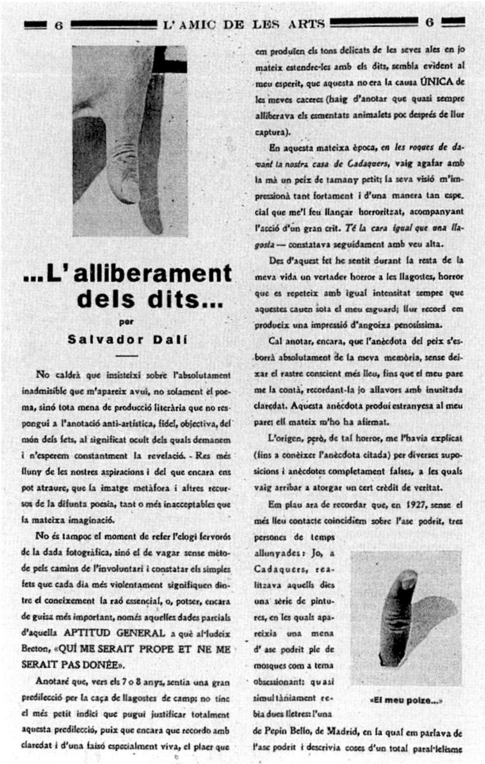

6 L' AMIC DE LES ARTS 6

...L'alliberament dels dits...

por

Salvador Dalí

No caldrà que insisteixi sobre l'absolutament inadmisible que m'apareix avui, no solament el poema, sinó tota mena de producció literària que no respongui a l'anotació anti-artística, fidel, objectiva, del món dels fets, al significat ocult dels quals demanem i n'esperem constantment la revelació. - Res més lluny de les nostres aspiracions i del que encara ens pot atraure, que la imatge metàfora i altres recursos de la difunta poesia, tant o més inacceptables que la mateixa imaginació.

No és tampoc el moment de refer l'elogi fervorós de la dada fotogràfica, sinó el de vagar sense mètode pels camins de l'involuntari i constatar els simples fets que cada dia més violentament signifiquen dintre el coneixement la raó essencial, o, potser, encara de guisa més important, només aquelles dades parcials d'aquella APTITUD GENERAL a què al·ludeix Breton, «QUI ME SERAIT PROPE ET NE ME SERAIT PAS DONÉE».

Anotaré que, vers els 7 o 8 anys, sentia una gran predilecció per la caça de llagostes de camp; no tinc el més petit indici que pugui justificar totalment aquesta predilecció, puix que encara que recordo amb claredat i d'una faisó especialment viva, el plaer que em produïen els tons delicats de les seves ales en jo mateix estendre-les amb els dits, sembla evident al meu esperit, que aquesta no era la causa ÚNICA de les meves caceres (haig d'anotar que quasi sempre alliberava els esmentats animalets poc després de llur captura).

En aquesta mateixa època, *en les roques de davant la nostra casa de Cadaquers*, vaig agafar amb la mà un peix de tamany petit; la seva visió m'impressionà tant fortament i d'una manera tan especial que me'l feu llançar horroritzat, acompanyant l'acció d'un gran crit. *Té la cara igual que una llagosta* — constatava seguidament amb veu alta.

Des d'aquest fet he sentit durant la resta de la meva vida un vertader horror a les llagostes, horror que es repeteix amb igual intensitat sempre que aquestes cauen sota el meu esguard; llur record em produeix una impressió d'angoixa penosíssima.

Cal anotar, encara, que l'anècdota del peix s'esborrà absolutament de la meva memòria, sense deixar el rastre conscient més lleu, fins que el meu pare me la contà, recordant-la jo allavors amb inusitada claredat. Aquesta anècdota produí estranyesa al meu pare; ell mateix m'ho ha afirmat.

L'origen, però, de tal horror, me l'havia explicat (fins a conèixer l'anècdota citada) per diverses suposicions i anècdotes completament falses, a les quals vaig arribar a atorgar un cert crèdit de veritat.

Em plau ara de recordar que, en 1927, sense el més lleu contacte coincidiem sobre l'ase podrit, tres persones de temps allunyades: Jo, a Cadaquers, realitzava aquells dies una sèrie de pintures, en les quals apareixia una mena d'ase podrit ple de mosques com a tema obsessionant; quasi simultàniament rebia dues lletres: l'una de Pepin Bello, de Madrid, en la qual em parlava de l'ase podrit i descrivia coses d'un total paral·lelisme

«El meu polze...»

Fig. 1. "L'alliberament dels dits," published in *L'Amic de les Arts, March* 31, 1929

The Wounded Bird also relates to "My Girlfriend and the Beach," a 1927 prose piece in which the artist conveys his tactile response to the menacing, disturbing natural environment that he encountered while beach combing on the shore at Cadaqués with Frederico García Lorca: "Today, because we are very happy, we shall go to the beach in order to explode the most painful fibers of our physiologies, and, with the contracted surface of little apparatuses and sharp corals, rip the most feeble pulse of our membranes. Contracting our nerves and pressing our pupils with the tips of our fingers, we will feel the guttural joy of our veins cracking, and the thousand sounds of our blood leaping under the pressure of each new wound."[2] Both painting and text reflect the artist's fascination with the deliquescence of matter and his own unique sense of the physical and emotional dangers that accompany a trip to the beach.

The painted image of the isolated thumb may have provided the inspiration for Jacques-André Boiffard's 1929 photographs of brutally enlarged big toes that accompanied Georges Bataille's article on "The Big Toe" in the November 1929 issue of *Documents*, (see p. 94, fig. 1) which was itself indebted to Dalí's aforementioned "The Liberation of the Fingers" essay and the photographs of phallic digits that illustrated it (fig. 1).[3] Bataille's interest in the Spanish artist's work began when he saw Dalí and Luís Buñuel's 1929 film *Un Chien andalou*, whose opening sequence of a cloud neatly bisecting a moon is anticipated in the upper left-hand corner of this painting. M.R.T.

[1] Salvador Dalí, "L'alliberament dels dits" (The Liberation of the Fingers), *L'Amic de les Arts* no. 31 (Sitges: March 31, 1929), pp. 6-7.

[2] Salvador Dalí, "My Girlfriend and the Beach," 1927, reprinted in Haim Finkelstein, ed., *The Collected Writings of Salvador Dalí*, trans. Haim Finkelstein (Cambridge: Cambridge University Press, 1998), p. 25.

[3] Georges Bataille, "Le gros orteil" (The Big Toe), *Documents*, no. 6 (Paris: November 1929), n.p.

61. The Rotting Donkey, 1928

61. Oil, sand and gravel
collage panel
61 × 50 cm
24¹/8 × 19⁵/8 in.
Paris, Musée national
d'Art moderne,
Centre Georges Pompidou

The 'rotting donkey,' closely linked to the idea of the *putrefact*, first appears in Dalí's paintings the previous year, and was to figure again in the film *Un Chien andalou* which was shot in February 1929, as well as in *William Tell* (1930, cat. 78). Over these two years Dalí was engaged in a radical critique of the status of painting; he auditioned a procession of different styles and media offered by the avant-garde and began to recognize the possibilities of Surrealism. This he first became interested in through the works of Miró, Arp and Tanguy, but quickly experienced a crisis evident in the "anti-paintings" of 1928, large bare canvases scattered with spare ambiguous shapes and occasional objects (cat. 62). In his text "The new limits of painting" written early in 1928 he lays out the problems of the contemporary painter for whom freedom and the promise of a "new language" lack direction while the "assassination of painting" (which he embraced in the anti-paintings) logically leads to pure negativity. In the group of collage-paintings to which *L'âne pourri* belongs, he once again engages with extraordinary boldness the frontier world between abstraction and figuration. He takes advantage of new initiatives such as Masson's sand paintings of 1926-27, but not in the interests of the automatism that Masson was exploring (fig. 1).

The tight organization of this painting, despite the many parallels with the Surrealist work of Miró, Arp and Masson, already indicates a resistance to the automatism that was still the guiding principle of the Surrealist painters. The deliberate contrast between the textured areas and the smooth, hard and even surface of the painted areas is striking. An analysis of a fragment of pigment revealed that Dalí was already experimenting with different resins, as he later described in *50 Magic Secrets*. "The pink tones of this painting come from the mixture of 'dragon's blood,' a bright red gum or resin obtained from the fruit of a palm, and zinc oxide, a white pigment. The pigment is so completely ground that no grains are visible, and Dalí is effectively painting in enamel, without any use of oil. Such enamel dries swiftly to a glasslike hardness".[1] This very probably facilitated the miniaturist technique that characterizes his first Surrealist paintings, such as *Le Jeu Lugubre*.

Dalí uses sand in the wide foreground strand literally to represent itself, but thicker gravel outlines the forms in the central figure, which recalls the fleshy truncated Venus of *Cenecitas*, its legs poised in flight across the beach. Dangling horizontally across this Cubist creature is another figure outlined in black and white, its face sharply delineated in positive-negative forms recalling both Arp and Picasso. Much disguised, this might be a scene from a *Rape of the Sabine Women*, or possibly even a *Rape of Europa*, a distant mythologizing of Picasso's neo-classical beach scenes. Nibbling at the creature's leg is the rotting donkey itself, its skull buzzing with flies and a coral-red tail at its rear. D.A.

[1] Dawn Ades, *Dalí* (London: Thames and Hudson, 1982), p. 60.

Fig. 1. André Masson, *Figure*, 1926-27
New York (NY), The Museum of
Modern Art

62. Four Fishermen's Wives of Cadaqués[1], 1928

62. Oil on canvas
148 × 196 cm
58 1/4 × 77 1/8 in.
Madrid, Museo Nacional,
Centro de Arte Reina Sofía

Fig. 1. Joan Miró, *Pintura*,
in *L'Amic de les Arts,*
June 30, 1928

Fig. 2. Salvador Dalí,
Abstract Composition, 1928
Madrid, Museo Nacional
Centro de Arte Reina Sofía

In 1928, Dalí was preoccupied with questions of art, anti-art and the "assassination of painting."[2] Miró's famous denunciation of painting had been widely reported and Dalí, alert to the success of his fellow Catalan among the Surrealists in Paris, grappled with the issue in the texts he regularly published in *L'Amic de les Arts*. "This is a passionate period," he wrote in "New Limits of Painting," "because psychologically [painting] is beginning to arouse everyone at the very moment its most radical assassination is being carried out. You could say that nothing remains of earlier painting; not a single one of the concerns of early painters propels the hands of contemporary artists." [3]

Dalí responded to this challenge in a variety of ways, pushing his painting to the limits of representation, experimenting with automatism, incorporating readymade materials and championing film and photography. Among the most extreme of the works of this period is the group of bold, seemingly abstract canvases, striking in their disequilibrium, absence of spatial orientation and scale, with flat, rudimentary forms and large bare areas, to which *Four Fishermen's Wives of Cadaqués* belongs. Only one of these 'anti-paintings' was exhibited at the time: *Feminine Figure and Masculine Figure on a Beach*.

It was clear to Dalí that Surrealism, and especially the work of Miró and of Arp, offered ways of going beyond the traditional 'limits' of painting. Although after he joined the Surrealist movement in the summer of 1929 he distanced himself from the 'passive' mode of Surrealist automatism, during this exploratory period he credits it with the creation of a new mobile, dynamic world of ambiguous forms: "When inspiration and even the purest subconscious have revealed our individual truths, an organic world full of significant attributions invades the artist's figures."[4]

As his writing of the time confirms, Dalí was looking to Miró's recent paintings, such as those reproduced in the June 1928 issue of *L'Amic de les Arts* with their radically reduced patches of color and lines and also to the work of Hans Arp. He had been deeply impressed by André Breton's account of Arp's reliefs in *Le Surréalisme et la peinture*, and frequently alludes to their visual ambiguity.

Figures, often nude, on the beach, had long been a favorite theme of Dalí's and the representation of bodies and body fragments now become increasingly abstracted as well as erotically suggestive. Indeed, Dalí's stylistic experiments are inseparable from his fascination with the representation of sexual activity, and these paintings are like signs of "amorous simplifications."[5] The curious red shapes in *Four Fishermen's Wives of Cadaqués,* which are repeated in other paintings in this group, could be a highly condensed sign for the female body. The black shapes, some like digits, some frankly phallic, are painted on white patches which mimic collage; those elongated towards the top of the painting resemble anamorphic distortions, one of which is suspended from a tiny patch of blue sky or sea. In *Male and Female Figures on the Beach*, the sand rectangle is invaded by a white form like a convulsed hand, which creates a negative/positive effect of interlocked limbs or fingers. This switch between ground and figure, characteristic of Arp's woodcuts and reliefs of the 1920s, becomes one of the devices by which Dalí explores the idea of intercourse. In *Four Fisherwomen of Cadaqués*, Dalí sets in play a visual negative/positive switch which underlines the ambiguity of the forms; as the image oscillates, breasts, eyes, faces, genitals or crabs seem to appear. One of the few references traceable to the antipaintings in Dalí's voluminous memoirs fleetingly records that, after painting the seminal *Honey Is Sweeter than Blood*, he also produced "a sun dripping with light and bathing women fit to eat. This ardent work alternated with intense meditation."[6] This is a rare hint of the crisis Dalí was undergoing at the time. It also expresses with unusual clarity the combined impulses of eroticism and violence that continued to inform his work. D.A.

[1] This painting was exhibited at the Dalí retrospective at the Centre Georges Pompidou in 1979, when it was still in the painter's collection, with the title *Sun*. Descharnes entitles it *Sun, Four Fisherwomen of Cadaqués* (*Salvador Dalí: The Paintings*, Cologne: Taschen 1994) and in *Salvador Dalí: The Early Years* (London: South Bank Centre-Hayward Gallery, 1994) it has the present title.
[2] Miró's desire to 'assassinate painting' was quoted by Maurice Raynal in *Anthologie de la peinture en France de 1906 à nos jours* (Paris, 1927) and also spread by word of mouth. See also William Jeffett, *Dalí and Miró circa 1928* Salvador Dalí Exhibition Series 2003.
[3] Salvador Dalí, "Nous límits de la pintura," *L'Amic de les Arts* (Sitges: February, April, May 1928). This important essay appeared in three installments. *Oui: la Révolution paranoïaque-critique. Writings 1927-1933*, Trans. Yvonne Shafir in ed. Robert Descharnes, *Oui 1: The Paranoid-critical revolution, writings 1927-1933* (Boston: Exact Change, 1998), p. 40.
[4] *Ibid.*, no. 24, 30, April 1928, p. 37.
[5] *Ibid.*, no. 25, 31, May 1928, p. 41.
[6] Salvador Dalí and André Parinaud, *The Unspeakable Confessions of Salvador Dalí* (London: Quartet Books 1971), p. 75.

63. Sometimes I Spit with Pleasure on the Portrait of my Mother (The Sacred Heart), 1929

63. China ink on linen canvas glued on cardboard
68.3 × 51.1 cm
26⁷/8 × 20¹/8 in.
Paris, Musée nationale d'art moderne, Centre Georges Pompidou

Fig. 1. Péret insulting a priest, photo published in *La Révolution surréaliste,* no. 8, December 1, 1936,

Fig. 2. Joan Miró, *Un oiseau poursuit une abeille et la baisse*, 1927 Private collection

The sentence roughly scrawled across the surface of this canvas was the source of a bitter family quarrel. Dalí's father interpreted *Sometimes I Spit with Pleasure on the Portrait of my Mother* as a personal affront and a sacrilege against the memory of Dalí's mother. He had not seen the picture, which was in the Galerie Goemans exhibition that opened in Paris on November 20, 1929, but had evidently been informed of the inscription. He flew into a volcanic rage, and Buñuel, who had arrived in Figueres at Christmas 1929 on his way to film the opening scenes of *L'Âge d'or* at Cadaqués, witnessed Dalí's expulsion from the family home. "At first all I could hear were angry shouts; then suddenly the door flew open and, purple with rage, Dalí's father threw his son out, calling him every name in the book. Dalí screamed back while his father pointed to him and swore that he hoped never to see that pig in his house again."[1]

Although now known by this notorious inscription, the painting was exhibited with the title *Sacré Coeur,* "Sacred Heart." Written across the rudimentary ink drawing of the outline of Christ, the words have a less personal if equally iconoclastic connotation than the one immediately assumed by Dalí's father, step-mother and sister. As a new recruit to Surrealism, Dalí would have been well aware of the movement's virulent anti-cleri-

calism (publicly expressed for instance with the photograph in *La Révolution Surréaliste* of Benjamin Péret insulting a priest) (fig. 1) and wanted to establish his own credentials. The outline drawing of Christ with the sacred heart, raising his hand in blessing, was a familiar and immediately recognizable image; the unevenly written words, like graffiti, obliterate the holy image and subvert it. They may be taken as being spoken by Christ, or by the painter himself in relation to the Mother of God rather than to his own mother.

The starkness and emptiness of this work is as startling as its subject and stands out among the other paintings of 1929. The previous year Dalí had gone through a pictorial crisis, as he wrestled with the conflicting styles and ideas of the avant-garde, painting a series of large, almost abstract and very bare canvases. Whereas these responded to the biomorphism and minimal forms of recent work by Arp and by Miró, here he seems to be looking at Miró's mid-1920s paintings that include writing. *Photo: ceci est la couleur de mes rêves* (1925) and *L'oiseau poursuit une abeille et la baisse* (1927, fig. 2), for instance, similarly have phrases strewn over the canvas, not neatly lettered like the words on cubist pictures but expanding in childlike and uneven writing to create a dialogue between the visual form of words and the visual

Fig. 3. Francis Picabia, cover
drawing for *Littérature,* no. 4,
September 1, 1922

Fig. 4. Francis Picabia, cover
drawing for *Littérature*, no. 5,
October 1, 1922

images. Miró's challenge to pictorial integrity is
clear and heralds his much quoted desire to 'assassinate painting.' Dalí's *Sacré Coeur,* however, is
even more aggressively unmannered as a painting.
Despite the variability in the sizes and shapes of
the words, Dalí—for whom the introduction of
writing onto the painting is rare—makes no attempt to stretch the calligraphy into pure marks as
Miró does. The stiff formality of the outline of
Christ, stereotypical and like a tracing, emphasizes
the differences in the conventions of writing and im-
age-making rather than challenging them through
visual interplay like Miró. It is closer in many ways
to Picabia's outrageous cover drawings for the Dada
review *Littérature* whose deadpan style often mim-
icked popular catholic images, as in the Sacred
Heart cover (fig. 3). They are often crudely iconoclastic conjunctions of the erotic and the sacred,
as in *Nul n'est censé ignorer* (fig. 4).

This painting was acquired by André Breton after
the *L'Âge d'or* scandal in 1930. Could it have been
the picture exhibited in the foyer at Studio 28
during the film's run under the title *La Veuve*? At
some point following Dalí's rupture with Surrealism, Breton appears to have pasted onto it a newspaper clipping in which Dalí announced his return to the church.

There is no doubt about the depth and consequences of Dalí senior's anger. He wrote to both
Lorca and Buñuel—Dalí's own closest associates—to enlist them as allies. To Lorca he wrote "I
do not know if you are aware that I had to throw
my son out of the house… In one of the paintings
of his Paris exhibition he committed the vile act of
writing these insolent words: 'I spit on my mother.' Imagining that he was drunk when he wrote
them, I asked him to explain himself. But he
would not do so and insulted all of us again."[2] The
letter to Buñuel gives a terrible picture of the extent of his persecution of his son. "My son has no
right to embitter my life. Cadaqués is my spiritual
refuge, and …moreover this is my wife's resting
place and will be destroyed if my son, with his indecent conduct, befouls it." Having ordered the
Civil Guard to chase him out of Cadaqués, he is
now prepared, he tells Buñuel, to take any measures necessary to enforce his will. "…when the
measures I dispose of at the moment are no longer
sufficient, let us fight each other and then we will
see who wins and I can tell you that since I wish to
win whatever the cost I will do all I can to make
sure I win, getting people to help me to beat him
up, or seeking the opportunity to bestow the
blows myself without receiving any in return."[3]

In the light of such threats, Dalí's construction of
the vengeful paternal imago in his William Tell
paintings and in the poem "The Great Masturbator" (cats. 78, 109, 110) becomes considerably
less fanciful. Given Dalí's imminent appropriation
of mythical figures, it is possible that this first misapprehension of the meaning of his work was one
of the generative moments in his complex construction of identity. Despite the frankness of his
autobiographical writings, Dalí almost never alluded to this episode. On the publication of Ana
María's memoirs of her brother in 1949, he pointed out furiously that he had veiled the "TRUTH
ABOUT THE FAMILY QUESTION"[4] in *The Secret Life*
out of decency, and printed a memorandum that
he distributed widely: "I was expelled from my

family in 1930 without a cent. I have achieved my entire world-wide success solely with the help of God, the light of the Empordà and the heroic daily abnegation of a sublime woman, my wife, Gala."[5] D.A.

[1] Luis Buñuel, *My Last Breath* (London: Jonathan Cape, 1984), p. 115.

[2] Quoted in Ian Gibson, *The Shameful Life of Salvador Dalí* (London: Faber and Faber, 1997), p. 239.

[3] *Ibid.*, p. 257.

[4] *Ibid.*, p. 455.

[5] *La Vie publique de Salvador Dalí* (Paris: Centre Georges Pompidou, Musée National d'Art Moderne, 1980), p. 132.

64. The First Days of Spring, 1929

64. Oil and collage on panel
50.2 × 65 cm
19³/4 × 25⁵/8 in.
St. Petersburg (FL),
Salvador Dalí Museum

Dalí painted *The First Days of Spring* in the spring of 1929, and in November of the same year it was included in his first solo exhibition in Paris held at the Galerie Goemans. The painting presented a complex deployment of Freudian symbolism imbued with an autobiographical content.[1] André Breton wrote the enthusiastic preface for the Goemans exhibition catalogue: "Perhaps, with Dalí, it is the first time that the mental windows are wide open and that one feels oneself drawn into the savage sky's trap door."[2] Though Breton did not specifically mention *The First Days of Spring*, clearly the mention of 'mental windows' suggests a pictorial vista similar to the plunging perspective that so distinguishes this painting.

Dalí painted *The First Days of Spring* around the time of the production of the film *Un Chien andalou*

Fig. 1. Stills from the final scene of *Un Chien andalou*, 1929

(1929). Arguably the painting has several qualities related to cinema, a point that was not missed in Sebastià Gasch's review of the Goemans exhibition for the Barcelona newspaper *La Publicitat*: "We then affirm, uniquely, that the last works by the painter from Figueres, as his film, exalt the content in detriment to the formal container, reducing it to the minimum expression. And, as his film indicates, they [the last works] are the exclusive children of an unleashed subconscious, [liberated] from the guardianship of the conscience."[3]

Further, Gasch pointed out the importance of Verism in the paintings: "In these canvases, as in those of many Surrealists, *trompe-l'œil* is recuperated as a singular tendency. It is curious to record that the most intensely mysterious art achieves enigmatic results because of a vulgar verism. And this mystery is born most often because of the special manner of grouping objects…"[4]

In coming close to reality, therefore, Dalí undermined its seamlessness, opening up fissures in its surface by introducing enigmatic elements and bizarre juxtapositions. *The First Days of Spring* would offer a springboard to further speculation on the dismantling of rational constructions of reality. The painting presents several anecdotal scenes inspired for the most part by Freud's psycho-analysis. For example at right a little girl hands a gift to a bearded father figure in a gesture symbolic of sexual initiation. In the middle ground one suited male figure stands above another similarly dressed and holds the other's head back in what might allude to an act of male coupling. In the background a father and child holding hands suggest Dalí's early memories of paternal authority. At left in the middle ground a male figure is seated with its back towards us in reference to a distant and removed father. And in the foreground left is a shockingly sexualized couple: her head is an open female sex from which emanate a swarm of flies; his hands are joined in the form of a female sex and are located above a pail to which is attached an erect and phallic finger, which will appear again in three-dimensions in *Anthropomorphic Beach*. As Dawn Ades notes, Dalí and Buñuel made a bet about representing sex in the most blunt way possible. Similar provocative qualities, such as the suggestive representation of a woman's underarm hair, may also be found in *Un Chien andalou*. Without going into further detail regarding the painting, suffice it to say Dalí situates himself at the psychological center of these various narrative events by gluing a photograph of himself to the surface of the painting.[5]

In March 1930 the Galerie Goemans staged an important group exhibition of collages that included the Surrealists and their Cubist and Dada precursors in the field of *papier collé*: Arp, Braque, Dalí, Duchamp, Ernst, Gris, Magritte, Man Ray, Miró, Picabia, Picasso and Tanguy. For the catalogue,

published by José Corti, Louis Aragon wrote the essay "The Challenge to Painting." Aragon stressed the 'poor' nature of collage and its capacity thereby to discredit reality and introduce what he called the 'marvelous' into the everyday, "It is certain that the marvelous is born of the refusal of a reality but also of the development of a new relationship, of a new reality that this refusal has liberated." [6]

Aragon went on to speculate that this new relationship, born of the negation of reality, was indeed of an ethical order, and he tells us this new relationship is 'surreality.' [7]

Dalí's participation in the exhibition included *The First Days of Spring* with its presentation of Freudian scenes meticulously rendered as a dream landscape. Dalí, further, applied collage in the forms of a chromolithograph, different cut out images of paternal figures and a photograph of himself as a child, the effect being the construction of a mythology of the self. The collage elements were so woven into the pictorial fabric of the painting as to be confused with the paint itself and, likewise, the painted parts were confused with the collage elements. This was an apt means for establishing the confusion between dream and reality typical of the psychological discourse surrounding paranoia. Aragon seized on

exactly this point—what he called the 'double play' between paint and collage, illusion and a re-ordered reality—and he concluded that, if one were to think in terms of the relation of psychology and literature, each one of Dalí's paintings would have to be considered a novel, by which he meant that they were psychological narratives with Dalí as the chief protagonist. [8] In a moment of critical distance, Aragon rhetorically questioned Dalí's meticulous treatment of the details in his paintings, asking "What to think of Salvador Dalí's minutiae?" [9] Such doubts aside, with *The First Days of Spring* Dalí firmly established himself within the pictorial center of Surrealism. W.J.

[1] Dawn Ades and Fiona Bradley, *Salvador Dalí: A Mythology* (London and St. Petersburg, Florida: Tate Gallery Publishing and Salvador Dalí Museum Editions, 1998-99) and Robert Lubar, *Dalí: The Salvador Dalí Musem Collection* (Boston: Bullfinch, 2000).

[2] André Breton, "Première exposition Dalí" (1929) in André Breton, *Oeuvres complètes*, II (Paris: Gallimard, 1992), p. 308.

[3] Sebastià Gasch, "Les obres recents de Salvador Dalí," *La Publicitat* (Barcelona: November 16, 1929) in *Escrits d'art i d'avantguarda (1925-1938)*, ed. Joan Minguet, Sebastià Gasch (Barcelona: Edicions del Mall, 1987), pp. 122-123.

[4] *Ibid.*

[5] For more detailed analysis see Dawn Ades and Robert Lubar, *op. cit.*

[6] Louis Aragon, *La Peinture au défi* (Paris: José Corti, March 1930), p. 6.

[7] *Ibid.*, p. 10.

[8] *Ibid.*, p. 27.

[9] *Ibid.*, p. 28.

Fig. 2. Hieronymus Bosch,
The Garden of Earthly Delight,
ca. 1510
Madrid, Museo Nacional del Prado

65. The Great Masturbator, 1929

65. Oil on canvas
110 × 150 cm
43 1/4 × 59 in.
Madrid, Museo Nacional
Centro de Arte Reina Sofía,
gift of Dalí to the Spanish State

Salvador Dalí painted *The Great Masturbator* in the summer of 1929. The face in the centre that occupies nearly the whole canvas is thought to be a portrait of the artist himself depicted as the "great masturbator".[1] Some critics have even interpreted the juxtaposition of the grotesque face and the "petrified" couple portrayed on the right of the painting, who seem to be engaged in the act of fellatio, as a synthesis of the tensions and anxieties that were tormenting him during that period. And it was that same summer that Dalí met Gala and with her he had the possibility of experiencing a heterosexual relationship that freed him from his supposed addiction to onanism.[2] It is certainly true that this painting evokes the events of August 1929, but it must not be forgotten that shortly afterwards Dalí reproduced the same face to portray André Breton in the André Breton ex libris, the giant ant-eater, and that the same face is evidently similar to the representation of the "average bureaucrats" in another work that is chronologically not far apart. The theme of the bureaucrats, generally associated with the figure of Dalí's father and probably inspired by the face that de Chirico painted in (*The Child's Brain*) (fig. 2, p. 138), whose long eyelashes are to be found again in *The Great Masturbator*.[3] The profile of this ambiguous face is also found in other works of this period and in later paintings, if it is not as a self-portrait, it is definitely a clear "obsessive image" around which the painter develops an iconog-

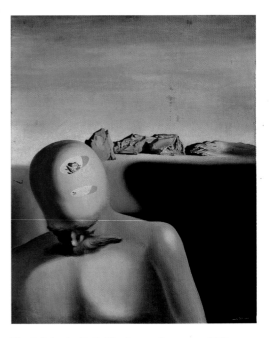

Fig. 2. Salvador Dalí, *The Average Bureaucrat*, 1930
St Petersburg (FL), The Salvador Dalí Museum

raphy that is nearly always baroque and complex. In the case of *The Great Masturbator*, most of the elements depicted can be traced back to the painter's origins. "Ever since my arrival at Cadaqués I had gone right back to my childhood," Dalí wrote referring to that summer.[4] His mind became filled with an infinite number of perceptions that he did his utmost to express in his painting with painstaking precision. The regression he speaks of can be found in the link between the three figures situated below the great masturbator's face; a line that ends in the distance, on the horizon, with an adult holding a child by the hand, a typical image in the paintings of the artist as a child executed during that period. Also the grasshopper, shells, colorful feathers, parched earth and ants are associated with this return to childhood. The "petrified" woman also derives from these personal reminiscences. It is not merely by chance that one of the concrete objects that inspired the painting was a modernist mirror that had always hung on a wall in the Dalí family home.[5] In general the childhood memories represented in the painting express fear, like the woman's face. If we consider that the second model that gave the artist inspiration for *The Great Masturbator* was the painting *Beata Beatrix* by Dante Gabriel Rossetti, and that for Dalí the Pre-Raphaelite woman was synonymous with "terror" and "repugnance," we will understand better the "petrified" pose of the female figure and the male body her lips are approaching.[6] A subtle connection links both of them to the lion's head that, with its mane standing on end, is reminiscent of a terrifying destructive Gorgon able to turn people to stone with her gaze. The

Fig. 1. Hieronymus Bosch,
The Garden of Earthly Delight,
(detail), ca. 1510
Madrid, Museo Nacional del Prado

fear of castration, symbolized according to Freud by Medusa's head, is accentuated by the red phallic tongue conspicuously pushing its way through the lion's sharp fangs. In this interplay of sexuality and death the volutes of the architectural ruins into which the couple on the right merge and the cold, desert plateau shrouded in a lugubrious atmosphere where the whole representation unfolds are not extraneous. This is not merely a psychopathological document, completely removed from the world of art as Dalí, following surrealist principles, wanted people to believe at the time. He always maintained that the anguished face was inspired by a rock at Cape Creus (a secluded place near Cadaqués), but recent studies have associated that face with the images in *The Creation of the World*, the left panel of the triptych *The Garden of Earthly Delights*) (fig. 1) by Hieronymus Bosch, a work that Dalí knew very well because it is held by the Prado Museum.[7] If we consider that, like Dalí's painting, the Flemish painter's work also represents immersion in the obscure depths of Man's origins – based on an interplay of sexuality and death – the reason why *The Great Masturbator*, years after it was painted, continued to menace André Breton's nights turning his dreams into nightmares becomes clear.[8] F.F.

[1] See, for example, Rafael Santos Torroella, *La miel es más dulce que la sangre*, Seix Barral, Barcelona, 1984, p. 23.

[2] Dawn Ades, *Dalí*, Thames and Hudson, London, 1982.

[3] The link between the face in this picture and the average bureaucrats is suggested by Santos Torroella, op. cit., pp. 59-60.

[4] Salvador Dalí, *Vita segreta di Salvador Dalí*, Longanesi, Milan, 1949, p. 200.

[5] Fèlix Fanés, *El gran masturbador*, Electa, Madrid, 2000, pp. 47-48.

[6] On Dalí and Dante Gabriel Rossetti see Hiroyuki Tanita, 'Dalí and the Pre-Raphaelites' in *The Journal of Pre-Raphaelite and Aesthetics Studies*, autumn 1988. Dalí wrote an article on the Pre-Raphaelite woman, "Le Surréalisme spectral de l'éternel féminin préraphaélite," in *Minotaure*, 15 June 1936.

[7] Joaquin Yarza, *El jardin de las delicias de El Bosco*, Tf. Editores, Madrid, 1998, p. 51.

[8] André Breton, "Les Vases communicants" (1932), in A. Breton, *Oeuvres complètes*, vol. II, Gallimard, Paris, 1992, p. 132.

66. Study for "The Great Masturbator," 1929

67. Study for "The Enigma of Desire and the Memory of the Child Woman," 1929

66. Watercolor on paper
14 × 9 cm
5 1/2 × 3 1/2 in.
Private collection

67. Yellow china ink on paper
31 × 24 cm
12 1/8 × 9 1/2 in.
Private collection

68. The Enigma of Desire, 1929

68. Oil on canvas
110 × 150.7 cm
43 1/4 × 59 3/8 in.
Munich, Bayerische
Staatsgemäldesammlungen,
Pinakothek der Moderne

Exhibited under the title *The Image of Desire* at Dalí's first solo show in Paris in 1929 at the Galerie Goemans, this was one of the two paintings of the eleven in the exhibition that contained a reference to his mother. The other, exhibited as *Sacré Coeur* (Sacred Heart), but now known by the large inscription across its surface, *Sometimes I Spit with Pleasure on the Portrait of my Mother*, outraged his father and led to their lengthy rupture (cat. 63). Apart from some early portraits, Dalí's mother very rarely appears in his work, but this absence was not indifference. Her death in 1921 was a terrible blow: "I worshipped her...and I could not resign myself to the loss of a being on whom I counted to make invisible the unavowable blemishes of my soul—she was so good that I thought that 'it would do for me too.' She adored me with a love so whole and so proud that she could not be wrong—my wickedness, too, must be something marvellous! ... With my teeth clenched with weeping, I swore to myself that I would snatch my mother from death and destiny with the swords of light that some day would savagely gleam around my glorious name!"[1]

There is something indescribably pitiful about the repeated invocation "*ma mère, ma mère,*" in the niches of the rock, pitted like the harsh cliffs of Cap Creus. This mournful refrain towers over the fragmentary images familiar from other paintings of 1929, though what it signifies remains enigmatic.

The supremely elegant composition of this large painting with its sharply structured space, cleanly detached objects and clear horizon line visible through the holes in the rock-figure is in dramatic contrast with the abject or aggressive objects themselves. In the nearer miniature configuration, a fish, grasshopper and the bust of a woman cluster with an adolescent figure draped round an older male, who grasps a knife. More distant, and significantly framed in the womb-hole, is a female torso, itself framed in a rock window. The foreground is dominated by the huge eroded rock which trails into (or grows from) Dalí's melting head and a fragment of the outmoded art nouveau architecture he championed. As in *The Great Masturbator* (cat. 65) his head lacks a mouth—an absence that terrified him. The deliquescent shapes (see Encyclopedia 'Soft structures') are formed from both hard and soft substances (flesh and stone), melding together, which emphasizes their troubling and repugnant character. The head is becoming inhuman, inanimate, deathly. Dalí wrote in "L'Amour": "If love incarnates dreams, let us not forget that one often dreams of one's own annihilation and that this, if one judges it according to oneiric life, would be one of man's most violent and tumultuous unconscious desires."[2] Repugnance, he goes on, is a mechanism to defend against the death drive, the desire for an-

nihilation: "Repugnance is a symbolic defence against the vertigo of desire for death."[3] Dalí also correlates abjection not just, like Kristeva, with a pre-oedipal phase of differentiation from the maternal body, but with the pre-natal: "The intra-uterine significance occupies a more important place every day in the study of dreams."[4] Perhaps at one level the rock with its womblike holes sucking at Dalí's head is the maternal body, and represents a return to the womb both desired and feared.

In his slightly later text *The Tragic Myth of Millet's Angelus* Dalí, now in the full flood of his psycho-analytically inspired paranoiac period, interprets the *Angelus* as the maternal variant of the myth of the threatening Father (cats. 117-121, 145). Although the maternal imago he constructs in this text has nothing to do with his real mother, in the process of examining childhood memories and fantasies he throws some light on the influence he believes she had, anxious and loving, on his sexual development. In one fantasy, the male/son is drowned in milk. The association of the fear of death with milk functions, he argues, as a symbolic defense against the danger of incest. He mingles what are probably real childhood memories with false ones. His mother forbade him from touching a poisonous plant which produced a substance known as Sainte Theresa's milk at the same period that he learned from school fellows that the penis if rubbed with this milk grew to huge proportions and could cause death. This convincing account of the terrorizing tales of childhood is followed by a false memory (doubtless inspired by Freud's psycho-analytical study of Leonardo) "of his mother sucking, devouring, his penis."[5] It was to his mother, he says, that he owed his "terror of the sexual act and the belief that it would bring about his total annihilation."[6]

The anxieties and desires that crackle in the 1929 paintings, with their deliberate Oedipal themes, could be seen to touch, in *The Enigma of Desire*, not just on paternal rivalries and taboos but on maternal ones as well. The sense of loss is combined with the sentiment of anxiety in the traumatically repeated words "my mother." D.A.

[1] Salvador Dalí, *The Secret Life of Salvador Dalí*, trans. Haakon Chevalier (London: Vision Press, 1968), p. 153.
[2] Salvador Dalí, "L'Amour," in *La Femme visible* (Paris: Éditions surréalistes, 1930), p. 66.
[3] *Ibid.*, p. 68.
[4] *Ibid.*, p. 66.
See also *The Haunted Self: Surrealism, Psychoanalysis, Subjectivity* (New Haven: Yale University Press, 2000), p. 163.
[5] Salvador Dalí, *Le Mythe tragique de l'Angélus de Millet, Interprétation 'paranoiaïque-critique'* (ca. 1932) (Paris: Jean-Jacques Pauvert, 1963), p. 57.
[6] *Ibid.*, p. 57.

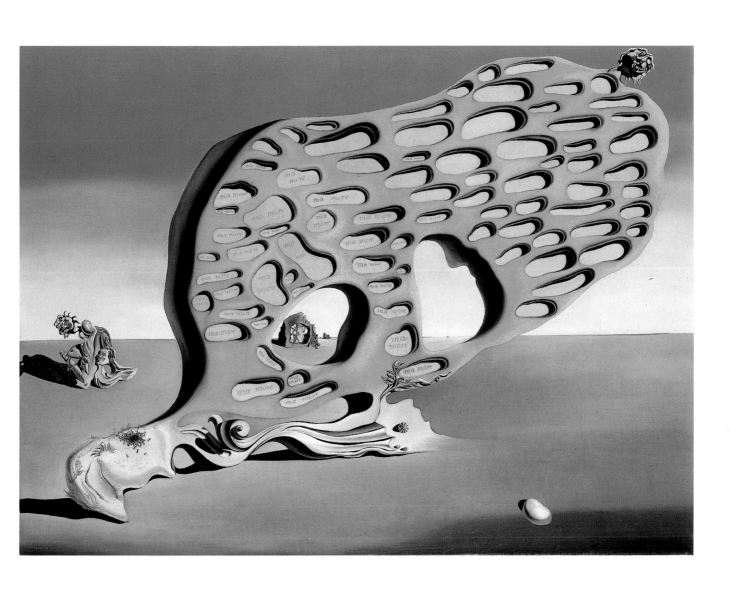

69. Accommodations of Desire, 1929

69. Oil and collage on board
22.5 × 35 cm
8⁷/8 × 13³/4 in.
New York (NY), The
Metropolitan Museum of Art,
The Jacques and Natasha
Gelman Collection

In an interview published in *The New Yorker* in July 1939, Dalí provided crucial information concerning the complex autobiographical references contained within this seminal painting. According to the artist's testimony, the setting is the Ampurdàn plain, near Figueres, his birthplace in Catalonia. Dalí remembered this place as a grim expanse of desertlike landscape, strewn with the fragmentary carcasses of donkeys and other animals, which led him to associate it with death and decomposition. Placed within this psychologically charged landscape are seven large stones or pebbles, upon which are painted the heads of roaring lions, a Freudian symbol of violence, passion, and authority. In the middle distance is a naked, androgynous figure, a self-portrait of the young Salvador, who clings to a bearded man with a lion coming out of his chest. According to Dalí, this man represents his father, an oppressive figure who made the young Salvador travel alone across the Ampurdàn plain on his five-mile walk to school. If he rebelled against this terrifying daily journey, his father would grab him by the hand and march across the plain, dragging his son behind him. Below the embracing father and son is a mustached young man—thought to be Dalí again—who holds his head in shame. To their left are a group of urns or jugs, one of which has flowered into a woman's head, which Dalí identified as his mother, who died of cancer when the artist was 16 years old.[1] As Ian Gibson has pointed out, "Dalí had never had to walk more than a few yards to school. As for the vast morbid plains of Catalonia, littered with the skeletons of asses, they sound more like the Sahara than the lush meadows of the Upper Empordà."[2] However, this false childhood memory was a key component of Dalí's psychosexual Oedipal scenario, repeatedly played out in his paintings of the late 1920s and early 1930s, which revolves around the artist's relationship with his loving mother, the woman-jug, and his formidable father, the ferocious notary-lion. However, Dalí's description of these symbolic representations in *The New Yorker* interview inexplicably leaves out an important aspect of this painting, namely the repressed desires that were awakened in him by the presence of Gala, his future wife, in Cadaqués during the summer of 1929. The artist's fear of intimacy and the sexual act meant that he was terrified by Gala's advances during the earliest days of their relationship, when they would go for long walks together among the olive trees and vines of the surrounding countryside. As Dalí later recounted, it was after one such outing that he painted the *Accommodations of Desire*, in which "lions' maws translate my terror before the revelation of the possession of a woman's cunt that would lead to the revelation of my impotence. I was getting prepared for the recoil of my shame. At this period, my laughing fits turned hysterical."[3]
The painting thus became a vehicle for exorcising his personal demons and sexual neuroses, especially regarding the fear and apprehension he felt over the im-

pending consummation of his relationship with the uninhibited Gala. Rather than simply representing his domineering father, as in other paintings of the time, "the terrorizing images of lions' heads" become multivalent images symbolizing, among other things, the artist's forbidden sexual desires, and the anxiety this caused him.[4] The lion's head, which the artist appears to have culled from a children's picture book of animals, is shown in various forms in the painting, including the small colored print that Dalí cut out and pasted on one of the pebbles. Dalí's expertise in working on such a small scale with a precise, miniaturist technique allowed him to seamlessly incorporate the collage element within the picture, which is difficult to distinguish from his own renderings of the storybook lion in oil paint. Other images on the pebbles directly express the artist's horror of his impending sexual union with Gala, which he believed would be "terribly violent and disproportionate to my physical vigor," while the predominance of red in the painting speaks to the heat of his passion and the rage and shame he felt concerning his perceived impotence.[5] These include the swarming ants that assume the shape of a vulva on the stone in the lower right-hand corner, and the small lion that replaces a woman's pubic area on the pebble above it. The lion thus becomes a sexually ambivalent symbol in this work, which conflates the artist's fear of his authoritarian father with his terror of female genitals and sexual intercourse to create one of his most memorable and celebrated compositions. *Accommodations of Desire* was included in Dalí's first solo exhibition at the Galerie Goemans in Paris in November 1929 and was reproduced in *La Révolution Surréaliste* in the following month, having been purchased by André Breton shortly before the exhibition opened.[6] M.R.T.

[1] Margaret Case Harriman, "Profiles: A Dream Walking," *The New Yorker*, vol. 15, no. 20 (July 1, 1939), p. 24. As Harriman concedes, the artist was reluctant to explain the work "because, to a Surrealist, trying to explain a picture is like trying to explain anything as instinctive as your reasons for pulling your hand away from a lighted match." However, Dalí's identification of the central protagonists and location of the picture is fundamental to our understanding of his early work.
[2] Ian Gibson, *The Shameful Life of Salvador Dalí* (London: Faber and Faber, 1997), p. 369.
[3] Salvador Dalí, *The Unspeakable Confessions of Salvador Dalí* (New York: William Morrow and Company, 1976), p. 92.
[4] Salvador Dalí, *The Secret Life of Salvador Dalí* (New York: Dial Press, 1942), p. 242.
[5] *Ibid.*
[6] The catalogue of the exhibition "Dalí," (Galerie Goemans, Paris, November 20-December 5), 1929, listed *Accommodations of Desire* as being in the collection of "A. Breton," confirming that he had acquired the work beforehand, see catalogue no. 2. The painting was subsequently reproduced in *La Révolution Surréaliste*, no. 12, (December 15, 1929), p.18.

70. Illuminated Pleasures, 1929

70. Oil and collage on board
23.5 × 34.9 cm
9 1/4 × 13 3/4 in.
New York (NY),
The Museum of Modern Art
The Sidney and Harriet Janis
Collection

Fig. 1. Max Ernst, *Pietà,*
or Revolution by Night, 1923
London, Tate

This disquieting painting continues the artist's quest to explore his sexual anxieties through the medium of oil paint and collage. Dalí's personal struggle is expressed in a plethora of disconcerting scenes, many of which appear to have been directly inspired by Sigmund Freud's psychoanalytical writings, such as the pair of hands struggling with a bloody knife that reference Freud's notion of castration anxiety. Many of these ciphers of the artist's personal obsessions are familiar from earlier works, especially the lion's head and woman-jug figure, which are thought to represent Dalí's domineering father and his beloved mother, who passed away eight years earlier and is now reduced to a Freudian receptacle with a ludicrous grin. However, the extraordinary concentration of imagery seen in the painting reveals the artist's increasing familiarity with the work of the artists associated with the Surrealist group in Paris. For example, the totem pole made up of multicolored birds' heads near the center of the composition is indebted to the work of Max Ernst, while the painting inside the box on the right, which depicts a large group of cyclists with smooth round stones or sugared almonds balanced on their heads, recalls the paintings of René Magritte.

This incongruous image is one of three paintings-within-a-painting, a pictorial device that was developed by Giorgio de Chirico during the First World War. Dalí may have known de Chirico's *Metaphysical Interior with Sanatorium*, of 1917, possibly through Gala, as at that time it was in the collection of her husband, the Surrealist poet Paul Eluard. This painting incorporates separate boxlike pictures, one of which contains a framed image of a landscape featuring a winding road, a gushing fountain, and a three-storied building. Like the box-framed pictures in Dalí's work, this painting-within-a-painting runs parallel to the picture plane, thus ensuring that the beguiling landscape scene within the box appears as real as the objects outside it. This disorienting effect is exacerbated in *Illuminated Pleasures* by the use of collage in the left-hand picture, in which a black and white print of a church façade provides the backdrop to a violent scene of a man firing a gun at a blood-filled object.

This symbolic imagery swirls around the central figure of Dalí's floating, disembodied head, which faces downward with eyes closed in an attitude suggested by the anthropomorphic geological structures of the rocks at Cap Creus on the Costa Brava. That the artist is shown fast asleep against a pale blue background suggests that what we are witnessing are painted memories or 'snapshots' of his dreams, whose terrifying nature is suggested by the nosebleed that trickles from his nostrils. Dalí en-

couraged such interpretations, claiming that he worked solely from dreams, or self-induced hypnagogic images, that came to him when he felt drowsy, or was about to fall asleep. "I do all my work subconsciously," he explained in 1934, "I never use models or paint from life or landscapes. It is all imagination. That is, I see everything in a dream as I am working, and when I have finished a picture, I decide what the title is to be. Sometimes it takes a long time before I can figure out what I have painted."[1]

In the case of this painting, Dalí was clear that the claustrophobic litany of images reflected his own family drama, in which the repressed desires that Gala had released in him were threatened by his feelings of shame and guilt, which were surmounted by his father's continuing disapproval of their relationship. Such a reading is supported by the image of the bearded paternal figure that cradles a frightened, fleeing woman in his arms, who attempts to grasp the swirl of blue water that emanates from the prone self-portrait, as if trying to capture Dalí's essence. However, this modern Venus also has a sinister side, denoted by her blood-stained hands, which, as Dawn Ades has persuasively argued, evokes the figure of Lady Macbeth trying in vain to wash the spots of blood from her hands in her imaginary guilt while sleepwalking.[2] The elderly father figure assisting the woman is drawn from Max Ernst's *Pietà, or Revolution by Night*, of 1923 (fig. 1), whose iconography refers not only to the Passion of Christ but also to the Greek myth of Oedipus, which according to Freud's interpretation was pregnant with unconscious incestuous feelings and repressed generational rivalries between father and son. This scene of parental violence and Oedipal guilt can be linked in Dalí's cosmogony to the image of the naked boy, hiding his face in shame, which can also be read as a self-portrait. Whereas the artist's earlier paintings had alluded to his sexual fantasies through veiled or abstract imagery, these images of pent-up family violence and repressed desires were now openly displayed, rather than hidden. As the artist later recalled, "pleasures, even criminal ones, in contrast to the Gothic period when they could be glimpsed only in the half-light of oil-lamps, can today be turned inside out like a stocking and displayed in broad daylight."[3] M.R.T.

[1] Anonymous, "Salvador Dalí Arrives," *New York Times*, November 15, 1934, p. 22.
[2] Dawn Ades, *Dalí and Surrealism* (London: Thames and Hudson, 1982), p. 81.
[3] Robert Descharnes, *The World of Salvador Dalí*, trans. Albert Field (New York: Harper & Row, 1962), p. 155.

71. Man of Sickly Complexion Listening to the Sound of the Sea or The two Balconies, 1929

71. Oil on wood panel
23.5 × 34.5 cm
9$^{1/4}$ × 13$^{5/8}$ in.
Rio de Janeiro, Museu
da Chácara do Céu,
Fundaçao Raymundo
Ottoni de Castro Maya

72. The Ants, 1929

SALVADOR DALI 1929

72. Gouache, ink and collage
11.5 × 16.4 cm
$4^{1/2} \times 6^{1/2}$ in.
Paris, Horacio Amigorena
Collection

73. Phantasmagoria, ca. 1930

73. Oil on panel
69 × 44 cm
27 1/8 × 17 3/8 in.
Beverly Hills (CA), J. Nicholson

The title of this important early painting aptly describes the shifting medley of real or imagined figures that haunted Dalí's work of this time. From the artist's writings and published statements we can tentatively identify the characters involved in this complex Oedipal scenario that was built around specific persons and events in his life, such as the death of his beloved mother and his strained relationship with his fearsome father. The two keys that face each other on the plinth that contains the artist's signature encourage the viewer to decode this imagery, much like a psychoanalyst would analyze a patient's dreams. The key is, of course, a standard Freudian symbol of the unconscious, which must be unlocked to gain access to the analysand's repressed desires, in the hope of finding the trigger for their emotional disorder. However, any attempt to deconstruct Dalí's mythic autobiography through the visual evidence of his paintings must be made with the proviso that the artist had a profound knowledge of the language and tropes of psychoanalysis. He was thus fully aware that he was utilizing the signature themes of Freudian psychoanalytical theory, such as Oedipal guilt, castration anxiety, and paternal retribution, to explore his childhood memories and sexual fantasies. Dalí was thus a conscious and knowing editor of his fears and desires, which he nonetheless presents in his paintings as unconscious fantasies, secrets, phobias, anxieties and perversions, in the confessional mode of the 'talking cure' of psychoanalysis.

The key that Dalí offers the viewer to unlock the veiled meaning of this painting comes from Sigmund Freud's psychoanalytical study of the biography of Leonardo da Vinci, in which the Viennese doctor considered the implications of the Renaissance artist's memory of a vulture that visited him in his cradle, opening his mouth with its tail.[1] This reference is made clear in the iconography of Dalí's golden-hued painting, which revolves around the familiar figures of his mother as a jug-receptacle, his father as a ferocious lion, and his own anamorphic self-portrait in the guise of "The Great Masturbator," to borrow the title of an eponymous work of the same year. We feel Dalí's physical and emotional pain in the form of a bloody nose, and a grasshopper that has attached itself to his face, as if in the sexual act of mounting or penetrating his mouth, much like the vulture's tail that had repeatedly struck Leonardo's lips. The artist's childhood fear of these insects had led him to associate them with abjection and horror, and the strategic placement of the grasshopper over his mouth renders the artist mute, thus conveying a sense of terror-stricken paralysis.[2]

The artist even added a terrifying, long-beaked bird into the composition, thus reinforcing the connection with Freud's celebrated essay on Leonardo. This bird can also be seen as a reference to the hidden vulture that Freud saw in Leonardo's *Virgin and Child with St. Anne*, of ca. 1508-10.[3] In this case, the bird of prey occupies the psychologically charged space between the artist's mother and father. One can almost hear the ear-piercing cry of this fantastic creature with its mouth open and tongue extended, although Dalí, echoing Freud's daring hypothesis concerning the riddle of Leonardo's character, leaves open the possibility that the bird represents a fusion of several repressed fantasies. It is thus unclear whether the vulture is protecting his mother from the sexual advances and violence of his father, or is there to reinforce the atmosphere of forbidden and incestuous desires that pervade the painting. Although this intense family drama threatens to permanently engulf the emotionally crippled artist, there is hope that his sense of paralysis and mute torment will be assuaged in the future, perhaps through the aid of Gala, his muse and liberator, whom he first met in the summer of 1929. In the distance, a statue of naked man points toward the horizon in a gesture laden with optimism, while to his right a giant peacock moth has alighted in an area beyond the leonine image of the artist's father. This moth perhaps signals the new life that Dalí would build for himself and Gala, as he emerged from the smothering cocoon of his overbearing family in Catalonia. M.R.T.

[1] Sigmund Freud, "Leonardo da Vinci and a Memory of His Childhood," reprinted in *The Freud Reader*, ed. Peter Gay (New York: W.W. Norton, 1989), pp. 443-481.
[2] Salvador Dalí first recounted the history of his violent terror of grasshoppers in his 1929 essay "The Liberation of the Fingers." According to this account, up until the age of seven or eight the artist had loved to chase and catch grasshoppers. But one day on the rocks in front of the family home at Cadaqués he caught a small fish, which he suddenly threw away in revulsion and screamed that it had the same face as a grasshopper. From that moment he acquired an intense phobia about grasshoppers, and as a result was mercilessly teased by his schoolfellows, see Dalí, "L'alliberaments dels dits" (The Liberation of the Fingers), *L'Amic de les Arts*, vol. 4, no. 31 (Sitges: March 31, 1929), p. 6, reprinted in *The Collected Writings of Salvador Dalí*, ed. trans. Haim Finkelstein (Cambridge: Cambridge University Press, 1998), p. 100.
[3] Dalí later made reference to Freud's 'discovery' in the catalogue for his 1939 exhibition at the Julien Levy Gallery, New York: "Sigmund Freud, in analysing the famous invisible vulture (which appears in that strangest of all pictures, Leonardo's *Virgin of the Rocks* [sic]) involuntarily laid the epistological and philosophical cornerstone of the majestic edifice of imminent 'paranoiac painting,'" see Salvador Dalí, *Dalí, Dalí!* (New York: Julien Levy Gallery, 1939), n.p. As Freud himself acknowledged, the hidden vulture was first discovered by a disciple of his named Oscar Pfister.

74. Paranoiac Woman-Horse
(Invisible Sleeping Woman, Lion, Horse)[1], 1930

74. Oil on canvas
50.2 × 65.2 cm
19³/4 × 25⁵/8 in.
Paris, Musée national d'art
moderne, Centre Georges
Pompidou, gift of the
Association Bourdon

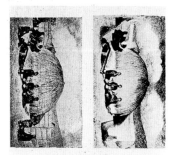

Fig. 1. Salvador Dalí, "The Invisible
Man," in *Le Surréalisme au service
de la révolution*, no. 1,
July 1930

Fig. 2. Salvador Dalí,
*"Communication: visage
paranoiaque,"* in *Le Surréalisme
au service de la révolution,* no. 3,
December 1931

This is probably the first completed example of Dalí's paranoiac "double images." His other major experiment in double images at the time, *The Invisible Man* (fig. 1), was still unfinished when it was exhibited at the Pierre Colle Gallery in 1931, where it was dated somewhat surprisingly 1929-32. *Paranoiac Woman-Horse* was exhibited for the first time in the foyer of Studio 28 during the showing of Buñuel and Dalí's film *L'Âge d'or* (November 28 – December 3, 1930). On 3ʳᵈ December, a mob from the League of Patriots and the anti-Jewish league attacked the cinema, throwing ink at the screen, smoke bombs into the audience and slashing the works by Dalí, Ernst, Man Ray, Miró and Tanguy in the foyer exhibition. The destruction was documented in the protest tract by the Surrealists, *L'Affaire de l'Âge d'or*. Following the severe damage to his painting, Dalí was invited by the Comte de Noailles to repaint it, which he willingly did, exhibiting at the 1931 Pierre Colle exhibition two new canvases on the theme: *Invisible Sleeping Woman, Lion, Horses* and *Sleeping Woman, Lion, Horses* (figs. 3, 4). The two slightly later versions are very interesting in their own right; neither replicates the original painting. The grisaille version concentrates on a straining couple that doubles as the head and breast of the sleeping woman. The other places a more voluptuous rendering of the female nude, with the lion's head strongly emphasized in black and white in a deep golden landscape, littered with distended objects that suggest anamorphic perspectives.

Dalí chose *Invisible Sleeping Woman, Horse, Lion* as the key example to demonstrate his new ideas about paranoia in the important text "L'âne pourri"(The Rotting Donkey), which was published in the first issue of *Le Surréalisme au service de la révolution* (July 1930) and was to form part of his book *La Femme visible* in 1930. "The double image (an example of which could be the image of a horse which is at the same time the image of a woman) can be prolonged, continuing the paranoiac process, the existence of another obsessional idea being sufficient for a third image to appear (the image of a lion, for example)…"[2]. Dalí understands paranoia as a "delirium of interpretation": a single configuration can be "read" or interpreted in different ways—depending, as he explained in "Communication: visage paranoiaque," on the particular interests or obsessions of the viewer (fig. 2).

Just as in "Communication: visage paranoiaque," where the double image originates in a postcard of an African hut, which he "mis-read" as a painting from Picasso's African period, while Breton, to whom he showed the picture, saw in it a portrait of the Marquis de Sade, the origins of the central figure in *Paranoiac Woman-Horse* lie, not in objects in the external world, but in other paintings. The sleeping woman is constructed of other elements in a manner resembling Arcimboldo (fig. 6); her over-

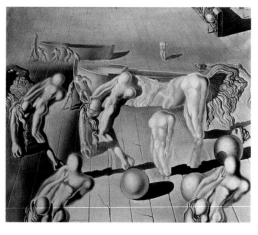

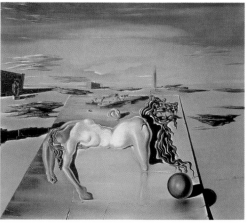

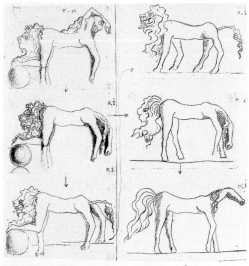

Fig. 20
Salvador Dalí

Figs. 3-4. Salvador Dalí, *Invisible Sleeping Woman, Lion, Horses* and *Sleeping Woman, Lion, Horses*, 1930
Paris, Private collection

Fig. 5. Salvador Dalí, *Sleeping Woman, Lion, Horses*, page from an unpublished film scenario, ca. 1931

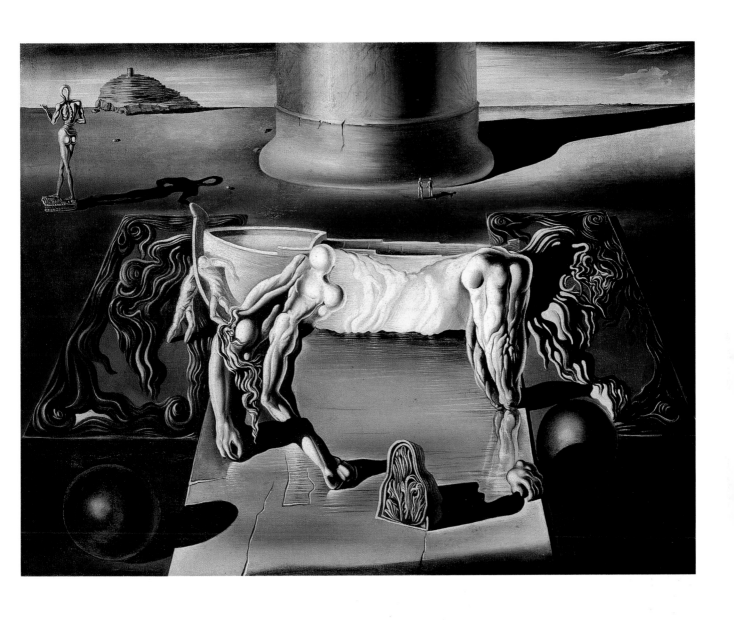

131

Fig. 6. Arcimboldo, *Summer*, 1563
Vienna, Gemäldegalerie

Fig. 7. Giulio Romano
(ca. 1499-1546), *Fight for the Body
of Dead Patroclus* (detail)
Mantua, ducal palace

Fig. 8. Heinrich Füssli,
Nightmare, 1781
Detroit, The Detroit Institute of Art

all posture resembles less a classic reclining female nude than the exaggerated figure with a long extended arm in Fuseli's *Nightmare* (1781) (fig. 8). The grotesque horse's head in Fuseli's painting, a visual pun on "night-mare," is fused by Dalí into the female figure. Fuseli's painting would have attract-

ed Dalí not just because it is redolent of the atmosphere of the gothic novel, which appealed to the Surrealists, but because it witnesses the early stirring of scientific interest in states of mind, dreams and what was to become known as the unconscious. Dalí's attention may have been drawn to it in the course of his research for a book, never published but often announced in the early 1930s, on *Surrealist Painting through the Ages*.

Another proposed source is a composition by Giulio Romano for the Trojan Room ("Sala di Troia") in the ducal palace in Mantua (fig. 7).[5] The body of the dead hero Patroclus carried by Achilles could have suggested both the reclining woman's pose and the strongly marked musculature of the configuration that produces both the woman's arm and the leg of another standing figure, whose head and shoulder are also her breasts. This ambiguous form is picked up in the more overtly sexualized nude couples in the second, grisaille version of *Invisible Woman* (fig. 3), whose postures recall the encounter of the female head and male torso in *The Great Masturbator* (cat. 65). The flowing manes of the horse/lion could plausibly originate in the classically influenced forms of Romano. A striking feature in the original *Invisible Sleeping Woman, Horse, Lion,* which does not appear in the two later versions, is the huge centrally placed column, whose base alone is visible. This recalls the curious composition of Veronese's *Last Supper*, where a

Fig. 9. Paolo Veronese,
The Last Supper, after 1581
Milan, Pinacoteca di Brera

similar column rears up prominently in the foreground (fig. 9).

When Dalí came to illustrate his ideas on paranoia and the double image for the short documentary film he planned on Surrealism, (which was never realized) he chose *Invisible Sleeping Woman, horse, lion* as his model (fig. 5). His scenario explains step by step how the double image is obtained, and the commentary reminds us how the mobility of film remained a constant lure for him: "Paranoiac activity offers us the possibility of systematizing delirium. Paranoiac images are due to the delirium of interpretation. Delirium which, in a dream, disappears on awakening, continues in reality in paranoiac images and is communicable objectively to everyone. We shall see how paranoiac delirium can make an oDalísque simultaneously a horse and a lion. The oDalísque enters, lies down languorously. Notice the movement of the horse's tail, which becomes again an odalisque and now a lion which fades into the distance. Here is a real phantom."[4] However, the schematic rendering of the core image in the scenario cannot do justice to the richly diverse and ambiguous ways in which Dalí

used the medium of paint to elaborate on the multiple associations of this first double image in its three versions. Although these first essays in the double image do not reach the slick precision of later examples such as *Endless Enigma* (cat. 183), their radical and experimental intervention in the relation between perception and representation opened a new chapter for Surrealism. D.A.

[1] *Dormeuse cheval lion invisibles (Invisible Sleeping Woman, horse, lion)* was the title under which the painting was listed in the catalogue in the brochure accompanying the film *L'Âge d'or.* It was subsequently entitled *Paranoiac Woman-Horse.*

[2] Salvador Dalí, "L'Âne pourri, à Gala Éluard," *Le Surréalisme au service de la révolution*, no. 1 (Paris: July 1930), p. 10.

[3] Claire Pélissié, "Une devinette de Salvador Dalí," *Revue de l'art* (Paris: 1992), p. 77.

[4] Dawn Ades, "Unpublished scenario for a documentary on Surrealism," *Studio International Journal of the Creative Arts and Design*, vol. 195, nos. 993-994, (London: 1982), pp. 62-77.

75. Study for "Invisible Sleeping Woman, Lion, Horse," 1930
76. Study for "Invisible Sleeping Woman, Lion, Horse," 1929

75. China ink and pencil
on paper
27 × 47 cm
10⁵/₈ × 18¹/₂ in.
Paris, Private collection

76. Mixed media
34.3 × 51
13¹/₂ × 20 in.
Figueres, Fundació
Gala-Salvador Dalí

77. Study for "Invisible Sleeping Woman, Lion, Horse," 1929

77. Pencil on paper
64.5 × 55 cm
25³/8 × 21⁵/8 in.
Private collection

78. William Tell, 1930

78. Oil and collage on canvas
113 × 87 cm
44 1/2 × 34 1/4 in.
Paris, Musée national
d'art moderne, Centre
Georges Pompidou

The legend of William Tell suddenly enters Dalí's work in 1930 as a new dramatic focus to the Oedipal myths familiar to the Surrealists but with a very personal significance for the painter. The story of the 14th-century Swiss patriot, a famous bowman, who refused to acknowledge the authority of the occupying Austrian forces and was condemned to shoot an arrow through an apple placed on his son's head, was re-interpreted by Dalí to become the vehicle for a threatening and cannibalistic myth of the Father. This idea makes an immediate appearance in several forms: with this painting and related works like *The Old Age of William Tell*, in the long poem "The Great Masturbator," which forms the third part of *La Femme visible* (fig. 1), and in the photograph by Buñuel of Dalí with the empty sea urchin shell posed on his shaved head, which Dalí adapted for the frontispiece to *L'Amour et la mémoire*.

Although the painting has the title *William Tell*, it neither illustrates the legend nor even refers explicitly to the chief motif Dalí drew from it in other contexts: the apple, or other edible object, placed on the son/victim's head. William Tell is, rather, drawn into the generalized myth of the Father: Saturn, who ate his own sons, Abraham, who tried to sacrifice his son Isaac, and God the Father, who did sacrifice his Son. In this painting, the immediate visual analogy is with the famous section of Michelangelo's Sistine chapel ceiling, with the finger of God pointing to his creation Adam, here transposed into a father and son whose gestures indicate mutual accusation and guilt.

Dalí's treatment of the paternal myth is as ambiguous, though in different ways, as that of Max Ernst in *Pieta or Revolution by Night*. In this key Surrealist image, as in de Chirico's *The Child's Brain* (fig. 2, p. 138), the Surrealist writer Robert Melville recognized the revelation of "the face of the Father."[1] Ernst subverts the classic Christian image of the Dead Christ, borrowing from a South German tradition that shows Him cradled not in the arms of the mother but of the Father. *Pieta* is informed by a familiarity with Freudian ideas and the dead or catatonic son, a recognizable self-portrait, has been interpreted in terms of a reversed oedipal myth.[2] Dalí, who follows Ernst's example in making his starting point a familiar Christian image, is no less conscious of the core psycho-analytical notion of Oedipal rivalry, but elaborates it in his own terms. The violence of the castration drama is at the fore in Dalí's painting, the father wielding a pair of scissors, just above a fountain, while the son's genitals are hidden by a collage of leaves. However, although the father is apparently the terrible perpetrator of the crime he is also a ridiculous figure: grinning, exposed and half-naked. Dalí's poem "The Great Masturbator" revels in the threateningly doubled, but also ludicrous figures of the two William Tells:

"Further away
beyond the face of the great Masturbator
rose
two huge sculptures of William Tell
One made
Of real chocolate
The other of false shit…"[3]

The combination of fear and mockery here is extremely telling and must be a reaction against the recent traumatic quarrel with his father, which result-

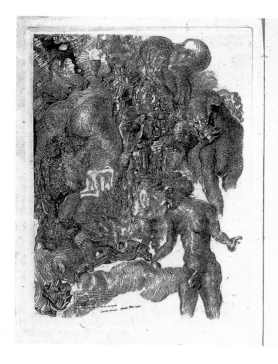

SALVADOR DALI

LA FEMME
VISIBLE

ÉDITIONS SURRÉALISTES
A PARIS
1930

Fig. 1. Frontispiece to
La Femme Visible, 1930

136

Fig. 2. Giorgio de Chirico,
The Child's Brain, 1914
Stockholm, Moderna Museet

ed in Dalí's banishment from the family home (see *Sometimes I spit...*, cat. 63). The intensity of these events has a Homeric quality: Dalí's father defends the sacred family hearth against the incursions of alien forces. Gala and Surrealism together seem to the father to have perverted the son and turned him against his own family. And the father reacts violently: Dalí is thrown out without a penny, harried by the local police and warned never to return to Cadaqués. In a style equally worthy of an epic hero, Dalí defies the paternal edict by not only remaining loyal to Gala, and to Surrealism, but also purchasing a small fishing hut in Port Lligat, the next bay to Cadaqués, where he will make his permanent home. These events are the immediate context for this powerful painting, in which the stereotype of the oedipal threat has become the mask for his personal drama. The ludicrously virile aggression of the father is fully matched by the aggression of the picture as a whole against him.

The fleeing horse, the rotting donkey in the piano and its effete virtuoso pianist are Dalí's signs of the *putrefact*, a character invented during his Residencia days in Madrid, who stood for the hated bourgeoisie, its sentimental tastes and hypocritical aesthetic enthusiasms. It had taken horrific physical form in the film *Un Chien andalou*, with the putrefying body of the donkey in the grand piano, hauled along as the final dead weight on the rope that holds the hero back from his lustful attack, here graphically replayed complete with concert pianist. The presence of the ghostly female figure, trapped but otherwise inviolate in a box beneath William Tell, may signify Gala, threatened but remote from the conflict.

Dalí's choice of this Swiss hero was probably influenced by the recent publication of an epic drama by the Catalan writer Eugenio D'Ors, *Guillermo Tell* (1926). Although an historical drama, the old legend as the bearer of patriotic ideas clearly had, for D'Ors, contemporary relevance to Catalonia and its subjugation under the Castilian yoke. Any political link is ambiguous, though Dalí's father's support for limited Catalan autonomy might have incidentally supported Dalí's identification of him with Tell. Although Dalí's treatment of the paternal imago does not very obviously source itself in the full Surrealist revolt against the trinity "*père, patron, patrie*" (father, boss, fatherland) his skepticism of politics may have a taken a foothold here.

The archetypal father/son relationship, whose real basis in Dalí's relations with his father is foreshadowed in his early portraits, had figured in 1929 paintings where an old man and a youth often appear locked in intense encounters, as in *The Font* (cat. 81) or *Lugubrious Game*. In the latter, the two figures in the lower right of the painting recall de Chirico's *Prodigal Son*, which was reproduced in *Valori Plastici*. In *William Tell*, however, the father

and son are separated. Their separation, which is paradoxically built on the linking gesture in Michelangelo's Sistine ceiling, is enforced by a third "point" which descends to meet the two straining fingers—the leg of the piano. This not only neutralizes the famous creational gesture, but also emphasizes the strangely empty core to this violent picture, the void of the blank horizon.

Buñuel, who claimed to have witnessed the violent expulsion of Dalí from his father's house, clearly kept sufficiently remote from their quarrel to make a short film, known as *Menjant Garotas* ("Eating sea urchins") at the time he was shooting scenes for *L'Âge d'or* in the environs of Cadaqués. It shows Dalí's father and step-mother at their seaside home. In one scene, Dalí's father appears with a huge pile of sea urchins on the table before him, which he slices and devours while drinking quantities of wine. It is an impressive and intimidating sight, and underlines the highly personal relevance of the sea urchin shell that Dalí, as the victim son of "William Tell," placed on his shaved head in Buñuel's photograph. In the frontispiece for *L'amour et la mémoire*, Dalí constructs a photomontage, splicing this photograph with one of Gala, his rescuer, sitting on the wall at Port Lligat.

By the time it was exhibited at Dalí's solo exhibition at the Pierre Colle Gallery in Paris in June 1931, *William Tell* belonged to the Surrealist leader André Breton, who kept it for the rest of his life. D.A.

[1] Robert Melville, "Three Moves in the Big Game," *View*, series 4, Autumn 1944, p. 78.
[2] Interpretations of *Pietà* have pointed in Freudian terms to the ambivalence of the relationship between son and father, which might indicate a death wish against the father turned back onto the son himself, or even desire for the father (Freud's case studies of The Wolf Man and of Schreber are cited). See Malcolm Gee, "Max Ernst, God and Revolution by Night," *Arts Magazine*, no. 55 (1981), pp. 85-91 and Dawn Ades, "Dalí and the Myth of William Tell," in Ades, Dawn and Fiona Bradley, *Salvador Dalí: A Mythology* (London: Tate Gallery Publishing, 1998).
[3] Salvador Dalí, "Le Grand Masturbateur," in *La Femme visible* (Paris: Éditions surréalistes, 1930), p. 43.

79. Study for "Memory of the Child Woman," 1932

79. China ink, lead point
and colored pencils on
watermarked paper
32.5 × 28 cm
$12^{7}/8$ × 11 in.
Paris, Musée Picasso

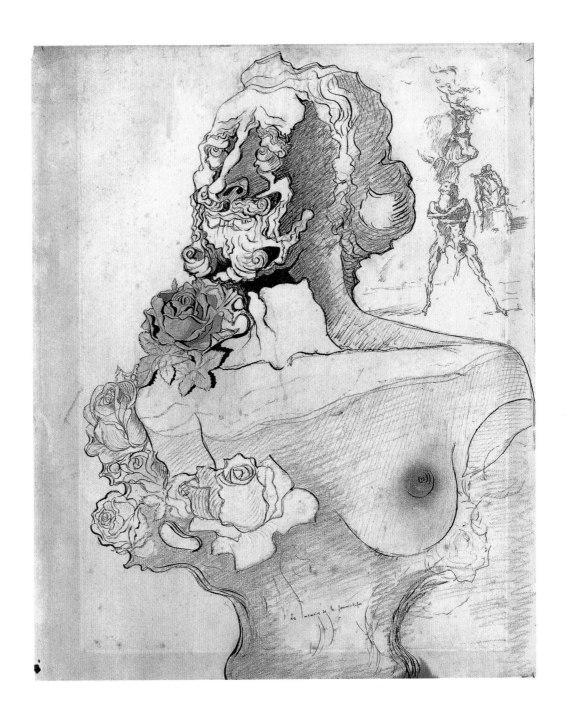

80. Premature Ossification of a Railway Station, 1930

80. Oil on canvas
31.5 × 27 cm
15¹/₂ × 10⁵/₈ in.
Alan Koppel Gallery, Chicago

This work evokes the eerily silent city squares of Giorgio de Chirico's metaphysical paintings, which share a similar vocabulary of disembodied shadows, exaggerated perspectives, and incongruous station clocks. Dalí's early poetic texts and critical writings reveal that he had admired the Greek-born artist's work since the early 1920s, having discovered his paintings through reproductions in the Italian avant-garde journal *Valori Plastici*, which ran from 1919 to 1921.[1] However, the artist's trips to Paris in the late 1920s, where he eventually settled at the end of the decade, would have provided Dalí with numerous opportunities to experience de Chirico's paintings firsthand, since close friends and colleagues such as André Breton, Paul Éluard, Max Ernst, and Jean Paulhan all owned major early works by the artist. De Chirico's *The Enigma of a Day* of 1914 was in Breton's collection when Dalí first arrived in Paris and a loose memory of this famous painting of a sun-drenched piazza, with its plunging perspectives, appears to inform *Premature Ossification of a Railway Station*. Dalí's veneration of de Chirico's work and ideas was no doubt influenced by his relationship with Gala, who had visited the artist's studio in Rome in 1923, where her then husband, Paul Éluard, had acquired some paintings.

The son of a railway engineer, de Chirico's thinly painted, luminous paintings often featured puffing steam locomotives and deserted train stations, whose mysterious empty spaces are suffused with a sense of loneliness and melancholy. De Chirico's work of the 1910s was hailed as an important precursor to Surrealist painting and Dalí quickly picked up on his use of deep space and deliberate

distortions, as seen in the deformed clock (which anticipates the limp watches he perfected in the following year in *The Persistence of Memory*) whose late hour does not accord with the sun-drenched sandy plain depicted in *Premature Ossification of a Railway Station*. Elsewhere, the illogical use of cast shadows, falling in different directions as if lit by multiple light sources, again points to de Chirico's subtle undermining of the rules that governed the use of perspective and other pictorial devices associated with painterly illusionism. In an essay written just two years before this work was completed, Dalí extolled the virtues of de Chirico's paintings, with their "bloodied perspectives" and "terrible calmness."[2]

Whereas de Chirico took his inspiration from the "nonsensical," anti-Positivist poetics of the German philosopher Friedrich Nietzsche, which awakened in him a new pictorial vocabulary based on intuition and revelation, rather than the external appearance of the world, Dalí's interest in challenging common sense, logic, reason, and causality came out of his profound understanding of the psychoanalytical writings of Sigmund Freud. This crucial difference manifests itself in the painting's title, which conjures up an image of the natural world turned to bone, where trees and people are frozen in time and petrified, literally stopped in their tracks like the train rails that plunge into the distance, only to be blocked by an oversized woman's shoe, one of Dalí's principal fetishes. This disquieting vision is quite different to the sense of premonition and foreboding found in de Chirico's early paintings, where the use of skewed perspectives and multiple viewpoints invokes a sense of uneasiness, rather than terror or paranoia. Although Dalí would continue to be interested in de Chirico's work—and by extension that of Arnold Böcklin, whose mythological paintings were greatly admired by both artists—throughout his career, this work is arguably the closest he came to imitating the older artist's troubling dream reality. M.R.T.

Fig. 1. Giorgio de Chirico,
The Enigma of a Day, 1914
New York (NY), The Museum
of Modern Art
© 2004, Digital image,
The Museum of Modern Art,
New York / Scala, Firenze

[1] The artist's 1927 essay "Sant Sebastià," for example, makes reference to de Chirico's *Evangelical Still Life* of 1917, which had been reproduced in *Valori Plastici*, nos. VII-VIII, July-August 1920, facing p. 81; see Salvador Dalí, "Saint Sebastià" (Saint Sebastian), *L'Amic de les Arts* vol. 2, no. 16 (Sitges: July 31, 1927), pp. 52-54, reprinted in Haim Finkelstein, ed., *The Collected Writings of Salvador Dalí*, trans. Haim Finkelstein (Cambridge: Cambridge University Press, 1998), p. 22.
[2] Salvador Dalí, "Nous limits de la pintura," Part I, *L'Amic de les Arts*, vol. 3, no. 22 (Sitges:February 29, 1928), pp. 167-169, translated in Haim Finkelstein, ed., *The Collected Writings of Salvador Dalí, ibid.*, p. 84.

81. The Font, 1930
82. Combinations (or The complete dalinian phantasm: hunts, keys, nails etc.), 1931

81. Oil and Collage
on wood panel
66 × 41 cm
26 × 16 1/8 in.
St. Petersburg (FL),
The Salvador Dalí Museum

82. Gouache on paper
14 × 9 cm
5 1/2 × 3 1/2 in.
New York (NY), Private
collection

This painting continues the construction of psycho-analytic and autobiographical content first explored in *The First Days of Spring* (1929, cat. 64), which latter work initiated Dalí's entrance in André Breton's Surrealism. Further psycho-analytic content is wedded to a devastatingly anti-clerical stance. The title refers to the Baptismal font in the background that doubles as a woman's face rendered in Art Nouveau style, with her mouth and forehead covered with ants. The space is a plunging perspective with a high horizon line reminiscent of de Chirico's metaphysical painting and heightening the unreal sense of the bizarre scene. In the middle ground is a vase in the form of a female resting on a plinth and facing a chalice and radiating host. A grasshopper, symbol of irrational fear, rests on the plinth on which there is a blood stain and a key, suggestive of unlocking the meaning of hermetic dream images.

Robert Lubar has pointed out the sexual symbolism of the two male figures in the foreground. One kneels and embraces the other who holds out one hand while covering his face with the other as if blinded by the light of the host. Are they engaged in the act of fellatio with the standing figure tyrannized by shame? Again as Lubar points out, the fantastic bird (perhaps a vulture) and the grasshopper resting on the head of the kneeling figure recall passages in Freud's essay on Leonardo, and the lion represents the "sign of paternal authority under which this nightmarish scene of desire, guilt, and retribution is enacted."[1]

The strange organic form with holes at the right introduces key imagery, screws, and ants, as well as a French postage stamp representing Marianne, a feminine ideal of desire. On top of this edifice rests another menacing grasshopper and more ants. The flowing, hairlike structure of this construction recalls Art Nouveau architecture. At the same time, as both Reynolds Morse and Ian Gibson have noted, it recalls the uncanny rock formations of Cap Creus. The doubling of such local images is typical of Dalí's painting of this period. The columns of course may be read as phallic symbols, but they likely derive from the Greek ruins in Ampurias located near Dalí's native Figueres. In this way Dalí again anchors the Freudian, and presumably universal, symbolism of desire in the local and personal dimension of autobiography. W.J.

[1] Robert S. Lubar, *Dalí: The Salvador Dalí Museum Collection* (Boston: Bulfinch Press, 2000), p. 60.

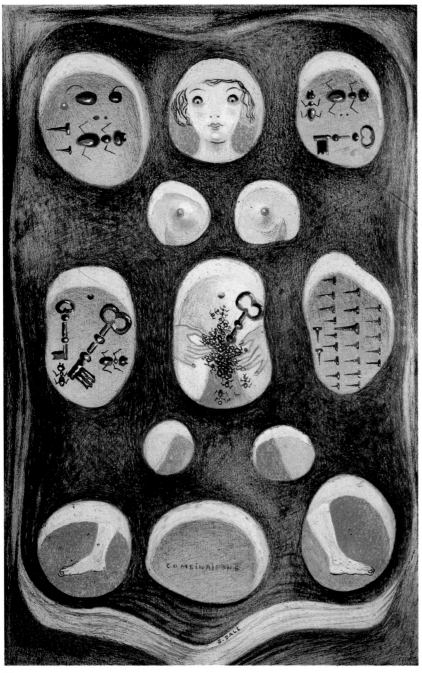

82

83. Projet pour le menu de la Société du roman philosophique, 1931

84. Dessin fait expressément pour Gala, 1931

83. China ink and pencil
on paper
26 × 20 cm
10 1/4 × 7 7/8 in.
Private collection

84. Ink on paper
25 × 17.5 cm
9 7/8 × 6 7/8 in.
Private collection

85. Des Douceurs fines pour les enfants, 1931   86. Automatisme rapide d'un rêve, 1931

85. China ink and pencil
on paper
27 × 18 cm
10⁵/8 × 7 in.
Private collection

86. China ink
25 × 16.5 cm
9⁷/8 × 6¹/2 in.
Private collection

87. Narcissus, 1931

87. China ink and pencil
on paper
23.5 × 18 cm
9¹/4 × 7 in.
Private collection

88. Reverie – Password: Mess up All the Slate, 1933

88. China ink on paper
28.2 × 21.3 cm
11 1/8 × 8 3/8 in.
Private collection

89. The Persistence of Memory, 1931

89. Oil on canvas
24.1 × 33 cm
9¹/2 × 13 in.
New York (NY),
The Museum of Modern Art
Given anonymously
© 2004, Digital image,
The Museum of Modern Art,
New York / Scala, Firenze

Dalí described the genesis of this painting in his 1942 autobiography, *The Secret Life of Salvador Dalí*, in which he claimed that the unforgettable limp watches were inspired by the remains of a very strong Camembert cheese. He had contemplated this cheese one evening after dinner, when he stayed at home with a headache while Gala went to the cinema with some friends. Having meditated on the "super-soft" qualities of the runny cheese, Dalí went to his studio where he suddenly realized how he should finish a lonely landscape featuring the rugged cliffs of the Catalan coast, illuminated by a never-setting sun, which had been sitting on his easel awaiting inspiration. "This picture represented a landscape near Port Lligat, whose rocks were lighted by a transparent and melancholy twilight; in the foreground an olive tree with its branches cut, and without leaves. I knew that the atmosphere which I had succeeded in creating with this landscape was to serve as a setting for some idea, for some surprising image, but I did not in the least know what it was going to be. I was about to turn out the light, when instantaneously I "saw" the solution. I saw two soft watches, one of them hanging lamentably on the branch of the olive-tree."[1] Within two hours he had added the startling imagery of the melting watches to this meticulously rendered landscape setting, and so created his most celebrated painting. Throughout his career Dalí explored his fascination with softness and malleability in numerous paintings, sculpture and works on paper, as well as in his critical writings. However, none has a more obvious sexual significance than the limp pocket watches in this painting, hanging flaccidly from the branch of the defoliated olive tree, drooping over the edge of a blocky architectural form, or draped over the amorphous creature sleeping in the foreground, which can be understood as a self-portrait from related works, such as *The Great Masturbator*, in which Dalí fuses his own features with those of the white granite rock above the Bay of Cullero on Cape Creus. A fourth timepiece, its watch case covered in swarming ants, rests dial-down on the plinth's surface, while a fly alights on the face of its neighbor, soon to become the butt of a thousand jokes about "time flies" that the artist could not have foreseen. The addition of the melting pocket watches animated the empty, desertlike expanse of the painting, while also highlighting as never before Dalí's avowed intention to use his "paranoiac critical" method to disrupt conventional notions of reality and the universe by exploiting moments of extreme irrational intuition. In this painting, which simultaneously renders events in both actual time and remembered time, the artist claimed, with some justification, to have paralleled Albert Einstein's scientific discoveries, especially those presented in his special and general theory of relativity, published in 1920, which overturned the old absolute notions of a cosmic order.[2] The soft watches, all stopped at different times, were thus an unconscious symbol of the relativity of space and time, which when seen together create a sensation of timelessness that is associated with the frozen temporal state of dreams and nightmares.

Although Gala would prophetically claim the work to be so extraordinary that "no one can forget it once he has seen it,"[3] *The Persistence of Memory* was left unsold when it was first shown in Dalí's solo exhibition at the Pierre Colle Gallery in Paris in the summer of 1931.[4] However, the young American art dealer, Julien Levy, acquired the painting shortly after the close of the show, paying the trade price of a mere $250.[5] It was only when the work was widely exhibited in the United States in the early 1930s that it gained the recognition it deserved as one of the most important paintings of the 20th-century.[6] The painting became an overnight sensation when it was included in a group exhibition entitled "Surréalisme" held at the Julien Levy Gallery in New York in January 1932.[7] That *The Persistence of Memory* stole the show is reflected by the fact that it was reproduced in virtually every review, or lampooned in cartoons that poked fun at watches that were as soft as melting butter or overripe cheese, and the strange monster with the long eyelashes in the foreground, who was invariably interpreted as a sleeping walrus or a fat snail.

Visitors to the Julien Levy Gallery were utterly perplexed, yet completely enthralled by what Levy called his "10 × 14 inches of Dalí dynamite."[8] Art critics were equally divided on the meaning of the painting, which some saw as a haunting metaphor for the ephemeral nature of mankind, our inevitable demise, and our subsequent obsession with the nature of time set against us, while others understood it as Dalí's own attempt to defeat time and achieve immortality through an enduring image of man's triumph over the forces of decay. The response of the critic for *Art News* is fairly typical: "Salvador Dalí is a clever painter with macabre yet forceful tendencies. His *Persistence de la Mémoire* is a curious medley of watch dials which droop and drip all over a charming landscape, one of the foreground timepieces being cosily crowded by ants! Page Mr. Freud!"[9] Psychiatrists were indeed drawn to the artist's pictorial investigations of memories, dreams, and the unconscious, but were likewise unable to reach an agreed conclusion on the painting: "The limpness of the clocks, one of them found, expressed impotence. Another felt that it was an excellent rendition of potence, because time, as symbolized in the clocks, meant power which could be transformed into anything, even saddles on which one might mount and ride off to victory in the distant hills."[10]

The popular and critical success of the work ensured that it did not stay in Levy's hands for long,

and in the following year he sold it to Mrs. Stanley B. Resor, who in November 1934 presented it to the Museum of Modern Art as an anonymous gift to celebrate the Museum's Fifth Anniversary.[11] In the post-Second World War era Dalí linked *The Persistence of Memory* to his continued interest in modern science, believing that his work was a powerful forerunner to the discovery of DeoxyriboNucleic Acid, or DNA for short, whose molecular structure was identified by Dr. Francis Crick and Dr. James Watson in 1953.[12] As he explained to Robert Descharnes, "soft watches, biologically speaking, are the giant Dalínian DNA molecules which constitute the factors of eternity. They are masochistic, because they are so eternal. Like filets of sole, they are destined to be swallowed by the sharks of mechanical time."[13] M.T.R.

[1] Salvador Dalí, *The Secret Life of Salvador Dalí*, trans. Haakon M. Chevalier (New York: Dial Press, 1942), p. 317.
[2] The artist told André Parinaud that *The Persistence of Memory* was "the fruit of wedding my genius to the tender Camembert, the expression of my notion of space-time, prophetically representing the disintegration of matter"; see Salvador Dalí, *The Unspeakable Confessions of Salvador Dalí (as Told to André Parinaud)*, trans. Harold J. Salemson (New York: William Morrow and Company, 1976), p.123.
[3] Dalí, *The Secret Life*, p. 317. Gala's response may even have inspired the title of the painting, which is aptly named, since the exquisite wrought scene is indelibly memorable.
[4] "Exposition Salvador Dalí," Galerie Pierre Colle, Paris, May 26-June 17, 1932.
[5] Julien Levy recounted the circumstances surrounding his purchase of the painting in Levy, *Memoir of an Art Gallery* (New York: G.P. Putnam's Sons, 1977), p. 71.
[6] Levy first lent the painting to a group exhibition entitled "Newer Super-Realism," which was on view at the Wadsworth Atheneum in Hartford, Connecticut, from November 15-December 6, 1931. It was then shown in his own "Surréalisme" exhibition at the Julien Levy Gallery, New York, in January 1932, which later traveled to the Harvard Society of Contemporary Art in Cambridge, Massachusetts, where it was on display from February 15-March 6, 1932. The painting was subsequently included in "Trends in Twentieth Century Painting," an exhibition held at the Slater Memorial Museum in Norwich, Connecticut, from April 11-26, 1932; and "An Exhibition of Literature and Poetry in Painting since 1850" at the Wadsworth Atheneum, Hartford, which ran from January 24-February 14, 1933. Finally the work was included in Dalí's first solo exhibition in the United States, which was on view at the Julien Levy Gallery from November 21-December 8, 1933, and was the only work to be reproduced in the small, pamphlet-like catalogue. Levy probably sold the painting to Mrs. Stanley B. Resor during the run of this exhibition.
[7] The "Surréalisme" exhibition was on display at the Julien Levy Gallery, New York, from January 9-29, 1932.
[8] Julien Levy, *Memoir of an Art Gallery*, *op. cit.*, p.80.
[9] Anonymous, "Surrealisme – Julien Levy Gallery," *Art News* (New York: January 16, 1932), p. 10.
[10] Anonymous, "Freudian Psychology Appears in First American Surrealist Show," *The Art Digest* (January 15, 1932), p. 32.
[11] Although the credit line read "given anonymously," the generosity of Mrs. Resor, a Trustee of the Museum of Modern Art, was openly acknowledged in numerous newspaper articles at the time, see, for example, Anonymous, "Surrealists' Art is Puzzle No More," *The New York Times* (New York: January 10, 1935), p. 21. According to this account, the painting "has puzzled many of the resolute who have climbed two flights of museum stairs to study it."
[12] "That is extraordinary, isn't it?" Dalí exclaimed when discussing the painting with Carlton Lake. "I foresaw the whole idea [of DNA molecules] and now they are getting round to proving it scientifically. It is in the genes—the key to life, the genetic code which transmits to each living cell"; see Lake, *In Quest of Dalí* (New York: G.P. Putnam's Sons, 1969), p. 22.
[13] Robert Descharnes, *The World of Salvador Dalí*, trans. Haakon Chevalier (New York: Harper & Row, 1962), p. 61.

90. The Dream, 1931

90. Oil on canvas
96 × 96 cm
37³/4 × 37³/4 in.
Cleveland (OH),
The Cleveland Museum of Art
John L. Severance Fund

As its title suggests, *The Dream* gives visual form to the strange and disturbing world of dreams and hallucinations to which the artist was prone. The green-hued female figure that dominates this work was based on a painting of the previous year, entitled *The Font* (cat. 81), which included a large, overflowing fountain in the background in the shape of a woman's head. In both works, the woman's mouth has been effaced by a pubislike expanse of flesh that is overrun by a horde of frenzied ants. This substitution of body parts looks back to the notorious film sequence in *Un Chien andalou*, where Pierre Batcheff terrorizes a girl by wiping his hand across his face, apparently removing the mouth and replacing it with smooth flesh, which then bristles with her own underarm hair. That the underarm hair has now been supplanted by swarming ants is in keeping with the artist's anxiety about ants as a symbol of death and decay, which dates back to a childhood memory of finding an injured bat crawling with ants.[1] The flowing hair and sealed eyelids of the petrified figure allude to the myth of Medusa, whose blinding stare turned all who dared to look at her to stone. This reference to the snake-haired Medusa is supported by the serpentine coils of the figure's wavy hair, whose tapering, wind-swept design is thought to have been based on an Art Nouveau pin box that Dalí owned.[2]

The bust of the woman with her eyes closed can be read as a public monument or statue dedicated to dreams and the unconscious, which had provided the artist with his unique iconography based on repressed sexual fantasies and childhood memories. The figures in the background, their faces covered in shame or guilt, speak to the hidden nature of sexual repression, which according to Freudian psychoanalytical theory could only be cured by unraveling the patient's dreams and revealing the source of their neurosis. The seated figure with his bloodied head in his hands was based upon the statue of Sefarí Pitarra (Frederic Soler), the founder of the modern Catalan theatre, seated on an elaborate Art Nouveau plinth in Barcelona. The figure perched atop the scroll-like plinth, with his blood-stained visage as a clear reference to Oedipal guilt, had first appeared in the 1930 painting *The Hand*, again showing how Dalí would revisit and cannibalize an earlier work to create a dark and disturbing new painting on the theme of sexual anxiety and repression, as revealed through dreams and dreamlike imagery. *The Dream* was one of only three paintings by Dalí that were included in the 1936 "International Surrealist Exhibition" in London, thus suggesting that the artist was satisfied with its desired blend of earlier motifs, whose roots can be found in his childhood memories of "Art Nouveau Catalonia" and their associations with his own perverse erotic fantasies. Dalí's participation in this exhibition was somewhat overshadowed by a famous suffocation incident in which the artist had a near death experience while delivering a lecture on the subject of "Authentic Paranoiac Phantoms" while wearing a deep-sea diving suit. After speaking for a few minutes from inside the diver's helmet, the artist began to suffocate and was about to pass out when Gala intervened and unscrewed the bolted down helmet. A photograph taken at the London exhibition shows Dalí, still wearing the diving suit, but not the helmet, apparently explaining the meaning of the painting to a circle of enraptured onlookers that included Gala, her former husband Paul Éluard, and the British Surrealist artist and collector, Roland Penrose (fig. 1). M.R.T.

Fig. 1. Dalí and Gala in front of *The Dream*, with Paul Éluard and Roland Penrose [Graphic Photo Union]

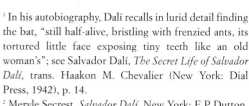

[1] In his autobiography, Dalí recalls in lurid detail finding the bat, "still half-alive, bristling with frenzied ants, its tortured little face exposing tiny teeth like an old woman's"; see Salvador Dalí, *The Secret Life of Salvador Dalí*, trans. Haakon M. Chevalier (New York: Dial Press, 1942), p. 14.
[2] Meryle Secrest, *Salvador Dalí*, New York: E.P Dutton, 1986, p. 129. This Art Nouveau object appears again in *The Hand (La Main)*, of 1930, now in the Salvador Dalí Museum, St. Petersburg, Florida.

91. Remorse, or Sphinx Embedded in the Sand, 1931

91. Oil on canvas
19.1 × 26.9 cm
7 1/2 × 10 5/8 in.
East Lansing (MI), Kresge
Art Museum, Michigan
State University, gift
of John F. Wolfram, 1961

In Dalí's 1942 autobiography, *The Secret Life of Salvador Dalí*, this painting was reproduced in a plate section entitled "Personal Magic: My Principle Fetishes." In the accompanying caption the artist wrote: "'Sphinx Embedded in the Sand' with a woman's slipper and a glass of warm milk underneath the skin of her back—the most active fetishes in my life."[1] This text provides valuable insights into the meaning of this enigmatic work, which until that time had been assigned the variant title of *Remorse*.[2] What at first sight look to be folds in the drapery of the dress that clings to the body of the blond-haired woman, who is buried waist deep in the sand, can now be identified as a high-heeled slipper and a glass of warm milk. These personal fetishes were identified by Dalí as "symbolically functioning objects" in a short article that appeared in *Le Surréalisme au service de la révolution* in December 1931, which described different kinds of Surrealist objects that represented the physical embodiment of repressed sexual fantasies, rather than dealing with the usual formal concerns of modern sculpture, which he viewed as redundant.[3] In the following year, the artist created an elaborate assemblage featuring one of Gala's red slippers, which contained a glass of milk and numerous other appendages, entitled *The Shoe – Surrealist Object Functioning Symbolically*, which translated the concerns of his earlier paintings into three dimensions (cat. 93).

Sphinx Embedded in the Sand shares the visual syntax of a large number of the "nostalgic landscapes" that the artist made around 1931, which typically feature the solitary figure of a man or a woman on a flat, open plain out of which just rugged rock formations. The face of the man or woman is always hidden, perhaps in shame or sorrow, or in this case melancholy, while the body is usually turned away from the viewer and seen only from the back. The mournful, head-in-hand pose of this figure, with its elongated black shadow, ultimately looks back to Albrecht Dürer's famous engraving *Melencolia I* of 1514 (fig. 1), that great allegory of the melancholic nature of the creative individual, and to later variations on the theme of solitude, melancholy and loss by artists such as Arnold Böcklin and Giorgio de Chirico, whose paintings Dalí greatly admired. This pared-down iconography allowed the artist to contrast the softness of the woman's smooth skin and silky drapery with the hardness of the geological landscape, which can be securely identified as the golden-orange hued rocky promontories of Cap Norfeu, near Cadaqués, on the Catalan coastline. The end result, then, is a stark portrayal of loneliness, melancholy, and repressed erotic desires, perhaps associated with the traumatic recent illness of Gala, who was suffering from pleurisy.[4] Gala's poor health threatened to disturb his newfound state of equilibrium—both personal and artistic—and plunge him back into the torturous depths of his childhood phobias and adolescent fears of sex and death. In a tribute to Gala, his Sphinx-like companion, he signed the painting "Olive Salvador Dalí," Olive being one of her nicknames based on the color of her skin. M.R.T.

[1] Salvador Dalí, *The Secret Life of Salvador Dalí*, trans. Haakon M. Chevalier (New York: Dial Press, 1942), plate vi.

[2] The painting had previously appeared under the title *Remorse* in the following publications: Anonymous, "Dalí – the Surrealist," *Vanity Fair*, vol. 43, no. 6, February 1935, p. 49; and Morrill Cody, "Dalí and the New Art," *Art and Artists of Today*, vol. 1, no. 6, June-July, 1938, p. 6.

[3] Salvador Dalí, "Objets surréalistes," *Le Surréalisme au service de la révolution,* no. 3 (Paris: December 1931), pp. 16-17.

[4] Dalí later recounted Gala's illness, and his own physical and psychological reaction to her suffering, in graphic detail: "Gala took to bed, burning up with fever. It was pleurisy. I was sick along with her, suffocating, choking, raving just as she did"; see Salvador Dalí, *The Unspeakable Confessions of Salvador Dalí (as Told to André Parinaud)*, trans. Harold J. Salemson (New York: William Morrow and Company, 1976), p. 104.

Fig. 1. Albrecht Dürer,
Melencolia I, 1514
Berlin, Staatliche Museen zu Berlin,
Kupferstichkabinett

92. Shades of Night Descending, 1931

92. Oil on Canvas
61 × 49.8 cm
24 × 19⁵/8 in.
St. Petersburg (FL),
The Salvador Dalí Museum

Dalí's paintings of the early 1930s often borrowed their setting from the Ampurdàn landscape. In *Shades of Night Descending* (1931), an apparently male figure with erect phallus is draped head to toe with a bedsheet. In the painting the fessured rocks cast long shadows. These elongated shadows reinforce psychological symbolism and suggest that these dream landscapes are also representations of something like a phallic ghost which we might liken to what Jacques Lacan called a "specular image"— that is the ghostlike image of unrepresentable self-annihilation.

A glass and a high-heeled shoe are visible beneath the shroud of the veiled figure. Robert Lubar speculates as to the female gender of this figure, "Although the sex of the figure is indeterminate, the contours of a glass and a high-heeled shoe beneath the surface of the clinging garment point to a female presence."[1] This reading does not account for the bulge below suggestive of an erect phallus and, therefore, male gender, although Lubar is certainly correct in pointing out the ambiguity of the figure's gender. The likely male gender complements the other phallic imagery in the painting and is not necessarily inconsistent with the presence of a woman's shoe, the latter possibly suggestive simultaneously of gender instability (transvestitism) and displaced desire or fetishism.

Shades of Night Descending may have originally belonged to Pierre Colle, because Pierre Colle's name is written on the verso of the stretcher bars, though it was not included in the catalogues of the 1931, 1932 and 1933 solo exhibitions held at the gallery. Lubar wonders if it may have been exhibited in Paris at the 1934 exhibition at Jacques Bonjean.[2] The painting was in the collection of Mr. Joseph Winterbotham (Burlington, Vermont) as early as 1933 when it was loaned for the Chicago World's Fair exhibition called "A Century of Progress held at the Art Institute of Chicago" (exh. cat. 772).[3] It then was given to the Art Institute of Chicago and was included in the Museum of Modern Art's 1941 Dalí retrospective (exh. cat. 11, p. 42), at which time it was still in the collection of the Art Institute of Chicago.[4] Later, perhaps around 1943, the Art Institute de-accessioned it in an exchange for *Invention of Monsters* (1937) with Durlacher Brothers (New York), from whom Reynolds Morse purchased it in September 1943 for $1,000.[5] W.J.

[1] Robert Lubar, *Dalí: The Salvador Dalí Collection* (Boston: Bulfinch, 2000), p. 65.
[2] Robert Lubar, *op. cit.*, p. 64.
[3] Salvador Dalí Museum Archives.
[4] James Thrall Soby, *Salvador Dalí* (New York: Museum of Modern Art, 1941), p. 42.
[5] Salvador Dalí Museum Archives.

93. Scatalogical Object Functioning Symbolically (The Surrealist Shoe), 1931

93. (1973 reconstruction of now-lost original, in an edition of eight plus four artist's proofs, each slightly different, by Max Clerac-Sérou of the Galèrie du Dragon under the supervision of Salvador Dalí)
Assemblage with lady's shoe, white marble, photographs, modeling clay, milk glass containing wax, brush without bristles, sugar cubes, spoons, matchbox, wooden scraper, hair and a gibbet
48 × 28 × 14 cm
19 × 11 × 5 1/2 in.
New York (NY), courtesy Timothy Baum
and Ekstrom + Ekstrom

Inspired by the recent sculpture of Alberto Giacometti, and to a lesser extent the readymades of Marcel Duchamp, Salvador Dalí launched a concerted effort in 1931 to get his friends and colleagues to produce erotically charged Surrealist objects. Updating the notion of the Surrealist *objet trouvé*, to which André Breton had devoted several pages in his 1928 novel *Nadja*, Dalí argued for "symbolically functioning" objects that were intended to awaken repressed desires within the viewer, in line with Sigmund Freud's definition of fetishism.[1] Freud saw fetishism as a pathological condition in which the fetishist, unable to acknowledge his or her attraction for some threatening or forbidden object of desire, finds gratification by displacing the impulse onto an object or body part, such as a glove or a foot. Replete with fetishistic vigor, Surrealist objects took the form of a three-dimensional collage of "found" materials that were chosen for their metaphorical, psychological or sexual connotations, rather than their visual or aesthetic value. In an article published in the December 1931 issue of *Le Surréalisme au service de la révolution*, Dalí identified six different categories of Surrealist objects and provided examples of those objects in a second column:

I Objects Functioning Symbolically
(automatic origin)
Suspended Ball
Saddle, Sphere and Leaves
Shoe and Glass of Milk
Sponges and Bowl of Flour
Gloved Hand and Red Hand

II Transubstantiated objects
(affective origin)
Soft Watch
Watch Made of Straw
III Objects To Be Thrown
(oneiric origin)
Figuratively
Physically
IV Wrapped Objects
(diurnal fantasies)
Handicap
Sirenion
V Machine Objects
(experimental fantasies)
Rocking Chair for Thinking
Association Board
VI Mould objects
(hypnagogic origins)
Automobile-Table-Chair-Lampshade
Forest[2]

The artist created at least a half dozen Surrealist objects during the 1930s and encouraged numerous other artists, such as Meret Oppenheim, Marcel Jean, Oscar Dominguez, Valentine Hugo, Roland Penrose, and Eileen Agar, to do the same.[3] Dalí's own efforts in this vein include this infamous assemblage, mentioned in the first category of Surrealist objects as simply "shoe and glass of milk," for which Dalí provided an elaborate description in the same article: "A woman's shoe, inside of which a glass of warm milk has been placed, in the center of a soft paste in the color of excrement. The mechanism consists of the dip-

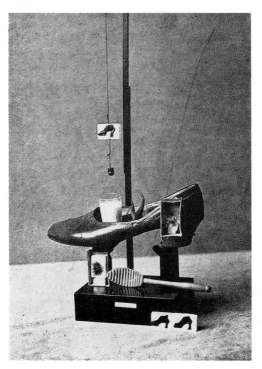
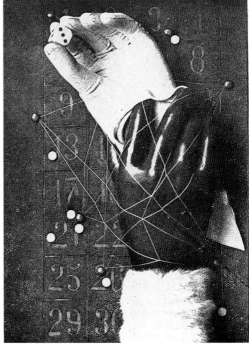

Fig. 1 Salvador Dalí, *Scatalogical Object Functioning Symbolically* (left) and object by Valentine Hugo (right), in *Le Surréalisme au service de la révolution,* no. 3, December 1931

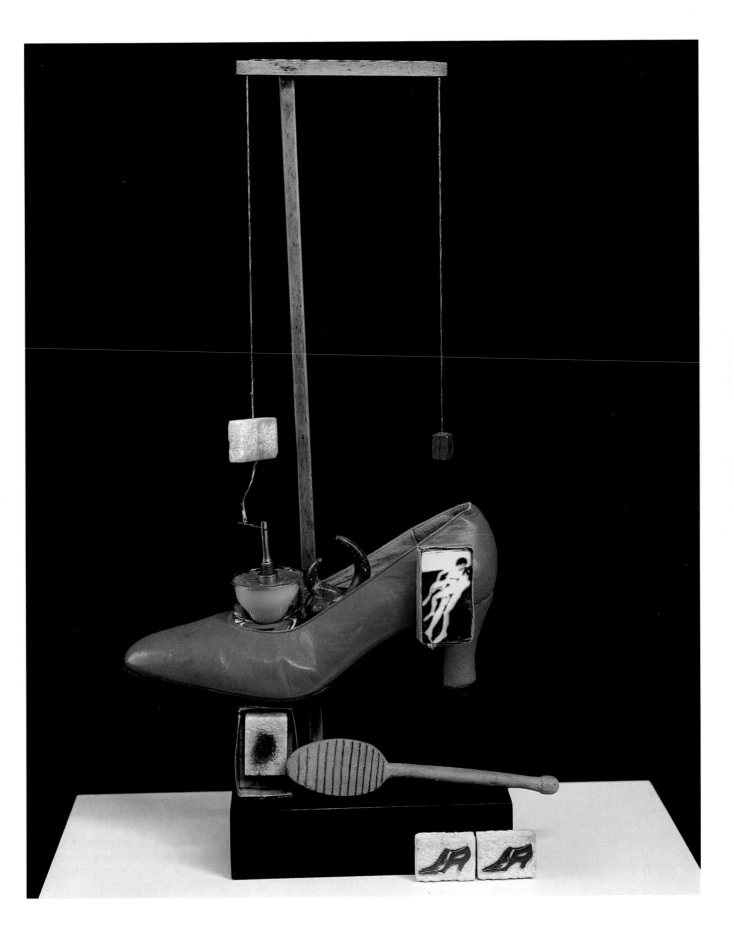

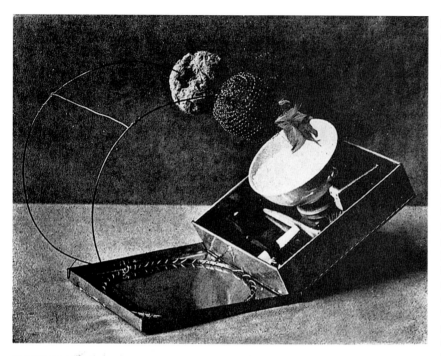

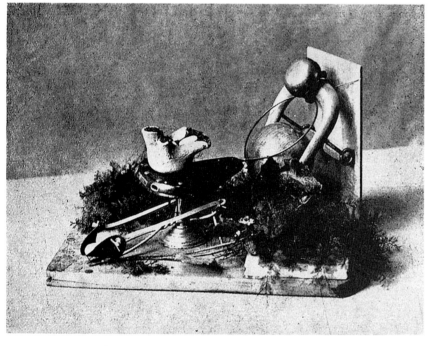

Fig. 2 Objects by Gala Éluard (top)
and by André Breton (above),
in *Le Surréalisme au service de
la révolution*, no. 3, December 1931

ping in the milk of a sugar lump, on which there is a drawing of a shoe, so that the dissolving of the sugar, and consequently of the image of the shoe, may be observed. Several accessories (pubic hairs glued to a sugar lump, an erotic little photograph) complete the object, which is accompanied by a box of spare sugar lumps and a special spoon used for stirring lead pellets inside the shoe."[4] This carefully worded explanation, whose language appears to have been borrowed from scientific experiment manuals, again points to the fetishistic nature of the work, which is activated through a process of substitution. Dalí's choice of a woman's shoe, which Krafft-Ebing in his *Psychopathia sexualis* had associated with masochism, ranks alongside other subversive items, such as gloves, zippers, feathers, hair, and fur, that recur in numerous Surrealist objects of the 1930s. These are all classic examples of a fetishist's object of displaced desire, in which the libido is transferred from the whole object of affection to a part, a symbol, or an article of clothing. As if to underscore the sexual nature of his assemblage, Dalí included a pornographic photograph and pubic hair, which, like the fake turd, serves to underline the fetishist's attraction to the base and the forbidden.

Dalí's reference to "Suspended Ball" underscores his profound interest in the work of Alberto Giacometti, which can be seen in numerous paintings and sculptures of the early 1930s, such as *The Architectural Angelus of Millet*, of 1933, with its clear reference to the sculptor's menacing *Man and Woman*, of 1928-29, or *Catalan Bread*, of 1932, which appears to have been directly inspired by Giacometti's phallic *Disagreeable Object*, of 1931. It also specifically relates to the feelings of sexual frustration aroused in him by seeing the Swiss artist's *Suspended Ball*, of 1930-31 (see p. 240, fig. 1), with its intimations of intercourse, violence, and the indeterminate nature of sexual difference.[5] This work, which consists of a ball with a slit in it, suspended over a sharp wedge shape, provocatively invites the viewer to place the ball in a swinging motion. However, the cleft in the ball does not quite fit in the wedge of the second curved object and this metaphor for frustrated desire, with sadistic undertones, motivated Dalí, as he freely admitted, to create his general catalogue of Surrealist objects, although he distinguished his own work from that of Giacometti on the grounds that *Suspended Ball* was still a sculpture. The connection between Giacometti's sculpture and this new phase of Surrealist objects was made explicit when André Breton published seven precise line drawings of the Swiss sculptor's work, including *Suspended Ball*, to accompany Giacometti's short essay "Objets mobiles et muets" (Moving and Mute Objects), in the same issue of *Le Surréalisme au service de la révolution* as Dalí's

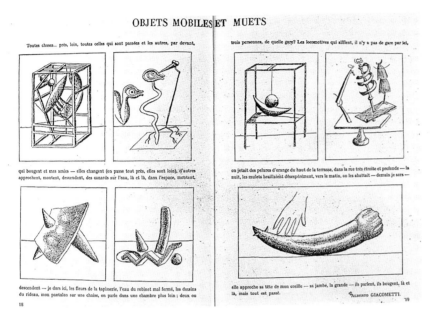

OBJETS MOBILES ET MUETS

Toutes choses... près, loin, toutes celles qui sont passées et les autres, par devant,

trois personnes, de quelle gare? Les locomotives qui sifflent, il n'y a pas de gare par ici,

qui bougent et mes amies — elles changent (on passe tout près, elles sont loin), d'autres approchent, montent, descendent, des canards sur l'eau, là et là, dans l'espace, montent,

on jetait des pelures d'orange du haut de la terrasse, dans la rue très étroite et profonde — la nuit, les mulets braillaient désespérément, vers le matin, on les abattait — demain je sors —

descendent — je dors ici, les fleurs de la tapisserie, l'eau du robinet mal fermé, les dessins du rideau, mon pantalon sur une chaise, on parle dans une chambre plus loin ; deux ou

elle approche sa tête de mon oreille — sa jambe, la grande — ils parlent, ils bougent, là et là, mais tout est passé.

ALBERTO GIACOMETTI.

18   '19

Fig. 3. Alberto Giacometti,
Suspended Ball, illustration
for "Objets mobiles et muets,"
in *Le Surréalisme au service de
la révolution,* no. 3, December 1931

"Objets surréalistes" essay, which immediately preceded it (fig. 3).[6] M.R.T.

[1] Dalí's proposal for the construction of Surrealist objects, as a new form of communal activity for the movement, is discussed at length in Dawn Ades, "Surrealism: Fetishism's Job," in *Fetishism: Visualising Power and Desire,* ed. Anthony Shelton, exhibition catalogue (London: The South Bank Centre, in association with Lund Humphries, 1995), pp. 73-78.

[2] Salvador Dalí, "Objets surréalistes," *Le Surréalisme au service de la révolution,* no. 3 (Paris: December 1931), pp. 16-17, reprinted in *The Collected Writings of Sal-vador Dalí* ed., trans. Haim Finkelstein (Cambridge: Cambridge University Press, 1998), p. 231. Translation slightly modified by the author.

[3] For more on the history and reception of Dalí's Surrealist objects see Joan R. Kropf, *Dalí Objects / Dalí Fetishes* (St. Petersburg, FL: Salvador Dalí Museum, 2002), pp. 7-24.

[4] Salvador Dalí, "Surrealist Objects," in *The Collected Writings of Salvador Dalí,* ed. Haim Finkelstein, op. cit., p. 234. Translation slightly modified by the author. As Steven Harris has argued, the combination of warm milk and dissolving sugar relates to Dalí's preoccupation "with what he described as the dipping of the male into the warm milk of the mother; he traced the genesis of this preoccupation in his *Mythe tragique de l'Angélus de Millet.* For Dalí, the Oedipal myth *was* the tragic myth of our time, the dipping into warm milk representing both terror and comfort, the loss of self and the fear of being devoured by the mother, which animated the whole chain of associations in that book, see Harris, *Surrealist Art and Thought in the 1930s: Art, Politics, and the Psyche* (Cambridge: Cambridge University Press, 2004), p. 46.

[5] Dalí was not alone in his admiration for *Suspended Ball.* Maurice Nadeau recalled how the disturbingly erotic sculpture caused a sensation among the Surrealist group: "Everyone who saw this object functioning experienced a strong but indefinable sexual emotion relating to unconscious desires. This emotion was in no sense one of satisfaction, but one of disturbance, like that imparted by the irritating awareness of failure"; see Nadeau, *Histoire du Surréalisme,* (Paris: Seuil, 1945), p. 176. Translation by the author.

[6] Alberto Giacometti, "Objets mobiles et muets," *Le Surréalisme au service de la révolution,* no. 3 (Paris: December 1931), pp. 18-19.

94. The Invisible Man, 1932

94. Oil on canvas
16.5 × 23.8 cm
6 1/2 × 9 3/8 in.
St. Petersburg (FL),
The Salvador Dalí Museum

In this work from 1932, Salvador Dalí has painted three loaves of bread within the interior of the one-room fishing shack that he and his wife Gala shared in the coastal village of Port Lligat, Spain. What would initially appear to be a rather peaceful tableau is laden with intense personal symbolism. The title of this painting is the same as that of a major picture begun in 1929 and was still unfinished in 1932, which was one of his first essays in the paranoiac-critical method. Bread had taken on a strongly anthropomorphic character for Dalí, and here clearly stands for a human presence.

The balanced loaf—featured in drawings, paintings, and sculptural assemblages by Dalí—refers to the Swiss myth of William Tell. In the myth, as punishment for not acknowledging the acting governor, Tell is forced to shoot an apple off his son's head at fifty paces in order to regain their freedom. When this is accomplished, it is revealed that there was a second arrow to be used on the king if Tell failed the attempt and killed his son. Dalí was fascinated by this tale, which he considered to have an oppressive and persecutory tone that ultimately symbolizes Oedipal desires, sacrifice, and castration. The upright loaf on the chair is a symbol particular to the artist. Writing in his autobiographical *The Secret Life of Salvador Dalí*, Dalí states that once he "was looking absentmindedly, though fixedly, at a piece of bread. It was the heel of a long loaf, lying on its belly, and I could not cease looking at it. Finally I took it and kissed the very tip of it, then with my tongue I sucked it a little to soften it, after which I struck the softened part on the table, where it remained standing. I had just reinvented Columbus's egg: the bread of Salvador Dalí."[1] This upright loaf clearly evokes a phallic imagery and most likely refers to the artists' estranged father. The cut loaf upon the table is obviously another representation of castration—the loaf has been truncated and then sliced into smaller segments that will never be part of the whole again.

The use of symbolic imagery by the Surrealists—and Dalí in particular—was inspired by Freud, and then supplemented with personal memories, or societal taboos that are drawn out of the disordered state of the human psyche. Here, Dalí has achieved that goal by combining images and motifs that he can change, supplement and complement as he sees fit. D.AR.

[1] Salvador Dalí, *The Secret Life of Salvador* Dalí (New York: Dial Press, 1942), p. 306.

95. The Birth of Liquid Fears, 1932
96. The Birth of Liquid Desires, 1932

95. Oil on canvas
55 × 38.5 cm
21⁵/₈ × 15¹/₈ in.
Hamburg, Private collection,
on loan to Kunsthalle

96. Oil and collage on canvas
96.1 × 112.3 cm
37⁷/₈ × 44¹/₄ in.
Venice, Peggy Guggenheim
Collection

The Birth of Liquid Desires is one of Dalí's most intricate and complex paintings. It echoes the great rock-self-portrait of *The Great Masturbator,* now transformed into a setting for his personal interpretation of the mythological theme of William Tell, linked to motifs inspired by Arnold Böcklin's *Isle of the Dead* (fig. 1). Dalí was contemplating at the time a detailed study of the *Isle of the Dead* for his unrealized "History of Surrealist Painting through the Ages." However, this study was never completed, and whereas his obsession with Millet's *Angelus* was to be fully explored in his book, *The Tragic Myth of Millet's Angelus*, no such key exists for the Böcklin theme. But there are hints in such texts as "Rêverie" of the significance of the *Isle of the Dead* for his iconography (see *The True Painting…* , cat. 98).

Dominating the composition of *The Birth of Liquid Desires*, and cutting it off frontally from the horizon, is a huge yellow rock whose curved upper edge resembles a violin or cello. The metaphor of body/musical instrument was given visual currency by Cubism, and the rock-body image is also familiar from Dalí's 1929 paintings such as *Enigma of Desire* (cat. 68) and *The Great Masturbator* (cat. 65). From the waist of the rock-cello, which is bifurcated by the head of the old man to create two breastlike gaps, rises a dark mass culminating in cypress trees. The conjunction of the yellow-gold rocks and the dark cypresses above vividly conjures up the cliffs and cypresses in the *Isle of the Dead* where the evening glow lights up the twin rocks of the mausoleum island, starkly bisected by a black clump of trees, the unknowable destination of the dead.

The central couple in *The Birth of Liquid Desires*

Fig. 1. Arnold Böcklin,
Isle of the Dead, 1880
Basle, Kunstmuseum

are identifiable as William Tell and Gradiva, familiar figures from Dalí's personal mythology. At first sight they appear to be locked in an embrace, but the old man, one hand raised in fear, is attempting to ward off "Gradiva" who has become a female spectre with a head of roses. This motif has shifting associations for Dalí, but could here symbolize decay rather than passion. The erect, white-robed spectre is positioned centrally, like the shrouded figure in the funeral boat of the *Isle of the Dead*, and seems thus to evoke death rather than love. A male and a female figure at each side of this couple, their faces hidden, perform mysterious, ritualistic gestures, one turning away into a dark cave within the yellow rock, the other pouring liquid from a jug through a hole into a basin. Planted in the basin is the gnarled, gray foot of the old man, with the implication that it is being washed or anointed; however, the female averts her head, as though the task repels her. The oblique reference could be to Christ washing the feet of the disciples before the Last Supper, an act of abasement that Dalí thus invokes but rejects. He makes a similar reference to biblical history, this time to the Old Testament, in *The Old Age of William Tell* (fig. 2), where the departing couple resemble Adam and Eve cast from Paradise. What they leave, however, is not the Garden of Eden but a secret scene with an old man engaged with two younger women, which recalls the tale of Lot and his daughters. These references to biblical legends and Christian myth are full of scorn and horror, mocking the figures of authority and sanctity.

As in *The Old Age of William Tell*, and the closely related painting *Memory of the Child Woman*, the old man in *The Birth of Liquid Desires*, the father figure, has female breasts, a feature which recalls Apollinaire's play *Les mamelles de Tiresias* but more particularly Freud's study of the 17th-century painter Christoph Haizmann, who imagined that he entered into a pact with the devil whom he represents with breasts. Dalí was undoubtedly familiar with Freud's paper, which was published in translation in *Revue française de psychanalyse.*[1]

The young man to the left of the couple, turned away from the viewer, stoops towards a dark mass; he resembles Sisyphus, whose torment in Hades was to push a heavy stone up a hill but never reach the top. This bewildering range of mythical touchstones is further extended with the collaged chromolithograph on the pedestal supporting "William Tell's" knee, of an ancient gem representing the scene of the flaying of Marsyas. This terrible legend of the piper\satyr's tragic challenge to the god Apollo for musical supremacy is probably incorporated by Dalí as another instance of the draconian methods of those in authority (the father) to suppress challenge or resistance (the son). The autobiographical character of these images is undeniable;

95

the pointed use of classical and biblical myth takes on peculiar poignancy in the light of Dalí's expulsion by his father and struggle to make a life for himself and Gala. As Dalí said of *The Old Age of William Tell*, "The crucial thing from my point of view was to tell, by any means possible, our story as myth."[2]

Dalí's method in *The Birth of Liquid Desires* could in some respects be compared to Hogarth's "modern moral subjects," where all details in the pictorial narrative are emblematic of the central subject. In Hogarth's *Marriage à la Mode*, for example, an image of Marsyas looms above the fiancés who are sacrificed to their parents' cupidity and ambition. Unlike Hogarth, however, any narrative here is ambiguous and many of the elements have multiple connotations. The (multifarious) symbols of paternal oppression are present as well as those of desire. That the two might be linked is part of the complexity of the image. In his poem "The Great Masturbator" Dalí describes in detail a series of imaginary images carved in relief on medals, like the collage of the "Marsyas" gem in *The Birth of Liquid Desires:*

"In one of these medallions
Was the image
Of a man
With slowed
Development
Endowed with an unhealthy
Complexion
And who symbolized
Simultaneously
The image
Of desire
The image
Of death
And even the image
Of dried shit…"[3]

In the upper corner, the chest of drawers from which the fountain begins to flow recalls Dalí's film scenario *Babaouo*: "a medium-size cupboard with open doors and drawers, revealing linens overflowing in a tumultuous disorder."[4] The spring gushing from the chest of drawers recalls the fountain en-

closed by a clump of cypresses, which he used to visit as a child, a memory that surges as he creates the setting for his erotic daydream, "Rêverie." "The emotion aroused by the points of the cypress trees was caused by the instantaneous association with another group of cypresses situated in a public place near Figueres, called "The Log Fountain." This group of ancient, dense cypresses surrounded a paved circle in the middle of which …flowed a rusty fountain."[5]. Almost invisible in the dark rock wall is the inscription "*Consigne: gâcher l'ardoise totale,*" which appears also as the title of an erotic drawing whose female protagonists are named after those in "Rêverie": Dulita, Matilde, Gala (or Gallo) and Elena (cat. 88).[6]

Spilling over a crack in the yellow rock are two fried eggs, objects which multiply in paintings of the period such as *Fried Egg on the Plate without the Plate* (cat. 100). These viscous objects are linked to Georges Bataille's *L'Histoire de l'oeil*, a book whose violent and extreme treatment of sexuality had a profound impact on Dalí. In *L'Histoire de l'œil* the fetishized eye and associated objects (egg, testicles) prompt associations with liquids, milk, water, blood, semen, which provoke both desire and repulsion.

The Birth of Liquid Desires is signed Gala Salvador Dalí and dated 1932; on the back is the inscription "*plaisirs liquides*" (liquid pleasures) probably in the hand of Gala, from whom the painting was purchased by Peggy Guggenheim in 1940. It was exhibited at the Pierre Colle Gallery in Paris in June 1933. *The Birth of Liquid Fears* contains, by contrast, a single dramatic motif, which can also be linked to the cluster of associated images in "Rêverie." The fountain gushes now from the cypress itself, round which a white cloth curves itself. The cloth, or perhaps shroud, is so sharply edged that it resembles the rocks at Cap Creus. Blanched by distance on the horizon is the little round hill topped by a tower visible from the bay at Port Lligat. The absence of any figures enhances the phallic character of the cypress, as if Dalí concentrates in it all the emotion of a hidden erotic scene. D.A.

[1] Sigmund Freud, "Une névrose démoniaque au XV11 siècle," *La Revue française de Psychanalyse*, no. 2 (Paris: 1927). This version does not contain Haizmann's images.
[2] Robert Descharnes, *Dalí de Gala* (Lausanne: Éditions Denoël, 1962), p. 157.
[3] "Le grand masturbateur," *La Femme Visible* , p. 48.
[4] *Babaouo: (scénario inédit…)* (Paris 1932), p. 36.
[5] "Rêverie," *SASDLR*, no. 4 (December 1931), p. 33.
[6] This gnomic phrase could be translated: "Command: spoil the total slate." The connection with the drawing was identified by Angelica Rudenstine in her excellent entry on this painting in *Peggy Guggenheim Collection, Venice* (Abrams, 1985), pp. 198-205, to which the reader is referred.

96

97. Agnostic Symbol, 1932

97. Oil on canvas
61 × 72.1 cm
24 × 23³/8 in.
Philadelphia (PA),
Philadelphia Museum of Art
The Louise and Walter
Arensberg Collection

Spoon imagery appears in several of Dalí's paintings in 1932, during which time the artist was exploring the "morphological esthetics of the soft and hard" through an elaborate symbolism involving fried eggs, ears of corn, and other food products.[1] In *Agnostic Symbol* a miniature gold pocket watch is presented in the hollow of a Louis XV spoon, as opposed to the pair of fried eggs that are offered in the spoons and kitchen utensils of other works from this period. The vastly elongated spoon emerges from a cracked wall, located in the upper right-hand corner of the canvas. This wall, which can also be read as a fresco-like painting-within-a-painting, is the only notable feature in this stark landscape environment, apart from the small rock that the iridescent spoon handle snakes around in the foreground. Stretched like elastic or chewing gum, the elongated spoon clearly relates to Dalí's theories of psychic cannibalism and edible beauty, although its precise meaning remains unclear. One possible solution would be the common saying "he must have a long spoon that must eat with the devil," made famous by William Shakespeare in *The Comedy of Errors.*[2]

The reference to agnosticism in the painting's title must be seen within the context of the Surrealist group's antipathy toward organized religion, which Dalí appears to have shared at this time, although he later renounced it in favor of his own brand of Catholicism that combined his fascination with nuclear physics and his faith in the "supreme reality" of God. Dalí seems to have been especially preoccupied with this issue in

1932, since a related work, now known as *Suez*, was originally entitled *Paysage Agnostique* (Agnostic Landscape). This barren landscape shares the reduced palette of warm browns and sickly greens used in *Agnostic Symbol*, as well as the long-handled spoon that is stretched across an enormous canal or trench like a tightrope.

Recent research into the provenance of this painting has revealed that Louise and Walter Arensberg acquired the work in July 1937 from the Stendhal Galleries in Los Angeles, which had, in turn, received *Agnostic Symbol* on consignment from the Paris-based Hungarian dealer Ladislas Szecsi. The painting quickly attained a deep personal meaning for Walter Arensberg, for whom the spoon coming forward from the distance to disclose its pill-sized watch like a secret "seemed especially to symbolize [his] own outlook."[3] According to Marie Kimball, who was a frequent visitor to the Arensberg household in the late 1940s, Walter "was a complete agnostic, and he never failed to touch on that subject in his amusing and lively way."[4] Arensberg's interest in agnosticism and cryptography may have led him to identify with this hermetic painting, which he later donated to the Philadelphia Museum of Art as part of his prized collection of modern and pre-Columbian art. M.R.T.

[1] Salvador Dalí, *The Secret Life of Salvador Dalí* (New York: Dial Press, 1942), p. 304.
[2] William Shakespeare, *The Comedy of Errors,* Act IV, Scene III.
[3] Fiske Kimball, "Cubism and the Arensbergs," *Art News Annual*, vol. 24, no. 7, November 1954, p. 178.
[4] *Ibid.* Marie Kimball was Fiske's Kimball's wife and accompanied him on his numerous trips to California in the late 1940s on behalf of the Philadelphia Museum of Art. As Director, Kimball successfully secured the acclaimed Arensberg Collection, which was bequeathed to the Museum in 1954.

Fig. 1. Salvador Dalí,
Surrealist Architecture, ca. 1932
Bern, Kunstmuseum Bern

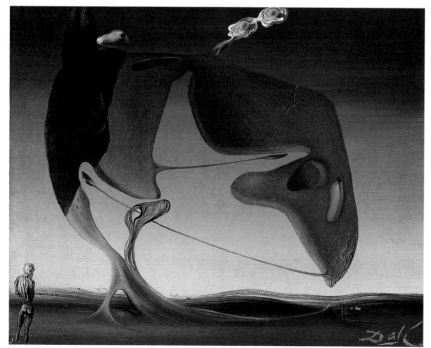

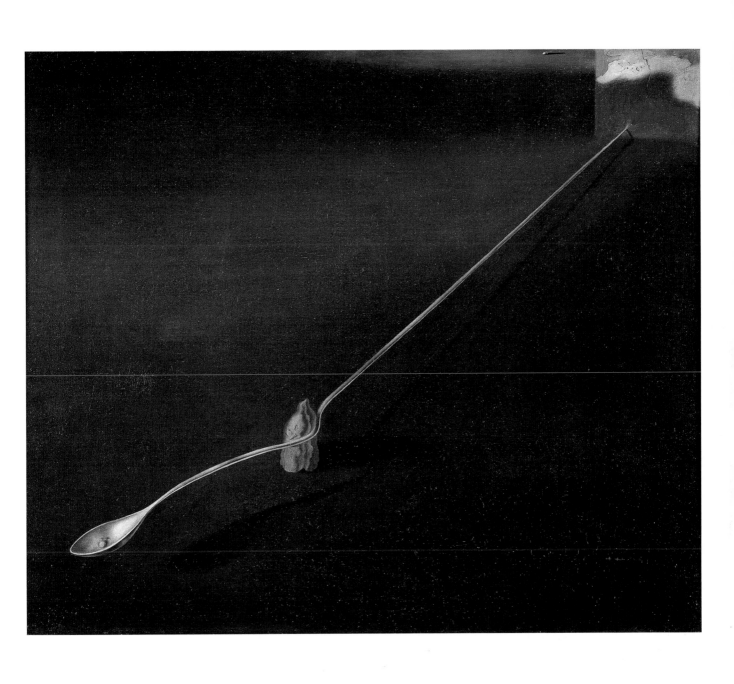

98. The True Painting of the "Isle of the Dead" by Arnold Böcklin at the Hour of the Angelus, 1932

98. Oil on canvas
77.5 × 64.5 cm
30¹/2 × 23³/8 in.
Wuppertal, Von der Heydt Museum

Fig. 1. Salvador Dalí,
The Isle of the Dead – Center Section – Reconstructed compulsive image after Böcklin, 1934
Private collection

Although the title of this painting refers directly to Böcklin's *Isle of the Dead* (see p. 164, fig. 1), the visual allusions are less direct than in such paintings of the same period as *Birth of Liquid Desires* (cat. 96) or *The Isle of the Dead – Center Section – Reconstructed compulsive image after Böcklin.* (fig. 1) Böcklin painted four versions of *The Isle of the Dead*, and Dalí was probably familiar at least from reproductions with those in the Kunstmuseum, Basel and at the Metropolitan Museum in New York (both of 1880).[1] Dalí refers in his text "Rêverie" (which he dates precisely, October 17, 1931) to a study he was making of the *Isle of the Dead*, which was to be a major section of his projected *History of Surrealist Painting through the Ages*.[2] He announced this book on several occasions in the early 1930s, for instance in *L'Amour et la mémoire* (1931), where he calls it *La Peinture surréaliste à travers les âges.*

Dalí's text "Rêverie" goes some way to explaining the relationship between *The True Painting of the "Isle of the Dead" by Arnold Böcklin at the Hour of the Angelus* and the "Isle of the Dead." He sets the scene for his erotic "reverie" by describing his minute preparations for a post-prandial rest after which he plans to "write part of a very long study of Böcklin, a study which has obsessed me for some time."[3] During the siesta he intends to reflect on certain contradictory elements in the *Isle of the Dead*, in particular on "the antagonism between the feeling of death and the absolute lack of anxiety as to notions of space, so striking with this painter."[4] He was especially preoccupied with the "frontality" of the *Isle of the Dead* and conjures up as clear an image as possible of the painting in order to resolve the problem. In doing so he recognizes that he mistakenly believed that the *Isle of the Dead* lacked "spatial trouble" because he had reduced this "trouble" to perspective alone. Dalí had himself already frequently used excessive or anamorphic perspective to reinforce sensations of anxiety, whether sexual or mortal. The absence of any very notable perspectival effects in *Isle of the Dead* had, Dalí notes, misled him into thinking it lacked "spatial trouble" altogether. He had been trying to connect the Böcklin with his long-standing study of perspective in Vermeer and de Chirico, in which he claimed to have found an unconscious preoccupation with death. Now he sees that the "frontality" he had noticed does indeed "indicate a strongly characterized spatiality."[5]

The True Painting concentrates its spatial drama on a contrast between perspective and dominant horizontal and vertical forms. Dalí does not eliminate perspective but simplifies and counteracts it. The parapet on the right recedes sharply (like that in *The First Days of Spring;* cat. 64) and there is a notional, central vanishing point where this recession meets an imaginary line from the violet box on the left, at the tip of the sunlit cliff. However, the parapet is so dark that the perspective effect is virtually cancelled out. Beside the parapet is an ambiguous dark brown form with a slightly wavering edge, which could be read as a curtain and thus emphasizes the flatness of the foreground plane. Although the distant rocks and the tiny figure in shadow do contribute to a sensation of depth, the effect of the dark band in the foreground and the cloudless evening sky is to hold the rocks in suspension, perhaps in an attempt to invest them with the "frontality" he saw in the *Isle of the Dead*. The resemblance between the rocky cliffs in Böcklin's painting and those of Dalí's familiar Cap Creus is deliberately emphasized.

Dalí's meditation on the *Isle of the Dead* in "Rêverie" is a prelude to an elaborately detailed imaginary erotic encounter. Sexual excitement here, as elsewhere—for example in the use of Wagner's "Love in Death" motif from *Tristan and Isolde* in the music accompaniment to the film *Un Chien andalou*—is bound up for Dalí with deathly forebodings. Here it is present both in the *fuite* of perspective and in the cup, from which spurts a long vertical stream that has turned instantly to rock or bone; the liquid of desire is calcified and ends abruptly in a dead point. D.A.

[1] Of the other two versions one is destroyed, and the other is in Leipzig.
[2] "Rêverie," *Le Surréalisme au service de la révolution*, no. 4 (Paris: December 1931).
[3] *Ibid.*, p. 31. At the beginning of the reverie itself, Dalí sees himself, as he is but noticeably older, with a beard, in the castle of some friends where he intends "to finish writing my study of Böcklin, which will be a chapter of the vast work I call for the moment 'Surrealist Painting through the ages'."
[4] *Ibid.*, p. 31.
[5] *Ibid.*, p. 32.

99. Nostalgia of the Cannibal, 1932
100. Fried Egg on the Plate without the Plate, 1932
101. Retrospective Bust of a Woman, 1933
102. Paranoaic Metamorphosis of Gala's Face, 1932

99. Oil on canvas
47.2 × 47.2 cm
18⁵/8 × 18⁵/8 in.
Hanover, Sprengel Museum

100. Oil on canvas
55 × 46 cm
21⁵/8 × 18¹/8 in.
Private collection

101. Porcelain display bust with
ears of corn, strip of cardboard
used as a necklace; gilded
sponge, and couple from Millet's
Angelus with wheelbarrow
and two calamai with quills
54 × 45 × 35 cm
21¹/4 × 17³/4 in.
Private collection, courtesy
Galerie Natalie Seroussi, Paris

102. China ink on Japon paper
29 × 21 cm
11¹/2 × 8¹/4 in.
Figueres, Fundació
Gala-Salvador Dalí

The *Nostalgia of the Cannibal* was exhibited in Paris in June 1933 at the Pierre Colle Gallery and in New York in November at Julien Levy's, with the title translated as *Cannibal Nostalgia*. At both exhibitions there was a subtitle in brackets, *image instantanée,* "instantaneous image." Dalí was intrigued by the differences between images that appear unbidden such as hallucinations, the obsessional delusions of paranoia and willed *rêveries* or "diurnal fantasies" like the one he described in detail in *Le Surréalisme au service de la revolution* in 1931 (see Writings by Dalí, "Rêverie"). The "instantaneous" image invokes the idea of the photograph, complete, unique and frozen with the click of a button. In the preface to the Pierre Colle Gallery catalogue, which consisted of a "letter" to Breton, Dalí runs through a list of different kinds of photo-image: "the 'continuous' photographic dream aspect, the photographic brain aspect, the instantaneous hand-made photographic aspect, that is to say instantaneous photography under the control of the most treacherous psychic automatism," and he ends with "the little, edible, photo aspect, the little edible, delicate aspect of a painter like Meissonier."[1] In his exhibition the following year at the Levy Gallery he prefaced the catalogue with the following words:
…"SNAP-SHOT PHOTOGRAPHS IN COLOr of subconscious images, Surrealist, extravagant, paranoiac hypnagogical, extra-pictorial, phenomenal, super-abundant, super-sensitive, etc… of CONCRETE IRRATIONALITY"…[2]
The *Nostalgia of the Cannibal,* as an "instantaneous image," would, he implies, be like a photograph of unconscious thought, thus related to psychic automatism. The conjunction of two of the objects recurrent in his work at this moment—ink well and fried egg—springs unpremeditated from his unconscious. They suddenly appear together in an alternating row on a large plinth void of inscription. The associations of such objects are usually additive—after their first appearance they appear in diverse juxtapositions that build up additional meanings. The pen and ink well arrived in his work, appropriately enough, embedded in the head of an "average bureaucrat," the bald and heavily mustached man whose head is often submissively bowed. Sometimes, as in the drawing *William Tell, Gradiva and the Average Bureaucrat* (cat. 110) he is placed beside the father figure William Tell, of whom he might be an alter ego—Dalí's father, one should remember, was a notary, a bureaucrat. The pen and ink well, which the average bureaucrat holds in his hands, is also a phallic symbol, symptom of the "latent content" of images.[3]
In 1932, Dalí exhibited two objects at the Pierre Colle gallery: *Hypnagogic Clock* and *Clock based on the Decomposition of Bodies. Hypnagogic Clock*

"consisted of an enormous loaf of French bread posed on a luxurious pedestal. On the back of this pedestal I fastened a dozen ink-bottles in a row, filled with "Pelican" ink and each bottle held a pen of a different color."[4]. The following year Dalí elaborated on the "bread and ink" combination in one of his most brilliant Surrealist objects: *Retrospective Bust of a Woman.* The discovery of the bronze pair of ink wells featuring the figures from Millet's *Angelus,* and bearing its original title *L'Abondance,* was a fine example of Surrealist objective chance on which Dalí immediately capitalized. He embedded the bronze object in a loaf of bread resting on the head of a porcelain bust of a woman, to which he added a celluloid strip of cartoon figures and a pair of maize cobs. He showed the resulting object in the Surrealist exhibition at Pierre Colle in 1933. (It is rumored that, when *Retrospective Bust of a Woman* was first exhibited, at the Salon des Surindépendents in 1933, Picasso's dog ate the bread). Edibility is one of Dalí's most complex tropes. Food is an offering to divert the cannibalist rage of the father: hence the chops on Gala's shoulder in *Portrait of Gala with Two Lamb Chops Balanced on her Shoulder,* 1933 (cat. 104) and the proof of his terrible appetites litter the ground in the *Study for "The Enigma of William Tell"* (cat. 105). Bread is also a symbol of the sacred: "What more degrading and beautiful," he wrote, "than to see the bread stain itself with spots of Pelican ink."
In *Nostalgia of the Cannibal* the black of ink and inkwell contrasts with the white of the eggs; the final yolk is pierced by the displaced pen. The egg is an even more over-determined symbol than bread or ink well in Dalí's object pantheon. Whole, it is a sign of birth and origins; broken, raw or cooked, its sticky viscosity could hardly be a greater contrast with the pure hard ovoid of the shell. It is thus a natural bearer of the hard-soft oppositions that structure so much of Dalí's thought and iconography.
Fried Egg on the Plate without the Plate has a special meaning in relation to his fantasies of intra-uterine memories. "The intra-uterine paradise was the color of hell, that is to say, red, orange, yellow, and bluish…above all it was soft, immobile, warm, symmetrical, double, gluey. Already at that time all pleasure, all enchantment for me was in my eyes, and the most splendid, the most striking vision was that of a pair of eggs fried in a pan, without the pan; to this is probably due that perturbation and that emotion which I have since felt… in the presence of this ever-hallucinatory image."[5] He could reproduce a similar image "by subjecting my pupils to a strong pressure of my fingers," which he interprets as a phosphene ("a luminous sensation resulting from pressure on the eye when the eyelids are shut")[6]; fists pressed on

172

99

100

Fig. 1. Gala in Paris in the apartment with functionalist furniture, ca. 1932

the orbits is characteristic of the fetal posture. These passages from *The Secret Life* bring together two texts of special importance for Dalí: Freud's *Beyond the Pleasure Principle* and Georges Bataille's *Histoire de l'œil* (History of the Eye). Freud's seductive meta-psychological theory of the death drive, the desire of all matter to return to an inanimate state, is summarized by Dalí in terms of a return to the womb: "It would seem that the death-wish is often explained by that imperialistic and constant compulsion to return where we came from."[7] The disquieting slippage from egg to eye ball recalls the metaphorical chain of eroticized objects in *History of the Eye*. Dalí forges these ideas together in a pre-natal vision that encompasses the fear of and fascination with the female genitals. The "instantaneous images" of *Nostalgia of the Cannibal* and *Fried Egg on the Plate without the Plate,* are as dense in associations as those of dreams. D.A.

[1] Preface "cher Breton," exhibition catalogue *Salvador Dalí,* Pierre Colle (Paris: 1933).
[2] *Dalí* exhibition catalogue Julián Levy Gallery (New York: 1934).
[3] Preface *Salvador Dalí* Pierre Colle Gallery 1931.
4 Salvador Dalí, *The Secret Life of Salvador Dalí,* trans. Haakon Chevalier (London: Vision Press, 1968), p. 21.
[5] *Ibid.,* p. 27.
[6] *Ibid.*
[7] *Ibid.*

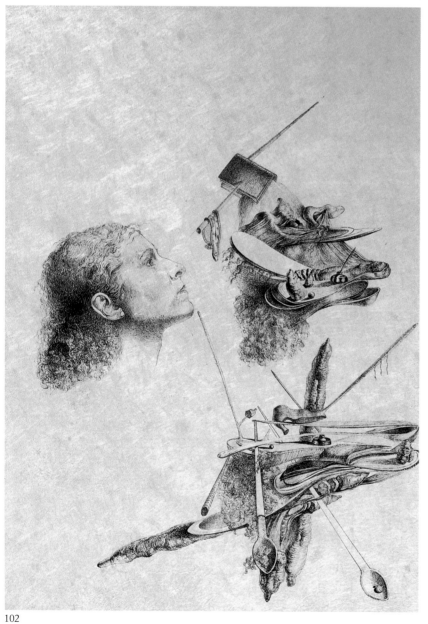

102

103. Study for "Portrait of Gala with Two Lamb Chops Balanced
on her Shoulder," 1933
104. Portrait of Gala with Two Lamb Chops Balanced on her Shoulder, 1933

103. China ink on wood panel
6.8 × 8.8 cm
2⁵/8 × 3¹/2 in.
Chicago (IL), The Art Institute
of Chicago

104. Oil on wood panel
6.8 × 8.8 cm
2⁵/8 × 3¹/2 in.
Figueres, Fundació
Gala-Salvador Dalí

105. Study for "The Enigma of William Tell," 1933

105. Pen and pencil
17.2 × 22.3 cm
6³/4 × 8³/4 in.
St. Petersburg (FL),
The Salvador Dalí Museum, on
loan from E. and A. Reynolds
Morse Collection

Fig. 1. Salvador Dalí,
The Enigma of William Tell, 1933
Stockholm, Moderna Museets

106. Gradiva, 1933
107. Andromeda, 1930-31

106. China ink on paper
63 × 45.5 cm
24³/4 × 17⁷/8 in.
Munich, Staatliche Graphische
Sammlung

107. Pen, ink on paper
72.39 × 54.61 cm
28¹/2 × 21¹/2 in.
Buffalo (NY), Albright Knox
Art Gallery, gift of A. Conger
Goodyear

This *Gradiva* (1933) drawing represents a female figure called Gradiva as viewed from behind. It borrows its treatment of the figure in part from Dalí's 1926 painting *Girl with Curls* (Salvador Dalí Museum) which represents the peasant girl Dullita described in Dalí's texts "Rêverie" and *The Secret Life of Salvador Dalí* (1942), the latter including an illustration bearing a resemblance to the figure in the 1926 painting. In this 1933 Gradiva drawing the treatment of the curving hips and buttocks, the thin waist and the flowing hair also follows the composition of *Girl with Curls* and may be identified also as Dullita. As Dalí explains in *The Secret Life*, Dullita was transformed into Gradiva and Gradiva in Gala. The subject of Gradiva fascinated Dalí from around 1931 when the French translation of Wilhelm Jensen's novel *Gradiva*, together with Sigmund Freud's analysis, was translated and published in French as *Délire et rêves dans un ouvrage littéraire: La "Gradiva" de Jensen* (Gallimard).

Jensen's novel *Gradiva*, first published in 1903 (Dresden and Leipzig: Reissner), tells the story of the young archaeologist Norbert Hanold, who becomes intrigued with the figure of a woman walking as represented in an ancient relief. Fascinated with how her foot is slightly lifted in stride, he becomes convinced that she was distinguished by a

uniquely elegant manner of walking. Baptizing her "Gradiva"—beautiful in walking—he then has a dream that she died in Pompeii at the time of the eruption of mount Vesuvius. His delusion takes him to the ruins of Pompeii where he sees a spectral female figure in the noonday sun that he takes to be Gradiva. Finally, he encounters this spectre and is shocked that she speaks German rather than Greek or Latin. In subsequent meetings, he gradually understands that, rather than a ghost, Gradiva is a real woman. At the end of the novel, the woman's identity, as a forgotten childhood sweetheart and neighbor, is revealed as is her name: Zoe Bertgang; Zoe means life, and Bertgang in German means much the same as Gradiva ('splendid in walking'). With this revelation comes a love and promise of marriage. For Freud the narrative represented the unveiling of repressed infantile desire and its fruition as a mature object-oriented love. Gradiva is no longer a delusion of the mind and is the real woman Zoe. Further, Zoe performs a therapeutic analysis on Hanold in that she represents the triumph of love over illusion.

Though Ian Gibson has indicated that Dalí was familiar with Freud through the Spanish edition of the complete works as early as the period 1924-26, it does not seem likely that he read Gradiva until 1931.[1] For this reason, earlier subjects were merged into the nascent Gradiva subject at the beginning of the 1930s. The earliest work clearly titled *Gradiva* was the 1931 painting on copper (now lost) which represented the female figure similar to the one he had composed in two drawings titled *Andromeda* (pen, ink, 1930; Albright-Knox Art Gallery and pencil, 1931; Private collection), both originally in the A Conger Goodyear Collection. A similar figure appears in *Guillaume Tell* (1930; cat. 78) on the bas-relief in the foreground, though there is no mention either of Gradiva or Andromeda in the title. While the title *Andromeda* is certain, because it was listed as number 13 in the Wadsworth Atheneum's *Newer-Super Realism* catalogue (Hartford, 1931), the date was not indicated in the catalogue. It is possible that the undated Albright-Knox drawing might date from 1931 like the signed and dated drawing from the private collection.[2] This Andromeda-Gradiva figure, is frontal and related to the subject of the painting *The Bleeding Roses* (1930), with the woman's sex represented as flowers and the blood referring to the operation which left Gala sterile, and to the two drawing studies for *The Invisible Man* (Salvador Dalí Museum and Private collection), in which the sex of the female figure is represented once again as blooming roses. In this *Andromeda* drawing, her body casts a spectral shadow against a classical building suggesting her double identity as relief sculpture. In the background a male figure embraces a Dullita

Fig. 1. Salvador Dalí,
The Invisible Man, 1929
Madrid, Museo Nacional
Centro de Arte Reina Sofía

178

Fig. 2. Salvador Dalí,
*The Bleeding Rose*s, 1930
La Coruña, Fundación Caixa Galicia

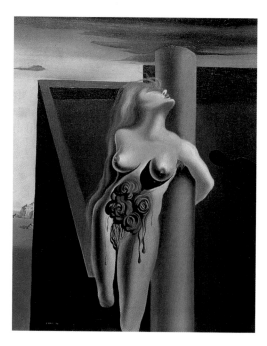

figure, presumably the physical embodiment of the spectral figure. Though these two figures remained identifiable as Andromeda and Dullita, with Dalí's reading of Jensen (1931), the two would coalesce into the composite personality of Gradiva.

The Munich drawing *Gradiva* (1933) introduces a variant on the treatment of the *Girl with Curls* and Dullita subjects. She stands nude in a rocky landscape with her back to us with a slightly twisting torso. We can see over her shoulder that she is engaged in scrutinizing a miniature skull held in the palm of her hands. So here the erotic fascination with Gradiva meets the more Baroque interest in the Vanitas or Memento Mori. Sex reminds us of death. In Jensen's novel there are numerous symbols of death. Gradiva was meant to have died at Pompeii and be reborn first as a relief and second as a real woman. Images of flowers pervade the novel, and range from the white asphodel associated with death to the red Sorrento roses symbolic of reborn love. Finally, the excavation of the past is the primary metaphor of the novel and arguably the one Freud found most intriguing. For Freud the novel was a parable of repression (understood as the buried layers of mental experience) and the uncovering of that repression as sublimated love. W.J.

[1] Ian Gibson, *The Shameful Life of Salvador Dalí* (London: Faber and Faber, 1997), pp. 115-117.

[2] There might be some confusion in the two drawings' exhibition history, which is exacerbated by their common provenance in the A. Conger Goodyear Collection and near identical dimensions. The Wadsworth Atheneum catalogue offers only a title without date and the generic description "drawing" making it difficult to discern which of these two drawings was in the exhibition. A drawing titled *Andromeda* and described as "ink" is listed in the *Fantastic Art, Dada and Surrealism* (Museum of Modern Art, 1936-37) exhibition catalogue with the date 1930 suggesting that this is most likely the Albright-Knox drawing. For the private collection version of the drawing and a proposed provenance see Christie's, *Impressionist and Modern Art* (Day Sale) and *Impressionist and Modern Works on Paper* (New York: Christie's), May 5, 2004, Lot, 158, p. 58.

108. Untitled (Gradiva), 1932

109. William Tell and Gradiva, 1930-31

108. Ink and pencil on paper
27.5 × 20.8 cm
10$^{7/8}$ × 8$^{1/8}$ in.
London, The Mayor Gallery

109. China ink
and pencil on paper
28 × 22 cm
11 × 8$^{5/8}$ in.
Private collection

110. William Tell, Gradiva and the Average Bureaucrat, 1932

110. China ink on cardboard
118 × 65 cm
$46^{1/2} \times 25^{5/8}$ in.
Private collection

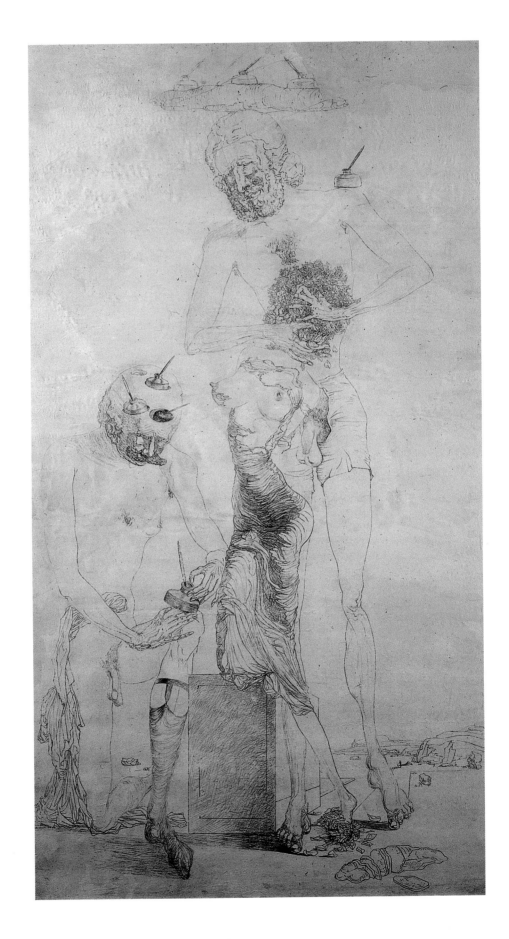

111. Salvador Dalí, Gala Éluard, Valentine Hugo, André Breton
"Exquisite Corpse," ca. 1932

111. Ink on paper
26.7 × 19.5 cm
10 1/2 × 7 7/8 in.
Milan, Fondazione
Antonio Mazzotta

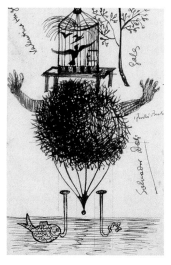

Fig. 1. Salvador Dalí, Gala Éluard,
André Breton and Valentine Hugo,
Exquisite Corpse, 1928
Private collection

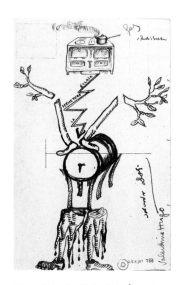

Fig. 2. Salvador Dalí, Gala Éluard
and Valentine Hugo, *Exquisite
Corpse*, March 21, 1932
Paris, Bibliothèque Littéraire
"Jacques Doucet"

With his vivid imagination and consummate skills as a draftsman, Salvador Dalí was especially adept at the exquisite corpse (*cadavre exquis*), a game that the Surrealists played by taking turns to produce a collaborative image through drawings and, occasionally, collage. Although often described as automatic drawings, these hybrid images are closer in spirit to automatic writing, since their power comes from juxtapositions that produce unforeseen and unplanned similarities and metaphors, rather than the "revelations"of André Masson's freely conceived automatic drawings. Based on an old parlor game, the exquisite corpse was defined in the *Dictionnaire Abrégé du Surréalisme* as: "Game of folded paper that consists in having a sentence or a drawing composed by several persons, each ignorant of the preceding collaboration.'"[1] These drawings and poems were created collectively during Surrealist café meetings or soirées, when pieces of paper were passed around among three or more members of the group. The first participant would make a drawing, fold over the sheet of paper for the next person, who would do the same without peeking at the first drawing, thus ensuring that the finished work would not conform to accepted notions of reality. The strange and often preposterous images that resulted continued the Surrealists' interest in utilizing chance procedures to unlock the secrets of the unconscious.

These drawings were made in March 1932, when Breton and Valentine Hugo visited Dalí and Gala in Cadaqués. Another *Exquisite Corpse* produced on this trip (fig. 2) bears the inscription of "March 21, 1932," thus suggesting that all of these drawings were made on, or around, that date. Dalí's contributions to these drawings reveal that he was an enthusiastic participant in the game, although much of his imagery is familiar from his standard repertoire of repressed sexual desires and childhood memories. Contrary to Breton's views about the communal aspect of the exquisite corpse, whose powerful images he believed bore the mark of a "uniquely collective authority" that could not be begotten by one mind alone, Dalí was the only player to sign all of his efforts in the Cadaqués drawings.[2] Even without his signature, it is hard not to recognize his hand in the sections depicting cypress trees and clocks in deep perspective, or the standing female nude with the large nipples.

The incongruous images that came out of this meeting of friends in Cadaqués follow the standard iconography of exquisite corpses, with their conglomerate bodies and scenes of death and violence, which often made reference to female torsos and cadavers, as implied by the name of the game. The firing gun and blood-spattered knife that Dalí renders in one of these works are fairly typical of this imagery, although it should be pointed out that he had already depicted a man firing a gun and a pair of hands struggling with a bloody knife in *Illuminated Pleasures* of 1929 (cat. 70). In that painting, the scenes of violence can be understood as referring to Freud's notion of castration anxiety, but this meaning is diluted three years later in the *Exquisite Corpse*, where the combination of the gun and knife read more like a cartoon representation of gangsters and knife-wielding assailants. Although much of Dalí's imagery in these works is recycled from earlier paintings, the curious scene of violent, flag-bearing revolution in one of the *Exquisite Corpse* drawings is especially noteworthy, since it contains the spectacle of a firing-squad execution. While ultimately indebted to Goya's *The Third of May, 1808*, painted in 1814, this chaotic scene of summary execution, death (in the form of two coffins), and destruction, set against the cacophonous backdrop of two steam locomotives hurtling towards the horizon, anticipates the horrors of the Spanish Civil War four years later, which the artist would memorialize in such gruesome paintings as *Autumn Cannibalism* of 1936 (cat. 165).

Although often dismissed as ephemera, these collaborative drawings were clearly important to the artist's subsequent development, especially during his time in the United States in the mid-1930s, when he would make frequent reference to them in posters and magazine illustrations. For example, Dalí's design for the *Invitation to the Bal Onirique*, the Dream Ball given by Caresse Crosby in New York on January 18, 1935, re-deploys the image of the naked woman with snails for feet and a baby carriage (with baby inside it) on her shoulders. This bizarre image appeared again in an article in *The American Weekly* in February 1935, entitled "New York as Seen by the "Super-Realist" Artist, M. Dalí," where the artist was given sole credit for this collaborative effort, now called *Woman's Infinite Variety*.[3] It is fascinating to note that having been commissioned to record his impressions of the vertiginous skyscrapers and exciting people of New York City the artist would have returned to an image created in distant Cadaqués three years earlier. M.R.T.

[1] *Dictionnaire Abrégé du Surréalisme* (Rennes: José Corti, 1969, reprinted from the 1938 edition issued by the Galerie des Beaux-Arts, Paris), p. 6. Translation by the author. The first Surrealist exquisite corpse is thought to have been made in late 1925 in the house of Marcel Duhamel in Paris, where Duhamel played the game with the poet Jacques Prévert and the painter Yves Tanguy. The name was born when the first sufficiently striking sentence that emerged read: "the exquisite corpse will drink the new wine,"; see André Breton, *Surrealism and Painting* (New York: Icon Editions, Harper & Row, 1972), p. 288.
[2] *Ibid.*, p. 290.
[3] Anonymous, "New York as Seen by the "Super-Realist" Artist, M. Dalí," *The American Weekly*, February 24, 1935, p. 3. The astonishing image of the woman with the perambulator head and snails' feet appears again in the artist's work in 1946, in one of his designs for Walt Disney's animated film *Destino*. This study for *Destino* is reproduced in the exhibition catalogue, *Dalí. Cultura de Masas* (Barcelona: Fundación "la Caixa," 2004), p. 114.

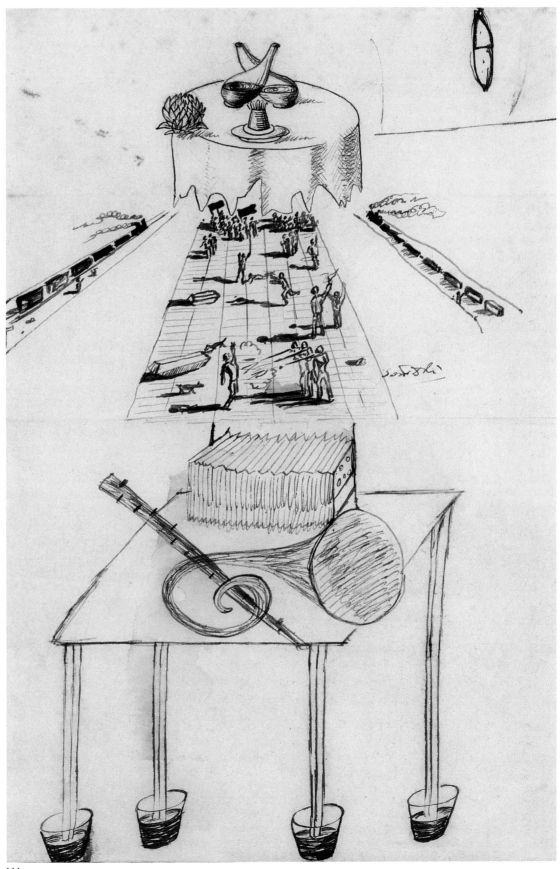

112. Pablo Picasso, "Three Bathers," 1933
113. Study for "Pablo Picasso, Salvador Dalí – Surrealist Figures," 1933

112. Copper engraving
19.4 × 26.9 cm
7⁵/8 × 10⁵/8 in.
Paris, Musée Picasso

113. Pencil on paper
32.3 × 26 cm
12⁵/8 × 10¹/4 in.
Figueres, Fundació
Gala-Salvador Dalí

114. Surrealist Figures – Print by Picasso with Interventions by Dalí, ca. 1933

114. Drypoint engraving
36 × 42.5 cm
14 1/8 × 16 3/4 in.
Paris, Musée Picasso

115. The Average Fine and Invisible Harp

115. Oil on canvas
21 × 16 cm
8¹/4 × 6¹/4 in.
Private collection

One of Dalí's most arresting works, *The Average Fine and Invisible Harp* depicts Dalí and Gala's home at Port Lligat in vivid detail. The enclosed bay, with beach and fishermen's shacks, the roof terrace and the shadows on the surrounding hills, have a concrete presence undisturbed by disquieting perspectives. Not that it is a tranquil picture. Dalí and Gala spent the summers of the early 1930s at Port Lligat, gradually converting and extending the one-story whitewashed house that Dalí had bought from Lídia Noguer's son, Bienvenido Costa Noguer when he was thrown out of his father's house. Life was primitive there, and the road from Cadaqués to Port Lligat in those days ran between abrupt rocks "where no car can get through. So it was necessary to carry everything on a donkey's back."[1] They saw few people apart from Lídia, her mad sons and the fishermen, and were always aware of the violent hostility of his father over the hill in Cadaqués a quarter of an hour's walk away. "Around us gray, cutting rocks, aridity, famished cats, wind, sickly vinestalks, exalted madmen in rags…"[2]

Lídia Noguer, "who possessed the most marvelously paranoiac brain aside from my own that I have ever known," had developed a passion for the prominent Catalan writer Eugenio D'Ors, to whom she wrote regularly and believed that she received coded answers in D'Ors newspaper column. One day she announced to Dalí that D'Ors had begun his article with the end of her letter. The article was on "Poussin and El Greco"; in her letter Lídia had "alluded to two popular characters in Cadaqués. One of them was called Pusa, and the other was a Greek deep sea diver, who was surnamed El Greco."[3] On this phonetic similarity Lídia build a systematic but delirious, paranoid interpretation of D'Ors article. It seems possible that the two men in *The Average Fine and Invisible Harp* might be Pusa and "El Greco"—the latter holds a fragment of an amphora such as lie on the sea bed around Ampurias. Behind them, the tiny figure of Gala clad only in her embroidered jacket slips away. Alternatively they might Lídia's own, crazed sons. "If Lídia was linked to reality, and of the most substantial kind, by multiple terrestrial and maritime ties, her sons on the other hand were really mad and ended much later by being committed to an asylum."[4] In *The Secret Life* Dalí recounts how, the year before he went to Paris, they had come in great secrecy to reveal to him their secret: they thought they had discovered radium at Cap Creus and "would spend moonlit nights hauling dirt in wheelbarrows from a great distance to bury the vein of the mineral so that no one might discover it."[5]

In several paintings of the early 1930s bodies sprout extended phallic protuberances, most famously in *The Enigma of William Tell* (see p. 177, fig. 1). There seem to be two kinds of these elongated forms: the fleshy, soft and bloated, and the hard distorted skull. The distortion in both soft and hard shapes may relate to anamorphosis, a type of perspective which distends images so that the "true form" can only be seen at an angle to the surface of the picture. This is not just an optical trick but "partakes of a detailed symbolism linked in general to deformation."[6] In *Meditation on the Harp* an elongated anamorphic skull stretches from the son's elbow, like the "hidden" death's head in Holbein's *The Ambassadors*. Dalí was also fascinated by recent scientific writings on morphology (see Encyclopedia. "Soft structures") and developed multiple associations around the idea of the ferocious pressure of space on form: "producing the swellings that burst from its life…" Here the huge swollen organ, at once monstrous and detumescent, contrasts dramatically with the hard stone and rock of buildings and landscape. D.A.

[1] Salvador Dalí, *The Secret Life of Salvador Dalí*, trans. Haakon Chevalier (London: Vision Press, 1968), p. 297
[2] *Ibid.*, p. 301.
[3] *Ibid.*, p. 266.
[4] *Ibid.*, p. 267.
[5] *Ibid.*
[6] Carl Einstein, "Saint Antoine de Padoue et l'enfant Jesus," *Documents* no. 4 (September 1929), p. 230.

Fig. 1. Salvador Dalí, *Skull with its Lyric Appendage Leaning on a Bedside Table which Should Have the Exact Temperature of a Cardinal's Nes* 1934 St. Petersburg (FL), The Salvador Dalí Museum

189

116. Angelus, ca. 1932
117. The Architectonic Angelus of Millet, 1933
118. Atavism at Twilight, 1933-34

116. Oil on wood
16 × 21.7 cm
6¼ × 8½ in.
Private collection, courtesy
Galerie Natalie Seroussi, Paris

117. Oil on canvas
73 × 61 cm
28¾ × 24 in
Madrid, Museo Nacional,
Centro de Arte Reina Sofía

118. Oil on wood,
14 × 18 cm
5½ × 7⅛ in
Bern, Kunstmuseum Bern

In 1932, Millet's *Angelus* suddenly presented itself to Dalí in a vivid mental image, without warning or conscious association. Its profound effect on him was quite out of proportion to the apparent character of this innocent devotional painting. Millet's peasant couple, who pause from their rural labor to pray at the sound of the Angelus bell from the distant church, their wheelbarrow and pitchfork lying idle, had become one of the most popular and massively reproduced Christian images. Its message of grave personal devotion, even among the lowliest in society, far away from ritual pomp, was familiar throughout Catholic Europe. But the painting for Dalí was charged now with a quite different emotional impact and had become "the most troubling, most enigmatic, densest and richest in unconscious thoughts that had ever existed."[1] He recalled that as a child at the Christian Brothers' school in Figueres, a copy of the *Angelus* had "produced in me an obscure anguish, so poignant that the memory of those two motionless silhouettes pursued me for several years."[2] It then "disappeared completely from my imagination." This sudden hallucinatory return of the *Angelus* inaugurated an extraordinary series of visual images as well as one of the most remarkable interpretations of a picture ever written: his book *The Tragic Myth of Millet's Angelus*.[3]

In *The Tragic Myth of Millet's Angelus*, Dalí analyses, in the manner of a Freudian case history, the encounters and fantasies—what he calls the "secondary delirious phenomena"—that accompanied his obsession with the painting. Following the description of these phenomena he interprets them with the aid of his paranoiac-critical method, with a quantity of associations and memories that gradually uncover the picture's hidden "meaning."

The secondary phenomena include suddenly recognizing the Angelus couple in the position of two stones he was playing with on the beach, but with the left, "male" one, perforated with holes and much smaller than the other; a fantasy in which the two figures are carved into the "delirious geology" of the rocks at Cap Creus, fissured and

eroded; glimpsing a porcelain tea set in a shop window decorated with the Angelus picture, which arouses a sensation of anguish; momentarily confusing a color lithograph of a pile of cherries with the postcard of the Angelus.

He begins the paranoiac-critical interpretation of these phenomena with a discussion of "the atavisms of dusk" which are rich in associations. The twilight world of the *Angelus* takes him back to youthful reveries when walking at dusk in the countryside round Figueres. Surrounded by the sounds of insects, grasshoppers and above all the praying mantis, he composed elegiac poems on the early epochs of the earth whose extinguished plants and animals were visible in the numerous fossils of the region that his father collected. Having more recently read Fabre, the "Facteur Cheval of entomology," he was struck by Fabre's nostalgic descriptions of the insects whose "antique" habits recalled previous ages. The dawn of the world, Dalí notes, appears to us as its twilight. These ideas return with another of the initial *rêveries*, when Dalí imagines visiting the Museum of Natural History in Madrid with Gala, and seeing in the insect room, in place of the diplodocus, the colossal figures of the Angelus. On leaving the Museum, Dalí sodomizes Gala at the door, a violent act "eminently tragic and disproportionate to my physiological and vital capacities," which Dalí, in his terror of the sexual act, used to believe would inevitably end in his death. "The fate of the male praying mantis always appeared to illustrate my own fate confronted with love."[4] The attitude of the woman in the *Angelus* resembled the "spectral and expectant attitude of the female praying mantis," the implications of which are finally revealed by Dalí in the final section of the *Tragic Myth*, with a long quotation from Fabre describing the female mantis's habit of devouring her mate not just after but during copulation.[5]

A further set of associations uncovers not only fear of death in love but a slippage of identity: the couple is not just husband and wife but also mother and son. The anguish caused by an "experimental" reverie in which he saw the male figure dipped and drowned in a bucket of milk, associated with a childhood fantasy that the pouch in which the female kangaroo carried her young was full of milk, together with the interpretation of the tea service decorated with the Angelus, is explained in terms of the notion of the male/son engulfed and obliterated by the maternal element. "It is worth noting that, in the analysis of the earlier delirious phenomenon where we saw the identification of Gala and myself with the Angelus couple, Gala in reality occupied the place of my mother, to whom I owe my terror of the sexual act."[6] The cherries that he momentarily confused with the Angelus couple "represent the stereotype

Fig. 1. Salvador Dalí,
*Archaeological Reminiscence
of Millet's "Angelus,"*1935
St. Petersburg (FL), The Salvador
Dalí Museum

190

116

of the son." "The identification with the cherries presents …the aggressive awakening of cannibalist desires: it is also highly charged with erotic factors"[7]; a postcard reproduced in the *Tragic Myth* typifies the rich symbolic resources of this fruit. For Dalí, the male, the son, appears "already dead." From the "insipid and stereotypical" image of the Angelus, Dalí thus conjures "the maternal variant of the immense, atrocious myth of Saturn, Abraham, the Eternal Father with Jesus-Christ and William Tell himself devouring their own sons."[8]

The mutations to which Dalí subjects the couple in his paintings respond to the new scenario provided by his paranoiac interpretation. Eroticism and extinction govern the transformations: the figures are turned to stone, or huge brick ruins (*Archaeological Reminiscence of Millet's "Angelus"*; fig. 1); the male figure is sometimes a skeleton and often pierced with holes (*Atavism at Twilight*), while the female looms over him. Dalí invests the two figures with sexual potency but inverts its normal operation: the male figure he presents as sexually aroused but passive and threatened, the female as expectant but aggressive.

In the *Architectural Angelus of Millet* the immense figures of the couple are turned to stone, fossil-like and white as chalk or milk. The male figure, with a calcified "bean" on top like William Tell's apple, dripping like a stalactite, supported by a crutch, pierces the female with a long spike that she already is in the process of engulfing. A dark shadow reaches up the canvas as at the approach of twilight, in which stand the minute figures of father and son, witnessing an ancient, atavistic drama. In *The Angelus* the two figures are outlined against what appears to be a deep, illuminated theatre backdrop. The father-son has a gaping hole in his chest and is partially naked. A drawing for this picture shows them holding a large sheet, as in *The Old Age of William Tell*, as if to shield an atrocious scene, or perhaps as a winding sheet. In the Prologue to *The Tragic Myth* written in 1962 Dalí triumphantly presents evidence, from an x-ray taken at his request of the painting by the Louvre, of a boxlike shape that Millet had painted over, which he argues is the coffin of the dead son over which the couple are praying and confirms his original paranoiac interpretation.

The Tragic Myth is not, it should be noted, a "psycho-analytical" interpretation relative to Millet himself, of whose life Dalí was totally ignorant; significantly, he notes that although the *Angelus* occupies his reveries, he never actually dreams of it. It is, rather, a "Surrealist experiment" in irrational knowledge, in which the active method of "paranoiac thought" meets the Surrealist notion of objective chance. Chance encounters and chance events are invested with exceptional emotional force, revealing an unconscious fear or desire within the subject. The delusional, but systematic, associations that follow are stimulated by the fantasies and reveries in which Dalí frequently indulged to produce a whole range of visual inventions around the *Angelus*.

As far as the "objective truth" is concerned, Dalí notes, his "paranoiac reveries" are no less productive than those of philosophy, of history and even those of "scientific investigation where experimental activity reaches the most ambitious degrees of objectivity." Such sciences as psychoanalysis itself, he argues, are "brilliantly systematised deliria."[9] He might have had in mind Freud's remark at the end of his "Psychoanalytical Notes on an Autobiographical Account of a Case of Paranoia" the Schreber Case: "It remains for the future to decide whether there is more delusion in my theory than I would care to admit, or whether there is more truth in Schreber's delusion than other people are as yet prepared to believe."[10] D.A.

[1] Salvador Dalí, *Le Mythe tragique de l'Angélus de Mil-*

Fig. 2. Salvador Dalí, *Atavistic Vestiges after the Rain*, 1934
Private collection

Fig. 4. Salvador Dalí, cover of *The The Tragic Myth of Millet's Angelus*

Fig. 5. Jean-Françoise Millet, *The Angelus*, 1857 Paris, Musée d'Orsay

let, Interprétation "paranoiaïque-critique" (ca. 1932), (Paris: Jean-Jacques Pauvert, 1963), p. 17.

[2] Salvador Dalí, *The Secret Life of Salvador Dalí*, trans. Haakon Chevalier (London: Vision Press, 1968), p. 64.

[3] Dalí had finished the manuscript of this book in the 1930s; a manuscript copy with corrections in Breton's hand exists in the FGSD archives. It was mislaid during the confusion of fleeing Paris after the outbreak of war in 1939 and when he recovered it in 1962 he decided to publish it as it stood, with the addition of a prologue and some notes. It was only with its appearance in 1963 that the full implications of Dalí's obsessional re-workings of the An-gelus theme could be clarified. In this sense it is similar to the publication of Duchamp's Notes to the Large Glass, *The Bride Stripped Bare by Her Bachelors, Even* in 1934, which for the first time gave a clue to the iconography of that mysterious icon. However, whereas Duchamp's Notes were heralded by and interpreted by Breton at the time, Dalí's *Tragic Myth of Millet's Angelus* fell into a relative

void, in that he had long since parted company with Sur-realism, which had provided its immediate context, and his celebrity status was not predicated on the kind of seri-ous and complex analysis this book constitutes. It is only relatively recently that its interest not just for Dalí scholars but also for anyone engaged in psycho-analytical theory in relation to art has been recognized.

[4] Salvador Dalí, *Le Mythe tragique*, p. 53.

[5] This habit, Dalí subsequently learned, was apparently true only of the Praying Mantis in captivity, as he notes in his caption to the photograph.

[6] *Le Mythe tragique*, p. 57.

[7] *Ibid.*, p. 73.

[8] *Ibid.*, p. 89.

[9] *Ibid.*, p. 91.

[10] Sigmund Freud, "Psychoanalytical Notes on an Auto-biographical Account of a Case of Paranoia" (the Schre-ber Case) in *Case Histories 11* vol. 9 (London: Pelican Freud Library, 1911), p. 218.

118

119. The Spectre of the Angelus, ca. 1934

119. Oil on canvass
22 × 16 cm
8⁵/8 × 6¹/4 in.
Private collection

Fig. 1. James Pradier, model for the sculpture *Hysterical and Aerodynamic Nude—Woman on the Rock* location unknown

Fig. 2. Salvador Dalí, *Hysterical and Aerodynamic Nude – Woman on the Rock*, 1934 Paris, Private collection

In *The Spectre of the Angelus*, Dalí introduces another element to his Angelus theme: Napoleon. He had painted a medallion representing the Emperor on the pedestal in *The Old Age of William Tell* (1931); here, like the peasant couple, Napoleon is formed from the clouds, a fragment of an equestrian portrait. Dalí opened *The Secret Life* with the assertion: "At the age of six I wanted to be a cook. At seven I wanted to be Napoleon. And my ambition has been growing steadily since."[1] Another treasured childhood memory was of the mate drinking ceremony in the third floor apartment belonging to an Argentinean family, above the Dalí home. There was "a picture of [Napoleon] in the center of the circle of glorious polychromes that adorned one end of a tin keg… Napoleon's image, reproduced on the mate keg, meant everything to me; for years his attitude of Olympian pride, the white and edible strip of his smooth belly, the feverish pink of those imperial cheeks, the indecent, melodic, and categorical black of the spectral outline of his hat, corresponded exactly to the ideal model I had chosen for myself, the king."[2] While there is no reason to doubt his childhood fascination, the description of Napoleon written in 1941 is colored by Dalí's evocation of Hitler that has a similarly ambiguous sexuality.

Dalí's interest in Napoleon might have been re-awakened by an article in the *Revue française de psychanalyse*, which Éluard had recommended to Gala and Dalí. "I'm sending a large package of journals: *Revue de Psychanalyse* in which you must read Frois-Wittman's article and the article on Napoleon," he wrote from Cannes in August 1930.[3] Dr Louis Jekels' "Le tournant decisive de la vie de Napoleon" was published in *Revue française de psychanalyse* in 1929. This psychoanalytical study examined Napoleon's career in the light of incidents from his early life and concluded: "Napoleon's unconscious adopted once and for all a negative attitude towards the father. It is against him that he was thenceforth to wage incessant and pitiless war."[4] Éluard, who remained intimate with Dalí and Gala and was familiar with Dalí's battle with his father, recognized Napoleon's potential to become another Oedipal hero in the painter's mythology.

In the foreground of *The Spectre of the Angelus* is a distorted female "spectre"—the type Dalí opposed to the "phantom" in his *Minotaure* text of 1934 "Les nouvelles couleurs du sex-appeal spectral." (See also *The Sign of Anguish*, cat. 122). "The spectral woman will be the folding woman," he wrote.[5] The head is elongated like an anvil or baguette, and its distended buttock is propped up by a crutch, like a female version of the Lenin figure in *The Enigma of William Tell*. The "spectre" has a general family resemblance to the illustrations for *Les Chants de Maldoror*, but also recalls

the sculpture *Hysterical and Aerodynamic Nude – Woman on the Rock* of 1934 (figs. 1, 2). The 19th-century marble nude by James Pradier has been altered so that parts of the anatomy and especially the head are stretched out as though compressed by the immense force of gravity. The "aerodynamic" of the title may be a later interpretation; the sculpture is probably related to the "*objets atmospheriques*" that Dalí exhibited at Pierre Colle in 1933. D.A.

[1] Salvador Dalí, *The Secret Life of Salvador Dalí* (New York: Dial Press, 1961), p.1.

[2] *Ibid.*, p. 5.

[3] Paul Éluard, *Lettres a Gala 1924-1948* , NRF 1984 p. 118.

[4] Dr Louis Jekels, "Le tournant decisive de la vie de Napoleon," *Revue française de psychanalyse*, 3rd Year no. 2, 1929, p. 348. The article was originally published in *Imago* (1914) and was translated from the German by Anna Ratisbonne, *Psychoanalysing Napoleon became something of a fashion*. In 1933, E. Bergler published "Motifs inconscients de l'attitude de Napoleon à l'égard de Talleyrand," *Revue française de psychanalyse,* vol. 6, no. 3-4, p. 408.

[5] Salvador Dalí, "Les nouvelles couleurs du sex-appeal spectral," *Minotaure*, no. 5, (1934), p. 22.

120. Gala and the Angelus of Millet Preceding the Imminent Arrival of the Conical Anamorphoses, 1933

120. Oil on wood panel
24.2 × 19.2 cm
9 1/2 × 75/8 in.
Ottawa, National Gallery
of Canada
Purchased 1975

This tiny, luminous and enigmatic painting belongs to a series of works from the early 1930s that explored the emotional fears that Jean-François Millet's *The Angelus* aroused in Dalí. This 19th-century painting, stemming from his childhood memory of seeing a reproduction of the work hanging in the corridor of his school in Figueres, held an intense fascination for the artist. However, whereas most people regarded *The Angelus* as a sacred image of rural piety, for Dalí it was a monstrous example of disguised sexual repression and violence.[1] In his book-length, paranoiac-critical interpretation of the painting, entitled *The Tragic Myth of Millet's "Angelus,"* which he began around 1932 but did not publish until 1963, Dalí argued that the work was encoded with latent images of castration and death.[2] According to this morbid scenario, the humble peasant woman and her husband, who revolves his hat between his fingers while he waits for his wife to finish her prayer, take on the sinister connotations of the bizarre mating ritual of the praying mantis, in which the husband is about to be devoured by his sexually aggressive mate after copulation.
The man's hat has been strategically placed to hide an erection, which Dalí understood as a sure sign that he anticipates and even welcomes her fatal embrace, which by extension related to his own fear of being absorbed, annihilated and eaten by his mother, a fear that the artist related to a false memory of his mother sucking or devouring his penis as a child.[3] In this painting, instead of being transformed by Dalí's paranoiac-critical method, Millet's *The Angelus* is reproduced without significant alteration, although the composition has been stretched horizontally so that the space between and at either side of the figures is greater than in the original and fully occupies the width of the open doorway above which the painting is positioned. The presence of a moderately faithful reproduction of *The Angelus* above the doorway in this painting offers a partial explanation for the proceedings below, in which the grotesquely grinning Gala, seen in the background in her richly embroidered, multi-colored jacket, assumes the role of the predatory, dominant female. Facing her across the table is the figure of Vladimir Ilyich Lenin, the leader of the Communist Revolution, recognizable by his bald head and facial hair, while the strange, lobster-headed character eavesdropping from behind the door has been identified as Maxim Gorky. Another "revolutionary" present in the room is André Breton, the poet and leader of the Surrealist group, who is portrayed in a plaster bust that sits on a high ledge overlooking Gala and Lenin. Although the ultimate meaning of this mysterious work remains unfathomable, the presence of Gala, Lenin, Gorky, and Breton under the sign of Millet's *Angelus* suggests that the painting was intended as an allegory of the artist's deepest anxieties and obsessions, which at this point centered around

mothers devouring their sons in a form of sexual cannibalism. This would explain the presence of the engulfing maternal figure of Gala, who is rendered with a minute, almost photographic, realism that is in stark contrast to the spherical heads of Gorky and Lenin (the "conical anamorphoses" of the painting's title),[4] and the petrified features of Breton, all of whom were key figures in Dalí's personal mythology of the time. These father figures thus relate to the artist's contemporaneous interest in "the immense and atrocious myth of Saturn, of Abraham, of the Eternal Father with Jesus Christ and of William Tell himself, all devouring their own sons."[5] The end result is one of the most complex and daring compositions that utilize the paranoiac-critical method and its importance in Dalí's oeuvre was recognized as early as 1941, when the painting was chosen for the catalogue cover of the artist's first retrospective exhibition at The Museum of Modern Art in New York. M.R.T.

[1] In his *Unspeakable Confessions*, Dalí mentions seeing the copy of *The Angelus* on the wall of the corridor leading to his classroom, which induced in him "an unhealthy anxiety that arose from the two motionless characters of the Millet picture with that dead space between them"; see Salvador Dalí, *The Unspeakable Confessions of Salvador Dalí (as Told to André Parinaud)*, trans. Harold J. Salemson (New York: William Morrow and Co., 1976), p. 29.
[2] Salvador Dalí, *Le mythe tragique de l'Angélus de Millet: Interprétation "paranoïaque-critique"* (Paris: Jean-Jacques Pauvert, 1963).
[3] *Ibid*, p. 57.
[4] The artist offered a description of "conical anamorphosis" in the following year: "Flat reconstitution of the deformation reflected in a very smooth cone. The best examples date to the 1900 period"; see Salvador Dalí, "The Latest Modes of Intellectual Stimulation for the Summer of 1934," "Derniers modes d'excitation intéllectuelle pour l'été 1934), *Documents 34: Numéro spécial Intervention surréaliste*, nouvelle série 1 (Paris), June 1934, pp. 34-35, reprinted in Haim Finkelstein, ed., *The Collected Writings of Salvador Dalí* (Cambridge: Cambridge University Press, 1998), p. 254.
[5] Salvador Dalí, *Le mythe tragique de l'Angélus de Millet: Interprétation "paranoïaque-critique,"* op. cit., p. 89, reprinted in Haim Finkelstein, ed., *The Collected Writings of Salvador Dalí, ibid*, p. 297.

121. The Phantom Cart, 1933

121. Oil on wood panel
16 × 20.3 cm
6¹/4 × 8 in.
New Haven (CT), Yale
University Art Gallery, gift of
Thomas Fine Howard, 1953

In his 1930 essay "L'Âne pourri" (The Rotting Donkey), Dalí linked his interest in paranoiac double images with a desire, shared by his Surrealist colleagues, "to systematize confusion and thereby contribute to a total discrediting of the world of reality."[1] This questioning of the veracity of the external world's appearance through multiple figurations and visible illusions can be seen in *The Phantom Cart*, where the contours of the driver and passenger of a *tartana*, or covered cart, can also be read as the two buildings of the small town toward which they are traveling, while the wheels double as stakes stuck in the sand. The minuscule "doubling" of buildings and figures successfully introduces a disquieting sense of doubt and confusion in the viewer, whose experience in looking at the work is akin to seeing a mirage or hallucination. The constantly shifting apparition of the two figures in the wagon and the towers of the town eventually metamorphose into a single entity in which, in the words of James Thrall Soby, "the cart becomes its own destination."[2] This optical illusion, which represents Dalí's first complete success in achieving a double image, is enhanced by the diffuse golden light of the setting sun that bathes the painting in atmospheric effects that are indebted to the 19th-century landscape tradition.

Dalí based this painting, which exists in several versions, on his memory of a childhood journey in a horse-drawn carriage to the Pichot family's farmhouse, called El Molí de la Torre (or Tower Mill), just outside the artist's hometown of Figueres, which he remembered slowly approaching at sunset. This identification with the Ampurdàn plain, in which El Muli de la Torre lies, is supported by the presence of an antique amphora in the painting's foreground, which can be understood as a reference to the rich cultural history of the region and more specifically to its archaeological ruins of major Phoenician and Roman cities. The fragment of the encrusted amphora recalls similar pictorial devices in Giorgio de Chirico's 1920s paintings of horses running wild along the shores of Thessaly, which feature archaeological remains, such as Greek temples and sunken columns, that create a delirious conjunction of classical antiquity and modernity. For Dalí, this interest in archaeology can also be linked to the unearthing of his innermost desires and fantasies, which had been repressed in adulthood, since the use of archaeology as a metaphor for the psychoanalytic project had become commonplace since the publication in 1909 of Sigmund Freud's *Delusions and Desires in Jensen's Gradiva*. M.R.T.

[1] Salvador Dalí, "L'Âne pourri," *Le Surréalisme au service de la révolution* (Paris: 1930), p. 9, reprinted in Haim Finkelstein, ed., *The Collected Writings of Salvador Dalí*, trans. Haim Finkelstein (Cambridge: Cambridge University Press, 1998), p. 223.
[2] James Thrall Soby, *Salvador Dalí* (New York: The Museum of Modern Art, 1941), p. 20.

122. The Sign of Anguish, 1932-36
123. The Sense of Speed, 1931
124. The Tower, 1934

122. Oil on panel
22.2 × 16.5 cm
8³/4 × 6¹/2 in.
Edinburgh, Scottish National
Gallery of Modern Art,
bequeathed by Gabrielle Keiller,
1995

123. Oil on canvas
33 × 24 cm
13 × 9¹/2 in.
Figueres, Fundació
Gala-Salvador Dalí

124. Oil on canvas
66.5 × 53.5 cm
26¹/8 × 21¹/8 in.
Zürich, Kunsthaus Zürich
gift of Erna and Curt Burgauer

Fig. 1. Works by Salvador Dalí
and Yves Tanguy reproduced in
Minotaure, no. 5, 1934

Fig. 2. Alberto Martini,
La Beauté feminine

The disquieting spaces of these landscapes, often with a single cypress tree, relate to Dalí's obsession with Böcklin's *Isle of the Dead* (see p. 164, fig. 1 and cat. 98). The long shadows and emphatic, but inconsistent, perspective also invoke the mood of melancholy in de Chirico's paintings. *The Tower* explicitly refers to the recurrent motif of a high tower rising against the sky in such paintings by de Chirico as *The Anguish of Departure* (1913-14), whose title is echoed in Dalí's *The Sign of Anguish*. The clock embedded in the shoe-shaped stone monument in *The Sense of Speed* likewise recalls de Chirico, whose station clocks brood over an atmosphere of loss and partings (see *Gare Montparnasse [The Melancholy of Departure]* 1914, MoMA).

As is so often the case with Dalí, however, a single image is open to multiple interpretations. Both *The Sense of Speed* and *The Tower* are also informed by Dalí's concept of the "symbolically functioning Surrealist object." The shoe was one of his chosen fetishes around which, in his first Surrealist object, he constructed an elaborate erotic scenario (see cat. 93). The old-fashioned shapes of the shoes in *The Sense of Speed* harks back to a collage in a letter to Lorca, in which he pasted reproductions of shoes from different epochs and cultures, reveling in the mixture of grotesque and good taste. In his short text on "Objets Surrealistes" Dalí imagines the proliferation of objects that lack utility but correspond to "the culture of desire." The shoe-monument in *The Sense of Speed*, which we must read as enormous, is a denizen of a future world prophesied by Dalí: "Museums will rapidly fill up with objects, whose uselessness, size and inconvenience will necessitate the construction, in deserts, of special towers to contain them.

The doors of these towers will be skillfully erased and in their place will flow a continual fountain of real milk, which will be avidly absorbed by the warm sand."[1]

The sense of hidden presences in *The Tower* is reinforced by the double image in the clouds, which can be read as breasts. Similarities between Dalí's open landscapes and Tanguy's paintings of this period were underlined in the Surrealist journal *Minotaure,* where groups of works by the two artists were reproduced on facing pages (fig. 1). Whereas Tanguy, however, often makes the division between land, sea and sky indistinct, Dalí retains a distinct horizon line, bounded by the plain and hills of the Ampurdàn. There is also an interesting comparison between Tanguy's abstract, biomorphic beings and the objects that people Dalí's canvases, most striking in the monstrous beans or maggots of *Melancholy*, reproduced in the top left hand corner of the page.

After *The Sign of Anguish* was reproduced in *Minotaure* and exhibited at the Julien Levy Gallery in New York in 1934, Dalí changed a couple of elements and signed and dated it on the back 1936.[2] The changes are not substantial but include, as Elizabeth Cowling has pointed out, the elimination of a "limb" from the cypress tree and the addition of a leafy branch across the

nude's shoulders.[3] The forked branch beneath the globular breast may be a memory of Dalí's childhood fantasy of touching the breasts of a young woman with his crutch, but the addition of the leafy twigs suggests the myth of Daphne who, pursued by Apollo, was saved by being transformed into a bush. The juxtaposition of female figure and leafy twigs also disturbingly resembles photographs of the praying mantis, which accompanied Roger Caillois' article "La mante religieuse," in the same issue of *Minotaure*.

Signs of disquiet invade the canvas; the horizontal plane of the decrepit building and its ruined window is spatially incompatible with the deep landscape to the left. The figure of the woman, which partially masks the edge of the building, can neither be located in the landscape nor in relation to the wall. The curious inconsistencies in the painting of the body, whose breasts, buttocks and back are unnaturally inflated and greenish in color, recall Dalí's ideas about opposing female sexualities, divided between "phantom" and "specter," which he described in "Les nouvelles couleurs du sex-appeal spectral," published in the same issue of *Minotaure* where the painting was reproduced. The "virtual" volume of phantoms and the shrouds enveloping them are analogous to fat and flesh, what he calls "anthropomorphic anguish." The terrifying fleshly fat "envelops, hides, protects, transfigures, incites, tempts, gives a deceptive idea of volume."[4] Dalí contrasts "Mae West's round and salivary muscles, terribly glutinous with biological afterthoughts" with a new form of sex appeal: the spectral. The anatomy of spectral woman can be disassembled and exhibited in parts, according to her will. "The 'dismantle-able body' is the aspiration and verification of feminine exhibitionism, which … permits each piece to be isolated and separately consumable."[5] (The following issue of *Minotaure* included Bellmer's photographs of his dismantled doll, "Poupée. Variations sur le montage d'une mineure articulée.") Dalí articulates his anxieties about female sexuality round the opposing poles of a soft engulfing mammary exuberance and the hard, dissected spectral body. The drooping linen cloths in this context, which could be taken to symbolize a fear of impotence, are also invested with some of the horror of the "virtual volume" of the phantom's shrouds, while the body is swollen with cannibalistic urges. D.A.

[1] Salvador Dalí, "Objets Surrealistes" in *Le Surréalisme au service de la révolution,* no. 3 (Paris: 1931), p. 17.

[2] The following is a revised version of the entry for *The Sign of Anguish* in Dawn Ades, *Dalí: Optical Illusions* (Yale University Press, 2000), pp. 86-88.

[3] Elizabeth Cowling, *Surrealism and After: The Gabrielle Keiller Collection* (Edinburgh: Scottish National Gallery of Modern Art, 1997), p. 87.

[4] "Les nouvelles couleurs du sex-appeal spectral" in *Minotaure,* no. 5 (Paris: 1934), p. 20.

[5] *Ibid.*

125. The Locust Child, 1933
126. Soft Skulls and Skull Harp, 1935

125. China ink and pencil
37.5 × 34 cm
14³/4 × 13³/8 in.
Private collection, courtesy
Galerie Natalie Seroussi, Paris

126. Engraving on paper
37 × 30.5 cm
14¹/2 × 12 in.
Private collection

127. Le revolver à cheveux blanc, 1932

128. Frontespice to "Le revolver à cheveux blanc," 1932

127. Copper engraving
16.8 × 11.5 cm
6$^{5/8}$ × 4$^{1/2}$ in.
Private collection

128. Etching
15 × 21 cm
5$^{7/8}$ × 8$^{1/4}$ in.
Private collection

Le Chants de Maldoror

Isidore Ducasse, Comte de Lautréamont, *Les Chants de Maldoror*. Albert Skira, Paris, 1934. 42 etchings by Salvador Dalí. 207 pages, printed in black ink on Vélin d'Arches paper. 33 by 25 cm. Deluxe edition of the 1869-74 French text by Isidore Ducasse. Paper chemise inside black velvet-covered board casing stamped with title in blue letters. Fifty-four, four-page folios. The colophon sites an edition of 200, forty of which have an additional suite with remarques, and ten books that were not for sale. Of these, only sixty copies of the book and forty additional suites were printed but not signed. In 1974 Pierre Argillet printed 100 copies of the book and 100 additional suites with all prints signed by the artist.

The colophon of the book reads:
"CETTE ÉDITION des *Chants de Maldoror*, illustrée de quarante-deux eaux-fortes originales de Salvador Dalí; a été achevée d'imprimer le trente et un juillet mil neuf cent trente-quatre, à Paris, sur les presses de Philippe Gonin pour la typographie, et par Roger Lacourière pour les gravures./ Tirage limité à deux cents dix exemplaires, sur vélin d'Arches, tous numérotés à la presse et signés par l'Artiste. / Quarante exemplaires numérotés de 1 à 40, contenant chacun une suite avec remarques; Cent soixante exemplaires numérotés de 41 à 200. Dix exemplaires hors commerce, numérotés en chiffres romains de I à X, réservés à l'Artiste et aux Collaborateurs. / Les cuivres ayant servi au tirage des illustrations ont été rayés par l'Artiste, en présence de l'Éditeur."

Of the fifty-four, four-page folios gathered unbound in a paper chemise, a first folio is printed with a first and second title page, edition number and artist's signature. The second folio is not printed. The third folio indicates the pagination for the six songs of the work and a colophon. The following 51 folios are printed with the text. At the start and end of each of the six song sections is an etched illustration printed on the text folio, twelve in total. Thirty, single sheet etchings are presented loose in the text folios. It is not clear in what manner the thirty engraved sheets were intended to correspond with the fifty-one folios. The text folios are paginated, but the single sheet prints are not. These prints are from plates measuring 22.5 by 17 cm. The block of 14 pt. text corresponds to the size of the plates.
Löpsinger[1] reports that prepublication details predicted a book with 52 etchings. This number suggests that a formal correspondence of one print to each folio was intended, perhaps with the elegant nude as a frontispiece invoking Dalí's muse, to be included in the title or signature folio; the reduced number of engravings left the book with a formal imbalance.

Both artist book and initial publication of the text were issued piecemeal: the text printed in 1869 was withheld from the market for revisions and Dalí's illustrated version was issued in several stages. Curiously, Ducasse himself had the same interrupted release, being disinterred the year after his death and reburied in another Parisian cemetery.[2]

The prints
In this suite of etchings, each from a plate the same size and each printed in black, Dalí presents many of the images already generated in his painting to date as well as those elaborated later on: furniture, pens with their ink bottles, piano, bones on the ground, bones vertically stacked, bones creating images of flesh, intricate coiffures, skulls, posts, crutches, pillows and bundles, geometric bases, forks and spoons, soft watches, the Angelus figures and paraphernalia, vast plains, mountains, a sewing machine, a car.
In many plates there is a central image composed of human or anthropomorphized assemblages, diverse elements in an Arcimboldo-like accretion of organic and domestic forms. The compositions are moribund and the energy centripetal: the clumping of severed body parts standing limpidly in the vast spaces and among the rays of the sun. Here and there an anamorphic skull bulges up, a lone element in the space of the plate. Elsewhere, the ground is highly integrated into the composition, holding the objects' shadows and diminishing along fine perspectival lines to the horizon. Nothing can be said to be happening on a narrative level in the series, yet the elements of each composition hum with a metamorphic energy. Within the compositional stasis the elements pierce, stack, press, droop, deform, bundle, cut, tear, nail, clamp, and stitch. The violence of the actions and the pervasive transformational process depicted provide the thematic and temperamental coherence with the songs of Maldoror.
The objects and organic forms are composed by stippling and short parallel linear strokes, or, and often in the same plate, by short concentric curvilinear strokes. These techniques give volume and density to the forms and are complemented with long crisp etched lines that curve elegantly.
The complex and uncertain methods of the making of the plates have attracted more attention than the prints as pictorial facts or their correspondence with the text in generating a total esthetic effect. Robert Rainwater writes, "Generally regarded without apology as original etchings by Dalí, as they are described on the book's colophon page, the illustrations for *Les Chants de Maldoror* have recently been demonstrated to be photo mechanically derived, at least in part."[3] Löpsinger describes them as "heliogravures reworked in drypoint."[4] "More extensive descriptions of Dalí's

129. Female Nude with Lamb Chops, ca. 1933   130. Study for "Le Chants de Maldoror," ca. 1933

129. Pencil on paper
21.5 × 15.8 cm
8$^{1/2}$ × 6$^{1/4}$ in.
Stuttgart, Staatsgalerie,
Graphische Sammlung

130. Pencil on paper
22 × 16 cm
8 $^{5/8}$ × 6$^{1/4}$ in.
Stuttgart, Staatsgalerie
Graphische Sammlung

working methods have proposed that the images for the prints were first made as celluloid engravings, and impressions of these intermediary prints made with graphite or soot were then photo mechanically transferred onto copper plates."[5] By "celluloid engraving" is meant a procedure that served Picasso, Dalí, Rouault, and innumerable subsequent 20th-century artists. In this procedure and its variants, the artist scrapes the surface of the transparent sheet with a sharp point, rubbing an opaque material into the opened surface, or draws with pigment. This sheet, drawn or scribed, serves as a positive film for any light-based etching techniques. The method is extremely flexible as the artist can add or subtract elements to amend the image both prior to etching the plate and in further iterations after the plate is etched.

Rainer Mason suggests that the possibility of other hands in Dalí's prints is more troublesome than the

signing of thousands of blank sheets in his later career.[6] In those plates that appear to be developed initially as drypoints he finds a style that is "nervous, detailed, frequentative"[7] and in those that begin with photogravure he senses a hand lacking a living force and weight[8] Mason, who has looked at the prints with intelligence and connoisseurship, perceives the presence of an understructure beneath the strong lines, a wispy substance humming beneath the surface.[9] In his catalog, Mason presents proof of this initial state of the plate printed in graphite, some of which have been reworked with ink. Yet, as Larry Saphire points out, the existence of drawing studies that differ subtly but significantly from the etched version of the same image probably indicates that Dalí did not use a photomechanical method to realize the image on the plate.[10] Saphire reasons that only the existence of drawings formally identical to the finished etching could demonstrate the use of photomechanical processes. The system thus described by Mason consists of many elaborate stages. In this method the print is derived from a drawing or an engraving on celluloid that is transferred to the plate by heliogravure. This plate is then printed as a proof on paper to which additions handmade to the proof, the plate etched again integrating those changes, and finally the plate finished with drypoint or hardground etching. These stages provide for the artist's considered development of the image. So whether begun in photogravure or not, these prints demonstrate Dalí's utilization of one of printmaking's key esthetic qualities, that of amendment and elaboration through successive states of the image.

The sequential states also allow the introduction of diverse material, with a different moment or weight, such as the introduction into a plate depicting double Angelus figures (Löpsinger #28) of Meissonnier's Napoléon in outline form perhaps traced from an earlier mechanical reproduction of the work. Since some part of the making of these plates is likely to remain a mystery, it is useful to consider the disposition of the artist as we imagine the origin of the prints. On the one hand, we know that Dalí welcomed collaboration (even going so far as considering his entire works a collaboration with Gala); on the other hand, it is difficult to imagine an artist with such facility in drawing to have any resistance to directly marking an etching plate.[11] If Dalí used printmaking as a flexible matrix for the introduction and integration of diverse techniques and materials, including even the hands of collaborators, his procedures predict those of later 20th- and 21st-century artists.[12]

Rainwater prudently puts the matter to rest in his remark, "By whatever means, the particular vision conveyed in the prints in *Les Chants de Maldoror* is convincing and well recognized as having originated with Dalí."[13]

Fig. 1. Salvador Dalí,
Bureaucrat and gramophone, 1933
Berlin, Stiftung Sammlung
Dieter Scharf

The text

Les Chants de Maldoror was printed in 1869, but held out of distribution for fear of censorship.[14] The book was not distributed until after the author's death in 1870 at the age of 24. An 1890 edition with an introduction by Genonceaux advanced a celebration of the work that accelerated during the 1920s and 1930s remarkably. In each new edition the editor celebrates the vigor of the work and speaks of a special problem to be addressed in reading *Les Chants de Maldoror*. Each articulation of that problem is somewhat different, but is based on the attempt to reconcile the level of alienation and violence in the work with the practice of literature. In his introduction to the Edition de la Sirène, Paris 1921, Remy de Gourmont emphasizes the madness of the writer.[15] "He was a young man with a furious and unexpected originality, a sick genius and even, frankly, a mad genius." De Gourmont identifies the literary sources of the work as Anne Radcliffe, Maturin and the Bible. Ducasse himself wrote that he intended a work in the manner of Byron and Conrad, however more terrible: "In his thoughts, this book was something in the manner of Byron's *Manfred* and Conrad and Mickiewicz, but much more terrible nonetheless."

Edmond Jaloux writes of the almost perfect literary and artistic fulfillment ("a world with a tragic grandeur, a world that is closed, impermeable, incommunicable, a veritable sphere that will belong to him forever,") in parallel with a state of terror perversity, cruelty and morbidity.[16] Jaloux finds sufficient explanation in Ducasse's youth for the presence of malevolence that he then considers "the puerile reverse of things."[17] He likens the work to a *Divine Comedy* written by an adolescent of extraordinary intuition, full of darkness and punishment, and centripetal gloom, but without narrative structure or theological order.[18]

Breton, whose celebration of Ducasse is unfettered, remarks that the incandescence of the writing approaches a theoretical limit. He writes that the "verb," the active diction, brings Ducasse to the limit at which things can relate to things, words to words.[19] Yet Breton finds a redemptive shiver in this disjuncture of sense and reason. Ducasse's language is, he says, "at once a solvent and a generative plasma without equals."

Gaston Bachelard admires "the energy of aggression" and the "discontinuous, hostile acts" as the essence of poetry. [20] "They have been called a reckless venture into bad taste produced by a frenzy of unwholesome and puerile originality. In fact they are totally incomprehensible from the limited perspective of a static theory of imagination that allows only finished forms. But a reader who is willing to stay with this animalizing phenomenology will read with a different eye. He will recognize in it the movement of a special force, the thrust of a characteristic life."

Dalí certainly found these Ducassian elements appealing: the rejection of the bourgeois by a prodigious and youthful talent, a grotesque vision of nature together with horror and fascination for it, the energy that convolutes and deforms, puerile obsession, aggressive posturing, the rejection of a human discourse in favor of an existential one, the curious absence of ordinary human emotions, and, of course, the self-identification of nobility. Dalí remarks in *The Secret Life* that he bought a dinner jacket in Paris from a tailor on the street where Lautréamont lived.[21]

Yet there is another problem presented by the text, one or reconciling the verbal and the visual; *Les Chants de Maldoror* is not formally a poem. It is prose consisting of approximately 80,000 words with poetic qualities. Aspirations to poetry are evident on every page, as well as in its title, and are defined by diction, tone, rhetorical devices, and sensibility. In this passage, Ducasse uses apostrophe, alliteration and repetition:

"Vieil Océan, tes eaux sont amères…je te salue, vieil Océan.—Vieil Océan, ô grand célibataire, quand tu parcours la solitude solennelle de tes royaumes flegmatiques..je te salue, vieil Océan.".[22]

The six sections of *Les Chants* lack any typographic units that provide a rhythm and structure to the printed page. If the prose format shows an overwhelming attribution of form by unparceled—if not unmeasured speech—it also homogenizes the language with regard to its spatial deployment on the page and makes it difficult to assert any correspondence of image and text. The lack of correlation between the thirty loose prints and the fifty-one text folios is a result of the difficulty of penetrating the hermetic body of prose with the printed images, as well as of financial issues. In the generative plasma, to use Breton's term, of the language, the principal correspondence that Dalí can establish is one of sensibility, of the surprising agglutination of deforming objects in metamorphosis. In creating an extended series of these images, Dalí nears a correspondence with the essential quality of Ducasse's transformative language and superabundance of images. H.H.

[1] Ralf Michler and Lutz W. Löpsinger, *Salvador Dalí: Catalogue Raisonné of Etchings and Mixed-Media Prints 1924-1980* (Munich: Prestel Verlag, 1994), p. 128.

[2] L. Genonceaux, Preface de *Les Chants de Maldoror* (Paris: Edition Genonceaux, 1890).

[3] Robert Rainwater, *Au rendez-vous des amis: Surrealist Books and the Beginning of Surrealist Printmaking* in *Visionary States: Surrealist Prints from the Gilbert Kaplan Collection* (Los Angeles: Grunwald Center for the Graphic Arts, University of California, Los Angeles), p. 26.

Fig. 2. Salvador Dalí,
Mobile Figures, 1934
Berlin, Stiftung Sammlung
Dieter Scharf

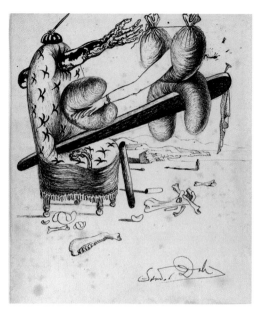

[4] Löpsinger, p. 128.

[5] Rainwater, p. 26.

[6] Rainer Michael Mason, Vrai Dalí / Fausse Gravure: l'oeuvre imprimé 1930-34 (Genève: Cabinet des estampes du Musée d'art et d'histoire), p. 63.

[7] *Ibid.*, p. 52.

[8] *Ibid.*, p. 62.

[9] *Ibid.*, p. 62.

[10] Larry Saphire, "Dalí the Obscure: An Analysis of his Printmaking 1934-47," paper presented at "Persistence and Memory: New Critical Views of Dalí at the Centennial," St. Petersburg, Florida, March 20, 2004.

[11] William Jeffett in conversation, St. Peterburg Florida, December 2003.

[12] The history of 20th-ventury printmaking may be viewed as a study in collaboration and the amplification of the iconographic resources of printing media.

[13] Rainwater, p. 26.

[14] Préface de L. Genonceaux in Comte *de Lautréamont, Isidore Ducasse, Oeuvres Complètes,* Paris: Librairie José Corti, 1961), p. 9, "due to a sometimes violent style that made the publication perillous." This refers to imperial censorship of the time.

[15] Introduction de Remy de Gourmont, in *Comte de Lautreamont, Isidore Ducasse, Oeuvres Complètes*, Paris: Librairie José Corti, 1961), p. 17.

[16] Preface d'Edmond Jaloux, in *Les Chants de Maldoror*, (Paris: Edition Librairie Jose Corti, 1938), p. 25.

[17] *Ibid.*, p. 25.

[18] *Ibid.*, p. 28.

[19] André Breton, Introduction to *Comte de Lautréamont Oeuvres complètes* (Paris, GLM, 1938).

[20] Gaston Gachelard, *Lautréamont*, trans. Robert S. Duprée (Dallas: The Dallas Institute Publications, 1986), p. 2.

[21] Salvador Dalí, *The Secret Life of Salvador Dalí,* trans. Haakon M. Chevalier (New York: Dial Press, 1942), p. 209.

[22] De Gourmont, p. 18.

131. Le Chants de Maldoror, 1934

131. Forty-two etchings
printed in black ink on vélin
d'Arches paper
33 × 25 cm
13 × 9 7/8 in.
St. Petersburg (FL),
The Salvador Dalí Museum

131. Le Chants de Maldoror, 1934

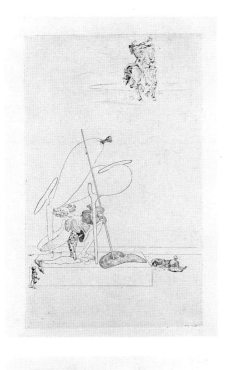

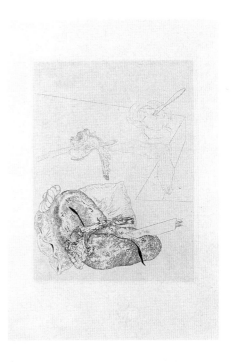

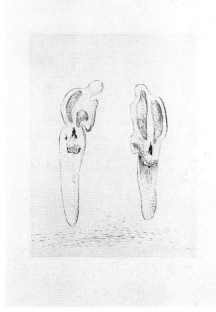

131. Le Chants de Maldoror, 1934

131. Le Chants de Maldoror, 1934

132. Morning Ossification of the Cypress, 1934

132. Oil on canvas
82 × 66 cm
32 1/4 × 26 in.
New York (NY), Collection
of Gilbert Kaplan

This enigmatic work was inspired by the paintings of the 19th-century Swiss-German artist, Arnold Böcklin, whose depictions of centaurs, unicorns, sleeping nymphs and other mythical subjects were imbued with a brooding atmosphere of mystery and foreboding. Giorgio de Chirico and Marcel Duchamp had greatly admired Böcklin's paintings since the early 1910s, having both discovered the artist's dreamlike evocations of ancient Greece while staying in Munich. By the mid-1930s, Böcklin's vividly imagined re-creations of scenes from classical antiquity were hailed as an important precursor to Surrealist painting and Dalí was particularly drawn to the Romantic Symbolism of the artist's melancholic painting *Isle of the Dead*, of 1880 (see p. 164, fig. 1), whose tall cypress trees set against a deadly calm expanse became a recurrent motif in his own work from 1931 onwards.[1]

The petrified horse that takes flight against a blue sky filled with "Böcklinian clouds and storms"[2] in *Morning Ossification of the Cypress* can also be understood as updating the Swiss-German artist's mythological paintings, since it appears to make reference to the Greek myth of Pegasus, the winged horse who is often depicted in the company of Perseus, Andromeda, or Bellerophon. Although rider-less and without wings, the fossilized stone horse that is about to leap from its hollowed-out perch in Dalí's painting ultimately looks back to earlier representations of the wondrous stallion by artists such as Odilon Redon and Frederick Lord Leighton. Indeed, Leighton's depiction of an energetically leaping Pegasus in his *Perseus Hastening to Free Andromeda*, of ca. 1895, is highly suggestive of the sort of academic rendition of antiquity that the artist may have been looking at for inspiration in his own version of the Greek myth.

The flying white steed had earlier appeared in Dalí's painting *William Tell*, of 1930 (cat. 78), and is thought to symbolize the liberation of repressed desires and unbridled sexual energy. As A. Reynolds Morse has pointed out, Dalí's leaping horses were based upon the decorative Pegasus in flight in the auditorium of the Palau de la Música Catalana (Palace of Catalan Music), designed by Lluís Domènech i Montaner, where the artist often went as a child and a young man. According to Morse, the aerial horse "is up near the ceiling on the right of the stage, and is a distinctive feature of the ornate decor of the splendid Palace of Catalan Music."[3] According to Greek mythology, Pegasus had opened up the Hippocrene spring on Mount Helicon (the Mountain of the Muses) by stamping his hooves, thus becoming a symbol of poetic and artistic inspiration. The Hippocrene spring may provide another clue to the painting's meaning, since Dalí's contemporaneous writings reveal how he equated Böcklin's elongated cypress trees with his childhood memory of the "Font del Soc," the cypress-

surrounded spring between Figueres and Vilabertran to which the family had enjoyed walking when Salvador was a boy.[4] M.R.T.

[1] In a prose piece entitled "Reverie," (see Writings by Dalí), which was written in Port Lligat on October 17, 1931, Dalí reports that: "I intend to write a section of a very long study of Böcklin, a study which has preoccupied me greatly for some time now … Friends have lent me for about ten days a large manor-farmhouse, where I intend to finish writing my study of Böcklin, which will constitute one chapter in a huge work that I name, for the time being, *Surrealist Painting Throughout the Ages*"; see Haim Finkelstein, ed., *The Collected Writings of Salvador Dalí* (Cambridge: Cambridge University Press, 1998), pp. 150-153.
[2] *Ibid.*, p. 153.
[3] A. Reynolds Morse, *Dalí's Animal Crackers* (St. Petersburg, Florida: Salvador Dalí Museum, 1993), p. 136.
[4] Ian Gibson, *The Shameful Life of Salvador Dalí* (London: Faber and Faber, 1997), p. 295.

133. Imperial Monument to the Child Woman, 1934

133. Oil and collage on canvas
140 × 80 cm
55 1/8 × 31 1/2 in.
Madrid, Museo Nacional,
Centro de Arte Reina Sofía

A virtual compendium of Dalí's imagery is embedded here in the monumental rock and in the landscape round its base. Although usually dated 1929, the presence in this painting of so many complete motifs from works not only of 1929 but also from the early 1930s indicates a later date. Among these are the tower of niches with keys and ants from *The Font* (1930, cat. 81); the "Javanese Mannequin" in the right foreground from the painting of 1934 (cat. 134); and the couple from Millet's *Angelus*, which began to obsess him from ca. 1932. The painting was exhibited at the Julien Levy Gallery in New York in 1934 with the title *Imperial Monument to the Child Woman, Gala (utopian fantasy)*, but was undated. At Dalí's solo exhibition at Alex Reid & Lefevre Gallery in London, June-July 1936, however, it was exhibited with its present title and dated 1934, which is convincing. If, as seems likely, it was Dalí who gave this painting the earlier date, it may have been because he instinctively wished to acknowledge the key role of Gala, whom he met in 1929, in the creation of the unique personal iconography that dates from that year.

This painting was, Dalí said, a "sacrifice of all the childish '1900' terrors of my childhood" to Gala, the child-woman.[1] The monument is partly constructed of the soft shapes of art nouveau architecture and partly of the rock formations of Cap Creus; at its base on the right the flowing curves become waves which sweep back onto the monument and recall Dalí's description of a house built by Gaudí "according to the forms of the sea, 'representing' waves on a stormy day."[2] That the soft morphology of 1900, "Modern Style" architecture, "majestic flowering of unconscious irrational-erotic tendencies," was a source of terror as well as fascination for Dalí is evident here. Leering from the top of the monument is a cluster of terrifying heads, which had also appeared ringed with phosphorus in a cypress tree in the 1932 painting *Phosphene of Laport – Homage to the Italian Physicist Giambattista della Porta*. Protruding from the rock beside them is a string of images: vulture, jug-woman, roaring lion, familiar from 1929 paintings like *Lugubrious Game* or *Accommodations of Desire* (cat. 69). The monument culminates in an ossified figure holding its head in its hand. This posture of shame and despair is frequent in works of 1929, and is here repeated again by a bearded gray-haired man. These figures and symbols accumulate to express the sexual anxieties and fear of woman that the advent of Gala dissolved for Dalí.

In contrast to these oppressive images, the swooning woman at the left, who rises from a strange stone flower and whose single bare breast may also identify her with Gala, recalls the collage *Phenomenon of Ecstasy*, which included photographs of "hysterical" women and heads from Gaudí's sculpture-architecture. Dalí invokes its melting metamorphic possibilities in "De la Beauté terrifiante et comestible de l'architecture modern style":

"woman-flower-skin-peyotl-jewels-cloud-butterfly-mirror."[3]

Not only the Angelus couple but also the Mona Lisa and Napoleon people this dense canvas. Dalí frequently expressed his own imperialist ambitions through the figure of the Emperor: he opens *The Secret Life* with "At the age of six I wanted to be a cook. At seven I wanted to be Napoleon. And my ambition has been growing steadily ever since."[4] A specific childhood memory also attached to Napoleon. The voluptuous pleasure of communally drinking maté with Argentinian friends, who worshipped him as he was worshipped at home and had a very beautiful daughter, was enhanced by the image of Napoleon on the keg of maté[5]

The vulture mentioned above, which also appears in *The Font*, is a reference to Freud's essay on Leonardo, and thus at a remove from the Mona Lisa. In his commentary on the "documents" accompanying his first published essay on the Angelus, "Interpretation Paranoiaque-critique de l'*Angelus* de Millet," Dalí writes: "The configuration constituted by the child's mouth and the famous invisible vulture interpreted by Freud in Leonardo's painting coincides intentionally with the child's head in Millet's Harvesters."[5]

Dalí intended this painting as a "daybreak in the style of Claude Lorrain with modern style morphology corresponding to the worst Barcelona taste."[6] The glowing Claudian sunrise melting earth and sky in the background does suggest a new day in contrast with the massed fears and obsessions of the past in the shadow of the great modern style monument. However, these include not just the anxieties of childhood but also the new obsessional myths that he was in the process of elaborating. Dalí had just completed his series of prints, *Les Chants de Maldoror*, with the Angelus couple as chief protagonists, and their tiny figures here in the distance are a reminder of his complex interpretation of the peasant couple, which at one level corresponds to Dalí and Gala themselves. D.A.

[1] Robert Descharnes, *Dalí de Gala* (Lausanne: Éditions Denoël, 1962), p. 156.

[2] Salvador Dalí, "De la Beauté terrifiante et comestible de l'architecture modern style," *Minotaure* no. 3 (Paris: December 1933), p. 73.

[3] *Ibid.*, p. 73.

[4] Salvador Dalí, *The Secret Life of Salvador Dalí*, trans. Haakon Chevalier (London: Vision Press, 1968), p. 1.

[5] "Interprétation paranoïaque-critique de l'image obsédante 'L'Angélus' de Millet," *Minotaure*, no. 1 (Paris: June 1933), p. 67.

[6] Robert Descharnes, *Dalí de Gala*, p. 156.

134. Javanese Mannequin, 1934

134. Oil on canvas
65 × 54 cm
25 1/2 × 21 1/4 in.
St. Petersburg (FL),
The Salvador Dalí Museum

A convincing explanation for the title of this picture is lacking. The meaning of the image must be inferred from its family resemblance to other works by Dalí of a similar date and by its proximity in time to his trial and attempted exclusion from the Surrealist group.

First in a line of parentage is *The Enigma of William Tell* (see p. 177, fig. 1) of which *Javanese Mannequin* is easily recognizable as a pictorial offspring. The Oedipal drama that Dalí saw as enacted in the legend of William Tell carries over to the relationship of filiation that exists between these works. If *The Enigma of William Tell* represents the feared and hated father who ponders the fate of the infant ambiguously cradled in his arms, then it follows that *Javanese Mannequin* portrays the Oedipal son. Completing the Oedipal triangle is *The Spectre of Sex Appeal* (cat. 135), a picture of similar date to *Javanese Mannequin* that was inspired by Dalí's musings on the male and female couple in Millet's *Angelus*. Affinities with *Javanese Mannequin* are evident in the treatment of the main assemblage figure, a hallucinatory phantasm that looms not entirely reassuringly before Dalí as a small child dressed in a sailor's suit. It can be identified as a maternal counterpart to the paternal imago in *The Enigma of William Tell*.

There were good reasons for Dalí to dramatize his personal situation in early 1934 in terms of Oedipal conflict. Coming on top of the disinheritance by his own father, an event that lies behind the series of pictures on the William Tell theme, the actions taken by André Breton to expel Dalí would have been tinged with Oedipal significance. Dalí's latest provocation had been to display *The Enigma of William Tell* at the "Salon des Indépendents" that opened on February 2, 1934. The undignified portrayal of Lenin as William Tell with a hugely elongated buttock supported by a crutch threatened to scupper efforts by the Surrealist leader to patch up relations with the French Communist Party. At a hastily convened gathering in Breton's apartment, Dalí was far from contrite about the charges brought against him, robustly defending his right to uncensored expression of fantasy over which he purported to have no control.

My conjecture is that *Javanese Mannequin* was painted in the wake of these events and that it reflects Dalí's embattled position. The picture was first exhibited at the Galerie Jacques Bonjean from June 20-July 13, 1934. Dramatic lighting isolates the main figure against a somber background, a pictorial device adapted from *The Enigma of William Tell* that conveys a brooding, solitary atmosphere. Dalí may have been ostracized but he remained resolutely defiant. Most pointedly, the image flaunts the very same buttock that only recently had caused such offense, as if cocking a snook at his accusers. Reputedly, at his show-trial Dalí informed Breton

that were he to dream of sodomizing the Surrealist leader he would be obliged to paint it the next day, a promise the Jarryesque *surmâle* in *Javanese Mannequin* seems ready to make good on.

Dalí once remarked that Sigmund Freud defined the hero as he who revolts against paternal authority and finishes by vanquishing it. The close relationship of *Javanese Mannequin* to the contemporaneous *Maldoror* suite of etchings might suggest that Dalí identifies with Maldoror as a rebellious outlaw. Remarks in *The Secret Life* confirm the depth of his perceived affinity with a venerated Surrealist precursor in whose writing can be found an important source for the prevalent imagery of decay and putrefaction in Dalí's work, as well as a startlingly precise anticipation of the idea of a *cadavre exquis* assemblage of rotting flesh and other debris, which in *Javanese Mannequin* signifies Dalí's abjection. A tiny but troublingly enigmatic detail is the pearly luminescent object that sits atop the oversized phallus. Is it possibly "the white truffle of death," as Dalí refers to the gleaming white shade in Böcklin's *Island of the Dead* (see p. 164, fig. 1), or its displacement, a kneaded ball of bread that he inserts under his foreskin in "Rêverie" (whose publication had been a previous source of friction with Communist Party officials)? Such an interpretation would be in keeping with the contrived mood of anguish in this exquisitely crafted picture, a favorite of the collector Reynolds Morse. D.L.

135. The Spectre of Sex Appeal, 1934

135. Oil on panel
18 × 14 cm
7 1/8 × 5 1/2 in.
Figueres, Fundació
Gala-Salvador Dalí

In this tiny picture the huge, headless and decaying female corpse towers over the minute figure of Dalí as a child dressed in a sailor suit. The play of internal scale against the actual size of the image is one of Dalí's most successful manipulations of the miniature. It is also one of the most horrific expressions of the fear of woman ever conjured up by a male painter; although explicitly a distant memory given the presence of the child-Dalí, it may have been prompted by the sudden rush of associations clustered round Millet's *Angelus*, which Dalí had recently interpreted as the female version of the myth of the threatening Father. The closest parallels to the image appear among the etchings Dalí made for *Les Chants de Maldoror* (cat. 131), in which the *Angelus* theme is strongly present.

Dalí later called this painting *Spectre of the Libido*, and described it as follows: "The little Dalí is terrified by the gigantic spectre of the eternal feminine, at the anguishing hour when she bathes. The eternal amphibious-feminine is perhaps a phobia."[1] His enjoyment of the "amphibious phobia," play on words aside, this account of the fear of the eternal feminine, links into his increasingly complex analysis of sexuality and also recalls real enough scenes from his childhood. The setting of the painting is one of the bays on the headland at Cap Creus, an ideal bathing place with clear waters, full of marine life by comparison with the bare rocks. Dalí witnessed here female members of his family and friends swimming, and thus perhaps female bodies uncovered for the first time, or at least covered in a more revealing and disturbing way by sagging swimming costumes. The sacks and pillow that stand in for soft breast and bellies recur in the etching for Maldoror *Desir de suavité* (desire for softness), though desire is closely allied as here with repulsion. The substitution of sagging cloth for flesh emphasizes the mystery of what is hidden beneath the skin. The sacks also for Dalí were part of a rural eroticism that he found everywhere in Millet's paintings; in Millet's *Angelus* itself the two sacks in the wheelbarrow behind the female peasant take on "the exact position of those in the illustration *Kiss in a Wheelbarrow*."[2] Here, however, the female body rather than engulfing a male is iconlike and apart, like the later great body-construction allegorizing the Civil War (cats. 160-161). But whereas the woman in Millet's *Angelus*, for all her alarming resemblance to the praying mantis, remains part of the "woman as nature" myth, in a rustic context where plowing and sowing are daily imprinted with sexual meaning, here there is nothing fertile. Positioned between water and rock, the brown matter draped round her echoes the russet and gold of the hard and mineral scarps behind her. The specter of the libido is composed of hard and soft matter, the leprous flesh of one leg revealing its skeleton in a way which curiously resembles the single bony foot of the Mexican war god Tezcatlipoca.

If "Libido" is a Freudian term, signifying "the cathexes of energy which the ego directs towards the objects of its sexual desires"[3] (commonly known as sex appeal), "Spectre" belongs to a new idea Dalí was in the process of developing about female sexuality. In "Les nouvelles couleurs du sex-appeal spectral" in *Minotaure* in 1934, he distinguishes minutely between the attributes of the "spectre" and of the "phantom." The latter readily betrays Dalí's ambivalence towards female flesh. "The phantom materialises via "the simulacrum of volume." The simulacrum of volume is the envelope… The envelope dematerialises the content, the volume, renders it virtual, anguishing."[4] Flesh itself "envelopes, hides, protects, transfigures, incites, tempts, gives a deceptive notion of volume." By contrast, the "anatomy of spectral woman can be disassembled, taken apart and exhibited separately, according to her will: 'The dismantle-able body is the aspiration and the verification of female exhibitionism.'"[5] Its illusory volume is decomposed and it is evidently more to Dalí's taste (Gala is an example of the "spectral"). Dalí reproduces the work *La Beauté feminine* by Alberto Martini (see p. 202, fig. 2) as the example of a spectral representation: "admirable model of the 'acute spectre,' torn, open eyes, crowned…" Also illustrating this text is a lost painting, *The Enigma of William Tell* (see p. 177, fig. 1), in which the child-Dalí with enlarged bony penis, identical to the figure in *The Spectre of Sex Appeal*, stands beside the "phantom" nurse with her massive immobile back. *The Spectre of Sex Appeal*, however, seems to be an amalgam of phantom and specter, both objects of terror to Dalí.

The child leaning on his hoop contemplates this massive body propped on crutches; the crutch was one of Dalí's oldest fetish-objects, the tool of sexual fantasies and "crimes" that he describes in *The Secret Life*. Calling it there "the symbol of death" and "the symbol of resurrection," it retains its ambiguity as the prop of the decomposing and decadent throughout his work.[6] *The Spectre of Sex Appeal* was exhibited at the Julien Levy Gallery in New York in 1934. The exhibition was a sensation: "fashionable, very disputed and very difficult" according to the critic Henry McBride, who welcomed Dalí's "highly finished miniatures" as a contrast to "this cursed Cubism" then prominently on show at the Museum of Modern Art in Alfred Barr's *Cubism and Abstract Art*.[7] D.A.

[1] Robert Descharnes, *Dalí de Gala* (Lausanne: Éditions Denoël, 1962), p. 51.
[2] Salvador Dalí, *Le Mythe tragique de l'Angélus de Millet, Interprétation "paranoiaïque-critique"* (ca. 1932), (Paris: Jean-Jacques Pauvert, 1963), p. 17.
[3] Sigmund Freud, *Introductory Lectures of Psychoanalysis* (New York and London 1977), p. 414.
[4] Salvador Dalí, "Les nouvelles couleurs du sex-appeal spectral," *Minotaure*, no. 5 (Paris: May 1934), p. 20.
[5] Dawn Ades, *Dalí's Optical Illusions* (New Haven and London: Yale University Press, 2000), p. 88.
[6] Salvador Dalí, *The Secret Life of Salvador Dalí*, trans. Haakon Chevalier (London: Vision Press, 1968), p. 111.
[7] Henry McBride, "The Subconscious in Art," *The Sun Saturday* (November 24, 1934).

136. Untitled, Dreams on a Beach, 1934

136. Oil on wood
9 × 7 cm
3^{1}/2 × 2^{3}/4 in.
Private collection

137. The Alert, 1938

137. Oil on wood
24 × 19 cm
9 1/2 × 7 1/2 in.
Berlin, The Ulla and Heiner
Pietzsch Collection

138. Paranoiac-Astral Image, 1934

138. Oil on panel
15.8 × 22.1 cm
6¹/4 × 8³/4 in.
Hartford (CT), Wadsworth
Atheneum Museum of Art
The Ella Gallup Sumner and
Mary Catlin Sumner Collection
Fund, 1935

This work is part of a series of small panel paintings made by Dalí between 1934 and 1936 that feature the immense sandy beach at the Bay of Rosas on the Costa Brava. These works, in which figures from the artist's childhood appear like hallucinations on an infinite stretch of shoreline, are characterized by an intense luminosity and a hand-colored, photographic realism that imparts a heightened sense of drama to the compositions. A key to understanding this series of paintings is found in a 1944 letter from the British collector Edward James to James Thrall Soby, in which Dalí's former patron supplied a detailed description of the artist's childhood memories that informed these shimmering shorescapes, many of which he owned.[1] According to James, these paintings often featured family members, such as his cousin (in fact she was his aunt) Carolinetta Barnadas Férres, a frail and poetic figure, who can be seen hovering in the background of this work. Carolinetta had died tragically of tuberculosis when the artist was still a teenager and he vividly remembered the news of her death reaching his family by letter. It may be for that reason that Dalí always depicted the consumptive Carolinetta in flowing, whisplike drapery, forever associating her in his imagination with the shrouded spectral figure on the boat approaching Arnold Böcklin's *Isle of the Dead* (see p. 164, fig. 1). The artist himself appears in the figure of the small boy in the sailor suit, seated in a boat opposite an unidentified woman, while on the left-hand side the imposing figure of the artist's father strides purposefully towards the viewer.[2] The four evenly placed figures appear like apparitions on the vast bleached expanse of sand, which is bathed in the brilliant white light of the Mediterranean that enhances their sense of phantom-like dematerialization.

Dalí intended these ghostly figures to appear instantaneous, as if they were images from elsewhere (family photograph albums?) projected onto the extraordinarily wide, empty, open landscape of the Costa Brava, which can be identified by the fragment of an amphora in the foreground. The amphora evokes the ancient past of Catalonia, especially the art and artifacts of the Phoenician and Greco-Roman civilizations that once inhabited the region. This archaeological detail echoes the artist's interest in mining his own biography in his mature paintings, which are informed by his childhood souvenirs of the people and places in Catalonia where he grew up. In *Paranoiac-Astral Image*, the hallucinatory appearance of the four figures is enhanced by the fact that each person appears to exist in a different time-space from the rest of the picture. The elongated shadow of the artist's father, for example, is completely out of proportion with the shadows cast by the boat and the figure of Carolinetta, while the piece of cloth that billows upwards from his hat is blown in a different direction

from the scarf that trails behind Dalí's deceased aunt. These temporal disjunctions were perhaps the result of the collagelike working methods employed by the artist at this time. Dalí appears to have used individual images of family members and childhood acquaintances as source materials for these paintings, in which single or grouped figures from separate photographs were transferred to the canvas, either through direct observation or with the aid of a slide projector. This would account for the discrepancies in scale and time that we see in this work, in which the faded figures correspond with the fleeting experience of memory itself. M.R.T.

[1] Edward James, letter to James Thrall Soby, 1944, The Museum of Modern Art, New York, James Thrall Soby Archive, p. 1. This letter contains a dictated transcript of notes pertaining to Salvador Dalí's childhood memories.
[2] Although long-identified as Dalí's father, this mysterious figure also bears an uncanny resemblance to Pepito Pichot, whom Ian Gibson has described as the artist's second father, who "was always at hand for excursions and visits to places of entertainment. Typically, when the French pilot Henri Tixier visited Figueres in the summer of 1912 to give a display of aerobatics, it was with Pepito that a sailor-suited Salvador was photographed at the improvised airfield outside the town at the Camp dels Enginyers"; see Gibson, *The Shameful Life of Salvador Dalí* (London: Faber and Faber, 1997), p. 47. This photograph of Pepito Pichot, reproduced as plate 21 in Gibson's book, shows a strong likeness to the man walking towards the viewer in *Paranoiac-Astral Image*.

139. Weaning of Furniture-Nutrition, 1934

139. Oil on canvas
18 × 24 cm
7 1/8 × 9 1/2 in.
St. Petersburg (FL), The
Salvador Dalí Museum

The title of this work *The Weaning of Furniture-Nutrition* offers a clue to the identity of the nurse and Dalí's portrayal of her in this manner. This small panel features Dalí's childhood nurse, Llucia, to whom he was very attached. Her pose is that assumed for centuries by the old women mending fishing nets on the familiar beach of Port Lligat with the terraced hills in the background. She is, then a dual image representing both his nurse and an old woman net mender.

Dalí takes the "weaning" metaphor a step further. As a child, Dalí associated his night table and the bottle with his nurse and saw them as an intrinsic part of her being. So in this work he "weaned" them physically out of her body, suggesting that his nurse and these inanimate objects were two parts of the same identity, the furniture fitting in a rectangular hole carved in her back. Their removal creates a void that requires a crutch. Dalí's crutch often symbolizes death or impotence. In this painting the crutch takes on a new meaning and becomes a symbol of solemnity rather than a prop of any kind.

According to Dr. Robert Lubar, Dalí strongly associated these times with his nurse, suggesting "a nostalgic desire to return to the maternal body, to a moment of primal unity before the self and its objects are differentiated."[1] Certainly, it is a natural tendency, especially of children, to strongly associate material objects with certain people. "Weaning," in this case, to detach from a person that to which he is accustomed or devoted.

The painting was first exhibited in Barcelona at Galeries d'art Catalonia, October 1934, and then in New York at the Julien Levy Gallery from November 21 to December 10, 1934. The painting's history is intriguing as well since it came narrowly close to destruction at the hands of the Nazis. If it were not for the quick thinking of the painting's owner, Jocelyn Walker (Mrs. Charles Potter), the painting would have been lost. Apparently upon fleeing the Channel Islands, where she lived, she concealed the small painting in her coat and was able to spirit it away to safety. J.K.

[1] Robert Lubar, *Dalí: The Salvador Dalí Museum Collection* (Boston: Bulfinch Press, 2000), p. 97.

140. Cardinal, Cardinal!, 1934

140. Tempera and oil
on wood panel
16 × 22 cm
6 1/4 × 8 5/8 in.
Utica (NY), Munson-Williams-
Art Institute

This strange and perplexing work was first shown in an exhibition of five of Dalí's most recent paintings that was held at the Galeries d'Art Catalònia in Barcelona in October 1934.[1] At that time the painting was known under its variant title of *Cadernera, Cadernera (Goldfinch, Goldfinch)*, which was changed to *Cardinal, Cardinal!* when the work was exhibited at the Julien Levy Gallery, New York, later that year.[2] Since the plumage of the male bird with the bright red head and yellow wing patch, seen in the lower left-hand corner of the painting, corresponds with that of the European goldfinch (carduelis, carduelis) one must assume that the original title was correct. None of the five birds in Dalí's painting even remotely resembles the cardinal, a North American bird whose name derives from its distinctive scarlet-hued plumage, which bears a close likeness to the brilliant red of a cardinal's robes. There are several possible reasons as to why the title was changed, the most plausible being that an American translator made an innocent mistake in mistranslating the Catalan *Cadernera, Cadernera (Goldfinch, Goldfinch)* as *Cardinal, Cardinal!* As an anti-Clerical Surrealist at this time, Dalí would no doubt have enjoyed the sacrilegious connotations of conflating the image of a topless Gala Éluard with that of a cardinal, a high ecclesiastical official in the Catholic Church. This may justify the addition of the explanation point, since it emphasizes the outrageousness of the new title, which the artist decided to retain in both this painting, and another work from 1934, now known as *Skull with its Lyric Appendage Leaning on a Bedside Table which Should Have the Exact Temperature of a Cardinal's Nest*. It should also be pointed out that the repetitive nature of both titles was probably intended to read like one of the double-barreled Latin names for birds found in an ornithologist's handbook.

As is typical of the artist's works of the early 1930s, the painting is dominated by the haunting presence of Gala, who appears like a phantom or apparition, having evidently been painted from a recent photograph of her posing with her breasts bared and a broad smile on her face. In the original photograph she may have been holding a fish, but in the finished painting she appears to hold up a wet or stained piece of cloth, as opposed to the bloody rag that frequently appears in earlier paintings. The half-nude Gala's sexually ambiguous persona is underlined in this work by her skimpy shorts, which as Dalí's biographer, Carlton Lake, has noted, "bulge at the front in a most extraordinary way for a woman."[3] Dalí regarded Gala as his savior, having liberated him from his repressed fears and sexual anxieties, but her fleeting appearance here may reflect his anguish that one day she might leave him. Gala's transparent body, through which shines the golden sunlit sands of the desertlike landscape behind her, is in stark contrast to the pecking birds in the foreground, which resemble the frozen cut-out images of birds used to illustrate children's books. This montage-like juxtaposition of disparate, second-hand

source material, based on faded photographs or reproductions in books, is heightened by the third element of the painting, namely the gloomy group of anonymous fishermen arranged in a pyramid-like configuration in the center of the composition. These ghostly characters, whose bowed heads conceal their faces, gather around a bedside table in the shade of a ruin, which can be identified as the old barracks at Port Lligat.[4] Like Gala, the bodies of the Port Lligat fishermen are transparent, at times allowing the dark wall behind them to penetrate their torsos. But whereas her flimsy appearance simulates the effect of a faded photograph or a double exposure, the streakily painted male protagonists look back to the work of Jacopo Tintoretto and other 16th-century Venetian painters, who often created similarly dematerialized figures whose forms are picked out of the darkness by carefully delineated highlights. Seen together, this arrangement of hand-painted color photography, simulated children's book illustration, and "painterly" painting, combines to produce one of Dalí's most intriguing and compelling works that continues his interest in questioning conventional notions of reality.
M.R.T.

[1] Dalí's one-man show at the Galeries d'Art Catalònia was on view from October 2-4, 1934. The exhibition was organized by the important Catalan art dealer Josep Dalmau, who had earlier introduced the work of Pablo Picasso and Marcel Duchamp to audiences in Barcelona. The painting was listed in the catalogue as "no. 2 *Cadernera-Cadernera*," and since this exhibition was billed as presenting "les cinc últimes pintures de Dalí" (the five most recent paintings by Dalí), *Cardinal, Cardinal!* was almost certainly completed shortly before the exhibition opened.

[2] *Cardinal, Cardinal!* is listed as no. 14 in the catalogue of the "Salvador Dalí" exhibition, which was on display at the Julien Levy Gallery, New York, from November 21-December 10, 1934.

[3] Carlton Lake, *In Quest of Dalí* (New York: G.P. Putnam's Sons, 1969), p. 301.

[4] Dalí had been scheduled to give a lecture at the Llibreria Catalònia on October 5, 1934, the day after his exhibition closed. This lecture, entitled "Misteri Surrealista i fenomenal de la tauleta de nit" ("Surrealist and Phenomenal Mystery of the Bedside Table"), was to have discussed the significance of the bedside table, a recurring motif in his work of the early 1930s, but the event was cancelled due to the revolutionary general strike that took place in Barcelona on October 4, 1934, with thousands of people taking to the streets to proclaim a Catalan Republic in defiance of the central government, see Ian Gibson, *The Shameful Life of Salvador Dalí* (London: Faber and Faber, 1997), pp. 331-332. In an interview with Just Cabot later that year, Dalí explained that his lecture was to have ended with an explanation of the bedside table, which he related to the evolution of the idea of space in physics, from Euclid to Einstein, see J. Cabot, "Abans d'anar a Nova York. Una conversa amb Dalí" (Before going to New York. A Conversation with Dalí), *Mirador* (Barcelona), October 18, 1934, n.p.

141. Study for "Cardinal, Cardinal!," 1934

141. Pencil on paper
15 × 20 cm
5⁷/8 × 7⁷/8 in.
Private collection

142. Spectre of Vermeer, ca. 1934

142. Oil on canvas
22.2 × 17.1 cm
8³/4 × 6³/4 in.
Private collection

143. The Angelus of Gala, 1935

143. Oil on wood panel
32.4 × 26.7 cm
12³/4 × 10¹/2 in.
New York (NY), The Museum
of Modern Art, gift of Abby
Aldrich Rockefeller, 1937
© 2004, Digital image,
The Museum of Modern Art,
New York / Scala, Firenze

When *The Angelus of Gala* was donated to The Museum of Modern Art, New York, in 1937 it was described by the artist as a double portrait in which "the two selves of the woman come face to face."[1] The woman depicted is, of course, his wife Gala, "that soft motor which makes my paranoiac-critical method function," who is shown twice.[2] The first portrait shows Gala with her back to the viewer, seated on a boxlike structure and wearing a multi-hued silk jacket whose intricate decorative pattern has been rendered with a meticulous, almost photographic attention to detail that is reminiscent of the paintings of Vermeer. This portrait of Gala, which looks back to the artist's earlier representations of his sister, Ana María, seated from the back, confronts another view of herself facing the viewer. This second image depicts the artist's wife, incongruously seated on a wheelbarrow with her hands clasped in her lap, while dressed in the same brocaded jacket. Although it is tempting to read this image of Gala as a mirrored reflection of the woman that we see from the back, the low viewpoint and the wheelbarrow that she perches on confirm the artist's statement that this is a separate portrayal.

The importance of this painting in Dalí's oeuvre was underlined in 1935, when a color plate of the work was used as the frontispiece for the artist's *Conquest of the Irrational*. This book, which was simultaneously published in French and English, contains a lengthy passage concerning Dalí's attempt to use his paranoiac-critical method to uncover "the delirious fact which constitutes the obsessional character of Millet's *Angelus*," which may explain the prominent place given to the painting in the publication.[3] Of all of Dalí's paranoiac interpretations of Millet's *The Angelus*, this work is perhaps the most disturbing. A modified version of the Millet painting hangs on the wall behind Gala's head, which shows the two peasants sitting on a wheelbarrow, thus repeating her own seating arrangement. The artist considered the wheelbarrow to be a fetish object, since he believed that agricultural workers, worn down by overwork, tended to eroticize their working tools.[4] The male farm laborer is depicted with his head bowed, covering his groin with his hat, while the woman is shown in profile, with her clasped hands raised in prayer. These configurations follow the basic composition of Millet's painting, although the size of the woman, who in Dalí's work is the larger figure of the two, represents a significant departure from the original. Her exaggerated scale and posture are deliberately intended to evoke the attitude of the praying mantis, "prior to her cruel coupling with the male that will end in his death."[5]

This threatening scenario is played out again below, where Gala, the beatific Madonna of his later religious paintings, is shown in an unusually cruel manner, with a pinched mouth and fierce expression, who stares aggressively at her double. That Gala takes on the terrifying form of the hostile *femme fatale* of *The Angelus* suggests that the ambiguous figure that we see from the back might represent the artist himself. This reading is perhaps supported by a much-later stereoscopic painting, entitled *Dalí from the Back painting Gala from the Back eternalized by Six Virtual Corneas provisionally reflected in Six Real Mirrors* of 1972-73 (cat. 247), which depicts the artist, seated at his easel with his back to the viewer, at work on a portrait of Gala, who is shown from the back and also reflected in a mirror. Dalí thus combines the emotional fears aroused by *The Angelus*, which he uniquely understood in terms of disguised sexual repression and violence, with his anxieties over the sexually aggressive Gala, who by 1935 had become his wife, muse, business manager, artistic advisor, cook, secretary, and nurse, thus dominating every sphere of his life and work.
M.R.T.

[1] Anonymous, "An Anonymous Gift to The Museum of Modern Art," *The New York Times*, October 12, 1937, p. 23.
[2] Salvador Dalí, *Diary of a Genius*, trans. Richard Howard (London: Creation Books, 1994), p. 156.
[3] Salvador Dalí, *Conquest of the Irrational* (New York: Julien Levy, 1935), p. 18.
[4] Salvador Dalí, *The Unspeakable Confessions of Salvador Dalí (as Told to André Parinaud)*, trans. Harold J. Salemson (New York: William Morrow and Company, 1976), p. 155.
[5] *Ibid.*

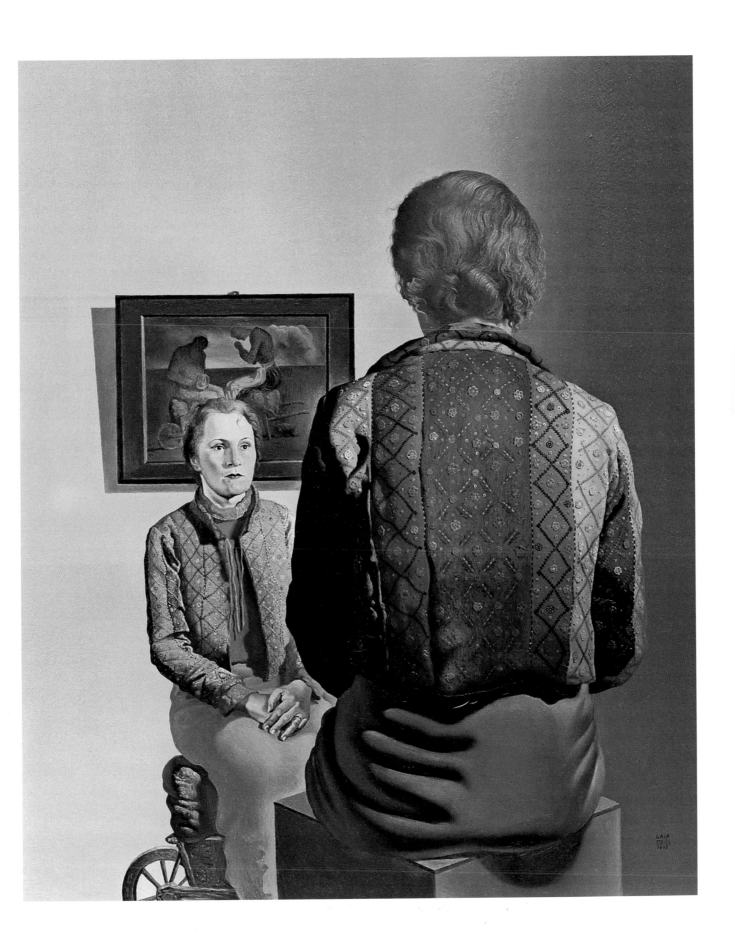

144. Graphite pencil
and ink on paper
54.6 × 40 cm
21$^{1/2}$ × 15$^{3/4}$ in.
Houston (TX), The Menil
Collection

Shortly after his arrival in New York in November 1934, Salvador Dalí was commissioned to produce a series of illustrated texts for *The American Weekly*, a popular magazine with a wide readership, whose editors immediately recognized the artist's innate talent for scandalous publicity and self-promotion. Dalí eventually published seven illustrated articles between December 1934 and July 1935, whose content was intended to reflect his impressions of daily life in the United States.[1] The drawings that accompanied them reveal his intense fascination with the sights he encountered in New York, with its vertiginous skyscrapers and streets filled with throngs of people. In "New York as Seen by the "Super-Realist" Artist, M. Dalí," published in the February 24, 1935 issue, Dalí depicts his response to Central Park, where he claimed to have encountered phantoms and a strange rock in the shape of an anamorphic skull. While other issues dealt with his reaction to Broadway and its shows, or the changing face of the city during night and day, the Central Park spread anticipates *Gangsterism and Goofy Visions of New York* in that it contains a self-portrait of Dalí asleep, with his mouth covered by a swarming mass of ants, which can be related to the fear and anxiety he felt "After Reading about New York Crimes" through an accompanying caption.

"Gangsterism and Goofy Visions of New York by M. Dalí, Super-Realist" appeared in the May 19, 1935 issue of *The American Weekly*, and represents the penultimate work in Dalí's series of artistic interpretations of American life. The surviving

drawing reads like a storyboard for a movie, in which three distinct scenarios are played out in three frames that read across the page. The bottom level is filled with familiar images from the artist's arsenal of repressed desires and paranoiac imagery, such as the archer from the myth of William Tell, or the cherries from the tragic myth of Millet's *Angelus*. These cherries are placed in a configuration involving a wedge of fruit dangling over a sliced apple that can be understood as a humorous reference to the geometric forms in Alberto Giacometti's *Suspended Ball* of 1930-31 (fig. 1). The scenario in the central panels relates to the artist's ongoing investigation into double images, whereby an exposed patch of bricks in a wall takes the shape of a man with a stone on his head, leading the viewer to mistake it for a passerby who picks up a stone and walks off. Unlike the lower layers, which show the artist's continued fascination with Surrealist themes and imagery that had occupied him since at least the early 1930s, the uppermost level reveals Dalí's newfound interest in gangsters and gangsterism, an obsession that he shared with millions of Americans who believed that rampant crime was a defining element of their society. The Prohibition-era gangster represented the paragon of modern criminality and became the subject of innumerable newspaper and magazine articles, scores of novels and plays, and more than a hundred Hollywood movies.[2]

The world of the organized gangster as a film subject did not develop until the latter part of the 1920s, although an early appearance of the urban hoodlum on the screen can be traced back to D. W. Griffith's *The Musketeers of Pig Alley* of 1912. By the time Dalí arrived in the United States the gangster was firmly ensconced as a romantic, yet self-destructive, character in popular culture, thanks in large part to gritty, violence-laden Prohibition gangster films such as *Little Caesar*, of 1930, *The Public Enemy*, of 1931, and *Scarface*, of 1932. These movies established the prototype of the high-living gangster, synonymous in the public mind with fast cars, easy money, fancy clothes, loose women, boozing, swank nightclubs, and reckless, uninhibited behavior. Dalí's image of two dapper hoods battling through a door conforms to the mass media stereotype of the gangster as a stylishly attired, ruthless criminal, who is often accompanied by beautiful but dangerous women. The scene is strongly reminiscent of Paul Muni's portrayal of Chicago mobster Al Capone shooting it out through a glass plate window in *Scarface*, while the seductive "moll" who wields a knife above the seated gangster's head may have been based on Ann Dvorak's sultry, flirtatious, sexually eager character Cesca in the same movie. The artist would naturally have been drawn to the

Fig. 1. Alberto Giacometti,
Suspended Ball, 1930-31
Basle, Öffentliche Kunstsammlung

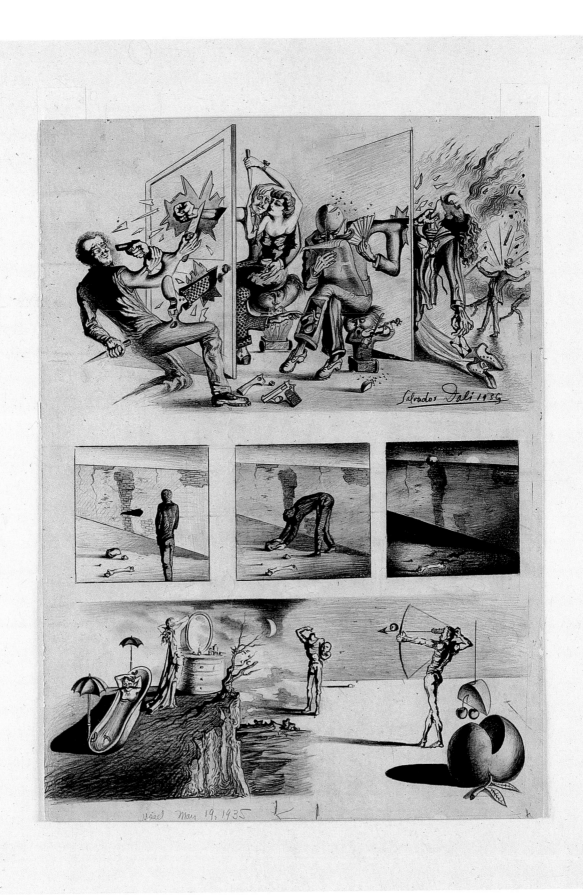

cycle of Hollywood gangster films that appeared in the 1930s, with their thrilling car chases, shocking violence and bloodshed, and complete lack of sentimentality. The tense struggle that he depicts in this drawing was undoubtedly informed by the antisocial activities performed on screen by actors such as James Cagney and Edward G. Robinson, whose charismatic gangsters display a thorough disrespect for authority and a zest for action and forbidden pleasures that separates them from the moral and ethical codes of society. Dalí no doubt identified with these outsiders, whose amoral daring and alarming exploits made them dangerous to the status quo. Indeed, the artist's own deviant behavior, sartorial elegance, and thirst for power and success may have led him to sympathize with these dangerous criminals, who were simultaneously reviled and celebrated at the time as archetypal American dreamers and transgressors of society's rules.[3] M.R.T.

[1] The series began with "Written by a Madman, Illustrated by a Super-Realist" in the December 16, 1934 issue of *The American Weekly*. This was followed by "New York as Seen by the 'Super-Realist' Artist, M. Dalí" on February 24, 1935; "How Super-Realist Dalí saw Broadway" on March 17, 1935; "The American City Night and Day by M. Dalí" on March 31, 1935; "American Country Life interpreted by M. Dalí" on April 28, 1935; "Gangsterism and Goofy Visions of New York by M. Dalí, Super-Realist" on May 19, 1935; and finally "Crazy Movie Scenario of M. Dalí, the Super-Realist" on July 7, 1935.

[2] David E. Ruth, *Inventing the Public Enemy: The Gangster in American Culture, 1918-1934* (Chicago: University of Chicago Press, 1996), p. 1.

[3] As Jack Shadoian has argued, the gangster is a paradigm of the American Dream: "Our involvement with the gangster rests on our identification with him as the archetypal American dreamer whose actions and behavior involve a living out of the dream common to most everyone who exists in the particular configurations and contradictions of American society, a dream in conflict with the society"; see Shadoian, *Dreams and Dead Ends: The American Gangster/Crime Film* (Cambridge, Massachusetts: The MIT Press, 1977), p. 2.

145. Oil on canvas
40 × 30 cm
15³/4 × 11⁷/8 in.
Berlin, the Ulla and Heiner
Pietzsch Collection
Project for the poster
of an unrealized film

146. The Vertebrated Cavern – Series of Decals, 1936
147. Two Figures, 1936

146. Gouache on black paper
24 × 16 cm
9 1/2 × 6 1/4 in.
Jacques Herold Collection

147. Gouache on black paper
21.3 × 33.7 cm
8 3/8 × 13 1/4 in.
Wuppertal, Von der Heydt
Museum

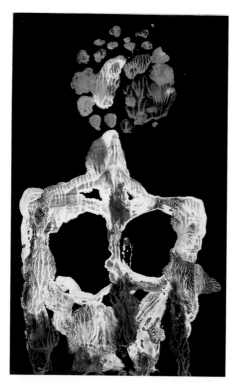

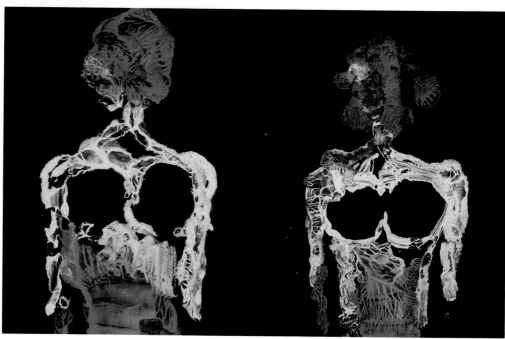

148. Untitled (Woman with Flower-head), 1937
149. Animated Surrealist Landscape, 1936

148. Ink and gouache on paper
38.5 × 50 cm
15¹/8 × 19³/4 in.
Private collection

149. Ink on paper
16.5 × 21
6 ¹/2 × 8¹/4 in.
Private collection, courtesy
Galerie Natalie Seroussi, Paris

150. The Chemist of Ampurdàn in Search of Absolutely Nothing, 1936

150. Oil on panel
30 × 52 cm
11³/4 × 20¹/2 in.
Essen, Museo Folkwang

Fig. 1. Victor Eisenmenger, inventor of the cardiac massage device

In the mid-1930s Dalí began to propagate the false notion that the Ampurdàn plain in his native Catalonia was a barren waste, devoid of vegetation, and strewn with the carcasses of dead and rotting donkeys.[1] This painting would appear to support his recollection of the vast open plain of the Alt Empurdá, which extends from Figueres to the snow-covered peaks of the Pyrenees, as a sun-baked, desolate landscape, comprising rocky outcrops in the foreground, a large building in the middle ground, and a distant town, framed by a mountain, in the background. Although Dalí described the Ampurdàn plain to friends and newspaper reporters as "a grim expanse of lonely land, depressed in spots by the bones of dead asses,"[2] in reality the fertile countryside surrounding his hometown was in fact made up of lush meadows, which he had earlier extolled as an abundant garden filled with poetry.[3] The fact that this fictitious barren landscape also served as the setting for *Soft Construction with Boiled Beans (Premonition of Civil War)* (cat. 162), painted in the same year, may provide an explanation as to why the artist began to associate the Ampurdàn plain with death and decomposition at this time, since it coincides with the internecine violence and political turmoil that broke out in his native Spain in 1936.

The contemporary political significance of the work is also supported by the image of the standing man staring downward on the far left of the painting, who appears to explore the ravaged terrain like a scientist inspecting the geological features of the landscape for evidence of volcanic activity. A recurring figure in Dalí's work at this time, the so-called "Chemist of Ampurdàn" was based on an illustration in a scientific magazine of a doctor demonstrating a heart-massage apparatus (fig. 1).[4] The caption of the photograph reads "Mode d'emploi de l'appareil Eisenmenger," which has led previous scholars to erroneously relate the recurring figure in Dalí's painting with the noted Austrian physician, Victor Eisenmenger (1864-1932), who invented the machine advertised in the magazine illustration.[5] The doctor controlling the medical apparatus with his foot in the photograph may indeed be Eisenmenger, but Dalí forever associated the stooped figure in his paintings with "the nostalgic pharmacist of the provincial town," a reference to his hometown of Figueres, rather than the renowned cardiologist.[6] Employing his paranoiac-critical method to dazzling effect, Dalí identified this chemist as a Signor Deulofeu, who was indeed the pharmacist for the town of Figueres when he was growing up. With convoluted logic, the artist then transferred this identity onto the chemist's famous son, the Catalan mathematician Alexandre Deulofeu (1903-78), whose astonishing 1929 book, *La pau al mòn per la matemàtica de la Història* (The Mathematics of History), he greatly admired.[7] The fact that Alexandre Deulofeu lived at no. 11 Monturiol Street, the street

where Dalí was born, allowed the artist to create another link in this elaborate chain of coincidences related to the inquisitive apothecary's identity by connecting the image with Narciso Monturiol (1819-85), the Catalonian physicist and inventor. A pioneer of underwater navigation, Monturiol became a hero to the Catalan people on June 28, 1859, when he launched the "Ictineo," the first fully operable submarine, in the bay of Barcelona, where it remained submerged for more than two hours. The unifying element between this inventor, mathematician, and chemist, apart from the fact that they were all born or lived in Figueres, is the notion of Catalonia as the cradle of European civilization and scientific progress. The fact that the Catalan language and culture were now under threat from a barbaric civil war that would see the region tear itself apart through reciprocal killings, rapes, and other atrocities sheds new light on Dalí's paintings of the time, the barren wastelands of which appear to predict an apocalyptic future for this once fertile landscape. M.R.T.

[1] See, for example, Julien Levy's account of Dalí's allegedly terrifying daily journey as a child across the Ampurdàn plain, which was clearly based on false information supplied by the artist himself, as part of his efforts to fashion a mythical persona to help promote his work in the United States. "As a boy," Levy reports, "he walked to school across the vast morbid plains of Catalonia, the bleached bones of the dead ass to right and left, always beside him his terror, his father, and always within him that frantic, repressed energy, equal to the energy of madness"; see Levy, *Surrealism* (New York: The Black Sun Press, 1936), p. 23.
[2] Margaret Case Harriman, "Profiles: A Dream Walking," *The New Yorker*, vol. 15, no. 20, July 1, 1939, p. 24. Harriman's article was based on an interview with Dalí in New York that took place shortly before the magazine's publication.
[3] An entry in the artist's diary, dated May 16, 1920, reads: "L'Empordà es un jardi, un jardi frondos. Omple de poesia"; see Salvador Dalí, *Un Diari, 1919-1920. Les Meves impressions i records íntims*, ed. Fèlix Fanés (Barcelona: Edicions 62, 1994), p. 102.
[4] The Chemist of Ampurdàn also appears in paintings such as *A Chemist Lifting with Extreme Precaution the Cuticle of a Grand Piano* and *Soft Construction with Boiled Beans (Premonition of Civil War)*, both made in 1936.
[5] This hypothesis was first advanced in the exhibition catalogue, *Dalí* (Rotterdam: Boijmans Van Beuningen Museum 1970), n.p. (exh. cat. no 48).
[6] Salvador Dalí, "Les nouvelles couleurs du sex appeal spectral" ("The New Colors of Spectral Sex-Appeal"), *Minotaure*, no. 5 (Paris: February 1934), pp. 20-22, reprinted in Haim Finkelstein, *The Collected Writings of Salvador Dalí*, trans. Haim Finkelstein (Cambridge: Cambridge University Press, 1998), p. 206.
[7] Robert Descharnes, *Salvador Dalí: The Work, The Man*, trans. Eleanor R. Morse (New York: Harry N. Abrams, 1984), p. 194.

151. Suburbs of the Paranoiac-Critical Town: Afternoon on the Outskirts of European History, 1936
152. Study for "Paranoiac-critical city suburbs," 1935

151. Oil on wood panel
46 × 66 cm
18$^{1/8}$ × 26 in.
Private collection

152. Ink and pencil
32 × 22.8 cm
12$^{5/8}$ × 9 in.
Berlin, Stiftung Sammlung
Dieter Scharf

Fig. 1. Salvador Dalí,
Nostalgic Echo, 1936
Spain, Private collection

When this disquieting painting was exhibited at the Julien Levy Gallery in New York, in December 1936, it was hailed by the noted art critic Henry McBride as "the incontestable masterpiece of Surrealism to date; and that statement is intended to convey the information that it also overtops anything that the old master in this line, Hieronymous Bosch, ever put forth in the way of horror."[1] McBride identified the "jittery" uneasiness he felt while examining the painting's iconography with "our present predicaments," meaning the unchecked rise of Fascism in Europe, which threatened to plunge the world into global conflict.[2] The painting, virtually a manifesto of Dalí's artistic ideas and concerns at that time, was made during his stay on the estate of the Catalan mural painter José Maria Sert near Palamós on the Costa Brava. As McBride intuited, the work can also be understood as a complex allegory of the turbulent political situation in Europe in the mid-1930s, albeit filtered through the artist's paranoiac-critical method, which gave free reign to his vivid imagination and extraordinary technical facility.

The central image of the artist's wife, Gala, invitingly holding forth a bunch of grapes, is framed on either side by a confusing array of incongruous objects, fragmented vistas, and eerie townscapes that reverberate with Dalí's personal history and his sense of place, all of which are alluded to in the painting's enigmatic title.[3] As the artist later reminisced, the grapes refer to the first summer he spent with Gala, in 1929, in which his passion grew daily and he "became delirious with fear and anxiety, possessed of the strange happiness that perhaps binds the victim to the executioner. It was grape-gathering time. Gala sat in the sun on a retaining wall and ate the muscadines I had just given her. I watched, fascinated, as her hand carried the fruits from the bunch to her mouth."[4] Although Dalí claimed that he had only to close his eyes to recapture this image of Gala gleaning the ripe fruit, the grapes may also refer to Pliny the Elder's story of the ancient Greek painter Zeuxis, who painted a bunch of grapes with such *trompe-l'œil* illusionism that birds flew down to eat them. The use of eye-deceiving realism had been a trademark of Dalí's mature work, seen in this painting in the extraordinary richness of detail with which he renders individual elements, such as the grapes, the skull and amphora on the green cloth-covered table in the foreground, and the equestrian statue in the middle distance. A page of preparatory sketches for the painting reveals how the artist wove a close network of associations between these elements. They are linked by a series of visual rhymes between the rotund hindquarters of the horse, the spherical grapes and the elongated skull, which may have been drawn from the work of Salvator Rosa.[5] The recurrence of these shapes fosters an atmosphere of formal ambiguity that permeates the entire painting, which is truly irrational in its temporal and physical dislocations.

The architectural spaces shown in the painting's tripartite arrangement remain faithful to the artist's roots, since all three settings take place in Catalonia. On the left is a building from Palamós, near where Dalí was staying when he painted this picture; in the center, framed by the decaying archway, is the village of Vilabertràn, just outside his hometown of Figueres, while on the right is the picturesque main street of Cadaqués, the Calle del Cal, which is again seen through an archway. The disorienting juxtaposition of these three separate pictorial spaces invokes the work of Giorgio de Chirico, who had earlier imparted a similarly disjointed sense of historical continuity in his Metaphysical paintings, which often combined images of modern steam locomotives, Renaissance architecture, and classical sculpture to create a

151

disturbingly ambiguous sense of time and place. The girl skipping rope that we see through the central archway is also a direct descendant of the child spinning the hoop in de Chirico's *Mystery and Melancholy of a Street* of 1914, while the swaying bell in the belfry behind the girl that functions as her "anthropomorphic echo" can be traced to an etching from the *Bizzarie di varie figure* cycle by the 17th-century Italian artist Giovanni Battista Bracelli. M.R.T.

[1] Henry McBride, "The Battle of the Surrealists," *The New York Sun*, December 19, 1936, reprinted in Daniel Catton Rich, ed., *The Flow of Art: Essays and Criticisms of Henry McBride* (New York: Atheneum, 1975, p. 342. The exhibition, simply entitled "Salvador Dalí," took place at the Julien Levy Gallery, New York, from December 10, 1936 to January 9, 1937.

[2] *Ibid.*

[3] The painting has been known under numerous different titles over the years. The work was first shown under the abbreviated title of *Suburbs of the Paranoiac-Critical Town* in the artist's one-man exhibition at the Alex Reid & Lefevre Gallery in London, which ran from June 25 to July 18, 1936, see cat. no. 26. However, when it was exhibited in New York later that year a poor translation from the French meant that it was listed in the "Souvenir-Catalogue" of Dalí's show at the Julien Levy Gallery under the title of *Suburbs of the "Paranoiac-critical" Afternoon (on the Outskirts of European History)*, see cat. no. 12. This exhibition was on view from December 10, 1936, to January 9, 1937.

[4] Salvador Dalí, *The Unspeakable Confessions of Salvador Dalí (as Told to André Parinaud)*, trans. Harold J. Salemson (New York: William Morrow and Company, 1976), p. 93.

[5] This type of skull is a common feature of Salvator Rosa's paintings and etchings. Dalí was surely familiar with the artist's celebrated *Democritus in Meditation* of ca. 1650, which contains the clean picked skull of a horse, along with the skulls and skeletons of other animals and humans that combine to create a *Vanitas* on a grand scale whose melancholic atmosphere is akin to his *Suburbs of the Paranoaic-Critical Town*.

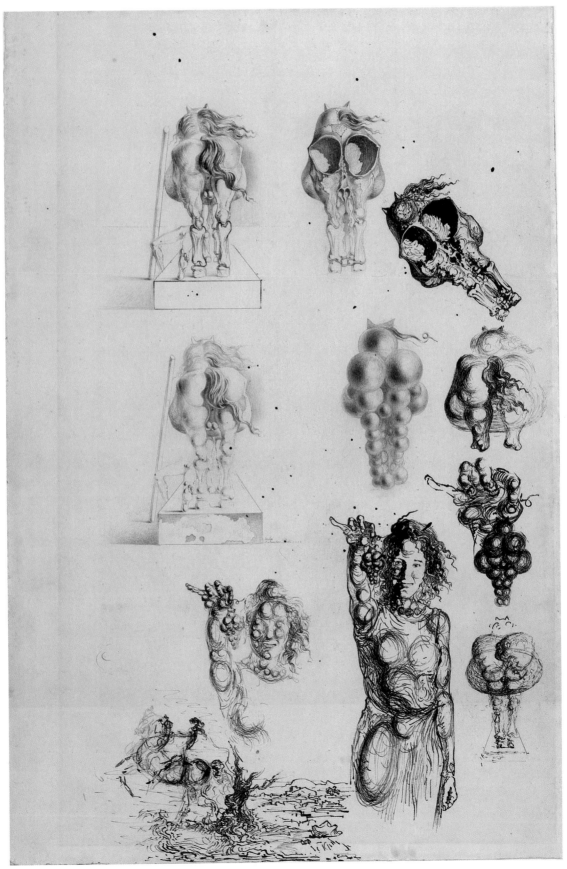

153. Surrealist Composition with Invisible Figures, ca. 1936

153. Oil on cardboard
60.9 × 45.8 cm
24 × 18 in.
Figueres, Fundació
Gala-Salvador Dalí

Some time in the mid 1930s Dalí re-painted the lower half of this picture, which had been reproduced in its original state in *L'Amic de les Arts* in April 1927 with the title *Seascape with woman bathing*.[1] The original was one of a small group of works related to one of Dalí's favorite subjects, bathers, but which give pride of place not to the human figure but to the rocks themselves at Cap Creus (see *Penya-Segats*, cat. 49). The woman's body, exposed through the clinging costume, might be the source, though horribly transformed, for the *Spectre of Sex Appeal* (cat. 135). She hides her face as though to escape identification.

In its second state, the rocks and bather have been replaced by a flat platform with a bed and chair imprinted with the ghostly traces of two figures, and a curious pillar with mosaic base like that in *First Days of Spring* supporting a huge, glowing, ruby. The jewel could be taken to symbolize the female sex, whose association with blood for Dalí is luridly reflected in the color. At the same time its hard, crystal, character contrasts with the cluster of ants gathered in the folds of the sheets where the woman's sex would be, setting up an opposition between desire and disgust, permanence and decay.

But desire and disgust can be disturbingly linked; as Dalí writes in *La femme visible*: "All that psychophysiology has taught us about the phenomenology of repugnance leads us to believe that desire could easily overcome unconscious symbolic representations. Repugnance would be a symbolic defense against the intoxication of the death drive. One experiences repugnance and disgust for what one wishes to get closer to, and from this comes the irresistible 'morbid' attraction, conveyed often by incomprehensible curiosity, of what appears to us repugnant."[2] Dalí here draws not only on Freud's *Beyond the Pleasure Principle*, and its controversial theory of the death drive, but also, as recent research has shown, on an essay by the Hungarian writer Aurel Kolnai, "Der Ekel" (Disgust) which appeared in a Spanish translation in 1929.[3] Kolnai argues that "our psychic ambivalence regarding death lies behind most reactions of disgust"[4] (see Encyclopedia "Disgust"). Dalí must have found striking confirmation of his obsession with putrefaction in Kolnai, for whom it was not only one of the chief objects of disgust, but also exhibits a "vital exuberance."[5] The glittering iridescence of flies is thus visual confirmation of the paradoxical appeal of the repugnant, and can be turned into their very opposite: precious stones.

"Nothing can stop me from recognizing the multiple presence of simulacra in the example of the double image, even if one of its states adopts the appearance of a rotting donkey and even if such a donkey is truly and horribly decayed, covered with thousands of flies and ants, and, as in this case one cannot consider the significance of the distinct

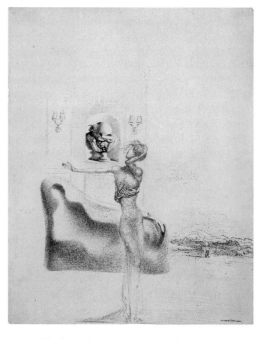

Fig. 2. Salvador Dalí, *Woman in front of a Bust with Drawers,* 1936
Berlin, Stiftung Sammlung Dieter Scharf

states of the image outside the notion of time, nothing can convince me that this cruel putrefaction of the donkey is anything other than the blinding reflection of new precious stones.

And we do not know whether, behind the three great simulacra which are excrement, blood and decay, the *desired* 'land of treasures' is not hidden."[6] The absent figures of the man in the chair and the woman on the bed might be Dalí and Gala themselves, and a specific incident might underpin Dalí's more general meditations on desire and death: Gala's operation (in 1932) that left her sterile and which he elsewhere symbolizes with bleeding roses.

[1] M. A. Cassanyes, "L'Espai en les pintures de Salvador Dalí," *L'Amic de les Arts*, no. 13 (Sitges: April 30, 1927), p. 31.
[2] Salvador Dalí, "L'Amour," in *La Femme visible* (Paris: Éditions surréalistes, 1930), p. 67.
[3] See David Lomas, *The Haunted Self: Surrealism, Psychoanalysis*, Subjectivity (New Haven: Yale University Press, 2000), and Robert Radford, "Aurel Kolnai's "Disgust": a source in the art and writing of Salvador Dalí," *Burlington Magazine*, no. 1150 (January 1999), p. 32.
[4] David Lomas, *The Haunted Self*, p. 176.
[5] *Ibid.*, p. 176.
[6] Salvador Dalí, "L'Amour," in *La Femme visible*, p. 17.

Fig. 1. Salvador Dalí,
Llane's Rocks, 1926, reproduced
in *L'Amic de les Arts*

154. "Geodesic" Portrait of Gala, 1936

154. Oil on panel
21 × 27 cm
8¼ × 10⅝ in.
Yokohama (Japan),
Yokohama Museum of Art

The *"Geodesic" portrait of Gala* was shown at both Dalí's solo exhibition at the Alex Reid & Lefevre Gallery in London in June 1936, which coincided with the "International Surrealist Exhibition" at the Burlington Galleries, and later that year at the Julien Levy Gallery in New York.[1] The catalogue for both exhibitions announced "Snapshots in color" prompted by such disturbing objects and images as "morphological specters," "caprices within the womb' and 'diurnal phantasies." Among these phantoms, dreams and paranoiac images of concrete irrationality, this portrait of Gala seems to stand out as a palpable and earthy presence. The blank, dark background, concentration on the intricate physical surfaces, the gleams of light and the brown, gold and russet tonalities resemble the still life *Basket of Bread* (cat. 51). It is a "lost-profile" portrait, with no discernable features and only the pure line of the cheek and brow visible, and it is strikingly similar to early portraits of his sister Ana María, such as the 1925 painting *Girl seated from the back.* As in the latter, the jacket slips to reveal a naked shoulder and neck. Unlike other portraits of Gala of the period, such as the lovely *Sugar Sphinx*, where Gala, seated again from the rear, gazes onto an evening landscape with the *Angelus* couple partially concealed among cypresses, or the *Angelus of Gala* (cat. 143) a double portrait in which she is again juxtaposed with an Angelus image, there are no visible associations with Dalí's obsessional themes.

Nonetheless, there is a strong sense of a hidden meaning, underlined by the title, which points to a connective idea in the carefully detailed structures of the segmented cap and the seams and quilting of the embroidered jacket, which frame Gala's body. "Geodesic" denotes "an artificial structure composed of a large number of identical components, especially a dome." This architectural dimension is confirmed by the study for the painting (fig. 1), in which Dalí has drawn a circular building with dome and staircase, mirroring the morphology of Gala's head in a clearly paranoiac process. Whether or not he planned to make of this a double image is unknown, but it reveals Dalí's perception of the architectonic within the image of Gala. The finely proportioned shell of the building echoes Gala's head, its monumental scale emphasized by the two tiny figures below.

The association between bodies and buildings was long and diverse in Dalí's work. In 1945 he returned to the subject in *My Wife Nude, Contemplating her own Flesh becoming Stairs, Three Vertebrae of a Column, Sky and Architecture* (cat. 207). It is interesting that already in the study for *Geodesic Portrait* the building resembles classical architecture rather than the Art Nouveau or Modern Style that Dalí championed in the 1930s. The openings and entrances to buildings carry obvious sexual connotations, but Dalí was also fascinated by analogies be-

tween buildings and creatures with exo-skeletons such as lobsters and sea urchins, whose outer crust, unlike the human body, protects the soft flesh. In *Geodesic Portrait* this sense of the vulnerability of the body is emphasized by the bare shoulder, while the jacket and cap provide a protective "architectonic" shell.

In a later statement Dalí plays on another potential application of the term "geodesic." He remarked that "The Persian ornamentation of Gala's back represents the electronic units of my brain."[2] He seems to be suggesting an analogy between the synapses in the brain ("the minute gaps across which nerve impulses are transmitted by means of a chemical substance known as neurotransmitter") and the structure of a dome. This leap from the minute to the mighty is characteristic of the dramatic use of scale in Dalí's work, but also underlines the way he projects himself onto the figure of his beloved Gala.

In the same commentary on this painting he goes on to say: "In the hat there is already the horse-shoe of our luck, figuring the distinctive crescent moon of the effigy of Helen." In Dalí's proliferating myths, Gala (whose real name was Elena Dmitrievna Diakona), becomes Helen, "univitelline" twin of Pollux. From the union between Zeus in the guise of a swan and the mortal Leda, two double-yolked eggs were hatched, producing two pairs of twins: the mortal Pollux and immortal Castor, and the immortal Helen and mortal Clytemnestra. Dalí refers to himself and his "twin" Gala as both Pollux and Helen and also occasionally as Pollux and Castor.[3] The reference to the moon, which is not normally associated with Helen, slips in an allusion to a further set of twins, this time born to Zeus by Leto: Apollo and Artemis, who was indeed a moon goddess. D.A.

Fig. 1. Salvador Dalí, *Study for "Geodesic Portrait of Gala,"* 1936
Private collection

[1] The title as it was listed in the catalogue; by the time of the Levy exhibition, in December 1936, the painting was in the "Collection of Gala Dalí."

[2] Robert Descharnes, *Dalí de Gala* (Lausanne: Éditions Denoël, 1962), p. 99.

[3] See Fiona Bradley, "Gala Dalí: the Eternal Feminine" in Ades, Dawn and Fiona Bradley, *Salvador Dalí: A Mythology* (London: Tate Gallery Publishing, 1998).

155. Oil on wood
87 × 66 cm
34 1/4 × 26 in.
Private collection

Fig. 1. René Magritte,
Representation, 1937
Edinburgh, Scottish National
Gallery of Modern Art

The two pairs of shaped panels, which bear the same title, are closely related to the theme of the *Angelus*. The better known of the two works, the version now in the Boijmans Museum, obviously represents a male and female couple, the latter with her head inclined and hands shrouded in the tablecloth raised in prayer resembles the female peasant in Millet's painting. However, the other version, while so similar in many respects, represents not a man and woman but two men. Both outlines of the two heads have clearly demarcated ears, like those in Dalí's early self-portrait drawings. They resemble the pairs of heads in such early paintings as *Honey Is Sweeter than Blood* (see p. 90, fig. 3), which represented Dalí and Lorca. What, if any, couple is in question here is more of a mystery.

That Dalí on one level identified himself and Gala with the male and female couple in the *Angelus* is suggested both by *The Tragic Myth of Millet's Angelus* and by the sequence of photographs by Cecil Beaton of Dalí and Gala posing with the paintings. These photographs are also a moving testimony of their own relationship; rather than mimicking the *Angelus* pose itself they embrace the paintings but lean eagerly towards each other (see p. 495). This is not to say that the couple "represent" Dalí and Gala—rather that as archetypes of mother/wife and son/father this is one possible identification. If the two male heads follow the same logic, it seems like-

ly that they too represent an archetypal male pair, and in Dalí's mythology this would be father and son, the "William Tell" theme. Given the greater difference in size between the two busts, this seems more probable than that they are either a recollection of the portraits of Dalí and Lorca, or a gesture towards his new patron, James himself.

The Boijmans painting was bought by Edward James from the Alex Reid & Lefevre Gallery exhibition in London in 1936. Dalí had met James at the latest at the end of February 1935, and by the time of his London show, which coincided with the "International Surrealist Exhibition" at the Burlington Galleries, Dalí, Gala and James had become close friends In David Sylvester's Magritte catalogue raisonné *A Couple with their Heads Full of Clouds* is mentioned as a source for Magritte's shaped canvas of the female torso of 1937, *Representation* (fig. 1), and the catalogue states that James had commissioned the work from Dalí. However, it is unlikely that James would have purchased the painting from the Gallery had he also commissioned it.

The precise date and circumstances of the second pair's creation are unknown, though it seems likely it was painted after the version acquired by James. It was given to the Italian composer Scelsi and remained in his possession, in Rome, until his death. D.A.

Fig. 2. Cover of *Métamorphose de Narcisse*, Éditions surréalistes, Paris 1937

Fig. 3. Salvador Dalí, *A Couple with their Heads Full of Clouds*, 1936 Rotterdam, Boijmans Van Beuningen Museum

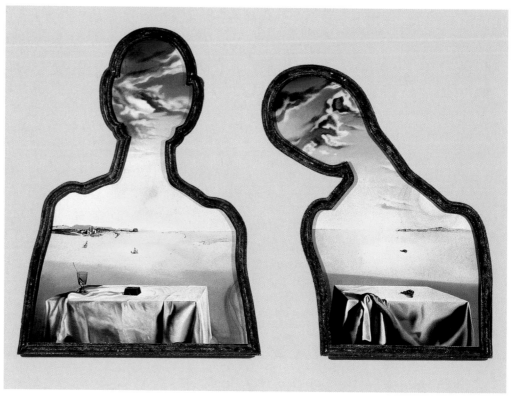

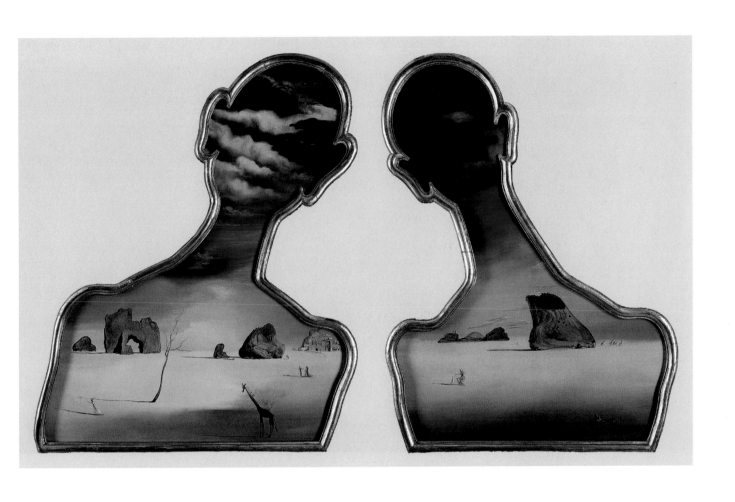

156. Venus de Milo with Drawers, 1936
157. The Anthropomorphic Cabinet, 1936
158. The City of Drawers-Study for "The Anthropomorphic Cabinet," 1936

156. Original plaster of 1936 with metal knobs on the drawers and white fur tuft covers
98 × 32.5 × 34 cm
38 1/2 × 12 3/4 × 13 3/8 in.
Private collection

157. Oil on panel
15.4 × 44.2 cm
6 × 17 3/8 in.
Düsseldorf, Kunstsammlung Nordrhein-Westfalen

158. Pen and India ink on gravure paper
32 × 41.5 cm
12 5/8 × 16 3/8 in.
Private collection

In 1936, likely with the technical assistance of Marcel Duchamp, Salvador Dalí modified a plaster cast of the Venus de Milo, one of the most famous of ancient sculptures in the Louvre, by introducing a series of drawers with the knobs covered in ermine fur in his sculpture *Venus de Milo with Drawers*.[1] The fur material is both tactile, and alongside the white surface of the Venus sculpture, suggests an icy eroticism that may be indebted to Sacher-Masoch's novel *Venus in Furs* (1870), whose title in French is *Venus à la fourrure*.[2] Though the *Venus de Milo with Drawers* is linked with Dalí's interest in the Surrealist object, it was not exhibited publicly in the 1930s. Surprisingly it appeared in neither Charles Ratton's "Exposition surréaliste d'objets" (Paris, 1936) nor in the "International Surrealist Exhibition" (London, 1936), though in the former Magritte's *Les menottes de cuivre*—a work also based on the Venus de Milo—was included. Nevertheless, according to Robert Descharnes, Dalí presented this work twice at private parties held at home in 1936 and 1939, so it was not entirely unknown.[3] Its public history begins relatively late, but rapidly it became an icon of the later Surrealism of the 1960s. The bronze version was cast in 1964 by Max Clarac-Sérou, and that same year it was exhibited in the Surrealist exhibition organized by Patrick Waldberg at the Galerie Charpentier in Paris.[4] Painting the bronze conceptually negated the weight and richness associated with the material and at the same time evoked the memory of the marble Venus. Dalí's interest in the subject paralleled the Venus de Milo's appearance in the contemporary New Realism practiced by Niki de Saint-Phalle, Arman and Miralda: artists promoted by the French critic Pierre Restany. Indeed, Dalí's renewed interest in the subject reveals as much his engagement with contemporary preoccupations as a return to the Surrealism of the 1930s.

In *The Anthropomorphic Cabinet* (1936) the female figure is more lifelike, and unlike the Venus statue, she is depicted reclining. Her head leans forward over the partially open drawers, and her hair falls forward so as entirely to obscure the face. The treatment of the hair recalls that of Gradiva's hair in other drawings and paintings of the period 1931-33, one also related to his earlier erotic representation of the peasant girl Dullita in paintings such as *Girl with Curls* (1926; Salvador Dalí Museum, St. Petersburg, Florida). Dalí's interest in Gradiva took inspiration from Wilhelm Jensen's 1903 novel and Sigmund Freud's psycho-analytic interpretation of Jensen's novel (1907) published in French as *Délire et rêves dans un ouvrage littéraire : la "Gradiva" de Jensen* (1931).[5] As Gradiva was an ancient relief turned into a real woman, so here woman is represented as a statue representing the goddess of love. The bizarre transformation of the figure contrasts with the realistic, archaic and

slightly Victorian street setting in the right background.

Dalí was inspired by the typically English piece of furniture called "chest of drawers," and in this painting made a word play on the anatomical meaning of chest and the piece of furniture. This poetic slippage amounted to making the human form into a piece of furniture, a poetic confusion worthy of Lautréamont. According to Conroy Maddox it was Dalí's time in England that inspired this motif,

Dalí's patron, Edward James, bought many of Dalí's works during that period, and Dalí was a frequent guest at James' house. At that time his English was practically non-existent, which could account for the misunderstanding that arose upon hearing someone talk of "a chest of drawers." Interpreting this quite literally, Dalí in *The Anthropomorphic Cabinet*, as well as a number of drawings, was to show a reclining woman out of whose chest appeared numerous half-opened drawers.[6]

That both *The Anthropomorphic Cabinet* and its drawing study *The City of Drawers* (see below) were initially in the possession of Edward James makes Maddox's comments all the more telling. Further, the drawers suggest the obscure recesses of the human mind, in the sense of Freud's conception of the unconscious.

The City of Drawers (1936) is the most elaborate of the drawing studies for *The Anthropomorphic Cabinet*. It reveals the realistic street scene in the background and the treatment of the figure closely parallels that of the figure in the painting complete with the Dullita-Gradiva treatment of the hair. In addition, there is an element to the drawing absent from the painting. Two other female figures with drawers appear in the middleground between the street scene and the figure in the foreground. One is standing while the other sits on a chair beneath which there are three drawers. Two other drawers are located nearby. Again the elision of the body and the drawers, that is the body with furniture, together with the chair, another piece of furniture related to the form of the human body, suggests a poetic slippage worthy of the transformations to be found in Lautréamont's *Chants de Maldoror*. W.J.

[1] Robert Descharnes in *D'après l'antique* (Paris: Louvre, 2000), p. 463.

[2] See *The Collected Writings of Salvador Dalí*, ed. Haim Finkelstein (Cambridge: Cambridge University Press, 1998), p. 408.

[3] Robert Descharnes, *op. cit.*, p. 463.

[4] *Le Surréalisme, source, histoires, affinities* (Paris: Galerie Charpentier, 1964).

[5] Sigmund Freud, *Délire et rêves dans un ouvrage littéraire: la "Gradiva" de Jensen* (Paris: Gallimard, 1931).

[6] Conroy Maddox, *Salvador Dalí 1904-1989: Eccentric and Genius* (Cologne: Taschen, [1979], 1990), p. 78.

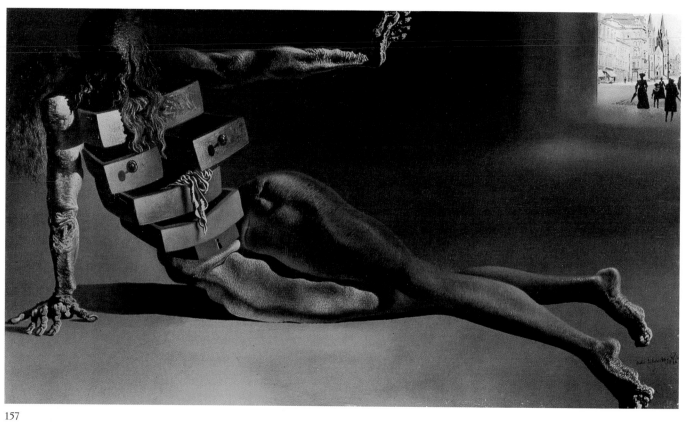

157

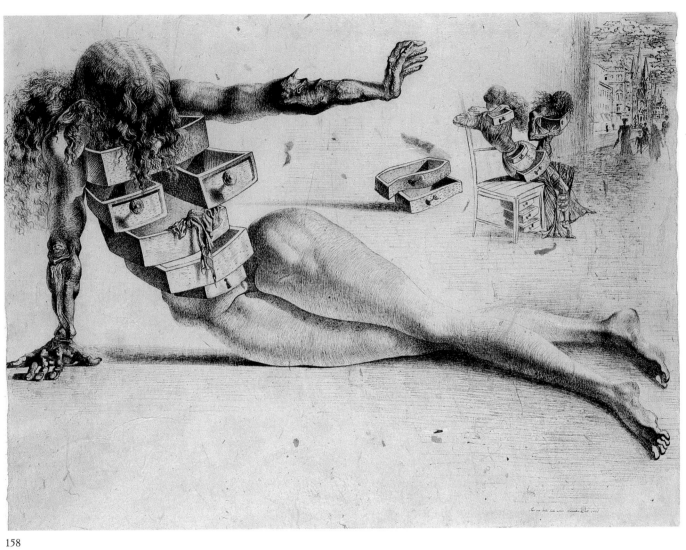

158

159. Soft Construction with Boiled Beans (Premonition of Civil War), 1936

159. Oil on canvas
101.3 × 100 cm
39⁷/8 × 39³/8 in.
Philadelphia (PA), Philadelphia
Museum of Art, The Louise and
Walter Arensberg Collection

With its flair for detail as gruesome as it is meticulous, Salvador Dalí's Surrealist painting style might well have been invented for the depiction of the unique horrors of the Spanish Civil War. This painting, however, is one of only a handful in which Dalí turned his attention to the social and political tragedy that was about to beset his homeland. Like Picasso's *Guernica*, painted one year later, it addresses the Spanish Civil War that began on July 17, 1936 when General Francisco Franco led a *pronunciamiento*, or military coup, against the democratically elected Popular Front government of the Second Spanish Republic. Over the decades, both *Soft Construction with Boiled Beans* and *Guernica* have come to serve as universal icons decrying human hatred and destruction. However, there are fundamental differences between the two works. Picasso, who had publicly sided with the Republican forces in their attempt to resist the Nationalist's armed insurrection, sought to convey the horrific carnage inflicted upon the Basque town of Guernica, which had been bombarded by German warplanes in support of General Franco. Dalí's message, on the other hand, is far more ambiguous and apolitical, reflecting his belief that the Spanish Civil War was an inevitable occurrence involving instinctual forces, a "phenomenon of natural history," rather than a political event of international significance.[1]

Dalí's own words, as singular as his pictorial language, perhaps best describe the mood of this overwrought picture, which shows "a vast human body breaking out into monstrous excrescences of arms and legs tearing at one another in a delirium of autostrangulation. As a background to this architecture of frenzied flesh devoured by a narcissistic and biological cataclysm, I painted a geological landscape, that had been uselessly revolutionized for thousands of years, congealed in its 'normal course.' The soft structure of that great mass of flesh in civil war I embellished with a few boiled beans, for one could not imagine swallowing all that unconscious meat without the presence (however uninspiring) of some mealy and melancholy vegetable."[2]

Dalí's fellow Surrealists reveled in the desecration of the human body, whether in painting, sculpture, or photography, but none had yet descended to such depths of tortuous anatomy. The ecstatic grimace, the taut neck muscles, the elasticized torso, and the petrifying fingers and toes all conspire to create a vision of disgusting fascination. So persuasive is the construction's visceral presence that it appears to be an authentic natural phenomenon, an eighth wonder of the world, rather than merely a human figure or an imagined apparition. With the limp phallic form draped over the truncated hip, Dalí deployed his signature device of 'soft forms,' while the scattered beans of the title exemplify the bizarre incongruities of scale he used to conjure the workings of the unconscious mind. Dalí's frenzied vision of cannibalistic mutilation ultimately looks back to the work of his compatriot Francisco José de Goya y Lucientes, whose *Saturn Devouring One of His Children* of ca. 1820 (see p. 266, fig. 1) may have inspired him to embrace his own nightmarish vision of Spain on the brink of self-inflicted annihilation.

The decomposing figure, its face racked in pain, is set within a desolate landscape that can be identified as the plain of Ampurdàn, in northern Catalonia, from the artist's related painting, *The Chemist of Ampurdàn Looking for Absolutely Nothing*. Although in reality the Ampurdàn plain was a fertile stretch of countryside filled with lush greenery, this terrain was irrevocably associated in Dalí's mind with death and decomposition, and in his paintings of the 1930s it takes the form of an uninhabitable expanse of rocky, desertlike landscape. The tiny bearded figure visible behind the monster's curling hand also appears in this contemporaneous painting, having been drawn from an illustration in a scientific magazine of a doctor demonstrating a heart-massage apparatus. In this work, however, the doctor inspects the ravaged landscape and putrescent entrails with the clinical detachment that Dalí himself aspired to in his own quasiscientific examination of his country's inexorable slide into internecine combat. The artist believed that his savage image of Spain ripping itself to pieces prophetically foretold the reciprocal killings and atrocities committed by either side in this bloody conflict. As the artist later explained, "the Spanish corpse was soon to let the world know what its guts smelled like."[3]

In recent years, critics have questioned whether the painting was prophetic of the Spanish Civil War, as Dalí had claimed, believing that he might have renamed the painting with fitting opportunism for his exhibition at the Julien Levy Gallery in New York in December 1936, which took place some six months after the hostilities broke out.[4] The work was first shown at the Alex Reid & Lefevre Gallery in London in June 1936 under the title of *Soft Construction with Boiled Apricots* (the English translator no doubt confusing "abricots" with "haricots").[5] However, when the painting was reproduced in color in the July 15, 1936 issue of *Minotaure* it was renamed *Spain. Premonition of Civil War*.[6] It was not until the painting was shown in an international exhibition at the Carnegie Institute in Pittsburgh in 1937, where it won fourth prize, that the work received the title it bears today.[7] Although there can be no doubt that Dalí renamed the work to highlight his powers of intuition, the fact remains that the first studies for this large canvas were begun as early as

1934-35. These drawings often focus on the single foot of this monstrous figure, with its grotesquely extended big toe, which had to convincingly support its weight. As in the finished painting, the dislocated limbs of the agonized Titan in these drawings are manipulated and stretched to form a rough outline of the map of Spain, thus confirming that Dalí's vision of his country as a decomposing figure tearing itself apart long preceded the outbreak of the Spanish Civil War. M.R.T.

[1] Robert Descharnes, *Dalí de Gala* (Lausanne: Edita S.A., 1962), p. 169. Dalí made this statement in relation to the painting *Autumnal Cannibalism*, which he described as expressing "le pathos de la guerre civile considérée comme un phénomène d'histoire naturelle."

[2] Salvador Dalí, *The Secret Life of Salvador Dalí*, trans. Haakon M. Chevalier (New York: Dial Press, 1942), p. 357.

[3] Salvador Dalí, *The Unspeakable Confessions of Salvador Dalí (as Told to André Parinaud)*, trans. Harold J. Salemson (New York: William Morrow and Company, 1976), p. 138.

[4] The "Dalí" exhibition opened at the Julien Levy Gallery, New York, on December 10, 1936, and ran through January 9, 1937. The painting was listed in the catalogue as number 16, under the title *Soft Construction with Boiled Beans, 1936. (Premonition of Civil War)*.

[5] The "Salvador Dalí" exhibition took place at the Alex Reid & Lefevre Gallery, London, from June 2 to July 18, 1936.

[6] See *Minotaure*, no. 9, October 15, 1936, p. 42. The painting had been reproduced without a title—the caption simply read "Salvador Dalí" and "1936"—in an earlier issue of the magazine, see *Minotaure*, no. 8, June 15, 1936, p. 11. Although this apparent discrepancy would appear to support Ian Gibson's claim that Dalí "strategically renamed" the work to coincide with the outbreak of the Spanish Civil War, I would argue instead that the painting, and the numerous studies that preceded it, suggest that Dalí was simply responding to the volatile nature of the political situation in his native land, rather than to any specific event. General Franco's military coup in North Africa, which provided the catalyst for the conflict in his homeland, simply confirmed what Dalí had believed all along, which was that the Spanish people were prone to mutually destructive violence. See Gibson, *The Shameful Life of Salvador Dalí* (London: Faber and Faber, 1997), p. 363.

[7] The painting was shown in the "35th Annual International Exhibition of Paintings," which took place at the Carnegie Institute, Pittsburgh, from October 14-December 5, 1937, exh. cat. no. 288. A sticker on the back of the painting confirms that the work was lent by the Julien Levy Gallery, New York.

160-164. Studies for "Premonition of Civil War," 1934-35

160-164. Pen, pencil and China
ink on paper
23 × 18 cm
9 1/8 × 7 1/8 in.
Valladolid, Museo de Arte
Contemporáneo Espagnol
Patio Herreriano

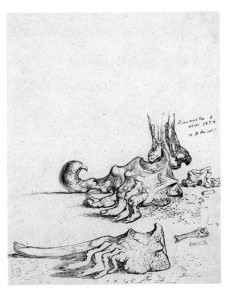

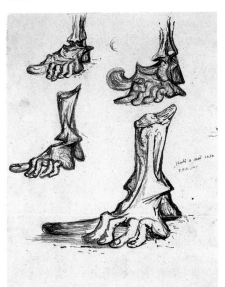

165. Autumnal Cannibalism, 1936

165. Oil on canvas
59.9 × 59.9 cm
23⁵/8 × 23⁵/8 in.
London, Tate, purchased 1966

In conversation with Robert Descharnes in the early 1960s Dalí reportedly said of *Autumnal Cannibalism*: "These Iberian creatures mutually devouring each other in autumn express the pathos of civil war considered as a phenomenon of natural history."[1] These words attributed to Dalí—the only known comment by the artist specifically on this work—have been taken by many to signify that the painting was an immediate and sympathetic response to the Spanish Civil War.

It is not known for certain when the painting was executed, but it seems probable that it was completed after the outbreak of war in July 1936. A related drawing, dated 1936 and showing two figures made up of curvilinear shapes (or "omelettes," as Dalí sometimes called them), seated on two draw-

ers, was sold in the summer of that year, suggesting that the idea for the painting predated the war. However, as *Autumnal Cannibalism* was not included in Dalí's solo exhibition at Alex Reid & Lefevre Gallery, London, in the summer but was shown in New York in December 1936 (when already owned by the collector Edward James), it can be assumed perhaps that "autumnal" in the title refers to the season in which the picture was painted.

As a high profile Spaniard, Dalí was under intense pressure to declare his allegiance to one side or the other of the civil war in these months. He later spoke of "the hyena of public opinion slinking around me," demanding "that I make up my mind at last, that I become Stalinist or Hitlerite." However, Dalí wanted to avoid being drawn on this subject

Fig. 1. Francisco José de Goya y Lucientes, *Saturn Devouring One of His Children*, ca. 1820 Madrid, Museo Nacional del Prado

at all costs. "Horror and aversion for every kind of revolution assumed in me an almost pathological form. Nor did I want to be called a reactionary... I simply continued to think, and I did not want to be called anything but Dalí."[2]

In using the word cannibalism in the title of this painting, however, Dalí ensured that the canvas would be seen as a condemnation of the barbarism of current events. Dalí himself saw the word "cannibalism" as an appropriate metaphor for the Spanish Civil War, describing the conflict in 1941 as the "great armed cannibalism of our history."[3]

As Dalí would have known, cannibalism—a taboo topic rarely addressed in art—was a theme particularly associated with the work of the great eighteenth—and 18th-19th-century Spanish painter Goya, and this may have influenced the genesis of the 1936 work. In a famous late picture *Saturn Devouring One of His Sons* (ca. 1821-23) Goya depicted a naked giant with a crazed expression about to consume the already bloody corpse of a smaller male figure (fig. 1). This image is sometimes seen as a source for Dalí's earlier *Soft Construction with Boiled Beans* (1936), a work that Dalí subsequently dubbed *Premonition of the Civil War* (cat. 159). More generally, Goya's graphic scenes of murder and mutilation in *The Disasters of War* etchings of 1810-20, prompted by the outbreak of war in Spain with France in 1808, were seen by some as a topical point of reference for contemporary events: the series was reissued in London in 1937 as a protest against fascist atrocities in Spain.

Beyond the title, however, there is little in *Autumnal Cannibalism* that links it obviously to the war. There is no sign of struggle or brutality: the couple use utensils to slice and spoon in a surprisingly polite manner, and they support one another in a languid and affectionate embrace. Furthermore, the imagery comprises a number of Dalínian motifs that ostensibly have nothing to do with the political crisis of the period. With an apple on his head, the male figure appears to be the son of William Tell and therefore, in terms of the artist's personal mythology, Dalí himself; consequently, the female partner may be assumed to represent Gala. The double image of a head in the clouds and the concept of figures emerging from drawers (and *vice versa*) have antecedents in other works. Even the theme of cannibalism had a precedent in Dalí's illustrations for the 19th-century text *Les Chants de Maldoror* of 1932-34.

Dalí's reported comment that *Autumnal Cannibalism* expressed a view of war as a phenomenon of nature perhaps invites more consideration than hitherto it has been given. To interpret the theme of cannibalism *ipso facto* as condemnatory of the war in Spain is to miss the perversity of Dalí's refusal to take a political or moral stance in relation to the gustatory activities of the amorous couple. If we take him at his word, it would seem that in late 1936—or at least by the early 1960s, as reported by Descharnes—Dalí viewed the war in Spain with the detachment of a naturalist studying the behavior of animals. In this light, the "cannibalism" of war was to be seen, as far as Dalí was concerned, as just another aspect of human nature—and, potentially at least, a matter of indifference. J.M.

[1] Robert Descharnes, *Dalí de Gala* (Lausanne: Éditions Denoël, 1962), p. 169.
[2] Salvador Dalí, *The Secret Life of Salvador Dalí* (London: Vision Press, 1948), p. 360.
[3] *Ibid.*, p. 357.

166. Drawers Cannibalism (Composition with Drawers), 1937

166. China ink on paper
54.5 × 75.8 cm
21 1/2 × 29 7/8 in.
Cambridge (MA), The Fogg
Art Museum, gift of
Dr. and Mrs. Allan Roos

167. The Metamorphosis of Narcissus, 1937

167. Oil on canvass
50.8 × 78.3 cm
20 × 30⅞ in.
London, Tate,
purchased 1979

Fig. 1. Caravaggio, *Narcissus*,
ca. 1600
Rome, Galleria nazionale
d'Arte antica

When Dalí's long-standing ambition to meet Sigmund Freud was at last realized in 1938, the picture he chose to take with him on his visit was *The Metamorphosis of Narcissus*. The reasons why Dalí was drawn to represent the myth of Narcissus are several, but we must count among them the complex interweaving of truth and deception, desire and the power of illusion that are enacted in the story of the self-infatuated youth who fell in love with his own reflection. *The Metamorphosis of Narcissus* is a supreme demonstration of Dalí's virtuosity in *trompe-l'œil* illusionistic painting, as Freud acknowledged. The picture replicates for the viewer something of the predicament of Narcissus himself as we too are transfixed by the compelling power of an image.

At center stage is the famous double image. *Metamorphosis of Narcisisus* introduces a new variation on the long-standing Dalínian motif of the double or reversing image by reduplicating the individual components and splaying them apart, a decision he took only at the stage of working on the final picture since none of the preparatory studies show evidence of it. Overall, it would seem that Dalí has adhered closely to an interpretation by Otto Rank in his essay on *The Double*, in which the death significance of the double is intimately connected with its narcissistic meaning. Rank, a prominent disciple of Freud, sees the Narcissus fable as a latter-day poetic expression of archaic superstitions that attribute to reflections and other doubles a diabolical power to steal life away.

An essay by Dalí from 1934-35 contains a description of the Roman *Spinario*, a well-known sculpture of a boy picking a thorn from his foot, that applies almost verbatim to the figure of Narcissus on the left of the picture: "Observe him, bent over his thorn, with the same fossil immobility of Narcissus, he, too, bent over the silvery comedo of his own death." Dalí intended that Narcissus should gradually disappear as one gazed at him and a sequence of images in a poem he wrote to accompany the picture narrate his stepwise dissolution. As he succumbs to death's siren call, Narcissus unconsciously yearns to re-create the blissful solitude of life *in utero*. Crouching in what can best be described as a fetal position his body is bathed in a warm ethereal glow.

The extraordinary apparition on the right of the picture of a hand holding an egg, from which sprouts a narcissus flower is one of the most startlingly original products of Dalí's imagination. Whilst in general terms this configuration recalls Max Ernst's *Oedipus Rex*, the dread evoked by details such as a crack running the full length of the thumbnail aligns it more with the scene of a severed hand swarming with ants in *Un Chien andalou*. The enlarged hand could refer to the act of masturbation, as it does elsewhere in Dalí's work, though

connotations of death predominate. *The Secret Life* recounts an incident that occurred some months before on Dalí's first trip to Italy in which his right hand swelled up from infection after a needle-sharp object had lodged under a fingernail. Delirious with fever, Dalí writes: "I imagined my hand already separated from my arm, a prey to the livid first symptoms of decomposition."[1]

From his reading of the Leonardo case, Dalí knew of the link that Freud makes between narcissism and homosexuality. Allusions to his intense friendship with the poet Federico García Lorca have been suggested by various commentators, but another model possibly for our suicidal Narcissus in the grip of the death drive is the writer René Crevel whose tragic death in 1935 deeply upset Dalí. The homoerotic content of the Narcissus myth has long been a factor in its representation by artists. Had Dalí seen Caravaggio's *Narcissus* on his travels through Italy he surely would have noticed a double image worthy of himself: a curiously inept depiction of the right knee, which looks strangely like a buttock. Dalí goes one better, twinning the flexed knee of Narcissus with its reflection so that both are visible together. The same analogy of knees and buttocks occurs later in a passage from *The Secret Life* that recalls Dalí's feelings for a schoolboy nicknamed Buchaques, and it is revealing of its significance that Dalí chose to project this precise detail in a lecture he gave at the Sorbonne in 1955.

It is only in the final stanza of Dalí's poem *The Metamorphosis of Narcissus* that the metamorphosis takes place:
"When this head splits
When this head cracks
When this head shatters
it will be the flower,
the new Narcissus,
Gala -
my narcissus.

Gala is the intercessor whose love rescues Dalí from the fate that befell the original Narcissus. This ending reaffirms the faith Surrealism put in the transformative power of love and moreover accords with a Freudian developmental narrative where narcissism is a transitional moment *en route* to mature heterosexual object love. And yet a closer look reveals in fact a far more ambiguous resolution of the narcissistic scenario in Dalí's rendition of the myth. As "my narcissus" Gala is enlisted into the class of narcissistic love objects and he creates in her a narcissistic double of himself. D.L.

[1] Salvador Dalí, *The Secret Life of Salvador Dalí*, trans. Haakon Chevalier (London: Vision Press, 1968).

168. Sleep, ca. 1937

168. Oil on canvas
50.2 × 76.7 cm
19³/4 × 30¹/8 in.
Private collection

Sleep is one of Dalí's most powerful and memorable images. The monumental head fills the foreground of a limpid landscape which embodies what James Thrall Soby called the "new and deliberate lyricism" of the Rosas beach scenes, such as *Paranoiac-Astral Image* (cat. 138).[1] This head is a dramatic revision of the earlier flaccid self-portrait heads such as those in *The Great Masturbator* (cat. 65) or *The Persistence of Memory*. Unlike *The Great Masturbator,* however, whose face droops to the ground in abasement, here it is erect and lifted delicately into the air by spindly crutches. Its features are strongly marked: whereas in the earlier examples the mouth is absent, horribly effaced, here the lips are exaggerated and protruding. Fastened to the back of the head is a frilled cloth recalling the white linen *mantelets* of the cyclist in *Un Chien andalou*. The luminosity of the pale background against which the head is sharply detached is enhanced and framed by the deep blue at the top and a dark shadow filling the foreground. The crutches cast long thin shadows and a pale moon is visible in the darkening sky. The head in *Sleep* has been compared to a famous eroded rock at Cap Creus known as the "Sleeping Rock." But the head is smooth and its soft skin lengthens out and drapes over the crutch at the far right as though it were an empty sack or a deflated balloon. The overall shape, however, also resembles that of the grand pianos in paintings such as *Skull with its lyrical appendages...* Condensed into the single configuration of the head are thus several forms with complex associations. But it is not the associations and potential interpretations of a dream that are important here, but rather the idea of "condensation" itself. Condensation, for Freud, was "the first achievement of the dream-work."[2] In the manifest content of a dream, people or objects are often composites—that is they unite in a single element what turn out to be several different elements. "The dream work," Freud writes, "tries to condense two different thoughts by seeking out (like a joke) an ambiguous word in which the two thoughts may come together."[3] In this sense Dalí here is not representing the content of a dream, latent or manifest, so much as a brilliant visualization of the psychic mechanism of the dream-work. Of *Sleep,* he said: "For sleep to be possible, a whole system of crutches in psychic equilibrium is essential. If only one is missing, one would wake up and above all the little boat would disappear immediately."[4] The crutches here could therefore stand for the dream-work itself, all those mysterious operations of the unconscious mind which sort, translate and encode hidden wishes and desires and perform strange feats of condensation and displacement in order to prevent the surfacing of anxieties so acute that the sleeper might awaken. The little boat, floating tenant-less over a magical scene where shore and sky are merged in a white calm, is one of the el-ements, like the dog and the miniature vision of Cadaqués with a shrouded figure emerging behind its mass, which might be the "ground bass" of a dream, all beautifully in balance.

Sleep was exhibited in the "International Surrealist Exhibition" in Paris in 1938 (January-February) and was in Edward James's collection by 1939 when it was lent to Dalí's exhibition at the Julien Levy Gallery in New York (exh. cat. no. 19). James noted for insurance purposes that it was purchased for $1400, which suggests it could have been bought before the 1937-8 contract that gave him exclusive rights to Dalí's production, although it could equally have entered his collection under the terms of the contract.[5] D.A.

[1] James Thrall Soby, *Salvador Dalí* (New York: Museum of Modern Art, 1946), p. 15.
[2] Sigmund Freud, *Introductory Lectures on Psychoanalysis,* trans. James Strachey (New York: Norton & Co. 1966), p. 171.
[3] *Ibid.* pp. 172-173.
[4] Robert Descharnes, *Dalí de Gala* (Lausanne: Edita S.A., 1962), p. 65.
[5] I am grateful to Sharon Michi-Kusunoki, Edward James Archive, for this information.

169. Inventions of the Monsters, 1937

169. Oil on canvas
51.4 × 78.1 cm
20 1/4 × 30 3/4 in.
Chicago (IL), The Art Institute
of Chicago
Joseph Winterbotham
Collection

Fig. 1. Angelika Kauffmann, *Cupid Wiping Away Psyche's Tears*, 1807
Zürich, Kunsthaus Zürich

When the Art Institute of Chicago acquired this painting in 1943, Dalí sent the following telegram congratulating the Museum and commenting on the work's genesis and symbolism: "I am pleased and honored by your acquisition. According to Nostradamus the apparition of monsters presages the outbreak of war. This canvas was painted in the Semmering mountains near Vienna a few months before the Anschluss [the annexation of Austria by Nazi Germany in March 1938] and has a prophetic character. Horse women equal maternal river monsters. Flaming giraffe equals cosmic masculine apocalyptic monster. Cat angel equals divine heterosexual monster. Hourglass equals metaphysical monster. Gala and Dalí equal sentimental monster. The little blue dog alone is not a true monster. Sincerely, Salvador Dalí."[1]

This detailed description provides invaluable insights into the content and meaning of this mysterious and darkly ominous work, which we now know was painted in the small ski resort of Semmering in the Austrian Alps towards the end of 1937.[2] Despite his apolitical stance during the Spanish Civil War, which he saw as a natural phenomenon of history involving basic and instinctual forces, the artist was not immune to the contemporary political reality of Europe in the late 1930s. Dalí's reference to the 16th-century French astrologer and physician Nostradamus (Michel de Nostredame, 1503-66), whose cryptic quatrains are thought by some people to predict the future rise of tyrants, the collapse of empires, and the outbreak of wars, suggests a kinship with his own work, which he believed was capable of similar acts of prophesy and divination. The artist regarded the slightly earlier *Soft Construction with Boiled Beans…*, for example, as a premonition of the turbulent civil war in his native Spain, while *Inventions of the Monsters* was clearly associated in his mind with the impending catastrophe of the Second World War. Dalí intuitively believed that this conflict would lead to the collapse of European tradition and culture, as well as to untold human suffering, which perhaps explains the overt references to classical mythology and Christian iconography in the painting, all of which are threatened by the approaching apocalypse that takes the form of a burning giraffe in the far distance.

The painting addresses the imminent threat of chaotic upheaval and warfare through pictorial devices that are both subtle and complex. This can be seen in the deliberately asymmetrical composition, in which the figures are shifted to the left-hand side of the canvas like the contents of a ship listing in a storm, which is as disturbing as the double-headed monsters themselves. The viewer is invited to witness the events that unravel before their eyes by the petrified hand that mysteriously emerges from the lower left-hand corner of the painting and points admonishingly to the scene before us. Here, a sibylline figure gazes from black eye sockets at the butterfly and hourglass she holds in her hands, while an ossified hand holding a ball stands on the table beside her. The butterfly and the hourglass can be interpreted as symbols of *memento mori*, or visual reminders of death and mortality, and the transitory nature of worldly possessions and beauty. This multitude of hands recalls the paranoiac double image of the crouching Narcissus and his double, a stony hand holding a cracked egg from which sprouts a narcissus flower, in *Metamorphosis of Narcissus*, which Dalí completed earlier that year. Like all of the hybrid monsters in the work, this figure has a composite head that is formed by combining a profile and frontal view into a single entity. Behind her can be seen a double portrait of Gala and Dalí, who appear to be caught in a happily shared moment, as they contemplate with apparent amusement and fascination the array of objects before them on the table, which include a loaf of bread, a fossilized hand holding an egg, and a small portrait bust. In the center of the picture is a kind of altar supporting the bust of a naked woman, whose head merges with that of a horse, thus associating her with the horse women bathing in the top left-hand corner, whose strange poses were derived in part from the centaurs found in the work of Piero di Cosimo. Centaurs are often thought to represent the bestial side of man's nature, as opposed to the rational or intellectual side, and these hybrid "horse women" may have been invented as a response to the perceived threat to European civilization by barbaric forces. What the artist refers to as a "cat angel" leans against the altar, seemingly engaged in conversation with the bust of one of the horse women, in a pose derived from earlier representations of Cupid and Psyche. In what is now the empty lower right-hand corner of the painting was the solitary figure of the blue dog, which is sadly no longer visible to the naked eye since it was evidently painted with a fugitive, or chemically unstable, pigment that quickly faded after the completion of this intriguing work.[3] M.R.T.

[1] This telegram, which is housed in the archives of the Art Institute of Chicago, was first published in full in October 1943; see Anonymous, "Dalí's Heterosexual Monster Invades Chicago," *The Art Digest*, vol. 18, no. 2, October 15, 1943, p. 13.

[2] According to Robert Descharnes, Dalí began the painting "in Paris, in his studio on rue de la Tombe-Issoire and resumed work on it in Austria while he was spending a short time at the winter-sports resort of Semmering, south of Vienna"; see Descharnes, *Dalí*, trans. Eleanor R. Morse (New York: Harry N. Abrams, 1976), p. 120.

[3] The little dog was described as "barely visible against the somber background" in a newspaper article published shortly after the work was acquired by the Art Institute of Chicago, thus confirming that the fading is not a modern phenomenon; see Sydney J. Harris, "It's Confusing, It's Amusing – It's Dalí's Art," *Chicago Daily News*, October 8, 1943, p. 10.

170. Palladio's Thalia Corridor, 1937

170. Oil on canvas
116.5 × 89.5 cm
45$^7/8$ × 35$^1/4$ in.
Mie (Japan), Mie Prefectural
Art Museum

The writhing mass of elongated figures that recede into the distance of this painting was deliberately made to resemble the *trompe-l'œil* proscenium of the Teatro Olimpico at Vicenza (fig. 1). This spectacular theater design was the last major work of Andrea Palladio (1508-80), whom Dalí considered to be the world's greatest architect. The artist's appreciation of Palladio's work was greatly enhanced around 1937-38, when he visited Italy for an extended period in order to recuperate from a bout of nervous exhaustion brought on by the traumatic events of the Spanish Civil War. It was while staying with close friends such as Edward James and Lord Berners that the artist began to take a new interest in the art and architecture of the Italian Renaissance and the Baroque.[1] As Dalí later recalled, the architecture of Palladio and Donato Bramante "impressed me more and more as being the startling and perfect achievement of the human spirit in the realm of esthetics, and I was beginning to feel the desire to go and see and touch these unique phenomena, these products of materialized intelligence that were concrete, measurable, and supremely non-necessary."[2]

In order to study the work of Palladio firsthand, the artist visited Vicenza, in the north of Italy, where he was so impressed by the dramatic perspective recession of Palladio's architectural scenery that he declared the Teatro Olimpico to be "the most mysterious and divine 'esthetic' spot" in the world.[3] *Palladio's Thalia Corridor*, and related paintings such as *Palladio's Corridor of Dramatic Surprise*, of 1937-38, reveal the lessons that the artist learned from the Baroque

architect, whose work was undergoing a thorough re-evaluation during the period of Dalí's Italian sojourn. Palladio's reputation had waned during the second half of the 19th-century, due to a fervent anticlassical reaction to his borrowings from the buildings of pagan antiquity. This arid Neoclassical view of Palladio, promoted by critics such as John Ruskin, was challenged during the 1930s, thanks in large part to a landmark essay by Giulio Argan entitled "Andrea Palladio e la critica neoclassica."[4] Argan took issue with earlier critics whom he believed had misrepresented Palladio as a sober, self-controlled architect, interested solely in classical order and serenity. Argan argued instead that his building designs, which often incorporated dazzling visions of color and light molded in dramatic spatial sequences, revealed Palladio to be an expressive artist capable of Mannerist distortions. The great burst of scholarship and public debate that followed the publication of Argan's essay in 1930 may have penetrated Dalí's circle of friends in Italy, perhaps explaining his sudden interest in Palladio's illusionistic treatment of space, which coincided with his own investigation into double images and other pictorial devices designed to manipulate the viewer in his paintings of the late 1930s.

The dramatically foreshortened corridors that appear to open from the proscenium in the Teatro Olimpico are clearly evoked in Dalí's painting, in which the two rows of standing figures form a plunging perspective that ends in the figure of a girl skipping rope in the far distance. These distorted personages owe a debt to the elongated figures found in the work of El Greco, while the use of

Fig. 1. The proscenium of the Teatro Olimpico by Palladio, Vicenza

Fig. 2. Jacopo Tintoretto,
*The Finding of the Body
of Saint Mark*, ca. 1562
Milan, Pinacoteca di Brera

space was connected in his mind with Palladio's virtuoso use of perspective at Vicenza. Like Tintoretto, Dalí picked his colorful figures out of the darkness with highlights made using bold brushstrokes that barely delineate their forms. Dalí's references to Tintoretto and El Greco in this work mirror Argan's conception of Palladio as a Mannerist artist, while the title, with its nod to Thalia, the Greek muse of comedy, underlines the artist's predilection for theatricality and spectacle that made him especially receptive to Palladio's "enflamed proscenium of torrential beauty."[5] M.R.T.

chiaroscuro looks back to the paintings of Jacopo Tintoretto. The tall figure with an upraised hand that heads the procession on the left-hand side of Dalí's painting is a direct quotation from Tintoretto's *The Finding of the Body of Saint Mark* of ca. 1562 (fig. 2), which the artist would have seen in the Brera in Milan. Dalí may have been drawn to this work because its deeply recessed architectural

[1] For more on Dalí's visit to Lord Berners in Rome (and briefly to Sicily), and his stay with Edward James at the Villa Cimbrone at Ravello, see Ian Gibson, *The Shameful Life of Salvador Dalí* (London: Faber and Faber, 1997), p. 419.
[2] Salvador Dalí, *The Secret Life of Salvador Dalí*, trans. Haakon M. Chevalier (New York: Dial Press, 1942), p. 352.
[3] *Ibid.*, p. 208. Dalí also experienced Venetian art and architecture for the first time during this Italian sojourn, when he visited his own friend Coco Chanel in Venice around the same time as his trip to Vicenza.
[4] Giulio Carlo Argan, "Andrea Palladio e la critica neoclassica," *L'Arte*, vol. XXIII, 1930, pp. 327-346. For a detailed analysis of the critical reception of Palladio's work during this period, see Deborah Howard, "Four Centuries of Literature on Palladio," Review Essay, *Journal of the Society of Architectural Historians*, vol. XXXIX, no. 3, October 1980, pp. 224-241.
[5] Salvador Dalí, "Dalí, Dalí!," artist's statement in the catalogue of the Salvador Dalí exhibition held at the Julien Levy Gallery, New York, March 21-April 18, 1939, n.p., reprinted in Haim Finkelstein, ed., *The Collected Writings of Salvador Dalí* (Cambridge: Cambridge University Press, 1998), p. 336.

171. Untitled (Vision of Eternity), 1936-37

171. Oil on canvas
207 × 118.1 cm
$81^{1/2} \times 46^{1/2}$ in.
Chicago (IL), The Art Institute
of Chicago

172. Harpo Marx, 1937

172. Graphite and ink
on coated card stock
45.1 × 35.6 cm
17³/4 × 14 in.
Philadelphia (PA),
Philadelphia Museum of Art
The Henry P. McIlhenny
Collection in memory
of Frances P. McIlhenny, 1986

Fig. 1. Harpo Marx photographed
in 1937

In his 1932 essay, *A Short Critical History of Cinema*, Dalí placed the Marx Brothers' movie *Animal Crackers* "at the summit of the evolution of comic cinema."[1] The artist went on to describe the deep kinship he felt with the "concrete irrationality" of the Marx Brothers, whose humorous antics he likened to his own Surrealist art practice, before singling out Harpo Marx for special praise: "The one with the curly hair, whose face is that of persuasive and triumphant madness, as much at the end of the film as during the too short moment when he interminably plays the harp."[2] Dalí's admiration for the horn honking, trench-coated Harpo, the stage persona of Adolf Marx, the second-oldest and most charismatic of the Marx Brothers, led him to seek out his screen idol when he visited Europe in the summer of 1936. This meeting with the silent actor, which took place at a party in Paris, was by all accounts a great success and Dalí decided to cement their friendship with a hand-made Christmas present that he sent to Harpo in December of that year. The artist designed an elaborate harp assembled with barbed-wire strings and adorned with teaspoons and forks for tuning knobs.[3] Harpo Marx was so delighted with this strange musical instrument that he immediately sent the artist a photograph of himself with bandaged fingers, thus pretending that he had unwittingly plucked the barbed-wire strings with his bare hands. The photograph was followed by a telegram informing Dalí that he was a great admirer of *The Persistence of Memory* and that, if ever the Spanish artist visited Southern California, he would be "happy to be smeared by you."[4]

Dalí did not wait long to take Harpo up on his intriguing invitation, arriving in Hollywood in January 1937, where he announced to newspaper reporters that he intended to make a portrait of the sweet-natured comedian. As one art critic speculated at the time, "it is not stated whether Dalí will endeavor to balance two broiled chops on the silent redhead's shoulders or to merely infest his countenance with ants, but one thing is certain, the stunt will be worth many columns of publicity for both artist and subject."[5]

Their first meeting took place in the garden of Harpo's Los Angeles home, which confirmed Dalí's impression that the comedian was the most fascinating and surrealistic character in Hollywood: "He was naked, crowned with roses, and in the center of a veritable forest of harps (he was surrounded by at least five hundred harps). He was caressing, like a new Leda, a dazzling white swan, and feeding it a statue of the Venus of Milo made of cheese, which he grated against the strings of the nearest harp."[6] Although Dalí's vivid imagination no doubt exaggerated the events of that day, it is clear that Harpo enjoyed playing the buffoon around the Spanish artist and raised his manic energy to new levels of hysterical frenzy.

This exquisite pencil and ink drawing is one of two known portraits of Harpo Marx that Dalí completed in February 1937. The portraits were made from quick sketches carried out during the intervals of the making of the latest Marx Brothers' film, *A Day at the Races*, in which Harpo played the role of Stuffy.[7] These animated sessions were documented in numerous photographs, which show Dalí intently sketching a beaming Harpo (figs. 1, 2), or re-creating the earlier photograph of the comedian's bandaged fingers, in which a grimacing Harpo strums the barbed-wire strings of this instrument of torture under Dalí's fierce gaze. In the finished drawing, Harpo is shown with a beatific smile and wide, unblinking eyes, as he plays the harp with his long, graceful fingers. Dalí painstakingly observed every fold of the comedian's trademark trench coat, while his curly locks were lovingly delineated with the de-

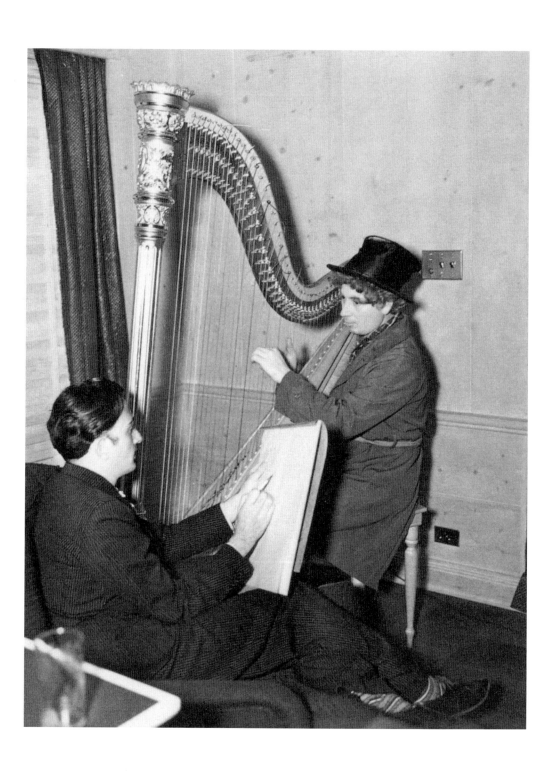

Fig. 2. Salvador Dalí intently
portraying Harpo Marx in 1937

tailed illusionism that the artist had perfected. This conventional image of the celluloid clown was then embellished with familiar Dalínian props, such as the piece of tonguelike meat draped over the top of the harp, or the lobster and apple that rest on Harpo's head, which relate to the artist's earlier interest in the themes of edible beauty, cannibalism, and the legend of William Tell.

The two men become so friendly during these sittings that they began working together on a scenario for a short film entitled *Giraffes on Horseback Salad*. All that remains of their collaboration is about a dozen sketches and some notes for a scene in which Harpo, playing the Emperor Nero, is restrained by chains and put on trial for using money for evil purposes. Encouraged by Harpo's initial interest in the project, Dalí continued to work on the screenplay when he returned to Europe in March 1937. In an enthusiastic letter to Harpo, written at the Arlberg-Wintersporthotel in Zürs, Dalí confidently predicted that the film's "sensational scenario made expressly for your genius, with extraordinary decorations and a very lyrical music, like Cole Porter's, would be something hallucinatory which in addition to amusing us could make a successful revolution in the cinema."[8] Sadly, like so many of Dalí's film projects, *Giraffes on Horseback Salad* was never realized. M.R.T.

[1] Salvador Dalí, "Abrégé d'une histoire critique du cinema" (A Short Critical History of Cinema), in *Babaouo: Scenario inédit précédé d'un Abrégé d'une histoire critique du cinema et suivi de Guillaume Tell ballet portugais* (Paris: Éditions des Cahiers Libres, 1932), pp. 11-21, reprinted in Haim Finkelstein, ed., *The Collected Writings of Salvador Dalí*, trans. Haim Finkelstein (Cambridge: Cambridge University Press, 1998), p. 140.

[2] *Ibid.*, p. 141. Translation slightly modified by the author.

[3] Marie Seton, "S. Dalí + 3 Marxes =," *Theatre Arts Monthly*, vol. 23, October 1939, p. 734.

[4] Harpo Marx, undated telegram to Salvador Dalí, in Meredith Etherington-Smith, *Dalí* (London: Sinclair-Stevenson, 1992), p. 262.

[5] Anonymous, "Dalí Goes Hollywood," *Art Digest*, March 1, 1937, p. 17.

[6] Salvador Dalí, "Surrealism in Hollywood," *Harper's Baazar*, June 1937, p. 68.

[7] The other drawing was reproduced in *Time* magazine in December 1938, where it was accompanied by the following detailed description: "In the centre foreground sits Harpo staring, sadly strumming on his harp. His hair is golden fuzz, interwoven with fuchsia flowers and gay green leaves. He is not surprised by the company of three attentive giraffes—their backs on fire. In the distance are eight more giraffes, also burning, trying to get away from their own heat by running"; see Anonymous, "Dalí's Harpo," *Time*, December 12, 1938, p. 50. When Dalí was asked why his portrait of the comedian included giraffes, from whose necks issued tongues of flames rendered in bright orange pastels, he answered: "Slapstick humor. How could that better be expressed than by these giraffes with their burning necks"; see S.J. Woolf, "Dalí's Doodles Come to Town," *The New York Times Magazine*, March 12, 1939, p. 16.

[8] Meredith Etherington-Smith, *Dalí*, op. cit, p. 262. Dalí sent a draft of this letter to Edward James, requesting that he translate it into English. It is not known if the letter, which is now preserved at the Edward James Foundation, West Dean, was ever sent to Harpo.

173. Mae West Lips Sofa, 1938

173. Wood carcass upholstered in pink satin
86.5 × 183 × 81,5 cm
34 × 72 × 32 1/8 in.
Chichester, The Trustees of The Edward James Foundation

Fig. 1. Salvador Dalí, *Mae West's Face which May Be Used as a Surrealist Apartment*, 1934-35
Chicago (IL), The Art Institute of Chicago

In 1936 Edward James proposed an idea to Dalí for constructing an entire Surrealist environment in the drawing room of his London home. Although the project was abandoned, Dalí and James began together to invent ambitious Surrealist schemes for interiors. Dalí had already painted the gouache *Mae West's Face which May Be Used as a Surrealist Apartment* in 1934-35. James suggested that the lips be manufactured as a sofa, and supervised both the creative and practical aspects of their production. He commissioned two design firms to manufacture a total of five sofas in the shape of Mae West's lips. Whilst these objects have regularly been dated to 1936, manufacturing receipts from this period firmly place their completed production in the year 1938. Of the five sofas there were three different versions, one upholstered in satin to match the shade of Schiapparelli's shocking pink lipstick, two in a red felt with a pink felt base,[1] and two in red felt with a black wool fringe which lined the outer edge of the bottom lip.[2] The *Mae West Lips* sofa was probably born in the dining room of James's London home when Dalí was his guest in 1936. There James and Dalí discussed a plethora of ideas around paranoiac furniture, as witnessed in Dalí's sketches, *The Birth of Paranoiac Furniture*,[3] which James then planned to manufacture.[4] Dalí attributed his inspiration for the sofa to the jagged rocks of Cadaqués on which it was uncomfortable to sit, which he linked, in *The Secret Life,* to the balconies on one of Gaudí's façades, for instance, La Pedrera.[5]

The first reference to the production of the sofas dates from February 1938. Dalí and James presumably worked together on the original design which was passed to James's Decorative Contractors, Green & Abbott of London as well as to Edward Carrick, the Director of the Associated Artist-Technicians.[6] James decided on both the final shape and fabric for each object. Originally, James gave instructions for the sofa intended to match the color of Schiapparelli's lipstick to be upholstered in satin, and then, following a conversation with Dalí, a Moroccan leather dyed pink which Green & Abbott went to great lengths to locate.[7] However, after a conversation James had with Elsa Schiapparelli through which he learned that she hated the idea of a leather sofa, James made the decision to upholster the lips in satin, as he had originally intended: "The point of this letter really is to tell you that I was under a misapprehension when I telephoned about the leather for the couch. Dalí had said to me *cuivre* with a v … he had said that Elsa Schiapparelli had decided that it would be nice in *cuivre*. I of course had understood *cuir* ('leather') because a sofa shaped like a mouth or not shaped like a mouth in copper would be quite impossible. The error came through her having told Dalí that she told me to have the notched timber chairs cast in brass: and he made the confusion by thinking that the metal was for the sofa and not for the chairs. And when I heard him say *cuivre* I translated this into *cuir*. … When on the evening following my telephone conversation with you, I talked to Elsa herself, I found that she hated the idea of leather for the sofa and would much prefer it in faced-cloth or satin as we had decided.

… So 'as you were' about the leather; and go ahead with your satin as always."[8] From James's correspondence, it appears that three of the sofas were made by Green & Abbott and two by Edward Carrick. Green & Abbott apparently made the satin sofa as well as the two with the black worsted fringe: "Only keep in mind about the black worsted ruche and fringe for the other sofa which is going to be in felt—because I doubt very much whether your rivals … are sufficiently good upholsterers to be able to produce what I want in the way of a black wool fringe to look like the embroidery upon the epaulettes of a picador or the breeches and hat of a toreador."[9] The pink satin sofa was completed in February and sat in the dining room of James's Wimpole Street home while the two red felt sofas were at Monkton.[10] S.M.K.

[1] Salvador Dalí and Edward James, *Mae West Lips Sofa*, 1938, wood carcass upholstered in deep pink and light pink felted woven wool fabric, 92 x 213 x 80, one purchased from James on 12 January 1983 by the Royal Pavilion, Libraries & Museums, Brighton & Hove, and the other purchased by the Boijmans Van Beuningen Museum in Rotterdam from the sale at Christie's on 8 October 2003, formerly in the collection of Edward James. The sofa purchased by the Boijmans was sold in October 1984 through the Robert Fraser Gallery in London.

[2] Salvador Dalí and Edward James, *Mae West Lips Sofa*, 1938, wood carcass upholstered in red wool fabric with black fringing, 79×206×91.5, both sofas are the property of The Trustees of The Edward James Foundation, Chichester.

[3] Salvador Dalí, *The Birth of the Paranoiac Furniture,* ca. 1937-38, black chalk and yellow gouache, 62.2×47 cm, sold through the Mayor Gallery in January 1984.

[4] Dalí and James's discussions resulted in a series of sketches for the production of paranoiac furniture which James planned to install in his Wimpole Street home. Some of these sketches were given to Green & Abbott but unfortunately, were never returned. It can, however, be ascertained from archival material, that James had commissioned a full-size "torso set of drawers" to be made from one of Dalí's sketches. In a letter from James's decorative contractors dated July 18, 1938, John Hill stated that they had drawn out the chest of drawers but felt it would be more successful if Dalí were to draw it to scale: "We have drawn out the torso chest of drawers full size, and will telephone tomorrow morning to see if you can see me if I bring it round. I feel it would really be more satisfactory if Dalí drew the full size, as it will depend so much on the proportion and movement of the figure." John A. L. Hill from Green & Abbott, Ltd., letter to Edward James, July 18, 1938 (EJA, Box: *Green & Abbott, Ltd.*).

[5] Salvador Dalí, *The Secret Life of Salvador Dalí,* trans. H.M. Chevalier (New York: Dover Publications, Inc., 1993), p. 279.

[6] Edward Carrick, Associated Artist-Technicians, invoice to Edward James for the building and upholstering of the sofa, 3 March 1938 (EJA, Box: *Associated Artist-Technicians*).

[7] Edward James, letter to J. A. L. Hill of Green & Abbott, Ltd., 20 January 1938 (EJA, Box: *Green & Abbott, Ltd., 1938*).

[8] *Ibid.*

[9] *Ibid.*

[10] Green & Abbott, Ltd, invoice to Edward James, 31 July 1938 (EJA, Box: *Green & Abbott, Ltd*).

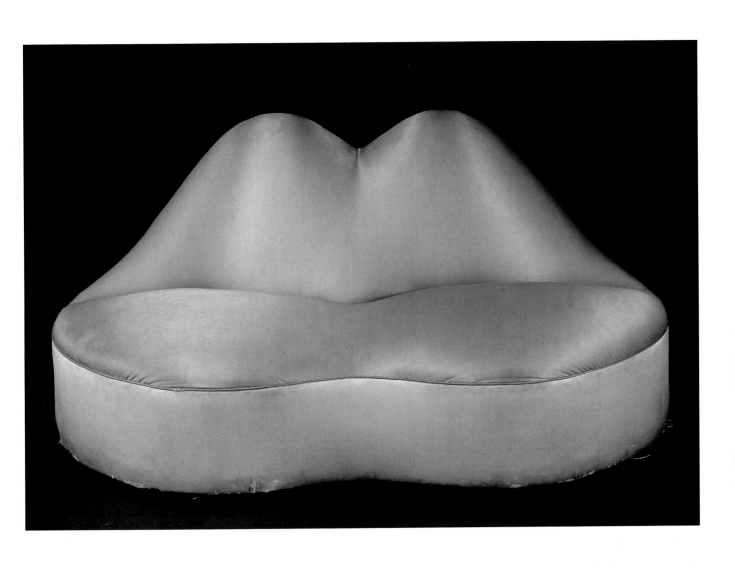

174. Lobster Telephone, 1938
175. Lobster Telephone, 1938
176. Raoul Ubac, Lobster Telephone by Salvador Dalí, in the "International Surrealist Exhibition," Galerie des Beaux-Arts, Paris, 1938

174. Assemblage
(painted plaster, plastic
and metal)
19 × 31 × 16 cm
7$^{1/2}$ × 12$^{1/4}$ × 6$^{3/8}$ in.
Chichester, The Trustees of
The Edward James Foundation

175. Assemblage
(painted plaster, plastic
and metal)
19 × 31 × 16 cm
7$^{1/2}$ × 12$^{1/4}$ × 6$^{3/8}$ in.
Chichester, The Trustees of
The Edward James Foundation

176. Silver gelatin print
23.4 × 17.3 cm
9$^{1/4}$ × 6$^{3/4}$ in.
New York (NY),Timothy Baum
Collection

Fig. 1. *The Dream of Venus*,
photograph by Georges Platt Lyne
(on the right in the photo) with
Edward James, Gala, Salvador Dalí
and a model

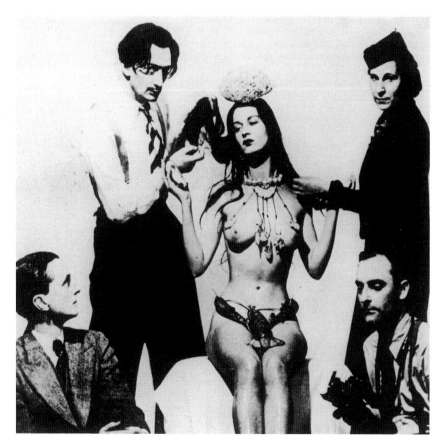

The *Lobster Telephone* is one of the best-known icons of the 20th-century. A collaboration between Dalí and his patron and co-creator, Edward James, the telephone emerged from a conjunction between the idea of the Surrealist object, which Dalí had launched in 1931, and the exploration of interior design as a new and creative means of expressing Surrealist ideals. From this exploration grew paranoiac-critical environments, furniture, and Surrealist assemblages. Dalí has been credited, as a result, with "single-handedly bringing a new dimension, a new lift, to an aging Surrealism."[1] The correspondence in The Edward James Archives tells a slightly different version of the story, however, one in which the inspiration for the schemes sometimes came from James.

In June of 1936, Dalí was James's houseguest in his London home at 35 Wimpole Street. From this visit resulted a host of ideas for the production of Surrealist objects and furniture. Anecdotally, James recorded that the idea of the *Lobster Telephone* grew out of an incident that occurred during this visit. According to James, he, Dalí and some other friends were sitting on the bed eating lobsters and tossing the shells to the side. One, he said, landed on the telephone.[2] This, presumably, reminded James of a visit he had made earlier in the year to a rather aristocratic lady who sat in her bed as the other guests sat in chairs around her. In an ice bucket by the side of the bed was a lobster and unbeknownst to her, a telephone. When the telephone rang, the hostess picked up the lobster by mistake.[3] James related this incident to Dalí who later wrote, in *The Secret Life*:

"I do not understand why, when I ask for a grilled lobster in a restaurant, I am never served a cooked telephone. I do not understand why champagne is always chilled and why, on the other hand, telephones, which are habitually so frightfully warm and disagreeably sticky to the touch, are not also put in silver buckets with crushed ice around them."[4]

Among the objects Dalí exhibited at the 1938 "International Surrealist Exhibition" in Paris (January-February) was *Aphrodisiac Telephone*, presumably the prototype of those shortly to be manufactured. Interestingly, André Breton also mentions the telephone in his entry on Dalí for *Anthologie de l'humour noir* (1940) wherein he writes of a telephone which was painted red with a live lobster as a handset. Whilst the juxtaposition of these two unlikely elements project, at first glance, a shell of innocence and humor, this feeling is eviscerated by the strong sexual connotations of the finished object. Lobsters, it should be noted, are often considered to possess aphrodisiac qualities that are thought to enhance the power and charm of men and the fertility of women. In dream analysis, the image of a lobster is interpreted as a phallic symbol. Dalí himself was renowned for his love of shellfish, more particularly because of the fact that the hard, rigidity of the exoskeleton acted as a womb that protected the softness and more amorphous character of its internal organs.[5] With the *Lobster Telephone*, which is understood to be female, the lobster is placed on the phone so that the tail, and hence, the sexual organs, are situated directly over the mouthpiece.

James commissioned from his Decorative Contractors, Green & Abbott of London, the manufacture and hand-painting of ten lobsters.[6] Although the actual date when the production of the lobsters commenced is not known, they were certainly completed by July 1938. As indicated on Green & Abbott's invoice dated August 11, 1938, it would seem that initially, four lobster telephones were painted red and six white. Of the four red phones, three were covered with white paint and then repainted back to the original red.[7] James supervised the production of the lobsters, suggesting and approving the color schemes for the shell:

"With regard to the telephone lobster, the Studio are painting them now, and they will be varnished and hard, I think, by Thursday."[8]

With the inevitability of the Second World War fast approaching, the motif of the telephone appeared frequently in Dalí's work. *Beach with Telephone, The Sublime Moment, Imperial Violets* (cat. 133), *The Enigma of Hitler* (cat. 186), *Telephone in a Dish with Three Grilled Sardines at the End of September,*

174

175

and *Landscape with Telephones on a Plate* (cat. 189),[9] all featured a telephone receiver broken, castrated, or collected together in a bizarre gathering of disconnected phalluses. S.M.K.

[1] A. Reynolds Morse, "Dalí's Surrealist 'Sculptures,'" *Dalí – Espace Montmartre* (Paris: 1989), p. 16.

[2] Edward James, undated fragment (EJA, Box: *Edward James Biographical – Undated*).

[3] Martin T. Heymann, Agent to Edward James, in conversation with Sharon-Michi Kusunoki (October 7, 2003).

[4] Salvador Dalí, *The Secret Life of Salvador Dalí*, trans. Haakon M. Chevalier (New York: Dover Publications, Inc., 1993), p. 271.

[5] *Ibid.*, p. 9.

[6] Salvador Dalí, *Lobster Telephone*, 1938, designed by Salvador Dalí, made by Green & Abbott, London, assemblage, plaster and other materials, 19 × 31 × 16 cm, present locations believed to be as follows: Painted Lobsters—Tate Gallery, London; German Telephone Museum (Deutsches Postmuseum, Frankfurt-am-Main); National Gallery of Australia; The Trustees of The Edward James Foundation, Chichester, England. White Lobsters – Boijmans Van Beuningen Museum, Rotterdam; Dalí Museum, St. Petersburg, Florida, USA; Minnesota Institute of Art, Minneapolis, Minnesota, USA; one in Johannesburg, actual whereabouts unknown; one in Portugal actual whereabouts unknown; The Trustees of The Edward James Foundation, Chichester, England.

[7] Green & Abbott, Ltd, invoice to Edward James, August 11, 1938 (EJA, Box: *Green & Abbott, Ltd*). The painted lobsters were placed on black telephones and the white lobsters were placed on white telephones. Whilst the original telephones do not exist, it can be ascertained that the phones were placed on a Siemens Brothers 332, which was introduced in 1936 with a "cheese tray" in the base, which contained dialing instructions, a built-in bell and a side cord entry.

[8] John A. L. Hill of Green & Abbott, Ltd., letter to Edward James, July 18, 1938 (EJA, Box: *Green & Abbott, Ltd.*).

[9] Salvador Dalí, *Beach with Telephone*, 1938, oil on canvas, 73.6 × 92 cm, London, The Tate Gallery, formerly in the collection of Edward James; *The Sublime Moment,* 1938, oil on canvas, 38 × 47 cm, Stuttgart, Staatsgalerie Stuttgart; *Imperial Violets*, 1938, oil on canvas, 99.5 × 142.5 cm, private collection, formerly in the collection of Edward James who donated it to The Museum of Modern Art, New York, since sold; *Telephone in a Dish with Three Grilled Sardines at the End of September,* 1939, oil on canvas, 45.7 × 54.9 cm, St. Petersburg, Florida, The Salvador Dalí Museum, on loan from the Morse Charitable Trust; *Landscape with Telephones on a Plate*, 1939, oil on canvas, 22 × 30 cm, Madrid, Galería Theo, formerly in the collection of Edward James.

176

177. Study for "Self-Portrait in Impressions of Africa," 1938
178. Study for "Self-Portrait in Impressions of Africa," 1938
179. Impressions of Africa, 1938

177. Pencil and India ink
on paper
63 × 48 cm
24³/4 × 18⁷/8 in.
Rotterdam, Boijmans
Van Beuningen Museum

178. Pencil on paper
52 × 33 cm
20¹/2 × 13 in.
Rotterdam, Boijmans
Van Beuningen Museum

179. Oil on canvas
91.5 × 117.5 cm
36 × 46¹/4 in.
Rotterdam, Boijmans
Van Beuningen Museum

Dalí painted *Impressions of Africa* in Rome in March 1938 at the Villa Cimbrone (Foro Romano), the house of the Lord Berners, a close friend of his patron Edward James. Unable to return to their home at Port Lligat because of the Spanish Civil War, Dalí and Gala moved round Europe staying in hotels or with their high society friends. This peripatetic lifestyle never interfered with Dalí's passionate commitment to his work, and the contract with Edward James by which James purchased his entire production between June 1937 and June 1938 assured them security. It was one of Dalí's most fruitful periods.

The title of this painting refers both to Africa itself and to Raymond Roussel's play *Impressions d'Afrique*. Just before settling in Rome, Dalí and Gala had visited Sicily, where he found "mingled reminiscences of Catalonia and Africa."[1] He was also fond of alluding to his own supposed Moorish antecedents, but there may have been a more topical allusion in that Franco's invasion of the Spanish Republic in 1936 had been launched from the country's North African colonies.

The curious method Roussel had used in *Impressions d'Afrique* to generate events and images via linguistic games had already fascinated Marcel Duchamp. Homonyms or near homonyms were milked to create a kind of parallel world. One example was *mou á raille* and *mou á rail* (*mou* meaning both soft and entrails, and *rail* meaning rails), together with *baleine á îlôt* and *baleine á ilote* (*baleine* meaning whale or whalebone, *îlôt* small island, *ilote* helot.) This gave Roussel "the statue of the slave made of whalebone corsets running on rails of calves' lights."[2] The irrational universe created by these puns was in some ways a verbal equivalent to Dalí's paranoiac-critical method, and its double images. Threaded through this painting are other specific allusions to *Impressions d'Afrique*, such as the red cloth in which, in the play, the emperor's son Rhejed is carried off by a giant black-plumaged bird. This incident that recalls the abduction of Ganymede, Zeus's favorite, by an eagle could be construed as a distant compliment to Dalí's patron James with Dalí himself as a Surrealist Ganymede.[3]

Impressions of Africa contains some of Dalí's most intricate double images, but it is also a homage to Italian painting. The red cloth is a generalized reference to the crimson draperies of the Baroque as well as, perhaps, to the red flag of the revolution. The dramatic chiaroscuro and foreshortening of the outstretched hand, meanwhile, recall Venetian paintings such as Titian's *Transfiguration of Christ* in the church of San Salvador. The hand reaching towards a vision as well as into the spectator's space commands attention here just as in Titian's altar piece.

Dalí also draws on the device in Velazquez' *Las Meninas* where the presence of the artist and his easel renders mysterious the nature of the scene being represented. What is "seen," what Dalí is "fixing" on his canvas, is visualized in the images above his head: first Gala's head, whose eyes become the arcades of a building, and then multiply in ever more minute and intricate double images: cave, bushy tree, a donkey's head which is also a priest. To the right of the canvas, figures with basket and guitar who may be Port Lligat fishermen or gypsies melt into and double as the rocky beach. Between them is a figure of uncertain gender, its head also a cavity of the rock behind, wearing what appears to be the remnants of a matador's costume, holding in its hand a limp red cloth. All seem to be stereotypical images of traditional Spain.

The two self-portrait drawings, studies for the painting, are starkly contrasted. One concentrates in fine detail on the hand and eye of the artist, the other, more heavily drawn, emphasizes Dalí's body and his loosened clothes.[4] D.A.

[1] Salvador Dalí, *The Secret Life of Salvador Dalí*, trans. Haakon Chevalier (London: Vision Press, 1968), p. 363.
[2] Raymond Roussel, *Comment j'ai ecrit certains de mes livres* (Paris 1938), p. 9.
[3] Piet de Jonge, correspondence with the author, 1999.
[4] This is a revised version of the entry for *Impressions of Africa* in Dawn Ades, *Dalí's Optical Illusions* (New Haven and London: Yale University Press, 2000).

177

178

179

180. Study for Spain, 1936
181. Spain, 1938

180. Pencil and China ink
on paper
77.5 × 57.7 cm
30 1/2 × 22 3/4 in.
Figueres, Fundació
Gala-Salvador Dalí,
gift of Dalí to the Spanish State

181. Oil on canvas
91.8 × 60.2 cm
36 1/8 × 23 3/4 in.
Rotterdam, Boijmans
Van Beuningen Museum;
formerly Edward James
Collection

The full-length allegorical figure of Spain takes shape within a bleak sandy desert. This may be the familiar Ampurdàn plain, which Dalí does render as a waste in some paintings; however, distant features here such as the palms and arcaded buildings, as well as the lion, suggest rather North Africa. The Spanish Civil War had begun with the invasion of Spain by Franco's troops from her African colonies. By 1938, the right-wing, Nationalist Franco was in control of most of the country.

The woman's posture, drapery and gently tilted head give her a (ghostly) classical appearance. One arm leans on a high chest with a single open drawer from which dangles a shabby red cloth: it might be bloodied, or the red flag, pointing in any case at the violence unleashed by the political extremes of right and left. The other light touches of color in this monochromatic picture are her lips, formed of a pink jacket and the turbaned heads of two lancers that are also her nipples. Dalí first created a double image of a woman's head in the form of warring horsemen two years earlier, in *Paranonia* (Dalí's mis-spelling of Paranoia) 1936. The head of the muse "Paranonia" is very close to that of *Spain*. But the "battle" in *Paranonia* probably refers less to external events than to the turbulent forces of the unconscious, which Breton had evoked in the first *Surrealist Manifesto*. "If the depths of the mind contain strange forces capable of augmenting those on the surface or of fighting victoriously against them, there is every interest in seizing them…"[1] Paranoia would be an instance where the mysterious and violent working of the unconscious mind, normally kept safely at bay by reason and consciousness, break through into the "real world." The eyes of the muse in *Paranonia,* which are also the bright buttocks of horses, gleam white as though she is gazing out in horror or shock. In *Spain*, Dalí has toned down the woman's features so that she appears to be sadly meditating.

Dalí bases his battle and horsemen on Leonardo, in particular on the sketchy background scene in the unfinished *Adoration of the Magi* (started in 1481). He thereby also acknowledges, as Max Ernst had earlier, Leonardo's famous lesson on invention: "Do not despise my opinion, when I remind you that it should not be hard for you to stop sometimes and look into the stains of walls, or ashes or a fire, or clouds, or mud or like places, in which, if you consider them well, you may find really marvelous ideas. The mind of the painter is stimulated to new discoveries, the composition of battles of animals and men, various compositions of landscapes and monstrous things, such as devils and similar things, which may bring you honor; because by indistinct things the mind is stimulated to new inventions."[2] Dalí did sometimes read images into the formless matter of clouds or stains, but his paranoiac critical method more often operated in terms of an obsessional misreading of another specific image, creating, as in this case, a switch between two completely different images that cannot be perceived simultaneously. Dalí might also have been stimulated by details of Uccello's *Battle* published in *Minotaure* in 1935. *The Head of a Woman in the Form of a Battle*, also of 1936, is based on similar double readings of fighting and fleeing figures, though the woman's head is tilted at a different angle. The first sketch for the full figure of *Spain* (cat. 181) also dates from 1936.

With *Spain*, given the title, Dalí now evidently has the Spanish Civil War in mind although the Leonardesque horses and riders also evoke ancient battles. *Spain* might therefore be a counterpart to the terrifying image of self-destruction in the *Soft Construction with Boiled Beans – Premonition of Civil War*. When this was reproduced in *Minotaure* no. 9 in July 1936 it had the title *Spain, Premonition of Civil War*. In place of the grotesque cannibalist limbs of *Soft Construction* the ghostly allegory suggests the memories and the long history of Dalí's torn country.

The painting was exhibited at the Julien Levy Gallery in New York in 1939, and subsequently entered the collection of Edward James. D.A.

[1] André Breton *Manifeste du Surréalisme* (1924) (Paris: NRF, 1967) p. 19.
[2] *The Notebooks of Leonardo da Vinci* selected and edited by Irma A. Richter (Oxford: 1998), p. 182.

180

Fig. 1. Salvador Dalí,
The Great Paranoiac, 1936
Rotterdam, Boijmans
Van Beuningen Museum,
formerly Edward James Collection

182. Study for "The Endless Enigma," 1938
183. The Endless Enigma, 1938

182. Pencil on panel
20 × 25 cm
7⁷/₈ × 9⁷/₈ in.
Figueres, Fundació
Gala-Salvador Dalí

183. Oil on canvas
114.3 × 144 cm
45 × 56⁵/₈ in.
Madrid, Museo Nacional,
Centro de Arte Reina Sofía

As its title suggests, this work, composed of no less than six different subjects, is by far the most complex and enigmatic of the multiple-image paintings that Dalí made in 1938. The artist painted *The Endless Enigma* while vacationing at the La Pausa estate of the couturier Coco Chanel, which was located at Roquebrune on the Côte d'Azur. This summer home provided the necessary space and quietude for Dalí to continue his research into paranoiac double images on a large scale. When *The Endless Enigma* was first shown in the 1939 exhibition of Dalí's multiple-image paintings at the Julien Levy Gallery on East 57th Street in New York it attracted vast crowds, who lined up around the block to marvel at its visual complexity and cryptic illusionism. As *Life* magazine reported at the time, "for general popularity there hasn't been such an exhibit since Whistler's *Mother* was shown in 1934."[1] In his statement for the exhibition catalogue, the artist declared that: "the first 'systematic research' of the problem, I may state, begins with the picture featured in my present exhibition, *The Endless Enigma*. Therein appear, instead of a double image, six different images—thence to the limits of imminent metamorphoses."[2] To illustrate his point, Dalí reproduced the six different states of the work, all loosely sketched in red ink on tracing paper, which revealed the artistic process through which the image was constructed. By separating the work into its various constituent elements, the reader could disentangle the painting's convoluted iconography of overlapping images into its successive stages of completion.

The six individual segments that eventually coalesce into a single, seamless image in the finished painting were also reproduced in line engravings in the cata-

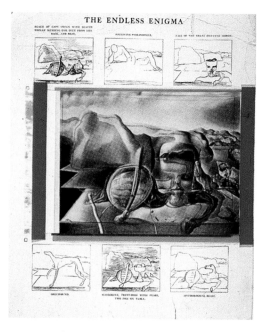

Fig. 1. Page from the exhibition catalogue at the Julien Levy Gallery, New York, 1939

logue, which Dalí labeled with the following titles: *Beach of Cap Creus with Seated Woman Mending Sail from the Back and Boat; Reclining Philosopher; Face of the Great One-Eyed Moron; Greyhound; Mandoline, Fruit-Dish with Pears, Two Figs on a Table;* and *Mythological Beast.* Some of these motifs, such as the fruit-dish, the beach and rock formation at Cape Creus, and the face of the Great One-Eyed Moron, are common features of the 1938 double-image paintings. As Ian Gibson has argued, Dalí probably intended the hallucinatory face that emerges through figure-ground reversal from the mountainous landscape to be that of the Spanish poet Federico García Lorca, who had been one of the artist's closest friends during his student days and his subsequent involvement in the Catalan avant-garde.[3] In September 1936, the poet was shot and killed in his native Granada by Fascists loyal to General Franco's nationalist forces and his death haunted Dalí, who included his visage in two other double-image paintings that year. Other subjects are unique to this painting, such as the mythological beast and the greyhound, which were perhaps drawn from the numerous photographs of dogs that hung on the back wall of the artist's studio at Roquebrune, as seen in a 1938 photograph of the artist standing beside his then unfinished *Endless Enigma* (see p. 496). M.R.T.

[1] Anonymous, "New Yorkers Stand in Line to See his Six-in-One Surrealist Painting," *Life*, April 17, 1939, pp. 44-45.
[2] Salvador Dalí, "Dalí, Dalí!," in the catalogue of the Dalí exhibition held at the Julien Levy Gallery, New York, March 21-April 18, 1939, n.p.
[3] Ian Gibson, *The Shameful Life of Salvador Dalí* (London: Faber and Faber, 1997), p. 385.

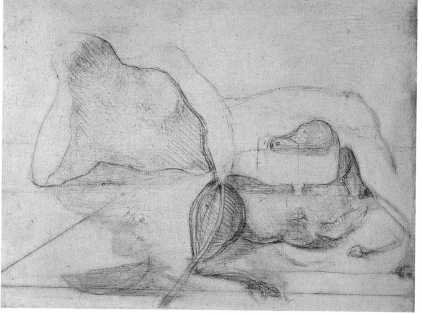

182

183

184. Apparition of Face and Fruit Dish on a Beach, 1938

184. Oil on canvas
114.5 × 143.8 cm
45 1/8 × 56 5/8 in.
Hartford (CT), Wadsworth
Atheneum Museum of Art
Ella Gallup Sumner and Mary
Catlin Sumner Collection Fund

This dazzlingly complex work is one of a series of paintings that Dalí made in 1938 in which he projected multiple images into elaborate, episodic compositions featuring commonplace surroundings and objects. When these paintings were exhibited at the Julien Levy Gallery in New York in March-April 1939 they were greeted with great popular and critical acclaim, thus cementing the artist's reputation in the United States as the leading painter of the Surrealist group. Indeed, A. Everett "Chick" Austin, Jr., the illustrious director of the Wadsworth Atheneum, purchased this work directly from the Levy Gallery exhibition for his Museum for the then princely sum of $1,750.[1] The commercial success of Dalí's recent work disturbed André Breton, who probably had works such as *Apparition of Face and Fruit Dish on a Beach* in mind when he wrote in 1939 that the artist was "concocting entertainments on the level of crossword puzzles."[2] This harsh criticism of Dalí's refinement of the paranoiac-critical method into ever more elaborate equivocal visual illusions, which would reach its apogee in the six composite images that make up *The Endless Enigma*, may have stung the Spanish artist, who would never again attempt such mind-bogglingly intricate compositions, although the double image would remain an important aspect of his work for the rest of his career.

As in all of the 1938 multiple image paintings, this work contrasts deep, open spaces with smooth, malleable shapes to create a visual drama fraught with tense psychological overtones. The painting's embedded imagery can be read simultaneously as a landscape with a beach, a standing dog, or a hallucinatory face, all of which are integrated into the central image of a tabletop still life featuring a fruit dish with pears. The work is filled with ingenious vignettes, such as the dog's eye, which doubles as a tunnel through a hillside, or its collar, which is made up of an aqueduct and its reflection in the water, that reveals Dalí to be at the height of his creative powers in this series of multiple image paintings.

Although Breton's allusion to "crossword puzzles" is not without merit, even if it does speak to his fears about mass entertainment and popular culture, it should be pointed out that Dalí's paintings never slip into the sort of gimmicky stunts of illusionism,

Fig. 1. Salvador Dalí, *Apparition of Face and Fruit Dish on a Beach* (detail), 1938

seen for example in the contemporaneous work of M.C. Escher. The repetitive designs and paradoxical nature of Escher's visual illusions are far removed from the Spanish artist's working practice, which was more akin to the imaginative exercises of Leonardo da Vinci, whom he invoked in his catalogue essay for the 1939 Julien Levy Gallery exhibition: "Leonardo da Vinci proved an authentic innovator of paranoiac painting by recommending to his pupils that, for inspiration, in a certain frame of mind they regard the indefinite shapes of the spots of dampness and the cracks on the wall, that they might see immediately rise into view, out of the confused and the amorphous, the precise contours of the visceral tumult of an imaginary equestrian battle."[3] Dalí even included a subtle homage to Leonardo's *Battle of Anghiari*, of ca. 1504-5, in *Apparition of Face and Fruit Dish on a Beach*, which includes a cavalry combat scene below the dog's muzzle. M.R.T.

[1] Eugene R. Gaddis, *Magician of the Modern: Chick Austin and the Transformation of the Arts in America* (New York: Alfred A. Knopf, 2000), p. 315.
[2] André Breton, *Surrealism and Painting*, trans. Simon Watson Taylor (New York: Icon Editions), 1972, p. 147.
[3] Salvador Dalí, "Dalí, Dalí!," in the catalogue of the "Dalí" exhibition held at the Julien Levy Gallery, New York, March 21-April 18, 1939, n.p.

185. The Transparent Simulacrum of the Feigned Image, 1938

185. Oil on canvas
72.5 × 92 cm
28¹/2 × 36¹/4 in.
Buffalo (NY), Albright-Knox
Art Gallery,
Bequest of A. Conger Goodyear,
1966

As its title suggests, this painting utilizes the conceit of the double image, in which one image takes on the semblance of another after being stared at intently, that by 1938 had become one of the central techniques of Dalí's "paranoiac-critical" method. The reference to images that are transparent, simulated, or feigned is borne out in the shifting ambivalence of the painting's iconography, which at first glance can be read simply as the sandy beach and cove of Cap Creus near Port Lligat, surrounded by mountains in the far distance. Upon closer inspection, the deceptive calm of this Catalan coastal landscape yields another, previously hidden, layer of imagery, casting doubt on the authenticity of similar images that are made with conventional pictorial devices, such as perspective and chiaroscuro, to create the illusion of a three-dimensional world on a flat canvas support. The fraudulent nature of Dalí's double images accentuates the atmosphere of uncertainty and irrationality that was already a prominent feature of his earlier paintings, and ultimately discredits and shatters accepted notions about the supposed reality of the images of the external world.

The troubling succession of images seen in this painting is brought about through Dalí's expert manipulation of landscape elements, especially the open vista of the lake and mountains, which can also be read as a tabletop still life, made up of a bowl of pears in a shallow dish and a crumpled cloth in the foreground. There can be no doubt that Dalí had an innate ability to perceive hidden or composite images in paintings, photographs, and even the natural world. As the artist later explained, "my paranoiac force projected a series of systematic images that I consciously apprehended and tried to concretize. I am neither copyist nor image maker, but am delirious."[1] Taking advantage of the slightest coincidences of shapes and colors, Dalí was able to ingeniously transform one image into another. These double images often proliferate into multiple configurations, as in the tablecloth/beach towel that subsequently metamorphoses into a bird flying across the lower half of the canvas. Along the right-hand side of the painting floats an apparition of the head of Dalí's wife, Gala, who is continually invested in the artist's paintings with mythical connotations and whose inspirational role is acknowledged through the double signature "Gala Salvador Dalí."

In his important early essay "The Stinking Ass," Dalí argued that the viewer's ability to discern these concealed images depended upon the degree of their paranoiac faculties, since "the attainment of such a double image has been made possible thanks to the violence of the paranoiac thought which has made use, with cunning and skill, of the required quantity of pretexts, coincidences, and so on, taking advantage of them so as to reveal the second image, which, in this case, supercedes the obsessive idea."[2]

Dalí later claimed that his interest in the phenomenon of hidden or double images was directly inspired by the work of earlier artists, such as the composite heads of Giuseppe Arcimboldo and the fantastic etchings of Giovanni Battista Bracelli, both of which featured highly inventive double configurations. In the catalogue essay for his 1939 exhibition at the Julien Levy Gallery in New York, where *The Transparent Simulacrum of the Feigned Image* was first shown, Dalí extolled the virtues of his artistic forebears: "It was in 1929 that I first drew the attention of my Surrealist friends to the importance of the paranoiac phenomenon and especially to those images of Arcimboldo and Bracelli composed of heteroclite objects, and to the romantic detritus that expands and flowers into those compositions of double configuration."[3] However, the Spanish artist went beyond these earlier antecedents in his quest to superimpose multiple images, whose potentially infinite number of simultaneous transformations was limited only by each individual's paranoiac capacity according to Dalí.[4] M.R.T.

[1] Salvador Dalí, *The Unspeakable Confessions of Salvador Dalí (as Told to André Parinaud)*, trans. Harold J. Salemson (New York: William Morrow and Company, 1976), p. 142.
[2] Salvador Dalí, "The Rotting Donkey" ("L'Âne pourri"), in Haim Finkelstein, ed., *The Collected Writings of Salvador Dalí*, trans. Haim Finkelstein (Cambridge: Cambridge University Press, 1998), p. 223. This essay was probably written in 1929 and was first published in *La Femme visible* (Paris: Éditions surréalistes, 1930).
[3] Salvador Dalí, "Dalí, Dalí!," artist's statement in the catalogue of the Salvador Dalí exhibition held at the Julien Levy Gallery, New York, March 21-April 18, 1939, n.p., reprinted in Haim Finkelstein, ed. *The Collected Writings of Salvador Dalí, ibid.*, p. 335.
[4] *Ibid.*, p. 224.

186. The Enigma of Hitler, 1938
187. The Sublime Moment, 1938

186. Oil on canvas
51.2 × 79.3 cm
$20^{1/8} \times 31^{1/4}$ in.
Madrid, Museo Nacional,
Centro de Arte Reina Sofía

187. Oil on canvas
38 × 47 cm
$15 \times 18^{1/2}$ in.
Stuttgart, Staatsgalerie Stuttgart

The Sublime Moment and *The Enigma of Hitler* premiered together in New York, at Dalí's enormously popular 1939 exhibition at the Julien Levy Gallery. In both paintings, an olive branch supporting a large telephone receiver looms over a soup dish set amidst one of the artist's emblematic Catalan landscapes, while the telephone's earpiece transforms into what might be read as a lobster claw or perhaps a bite. *The Sublime Moment*'s "soft" extension of the dish—crowned with a snail and supported by a crutch—exudes a liquid threatening to drip into the two fried eggs beneath it. This unidentified secretion reappears in *The Enigma of Hitler*, where it emanates from the telephone's mouthpiece, while the *Sublime Moment*'s dilapidated dish becomes an ethereal gray umbrella mimicking the shape of a small bat hanging to its left; near the center of the plate, in lieu of fried eggs, is the small portrait of Hitler that gives the painting its title—a newspaper photo Dalí adroitly reproduced in paint.

Dalí's erotic fascination with Hitler was first revealed in a 1933 letter to André Breton suggesting the "Hitler phenomenon" be considered in the realm of Surrealist discourse.[1] At his ensuing Surrealist "trial" in February 1934, he (temporarily) convinced his fellow-Surrealists that his scandalous allusions to political figures were innocuous, as his interest was purely paranoiac and apolitical. He similarly contended *The Enigma of Hitler*—painted during a four-month stay at Coco Chanel's villa La Pausa in Roquebrune, Cap Martin—was void of any "conspicuous political significance," admitting only that it had been inspired by a dream sequence surrounding the Munich Agreement: the pact on September 29, 1938, in which France and Britain attempted to appease Hitler, but only succeeded in furthering German control in Europe.[2] Notwithstanding Dalí's apolitical claims and his work's paranoiac precedent, the telephone with its cord cut, in combination with *The Enigma of Hitler*'s impending tempest and the artist's description in *The Secret Life* of Prime Minister Neville Chamberlain's batlike umbrella as "sinister" and "extremely anguishing," has been read to infer Dalí's exasperation with Chamberlain's passive attitude towards Hitler and the failure of "telephone diplomacy."[3] Although this interpretation is consistent with the politically-active British Surrealists, who marched in protest against Chamberlain in 1938, it is neither consistent with Dalí's avowal that his "Hitlerian vertigo contained nothing of a political nature," nor does it account for the number of paintings he exhibited in 1939—such as *The Sublime Moment* and *Imperial Violets* (1938, cat. 133)—that share similar motifs without conspicuous political allusions.[4] More revealing for both, perhaps, is his 1973 profession that the *Enigma of Hitler*, "brought together all the elements of my ecstasy."[5] Indeed, both *The*

Sublime Moment and *The Enigma of Hitler* are compendia of Dalí's 1930s paranoiac motifs—the *Angelus*, *Les Chants de Maldoror*, the eroticism of Hitler and the myth of William Tell—, with neither taking any clear ideological stance.

Few "elements of ecstasy" are as enduring in Dalí's corpus as the peasant couple from Jean-François Millet's painting *The Angelus* (1859), which influenced, among other works, his 1933-34 illustrations of Lautréamont's *Les Chants de Maldoror*.[6] Proclaiming the *Angelus* to be the most capable means of illustrating *Maldoror*, Dalí paired Lautréamont's famous umbrella and sewing machine with the masculine and feminine figures of the *Angelus*, respectively.[7] "The umbrella," Dalí writes, "… besides its flagrant and well-known symbol of erection, can be none other than the masculine figure in the Angelus… Facing him, the sewing machine, feminine symbol known to all…"[8] This metaphoric representation can be grafted onto *The Enigma of Hitler* as well: Chamberlain's phallic umbrella, nearly identical to that appearing in Dalí's 1945 *Homage to Lautréamont*, hangs limply from an olive branch with flaccidity reminiscent of the famous soft watch draped over an almost identical branch in *The Persistence of Memory* (1931). This sense of impotence, mirroring the castration anxiety he famously interpreted in *The Angelus*, may well have struck Dalí as "anguishing"—indeed, probably more so than Chamberlain's political weakness, for which the limp umbrella is nonetheless a poignant symbol.

Dalí further equates the umbrella with the bat: a source of distress identified in *The Secret Life* with one of his earliest "memories" of putrefaction, when his twenty-year-old cousin shot a bat in the wing and gave the wounded animal to the five year-old Dalí; the next morning, he awoke to find the tortured bat half-alive but "bristling with frenzied ants"; overcome with pity, he took up the bat to kiss it, but instead ferociously bit into the hapless creature—a sadistic act worthy of Maldoror that may inform *The Enigma of Hitler*'s second bat, perched birdlike on the right edge of the dish and consuming an amorphous "soft-oyster"—the only apparently edible item on the plate save five boiled beans.[9] Certainly, Dalí recognized the bat's Maldororean potential, evidenced by his unfinished *Landscape After de Chirico* (1935-38), which pairs bats with Lautréamont's exhaustingly overdetermined sewing machine. *The Sublime Moment*'s downward-hanging plate buttressed by a crutch evokes similar putrescence; like the bat, the crutch is also a symbol from Dalí's childhood, described in *The Secret Life* as a fetishistic scepter that, after being contaminated by a deceased hedgehog, "transformed into a frightful object synonymous with death."[10]

While the masculine component of the *Angelus*

186

couple is relatively easy to construe in *The Enigma of Hitler* through the overtly phallic umbrella, the female component, Hitler on the plate, is traced implicitly through Dalí's gendered associations tied to shellfish: the "soft oyster" consumed by the bat, and its "hard" counterpart on the lower right side of the dish. Declaring all "self-respecting food" preserves its form, Dalí writes in *The Secret Life* that, having attained the basic requirement of structure (e.g., shell, bone, etc.), "nothing can be regarded as too slimy, gelatinous, quivering, indeterminate or ignominious to be *desired*, whether it be the sublime viscosities of a fish-eye, the slithery cerebellum of a bird, the spermatozoal marrow of a bone or the *soft and swampy opulence of an oyster*."[11] This gustatory praise of the "hard" that protects the edible, desirable "soft" informs, in *The Sublime Moment*, the fried eggs (extracted from eggshells), as well as the snails, which had appeared earlier that year as part of his *Rainy Taxi*, exhibited at the Exposition intérnationale du surréalisme at the Galerie des Beaux-Arts. *The Enigma of Hitler* takes the analogy further, depicting alongside the aphrodisiacal oysters the most idiosyncratic of his "armored" desiderata: the feminized projection of the Führer himself. Recalling Dalí's embodiment of Nazism as a corpulent wet-nurse in *The Weaning of Furniture Nutrition* (1934), who appears also in the background of *The Enigma of Hitler*, he tells André Parinaud: "[Hitler's] fat back, especially when I saw him appear in the uniform with Sam Browne belt and shoulder straps that tightly held in his flesh, aroused in me a delicious gustatory thrill originating in the mouth and affording me a Wagnerian ecstasy. I often dreamed of Hitler as [of] a woman. His flesh, which I had imagined whiter

Fig. 1. Costume for the "Dream of Venus" pavilion; photo by Horst P. Horst

than white, ravished me."[12] Thus, Dalí describes his Hitlerian ecstasy as predominantly oral, and *The Enigma of Hitler* is appropriately saturated with images of ingestion. In an analogy that would become popularized in later critical studies of fascism, Dalí links the oyster's shell with the Nazi uniform: both protect succulent, feminized, *desirable* flesh beneath an armored exterior.[13]

The oyster's minor role in Dalí's "Dream of Venus," a Surrealist Pavilion Julien Levy spearheaded for the 1939 New York World's Fair following the success of the 1939 exhibition, re-enforces this feminine representation of the Führer. For this project, Dalí decorated his "mermaids" with phallic lobsters and jewelry made from mussels. One piece—a beaded necklace attached to six large hooks piercing mussels (fig. 1)—may inform the bat's sensuous "suckling" in *The Enigma of Hitler*, given the metaphor resulting from the mussels' proximity to the model's breasts. This consumption—in the legacy of his 1937 *Cannibalism of Objects* (fig. 2)—evidences Dalí's yearning to make edible that which is desired.[14] Paired in *The Enigma of Hitler* with an aphrodisiacal oyster analogous to a female breast, then, Hitler is presented not only as female (i.e., a soft female breast), but also *so erotically desired as to be consumed*.

If one is persuaded the umbrella may connote Chamberlain in a more paranoiac than political rapport with the portrait of Hitler, what is one to make of the oversized telephone receiver? Like oysters and umbrellas, it also feature prominently in Dalí's 1939 "Dream of Venus" décor and, although one critic cleverly described the space as "hung with enough umbrellas to recapture the spirit of Munich," in no circumstance did Dalí either present a strong opinion on the Munich Agreement or explicate the telephone's significance.[15] Instead, he writes several lines on the telephone in *The Secret Life* that eschew political in favor of gustatory associations:

"I do not understand why, when I ask for a grilled lobster in a restaurant, I am never served a cooked telephone; I do not understand why champagne is always chilled and why on the other hand telephones, which are habitually so frightfully warm and disagreeably sticky to the touch, are not also put in silver buckets with crushed ice around them."[16]

That the telephone features in so many works without any conspicuous connection to Hitler, yet almost always in connection to food, suggests its significance is beyond the common interpretation of "telephone diplomacy." In light of the themes of predation that have been discussed, it may, in part, be a veiled allusion to the Fascist army's 1936 victory in Toledo. On July 21, 1936, after three days of street battles against leftist Republicans, about 1,000 Civil and Assault Guards, Falangists, and infantry cadets took hostages and retreated into the

Fig. 2. Salvador Dalí,
*Cannibalism of Objects – Woman's
Head with Shoe*, 1937
Private collection

Alcázar, a historic Spanish fortress occupied by the Military Academy. Republican forces besieged the Alcázar for nearly two months, but the Nationalists, under the command of Colonel José Moscardó, the Commandant of the Academy and commander of the Nationalist garrison, staunchly resisted. On September 28, 1936, Nationalist reinforcements arrived to Toledo and, on September 29, successfully rescued the Alcázar defenders. One of the more colorful anecdotes to come out of the battle was that Moscardó had received a phone call from Republican forces relaying that they had captured his son, Luis, and hoped to use him as a hostage to extort the Nationalists' surrender. Moscardó allegedly condemned his son to death by firing squad rather than concede to the Republicans' demands.

The Alcázar became a powerful propagandist tool under the victorious Fascist regime, and Moscardó's famous phone call became a symbol of the valor of the Spanish state.[17] The 1939 re-edition of Henri Massis and Robert Brasillach's 1936 book *Les cadets de l'Alcazar* not only opened with the legend of Moscardó and his famous phone call, but also included photographs of the celebrated telephone, which was put in a special position of prominence after the Alcázar was reconstructed as a memorial in 1944.[18] Although one cannot suggest that the telephone in Dalí's work—debuting (coincidentally?) with the 1936 *Lobster Telephone*—is invariably a reference to Moscardó's celebrated conversation, particularly as the telephone did not achieve its position of reverence until after the War, Dalí would have undoubtedly appreciated the Colonel's sacrifice, which echoed one of his favorite tropes, the myth of William Tell, which he identified with other circumstances of the son being "conquered" by the father (e.g., Saturn devouring his children, God the Father sacrificing Jesus Christ, Abraham's near-sacrifice of Isaac).[19] In *The Secret Life*, Dalí posits that his images of food paired with the William Tell myth are, like Abraham's ram and William Tell's apple, meant as the "expiatory victims of abortive sacrifice": food is presented as a distraction, keeping the anthropophagous father-figure from devouring his son (e.g., the raw steak in *The Enigma of William Tell*, 1933).[20] Dalí's recurring juxtaposition of the telephone with food, then, might suggest his regard for Moscardó as a cannibalistic William Tell, and the accompanying food (e.g., oysters, grilled fish, and eggs) as attempts to entice the Colonel from his infanticide. This is especially poignant *a propos* oysters, which are commonly served raw: "Ram and apple, like the sons of Saturn and Jesus Christ on the cross, were raw—this being the prime condition for the cannibalistic sacrifice."[21] Whilst enforcing Hitler's femininity with regards to the umbrella in *The Enigma of Hitler*, then, the oyster may also be in dialogue with the telephone as a substitute victim.

Just as Dalí's rendering of Hitler does not implicate him as a Nazi sympathizer, however, so the telephone, if read as a Spanish Nationalist symbol, should not necessarily imply his admiration for the "New Spain" developing under Franco so much as a variant on the William Tell narrative. "For Dalí, [Surrealist activity] was inevitably an end to itself and therefore in some way inoculated against the real world. Hitler was not in his view different in kind from William Tell or his nurse, because all that mattered was their existence in his mind as dream subjects."[22] Although these paintings arguably present major world events—Hitler, Chamberlain and the Spanish Civil War—literally "on the same plate," Dalí's position remains detached: in his words, "Dalínian and only Dalínian!"[23] E.H.K.

[1] Salvador Dalí, "Lettre à André Breton" (Paris: Galerie Pierre-Colle), exh. cat. (June 11, 1933). Published in English in *The Collected Writings of Salvador Dalí*, ed., trans. Haim Finkelstein (Cambridge: Cambridge University Press, 1998), p. 249.

[2] Salvador Dalí, "The Myth of William Tell" (1952). From a manuscript in the collection of the Humanities Research Center. Austin, Texas. Published in *La Table Ronde*, no. 55, July 1952, pp. 21-28. Published in English in *The Tragic Myth of Millet's Angelus* (St. Petersburg: Salvador Dalí Museum, 1986), pp. 197.

[3] Salvador Dalí, *The Secret Life of Salvador Dalí*, trans. Haakon M. Chevalier (New York: Dover Publications, Inc., 1993), p. 371. Originally published by New York: Dial Press, 1942.

[4] Dalí, "The Myth of William Tell," pp. 193.

[5] André Parinaud, *The Unspeakable Confessions of Sal-*

vador Dalí, trans. Harold J. Salemson (New York: William Morrow and Company, Inc., 1976), p. 125. Originally published in French as *Comment on devient Dalí* (Paris: Éditions Robert Laffont, 1973).

[6] See David Lomas, *The Haunted Self* (New Haven: Yale University Press, 2000).

[7] Salvador Dalí, "Explanation of an Illustration from the *Chants de Maldoror*'" (1934). Translated and published in English as an appendix to Salvador Dalí, *The Tragic Myth of Millet's Angelus* (St. Petersburg: Salvador Dalí Museum, 1986), p. 151.

[8] *Ibid*., p. 156. As David Lomas has criticized, this gendering of the Maldoror couple à la *The Angelus* is potentially hetero-centric; indeed, Lautréamont's original reference is potentially homo-erotic, as it is, in fact, a male's (Maldoror's) longing description of another male (Mervyn).

[9] Dalí, *The Secret Life of Salvador Dalí*, p. 14.

[10] *Ibid*., pp. 89-90, 111.

[11] *Ibid*., p. 11. Emphases added.

[12] Parinaud, p. 153.

[13] See, for example, Klaus Theweleit, *Männerphantasien, vol. I, Frauen, Fluten, Körper, Geschichte* and *Männerphantasien, vol. II, Männerkörper: Zur Psychoanalyse des weissen Terrors* (Verlog Roter Stern, 1977 and 1978).

[14] Also known as *Woman's Head with Shoe*. See also Pierre Roumeguère, "Cannibalism and Aesthetic," preface to Max Gérard, *Dalí... Dalí... Dalí...* (New York: Harry N. Abrams, 1974). Originally published in French by Draeger (Paris), 1974. Note also Dalí's enthusiasm for holography in 1971, which, he said, would allow him to accomplish one of his heart's "dearest desires": to eat the adored being Gala' in Parinaud, p. 352.

[15] "Freud + Minsky = Dalí," *Art Digest* 13 (July 1, 1939), p. 12.

[16] Dalí, *The Secret Life of Salvador Dalí*, p. 271.

[17] See Marko Daniel, *Art and Propaganda: The Battle for Cultural Property in the Spanish Civil War*. Unpublished PhD, University of Essex (Colchester, England), 1999.

[18] Henri Massis and Robert Brasillach, *Les cadets de l'Alcazar* (Paris: Plon, 1936, 1939).

[19] See Dawn Ades, "Dalí and the Myth of William Tell," *Salvador Dalí: A Mythology* (London: Tate Gallery Publishing, 1998).

[20] Dalí, *The Secret Life of Salvador Dalí*, p. 319.

[21] *Ibid*.. The William Tell myth may have struck Dalí as particularly "agonizing" during the period in which he executed *The Enigma of Hitler*, as it evoked his own paternal relationship—ruptured in 1929 following his entry into the Surrealists and his execution of the 1929 painting, *Sometimes I Spit With Pleasure on the Portrait of My Mother*, and to remain unreconciled until his return to Catalonia in 1940.

[22] Dawn Ades, *Dalí* (London: Thames and Hudson, Ltd., 1982), p. 108.

[23] Dalí, *The Secret Life of Salvador Dalí*, p. 360.

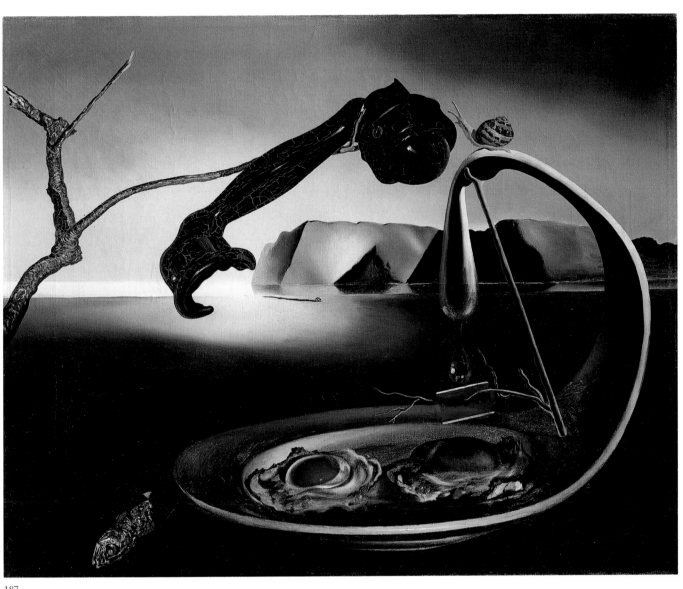

187

188. Two Pieces of Bread Expressing the Sentiment of Love, 1940

188. Oil on canvas
81.3 × 100.3 cm
32 × 39$^{1/2}$ in.
Figueres, Fundació
Gala-Salvador Dalí,
gift of Dalí to the Spanish State

189. Landscape with Telephones on a Plate, 1939

189. Oil on canvas
22 × 30 cm
8 5/8 × 11 3/4 in.
Private collection

190. Imperial Violets, 1938

190. Oil on canvas
100 × 142.5 cm
39³/8 × 56¹/8 in.
Arango Collection

This painting belongs to a series of works featuring black telephones that were inspired by dreams occurring at the time of the ill-fated Munich Agreement of September 29, 1938, the treaty that led British Prime Minister Neville Chamberlain to deliver the empty promise of "peace in our time." The telephone receiver is a direct allusion to Chamberlain's widely reported phone calls to Adolf Hitler in 1938, which culminated in the short-lived Munich Agreement. However, the pervading sense of melancholy and despair that characterizes these rather gloomy canvases anticipates the breakdown of dialogue between the Great Powers and the inevitability of global warfare. The contemporary political significance of the paintings is supported by *The Enigma of Hitler* (cat. 186), perhaps the best known and most controversial work from this series, which depicts a battered, oozing telephone suspended over a plate that contains a small, crumpled and torn photograph of the Führer, while a shadowy umbrella, clearly an allusion to Chamberlain, hangs on the right, like a bat suspended upside-down.

The telephone was a familiar fetishistic object in Dalí's oeuvre by the late 1930s, but its reoccurrence in these paintings relates to the artist's current preoccupation with the impending threat of world war, signified by the disconnected receiver in *Imperial Violets*, where it suggests the probable outcome of the conversations between Chamberlain and Hitler. Like other works in the series, the painting depicts a black telephone in a dish against a dark mountainous landscape background, which also frames a boat and white house in the middle distance that can be identified as the Dalí family home on the beach of Llaner in Cadaqués. The partially-eaten grilled sardines (with their long association with Spanish cuisine) to the right of the plate are also symbolic of Dalí's private anxieties at this time, while the man pulling the child across the flat expanse of barren land probably represents his false childhood memory of his father forcibly taking the young Salvador to school.

The enigmatic title has been assumed to refer to Hitler's imperial aspirations, as well as Chamberlain's false hopes of a peaceful outcome to the looming crisis over Nazi Germany's expansionist policies, since the violet is a symbol of devotion. However, Dalí later recalled that the title came from a French film he saw in Monte Carlo, while staying with Coco Chanel at her villa in Roquebrune, Cap Martin, in the winter of 1938-39.[1] The film in question is *Violettes impériales*, directed in 1923 by Henry Russell, which tells the story of Violetta, played by Raquel Meller, a Seville flower seller and woman of the streets, who attempts to steal from a wealthy woman, whom we later find out is Eugenie de Montijo, the fiancée of the French Emperor Napoleon III. The noblewoman, played by Suzanne Bianchetti, forgives the flower girl her indiscretion and the two become close friends as their lives become forever connected in the court life, romance, and political intrigue that take place during the rest of the film. The lavish Spanish costumes and scenery may have led Dalí to connect this film with his recently completed work, although a more likely solution is Henry Russell's innovative use of toning throughout the film, including an unusual green tint for the night scenes that resembles the somber tonal range of the artist's painting.

Imperial Violets was first shown in February 1939 at 88, Rue de l'Université in Paris, in a private viewing of works that were about to be shipped to New York for Dalí's exhibition at the Julien Levy Gallery.[2] Following the close of the New York exhibition in April 1939, the painting entered the collection of Edward James, in accordance with his contractual arrangement with the artist. In 1941, the English collector donated *Imperial Violets* to the Museum of Modern Art in New York, in time for the work to be included in their Dalí retrospective exhibition, which opened on November 18, 1941. In the early 1970s the painting was de-accessioned by the Museum of Modern Art, which by that time had amassed an impressive collection of the artist's key works, including *Illuminated Pleasures*, of 1929, *The Persistence of Memory*, of 1931, and *The Angelus of Gala*, of 1935. The painting was subsequently sold at auction in New York in October 1975, and has remained in private hands ever since.[3] M.R.T.

[1] Exhibition catalogue, *Dalí* (Rotterdam: Boijmans Van Beuningen Museum, November 21, 1970-January 10, 1971), catalogue number 64, n.p.
[2] Ian Gibson, *The Shameful Life of Salvador Dalí* (London: Faber and Faber, 1997), p. 387.
[3] Sotheby Parke Bernet, New York, *Important Impressionist and Modern Paintings and Sculptures*, October 22, 1975, lot. 163.

191. The Dream of Venus, 1939

191. Oil on canvas on Masonite
(four panels)
240 × 480 cm
94 1/2 × 188 7/8 in.
(the whole composition)
240 × 120 cm (each panel)
Hiroshima (Japan), Hiroshima
Prefectural Art Museum

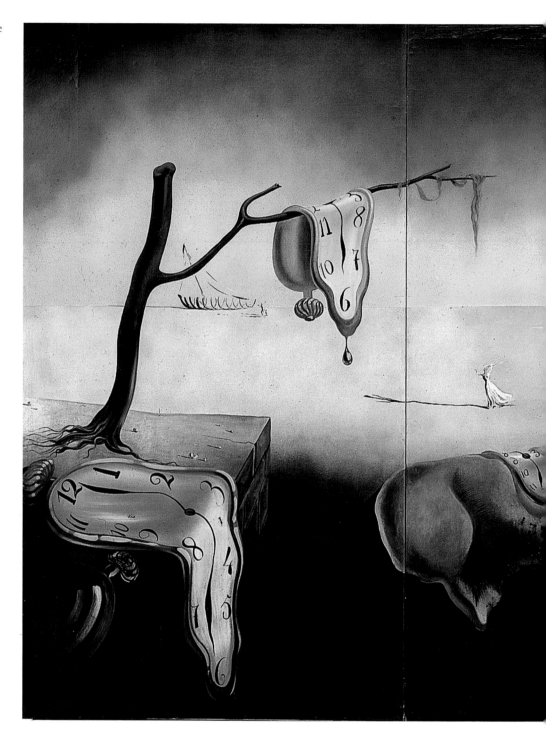

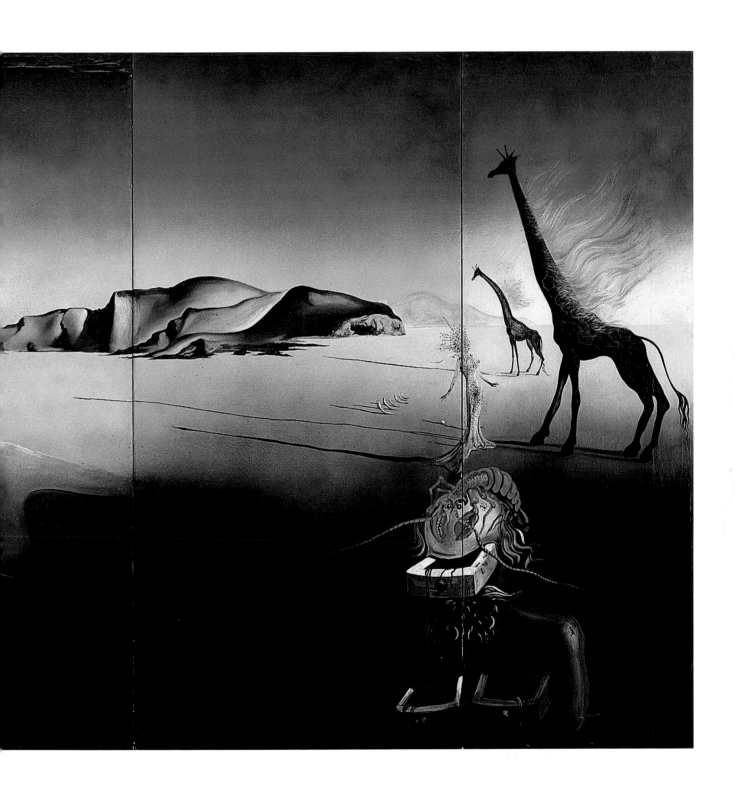

192. Design for set curtain for "Bacchanale," 1939
193. Study for "Bacchanale," 1938-39

192. Oil on canvas
46 × 61 cm
18¹/8 × 24 in.
Private collection

193. Pencil on cardboard
35.3 × 23 cm
13⁷/8 × 9¹/8 in.
Figueres, Fundació
Gala-Salvador Dalí

PARANOIA IN THE BALLET

Above is a scene from Salvadore Dalí's "Bacchanale," a "paranoiac" version of the Venusberg scene from "Tannhauser" which the Ballet Russe will present in San Francisco this week. Lower (left) is Marina Franca as an actress in the ballet "Ghost Town." On the right is Leonide Massine, director of the company and its greatest dancer.

Fig. 1. A review of the ballet *Bacchanale* with the photographs of a scene, a dancer, and the choreographer Léonide Massine

Bacchanale is the first of nine ballets designed by Dalí to be produced in New York from 1939 to 1949. It was also his first set design for Les Ballets Russes de Monte Carlo. Dalí was staying with Gabrielle Chanel in Roquebrune when he met Léonide Massine's ballet company that was to leave Europe just before the war. He was presumably intrigued by the idea of working for Les Ballets Russes—as had Joan Miró, Juan Gris, Pablo Picasso and many others before him.

Bacchanale received its world première as the middle part of a triple bill at the Metropolitan Opera House. It was preceded by *Rouge et Noir*, with designs by Matisse, and followed by *La Boutique Fantasque*, designed by Derain. The production went subsequently on an extensive tour throughout the US.

Dalí chose the *Venusberg* music from Wagner's *Tannhäuser* opera as the summit, as he expressed it, of Wagner's theatrical ascension. The scenario concerns Ludwig II, the King of Bavaria, and his delusion that he embodied Wagnerian characters. The action is mounted on a set dominated by the figure of a swan, from which enter several of the dancers, and notably Venus, with above it the temple from Raphael's *Betrothal of the Virgin* (fig. 2) and a road which, according to Dalí, leads not only to but also from Rome. The other characters are the Knight of Death, in the form of an unopened umbrella, Lola Montez, Sacher Masoch and his wife, the Three Graces, and various nymphs, fauns, cupids, bacchantes and satyrs.

In the program Dalí gives an account of his ballet: "The setting represents Mount Venus (the Venusberg near Eisenach), the background showing Salvador Dalí's birthplace, the Ampurdàn plain, in the center of which rises the temple as seen in *The Betrothal of the Virgin* by Raphael. Thus the Italian paving leading to the temple is laid on Catalonian soil.

'In the Tannhauser libretto Wagner mingles symbol and psychology, the fantastic and the real, with the scenic action.' (Larousse Dictionary)

'I have adopted this formula for my own scenario, substituting for 'psychology' the term 'psychoanalysis' which was unknown in Wagner's epoch. – Salvador Dalí.

The *Tannhauser Bacchanale* is shown here through the deliriously confused brain of Ludwig II of Bavaria who 'lived' all of Wagner's myths with such profound visual hyperesthesia as to verge on madness. As the real protagonist of the ballet, he identifies himself with those legendary heroes, and the plot represents the hallucinations and emotions he was prey to.

The opening chords of the overture evoke the departure of the pilgrims, and Louis in the form of Tannhauser approaches Venus. Blinded by the effulgent image, Louis flounders in the darkness of the most obscure of myths—Tobias and the Angel. Venus is metamorphosed into a fish, and the fish into a dragon. Louis lifts Lohengrin's sword and skewers the dragon. But this heroism proves a boomerang, for the entrails touch his eye-lid and his sight is further darkened by hypnagogic visions. At the supreme moment, wearing Lohengrin's helmet, Louis dies, his last vision being that of Leda tenderly embracing the swan (the classical symbol of heterosexual love). The object and subject of Louis's real death are present when his body is discovered: a parasol and the image of Lola Montez both scintillating like real skulls."

In a metaphorical text Dalí explains the intentions of his first ballet:

Geological foundations of VENUSBERG
I am writing this text in the shadow of the light of a little forest in Siberia, something similar to an illuminated clearing. It is Gala. (GALOUTCHKINETTA)
Perhaps, and without perhaps, every passing day makes me feel myself, so to speak, and this the moment to state, nailed to my own geology.
And precisely for this reason, if my feet have always touched, touch and will touch the earth of the Empordà plain (my birthplace, that of Christopher Columbus, the discoverer of America, Narcisse Monturiano, who manufactured the first submarine … not to mention others …) my brain and my eyes have always been attracted by mountains And of all mountains, that of Wagner produced the greatest effect upon me. And if it is true, clear as the day, that one perceives the mountains best only from the valley, that of Wagner, I assure you, can be clearly seen only from the Empordà plain, since Wagner is the apotheosis of Romanticism, and the Empordà is the most realistic valley in the world.
Wagner is so great, he has not yet ceased to grow, that is to say, none have as yet seen him. One knows of him only the music as it sounds in the real mountains, where, being too close, one can know it but through the murmur of cascades and the singing of nightingales, whom they train.
One thing is certain. Usually music requires, above and before all, not to be touched, but to be listened with closed eyes, the ears plunged in a half dream, and the eyes directed more inside than outside. Wagner, on the contrary, is one of the rare musicians who insists by the sound of trumpets to be seen as well as heard with both eyes and ears wide open to enchantment, since nobody before him had such a disorderly and grandiose passion for extra musical elements springing from his own heart. Nobody had a more complete idea of theatrical lyricism with its images, myths and make-believe, and this to such a point that we can affirm without fear of being mistaken: Wagner is not only a mountain of geological melodies, but also, and particularly, a real mountain of mythological images and hallucinations.

192

Fig. 2. Raphael, *Betrothal of the Virgin*, 1504
Milan, Pinacoteca di Brera

Fig. 3. *Drawing for "Bacchanale"* – *Ludwig II of Bavaria*, 1939
Private collection

A scene from "Bacchanale," controversial ballet designed by Surrealist Salvador Dali, is shown in rehearsal. Nini Theilade, as Venus, is shown talking with a knitting faun and boy.

Fig. 4. A scene of the ballet
Bacchanale

If Wagner is the most difficult mountain to be observed distinctly, not only due to the lyric vapor in which he so often drowns, but also because of his non prehensible morphology, the contours of Venusberg, one of the last mountains ascended by Wagner, are much more difficult to delimit. For it was in Venusberg that Wagner made a meeting for himself with the unique, real and substantial Bacchanal of the imagination.

For all these reasons have I chosen Venusberg as the summit of my first theatrical ascension.

You will see there what is seen in all other ballets: love, death, vice, virtue … all the usual and common happenings, etc.

You will also see the road passing through the grotto of Venusberg, the one that proves that all roads not only lead to Rome, but also serve for the return. You will see Louis II, Venus, Leda, the Swan, Sacher Masoch and his wife, Lola Montez …etc. You will see the Nordic and hunchbacked foresters, worth their weight in gold, since their humps are filled with real gold. Finally, you will see the Three Graces, with so many graces attached to their anatomies that it is incredible.

And all this and many other things will you see lighted by the rising sun of the latest particular sciences of our epoch, especially psychoanalysis. Thus, if I exalt and render actual Wagner's genius on the one side, I consider that on the other, I pay my tribute to Freud, who has permitted me to see Wagner. (Salvador Dalí, 1939)

A few years later Dalí recalls the making of *Bacchanale* in his *Secret Life* and in his *Dalí News*:

"As with everything else, my *Mad Tristan*, which was my best theatrical work, 'could not be played,' and became transformed into *Venusberg*, and *Venusberg* into the *Bacchanale*, which became its definite version. This was a ballet that I invented for the *Monte Carlo Russian Ballet*. I got along very well with Leonid Massine, who had been a hundred per cent Dalínian for a long time—it was precisely he who was predestined to do the choreography of the *Dance of the Crutches*. Prince Chervachidze, who with the Comte de Noailles is the purest representative of the authentic aristocracy of Europe, executed my stage sets with a professional conscience hardly deserved by our gimcrack modern epoch, always in a hurry and lacking of scrupulousness, in which everything is half done and badly done. I also had the good fortune to have Chanel take upon herself the designing of the costumes. Chanel worked on my show with a wholehearted enthusiasm and created the most luxurious costumes that have ever been conceived for the theater. She used real ermine, real jewels, and the gloves of Ludwig II of Bavaria were so heavily embroidered that we felt some anxiety as to whether the dancer would be able to dance with them.

But once more the work was to fail. The moment the war broke out the ballet company hurriedly left for America before Chanel and I had finished our work. In spite of the cables we sent to try to delay the performance, the *Bacchanale* appeared at the Metropolitan with improvised costumes, and without my having seen even a single rehearsal! Nevertheless it was, it appears, an immense success." (Salvador Dalí, *Secret Life*, 1942)

"I have never found in my life anything heavier and more difficult to stir than a choreograph. Nevertheless, I have already supported the weight of five ballets. "Bacchanale," with Wagners music, Apotheosis of the Crutches, Siren with the Head of a Fish, Louis II of Bavaria falling dead in the centre of four lugubrious umbrellas planted in the earth, and which, opening all four at a time synchronized to the collapse of the body, provoked the enthusiasm of the public. It was one of my quite good theatrical ideas. John Martin, critic of the New York Times liked "Bacchanale". I also, even though being in Paris at that time, I never saw it." (Salvador Dalí, *Dalí News,* no. 1, November 20, 1945)

"Little more than a series of impudent and spectacular surprises, a lot of oversophisticated nonsense" (John Martin, cit. in *Tribune Oakland*, 26th January 1940)

"However, if Dalí's treatment of the subject is two-fifth's artistry and three-fifths plain theatrical hokum, the amount of ingenuity and sheer creative energy that have gone into the making of both elements is sufficient to insure a diverting experience. Dalí has evolved a theatrical spectacle that is bold, preposterous, exciting and delightful by turns – but never dull. Occasionally it even manages to provide a fairly believable visual counterpart to Wagner." (Irving Holodin, *cit.* in *Tribune Oakland*, 26th January 1940)

"As a production affording entertainment, excitement, amusement, befuddlement, mystification and extraordinary cerebral exercise *Bacchanale* has no rival in the Ballet Russe's repertory. Its Freudian implications, freely suggested on stage, cross it off Junior's list. A forty-minute intermission, necessary to arranging the stage, almost crossed it off mine." (O. C., *New York Post*, November 10, 1939)
T.S.

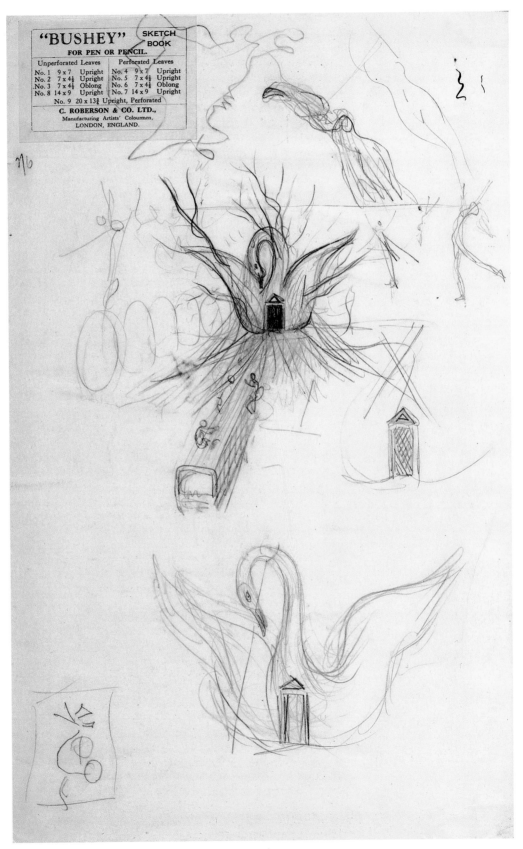

193

194. Book Transforming Itself into a Nude Woman, 1940

194. Oil on canvas
41.27 × 51 cm
16¹/4 × 20¹/8 in.
Private collection

This intense and enigmatic painting has not been publicly exhibited since the summer of 1941, when it was shown at the Arts Club of Chicago.[1] This Dalí exhibition had originated in New York several months earlier, where *Book Transforming Itself into a Nude Woman* was first shown in the artist's sixth (and final) exhibition at the Julien Levy Gallery.[2] The slump in the New York art market had forced Levy to travel this exhibition to venues in Chicago and Los Angeles in the hope of further sales. This "caravan of art," as Levy called it, ended in success when *Book transforming Itself into a Nude Woman* was purchased by a New York collector shortly after the close of the Chicago exhibition on June 14, 1941.[3] The painting did not travel to the Los Angeles venue of the exhibition, which opened in September 1941,[4] and subsequently disappeared from public view for several decades. As a result, the work was not included in the artist's *catalogue raisonné*, compiled by Robert Descharnes, or in any subsequent exhibition devoted to Dalí.

On view for the first time in over half a century, this compelling allegory of artistic creation and inspiration can tell us a great deal about Dalí's working methods and thematic interests in the work he produced shortly after the outbreak of the Second World War. As the evocative title suggests, the painting is dominated by a large open book, whose puffed up blank pages are in the process of metamorphosing into a reclining woman. The plump, pink-hued buttocks of this recumbent female figure are separated by the shiny blade of a knife. This sadistic detail recalls the artist's *Autumn Cannibalism*, of 1936, where human flesh is similarly sliced, cut and scooped by eating utensils. The book's Pygmalion-like metamorphosis from paper into the skin and bones of the "whole" woman is witnessed by an inquisitive, bald-headed figure, familiar from earlier paintings such as *Philosopher Illuminated by the Light of the Moon and the Setting Sun*, of 1939. The anatomy of this dark-skinned figure, who is supported by a crutch as he holds aloft a skull-like orb, echoes that of the woman-book, while his spherical dome rhymes delightfully with the large seashell on the right-hand side of the picture.

Elsewhere, another blank paged book lies open with a ribbonlike bookmark that falls limply off the foot of the page. This phallic symbol may have been derived from the flaccid red page marker that emerges from the yellow book in Giorgio de Chirico's *The Child's Brain*, of 1914 (fig. 2), a work of talismanic importance for the Surrealist group. Purchased by André Breton in 1919, de Chirico's painting was immediately hailed by Surrealists such as Breton and Max Ernst as a Freudian fantasy involving the artist's father. With his eyes closed, the pale-skinned father figure is shown naked from the waist up and appears to be masturbating from behind a half-drawn lace curtain. This reading is suggested by the hidden position of his hands and the expression of apparent erotic contentment on his ghostly visage, while the strategically placed thin strip of red fabric that emerges from the pages of the book in the immediate foreground has long been understood as a surrogate penis.

Dalí had made numerous references to *The Child's Brain* (see p. 138, fig. 2) in his paintings of the early 1930s, especially in his works on the theme of William Tell, which often contain scenes of his father, Salvador Dalí Cusí, involved in partially hidden sexual acts. The artist's father is also present in *Book Transforming Itself into a Whole Woman*, where he takes the form of the solitary inkwell holding a red pen that separates the two books. As Dalí's earlier paintings attest, the inkwell was indelibly linked in his mind with the profession of his father, who was a notary in Figueres. Although undoubtedly a symbol of parental authority, the inkwell, and the empty pages of the two books that frame it on either side, can also be understood as a reference to the mysterious and transformative power of artistic creation, while the idea of woman as the source of inspiration was a familiar trope in Dalí's work. The artist's unshakable faith in painting's ability to transcend the mundane realities of the outside world, as well as his personal conflicts, is never more apparent than in this work, painted "during these chaotic times of confusion, of rout and of growing demoralization," which had forced him to flee Europe for the safety of the United States.[5] Dalí and Gala arrived in New York on August 16, 1940, but shortly thereafter traveled to Virginia, where they stayed with Caresse Crosby at her Hampton Manor estate. This painting was probably completed at Hampton Manor, since it reflects the artist's joint literary and artistic aspirations of that time, when he was writing his memoirs, later published as *The Secret Life of Salvador Dalí*.[6] M.R.T.

[1] The "Salvador Dalí" exhibition at the Arts Club of Chicago ran from May 23-June 14, 1941. *Book Transforming Itself into a Nude Woman* was listed as no. 16 in the catalogue, just as it had been in New York.

[2] The exhibition at the Julien Levy Gallery, New York, was on display from April 22-May 19, 1941.

[3] Julien Levy, *Memoir of an Art Gallery* (New York: G. P. Putnam's Sons, 1977), p. 255.

[4] The final venue of the exhibition was the Dalzell Hatfield Galleries in the Ambassador Hotel, Los Angeles, which hosted a reduced version of the show from September 10-October 5, 1941.

[5] Felipe Jacinto (Salvador Dalí), "The Last Scandal of Salvador Dalí," (New York: Julien Levy Gallery, 1941), reprinted in Haim Finkelstein, ed., *The Collected Writings of Salvador Dalí* (Cambridge: Cambridge University Press, 1998), p. 337.

[6] Salvador Dalí, *The Secret Life of Salvador Dalí*, trans. Haakon M. Chevalier (New York: Dial Press, 1942).

195. Daddy Longlegs of the Evening – Hope! (including: soft airplane vomited by a cannon, ants, victory born of a broken wing, violoncello in white mastic, and an angel who weeps), 1940

195. Oil on canvas
40.5 × 50.8 cm
15⁷/8 × 20 in.
St. Petersburg (FL),
The Salvador Dalí Museum

Writing under the pseudonym of Felipe Jacinto in the catalog for Julien Levy's 1941 exhibition of his works, Salvador Dalí expressed his intention to "Find the unique attitude toward his destiny: to become classic," and also stated "Finished, finished, finished, a thousand times finished—the experimental period." The paintings in the exhibition—which included *Daddy Longlegs of the Evening – Hope!*—reflected this statement of intent, as they show a transition between the more personal "hand-painted dream photographs" of his Surrealist period, and begin to address important contemporary, historical, religious, and scientific issues found in his later classic period.

The title—taken from a French legend that says seeing a daddy longlegs at dusk brings good fortune—is the only optimistic element of the painting. The twilight that illuminates the composition instills an ominous sense of foreboding that illustrates Dalí's premonition of how the growing conflict in Europe will soon encompass the rest of the world. The spider of the title rests upon the face of the eviscerated figure—evoking the horrors of the recent Spanish Civil War—draped over the branches of the olive tree. The face is Dalí's own, which he referred to as *"the great masturbator,"* and is based upon a rock formation near his home in Port Lligat on Cap Creus called the Rock of Cullero. The included parenthetical title offers several clues to the meaning of the various elements found in the painting. The inkwells and the olive tree offer conflicting symbols of peace—the inkwells express the possibility of peace, but the cut branches indicate the opposite. The "soft airplane vomited by a cannon" as well as the Greek statue *The Winged Victory of Samothrace* (Musée du Louvre, Paris) "born of a broken wing," are indicators of the prominent presence that air power will play in modern warfare, as realized from its extensive use in the Spanish Civil War. The rearing horse, meanwhile, reminds us that cavalry was previously the dominant military force. Ants are a personal symbol used by Dalí to indicate decay, and the "violoncello in white mastic" alludes to the transitory nature of music—as well as to life itself. The "angel who weeps," with its hand covering its eyes in anguish, is one more sign of the inevitability, and subsequent horrors, of war.

With this painting—and its combination of contemporary, classical, and personal imagery and symbolism—Dalí has fully expressed his fears and views of the imminent escalation of the conflict in Europe and its effects on the world as a whole, and also entered a new phase in his artistic career. D.AR.

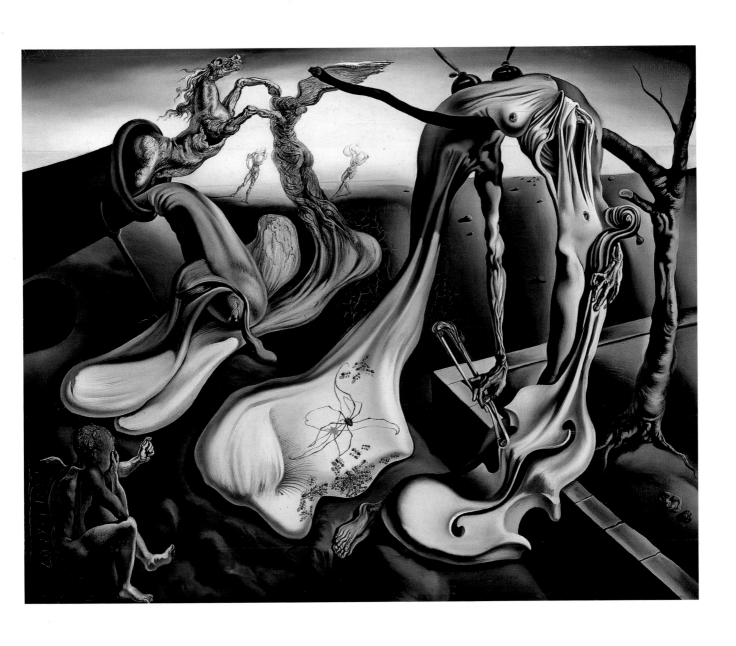

196. Slave Market with the Disappearing Bust of Voltaire, 1940

196. Oil on canvas
46.5 × 65.5 cm
18 1/4 × 25 3/4 in.
St. Petersburg (FL),
The Salvador Dalí Museum

This astonishing painting demonstrates the technical skill Dalí had achieved by 1940 in creating paranoiac-critical images, or optical illusions intended to undermine his audience's trust in the rational world. While in his paranoiac-critical image paintings of the late 1930s, such as *Impressions of Africa* and *Apparition of a Face in a Fruit Dish*, groupings of double images would only reveal themselves fully over time, *The Slave Market*'s power arises from the monumental singularity of its hallucinatory double image. Its immediacy achieves the systematized confusion the artist called for a decade earlier in his essay "L'Âne pourri".[1]

Painted at the Villa Flamberge in Arcachon, France, during the Nazi invasion of Paris, *The Slave Market* was first exhibited in April 1941 at the Julien Levy Gallery in New York, when the Dalís were exiled to the U.S. as they prepared for the artist's November retrospective at The Museum of Modern Art. The Julien Levy Gallery lists the title as *Slave Market (with Apparition of the Invisible Bust of Voltaire)*. Singled out for reproduction in the December 1, 1941 issue of *Art News*, it is described as "the best possible advance summing-up of Dalí's current retrospective…," revealing the artist's debt to Böcklin and to refined draftsmanship.[2]

Voltaire (1694-1778) is the celebrated 18th-century French skeptical philosopher, satirist, historian, who represented a dominant rational skepticism alien to Dalí's world. His rational skepticism made him an enemy of the Surrealists, and in Dalí's composition, Voltaire's threatening rationalism is associated with slavery, and the vision of Voltaire is dispelled as an apparition. In 1778, French sculptor Jean-Antoine Houdon (1741-1828) captured a variety of likenesses of the 84-year-old philosopher, who had just returned to France from exile and received a hero's reception. He became Houdon's most popular subject, and several versions exist of this celebrated *Bust of Voltaire* (1781).[3] It is not clear from which version Dalí worked: he made a black and white sketch that reduced the bust to a series of patterns, informing his oil painting.[4] In the painting, Dalí places an image of his wife on the left, leaning on a red tablecloth, her stare fixed on the bust of Voltaire. Before her gaze, Voltaire's bust both emerges from and dissolves into the chance arrangement of the central figures standing in the middle landscape. Two women in 17th-century Spanish dress stand in a slave market, and it is their features that create the illusion of Voltaire. The outline of Voltaire's head is formed by the negative space of the archlike opening in the ruined wall; with the women's heads for his eyes, their white collars form his upper cheeks and nose, the dark part of their clothing forms the shadows cast by his nose and cheeks, and the white ruffled sleeves of the right-hand woman form Voltaire's chin. The fruit dish also furthers the dual illusions: the apple in the center bowl appears to be the rear of the figure in the background, while the pear in the dish fuses into the hill in the distance.

Following Dalí's banishment from Surrealism, André Breton chose to criticize optical works like *The Slave Market* as trivial diversions, referring to them as "entertainments on the level of *crossword puzzles*."[5] Yet Dalí made several statements that indicate how this work furthers his critique of rationality, a goal still fundamental to Surrealism. In his *Unspeakable Confession*, Dalí says that, "The illustrious Monsieur de Voltaire possessed a peculiar kind of thought that was the most refined, most rational, most sterile, and misguided not only in France but in the entire world."[6] And in the *Secret Life*, the artist states, "Through her patient love, Gala protects me from the ironic and swarming world of slaves. Gala in my life destroys the image of Voltaire and every possible vestige of skepticism."[7] Far from being simply a visual game, *The Slave Market* uses optical phenomena to undermine the enslaving project of rationality identified with Voltaire and rational perception.

In *The Secret Life*, Dalí compares the perception of such double images with camouflage.[8] Since its ambiguous patterns successfully create figure and background confusion, *The Slave Market* has been used in various psychology textbooks and articles in order to explain how the mind processes perspective reversals. For example, in 1971, *Scientific American* used the painting to illustrate how human perception comprehends double images, arguing that each image can be seen independently, but they can never be seen simultaneously.[9] In the physical structure of the optical perception system, optical neurons can only reverse such images, but cannot hold them together. P.T.

[1] Salvador Dalí, "L'âne pourri," in *La Femme Visible*, July 1930; trans. H. Finkelstein, *The Collected Writings of Salvador Dalí* (Cambridge: Cambridge University Press, 1998), p. 223.
[2] "Prelude to Dalí: 'The Slave Market with the Disappearing Bust of Voltaire,'" *Art News*, vol. 40, December 1-14, 1941, p. 25.
[3] Versions include those in the Metropolitan Museum of Art, the National Gallery of Art, Washington, DC, and the Victoria & Albert Museum in London.
[4] Robert Lubar, *Dalí: The Salvador Dalí Museum Collection*, p. 123; Dawn Ades, *Dalí* (London: Thames and Hudson, 1982), p. 136; Christopher Masters, *Dalí* (London: Phaidon Press Ltd., 1995), p. 100.
[5] André Breton, "The Latest Tendencies in Surrealist Painting," *Surrealism and Painting*, trans. Simon Watson Taylor (New York: Icon Editions, 1965), pp. 146-147.
[6] Dalí, with André Parinaud, trans. Harold J. Salemson, *The Unspeakable Confessions of Salvador Dalí* (New York: Quill, 1981); quoted in Eric Shanes, *Dalí: The Masterworks* (New York: Portland House, 1990), p. 102.
[7] Dalí, *The Secret Life of Salvador Dalí*, trans. Haakon M. Chevalier (London: Vision Press Ltd., 1981); quoted in Robert Descharnes, *Salvador Dalí: The Work, The Man*, trans. E. R. Morse (New York: Harry N. Abrams, Inc., 1984), p. 267.
[8] Dalí, *Secret Life*, p. 69, footnote # 1.
[9] Fred Attneave, "Multistability in Perception," *Scientific American*, vol. 225, no. 6, December 1971, pp. 63-71.

197. Design for set curtain for "Labyrinth" I, 1941
198. Design for set curtain for "Labyrinth" II, 1941

197. Oil on canvas
39 × 64 cm
15³/8 × 25¹/8 in.
Private collection

198. Oil on canvas
64 × 79 cm
25¹/8 × 31¹/8 in.
Private collection

Labyrinth, Dalí's second ballet for Les Ballets Russes de Monte Carlo, was first performed at the Metropolitan Opera House in New York on October 8, 1941, with choreography by Léonide Massine. It went on a tour to Chicago, San Francisco and many other cities in the US.

Dalí's libretto is set to the music of Franz Schubert's 7ᵗʰ Symphony, and deals with the ancient myth of Theseus and Ariadne.

The maquette for the first backdrop, a colossal, naked bust with its head inclined that stood at the entrance to the labyrinth of cypresses, refers to Böcklin's *The Isle of the Dead* (see p. 164, fig. 1). This work became a Leitmotiv in Dalí's oeuvre after he saw it at the Metroplitan Museum in 1934. On the maquette for the second backdrop, inspired by the gloomy necrophile atmosphere of the Böcklin painting, Dalí depicts the other side of the island, with its living bodies decomposing into phosphorescent corpses and bones (*Javanese Mannequin*, 1934, cat. 134; *The Spectre of Sex Appeal*, 1934, cat. 135). A throne of bones in the landscape's center foreground is surrounded by metamorphosing cypresses, their long shadows recalling the late afternoon light in de Chirico's metaphysical paintings. We now see the colossal bust from the back on the distant horizon.

For a revival of *Labyrinth* at the Pittsburgh Ballet Theatre in 1942, Dalí designed a new backdrop for the final scene of Theseus fighting the Minotaure (Pittsburgh Museum of Art), referring to Picasso's treatment of the Minotaure theme in the *Suite Vollard*.

Fig. 1. Salvador Dalí, drop curtain for *Labyrinth*

"'Labyrinth,' which is the major production of the current Ballet Russes de Monte Carlo Season, is major from the scenic angle and definitely minor as to dance. The Surrealist sets and costumes by Salvador Dalí are more magnificent than any other ballet has disclosed so far. Strangely enough they are not silly, and although the opening scene reveals a tremendous cracked skull and a chest with a doorway in it, the effect is one of archaic grandeur. This is a perfect setting for the days of mythological Theseus and his Greek compatriots, and the second scene, where the hero fights the Minotaur, is one of macabre inventiveness, highlighting a throne of human skulls. As far as Dalí is concerned , 'Labyrinth' is something to see.

The dance aspect of this new work is another matter. Leonide Massine has attempted to create still another symphonic ballet, ... but Schubert and Dalí being two worlds apart, Massine succeeds in falling between them. His choreography is neither a stirring visualization of the Schubert score nor is it dramatic enough to cope with the overpowering splendor of the Dalí backgrounds. ... 'Labyrinth' is really a Dalí art exhibit." (Walter Terry, *New York Herald Tribune*, October 19, 1941)

Fig. 2. A scene of the ballet *Labyrinth*

"'Labyrinth,' the new 'Surrealist' ballet by Salvador Dalí ... is quite orthodox. Give the Devil a bad name and he gets a lot of free publicity. Take Dalí at its his own word that he is 'paranoical,' and he causes a popular uproar. ...

Dalí's paintings are quite 'academic' in their fundamentals and would not be out of place in the old Paris 'Salon of Bouguereau,' except for bizarre trimmings—and except they are better painted than the 'lovely' nudes of Bouguereau and his associates, who kept Cézanne, Van Gogh and their fellows out of the annual salon.

In the case of 'Labyrinth' the bizarre elements are not 'outlandish' to the habitual theatergoer. You have seen them all in 'Wizard of Oz' (stage and screen), Maeterlincks 'Blue Bird', Walt Disney's 'Fantasia' ...

All this does not detract from Dalí's triumph—and it is a triumph decidedly, just as are his paintings—but it does cut out the cheap excitement on which so much that is good in 'Surrealism' unfortunately rests in popular estimation.

Dalí has taken quite seriously the ancient Greek myth of Theseus slaying the Minotaur and finding his way back out by 'the thread of Ariadne.' Indeed he has made of it a social preachment, a bit obvious—but then the Greeks themselves, in their charming tales of gods, monsters and heroes, were obvious. ...

'Labyrinth' is a gorgeous spectacle, seethingly alive in its settings, gay and fantastic in its costuming, and thrilling in its dancing ...

In the blending and harmonizing of vivid and traditionally 'clashing' colors in costuming and setting, the same skill is exerted and the same satisfactory result obtained as in Dalí's paintings. 'Labyrinth' is not difficult as a whole, any more than in its elements—the music of Schubert, the tale of Theseus and Ariadne, and the eye-filling effects that would not be out of place in an ancient Italian or French masque festival or a modern *mardi gras*." (C.J. Bulliet, *News*, Chicago, December 29, 1941)

197

Fig. 3. Salvador Dalí, *Study for a backdrop of "Labyrinth" – Theseus Fighting the Minotaure*, 1942 Figueres, Fundació Gala-Salvador Dalí

"Boiled lobsters played no part in the costuming, ballerinas posed without benefit of crutches, and such umbrellas as the house may have held were all in the check room. For with 'Labyrinth' Dalí asserts his love of tradition, and the book he has provided for the ballet interprets the ancient Greek myth of Theseus, Ariadne's thread, and the slaying of the Minotaur as the search of the modern world for a return to the solid ground of established things, intellectually, spiritually and esthetically. When Salvador Dalí begins to talk about tradition he reminds one a little of the dusky preacher who, when asked to define the difference between orthodoxy and heterodoxy, replied, 'Orthodoxy is my doxy, heterodoxy is your doxy.'

Heterodoxy has been the Spanish artist's doxy in more senses than one for a good long time, and when he goes orthodox, at least in 'Labyrinth' some of the things he does best are put aside. The incredible fantasy, the bewildering fertility of strange and odd and sinister ideas that accounted for the fascination of his older ballet 'Bacchanal' are largely absent from this new piece. Perhaps when one becomes better acquainted with it, classical ideas of equal value will become apparent. On first contact one is rather inclined to feel that although tradition can be the foremost challenge and spur to the creative imagination, it can also be the excuse for continuing to do the same old business at the same old stand. Dalí's backdrops, with the characteristic anthropomorphic architecture, clouds and mountains, are very beautifully painted, and his costumes fill the stage with color, even though a few of them seem to have been held over from the two-bit peep show called 'A Dream of Venus' which he concocted for the New York Fair." (Alfred Frankenstein, *San Francisco Chronicle,* January 28, 1942)

"My ballet *Labyrinth*, with Schumann's music, [was too] confused and improvised, notwithstanding the sensational costume of a cock. John Martin did not like it. Neither did I." (Salvador Dalí, *Dalí News,* no. 1, November 20, 1945)

"The fact becomes clear. Dalí needs a stage with greater urgency than he needs an art gallery. His surrealism (which framed for the wall, has long since settled into formula), thrives in wide open spaces. There its sophistication, no longer just a well-memorized *dernier cri,* acquires an effect of preciosity that is in a sense monumental." (*The New York Sunday Times*, November 5, 1945)

In 1973, Dalí installs a copy of the set curtain with the colossal bust on the former stage of his Teatro-Museo in Figueres. T.S.

198

199. Ruin with Head of Medusa and Landscape (dedicated to Mrs. Chase), 1941

199. Oil on cavas
36 × 25.4 cm
14 1/8 × 10 in.
Madrid, Juan Abelló Collection

200. Soft Self-portrait with Fried Bacon, 1941

200. Oil on cavas
61.3 × 50.8 cm
24¹/8 × 20 in.
Figueres, Fundació
Gala-Salvador Dalí

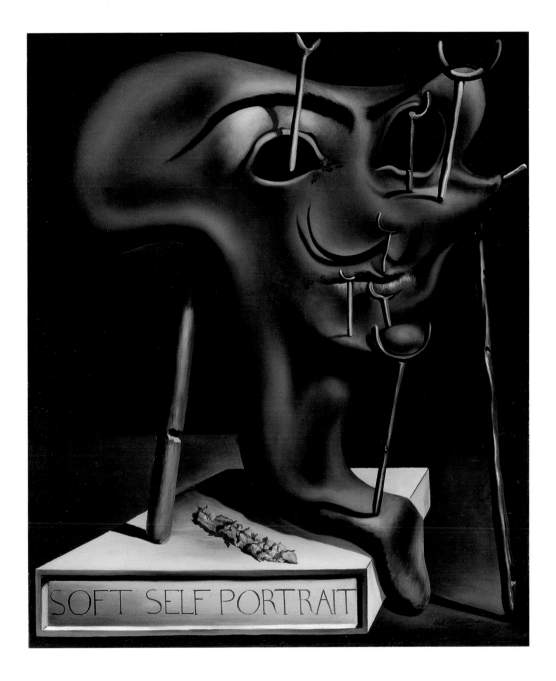

SOFT SELF PORTRAIT

201. Woman with Cap, 1934
202. Surrealist Animal, 1934
203. Soft Watch Unflated, 1934
204. Artist Painting à la Dürer, 1934

201. Ink on paper
22 × 16.5 cm
8$^{5/8}$ × 6$^{1/2}$ in.
Barcelona, Private collection

202. Ink on paper
9 × 9 cm
3$^{1/2}$ × 3$^{1/2}$ in.
Barcelona, Private collection

 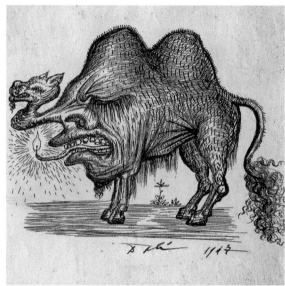

203. Ink on paper
9 × 9 cm
3$^{1/2}$ × 3$^{1/2}$ in.
Barcelona, Private collection

204. Ink on paper
22 × 30 cm
8$^{5/8}$ × 11$^{3/4}$ in.
Barcelona, Private collection

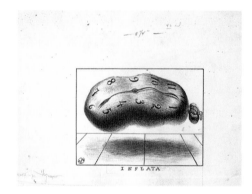 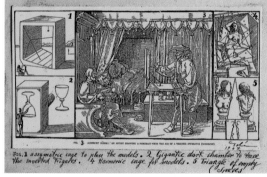

205. Sketch (tree, well, turtle-telephone), 1949

205. Ink on paper
28 × 35 cm
11 × 13³/4 in.
Mexico, JAPS Collection

206. Dream Caused by the Flight of a Bee around a Pomegranate, One Second before Awakening, 1944

206. Oil on canvas
51 × 41 cm
20$^{1/8}$ × 16$^{1/8}$ in.
Madrid, Museo
Thyssen-Bornemisza

Fig. 1. Detail of the left-hand panel of Hieronymus Bosch's *Temptation of Saint Anthony*, ca. 1501 Lisbon, Museu Nacional de Arte Antiga

In one of Dalí's best-known works from the post-Second World War era, a reclining nude hovers above one of the flat rocks at Port Lligat that in turn floats upon the Mediterranean Sea. This state of immobility and suspended animation can be related to the artist's newfound interest in nuclear fission and atomic energy, which had replaced his earlier fascination with Freudian psychoanalysis. As the title of this painting suggests, however, dream imagery was still at the core of his esthetics, as demonstrated by the alarming cavalcade of ferocious creatures and dangerous weapons that threaten the sleeping female figure. In a chainlike succession of images, a pomegranate bursts open to release a giant red snapper that in turn disgorges two raging tigers, whose leaping forms were derived from a Ringling Bros. and Barnum-Bailey, circus poster.[1] Closest to the gravity-defying female nude is a bayoneted rifle that is about to pierce her arm, while in the middle ground, near the horizon, an elephant carrying an obelisk on its back strides across the brilliant blue sea on stilted legs. This hybrid creature, a variation on Bernini's elephant-monument, was for Dalí a symbol of war and destruction, and its presence in this painting helps to convey a mood of terror and confusion appropriate for such a nightmarish vision. The disconcerting image of an enormous fish spewing forth a pair of leaping tigers appears to have been directly inspired by the work of Hieronymus Bosch. The left-hand panel of Bosch's *Temptation of Saint Anthony* triptych, now in the Museu Nacional de Arte Antiga in Lisbon, contains a similar image of a demonic fish eating a smaller fish (fig. 1). The presence of this devilfish in the Lisbon triptych subverts the traditional religious iconography of the fish as a symbol of Christianity, while also referencing the Flemish proverb, frequently illustrated by Pieter Brueghel, which translates as "the big fish eat the little fish." Dalí had long been fascinated by this menacing fish-eating creature, encased in a scorpion-like shell with a cathedral tower on top, whose grasshopper legs supported his own irrational fear of this insect, and his own painting builds upon Bosch's consummate ability to render the strange and the fantastic with great imaginative power.[2] This work was inspired by a dream that Gala, the model for the outstretched nude in the foreground, reported to Dalí, in which an associative chain of bizarre images was stimulated by the buzzing of a bee around a ripe pomegranate.[3] The pomegranate is a traditional symbol of the Virgin Mary, due to its association with the Greek myth of Persephone, the virgin goddess abducted by Pluto, thus relating the painting to other depictions of Gala as the Mother of God in Dalí's work of the 1940s and 1950s. It is also a Christian symbol of fertility and the painting is crammed with images of unbridled eroticism, including the luscious pomegranate in the far distance that spills its seed into the ocean below in what the artist described as an act of "creative biology."[4]

The small pomegranate and bee in the foreground—the catalysts for Gala's troubling dream narrative—hover below her prone and naked body, casting a heart-shaped shadow on the rocks below. This delightful touch allows Dalí to express his love for Gala, while at the same time assailing her with the pair of snarling tigers and the hunting rifle, which in a humorous reversal of logic and causality is aimed directly at her arm, rather than at the pouncing wild cats. Like the strange disjunctions in scale and perspective that are found throughout the painting, this perplexing detail only makes sense within the context of Gala's dream. In her deep sleep she remains as oblivious to their menacing presence as she is to the stalking, insect-legged elephant or the larger pomegranate, whose split core released the strange procession of images in the first place. As Dalí later explained to Robert Descharnes, it was only the bayonet, whose sharp point mirrors the sting of a bee, that has the power to wake her from her slumber: "Imagine the first time Freud discovered the typical dream with a long, argumentative plot, the consequence of a momentary accident causing the awakening of the dreamer. Just as the falling of a rod on the sleeper's neck simultaneously causes his awakening and a long dream ending in the blade of the guillotine, here the sound of the bee causes the prick of the spear which will awaken Gala."[5] M.R.T.

[1] This poster is reproduced in Karin V. Maur, ed., *Salvador Dalí, 1904-1989* (Stuttgart: Staatsgalerie, 1989), p. 294.
[2] Dalí referred to Bosch's image of a devilfish as early as 1927, see Salvador Dalí, "Two Pieces in Prose," (Christmas in Brussels [An Ancient Tale]), "Dues proses," (Nadal a Brusselles [Conte antic]), *L'Amic de les Arts* (Sitges) vol. 2, no. 20, November 30, 1927, p. 104, reprinted in Haim Finkelstein, *The Collected Writings of Salvador Dalí*, trans. Haim Finkelstein (Cambridge: Cambridge University Press, 1998), p. 26.
[3] That Gala's dream provided the point of departure for the painting is clear from the variant title of the work, used when it was first shown at the Bignou Gallery, New York, in 1947, where it was listed in the catalogue as: *One Second before the Awakening from a Dream Provoked by the Flight of a Bee around a Pomegranate*. See *New Paintings by Salvador Dalí*, exhibition catalogue (New York: Bignou Gallery, 1947), cat. no. 2. This exhibition was on view from November 25, 1947, to January 3, 1948.
[4] Robert Descharnes, *Salvador Dalí: The Work, The Man*, trans. Eleanor R. Morse (New York: Harry N. Abrams, 1984), p. 288.
[5] *Ibid.*

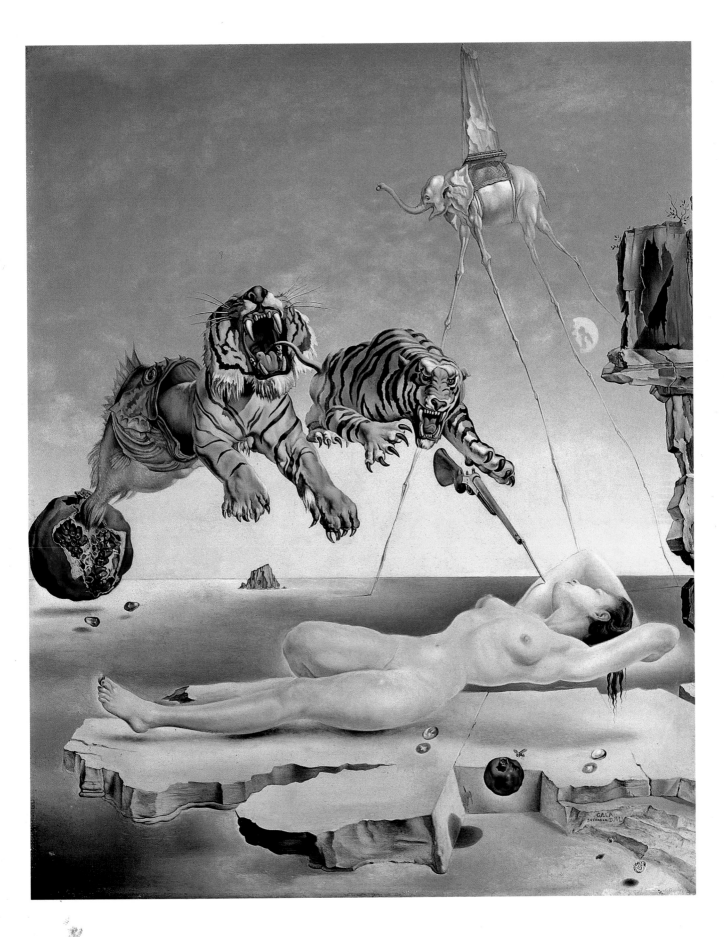

207. Study for "My Wife, Nude, Contemplating Her own Flesh Becoming Stairs, Three Vertebrae of a Column, Sky and Architecture," 1945
208. My Wife, Nude, Contemplating Her own Flesh Becoming Stairs, Three Vertebrae of a Column, Sky and Architecture, 1945

207. Pencil on paper
30 × 27 cm
11³/4 × 10⁵/8 in.
Figueres, Fundació
Gala-Salvador Dalí, gift of Dalí
to the Spanish State

208. Oil on wood panel
61 × 65 cm
24 × 25⁵/8 in.
San Francisco (CA), Private
Collection, on long-term loan
to the San Francisco Museum
of Modern Art

This painting was first shown in Dalí's solo exhibition at the Bignou Gallery on 32 East 57th Street in New York, which opened in November 1945.[1] The exhibition was accompanied by the publication of the *Dalí News*, the artist's self-promoting spoof newspaper whose title was a deliberate pun on the New York *Daily News*, which proclaimed in screaming headlines that Dalí had defied Homer and that Richard Wagner was dead. In a deliberately provocative gesture, the artist reproduced this portrait of his naked wife in the"Sports" section of the newspaper.[2] For this occasion, the artist also debuted eleven new oil paintings that he made "during nine consecutive months of strict seclusion" spent working in his improvised studio at the luxurious Del Monte Lodge in Pebble Beach, California.[3] This burst of intense creativity coincided with several important events in contemporary history, including the dropping of the first atomic bomb on Hiroshima and the end of the Second World War, which had an enormous impact on the artist's work and ideas. As Dalí revealed in a newspaper interview conducted shortly before the opening of the Bignou Gallery exhibition, the post-war political situation, combined with the latest advances in sci-

ence and technology, had led him to embrace the serene perfection and order of Italian Renaissance painting: "There comes a time when you have to stop experimenting and begin to realize. Constant experiment is sterility, Surrealist experiment no less than any other kind."[4] However, this shift away from Surrealist art practice in favor of the techniques and pictorial devices of the art of the past did not mean that he had to curb the unique flights of imagination that had heretofore characterized his artistic output. "At the same time," he explained, "the more classical I grow in the arrangement of subjects, the more irrational and inexplicable the subjects themselves become."[5]

According to the artist, *My Wife, Nude...* was "painted on wood during a period of four weeks, [working] two hours a day."[6] The painting depicts the artist's wife Gala, seen from the back, a familiar trope in the artist's work that looks back to his adolescent obsession with the backs of Dullita and his sister, Ana María, whom he painted seated from behind, with her body turned away from the viewer. This obsession was subsequently transferred to Gala, as can be seen in the *Geodesic Portrait of Gala*, of 1936, and other related works. Nine years later, in this portrait, Gala is shown looking across a barren landscape at a hollow, pavilion-like structure that mirrors, or rather duplicates, the shape of her own voluptuous body, becoming in effect her own skeleton. Although rooted in Freudian clichés of woman as enclosure or shelter, this correlation between flesh and architecture also reflects Dalí's interest in metamorphosis and decay, and may relate to a childhood experience of seeing the skeletal remains of an insect: "I saw, at the age of five, an insect eaten by ants, of which there remained only the clean and translucent shell. Through the holes of its anatomy, one could see the sky. Each time I wish to approach purity, I see the sky through the flesh."[7]

To the left of Gala is a single dandelion, a symbol of evanescence, whose stem repeats the curvaceous outline of her back, behind which lies a wall in which is set a Grecian stone head, whose presence serves to underline the classical nature of Dalí's new painting. The incorporation of a sculpted image within an image was one of the trademarks of Giorgio de Chirico's metaphysical paintings, such as *The Song of Love*, of 1914 (fig. 1), which includes a plaster bust of the *Apollo Belvedere* hanging on a similarly slanting wall. Dalí would surely have known this work, given his admiration for de Chirico's early work, since it had been widely reproduced in avant-garde magazines in the 1920s and 1930s.[8] The artist may even have seen the painting in Paris before the Second World War, since at that time it was owned by Marcel Raval, the editor of the literary and art journal *Les Feuilles libres*.

The antique bust also looks back to the Renaissance conceit of juxtaposing painted sitters with their

207

208

337

Fig. 1. Giorgio de Chirico,
The Song of Love, 1914
New York, The Museum
of Modern Art
© 2004, Digital image,
The Museum of Modern Art,
New York / Scala, Firenze

Fig. 2. Titian, *Portrait of
a Woman (La Schiavona)*, ca. 1511
London, National Gallery

sculptural likeness, perhaps best exemplified by Titian's *Portrait of a Woman (La Schiavona)*, of ca. 1511 (fig. 2), in which the sculptural relief on the parapet gives a profile view of the Slavonian sitter's head. Dalí thus updates and extends the Renaissance idea of the *paragone*, the comparison of the arts, in which sculpture and painting compete with each other for supremacy.[9] The empty shell of the domed building that we see over Gala's shoulder introduces architecture into this battle of the visual arts, in which painting ultimately emerges victorious, due to its appropriation of sculpture's (and architecture's) claim to greater permanence and multidimensionality, through the representation of more than one fixed view of the subject. M.R.T.

[1] "Recent Paintings by Salvador Dalí," Bignou Gallery, New York, November 20-December 29, 1945.
[2] See "Painting by Salvador Dalí" in the 'Sports' section, *Dalí News*, vol.1, no. 1, Tuesday, November 20, 1945, p. 3.
[3] Salvador Dalí, "Foreword to the Catalogue," *Recent Paintings by Salvador Dalí* (New York: Bignou Gallery, 1945), n.p.
[4] Alfred Frankenstein, "Dalí 'Stops Experimenting'—But He's Still Enigmatic," *The San Francisco Chronicle*, November 19, 1945, p. 6.
[5] *Ibid.*
[6] Edward Alden Jewell, "Dalí, an Enigma? Only His Exegesis," *The New York Times*, November 21, 1945, p. 19.
[7] Salvador Dalí, "My Wife, Nude, Contemplating Her own Flesh Becoming Stairs, Three Vertebrae of a Column, Sky and Architecture," in *Recent Paintings by Salvador Dalí*, exh. cat. (New York: Bignou Gallery, 1945), n.p., exh. cat. no. 4.
[8] The work was discussed and reproduced, for example, in an article written in 1924 by the Surrealist writer René Crevel, a close companion of Dalí during his early years in Paris, see Crevel, "La minute qui s'arrête ou le bienfait de Giorgio de Chirico," in *Sélection: Chronique de la vie artistique*) Anvers, year III, no. 7, May 1924, pp. 145-150, 161-165.
[9] For an excellent discussion of the *paragone* in Titian's *La Schiavona* see David Rosand, "The Portrait, the Courtier, and Death," in Robert W. Hanning and David Rosand, eds., *Castiglione: The Ideal and the Real in Renaissance Culture* (New Haven and London: Yale University Press, 1983), p. 104.

209. Gala Nude Seen from Behind, 1960

209. Oil on canvas,
41 × 31.2 cm
16$^{1/8}$ × 12$^{1/4}$ in.
Figueres, Fundació
Gala-Salvador Dalí

210. Study for "Portrait of Madame Isabel Styler-Tas," 1945

210. Pencil on paper
39.8 × 28.3 cm
15⁵/8 × 11¹/8 in.
Berlin, Staatliche Museen zu
Berlin Preußischer Kulturbesitz,
Kupferstichkabinett

211. Portrait of Madame Isabel Styler-Tas (Melencolia), 1945

211. Oil on canvas
65.5 × 86 cm
25³/4 × 33⁷/8 in.
Berlin, Staatliche Museen zu
Berlin Preußischer Kulturbesitz,
Neue Nationalgalerie

212. The Temptation of Saint Anthony, 1946

212. Oil on canvas
89.5 × 119.5 cm
33⁷/8 × 47 in.
Brussels, Musées Royaux
des Beaux-Arts de Belgique,
gift of Mme Anne-Marie
Robiliart, 1965

In 1946, Dalí entered a competition organized by the American film producer Albert Lewin, who was looking to include a cinematic shot of a painting on the theme of the temptation of Saint Anthony in a forthcoming movie based on Guy de Maupassant's novel *Bel-Ami*. Twelve noted American and European artists were eventually chosen to participate in the competition, including a number of prominent Surrealist painters, such as Max Ernst, Paul Delvaux, and Dorothea Tanning, along with visionary artists like Stanley Spencer, Ivan Albright and Horace Pippin. This emphasis on artists whose work dealt with the realm of the imagination, rather than abstraction, reflected not only the religious subject matter of the painting contest, but also the personal bias of the jury, which was made up of Alfred H. Barr, Jr., the Director of the Museum of Modern Art in New York, the art dealer Sidney Janis, and Dalí's close friend and colleague, Marcel Duchamp. Although the jury awarded first prize to Max Ernst, whose painting was the only color image in the entire black-and-white film of *The Private Affairs of Bel-Ami*, Dalí's work went on to achieve considerable fame after it was shown in a touring exhibition in the United States of eleven of the twelve entries (Leonor Fini having failed to make the exhibition deadline), which later traveled to the Palais des Beaux-Arts in Brussels in 1947.

After successfully working on Alfred Hitchcock's *Spellbound*, Dalí knew better than most what a Hollywood producer would look for in presenting an avant-garde painting on film. The artist drew on a wide range of visual sources, including the night-marish atmosphere of Hieronymus Bosch's painting *The Temptation of Saint Anthony* in the Prado, to create his image of the naked ascetic, who is harassed by fantastic visions of sexual lust and desire that emerge from the clouds in what Dalí called "the paranoiac hallucinations of his temptation."[1] Saint Anthony's temptation takes the form of a monstrous cavalcade of giant elephants perched on spiderlike legs, which are led by a rearing white horse, whose hooves threaten to crush the hermit below. The load-bearing elephants are clearly derived from Gian Lorenzo Bernini's sculpture of an almost life-size marble elephant, carrying a small Egyptian obelisk on its back, which was erected in 1667 on the Piazza della Minerva in Rome (fig. 1). The monastic saint is almost overcome by this procession of pachyderms on stilts, and the promise of sensual delight that they carry on their backs, including a humorous nod to his old rival René Magritte in the framed female torso that emerges from the building behind the obelisk. However, he steadies himself on a rock, while brandishing a crucifix to exorcise this demonic vision. Saint Anthony's triumph is foreshadowed by the appearance of El Escorial, King Philip II of Spain's vast castle-monastery, in the clouds, which for Dalí symbolized divine order's power over earthly temptations.
M.R.T.

[1] Salvador Dalí in *The Temptation of Saint Anthony: Bel Ami International Competition and Exhibition of New Paintings by Eleven American and European Artists, 1946-1947* (Washington, D.C.: The American Federation of the Arts, 1946), p. 19.

Fig. 1. Gian Lorenzo Bernini's elephant-monument carrying an Egyptian obelisk, Piazza della Minerva, Rome

213. Leda Atomica, 1947-49

213. Oil on canvas
61.1 × 45.3 cm
24 × 17⁷/₈ in.
Figueres, Fundació
Gala-Salvador Dalí

The mysterious levitating objects in *Leda Atomica* exhibit Dalí's dilettante understanding of the discontinuity of matter, which he considered among the paramount discoveries of the modern epoch. Just as particles do not touch at the atomic level, so *Leda Atomica* is void of physical contact; even the sea hovers above the land—a device that would figure into other later works including *Dalí Nude, in Contemplation before the Five Regular Bodies Metamorphized into Corpuscles, in which Suddenly Appear the Leda of Leonardo Chromosomatized by the Visage of Gala* (1954). The effect is both scientific and spiritual, recalling the number of Catholic saints said to have risen from the ground in a state of spiritual ecstasy—most notably Saint Joseph of Cupertino.

According to classical mythology, Leda was seduced by Zeus in the form of a swan, and, on the same night, made love to her husband, Tyndareus. Leda consequently bore two sets of twins: Helen (to become Helen of Troy) and Clytemnestra, and the Dioscuri—Castor and Pollux. Helen and Pollux—being the children of Zeus—were immortal, while the children of Tyndareus—Castor and Clytemnestra—were mortal.[1] Dalí identified with Leda's offspring, suggesting that he and Gala were twin souls—an especially appropriate analogy given Gala's Christian name, Helena Dimitrievna Diakonova. It is not as Helen, however, but as Leda herself that Gala appears in *Leda Atomica*—perhaps suggesting her role as a substitute for the artist's dead mother.[2] Her left-hand with conspicuous wedding band sweetly caresses the head of the Zeus-swan—the lone element in the painting that fails to cast a shadow, thereby indicating its ethereality.

In his intensive study, *Léda Atomica: Anatomie d'un chef-d'oeuvre*, Jean-Louis Ferrier presents *Leda Atomica*'s levitating elements as an extension of Dalí's idiosyncratic paraphilia, "clédalism" (see Encyclopedia)[3]—an interpretation supported by Ian Gibson's etymological observation, "If we knock off the initial 'C' of clédalism we find ourselves looking at the word 'lédalism,' in which 'léda' and 'Dalí' overlap."[4] Ferrier presents clédalism not as a perversity, but rather as a spiritualized sexuality emphasizing love over lust and therefore in keeping with *Leda Atomica*'s tender serenity; it is the "archetype of the sublime sexual act!" Ferrier writes. "That which is unconsummated!"[5] While Dalí's 1961 *Leda and the Swan* (fig. 3), described by the artist as 'spermatic,' exaggerates the Leda myth's carnality, as captured by such artists as Michelangelo (1530), Correggio (1532) and Rubens (1601), *Leda Atomica* eschews concupiscence in favor of a more Apollonian subject, akin to Leonardo's 1508 painting, *Leda and the Swan*.

In his 1946 publication, *The Geometry of Art and Life*, the mathematician, Matila Ghyka (see Encyclopedia), dissects the geometric organization of

Fig. 3. Salvador Dalí, *Leda and the Swan*, 1961
Figueres, Fundació Gala-Salvador Dalí

Leonardo's *Leda*, revealing two superimposed 'Golden rectangles' based on Luca Pacioli's 'Divine Proportion,' which Leonardo originally illustrated (fig. 1). Similarly, Dalí carefully worked out the design for the 'Golden pentagon' in which his Leda is inscribed on a page from *The Geometry of Art and Life*, and the mathematical formula—$p_r = (R/2) * \sqrt{(10-2\sqrt{5})}$—, used to calculate the side of a regular pentagon, appears in the lower right corner of one of Dalí's more advanced studies (fig. 2).[6] Thus, *Leda Atomica* can be compared with Leonardo's painting in both subject and structure—a parallel Ghyka perhaps also recognized, describing Dalí in his memoirs, "I had the impression that since Leonardo's, no pencil had expressed so much dynamic beauty through its lines and arabesques."[7] E.H.K.

[1] Rosa M. Maurell, "Mythological References in the work of Salvador Dalí: the myth of Leda" in *Hora Nova*, May 30, 2000.
[2] Ian Gibson, *The Shameful Life of Salvador Dalí* (New York and London: W.W. Norton & Co., 1998), p. 495. Originally published by Faber and Faber (London), 1997.
[3] Jean-Louis Ferrier, *Léda Atomica: Anatomie d'un chef-d'oeuvre* (Paris: Denoël/Gonthier, 1980), p. 34. Translation mine.
[4] Gibson, p. 495.
[5] Ferrier, p. 34.
[6] Matila Ghyka, *The Geometry of Art and Life* (New York: Dover Publications, 1977), p. 17. Originally published in English by Sheed and Ward (New York), 1946.
[7] Matila Ghyka, *The World Mine Oyster* (London: William Heinemann Ltd., 1961), p. 303. Originally published in French (La Colombe: Éditions du Vieux Colombier), 1956.

Fig. 1. The analysis of Leonardo da Vinci's *Leda and the Swan* conceived by Matila Ghyka

Fig. 2. Salvador Dalí, *Study for "Leda Atomica,"* 1947

214. The Madonna of Port Lligat (first version), 1949

214. Oil on canvas
49.5 × 38.3 cm
18 1/2 × 15 1/8 in.
Milwaukee (WI), The Patrick and Beatrice Haggerty Museum of Art, Marquette University, gift of Mr. and Mrs. Ira Haupt, 1959

Dalí's newfound enthusiasm for the Catholic religion was reciprocated on November 23, 1949, when he was granted a special audience with Pope Pius XII, to whom he presented his first version of *The Madonna of Port Lligat*. The artist had hoped that his pilgrimage would persuade the Vatican to offer him a special dispensation to marry Gala, whose first husband, the Surrealist poet Paul Éluard, was still alive.[1] Although the artist's marriage to Gala would not be sanctioned until after Éluard's death in 1952,[2] the painting apparently met with the Pontiff's approval and in the spirit of a Holy Year he blessed the work, thus paving the way for the artist's gradual acceptance by the Catholic Church, despite his vehement anti-clerical stance of the 1920s and 1930s.[3] However, as this painting demonstrates, it would be a mistake to regard Dalí's renewed inter-

Fig. 1. Carlo Crivelli, *Madonna and Child Enthroned with Donor*, ca. 1470 Washington, National Gallery of Art

est in the Catholic faith as a reactionary move away from his earlier interest in modern art and modernity. The artist's embrace of spirituality, and his related efforts to reinvigorate modern painting through the utilization of the techniques and religious iconography of the art of the Italian Renaissance, were inextricably linked with his understanding of recent scientific discoveries, most notably atomic energy and particle physics. The dropping of the first atomic bomb on Hiroshima in 1945 exerted a profound influence on Dalí, whose subsequent paintings attempted to replicate nuclear fission through the dematerialization of figures and objects, which are often suspended in space and fragmented to demonstrate the dissolution of gravity and the divisibility of matter.

The artist called this hybrid of atomic age physics and Catholic doctrine 'Nuclear Mysticism' and its application can be seen in this painting, where the changes in matter resulting from an atomic explosion are parallel to the physical and spiritual transformation of the praying Madonna who carries the Christ Child in the rectangular window space of her perforated belly. The painting depicts Gala as the Virgin Mary in a luminous blue-colored landscape setting that is immediately recognizable as the rocky bay of Port Lligat, the tiny Catalán fishing village on the Costa Brava where she first appeared to him, and where the couple had resettled in the previous year.

Indeed, the work has its origins in an earlier drawing entitled *Port Lligat Madonna Help Me*, whose title underscores the role of Gala as the artist's savior and which was reproduced as a frontispiece to the artist's 1948 technical treatise, the *50 Secrets of Magic Craftsmanship*.

Although much of the iconography follows Christian tradition—with the fish as a symbol of Christ, the seashells representing pilgrimage or baptism, and the lemons being associated with fidelity in love—the fragmentation of the figures and their surroundings is unique to Dalí's conception of the theme. The Madonna's physical body is pierced and dismembered, although her separated body parts are held in balance and in their correct anatomical positions, which are then framed by the disintegrated throne-like architectural elements that surround her.

The composition is clearly based on Piero della Francesca's *Madonna and Child with Angels and Six Saints*, of 1470-75 (fig. 2), in the Pinacoteca di Brera in Milan, which also features the Virgin Mary seated on a throne with her hands clasped together and forming an arch above the infant Jesus. Both Madonnas are prominently centered under an arch beneath which a dazzling white egg hangs by a thread from a large seashell, although Dalí inverts his own scallop shell in the manner of Carlo Crivelli's *Madonna and Child Enthroned with Donor* of ca. 1470 (fig. 1).[4] In the following year, the artist articu-

Fig. 2. Piero della Francesca,
Montefeltro Altarpiece (detail),
1470-75
Milan, Pinacoteca di Brera

lated his desire to revive "the dazzling perfection of the masters of the Renaissance" in a syndicated article published in the United States entitled "The Decadence of Modern Art."[5] Modern painting, he claimed, had been made obsolete through the invention of high-speed photography, which had forced artists like Picasso and Matisse to create "pseudo-decorative abstract modern art." Yet if painting was to survive, he argued, younger artists must return to classic principles of technique, skill, and craftsmanship in order to attain the perfection and uniform brilliance of the work of Raphael, Leonardo, and presumably his own efforts at reviving the splendor of Renaissance painting as seen in *The Madonna of Port Lligat*. M.R.T.

[1] Salvador Dalí, *Diary of a Genius*, trans. Richard Howard (London: Creation Books, 1994), p. 133. This audience with the Pope was arranged through Ruis Jimenez, a Minister of National Education in the Spanish Government, who was formerly the Spanish ambassador to the Vatican. As Dalí later confessed to Brassaï, this meeting was vital to him, not only because he wanted the Pontiff to grant him special dispensation to marry Gala, but also because he wanted to convince the Spanish Catholic Church of the sincerity of his recent religious work. "Scandalized by my more or less erotic or scatological painting, the Spanish clergy was casting a cold eye on my new mystical work. They suspected some hoax or blasphemy when they looked at my Virgins. So I said to myself, 'If Pius XII blesses my painting, if I can get Vatican approval, my Catholic detractors will all be silenced'"; see Brassaï, *The Artists of My Life, trans. Richard Miller* (New York: Viking Press, 1982), p. 35.

[2] Salvador Dalí and Gala Éluard were finally married in a religious ceremony on August 8, 1958, which took place in a small chapel outside Gerona.

[3] According to Dalí, the Pope showed "extraordinary comprehension" of his effort; see Anonymous, "Toward Raphael," *Time*, April 17, 1950, p. 65.

[4] When Dalí made his own *Madonna*, this Crivelli painting was in the collection of Samuel H. Kress, who donated it to the National Gallery of Art, Washington, D.C., in 1952. The art critic Emily Genauer was the first person to notice a connection between the artist's painting and that of Crivelli. However, Genauer connects the iconography of Dalí's painting with the Christ Child seated on a pillow amid cracked masonry in the Venetian Renaissance artist's *Madonna and Child* in the Metropolitan Museum of Art, New York; see Genauer, "The Salvador Dalí Madonna," *This Week Magazine*, April 9, 1950, pp. 8-9.

[5] Salvador Dalí, "The Decadence of Modern Art," *American Weekly*, August 20, 1950, p. 16. This polemical article also appeared in the same year in the *Philadelphia Evening Bulletin*, the *New York Journal American*, and the *Washington Times Herald*.

215. The Madonna of Port Lligat, 1950

215. Oil on canvas
366 × 244 cm
144 1/8 × 96 in.
Fukuoka (Japan),
Fukuoka Art Museum

In 1950, Dalí painted a second and final version of *The Madonna of Port Lligat*, an immense painting that he regarded as his greatest work to date. The work was painted on such a colossal scale that it took the artist five months to complete and, when the work was shipped to New York for its debut exhibition in November 1950, it was too large to fit on the elevator or stairs and had to be hoisted by ropes to the sixth-floor Carstairs Gallery.[1] As the artist gleefully explained to newspaper reporters at the time, this larger version was 'completely changed' from the earlier study, with the focal point no longer on the rapturous face of the Madonna, but instead on the Christ child, in the center of whose body now appeared the bread of the Eucharist.[2] Dalí's explanation for this modification of his original conception was that "modern physics has revealed to us increasingly the dematerialization which exists in all nature and that is the reason why the material body of my *Madonna* does not exist and why in place of a torso you find a tabernacle 'filled with Heaven.' But while everything floating in space denotes spirituality it also represents our concept of the atomic system—today's counterpart of divine gravitation."[3]

Although the basic iconography of the painting, drawn from the Italian Renaissance altarpieces featuring an enthroned Madonna by Piero della Francesca and Carlo Crivelli, remained the same as the 1949 version, the vibrant blue color scheme of the earlier work was replaced by a darker blue-gray palette, while the increased scale of the final painting required a plethora of new symbols to be added. Some of these were familiar to Dalí's repertoire, such as the basket of bread that is suspended beside Gala. However, other objects represented new obsessions, like the cuttlefish bones that double as angel wings in which the figure of Gala can at times be discerned. Another important feature of the painting is the first appearance of the rhinoceros, a recurring motif in Dalí's late work, which stands in the shadows of the recessed, predella-like space beneath the Madonna's foot. The shadow of the rhinoceros emphasizes its disconnected, levitating horn, a minor detail that nonetheless signals the genesis of what would become the artist's quintessential atomic emblem. Once again, Gala was depicted as the Virgin Mary, while Juan Figueres, a six-year old boy from Cadaqués, was used as the model for the infant Jesus.[4] Both figures are suspended in midair, like particles of atomic matter, while directly above their heads a symbolic ostrich egg hangs by a thread. This is a medieval symbol of the immaculate conception, based on the myth that the female ostrich hatched its eggs by exposing them to sunlight without being impregnated by the male bird.

The artist later spoke of "the egg of Euclidean perfection that Piero della Francesca suspended over the head of the Virgin. That egg to me became the sword of Damocles."[5] This reference adds a new meaning to the artist's appropriation of Piero's egg, which had previously been thought to be a symbol of Platonic idealism, perfection, equilibrium, and eternity, and which Dalí viewed as one of the greatest mysteries of Italian Renaissance painting. In his 1948 book *50 Secrets of Magic Craftsmanship*, Dalí compared the egg that is "gravely suspended over the head of the Virgin Mary" to the world that gravitates beneath the vault of Heaven, which represented the unity of the Catholic Church, and the prominent role of the Madonna in that world sphere.[6] Much like the egg and shell in Piero's *Madonna and Child with Angels and Six Saints* in Milan, which appear to exist in an indeterminate space, everything in Dalí's painting hovers in a kind of suspended animation that creates a heightened sense of other-worldliness, as science, art, and religion coalesce in a static image of Gala as the mystically transcendent Holy Mother of God.[7] M.R.T.

[1] "'The Madonna of Port-Lligat' by Salvador Dalí," was on view at the Carstairs Gallery, New York, from November 27, 1950 – January 10, 1951. The exhibition was held in honor of the Diamond Jubilee of the Philadelphia Museum of Art. For more on the artist's discovery that the painting was too large to fit in the gallery, which was located on the sixth floor of a New York townhouse, and the subsequent decision to hoist the work through an upstairs window, see Anonymous, "Madonna in Mid-Air," *Life*, vol. 29, no. 25, December 18, 1950, pp. 48-50. Dalí was disappointed that the window was removed for the job, since he had hoped that the crate would be smashed right through.

[2] Judith Crist, "Dalí here with 'Greatest' Work, But It's Too Big to Get in Gallery," *New York Herald Tribune*, November 11, 1950, p. 11.

[3] Anonymous, "Toward Raphael," *Time*, April 17, 1950, p. 65.

[4] M.F.L., "Young Juan's Moment of Fame," *Cleveland Plain Dealer, This Week Magazine Section*, April 29, 1951, p. 14.

[5] Salvador Dalí, *Diary of a Genius*, trans. Richard Howard (London: Creation Books, 1994), p. 154.

[6] Salvador Dalí, *50 Secrets of Magic Craftsmanship*, trans. Haakon M. Chevalier (New York: The Dial Press, 1948), p. 170.

[7] The painting was later the subject of a poem written by a Spanish priest who understood the work as reconciling "different planes of knowledge and experience in art, science, and theology"; see Fray Angelico Chavez, *The Virgin of Port Lligat* (Fresno [CA]: Academy Library Guild, 1956), p. XVII.

216. Gala as Madonna of Port Lligat, 1950

216. Photo with gouache
and pencil on cardboard
12.5 × 10 cm
4⁷/8 × 3⁷/8 in.
Private collection

217. The Christ of Saint John of the Cross, 1951
217 bis. Study for "Christ of Saint John of the Cross," 1950

217. Oil on canvas
205 × 116 cm / 80³/4 × 45³/4 in.
Glasgow, The Glasgow
Art Gallery

217 bis. Sanguine on paper
75.7 × 101.7 cm / 29³/4 × 40 in.
St. Petersburg (FL),
The Salvador Dalí Museum

Fig. 1. The drawing of the crucifixion realized by Saint John of the Cross (1542-91) during an ecstasy, St. Petersburg (FL), The Salvador Dalí Museum

The distinctive viewpoint from which he depicts the Crucifixion was inspired by a 16th-century drawing purportedly by Saint John of the Cross himself (fig. 1), which Dalí was shown by the French Carmelite, Bruno de Jésus-Marie, a biographer of the Saint. "This drawing so impressed me the first time I saw it," Dalí recalled, "that later in California, in a dream, I saw the Christ in the same position, but in the landscape of Port Lligat, and I heard voices which told me, 'Dalí, you must paint this Christ'."[1] In both versions, Christ is seen from above with His head bent forwards; however, in St John's drawing, the Crucifix is represented at an oblique angle. Dalí refers to his oneiric vision of Christ again in a 1950-51 rudimentary gouache study for the painting, on which he notes that the triangle and circle—derived from Pacioli's 'Divine Proportion' (see Encyclopedia, 'Ghyka')—'aesthetically' encapsulated his previous experiments; he adds emphatically, "AND I PUT MY CHRIST IN THAT TRIANGLE."[2]

Saint John of the Cross (1542-91)—mystic, poet, and associate of Saint Teresa of Avila—was a reformist member of the Carmelite Order, by which he was harshly treated. Only after his death did he achieve recognition as one of the greatest of Christian mystical writers; he is the patron saint of Spanish poets and mystics and was named a Doctor of the Catholic Church by Pope Pius XI in 1926. Dalí illustrated his 1951 *Mystical Manifesto* with two drawings of *The Christ of Saint John of the Cross*, pronouncing in the text that his ensuing painting of

Christ would contain "more beauty and joy than anything that will have been painted up to the present. I want to paint a Christ that will be the absolute contrast in every respect to the materialist and savagely antimystical Christ of Grünewald."[3] Grünewald's 1515 depiction of the Crucifixion in the Isenheim Altarpiece presents a mortal, dying Christ, with a bloodied body and agonizing expression (fig. 2); Dalí countered such attempts to "obtain emotion through ugliness" by painting Christ as "beautiful as the God that He is."[4]

Despite his aspirations for an idealized Deity, Dalí's anti-materialist Christ is, in fact, based on an all-too-human model: the athletic Hollywood stand-in, Russ Saunders, whom the artist arranged to have tied to a wooden panel and photographed.[5] Notwithstanding its human model, *The Christ of Saint John of the Cross* lacks all the traditional attributes suggestive of Christ's mortal anguish: the crown of thorns, the bloody gash at His side, and the nails in His hands and feet that appear dominantly in Saint John of the Cross' original drawing. Dalí admits originally intending to include these elements, although he planned to replace Christ's blood with red carnations and jasmine flowers (one suspects the effect might have been akin to his 1930 painting, *The Bleeding Roses*); towards the completion of the painting, however, Dalí apparently had a second dream in which he saw his picture "without the anecdotal attributes but just the metaphysical beauty of Christ-God."[6] The result is a decidedly

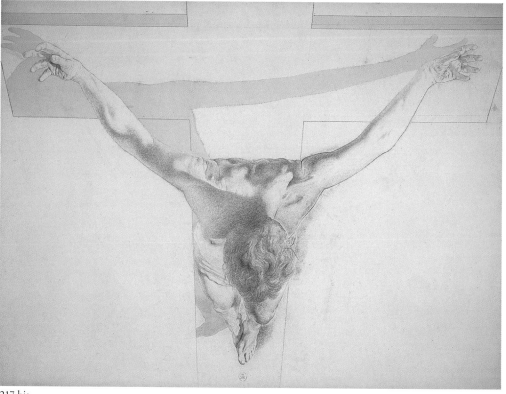

217 bis

217

Fig. 2. Matthias Grünewald,
Crucifixion, 1515
Colmar, Musée d'Unterlinden

more spiritualized Savior Who is not nailed to the Cross but rather hovers against it—an effect repeated in Dalí's 1954 *Crucifixion, Corpus Hypercubicus* (cat. 225) and his 1958 *Ascension* (cat. 234), in which Christ rises into Heaven without any traces of mortality or stigmata. E.H.K.

[1] Salvador Dalí, "A Letter from Salvador Dalí," *Scottish Art Review*, vol. IV, no. 1, Glasgow, 1952, p. 5.

[2] "Nuclear Mysticism," *Scottish Art Review*, vol. IV, no. 2, summer, 1952, p. 28. This issue was dedicated to Dalí's *Christ of St John of the Cross*, which had been controversially purchased by the Glasgow City Art Gallery and Museum.

[3] Salvador Dalí, *Manifeste Mystique* (Paris: Robert J. Godet, 1951). Published in English in Haim Finkelstein, *The Collected Writings of Salvador Dalí* (Cambridge: Cambridge University Press, 1998), pp. 365-366.

[4] Dalí, "A letter from Salvador Dalí," p. 5.

[5] Ian Gibson, *The Shameful Life of Salvador Dalí* (New York and London: W.W. Norton & Co., 1998), p. 517. Originally published by Faber & Faber (London, 1997).

[6] Dalí, "A letter from Salvador Dalí," p. 5.

218. Christ, 1951

219. Christ, 1952

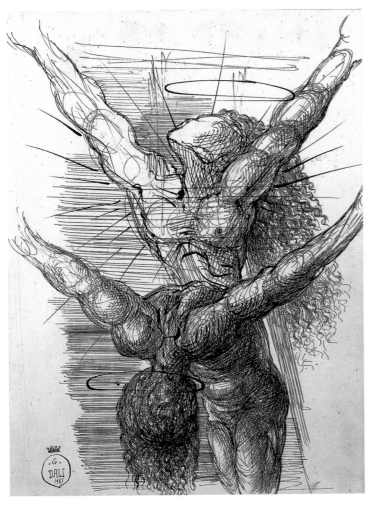

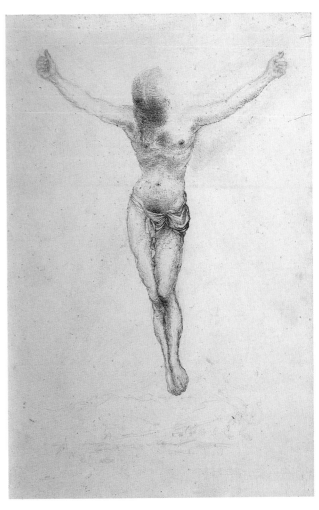

218. Ink on paper
28 × 23 cm
11 × 9$^{1/8}$ in.
Private collection

219. Pencil and charcoal
on paper
40.2 × 51.4 cm
15$^{7/8}$ × 20$^{1/4}$ in.
Figueres, Fundació
Gala-Salvador Dalí,
gift of Dalí to the Spanish State

220. Raphaelesque Head Exploding, 1951

220. Oil on canvas
43 × 33 cm
16 7/8 × 13 in.
Edinburgh, Scottish National Gallery, on permanent loan from Miss Stead-Ellis, Summerset

Fig. 1. Salvador Dalí, *The Wheelbarrows (Pantheon Formed by Twisted Wheelbarrows)*, 1951 St. Petersburg (FL), The Salvador Dalí Museum, on loan of E. and A. Reynolds Morse Collection

Raphaelesque Head Exploding is among the first of Dalí's paintings to completely fracture its subject into a coruscating cloud of paranoiac 'particles.' As in his contemporaneous watercolor, *The Wheelbarrows* (fig. 1), the figure is superimposed onto the interior of the Pantheon in Rome, where Raphael is buried. Sunlight pours through the building's famous oculus, creating a sense of divine illumination enhanced by the thinly-painted background that reveals a pencil-sketched halo and further 'atomizations'—the legacy of the levitating elements that had appeared in Dalí's art since 1947 (see *Leda Atomica,* cat. 213). Disintegrating wheelbarrows feature in both images—within the churning consistency of *The Wheelbarrows* and in the lower left corner of *Raphaelesque Head Exploding*; these instruments of rural labor connote the hybrid of sanctity and concupiscence Dalí read into Millet's *Angelus* and the subject of his recently-composed but unrealized 'paranoiac film,' *Wheelbarrow of Flesh* (1948).[1] The wheelbarrow is further flanked by swirling cones adopting the semblance of diminutive rhinoceros horns (see Encyclopedia), a paradoxical emblem he interpreted in the 1950s as both pious and aphrodisiacal.[2]

Dalí described *Raphaelesque Head Exploding* as his "interpretation of the creation, destruction and reintegration of the Universe as conceived by the 'Eternal Mind,'" adding, "Surrealism is disintegration. My paintings now show the spirit of reintegration."[3] With their figures comprised of specific loaded symbols, Dalí's atomic constructions are the legacy of his 1930s paranoiac canvases, for example *The Great Paranoiac* (1936; see p. 296, fig. 1) and may also be compared to the Renaissance paintings of Giuseppe Arcimboldo (1530-93), whose works, Dalí knew, were admired by King Philip II and housed in the Escorial Palace alongside works by that other antecedent to his Surrealist phantasms, Hieronymus Bosch.[4] Despite invoking a paranoiac sensibility, however, the atomic works' agenda is neither the discrediting of reality—as he described the paranoid critical method's capacity in 1930—nor its abstraction, though there is arguably an abstruse nod to Abstract Expressionism, the dominant movement of the period;[5] rather, with his ambition to "paint the beauty of angels and of reality" using "pi-mesons and the most gelatinous and indeterminate neutrinos," Dalí sought to penetrate reality, revealing the invisible vivacity underlying illusory continuity.[6] "What distinguishes our age from the Renaissance," he told Carlton Lake in 1964, "is that now for the first time we realize that matter, instead of being something continuous, is discontinuous…[I]f one wanted to give an accurate representation of a table, instead of being compact the table should resemble something like a swarm of flies."[7] E.H.K.

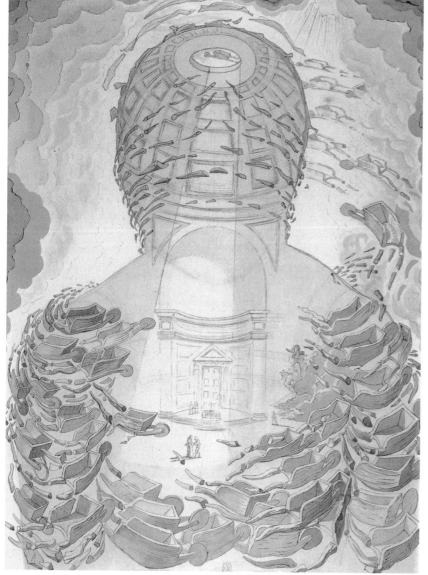

[1] See Salvador Dalí, *Le Mythe Tragique de 'L'Angelus' de Millet, Interprétation Paranoïaque-Critique* (Paris: Société Nouvelle des Éditions Pauvert, 1963). In *Wheelbarrow of Flesh*, Dalí presents the rural instrument in nine different functions: table for food, nuptial bed, coffin, cupboard, cradle, bird's nest, cat's bed, flesh wheelbarrow, and, most significantly given his mystic preoccupations, altar and cross (Salvador Dalí, *Wheelbarrow of Flesh* [1948], unrealized film script, Fundació Gala-Salvador Dalí).
[2] Salvador Dalí, *Diary of a Genius*, trans. Richard Howard (New York: Prentice Hall Press, 1986), p. 36. Originally published in French as *Journal d'un génie* (Paris: La Table Ronde, 1964). Dalí would describe the combination of contradictory elements as "an absolutely constant and characteristic element of Dalínian thought" in Salvador Dalí, *Les Dîners de Gala* (Paris: Draeger, 1973), p. 11.
[3] David Camelon, "Dalí's 'exploding angel,'" *The American Weekly* (February 10, 1952), p. 15. Dalí's would soon

contradict his statement with the title of his painting, *The Disintegration of the Persistence of Memory* (cat. 224), which reinterpreted his Surrealist tableau via his new 'atomic' perspective.

4 Indeed, Dalí reported painting *The Great Paranoiac* following a conversation with José Maria Sert on the subject of Arcimboldo. See Robert Descharnes, *Dalí de Gala* (Lausanne: Edita, 1962), p. 34.

5 Salvador Dalí, "L'Âne pourri*," La femme visible* (Paris: Éditions surréalistes, 1930), p. 11-20. Dalí much later praised the 'swift gestures' of certain action painters (e.g., William De Kooning and Georges Mathieu), which, he argued, corresponded to Max Planck's 'quantum of action' (Salvador Dalí, "Ecumenical 'chafarrinada' of Velázquez," *Art News*, vol. 59, no. 10, [February 1961] p. 30)—an interpretation De Kooning flatly contradicted (*Surrealist Intrusion in the Enchanters' Domain* [New York: D'Arcy Galleries, 1960], p. 24). Dalí also reported showing De Kooning some enlargements of a painting by Diego Velázquez, which the action painter allegedly called *Action Painting raised to the sublime!* (Salvador Dalí, "De Kooning's 300,000,000th Birthday," *Art News* 68 [New York: April 1969], pp. 57, 62-63).

6 Salvador Dalí, *Anti-Matter Manifesto* (New York: Carstairs Gallery, 1958-59).

7 Carlton Lake, *In Quest for Dalí* (New York: G.P. Putnam's Sons, 1969), p. 48. Although Dalí's understanding of matter's discontinuity provided the foundation for over a decade of his atomic paintings, the notion itself was not especially contemporary; indeed, Democritus of Abdera had posited in the 5th-century B.C.E. that matter was comprised of 'invisible' particles in motion, and Dalí's explication to Lake cited not a cutting-edge "Atomic Age" journal but a 1928 popular science book, *The Nature of the Physical World*, by the English astronomer, Sir Arthur Eddington. Eddington's text includes a famous comparison between an average/"common sense"/"substantial" table, and a "scientific" table comprised of atoms, electrons, etc. In this same text, Eddington describes stepping into a room, writing, "The plank has no solidity of substance. To step on it is like stepping on a swarm of flies. Shall I not slip through? No, if I make the venture one of the flies hits me and gives a boost up again; I fall again and am knocked upwards by another fly; and so on" (Arthur S. Eddington, *The Nature of the Physical World*, Gifford Lectures 1927, [Cambridge: Cambridge University Press, 1928], 342). Thank you to Dr. Gavin Parkinson for providing me with the origin of Eddington's comparison.

221. Corpuscular Madonna, 1952

221. Pencil, sepia-color
and China ink
55.8 × 43.2 cm
22 × 17 in.
Birmingham (AL), Birmingham
Museum of Art, gift of Mr.
and Mrs. Charles W. Ireland

222. Rocks, 1951

222. Watercolor on paper
14 x 27.5 cm
5¹/2 × 10⁷/8 in.
Switzerland, Private collection

Fig. 1. Salvador Dalí, *The Simoniacs (illustration for the "Divine Comedy")*, 1951

This is an illustration of canto 33 of Dante's *Divine Comedy*. In this canto, Count Ugolino della Gherardesca reveals the reason for his punishment to Dante and Virgil: he had been imprisoned in a tower with his sons and left there to die of hunger. When they died, in order to survive, he was obliged to eat their flesh. Such a terrible tragedy caused his soul to turn to stone:
"Father, much less pain 'twill give us
If thou do eat of us; thyself didst clothe us
With this poor flesh, and do thou strip it off."...
And there he died; and, as thou seest me,
I saw the three fall, one by one, between
The fifth day and the sixth; whence I betook me,
Already blind, to groping over each,
And three days called them after they were dead;
Then hunger did what sorrow could not do."
In 1951, the Italian government decided to publish a special edition of the *Divine Comedy* on the occasion of the seven-hundredth anniversary of the birth of Dante. Dalí was commissioned to illustrate the text and, from 1951 to 1960, he executed 101 watercolors. In 1954, the Istituto Poligrafico dello Stato published, in a lithographic edition, full-size reproductions of seven of the watercolors. The reactions to this were immediate: the Communists protested because of the excessively high fee being paid to Dalí, which, in their opinion would have been better spent on socially useful works, while the Italian patriots were indignant that the task of illustrating the most outstanding work in their country's literature should have been given to a Spanish artist. In the end Dalí was relieved of the assignment, although there is every reason for thinking that he was remunerated as agreed.
From April 1959 to November 1963, Joseph Foret, in a luxury edition limited to 33 copies, and Jean Strade, artistic director of Les Éditions d'Art Les Heures Claires, Paris, with an edition of 1,465 copies, published the *Divine Comedy* using 3,500 separate wood blocks to reproduce the watercolors as wood engravings.
In this scene, Dalí depicts, in the foreground, the long shadows cast by Dante, with his prominent nose, and Virgil while they observe an allegorical representation of the father facing the skull of one of his sons. The count, in the background, is derived from a stage set Dalí designed in 1941 for the ballet *Labyrinth*. The position of the father's head expresses a sense of heaviness and, at the same time, recalls the pose in which Goya portrayed Cronus as he devoured his sons. In the center of the composition stands a large rock in the form of a skull that is being consumed from within by an army of ants, visible in the fissures. R.M.P.

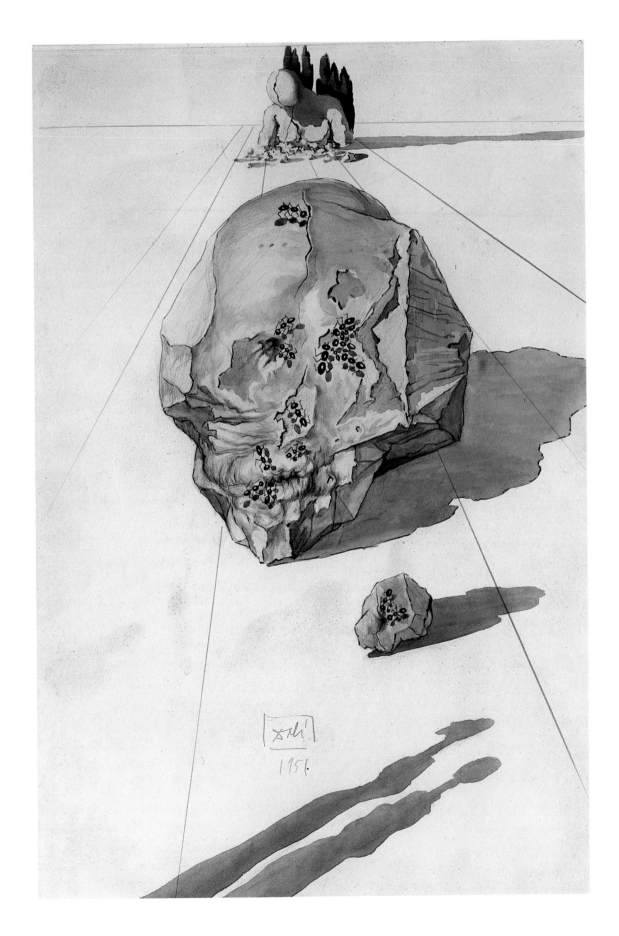

223. Nuclear Cross, 1952

223. Oil on canvas
78 × 58 cm
30³/4 × 22⁷/8 in.
Private Collection

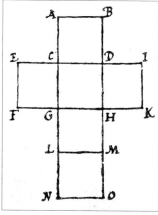

Fig. 1. Salvador Dalí,
Arithmosophic Cross, 1952
Location unknown; formerly
New York (NY), Carstairs Gallery

Fig. 2. Diagram by the mathematician
Juan de Herrera

Nuclear Cross is among the most striking of a number of variations on the Christian symbol Dalí—a self-proclaimed 'specialist in crosses (the greatest who ever existed)'—executed in the 1950s.[1] The painting depicts the circular end of a bread loaf—a clear allusion to the Sacrament, recalling also his 1950 *Madonna of Port Lligat* (cats. 214, 215)—surrounded by 950 diminutive cubes carefully drawn by his close friend, Emilio Puignau, a thirty-nine year-old builder whom Dalí and Gala hired in 1934 to renovate their newly-purchased fisherman's hut in Port Lligat.[2] Upon his return to Catalonia in 1948, Dalí reconnected with Puignau and, in 1951, asked the builder, who was again busy with the artist's renovations, to do him the 'favor' of making the preparatory designs for *The Christ of Saint John of the Cross*, based on drawings and various photographs.[3] Puignau was astonished—as he was not a professional draftsman—but honored by the task, carrying it out so to Dalí's satisfaction that he was soon asked to lay out the cubes for *Nuclear Cross*. Dalí described his vision of the painting to Puignau as a cross 'disintegrating ...as all matter is broken up into molecules and all molecules into atoms'—an explanation the builder admitted not understanding. He nonetheless committed several days and nights to sketching Dalí's many cubes, later jocularly describing the labor as his own veritable 'cross.' When a print of the finished painting was issued, Dalí dedicated a copy, "To Emilio Puignau, Responsible for the little cubes."[4]

In his 1944 novel, *Hidden Faces*, Dalí broadly positioned Christianity in opposition to Nazism, describing a withering and defeated Hitler spouting venomous blasphemies against Christ; "Why did not destiny allow Jesus to live in my time of domination, so that I might have strangled him with my own hands!" Hitler screams.[5] Following the 1951 inauguration of the "new era of mystic painting," as pronounced by the *Mystical Manifesto*, Christ and Spain became integrally entwined in Dalí's work, perhaps indicative of Franco's 'national Catholicism' and propagandistic self-promotion as a Catholic crusader; the cross thence became, for Dalí, an emblem of Spain's resistance to Hitler—"the total contrary of the swastika." "There can be no doubt," he wrote in 1956, "that Germany, in spite of its superhuman efforts to be vanquished, lost the war, and that it was Spain which, without taking part in the conflict, without doing anything, humanly alone, with its Dantesque faith and the help of God, was made to win, won, is still winning

and will spiritually continue to win this same war."[6] Dalí's concomitant fervor for Spain and the Church inspired many of his paintings of the 1950s, including *Arithmosophic Cross* (1952; fig. 1) and *Corpus Hypercubicus* (1954; cat. 225), both of which, along with *Nuclear Cross*, owe part of their inspiration to Juan de Herrera's (1530-97) *Treatise on Cubic Form*, a largely overlooked essay Dalí extolled, written by the mathematician who replaced Juan Bautista de Toledo as architect of the Escorial Palace (see Encyclopedia).[7] An ardent Vitruvian, Herrera believed "the whole harmony of the universe consists in the principle of proportion and the principle of comparison, for lacking these, there can be no relations between the creator and his creations nor [internal relations] among different creatures";[8] his treatise is thus a unique combination of geometry and piety, employing Euclid's postulates on the cube to illuminate the combinatory diagrams of the Catalan theologian, Ramón Llull (fig. 2). The cubic cross—spiritually rooted in Herrera and Llull and buttressed with notions of modern science—was a poignant symbol of Dalí's aspirations for Spain's mystical hegemony in the wake of Nazism. Designed for the 'Atomic Age,' it was at once Spanish, Catholic and corpuscular. E.H.K.

[1] Salvador Dalí, *Diary of a Genius*, trans. Richard Howard (New York: Prentice Hall Press, 1986), p. 137. Originally published in French as *Journal d'un génie* (Paris: La Table Ronde, 1964).

[2] Emilio Puignau, *Vivencias con Salvador Dalí* (Barcelona: Éditorial Juventud, S.A., 1995), p. 62.

[3] *Ibid.*, p. 60.

[4] *Ibid.*, p. 64.

[5] Salvador Dalí, *Hidden Faces*, trans. Haakon M. Chevalier (London: Nicholson and Watson, 1947), p. 340. Originally published by Dial Press (New York: 1944).

[6] Salvador Dalí, *Diary of a Genius*, pp. 137-138. In 1960, Dalí identified the "development of the Spanish Empire towards God" as the narrative of his monumental 1958-59 canvas saturated with crosses, *The Dream of Christopher Columbus* ("New Dalí 'Nuclear-Mystical' Canvas Unveiled," *New York Times* [New York, 13 January 1960]).

[7] Juan de Herrera, *El discurso de la figura cúbica* (Madrid: Simons y Godoy, Ed. Nacional, 1976).

[8] *Ibid.*, pp. 142. Quoted in English in Catherine Wilkinson Zerner, *Juan de Herrera: Architect to Philip II of Spain* (London and New Haven: Yale University Press, 1993), p. 42. Upon his death in 1597, Herrera left money to go towards founding a Llullist school in his hometown (43).

224. The Disintegration of the Persistence of Memory, 1952-54

224. Oil on canvas
25 × 33 cm
9⁷/8 × 13 in.
St. Petersburg (FL),
The Salvador Dalí Museum

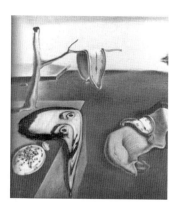

Fig. 1. Salvador Dalí and Philippe Halsman, *Surrealism It's Me*, 1954

The Disintegration of the Persistence of Memory—Dalí's atomization of his 1931 masterpiece, *The Persistence of Memory* (cat. 89)—was first exhibited at Carstairs Gallery, New York, from December 1954 to January 1955. The painting's then prolix title, *The Chromosome of a Highly Colored Fish's Eye Starting the Harmonious Disintegration of The Persistence of Memory* , emphasized the mysterious levitating fish, whose glowing eye possibly takes the place of the orange stopwatch teaming with ants—both among the few elements not shared by the two images. The painting is otherwise a close variation on the 1931 original, even in its identical dimensions; a soft self-portrait in the legacy of *The Great Masturbator* (1929; cat. 65)—here rendered in translucent violet—appears draped with a soft watch amidst a 'disintegrating' seascape based on the view from Dalí's studio at Port Lligat. The rectangular blocks—the meticulous work of the artist's builder and part-time studio assistant, Emilio Puignau (see *Nuclear Cross*; cat. 223)—and the rhinoceros horns floating through space suggest the world's 'harmonious' disintegration into atomic particles, the ramifications of which are so pervasive they have even affected the idyllic serenity of Dalí's isolated fisherman's hut.

By the time Dalí executed *The Disintegration of the Persistence of Memory The Disintegration of the Persistence of Memory* , its 1931 predecessor was well-established in popular consciousness, particularly in the United States; indeed, according to *Dalí News*, a self-apotheosizing 'newspaper' he published in 1947 to coincide with his Bignou Gallery exhibition, more U.S. cartoons were devoted that year to *The Persistence of Memory* than to any other subject.[1] "Journalists from coast to coast wrote stories about 'Limp Watches,'" recalled Julien Levy, the New York gallerist who purchased *The Persistence of Memory* for $250—more than he had ever paid for a painting—at its 1931 debut at the Pierre Colle Gallery in Paris.[2] The work's subsequent appearances at the 1933 Chicago World's Fair and 1936 Museum of Modern Art (New York) exhibition, "Fantastic Art, Dada and Surrealism," secured *The Persistence of Memory* as the archetypal Surrealist tableau, bringing Dalí enormous fame in the United States and the barrage of commercial projects that led André Breton to dub him with the biting anagram, 'Avida Dollars.' As his signature piece, *The Persistence of Memory* was publicly quoted by Dalí in such projects as the backdrop for his 1939 *Dream of Venus* Pavilion at the New York World's Fair, and in the malleable wagon wheel appearing in his 1944 dream sequence for Alfred Hitchcock's movie, *Spellbound*; he even had himself cast as a soft watch by the photographer Philippe Halsman in 1954 (fig. 1).

In suggesting the famous melting clocks merited revision through the lens of quantum mechanics, Dalí gave the painting his highest praise, placing it in the esteemed company of Vermeer's *Lacemaker* (cat. 228), which he 'rhinocerized' in 1955, and various works by Diego Velázquez, after whom he executed, among others, the 1958 painting, *Velázquez Painting the Infanta Marguerita with the Lights and Shadows of His Own Glory*. Dalí said he intended the soft watches as an illustration of the 'anguishing' revelations in time and space, specifically Einstein's 1905 challenge to the concept of Absolute or Universal Time. Following the 1945 detonation of the atomic bomb at Hiroshima—an explosion, he said, that shook him "*seismically*," after which the atom became his "preferred subject for consideration"—, his fervor for Einstein gave way to a new 'father figure,' atomic physicist Dr. Werner Heisenberg.[3] The nuclear fragmentation of the relativistic soft watches, described by Dalí in 1935 as the "tender, extravagant, solitary paranoiac-critical camembert of time and of space" (see Encyclopedia, 'cheese'), may therefore allude to progresses in the hard sciences and Einstein's outspoken refusal to accept quantum theory, to which Dalí posited the two might be reconciled through religion.[4] "When Einstein revealed the fourth dimension of time using theories of relativity, he offered us a means of being raving in order to meet God," he says in 1973. "…All the mystics, be they religious, nuclear, hallucinogenic, or of gold, have the same divine Heaven that my painting celebrates my painting…: the union of time and space that is the secret of God."[5] This devout unity between relativity theory and quantum mechanics adds a compelling dimension to Dalí's other depictions of atomized soft watches, including *Soft Watch at the Moment of First Explosion* (1954), the enigmatic title of which may connote the 'Big Bang,' believed by many to be the origin of the universe and the point at which Einstein's theories of general relativity—in the painting, quite literally—'fall apart,' revealing, for Dalí, swirling logarithmic rhinoceros horns (see Encyclopedia) and, thus, nature's underlying order—God's presence within both the macro and microcosms.
E.H.K. and J.K.

[1] Salvador Dalí, *Dalí News, monarch of the dailies* (New York) vol. I, no. 2, 1947.
[2] Julien Levy, *Memoir of an Art Gallery* (New York: G.P. Putnam's Sons, 1977), pp. 76-83.
[3] André Parinaud, *Comment on devient Dalí* (Paris: Éditions Robert Laffont, 1973), p. 265. See Salvador Dalí, *Anti-Matter manifesto* (New York: Carstairs Gallery, 1958-59).
[4] Salvador Dalí, *La conquête de l'irrationnel* (Paris: Éditions surréalistes, 1935), p. 25.
[5] Parinaud, p. 276.

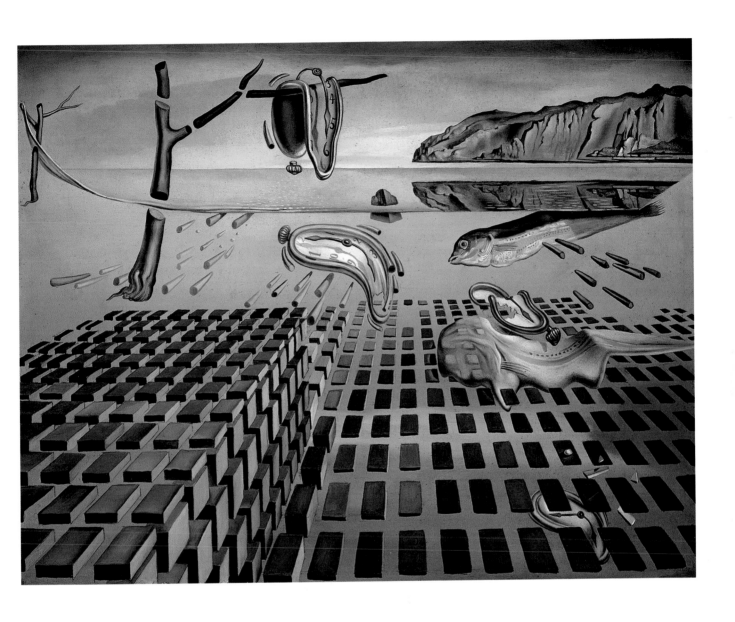

225. Crucifixion (Corpus Hypercubicus), 1953-54

225. Oil on canvas
194.4 × 123.9 cm
76 1/2 × 48 3/4 in.
New York (NY),
Metropolitan Museum of Art,
gift of the Chester Dale
Collection, 1955

Fig. 1. Salvador Dalí with a
hypercube made out of olive wood
photographed by Francesc
Català-Roca, 1951

When Dalí arrived in the port of Le Havre on March 27, 1953, having just completed a transatlantic crossing from New York on the ocean liner *America*, he announced to the awaiting newspaper reporters his plans for a sensational new painting: "an exploding Christ, nuclear and hypercubic."[1] Dalí began work on this immense canvas in the spring of 1953, but did not complete the painting until the following year, due to the enormous technical and compositional problems inherent in making "the first painting whose conception is genuinely based on cubist elements unfolding in the fourth dimension."[2] The artist's struggle with the work is recorded in the pages of *Diary of a Genius*, in which he mentions the technical failures that beset the work. "While I was painting the draperies better than ever," he reported on September 16, 1953, "I also tried, because of a chimerical desire for absolute perfection, to paint with almost no paint on surfaces saturated with amber. I wanted to attain the utmost mastery, the maximum of the quintessence of dematerialization. The result was disastrous. For an hour, the area I had painted was superb; but on drying, the amber absorbed the colored part and everything turned the color of dark amber and was covered with stains."[3]

Dalí eventually overcame these technical set backs to create an astonishing image of the crucified Christ, suspended in midair, while Gala stands at the foot of the cross wearing a sumptuous yellow robe that resembles that of the penitent Mary Magdalene in traditional Christian iconography. The painting is indebted stylistically to the Spanish painters Francisco de Zurbarán and Diego Velásquez, who both painted the central figure of Christ on the cross against a dark background that served to throw the figure into relief and heighten the emotion of the scene portrayed.[4] However, the painting's most unusual feature, the fourth-dimensional hypercube, i.e. the eight cubes out of which the cross is constructed, was inspired by the ideas of the late-13th-century Catalan philosopher and mystic Raymond Lull, as well as a manuscript written by the 16th-century Spanish architect Juan de Herrera.[5] According to Dalí, his work with the unfolded hypercube was the culmination of Lull's manipulation of two-dimensional forms and the three-dimensional researches that Herrera presented in his aesthetic treatise *Tratado de la figura cúbica* (Discourse on Cubical Form). The artist was fascinated by Herrera, who completed El Escorial, Philip II's austerely classical castle-monastery outside Madrid, that Dalí had earlier made reference to in *The Temptation of Saint Anthony*, of 1946, and believed that his use of the hypercube was a natural extension of the ideas of Lull and Herrera.

The cross is an octahedral hypercube, an eight-sided cubic cross (the back cube being hidden from view), with the body (corpus) of Christ identifiable as the ninth cube. This structure, essentially a cube projecting cubes out of each of its faces, with an additional cube coming out of the bottom face, to form a cross, was explicitly borrowed from the Hypercube, or Tesseract, that was developed by the British mathematician Charles Howard Hinton in the 1880s, and popularized by the 20th-century American architect and fourth-dimension theorist Claude Bragdon.[6] However, for Dalí, the modern notion of the Hypercube was only made possible by the discoveries of his fellow countrymen, Lull and Herrara, as well as Pablo Picasso, whose Cubist paintings were also invoked in the artist's discussions of *Crucifixion (Corpus Hypercubicus)*. Dalí was photographed in 1951 clutching to his chest a hypercube made out of olive wood, and in 1976 Thomas Banchoff presented the artist with a metal version, which allowed him to physically re-enact the rotating and folding movement of the painted cross in his painting. The hypercube represented

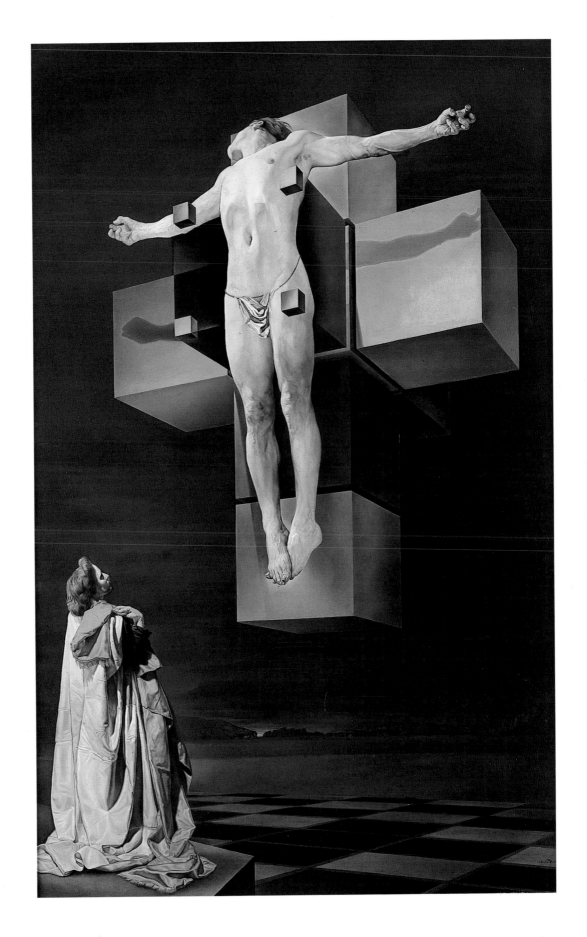

for Dalí an octahedron seen in the fourth dimension and he compared what he considered to be the explosive movement of the cubes in higher space to the convex and concave spatial ambiguities of Picasso's Cubist paintings as he understood them .[7]

While Dalí's ambitious and idiosyncratic *Crucifixion* was dismissed by most art critics as irrelevant kitsch, Chester Dale, the distinguished collector of Impressionist and modern French paintings, was overwhelmed when he saw the work for the first time at the Carstairs Gallery in New York, in December 1954. When asked to explain why he was "bowled over" by the painting, Dale replied: "I can't explain it except in one way—when it hits me, it hits me hard. It is a very honest picture, very great."[8] Dale decided to purchase the work on the spot, reportedly paying $15,000 for it, which he then donated, along with a painting by Amedeo Modigliani, to the Metropolitan Museum of Art, New York, in the same year. [9] The painting was initially hung in the Museum's great entrance hall, where it immediately attracted throngs of visitors, who were curious to see the artist's much publicized religious painting. The Metropolitan Museum even changed the title from *Corpus Hypercubicus* to *Crucifixion*, believing that this new name would be easier for the general public to understand, and proclaimed the work to be "an outstanding modern religious painting, very serious, with little surrealistic eccentricities."[10] However, it was left to Dalí to have the last word on the subject: "Juan Gris created beautiful cubism and Picasso continued it. Now myself (sic) has created one complete hypercubist painting."[11] M.R.T.

[1] Roger Campion, "Passager de l'"America': Salvador Dalí nous est revenu avec un christ 'Hypercubique' et un message pour Picasso," *Le Havre Libre* (Le Havre: March 30), 1953, p.1. Dalí also informed the reporters that his Christ would explode into 88 pieces, an idea he would later abandon in the finished painting, see Anonymous, "! Elo ! Elo ! Elo !," *The Register-Guard* (Eugene, Oregon: April 1, 1953), p. 5.

[2] Ramón Gómez de la Serna, *Dalí*, trans. Nicholas Fry (Edison, New Jersey: Wellfleet Press, 2001), p. 41.

[3] Salvador Dalí, *Diary of a Genius*, trans. Richard Howard (London: Creation Books, 1994), p. 100.

[4] Dalí remembered a reproduction of *Christ on the Cross* by Velázquez hanging in his parents' bedroom, alongside a photograph of his dead brother, when he was growing up. This suggests that the theme held a deep fascination for the artist that went beyond his newfound interest in Catholicism. See Salvador Dalí, *The Unspeakable Confessions of Salvador Dalí (as Told to André Parinaud)*, trans. Harold J. Salemson (New York: William Morrow and Company, 1976), p. 241.

[5] For more on the relationship between Lull's ideas and Herrera's *Tratado de la figura cúbica* see Catherine Wilkinson-Zerner, *Juan de Herrera: Architect to Philip II of Spain*, (New Haven: Yale University Press, 1993), p.43.

[6] Claude Bragdon, *A Primer of Higher Space: The Fourth Dimension to which is added Man The Square: A Higher Space Parable* (Rochester, New York: Manas Press, 1913), plate 4.

[7] Thomas F. Banchoff, *Beyond the Third Dimension: Geometry, Computer Graphics, and Higher Dimensions* (New York: Scientific American Library, 1990), pp. 105-106. This metal hypercube model is now on permanent exhibit at the Teatre-Museu Dalí in Figueres, Spain.

[8] Anonymous, "Dalí Makes Met," *Time*, January 24, 1955, p. 72.

[9] Anonymous, "Museum Acquires Its First Dalí; 'Crucifixion' to Be Shown Today," *New York Times* (New York: January 14, 1955), p.23

[10] Press release, Metropolitan Museum of Art, reprinted in Anonymous, "Dalí Makes Met," op. cit., p. 72.

[11] *Ibid.* Dalí's willfully perverse suggestion that Juan Gris invented Cubism has to be understood within the framework of his lifelong rivalry with Picasso and his desire for scandal and provocation.

226. Head Bombarded with Grains of Wheat
(Particle Head Over the Village of Cadaqués), 1954

226. Oil on cardboard
26.6 × 17.8 cm
10 1/2 × 7 in.
Private Collection

Like many of Dalí's early 1950s atomic paintings, *Head Bombarded with Grains of Wheat* presents a coruscating swarm of particles coalescing to form an idealized face over the Catalan village of Cadaqués. Dalí became captivated with atomic physics following the detonation of the atomic bomb on August 6 1945. "Thenceforth, the atom was my favorite food for thought," he reported.[1] It is possible that he partially adopted this interest as an oppositional response to the Surrealists—from whom he was now officially 'excommunicated'—, who once celebrated atomic physics but now—post-explosion—considered it irresponsible and destructive. Although Dalí claimed that many of his ensuing landscapes expressed "the great fear inspired in me by the announcement of that explosion," only the diminutive bomber in his tenebrous 1945 canvas, *Melancholic, Atomic, Uranic Idyll* (fig. 2) seems truly sympathetic to the destruction resulting from the Enola Gay's ten-kiloton weapon.[2] He quickly abandoned such uncharacteristic political commentary, recognizing the atomic bomb as an element of the modern age that required objective assimilation towards making art 'contemporary.' "The artist must express the cosmology of the epoch in which he lives," he told a reporter in 1952. "Since we now live in the atomic age … it is up to artists to work out a way of putting across an up-to-date message."[3] Dalí's artistic aim resulted in unique hybrids of academic painting with allusions to nuclear physics, particularly the discontinuity of matter (see *Leda Atomica,* cat. 213). Initially manifesting as levitating, but solid, elements (e.g., his 1950 *Madonna of Port Lligat* [see cat. 215]), in the 1950s the objects themselves disintegrated as he endeavored to render the vivacious particles that lie beneath the chimera of continuous form. "What distinguishes our age from the Renaissance," he told Carlton Lake, "is that now for the first time we realize that matter, instead of being something continuous, is discontinuous… [I]f one wanted to give an accurate representation of a table, instead of being compact the table should resemble something like a swarm of flies."[4]

Unlike the double-images common to his 1930s painting, Dalí designed his molecular 'swarm' to be readable only as a figure, albeit one comprised of paranoiac elements; these include, for example, the 'rhinoceratic' cones and wheelbarrows quoted from Millet's *Angelus* in his 1951 painting, *Raphae-*

Fig. 2. Salvador Dalí, *Melancholic, Atomic, Uranic Idyll,* 1945
Madrid, Museo Nacional Centro de Arte Reina Sofía

lesque Head Exploding. In *Head Bombarded with Grains of Wheat*, the figure's bust consists of spiny grains of wheat, explicitly along the neck and shoulder. The ear of wheat—appearing notably in Dalí's mystical 1947 painting, *Wheat Ear* (fig. 1), and his 1950 *Madonna of Port Lligat*—may allude to Christ's identification with wheat as a symbol for His sacrifice and resurrection: "Verily, verily, I say unto you, Except a corn of wheat fall into the ground and die, it abideth alone: but if it die, it bringeth forth much fruit."[5] In rendering a figure 'atomically' comprised of elements metaphorical to Christ, Dalí illustrates his opinion that matter is spiritualized on the subatomic level—indeed, that God might be the "substance being sought by nuclear physics."[6] E.H.K.

Fig. 1. Salvador Dalí,
Wheat Ear, 1947
Private collection;
formerly Coco Chanel Collection

[1] André Parinaud, *The Unspeakable Confessions of Salvador Dalí* (New York: William Morrow and Company, Inc., 1976), p. 216. Originally published in French as *Comment on devient Dalí* (Paris: Éditions Robert Laffont, 1973).
[2] *Ibid.*
[3] Clete Wiley, "Dalí, Showman of Art, Tells of His Nuclear Mysticism," *Waterloo Daily Courier* (Waterloo, Iowa, USA), February 6, 1952, original page unknown.
[4] Carlton Lake, *In Quest for Dalí* (New York: G.P. Putnam's Sons, 1969), p. 48.
[5] John 12:24
[6] Bruno Froissart, "Salvador Dalí et le monde angélique," *100 Aquarelles pour la Divine Comédie de Dante Alighieri par Salvador Dalí* (Paris: Musée Galliera, 1960), p. 54.

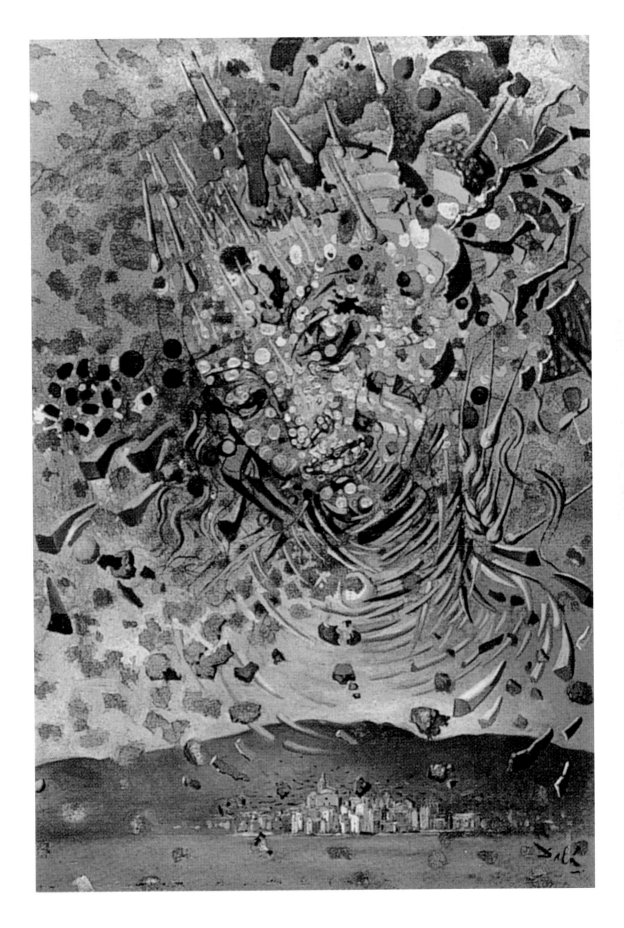

227. The Lacemaker (after Vermeer), 1954-55

227. Oil on canvas
23.5 × 19.7 cm
9¼ × 7¾ in.
New York (NY),
The Metropolitan Museum
of Art, The Robert Lehman
Collection, 1975

Dalí first met Robert Lehman during his first visit to the United States in 1934, when he went to see the American banker's famed collection of old master paintings in the Lehman family house on 7 West 54th Street in New York. The collector later recalled that the artist had been thrilled to see his Goya, an imposing double portrait of the *Condesa de Altamira and Her Daughter, Maria Agustina*, of 1787-1788, but wondered why Lehman had never acquired a work by Vermeer, the 17th-century Dutch painter whose detailed naturalism had obsessed Dalí throughout his early career? Lehman explained that he had searched the world for such a painting to complete his collection, but due to the scarcity of Vermeer paintings in private hands he had never found a suitable work for sale. The collector then impulsively asked Dalí if he would make a copy of a Vermeer for him, to which the artist replied, "That would be impossible. It couldn't be done."[1]

The two men met frequently over the course of the next two decades, but it was not until 1954 that Lehman reminded Dalí of their earlier conversation about copying a Vermeer. The artist informed him that he had recently begun a painstakingly accurate copy of Vermeer's *The Lacemaker* of ca. 1669-70 (fig. 1), which he would sell to the banker for $5,000, the price of an original Dalí painting, rather than a mere replica.[2] Lehman agreed and, in February 1956, he officially commissioned Dalí to make a copy of the Vermeer in "completely classical technique" for his collection.[3] Two years earlier, in December 1954, the artist had received permission from the Louvre to make a copy of Vermeer's *The Lacemaker*. The Museum provided the artist with a small room in which to execute his exact replica, while the conservation staff and curators provided Dalí with a technical analysis of the fine brushes and pigments used by Vermeer, as well as measurements and information regarding the painting's support, which consists of a slightly open, plain weave canvas, with a thread count of 12 × 12 cm (43/4 ×, 43/4) that had been glued to an oak panel. The artist then ordered his own brushes, colors, and canvas according to these precise specifications. Before starting work on the canvas, however, Dalí is also reputed to have read books on perspective, religion, and cartography (to try to understand why Vermeer so frequently incorporated maps in his compositions) that would have been available to the Dutch artist,

in a bid to enter into the mindset of his artist hero. Having prepared for months, the artist finally began work on his copy of *The Lacemaker* in New York in the winter of 1954-55, and completed the painting in Port Lligat, where he had gathered around fifty reproductions of the Vermeer, in the following year.[4] It is thus unclear what work, if any, Dalí carried out on the painting before delivering it to Lehman in April 1957, aside from adding his own signature in a self-consciously antiquated calligraphy in the top right corner. This signature, located in the exact same spot where Vermeer had placed his own ligature, closely resembles the Dutch artist's now faded lettering.[5] The copy was almost flawless, except for the coarse texture of the canvas, which bothered both artist and collector. It was later ascertained that the original Vermeer canvas had shrunk flat over the centuries, partly as a result of being lined by conservators at the Louvre, thus giving it the smooth surface one sees today. Although Dalí requested that his own work be relined, pressed and flattened in the same way, its textured surface remains much coarser than the Vermeer original and will have to wait for the ravages of time to iron out the roughness of the canvas weave. M.R.T.

[1] Fleur Cowles, *The Case of Salvador Dalí* (London: Heinemann, 1959), p. 253.

[2] Fleur Cowles, "Which Vermeer Is the Dalí?," *Telegraph Sunday Magazine*, no. 190, May 18, 1980, p. 18.

[3] Robert Lehman, Letter to Salvador Dalí, February 25, 1956, p. 1. Archives of the Robert Lehman Collection, Metropolitan Museum of Art, New York.

[4] The dating of the painting's execution was provided by Robert Descharnes in a fax to the Metropolitan Museum of Art, dated December 12, 1993, Archives of the Robert Lehman Collection, Metropolitan Museum of Art, New York. The artist remembered gathering "some fifty-odd reproductions of the Vermeer, that I hung all over my olive grove; and even on the beach, when I went bathing with Gala"; see Salvador Dalí, *The Unspeakable Confessions of Salvador Dalí (as Told to André Parinaud)*, trans. Harold J. Salemson (New York: William Morrow and Co., 1976), p. 232.

[5] Robert Lehman wrote to the artist to thank him for his visit and that of Mrs. Dalí, while also enclosing a check in "payment for the painting of Vermeer"; see Lehman, Letter to Salvador Dalí, April 9, 1957. Archives of the Robert Lehman Collection, Metropolitan Museum of Art, New York.

Fig. 1. Jan Vermeer, *The Lacemaker*,
ca. 1669-70
Paris, Musée du Louvre

228. Paranoiac-Critical Study of Vermeer's "Lacemaker," 1954-55

228. Oil on canvas
27.1 × 22.1 cm
10⁵/8 × 8³/4 in.
New York (NY), The Solomon
R. Guggenheim Museum,
anonymous gift, 76.2206

Dalí's fanatical obsession with the work of Johannes Vermeer, especially the Dutch artist's *The Lacemaker* (see p. 374, fig. 1), dates back to his early childhood.[1] In 1926, having begun to experiment with a meticulous and transcendent realism akin to that of Vermeer, the artist traveled to Holland to see his work in museums and public collections. This trip greatly enhanced his understanding of Vermeer's painting, which he described two years later as an art of perception and looking that reached "the highest, most humble and most dramatic probity."[2] The earliest direct reference to Vermeer's famous panel painting in his own work came in 1929, when the artist included a shot of *The Lacemaker*, seen reproduced on the open page of a book, in the film *Un Chien andalou*.[3] The serene and beautifully ordered world of Vermeer haunted Dalí, who made a number of variations of *The Lacemaker*, including this 'rhinocerontic' copy which he began at the Louvre in Paris December 1954.[4] Dalí used a heavy canvas support for this version of the Vermeer painting, thus challenging himself to re-create the Dutch artist's minute brushstrokes and jewel-like colors on such a rough surface. Like the representational copy he made of the Vermeer, now in the Robert Lehman Collection at the MoMa (New York), this work was based on direct observation of the original painting in the Louvre. Whereas the Lehman painting sought to replicate the immaculate craftsmanship and sustained purity of mood, color and light of the original, in this first version, which was made as its title suggests using the artist's paranoiac-critical method, the insistence on perfection and color harmony is replaced by a dynamic composition in which the lacemaker's face is surrounded by exploding conical forms that resemble the horns of a rhinoceros. Dalí had surprised the staff at the Louvre when, following an hour of meditation, he accurately re-created *The Lacemaker* using the curved and spiral forms of the rhinoceros horn, which formed the underlying composition of this painting. Dalí had been enthusiastically studying the rhinoceros since 1950, when his close friend Arturo López-Wilshaw presented him with a walking stick whose handle was formed from the animal's horn.[5] The artist's obsession led him to start 'seeing' the animal's horns in his own paintings, and those of other artists, including Vermeer. Although a traditional symbol of purity, related to the unicorn, the artist was aware of the sexual connotations of the rhinoceros horn, which is made up of a keratinous material that has long been considered an aphrodisiac. On December 17, 1955, Dalí gave a lecture entitled "Phenomenological Aspects of the Paranoiac-Critical Method" at the Sorbonne in Paris that expounded upon the connections he had drawn between Vermeer's *The Lacemaker* and rhinoceros' horns in his *Paranoiac-Critical Study of Vermeer's "Lacemaker"*: "These horns being the only ones in the animal kingdom constructed in accordance with a perfect logarithmic spiral, as in this painting, it is this very logarithmic perfection that guided Vermeer's hand in painting *The Lace Maker*."[6] Dalí thus claimed that through his discovery of a morphological resemblance between the Vermeer painting and the suspended, curved horns of a rhinoceros he had penetrated the crystalline outer surface of the *The Lacemaker* to reveal its underlying scientific structure. According to his theory, these curvilinear forms could be compared to the mathematically self-perpetuating logarithmic spiral, an idea Dalí also explored in a contemporaneous film that he worked on with Robert Descharnes entitled *The Prodigious Story of the Lacemaker and the Rhinoceros*. In order to verify his quasi-scientific discoveries, Dalí even organized a mock 'battle' staged in the rhinoceros enclosure at the Vincennes Zoo in May 1955, in which the artist confronted an African black rhinoceros rhinoceros by the name of François with numerous copies of *The Lacemaker*. To Dalí's great delight the animal proceeded to use its horn to tear to pieces an oversized copy of the *Lacemaker*, thus confirming in his mind the affinity between the lumbering beast and Vermeer's painting. This carefully orchestrated media event also included the bizarre image of Dalí painting the *Paranoiac-Critical Study of Vermeer's "Lacemaker"* while seated on a wheelbarrow, a reference to his interpretation of Millet's *Angelus*. The day finally ended with the artist simulating the charging rhinoceros by brandishing a narwhal's tusk, which he used as a lance to pierce and crashed through another reproduction of the Vermeer painting like a modern Don Quixote chasing after his windmill. M.R.T.

[1] Salvador Dalí, *Diary of a Genius*, trans. Richard Howard (London: Creation Books, 1994), p. 112.

[2] Salvador Dalí, "Nous límits de la pintura," (part 1), *L'Amic de les Arts*, no. 22 (Sitges: February 29, 1928), pp. 167-169; translated in H. Finkelstein, ed., *The Collected Writings of Salvador Dalí* (Cambridge: Cambridge University Press, 1998), p. 81.

[3] See Stuart Liebman, "Un Chien andalou: The Talking Cure," in Rudolf E. Kuenzli, ed., *Dada and Surrealist Film* (New York: Willis Locker & Owens, 1987), pp. 152-153. According to Liebman, *La dentellière*, the French title of the Vermeer painting, would connect this work with other images of teeth in the film. Although the reference is less direct, it could be argued that the artist's earlier paintings and sketches of his sister, Ana María, sewing were also inspired by Vermeer's *Lacemaker*.

[4] Dalí in conversation with V. E. Barnett, April 1978, in Barnett, *Handbook: The Guggenheim Museum Collection 1900-1980* (New York: 1980), p. 313.

[5] Salvador Dalí, *Diary of a Genius*, op. cit., p. 47. This cane was in Dalí's possession as early as May 1950, when he showed it during an interview in Paris: "I've always been a fetishist." … "This cane never leaves my hands. It was given to me by Arturo Lopez. The handle is trimmed in rhinoceros—the symbol of mystery." He held the cane aloft. "You see, it's like an antenna"; see M.Horton and J. Appleton, "Mostly About People," *International Herald Tribune* (Paris), May 15, 1950, n.p.

[6] Robert Descharnes, *The World of Salvador Dalí* (New York and Evanston: Harper & Row, 1962), p. 54.

[7] Dalí announced his intention in a telegram to Georges Mathieu, sent from New York in 1955. Ibid, p. 52.

[8] Anonymous, "Dalí marie pour se libérer une dentellière et un rhinocéros," *Paris Match* (Paris) May 14, 1955, no. 319, p. 78.

229. Young Virgin Auto-Sodomized by the Horns of Her Own Chastity, 1954

229. Oil on canvas
40.5 × 30.5 cm
16 × 12 in.
Private Collection

As one of the most significant works of Dalí's 'Atomic Period' (1945-ca. 60), *Young Virgin Auto-Sodomized by the Horns of Her Own Chastity* presents the artist's attraction to rhinoceros horns at its zenith, with the emblem simultaneously serving as a structural device and as a sodomizing phallus, in addition to connoting the myriad of religious and morphological subtexts he had applied to it since his purported 1952 discovery that all his paintings could be deconstructed into assemblages of rhinoceros horns (see Encyclopedia).[1] Recalling his depiction of his sister, Ana María, in *Figure at a Window* (1925) and anticipating his portrait of Gala nude at the window in his 1974-75 *Gala Contemplating the Mediterranean Sea which at Twenty Meters Becomes the Portrait of Abraham Lincoln – Homage to Rothko*, the painting presents a blonde nude based on a photograph in a late 1930s sex magazine, leaning out of a window that looks onto the sea.[2] Her buttocks consist of four converging horns, which Dalí would revisit with his mysterious painting, *Goddess Leaning on Her Elbow …* (cat. 236). As the horns simultaneously comprise and threaten to sodomize the callipygian figure, she is effectively (auto-)sodomized by her own constitution. Upon its completion, Dalí presented his painting as a gift to the Argentinean jeweler, Carlos Alemany, who executed Dalí's jewelry designs under the artist's supervision in New York beginning in the early 1940s.[3] Through the legend of the unicorn and its associations within Christian allegory, Dalí imbued the rhinoceros horn with the connotation of chastity—a counterintuitive subtext given its phallic morphology and fabled aphrodisiac qualities. By virtue of this association, the 'young virgin' may be linked to the Virgin Mary—a divinity further hinted at by the fact that, as with the Zeus-swan in *Leda Atomica* (cat. 213), the 'virgin' casts no shadow, despite the strong lighting and shadows cast by the balcony railing and the dominant, penile rhinoceros horn hovering behind H/her. In amalgamating the Virgin with a pin-up model, high art with mass culture, and the sacred with the profane, the painting generates a paradoxical hybrid, foreshadowing what Dalí would later dub 'chaste eroticism.'[4] "Paradoxically," he said in 1958, "this painting, which has an erotic appearance, is the most chaste of all."[5] E.H.K.

[1] Salvador Dalí, *Diary of a Genius*, trans. Richard Howard (New York: Prentice Hall Press, 1986), p. 36. Originally published in French as *Journal d'un génie* (Paris: La Table Ronde, 1964).

[2] Robert Descharnes, *Dalí, L'héritage infernal* (Paris: Éditions Ramsay/La Marge, 2002), p. 72.

[3] On the painting's overlap Dalí wrote, "*Para mi amigo Carlos Alemany como prueba de nuestros años de tenacidad e collaboracion*" (For my friend Carlos Alemany as proof of our years of tenacity and collaboration). Special thanks to Richard Rosenzweig of Playboy Enterprises, Inc., which owned the painting from 1971 until 2003, for alerting me to this dedication and for allowing me to see the work in 2003 as it hung in the Playboy Mansion in Beverly Hills.

[4] Salvador Dalí, *Les Dîners de Gala* (Paris: Draeger, 1973). One perhaps also recalls the chapter in André Parinaud's *Comment on devient Dalí*, "How to become erotic while remaining chaste" (New York: William Morrow and Company, Inc., 1976). Originally published in French as *Comment on devient Dalí* (Paris: Éditions Robert Laffont, 1973).

[5] A. Reynolds Morse, *Dalí: A Study of His Life and Work* (Greenwich: New York Graphic Society, 1958), p. 81.

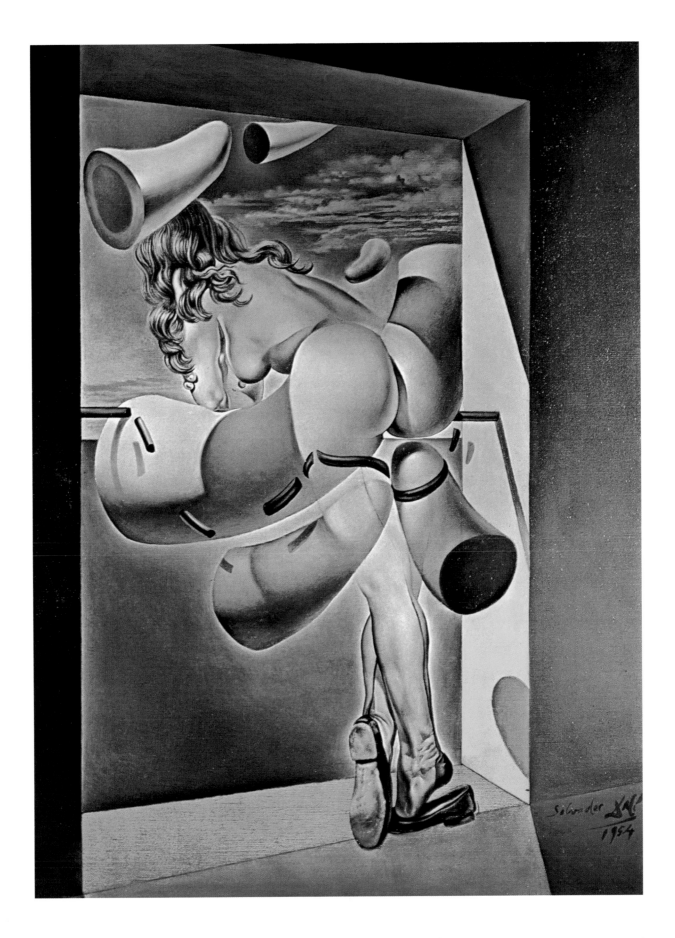

230. Still Life – Fast Moving, 1956

230. Oil on canvas
125 × 160 cm
49 1/8 × 63 in.
St. Petersburg (FL),
The Salvador Dalí Museum

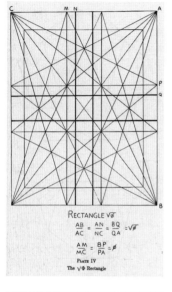

RECTANGLE √ø

$$\frac{AB}{AC} = \frac{AN}{NC} = \frac{BQ}{QA} = \sqrt{\phi}$$

$$\frac{AM}{MC} = \frac{BP}{PA} = \phi$$

PLATE IV
The √Φ Rectangle

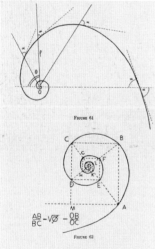

FIGURE 61

$$\frac{AB}{BC} = \sqrt{\phi} = \frac{OB}{OC}$$

FIGURE 62

Fig. 1. The rectangle of the square root of "phi" according to Matila Ghyka

Fig. 2. The square root of the spiral of "phi" according to Matila Ghyka

Emblematic of Dalí's emerging Nuclear Mysticism, this large painting was the sixth in the series of monumental history canvases Dalí began in 1948, and it is the first to depart from their strictly religious subjects. Taking five months to prepare and paint, the composition is a post-atomic variation on Dutch artist Floris Van Schooten's (1590-55) *Table with Food* (1617), in the Prado Museum Collection. Van Schooten's work is shattered into individual objects that float and rotate in space, disintegrating yet held in a suspended balance. All objects are flying apart, but nothing touches anything else. Dalí used the term 'divisionism' to describe this structural approach to his 1950s work where objects metaphorically break down into a series of floating particles held in suspension. This process has also been termed 'corpuscular,' describing how Dalí breaks down the composition into smaller particles.[1]

Presenting a paradoxically harmonious chaos, as underlined by the title's word play 'still life – fast moving,' this painting suggests that while the atomic bomb destroys reality, it reveals a divine cosmic order on the subatomic level. All of the objects in the painting are beginning to disintegrate as the result of the atomic bomb, but they are disintegrating in a harmonious arrangement. In Dalí's words, *Still Life – Fast Moving* is "[an] explanatory painting where one can observe the dynamic and irrational dividing of a fruit dish following the coefficients of uncertainty of Heisenberg in opposition to the positive security which cubist pictures once tried to offer us."[2] By referring to Heisenberg, Dalí declares his interest in modern physics and his stance against the post-Euclidean perception developed by modernist artists before Hiroshima. Prior to his interest in Heisenberg, Dalí referred to Albert Einstein's 'space-time' concept, a key aspect of his 'Special Theory of Relativity,' (see Encyclopedia) which is illustrated in the halted motion and spatial separation of the objects in the painting.[3]

As Robert Lubar convincingly argues, Dalí employs an illusionistic Renaissance space only to undermine it by presenting each object in sharp focus, eliminating atmospheric perspective, and further by unhinging the shadows from any singular light source.[4] Dalí creates a space where objects exist in a continuum with no fixed perspective, a post-atomic world of dynamic suspension that he presents in opposition to the flatness of the picture plane developed from Cubism through Abstract Expressionism. By employing divisionism, Dalí argues that "Cubism ... and the tradition of abstract art it spawned correspond to a conception of space that nuclear physics has rendered obsolete."[5] In a typical show of bravura, Dalí asserts that the small fragments of color at the lower left represent the "final bits of meaningless particles left over from [my] sin-

gle-handed assault on abstract-expressionism."[6]
This work reveals Dalí's obsession with underlying forms of order. Spiral structures can be found throughout, from the rhinoceros horn held in the upper left to the twisting compotier in the center to the cauliflower floret to the right, which resembles a meteor. For Dalí, the spiral was the most perfect form found in nature, a symbol that he employed to represent cosmic order. The golden spiral, derived from the golden section, can be found in both natural and manmade forms in the work. Both the cauliflower and rhinoceros horn are natural forms with the common morphology of the logarithmic spiral. In contrast, the double helix shape of the balcony rail refers to the double helix spiral shape of the DNA molecule discovered by Francis H. C. Crick and James Dewey Watson in 1953, for which they received the Nobel Prize in 1962. This connection between the genetic code and its double helix spiral would lead Dalí to refer to the DNA molecule as the "genetical persistance [sic] of human memory,"[7] a tidy reference to his own *Persistence of Memory* from 1931.

Such underlying order and unity ultimately inform Dalí's strategy for his overall composition. While it may appear chaotic initially because of the multitude of disparate objects, for the overall composition the objects obey a greater mathematical order derived from the golden section. Dalí was fascinated by *The Geometry of Art and Life*, a study of esthetic proportions by the Romanian mathematician, Matila Ghyka[8] (see Encyclopedia). For this composition, Dalí arranged all of the objects on a grid derived from Ghyka's study, a grid based on the harmonic division of the rectangle of the square root of 'phi.'[9] Based on the golden section, these proportions define Dalí's arrangements of objects, in turn providing a greater aesthetic unity to the contained chaos. P.T.

[1] Robert Descharnes, *Salvador Dalí: The Work, The Man*, trans. Eleanor R. Morse (New York: Harry N. Abrams, Inc., 1984), pp. 317-322.

[2] A. Reynolds Morse, *Salvador Dalí: A Panorama of His Art* (Cleveland: The Salvador Dalí Museum, 1974), p. 186.

[3] "Space-Time" is a way of describing the geometry of the universe after Einstein's Theory of Relativity. Time added to space becomes the forth dimension.

[4] Robert S. Lubar, *Dalí: The Salvador Dalí Museum Collection* (Boston: Bulfinch Press, 2000), pp. 141-142.

[5] *Ibid.*

[6] Morse, p. 189.

[7] Salvador Dalí, quoted in Carlton Lake, *In Quest of Dalí* (New York: Putnam, 1969), p. 16.

[8] Matila Ghyka, *The Geometry of Art and Life* (New York: Dover Publications, Inc., 1977), p. 31.

[9] Ghyka, pp. 30-31.

231. Skull of Zurbarán, 1956

231. Oil on canvas
100.3 × 100.3 cm
39¹/² × 39¹/² in.
Washington,
The Hirshhorn Museum
nd Sculpture Garden
gift of Joseph H. Hirshhorn
Foundation, 1966

Dalí's haunting homage to the Spanish Baroque painter Francisco de Zurbarán continued his interest in using morphology to create double images whose meaning can be understood on many levels. In this work, the stark architectural elements and the group of white robed figures, bent in prayer or veneration, transform themselves into a massive skull with teeth, a frequent motif in Zurbarán's paintings, seen in his numerous depictions of Saint Francis meditating over a skull in a cavelike setting. As the title suggests, the hovering image of the shape-shifting church interior can also be read as the cranium of the 17th-century painter, while the cubic building structure may represent an apse, before which several hooded, monklike figures appear to mourn, or even a mausoleum for the artist's remains. This monastic architecture takes the form of a series of ascending sets of stacked cubes that may have been inspired by the artist's close reading of Juan de Herrera's *Tratado de la figura cúbica (Discourse on Cubical Form)*, a 16th-century esthetic treatise that had earlier informed paintings such as *Crucifixion (Corpus Hypercubicus)* of 1953-54. The ambiguous arched form in the middle of the painting can be read as both an entrance into a recessed space and the nasal cavity of the gigantic skull. In addition, the shape appears to involve a visual pun on the peaked hoods worn by the monks in Zurbarán's paintings of Saint Francis of Assisi.

Dalí's admiration for the 17th-century painter dates back to his student days and first manifested itself in his own work in 1926 in the *Basket of Bread* (cat. 51), where the detailed illusionism and dramatic light effects referenced the Spanish tradition of still-life painting known as the *bodegòn*, of which Zurbarán was a recognized master. The *memento mori* device of the skull was associated with the *vanitas* theme in Spanish Golden Age painting, where it was known as *desengaño del mundo* (Disillusionment of the world). This painting may have been inspired by the Baroque artist's less well-known images of Saint Francis standing alive on top of his tomb, as he was found in 1449 by Pope Nicholas V, when he visited the crypt in the basilica at Assisi where the ascetic monk had been buried two hundred years earlier. In one of these variants, now in the Museum of Fine Arts in Boston, Zurbarán had painted the solitary hooded figure with a bold black shadow that gives the sensation of a double image, which must have fascinated Dalí, who repeated the curved design of the crypt's nichelike interior in his own austerely geometric setting (fig. 1). *Skull of Zurbarán* was first shown at the Carstairs Gallery, New York, in 1957, where it was purchased by the New York collector Joseph Hirshhorn, who admired the sinister subject matter and technical virtuosity of this perfectly square painting. M.R.T.

Fig. 1. Francisco de Zurbarán,
Saint Francis, 1640-45
Boston, Museum of Fine Arts

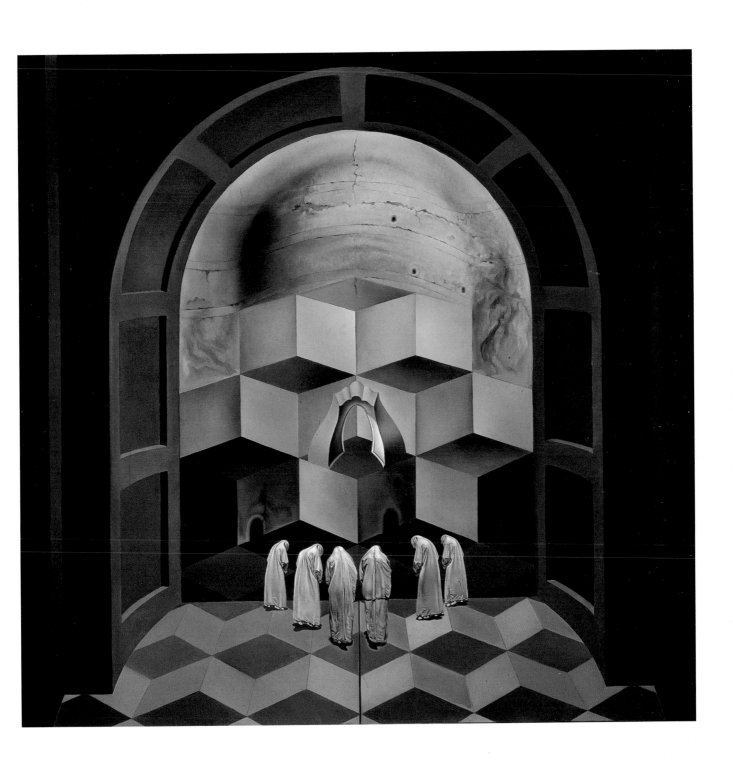

232. Music – The Red Orchestra – The Seven Arts, 1957

232. Oil on canvas
84 x 116 cm
33 1/8 × 45 5/8 in.
Private Collection

In 1943, after buying the Ziegfeld Theater in New York, the American impresario Billy Rose commissioned Dalí to paint a series of canvases for the foyer. The theatre was inaugurated with Rose's revue *The Seven Lively Arts*, which also provided the subjects for the decorative cycle: *The Concert*, *The Opera*, *The Ballet*, *The Theater*, *The Cinema*, *The Radio*, and *Boogie-Woogie*.

Dalí executed the seven canvases in about six weeks in one of the offices of the Ziegfeld Theater, which was temporarily converted into a studio for this purpose. In his memoirs, Billy Rose recalls that, in the course of a decade, millions of people flocked to see these works.

In April 1956, the paintings were destroyed in a fire in Rose's country house, where they had been taken. In 1957, in exchange for the compensation Rose received from the insurance company, Dalí repainted the entire series again in two months in his suite at the St. Regis Hotel in New York, replacing, however, *Boogie-Woogie* with *Rock and Roll*.

The new version of the allegory of *The Concert* was based on the composition of the 1943 painting—although there were a few minor variations—with the piano as a spring in the center of the work. This motif had already appeared in 1934 in the picture *The Mysterious Sources of Harmony*, and ten years later was the central element in the backdrop for the ballet *Sentimental Colloquy*, presented by the American Ballet Theater in New York in 1944. It is possible that the ironical elements of the picture reflect the lesser importance that Dalí, in appearance at least, attributed to music compared to the other arts.[1] T.S.

[1] Louis Pawels, *The Passion According to Dalí* (St. Petersburg, 1985), p. 150.

Fig. 3. Salvador Dalí, *Music – The Red Orchestra – The Seven Arts*, 1944
Destroyed in a fire in April 1956

Fig. 1. Salvador Dalí,
The Gran Opera, 1957
Private collection

Fig. 2. Salvador Dalí, *Study for "Sentimental Colloquy,"* 1944
St. Petersburg (FL), The Salvador Dalí Museum, on loan from E. and A. Reynolds Morse

233. The Sistine Madonna, 1958

233. Oil on canvas
224.6 × 191.3 cm
88 1/2 × 35 3/8 in.
New York (NY), The
Metropolitan Museum of Art
H.J. Heinz Collection.

Dalí's interest in *trompe-l'œil* and other forms of optical illusions reaches its apogee in this remarkable painting, which places a detail of Raphael's *Sistine Madonna* within the convolutions of the human ear.[1] In doing so, the artist made reference to the Catholic doctrine of the virgin birth of Jesus, thought by theologians in medieval times to have similarly occurred by way of the ear. The painting thus successfully reworks the old theme of the insemination of the Virgin Mary by the word, as it were, as graphically represented in early Renaissance paintings of the Annunciation in which actual phrases move across the painted surface from the lips of the archangel Gabriel to the ear of the patient Madonna.[2] Dalí also related the painting to alchemistic transmutations, as well as the passage involving Pantagruel's birth through the ear in François Rabelais' *Gargantua and Pantagruel*, of 1534.[3] This was no ordinary ear, however, since Dalí took it from a photograph of Pope John XXIII that was reproduced in *Paris Match*, which he then enlarged to the point where the halftone dots introduced by the printing process are unable to carry information about details of form and break down into a matrix of blobs. He then used a stencil to transfer the greatly magnified image to canvas, before using the moiré technique to superimpose the different layers of imagery. The end result is a visually ambiguous painting whose content and meaning continually shift with the movement of the viewer. From close up, we see an abstract grid, from a little further away the image of the Madonna and Child can be discerned, and from a far distance we see the

great ear, more than two meters high, of the Pontiff. Dalí's attempt to imitate the processes of modern industrial printing systems was not lost on younger artists, such as Andy Warhol, Roy Lichtenstein, Chuck Close, Richard Hamilton, Gerhard Richter and Sigmar Polke, who would all experiment with the effects of blown-up images from newspapers, cartoons and magazines.[4] Like Dalí, these artists were intrigued by the halftone illustrations, where the lights and shades of photographs are made up of hundreds of 'benday' dots, which are only revealed when the image is enlarged.[5] Whereas contemporary artists employed screened dot-patterns and other methods of commercial printing as a commentary on mass-media culture, Dalí's dematerialized *Sistine Madonna* reflects his continued fascination with nuclear physics, especially the concept of 'anti-matter,' in which particles of matter disappear on contact with particles of anti-matter, releasing tremendous energy. As the variant title of the work suggests, the work offers a kind of visual play on the structure of atomic particles, since the image dissolves and reorganizes itself in a constantly shifting screen: *Quasi-gray picture which, closely seen, is an abstract one; seen from two meters is the Sistine Madonna of Raphael; and from fifteen meters is the ear of an angel measuring one meter and a half; which is painted with anti-matter: therefore with pure energy.*[6]

Although rooted in the artist's efforts to reconcile modern art with religion and science under the banner of 'Nuclear mysticism,' this painting can also be understood as paying homage to Raphael and the great classical tradition in painting. Raphael's *Sistine Madonna*, of 1512-13 (fig. 1), is one of the best-known and most widely reproduced paintings in the history of art. Indeed, it may have been the universal fame of this painting that drew the artist's attention to the work after the Second World War, since a reproduction of Raphael's work hung in his studio at the St. Regis Hotel in New York in the late 1940s.[7] This would place the work within the context of the artist's copies and variations of other paintings of enormous popular appeal, such as Jean-François Millet's *The Angelus* and Jan Vermeer's *The Lacemaker*, for which he provided a unique 'paranoiac-critical' interpretation of their meaning.

Dalí completed the painting's optical illusion by perversely superimposing on the surface of the picture a group of impeccably painted *trompe-l'œil* objects, which consist of two pieces of folded paper, one supporting a cherry on the end of a piece of string, the other receiving its shadow. The hyper-reality of these suspended still life elements looks back to the precisely calculated *bodegónes*, or kitchen pictures, of Juan Sánchez Cotán. In Cotán's *Still Life with Quince, Cabbage, Melon, and Cucumber*, of ca. 1602 (fig. 2), for example, the apparently

Fig. 1. Raphael, *Sistine Madonna*, 1512-13
Dresden, Gemäldegalerie

Fig. 2. Juan Sánchez Cotán,
Still Life with Quince,
Cabbage, Melon, and Cucumber,
ca. 1602
San Diego (CA), San Diego
Museum of Art, gift
of Anne R. and Amy Putnam

weightless edibles that dangle on pieces of string take on a geometrical order that can be compared to Dalí's own interest in logarithmic curves and other mathematical principles in his late paintings. Like the benday dots, which draw attention to the mass-produced derivation of Dalí's image of the Pontiff's giant ear, these elements reinforce through their heightened realism the deceptive nature of the double image of the ear-Madonna.

When *The Sistine Madonna* was first shown at the World's Fair in Brussels in April 1958, and at the Carstairs Gallery in New York later that year, it was largely overlooked by critics and artists, who felt ill equipped to comment on the success or failure of the work due to their unfamiliarity with technical terms such as 'pi-mesons' and 'indeterminate neutrons' invoked by the artist to describe his anti-matter painting.[8] It was only when Marcel Duchamp included the work in the "Surrealist Intrusion in the Enchanters' Domain," an international Surrealist exhibition held at the D'Arcy Galleries in New York in 1960, that it received the *succès-de-scandale* that Dalí had hoped for.[9] Andrè Breton, José Pierre and over 20 other members of the Surrealist group protested the deliberate intrusion of Dalí's "portentous *Madonna*, painted in his most clerical manner, and which its large dimensions, added to its recent execution, should have excluded from such a gathering."[10] The Surrealists responded with a pamphlet

entitled "We Don't Ear It That Way," that in a humorous take-off of Duchamp's *L.H.O.O.Q* added a moustache and goatee to a reproduction of Gala's head from *Assumpta Corpuscularia Lapislazulina*. Although intended to discredit Dalí, whom the tract violently attacked as "Hitler's former apologist, the fascist painter, the religious bigot, and the avowed racist, friend of Franco," this protest simply gave the artist and his monumental painting some much-needed publicity, and in the process drew the attention of a younger generation of artists to his provocative new work.[11] M.R.T.

[1] Dalí's obsession with the human ear can be traced at least as far back as 1933, when his photo-collage *Le Phénomène de l'extase (The Phenomenon of Ecstasy)*, which contains a profusion of images of the ear, accompanied his article of the same title in *Minotaure*, nos. 3-4 (December 1933), pp. 76-77.

[2] The Annunciation was also often portrayed as the penetration of the dove (representing the Holy Ghost) into Mary's ear. It has been suggested that because of the resemblance between the shape of the external ear and the spiral coil of a snail's shell (in human anatomy, the words 'helix' and 'antihelix' are used), there came to be a symbolic association linking the ear, the snail, and birth (which resembled the emergence of the snail from its shell), leading to the idea that some gods and demigods had been born from out of their mothers' ears, see Hans

Biedermann, *Dictionary of Symbolism: Cultural Icons and the Meanings Behind Them*, trans. James Hulbert (New York: Meridian Books, 1994), p. 110.

[3] Salvador Dalí, "Ear with Madonna," in Robert Descharnes, *The World of Salvador Dalí*, trans. Haakon Chevalier (New York: Harper & Row, 1962), p. 192.

[4] Andy Warhol's 1985 painting *Raphael I - $6.99* may have been directly inspired by Dalí's *Sistine Madonna*, since it takes as its point of departure a commercial reproduction of Raphael's altarpiece in Dresden, complete with its exceedingly low price-tag.

[5] Named after its inventor, the newspaper printer Benjamin Day, the benday dot system involves the modulation of color, light and shadow through the placement and size of a homogeneous matrix of dots.

[6] This title was used when the painting was first shown in New York, see *Salvador Dalí*, exh. cat., (New York: Carstairs Gallery, 1958), n.p.

[7] A reproduction of Raphael's *Sistine Madonna* can be clearly seen hanging in the background of a photograph of Dalí and Gala at the St. Regis Hotel, taken around 1948. This image is reproduced in Robert Descharnes, *Salvador Dalí: The Work, The Man*, trans. Eleanor R. Morse (New York: Harry N. Abrams, 1984), p. 295.

[8] The Brussels World's Fair was on view from April 17-October 19, 1958. The painting then traveled to New York for Dalí's exhibition at the Carstairs Gallery, which was on display from December 6, 1958 to January 20, 1959, and which he "dedicated to Gala, my Sistine Madonna." Dalí used the occasion of this exhibition to launch his *Anti-Matter Manifesto*, which argued that "if the physicists are producing anti-matter, let it be allowed to the painters, already specialists in angels, to paint it. In the Surrealist period I wanted to create the iconography of the interior world - the world of the marvelous, of my father Freud. I succeeded in doing it. Today the exterior world—that of physics—has transcended the one of psychology. My father today is Dr. Heisenberg. It is with pi-mesons and the most gelatinous and indeterminate neutrinos (sic) that I want to paint the beauty of the angels and of reality"; see Salvador Dalí, *Anti-Matter Manifesto*, artist's statement in *Salvador Dalí*, exh. cat., (New York: Carstairs Gallery, 1958), reprinted in *The Collected Writings of Salvador Dalí*, ed., trans. Haim Finkelstein (Cambridge: Cambridge University Press, 1998), p. 366. Margaret Breuning's baffled response to the painting is fairly typical of the critical reaction to the artist's attempts to integrate the latest scientific developments, such as those proposed by the German physicist Werner Karl Heisenberg, into his work, see Breuning, "Dalí and anti-matter," *Arts*, vol. 33, no. 4, January 1959, p. 52.

[9] The painting was included under the title of *L'oreille anti-matière*, see *Surrealist Intrusion in the Enchanters' Domain*, exh. cat. no. 32 (New York: D'Arcy Galleries, 1960). The exhibition was on view from November 28, 1960 to January 14, 1961.

[10] "We Don't Ear It That Way," leaflet published by the Surrealist group in Paris, and signed by 25 members, in protest at Duchamp's inclusion of Dalí's work in the international Surrealist exhibition held at the D'Arcy Galleries in New York in 1960.

[11] *Ibid.*

234. Ascension, 1958

234. Oil on canvas
115 × 123 cm
45 1/4 × 48 1/2 in.
Mexico, JAPS Collection

Fig. 1. Theodore Cook,
Helianthus Annuus, 1979

Fig. 2. Salvador Dalí, *Assumpta
Corpuscularia Lapislazulina*, 1952
John Theodoracopoulos Collection

The visually striking foreshortening of Christ, along with the painting's triangular composition and Port Lligat seascape, evokes *Christ of Saint John of the Cross* (1951) (see *Study for "The Christ of Saint John of the Cross"*). Given that Christ's Ascension into Heaven is the counterpoint to his Crucifixion (cat. 217), it is especially appropriate that Dalí's compositions are so formally similar. He may have been particularly inclined to depict the *Ascension* in 1958, the year he and Gala finally married in the Catholic Church.

The yellow orb into which Christ rises resembles the spiraling florets of a sunflower—one of Dalí's logarithmic exemplars as featured in his 1955 Sorbonne lecture, "On the Phenomenological Aspects of the Paranoid Critical Method."[1] As with many plant species, the florets of the sunflower are arranged in opposite sets of logarithmic spirals that radiate from a common centre (fig. 1). In sunflower florets, the ratio of clockwise to counter-clockwise spirals is 21:34, corresponding to two adjacent numbers in the Fibonacci sequence—the arithmetical series in which each number is the sum of the preceding two numbers (i.e., 1, 1, 2, 3, 5, 8, 13, 21, 34…etc.).[2] As the Fibonacci sequence approaches infinity, the ratio of a given number to its preceding number more closely approximates the ratio $(1+\sqrt{5})/2$—dubbed 'the Divine Proportion' by Luca Pacioli and commonly referred to by the Greek symbol, *Phi* (Φ) (see Encyclopedia, Ghyka). Pacioli's 'Divine Proportion,' permeates his *Ascension*, both in the logarithmic sunflower-orb and the triangular positioning of Christ.[3]

Gala's role is ambiguous. Her juxtaposition with the dove suggests she may represent the Holy Spirit, or, by virtue of her enigmatic tear, the weeping Mary Magdalene—the first recorded witness to Christ's resurrection. It is in interpreting her as the Virgin Mary, however, that the most convincing case can be made for *Ascension*'s puzzling perspective and relationship with *The Christ of Saint John of the Cross*.

In his *Diary of a Genius*, Dalí makes two comments *a propos* the Assumption of the Virgin. Firstly, he declares the Assumption an 'Ascension'—a deliberate (mis)use of the term.[4] Although the Assumption of Mary and the Ascension of Christ are, according to Catholic doctrine, different—Jesus *ascended* by virtue of His own power, while the Virgin Mary was *assumed* into Heaven by the power of God—, Dalí describes both as 'Ascensions' because, he explains, the Virgin, like Christ, rose by virtue of Her own power. "The Virgin does not ascend to Heaven while praying," he explains. "She ascends by the very strength of her antiprotons."[5] Dalí thus employs the notion of particles with corresponding anti-particles that, when collided, annihilate one another, creating kinetic energy; the resulting intra-atomic explosions 'rocket' the Virgin skywards: "…the Virgin is wholly the superwoman who, according to the dream of the five bags of chick peas, will fall to Heaven"[6]—a paradoxical description derived from his idea for obtaining a photographic Assumption, Dalí proposes pouring out a large bag of chickpeas from a height of thirty-five feet. As the chickpeas are falling to the ground, one should project an upturned image of the Virgin onto the cascade. The chickpeas, separated from one another "like the corpuscles of the atom," will each reflect a portion of the image, and, as the image is rushing upside-down, the effect will be akin to an atomic Assumption as illustrated by his 1952 painting, *Assumpta Corpuscularia Lapislazulina* (fig. 2).[7] Given his admiration for Antonio Gaudí, one might suggest an affinity between Dalí's inverted Assumption 'falling to Heaven' and Gaudí's technique of designing his buildings based on inverting the folds of suspended drapery (e.g., his designs for the crypt chapel of *Santa Coloma de Cervelo, Colonia Güell*). Dalí goes on in *Diary of a Genius* to describe the Assumption (i.e., 'Ascension') of the Virgin as an elevator that rises "because of the weight of the dead Christ."[8] *Ascension*'s vacillating perspective captures this inverse relationship; seen from below, Gala—the Virgin—ostensibly falls towards the earth as Christ rises, His arms spread in the position of His Crucifixion. However, given Dalí's conflation of 'Ascension' and 'Assumption,' it may not be merely Christ Who ascends as the Virgin 'falls' but also the inverse. In this case, the viewer is positioned not below but above Christ, looking downwards onto a triangular Crucifixion hovering over Port Lligat, *The Christ of Saint John of the Cross*. E.H.K.

[1] See *La Vie publique de Salvador Dalí* (Paris: Centre Georges Pompidou, 1979), pp. 144-145.

[2] H.E. Huntley, *The Divine Proportion: A study in mathematical beauty* (New York: Dover Publications, Inc., 1970), p. 64.

[3] Salvador Dalí, "A Letter from Salvador Dalí," *Scottish Art Review* (Glasgow), vol. IV, no. 1, 1952, p. 5.

[4] Salvador Dalí, *Diary of a Genius*, trans. Richard Howard, (New York: Prentice Hall Press, 1986), p. 40. Originally published in French as *Journal d'un génie* (Paris: La Table Ronde, 1964).

[5] *Ibid.*, p. 48.

[6] *Ibid.*.

[7] *Ibid.*, p. 40.

[8] *Ibid.*, p. 55.

235. The Virgin of Guadalupe, 1959

235. Oil on canvas
200 × 130 cm
78³/4 × 51¹/8 in.
Private Collection

Dalí's *Virgin of Guadalupe* reinterprets the venerated wooden statue of the Madonna and Child clad in crimson brocade robes, said to have been carved by St. Luke and given as a gift from Pope St. Gregory the Great to St. Leander, the Bishop of Seville. The statue was buried in the northern Spanish province of Estremadura by pious Visigoth knights following the Saracens' victory over Don Rodrigo in 711 C.E., where it remained protected for over six-hundred years until a cowherd, Gil Cordero, purportedly following an apparition of the Virgin, unearthed it in 1326.[1] Beautifully preserved despite its entombment, it was enshrined within a Franciscan friary along the Wolf River—*Guadalupe* in Arabic—and thenceforth known as the Virgin of Guadalupe. The statue is adorned with a majestic crown surrounded by a golden halo, which, in Dalí's rendition, becomes the spiraling florets of a sunflower, signifying his developed understanding of natural growth patterns that follow the *Phi* calculation. As in his 1958 painting, *Ascension* (cat. 234), the sunflower evokes, for Dalí, Divine Geometry and his position that such logarithmic phenomena evidence the influence of God; the Virgin's royal crown can also be traced within the sunflower's florets. The body of Dalí's Virgin is comprised of a heavenly host of angels—reminiscent of the angelic ladder said in the Bible to have appeared to Jacob—, flanked by two kneeling apostles, quoted from his 1955 painting, *The Sacrament of the Last Supper*. Characteristically, Gala is cast as the Virgin, while her pink and white cloak, the infant Jesus and the tumultuous clouds are taken directly from Raphael's *Sistine Madonna* (1513-14; see p. 386, fig. 1)—a painting Dalí had concealed the year before within the 'atomized' ear of Pope John XXIII in his own *Sistine Madonna* (1958).

The roses encircling Dalí's Virgin of Guadalupe are a traditional symbol of the Virgin Mary and may also allude to her reported 1531 appearance on Tepeyac Hill, outside Mexico City. According to tradition, the Virgin of the Immaculate Conception—dressed in a red robe and blue mantle decorated with stars that are conspicuously absent in Dalí's rendition, though they also appear on the red mantle of the Spanish statue—appeared to a humble indigenous Mexican, Quauhtlatoatzin, who had been baptized into Christianity six years earlier as Juan Diego. The Virgin told St. Diego to approach the Bishop, Juan de Zumárraga, and have a temple built in her honor on the rocky hilltop. When the skeptical Zumárraga asked for proof, St. Diego returned to the Virgin, who told him to fill his *tilma*—a long cloak used by indigenous Mexicans—with red Castilian roses, which were miraculously blooming despite the cold of winter. When he returned to the Bishop, he unfolded the *tilma* to find, beneath the fresh roses, a painting of the Virgin standing atop a crescent moon.

The Virgin was said to have spoken to St. Diego in the Aztec language, Náhuatl—calling herself *coatlax-opeuh*, pronounced very much like 'Guadalupe' and translated to mean, "who crushes the serpent," referring perhaps to the Aztec serpent-God, Quetzalcoatl; she was believed by many Aztecs to be an apparition of the goddess, Tonantzin, whose temple had previously been located on Tepeyac Hill, but the conquering Spaniards dubbed her 'Guadalupe,' perhaps because many of them—including the conquistador, Hernán Cortés—came from Estremadura. The miraculous *tilma* and reports of a dark-skinned, Náhuatl-speaking 'Virgin of Guadalupe' proved an extraordinarily powerful tool for the Church towards converting the Aztecs to Catholicism; thousands of Aztecs traveled to see the image enshrined on Tepeyac Hill, and, within ten years of St. Diego's vision, nearly nine-million Aztecs had turned to Christianity. In 1737, The Virgin of Guadalupe was named Patroness of Mexico City, and ten years later this patronage was extended to all of New Spain. She was declared Patroness of Latin America in 1910 by Pope Pius X and Patroness of the Americas in 1946 by Pope Pius XII, thus extending her influence to Anglophone North America as well.

The Virgin of Guadalupe's role in spreading Spanish Catholicism to the Americas hints at a possible connection between Dalí's 1959 *Virgin of Guadalupe* and his nearly-contemporaneous 1960 canvas, *The Dream of Christopher Columbus*, beyond their mutual grandiose religiosity and exaggerated verticality. Indeed, the documents authorizing Columbus's first sea voyage were signed at the Friary of Santa Maria de Guadeloupe in the presence of the Catholic monarch, Queen Isabella, and the first Native Americans to convert to Catholicism were subsequently baptized there. Gala reappears in *The Dream of Christopher Columbus* as the Virgin of the Immaculate Conception, whom Dalí identifies as the "patroness of Spain," while the unmistakable figure of his *Christ of Saint John of the Cross* (1951), based on the drawing by the pious Spanish mystic, looms in the background.[2] Together with *The Virgin of Guadalupe*, these paintings celebrate what Dalí described in 1960, vis-à-vis *The Dream of Christopher Columbus*, as "the development of the Spanish empire towards God," extolling Spanish Catholic imperialism, from Columbus—whom Dalí believed to be a Catalan from the city of Girona, near Figueres—to Cortés.[3] E.H.K.

[1] Zsolt Aradi, *Shrines to Our Lady Around the World* (New York: Farrar, Straus and Young, 1954), p. 46.
[2] Robert Descharnes, *Dalí de Gala* (Lausanne: Edita S.A., 1962), p. 70.
[3] "New Dalí 'Nuclear-Mystical' Canvas Unveiled," *New York Times* (New York, January 13, 1960). Dalí refers to Columbus's Catalan origins in Descharnes, p. 70. For more on this argument, see *The Catalan Contexts of Columbus: Proceedings of the Third Catalan Symposium*, ed. Josep M. Solà-Solé (New York: Peter Lang, 1994).

236. Goddess Leaning on Her Elbow – Continuum of the Four Buttocks or Five Rhinoceros Horns Making a Virgin or Birth of a Deity, 1960

236. Oil on canvas
92.5 × 153 cm
36$^{1/2}$ × 60$^{1/4}$ in.
Barcelona, Generalitat
de Catalunya, Departament
de Cultura

Among Dalí's most enigmatic canvases, *Goddess Leaning on Her Elbow...* presents the limitations of space as represented by a 'four-buttock continuum'—rhinoceros horn/buttocks that converge from all sides of the canvas onto a precariously placed nail. Although the painting was completed in 1960, Dalí cites a four-buttock continuum in his *Diary of a Genius* as early as August 1952, when he writes, "I am grateful to modern science for corroborating by its researches that most pleasant, sybaritic, and antiromantic notion that "space is finite." My emotion has the perfect shape of a four-buttock continuum, the tenderness of the very flesh of the universe."[1] He goes on to describe his 1955 paranoid-critical 'rhinocerization' of Vermeer's *Lacemaker*, noting that his intention was to "depict [*The Lacemaker*] between four crusts of bread, as if she had been born of a molecular encounter according to the principle of my four-buttock continuum."[2] (see cat. 230)

That the universe was finite implied that it could be depicted—a welcome revelation for Dalí, whose painting chronically sought to render material the 'irrationality' of the universe. Dalí's choice to represent finite space with such an unusual symbol makes the work exceptionally difficult to penetrate, however. The painting's mystery is only augmented by its alternative subtitles: *Continuum of the Four Buttocks*, *Five Rhinoceros Horns Making a Virgin* and *Birth of a Deity*. Further, the 'Goddess leaning on her elbow' from the painting's main title is not even represented.

Goddess Leaning on Her Elbow... is most closely related to Dalí's 1954 canvas, *Young Virgin Auto-Sodomized by the Horns of Her Own Chastity*. In both paintings, strikingly similar rhinoceros horns

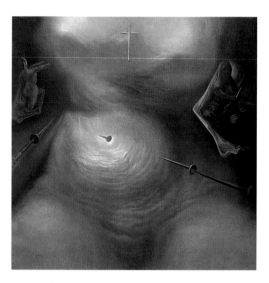

Fig. 2. Salvador Dalí, *The Life of Mary Magdalene*, 1960
Private collection

coalesce against a blue seascape to form the *derrière* of a 'virgin' (hence the 1960 painting's subtitle, *Five Rhinoceros Horns Making a Virgin*). The rhinoceros horn was a heavily-laden Dalínian symbol (see Encyclopedia), the religious subtext of which accounts for the 1954 ephemeral 'virgin' being 'sodomized by her chastity' (i.e., by a rhinoceros horn connoting chastity), as well as Dalí's observation that "this painting which has an erotic appearance is the most chaste of all."[3] The rhinoceros horn also abstrusely links the unidentified 'young virgin' with the Virgin Mary, who may be interpreted in 1960 as the 'Goddess leaning on her elbow,' just as the 'young virgin' / Virgin bends forward against her elbow in the 1954 painting.

Contributing to the veiled religious allusions in *Goddess Leaning on Her Elbow...* are the numerous painted nails, evoking the nails with which Christ was hung on the Cross. Nails appear in Dalí's work chiefly after his 1959 detonation of the nail-filled 'Bomb of the Apocalypse'—an event the artist staged towards producing his contributions to Joseph Foret's monumental book, *The Apocalypse of Saint John;*[4] the abundance of nail 'wounds' in the resulting images for Foret's book both suggest Christ's stigmata and obfuscates the figures in 'molecular' clouds that could be interpreted as quasi-atomic. The religious argument for the nail in *Goddess Leaning on Her Elbow...* is supported by its appearance in other works from 1960, including *The Life of Mary Magdalene* (fig. 2) and *Hyperxiological Sky* (fig. 3), though here, as in *Goddess Leaning on Her Elbow...*, the nails are painted rather than in relief—an arguably less powerful visual effect, though one made up for in *Goddess Leaning on Her Elbow* by the nail's perilous placement among the converging buttocks.[5] Perhaps the nail representing

Fig. 1. Salvador Dalí,
Rhinoceratic Gooseflesh, 1956
Private collection;
formerly B. Pagliai Collection

Fig. 3. Salvador Dalí,
Hyperxiological Sky
Private collection

Christ is the 'Deity' to Whom the rhinoceratic virgin(s) gives birth. Alternatively, the Deity may be Venus, who is also not explicitly represented in *Goddess Leaning on Her Elbow…* but who features in Dalí's 1956 canvas, *Rhinoceratic Gooseflesh* (fig. 1), in which a nude torso rises from the sea on a shell evoking Botticelli's *Birth of Venus* (ca. 1485). *Rhinoceratic Gooseflesh* is a reminder that Dalí copiously studied the phenomenon of 'gooseflesh'— the familiar response to cold or certain emotional states that causes the smooth muscles of the dermis to contract, making the skin pucker and body hairs stand erect.[6] In the 1950s, Dalí interpreted the erect hair follicles as diminutive rhinoceros horns. Perhaps this informs the enigmatic quotation from *Diary of a Genius* in which Dalí recounts hearing of space's materiality, describing his emotions as adopting "the perfect shape of a four-buttock continuum, the tenderness of the very flesh of the universe." In other words, one may understand, the materiality implied by finite space so excited Dalí that he simply got 'gooseflesh'—a 'rhinoceratic' phenomenon in the micro-cosmos resembling the artist's unique, callipygian conception of the macro-cosmos. E.H.K.

[1] Salvador Dalí, *Diary of a Genius*, trans. Richard Howard (New York: Prentice Hall Press, 1986), p. 53. Originally published in French as *Journal d'un génie* (Paris: La Table Ronde, 1964). Dalí goes on in *Diary of a Genius* to report making a plaster cast of his four-buttock continuum (also in 1952), though this sculpture has ostensibly been lost since then (Dalí, *Diary of a Genius*, p. 54).

[2] *Ibid.*, pp. 138-139.

[3] A. Reynolds Morse, *Dalí: A Study of His Life and Work* (Greenwich: New York Graphic Society, 1958), p. 81.

[4] Foret's book, which weighed nearly five-hundred pounds and required seven people to carry it, was illustrated by Bernard Buffet, Leonor Fini, Foujita, Georges Mathieu, Trémois, Zadkine and Dalí. Various descriptions and references to the immense tome can be found in Carlton Lake, *In Quest of Dalí* (New York: G.P. Putnam's Sons, 1969).

[5] *Hyperxiological Sky*, with its subject and coloration strikingly similar to *Continuum of the Four Buttocks…*, cites the Catalan philosopher, Francesc Pujols, a self-proclaimed Llullist and close friend of Dalí, and his science-based religion, 'hyperxiology.'

[6] It was around this period that Dalí's *Surrealist Composition* (1928) was renamed *Inaugural Gooseflesh*.

237. Portrait of Juan de Pareja Adjusting a String on his Mandolin, 1960

237. Oil on canvas
76.5 × 87.6 cm
30 1/8 × 34 1/2 in.
Minneapolis (MN),
The Minneapolis Institute
of Arts

238. The Trinity (Study for "The Ecumenical Council"), 1960

238. Oil on canvas
58.4 × 66 cm
23 × 26 in.
Vatican City, Musei Vaticani

Fig. 1. Salvador Dalí,
The Ecumenical Council, 1960
St. Petersburg (FL), The Salvador
Dalí Museum

Dalí's *The Trinity* debuted in 1960 at Carstairs Gallery, New York, together with the mammoth canvas, *The Ecumenical Council* (1960; fig 1) for which it was a study. *The Ecumenical Council* honored Pope John XXIII's meeting that year with the archbishop of Canterbury in a gesture promoting Christian unity. Dalí enthusiastically approved of Angelo Giuseppe Cardinal Roncalli's 1958 election as head of the Catholic Church, famously enlarging a *Paris Match* photograph of the Pontiff's ear for his *trompe-l'œil* painting, *The Sistine Madonna* (1958). The Pope had announced the upcoming Ecumenical Council on January 24, 1959, inspiring Dalí to request an audience on May 2, 1959 to discuss a commission he had received to design a cathedral in Arizona; Dalí envisioned this cathedral—which would go unbuilt—in the shape of a pear because, he explained, the pear symbolized the Resurrection in the Middle Ages and was thus an appropriate metaphor for the forthcoming Council.[1]

By the painting's title, which denotes the Christian doctrine that the Father, Son and Holy Spirit are united in one God, one supposes the left-hand fig- ure holding the crucifix to be Christ, with God the Father in the center—portrayed in the completed *Ecumenical Council* under an arch in St. Peter's Basilica, Rome—and the Holy Spirit on the right, identified with the dove in both *The Ecumenical Council* and the 1958 painting, *Ascension* (cat. 234). The identities of these figures, however, particularly in this less-developed tableau, are more ambiguous, with none displaying the attributes by which God, Christ and the Holy Spirit are traditionally recognized: the central figure's agonized posture— possibly inspired by the bare-chested characters appearing in Baroque paintings by Luca Giordano (1632-1705)—more readily evokes a naked, suffering Christ than the resplendent God the Father, while the right figure's humbly-crossed hands in rapport with the evangelical left-figure bring to mind traditional renderings of the Annunciation, in which the archangel Gabriel tells Mary—often in the presence of God, Who oversees the event from above, and the dove of the Holy Spirit—that she will give birth to Christ. Contributing to the ambiguity, these two figures express strongly feminine characteristics—perhaps denoting the androgyny said of divine beings, though this fails to explicate the central character's prominent testicles. Their robes and stances resemble Dalí's contemporaneous depiction of *Beatrice* (1960), with nebulous countenance, outstretched hand and clumsily-rendered foot, or his effeminate Christ with upraised hand in *The Last Supper*, while their haphazardly-sketched drapery nods to Velázquez's '*refregados*' and '*chafarrinadas*,' which Dalí would translate in 1961 as 'stains or spots' (see Encyclopedia 'Velázquez') and link to such 'action artists' as Georges Mathieu (see Encyclopedia).[2]

Although nondescript in *Trinity*, the two side-figures possess a strikingly similar countenance in the completed *Ecumenical Council*—one perhaps also shared by the central figure, whose face is masked by an outstretched hand. Although this only advances questions in identifying the painting's three personages, it is perhaps informed by the three-in-one doctrine of the Trinity; indeed, the three figures may appear to share the same face precisely because They are, according to dogma, three distinct beings joined in One. Always striving to make the ineffable concrete, Dalí was well-suited to illustrate this notion central to Christianity; his painting is as enigmatic as the paradoxical Trinity itself. E.H.K.

[1] Ian Gibson, *The Shameful Life of Salvador Dalí* (New York and London: W.W. Norton & Co., 1998), p. 547. Originally published by Faber and Faber (London), 1997.
[2] Salvador Dalí, "Ecumenical 'chafarrinada' of Velázquez," *Art News*, vol. 59, no. 10 (New York: February 1961) p. 30.

239. Fifty Abstract Paintings Which as Seen from Two Yards Change into Three Lenins Masquerading as Chinese and as Seen from Six Yards Appear as the Head of a Royal Bengal Tiger, 1963

239. Oil on canvas
200 × 229 cm
78³/4 × 90¹/8 in.
Figueres, Fundació
Gala-Salvador Dalí

The sesquipedal title of this 1963 tableau is explicitly self-descriptive: fifty individual abstract canvases in alternating black and gold, along with two red and white works towards the center, form the three triangular figures of Vladimir Lenin, sporting exaggerated Asian attributes (i.e., Fu Man Chu moustaches, and almandine eyes derived from painted cuts in the painting's surface). These three figures are easily recognized in the mouth and beneath the eyes of the conspicuous harlequin tiger that unifies the work, purportedly best viewed from a distance of six yards.

In contrast to Dalí's famous double-images, which can be seen from any distance, *Fifty Abstract Paintings...* reveals its multiple subjects depending on one's position in relation to it, a mechanism he employed in such other works as *The Sistine Madonna* (1958; cat. 233)—in which a series of 'atomic' dots comprise Raphael's *Sistine Madonna* and, further away, the enormous ear of Pope John XXIII—and *Gala Contemplating the Mediterranean Sea which at Twenty Meters Becomes the Portrait of Abraham Lincoln – Homage to Rothko* (1976). Both these are arguably more refined than *Fifty Abstract Paintings...*, though Dalí's assimilation and subversion of abstraction, which he had ferociously attacked in his 1956 book *Les Cocus du vieil art moderne*, compellingly substantiates what might otherwise be viewed as merely a large-scale *trompe-l'œil*. Indeed, whereas the 1950s saw Dalí comparing Jackson Pollock's famous drip paintings to indigestion, the artist refocused his attack in the 1960s, enlarging details of outmoded academic works to reveal their veiled abstract sensibilities;[1] in 1967, for example, he described how the motion of the grass in Meisonnier's *Friedland 1807* "might almost be a Pollock."[2] He similarly claimed to have shown details from a painting by Diego Velásquez to Willem De Kooning, whom he identified in 1969 as "the initial point of the *pompier* art of the future," to which De Kooning allegedly exclaimed, "That's Action Painting raised to the sublime!," surely informing Dalí's 1961 statement, "Velasquez started with figurative representation, to end up with '*taches*.' And today, with *taches* as a starting point, one should aim at sublime figures."[3] In *Fifty Abstract Paintings...*, Dalí demonstrates how abstract painting, in his opinion, is already established within the academic genre; taking nonfigurative painting as a 'starting point,' he develops a complex canvas that forms the abstract from the nonfigurative, the realistic from the abstract.

There is inevitable innuendo attached to Dalí's representations of Lenin 'masquerading as Chinese' concealed within the colossal head of a Bengal tiger, though, as with all his political allusions, his own stance remains nebulous. Lenin had been among Dalí's dream-subjects for over three decades, cryptically appearing in the 1931 painting *Partial Hallucination. Six Apparitions of Lenin on a Grand Piano*, as well as his scandalous *Enigma of William Tell* (1933), in which he is portrayed as a cannibalistic father figure wielding an embarrassingly extended buttock. In 1963, however, three years after Nikita Khrushchev attacked the People's Republic of China at the congress of the Romanian Communist Party, thereby publicizing the Sino-Soviet split, Chinese Lenins evoked less Dalí's paranoid-critical phantasms than the Marxist-Leninist Mao Zedong, in whom Dalí would express an enthusiastic interest throughout the 1960s. Following Stalin's death in 1953, Mao viewed himself as heir to leading the global Communist movement; he thus quietly resented Khrushchev's 1956 denunciation of Stalin at the 20th Congress of the Soviet Party, as well as the Soviet Union's 1959 refusal to help China develop its nuclear arsenal. Khrushchev meanwhile enjoyed a successful summit with U.S. President Dwight Eisenhower, leading Mao to conclude the Soviet was acquiescing to "American imperialism," which he not insignificantly castigated as a "paper tiger."[4] Dalí's 1963 amalgamation of abstract canvases with Communist China, Soviet Russia and an all-encompassing 'paper tiger' thus solicits many questions, not least regarding the U.S. government's alleged use of American Abstract Expressionism as a cultural weapon of the Cold War.[5] Pulling its subject from the day's headlines, as was Dalí's fashion, *50 Abstract Paintings...* playfully engages its audience with optical trickery whilst concurrently suggesting the seriously tenuous relations among the Soviet Union, the People's Republic of China and the United States, all at the brink of nuclear war. E.H.K.

[1] Salvador Dalí, *Dalí on Modern art: the Cuckolds of Antiquated Modern Art* (New York: Dial Press, 1957), p. 19. Originally published in French as *Les Cocus du vieil art moderne* (Paris: Fasquelle, 1956).
[2] Carlton Lake, *In Quest of Dalí* (New York: G.P. Putnam's Sons, 1969), p. 169.
[3] Salvador Dalí, "De Kooning's 300,000,000th Birthday," *Art News* 68 (New York: April 1969): pp. 57, 62-63. Salvador Dalí, "The Secret Number of Velasquez Revealed," *Art News,* vol. 59, no. 9 (New York: Jan. 1961) pp. 45, 61. "Taschisme" refers to the French equivalent of American Action Painting, led by artist Georges Mathieu (see Encyclopedia):
[4] Mao Zedong, "U.S. Imperialism is a Paper Tiger" (July 14, 1956). Published in *Selected Works of Mao Tse-tung* (Peking: Foreign Languages Press, 1977), vol. V, pp. 308-311.
[5] See Frances Stonor Saunders, *Who Paid the Piper? The CIA and the Cultural Cold* War (London. Granta Books, 1999).

240. Portrait of My Dead Brother, 1963

240. Oil on canvas
69 × 69 cm
27 1/8 × 27 1/8 in.
St. Petersburg (FL),
The Salvador Dalí Museum

Dalí was 59 years old when he painted this enigmatic work concerning his relationship with his dead brother. In the 1970 publication *Dalí by Dalí*, the artist says that his "despairing parents...committed the crime of giving the same first name to the new Dalí that their dead son had born."[1] While Salvador was named after his father, Salvador Dalí Cusi, he also shared this first name with his absent brother, Salvador Galo Anselmo Dalí, the first born son of the Dalí family. He died of catarrh with gastroenteritis infection at 21 months of age, just nine months and eleven days prior to the artist's birth. Surprisingly in *The Secret Life,* the artist gets the three essential facts of his brother's life incorrect: he claims that his brother died at the age of seven, that he died three years prior to the artist's birth, and that he died of meningitis.[2] Such errors continue with this portrait of the brother he didn't know.

Related to Dalí's more clearly demarcated double image paintings, this portrait emerges from a shower of dark and light cherries falling from the heavens, resembling the Benday dots associated with the young Roy Lichtenstein. According to Dalí, "the cherries represent the molecules, the dark cherries create the visage of my dead brother, the sun-lighted cherries create the image of Salvador living."[3] Thus Dalí suggests that the face is a composite portrait of both the brother and himself through the symbolic combination of dark and light cherries. This combination is emphasized with two cherries sharing a single stem, and the molecular structure on the nose, which combines both dark and light cherries into one structure. Yet this painting can also be seen as a *doppelgänger*.[4] In *The Secret Life*, Dalí amplifies the fundamental strangeness of his shared identity premise, attributing qualities to his absent brother that he could never have possessed.[5] Asserting that his parents wanted him to be a replacement for his dead brother, this specter became a threat to Dalí's fundamental Narcissism, compelling him to cultivate his eccentric exhibitionistic behavior to prove that he was different from the first, supposedly better-loved version of Salvador Dalí, and thus was unique. Influenced by the theories of his friend Dr. Pierre Roumeguère, the psychiatrist whom Dalí saw from 1954 to 1958, the artist began referring to himself and his dead brother as the Dioscuri, Castor and Pollox, the two Greek twins. Although Dalí's brother was dead, he still remained a specter in his life. In an interview with Alain Bosquet, the artist says, "Every day, I kill the image of my poor brother...I assassinate him regularly, for the 'Divine Dalí' cannot have anything in common with this former terrestrial being."[6] The conquistadors holding lances at the bottom right assist Dalí with dispelling the visage of the former Salvador. The conquistadors direct the attention to the 'progress of man' iconography Dalí employs, for the Spanish-style guards in the lower right point their lances at the strange seated figures who resemble astronauts. In turn these astronauts begin to walk in a way that resembles primates (forming the ear on the right), presenting the stages of human progress. On the bottom left, Dalí inserts several figures, including the ghostly image of Millet's *Angelus* couple and a wheelbarrow, obliquely returning to the theme of sexual desire and death from the 1930s, with the parental couple standing over the sacks of potatoes, referring to Dalí and his brother.[7]

When he exhibited the work, Dalí wrote this cryptic description: "The Vulture, according to the Egyptians and Freud, represents my mother's portrait."[8] The bird he refers to is hidden within the brother's dark hair on the upper left side of the face, its eye and beak indicating its presence. By describing the bird as a vulture, Dalí connects his portrait with Freud's study of Leonardo da Vinci, where Freud mistakenly connects Leonardo's one recorded dream of a bird alighting on his mouth with an Egyptian name for vulture, interpreted as a symbol of the Mother.[9] Elsewhere Dalí amplifies this connection by interpreting the vulture/mother as the goddess Leda (Gala), the mother to the twins Castor and Pollux (the twin Salvadors).

A final compelling aspect of this work is the source of the model. The brother portrayed should be either a 21-month old boy or a seven year old boy as Dalí proposes in *The Secret Life*. Yet here Dalí presents the viewer with a more mature boy, ironically bearing little resemblance to Dalí. The source for the brother's face is unknown, probably taken from an anonymous newspaper photograph.[10] Often the portrait has been compared to Charles Lindbergh, because the figure's ear also appears to be bleeding, perhaps a reference to the Lindbergh baby kidnapping and a reference to the scandal the Dalís created in 1935 when Gala appeared at a New York ball wearing a head dress with a dead baby and airplane. The seemingly absent ear also suggests Van Gogh, who, like Dalí, had a dead brother whose name he shared. This anonymity of the sitter appears to be Dalí's desired effect. P.T.

[1] Dr. Pierre Roumeguère, "The Cosmic Dalí: The 'Royal Way' of Access to the Dalínian Universe," *Dalí by Dalí*, trans. Eleanor Morse (New York: Harry N. Abrams, Inc., 1970), p. III.

[2] Salvador Dalí, *The Secret Life of Salvador Dalí*, trans. Haakon M. Chevalier (London: Vision Press Ltd., 1981), p. 2

[3] Dalí, *George Keller Presents Dalí*, exhibition catalogue, Knoedler Gallery, New York, November 26-December 26, 1963.

[4] Doppelgänger: from German meaning 'double walker,' a ghostly double or counterpart of a living person; often possessing evil traits, and suggesting the uncanny.

[5] Dalí, *The Secret Life*, p. 2.

[6] Salvador Dalí, with Alain Bosquet, *Conversations with Salvador Dalí* (New York: E. P. Dutton, 1969), p. 32.

[7] Dr. Pierre Roumeguère, p. ix.

[8] Dalí, *George Keller Presents Dalí*, Knoedler exhibition catalogue, November 26-December 26, 1963.

[9] Sigmund Freud, *Leonardo da Vinci: A Study in Psychosexuality*, trans. A. A. Brill (New York: Vintage Books, 1947).

[10] Carlos Rojas, *Salvador Dalí: Or the Art of Spitting on Your Mother's Portrait* (Pennsylvania: Pennsylvania State University Press, 1993), p. 62; Dr. Karen Maur, *Salvador Dalí* (Exhibition Catalogue, Stuttgart Statsgalerie, Kunsthaus Zürich, 1989).

241. The Railway Station at Perpignan, 1965

241. Oil on canvas
295 × 406 cm
116 1/8 × 159 7/8 in.
Cologne, Museum Ludwig

Gala looking at Dalí in a state of anti-gravitation in his work of art "Pop, Op, Yes-Yes, Pompier" in which one can contemplate the two "anguishing" characters from Millet's "Angelus" in a state of atavistic hibernation, standing out of a sky which can suddenly burst into a Gigantic Maltese Cross, right in the heart of the Perpignan Railway Station, where the Whole Universe Must begin to converge [1]

The Railway Station at Perpignan is the climax of a long-elaborated personal mythology structured around Millet's *Angelus,* which had obsessed Dalí since the early 1930s. It had recently re-occupied his attention with the recovery and 1963 publication of the manuscript of his book, *The Tragic Myth of Millet's Angelus,* which had been lost when he and Gala fled Paris in 1939 at the outbreak of war. His brilliant but shocking paranoiac-critical analysis of the popular image of pious devotion is the key to a number of early paintings, including *The Architectural Angelus of Millet* (1933, cat. 117) and *Imperial Monument to the Child Woman* (1929, cat. 133). The *Angelus* couple reappear here, now firmly linked to the personae of Dalí and Gala themselves and in association with a place of cosmic importance to Dalí: Perpignan Railway Station.

The impressive conjunction here of symmetry and dynamism in the horizontal and vertical disposition of the figures and the zoom effect of the shifts in scale perfectly embody the 'projective dynamism' that structures Dalí's vision. The latent familial drama he read into the *Angelus* involved slippages of identity, with encounters between husband and wife, mother and son and also the Oedipal father and son. The schema of the painting is dramatic but tightly controlled; the canvas is divided diagonally into four quarters by a Maltese cross, with the two protagonist couples in horizontal and vertical alignments. The peasant couple, now restored to their normal appearance after the various metamorphoses into skeletons, rocks and ruins to which Dalí had earlier subjected them, frame the canvas at right and left. Gala, seen squatting from the rear at the bottom of the painting, confronts the doubled portrait of Dalí—quoted from Philippe Halsman's 1964 photograph, *Port Lligat Ascension*—, which appears dramatically suspended at the top and again at the heart of the canvas, superimposed over the almost invisible figure of Christ on the Cross.[2] This twinning of Dalí with Christ brings to mind his oft-cited myth of William Tell, with the painting's 'invisible Son'—the figure of Christ as 'conquered' by the Eternal Father—evoking both Dalí's own identification with the sacrificial son (according to which, in 1952, he recognized his own father, André Breton, and Pablo Picasso as his three sav-

age 'Fathers'), as well as that other lost son whose existence in the *Angelus* he had posited in *The Tragic Myth.*[3]

Two further, rather ghostly, scenes to right and left introduce his notion of the eroticized nature of the instruments of rural labor and make a triangular link to the figure of Gala squatting on a wheelbarrow. The scene to the right is Dalí's only representation of a 'false memory' of a sexual encounter with Gala that, in a long reverie described in *The Tragic Myth,* is inserted into an adolescent fantasy. He imagines—or 'remembers'—visiting with Gala at dusk the Natural History Museum in Madrid. In the insect hall, they contemplate fearfully a colossal sculpture of the *Angelus* couple, and, upon leaving the museum, Dalí fulfils his infantile theories of the terrifying physical brutality of the erotic act in sodomizing Gala. These, he recalls, had returned to him forcefully when he first met Gala, "whose love had achieved a true psychic cure."[4] Gala is wife, mother, lover, muse and also Narcissistic twin: "You are me, you are the pupil of my eyes and of your eyes."[5]

What appears to be the luggage car of a train looms in the painting's upper quadrant, bridging Dalí's established paranoiac *Angelus* narrative with his newfound obsession with the ostensibly mundane train station that he would later extol as "the most important discovery of my paranoid-critical method."[6] At Perpignan, the nearest major railway station to Port Lligat, Dalí's paintings were "shipped, wrapped, packed, crated like a reliquary" every autumn before he and Gala embarked for Paris.[7]

While Gala attended to the crates' inspection and insurance, Dalí perused various scientific periodicals that galvanized his creativity; among the myriad of inspirations he credited to the Station's waiting room was the notion to dissolve wasps in oil in order to get a better bonding agent, as well as the possibility of achieving three-dimensional painting through moiré.[8] Every autumn, he reported experiencing a creative epiphany at Perpignan Station—a sensation that would gradually subside as he neared Lyons.[9] Obsessed with uncovering the impetus for this deluge of ideas, he meticulously measured and had photographed the Station's every detail, noting its elliptic cupola—"an obvious monarchical symbol"—and the lines of the tiled floor that paranoiacally evoked a cauliflower, one of his logarithmic exemplars.[10] "I long thought it was because genius needed a trivial place in which to assert itself," he recalled. "The Parthenon and Niagara Falls are too overwhelming! The absurd and the anodyne are better handmaidens to enlightenment."[11]

The Railway Station at Perpignan cites one such especially powerful 'cosmogonic ecstasy,' experienced on 19 September 1963, when the structure

of the universe, he claimed, revealed itself to be analogous to the Perpignan railway station.[12] Elated with his discovery, he hailed a taxi and asked the driver to encircle the Station.

A light like fire, egg-yolk yellow and golden red, passed through and through the building, again bursting forth through the enflamed glass windows on all the facades around it, making the windows of the Hotel de l'Europe blaze. Raising my eyes in the midst of all this dazzlement, I saw the electric cables of the streetcar above the square forming a perfect circle to allow the cars to turn around before they start out again on the boulevard. Thus, the glass roof of the railway station, pierced by the royal light of the sun, was further adorned by the crackling monarchical crown of the cable in the sky.[13]

His description of the building at sunset informs the painting's fiery coloration and grandiose radiance, as the 'universe'—established by the horizontal and vertical axes that merge into a Crucifixion, as well as the diagonal rays of light forming the Maltese cross—converges on Christ's blinding luminosity, recalling the 1951 'cosmic dream' in which he saw Christ as the 'atomic nucleus' and 'the unity of the universe,' thence inspiring his famous *Christ of Saint John of the Cross* (cat. 217). The sense of divine revelation is echoed in the painting's floating elements, which—in conjunction with the painting's religious subject—evoke the physical levitation believed to accompany religious ecstasy. Notwithstanding this and Dalí's earlier inclusion of such elements to connote the discontinuity of matter (see *Leda Atomica,* cat. 213), his two hovering self-portraits denote 'antigravitation' as conceptualised by Dr. Marcel Pagès, the Perpignan-based medical doctor who, in 1960, patented a 'machine for cosmic flights' based on his theory that a machine able to manufacture an electromagnetic field could reverse the gravitational force, thereby repelling gravity; attesting to Pagès' significance, Dalí and Gala visited the Doctor in Perpignan on 27 August 1965, in an elaborately orchestrated journey from Port Lligat to Perpignan—a voyage to "the center of the world."[14]

The subtitle, *Popop-Yes-Yes-Pompier*—an amalgam of Pop Art and Op Art, which, Dalí suggested, would lead to a resurrection of and expansion upon the 19th-century French academic painting that art critics had almost unanimously deemed minor or outmoded—, illuminates less *The Railway Station at Perpignan*'s weighty and idiosyncratic iconography than Dalí's self-positioning within (or, rather, outside) the context of 1960s contemporary art. Following his vehement attacks on Abstract Expressionism, Dalí expressed his approval of Pop Art, recognizing it in 1976 as the "*affirmation* of reality" opposed to abstraction, which was the "*negation* of reality." [15] Positing

that Vermeer—with his photorealistic naturalism—was an antecedent to the movement he described as "part of the healthy trend away from abstract expressionism…back to the maximum of visual reality," he expressed his hope that Pop Art—while not the ultimate realization of his vision—would be a harbinger of what he presaged as the future of painting: "very objective…in the style of Meissonier," but informed by the new cosmology afforded by the latest scientific advancements;[16] "After Pop Art and Op Art, optical, cybernetic art," he declared. "But after these will come the super-Meissonier monarchists."[17] D.A. and E.H.K.

[1] This is the sub-title of the picture in the fold-out catalogue for the exhibition "Dalí's Best Paintings to Date" at the Knoedler Gallery, New York, (1965).

[2] Today, there is a sculpture of Dalí in this pose on the roof of the Perpignan Railway Station.

[3] Salvador Dalí, "Le Mythe de Guillaume Tell: Toute la Vérité sur Mon Expulsion du Groupe Surréaliste," lecture published by the University of Texas, June 9, 1952.

[4] Salvador Dalí, *Le Mythe Tragique de l'Angelus de Millet* (Paris: Jean-Jacques Pauvert, 1963), p. 51

[5] Salvador Dalí, *Diary of a Genius*, trans. Richard Howard (New York: Prentice Hall Press, 1986), p. 113, entry for September 17, 1953. Originally published in French as *Journal d'un génie* (Paris: La Table Ronde, 1964). Quoted in Fiona Bradley's study "Strategies of Encounter in Dalí's *La Gare de Perpignan*" (unpublished).

[6] Salvador Dalí, "La Découverte la plus importante de ma méthode paranoiaque-critique: la gare de Perpignan" (31 October 1983). Published in Robert Descharnes, *Dalí, l'oeuvre et l'homme* (Lausanne: Edita, 1984), p. 423.

[7] Salvador Dalí, "The Railway Station at Perpignan," published as an appendix to Louis Pauwels, *The Passions According to Dalí* (St. Petersburg: Salvador Dalí Museum, 1985), p. 136. Published originally in French as *Les Passions selon Dalí* (Paris: Éditions DeNoël, 1968).

[8] Salvador Dalí, "Résumé d'histoire et de l'histoire de la peinture" (1965). Published in Robert Descharnes (ed.), *Oui 2: l'Archangelisme scientifique* (Paris: Éditions Denoël, 1979), p. 153.

[9] Dalí, "The Railway Station at Perpignan," p. 139.

[10] *Ibid.*, p. 142.

[11] André Parinaud, *The Unspeakable Confessions of Salvador Dalí* (New York: Marrow; London: W. H. Allen, 1976), p. 156. Originally published in French as *Comment on devient Dalí* (Paris: Robert Laffont, 1973).

[12] Dalí, *Diary of a Genius*, p. 218.

[13] Dalí, "The Railway Station at Perpignan," pp. 140-141.

[14] Georges-Henri Gourrier, Bernard Revel and Grégory Tuban, *Dalí, Voyage au centre du monde/Viatge al centre del món/Viaje al centro del mundo* (Perpignan: Éditions

mare nostrum, 2003). See also Patrick Gifreu, *Dalí, un manifeste ultralocal* (Perpignan: Éditions mare nostrum, 1997), and Marcel J.J. Pagès, *Le Défi de l'antigravitation : techniques antipondérales, utilisation de l'énergie de l'espace* (Paris: Chiron, 1974).

[15] Salvador Dalí, "Eureka," (Paris: Hôtel Meurice, October 1976). Printed in *Oui 2*, pp. 198-199. Note that Dalí's relationship with abstraction was not altogether adversarial, as evidenced by his veneration of Georges Mathieu and William De Kooning, whose "swift gestures," he argued, corresponded to Max Planck's "quantum of action." See Salvador Dalí, "Ecumenical 'chafarrinada' of Velázquez," *Art News*, vol. 59, no. 10, New York, Feb. 1961, p. 30. Indeed, Dalí even declared De Kooning as "the initial point of the pompier art of the future," connecting his "spasmodic impastos" with the "brutal brushstrokes" of Velázquez. See Salvador Dalí, "De Kooning's 300,000,000th Birthday," *Art News,* vol. 68, New York, April 1969: pp. 57, 62-63.

[16] "Playboy interview: Salvador Dalí, a candid conversation with the flamboyantly eccentric grand vizier of surrealism," *Playboy,* New York, July 1964, p. 46.

[17] Pauwels, p. 67. A very similar statement appears in the catalogue to Dalí's 1967 *Hommage à Meissonier.*

242. The Face (Sketch for "The Hallucinogenic Toreador"), ca. 1968-70
243. The Whole Dalí in a Face, 1975

242. Oil on paper
55.5 × 44 cm
21⁷/8 × 17³/8 in.
Figueres, Fundació
Gala-Salvador Dalí

243. Collage on postcard
28 × 22 cm
11 × 8⁵/8 in.
Private collection

This painting is a preliminary study for Dalí's monumental canvas, *The Hallucinogenic Toreador* (fig. 1)—a painting inspired in 1968, when he saw the nose, mouth and cheek of a bullfighter within an illustration of the *Venus de Milo* (130-120 B.C.) on a box of pencils manufactured by Venus Esterbrook Ltd. Dalí invested nearly fifteen months of diligent work into *The Hallucinogenic Toreador* between 1969 and 1970, aspiring for it to encapsulate all his previous experiments since the 1930s; the result is one of his most developed paranoiac double-images, as the shadows of *Venus* form the toreador's hair and vague countenance, easily identified here by the ear, and outward-looking yet eerily empty eyes that do not appear in the larger version. Another paranoiac *Venus* appears behind the bust, forming the shape of a bullfighter's body with upraised cape. This ethereal figure consists of swarming flies that reappear prominently in the painting's foreground, originating in the eye of the spectral bull and forming a line to the figure of Dalí as a child in the lower-right corner, dressed in his blue sailor suit and holding a hoop, as in several 1930s images including *The Spectre of Sex Appeal* (1934, cat. 135). As Dalí was quick to explain, the flies refer to the miracle of Saint Narcissus, the patron saint of the Catalan city of Girona (situated between Figueres and Barcelona); according to legend, when French troops invaded Girona in 1285, a swarm of flies emerged from St. Narcissus' tomb in the cathedral and attacked the soldiers, who were forced to retreat. The miracle allegedly reoccurred on 12 July 1653, when Girona was again besieged by the French.[1] There is a painting commemorating this legend in the Girona Cathedral, and today one can even buy fly-shaped chocolates along the city's Rambla.

Luís Romero's 1975 monograph, *Todo Dalí en un rostro*, chronicles the completion of *The Hallucinogenic Toreador* and dissects each of the painting's twelve square meters.[2] Although several elements Romero describes do not appear in *The Face* (e.g., the 'Dioscuric,' stereoscopic cherries and the cubist corner inspired by Juan Gris), among the features that do appear in both this and the larger painting are the bullfighter's distinctive white shirt, red jacket and bright green necktie. Ian Gibson has speculated that this colored necktie may allude to Federico García Lorca's line from *Sleepwalking Ballad*, "Green how I love you green";[3] although the painting is likely connected to Lorca's 1934 poem, *Lament for the Death of a Bullfighter*, written to mourn the death of the toreador, Ignacio Sánchez Mejías, the green—which Dalí recognized in the late 1960s as a symbol of bad luck—could be merely emblematic of the toreador's ultimate misfortune.[4] A more convincing allusion to Lorca is the small dog in the painting's bottom center, which Dalí identifies as 'The Andalousian Dog,' referring to his 1929 film with Luis Buñuel.[5]

The *Venus de Milo* is a recurring subject in Dalí's oeuvre, identified with eroticism, psychoanalysis, religion and Pop Art. In *The Secret Life of Salvador Dalí*, the artist recalls the makeshift 'studio' of his youth—set up in the family's laundry room—, where he sculpted a copy of the *Venus de Milo* in clay; "I derived from this my first attempt at sculpture an unmistakable and delightful erotic pleasure," he writes.[6] He returned to the *Venus de Milo* with his 1936 sculpture, *Venus de Milo with Drawers*, suggesting the Freudian view that the human mind is "full of secret drawers that only psychoanalysis is able to open."[7] By the mid-1960s, Dalí's *Venus de Milo with Drawers* was additionally burdened with religious subtext; "With the addition of drawers," he told an interviewer in 1964, "it is possible to look inside the body of the *Venus de Milo* to

243

242

Fig. 1. Salvador Dalí, *The Hallucinogenic Toreador*, 1968-70 St. Petersburg (FL), The Salvador Dalí Museum, on loan from the Morse Charitable Trust

ment of Renaissance aesthetics.[11] "…[I]t was in coming across the debris of ancient sculptures, that the 16th-century cultural revolution, rightfully named the Renaissance, took place," he writes.[12] In the figure of himself as the bullfighter, Dalí amalgamates his paranoid-critical method, his 'atomic' fascination with flies and *The Venus de Milo*—one such 'ancient sculpture' destined to be aesthetically unearthed—, suggesting his hope that a 'cultural revolution' would abolish Abstract Expressionism in favor of a naturalistic aesthetic informed by contemporary science.[13] E.H.K.

[1] Luís Romero, *Todo Dalí en un rostro* (Barcelona: Editorial Blume, 1975), pp. 81-90.

[2] See also Luís Romero, *Torero allucinogen* (Barcelona: Editorial Mediterrània, 1990).

[3] Ian Gibson, *The Shameful Life of Salvador Dalí* (New York and London: W.W. Norton & Co., 1998), p. 597. Originally published by Faber and Faber (London: 1997).

[4] Amanda Lear, *My Life with Dalí* (London: Virgin Books, Ltd., 1985), p. 22. Originally published in French as *Le Dalí d'Amanda* (Paris: Favre, 1984).

[5] Romero, *Todo Dalí en un rostro*, p. 93. On Lorca's connections with *Un Chien andalou*, see Gibson, pp. 244-248.

[6] Salvador Dalí, trans. Haakon M. Chevalier, *The Secret Life of Salvador Dalí* (New York: Dover Publications, Inc., 1993), p. 71. Originally published by Dial Press (New York: 1942).

[7] Robert Descharnes and Gilles Néret, *Dalí* (New York: Taschen, 1998), p. 276. Originally published in French as *Salvador Dalí, 1904-1989. L'Oeuvre peint* (Cologne: Benedikt Taschen, 1993, 1998).

[8] *Playboy interview: Salvador Dalí, a candid conversation with the flamboyantly eccentric grand vizier of Surrealism. Playboy* (New York: July 1964), p. 44.

[9] Salvador Dalí, Preface to Robert Descharnes and Clovis Prévost, *Gaudí the Visionary* (New York: Dorset Press, 1989). Originally published in French as *La vision artistique et religeuse de Gaudi* (Lausanne: Edita S.A., 1969).

[10] Gibson, p. 597. The sketch appears in Romero, *Todo Dalí en un rostro*, p. 217.

[11] Salvador Dalí, "Ma révolution culturelle," 1968. English translation in Haim Finkelstein, *The Collected Writings of Salvador Dalí* (Cambridge: Cambridge University Press, 1998), pp. 374-376.

[12] *Ibid.*, 375.

[13] Romero notes Dalí's description of a swarm of flies as 'atomic' (Romero, *Todo Dalí en un rostro*, p. 340).

the soul."[8] One wonders whether this might inform the backwards-facing *Venuses* in *The Hallucinogenic Toreador*, whose bodies are opened in the manner of his 1934 *Weaning of Furniture Nutrition* and his 1949 and 1950 versions of *The Madonna of Port Lligat* (cat. 214, 215). Yet more contemporaneous with *The Hallucinogenic Toreador*, Dalí includes the *Venus de Milo with Drawers* as an antecedent to Pop Art in his 1968 preface to *Gaudí: The Visionary*, by Clovis Prévost and Robert Descharnes.[9] Indeed, the rudimentary dot/'flies' comprising the bullfighter's hat and cape in *The Hallucinogenic Toreador* may call to mind Pop artist Roy Lichtenstein's Benday dot paintings, though a more cryptic allusion to Pop Art may be Dalí's disclosure that the small toreador in the background is himself, who "has become a young bullfighter dreaming of offering Gala the bull of his Cultural Revolution."[10] Dalí's reference to Mao Zedong's 'Cultural Revolution' in China (1966) is misleading; as his May 1968 tract, 'My Cultural Revolution,' written in support of the rioting Sorbonne students in Paris, illustrates, Dalí's 'cultural revolution' was not a Left-wing political movement but, on the contrary, a reestablish-

244. Dawn, Noon, Sunset and Dusk, 1979

244. Oil on canvas
122 × 246 cm
48 × 96$^{7/8}$ in.
Figueres, Fundació
Gala-Salvador Dalí

245. Study for the Commemoration of the First Cilindric Crono-hologram of Alice Cooper, 1973

245. Pastel, sanguine
and ink on paper
31.9 × 43 cm
12⁵/8 × 16⁷/8 in.
Figueres, Fundació
Gala-Salvador Dalí

246. First Cilindric Crono-hologram. Portrait of Alice Cooper's Brain, 1973

246. Hologram with white light
realized by Selwyn Lissack

247. Dalí from the Back Painting Gala from the Back Eternalized by Six Virtual Corneas Provisionally Reflected in Six Real Mirrors, 1972-73
248. Gala's Christ, 1978

247. Oil on canvas,
stereoscopic work
in two components
Each 60 × 60 cm
23⁵/8 × 23⁵/8 in.
Figueres, Fundació
Gala-Salvador Dalí

248. Oil on canvas,
stereoscopic work
in two components
Each 100 × 100 cm
39³/8 × 39³/8 in.
Mexico, JAPS Collection

Along with *Gala's Christ*, this painting is an example of Dalí's numerous 1970s experiments with stereoscopy, the science concerning pairs of two-dimensional images that appear to exist in three dimensions through binocular viewing. Stereoscopy was first described in 1832 by the English physicist Sir Charles Wheatstone who developed a mirror stereoscope that created three-dimensional images from drawings. By presenting the same scene from slightly different angles that correspond to the angles of vision, the brain combines the separate perceptions and interprets the illusion of depth. With the advent of photography in 1837, stereoscopy was able to convey realistic, three-dimensional scenes, and stereoscopes became popular Victorian gadgets. Dalí describes his childhood infatuation with one of these 18th-century 'optical theaters' at the home of his schoolmaster, Señor Traite.[1] However, it was not until a 1969 exhibition of the Dutch master Gérard Dou (1613-75) at the Petit Palais in Paris, that Dalí realized stereoscopy's application to his own painting. Amanda Lear recalls accompanying Dalí to the exhibition and, later, perusing a book of Dou's paintings, where she noticed Dou had depicted many of his subjects more than once. Dalí explained that it was normal for painters to redo the same subject, to which Lear asked, "So why didn't they copy it exactly? Look, the space between the woman and the window is larger in this painting than in the other one."[2] Dalí excitedly suggested Dou might have been creating stereoscopic canvases, noting that "no one has ever noticed this before because no two of his paintings have ever been exhibited side by side."[3] Soon after, Dalí described Dou definitively as "the first stereoscopic painter," relaying his hypothesis to Luis Romero that Dou's pioneering stereoscopy in the 17th-century developed out of the Dutch preoccupation with optics that had produced Vermeer, Cornelius van Drebbel—the inventor of the submarine—, and Antoni van Leeuwenhoek, who developed the microscope.[4] Although it is extremely unlikely that Dou was attempting to execute stereoscopic paintings, the connection between 17th-century Dutch painting and photographic realism is well-established and not unique to Dalí. The renewed interest in Dutch painting in 1860s France coincided with the camera's first impact on art, and Dalí had praised Vermeer's 'photographic eye' as early as 1927.[5] In the early 1970s, Dalí's affinity for naturalism led him to applaud American Hyperrealist.[6] Fascinated with creating art in the third and fourth-dimensions and freshly disappointed with the limitations of holography, Dalí was inspired by Dou and Hyperrealist trends to attempt access to the third dimension through stereoscopy. For stereoscopy to work, the pairs of canvases have to be painted from points of view that are at exactly the correct distance apart for the images to overlap and exaggerate a 3-D effect. It is a testament to Dalí's virtuosity that he was able to successfully create the 3-D effect in his stereoscopic paintings, some of which are over two meters tall. The coloration of the images is also important; "Do you realize that one can create colors which don't exist, color which the brain is only imagining?" Dalí asked Amanda

Lear. "You paint a sky in blue-gray tones on the right and on the left you paint the same thing using pale-pink and apricot shades. These two skies superimpose in your brain and you see a viable image of an extraordinary amethyst and eau-de Nil tint which does not exist."[7] Dalí's example describes the disparate hues one sees in the pair, *Dalí from the Back Painting Gala…*. With this, Dalí aims for a *trompe-l'œil* beyond the chimera of depth; he strives for the color itself to be illusory, blending in the brain rather than on the canvas.

The self-portrait in *Dalí from the Back Painting Gala…* recalls such historical antecedents as Velázquez's *Las Meninas* (1656), in which a mirror like that featured in *Dalí from the Back Painting Gala…* reflects the image of King Philip IV and Queen Maria Anna. While *Gala's Christ* is arguably less skillfully rendered than *Dalí from the Back Painting Gala…*, its stereoscopic success confirms the time and energy Dalí dedicated to its completion. Dalí painted *Gala's Christ* as a gift for his wife, and the pair of canvases hung in the Castle at Púbol until Gala's death in 1982. The model for the auburn-haired Christ may have been Gala's junior love-interest, Jeff Fenholt, who performed as Jesus in the Broadway musical, *Jesus Christ Superstar*.[8] While *Dalí from the Back Painting Gala…* exemplifies Dalí's technical skill in the legacy of Vermeer and Dou, *Gala's Christ* connotes the artist's religious preoccupations. As his pursuit of naturalism adopted a decidedly spiritual subtext, so Dalí's foray into stereoscopy was ideologically beyond an optical parlor trick. "Binocular vision is the Trinity of transcendent physical perception," Dalí stated in *Ten Recipes for Immortality* (1973). "The Father, the right eye, The Son, the left eye and the Holy Ghost, the brain…"[9] E.H.K.

[1] Salvador Dalí, *The Secret Life of Salvador Dalí* (New York: Dover Publications, 1993), p. 41.

[2] Amanda Lear, *My Life with Dalí* (London: Virgin Books, Ltd., 1985), p. 200.

[3] *Ibid.*, p. 201.

[4] Luis Romero, *Dalí* (Secaucus, NJ: Chartwell Books, Inc., 1975), p. 160.

[5] See Salvador Dalí, "The Photographic Data," *Gaseta de les Arts* 2(6), (Barcelona: February 1929): pp. 40-42. Translated and published in English in ed., trans., Haim Finkelstein , *The Collected Writings of Salvador Dalí* (Cambridge: Cambridge University Press, 1999), pp. 68-69. Also, Salvador Dalí, "Photography: Pure Creation of the Mind," *L'Amic de les Arts*, 2 (18), (Sitges: September 30, 1927), pp. 90-91. Translated and published in English in Finkelstein, pp. 45-47.

[6] Salvador Dalí, preface to Linda Chase, *Les Hyperrealistes americains* (Paris: Filipacchi, 1973).

[7] Lear, p. 201.

[8] "Salvador Dalí: Le Christ de Gala," *The Art of the Surreal (Evening Sale)* (London: Christie's, 4 February 2002), p. 102.

[9] Salvador Dalí, *Dix recettes d'immortalité.* (Paris: Audouin-Descharnes, 1973). Cited in English in Robert Descharnes, *Dalí, the Work, the Man* (New York: Harry N. Abrams, 1984), p. 409. Published originally in French as *Dalí, l'oeuvre et l'homme* (Lausanne: Edita, 1984).

247

249. The Swallow's Tail (Series on Catastrophes), 1983

249. Oil on canvas
73 × 92.2 cm
28³/4 × 36¹/4 in.
Figueres, Fundació
Gala-Salvador Dalí

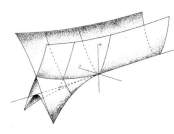

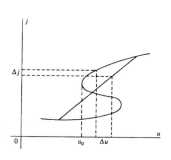

Fig. 1. Diagrams by René Thom
from *Stabilitè structurelle
et morphogénèse*

The Swallow's Tail, completed in May 1983, is considered by many to be Dalí's last painting. It is the final work in a series based on 'catastrophe theory,' as sired by the French mathematician, René Thom (1923-2002). Thom was internationally renowned for his work on topology—the branch of mathematics that studies the shapes and symmetries of abstract geometric figures or solids—and was awarded the Fields Medal in 1958. Thom's pioneering applications of geometric models to disciplines that traditionally resisted mathematical treatment culminated in his 1972 book, *Structural Stability and Morphogenesis*, which outlined his efforts to qualitatively model continuous actions (e.g., sailing along the smooth surface of a lake) that suddenly give way to discontinuous changes, or 'points of catastrophe' (plunging over a waterfall).[1] Thom suggested that in four-dimensional phenomena, there are seven possible equilibrium surfaces and thus seven possible discontinuities, or 'elementary catastrophes;' Thom named these seven elementary catastrophes: 'fold,' 'cusp,' 'swallow's tail,' 'butterfly,' 'hyperbolic umbilic,' 'elliptic umbilic,' and 'parabolic umbilic.'[2] The shape of Dalí's *Swallow's Tail* is taken directly from Thom's 4-dimensional graph of the same title, combined with a second catastrophe graph, the s-curve that Thom dubbed, 'the cusp' (fig. 1).

Given Dalí's enduring study of morphology, as exemplified by his numerous allusions to D'Arcy Thompson's *On Growth and Form*, and his obsession with the latest developments in modern science, it is unsurprising that the artist was attracted to Thom's work on morphogenesis—the multifarious field of biology concerned with the appearance of new organic forms in the course of evolution.[3] Dalí was especially drawn to Thom's geometric graphs of the seven elementary catastrophes, perhaps because they—like so many of his own canvases—sought to render concrete what had previously been determined 'discontinuous' and, thus, irrational. In his speech, "Gala, Velázquez and the Golden Fleece," presented upon his 1979 induction into the prestigious *Académie des Beaux-Arts* of the *Institut de France*, Dalí recollected his first and only meeting with Thom, at which Thom purportedly told Dalí that he was studying tectonic plates. This provoked Dalí to question Thom about the railway station at Perpignan, France—which the artist had declared in the 1960s to be the center of the universe (see *The Railway Station at Perpignan*, cat. 243). Thom reportedly replied, "I can assure you that Spain pivoted precisely—not in the area of— but exactly there where the Railway Station in Perpignan stands today." [4] Dalí was immediately enraptured by Thom's statement, as it buttressed his own delirious claims.

Citing Thom's work on tectonic plates, Dalí painted his penultimate canvas, *Topological Abduction of*

Europe – Homage to René Thom (March 1983) (fig. 2), the lower left corner of which features Thom's equation for the 'swallow's tail'—[$V=x^5/5+(ux^3)/3+(vx^2)/2+wx$]—, a diminutive illustration of the graph, and the term, *queue d'aronde* (French for swallow's tail). The seismic fracture that transverses *Topological Abduction of Europe* reappears in *The Swallow's Tail* at the precise point where the y-axis of the swallow's tail graph intersects with the s-curve of 'the cusp'—a graph featuring more evidently in Dalí's untitled painting on catastrophes from 1983 (fig. 3). Here again, Thom's model is presented alongside the elegant curves of a cello and the instrument's f-holes, which, especially as they lack the small pointed side-cuts of a traditional f-hole, equally connote the mathematical symbol for an integral in calculus: ∫.

In "Gala, Velázquez and the Golden Fleece," Dalí describes Thom's theory of catastrophes as "the most beautiful aesthetic theory in the world," stating that Thom's geometric figures fascinated him "from a purely aesthetic point of view."[5] This is a significant revelation, for presumably Dalí—despite his avid interest in science and geometry—would have had difficulty understanding Thom's complex mathematics. That Dalí admits to appreciating Thom's models on a purely aesthetic basis suggests that his decision to focus primarily on the swallow's tail was more an aesthetic judgement than one informed by Thom's writing (which Dalí nonetheless certainly read). In a short 1983 essay, "The Most Important Discovery of my Paranoiac-Critical Method: the Railway Station at Perpignan," Dalí reveals that the swallow's tail had adopted particular paranoiac significance as he constructed the calligraphy for his 29-page *Treatise of Catastropheiform Writing* in October 1982. "At the moment that I was writing it," he recalls, "I had four hallucinations in which the French scholar, René Thom, appeared and explained to me the phenomena of morphogenesis with a venerable and paternal attitude." He continues: The most stupefying part of this anticipation… is that one of the six catastrophes of René Thom that appeared in my hallucination is the one that he called *the swallow's tale*. And now, at this precise instant, I realize with stupefaction that since my childhood, my constant dream has been the divine negentropic entasis of the swallow's tail, undoubtedly already dreamed by my own moustaches as photographed by Man Ray on the cover of *Time* magazine in December 1936.[6]

Dalí thus seems to have chosen the swallow's tail from among Thom's other graphs based on hallucinatory suggestion and its antennae-like shape, which indeed evokes the artist's upturned moustache. Contributing to the moustache effect in *The Swallow's Tail* are two mirrored ∫-symbols just above the center of the canvas that mimic a downturned handlebar moustache.

Prior to his 1984 self-imposed isolation in the Torre

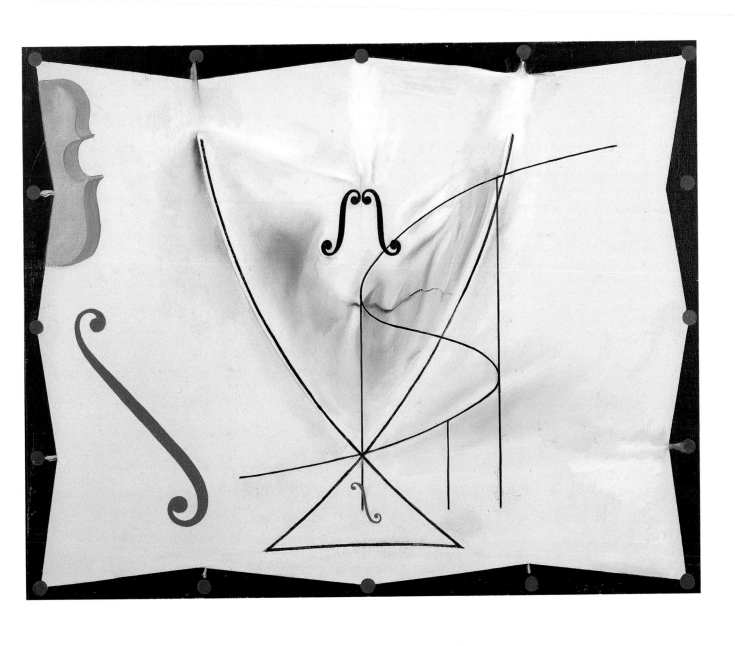

Fig. 2. Salvador Dalí, *Topological Abduction of Europe – Homage to René Thom*, 1983
Figueres, Fundació Gala-Salvador Dalí

Fig. 3. Salvador Dalí, *Untitled – Series on Catastrophes,* 1983
Figueres, Fundació Gala-Salvador Dalí

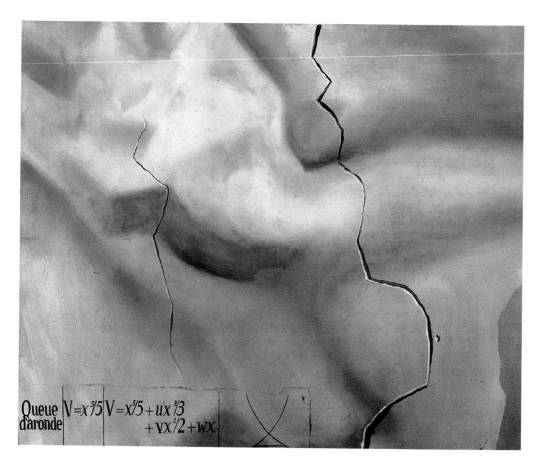

Galatea, Dalí would tell the rare visitors he received at the castle at Púbol, "All that I do henceforth will be concentrated on the phenomenon of catastrophes."[7] Given Dalí's tragic final decade, it is poetic that his final canvases would reflect Thom's 'points of catastrophe.' Dalí fell into severe depression following Gala's death in 1982, refusing to eat due to a psychological inability to swallow; he was thus fed through a tube in his nose. His now trembling right hand—described by his doctor as a result of old age rather than Parkinson's disease—made it difficult for him to paint the fine details for which he was famous, though close friends contend that the artist's hand steadied long enough for him to render the graceful curves of *The Swallow's Tail*.[8] Following a string of ailments and a bedroom fire in 1984 that caused first and second-degree burns on approximately 18% of Dalí's body, the artist died of "cardiac insufficiency, associated with pneumonia, professing irreversibly to severe respiratory insufficiency and cardio-respiratory failure," on 23 January 1989.[9] As one so fearful of death—ever conceiving imaginative means to extend his life indefinitely—, Dalí may have appreciated Thom's words on the subject, which blend scientific language with, perhaps unintentional, *humour noir*; "Everyday life, on the physiological plane, may be a tissue of ordinary catastrophes," Thom writes, "but our death is a generalised catastrophe."[10] E.H.K.

[1] George Johnson, "René Thom, 79, Inventor of Catastrophe Theory, Dies," *The New York Times*, 10 November 2002.

[2] See René Thom, *Structural stability and morphogenesis. an outline of a general theory of models*, trans. D.H.Fowler (Reading, Mass., London: Benjamin, 1975). Originally published in French as *Stabilité structurelle et morphogénèse*, 1972.

[3] André Parinaud, *The Unspeakable Confessions of Salvador Dalí* (New York: Marrow, 1976), p. 237. Originally published in French as *Comment on devient Dalí* (Paris: Robert Laffont, 1973). See also René Thom, *Mathematical Models of Morphogenesis* (Chichester: Ellis Horwood, 1983).

[4] Salvador Dalí, "Gala, Velásquez and the Golden Fleece" (9 May 1979). Reproduced in-part in Robert Descharnes, *Dalí, the Work, the Man* (New York: Harry N. Abrams, 1984), p. 420. Originally published in French as *Dalí, l'oeuvre et l'homme* (Lausanne: Edita, 1984).

[5] *Ibid.*

[6] Salvador Dalí, "The Most Important Discovery of my Paranoiac-Critical Method: the Railway Station at Perpignan," 31 October 1983. Reproduced in Descharnes, *Dalí, the Work, the Man*, p. 423.

[7] Descharnes, *Dalí, the Work, the Man*, p. 424.

[8] Ian Gibson, *The Shameful Life of Salvador Dalí*, (New York and London: W.W. Norton & Co., 1998), pp. 656 and 666. Originally published by Faber and Faber (London, 1997).

[9] *Abc* (Madrid), 24 January 1989: p. 29. Quoted in *Ibid.*, p. 678.

[10] Thom, *Structural stability and morphogenesis. An outline of a general theory of models*, p. 251.

L'Amic de les Arts

The journal *L'Amic de les Arts* played a fundamental role in the diffusion of Catalan culture. Issued monthly in the Catalan language, this periodical devoted to the arts and literature received contributions from various artists, including Joan Miró, and the poet and dramatist Federico García Lorca, as well as Dalí. Published at Sitges (a seaside town not far from Barcelona, which the birth of Modernism transformed into an important cultural center), was edited by the writer Josep Carbonell, while its political line was laid down by the poet Josep Vincenç Foix. In the 1920s the journal reflected the eclectic modernity deriving from the political ideology of those who wrote for it. "The Catalan and Catalanist revolution," Foix wrote, "is in its essence Futurist, thus anti-traditionalist, modern, and European" and, moreover, "it accepts and even encourages risk and adventure in all the manifestations of thought and the products of artistic and literary creativity." "Risk" and "adventure" guide a number of the cultural proposals of the journal, which, although it was moderately Catholic, introduced the works of such writers as the Comte de Lautréamont (the pen name of Isidore Lucien Ducasse) to Catalonia and the Surrealist poets, and, despite its radical Catalanism, it did not close the door on the most interesting aspects of Spanish culture and the avant-garde that expressed itself through the voice of the poet Federico García Lorca and the writer Ernesto Jiménez Caballero, editor of *La Gaceta Literaria*. And it was "risk" and "adventure" that induced Dalí to contribute to the journal and organize—together with the critics Sebastià Gasch and Lluís Montanyà—a small group (the "anti-artistic group") interested in creating artistic ferment, the activities of which culminated in the drawing up of the *Manifest Groc*. "Sant Sebastià," the first written work published by Salvador Dalí in *L'Amic de les Arts*, appeared in print in July 1927. Four months later, the painter was already a member of its editorial committee, and in March 1929 he undertook the task of editing what was to be the last number of the journal, the contents of which, because of their radical and avant-garde nature, were very different from the previous ones.

Between his first contribution to the journal and its last edition, Dalí wrote more than twenty articles for the monthly: some of these were particularly lengthy and were published in installments in a number of is-

sues. These texts provide an opportunity for reconstructing Dalí's evolution from a mechanistic position strongly influenced by Le Corbusier's journal *Esprit nouveau* to the espousal of opinions very close to those of André Breton and his friends, whom the painter knew through *La Révolution surréaliste*. F.F.

Art Nouveau see Modernism

Gaston Bachelard (1884-1962)

The son of a shoemaker, Bachelard worked in the postal service before embarking on an outstanding academic and publishing career, lecturing mainly at the Sorbonne on physics, philosophy, and the study of poetry. He is best known in the anglophone world for his later, widely-read lyrical volumes *The Poetics of Space* (1958) and *The Poetics of Reverie* (1960) which are usually believed to constitute the chief link between his thought and that of Dalí and the Surrealists. But in the 1930s, Bachelard was friends with Surrealists Roger Caillois and Pierre Mabille, and was on the editorial board of *Recherches philosophiques*, to which Caillois, Georges Bataille, Pierre Klossowski, and others close to Surrealism contributed articles. His books of that period on the history and philosophy of science, such as *Le Nouvel esprit scientifique* (1934) and *La Philosophie du non* (1940), introduced the notion of "epistemological breaks," which, Bachelard claimed, underlay the apparently continuous accrual of knowledge, historically demarcating intellectual generations, collective sympathies, and conceptual frameworks. Every individual in Surrealism and its wider milieu read *Le Nouvel esprit scientifique*, most factoring the idea of the *coupure épistémologique* into their writings. The concept surfaces in articles and texts by Dalí of 1935 such as "Non-Euclidean Psychology of a Photograph' and 'The Tears of Heraclitus," situating Surrealism and modern physics together in a non-classical, non-Cartesian, non-Newtonian, non-Kantian epistemology, whilst along similar lines in a letter to the poet Paul Éluard of that time, Dalí insisted that the new Surrealist "religion" should be "based on the progress of scientific knowledge (especially the new ideas of space, which were inaccessible not only to the Greeks but also to Christianity)...." The scale of the Surrealists' reception of Bachelard's writings was overlooked or forgotten, though after the Second World War the same ideas were deployed in their

respective fields by Louis Althusser, Georges Canguilhem, Michel Foucault, and Michel Serres among others, changing the course of French philosophy and sealing Bachelard's reputation. G.P.

Georges Bataille (1897-1962)

There is a remarkable coincidence of ideas between Georges Bataille and Salvador Dalí, although because of the strained relations between the Surrealists and Bataille, who described himself as "Surrealism's old enemy from within," and Dalí's whole-hearted colonization of Surrealism, this has received less attention than it deserves. Dalí retained a strong admiration for Bataille until the end of his life, especially for his *Story of the Eye;* perhaps he and Buñuel knew this violent, erotic tale before making their film *Un Chien andalou* is uncertain.

In the review *Documents* (1929-30), which drew a number of disaffected Surrealists into its orbit, Bataille waged a campaign against what he saw as Surrealism's poetic evasions and idealist aspirations. Confronting horror and recognizing not only its link at the extremes to seduction but also its capacity to break with stifling conformity, Bataille challenged the Surrealists' notion of liberation. For Bataille, Dalí's paintings and *Un Chien andalou* had a capacity to shock and a level of horror unique in contemporary art. In his "Dictionary" entry on "Eye" in *Documents* he discusses the film's power of attraction following the notorious opening sequence of the razor slicing an eye, where fascination and horror converge.

Bataille gave Dalí considerable prominence in *Documents:* the first Parisian review to do so. In the same issue as "Eye" (no. 4 September 1929) three works by Dalí are reproduced: *Honey Is Sweeter Than Blood, Bather* and *Female Nude*. Following the journal's radical policy of juxtaposing heterogeneous cultural materials, the former is reproduced together with two pages of brutal and violent images from a pulp crime magazine, *L'œil de la police*. Dalí's two *Bathers*, which were exhibited in "Abstract and Surrealist Art" in Zurich, are juxtaposed with an anamorphic image of Saint Anthony of Padua, analyzed in the same issue by Carl Einstein. The formal likeness between this image, whose anamorphic deformation is expressive of ecstatic devotion, and Dalí's *Bathers* underlines the iconoclasm of the journal. Shortly after this Bataille published his famous article on *The Big Toe* that has striking similarities with a text by Dalí in *L'Amic de les Arts* in March 1929, "L'alliberaments dels dits" (The Liberation of Fingers), illustrated with isolated digits.

The clash between Bataille's and Breton's Surrealism, of which Dalí becomes a sign, reached its peak in the article "Le Jeu lugubre" (no. 7, December 1929). Bataille, refused permission to reproduce Dalí's painting of this title, reproduces instead a schematic drawing in which he points out in Freudian terms the psycho-sexual complexes which he claims the painting reveals. He asks how one can take seriously the suggestion that with this painting, for the first time, "the mental windows are thrown open wide," a quotation from Breton's preface to Dalí's first exhibition in Paris that October. D.A.

Bread

Dalí turned the idea of bread as "the staff of life" on its head. He discovered what he called "the enigma of bread: it could stand up without having to be eaten!" Unlike his still lives of *Baskets of Bread*, the propped baguettes in *The Invisible Man* or *Anthropomorphic Bread* turn this classic emblem of the sacred and the nutritious into symbols of other things. Dalí also taunted Paris society, eager for novelty, with projects for baking a loaf fifteen meters, twenty meters, forty five meters long, to be placed in the Palais Royal, or Versailles, or the Savoy-Plaza. Was he a communist, they wondered? Or was it just Surrealism? In this period in the early 1930s, Surrealism was going through a crisis in terms of its political commitment, and Dalí was often at the center of the movement's problems with the French Communist Party. His erotic text "Rêverie" (Daydream) published in *Le Surréalisme au service de la révolution* was the cause of disciplinary measures by the PCF; although Breton defended him to the PCF just as he defended Aragon's propaganda poem "Front rouge" to the French authorities, the Surrealists found Dalí's resistance to revolutionary discipline and his awkward interest in Hitler a constant cause of conflict. In this context, Dalí's obsession with bread, which he persistently renders useless and aesthetic, has a pointedly defiant character. He used to carry a copy of Prince Kropotkin's anarcho-communist tract *The Conquest of Bread* around with him. This would have been anathema to the PCF. Kropotkin's detailed economic solution to the problem of bread for all (he proves that with a rational culture, intensive farming

and the use of the 100,000 unemployed it would be easy to produce bread freely for the 3-4 million inhabitants of Paris and its regions) is linked to the abolition of state authority. Dalí's giant and mysterious loaves that he proposed placing in unexpected sites in the cities is like a paranoiac reverie on such utilitarian utopianism, "the bread of the revenge of imaginative luxury on the utilitarianism of the rational practical world." *The Conquest of Bread*, moreover, may well have inspired the title of his famous text *Conquest of the Irrational*. D.A.

André Breton (1896-1966)

Breton, poet, thinker and charismatic leader of the Surrealist movement, welcomed Dalí as a new recruit in 1929 by writing the preface to his first one-man exhibition in Paris at the Galerie Goemans. Having launched Surrealism in 1924, with a *Manifesto* that paid special homage to Freud and what the Surrealists took as psychoanalysis's promise of the liberation of the imagination, Breton asserted Surrealism's right to intervene in every aspect of human life. He sought above all to reconcile the ideas of Freud and of Marx, but found it increasingly difficult to convince the French Communist Party of Surrealism's commitment to the revolution while at the same time maintaining their explorations into the human unconscious. Surrealist poetry and art, often violent and erotic, was anathema to the PCF; Dalí was one of the prime culprits and his waywardness also took the form of an interest in Hitler. Breton, trying to maintain the purity of the movement with what seemed like increasingly Stalinist methods, made an attempt to exclude Dalí, but the latter persuaded him that far from indicating support for Hitler his interest in him was a pathological phenomenon. It was not until 1939 that Breton finally excluded Dalí, for both his political views and unabashed commercialism, coining the memorable anagram "Avida Dollars." Nonetheless, he included Dalí's text "Les nouvelles couleurs du sex-appeal spectral" in the 1940 edition of *Anthologie de l'humour noir*, and wrote favorably of his originality, his paranoiac-critical method and of his invention of objects that become the concrete vehicles of humor.

Surrealism was a close and collaborative community and Dalí's imaginative ferment supported it through the 1930s. Dalí drew the frontispiece for Breton's *Second Surrealist Manifesto* when it was published as a book in 1930 and contributed drawings to Breton

and Éluard's *L'Immaculée conception*, which included texts simulating mental illnesses—a subject of great interest to Dalí. Breton corrected the manuscript of Dalí's *Le Myth Tragique de l'Angelus de Millet*, trying, as Gala so frequently did, to put in order Dalí's wild orthography and bubbling grammar.

Breton wrote to Dalí in January 1931 that the inscription on the ex-libris he had commissioned should read "André le tamanoir" (great ant-eater) rather than "André le fourmilier" (fig. 2). Robert Browning, in his poem "Sludge the Medium," identifies himself with the ant-eater, "placid as it lies in wait but swift to seize its prey": just the attitude of the poet. D.A.

Cadaqués

Cadaqués is located in the region of Alt Empordà, in the northeast of the province of Girona, in Catalonia. The area surrounding it is bounded to the north by Cap Creus, to the south by Cala Jònculs, to the east by the Mediterranean Sea, and to the west by the Pení Mountain (613 meters). Practically isolated from the rest of Spain, Cadaqués enjoyed a period of great prosperity thanks to the wine trade during the 18th-century, and it engaged in commerce with the whole Mediterranean basin (including Greece) and the New World, especially Cuba. However, the introduction of steamships, which favored the port of Barcelona, and the phylloxera blight, which devastated the vineyards, led to the town's economic decline. It was only in the 1960s, with the advent of mass tourism, that the town was able to recover from this crisis. The vineyards were replaced by olive groves, which eventually occupied eighty-seven per cent of the entire cultivable land in the area, although they were severely damaged by the frosts of 1956. In order to understand the extent of Cadaqués's economic power in its period of greatest splendor, it is sufficient to consider that, at the beginning of the 19th-century, of the town's 2,000 inhabitants, 469 owned boats carrying crews.

Cadaqués's isolated position has helped to preserve the wild natural beauty of this corner of Catalonia, which in the early 20th-century became the favorite vacation resort for many artists, including the Pichot family, who in 1908 gave hospitality to the Dalís—shortly afterwards they bought their own house there—and, in 1910, the Picassos. In their turn, the Dalís provided accommodation for many of the leading creative figures of the period; Federico García Lorca in 1925

Fig. 1/cat. 250
Salvador Dalí, *Federico
in the Café de Oriente with a Guitar*,
ca. 1924
Pencil on paper,
18.7 × 11.5 cm
7³/8 × 4¹/2 in.
Munich, Staatliche
Graphische Sammlung

Fig. 2/cat. 251
Salvador Dalí, *André Breton:
The Great Ant-eater,* 1929-31
Pen and ink on paper
4.3 × 6.3 cm
1⁵/8 × 2¹/2 in.
Barcelona, Mas Peinado Collection

Fig. 3/cat. 252
Salvador Dalí, *Ex-libris
for Federico García Lorca,* 1926
Watercolor on a postcard
16 × 16 cm
6³/8 × 6³/8 in.
Private Collection

1

2

3

and 1927; Gala and Paul Éluard, Luis Buñuel, René Magritte, and Camille Goemans in 1929; André Breton, Max Ernst, Man Ray, and others in 1930. From the 1950s onward Cadaqués became the meeting point for artists such as Marcel Duchamp, Joan Josep Tharrats, Modest Cuixart, Joan Ponç, Richard Hamilton, and many more besides.

From 1918 to 1926, during his summer vacations Dalí portrayed Cadaqués more than eighty times. After his father expelled him from the family home in 1929, the artist acquired a fisherman's cottage from the children of his friend Lídia Noguer i Sabà in the nearby secluded village of Port Lligat, which became his new home. This house was also depicted in numerous works of both his early Surrealist phase and his mystic period (after his return from America in 1948). And Dalí never ceased to regard Cadaqués as the most beautiful place in the world. R.M.P. and V.A.M.

The Catalan Avant-Garde

In March 1928, Dalí signed the *Manifest Groc* (Yellow Manifesto) along with the writer Lluís Montanyà and the art critic Sebastià Gasch, indicting the provincial state of Catalan arts and letters. Subtitled the "Catalan Anti-artistic Manifesto," the *Manifest Groc* was a call to arms to Catalan artists and intellectuals to militate actively on behalf of modern culture and the international avant-garde. Denouncing the hackneyed clichés of fin-de-siècle sentimental poetry, contemporary pastiches of ancient painting and sculpture, and "the total lack of preparation on the part of critics with regard to the art of today and yesterday's art,"[1] the authors of the manifesto put forth the cause of contemporary developments in fashion, transportation, technology, sports, popular music, and film. Citing Pablo Picasso, Juan Gris, Amédée Ozenfant, Giorgio de Chirico, Joan Miró, Jacques Lipchitz, Constantin Brancusi, Jean Arp, Le Corbusier, Pierre Reverdy, Paul Éluard, Louis Aragon, Robert Desnos, Tristan Tzara, Jean Cocteau, André Breton, Federico García Lorca, and Maurice Raynal as partners in this enterprise, Dalí, Montanyà, and Gasch sought to install a national culture of modernity in Catalonia that would be in line with the most recent tendencies of contemporary thought.

The relatively late date of the Yellow Manifesto may appear remarkable, given the tradition of avant-garde art that had developed in such European capitals as Paris, Munich, Berlin, Moscow, and Milan in the early years of the 20th-century. But Dalí and his colleagues immediately understood that the course of the Catalan avant-garde was by no means assured, and that public hostility, in addition to a still largely underdeveloped market system in Barcelona, provided serious obstacles to its success. To this end, Dalí had only to recall that Picasso, whom Catalan critics claimed as a native son, had built his reputation in Paris, and that Miró had likewise traveled to the French capital in 1920 with the expressed goal of becoming an "international Catalan" in the face of incomprehension at home. Indeed, Dalí himself would continue this pattern of artistic emigration when he joined the Parisian Surrealist group as a full member in the autumn of 1929.

Throughout the 1910s and the 1920s, the Catalan avant-garde represented the minority efforts of a small coterie of artists, poets, intellectuals, and impresarios in Barcelona. In 1906, the art dealer Josep Dalmau, a former member of the Quatre Gats circle where Picasso had celebrated his first one-man exhibition in February 1900, opened a small gallery on the Carrer del Pi in Barcelona's Barri Gòtic, before moving on to larger quarters. Over the next 20 years, Dalmau played host to a wide range of international avant-garde artists, including: Kees van Dongen and Celso Lagar (1915), Albert Gleizes (1916), Sergei Charchoune and Helena Grunhoff (1916 and 1917), and Francis Picabia (1922). Dalmau also gave Miró and Dalí their first one-man shows (in 1918 and 1925, respectively), launching the careers of both artists. Through Dalmau and poets associated with his circle—most notably Josep Maria Junoy—Catalan artists were introduced to recent developments in avant-garde painting and literature, an experience that, in Dalí's case, was supplemented by the artist's access to advanced literary and artistic journals such as *Esprit nouveau* and *La Révolution surréaliste*, which he acquired through his uncle Rafael, who was a book dealer.

By the time Dalí co-authored the *Manifest Groc*, he had already made one brief trip to Paris and was fully conversant with the most recent international developments in painting and poetry. His disdain for the Catalan cultural establishment increasingly assumed the form of vitriolic and very public attacks on specific institutions—most notably the Autumn Salon held at the conservative Sala Parés in 1928[2]—and on Catalan intellectuals, generally.[3] There is, however, a double-edge to Dalí's criticism as throughout the early 1930s the artist continued to contribute to Catalan cultural initiatives, lecturing at such institutions as the Ateneu Barcelonés in 1930 and celebrating another one-man exhibition at the Galeria d'Art Catalònia in Barcelona from December 8-21, 1933 under the auspices of the newly-formed organization A. D. L. A. N. (An acronym for "Amics de l'Art Nou," or "Friends of the New Art"). Nevertheless, Dalí's attentions were increasingly directed beyond the borders of his native land and his adopted city of Paris to venues abroad. Immediately preceding his Barcelona show, Dalí celebrated his first exhibition in New York at the Julien Levy Gallery from November 21 to December 8, establishing his critical fortune in America and leaving the Catalan avant-garde behind. R.S.L.

Catalonia

The autonomous community of Catalonia is located in northeastern Spain on the Mediterranean Sea, bordered by Aragon to the west, France and Andorra to the north, and Valencia to the south. The region is comprised of four provinces—Barcelona, Girona, Lleida, and Tarragona—and covers an area of approximately 12,328 square miles. It is the wealthiest and most highly industrialized community in modern Spain. Catalonia's climate and topography are varied, from the deep valleys and majestic, snow covered peaks of the Pyrenees to the north, to the vast, fertile plains of the Empordà in the area surrounding Dalí's native city of Figueres in the province of Girona, and the arid, mountainous terrain of the Camp de Tarragona south of the capital city of Barcelona. Just as Dalí's contemporary Joan Miró made the flora and fauna of the Tarragona countryside a leitmotif of his art, so too did Dalí mythologize his native landscape: the villages of Figueres and Cadaqués, the Bay of Roses, and the extravagant rock formations of Cap Creus are stock elements in his work.

Catalonia has always been a crossroads for diverse peoples and cultures. The native population was conquered first by the Romans, and, in the 5th and 8th centuries, Catalonia was occupied by Goths and Moors. In the Middle Ages the principal cities of Girona and Barcelona were home to Jews, Christians, and Muslims, and in the 13th and 14th centuries, under the united crown of Catalonia and the Kingdom of Aragon,

Catalan maritime and commercial interests dominated the western Mediterranean, with influence extending as far east as Greece and as far south as Sicily. With the unification of Spain following the marriage of Ferdinand of Aragon to Isabella of Castile in the 16th-century, Catalonia lost many of its privileges and much of its economic influence, a process that reached an unhappy finale in 1714 when Catalonia, siding with the Hapsburgs in the War of the Spanish Succession, lost the last remnants of its autonomy under the victorious Bourbon ruler, Philip V.

Strong nationalist sentiment in Catalonia reemerged in the mid-19th-century, as the region underwent a process of industrialization and as a nascent bourgeoisie sought economic self-definition through culture. The ancient Catalan tongue, an independent romance language that derives from the Latin vulgate, once again became a medium of literature and poetry during the cultural *Renaixensa* that began in the 1850s. Initially a nostalgic and folkloric movement, Catalan nationalism, however, soon entered into a political phase, as Catalan industrialists sought to maintain greater protection of their interests. Following Spain's defeat in the Spanish-American war of 1898, and the ensuing "National Disaster" in which the nation lost the last vestiges of its colonial possessions in Cuba, Puerto Rico, and the Philippines (major export markets for Catalan industry), Catalan political nationalism entered a decisive phase in the contest with the central government in Madrid. Over the next two decades, as Catalans consolidated their power in the constituent Cortes, a far-reaching series of cultural and political initiatives was undertaken: the Catalan language was standardized as a modern literary and administrative medium and a dictionary was published; a national museum of Catalan art and a Catalan national library were established, and, in 1914, the Mancomunitat de Catalonia was formed to place the region's four provincial governments under a single, centralized authority, harking back to the role played by the medieval Generalitat de Catalunya in the bygone days of Catalan political hegemony. By the time of the Second Republic (1931-39) and the Spanish Civil War (1936-39) Catalan interests assumed center stage in Spanish political life. With the victory of General Francisco Franco's forces in 1939, however, Catalonia again lost many of its privileges, and its citizens and institutions were subject to censorship and repression. With the death of Franco in 1975 and the succession of King Juan Carlos I to the throne, a constitutional monarchy was established in Spain in which the autonomous community of Catalonia was ratified by a regional plebiscite. R.S.L.

Cheese

The changing significance of cheese in Dalí's oeuvre reflected his current preoccupations, from scientific principles in the 1930s to religious mysticism in the 1960s and 1970s. In *The Secret Life* (1942), he explains how a melting wheel of Camembert provided the inspiration for his famous soft watches, debuting in *The Persistence of Memory* (1931). "We had topped off our meal with a very strong Camembert," he writes, "and after everyone had gone I remained for a long time seated at the table meditating on the philosophic problems of the "super-soft" which the cheese presented to my mind. I got up and went into the studio, where I lit the light in order to cast a final glance, as is my habit, at the picture I was in the midst of painting… I was about to turn out the light, when instantaneously I "saw" the solution. I saw two soft watches, one of them hanging lamentably on the branch of the olive tree…" His earlier description in *Conquest of the Irrational* (1935) of the soft watches, as "nothing but the soft, extravagant, and solitary paranoiac-critical Camembert of time and space," alludes also to the crucial paranoiac connection between soft cheese and the Einsteinian dilation of relativistic time. The softness of the cheese also elicited for him a visceral sense of rot and putrescence; hence, his 1944 novel, *Hidden Faces*, describes a macabre scene as a "Dantean gruyère."

By the 1960s, Dalí's use of the cheese metaphor turned from the grotesque and scientific to the pious; he writes in his essay, *Le divin fromage*, introducing his illustrations of Dante's *Divine Comedy* (1960), "I want my watercolors for Dante to be like light marks of the humidity of a divine cheese… the mystique is the cheese; Christ is cheese, better yet, mountains of cheese!" He credits this unusual metaphor—repeated in *Diary of a Genius*—to Saint Augustin, who, he says, recounts Christ's words, "*montanus coagulatus, montanus fermentatus,*" which should be understood as a "veritable mountain of cheese" "véritable montagne de fromage." His reference is to Book IX of Augustin's *Confessions*, which quotes Psalms 67:22-23, "that mountain flowing with milk, that fruitful mountain"—literally, *monte in-*caseato, "the mountain of curds"; the Latin Vulgate employs the word, "*coagulatus,*" which, as the 16th-century Augustinian Spanish mystic, Fra Luis de León—whose book, *De los nombres de Cristo*, Dalí owned—, explains, originally means "cheese." It designates also what is "deformed"… If we add to it the name "mountain"…, it signifies, as Saint Augustin read it, "mountain of cheeses"… or as certain people now translate it, "mountain of humps." Armed with this allegory, Dalí reinterpreted the "prophetic" value of his soft watches as "a prefiguration of Christ, because they resemble the soft cheese that obsessed me," and Dalí has discovered that the body of Jesus is the same as cheese. This is not only Dalí; the first man who talked about this was Saint Augustine, who once compared the body of Christ to mountains of cheese. So Dalí has merely reintroduced the concept of cheese back onto the body of Christ. "In the communion, there have always been the bread and the wine for the body and the blood. In the same way, the soft watches, like soft cheese, are the presence of the body of Christ in my painting." E.H.K.

Cinema

Just what were Dalí and Buñuel playing at with their 1929 short, *Un Chien andalou*? What was their game? For one they were hoping to take Paris by storm—to leave their mark on its ultra-sophisticated intelligentsia by outraging it, a technique familiar since the 1860s, although less so in film culture. For Dalí the movie would demonstrate his versatility, its Studio 28 public opening October 1, 1929 neatly coinciding with his first solo painting show in Paris. (And Buñuel, he'd get to do the movie he'd trained for at Jean Epstein's film school, and to pay Epstein back for certain slights).

Un Chien andalou's opening sequence—one of the great starts in movie history—announced an aesthetic program predicated on exuberant perversity at the level of both form and content. Theory-wise, the two Spaniards had long been waxing lyrical about photogenia, segmentation, the virtues of "standardized" Hollywood cinema, especially the comedies of Langdon and Keaton and the melodramas of Lubitsch and Stroheim. And railing against the vices of the formalist "art film": Lang, Gance, Léger and even Man Ray. However, the only viable venue for a wacky "anti-artistic" montage movie like theirs was the art house. As chance would have it both the art film and its "other" were on the verge of obsolescence: the arrival of sound would see them off.

Dalí and Buñuel's biggest hopes, though, were pinned on their insurrectionary short functioning as a calling-card to get them invited into a group they'd admired from afar: the Surrealists. And the movement, which was living through the ideological crisis outlined in Breton's *Second Manifeste*, needed them, needed their inventiveness, their belligerence, and, once they'd been put straight on who their real friends were—certainly not that Bataille/Prévert lot—their orthodoxy. Which is why, when the co-scenarists came to speak about their cinematic squib, they parroted one of Surrealism's founding myths, automatism, and emphasized the magical spontaneity of *Un Chien andalou*'s writing. A mystification, of course, since to arrive at a professional shooting script—and Buñuel did, even then, like to stick to his *découpage*—a lot of aesthetic secondary elaboration was required.

Un Chien andalou is an absurdist Freudian comedy about libidinal gratification, its tragic vicissitudes and endless deferral, yet it's an apolitical movie and as such doesn't exemplify the Freudo-Marxism promulgated in the *Second Manifeste*. *L'Âge d'or*, the Sur-Surrealist movie, would do that. Initially planned as a sound remake of *Un Chien andalou*, and paid for by the film-loving Vicomtes de Noailles, Buñuel and Dalí's second scenario again centered on a tragicomic romance, but framed this within a much more class-conscious discourse. The sociopolitical jokes in *L'Âge d'or* are more than likely Buñuel's, the sexual ones Dalí's. *L'Âge d'or* came out at three times the length of its predecessor, but as a collaboration it was twenty times less gratifying, in part due to the antipathy between Buñuel and Gala, who'd arrived on the scene after the first showings of *Un Chien andalou*. Many of the tactics of the latter were reused in its follow-up: the "beside-the-point" prologue and epilogue; shots and shot-sequences with an over-determined, irrational content; narrative incongruities and non-sequiturs; embedded narrative continuities that only repeated viewings bring to light; contradictory continuity cuts within a sequence; the use of mendacious and/or paradoxical intertitles leading to spatio-temporal "matching mismatches," to disorienting ellipses; the in-joke as a generator of imagery, and so on. What is new in *L'Âge d'or* are the colliding aesthetics and textures which come with the interpolation of found footage; the statelier

cutting, at half the speed of *Un Chien andalou*'s; the less arty camerawork (no slow-motion soft-focus shots); and especially, in line with psychoanalysis, the planted parapraxes, the bungled actions, the visualized symptoms—a manifest latent content, if you like. Interestingly, the director rejected Dalí's ideas for a number of the kind of lap-dissolves used in their first film—a sea-urchin metamorphosing into a hairy armpit, for instance—lap-dissolves that are one source of the visual punning of paranoia-criticism. As for its use of sound, the *sonore et parlant* movie is less innovative than is often claimed, being already technically outmoded, a mishmash of sound effects, talking heads and of silence alleviated by music. In any event *L'Âge d'or*, which was again showing at Studio 28, was banned in December 1930 after the ultra-Right put the boot in.

For decades the received idea was that Dalí had almost no part in the writing of *L'Âge d'or*. Today, we know different. Whose pet subjects were hysteria, scatology and onanism, all present in the film: Buñuel's or Dalí's? I'd even argue that *L'Âge d'or* is a *more* Dalínian opus than *Un Chien andalou*. Whatever, it's the film that marks the beginning of the end of a perfect marriage. Miffed at being left to face the flak alone—Buñuel was in Hollywood, putting his pro-Taylorist ideas to the test for several months—Dalí's ire increased when he heard in March 1932 that his amigo, a card-carrying Communist by now and on the point of breaking with Surrealism, was to bowdlerize *L'Âge d'or*, recycle it as a worker-friendly short. Four months later Dalí published *Babaouo*, a *L'Âge d'or*-style scenario which mocked Buñuel's plans to make agit-prop movies, with, in the same volume, a capricious "critical history of the cinema" in which, taking his "anti-artistic" film ideas of 1928-29 to a logical conclusion, Dalí lauded a *pompier* cinema founded on minimal (or no) editing and an immobile camera, the better to objectify the world's "concrete irrationality."

Comedy film remained the acme of such irrationality, although now, five years into the sound era, it was the Marx Brothers, particularly the mute Harpo, who were paradigmatic. Later, in 1937, Dalí talked with the curly-haired clown about doing a movie together, *Giraffes on Horseback Salad*, a mock-Surrealist title for a mock-Surrealist movie by a mock-Surrealist creator.

Early in 1939, Buñuel, penniless in Los Angeles after the end of the Spanish Civil War, contacted the ultra-famous, well-heeled Dalí

in New York to propose they write a script together. He was turned down. During his subsequent forays into Tinseltown, Avida Dollars would be commissioned to invent brief nightmare sequences for films by Archie Mayo (1942), Hitchock (1945) and Minnelli (1950), proof that the "cinematic Surrealism = filmed dreams" equation was still hegemonic in the popular mind. A five-minute cartoon for Disney, *Destino* (1946), for inclusion in a *Fantasia*-like compilation got shelved; Walt's nephew Roy would make it fifty-seven years later. Dalí was to tinker with personal projects such as *The Flesh Wheelbarrow* (1949-54), *The Prodigious Adventure of the Lacemaker and the Rhinoceros* (1954-62) and *Voyage in Upper Mongolia* (1975), and footage was shot for the last two, but the images were largely disappointing. The Catalan was a great ideas man, yet he needed a director as brilliant, indulgent and professional as Buñuel to get anything substantial on the screen. P.H.

Clédalism

Dalí describes his unique paraphilia, "clédalism"—first introduced in his 1944 novel, *Hidden Faces*—, as the completion—along with Sadism and Masochism—of the "passional trilogy" inaugurated by the Marquis de Sade, reflecting "synthesis and sublimation" in an "all-transcending identification with the object." Its ambition is simultaneous orgasm triggered merely by facial expressions, which is to say without any physical interaction. The appellation is taken from the surname of the novel's aristocratic character, Solange de Cléda, whose name, in turn, is derived from "Clé-Dalí"—the "key (French *clé*) to Dalí.' E.H.K.

Crutches

The crutch was one of Dalí's most fruitful symbols. Some of his earliest childhood erotic fantasies and experiments, according to his autobiography, center on a crutch he found in an attic at the Pichot's country home El Muli de la Torre. The crutch immediately became his new fetish object, replacing the "old mattress beater with leather fringes which I had adopted a long time ago as a scepter." In the episode Dalí called "The Story of the Linden Blossom Picking and the Crutch" in *The Secret Life* (pp. 89-111), it is first contaminated by a rotting hedgehog that Dalí pressed with its bifurcated end, then, ritually cleansed by water and the linden blossoms, becomes the tool first for digging at a melon which is the substitute for the blossom picker's breasts, then for encircling the slim waist of "Dullita." Whether real or imagined, the erotic encounters are fuelled by feverish and ritualistic fantasies similar to his 1931 text "Rêverie" (Daydream) and already mark what Dalí would later recognize as his fetishism, with the sexual *frisson* displaced onto an inanimate object.

Crutches make their first appearance ca. 1932 in paintings like *The Average Fine and Invisible Harp* and *Meditation on the Harp,* but could have been prompted by the bifurcated branch supporting the soft watch in *Persistence of Memory.* The soft structures and monstrous physical appendages that proliferate in his work of the 1930s necessitated, in Dalí's logic, the crutches, but these then took on further metaphorical significance that shifts with his own changing allegiances. Crutches symbolize his ambition to shore up the decaying social order of old Europe. Addressing the "aristocracy," Dalí wrote in *The Secret Life* "With the pride of your one leg and the crutches of my intelligence, you are stronger than the revolution that is being prepared by the intellectuals." (p. 262)

Dalí defined the crutch for the *Dictionnaire abrégée du Surréalisme* as follows: "Wooden support derived from Cartesian philosophy. Generally used to hold up the *morbidez* of *soft structures.*" The twin prongs of the crutch perhaps reminded Dalí of Descartes' dualistic account of human beings as hybrid entities made up of physical body and immaterial soul. In the *Passions of the Soul,* which Dalí certainly knew, Descartes argued that the pineal gland in the brain was "the seat of the soul." Descartes also famously likened the whole of philosophy to a tree, whose roots are metaphysics, trunk physics, and branches, the particular sciences such as mathematics. D.A.

René Crevel (1900-35)

The writer René Crevel was one of Dalí's most faithful friends in the Surrealist group. Philippe Soupault described him as a trembling person ("He trembled form head to foot"), an expression that helps us to understand the portrait that Dalí painted of Crevel in 1934, *The Man with the Cigarette,* in which a profusion of brushstrokes gives the impression of a person trembling like a leaf. They probably first met toward the end of 1929, after Dalí joined the Surrealist group, although the painter had quoted Crevel in his writings of 1927.

"Tell Dalí," Crevel wrote to Gala (Paul Éluard's wife had now become the painter's companion) at the end of 1930, "that for years nothing has pleased me as much as his "invisible man." If I am better in the autumn [Crevel suffered from a lung disorder], I'll try to come and see you in Spain." In fact, the visit only took place in the summer of 1931, shortly after the proclamation of the Spanish Republic. After a few days in Cadaqués, Dalí and Crevel left for Barcelona where, on September 18, they took part in a meeting organized by the Bloque Obrero y Campesino (B.O.C., Workers and Peasants Bloc), an anti-Stalinist splinter group to the left of the Communist Party. This meeting resulted in *Dalí ou l'antiobscurantisme,* a booklet, written and published by Crevel in the same year, which consisted of a description of the modern hell: intellectualism, mechanism, nickel furniture, pictures by Léger, organization of work, and the Taylor system. In other words, the "moral, intellectual, and physical cloaca through which crippled wills glide until they reach a state of ecstasy for having done their duty." This was, in Crevel's opinion, the modern world that was opposed by Dalí, a revolutionary and subversive, who not only challenged the specialization in which "obscurantism" sought to include him, but, with its corresponding element, the "activity having a moral tendency," he began "a new course in the history of mankind."

Despite the numerous tensions and conflicts within the Surrealist group caused by Dalí's political stance, Crevel never ceased to defend him. When the writer committed suicide—on 20 June 1935—Dalí was deeply shocked. In *The Secret Life of Salvador Dalí* he attributed Crevel's terrible decision to the impossibility of resolving "the dramatic contradictions of the ideological and intellectual problems that faced the postwar generation"—in other words, he ascribed it to the difficulty of combining communism with Surrealism. F.F.

Daydreams

Dalí studied not only dreams (he discovered Freud's *Interpretation of Dreams* as a student) but also daydreams, hallucinations and fantasies and was familiar with contemporary theories concerning the mechanisms that governed mental imagery of this kind. His text "Rêverie" (1931), notorious as the cause of a serious rift between the Surrealists and the French Communist Party, who regarded it as plain pornography, had its origins in an article by the French psychologist Hesnard in the major organ of the Société psychanalytique de Paris, *Revue française de psychanalyse,* (which enjoyed Freud's patronage), entitled "Contribution à l'étude des Phantasmes érotiques" (Volume 4, no. 3, 1931, p. 524) Hesnard's description of erotic phantasms perfectly matches Dalí's "Rêverie": they are "images, imaginary representations of objects or concrete situations, whose essential character is to procure, for the subject, erotic arousal, which is conscious and more or less intentional." In "Rêverie," Dalí details his elaborate preparations for the daydream, which concerns the sexual initiation of a young girl, Dullita, as well as its lengthy unfurling, which he consciously directs. "Erotic phantasms are sometimes frankly and freely voluptuous, and the patient caresses them in a waking dream that lasts for hours." The fact that Dalí's "Rêverie" was published (*Le Surréalisme au service de la révolution* no. 4 1931) shortly after Hesnard's text is no coincidence; the irony is that this highly erotic text is an experiment in scientific theory. It could be seen in the same light as Breton and Éluard's experimental writing "Les Possessions," which simulated mental states. Such "phantasms" represent for Hesnard "an essential, normal narcissistic element in sexuality," a view that must have intrigued Dalí who, a few years later, was to paint *Metamorphosis of Narcissus.* D.A.

Willem De Kooning (1904-97)

Salvador Dalí's admiration for the gestural paintings of Willem De Kooning, the Dutch born, American Abstract Expressionist, was both genuine and profound. Although Dalí was severely critical of the work of other abstract artists of his generation, most notably Jackson Pollock, he praised De Kooning as "the colossus straddling the Atlantic with one foot in New York and the other in Amsterdam, whose paintings suggest the geological dreams of the earliest ages and the cosmic happenings that record the adventures of the planet." Dalí probably had in mind De Kooning's *Excavation,* of 1950, which generated great excitement when Alfred Barr included the work in the XXV Venice Biennale in the summer of that year. The title of this monumental painting refers to the artist's creative process, which involved the intensive building up of the richly painted surface and the scraping down of its paint layers until the desired effect was achieved. This working method created an all-over composition of loose, sliding planes that is punctuated by flashes of blue, red, yellow, and pink, and replete with shapes suggestive of eyes, teeth, and noses, whose presence recalls a layer of geological stratum in which archaeological material, such as skeletons, fossils and artifacts, is found on excavation.

In his "dazzlingly veracious" article "De Kooning's 300,000,000th Birthday," published in *Art News* in April 1969, Dalí praised the Abstract Expressionist as "the greatest, the most gifted and the most authentic finial point of modern painting, and the initial point of the *pompier* art of the future." While once again comparing the surfaces of his paintings with earthquakes and prehistoric geological events, Dalí hailed De Kooning as the successor to Diego Velázquez de Silva and Spanish Baroque painting, as well as the academic painting of French *art pompier*, whose revival he claimed was imminent. In the following year, the artist once again connected the violence of De Kooning's "intimate visions" with the "molecular energy of Meissonier." This attempt to position De Kooning, who had received exhaustive academic training in the Netherlands, as the inheritor of the classical tradition of Velázquez and Meissonier was also bound up with Dalí's understanding that De Kooning's "swift gestures" corresponded to the quantum physics of Max Planck. The Abstract Expressionist painter flatly denied this atomic interpretation in the catalogue for the "Surrealist Intrusion in the Enchanters' Domain" exhibition, held in New York in 1960: "The space of science—the space of the physicist—I am truly bored with by now. Their lenses are so thick that, seeing through them, the space gets more and more melancholy. All that it contains is billions and billions of hunks of matter, hot or cold, floating around in darkness echoing the great scheme of aimlessness."

Undeterred, Dalí's own evocation of quantum particles, in paintings such as *Saint Surrounded by Three Pi-Mesons*, of 1956, and *Velázquez Painting the Infanta Margarita with the Lights and Shadows of his Own Glory*, of 1958, nonetheless employed the raw and expressive virtuoso brushwork that characterized De Kooning's action painting. Determined to prove his point, Dalí purportedly showed the artist some enlargements of details from a Velázquez painting, to which he claimed that De Kooning declared, "That's Action Painting raised to the sublime!" M.R.T.

Disgust

On first joining the Surrealists, Dalí published a manifesto setting out his provocative aesthetic credo. Titled "L'Âne pourri" (The Rotting Donkey, 1930), it warns "art critics, artists, &c., that they need expect nothing from the new Surrealist images but disappointment, distaste and repulsion." More consistently than any other artist in the period, and in a way that chimes with the preoccupations of a good many contemporary artists, Dalí's work in the decade of the 1930s explores the terrain of the abject: blood, shit and putrefaction.

Dalí acknowledged as a vital theoretical support for his speculations in this area an essay on the phenomenology of disgust by the Hungarian-born philosopher Aurel Kolnai (1901-73), first published in German in 1929 ("Der Ekel," *Jarhbuch fur Philosophie und phaenomenologische Forschung*, edited by Edmund Husserl, Halle, 1929, pp. 515-569). Soon afterwards the essay became available in a Spanish translation by Ortega y Gasset in the *Revista de Occidente* (1929), the version one presumes Dalí consulted. Recent scholarship and translations into French and English have brought recognition to an essay that, well before Sartre's *La nausée*, undertook to investigate the hitherto neglected subject of disgust.

The list of disgusting things enumerated by Kolnai reads like an inventory of Dalínian obsessions. Chief amongst them is putrefaction, the most fundamental object of disgust according to Kolnai. The disgusting aspect of excreta is linked with the decay of living matter. "Everything disgusting 'sticks' in some manner to the subject, surrounding it by its proximity, by its emanation," writes Kolnai. He notes that tactile sensations linked to viscous materials, and simply "the soft," are especially liable to incite feelings of disgust. Kolnai makes a point of remarking that strong-smelling cheese contains something that must be called putrid; one is reminded here of the genesis of Dalí's famous "soft" watches. One of the more novel aspects of Kolnai's account is his evocation of a sort of "vital exuberance," a paradoxical intensification of life in the midst of rankness. He speaks of an *éclat* and tumultuous excess in decomposition where even colors are more vivid than usual. Dalí, for his part, recalls seeing a decaying donkey swarming with ants and blow flies which he mistook for sparkling gemstones, and it is tempting to connect the lightning flash atmosphere

and intense, saturated coloring of certain key pictures with this abrupt short-circuiting of life.

Of interest is Kolnai's explanation of disgust as one of a series of so-called reactions of defence. Noting that disgust is often accompanied by a macabre seduction, seeming to comprise an integral part of the affect, he asserts that "the invitation actualizes the defence." On this point, Dalí virtually paraphrases Kolnai, writing that: "One exhibits repugnance and disgust for that which at root one desires to approach and from this arises an irresistible "morbid" attraction, translated often by incomprehensible curiosity for that which appears as repugnant." Kolnai proceeds to argue in a key section of his essay on "The relation of disgust to life and death" that our psychic ambivalence regarding death lies at the basis of most reactions of disgust (presumably this is why he considers putrefaction as a fundamental cause). Once again, Dalí accurately conveys the bones of Kolnai's argument when he suggests that "repugnance [is] a symbolic defense against the vertigo of the death drive."

Kolnai is circumspect about what he sees as the reductionism of psychoanalysis, whereas for Dalí the usefulness of Kolnai's account lies in its essential compatibility with his interests in that direction. In *Civilization and its Discontents*, Freud propounds a sort of evolutionary fable in which man's assumption of an upright posture leads to various fateful consequences: vision is privileged and there is a concomitant devaluation of other sensory modalities, notably olfaction. The genitalia, previously hidden beneath the body, are now exposed and visible, giving rise to feelings of shame and repugnance. As a consequence of the depreciation of smell there is a reversal in the attitude towards excreta, which, Freud notes, arouse no disgust in children or animals, but for the adult are "worthless, disgusting, abhorrent and abominable." Dalí exhibits shame but wallows in abjection, a dialectic of repression that owes more to his understanding of Freud than to Kolnai, as does his contention that the *treasure land* the Surrealists hankered after lies hidden behind objects of disgust.

Dalí's phenomenology of repugnance was a heretical version of the Surrealist doctrine that immediately brought him into conflict with the mainstream Surrealists. In *Diary of a Genius* he recalls the consternation that greeted *The Lugubrious Game*, his reception piece among the Surrealists, at the foreground of which is a male figure with shit-smeared pants. One factor contributing to sensitivities on this score was the crossfire, at its bitterest when Dalí joined the Surrealists, between them and Georges Bataille, whom Breton had denounced in the *Second Manifesto* as an "excremental philosopher." Like Dalí, reactions of disgust are at the center of Bataille's reflections and it transpires that he too was indebted to Kolnai. The intimacy that Kolnai says exists between the subject and the object of disgust is reflected in Bataille's assertion that: "There exists a manner of being rotten, the sheer *presence* of a cadaver decomposes the living being." References in Bataille's published writings to a thematic of putrefaction (*pourriture*) correspond closely with Dalí's arrival in Paris. It is, moreover, to the slit eye episode in the Dalí-Buñuel film *Un Chien andalou* that Bataille refers as approximating to that ambivalent point described by Kolnai where the extremes of seduction and horror collide. Bataille's notion of the formless (*informe*), a key term in his philosophical lexicon, recalls Dalí's preoccupation with soft forms (*super-mou*) which in the case of the latter most certainly was indebted to Kolnai.

The landscape of scatological delights proffered by Dalí runs emphatically counter to the quest for transcendence and purity in the dominant Modernism of the 1930s. It points moreover to a possibly unexpected affinity between Dalí and contemporary art practice. The eclipse of Modernism, with its associated bodily and sensorial hierarchy, has seen a riotous liberation of the abject body and an invasion of the clean white spaces of the modern art gallery by dirt and bodily effluvia. Could it be that the abject in Dalí provides an avenue for his art historical rehabilitation? One contemporary artist at least has found inspiration in Dalí's notion of the *putrefact*. The British artist Glenn Brown works with appropriated imagery and his art reflects upon the mediation of reality by reproduction in our postmodern world. Brown relates the colors of putrefaction to the decay that is an inevitable byproduct of the always-already-reproduced status of the postmodern image. His manipulated copies of works by Dalí, notably his version of *Soft Construction with Boiled Beans*, are alert to the overripe garish intensity of color in the original that was one of the essential lessons Dalí learnt from Kolnai. D.L.

Eugenio D'Ors (1881-1954)

After graduating in law from Barcelona University, Eugenio D'Ors obtained a research doctorate from Madrid University, submitting a thesis entitled "Ideal Genealogy of Imperialism." In Barcelona he was a member of the modernist coterie and frequented the legendary café Els Quatre Gats. In 1906, under the pseudonym of Xènius, he began to publish *Glosari*, a series of short articles on philosophical themes that, however, had a practical objective, in the Catalan nationalist newspaper *La Veu de Catalunya*. All the intellectuals of the period faithfully followed the *Glosari*: reading D'Ors's articles, they adopted such concepts as "elevating the anecdote to a category." D'Ors proposed civic ideals into which he introduced the theory of arbitrariness and, at the same time, elaborated an aesthetic theory that he called "Noucentisme." This was based both on the overcoming of the modernist symbolism and on a new field of artistic inquiry that was concerned with the recognition of the individual's own origins: Mediterranean and, for the Catalans, also classical.

After spending a period of time in Cadaqués as a guest of Lídia Noguer, the writer published a series of articles under the title *La Ben Platada*, and Lídia, in her erotomaniac folly, identified with the book's protagonist, whose absurd ideas are thought to have later influenced Dalí's paranoiac-critical method. The autonomous government of Catalonia entrusted D'Ors with a number of assignments such as the organization of the Pedagogical Council, the secretariat of the Institut d'Estudis Catalans (Catalan Studies Institute), the philosophy course, and the direction of the Escuela de Bibliotecas (Library School), a post from which he was dismissed in 1921 as the result of strong disagreement with the conservative government.

D'Ors was one of the first dedicated admirers of Dalí, while the artist, on his part, assimilated much of the writer's theories on structure and arbitrariness, using archetypal expressions—such as "Oh clarity!"—in the articles published in the journal *L'Amic de les Arts*. Dalí read D'Ors's *Tres horas en el Museo del Prado* (1922) and the fragments of the tragedy *William Tell* (1922). In fact, it was D'Ors who, after seeing in Paris the work in which Dalí insulted his mother, wrote the article in *La Gaceta Literaria* that, together with other aggravating circumstances, led Don Salvador to expel his first-born from the family home.

During his years in exile, Dalí identified strongly with D'Ors's work *Introducción a la vida angelica. Cartas de una soledad*, published in Buenos Aires in 1939. And in 1954 he illustrated the writer's posthumous work *La verdadera historia de Lídia de Cadaqués*. R.M.P. and V.A.M.

Escorial

El Real Monasterio de San Lorenzo del Escorial is an enormous complex situated on the south-eastern slope of the Sierra de Guadarrama, about twenty-seven miles north-west of Madrid. It was built during the "Golden Age" of Spain, under the auspices of King Philip II, to commemorate the 1557 Spanish victory over the French at the battle of St-Quinten. The complex was originally designed by the architect, Juan Bautista de Toledo, who drew the plans for the monastery and began its construction in 1563. Bautista died in 1567 and was succeeded by the master-draftsman and mathematician, Juan de Herrera, under whose supervision most of the work was completed by 1584.

Dalí's pronounced his admiration for the Escorial in his 1941 essay, "The Last Scandal of Salvador Dalí," in which he included it among Bramante and Raphael as an exemplar of the "pitiless and inquisitorial process to which matter is submitted" to create beautiful form. Dalí's choice of examples represents the aesthetic models for his budding "classicism": Donato Bramante's Tempietto is among the most remarkable buildings of the High Renaissance; Dalí expressed amaranthine admiration for Raphael and his High Renaissance classicism; and the Escorial, with its harsh austerity, was directly responsible for the propagation of classicism throughout Spain. Dalí returned to these examples in his 1951 *Mystical Manifesto,* writing, "The most beautiful architectural works of the human soul are the Tempietto de San Pietro in Montorio by the divine Bramante in Rome, and the monastery of El Escorial in Spain. Both were shaped in the same 'incorruptible mode: ecstasy.'"

In the 1950s, Dalí's exaltations of the Escorial were eclipsed by his praise for its later architect, Juan de Herrera. Dalí credited Herrera's largely overlooked essay, *El discurso sobre la figura cúbica (Treatise on Cubic Form)* (ca. 1570-80), as the inspiration for his 1954 tesseract-crucifixion, *Corpus Hypercubicus*, no less his 1960 painting, *A Propos of the "Treatise on Cubic Form" by Juan de Herrera*. Herrera's dissertation, unpublished during his lifetime, addresses Euclid's postulates *a propos* the cube, utilizing these geometric properties to elucidate the combinatory logic of Ramón Llull (1235-1316). Herrera's text integrated Alberti's image of the intellectual designer with the contemporary view of science, and folded science into Llull's sacred philosophy; the result was a fragile construction that was both classical and Catholic. E.H.K.

Figueres

Salvador Dalí's birthplace, Figueres is situated between Barcelona and the French border in the center of the Empordà Plain, the landscape in which many of the artist's works are set. During Dalí's childhood and adolescence Figueres was a town open to reformist ideas with a very lively intellectual milieu that comprised his father, who was a notary there. Dalí went to various local schools, including the Institut (middle and high school), the oldest in Spain. It was in Figueres that he started his artistic career: here he attended Juan Núñez Fernández's drawing lessons, staged his first exhibition of painting and helped to edit various journals. Federico García Lorca and Luis Buñuel were his guests in the town.

Figueres always played an important role in Dalí's life: it was no coincidence that he decided to create his last great work here—the Dalí Theater-Museum. "Where should the most bizarre and solid of my works be located if not in my town? Where, if not here?" Inaugurated on September 28, 1974, the Theater-Museum is an extremely significant place for those wishing to understand the artist's life and works. It is a space that Dalí wanted to transform into the mecca of art and it was here that the artist decided to be buried. Also in Figueres was what was to be the artist's last home, Torre Galatea, a building attached to the Theater-Museum where he lived from 1984 until his death on January 23, 1989. In order to fully comprehend the role Figueres played in Dalí's life it is important to remember one of Montaigne's aphorisms that the artist liked to quote, according to which, it is from the local situation that one arrives at the universal one. M.A.

General Franco (Francisco Franco Bahamonde, 1892-1975)

Franco: "the phallus that will penetrate Spain..."
Ernesto Gimènez Caballero, 1938
"My son considered himself a statesman and a politician of the first class because that is what his adulators have made him believe, but it was just laughable."
Don Nicolás José Saturnino Franco Salgado-Araujo

Dalí's political position shifted towards the right by the spring of 1939, when André Breton finally expelled him from the Surrealist movement (*Minotaure*, May, 1939). These events were likely provoked by the exhibition of *The Enigma of Hitler* (1939) in New York, but, also, Dalí was the only Spanish artist of an international reputation not to participate in the 1937 Spanish Pavilion, where Picasso's *Guernica* made a powerful anti-war and pro-Republican statement. This exhibition took place in the wake of the destruction of the Basque city Guernica, at a moment of crisis, when the tide of civil war began to turn against the democratic second Republic (1931-39). Under Francisco Franco's guidance, and deploying the ruthless Moroccan Army, the uprising of the Generals (July 1936) would quickly lead to the military demise of the Republic and the bloody conclusion of the civil war (1939). The "Generalísimo" coldly killed all who opposed him, making no distinction between enlisted person and civilian, a calculated terrorism which was highly efficacious. Liquidations of leftists and forced labor continued in the immediate post-war years. (I. Lafuente, *Esclavos para la Patria: La explotación de los presos bajo el franquismo*, 2002)

With the coming of Second World War (1939) and the ensuing occupation of France (June 1940), Dalí departed Paris travelling via Portugal and arrived in New York in August 1940. Dalí's myth-making and autobiographical *The Secret Life* (1942) appeared one year following Franco's own megalomaniac and idealized autobiography: the novel/film-script *Raza* (1940-41). Franco's libertine and dissolute father, Don Nicolás José Saturnino Franco Salgado-Araujo, paralleled Dalí's own Republican and atheist father—but Franco's father never accepted the authoritarianism of his son—and in his novel the *Generalísimo* re-constructed his father as a hero, that is, according to his own desires and social ambitions.

Dalí's portrait of Franco's official representative to the U.S., *Portrait of Ambassador Cárdenas* (1943), depicts Juan Francisco de Cárdenas in the foreground of an expansive Spanish landscape dominated by El Escorial. Cárdenas holds a book, suggesting the erudition of Spain, and his identification with El Escorial evokes the eternal values of an Imperial and Catholic Spain. No signs of the recent conflict are evident, only the presentation of a pastoral and idyllic rural

scene and the grandeur of the Catholic Kings. The painting was significantly painted at a time when Cárdenas was seeking to broker trade normalization between the Regime and the U.S. Breton, in exile in New York, publicly protested in the pages of the Surrealist review, Dalí's decision to paint this portrait: "… liberty is at once wildly desirable and completely fragile, which gives it the right to be jealous. In order to fall into disgrace with it, there is no need to stink, like de Chirico fifteen years ago…, like Avida Dollars [Salvador Dalí], of the obsequious academicism with the portrait of the Spanish ambassador, that is of Franco's representative, of he to whom the portrait's author owes the oppression of his country, not to mention the death of his best friend when he was a young man, the great poet García Lorca,—Franco about whom we know what terms he is on with life, with the spirit as with freedom." ("Situation du Surréalisme entre les deux guerres, 2-3, March 1943, p. 49).

Dalí remained in America until 1948, when he returned to live in Spain. In 1949, he had an audience with Pope Pius XII, in which he asked the Pope to condone the new religious direction of his work represented by *The Madonna of Port Lligat*. This meeting also initiated the process of seeking permission to marry Gala in the Church, but this marriage would not take place until August 1958. These moves were devised to increase Dalí's standing with the Franco Regime. In November 1951, Dalí gave a Madrid speech in support of Franco, whom he lauded as a leader "who has established clarity, truth and order in the country at the most anarchical moments of the world. This seems to me to be a sign of great originality." Receiving applause, he further recounted a telegram sent to Picasso, "Spain's spiritual nature is the furthest extreme from Russian materialism... We believe in the absolute, Catholic freedom of the human soul. Know then that despite your communism we consider your anarchical genius as the inseparable patrimony of our spiritual empire and your work as one of the glories of Spanish painting. God keep you. Madrid, 11 November 1951. Salvador Dalí." (Max Gallo, *Spain Under Franco,* New York 1974, p. 216)

In 1955, Dalí was granted a two-hour conversation with the Pope, but this time it was an informal and non-official meeting, and therefore it was not reported in the press. Finally, he was granted an official audience with Franco on July 16, 1956 at the Bardo

Palace, with a photograph documenting the meeting reproduced in the Spanish press. This was the final stage of official rehabilitation for former exiles. That this event coincided with the publishing of Dalí's *Les Cocus du vieil art moderne* (1956) reveals that rehabilitation involved also the public renunciation of his earlier vanguardism. Following a lunch meeting with Franco, Dalí publicly proclaimed, "I have reached the conclusion that he [Franco] is a saint." (Paul Preston, *Franco*, [1993], 1995, p. XVII.)

Dalí's visible support of Franco was not limited to the 1950s and continued even in the last days of the Dictatorship, at a time when it was increasingly obvious that social and political transformation was imminent. The exiled Spanish painter Eduardo Arroyo recognized this in his bitterly satirical *Portrait du nain Sebastián de Morra, Bouffon de cour né à Figueres dans la première moitié du XX siècle* (1970), where he cast Dalí in the role of Velázquez's dwarf. In 1974, Dalí painted Equestrian Portrait of Carmen Bordiu-Franco, a formal portrait of the Caudillo's niece set, like the Portrait of Ambassador Cárdenas, against the backdrop of El Escorial. Though ill, in September 1975, Franco executed five Basques charged with membership in ETA (Basque Land and Freedom) and staged massive pro-Falangist demonstrations in Madrid rejecting foreign criticism as "a Masonic left-wing conspiracy." (Preston, p. 776) The response of the international community was unanimous in protesting the Regime's abysmal human rights record, which, according to Amnesty International, still included torture. When asked by Agence France-Press of his opinion on the executions, Dalí was equally enthusiastic and glib:

"The success he's [Franco's] had today, with a crowd of more than two million people acclaiming him the greatest hero of Spain..., could never have happened if there hadn't been these incidents [the executions]. The hostility of the other countries has made him thirty years younger... He's a wonderful person... We'll see then that Spain is a country where, in a few months, there will be no more terrorism because they're going to be liquidated like rats. Three times more executions are needed." (S.D., "Franco est un être merveilleux," *Le Monde* et. al. in I. Gibson, *The Shameful Life of Salvador Dalí*, London 1997, p. 561)

Dalí's timing was again bad, for Franco would shortly die (November 20, 1975) of the Parkinson's disease which had gradual-ly destabilized his control over his body. Somehow this was an appropriate metaphor for a totalitarian guilty of submitting a generation of Spaniards to his control. Equally, Franco's death foretold Dalí's own sad demise from the same disease more than a decade later. Arroyo's obituary on Dalí concluded, "His relationship with General Franco was warm and servile. He even made some portraits of the general's family; without a doubt his best work since 1939, the end of the Spanish w ar." (in F. Calvo Serraller, *Diccionario deideas recibdas del pintor Eduardo Arroyo*, 1991, p. 68) W.J.

Sigmund Freud (1856-1939)
André Breton reflected that no one was better versed in psychoanalysis than Dalí who used it not in order to cure his complexes but to nourish and preserve them. Dalí read Freud avidly through the 1920s as volumes in a Spanish edition of the *Complete Works* became available, acquiring a sound instruction in neurosis and perversity. He arrived among the Surrealists as a fully-fledged *pervers polymorphe* according to his own estimation and for the next decade or more the Freudian corpus supplied him with staple motifs for many of his best-loved pictures. The Oedipus complex, castration anxiety, incestuous wishes, the death instinct, birth trauma, and so much more: in outrageously exhibitionist fashion, Dalí paraded for all and sundry to see the dirty linen of the analytic session.

Not everyone was won over by this Meissonier of the unconscious. Writing under the banner "Freudian Conformities," the left wing critic Emmanuel Berl describes a new academicism in which the phallus simply replaces the fig leaf of traditional painting. Surveying the Paris art scene in 1930, he imagines a cry emanating from all the fashionable art dealers: "*Beaux complexes à vendre, beaux complexes!*" One of the most frequent accusations leveled against Surrealism by its critics was that it is too conscious. Eugène Tériade wrote in *Cahiers d'Art* in 1930 that the "return to instinct" undertaken by the Surrealists is self-defeating for the very reason that everything was conscious calculation and premeditation. Tériade claims with an air of triumphalism that there is more unconscious in works of art made before Freud than in those made according to his dicta.

Breton, too, had reservations about Dalí's immoderate use of psychoanalysis. Discussing the symbolically functioning object as advocated by Dalí in which the sexual symbolism is extremely overt, he remarks that: "The willing incorporation of latent content—decided on in advance—in the manifest content serves here to weaken the tendency to dramatize and magnify, which the censor imperiously uses with such success in the opposite case." What Breton implies is that the artist or poet must not preempt unconscious censorship, because poetic creation occurs in the transmutations which the unconscious wish undergoes in the course of becoming conscious. A degree of *un*awareness is hence preferable to Dalí's ultra-lucidity. (Breton's views are, in fact, consonant with sentiments expressed by Freud in a letter to Stefan Zweig the day following his meeting with Dalí.)

An examination of the status of paranoia in Dalí's system suggests that the relationship to Freud and psychoanalysis may not be completely straightforward. Considered as a hermeneutical method, as a form of interpretation, paranoia bears more than a passing resemblance to psychoanalysis itself. Both interpret the unconscious, claim to speak the truth of the unconscious. Freud comments that: "Paranoia decomposes just as hysteria condenses. Or rather, paranoia resolves once more into their elements the products of the condensations and identifications, which are effected in the unconscious." Paranoia is analogous, in this respect, to the work of psychoanalytic interpretation which consists in painstakingly unpicking the disguises undergone by an unconscious wish in order to bypass the ever-vigilant censor on the road to becoming conscious. The parallels do not stop there. Just like the psychoanalyst, paranoiacs have a propensity to divine occult or secret meanings and connections in the most insignificant and unpropitious of circumstances: "There where others see only a coincidence, they, due to their interpretive clairvoyance, know how to unravel the truth and the secret rapports among things." Thus, it is possible to regard the delusions of a paranoiac as holding a mirror up to psychoanalysis—an irony not lost on Freud who, in the course of his analysis of the paranoiac Schreber, writes that "It remains for the future to decide whether there is more delusion in my theory than I should like to admit, or whether there is more truth in Schreber's delusion than other people are as yet prepared to believe."

Considered in this light, paranoia is a kind of mad parody of the rational science of psychoanalysis. Apparently, Dalí was well

4

5

Fig. 4/cat. 253
Salvador Dalí, *Portrait of Sigmund Freud*, 1938
Pen and ink on paper
34.5 × 28 cm
13⁵/8 × 12¹/8 in.
London, The Freud Museum

Fig. 5/cat. 254
Salvador Dalí, *Portrait of Sigmund Freud*, 1938
China ink and gouache on paper
35 × 25 cm
13³/4 × 9⁷/8 in.
Figueres, Fundació
Gala-Salvador Dalí

apprised of this ambiguity since he exploits it to the full in his textual-cum-pictorial analysis of Jean-François Millet's *The Angelus* which, carried out over several years, is the most sustained and comprehensive attempt to implement the paranoiac-critical method as a mode of exegesis. Written in the 1930s but not published until 1963, *Le Mythe tragique de l'Angélus de Millet* is one of his most brilliant accomplishments. Dalí's strenuous efforts to persuade the reader of the unpremeditated character of his analysis are somewhat disingenuous as it is certainly the case that this exercise in paranoiac interpretation was modeled if not on the Schreber case, then certainly on Freud's case-study of Leonardo to which his 1933 article on the *Angelus* explicitly refers. Dalí's and Freud's interpretations both deal with very famous paintings and use this fame as a guarantee of the general validity of their readings. The *Angelus*, Dalí notes, is one of the most widely reproduced images in France, a petit-bourgeois icon likely to crop up on anything from tea-cups to tea cozies. Dalí treats the patent overestimation of this drab naturalist image as symptomatic, and, like Freud with the Mona Lisa, he embarks on a search for the unconscious determinants of its otherwise enigmatic appeal. Like the paranoiac, Dalí's interpretations are full of self-reference, unlike Freud who prefers the pose of detached, scientific observation. But Dalí, no less than Freud, is anxious to persuade the reader of the concrete, verifiable truth of his reading, however irrational it might appear.

"How can one refuse to envisage sciences such as psychoanalysis as being 'mildly systematized delusions,'—naturally without intending by that anything pejorative—?" asks Dalí. Nothing was left unscathed by his corrosive humor; certainly not Freud himself who in a very fine pen and ink portrait is portrayed by Dalí with the cranial morphology of a snail. Dalí's mad parody of Freud might be seen as undermining whatever claim psychoanalysis has to serious attention. As it becomes absorbed into his ever-expanding delirium, what is left except to affirm the paranoiac structure of *all* knowledge, as Lacan did? D.L.

Gala

Elena Dmitrievna Diakona came from Russia to marry the poet Paul Éluard in 1916. They had met at a sanatorium near Davos in 1912 when both were seventeen years old; in 1918 their daughter Cecile was born. Their infidelities were mutually tolerated, both

holding to the principle of absolute freedom in love. There was an affair in the early 1920s with Max Ernst, who moved in with the couple in Paris when he arrived as a refuge from Germany.

Fierce, intelligent, highly educated and intensely private, she appears always as the muse of artists and poets; rumors that she had written her autobiography appear unfounded. But it is as the lifelong companion and inspiration of Dalí that she has been immortalized. They met when she and Éluard, Magritte and his wife, and Goemans visited Cadaqués in the summer of 1929. Central though she was to the mythical identities Dalí constructed for them both, there is nothing mythical about the way she saved the 25-year-old painter from the sexual neuroses so graphically described in his paintings of 1929 and which seemed to be bringing him to the edge of a severe breakdown. Dalí tells the story of his "recognition" of her in *The Secret Life*: "It was she! Galuchka Rediviva!" From that moment Gala ordered his life and ensured his success. "I call my wife Gala, Galuchka, Gradiva (because she has been my Gradiva), Olive (because of the shape of her face and color of her skin)... Lionete, because she roars like the MGM lion when she gets angry, Squirrel, Tapir, Little Negus... I also call Gala Noisette Poilue—Hairy Hazelnut... and also Fur Bell (because she reads aloud during my long sessions of painting, making a murmur as of a fur bell by virtue of which I learn all the things that but for her I should never know." One of the first things she did was to organize the disordered pages of the texts that became *La Femme Visible* (1930), and the many careful copies of Dalí's wild scripts in the archives at the Gala-Salvador Dalí Foundation are testament to her continuing role as amanuensis. Despite Dalí's dependence on her, as muse, mistress, nurse, mother, and manager, and her evident importance in the development of his work, acknowledged by him when for a period he signed his paintings with their joint names, she has not had a good press, being blamed often for the couple's naked pursuit of money and fame. She made two Surrealist objects in her own right, neither of which has survived. D.A.

Antoni Gaudí (1852-1926)

Born into a family of coppersmiths, Gaudí attributed his personal vision and understanding of architectural space to the tradition of this trade. After he graduated in 1878, and until 1882, his activity, guided by

profound ideals of cooperation, was based on solid principles of urban design and social policy. He collaborated with Josef Fontseré on the realization of the Parc de la Ciutadella in Barcelona and he designed various lamps for the city streets, such as those still standing in Plaça Reial.

From 1883 to 1900, the year when he started work on the Sagrada Familia, Gaudí's professional efforts were concentrated on his attempt to abandon the historicism then prevalent in architecture in order to introduce structural plasticity in which greater emphasis was laid on the building materials. His most outstanding buildings from this period include the Casa Vicenç (1883-85), the Güell pavilions (1884-87), the Palau Güell (1896-91), the Bishop's Palace in Astorga (1887-94), the Casa Calvet (1898-1904), and Bellesguard, a work characterized by his highly idiosyncratic use of Islamic, Gothic and Baroque elements.

Gaudí's most creative and innovative period was between 1900 and 1917, and during this time he realized the projects in which his most personal style manifested itself: Parc Güell (1900-14), the remodeling of the Casa Batlló (1904-06) and the crypt of the Colonia Güell Church (1908-15), Casa Milà (called "La Pedrera" [the quarry], 1906-10), and the work on the Sagrada Familia.

From 1918 until his accidental death in 1926 (he was run over by a streetcar), he focused particularly on his search for a figurative and structural synthesis that, insofar as it was a supreme geometrical form, would allow him to create his fourth design for the nave of the Sagrada Familia, and he devoted himself to finishing the towers on the Nativity façade of the east transept.

An apparently contradictory figure, a mystic who sympathized with the working classes, a Catalanist, and pan-naturalist, indifferent to the avant-garde architectural movements, Gaudí was soon forgotten or despised by the classicists and modernists until 1933, when an article written by Salvador Dalí for the Parisian Surrealist journal *Minotaure*, "De la beauté terrifiante et comestible de l'architecture modern style" (On the terrifying and edible beauty of Art Nouveau architecture), marked the beginning of his vindication. The article is illustrated with splendid pictures by Man Ray, who, on Dalí's request, went expressly to Barcelona to photograph the Parc Güell, the Casa Milá, and other works by Gaudí.

After his return from exile in America (in 1948), Dalí allowed himself to be portrayed

Fig. 6/cat. 255
Gala's brocade jacket
New York, Timothy Baum Collection

Fig. 7/cat. 256
Salvador Dalí, *Study for
"Gala wearing a Turban,"* 1939
Pencil on paper
33.4 ×22.4 cm / 13$^{1/8}$ × 8$^{3/4}$ in.
Figueres, Fundació
Gala-Salvador Dalí

Fig. 8/cat. 257
Salvador Dalí, *Female Nude
(Study for "Honey Is Sweeter
than Blood"),* 1941
Pencil on paper
56 ×43 cm / 22$^{1/8}$ × 16$^{7/8}$ in.
London, The Mayor Gallery

Fig. 9/cat. 258
Salvador Dalí, *Geometrical Female
Figure with Crutches,* 1937
Pencil on paper
63 ×48 cm / 24$^{3/4}$× 18$^{7/8}$ in.
Berlin, Galerie Brusberg

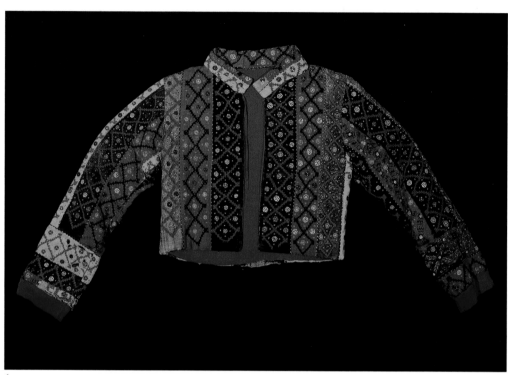

6

7

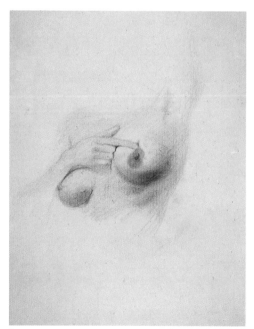

8

9

in the Parc Güell on various occasions: in 1953, by Francesc Català-Roca, for an article in *Revista*; in 1956, by Brangulí, to document his happening-cum-tribute-cum-lecture dedicated to Gaudí, during which he painted a huge canvas in tar with the outline of the Sagrada Familia, while a number of Xiquets de Valls (boys who formed the "human castles" typical of the Catalan tradition) created a human tower.

Subsequently, Dalí wrote the preface to a special edition of *La visió artística i religiosa de Gaudí* (The artistic and religious vision of Gaudí) by Francesc Pujols (1969, originally published in 1927), as a tribute to his two dear friends. But, in reality, what Dalí admired in Gaudí was his angelic vision of structures, thanks to which the Catalan architect believed he did not need plans for his buildings because he saw things from their interior. In his most improbable architectural designs, Dalí was a faithful disciple of Gaudí in his attempt to construct by emulating the most elementary laws of nature. R.M.P. and V.A.M.

Matila Ghyka (1881-1965)

Sailor, diplomat, mathematician, poet and novelist, Matila Ghyka was a descendent of Gregory Ghyka X, the last reigning Prince of Moldavia before it merged with Wallachia in 1859 to become the kingdom of Rumania. His research into aesthetics focused primarily on the "Golden Number"—the ratio $(1+\sqrt{5})/2$, frequently referred to by the Greek symbol, *Phi* (Φ). His book, *Le nombre d'or* (1930), elaborating on Luca Pacioli's Renaissance work on the "Divine Proportion," remains an especially important landmark in aesthetic theory. In approximately 1946, Ghyka—then a professor at the University of San Diego—met Dalí at a dinner party, soon after which Ghyka mailed Dalí a copy of his recent American publication, *The Geometry of Art and Life* (1946). When the two met just two weeks later, Ghyka was impressed with the extent to which Dalí had digested his ideas, particularly those based on the knowledge and handling of proportions and of the regular polyhedra. Dalí would come to own numerous books by Ghyka, including *Esthétique des proportions* (1927), *Essai sur le rythme* (1938), *The Geometry of Art and Life* (1946) and *Practical Handbook of Geometric Composition and Design* (1952). E.H.K.

Werner Karl Heisenberg (1901-76)

Heisenberg was one of the greatest physicists of the 20th-century and, along with Niels Bohr, Erwin Schrödingern and Max Planck, one of the physicists Dalí most revered. Heisenberg was awarded the Nobel Prize in Physics in 1932 and is best known for his 1927 "Uncertainty Principle," which stated that the more precisely the position of a subatomic particle is determined, the less precisely the momentum is known in that instant, and vice versa.

In the Preface to the catalogue for his 1958-59 exhibition at New York's Carstairs Gallery, christened the *Anti-Matter Manifesto,* Dalí confirmed the paramount importance of physics to his contemporary work by displacing Freud—emblematic of his former Surrealist production's emphasis on the subconscious—as his "father" in favor of Werner Heisenberg: "In the Surrealist period," he writes, "I wanted to create the iconography of the interior world—the world of the marvelous, of my father Freud. I succeeded in doing it. Today the exterior world—that of physics—has transcended the one of psychology. My father today is Dr. Heisenberg." His digestion of Heisenberg's ideas is demonstrated by his 1956 painting, *Still Life – Fast Moving*, which Dalí described as an explanatory painting following the coefficients of Heisenberg's Uncertainly Principle. As the Uncertainty Principle states that the location and momentum of a subatomic particle cannot be simultaneously ascertained, so the spinning fruit dish in *Still Life – Fast Moving* is vaguely ephemeral while its unmoving counterpart remains solid. Similarly, the motionless apple casts a shadow connoting its materiality, while its "fast moving" equivalent casts no shadow because, citing Heisenberg, its speed prohibits it from being precisely located. E.H.K.

Hologram

In 1971, Dalí began experimenting with holograms as a medium towards capturing the illusion of three-dimensional painting. His first experiments with holography premiered at New York's Knoedler Gallery in April 1972, with the Nobel Prize-winning inventory of holography, Dr. Denis Gabor, writing the exhibition's catalogue. Dalí's first "three-dimensional collage" hologram, *Holos! Holos! Velázquez! Gabor!* (1972-73)—constructed by overlapping a flat hologram of Velázquez's *Las Meninas* with another of a card game—was included in the Knoedler Gallery exhibition.

Pushing the envelope of his pioneering medium, Dalí expanded into highly-costly cylindrical holograms, presenting his first so-called "chrono-hologram" in May 1973 at Paris' Hotel Meurice. Among only a handful of revolving 360-degree holograms Dalí executed with the aid of hologram expert, Selwyn Lissack, *First Cylindric Chrono-Hologram Portrait of Alice Cooper's Brain* (1973) features rock star Alice Cooper decorated with $2 million in jewels and biting the head off a diminutive *Venus de Milo*. Although Gabor foresaw the possibility of creating holograms that did not rely on photography and could be produced in natural colors, holographic technology was slow to advance. Dalí therefore quickly abandoned the medium in favor of stereoscopy, which allowed him to project any image he imagined in any hue into the third-dimension. E.H.K.

Edward James (1907-84)

In 1939, at the age of thirty-two, Edward James's collection of Surrealist art numbered in excess of two hundred and fifty works, over one hundred and eighty of which were by Salvador Dalí. Although a great patron of the arts and a creator in his own right, Edward James remains a relatively unknown figure both internationally and in his native Britain. Born in Scotland in 1907, Edward James was the son of William James, a wealthy landowner, and his wife, Evelyn, the daughter of Sir Charles Forbes, a Scottish aristocrat. Throughout his life he devoted his time, energy, and considerable fortune, his father having died in 1912, to leading an artistic and literary life. He supported many artists, especially during the 1930's when he was also briefly involved with the Surrealist journal *Minotaure*. He bought their work, encouraged them with money and with an acute critical view. In assisting musicians such as Darius Milhaud, Igor Stravinsky, and Kurt Weill, writers such as John Betjeman, and Dylan Thomas, and financing innovative ballets such as "Les Ballets 1933" founded by George Balanchine and Boris Kocho, Edward James was an important influence on 20th-century culture. Latterly, his construction of a surreal Garden of Eden at Xilitla in the Mexican jungle is now recognized as an artistic, architectural and structural achievement. Throughout his life, Edward James also wrote poetry and novels; at their one meeting in 1936, Federico García Lorca christened him the "humming bird poet."

Edward James was educated at Eton and Oxford, but left before graduating. In 1929, James met the Austrian ballet dancer, Ottilie (Tilly) Losch and they married in 1931. The marriage failed and following his divorce in 1934, he traveled extensively throughout Europe, spending a great deal of time in France. Through James's friendship with the Vicomte and Vicomtesse de Noailles, he was introduced to the Parisian "avant-garde" of the 1930s and he developed close friendships with artists, most particularly Salvador Dalí, René Magritte, Leonora Carrington, Leonor Fini, and Pavlik Tchelitchew. Between 1935 and 1940, James's milieu was dominated by his friendship with Salvador Dalí with whom he had an extremely close and collaborative relationship, with James both patron and involved participant in the process of Dalí's artistic production, e.g. *Lobster Telephone* and *Mae West Sofa*. In 1936, worried that Dalí was being forced to sacrifice the quality of his art in order to survive, James drew up a contract with him that gave Dalí a regular and monthly allowance of £200 (£2,400 a year). Much has been written about the contract between James and Dalí, most literature dating the contract from 1936. In actuality, although the contract was signed in 1936, it did not commence until 1937 and ran for a period of one year from June 1, 1937 to June 1, 1938.

In 1964 James bequeathed his estate to a foundation bearing his name and in 1971, West Dean College opened under the auspices of The Edward James Foundation. West Dean College is now an established center for education in conservation and the visual arts. S.M.K.

Jewels

The history of the jewels goes back to the beginning of the 1940's, when Salvador Dalí became associated with Ertman and Alemany, two jewelers established in New York. Dalí designed the jewels that were produced between 1941 and 1958 and he supervised the whole process. The Catherwood Bryn Mawr Foundation provided the finance. In 1958, the Owen Cheatham Foundation bought the jewels from the Catherwood Foundation and, through the acquisition of new pieces, extended the collection until 1970. The Owen Cheatham Foundation loaned the collection of jewels to charitable, educational and cultural organizations for them to raise funds through their exhibition all around the world. In 1981, the whole collection was sold to Akram Ojeck who loaned them to his own Foundation, TAG Oeuvres d'Art, S.A. In 1986, the jewels became the property of the Japanese magnate, Masao Nangaku, through whose custody they were

then exhibited at the Minami Jewels Museum in Kamakura. In June 1999, the jewels were acquired by the Gala-Salvador Foundation and they are exhibited to the public in specially designed halls.

As Dalí explained in his *Comments on the jewels*, 1959, "My jewels are a protest against emphasis upon the cost of the materials of jewelry. My object is to show the jeweler's art in true perspective—where the design and craftsmanship are to be valued above the material worth of the gems, as in Renaissance times."

And in a truly significant manner, Dalí points out: these jewels "were created to please the eye, uplift the spirit, stir the imagination, express convictions. Without an audience, without the presence of spectators, these jewels would not fulfill the function for which they came into being. The viewer, then, is the ultimate artist. His sight, heart, mind—fusing with and grasping with greater or lesser understanding the intent of the creator—gives them life." M.A.

Hermann Keyserling (1880-1946)

Count Hermann Keyserling was a fashionable figure in European philosophical circles during the 1920s and early 1930s. Born to an Estonian aristocratic family, and taking up philosophy around 1908, he founded The School of Wisdom in Darmstadt (1920). A close associate of Carl Gustav Jung, he hosted Jung's lectures in Darmstadt and published Jung's "The Structure of the Psyche" (1927) in *Mind and Earth* and included Jung's "Marriage as a Psychological Relationship" in *The Book of Marriage* (ca. 1926). Keyserling's books were rapidly translated from German into English, French and Spanish. His celebrated *Travel Diaries of a Philosopher* (ca. 1919), published in French as *Journal de voyage d'un philosophe* (1930), recounts his 1911 journey around the world. The book reveals a philosophical interest in world religions and an engagement with the then fashionable theosophical school.

André Breton read an abbreviated version of Keyserling's *Travel Diaries* published in the *Cahiers du mois* (February-March 1925) and mentions him in an important footnote to his 1926 "Légitime défense." Here, Breton lays out for the first time the idea of the interpenetration of different states of reality, an idea later explored in *Le Surréalisme et la peinture* (1928), *Second manifeste du surréalism* (1930) and *Les Vases communicants* (1932). Breton's thinking in this matter was fully in accord with Keyserling's unitary

metaphysics: "We are in complete agreement with Count Hermann Keyserling, along the tracks of a *métaphysique monotone*. It only refers to Being one, where God, the spirit, and the world come together, of the one that is the deepest essence of all multiplicity. It, too, is only pure intensity; its only aim is life itself, this *in-objectif* whence objects spring forth like incidents." (*OC* II, p. 293)

Dalí first cites Keyserling in his "Realidad y sobrerrealidad" in *La Gaceta Literaria* (Madrid, October 1928), writing of "the receptivity of Keyserlingian-motorist elementality..." (H. Finkelstein, 1998, p. 98). Dalí was more than familiar with the intellectual propositions of the German philosopher, for Josep Carbonell's three-part article on Keyserling, had appeared in *L'Amic de les Arts* (April, May, June, 1928). Dalí was one of the permanent editors of the review, and in each of these numbers he also published an article. Carbonell's "Butlletí: Contribució a la recerca d'un nou classicisme" depended on the *Travel Diaries*. Carbonell, the director of the review, adopted Keyserling's idea of the "chauffeur" as an archetype of modern, materialist man, exactly the reference Dalí would make in "Realidad y sobrerrealidad." Contemporary society was understood as a mechanistic form of technical domination. This "chauffeur" mentality was also primitivist. Carbonell viewed Keyserling as an anti-intellectual preoccupied with primitive instincts. In the 1920s, Keyserling's politics were both anti-fascist and anti-bolshevist; both were mass movements embodying the materialism of the "chauffeur." For Carbonell, Keyserling sought a recovery of the spiritual values of the pre-modern era, those ignored by the age of progress, without necessarily advocating a return to archaic political structures. The new spirituality would be classical, and this classicism would be universal, what Keyserling called "ecumenicism." Art would be elevated to religion and this religion was Surrealism. De Chirico, Tanguy, Miró, and Dalí represented examples of this elevation: "...art elevated to religion... and in the most recent art, surrealist, metaphysical, even, and pure *primitivist* metaphysic... transformer of the most meager realities (oh! Chirico, oh! Tanguy, oh! Miró, oh! Dalí you that in some other aspects advance your companions)...". It is revealing that Carbonell specifically mentioned Dalí as an example of this new ecumenicism of culture. However, both Keyserling and Carbonell warn us that the "chauffeur" type, despite its modernity, would not save the world. A recovery of historical culture and a new immersion of the tree of humanity in metaphysical depths, in the religious side of life, was necessary to bring about a cultural renovation. Clearly, Keyserling had sociological and political interests. Dalí again quotes Keyserling in a perplexing letter to Breton, dated 1935, where he proposes the creation of a new religion and speculates as to a future racial war: "Keyserling rightly says that in order for the European war to be won by races of color, it is necessary to decide to participate and dig away at the antagonisms with a goal to dominate one or the other, domination and submission to the slavery (which is perhaps not impossible if all whites were to join forces fanatically), which could lead to immense possibilities of immediate illusions for white men in a mythical manner which could identify itself with the new crime of sons against this obscure thing." (In Calmels Cohen, *André Breton: Livres II* [Paris, April 9-11, 2003], Lot 1136, now owned by the Fundació Gala-Salvador Dalí, Figueres.) Dalí may be extrapolating this idea from Keyserling's 1928 *Das Spektrum Europas*, translated into English as *Europe* (1928) and into French as *Analyse spectral de Europe* (1931). Nowhere in this work does Keyserling speculate about a future racial war, nor does he foresee conflict with the Third World. Neither is he racist, and he firmly rejects anti-semitism, writing "only a highly cultivated people like the Jews could endure thousands of years of slavery without being broken" (p. 260) and of "the real tragedy of the Jewish destiny" (p. 333). Keyserling, in *Europe*, rejects classical 19th-century nationalism, "the excrescences of nationalism can be rightly evaluated only as the symptoms of disease" (p. 350). He proposes a pan-Europeanism based not on internationalism but on each European people finding its common identity through becoming more fully itself. Europe will save the future from the primitive materialism of America, "To Europe... has the task been entrusted to guard the sacred fire of the spirit from extinction during the long night of the spirit which now lies before mankind" (p. 390). Keyserling's muddled reflections on spirituality may have been one model for Dalí's desire to create a new religion with the Surrealists as its high priests, and the vocabulary of crisis would have appealed to the paranoid political climate typical of popular philosophy of the late 1920s. On the other

hand, Dalí's 1935 letter to Breton was rapidly contradicted by another ca. 1936 manuscript in which he called for a violent revolution of the Third World against the colonizer, in a reflection on two African types: "Against these social reasons, let us no longer oppose the lyric and pitiable black, the Chaplin of blacks, the shameful Ghandis of blacks, instead let us oppose the cruel black [,] the Dzerjinsky of blacks! Long live the armed revolution and the vengeance of blacks outside everything that pretends to deviate the magnificent justice of these next murders in favor, once again, of the dirty and optimistic masochism of the vile Jesus Christ." [In Renaud-Giquello & Associés, *Dadaïsme Surréalisme International* (Paris, May 15, 2004), Lot 61, current location unknown.] Breton would have sympathized with this anti-colonial and anti-clerical tone; however ironically, it was precisely because of the above 1935 letter citing Keyserling that Breton finally would exclude Dalí from the movement in May 1939 (*Minotaure*, nos. 12-13) in "Des tendances les plus récentes de la peinture surréaliste": "... Dalí is beginning a very rapid decline... Dalí professes in February 1939—it is from him that I have taken the time to assure myself that any sort of humor was excluded from this propos — that all the current discomfort in the world is *racial* and that the solution that must be enforced is, by all the peoples of the white race, to reduce all peoples of color to slavery. I do not know what doors any such declaration could open... but I know what doors it closes to him. I do not see how, after that, we can continue to consider his message in independent circles...." (p. 17) That Breton waited from 1935, when he received Dalí's letter, until early 1939 to do this, and that he kept Dalí's 1935 letter in his personal copy of *Minotaure* until his death, is at best curious. Arguably, Breton's definitive censure of Dalí, though much delayed, was prompted by the latter's plan to exhibit *The Enigma of Hitler* (1939) in New York. Whereas Keyserling was a conservative reactionary, Breton was progressive and radical. And Dalí stood somewhere in the no-man's land located between the twin fronts of tradition and revolution. W.J.

Jacques Lacan (1901-81)

The first issue of the Surrealist magazine *Minotaure* published in June 1933 contained an article by Dalí on the subject of paranoia considered from a Surrealist point of view. Since joining the group, Dalí had

promoted the view that his painting method was rooted in the condition of paranoia. It is by a distinctly paranoiac process of thought, Dalí claimed, that his double and multiple images were generated. Crucially, from the vantage point of its utility to Surrealism, he asserted that this paranoiac process is at the service of our unconscious desires and furthermore that it is an inherent capacity open to any individual. The paranoiac-critical method was Dalí's big idea, with a range of applications that steadily grew, but what, precisely, he meant by paranoia, and how his use of the term relates to prevailing medical concepts, is rather difficult to pin down. Between the first exposition of his theories in "L'Âne pourri" (The Rotting Donkey, 1930) and the *Minotaure* article, a thesis was published on the subject of paranoia that gave authoritative backing to certain of Dalí's views. Its author was a brilliant young psychiatrist, Dr Jacques Lacan, who went to become the most famous French psychoanalyst of his era. Lacan founded a school of psychoanalysis and has also been highly influential as a theorist of postmodernism. But at the time of writing his doctoral thesis, Lacan was still functioning within a medical psychiatric framework. *On Paranoiac Psychosis in its Relations to the Personality* (1932) is an attempt to integrate psychoanalytic conceptions of paranoia which, it is argued, permit a comprehensive and holistic understanding of the paranoiac delirium. Unlike the organicist theories generally accepted by the medical establishment that paid scant regard to the actual content of the delirium, Lacan's analysis of a patient called Aimée aimed to show that the paranoiac delirium was a meaningful product of the unconscious that has a relation to the whole personality. This was music to Dalí's ears when he read it. During the early 1930s, Lacan took more than a passing interest in Surrealism, which had been at the forefront of the introduction of psychoanalysis into French culture. Recent scholarship has rightly emphasized the formative influence of Surrealism on Lacan. The convergence with Dalí owing to their shared interest in paranoia is especially marked, and for a time it seems as if they held each other in mutual admiration. Back to back with Dalí's article in the first issue of *Minotaure* (which refers admiringly to Lacan's thesis) is an essay by Lacan on paranoia. The juxtaposition of Surrealist and psychiatric perspectives was carefully orchestrated. Like Dalí, Lacan is willing to entertain the notion that the paranoiac delirium is a potentially creative mental state. He writes: "the delirium reveals itself in effect extremely fecund in phantasms of cyclic repetition, of ubiquitous multiplication, of periodic recurrence without end of the same events, in doubles and triplets of the same persons, sometimes in hallucinations of doubling (*dédoublement*) of the personality of the subject. " This observation based on clinical material is remarkably similar to views outlined by Dalí in his 1930 essay on the paranoiac process. A case of imitation being the sincerest form of flattery? At any rate, Dalí reports that after the *Minotaure* issue came out Lacan telephoned and was insistent that they should meet, expressing astonishment at Dalí's knowledge of the condition. For his part, Dalí admits to being flattered, to be taken seriously at last in strictly scientific circles, and he readily agreed. He recalls that they conversed for two hours with a high measure of agreement and then parted with a promise to keep in touch. Whether they did so is not documented, though Dalí, in his paranoiac-critical interpretation of Millet's *Angelus*, written in the 1930s though not published until 1963, refers to a patient examined by Lacan who presumably relayed the information to him.

The lack of firm evidence for more than occasional contact between the pair apart from the one documented episode must throw doubt on the opinion of some scholars that Dalí's *Metamorphosis of Narcissus* of 1937 illustrates—or affords a visual parallel to—Lacan's mirror stage hypothesis. Against such a view, it should be noted that while Lacan may have presented his paper on the *stade du miroir* at a congress at Marienbad in August 1936, his best-known contribution to classical Freudian theory did not appear in print until considerably later and only in a revised form. Hence it is debatable whether Dalí would have known about it, and anyway the main elements of the picture—in particular, the figure of Narcissus mirrored in the lake—had demonstrably coalesced in his imagination well before this date. The centrality of narcissism to a psychoanalytic account of subjectivity is something of which Dalí would have been well aware from his reading of Fritz Wittels' intellectual biography of Freud. Wittels devotes an entire chapter to the subject, remarking that: "To-day, few analysts deny that the fiction of the ego is created by narcissism." Such views were plainly not the preserve of Lacan.

On the other hand, there is a striking parallel between Dalí and Lacan as regards their exploration of themes of sadism and aggressiveness. Lacan's concern with the issue of aggressivity during the 1930s arises out of his investigation of paranoia that had revealed aggression to be an intrinsic, quasi-structural property of the human condition. Aimée, the paranoiac whose case was analyzed by Lacan in his doctoral thesis, had attempted to stab an actress whom she believed was trying to persecute her. Lacan argued that since Aimée had wanted to be successful and famous like the actress she attacked, the persecutor was actually a projection of her ego ideal, a double or rival of whom she had developed a consuming hatred. Dalí's *Maldoror* etchings supply us with a pictorial counterpart to this state of affairs. It is noteworthy that the two figures shown as throttling or devouring each other in several of the etchings are nearly identical, one the mirror image of the other. In light of Dalí's familiarity with Lacan's doctoral thesis, and his subsequent *Minotaure* article on the Papin sisters, it might well be significant too that they are both female.

Explicit references to Dalí occur only sporadically in Lacan's published writings. The 1964 lecture on the "Anamorphosis," a text that one might surmise is more than superficially indebted to Dalí, refers somewhat flippantly (with reference to the anamorphic skull in the foreground of Holbein's *Ambassadors*) to "that flying form in which Holbein has the cheek to show me my own soft watch." An article by Dalí in *Minotaure* no. 6 (winter 1935) had reproduced the anamorphic skull from Holbein's painting, a clear influence on works from the same date. In a manner that prefigures Lacan's interpretation of the anamorphosis as a symbolic representative of lack, i.e. castration, within the perspectival field (he dubs it cheekily "the phallic ghost"), Dalí saw the anamorphosis as having an intrinsic connection with death. Similarly, Lacan's *Seminar XX* (1973-74), "Encore," which posits a feminine *jouissance*, or pleasure, "beyond the phallus" as exemplified by female saints and religious mystics, harks back to Dalí's obsession with the phenomenon of ecstasy. The well-known excesses of Lacan's writing style, the buffoonery and high jinks, and a propensity for scientific or mathematical analogies that smack more of willful obfuscation than a desire to illuminate, all these things bear more than a passing resemblance to Dalí. But whether these tantaliz-

ing parallels are a result of subterranean influence would be no easier to disentangle than one of Lacan's famous Borromean knots. D.L.

Julien Levy (1906-81)

The pioneering art dealer, author and filmmaker Julien Levy was a powerful advocate for Salvador Dalí's work in the United States during the 1930s and early 1940s. As early as 1926, while a student at Harvard University, Levy had become interested in modern art and had persuaded his father, Edgar A. Levy, to purchase Constantin Brancusi's white marble *Bird in Space* from an exhibition in New York. It was during a visit to the 1926 Brancusi exhibition at the Brummer Gallery that Levy first met Marcel Duchamp, who had helped with its organization, and the two men soon became close friends. It was Duchamp, along with Alfred Stieglitz, who would exert the greatest formative influence on Levy's future dealings in the New York art world. Taking Duchamp's advice, Levy abandoned his studies and moved to Paris in February 1927, where he quickly immersed himself in the international avant-garde art movement. Following his return to the United States four years later, Levy opened the Julien Levy Gallery at 602 Madison Avenue in New York on November 2, 1931, using funds inherited from his mother with additional help coming from his father, a powerful Manhattan real estate developer. This would be the first of four locations for the gallery, which between 1931 and 1949 hosted a succession of groundbreaking exhibitions, featuring artists such as Max Ernst, Dorothea Tanning, Arshile Gorky, Joseph Cornell, Eugene Berman, Pavel Tchelitchew, Yves Tanguy, Paul Delvaux, Matta, and most notably Salvador Dalí. Several emerging American artists had their first solo exhibitions at the Julien Levy Gallery, while the vast majority of the more established European Surrealists were given their debut shows in the United States thanks to Levy's uncompromising vision. Through these innovative exhibitions, Levy helped to introduce the American public to Surrealism and Neo-Romanticism, at a time when few other New York galleries were prepared to exhibit modern art.

Levy was introduced to Dalí and Gala in the summer of 1931 through Max Ernst, whom the young dealer had met in the previous year. The quartet spent a memorable weekend at Caresse Crosby's "Moulin du Soleil" near Senlis, just north of Paris, where Levy was greatly impressed by the Catalan artist's provocative work and outrageous personality. Soon after this encounter, he acquired *The Persistence of Memory* from Pierre Colle's gallery in Paris, paying a mere $250 for what is today considered to be the artist's greatest work. In January 1932 Levy included the painting in a group exhibition entitled "Surréalisme," thus becoming the first commercial gallery to present Dalí's work in the United States. *The Persistence of Memory* stole the show and created a scandalous sensation among visitors and the popular press that would secure the reputation of the Julien Levy Gallery as the premier center for Surrealism in New York. Between November 1933 and May 1941, Levy honored Dalí with six one-man exhibitions at his gallery, and tirelessly promoted his work through beautifully designed catalogues and translations of his critical writings, as well as important sales to prominent American private collectors and Museums. It was also through Levy that Dalí received a commission to design his *Dream of Venus* pavilion for the 1939 New York World's Fair. Although Dalí switched his allegiance to other galleries in New York when Levy enlisted for military service in the United States Army during the Second World War, the American dealer never lost his passion for the artist's work and the treasury of his complicated mind. M.R.T.

Federico García Lorca (1898-1936)

Federico García Lorca and Dalí met at the Residencia de Estudiantes (student hall of residence) in Madrid, where the young painter stayed in the autumn of 1922 to study at the Academia de San Fernando. In the hall of residence—which had been built as a result of the education reform in Spain—Dalí also met Luis Buñuel, Pepin Bello, Eugeni Montes, José Moreno Villa, and many other people later to become famous, but it was with Lorca that he developed the closest friendship. An interesting collection of letters and a Cubist portrait of the poet that Dalí must have painted around 1923 bear witness to this relationship. The painting was probably exhibited at the first Salón de los Artistas Ibéricos (Madrid, May 1925) with the title *Still Life*. Immediately after the show, however, Lorca started to write his "Oda a Salvador Dalí," which was published in the *Revista de Occidente* in April 1926.

Nearly a year before, during the Easter holiday of 1925, Lorca had been to Figueres and

Cadaqués, where the Dalí family gave him a very warm welcome. The poet, who had just completed his historical drama *Mariana Pineda*, gave a public reading of the work in Figueres, and then repeated it in Barcelona. Lorca's friendship with Dalí enabled him to frequent Catalan artistic and literary circles, where he made various friends. Because he was unable to find a theater impresario who was interested, *Mariana Pineda* was staged for the first time in 1927 in Barcelona thanks to the Catalan actress Margarita Xirgu, and the poet asked Dalí to design the sets for the work. These were highly acclaimed, unlike the painter's other works in this period, which gave rise to animosity and controversy. The following day (25 June 1927) the Galeries Dalmau inaugurated an exhibition of the poet's drawings, sponsored by his Catalan friends, which Dalí reviewed in a very interesting article that appeared in *La Nova Revista*.

This period—during which the poet went once again to Figueres, where Dalí was doing his military service, and also to Cadaqués—marked the culmination of the friendship between the two young men. A number of critics, including Rafael Santos Torroella, have identified a reflection of this close relationship in a series of paintings Dalí executed toward the end of 1927 in which they claim to see hidden portraits of the poet (especially in *Still Life. Invitation to Sleep*). But when Dalí started to take an interest in Surrealism, a wide divergence of opinion between him and Lorca became evident, especially following the publication of the poet's *Romancero gitano* (Gypsy Ballads) in 1928, a book that Dalí considered to be too distant from his new aesthetic canons. From then onward, relations between Dalí and Lorca began to deteriorate and they went their separate ways. F.F.

Maldoror

"Beautiful as…the chance meeting on a dissecting table of a sewing machine and an umbrella!" This phrase, in nearly every text by or about the Surrealists, actually originates in a work by one of their admired precursors. *Les Chants de Maldoror* is an epic poem by Isadore-Lucien Ducasse (1846-70) who wrote under a pseudonym, the Comte de Lautréamont. Only published after his death in 1890, the book was relatively unknown until discovered by the Surrealists who helped rescue it from oblivion. The extreme, unprecedented use of poetic language captivated André Breton and opened

the way for him and other Surrealist writers. Beyond that, Maldoror (the eponymous narrator) is a potent symbol of revolt, defiance and blasphemy who spoke to the mindset of the Surrealist generation.

A letter from Dalí to Charles de Noailles of January 28, 1933 excitedly relates the news that he is about to sign a contract with the Swiss-based publisher Albert Skira to illustrate *Les Chants de Maldoror*. The etchings Dalí produced rank among his most brilliantly inventive work but have little obvious connection with the *Maldoror* text. They revolve around the peasant couple from Millet's *Angelus* who Dalí would have us believe are an exact pictorial equivalent to the famous metaphor. A psychic drama of unimaginable ferocity is brewing within this deceptively bland image, Dalí maintains, and it is this supposedly latent content that his etchings make explicit. The coupling of linguistic terms become paired figures on a sort of raised sculptural plinth, or dissecting table, enacting what appears to be an exhaustive set of permutations on the theme of sado-masochistic eroticism. Lovers forage with knives and forks, hacking and tearing at their own and each other's flesh. A book-length study by Léon Pierre-Quint, Le Comte de Lautréamont et Dieu, accords with Dalí's illustrations in identifying sadism as a central theme of *Les Chants de Maldoror*. Oral cannibalism is especially salient in the images as well as text. A further area of correspondence concerns the sumptuous tableau of the foul and disgusting offered by Lautréamont. The etchings show Dalí vying with passages of poetic description such as the following:

"I am filthy. Lice gnaw me. Swine, when they look at me, vomit. The scabs and sores of leprosy have scaled off my skin, which is coated with yellowish pus […] From my neck, as from a dungheap, an enormous toadstool with umbelliferous peduncles sprouts. Seated on a shapeless chunk of furniture, I have not moved a limb for four centuries. My feet have taken root in the soil forming a sort of perennial vegetation—not yet quite plant-life though no longer flesh—as far as my belly, and filled with vile parasites. My heart, however, is still beating. But how could it beat if the decay and effluvia of my carcass (I dare not say body) did not abundantly feed it?"

The sheer abundance of imagery of this kind in *Maldoror* raises a question as to whether it may have given a direct impetus to Dalí's earliest forays into this territory .

Dalí first encountered Lautréamont around the time he met Garcia Lorca, in 1925 or thereabouts, and he implies that it had a similarly fateful impact. By that date, a Spanish translation, *Los Cantos de Maldoror*, with a prologue by Ramòn Gómez de la Serna, was available. The no longer extant picture *Honey Is Sweeter than Blood* of 1927 is a crucial marker for the first stirrings of Dalí's interest in the subject of putrefaction, which by 1930 had become a pivotal obsession. Closely allied themes of mutation and metamorphosis also abound in works from the same period around 1927, of which *Bird...Fish* is a typical example. Again, this theme could derive from Lautréamont, either from *Maldoror* itself or filtered via the influence of Masson's sand paintings (the latter strongly Maldororian in flavor). Ceaseless metamorphoses from man to animal, from animate to inanimate, are quite the order of the day in *Les Chants de Maldoror*.

The renowned excesses of Dalí's writing style and his humor are other areas where an unmistakable influence of *Maldoror* can be discerned. Léon Pierre-Quint included a chapter on humor in his book on Lautréamont, which would have caught Dalí's eye no less than the one on sadism. Pierre-Quint sees the comic in Lautréamont as an instrument of revolt. It has a tone that he says is close to sarcasm and the laughter it provokes is actually a grimace—an observation that finds a ready counterpart in Dalí's painting. There is much in Dalí that puts one in mind of Lautréamont's ambition to cretinize the reader. *The Secret Life*, his confessional autobiography, is littered with episodes of gratuitous cruelty recounted without any hint of shame or remorse that seem to be modeled on similar episodes in *Les Chants de Maldoror*. In the *Maldoror* etchings, it is the cohabitation of sadism with the comic that is so perverse and, by the same token, so redolent of Lautréamont. The jarring transitions that occur when a technical, scientific vocabulary is interspersed with a more conventional literary one are, Pierre-Quint claims, a source of Lautréamont's humor. Dalí, for his part, reckoned Surrealists were like sturgeons, swimming between the warm water of science and the cool water of art, and delighted in couching his speculations in the arcane jargon of psychiatric textbooks.

Amongst the offshoots of the *Maldoror* etchings are two major paintings, *Autumnal Cannibalism* and *Soft Construction With Boiled Beans*. It required little effort for Dalí to inflect these works, both of which incorporate themes of sadism and oral cannibalism from the etchings, as allegories of civil war in Spain. Deeply problematic from a political point of view, but strongly reminiscent of the way violence is portrayed in Lautréamont, is the distanced, amoral stance Dalí adopts towards the orgy of destruction unleashed by the conflict: "These Iberian beings mutually devouring each other correspond to the pathos of the civil war considered as a pure phenomenon of natural history," he writes. D.L.

Manifest Groc ("Yellow Manifesto")

In March 1928, Salvador Dalí, Sebastià Gasch, and Lluís Montanyà—the three members of the editorial committee of *L'Amic de les Arts*—published the *Manifest Groc* ("Yellow Manifesto"). Also known as *Manifest antiartistic català*, it was an apology for mechanism and the contemporary culture deriving from it. The milieu of the Catalan intellectuals—described as "grotesque" and "utterly sad"—was contrasted with a form of art close to the "new reality" that had given rise to the "modern spirit": the cinema, sports, jazz, automobiles, fashion parades, engineering, ocean liners, phonographs, cameras, newspapers, and so on. Art could only be described as such if it was "in tune with this spirit, in tune with the times." The promoter of the *Manifest Groc* was the art critic Sebastià Gasch—one of the leading experts on modern art in Spain at that time—but Dalí's contribution proved to be of fundamental importance in the final version. Although it did not say anything new—as the painter himself is alleged to have admitted to a journalist—the document at least trusted that "the avant-garde movement, now established all over the world, would arouse interest in our country as well." The text, which was intended, first and foremost, to awaken the consciences of the Catalan cultural milieu, reveals the signatories' great admiration for the theories of Amédée Ozenfant and Charles-Édouard Jeanneret (better known as Le Corbusier), disseminated by the periodical *Esprit nouveau*. In the last part of the manifesto, devoted to the "great artists of today," the very diverse nature of the names selected reveals that the members of the group were not in complete agreement and that the list was the result of omissions and compromises. In the months following its publication, Dalí would certainly have had to face up to his own contradictions—for example, his veneration for both Breton and Le Corbusier at the same time was in no way tenable. When Le Corbusier had an opportunity to read the manifesto during a visit to Barcelona in 1928, he expressed ironic surprise on seeing his name next to the father of Surrealism, a combination that would have been unthinkable in Paris. After being translated into Spanish, the manifesto was published in *Gallo* (no. 2, April 1928), a literary magazine founded by Federico García Lorca in Granada. F.F.

Ernest Meissonier (1815-91)

(Jean-Louis) Ernest Meissonier was an academic painter of historical genre scenes whom Dalí increasingly extolled. Meissonier's predominantly small scale and attention to detail attracted many collectors, and he quickly emerged as among the most expensive artists in France. In 1859, Napoleon III invited him to join the Imperial staff on expedition to Italy; Meissonier's subsequent depictions of Napoleon's military campaigns were generally painted on a far larger scale than his earlier works.

Dalí credited Meissonier as the inspiration for his miniaturist technique, writing to André Breton in 1933 that Meissonier's "photographic" skill struck him as "the most complicated, intelligent and extrapictorial means" towards depicting his "irrational" phantasms. Dalí's fervor for Meissonier increased exponentially in the 1960s with the advent of Pop Art, culminating with his November 1967 *Homage to Meissonier* event at Paris' Hotel Meurice, which included the debut of his enormous canvas, *Tuna Fishing* (1966-67). Dalí prognosticated that Meissonier's—and, by association, his own—reputation as a banal academic painter would be rehabilitated as tastes gradually moved away from abstraction. "After Pop Art and Op Art," he told Louis Pauwels in 1968, "optical, cybernetic art. But after these will come the super-Meissonier monarchists." E.H.K.

Modernism

Dalí made his first public pronouncement in favor of Modernism—"it is what comes closest to what we are able to love with sincerity"—during the lecture entitled "The Moral Position of Surrealism" that he gave in the Ateneu Barcelonés (the Barcelona cultural center) in March 1930. The rediscovery of Modernism, that is Art Nouveau or *fin-de-siècle* architecture, not to be con-

10

11

12

13

Fig. 10/cat. 259
Ana María and Salvador Dalí
in Cadaqués, 1927
Madrid, Fundación
Federico García Lorca

Fig. 11/cat. 260
Photomontage:
Salvador Dalí in Barcelona, 1930
Madrid, Fundación
Federico García Lorca

Fig. 12/cat. 261
Ana María Dalí in Cadaqués, 1927
Madrid, Fundación
Federico García Lorca

Fig. 13/cat. 262
Federico García Lorca
and Salvador Dalí in Cadaqués, 1927
Madrid, Fundación
Federico García Lorca

fused with the later Greenbergian "Modernism", coincided with the painter's adherence to the Surrealist movement. In "L'âne pourri," his first essay published by the journal *Le Surréalisme au service de la révolution*, Dalí wrote: "No collective effort has ever managed to create a world of dreams as pure and disturbing as that evoked by the modernist buildings that, by going beyond the boundaries of architecture, represent authentic realizations of solidified desires." With this statement of principles, the artist distanced himself from the aesthetics of *L'Espirit nouveau*, which, until then, had played a fundamental role in his work, and the functionalist architecture that, from then onward, he regarded as being merely a form of "stupidity" and "self-castigation."

From 1930 to 1933 references to the Noucentista style proliferated in Dalí's works: the abundance of ornamental elements, the sinuous curves, and the fibrous structures that appear in a number of oil paintings such as *The Lugubrious Game, The Great Masturbator, Imperial Monument to the Child-Woman*, and *Profanation of the Host*. Similar references are also to be found in his writings of this period—for example, in "The Great Masturbator" (1930) he alludes to the "multicolored decorative windows with motifs of metamorphoses that exist only in those abominable modernist interiors." In the text "L'amour" (Love, 1930) there is a list of "preferences" that also comprises "the anti-natural splendor of all the deviations from the Greco-Roman culture culminating in Art Nouveau." Dalí's interest in Modernism finally took concrete form in a dense and stimulating essay, illustrated with photographs by Man Ray and Brassaï: "De la beauté terrifiante et comestible de l'architecture modern style" (On the terrifying and edible beauty of Art Nouveau architecture), published in 1933 by the Parisian Surrealist journal *Minotaure*.

Dalí's passion for Gaudí's architecture was viewed favorably by André Breton and Paul Éluard who had already stressed the importance of this style for Surrealist aesthetics, associating it with the "spirit of their childhood." In effect, their interest in outmoded objects was a peculiarity of the two writers, as Walter Benjamin also maintained in his *magnum opus*, the unfinished *Arcades Project*: he asserted, in fact, that the reappraisal of the past was one of the distinctive features of Surrealism. If the first person "to speak of the ruins of the bourgeoisie" was Balzac, Benjamin stated, it was necessary to

recognize that it was Surrealism that first offered "a new perspective" on these ruins, transforming them from commodities into "elements of a dream." Louis Aragon, for example, found the now unfashionable shopping arcades of the cities dreamlike. There is, therefore, nothing strange in the fact that Dalí compared modernist architecture to dreams, an association that is certainly not original because the French neurologist Jean Martin Charcot (1825-93) had already identified a relationship between modernism and hysteria, and Dalí was no doubt aware of this, as appears evident in the photomontage *The Phenomenon of Ecstasy* (1933), in which portraits of hysterical women are juxtaposed with ornamental elements of modernist architecture. F.F.

Music

When still a romantic youth who wrote "private diaries," Dalí adored classical music, especially Schumann, Romanticism, and Mozart. The artist's father was a true music lover, as well as being a devotee of the *sardana*, the Catalan national dance. Dalí's father, a notary in Figueres, owned a gold *tenora*—an oboe-like instrument used in the *cobla*, the band accompanying the dance—belonging to Pep Ventura, the father of the modern *sardana*.

Dalí's stay in the Residencia de Estudiantes (student hall of residence) in Madrid marked a radical change in Dalí's musical tastes. Rejecting those transmitted to him by his father, he turned to more frivolous and fashionable types of music, in vogue among his new friends in Madrid: the foxtrot, the Charleston, the tango, and any other type of lively modern rhythm. There are still photographs of the young Dalí, elegant in his slipover, frenetically dancing the Charleston. For him, this musical genre was an excellent antidote to the romantic sentimentalism impregnating the majority of the artistic creations at the time.

Nevertheless, he never forgot the songs that his mother and aunt had taught him when he was a child—for instance, *La filla del marxant* (The Merchant's Daughter) and *La dama d'Aragó* (The Lady of Aragon). Indeed, he continued to sing them with his friend Federico García Lorca, even if he regarded them with irony and was aware of the vulgarity that often characterized the lyrics of traditional music.

When he moved to Paris, Dalí shared total contempt for any kind of classical music with Breton and his Surrealist followers.

Abandoning all forms of "high culture," he only took an interest in a number of so-called minor forms. In 1929 Dalí wrote: "Music is synonymous with sheer boredom." This should not, however, lead us to think that the use of music as an accompaniment to the images in his films was in any way intended to show disdain: for *Un Chien andalou* he chose excerpts from Wagner's opera *Tristan and Isolde* and tangos, while for *Babaouo*, a scenario that was never filmed, he wanted to use a *sardana*, *Per tu ploro*, and the Cuban song *El manisero* (The Peanut Vendor). The rediscovery of Wagner and the Italian opera coincided with the awakening of Dalí's interest in modernist aesthetics.

In the late 1930s and in the 1940s Dalí designed the stage sets for such ballets as *Bacchanale* (New York, 1939), inspired by the Mount of Venus in Wagner's *Tannhäuser*; *Sentimental Colloquy* (New York, 1944), with music by Paul Bowles; *Salome* (London, 1949), by Richard Strauss, and a great flop: Alessandro Scarlatti's *La dama spagnola e il cavaliere romano* (The Spanish Lady and the Roman Cavalier), followed by the ballet *Gala* (Venice, 1961).

Dalí never organized musical entertainment, but, while he painted, he liked to listen to classical music on the radio (if it was not the period of the Tour de France, which he followed with great interest), or else he played "The Death of Isolde" over and over again on an old phonograph. Because the record was damaged, thus distorting one of the most sublime passages, the painter Joan Josep Tharrats suggested he should change it, but Dalí replied: "I regard myself as lucky because I can enjoy Wagner's music in a way that not even the composer himself would have dared to imagine." In a way, this was a forerunner of the scratching technique later adopted by disk jockeys.

Dalí was also in touch with a number of rock stars such as John Lennon, with whom he wanted to organize a pilgrimage to Santiago de Compostela, and Alice Cooper, to whom he dedicated a hologram.

In 1974, deeply impressed by a performance of the sacred drama *El misterio de Elche*, the artist decided to compose his own personal mystery play that then gave birth to the opera *Être Dieu*, with the libretto by Manuel Vázquez Montalbán and music by Igor Wakhévitch: although it was never performed, a recording was made. Anarchic in style and partly improvised, the opera exalts the virtues of absolute monarchy and despotism.

For his old friend Luis Buñuel, Dalí made a

video with the interminable Catalan popular song *La filla del marxant*, conceived as a project for a future film. Another of his favorite musical works was the licentious operetta *La Corte del Faraón*, which he liked to sing in a duet with his friend Nanita Kalaschnikoff, or Luis XIV, as he called her. In the last years of his life, Dalí often listened to tangos by Carlos Gardel, excerpts from *Tristan and Isolde*, Bach's violin suites played by the Catalan musician Gonzalo Comellas, and a serenade by Enrico Toselli, specially recorded for him by the violinist of Maxim's of Paris. It is said that Dalí breathed his last to the sad notes of this serenade. R.M.P.

Natural History

As a young child, Dalí had a startling gift for observing the natural world that he later dramatizes in *The Secret Life*. The famous phobia for grasshoppers, which he was to interpret in psycho-analytical terms, began in his studies of the insects in the countryside round Figueres. At the age of nine he discovered a tiny beetle that imitated the leaves of a seaside plant. "I believed I had just discovered one of the most mysterious and magic secrets of nature. And there is no shadow of a doubt that this sensational discovery of mimesis influenced from then on the crystallization of the invisible and paranoiac images which people most of my present paintings with their phantasmal presence" (*The Secret Life*, p. 69). Like Dalí, the Surrealists were fascinated both by the phenomenon of mimesis and the curious habits of the praying mantis that revealed nature in a convulsive and occult form. Dalí also discovered the "plant-animals" that inhabit the sea and that upset the normal taxonomies ("animal, vegetable, mineral"). His father was an amateur geologist and instructed Dalí in the fossils of the region; the dinosaur hall of the Natural History Museum in Madrid was to be the scene for one of the fantasies associated with the Angelus. D.A.

Lídia Noguer Sabà (1866-1946)

It was said that Lídia, a fisherman's wife of Cadaqués, the daughter of Dolors Sabà, the *Sabana*, was a witch. It was her boarding house where Picasso and Fernando Olivier stayed in 1910 when they came to see their friend Ramon Pichot in Cadaqués. About six years earlier Eugenio D'Ors had been a guest there and Lídia fell in love with him; this was a passion that lasted for the rest of

her life and turned into a sort of madness. In her paranoia, Lídia became convinced that the articles that D'Ors published in various journals in that period—for example, *L'Esquella de la Torratxa* and *La Campana de Gràcia*—were coded messages written explicitly for her. "Lídia la Bien Plantada"—the name of the protagonist of D'Ors's novel *La Ben Plantada* (1911) with whom the woman had identified—became her nickname.

Dalí first met Lídia when, as a little boy, he listened to the stories the woman recounted to the children of Cadaqués. Federico García Lorca was fascinated by this strange character when, in 1925, he visited the seaside town with Dalí. And in 1929, when the painter decided, against his father's wishes, to live in Cadaqués with Gala, Lídia was the only person to help him: she sold him a fisherman's cottage in Port Lligat and often went to see the couple.

With the passing of time, Lídia was left alone in her little house by the beach of Sa Conca, with the books by Eugenio D'Ors that she read over and over again. After she had fallen sick and been reduced to poverty, it was thanks to the help of Dalí's sister, Ana María, that Lídia was admitted to the Gomis old people's home in Agullana, where she ended her days receiving adequate care and attention.

On hearing of Lídia's death, D'Ors dedicated a tombstone to his deceased friend with an epitaph: "Here lies / if the tramontana allows it / Lídia Noguér de Costa / the sibyl of Cadaqués / who by magic inspiration / dialectically was and was not / at the same time Teresa / la Bien Plantada, / the angels / in her name entreat / goats and anarchists." Because of the word "anarchists," however, the *guardia civil* prevented the tombstone from being placed on Lídia's grave. Dalí managed to trace it around in 1972 and finally, in 1989 (the year of his death), it was put in its rightful place.

Lídia's name recurs frequently in Dalí's writings. The artist was fascinated by her, as is demonstrated by a number of passages in *The Secret Life of Salvador Dalí*—for instance, "Lídia had the most remarkable paranoiac mind that I have ever come across, except for my own." M.A.

Nuclear Mysticism

Dalí's nebulous philosophical and artistic tenet, "Nuclear Mysticism," developed out of his 1940s zeal for classical painting, atomic science and Catholicism, citing a legacy of medieval—particularly Spanish—mystics

for whom science, art, mysticism and religion were one. Although already experimenting with amalgamating these elements in such paintings as *The Madonna of Port Lligat* (1949), Dalí officially inaugurated "the new era of mystic painting" with his 1951 *Mystical Manifesto*—a grandiloquent tract pronouncing his destiny to save modern art from its "lack of faith." His ensuing paintings would reflect his simultaneous passions for physics and Catholicism.

"The role of my country is essential to the great movement of 'nuclear mysticism' that must characterize our times," Dalí wrote in a 1952 entry in his *Diary of a Genius*, and, indeed, the emphasis on Spain in his evolving cosmology cannot be overestimated. In his pseudo-scientific explications of Catholic dogma, Dalí was surely looking to the Catalan philosopher, Francesc Pujols (1882-1962), whose writing chronicled the "Catalan tradition" of seeking religious "truth." Pujols—a self-proclaimed disciple of Ramón Llull (1235-1316) but vehement anti-Catholic—predicted that it would be Catalonia's destiny to introduce a new science-based religion, baptized *"hiparxiologia."* In 1968, Dalí professed to Louis Pauwels that he was engaged in becoming "the Catalonian archetype of Pujols"; from such allusions, one can extrapolate that Dalí's idiosyncratic explications of religion were not simply the hollow publicity stunts they are widely taken to be but rather reflected a sincere—albeit ambitious—desire to fulfill Pujols' Catalán-centric prediction of finding the truth of the Faith.

Although Dalí's explicit references to Nuclear Mysticism waned into the 1960s, its influence can be construed in his art and writing through the 1960s and 1970s, through his interest in "hyperrealist" technique buttressed by scientific knowledge, his increasingly fervent Spanish nationalism, and his allusions to hierarchy in both the aesthetic and political spectra. Perhaps the legacy of Nuclear Mysticism is most explicit in his 1976 text, "Eureka," in which he chronicles modern art's engagement with reality, concluding with his vision of the future of painting: "Metaphysical Hyperrealism." Dalí does not define "metaphysical hyperrealism," but one can be certain of its Nuclear Mystic heritage, for, as he would frequently posit, his cosmology never refuted his previous ideas; "I have repudiated nothing," he wrote in *Diary of a Genius*, "on the contrary, I have reaffirmed, sublimated, hierarchized, rationalized, dematerialized, spiritualized everything." E.H.K.

Paranoia see Freud and Lacan

Perpignan

The train station at Perpignan, France, is among the most significant, recurring and enigmatic emblems in Dalínian cosmology. As the nearest major railway station to Port Lligat, it was from here that his paintings were shipped every autumn before he and Gala embarked for Paris. As Gala attended to the crates' inspection and other practical matters, Dalí perused various scientific journals that galvanized his creativity. Among the numerous inspirations he credited to the railway station's waiting room was the idea to dissolve wasps in oil in order to get a better bonding agent, and the possibility of achieving three-dimensional painting through moiré. Dalí struggled to understand the impetus for his epiphanies and studied the Perpignan station thoroughly. In the ceiling he discovered, among other facets, an elliptic cupola—'an obvious monarchical symbol'—, and also found the lines in the tiled floor evoked for him a cauliflower, one of his logarithmic exemplars.

On September 19, 1963, Dalí experienced an especially powerful "cosmogonic ecstasy" at the station in which he saw the waiting room resembling the layout of the universe—a vision he immortalized in his 1965 canvas, *The Railway Station at Perpignan*. This delirious notion was enforced a year later, when he discovered that Pierre Méchain had established the standard meter in 1796 just north of the city. The meter had returned to contemporary consciousness in 1961, when it was redefined for accuracy as "1650763.73 wavelengths in a void of the radiation corresponding to the transition between the levels of $2p_{10}$ and $5d_5$ of the krypton atom 86"—a definition Dalí employed in his writing, usually without explanatory context. "[T]his precision to the thousandth of a micron," he writes in 1968, "is insignificant compared to my ability to conceive that the *x* of the radiations of krypton is an equivalence of God," referring perhaps to an abstruse connection he construed between the x-shaped meter cast in 1870 by the International Meter Commission and the golden cross of Saint Catherine of Siena.

In his 1979 speech, "Gala, Velázquez and the Golden Fleece," presented upon his induction into the prestigious *Académie des Beaux-Arts* of the *Institut de France*, Dalí relayed a conversation with the French mathematician, René Thom (see *Swallow's Tail*, cat. 249). Thom purportedly revealed to him

that, when the central Atlantic Ocean and the Bay of Biscay opened 132 million years ago, the Iberian Peninsula rotated precisely at the point of Perpignan—a geological event Dalí would evoke in his 1983 canvas, *Topological Abduction of Europe – Homage to René Thom*. This was only further proof for him of the Perpignan station's importance, leading him to declare it in 1983 the most important discovery of his paranoid-critical method. E.H.K.

Perversion

Coprophilia, exhibitionism, fetishism, masochism, onanism, sadism, sodomy, voyeurism: a list of the assorted sexual aberrations that Dalí at one time or other laid claim to would fill an encyclopedia. With a candor that alarmed even his friends among the Surrealists, he declared himself a connoisseur of the perverse: "I wish it to be known," he writes in *La femme visible* (1930), "that in love I attach a high value to everything generally named perversion and vice."

The first modern use of the term perversion has been located to 1846. Only in the latter part of the 19th-century do the sexual perversions emerge as a field of study. That was a time when, as Michel Foucault has written, psychiatrists compiled a new herbal and bestowed strange baptismal names on individuals and their sexual practices. The perversions were regarded as any deviation of a sexual instinct from its biological function of propagating the species. The variety of human sexuality was subdivided into a normative heterosexuality and a series of functional disturbances, of which the major forms were fetishism, masochism, sadism, and homosexuality. Richard von Krafft-Ebing's *Psychopathia Sexualis* (1886), the most famous textbook of the perversions by one of the pioneers of sexology, was read well into the 20th-century and circulated far beyond the medical specialists for whose instruction it was intended. Stuffed with illustrative case histories, it makes fascinating reading as well as a rich sourcebook for anyone seeking to actively cultivate perversity.

Dalí owed a great deal to Freud's conceptual revision of the perversions in the first of his *Three Essays on Sexuality* (1905). Freud loosens the bond between the sexual instinct and its object or aim that underlay definitions of normal and pathological function in the work of Krafft-Ebing, his colleague at the University of Vienna. For Freud the normal outcome of sexual development is just as much in need of explanation as the so-called

deviations. Freud described the sexual instinct (or libido) as an amalgam of component drives that, as it were, fall apart in the sexual perversions. This leads him to state that: "The omnipotence of love is perhaps never more strongly proved than in such of its aberrations as these." Freud also posited a state of polymorphous perversity in the infant before the instincts come under the restrictive and controlling authority of the Oedipus complex. Dalí comically illustrates the psychoanalytic theory of infantile sexuality with a found photograph of an innocently smiling baby to which he added a rat dangling from its mouth and smattered blood over its face and white costume. To the title on the photograph *Contentment* he has added in brackets "Le Pervers Polimorf [sic] de Freud." Dalí himself clung to the polymorphously perverse disposition.

Dalí was entitled to see his championing of the sexual perversions as a legitimate expression of Surrealist doctrine. André Breton claimed the omnipotence of desire as Surrealism's "sole article of faith" and the Marquis de Sade, whose name Krafft-Ebing applied to one of the major perversions, was a potent symbol of revolt and a presiding deity of the movement. Dalí came to Surrealism already imbued, he says, with the spirit of Sade whose influence is evident in pornographic drawings produced after he joined the group, notably the frontispiece etching for *La femme visible*. Dalí's claim in that book that perversion and vice are revolutionary forms of thought and activity evokes Sade and the Surrealist faith in desire as a force pitted against the repressive institutions of family, church, and state. A viewpoint compatible with Dalí's is expressed by the dissident Surrealist Georges Bataille in a review of a French edition of Krafft-Ebing's *Psychopathia Sexualis* printed in *La Critique sociale* 1931. Bataille argues that the perversions, as desublimated sexual desire, are a force of antagonism and discord opposed to laws and conventions of the reigning social order in a dialectic without resolution.

Dalí's determination to play the polymorphous pervert soon brought him into conflict with the orthodox Surrealists, however, who looked askance at his more *outré* appetites and predilections. Dalí implies that this was due to prudishness. While that may have been a factor in the reactions that greeted his picture *The Lugubrious Game*, for example, in some of Dalí's antics one senses a trivialization of the Surrealists' emancipatory project. For Dalí, the expression of perverse sexual desire is uncoupled from the objective of social and political revolution that in the early 1930s was at the forefront of Breton's concerns. Nevertheless, it is in Dalí that one finds one of the profoundest meditations on shame and disgust—byproducts of social convention that act like "dams" upon sexual development (Freud)—in contemporary culture. And although he was strangely reticent about admitting to any homosexual tendencies, his affirmation of a perverse subject position inevitably undercut the heterosexist ideology of love that, from a contemporary vantagepoint, appears as one of the main limitations of historical Surrealism. D.L.

Pablo Ruiz Picasso (1881-1973)

Pablo Picasso and Surrealism's founder André Breton were Dalí's two spiritual and artistic "fathers." Identifying them with the William Tell of myth, he casts himself in the role of the son, the hero, who, as Freud said, "rebels against paternal authority and conquers it." Dalí was a passionate admirer of Picasso through the 1920s, as he explored the new languages of avant-garde painting. Picasso's inventiveness was a model and challenge. Unlike the dadaists and surrealists Dalí did not experience Picasso's startling switches from the radical formal inventions of Cubism to a neo-classical realism as a betrayal, but as proof of the protean possibilities of modern painting. Visiting his famous fellow Spaniard in Paris in 1926 Dalí received encouragement; in 1929 Georges Bataille approved Dalí's painting as being even uglier than Picasso's. Dalí's text "Picasso's Slippers" of 1935 expresses both homage and rivalry. The aftermath of the Spanish Civil War divided them irrevocably; Picasso refused to return to Spain while Franco was in power, while Dalí made his peace with the regime. After the war Dalí continued, nonetheless, to solicit Picasso's attention, and sent him a postcard every July with the cryptic message "In July neither women nor snails." D.A.

The Pichot Family

The Pichot family had a very special relationship with the Dalís: Salvador Dalí's father (Salvador Dalí i Cusí) had met José Pichot (known familiarly as "Pepito") at the University of Barcelona when they were both students at the law faculty. When he graduated, Dalí i Cusí took the competitive examination to become a notary, while Pepito Pichot left university before completing his studies to marry his aunt Angela, the sister of the patriarch Ramón Pichot Mateu's wife. Both these ladies were heiresses to Antoni Gironés, a wealthy citizen of Cadaqués. The Pichot's salon was one of the most fashionable and entertaining in Barcelona. The painter Ramon Pichot Gironés was a close friend of Picasso's, while Ricard Pichot was a cellist, Luis Pichot a violinist, and the singer María Pichot—her stage name was María Gay—was regarded as one of the best Carmens of all time.

When Pepito Pichot and his wife moved to Figueres they tried to persuade their friend Dalí to make the same choice. In fact, a few months later, after being appointed state notary for this town, he followed his friend's advice. Pepito was like a second father to Salvador junior: in 1916, after the boy had passed his high school entrance examinations, he invited him to his country estate near Figueres, where Salvador discovered Ramón's Impressionist painting and the innocent eroticism of Pepito's adopted daughter, Julita (Dullita), the subject of the daydreams forming the basis of "Revêrie" (Daydream, 1931), a text that scandalized the Surrealists.

Pepito's wife, Angela, inherited a house in the Cala di Es Sortell on the outskirts of Cadaqués, where the notary and his wife were invited in 1908. A native of Cadaqués, Don Salvador decided to rent a house nearby, next to the Llané Beach, which then became the Dalí's home. The Pichots, a family of musicians and painters, were in the habit of staging concerts for the public on their boat around which specially trained swans swam: these were the "nights of white calm" in which everything appeared to be phantasmagorical.

In 1972, Salvador Dalí made contact with the Pichot family again through the painter Antoni Pichot Soler (b. Figueres, 1934), who subsequently Catalanized the spelling of his surname as Pitxot. The son of the cellist Ricard Pichot, Antoni studied in San Sebastian under the painter Juan Núñez Fernández, who had also been Dalí's teacher. In the following years, Pitxot helped Dalí set up the Theater-Museum, of which he is still the director. R.M.P.

Pitxot, see *Pichot*

Politics

André Thirion, charged with organizing the celebration of the 10th anniversary of the French Communist Party in Bellevoise, invited Dalí to design the exhibition. Thirion had access to the party's archives, including the startling 1925 telegram from Jacques Doriot to Abd El-Krim congratulating him on his success in fighting against the French in the Moroccan War. Though the exhibition never happened, Dalí made two suitably provocative preparatory drawings, relevant to Surrealism's engagement with radical politics. The first referred to Doriot's telegram and consisted of a red arrow and a large bloodlike spot. Dalí's annotation explained that the red spot would be made of newspapers, magazines and photographs and the arrow and the blood made as large as possible. The other drawing represented a pile of goods, including financial documents, in a large conflagration, whose flames were transformed into a red flag bearing the letters: URSS (USSR). These drawings recall Dalí's youthful ca. 1920 drawings *USSR – Long Live Russia – Death to Wars and Trotsky*; these works were executed at the time of the 1919-20 labor wars between industry bosses and anarcho-syndicalist labor unionists. Dalí's sympathies with post-1917 events in Russia, with the failed 1919 Sparticist revolt in Germany and with anarchist "terrorism" are clearly evident in his 1919-20 diary.

Dalí joined Surrealism in late 1929. His *Sometimes I Spit With Pleasure on the Portrait of My Mother* (1929) and his film *Un Chien andalou* (1929), where he provocatively plays the role of one of the "rotting" priests, established his anti-clerical credentials. The same year he announced Surrealism's allegiance with the Communist Party in his "Documental-Paris" published in *La Publicitat* (Barcelona): "the Surrealist movement has always been, politically, an unconditional supporter and has always been for a long time incorporated in the Communist Party" (28 June 1929) (H. Finkelstein, p. 117). Dalí was perceived in Spain as a Bolshevist, "at the point of registering in the Communist Party," according to Ernesto Giménez Caballero (*La Gaceta Literaria*, Madrid, November 1, 1931). Often his agitprop was directed towards Catalonia rather than Paris. At the invitation of his friend, the labor militant, Jaume Miravitlles, Dalí delivered his talk "El surrealismo al servicio de la revolución" (Surrealism at the Service of the Revolution) at the meeting of the Labor and Agricultural Workers' Block: Joaquín Maurin's revolutionary Communist and Catalanist movement. Dalí proclaimed his solidarity with the Labor and Agricultural Workers' Block and revolutionary Communism (F. Fanés, 1997, pp. 253-254). The critic Sebastià Gasch challenged Dalí's political posturing in his "L'esperit nou" (The New Spirit) in *La Publicitat* (April 1932): "Being communist and Supperrealist is a blatant contradiction," calling Dalí's painting "putrefaction in its pure state…". Dalí's vitriolic rupture with Gasch led to a permanent break with Miró, who until then was one of Dalí's strongest supporters.

Dalí's texts devoted to sexual fantasy (e.g. "Rêverie," Daydream, 1931) were received badly by the more puritanical of the communist Surrealists, especially by Aragon. But his representation of Lenin with a giant phallic buttock in *The Enigma of William Tell* (1933: Moderna Museet) went beyond the pale, and presumably beyond the more acceptable depiction of the father of the Revolution in *Partial Hallucination: Six Apparitions of Lenin on a Grand Piano* (1931). Worse, Dalí committed it for exhibition at the Salon des Indépendants, scheduled to open February 2, 1934. Breton summoned Dalí to respond to a list of charges (letter, January 23) including the disrespectful presentation of the image of Lenin and, more damning, sympathy for Hitlerism. Dalí responded (January 25), stating that the Lenin figure represented his own castrating father and was not disrespectful; regarding Hitlerism, he denied any sympathy ("I am neither de facto nor intentionally Hitlerian"), and he called for a more revolutionary challenge to Hitler than that offered by dialectical materialism and the Communist Party. Simultaneously, Breton was considering how Hitlerism could be analyzed by Surrealism ("Enquête intérieure sur las positions politiques," *OC*, II, 1992, p. 580). Irrational mystification had to be exposed; the underlying foundation of Hitlerism was an irrational response to despair, political humiliation (the Versailles treaty) and mass unemployment. Dalí's position was too close to the irrationalism of Hitler's charismatic methodology for Breton to accept it. Another undated letter sent to Breton by Dalí (ca. January 25) did not calm Breton's anxiety, for Dalí speculated that "racial struggle" preceded class struggle. Dalí intended to confront Hitlerism's psychic mechanisms in order to dominate it, and he went on offering his observations on the genesis of racial struggle ("Races [probably] came before classes…. It appears that they exist and existed throughout the "BATTLES OF THE RACES" in history"). Breton's

response (February 3) informed Dalí of the exclusion vote by the Surrealists for "anti-revolutionary acts" and his "glorification of fascism" (K. Von Maur, *Breton and Dalí*, 1991, p. 201). During these early February days, Breton corresponded notably with Éluard and Tzara: the former responding that he hoped Dalí could restrain his delirium and wondered if the problem derived from the Surrealists' own weakness in taking unified positions; the latter expressing strong reservations about "Dalí's racist activity" but stating his confidence that Breton would resolve the issue so that Dalí could continue his brilliant contribution to the movement. Éluard simultaneously confided the extent of his concerns in several letters to Gala (*Lettres à Gala*, 1984, letter n. 188). Dalí was summoned to Breton's apartment on February 6, and he narrowly avoided exclusion with the agreement to sign a document rejecting Hitlerism and supporting the Revolution. The violent right-wing riots on February 7, instigated by Colonel Roque's Croix de Feu which brought over 100,000 militants onto the street, and the near storming of the Chamber of Deputies, explain the Surrealists' sense of urgency in the previous uneasy days. The Republic had narrowly escaped a fascist coup d'état. Breton quickly issued an "Appel à la lutte," denouncing the fascist peril and calling for solidarity with the general strike on the 12th which, though less violent, provoked the resignation of Prime Minister Edouard Daladier. These events foreshadowed the Surrealists' support for the Front Populaire.

Dalí planned and drafted the notes for two more lectures in Barcelona in 1934, for April and October (F. Fanés, 1999, pp. 255-263). 1934 was a politically incendiary year in Spain. Throughout the year Largo Caballero, "the Spanish Lenin," and his Socialist Left, along with the General Workers' Union called for Revolution. He formed the Workers Alliance (Alianza Obrero) devised to unite working class parties. In Catalonia, Maurin's Labor and Agricultural Workers' Block, to which Dalí had proclaimed allegiance (in 1931), established an Antifascist Worker Alliance with the Socialist Union of Catalonia, Party of Socialists of Catalonia, dissidents from the anarcho-syndicalist labor unionists, the agrarian Union de Rabassaires and Andrés Nin's Communist Left. By early in the year, Nin was in contact with Largo Caballero. Dalí reflected the revolutionary atmosphere of Barcelona in his lec-

ture "Por un tribunal terrorista de responsabilidades intellectuales" (For terrorist tribunal of intellectual leaders) held at the Ateneo Eciclopédico Popular (April 11), where he called for "legitimate direct action!" In June there was a failed agrarian strike, and Largo Caballero formed a secret Revolutionary Committee. In Madrid, militant gangs of Socialist Youth waged street warfare against the youth wing of the Falange (Fascists). The Madrid government declared the Generalitat of Catalonia's reformist Catalan Law of Agricultural Contracts unconstitutional, the debate resulting in the collapse of the Samper (Madrid) government and the formation of a new government on October 1 led by (the Radical) Lerroux, which included Gil Robles' Catholic right Confederation of the Autonomous Right. The Catholic right Confederation's participation was the match that lit the tinderbox of Revolution. In Madrid the Workers' Alliance called a general strike (October 5). In Barcelona, the Catalan Republican Left president of the Generalitat, Luis Companys, declared a rebellion against the Lerroux government, and on the evening of October 6th proclaimed a Catalan Republic within the Federal Republic of Spain. The uprising was quickly suppressed by the army unit stationed in Barcelona with 45 people killed. In Asturias 30,000 strikers took to the street. Colonel Juan Yagüe's Moroccan Army, under orders from General Franco, brutally put down the uprising with 4,000 casualties and 900 workers killed. Shortly after arriving in Barcelona for his exhibition in early October, and without giving his scheduled lecture "El misterio surrealista y fenomenal de la mesa de noche" (The Surrealist and phenomenal mystery of the bedside table) because of the turmoil, Dalí promptly made a hasty retreat to Paris.

Dalí began the preliminary drawings for *Soft Construction with Boiled Beans (Premonition of Civil War)* (1936) in May 1934. Here the composition is fully worked out, suggesting a visceral response to the revolutionary sentiment of the spring of 1934, if not the October Revolution in Spain. The painting depicts a contorted pair of figures locked in a mortal embrace; the hand of one crushes an attenuated and phallic breast from which emerges, in a painful grimace, a tortured head. A slab of raw beef suggests the castrating appetite of paternal power. The night stand propping up the arm of the lower figure introduces an autobiographical element and recalls the subject of Dalí's undelivered talk. The presence of the elegantly dressed

"Ampurdàn scientist" examining this grotesque metamorphosis suggests the need for scientific exploration of irrational phenomena as much as the contrast between the brutality of the scene and the tame order of liberal bourgeois society, one which masked the social tensions leading to civil war. Clear references to Goya suggest a self-consuming appetite motivated by dark obsessions. The definitive drawing and the painting were only completed in early 1936, before the onset of civil war in July, though the subtitle was added when it was reproduced in *Minotaure* (October 1936) with the title *Espagne, prémonition de guerre civil*.

Autumnal Cannibalism (1936) was executed after the uprising of Franco and the Generals in July 1936. The structure of the composition evokes art nouveau architecture, the very architecture which Dalí proclaimed as a bearer of "the immense 'cannibalisms of history' often illustrated by the real, grilled and flavorful lamb chop that marvelous dialectic materialism placed, like a true William Tell, on the very head of the politician" (*Minotaure*, 3-4, December 1933, pp. 103-104). Perhaps the figures in *Autumnal Cannibalism* represent politics and the apple represents the psycho-analytic inversion of politics, what amounts to a shift from political commitment to a narcissistic reflection on political events.

Dalí's series of telephone paintings (1938-39) reflected the frantic diplomatic efforts preceding the Munich Agreement (September 1938). *Debris of a Motorcar Giving Birth to a Blind Horse Biting a Telephone* (1938) presents a motorcar metamorphosed into a horse. This visual pun on "horsepower" represents the disjunction between the modern, technological warfare provided to the fascist uprising by Germany and the pre-modern (agrarian) economy limiting the resistance of the Republic. The spare electric light bulb illuminating the scene strongly recalls Picasso's *Guernica* (1937). When exhibited at the Spanish Pavilion at the Paris World's Fair (July 1937), *Guernica* quickly became the most emblematic anti-war painting referring to the Spanish Civil War. By contrast, Dalí's paintings can be read as a more generalized symbol of self-divided Spain in turmoil. Significantly, Dalí was the only Spanish artist of note absent from the Spanish Pavilion. The Munich Agreement represented the turning point of the Republic's military struggle against the Generals' uprising. Chamberlain naively believed he had solved the dispute over the Sudetenland, when he had conceded everything to Hitler. Daladier understood this, but remained powerless. Chamberlain hoped to apply a similar "solution" to the Spanish problem. The ensuing Czech crisis deflected international attention away from Spain at the worst moment of the disastrous and bloody battle of the Ebro Front, meaning France and England maintained an arms blockade to the Republic while Germany supplied the Fascists. The Munich agreement secured the same fate for Spain as Czechoslovakia, meaning the allies had abandoned the Republic. This was all implied in the symbolism of The Enigma of Hitler, despite Dalí's denial he had any awareness of the painting's meaning and his later claim that its imagery originated in a dream. This painting arguably prompted the final break between the Surrealists and Dalí, which took place with Breton's harsh judgement in "Des tendances les plus récentes de la peinture surréaliste" (The most recent trends in Surrealist painting; *Minotaure*, May 1939) on the grounds (again) of Dalí's understanding of "racial struggle" as the origin of global conflict. However, the most plausible explanation for the final rupture is Dalí's planned exhibition of *The Enigma of Hitler* at Julien Levy's gallery in New York which took place (March 21-April 18, 1939), immediately prior to Breton's *Minotaure* article. This event necessarily resuscitated Breton's memories of the controversial display of *The Enigma of William Tell*. Like 1934, 1939 was a decisive moment calling for a political clarity lacking in Dalí's ambiguous imagery. W.J.

Pompier

The French expression, *art pompier*, originated as a derogatory term referring to works of art produced under the influence of the 19th-century French Academy. It translates literally to "fireman art" and may allude to the helmeted soldiers who appear in certain academic painters' Neo-Classical battle scenes. The style, exemplified by such artists as Ernest Meissonier, Adolphe-William Bouguereau (1825-1905) and Édouard Détaille (1848-1912), was criticized by the budding proponents of Modernism, who viewed it as clichéd, conservative, and bourgeois.

The American art critic, Clement Greenberg, furthered the denigration of Academic art in 1939 when he vilified it as *kitsch*—the distasteful aesthetic that challenged "high art" (i.e., Abstraction). Dalí's unabashed copying from photographs, media prominence, and emphasis on figuration had already positioned him as a target for Greenberg's censure, and certainly the *art pompier* painting Dalí extolled—indeed, he owned several paintings by Meissonnier and Bouguereau, now on show at his Teatro-Museo Dalí in Figueres—was, and largely continues to be, maligned as *kitsch*; Millet's *Angelus*, too, which features so prominently in Dalí's work, was a *kitsch* element of French culture, with ubiquitous reproductions on teacups, pillowcases, inkwells, etc. In the 1960s, however, Pop Art challenged Greenberg's dichotomy by leveling the distinction between *kitsch* and "high art." Although Dalí approved of Pop Art, his interpretation of the Movement was idiosyncratic; he recognized Pop Artists as legacies of Vermeer's photo-realistic naturalism and of *pompier* art, suggesting they would lead to a period of objective painting informed by the latest scientific advancements. E.H.K.

Prints

Salvador Dalí's contribution to the graphic arts of the 20th-century can be placed within a clear historical framework, for Dalí's prints and his method of working relate to his classical roots. He used printmaking in the same manner as Raphael, who, wise to the fame that prints had brought Albrecht Dürer, worked with a master printer and publisher, ensuring enormous renown by the time of his early death. In the same way, Dalí, a natural publicist, assured his fame and renown through the print multiple. He worked in a variety of different media incorporating new methods and mixed techniques, but his special affinity was for etching to which he applied his brilliant draughtsmanship with outstanding results. Although there are a few early etchings, possibly done alongside his teacher Juan Nuñez, himself an accomplished engraver, it is clear that Dalí's printed oeuvre began in Paris, within the context of the French *livres d'artiste*.

Dalí's first important commission in 1933, with the publisher Skira, was for *Les Chants de Maldoror*. This book, hailed by the Surrealists as one of their own, fitted Dalí like a glove, and to its mesmerizing poetic violence and singular metaphors, he added his own imagery, as individual as the original text, yet quite distinct, of a visual beauty that was further accentuated by the miniaturist scale of the images themselves. Produced in the ateliers of Lacourière and Frélaut, this commission set the pattern for a lifetime of work with print workshops, in a spirit and tradi-

cat. 263
Postcards sent by Salvador Dalí
to Pablo Picasso

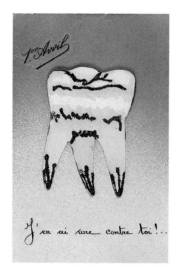 

April 1, 1929

October 17, 1949

 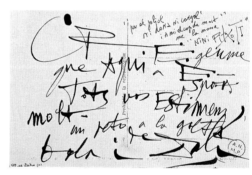

1952

 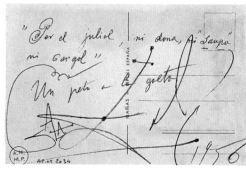

1956

1959

1961

1964

tion of collaboration between artist and artisan of which Dalí was proud, and that dated back to the Renaissance.

This method of working can be seen in the great number of different prints that Dalí made and that range from the heliogravures and collotypes of his major Surrealist period, including *L'Immaculée Conception* and *La Femme visible*, both of 1930, to the brilliant illustrations for *Le Tricorne* by Pedro de Alarçon (1959) and the *Divine Comedy* by Dante Alighieri (1960), which were produced as woodcuts. Dalí uses the wit and bite inherent to the print medium to great effect when he provokes the viewer's response, through the interplay of the fantastic and the surreal: in *Les Dix recettes d'immortalité* of 1973, disparate elements are woven together in a series that incorporates mirrors and cut-outs within a book-object. To *Les Songes drôlatiques de Pantagruel*, a series of satirical illustrations originally published in the 16th-century, Dalí adds his own imagery, fusing past and present in comic irreverence. In similar fashion, Dalí worked on Goya's *Caprichos* between 1973 and 1977. This suite of etchings and aquatints, produced by Goya in 1799, shows a strong critique of society through the brilliant use of satire, and Dalí's response, instinctively attuned to his Spanish predecessor, incorporates, through line and color, diverse source material in a provocative commentary composed of dissociative imagery.

When the print market began to flourish in the 1960's, in tandem with increased economic market possibilities for editors and buyers alike, Dalí's prints also multiplied. He was flooded with offers of work and it is clear from examination of his prints that Dalí's response to a proposal was dictated by his degree of interest in the subject matter. His graphic work ranges from the brilliant, witty and original to more journeyman imagery, on which less time was spent but which he undertook since it helped maintain his lifestyle. Here, Dalí subversively manipulates consumerism, of which both he and his public form part, by compelling the spectator to unveil his own knowledge through challenging his taste. In this sense he can be placed at the heart of 20th-century art, in line with Andy Warhol, whose use of the print both mirrors and reflects the society that it satisfies, and by which it is sustained. Dalí's roaming lifestyle, based over three countries and two continents, encouraged him to enter into business arrangements of confidence with his print workshops, presigning paper for certain editions. This was

an unfortunate decision since it spawned considerable fraudulent abuse. Unethical editors then gaily extended editions, capitalizing on a series of factors that they manipulated with ease: Dalí, a non-conformist in the art world was notoriously impractical; his imagery was extensive, and, above all, he was essentially uninterested in regimented certification of his work. (Here again he stands in line with Warhol, who rubber-stamped his signature on his prints.) Since Dalí had always courted publicity, it took time before he became aware that the negative publicity engendered by uncontrolled editions had spiraled out of control. The repercussions on his work were such that critical appraisal of his prints was seriously undermined. In consequence, it is only recently that Dalí's outstanding contribution to the world of graphic art is beginning to be thoroughly reappraised and recognized for its originality and inventiveness, reflecting the skill, commitment and knowledge of a truly subversive artist. J.MU.

Psychoanalysis see Freud, Lacan, Disgust, Perversion

Francesc Pujols (1882-1962)
The life of this self-taught writer and philosopher may be summed up by the popular saying, "Forty years of chatter and forty years spent demonstrating the empirical existence of God." Pujols published, in 1904, *Llibre que conté les poesies de Francesc Pujols*, with a prologue by Joan Maragall, a poet whose disciple he considered himself to be, and, in 1906, under the pseudonym of Augusto de Altozanos, the essay *El Nuevo Pascual o la Prostitución*, an explicitly provocative text. In 1908 he was appointed secretary of Les Arts i els Artistes group, the members of which could, in a way, be regarded as the exponents of what was known as the Noucentista style. Influenced by Neoplatonic philosophy and heir to the thought of Milà i Fontanals, Pujols was the editor and consultant of various cultural, artistic, and illustrated journals, such as *Papitu*, *Revista Nova*, *Vell i Nou*, *Picarol*, and *Mirador*. He was one of the members of the Consejo de Museos de Barcelona (Barcelona Museums Council) and secretary of the Ateneu Barcelonés (the Barcelona cultural center). In one of his most important works, *Concepte general de la Ciència catalana*, published in 1918, he sought to demonstrate the existence of a specific philosophical movement dating back to Ramón Llull of which he regarded himself as

being the present exponent. He called this system of thought "*iparxiologia.*" In 1926, he retired to the Torre de les Hores, his estate near Martorell, to devote himself to writing his essay *Història de l'hegemonia catalana en la política espanyola Durant el segle XIX*. In another outstanding text, *La visió artística i religiosa de Gaudí* (1927), he elected the Sagrada Familia as the new seat of a religion based on Catalan science.

With a subtle sense of humor laced with irony, Dalí approved of the complex philosophical system of Pujols, a scholar for whom he had great respect. In fact, he dedicated a statue to him, which was erected in front of the Theater-Museum in Figueres, and a painting. He also wrote the preface to a special edition of Pujols's *La visió artística i religiosa de Gaudí* (The artistic and religious vision of Gaudí) and illustrated a giftbook devoted to his friend, who, with his talent for anecdotes and powerful oratory, played a messianic role in Catalan cultural circles: "The day will come when Catalans, wherever they go, will be allowed to do what they like simply because they are Catalans." R.M.P. and V.A.M.

Quantum Mechanics
The set of equations and concepts covered by the term quantum mechanics constitutes the most successful model yet devised to explain the fundamental structure and behavior of the physical world. The beginnings of quantum mechanics can be dated to the turn of the 20th-century when a series of experiments by the German physicist Max Planck seemed to reveal that energy emission and absorption took place not continuously (as dictated by Newtonian mechanics), but discontinuously, in jumps of discrete measurable units or "energy quanta." Planck's discovery was generalized by Einstein in 1905 to affirm the quantization of light (reviving the notion of its particle composition) and electromagnetic radiation. Then in 1913, Niels Bohr used the same results to hypothesize a new design for the atom largely defined by "allowed orbits" between which electrons could jump once the atom absorbed or emitted energy (the former causing a jump to an outer orbit, the latter an inner orbit), again violating classical physics where the electron had not been fixed to predetermined radii. Even in its early form, the theory of quanta departed so radically from the traditional view of the physical world that most physicists—including Planck and Einstein—found it hard

to accept. Bohr presided over its full formulation, which was left to a younger generation of physicists to complete in the 1920s. Using a non-commutative mathematical system termed matrix calculus, and aided by the work of Wolfgang Pauli, Max Born, and Pascual Jordan, Werner Heisenberg discovered the first full version of quantum mechanics in 1925, eliminating "observation" based on analogy with objects on the macrocosmic scale and solving a set of continuing problems that had built up around the energy state of "Bohr's atom." Then the following year, Erwin Schrödinger broke with Bohr and Heisenberg, drawing instead upon the French physicist Louis de Broglie's wave description of matter to create a version of quantum mechanics called wave mechanics. Subsequently, towards the end of 1926, Paul Dirac was able to prove mathematically the equivalence of the two, having created a third version with "quantum algebra," which predicted precisely (and more elegantly) all of the findings around quanta so far, while including in its fabric Special Relativity and classical mechanics. The "official" acceptance of quantum mechanics is usually dated to 1927.

Predicting with great accuracy not only experimental findings in physics, but those in chemistry and molecular biology a well, the mathematics of quantum mechanics have immense application. However, the subatomic world it *describes* goes against the grain of common sense, throwing into question classical concepts such as "mass," "location," "velocity," and even "determinism," now thought to be unsuited to behavior and phenomena on the smallest scale. Rejecting or at least remodeling classical reason, these developments in physics held great interest for Dalí and the Surrealists. The writings of Gaston Bachelard, for instance, particularly his *Nouvel esprit scientifique* (1934), which outlines the "epistemological break" with Newtonian, Cartesian, and Kantian forms of reason forced by quantum mechanics, inflected the path taken by Dalí and the Surrealists in the 1930s. Dalí's articles for *Minotaure* and his *Conquest of the Irrational* (1935) demonstrate his knowledge of modern physics, and his later "nuclear mysticism" paintings acknowledge his fascination with the revolutionary quantum mechanical description of nature. G.P.

Relativity Theory
Forever associated with the name of Albert Einstein, Relativity Theory emerged out of a history of investigation into the velocity and propagation of light that goes back as far as Galileo. By the end of the 19th-century it had long been accepted that light had a speed that was measurable, and as increasingly refined experiments determined this quantity with greater exactitude scientists turned to focus their attention on the medium that allowed the distribution (propagation) of light waves. A ubiquitous, stationary ether had traditionally offered scientists a speculative object against which to set (and preserve) absolute time, space, and therefore motion. The failure of the Michelson-Morley experiments of 1881/1887 to discover an "ether wind" (to which the earth was subject due to its rotation) through the registration of variation in the intensity (or velocity) of light did not act as a deterrent to the idea. It was argued that the measuring devices used had been subject to the "Fitzgerald-Lorentz Contraction," shrinking in the direction of the motion of the earth, compensating for, and failing to show, the expected evidence of the effects of the ether on light speed.

In the wake of the findings of Hendrik Lorentz and the writings of Ernst Mach and Henri Poincaré, Einstein claimed in his 1905 paper "On the Electrodynamics of Moving Bodies" firstly that the laws of nature are consistent from one "frame of reference" to another and only relative motion between these is detectable, which affirmed that an absolute, fixed ether was undetectable and superfluous. Secondly, he stated that light was propagated at a definite velocity, c, irrespective of the state of motion of its source, a postulate leading to the counter intuitive conclusion that if a star and the earth were approaching each other at a combined velocity of 100,000 miles per second, the light leaving the star would still travel in our direction at light speed (186,000 miles per second), not at a rate of the sum of the two quantities. From these two revolutionary postulates, Einstein was able to develop equations explaining certain phenomena with greater precision than had been possible with Newtonian mechanics, and also make remarkable predictions later corroborated by experiment. The Special Theory of Relativity verified the Fitzgerald-Lorentz Contraction, and showed that the rate of temporal flow varied between positions in space and with the velocity of bodies in motion ('time dilation,' which abolished the notion of absolute time). It also accounted for an object's increased mass at a higher velocity, and showed how large a quantity of energy was equivalent to a small mass, given that the additional energy that accrues to the additional mass of an object increasing in velocity is equal to the increase in mass multiplied by the velocity of light squared. From this, Einstein deduced that in nuclear processes there would be a quantity of energy (E) associable with *any* mass (m) that can be found when the latter is multiplied by the square of the velocity of light (c^2): $E = mc^2$.

By the time Einstein extended his findings about constant relative velocities in the Special Theory to bodies moving with velocities varying with each other in the General Theory of Relativity in 1916, his work had found support from many of the major figures in physics. The technical difficulty of the General Theory meant that its reception was muted initially, but when it was validated experimentally in November 1919, Einstein's achievement was fully acknowledged within the physics community, while the physicist himself achieved instant celebrity around the world as the "new Copernicus." Countering common sense assumptions as to the behavior of time, space, and matter, Relativity held a peculiar interest for a nascent Surrealism in 1919. Dalí's earliest writings on paranoia-criticism are closely linked to his interest in concepts central to Relativity like the Fitzgerald-Lorentz Contraction, appearing among the texts of *La Femme visible* (1930). Together with images derived from paranoia criticism, the pliant warped forms, hybrids, and frames within frames which emerged at this time to characterize his mature painting style are all marked by the new world described by Relativity. Throughout the 1930s, in his texts for *Minotaure*, his book *Conquest of the Irrational* (1935), and his private correspondence, Dalí privileges Relativity as the harbinger of a new knowledge uncontaminated by Greco-Latin logic, Christian belief, or Enlightenment philosophy, equating its findings with the revolutionary modern age which had also borne psychoanalysis and Surrealism. In particular, his 1934 *Minotaure* text "Apparitions aérodynamiques des 'Êtres-Objets'" (Aerodynamic apparitions of "Beings-Objects") lauds the newly minted space and time inaugurated by Einstein, while his *Persistence of Memory* (1931) is the very image of "time dilation." G.P.

Residencia de Estudiantes
The Residencia de Estudiantes (student hall of residence) in Madrid was established in 1910 by the Junta Para Ampliación de Estudios e Investigaciones Científicas (Council for the Expansion of Studies and Scientific

Research), and together with the council itself, was one of the outstanding results of the innovative ideas of the Institución Libre de Enseñanza (Free Institute of Education), founded in 1876 by Francisco Giner de los Ríos, one of the mainstays of the Spanish Regenerationist movement.

From its foundation up to 1938, the Residencia—which in 1915 moved to its permanent site on the Colina de los Chopos in Madrid—was one of the most important cultural centers in Spain and also one of the most successful experiments of artistic and scientific exchange in Europe in the period between the two wars. Thanks to its first director, Alberto Jiménez Fraud, the Residencia de Estudiantes was open to all forms of creativity, thought, and interdisciplinary dialogue. The Residencia's main objective was to enrich university education by creating a lively intellectual environment and a sense of community among the students. Its distinguishing features were the promotion of a continuous dialogue between the sciences and the arts and the attention it paid to the international avant-garde movements. For all these reasons, the Residencia soon became the center from which modern culture spread throughout Spain, and its residents included many young men destined to become some of the most outstanding cultural figures in 20th-century Spain, such as the poet Federico García Lorca, the painter Salvador Dalí, the film director Luis Buñuel, and the scientist Severo Ochoa. Furthermore, Miguel de Unamuno, Manuel de Falla, Juan Ramón Jiménez, José Ortega y Gasset, Pedro Salinas, Eugenio D'Ors, and Rafael Alberti, just to mention a few names, spent time there either as residents or as visitors while they were in Madrid.

Important lectures and debates were held at the Residencia, which played a major role in the intellectual life of Europe in the interwar period. Prestigious visitors included André Breton, Filippo Tommaso Marinetti, Albert Einstein, Paul Valéry, Marie Curie, Igor Stravinsky, John Maynard Keynes, Alexander Calder, Walter Gropius, Henri Bergson, and Le Corbusier.

Dalí arrived at the Residencia de Estudiantes in September 1921 to study at the Real Academia de Bellas Artes de San Fernando (the Academy of Fine Art in Madrid). His aim—in reality imposed on him by his father—was to obtain a qualification that would allow him to earn a living by giving painting lessons. The first day he turned up with an intentionally eccentric appearance:

wearing a huge overcoat and a broad-brimmed hat, he had long untidy hair, sideburns with a bizarre cut, and a laconic air that was the cause of much hilarity among his companions. José Bello, the leader of the most dandyish faction in the Residencia and who did not have a high opinion of the young painter, found a number of Cubist drawings in Dalí's room. Greatly surprised, he invited him to join his group: wearing knee-breeches and a jacket made by an English tailor, and after having his hair cut at the Hotel Palace, he was taken out drinking in the most exclusive bars and clubs in Madrid. It was not long before Dalí abandoned his romantic pose in favor of an aloof, foppish attitude, adapting himself to the ideas of his friends Buñuel, Lorca, and Bello, with whom he began an intense creative exchange, giving rise to some of the most fruitful collaborations of the 20th-century. In October 1926, Dalí was expelled from the academy for the second time, on this occasion definitively: the Madrilenian phase of his life had drawn to a close. R.M.P.

Rhinoceros Horn

The rhinoceros horn was Dalí's Atomic Period (ca. 1945-60) symbol *par excellence*, connoting a myriad of religious and aesthetic associations. Although a diminutive rhinoceros with levitating horn appears in his 1950 *Madonna of Port Lligat*, the artist pinpoints his epiphanic discovery to July 5, 1952, when he reports to have surveyed his paintings and realized that all could be deconstructed into rhinoceros horns. Based on his entries in *Diary of a Genius* (1964), it would seem that Dalí's initial infatuation with the rhinoceros horn was strictly as a building block of imagery—like "Leonardo's eggs" and "Cézanne's cubes and cylinders"—, though it quickly adopted more symbolic significance. Indebted to such texts as D'Arcy Thompson's *On Growth and Form*, Dalí focused on the rhinoceros horn's morphology *a propos* the Golden Section and the related logarithmic spiral (see *Ascension*); by 1955, he had identified logarithmic spirals in rhinoceros horns, cauliflower heads, sunflowers and Vermeer's 17th-century painting, *The Lacemaker* (1669-70).

Cryptically citing the legend of the unicorn, Dalí further imbued the rhinoceros horn with the subtext of chastity—a deliberate irony given the horn's phallic shape and fabled aphrodisiac qualities. Indeed, many have suggested that the myth of the unicorn originated with the rhinoceros, and some

translations of the Old Testament have even translated what most now read as "wild ox" as "rhinoceros" or "unicorn." Unicorn horns, or "alicorns"—commonly rhinoceros horns or, more frequently, narwhal tusks—were highly valued in the Middle Ages for their alleged medicinal powers and capacity to protect against poisons. The alicorn's supposed purifying power led to the unicorn adopting within Christian allegory the connotation of chastity, and the animal became a symbol for the Virgin Mary. This informs several of Dalí's works from the 1950s onwards, including *Assumpta Corpuscularia Lapislazulina* (1952), *Young Virgin Auto-Sodomised by the Horns of Her Own Chastity* (1954), and the unfinished film with Robert Descharnes, *The Prodigious Adventure of the Lacemaker and the Rhinoceros*, in which Vermeer's *Lacemaker* "conquers" a live rhinoceros at Vincennes Zoo. E.H.K.

Saint Sebastian

Saint Sebastian is a recurring theme in Dalí's artistic output. The patron saint of Cadaqués and the artist's alter ego, Sebastian is the cardinal element of Dalí's aesthetic theory.

In the iconographic tradition, Saint Sebastian is usually depicted tied to a tree or a column while the Roman soldiers shoot arrows at him. It has almost been forgotten that the saint, who survived the torment of the arrows, was clubbed to death some years later. For this reason, in the 7th-century, when plague broke out in Rome, Saint Sebastian was chosen as the symbolic representation of immunity. For the same reason, numerous coastal towns like Cadaqués, where the plague could easily spread, chose Sebastian as their patron saint.

From the Renaissance onward Saint Sebastian became the protector of aesthetes and homosexuals because, despite the rigid Catholic censorship, the languid pose and ecstatic expression of this naked adolescent writhing under the blows of the arrows gives the spectator great visual pleasure.

Dalí used the figure of Saint Sebastian as a metaphorical representation of the friendship linking him to Federico García Lorca, the homosexual poet who wanted his relationship with Dalí to be something more than just a fraternal one. However, when Dalí formulated his first aesthetic theory in an essay published in the journal *L'Amic de les Arts* with the title "Sant Sebastià," (Saint Sebastian, July 1927), he based himself on the definition of irony suggested by

Fig. 14. Dress by Elsa Schiapparelli made of organza, Summer-Fall 1937 Philadelphia (PA), Philadelphia Museum of Art

Fig. 15/cat. 264
Evening Dress by Elsa Schiapparelli made of printed silk, Summer 1938 Philadelphia (PA), Philadelphia Museum of Art

Fig. 16. Salvador Dalí, *Veined Leaf*, 1953, yellow gold, 18 carats (13-14 carats inside), emeralds, rubies, 8.2 × 9.5 × 2 cm
Figueres, Fundació Gala-Salvador Dalí

Fig. 17. Salvador Dalí, *The Royal Heart*, 1953, yellow gold, 18 carats, rubies, sapphires, emeralds, aquamarines, peridots, garnets, amethysts, diamonds and pearls with a motor-driven mechanism simulating heartbeats, 24.5 × 12.8 × 9.5 cm
Figueres, Fundació Gala-Salvador Dalí

14

15

16

17

Heraclitus: "Nature likes to hide itself." Thanks to this lucid concept of irony, Dalí managed to make his first leap from the visible conventions to the infinite possibilities of a new aesthetic that were to have as their objective the "discredit of reality." "Irony… is nudity; it is the gymnast who hides behind Saint Sebastian's pain. And this pain exists because we are able to recount it."

Located on a promontory, the small hermitage of Saint Sebastian overlooks Cadaqués. On January 20 all the townspeople go there to pay homage to their patron saint, eat sea urchins, drink wine, and sing and dance the famous *patacades*, the improvised lyrics of which leave plenty of scope for popular ingenuity and irony. Dalí attempted to acquire the sanctuary shortly after his return to Catalonia (in 1948, when he came back from America): he wanted to make it a place of pilgrimage and decorate it himself with frescoes in honor of the martyr. Unfortunately, this plan came to nothing. R.M.P.

Elsa Schiapparelli (1890-1973)

On February 4, 1938—less than a month after the opening of the "Exposition internationale du Surréalisme"—the Paris *couturière* Elsa Schiapparelli presented arguably the most brilliant of her themed collections, the Circus Collection for Summer 1938. She described this collection in her 1954 autobiography *Shocking Life* as her "most riotous and swaggering" and its presentation in her salon at 21 place Vendôme was as surreal as the exhibit held at the Galerie Beaux-Arts. Circus performers raced through the 17th-century interior decorated by Jean Michel Frank, up and down the staircases, and in and out of the windows while mannequins sauntered through the rooms wearing some of Schiapparelli's most imaginative designs— tall peaked clown hats, circus tent veils, dresses printed with carousel horses and evening jackets embroidered with acrobats. The *couturière*'s collections were always topical and thus it was no surprise that the Circus Collection also contained references to the current "Surrealist Exhibition." Schiapparelli and Dalí worked together on several projects that season—designs for a slim black crepe evening dress padded with the silhouette of a skeleton, a hat in the shape of an inkpot with a quill thrust through its crown, and the evening ensemble seen here, an asymmetrically draped gown printed with an illusion of torn animal flesh and worn with a veil trimmed with appliquéd fabric 'tears.' Its inspiration may well have had its origin in Dalí's painting *Necrophiliac Springtime*, which Schiapparelli owned. This painting was one of three executed in 1936 with similar figures; the others were *The Dream Places a Hand on a Man's Shoulder* and *Three Young Surrealist Women Holding in their Arms the Skins of an Orchestra.* In all three paintings the boundary between clothing and flesh has dissolved making it impossible to distinguish one from the other. In the ensemble shown, originally worn by Schiapparelli, magenta *trompe-l'œil* slashes reveal layers of pink and black fur pulled to the underside of pale blue flayed skin (now faded to white). An identical gown and headdress was worn by the actress Ruth Ford who probably received it as a gift from Dalí's patron, Edward James. At the time James purchased clothes from Schiapparelli's salon for not only Ford but for her mother Gertrude and for Gala Dalí as part of his agreement with the artist. Although Schiapparelli's official collaboration with Dalí appears to have started with the designs for a coat and suit featuring pockets as bureau drawers shown in August 1936 for Winter 1936-37, the artist was without doubt already familiar with her earlier designs. Indeed Schiapparelli's decorative zippers designed both to reveal and conceal and her extremely pointed shoulders from the early 1930's, 'hands' used as belt buckles and fastenings and the aerodynamic shapes of the 'stormy weather' and 'typhoon' silhouettes were incorporated by Dalí into his own visual vocabulary from 1934. Schiapparelli's first introduction to the artist may well have been through her American assistant Bettina Shaw-Jones (later Bettina Bergery, the wife of French politician Gaston Bergery) who had joined the salon about 1928 and was responsible for its imaginative window displays. Bettina, whom Dalí described as resembling a praying mantis, was one of his best friends—he called her "the soul and biology of the Schiapparelli establishment." For their second collaboration shown in February for Summer 1937, Schiapparelli and Dalí designed a large red lobster which was both printed onto white cotton for beach wear and also made an erotically charged appearance on the skirt of a demure dinner dress worn by Wallis Simpson in May 1937 just prior to her marriage to the Duke of Windsor. The dress, one of eighteen Schiapparelli models Mrs. Simpson selected for her spring wardrobe, was consciously metaphorical as were several of her other choices, including the butterfly evening dress worn with a full length net 'cage' coat. Although Dalí drew the original lobster it was the master silk designer Sache who translated the design to fabric. Dalí's projects with Schiapparelli continued with two hat designs for the August showing for Winter 1937-38. One in the shape of a lamb chop complete with paper frill and another in the form of a high heeled shoe that was worn by both Gala Dalí and Daisy Fellowes. The collection also provided Dalí with the shocking pink knitted ski mask that he used for the mannequin he costumed for the street of mannequins in the "Surrealist Exhibition." Schiapparelli's inspiration for the mask had been a head covering she had seen in the Peruvian pavilion at the 1937 Paris Exposition. Although Schiapparelli and Dalí's collaboration on clothing and accessories ended with the Circus Collection, Dalí later provided the *couturière* with art work for advertisements and designs for perfume bottles including the label for *Shocking Radiance* perfume (1943) and the limited edition Baccarat bottle for *Le Roy de Soleil* perfume launched in 1947. D.B.

Erwin Schrödinger (1887-1961)

The Viennese physicist Erwin Schrödinger was one of the most important figures in the formulation of quantum mechanics in the 1920s. He was awarded the Nobel Prize for physics in 1933 for his discovery of a new form of atomic theory—wave mechanics— which attempted to replace the particle structure of the atom with a more elegant, vibrational account of its activity, ultimately achieving similar results through different concepts and mathematics to those reached by Werner Heisenberg (though unlike Heisenberg, Schrödinger thought "visualizability," or *Anschaulichkeit*, of subatomic processes desirable and possible). Dalí quoted Schrödinger at length towards the end of his *Mythe tragique de l'Angélus de Millet* (ca. 1938/1963) when he argued that both the spectator of a multiple-image painting forged through Dalí's method of paranoia-criticism and the modern scientific observer *create* a reality that they then take to be "objective." Dalí mentioned Schrödinger from time to time after this. Late in life, at the science conference "Chance on Trial" held at the Dalí Museum in Figueres in 1985, he attempted to resolve a heated dispute between the scientists Ilya Prigogine and René Thom by saying "I can see you disagree, but I would like that one day you come to an agreement in Schrödinger's name." Exactly what Dalí meant by this remains obscure. G.P.

Simulacrum

The concept of a copy *without* an original—the concept of the simulacrum—has gained popular currency from the discourse of postmodernism. It is remarkably prescient of Dalí, single-handedly and with the kind of fanfare that was already his distinctive trademark, to have introduced Surrealism to the notion of the simulacrum. He does so in the course of espousing the paranoiac-critical method whose superiority over the Bretonian Surrealist orthodoxy of psychic automatism he would soon be proclaiming. Altogether, the words "simulacra" and "simulacral" recur more than a dozen times smattered throughout "L'Âne Pourri," the manifesto statement of his new aesthetic credo, along with the other essays collected together and published as *La Femme visible* in 1930.

The simulacrum is a term that occurs but rarely in the aesthetic discourse of the interwar period apart from Dalí's ostentatious use of it (indeed that obscurity may have lent it some of its appeal). One exception is a small collection of poems entitled *Les Simulacres* by Michel Leiris with illustrations by André Masson. More directly relevant may be a selection of short texts titled *Simulacres* by the poet J.V. Foix that appeared in the Catalan avant-garde journal *L'Amic de les Arts* in November 1927. Dalí's use of the term simulacrum to denote the triumph of a mental image over external reality calls to mind a discussion in Hippolye Taine's *On Intelligence* (1871), a source that André Breton may have brought to his attention. For Taine, the mental image corresponding to a sensory perception is a sort of phantom or simulacrum (*'ce sont des simulacres, des fantômes ou semblants'*) in essence no different from the mere semblance of reality produced by hallucinations. Taine's conclusion that exterior perception is but a true hallucination surely would have appealed to Dalí's keen sense of paradox.

Though Dalí is alone among the Surrealists in referring explicitly to the simulacrum, the mode of representation it denotes—or rather the critique of representation it implies—is more widespread in Surrealist imagery, in a manner that links Surrealism to one of the main planks of Post-Structuralist thought. Michel Foucault, in his celebrated essay *This is Not a Pipe* (first published as an article in 1968), analyzed René Magritte's work in terms of a triumph of similitude over resemblance. Foucault likens resemblance to a finger pointing to a model, sovereign and unique, whereas similitude, he

came to realize, was analogous in its rupture of this mimetic relation to the Platonic simulacrum. A typical strategy employed by Magritte is to depict a painting-within-a-painting seamlessly joined to what it is meant to represent, the effect of which is to blur the distinction between model and copy. Another artist whose work is relevant to a culture of the simulacrum is Giorgio de Chirico whose evolving practice of pastiche and copying, including his own earlier metaphysical works, was anathema to Breton in the 1920s but much less so, one suspects, for Dalí.

Dalí first applies the term simulacrum to his reversing, double and multiple images, the individual components of which are intended to propagate sequentially according to the dictates of desire alone, independent of any model or external referent; indeed he confidently predicts that such a visual demonstration would serve to discredit reality. That the theme of the simulacrum continued to inform his fascination with optical illusions is evident in the latter part of the 1930s in a group of large paintings whose complex permutations of imagery Breton somewhat unfairly dismissed as mere picture puzzles. One of the more resolved and impressive of these works is titled the *Transparent Simulacrum of a Feigned Illusion*. Dalí gives an emphatically psychological slant to the theme of the simulacrum owing to his attachment to a Freudian conception of unconscious fantasy: "The new simulacra which paranoiac thought may suddenly unleash will not only have their origin in the unconscious, but, moreover, the force of the paranoiac power will itself be at the service of the unconscious." This subjective dimension is seen in his exploration of the theme of the double—the supreme form of the simulacrum because the double erases all distinction between model and copy—and in his attraction to the myth of Narcissus, the Greek youth who fell in love with a mere image that he mistook for reality. A subsidiary meaning of the Greek *phantasma* and the Latin term *simulacrum* is a ghost or phantom, yet another of Dalí's core obsessions. Ghostly veiled or shrouded figures, whose identity is rendered enigmatic or indeterminate, inhabit a good many pictures in the early 1930s as well as being the subject of an article in *Minotaure* in 1934. Behind Dalí's phantoms in a sort of receding perspective stand those of De Chirico and ultimately Böcklin whose *Island of the Dead* was im-

mensely important for him as a springboard for his own phantasmatic associations.

The simulacrum, and the related issue of simulation, draw together so many strands of Dalí's project as an artist and individual. The story is now well-known that Dalí had an elder brother also named Salvador who died just over nine months before he was born, and for whom he was a kind of surrogate in the eyes of his grief-stricken parents. He and his brother were, Dalí claims, indistinguishable, like two drops of water. In *The Secret Life* Dalí exploits this tale in order to portray himself as a simulacral replica of a non-existent original, or as the novelist Dominique Fernandez put it more evocatively, *the shadow of a ghost.* D.L.

The Secret Life of Salvador Dalí

Dalí wrote most of the over four hundred pages making up his autobiography, *The Secret Life of Salvador Dalí*, in 1940 and 1941. From the manuscript preserved in the Fundació Gala-Salvador Dalí, it appears that the artist dashed off the first version, and Gala then copied it out in clearer handwriting, correcting the spelling mistakes. Thus, Haakon Chevalier, who translated the book into English, made use of Gala's version, many parts of which were already typewritten. In December 1942, Dial Press published *The Secret Life*, illustrated with 130 pen drawings of varying complexity—displaying notable inventiveness and graphic skill—executed by the artist specifically for this edition. Even before publishing his autobiography, Dalí boasted a notable literary output, consisting of poems, articles, and essays that had appeared in various newspapers and journals. Some of these texts, published in booklets, such as *La femme visible* (1930), *L'amour et la memoire* (1931), and *Conquest of the Irrational* (1935), were only produced in very limited editions. Despite the fact that in these writings there were already autobiographical references—for example, in "L'Alliberament dels dits" and "Rêverie"—the idea that Dalí should have wished to commit his memoirs to paper at the age of thirty-seven is certainly surprising. Consisting of accounts deriving in equal parts from reality and from the author's imagination, *The Secret Life* is not so much an autobiography in the strict sense of the word as an interesting literary text in which the artist reveals curious analogies with the tradition that Georges Bataille described as "literature of evil." The latter comprised such writers as the Marquis de Sade, the

Comte de Lautréamont (Isidore Lucien Ducasse), and Joris Karl Huysmans (the author of *À Rebours*). On the other hand, in this book, for the first time Dalí defends his anti-modern stance—which was evident from the moment he adhered to the Surrealist movement—on conservative grounds. The praise of the monarchy, the Renaissance, and authority repeated throughout the book seems to be seeking to reproduce in a social context the tendency toward evil that had already been identified in the literary field. Written in a period of change in which Dalí was going through a creative crisis, it cannot be excluded that, with this book, he was seeking to give a new direction to his career by becoming a writer. And if this were so, the artist's autobiography should not be related to his previous output, but rather with the subsequent work, the novel *Hidden Faces*. Thus, perhaps *The Secret Life* ought to be regarded as a real literary project: a novel about the author's life heralded the novel about the society within which this life took place—in other words, *Hidden Faces*. F.F.

Soft Structures (*"les structures molles"*). Also "the super soft" (*"le super mou"*).

Dalí's account of his creation of the limp watches in *The Persistence of Memory*, 1931 (Museum of Modern Art, New York), is well known. One night, according to his *The Secret Life* written in 1941, he and Gala had finished their evening meal with a ripe Camembert. "After everyone had gone I remained for a long time seated at the table meditating on the philosophic problems of the "super-soft" that the cheese presented to my mind." Going to the studio that night he "saw" the solution to the unfinished landscape he was working on, and added three soft watches to the scene.

Soft watches were followed quickly by other objects rendered in strangely flaccid or extruded forms. Drooping violins, collapsing pianos, molten rock formations, soft skulls and elongated buttocks propped up on crutches became distinctive features of Dalí's paintings between 1931 and 1934. To some extent this preoccupation with soft structures sprang from Dalí's fascination with the "edible" and eroticized shapes of Art Nouveau that was announced in a text on ornamental art in 1931 and anticipated even earlier in such works as *The Great Masturbator* (1929). Nutritive and coprophilial fantasies also played their part in the dominance of soft structures within Dalí's work in these years.

However, a further factor that came into play in the mid-1930s was Dalí's knowledge of recent scientific writings in this field. In an article of 1936 on English Pre-Raphaelite painting, Dalí acknowledged a debt to what he called the "amazing" study of Edouard Monod-Herzen. In *Principes de morphologie générale* (1927), Monod-Herzen wrote about nature as a seething mass of form possibilities. A living creature, he claimed, was "subject to innumerable forces and pressures." It therefore had not one shape, but potentially an infinite number of shapes; it was a "milieu in movement." Monod-Herzen emphasized how quite different entities could share similar forms when subject to similar types of internal and external pressures: an illustration of the different shapes assumed by drops of cooled lava showed marked similarities to the shapes of amoebae.

This idea of the potential variability of forms may have lain behind Dalí's striking pronouncement in *The Secret Life*: "We know today that form is always the product of an inquisitorial process of matter, the specific reaction of matter when subjected to the terrible coercion of space, choking it on all sides, pressing and squeezing it out, producing the swellings that burst from its life to the most exact limits of the rigorous contours of its own originality of reaction."

Dalí frequently referred to natural morphology in his writings of the 1940s, focussing not on soft forms but on the spiral shapes that featured so often in standard texts on the subject. At some point, however, his mind returned to the implications of the soft forms announced in *The Persistence of Memory*. A Photostat of a text by Dalí about this painting—now in the files of the Museum of Modern Art and sent by Dalí, it is thought, in the winter of 1953-54, though possibly written earlier—indicates that he wanted to promote an interpretation of the painting that combined biology, theories of perception and psychoanalysis. Under the subheading "Morphology – Gestalt Theory – Mystery of Unduloids – Geodesic Lines," Dalí discussed, without much linking explanation, the patterns found in certain muscular fibers, the shortcomings of Gestalt theory and the exceptional nature of colloidal substances, before a discussion of the formation of his super-ego in this period under the separate heading "Psychoanalysis."

Unusually, Dalí provided in a footnote a list of French biological texts to support his discussion of natural morphology. These texts—R. Anthony, *Le Determinisme et l'adaption mor-*

phologique en biologie animale (1922), J. Ducloux, *Les Colloïdes* (1920), J. Loeb, *La Théorie des phénomènes colloïdaux* (1925), and C.H. Mauvin, *Les Etats physiques de la matière* (1910)—were distinctly mechanistic in their vision of the phenomenon of life. Loeb, for example, boasted how, as a result of advances in modern science, germination and the division of cells could be explained in terms of the differentials in osmotic pressure within cells, which were determined simply by chemical changes taking place within an organism. The texts also emphasized how the traditional distinction between the processes of growth in living entities and accretion in inorganic matter had been undermined by recent research into so-called "fluid crystals" and into colloidal particles (entities that did not follow the normal law of passing from a liquid to a crystalline state but that moved, Dalí noted, from a liquid state to either a gelatinous form or a granular structure).

The text suggests that at this point Dalí was attempting to assert that his invention of soft forms in 1931 was in tune with the latest research in biology and chemistry. As all the texts predate *The Persistence of Memory*, the note may even imply that Dalí wanted to suggest that these texts had also informed his thinking about "the philosophic problems of the 'super soft.'" J.M.

The Spanish Civil War

"The civil war had broken out!," Dalí wrote in *The Secret Life*. "I knew it, I was sure of it, I had foreseen it! And Spain, spared by the other war, was to be the first country in which all the ideological and insoluble dramas of Post-war Europe, all the moral and esthetic anxiety of the 'isms' polarized in those two words 'revolution' and 'tradition,' were now to be solved in the crude reality of violence and of blood." Defining his position somewhat disingenuously as a politically disengaged intellectual, Dalí insisted: "Horror and aversion for every kind of revolution assumed in me an almost pathological form. Nor did I want to be called a reactionary. This I was not: I did not 'react'—which is an attribute of unthinking matter. For I simply continued to think, and I did not want to be called anything but Dalí. But already the hyena of public opinion was slinking around me, demanding of me with the drooling menace of its expectant teeth that I make up my mind at last, that I become Stalinist or Hitlerite. No! No! No! And a thousand times no! I was going to continue to be as always and until I died,

Dalínian and only Dalínian! I believed neither in the communist revolution nor in the national-socialist revolution, nor in any other kind of revolution. I believed only in the supreme reality of tradition."[2]

Forced into self-imposed exile during the years 1936-39, Dalí traveled extensively with Gala throughout Europe and America, consolidating his patronage and international reputation. This was a period of feverish activity for Dalí, as the artist moved between venues in England, Italy, France, and the United States, expanding his artistic production beyond easel painting into the realm of fashion, entertainment, theatrical design, window dressing, and Hollywood films. His commercial activities and his retrospective denial of partisan engagement notwithstanding, Dalí was deeply disturbed by the recent course of events in Spain and the death of his friend, the poet Federico García Lorca, who was murdered by a fascist firing squad in Granada in the early months of the conflict. Unlike his compatriots Pablo Picasso, Alberto Sánchez, and Joan Miró, Dalí did not contribute work to the Republican Pavilion of the 1937 Paris International Exhibition, a stunning *mise-en-scène* for the Loyalist cause where Picasso's *Guernica* was displayed. Dalí's absence from the Pavilion is significant, given his notoriety in Surrealist circles and his prominence on the international art market. It is likely that internecine disputes among members of the French group, stemming in part from André Breton's accusations in 1934 that Dalí was a fascist sympathizer, were contributing factors. In response to these accusations, and with a characteristic sleight of hand, Dalí refused to view the Spanish Civil War in ideological terms, insisting years later that the image of "Iberian beings devouring each other" in his horrific *Autumn Cannibalism* of 1936, "express(es) the pathos of civil war considered (by me) as a phenomenon of natural history, as distinct from Picasso, who considered it a political one."[3]

In *Autumn Cannibalism* and *Soft Construction with Boiled Beans* of 1936, to which the artist later added the subtitle "Premonition of the Civil War," Dalí viewed the violence in his homeland through a paranoiac-critical lens, interpreting the conflict as a "narcissistic and biological cataclysm." "When I arrived in Paris," he wrote in *The Secret Life*, "I painted a large picture which I entitled *Premonition of the Civil War*. In this picture I showed a vast human body breaking out into monstrous excrescences of arms and

legs tearing at one another in a delirium of autostrangulation. As a background to this architecture of frenzied flesh... I painted a geological landscape that had been uselessly revolutionized for thousands of years, congealed in its 'normal course.' The soft structure of that great mass of flesh in civil war I embellished with a few boiled beans, for one could not imagine swallowing all the unconscious meat without the presence (however uninspiring) of some mealy and melancholy vegetable."[4] Returning to a theme he had first explored in 1934 in a series of etchings for a deluxe edition of the Compte de Lautréamont's *Chants de Maldoror*[5], Dalí now located his masochistic imagery in a concrete environment—the fertile plains of his native Empordà—underscoring the narcissistic trauma of self-annihilation as a quasi-geological and cyclical process of destruction and regeneration under the ever-present impulse of the death drive. R.S.L.

Surrealism see Breton

Diego Rodríguez de Silva y Velázquez (1599-1660)

Velázquez (or Velásquez) is widely considered Spain's greatest Baroque painter. Born in Seville, he was named the official painter to King Philip IV in 1623, under whose patronage he executed such well-known masterpieces as *Las Meninas* (1656) and *Portrait of Infanta Marguerita of Austria* (1660).

Dalí extols Velázquez as early as 1919 as "one of the greatest, perhaps the greatest, of all Spanish artists and one of the best in the world." Nearly thirty years later, in his 1948 book, *Fifty Secrets of Magic Craftsmanship*, Dalí rates Velázquez on par with Raphael and only slightly lower than Vermeer. One of the tiny fishermen in *The Christ of Saint John of the Cross* (1951) is quoted from Velázquez' study for *The Surrender of Breda* (1634), and Dalí's 1958 painting, *Velázquez Painting the Infanta Marguerita with the Lights and Shadows of His Own Glory*, is an explicit homage.

In 1960, Dalí participated in a group exhibition, "*O figura. Homenaje informal a Velázquez*," at the Sala Gaspar gallery in Barcelona. His exhibition later that year at New York's Carstairs Gallery, "The Secret Number of Velasquez Revealed," begot two articles in the periodical *Art News*, both published in early 1961. The first article, also titled, "The Secret Number of Velasquez Revealed," refers specifically to Dalí's 1960 painting, *The Maids-in-Waiting (Las Meni-*

nas). In *Maids-in-Waiting*, Dalí substitutes Velázquez's personages in *Las Meninas* for numbers corresponding to their general structures (e.g., the edge of the large canvas becomes a number seven). The resulting number, Dalí reveals in his essay, is 76,758,469,321—although the painting presents 77,758,469,321 instead; "Through this magic operation," Dalí writes in characteristic third-person, "Salvador Dalí affirms that he will do nothing less than save painting from chaos, demonstrating to the younger painters that from the actual '0 Figure' one must reach the 76,758,469,321 of Velasquez." Dalí's second essay, "Ecumenical 'chafarrinada' of Velasquez," celebrates Velázquez's brushstrokes, suggesting that his enduring beauty will eclipse the "experiments" of 20th-century painting. "Today," Dalí writes, "when no one is in accord with anything, especially with the present esthetic [sic] chaos, everything coincides on one unique phenomenon: VELÁZQUEZ. At the tricentennial of his death Picasso, Dalí, the *pompiers*, the Abstractionists, the followers of Action Painting, all consider Velázquez the most alive and most modern of painters."

Dalí's references to Velázquez persisted well into the 1970s, notably with his enthusiasm for the Roman Emperor Trajan. Trajan was born in Italica—10 kilometers from Seville—, inspiring Dalí to forge a paranoiac connection between the Emperor and Velázquez justified by an idiosyncratic link he construed between Trajan's Column in Rome and the double-helix of DNA. Dalí also evokes Velázquez in his collage hologram, *Holos! Holos! Velázquez! Gabor!* (1972-73), which superimposes Velázquez's painting of the Infanta Marguerita onto a poker game. As Dalí's interest in holography was primarily as a medium for artistic realism, it is unsurprising that he cites Velázquez, whose naturalism he had admired for so many decades. "Since Impressionism," Dalí writes in his 1976 text, "Eureka": "the entire history of modern art has revolved around a sole and unique objective: reality. And this might lead us to ask: What is new? Vélazquez." E.H.K.

Andy Warhol (1928-87)

The American Pop artist Andy Warhol was a great admirer of Salvador Dalí, whose iconic celebrity status he had succeeded in emulating by the early 1960s. Warhol later claimed that Dalí was one of his favorite artists "because he's so big," and this statement, which refers to

Fig. 18/cat. 265
Salvador Dalí, *At the Circus*,
ca. 1929
8.9 × 12.1 cm / 3¹/2 × 4¹/2 in.
New York (NY), Timothy Baum
Collection

Fig. 19/cat. 266
Salvador Dalí, *Untitled*
(Female Nude), ca. 1936
25.2 × 20.2 cm / 9⁷/8 × 8 in.
New York (NY), Timothy Baum
Collection

Fig. 20/cat. 267
Salvador Dalí, *Untitled*
(Study for the Ballet
"Romeo and Juliet"), 1942
Oil on canvas
69 × 79 cm / 27¹/8 × 31¹/8 in.
Mexico, JAPS Collection

Fig. 21/cat. 268
Salvador Dalí, *Untitled*
(Picasso with a Spoon), 1965
Photocollage
49.9 × 40 cm / 19⁵/8 × 15³/4 in.
Figueres, Fundació
Gala-Salvador Dalí

18

19

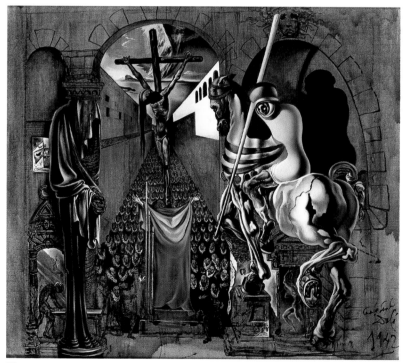

20

21

462

his fame, as well as the increasing scale of his canvases in the 1960s, underscores the fact that Dalí had provided him with the role model for the successful, publicity-oriented artist, whose knack for self-promotion ensured that every exhibition of his work was a sensational event. Warhol rarely acknowledged the profound debt his work owed to Dalí, but even a cursory glance at the older artist's pioneering ventures into commercial art, filmmaking, fashion, advertising, commissioned society portraits, and religious iconography reveals how much he learned from his example.

According to Ultra Violet, the two artists first met in New York in 1963. However, Warhol had an exceptional grasp of Dalí's work and ideas before this encounter, probably through his close friendship with the painter Philip Pearlstein, his classmate at the Carnegie Institute of Technology (now Carnegie Mellon University) in Pittsburgh in the late 1940s, who had a passionate interest in the Surrealist movement that would culminate in a doctoral thesis on Francis Picabia at New York University in 1953. Jack Wilson also remembered Warhol being "very much aware of Dalí" in the 1940s, and recalled that the artist first saw a screening of Dalí and Buñuel's film *Un Chien andalou* while at Carnegie Tech. Warhol's exhumations of Camp and Hollywood glamour in his underground movies of the 1960s were no doubt informed by Dalí's often scandalous forays into experimental cinema and television.

Dalí's earlier efforts to blur the line between high and low culture opened the door to Warhol's subsequent exploration of the media-saturated culture of the post-Second World War era, where fame had become increasingly attainable, but also increasingly transitory. There can be no doubt that Dalí's paintings, films, and even his hilarious newspaper, the Dalí News, informed Warhol's own efforts in this vein, such as Interview magazine, which began production in 1969, as well as his films, screen tests, and television programs. Dalí even sat for a Warhol screen test in 1966, which was eventually used as a backdrop for the multimedia performances by the Exploding Plastic Inevitable, which featured Warhol, the Velvet Underground, and Nico (Dalí was even advertised as a member of the band, although he never attended any of their concerts).

Whereas many modernist artists, particularly those devoted to formalist abstraction, felt uncomfortable with the new values and concerns of the 1960s, with its heady mix of mass-consumerism, sexual freedom, and social protest,

Dalí felt completely at ease in the company of hippies and other manifestations of the counter culture. Warhol also embraced that decade's mass-consumption of consumer products through his paintings and commercial work, especially in the publicity-entertainment industry. The fact that both artists had worked within the cultural-entertainment complex gave them a profound understanding of the mechanisms behind the aggressive marketing and seductive packaging of consumer products, which they extended to include the brand name merchandising of their own work and image. As their fame increased due to their skillful manipulation of mass-media outlets, such as television, popular magazines, and radio, both artists adopted instantly recognizable public personas, but whereas Dalí presented an image of outrageous excess, often accompanied by scandalous behavior, Warhol preferred to project a blank image akin to the cool, deadpan surfaces of his paintings of consumer products, celebrities, and scenes of death and disaster. In private, however, Warhol would abandon the mask of vacuous detachment and discuss sex, art and movies with Dalí, although the older artist's improbable accent, a mixture of Catalan, French and English, meant that he could not always follow his train of thought.

Warhol also shared Dalí's predilection for surrounding himself with an entourage of exotic, yet often self-destructive people, whose number included a fluctuating cast of transvestites, hermaphrodites, glamorous models, and minor actors. Such was the close relationship between the two groups that Warhol could never remember if "Dalí copied transvestites from me or I copied transvestites from Dalí." The Comtesse Isabelle de Bavière was originally part of the bizarre group that gathered around Dalí during his annual stay at the St. Regis Hotel in New York, before she changed her name to Ultra Violet and switched allegiance to the jet-set contingent of artists, groupies, hustlers, and celebrities that were drawn to Warhol's loft studio at 231 East 47th Street, which subsequently became known as "The Factory." As Warhol later lamented, his own retinue of artists, misfits and hangers-on failed to match the sycophantic "Court of Miracles" that Dalí gathered around him in New York: "It's like being with royalty or circus people. That's why I like being with Dalí – because it's not like being with an artist, he wouldn't be caught dead in a loft." The counter-cultural movement encouraged both artists to surround themselves with a sexually promiscuous, decadent atmosphere that was free from the constraints of conventional

bourgeois society, in line with their exploration of the forbidden and the repressed in their paintings.

Like Dalí, Warhol was a prolific artist who was constantly on the look out for new and exciting imagery, and often drew upon his friend's work for inspiration. A classic example of this act of appropriation can be found in Warhol's paintings and screenprints of the Chinese Head-of-State, Mao Zedong, begun in 1972, which clearly allude to Dalí's *Mao-Marilyn*, a composite photograph of the faces of Chairman Mao and Marilyn Monroe that he made with the help of Philippe Halsman around 1967. Warhol probably first came across this strange image, in which Mao looks like a drag queen, four years later, when it was used for the inner cover of the 1971 Christmas issue of the French edition of *Vogue*. When Hebe Dorsey asked Dalí why he combined the two portraits of Mao and Marilyn Monroe, he explained that: "the idea was to blend the two great matriarchal countries of the world, the United States and China. Those two civilizations are bound to have considerable impact on each other. For the next two years, people will talk about nothing else." It should also be pointed out that Dalí's choice of a 1952 photograph of Marilyn Monroe for this composite image might itself have been a subtle nod to Warhol's obsession with the deceased American screen actress.

At other times, Warhol simply followed in Dalí's footsteps, as when he designed a celebrated window display for Bonwit Teller, the exclusive department store on 57th Street in New York, in April 1961, some 22 years after Dali had accidentally crashed through the glass window of his own Surrealist display there. Both artists were adept at mining the annals of art history, especially in their late work when they became equally enthralled by the paintings of the Italian Renaissance. Warhol had made silkscreen versions of Leonardo's *Mona Lisa* as early as 1963, but in the mid-1980s he began work on an extensive series of pictures based on masterpieces by Botticelli, Raphael, Leonardo da Vinci, Uccello, and Piero della Francesca. The American artist's paraphrases of Leonardo's *The Last Supper* and Raphael's *Sistine Madonna* would have been unthinkable without the precedent of Dalí's own variations on the Old Masters. These works reflect their shared Catholic upbringing, although it remains unclear whether these artists were drawn to Italian Renaissance painting due to its religious iconography, or because of the universal fame and popular appeal of these majestic works of art. M.R.T.

Chronology

Montse Aguer

in collaboration with
Carme Ruiz and Teresa Moner

Chronology

1904

Salvador Felipe Jacinto Dalí Domènech is born in Figueres on May 11, the second son of Salvador Dalí Cusí, notary, and Felipa Domènech Ferrés. He is named after their first son who was born on October 12 1901 and died on August 1 1903.

1908

His sister, Ana María, is born. His father, Salvador, is a freethinker and instead of sending his son to a religious school, as befits the family's status, he enrolls him in the Escuela Pública de Párvulo (public school) of Figueres where he is put in Esteban Trayter's class. At home, the Dalís speak Catalan.

1910

The father's choice of school is not a success so he enrolls his son in the Colegio Hispano-Francés de la Inmaculada Concepción which had been inaugurated the previous year by the Christian Brothers. This is where Salvador learns French which will become his cultural language. During his six years at this school, he never shines as a student, in fact, he has to repeat his first year four times and his second year twice.

His first oil painting probably dates from this period: *Landscape (View of the environs of Figueres)*, 1910-14.

1912

At the beginning of July, the Dalís move to number 12, calle Monturiol, Figueres.

1913

It is probably during this period that Salvador starts reading art books or, more precisely, the *Gowan's Art Books* series. Three of these books are held in the Centre d'Estudis Dalínians of

Salvador Dalí with the jewel *El ojo del tiempo* in a photograph by Philippe Halsman, 1956

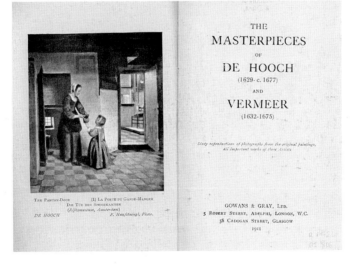

Salvador Dalí (first from the right) photographed in 1907 together with his sister Ana María (in the nurse's arms), his mother Felipa Domènech Ferrés (center) and his grandmother Maria Anna Ferrés, to whose right is his father Salvador Dalí Cusí. Caterina, Felipa's sister, is second from the left

The frontispiece of *The Masterpieces of De Hooch and Vermeer,* published by Gowans & Gray in 1911

the Fundació Gala-Salvador Dalí: *Ingres* (1913), *De Hooch and Vermeer* (1911), and *Boucher* (1911).[1]

1916

In the Summer, Salvador is sent away on holiday to the nearby El Molí de la Torre estate owned by the Pichot family. It is here, thanks to the collection of paintings belonging to the painter, Ramón Pichot (Barcelona 1871; Paris 1925), that Salvador discovers the French Impressionists. It is probably also Ramón Pichot, on whom Dalí later models himself. Pichot follows the Catalan Modernist and Symbolist movements and is a friend of Casas y Rusiñol. He divides his time between Cadaqués and Paris where he is a close friend of Pablo Picasso, who spent a long period in Cadaqués in 1910. His elementary school years over, he begins high school. In

the mornings, he goes to the Istituto de Figueres, the local school which teaches the official subjects, and, in the afternoons, he goes to the Marist Brother's College, which teaches more specialized subjects, to broaden his studies and deepen his knowledge.

Salvador also has lessons with Prof. Juan Núñez at the Escuela Municipal de Dibujo (Municipal School of Drawing) in Figueres. Juan Núñez (Estepona Malaga, 1877; Barcelona, 1963) is a draughtsman, an engraver and a painter trained in the classical school who, after studying at the Escuela Especial de Bellas Artes, Madrid, then won a scholarship to attend the Accademia Spagnola in Rome, where he lived for a few years. When he returned to Spain in 1906, he went to live in Figueres where he became a strong influence on his own pupils, thanks to his double duties as arts teacher at the high school and professor at the Escuela Municipal de Dibujo.

During 1916-17, Salvador Dalí begins sketching stories for his sister when she is ill.

Ana María Dalí in a photographic portrait by J. Carreras

467

Dalí (fifth from the left) with schoolfriends from the Institut de Figueres in 1916

Two of the illustrations for tales made by Dalí between 1916-17 for his sister

1917
Salvador's father organizes a viewing of his son's charcoal drawings at home.

1918
One of Salvador's drawings is published in the popular Catalan magazine, *En Patufet*.[2]

1919
Dalí takes part in an exhibition of several artists in the salons of the Societat de Concerts at the Figueres Municipal Theater, later to become the Teatre-Museu Dalí. It is Salvador Dalí's first official exhibition and he shares the space with two other Figueres painters: Josep Bonaterra Gras and Josep Montoriol Puig. A friend of Salvador's father, Joaquim Cusí, buys two of the paintings in the exhibition—Salvador's first sale. In the local publication, *Empordà Federal*, of January 11 1919, the critic Puvis sings Salvador's praises: "The man who can sense light as Dalí Domènech does, whose very being pulsates before the elegance of that fisherman, who at the age of sixteen dares to make such fiery and lush brush strokes as those in the Drinker, and who has as refined a decorative sense as that shown in his charcoal works, in particular the *Bulwark*, already belongs to that group of artists

who will always be in the public eye…We salute the new artist in the firm hope that in time our words—our own humble words—will become a prophesy: Salvador Dalí Domènech will become a great painter."[3]
Dalí collaborates with *Studium* magazine which that year, between January and June, publishes the works of a group of students and friends of the Figueres Institute, including drawings, a poem and the series of art books entitled *Los grandes maestros de la pintura*. The magazine's editor is Joan Xirau and the editorial staff are Ramon Reig, Jaume Miravitlles, Joan Turró, and Dalí himself who writes in an academic and scholarly style about the artists he admires: Goya (in January), El Greco (in February), Dürer (in March), Leonardo da Vinci (in April), Michelangelo (in May) and Velázquez (in June).[4]
Salvador, together with another group of friends from Figueres, is also involved in another magazine, this time the satirical *El sanyó Pancraci*; Salvador paints the imaginary portrait of this character. Only three editions of the magazine are published.
Dalí begins writing a diary in Catalan which is first published in 1994 under the title, *Un diari, 1919-1920: les meves impressions i records íntims*.[5]

1920
In this period, Dalí considers himself a mainly Impressionist painter, as reflected in his letter to his uncle, Anselm Domènech: "It is beginning to be clearer to me how difficult art is but I get a great deal of pleasure from art—more and more each time. I still admire the great French Impressionists: Manet, Degas and Renoir. May they help and guide me more clearly along my path!"[6]
Dalí begins writing the novel *Tardes d'estiu* (Summer Evenings). The novel begins by

Illustration for the calendar of *En Patufet* magazine, 1918

"The great Masters of painting. Velázquez," article by Salvador Dalí published in *Studium*, January 1, 1919

introducing the main character and sets the tone for the whole story: "Lluís was an orphan, his parents had died of the hereditary disease, consumption. The doctors had advised him to live in a mountain village and Lluís had chosen Horta Fresca— the prettiest and most picturesque—because he had a particularly artistic character and had devoted his life to painting. He was one of those romantic poets who live in the heart of Paris, who fall in love at the age of twelve and who

throw themselves into the Seine on a moonlit night because they are not understood."[7]
Dalí's father gives him an ultimatum: he can continue to be a painter on one condition: he must move to Madrid, to the Academy of Fine Arts, and study to be a teacher. Dalí accepts. His diary entry for April 12–16 states: "The following decision represents the highest and perhaps the most important point in my life, as it shows me which path I am to follow (with my family's approval): I will finish high school quickly, covering my last two years in one, if necessary. Then I will go to Madrid, to the Academy of Fine Arts. I intend to stay there for three years and work like mad. Even the Academy has a certain beauty. To sacrifice yourself to truth and cling on to it is never a bad thing. Then I will win a scholarship to study in Rome for four years and, when I return, I will be a genius and the world will admire me. Or maybe I will be despised and not understood, but I will still be a genius, a great genius... I'm sure I will."[8]
During the school year, Salvador studies and writes but in the Summer he dedicates himself to painting. The Dalís spend the Summer holidays in the fishing village, Cadaqués, because Dalí's father comes from there but also because of the friendship between the Dalí and Pichot families.
Salvador spends the whole school year thinking about going back to Cadaqués because that is where he can concentrate fully on his art. He writes in his diary, between June 15 and 19: "All I can think of these days is Cadaqués. I look at the calendar every day and get immense pleasure out of counting down the days to my departure... I am already getting all my things prepared, my painting equipment, and my eyes sparkle

when I look at the colors I keep in my cupboard, those shiny tubes of Can Teixidor in which I glimpse a whole world of hope."[9]
As there is not enough room to paint in the house in Cadaqués, the Pichot family let him use a room which Ramón Pichot had once used as a studio.

1921
January 6: Dalí and Joan Subias design the carriage of the Magi for the Figueres festival.
February 6: Dalí's mother dies.
May: Dalí designs the posters for the celebrations of the Holy Cross in Figueres.
October 15: Dalí's drawing, *Witches' Sardana*, is published in the special edition of *Empordà Federal* dedicated to Enric Morera and Pep Ventura.

1922
January 16-31: Dalí enters the "Concurs-exposició d'obres d'art originals d'estudiants" (Exhibition-competition of original art works by students) run by the Associació Catalana d'Estudiants which is held in the Galeries Dalmau, in Barcelona. He receives the university rector's prize for his work, *Market*. He also exhibits *Salomé*, *Smiling Venus*, *Dusk*, *Olive Trees*, *Tea "sur l'herbe,"* *Cadaqués* and *Celebration at the Hermitage*. The exhibition receives wide coverage in the press.[10]
Dalí finishes his studies with good grades as can be seen from the certificates from his school, the Instituto Técnico of Figueres.
May: he designs the posters for the program of the Holy Cross festival in Figueres .
July 2-16: Dalí exhibits fourteen works in the "Exposició d'artistes empordanesos" at the Salón de l' Orféo of Figueres, organized by the Orféo Germanor Empordanesa (section 3 of the Casino Menestral). The exhibition has

been organized to celebrate the inauguration of the Biblioteca Popular and the laying of the foundation stone of the Escuela Graduada.
Dalí applies for admission to the Escuela Especial de Pintura, in Madrid. While he is waiting for the reply, he writes to his uncle Anselm Domènech saying his greatest moment in Madrid up until then has been seeing the Velázquezes in the

Group photograph of the fifth grade at the Institut de Figueres, school year 1920-21

Cadaqués in the background, around 1921

469

Prado Museum, and that he is sure he will be admitted to the Escuela Especial.

He gets through the entry examination and moves to Madrid. He lives in the Residencia de Estudiantes where he becomes friends with a group of young students who later become important intellectuals and artists: Luis Buñuel, Federico García Lorca, Pedro Garfias, Eugenio Montes and Pepín Bello. He spends a lot of time visiting the Prado Museum while following his lessons with great interest, though he quite soon becomes disillusioned with them.

It is probably during this period that he first encounters Cubism, through both the Futurist catalogue that Pepito Pichot brings him from Paris and through the French art magazine, *Esprit nouveau*, to which Dalí has a subscription, thanks to his uncle Anselm Domènech who owned

Program for the celebrations for the festival of the Holy Cross in Figueres in 1922

an important bookshop in Barcelona.

Dalí decides to keep a notebook which he calls *Ninots. Ensatjos sobre pintura. Catalec dels cuadrus em notes* ("Essays on painting. Catalogue of paintings with notes"). The notebook is full of important information on Dalí's artistic development.[11]

Dalí has not been in Madrid long when his maternal grandmother, Maria Anna Ferrés, dies at the age of 80 on October 9. On December 22, 1922, his father marries Catalina Domènech Ferrés, sister of his first wife.

On December 30, the local press (*Alt Empordà*) announces that Dalí will be on the panel of judges to award the prize for the best carriages and the best children's lanterns (*fanalets*) in the Magi procession in Figueres on January 5.

1923

February 16: Carles Rahola gives a lecture at the Biblioteca Popular de Figueres on "Empordà in Muntaner's

Chronicle." For the occasion, a portrait in charcoal of Ramon Muntaner, by Dalí, is put up in the lecture room.

October 22: The Disciplinary Council of the Real Academia de San Fernando (Escuela Especial de Pintura, Escultura y Grabado) expels Dalí for a year. He is informed of this in a letter from the school secretary: "You are herewith informed that the Disciplinary Council, which met on the date above indicated, due to the scandal which occurred in the school courtyard on the afternoon of 17th of this month, and the insults directed at the teachers of said school and, as per the declarations made during a meeting of the said Council, and since it transpires that you are one of the most prominent participants in this act of serious lack of discipline, has decided to inflict upon you the punishment indicated in article 2, paragraph 10 of the University-scholastic disciplinary rules which amounts to a temporary expulsion from your current

course and consequent loss of rights to take the examinations for which you are enrolled."[12] The scandal to which the letter refers was a protest at the failure to appoint the prestigious painter Daniel Vázquez Diaz to the Chair of Painting—to the great disappointment of the students who supported him. Dalí was accused of being the leader of the student protest.

Return to Figueres. During these months, Salvador gets back into contact with Juan Núñez Fernández, a teacher from his earliest schooldays, and asks him to teach him the technique of engraving.

1924

January: one of Dalí's drawings from 1922 is published in issue no. 36 of *Alfar* magazine, La Coruña.

Some of his drawings are published in *España* magazine (issues of February 2 and March 15).

May 21: the young artist is arrested and put in the Figueres jail. The arrest is possibly a retaliation against his father's political activities; the latter being a man of liberal ideas who had put himself in the public eye during the previous year's elections in Figueres, which had been won by the Marquis of Olérdola. After nine days in prison, Dalí is transferred to the prison in Girona where he remains from May 30 to June 11, when he is finally released without charge.

September: Dalí returns to the Real Academia de San Fernando where he has to repeat the four subjects which he had not been able to complete the previous year due to his expulsion.

He continues to lead a happy and carefree life with his friends at the Residencia even though, as he says himself, "I avoided Lorca and the group, which increasingly grew to be his

FIGUERES
SANTA CREU DE 1922

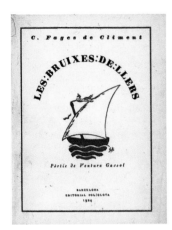

Cover of the book *Les bruixes de Llers* by Carles Fages de Climent, 1924

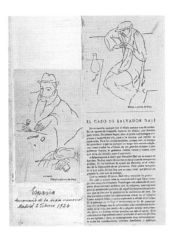

Illustrations for the article "El caso de Salvador Dalí," published in *España*, February 2, 1924

Illustration by Dalí published in "Alfar," January 1924

List of the works exhibited at the Galeries Dalmau

group. This was the culminating moment of his irresistible personal influence—and the only moment in my life when I thought I glimpsed the torture that jealousy can be."[13]
Dalí takes part in an adaptation of *Don Juan Tenorio* by Zorrilla, put on by Buñuel in the Residencia, on All Saints' Day. Buñuel's version is called *La profanación de Don Juan.* Buñuel plays Don Juan and Dalí his rival, Don Luis Mejía. Dalí illustrates *The Witches of Llers* by his friend, the poet Carles Fages de Climent.[14]

1925
Dalí spends Holy Week in Cadaqués with his friend Federico García Lorca. Soon afterwards, they start to write to each other.
Of the correspondence between the two artists only letters from Dalí to Lorca remain—barring a few rare exceptions. What we have helps us understand the deep and intense friendship binding the painter to the poet, and the great intellectual affinity between two young men who have a profound influence on each other. The relationship is maintained for several years and documented not only through their letters but also numerous portraits and

drawings which the two artists exchange over that time.
May 28: The inauguration of the "Primera Exposición de la Sociedad de Artistas Ibéricos" at the Palacio de Exposiciones del Retiro, Madrid. This exhibition, considered of fundamental importance for contemporary Spanish art, includes artists such as: Rafael Barradas, Norah Borges, José Moreno Villa, Ramón Pichot, José Gutiérrez Solana, José María Ucelay, Aurelio Arteta, Alberto Sánchez, Benjamín Palencia, and Ángel Ferrant. Dalí exhibits ten works, including *Portrait, Portrait of Luis Buñuel, Bather, Nude* and six still lifes.[15]
July-August: in a letter to Federico García Lorca, Dalí speaks of his current worries about painting: "Dear Friend, your letter brought me great joy. I think that 'The iron butterfly' sums up wonderfully the thinking on modern painting: everything must have the same consistency, eternity (rather than the same quality).
After Fauvism, it is the figures that still stand up, and nothing is as marvellous as feet pressed into the ground under the weight of the body, better than in Poussin. In Egypt you put both feet on the ground,

Xenius included, but from Egypt to the Mediterranean Polyclitas added the 'grace' of the free leg, and it is for this reason that Well Planted, when resting, stands on one leg. When I paint, I paint barefoot, I like to feel the ground in direct contact with my two feet. I am doing some experiments on constructing the atmosphere, or rather, on the construction of emptiness; I think the plasticity of emptiness is the thing of most interest but no-one has bothered with it even though this plasticity nearly always comes from the plasticity of mass.

I will keep you informed of the results of these experiments. I await your poems, for which I thank you very much. Kind regards to your brother. Here's a hug, SALVADOR."[16]

November 14-27: Dalí holds the first solo exhibition in the Galeries Dalmau, Barcelona, with seventeen paintings and five drawings. In the *La Veu de Catalunya* of November 27, Rafael Benet writes: "Dalí presents his own work in

A scene from the *Don Juan Tenorio* by Zorrilla, 1924

Federico García Lorca photographed in front of Dalí's *Still Life* (1924) Madrid, Fundación Federico García Lorca

Barcelona at the Galeries Dalmau, and enjoys great success with the intellectuals of the Ateneu, especially amongst the scholars. For the painters, however, the work of this worthy young man of 21 is not completely convincing…
In terms of temperament—we are led to suppose—Dalí has looked amongst the avant-garde theories for a hook to hang his own sensitivity on, desirous of things new, and of perfection. Nonetheless, our artist has perceived what is going on around him in a manner perhaps a little too cerebral: too much a

philosopher and not enough a painter. Due to the overall verticalist character and content of Dalí's art, at first sight, one has the impression of a complete lack of lyricism. If one looks more closely at the artist's work as a whole, including the more moderate works, one sees how this lyricism takes on a much more 'balanced' tone than one would have imagined. For this reason, Dalí appears to be more of an Italian Realist with 'Plastic Values' than a French-style Cubist, with the exception of Ozenfant. This affinity with Italy makes the young painter seem more of a decorator than a painter. In his less abstract tendencies one can see Neoclassicism in the manner of Casorati and even the more of 'academic' Ubaldo Oppi."

To celebrate Dalí's success with the Galeries Dalmau exhibition, two banquets are organized in his honor: one at the Hotel España, Barcelona, on November 21, and the other in Figueres on December 5.

1926
January 16: Inauguration of an exhibition dedicated to Catalan modern art, held in the Salón Permanente del Círculo de Bellas Artes, Madrid. It is the first of a series organized by the daily newspaper, *Heraldo de Madrid*. Dalí is among the forty-one artists participating in the event, showing two of his works: *Figure at a Window* and *Venus and Sailor (Homage to Salvat Papasseit)*.
In a letter dated March 1, Dalí's father, brimming with pride, writes of this event to his half-sister, Catalina Berta Cusí, born of his mother's first marriage, and to his brother-in-law, Josep Mª Serraclara: "We hear that you already know about our boy's success at the exhibition of Catalan modern art, organized in Madrid by the newspaper *Heraldo de Madrid*. The write-ups in the capital could not have been better for him. The painting of the window appeared in several Madrid periodicals, and the newspaper *Heraldo de Madrid* printed *Venus and Sailor* and an article analyzing and studying

the picture from all aspects. During the Madrid exhibition, the *Venus and Sailor* painting was bought by the eminent painter, Vázquez Díaz, for 500 pesetas. It is a seal of approval consecration, seeing as the buyer is a famous painter so, to help in such an extraordinarily horrible purchase, the boy offered it for the moderate sum of 100 duros.
In the first two weeks of April, the boy, the girl and Catalina are going to Paris. The boy wants to meet Picasso and see the pictures of the best contemporary artists. On their way back, they will pass by San Sebastian then go to Madrid. Once the boy has taken his third year exams, they will come back to Figureres."[17]
In this letter, Dalí's father refers to the exhibition's reviews in various Madrid newspapers, at the end of January. In the *Heraldo de Madrid* of January 26, Marjan Paszkiewicz writes:
"… One of the best exhibitors, in terms of promise if not result, was Dalí. Among the young who today practice the use of the paintbrush outside

Maruja Mallo, Ernestina Chamburch and Salvador Dalí, 1925

Salvador Dalí with Federico García Lorca and Pepín Bello at the Museo de Ciencias Naturales in Madrid, 1925

the Academy, Salvador Dalí is perhaps the one who shows the greatest gift for visual arts. A vast and youthful curiosity for new methods of painting lead him to tackle and resolve, with a rare graphic sense, the pictorial problems which continue to trouble various luminaries of modern art. In him, there is the constitution of the draughtsman in the broadest and noblest sense of the word. In line, Dalí finds an unlimited number of forms of expression without giving the feeling of a lack of color. In his *Venus*, the line adapts to the form; the form, however, does not bend to the plan of construction perhaps because this, coming from the now outdated Cubist formula, requires too many abstract elements and Dalí, who has an articulated sense of line, does not allow it to abandon completely the realist form. We have always believed that construction can become a pictorial element only in so far as it is a union of line and color. It must be a result and not a premise. In Dalí, construction has managed to transform itself into an imminent bias, easily explained by his inexperience and limited practice in working on nature; a bias in itself harmless or even beneficial for a shrewd character like his, as it pushes him to use his most salient ability: drawing. His meager use of color, which does not manage to add even a minimum of importance to the interpretation of the form, uncovers all the architectural framework of the *Venus* and makes it into a crude decorative project.

Figure at a Window is in a completely different line. It looks like an early Mantegna with its clarity and conciseness of profile. In this painting, the clarity is able to compensate for the imprecisions in the combining of line with light

Salvador Dalí in his studio in Figueres in 1926 alongside *Still Life* (1924)

The illustration *Venus and Sailor* published in *Heraldo de Madrid*, January 23, 1926

and color, by producing a pleasant sensation…"
The April edition of *Revista de Occidente* carries "Ode to Salvador Dalí" by Federico García Lorca.
April 11-28: Dalí leaves for Paris and Brussels accompanied by his aunt (stepmother) and sister. It is on this trip that Manuel Ángeles Ortiz, who Dalí knows through Lorca, introduces him to Picasso. Dalí shows him two of his works: *Girl from Figueres* and *Departure (Homage to the Noticiario Fox)*. In Paris, Dalí and Buñuel do the rounds of the galleries, go to the Spanish painters' meetings (*tertulias*) at the Café de la Rotonde, and visit the homes/studios of Millet in Fontainebleau, Versailles and the Louvre. After Paris, the three go to Brussels where they visit the Royal Museums.
June 14: Back at the Escuela Especial, Dalí refuses to be

«VENUS Y UN MARINERO», por Salvador Dalí.

*Heraldo de Madrid
23 enero 1926.*

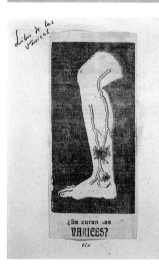

Libro de las varices, 1926

Cover of the book *L'oncle Vicents* by Josep Puig Pujades, 1926

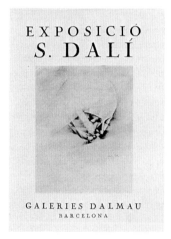

Dalmau exhibition catalogue, 1926

examined in the theory of Fine Arts saying that the examiners do not have the necessary competence to judge him and his preparatory work. As a result, after a meeting of the School Disciplinary Council, and in line with a royal decree, Dalí is definitively expelled from the Real Academia de San Fernando, on June 20. However, judging from his academic record, his time at the Academia was not all a waste of time.

Early Summer: In a letter to Federico García Lorca, Dalí starts speaking, for the first time, about the foundations of what will become one of his most transcendent articles, "Sant Sebastià": "I am writing to you about Saint Objectivity again, who is now called Saint Sebastian. Cadaqués is 'reason enough', to go further is already an excessive, but excusable sin; excessive depth could also be worse or could be ecstasy. I don't like things that I find extraordinarily likeable, I run away from things that could put me into ecstasy, like I run away from cars, ecstasy is a danger to intelligence…"[18]

Dalí returns to Figueres and devotes himself fully to his painting.

Dalí illustrates *L'oncle Vicents* by J. Puig Pujades, published by Políglota, Barcelona.

October: Dalí takes part in the "I Saló de Tardor" (First

Autumn Salon) held in the Sala Parés of the Establiments Maragall, Barcelona. He exhibits two pictures: *Woman Sewing* and *Penya-Segats (Woman by the Cliffs)*.

October 16-November 6: Salvador Dalí, together with other artists including Robert Delaunay, Raoul Dufy, Albert Gleizes, Francis Picabia, Rafael Barradas, Joan Miró, Manolo Hugué and Ramón Pichot, takes part in the "Exposició de Modernisme Pictòric Català confrontada amb una selecció d'obres d'artistes d'avantguarda extrangers" at the Galeries Dalmau. Dalí exhibits *Still Life*, known as *Still Life in Moonlight*, and two other works with the same title, *Mannequin*, one of which is known as *Mannequin (Barcelona Mannequin)*

In December, he completes two illustrations for *Conte de Nadal*, by J.V. Foix, published in the Sitges magazine, *L'Amic de les Arts*.

December 31-January 14, 1927: The Galeries Dalmau in Barcelona organize the second exhibition dedicated to Dalí. Twenty-three paintings and seven drawings are exhibited.

1927
February 1: Dalí begins his military service in the castle of San Fernando, Figueres.
February 28: Sebastià Gasch writes in the *L'Amic de les Arts*: "…We too, like Benet who wrote in *La Veu*, believe that the true Dalí, the strong, sincere Dalí, is the Dalí of the *Venus and Sailor* from the neo-Cubist Academy, and the *Penya-Segats (Woman by the Cliffs)*. In this style, the artist has produced works which are close to perfection. We do not think, however, that Dalí should violate his character because the character should not be betrayed without reason, and in this intelligent neo-Classicism, he should force

himself to go beyond what he has already achieved and allow a touch of humanity to penetrate his logic.
Lately, Dalí, who is not lacking in a little snobbery, has allowed himself to be guided by fashion and thrown himself unrestrainedly into the creation of canvasses in the style of the most recent works of Picasso…"
After the exhibition, Dalí receives a letter from Picasso's art dealer, Paul Rosenberg, who says he is interested in his work. Dalí does not reply. A little later, he writes to Federico García Lorca of his concerns: "Dear Federico, I

spent nearly a month in Barcelona with my exhibition and now I am back in Figueres. It is wonderful: I have a new set of gramophone records and lots of old and new things to read.

And lots of pictures at my *fingertips*, not in my *head*.

As you can see, I am 'inviting' you to my new type of Saint Sebastian which simply involves turning the Arrows into Soles. What makes Sebastian agonize deliciously is the principle of elegance. In him, there is a sense of anti-elegance which in *a cowardly way turns into convalescence*; but it had to be like that and I have been suggesting this to you for some time, perhaps with the new change, we will one day find the true cold temperature of the old Saint Sebastian's arrow. Rigol, the saint, spoke to me about you and many other things. I hope it is true that they are publishing your extraordinary books. Have you received a *Gaceta de les Arts* with the reproductions? Good-bye. *Greetings* to the people of distinction of the *Litoral*.

I hope to hear from you. Why don't you write to me much? The other evening, in Hospitalet, Barradas showed me a clownish portrait of you and Maroto. I nearly cried. What a truly wonderful Japanese Suchard chocolate you are!"[19]

March 12: The premiere of *La família d'Arlequí* (The Harlequin Family), at the Teatro Íntimo, Barcelona, a play written and directed by Adrià Gual. It is introduced as a "session of theatrical"; Dalí does the set-designing.

In a letter dated May 10, Dalí senior writes to his half-sister and brother-in-law, Josep Mª Serraclara, of his trip to Barcelona to see García Lorca's first work, *Mariana Pineda*, staged at the Teatro Goya on

June 24, and for which Dalí junior designed the sets and costumes: "In the Goya, Xirgu has put on a piece by the great Andalusian poet, Federico García Lorca, who is as great as he is unknown. The title of the work is Mariana Pineda; the heroine of Granada, where the poet was born and still lives. This young man will be much talked of, his health and lifespan permitting. Lorca wanted the boy to design the sets, two of which are wonderful for their grace, feeling and novelty. The boy has not completely finished or decided on the other two yet. … These sets are the first of the boy's works that have managed to make me understand clearly why he has received such praise from the intellectuals of Spain. It is something new in set-design and will draw a great deal of attention."[20]

The next morning sees the inauguration of an exhibition of the poet's drawings, in the Galeries Dalmau, sponsored by his Catalan friends. Salvador Dalí reports on it in the September edition of *La Nova Revista*: "… The poetic system of Lorca's drawings leans towards an organic immateriality, heralded by a most elegant and philological calligraphy. Lorca, who is profoundly Andalusian, has a very ancient sense of the relationship of color and architecture translated into that harmonious, uncontrolled asymmetry which characterizes the most pure of Oriental plastic arts."

July 31: Dalí publishes the "Sant Sebastía" essay, dedicated to Lorca, in *L'Amic de les Arts*. This article signals the start of an intense and regular collaboration with the magazine, which continues until 1929.

July: Dalí illustrates the article "Del cinema dins el sistema de les belles arts di Alexandre

Plana" published in *La Nova Revista* of Barcelona.

Dalí spends the Summer in Cadaqués. Lorca and Regino Sainz de la Maza go to visit him.

September: Joan Miró and his art dealer, Pierre Loeb, go to meet Dalí in Figueres. Both are deeply affected by his latest works, *Apparatus and Hand* and *Honey is Sweeter than Blood*. A few months later, Miró writes to him: "Dalí, my friend, I am so happy to have received your drawings.

You are without a doubt a very gifted man with a brilliant career ahead of you in Paris. Pierre wrote to me saying how much he had been affected. He seems well disposed towards you. He told me he had given some photos of your work to Zervos of the *Cahiers d'Art*. I think everything will work out well for you but you must never stop hammering away, not even for a moment.

Have you sent your latest drawing to Pierre? I would like you to. I would rather keep mine to show to other people in person. Before I close, I would like to ask you for photos of things of yours that belong to other stages or states of mind in your life. I think it is important that these things are also known. Anyway, don't stop persisting but don't get impatient. I wish you good health. Your good friend and companion—and pleased to be so.
Miró"[21]

Loeb, on the other hand, does not show the same interest as Miró. In fact, a little earlier, he had written: "Dear Sir, I looked at your photos with interest. You can send me more. I will consider taking up your work although I think you are still flitting, a little hurriedly, from one influence to another. I hope to see your own personality emerging. I am convinced that you will soon find your way and, with the gifts you have,

you will have a good career as a painter, I am sure.
In any case, I will closely follow your development.
Best regards,
Pierre"[22]

In the same period, Paul Rosenberg shows renewed interest in Dalí's work: "Sir, I did in fact write to you some time ago, at the time of your exhibition at the Galeries Dalmau, in Barcelona. I was very surprised not to have received a reply to my letter. I have the photos that said letter contained. I will study them carefully.

When you come to Paris, please do me the honor of coming to see me.
I await your news.
Yours sincerely,
Paul Rosenberg"[23]

October 8-21: Dalí takes part in the "II Saló de Tardor" organized by the Sala Parés in Barcelona, where he shows his *Apparatus and Hand* and *Honey is Sweeter than Blood*.

The October edition of *L'Amic de les Arts* carries an essay by Dalí entitled "Els meus quadros del Saló de Tardor."

1928

January: Dalí participates to the group exhibition "Manifestación de arte de vanguardia," held to mark the first anniversary of the magazine *La Gaceta Literaria*. Dalí contributes three drawings.

January 15: *La Gaceta Literaria* publishes a poem by Dalí dedicated "To Lídia of Cadaqués."

February: Lorca publishes the magazine *Gallo*, in Granada, of which there are two issues. Dalí draws the cockerel emblem and all the illustrations of the first issue.

In the same month, Filippo Tommaso Marinetti gives a lecture at the Teatre Tívoli of Barcelona. In an interview some time later, the Futurist writer and poet mentions Salvador Dalí as one of his followers in Catalonia.

March: Salvador Dalí, Lluís Montanyà and Sebastià Gasch publish the "Manifest Groc" (Catalan Antiartistic Manifesto) which their Granada friends translate and publish in the second issue of *Gallo* (April), describing it as "the most interesting thing about the Catalan youth of today."[24] The manifesto provokes a lot of negative reaction and most critics class it as Futurist, in other words, outdated.

May 13: *L'Amic de les Arts* magazine organizes "El Centaure," at the Ateneu in Sitges, a meeting attended by Josep Carbonell, J.V.Foix, Sebastià Gasch and Salvador Dalí. The aim of the meeting is to present the latest trends in contemporary art to the public. The most audacious speech is Dalí's, who, amongst other things, proposes the demolition of Barcelona's Gothic quarter and its substitution with reinforced concrete structures, the abolition of the sardana (a traditional dance) and a move to combat regionalism in all its forms.

May 21: Dalí takes part in the "Exposición Provincial de Bellas Artes" at the Casino Menestral Figuerense, opened during the celebrations of the Holy Cross festival. He contributes nine works: *Mannequin, Apparatus and Hand, Still Life, Still Life, Mannequin, Arlequín, Still Life, Honey is Sweeter than Blood* and *Mannequin*. The exhibition also includes a cycle of lectures finishing with a dissertation by Dalí on Surrealism. At the end of the lecture, when he is about to pronounce the closing words, the mayor of Figueres, Ramon Bassols, suddenly drops down dead.

September: Dalí's reticence in welcoming the publication of García Lorca's book, *Romancero Gitano* causes a

certain cooling in their relationship. In a letter which Santos Torroella dates to the beginning of September 1928, Dalí writes to his friend: "Dear Federico, I calmly read your book and cannot help but comment on a few things. Naturally, it is impossible for me to agree with even one of the opinions of the great, putrefied pigs who have commented on it. Andrenio, etc., etc. but I think that my opinions on poetry, *which are now starting to come together*, could be of interest to you. The best part of the book is the *last* part, the martyrdom of St. Eulalia, and the points about incest—*Rumor de rosa encerrada*. These things already contain much less theatricality, they are a lot less anecdotal than the others, etc.

The *worst thing* for me is the story of the gentleman who *goes to the river*. The grace, produced by a spiritual state based on an evaluation which has been sentimentally deformed by *anachronism*. The one about the cassock of the little saint, St. Gabriel, in his alcove; it seems to me, today, that in whatever production, I only admit *rage* in creating it, a sort of immorality: this is what has been done by the French, by the disgusting and inadmissable French *esprit*, Cocteau, etc., and by which we have all been tainted.

Your current poetry falls fully into the *traditional* category and I can see in it *the greatest poetic substance that has ever existed*: but!... utterly bound by the rules of ancient poetry, incapable, sadly, of moving us and satisfying our current desires. Your poetry is bound, hook, line and sinker, to the old poetry. You, perhaps, will think some of your images daring, or you may find a lot of your works rather irrational but I can tell you that your poetry is limited to *illustrating* the most

Salvador Dalí and Lídia Noguer in Cadaqués around 1928

stereotypical and conformist common ground. I am, for the record, convinced that, today, the effort in poetry only makes sense if it is cut off from the ideas that our intelligence has moulded artificially in order to give them their own precise, true significance.

In reality, there is no relationship between two dancers and a hive of bees, unless it is the same relationship as between Saturn and the little caterpillar asleep in its chrysalis; unless, *in reality*, there is *no difference* between the dancing couple and a hive of bees.

The hands of a clock (don't give any weight to my examples, I am not trying to be particularly poetic) start to have true value the moment they stop telling you the time, lose their "circular" rhythm and their arbitrary mission (to tell the time) which our intelligence has forced them to do, and they *escape* from that clock to go about in that place which corresponds to the sex of breadcrumbs.

You move between ideas that are acceptable and the anti-poetic. You speak of a horseman and presume he is mounted on a horse and

that the horse is galloping; *this is perhaps an exaggeration* because, in *reality*, you should *check* if it really is the horseman who is on top, if instead of reins they are not extensions of *his own hands*, if, in reality, the hairs on the horseman's balls don't travel faster than the horse and if the horse is not actually something immobile and attached to the ground with strong roots…, etc., etc. Imagine, then, what it is to arrive at the concept of a civilian guard, as you do. Poetically, a civilian guard does not exist unless it is a happy, beautiful figure, alive and resplendent in its good qualities and for the little protrusions sticking out from it, and for the little straps that are a visceral part of the same little beast, etc., etc. But you…—putridly— your civilian guard—what does it do? Bla, bla, bla, bla unreality, unreality.

–Anti-poetry–

The formation of arbitrary ideas about things.

You need to leave the little things *free* of the conventional ideas into which intelligence has forced them. Then these sweet little things will work on their own, in harmony with their true and *consubstantial* being. May they decide for themselves the direction in which their shadows fall! And maybe, the things we thought would cast the darkest shadow will not cast any shadow at all, etc., etc. Ugly-beautiful? Words that have ceased to have any meaning. Horror is another story, it is what provides us, far away from any *esthetic*, with the understanding of reality since lyricism is only possible in the more or less approximate ideas that our intelligence can have of reality.

An article dedicated to you is being published in the *Gaceta*. In it, I talk of these things as well as the importance of the strictly objective data obtained anti-artistically through a rigorous analytical method. But forget it; every day, I could write less, like this, by letter but instead write long and substantial articles, full of ideas. My little Federico, in your book, which I have brought with me to read in these mineral places, I saw you, little creature that you are, as an erotic bug, with the sex and *small* eyes of *your body*, your hairs and your fear of death, and your desire that, should you die, *the gentlemen should be told*; your mysterious spirit made up of little idiotic *enigmas* strictly in line with your horoscope; your thumb strictly in line with your penis and with the humidity of lakes of dribble from some species of *hairy planet*. I love you for what your book reveals you to be which is completely the opposite of what the putrids made of you. A Moorish gypsy with black hair, the heart of a boy, etc., etc., all this *Nestorian* Lorca, decorative, anti-real, non-existent which could only have been created by pigs of artists, a far cry from the hairs and bears and soft, hard and liquid characters that surround us, etc., etc.

You, beast with little nails, you from whom death will sometimes grab half your body or will rise up through your little nails to your shoulders in a completely useless effort! I have drunk of death upon your back, in the moments in which you absented yourself from your big arms which, if nothing else, were two wrinkled covers whose folds were unconscious of and unyielding to the ironing of the tapestries of the Residencia; … I love and admire you, the soul that you can see in your book, that big soul which, the day it loses its fear, will send to hell the Salinases, will finally abandon Rhyme, Art as understood by the pigs—you will do things that are fun, horrifying… [illegible], wrinkled, poetic, like no other poet has ever done before.

Good-bye. I believe in your inspiration, your sweat, your astronomic fate.

This Winter [?] I invite you to launch us into the *void*. I have been here for days now but I had lots of confidence.

Now I know something about *Sculpture* and REAL clarity, now, a long way away from any ESTHETIC.

Hugs.

DALÍ

Surrealism is *one* way to escape. The important thing is *the* Escape.

Through my style, I am keeping myself on the edge of Surrealism but it is something alive. As you can see, I don't talk about it like before; I have the pleasure of thinking very clearly about last Summer. Clever, eh?"[25]

Lorca admits to Sebastià Gasch that he thinks Dalí's letter is "intelligent and arbitrary" and, to his mind, it represents "an interesting poetic essay." Despite the distance that separates the two friends, there is no rancor between them, as can be seen from the fact that Dalí illustrates one of García Lorca's poems in *La Gaceta Literaria* of January 1, 1929, and from a letter the poet writes to Dalí on his return from New York (late Autumn 1930): "My dearest friend, Salvador, How long has it been since we met? I would love to talk to you and I really need to talk to you. I spent a wonderful year in New York and now I find that, since I don't know you, I don't know what to say… I want to talk to you. I have lived too long without communication of your friendship. Tell me what you think. Write me a long letter. Good-bye, yours as ever. Federico"[26]

October 6-28: Dalí takes part in the "III Saló de Tardor" set up in the Sala Parés. He contributes two works: *Big Thumb, Beach, Moon, and Decaying Bird* and *Two Figures on a Beach*, the latter later being known as *Unsatisfied Desires*. The gallery's director, Joan Anton Maragall, thinks it better not to exhibit the second work which he thinks obscene, as explained in a letter to the artist dated October 3: "Distinguished friend, I have just received your two canvases… I would be very embarrassed to exhibit one of

García Lorca and Dalí dressed as soldiers in 1928

them and I do not wish the Saló to be the object of any polemic which would discredit its success which I think it the responsibility of all of us to protect. I invite you to put yourself in my shoes and imagine what the public of Barcelona would feel were they to be invited to an exhibition in which they found work which mortified them. I invite you to put yourself in my shoes and

Salvador Dalí, *Bird-fish* with Cadaqués in the background, around 1928

Paul Éluard and Gala in Arosa, ca. 1929

understand how embarrassing it is for me to have to speak to you in such terms—as embarrassing as if I were to say nothing and exhibit the piece. I would be most grateful if you would relieve me of this obligation by allowing me not to exhibit this work despite the fact that I am very sorry about it. I trust in your help and await your reply by telephone or telegram.

Your most affectionate servant and friend."[27]

At first, Dalí wants to take back both canvasses and refuses to give the lecture but he later changes his mind and agrees to exhibit just the "permissible" work. The lecture "Catalan art and the most recent aspects of the young intelligencia" went ahead as planned on October 16 and caused much controversy. The text of the speeches was later published in *La Revista* (July-December 1928).

October 18-December 9: Dalí takes part in the XXVII International Exhibition of Paintings in Pittsburgh (the

Carnegie prize) with the following works: *The Basket of Bread, Seated Girl* and *Ana María*.

October 22-November 6: Dalí takes part in the opening of the Winter exhibition at the Galeries Dalmau, Barcelona, with three works: *Female Figure and Male Figure on a Beach, Female Nude* and *Two Figures on a Beach*. The last piece, which had been rejected by the "III Saló de Tardor', was exhibited only after the art dealer, Dalmau, had applied a cork to the appropriate point to avoid any controversy.
On November 24, Dalí senior writes to his half-sister, "There is no news. The boy is working on the next exhibition to be held in Paris. It will be in April or May and his whole artistic future depends on it. He has already finished the portrait of Miss Abadal. You will be able to see it, too, as it will be shown in Barcelona."[28]

1929
During January, Salvador Dalí and Luis Buñuel meet up in Figueres to work on the script of a film provisionally entitled

Dangereux de se pencher au dedans ("It is Dangerous to Lean in"). It is on this script that the director bases a film made in Paris between April 2 and 17. The film is finally called *Un Chien andalou* ("An Andalusian Dog").
One of Dalí's illustrations is used for the publication of "Degollación de los Inocentes" by García Lorca in *La Gaceta Literaria* of January 15, 1929. March 20: The "Exposición de pintura y escultura de españoles residentes en París" opens in the Botanical Gardens of Madrid, organized by the Sociedad de Cursos y Conferencias. The attention of the public and critics is particularly drawn to Dalí's five works: *Apparatus and Hand, Sterile Efforts*—later known as *Cenicitas (Little Ashes)*— *Female Nude, Honey is Sweeter than Blood, Female Figure and Male Figure on a Beach*.
Issue no. 31, the last issue, of the avant-garde magazine *L'Amic de les Arts* comes out on March 31. Its publication had stopped on December 31 of the previous year. Its concept and most of the text

were the work of Dalí whose articles were a profession of the Surrealist faith.
The painter goes to Paris in the first half of April and stays until the beginning of June to follow the making of the film, *Un Chien andalou*. His stay in Paris allows him to follow the advice Miró had given him in a letter dated March 3: "Most esteemed friend, I received your very interesting letter of the 2nd. I think your idea of holding an exhibition in Paris without first doing some ground work yourself is a mistake. If you don't do this, you will nearly certainly pass unobserved, so neutralizing your offensive and leaving yourself out of combat for a long time—bearing in mind that if you want an exhibition that makes a strong impression, you are not going to achieve it in a few weeks or even months. I think it would be a good idea if you came here for a few months to prepare the ground: you have good friends here and we will all do everything we can…"[29]
Miró introduces Dalí to the social life of the capital and puts him in contact with the Surrealist group whose activities Dalí already knows about through reading specialist magazines. He meets Magritte, Arp and Camille Goemans who introduce him to Paul Éluard. Dalí signs his first contract with Goemans to hold an exhibition in the Autumn. During his stay in Paris, Dalí writes seven articles for Barcelona's daily paper, *La Publicitat*. The series is called "Documental-París-1929" and Dalí writes of the discoveries he has made in the French capital that week, such as commentaries on new poets and paintings that had particularly moved him, and the word going round Paris on the film, *Un Chien andalou*.[30]
June 6: The preview of *Un Chien andalou* is held in the

Studio des Ursulines cinema. On July 3, the film is shown at the home of the Vicomte de Noailles and at the beginning of September, it is presented at the film festival in the Swiss town of La Sarraz where, according to Dalí, it won the praise of Sergej M. Eisenstein. The filmmaker, Jean Vigo, was deeply moved by the film and wrote, "Dishonor to those who, during their puberty, killed what they could have become and who look for it in earth and sea where the water drags our memories and our sorrows until, with the arrival of Spring, what they are decays. *Cave canem...* Beware of the dog, it bites..."[31]

On October 1, *Un Chien andalou* has its first public

Gala, Salvador Dalí and two fishermen at Cadaqués, around 1929

showing in Studio 28, an experimental salon with 400 places, owned by Jean Mauclaire.

Dalí spends the Summer in Cadaqués where he is joined by friends: Goemans with his companion Yvonne, René Magritte and his wife, Luis Buñuel, and Paul Éluard and Gala with their daughter, Cécile. In September, when the whole group returns to Paris, Gala stays behind for a few weeks.

At the end of September, Gala and Cécile leave Cadaqués bound for Paris. Gala takes *Lugubrious Game* with her, as requested by Éluard, and perhaps others of Dalí's paintings.

Once Gala has left, Dalí devotes himself to preparing new works for Goemans' exhibition and soon finishes

Portrait of Paul Éluard, *Accommodations of Desire* and *The Great Masturbator*.

October 6-November 3: Dalí takes part in the group exhibition "Abstrakte und surrealistische Malerei und Plastik" in the Kunsthaus, Zurich, contributing two pieces: *Bathers* and *Female Nude*.

November 25-December 5: The first Dalí solo exhibition in Paris opens at the Galerie Goemans. André Breton writes the prologue to the catalogue. Before the opening, the gallery sells some of Dalí's paintings, including *Lugubrious Game* to the Vicomte de Noailles, and *Accommodations of Desire* to André Breton.

Dalí is not there for the opening of the Paris exhibition because two days earlier he left for Barcelona and Sitges in the company of Gala.

The relationship between the painter and his family gets worse and worse and strong tension builds up between father and son. Dalí's relationship with Gala, begun that Summer, is doubtless the cause of the change that Dalí senior made to his will on September 26—which effectively disinherited his son. Moreover, a piece exhibited by Dalí at the Galerie Goemans in which an image of the Sacred Heart bears the inscription "Sometimes I spit with pleasure on the portrait of my mother" creates a great outcry in the family. (Eugenio D'Ors publishes an article in *La Gaceta Literaria* of December 15 on the outcry caused by the exhibition and the pieces presented there.) Buñuel, who was in Figueres to work with Dalí on *L'Âge d'or* is witness to a heated argument between father and son, as he explains in his memoirs, which ends with the latter being thrown out of his father's house. Despite this, Dalí and Buñuel go to Cadaqués where, from November 29 to

Salvador Dalí, Paul Éluard and Gala, ca. 1929-30

December 6, they work on the script of the new film, *L'Âge d'or* (originally called *La Bête andalouse*) which will be produced by the Vicomte de Noailles.

1930

January 10: Dalí and Gala go to the South of France where they spend a few months in a studio of the Hôtel du Château, in Carry-le-Rouet, near Marseille. Dalí begins painting *The Invisible Man* a piece he will continue working on until 1933 then leave unfinished. At the same time, he writes *La Femme visible* ("The Visible Woman"), which will be published at the end of the year.

March: When the Vicomte de Noailles learns that Goemans is about to close the gallery, he offers Dalí his help. The artist writes to him saying, "Now that I have understood, following our conversation, that it would not be difficult or too troublesome for you to give me a hand, I have decided to ask you to help me realize my plan to live in Cadaqués. I have just found out some facts and figures about this and I know that with 20,000 francs I could buy a small fisherman's cottage and also set it to rights in terms

Still from the film *Un Chien andalou*, 1929

The Fishing hut at Port Lligat sold to Dalí by Lídia Noguer, 1930

Gala at Port Lligat in the 1930s

of hygiene and comfort."[32]
The Viscount agrees to the request and, to give him some practical help, buys the oil painting *The Old Age of William Tell.*
Dalí buys a fisherman's cottage in Port Lligat from Lídia Noguer. He stays there every year from Spring to Autumn. Over the years, he adds new sections so that the final structure becomes Dalí's permanent residence. Dalí gives us clues as to the complex structure and surprising labyrinthine layout of his Port Lligat home, "Our house has grown just like a real biological structure, cell by cell. A new cell, or room, corresponds to each new impulse in our lives. The nucleus was supplied by Lídia's paranoid delirium; she paid us her respects by giving us the first cell.[33]
In his memoirs, *My Last Breath*, Buñuel minimizes Dalí's contribution to the script of *L'Âge d'or* and implies that he only accepted one of Dalí's suggestions: the scene in which a man is walking in the public

gardens with a stone on his head; he passes in front of a statue and the statue also has a stone on its head. Nevertheless, letters and changes to the script written in in pencil by Buñuel contradicts this and show how Dalí worked in close collaboration with the director right up until the start of the shooting of the film at the beginning of March.
Dalí and Gala leave for Barcelona: they board ship at Marseille on March 10. Once in Cadaqués, it seems the Hotel Miramar does not allow them to stay, according to Dalí senior who says the couple had to stay in a small pension.
Dalí senior's letter of March 18 to the Serraclara family, clearly shows how he wanted to distance himself from his son: "You will not receive anything from the boy just as I received nothing, not even best wishes. We have no news of him and have no desire to receive any. We have brought into the world a perverted son on whom you cannot depend for anything. Perhaps one day he will turn up using the excuse that he wants to visit you. Be very careful because if he comes it will only be to ask for money. If it should happen, do not give him anything because it would be an affront to us and, moreover, I would not pay you back for

what you gave him—and neither would he, for that matter. …"[34]
After a week of preparations to start the restructuring work on the fisherman's cottage, Dalí and Gala return to Barcelona where, on March 22, the painter gives the lecture "Posició moral del Surrealisme" (The Moral Position of Surrealism) in the Ateneu. The talk is published in issue no. 10 of the *Hèlix* magazine of Villafranca del Penedès.
When Dalí and Gala get back to Port Lligat, they are pursued by the Civil Police who were set on them by the terrible notary, Dalí senior. They only stay in Port Lligat for a few hours. Dalí's father writes to Buñuel asking him to tell his son never to return to Cadaqués. "My

esteemed Friend, I imagine you have received my letter of last Saturday. If you are still friends with my son, would you do me a favor. I do not write to him because I do not have his address.
Yesterday, I have been told, he passed through Figueres and went to Cadaqués with madame. He was lucky to have only stayed in Cadaqués for a few hours because, in the evening, as per their orders, the Civil Police paid him a visit. He saved himself some trouble because if he had stayed the night in Cadaqués he would have been in big trouble. Yesterday—evening or night— he left for Paris where I think he is staying for eight days. You will know madame's address; could you tell [my son] not to

go back to Cadaqués for the simple reason that he is not allowed to stay there even for two or three hours. Even more so because matters would become so complex that he would not even be able to go back to France.

Any damage he suffers will be his own fault (my son's) as I imagine you will inform him. My son has no right to spoil my life. Cadaqués is my spiritual refuge, my serenity is disturbed if my son is there. Moreover, it is the place where my wife is buried and it will be destroyed if my son sullies it with his indecent behavior.

I am not prepared to suffer again. For this reason, I have arranged everything so that I will not have to suffer violence this Summer.

As things stand today, the precautions I have taken should be enough to stop my son polluting us this Summer and next.

Should they prove not to be enough, I will use any means, including personal assault. My son will not come to Cadaqués, he must not come, he cannot come.

Neither this Summer nor the next, because I have other ways of preventing him from molesting me, but if the measures available to me are not enough then I want us to fight it out, just the two of us, then we will see who wins, and I can tell you, from the moment

Salvador Dalí in front of his reflection, 1930s

I decide I want to win at any cost, I will do anything to guarantee my victory. I will track down people who will help me to give him a thrashing or I will look for a chance to hit him myself without being hit back. It is not a case of being cowardly because the victim knows what I intend to do and, consequently, if he wants to come to Cadaqués, he can do anything he likes to defend himself or attack (whichever he thinks best).

His theories have completely convinced me. He thinks that in this world it is essential to do all the wrong possible and I am convinced of it. I cannot cause him any spiritual damage because he is completely corrupt but I can cause him physical harm because he is still made of flesh and bone. A hug from your most affectionate friend.
Salvador Dalí.[35]

March: The artist takes part in the collage exhibition at the Galerie Goemans in Paris which, soon afterwards, closes its doors for the last time. Dalí, who contributes the work, *The First Days of Spring*, exhibits together with other artists, including Arp, Braque, Duchamp, Ernst, Gris, Miró, Magritte, Man Ray, Picabia, Picasso and Tanguy. The introduction in the catalogue, "La peinture au défi," is written by Louis Aragon.

Dalí's involvement with the Surrealist group deepens, especially with André Breton who sees in the young painter the renewal of the movement which, in this period, is afflicted with internal struggles. Dalí does the title-page of the *Second manifeste du Surréalisme* (1930) and Breton himself dedicates the manifesto to him with these words: "To Salvador Dalí whose name, for me, is synonymous with revelation in the most resplendent sense of the word and always a little

Salvador Dalí in the 1930s

Salvador Dalí in the 1930s

dazzling, as I have always understood it, with my affection, my faith and my blindest hope."

April 4: Buñuel arrives in Cap Creus with his troupe to begin filming the bandit scenes. Dalí has decided not to go with him, probably to avoid meeting his father but perhaps because he was worried about Gala's health.

Buñuel makes the most of his stay in Cadaqués and films *Menjant garotes* (Eating sea-urchins).

April: Dalí and Gala leave for Torremolinos, near Malaga, where they have been invited

Salvador Dalí in the 1930s

Salvador Dalí in the 1930s

Gala with Lídia Noguer's two sons during the production of the film *L'Âge d'or*, ca 1930

by the poet, José María Hinojosa. They stay for five weeks. Dalí keeps working on the *Invisible Man*.

Dalí's departure is announced by the Malaga press on May 22, 1930. On the way back to Paris, Dalí and Gala pass through Madrid where they stay for a few days and are included in a film by Ernesto Giménez Caballero.

June: Dalí meets Alfred H. Barr, director of New York's Museum of Modern Art, at the Vicomte de Noailles' house. Barr shows an interest in his work and encourages him to go to the United States.

Stills from the film
L'Âge d'or, 1930

June 21: Dalí signs a contract with Pierre Colle to whom he has been warmly recommended by the Vicomte de Noailles.
June 30: The first showing of the final version of the film, *L'Âge d'or*, with sound, is given in the Noailles' private cinema. The Dalí's spend the Summer in Cadaqués.
Éluard sends the couple the first issue of *Le Surréalisme au service de la révolution* which includes Dalí's "L'Âne pourri" (The Rotting Donkey), and full-page frames from *L'Âge d'or* . René Char, Paul Éluard and his companion María Benz ('Nusch') go to see Dalí in Port Lligat.
October: Dalí and Gala return to Paris for the first night of *L'Âge d'or*, once again living in the apartment that Éluard has rented in rue Becquerel.
October 22: Charles and Marie-Laure de Noailles organize a private showing of *L'Âge d'or* in the Cinéma du Panthéon. Buñuel is noticeable for his absence. The film provokes indignation amongst many of the aristocratic friends of the Noailles. One week later, Buñuel moves to Hollywood.
November 23-December 3: On November 28, on the occasion of the premiere of *L'Âge d'or* at Studio 28, an exhibition is set up in the foyer of the cinema with pieces by Arp, Dalí, Ernst, Miró, Man Ray and Tanguy. Dalí shows *Host as Ring*, *Paranoiac Woman-Horse (Invisible sleeping woman, lion, horse)*, *Birth of a Deity* and *The Widow*. On December 3, some members of the League of Patriots and others from the anti-Jewish League break into the cinema during the show and, for revenge, throw paint onto the screen and destroy some of the exhibited works. Following the scandal, a press campaign run by various newspapers, including *Le Figaro* and *L'Echo de Paris*, demands that the showing of

the film be stopped. On December 10, the Prefecture officially prohibits its showing. This decision makes necessary a further communication from the Board of Censors which had previously authorized the film's showing.
December 15: Éditions surréalistes publishes Dalí's *La femme visible* which brings together L'Âne pourri" (The Rotting Donkey), a piece in which the artist defines the basis of his paranoid-critical method, "La chèvre sanitaire," "Le grand masturbateur" and "L'amour." Dalí does the illustration of the title-page and two engravings whilst André Breton and Paul Éluard write the prologue.
In Figueres, Josep Puig Pujades shows Dalí senior a copy of *La femme visible* which the journalist had probably received directly from the author. Dalí senior is so disgusted that he immediately changes his will so that now his son is completely and definitively disinherited.
Dalí designs two posters for the celebrations of the tenth anniversary of the foundation of the Communist Party in France. In one of these, which reminds one of the pro-Soviet sketches he made ten years earlier in Figueres, there is a red flag bearing the letters USSR flying over a bonfire in which symbols of the Bourgeoisie are burning.

1931
On January 2, a month after the Studio 28 saga, Nancy Cunard organizes a private showing of *L'Âge d'or* at the Gaumont Co. Theatre, in London.
April 14: Proclamation of the Second Republic of Spain. The Surrealists publish a pamphlet, *Au feu!*, in which they maintain that it is necessary to set light to the convents, and declare that the Republic has become a Bourgeois farce. Dalí and

Buñuel probably sign the pamphlet as "foreign comrades."

June 3-15: The Galerie Pierre Colle, Paris holds its first exhibition dedicated to Salvador Dalí. Twenty-seven works are exhibited: sixteen oils, seven pastels, a copper plate image and three objects in the modernist style. In the catalogue, the artist writes, "…ornamental art above all, the most stereotyped ornamental art, in particular the one that, with the least conviction,, repeats and mixes memories of distant and diverse styles, not without a touch of fantasy. It is in such ornamentation that the future will investigate the automatism which is disclosed painfully and with cruelty by each accident, each cessation, each bifurcation, each convergence, that is to say, each symptom of latent content, all unfailingly foul in the most exemplary fashion."

André Lhote writes about the exhibition in the July 1 edition of *Nouvelle Revue Française*, "Paradoxically, Salvador Dalí is showing his recent work in the same gallery (Pierre Colle) that hosts the work of J.E. Blanche. Dalí is to contemporary what Lalique and Gustave Moreau are to oneirism. His instrument ably chisels forms which are strongly

La Femme visible, 1930

inspired by those of the Modernism dear to our childhoods. His harmonies are willingly those of the anatomy tables where blood is king. Sulphur mixes its acid tones with the lilac of cold mucous membranes and the blue of veins which appear under dead skin. Let us now have a quick word about *Mots de liberté*: there are members which have been sadistically cut off, decapitated trunks, seething entrails and sexual organs which the spatula has dispersed around the four corners of the painting." Julien Levy, busy with preparations for the opening of a contemporary art gallery in Madison Avenue, New York,

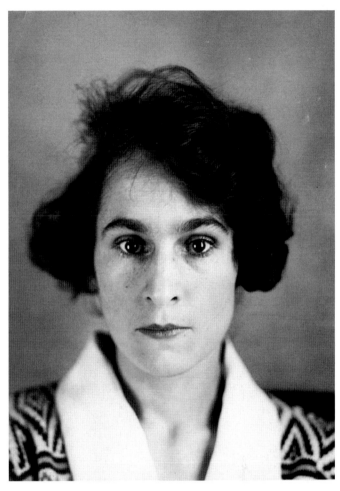

buys *The Persistence of Memory*, the work which is first exhibited in the United States in December, and introduces the continent to Dalí's art.

Gala in the photographic portrait by Man Ray (1927) reproduced in the frontispiece of *La femme visible* (1930)

Catalogue and list of works of the exhibition "Salvador Dalí," Galerie Pierre Colle, Paris, June 1931

July 21: Gala and René Crevel leave for the spa town of Vernet-les-Bains (in the west Pyrenees, at the foot of the Canigó) where Gala can rest and convalesce after her operation to remove a fibroma. Dalí joins her two days later and even Paul Éluard pays her a brief visit. Once Éluard leaves, on July 30, the three of them move to Port Lligat where Crevel works on the essay "Dalí ou l'anti-obscurantisme," which will be published in November by Éditions

483

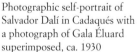

Photographic self-portrait of Salvador Dalí in Cadaqués with a photograph of Gala Éluard superimposed, ca. 1930

Salvador Dalí in ca. 1931 at Port Lligat in front of the painting *Inaugural Gooseflesh* (1928)

Gala and Salvador Dalí at Port Lligat in 1931

surréalistes, Paris. They then leave together for Barcelona where they go to see the works of Gaudí. Crevel writes in his essay, "Dalí in Barcelona showed me such *creations of solidified desires* as would have encouraged even Huysmans of *À rebours* fame
to undertake the path of artifice and subversion …
In the uniform oppression of the rich and docile quarters, subjected to the exigencies of an urbanization without imagination, they spurted out like lava being finally freed from an angry volcano. During Dalí's childhood, they represented not only rebellion but also one of the most peculiar and eloquent moments

of a permanent revolution."
Jaume (Met) Miravitlles invites them both to lecture in the Capcir Hall in Barcelona, on September 18, 1931, where the magazine *L'Hora*, the voice of the Workers' and Farmers' Coalition, is organizing a convention on the relationship between Marxism and Surrealism. Jaume Miravitlles, Dídac Ruiz and René Crevel take part in the debate with the lecture "Esprit versus reason," and Dalí with his speech, "Surrealism at the service of Revolution": "'Surrealism at the service of Revolution.' I apologize if my speech disappoints part of the audience whose masochistic pleasure it is to hear itself

constantly insulted. The change in tone is due only to the fact that previous lectures (like the one held in the Atenue in Barcelona, for example) were directed to an audience of intellectuals and artists whom I now find it absolutely inadmissable to address unless it is for the purpose of spitting in their faces. Today, I am addressing my friends, the Communists of Barcelona, instead, who are struggling for the revolution in whose service we Surrealists have been working for some time."[36]
November: The first Surrealist exhibition in the United States, "Newer Super-Realism" is held in Wadsworth Athenaeum, Harford (Connecticut). Fifty works are shown from various artists, including Giorgio de Chirico, Salvador Dalí, Max Ernst, André Masson, Joan Miró and Pablo Picasso. Dalí presents eight paintings: *The Feeling of Becoming, By the Sea, The Persistence of Memory, Diurnal Phantasies, Birth of a Deity, Man-Fish, Solitude* and *Landscape with Shoes and Two Drawings: Andromeda, Sun and Sand*.
December 15: Éditions surréalistes publishes "L'Amour et la mémoire," by Dalí, in which the artist expresses his feelings for Gala with great passion.

1932
January 9-29: Together with other artists, including Pablo Picasso, Marcel Duchamp, Man Ray and Max Ernst, Dalí takes part in the exhibition, "Surrealism: Paintings, Drawings and Photographs" at the Julien Levy Gallery, in New York. Dalí shows his *Persistence of Memory, Solitude* and *By the Sea*.
March 25: Dalí finishes his poem, *Je ne me sépare jamais de Gala*.[37]
April: An article by Sebastià Gasch appears in the magazine, *La Publicitat*, in which he

Dedication to Gala on the book
L'Amour et la mémoire, 1931

Photomontage with a photoportrait
of Dalí by Buñuel (1929) and one of
Gala from around 1930, used as the
frontispiece for *L'Amour et la mémoire*

Gala in 1931

right-hand side
Salvador Dalí and Gala with Paul
and Nush Éluard on the terrace
of Port Lligat in 1931

criticizes Dalí's painting and
that of Surrealists in general.
The article brings to an end the
friendship between the critic
and the painter of the
Empordà.
May 11: Dalí is once again in
Paris where a second exhibition
dedicated to him at the Galerie
Pierre Colle will be held from
May 26 to June 17. He shows
twenty-five works and two
Surrealist objects.
June: The magazine,
Nadrealizam Danas i Ovde,
publishes "Viva el
Surrealismo," part of "a
Surrealist story" by Salvador
Dalí, together with the inquiries
into desire to which Dalí,
Éluard, Breton and Crevel had
replied.
Dalí and Gala have lived in the
apartment of number 7, rue
Becquerel, at the foot of the
Sacré-Coeur, since the Spring
of 1930 but at the beginning of
July 1932, just before Gala and
Éluard's divorce comes
through—on 15th of the
month—the couple moves to
the opposite side of the city.
The move coincides with the
publication of *Babaouo*
(Éditions des Cahiers Libres),
a "compendium of critical
accounts of the cinema," and
the script of the film, *Babaouo*,
illustrated with seven
xylographs and a
diamond-etched copper plate
image. Dalí also designs the
film-bill.
In *La Publicitat* of July 28,
J.V. Fox announces that the
painter has just arrived in
Port Lligat and plans to stay
there for three months.
René Crevel goes to see Gala
and Dalí for the third time;
soon afterwards, André Breton
and Valentine Hugo also join
them. When the latter leave,
Dalí and Crevel leave for
Barcelona.
November 24: Christian Bérard
introduces Dalí to the writer
Julien Green, a future member
of the Zodiaco group. Four

days later, Green and his sister
go to see Dalí in his Paris
studio, rue Gauget.

1933
In a letter dated December 26,
1932, Dalí tells the
Vicomte de Noailles of the
birth of Zodiaco, an association
of collectors and friends set up
at the end of 1932 to give
financial help to the Catalan
artist by commissioning work
from him. From 1933, every
month, one of the members of
the group chooses a large
painting or a small one and two
drawings. Many of these works
are portraits of Zodiaco
members set in Surrealist
landscapes or interiors.
The members of the group are:
Caresse Crosby, the Countess
Cuevas de Vera, André Durst,
Prince Jean-Louis de Faucigny-
Lucinge and his wife, the writer
Julien Green and his sister,
Anne, the publisher René
Laporte, the Vicomte de
Noailles, Countess Pecci-Blunt,
Félix Rolo, Robert de Saint-
Jean, and Emilio Terry.
In a letter to the Viscount
of Noailles dated January 28,
Dalí tells of a contract he will
sign with Skira to illustrate
Les chants de Maldoror, by the
Count of Lautréamont, which
will be published the following
year. In 1948, in his book, *Vingt

ans d'activité*, Albert Skira will
tell of how it was René Crevel
who suggested he ask Dalí to
illustrate the poem.
In February, Gala and Dalí
return to Port Lligat.
May 27, 1933-October 31, 1934:
Dalí takes part in the Universal
Exhibition in Chicago where
he shows *Shades of Night
Descending.*
June: Publication of the first
issue of *Minotaure*, a magazine
edited by Albert Skira which
will count thirteen issues up
to the end of 1939. Dalí is an
assiduous collaborator.
Over the year, Dalí paints
*Gala and the Angelus of Millet
Preceding the Imminent Arrival
of the Conical Anamorphoses*
and *The Architectonic Angelus
of Millet*, two paintings from
the series inspired by *Millet's
Angelus*, and also a theme
which will appear in several of
Dalí's canvases, objects and
poems between 1932 and 1935.
June 7-18: The invitation to the
Surrealist exhibition at the
Galerie Pierre Colle, Paris,
reads peremptorily, "You must
go to the Surrealist exhibition."
The exhibition includes works
by many artists, including Arp,
Breton, Duchamp, Éluard,
Marie-Berthe Ernst, Magritte,
Valentine Hugo, Péret, Picasso,
Giacometti, Tzara, Man Ray,
Tanguy, René Crevel, Ernst,

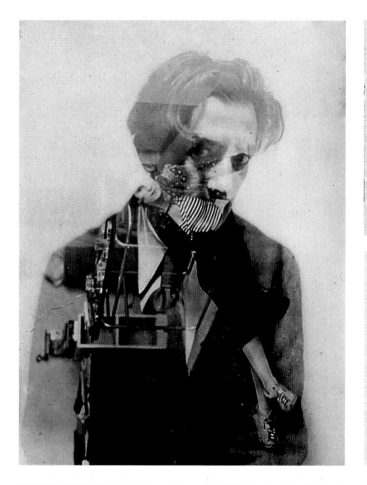

PIERRE COLLE, 29, RUE CAMBACÉRÈS, 29 – PARIS

EXPOSITION

SALVADOR DALI

Du 26 Mai au 17 Juin 1932
Vernissage le jeudi 26 Mai à 15 heures

CATALOGUE

1. La vieillesse de Guillaume Tell. *(Collection particulière)*
2. Objets surréalistes indicateurs de la mémoire instantanée.
3. Objet anthropomorphe indiquant la perte de mémoire.
4. Rencontre de l'illusion et de l'instant arrêté.
5. Objet enveloppé et objet hypnagogique.
6. Illusion sadique.
7. Effet surréaliste.
8. Hallucination affective.
9. Hallucination : Six images de Lénine sur un piano.

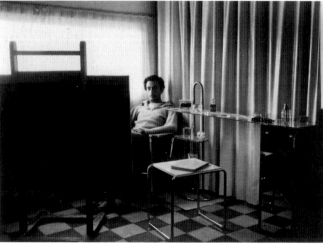

Henri Manuel, *Superimposed Dalí, Gala and functionalist furniture*, ca. 1932

Salvador Dalí in an interior with functionalist furniture, ca. 1932

Maurice Henry, Marcel Jean, René Char, Georges Hugnet and Joan Miró. Dalí contributes eight works: *Invisible Harp, Meditation on the Harp, Table of Demential Associations or Fireworks, Atmospheric Chair, Atmospheric Spoon, Egg on Atmospheric Plate, Retrospective*

Bust of a Woman and *Atmospheric Academy*.
June 19-29: The Galerie Pierre Colle holds its third exhibition dedicated to Dalí. In the catalogue, there is an open letter in which the artist explains to André Breton the origins of the Surrealist object: "As you will see, this process brings you, partially and contextually, to specifically Surrealist discoveries, which I will not dwell on; to the affective state of the 'object' and to the 'affective concerns about the objects'. In fact, the object is born of those sorts of paintings in which one would already have been able to recognize one's embryonic self. … It subsists only as an umbilical cord, to infuse strength to the accessories, ingredients and objects that are about to be born in it. One can therefore distinguish real stones from real shoes."

Catalogue of the exhibition "Salvador Dalí," Galerie Pierre Colle, Paris, May-June, 1932

August: Marcel Duchamp invites Man Ray to join him in Cadaqués as Dalí would like him to photograph Gaudí's works so he can use the photos to illustrate the article he will write for *Minotaure* ("De la beauté terrifiante et comestible de l'architecture modern style").
September 13: J.V. Fox announces in *La Publicitat* that Man Ray has just arrived in Catalonia to photograph Cap Creus and a few modernist buildings. On September 27, Man Ray writes Dalí a postcard informing him, "Dear Friend, I have been back in Paris a few days, now. In Barcelona, I took some photos which are not at all bad and I have given some of them to *Minotaure*. Exciting. As you are coming back soon,

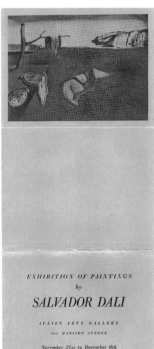

Salvador Dalí in the Paris apartment with functionalist furniture, ca. 1932

Salvador Dalí resting in Port Lligat, 1932

Catalogue of the exhibition "Salvador Dalí," Galerie Pierre Colle, Paris, June 1933

Catalogue of the solo exhibition, Julien Levy Gallery, New York, 1933

"La névrose extra-fine ondulante polychrome gutturale," the Antoni Gaudí's Park Güell in Barcelona photographed by Man Ray in 1933

I will set a series aside for you. Affectionate regards to you both, Man Ray."[38]

Dalí and Gala return to Paris. November 21-December 8: The Julien Levy Gallery of New York holds its first exhibition dedicated to Dalí, showing twenty-five of his works. In the catalogue, the artist writes, "This exhibition of my paintings coincides with a study which has become my present obsession (before its final integration in a book which I am about to publish, *Surrealist Painting Through the Ages*), a study of those delicate, substantial, and extraordinary phenomena which are Ludwig II of Bavaria, concrete irrationality, paranoia, 'art moderne,' heroism, immense solitude, illusion, *trompe-l'œil*, instantaneous photography, the paralyzing effect of too familiar objects, and also the great deception of a work of art, always negligible and lamentable and a thousand times more miserable beside the life and concrete thought of men…!"

December 8-21: Dalí contributes to an exhibition at the Galeria d'Art Catalònia of Barcelona with: two oil paintings, *The*

Enigma of William Tell and *The Birth of Liquid Desires*; three drawings, *Average Ensemble of Roses and Bureaucrats, Variation on the Horseman of Death* and *The Melancholy of the Beach*; twenty-seven engravings, twenty-five of which represent the first stage or drafts for *Les Chants de Maldoror* by Skira; seven photos of seven works: *The Great Masturbator, William Tell, The Memory of the Child-Woman,* known also as *Imperial Monument to the Child Woman, The Old Age of William Tell, Head, Babaouo* and *Surrealist Object*; and six photographs by Man Ray.

1934

January 22: André Breton writes a draft letter to Dalí in which he reproaches him for his latest public declarations which are very distant from the Surrealist doctrine.

January 30: Dalí and Gala get married in the registry office with Yves Tanguy and André Gaston as witnesses.

February 2-March 11: Dalí takes part in the "Exposition du Cinquantenaire" at the Salon des Indépendants in the

Gala in the 1930s

Grand Palais, Paris, with *The Enigma of William Tell* and *Cannibalism of Objects*. His presence is the sign of a certain contempt for the group of Surrealists who have decided not to participate. The portrayal of Lenin in *The Enigma of William Tell*, so far removed from that which had inspired *Apparition of Lenin*, had a strong effect on Breton. **February 5**: Breton gathers together a council to judge Dalí's behavior. It is the first attempt to expel him from the Surrealist group. André Breton together with his followers, Brauner, Ernst, Hérold, Hugnet, Oppenheim, Peret and Tanguy, prepare a letter to expel him. Crevel, Éluard and Tzara oppose it. Dalí writes to Breton as follows: "My Dear Friend Breton, I am sending you the / explanatory note that I promised you yesterday evening First, I am in solidarity with Nozière's publication, / and my collaboration with that work / stands as proof. Second, concerning the gossip going round / regarding my becoming a Fascist, I must / protest against these accusations which I deny / formally, and deny precisely in my broad paranoid-critical studies on / racism which could not be more

violently opposed to Hitlerism— and / which I would like to show you as soon as possible. Third, concerning my painting, / I refuse any notion that it denigrates / Lenin who, as you know, / is one of the people I [admire] most. / The subject that the picture may want to speak of / or signify is still / unknown to me, and enigmatic. / Only very rigorous scientific analysis / could resolve this question. Furthermore, I pray you, dear friend, consider me / unconditionally Surrealist./ Yours, Salvador Dalí"[39] **April 3**: The Julien Levy Gallery of New York organizes the exhibition "Drawings and Etchings to illustrate Lautréamont's *Chants de Maldoror* by Dalí." Dalí and Gala leave Paris for Port Lligat. **April 5**: Dalí gives lecture on Surrealism entitled, "Per un tribunal terrorista de responsabilitats intellectuals" (For a terrorist tribunal for intellectual responsibility), as part of an initiative organized by the Ateneu Enciclopèdic Popular of Barcelona. Dalí illustrates *Onan*, by Georges Hugnet (Éditions surréalistes, 1934) with an etching in which there is the following inscription: "Spasmographism obtained with the left hand whilst I

masturbate to death, to my bones, as far as the helix of the cup, with my right." At the beginning of May, Dalí and Gala are back in Paris. The Paris publisher, Skira, publishes, *Les chants de Maldoror*, by Isidore Ducasse, Count of Lautréamont, with forty-two etchings by Dalí. It is, without a doubt, Dalí's most important graphic work; he had been working on it since 1932. **May 12-June 3, 1934**: Dalí takes part in the exhibition "Exposition Minotaure" at the Palais des Beaux-Arts, Brussels, with *William Tell*, *Birth of a Deity*, *The Great Masturbator*, *Cannibalism of Objects*, *Painting* and *Retrospective Bust of a Woman*. **May 14-June 2**: Dalí takes part in the exhibition "Borès, Beaudin, Dalí" at the Zwemmer Gallery in London. **June 13-25**: Albert Skira's publishing house holds the exhibition "Salvador Dalí 42

Dalí upside down photographed by Man Ray in Port Lligat, 1933

Gala in the olive grove at Port Lligat in 1934

Watercolors and 30 Drawings for 'Les Chants de Maldoror'" in the Galeries Quatre Chemins, in Paris. **June 20-July 13**: The Galerie Jacques Bonjean presents an

Josep Maria, Roussie Sert and Salvador Dalí at Mas Juny, Palamós 1934

exhibition on Dalí in which the artist shows thirty-two paintings, two sculptures, four Surrealist objects and the engravings created for *Les Chants de Maldoror*.

October 2-4: The Galeria d'Art Catalònia in Barcelona organizes an exhibition which includes five works by Dalí. According to Alfred Barr, the exhibition "gets a growing group of Surrealists very excited."

On the occasion of the exhibition, a lecture by Dalí, entitled "The Surrealist and phenomenal mystery of the bedside table," is scheduled for October 5 but it does not take place because of the strike and controversy caused by the events of October 1934. For this reason, the Dalís return to Paris where the artist concentrates on his first studies for *Premonition of Civil War*.

October 18-December 9: At the annual "International Exhibition of Paintings" (Carnegie prize), in Pittsburgh, Dalí receives an honorable mention for his *Landscape with Enigmatic Elements*.

October 24-November 10: The Zwemmer Gallery, London, holds its first exhibition dedicated to Dalí (the first in the United Kingdom) with

sixteen paintings, twenty drawings
and seventeen engravings.

November 7: The Dalís set off for their first trip to the United States, accompanied by Caresse Crosby. They travel to New York on board the ocean liner *Champlain*. For the occasion, Dalí publishes an *octavilla* (stanza of 8 lines of 8 syllables) entitled, "New York Salutes Me."

November 21-December 10: A Dalí exhibition is held at the Julien Levy Gallery, New York. The artist shows twenty-two works.

Henry McBride defines the exhibition in *The Sun* as, " … in fashion, very controversial and difficult." Edward Alden Jewell writes in *Time Magazine*: "A craftsman, a man of art and a magician with the paintbrush, Dalí deserves to be considered one of the greats. In my opinion, he is, above all, a miniaturist whose small formats turn out best. The larger works are less convincing …"[40]

Dalí also designs the *Surrealist Poster* for the exhibition, the idea for which he got from an advertisement in a Catalan newspaper of January 12, 1920. During a press conference, Dalí reads a few lines of introduction in a Dalínian English, which Julien Levy later publishes in the book *Surrealism* (New York: Black Sun Press, 1936):

SURREALISM
aye av ei horror uv joks
Surrealism is not ei jok
Surrealism is ei strangue poizun
Surrealism is zi most vaiolent
and daingeros
toxin for dsi imaigineichon zad
has so far
bin invented in dsi domein
ouve art
Surrealism is irrezisteible and
terifai-ingli
conteichios
Biuer! Ai bring ou Surrealism
Aulredi meni pipoul in Nui
York jave bin infectid
bai zi laifquiving and

marvels sors of Surrealism
Dalí begins his collaboration with *The American Weekly* with "A Written by a Madman – Illustrated by a 'Super-Realist'," published on December 16. He realizes a series of drawings and articles in which he expresses various reflections on modern, urban life: "New York as seen by the 'Super-Realist' Artist M. Dalí" (February 24, 1935), "How Super-Realist Dalí Saw Broadway" (March 17, 1935), "The American City Night-and-Day by M. Dalí" (March 31, 1935) and "Gangsterism and Goofy Visions of New York by M. Dalí, Super-Realist" (May 19, 1935).

December 18-January 7, 1935: A Dalí exhibition is held at the Wadsworth Athenaeum in

Hartford (Connecticut). At the opening, Dalí gives a lecture during which, for the first time, he affirms: "The only difference between me and a madman is that I am not at all mad." The lecture is introduced by the director of the Wadsworth Athenaeum, A. Everett ('Chick') Austin. At the end, the film *Un Chien andalou* is projected for the public.

Salvador Dalí and Man Ray in a photo by Carl Van Vechten, Paris (Montparnasse) 1934

Photographic portrait of Salvador Dalí made by Georges Allié in 1934 for the article "Aparition aérodynamique des êtres-objets" published in *Minotaure* (no. 6, winter 1934-35)

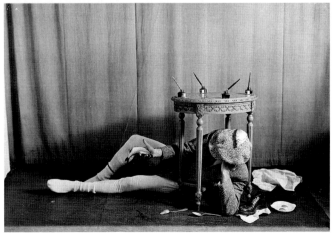

Salvador Dalí in a photo by
Carl Van Vechten, 1934

Catalogue of the exhibition "Dalí,"
Galerie Jacques Bonjean, Paris,
June-July 1934

Invitation to the exhibition
"Drawings and Etchings," Julien
Levy Gallery, New York, April 1934

1935
Dalí writes the script for the
film, *Les mystères surréalistes
de New York*, which will never
be made. Some of the ideas
in the script are repeated in his
articles written for
The American Weekly.
"…The Surrealist mysteries
of New York 1935

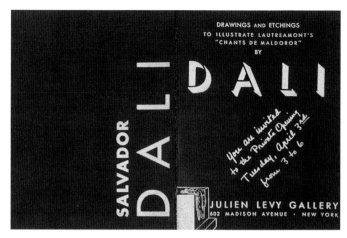

First of all, why do so many
cypresses stick out of the walls
of empty skyscrapers and,
above all, where are the rotten
tangos from my adolescence —
the authentically syphilitic
tangos, the tangos which
narcissistically bore the suicidal
tangos, which I listened to at
the Eden Concert in Barcelona,
sung by singers in ruins, in a
colossal, Argentine and criminal
dance-hall, more scoundrel-like
than anywhere else?
Likewise, where is the
minuscule and fragile
aerodynamic skull (sparkling in
the sun), twinkling with grains
of sand, which Gala found that
first winter of our love amongst
the wild fossils of Cap Creus?
But Gala is in New York and
that means that New York is a
mysterious and surre[a]list city
because Gala is the muse of my
imagination, no-one yet knows
the Surrealist mysteries of New
York except for Gala and
Salvador Da[l]í! …[41]
January 11: Dalí gives a lecture
on "Surrealist Paintings and
Paranoid Images" at the
Museum of Modern Art
(MoMA), New York.
January 19: Dalí and Gala
return to Europe. The night
before they leave, Caresse
Crosby and Joella Levy
organize a *bal onirique* (oneiric
ball) in their honor at Le Coq
Rouge, in New York. As
decorative scenery in the hall
they use a bath and a quartered

dead bull with a gramophone in
its belly. Dalí dresses up as a
mannequin and puts on a small
bra and Gala comes as a
cadavre exquis with a red
cellophane dress, and a
celluloid doll and a couple of
lobster-shaped objects on her
head.
At the end of January, Dalí
meets his future patron and
friend, Edward James, at a
concert organized by the
Princess of Polignac.
March 3: Dalí meets his family
again, after a long time, and
there is a reconciliation. Dalí had
not seen his father since 1929.
June: Dalí takes part in an
international exhibition on
Surrealism organized in Santa
Cruz, Tenerife.
June: Together with Hans Arp,

Invitation to the exhibition
"Les Chants de Maldoror," Galerie
Quatre Chemins, Paris, June 1934

Max Ernst, Marcel Duchamp, Alberto Giacometti, Valentine Hugo, Oscar Domínguez, Man Ray, Marcel Jean and Yves Tanguy, Dalí illustrates the programme of " Systematic series of lectures on the most recent positions of Surrealism" and designs two draft posters. According to the programme, Dalí should have read, *Je mange Gala*, a poem published by Ediciones Destino:

Birth of liquid desires
First song
I spend the week-end with
friends of Caresse Crosby in
Her windmill in the forest of
Ermanonville. I have been
suffering for a week
From a voluptuous desire
which gives me a slight
irritation.
In the stomach which I try
to accentuate by mixing all
The spiciest types of English
chutneys and sauces into my
Food. This gives me a thirst
of infinite sweetness.
A methodological thirst, a thirst
which, voluntarily and with
delight,
I try to satisfy as late as
possible, in order to accentuate
its action during my dreams
and fantasies.
I am lying on a chaise-longue
in the sun, my thirst
Is becoming invasive, Doric,
imperialist, darker than
emotions.
And salivary geometries,
and this because of the
overabundant
Quantity of alcohol drunk the
night before which hysterically
exasperated
My already fabricated and
ample thirst—
For hours I look at the high
and trembling top of an
Immense pair of poplars in
which shines an apotheosis
of greens and Guttural
freshness, extra-humid, and
super-trembling with
paradisiacal immediacy …" [42]

June 20: Dalí's friend, René Crevel, commits suicide.
July 20: Éditions surréalistes, Paris, sends Dalí's *La conquête de l'irrationel*, for printing and the New York gallery owner, Julien Levy, publishes the English edition, *Conquest of the Irrational*, translated by the poet, David Gascoyne.
September: Federico García Lorca and Salvador Dalí meet up again in Barcelona. Edward James invites Lorca to accompany the Dalís to Ravello, in Italy, but the poet does not accept as he is otherwise engaged. This will be the last time Dalí meets Lorca.

Gala, Salvador Dalí and Edward James in Rome in 1935

October 13-27: Together with Hans Arp, Giorgio de Chirico, Max Ernst, Paul Klee, René Magritte, Yves Tanguy, Man Ray and Joan Miró and other artists, Dalí takes part in a Surrealist exhibition in the Salle d'Exposition de la Commune de La Louvière, in Belgium.
October 17-December 8: Dalí takes part in the annual "International Exhibition of Paintings" at the Carnegie Institute in Pittsburgh.
November: Edward James invites the Dalís to London and

Salvador Dalí at Port Lligat in the 1930s

Salvador Dalí and Gala at Port Lligat in the 1930s

Salvador Dalí posing nude at Port Lligat in the 1930s

Salvador Dalí in two photos
by W. Vennemann, 1930s

Monkton, in West Sussex, where they are guests in this secluded country house, James's refuge. Dalí suggests painting the outside walls lilac and his friend follows his advice. He does not, however, agree with the artist's Surrealist ideas for the interior decorating.

December: Dalí illustrates the collection of poems by Paul Éluard, *Nuits partagées* (G.L.M., Paris), with two pictures.

December: Together with Valentine Hugo, Picasso, Miró, Man Ray, Tanguy and others, Dalí takes part in an exhibition of Surrealist pictures put on by the Galerie Quatre Chemins, Paris.

Dalí's "Les pantoufles de Picasso" is published in the special edition of *Cahiers d'art* (nos.7-10) dedicated to Picasso. In the text, he applies, to the letter, his paranoid-critical method: in reality, all he does is copy Sacher-Masoch's story, *La pantoufle de Sapho* (1859), and add a few small changes. In an interview with Alain Bosquet, Dalí explains, "It was enough to read the first chapter [of Sacher-Masoch's book] and substitute the name Sapho with that of Picasso."

1936

January 13: The Gallery Esteve, Barcelona, opens with an exhibition of Picasso, an event which coincides with a demonstration organized by the Associació Amics de l'Art Nou, which is transmitted on the radio. The people taking part include Salvador Dalí, Luis Fernández, Joan Miró, and Julio González. Dalí reads "Salvador Dalí té el gust d'invitar," published in *Cahiers d'art* (nos.7-10).

January 24: Dalí gives a lecture entitled "Surrealist Cannibalism and Hysteric Surrealism" in the Vieux-Colombier theater, Paris.

May 22-29: Dalí takes part in the "Exposition surréaliste d'objets" organized by the

Cover of *La Conquête de l'irrationnel*, 1935

Galerie Charles Ratton in Paris. All sorts of "objects" are exhibited, including: "Natural objects, Interpreted Natural Objects, Incorporated Natural Objects, Perturbed Objects, Found Objects, Interpreted Found Objects, American Objects, Oceanic Objects, Mathematical Objects, and Surrealist Objects." Dalí shows two Surrealist objects: *The Aphrodisiac Jacket* and *Monument to Kant*.

June 11-July 4: London's New Burlington Galleries organize "The International Surrealist Exhibition" and a cycle of lectures is held in parallel to this; they are opened by Breton on June 16 and closed by Dalí on July 1. According to the program, the themes to be treated by Dalí in his talk are Paranoia, The Pre-Raphaelites, Harpo Marx and Ghosts. During the lecture, he wears a diving-suit to express visually the idea that his work enters the depths of the unconscious. However, the experience only just avoids turning into a tragedy when, due to a technical problem, Dalí is nearly asphyxiated.

June-July: "Salvador Dalí" exhibition at the Alex Reid & Lefevre Gallery in London. Twenty-nine paintings and eighteen drawings are exhibited.

Salvador Dalí intently painting *The Metamorphosis of Narcissus*, ca. 1936-37

Salvador Dalí showing *The Dream* (1931) to Paul Éluard, Gala, and Roland Penrose, during the Surrealist exhibition in London, 1936 [Graphic Photo Union]

Gala and Salvador Dalí in a photo by Cecil Beaton, 1936

right-hand side
Cover of the catalogue of the exhibition "Salvador Dalí," Alex Reid & Lefevre Gallery, London, June-July 1936

Cover of the catalogue of the exhibition "The International Surrealist exhibition," Burlington Galleries, London, June-July 1936

Dalí is in London when news reaches him of the start of the Spanish Civil War and the death of Federico García Lorca, victim of the Franco regime. In his autobiography, *The Secret Life of Salvador Dalí*, the artist remembers the moment in these words, "When the revolution exploded, my great friend, the poet of the mala muerte, Federico García Lorca, died in front of a firing squad in Granada which was occupied by Fascists. His death was used for propaganda purposes. It was an ignoble act because they knew as I knew that Lorca was in essence the most apolitical person in the world. Lorca did not die as an emblem of political ideology, he died as the sacrificial victim of that total and integrated phenomenon which is the confusion of revolution which, as it developed, turned into the civil war. Besides, in the civil war, they did not kill people because of their ideas but for 'personal reasons', for personality reasons; and, like me, Lorca had personality enough to sell and, with that, more right than most Spaniards to be shot at the hands of Spaniards. The tragic sense of life that Lorca had was marked by the same tragic constant that marked the destiny of the whole of the Spanish people."[43]
The Dalís spend some time in Italy, in Cortina d'Ampezzo, staying at the Tre Croci hotel. In October, they return to Paris.
Dalí illustrates *Notes sur la poèsie*, by André Breton and Paul Éluard, published by G.L.M., Paris.
December 7: Dalí and Gala go to New York on board the *Normandie*: it is their second trip to the United States.
November 9-January 17: Dalí takes part in the group exhibition "Fantastic Art Dada Surrealism," at the MoMA, New York, with *Illuminated Pleasures* (1929), *The Font* (1930), *The Feeling of Becoming* (1930), *Andromeda* (1930), *Sun and Sand* (1930), *The Persistence of Memory* (1931), *Retrospective Bust of a Woman* (1933), *The Convalescence of a Kleptomaniac* (1933), *The Ghost of Vermeer of Delft, Which can be Used as a Table* (1934), the etching; *Paranoiac Face* (1935), *Paranoiac-critical Solitude* (1935), *Puzzle of Autumn* (1935) and *City of Drawers* (1936).

SALVADOR DALI

JUNE-JULY,
1936

ALEX. REID & LEFEVRE, Ltd.
LONDON

SURREALISM
CATALOGUE · PRICE SIXPENCE

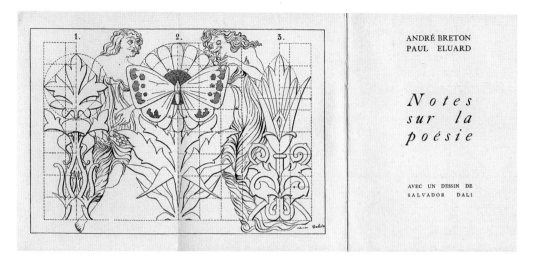

Frontispiece of the book *Notes sur la poésie* by André Breton and Paul Éluard, 1936

Cover of *Time* magazine December 14, 1936

Bonwit Teller, the famous department store on Fifth Avenue, New York, commissions a group of artists to design Surrealist windows for the opening of the exhibition, "Fantastic Art Dada Surrealism." Amongst all of them, it is Dalí's "She was a Surrealist woman, she was like a figure in a dream" that attracts the most attention from the public.

December 10: The Julien Levy Gallery of New York opens a Dalí exhibition with twenty-one of his paintings and twelve drawings. On the occasion of the exhibition a *Souvenir-catalogue* (catalogue-object) is realized.

December 14: Dalí appears on the front cover of *Time* magazine in a photograph of Man Ray. It is the start of Dalí's acclaim at international level.

December 21: Edward James and Dalí sign a contract in which James promises to buy all of Dalí's works produced between June 1937 and June 1938 for the sum of £ 2,400.
Dalí sends Harpo Marx a very Dalínian Christmas gift: a harp with barbed chords. Harpo replies with a photo of himself with bandaged fingers, and writes that if Dalí comes to Hollywood, he will be happy to sit for a portrait.

1937
February: Dalí leaves for Hollywood while the Marx Brothers are filming, *A Day at the Races*. Dalí paints Harpo's portrait and works with him on the script of the film, *Giraffes on Horseback Salad*, which is never made.
Dalí and Gala return to Europe on board the *Champlain*. They move to Zürs (Austria), staying for a period at the Arlberg-Wintersporshotel .
March 27: Dalí writes to Breton from the Hotel Berchof in Seefeld, Austria, about the gallery Breton will open in Paris, in May, "My idea is to call the shop Café, or even Café Gradiva. From the outside, it should look just like a butcher's, grim fake marble, golden horse heads from which hang two long tresses, longer than usual, like at the hairdressers… I have even written to Duchamp because I think that my project is within the scope of his concept of camouflage, and this might be useful to us."[44]
June 25: *Métamorphose de Narcisse* is published by

Éditions surréalistes of Paris. At the same time, the Julien Levy Gallery takes care of the publication of the English version in New York. Both publications are dedicated to Paul Éluard.
On the cover is a photograph from a series taken by Cecil Beaton the previous year. The series is of Dalí and Gala re-enacting *A Couple with their Heads Full of Cloud*. Dalí defines them as "The first poem and the first painting obtained by applying exclusively the integral application of the paranoid-critical method."
July: In an exhibition at the Galerie Renou et Colle, Paris, Dalí shows his portrait of Harpo Marx, the drawings for a film on which they are working together and *Mae West's Face which May be Used as a Surrealist Apartment*, with which he creates a Surrealist object, the design for the furniture of a room based on the lines on the actress's face. In 1937-38, Dalí makes, *Mae West Lips Sofa*, a work in which the lips of the woman are transformed into a sofa.

July 30-October 31: Dalí shows eight pictures in the exhibition, "Origines et développement de l'art international indépendant" organized by the Musée du Jeu de Paume, Paris.

In September, as they could not return to Cadaqués because of the civil war, the Dalís go to Ravello where they are the guests of Edward James in his Villa Cimbrone.

October: They return to Paris, to the apartment at no. 88 rue de l'Université. They put an enormous stuffed polar bear in the entrance hall, a gift from Edward James, as a welcome to their guests.

Dalí concentrates on designing material, clothes and hats for Elsa Schiapparelli. Many of the models will be made up like, for example, the shoe-hat, the ink-pot-hat, the skeleton dress and the tear-dress.

1938

January 17: The Galerie Beaux Arts of Paris opens the "Exposition Internationale du Surréalisme" organized by André Breton and Paul Éluard. In the catalogue, Dalí and Max Ernst are named as special advisers to the exhibition. Dalí's *Rainy Taxi* opens the exhibition: visitors are invited to go into a corridor, the "rue Surréaliste," lined with dummies representing various personalities, including Duchamp, Dalí, Miró, Man Ray, and Ernst. To complement the exhibition, the Galerie Beaux Arts publishes a "Concise Dictionary of Surrealism," written by Breton and Éluard. Dalí exhibits: *The Great Masturbator* (1929), *The Invisible Man* (1930), *The Birth of Liquid Desires* (1933), *Sleep* (1937), *The Enchanted Beach* (1937), *"En batet"* (1937), a few objects, including the *Aphrodisiac Telephone*, and various drawings. After the exhibition, Dalí and Gala leave for Rome, together with

Edward James, where they stay for two months as the guests of Lord Gerald Berners in his luxury home facing the Roman Forum. They take a brief trip to Sicily where the artist finds himself confronted with "jumbled reminiscences of Catalonia and Africa" and starts painting *Impressions of Africa*.

March 8-April 3: Dalí takes part in the exhibition, "Old and new 'Trompe-l'œil'" at the Julien Levy Gallery, New York. Dalí shows: *Javanese Mannequin* (1934), *Aerodynamic Chair* (1936), *Woman's Head in the Form of a Battle* (1936), *Double Profile* (1937), and *Portrait of Joella Lloyd* (1935).

Spring 1938: Dalí takes part in the "Exposition Internationale du Surréalisme" at the Robert Gallery, Amsterdam, organized by André Breton, Paul Éluard, Georges Hugnet, Roland Penrose, E.L.T. Mésens, and Kristians Tonny. Dalí shows: *The Average Bureaucrat* (1932, Paul Éluard collection), *Herb omelette* (1932, André Breton collection), *Hair* (1931, pastel, Valentine Hugo collection), and study sheets and etchings for *Les Chants de Maldoror* by Lautréamont.

July 19: Dalí visits Sigmund Freud in London and shows him *The Metamorphosis of Narcissus* painting. Dalí is accompanied by Edward James and Stefan Zweig, the person who had introduced them. The Centre de Estudis Dalínians of the Fundació Gala-Salvador Dalí has a letter from Zweig in its collection, written prior to this meeting. The Austrian writer tells Dalí that he can meet Freud as soon as the latter's health permits. In preparation for the

Man Ray, *Gala*, 1937

Cecil Beaton, *Salvador Dalí and Gala with "A Couple with their Heads Full of Clouds,"* 1937

Salvador Dalí while painting
The Enigma of Hitler, 1938
[Numa Blanc Fils]

right-hand side
Salvador Dalí intently painting
Impressions of Africa, 1938

Salvador Dalí in a photograph from
1938 that shows him with one of the
recurring iconographic motifs from
his work: the eggs in the frying pan
[Montecarlo Photo]

Salvador Dalí in Coco Chanel's
studio at the Villa La Pausa in
Roquebrune (Cap Martin), 1938.
On the easel *The Endless Enigma*
(1938)

Salvador Dalí portrayed together
with the painting *Spain,* 1938

visit, Dalí draws a series of
portraits in which Freud's head
is represented as a curl. Stefan
Zweig writes, "One day, during
one of my last visits (to Freud),
I took Salvador Dalí along with
me, who is, in my opinion, one
of the most gifted painters of the
new generation and whose
admiration for Freud is beyond
measure. While I was talking to
Freud, Dalí did a sketch. I have
never shown it to Freud because
Dalí had, with a certain
clairvoyance, already fixed an
image of death in him."
(*Yesterday's World, Memoires
of a European,* 1938)
Freud dies a year later.
After the London trip, Dalí
spends a few days in Italy
before settling for four months,
from September, at La Pausa,
Coco Chanel's villa in
Roquebrune, Monaco. Dalí

works on the ballet, *Tristan fou*
(later entitled *Venusberg* and
later still *Bacchanale*) and on his
next exhibition in New York.

1939
January: *Vogue* publishes Dalí's
article "First Prophecy on
Jewels." For the first time, the
painter talks about himself as a
designer of jewels. "At the same
time that afternoon clips with
lights in them (for instance, a
small ruby giraffe) will appear
in the most obscure corners at
cocktail parties, you may expect
the first mobile jewels for
evening—jewels that breathe,
that become convulsed, that
creep like ancient lizards; that
are scintillating, terribly sensual,
and swollen with sleep."
On February 2, before leaving
for New York, Dalí invites
various friends to visit his house
in rue de l'Université, Paris, to
see his latest creations for the
New York exhibition. The
works he shows are *Face of the
Great Cretinous Cyclops, The
Enchanted Beach (Long Siphon),
Imperial Violets,* and other
paintings and objects.
The last known letter from Dalí
to Breton is dated February 12
of this year. Dalí tells his friend
of his visit to Freud in London,
and confirms his great
admiration for him.
March: The New York
department store, Bonwit
Teller, gives Dalí some
exhibition space and Dalí
prepares two shop windows:
Day, and Night. At the end
of the work, the management
makes a few changes to them
without telling the artist. When
Dalí sees they have been
tampered with, he goes into one
of the windows and pushes a
bath-tub lined with Persian
lamb so that it crashes through
the glass. He is arrested and
later freed.
Cahiers G.L.M. carries out a
survey asking, "List twenty
poets from any country and
time in which you have seen the

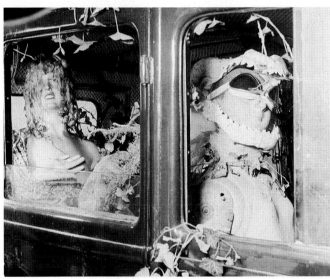

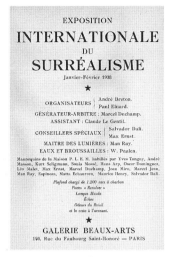

indispensable, that which does not require the eternity of your epoch but rather the mysterious course of your life." Dalí's answer appears in issue no. 9, "For me: Rubén Darío, Lautréamont, Éluard, Péret, Lorca, Góngora."

March 21-April 18: Dalí exhibits his work at the Julien Levy Gallery, New York. It is an enormous success. The day before it closes, *Life* magazine publishes an article on the exhibition, illustrated with a reproduction of *Endless Enigma* and the preparatory studies for this work. "… Almost in chorus, they (the critics)

admitted his ability as a draftsman and colorist and then roundly denounced his artistic explorations of the subconscious and irrational. Such critical abuse, however, seemed only to add to the length of the lines of curious New Yorkers fighting their way into the Dalí show. For general popularity there hadn't been such an exhibit since Whistler's *Mother* was shown in 1934. …" Dalí puts together a very original catalogue for the exhibition: on the cover, he shows a variation of the symbols of the Universal Exhibition of New York, *The*

Sphere Attacks the Pyramid, and inside, in addition to the list of exhibits, there is a reproduction of *The Endless Enigma* taken from the preparatory drawings. At the end, there is the "Dalí! Dalí!," text in which he mentions the artists whom he considers the forefathers of paranoiac painting which he defines simply and amusingly as follows: "Of a Cubist picture one asks: 'What does that represent?'–Of a Surrealist picture, one sees what it represents but one asks: 'What does that mean?'– Of a paranoiac picture one asks everything: 'What do I see?' 'What does that represent?' 'What does that mean?'"[45] *The Art Digest* of New York (April 1, 1939) publishes an article which summarizes all the comments made about the exhibition by the various city papers.

May: Dalí signs an agreement to take part in the Universal Exhibition of New York. He designs the "Dream of Venus" pavilion situated in the recreational area and defines it as "an exploration of the desert of man's unfulfilled desires and of his night-time and daytime dreams." The scenes created inside (mermaids, "refined corpses," Surrealist objects, dummies, etc.) are set out in the space and time of a dream. During April, Horst P. Horst and Georges Platt Lynes, two famous photographers, helped him design the costumes. In July, he publishes the "Declaration of independence of the imagination and the rights of man to his own madness," as a protest against the Universal Exhibition Steering Committee's decision preventing him from showing, on the outside of the pavilion, a reproduction of Botticelli's *Venus* transformed into an "inverted mermaid," with the head of a fish and the legs of a woman. Edward James, who

Catalogue of the exhibition "Exposition Internationale du Surréalisme," Galerie des Beaux-Arts, Paris, January-February 1938

Salvador Dalí in Coco Chanel's studio at the Villa La Pausa in Roquebrune (Cap Martin) in a photograph by W. Vennemann, 1938

Gala portrayed by André Caillet wearing Elsa Schiaparelli's hat-shoe inspired by a drawing by Salvador Dalí, 1938

left-hand side
André Caillet, *Rainy Taxi*, 1938

Rainy Taxi by Salvador Dalí photographed by Raoul Ubaca on the occasion of the "Exposition Internationale du Surréalisme," Galerie des Beaux-Arts, Paris, 1938

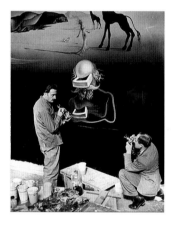

MORPHOLOGY

SPLASH OF MILK

Salvador Dali

*requests the pleasure of your company at the opening of his exhibition,
to see: "The Great One-Eyed Cretin", "The Sacred Siphon",
"The Imperial Violets" and other paintings and objects.*

Tuesday, March twenty-first
from three to six o'clock

Julien Levy Gallery
15 East 57 · New York

Invitation to the exhibition
"Salvador Dalí," Julien Levy
Gallery, New York, March 21, 1939

Salvador Dalí immortalized by
Eric Schaal while painting one
of the murals inside the Surrealist
pavilion, "Dream of Venus,"
New York, 1939

right-hand side
Salvador Dalí and Edward James
in front of the project made by the
painter for the façade of the "Dream
of Venus" pavilion, 1939

Salvador Dalí and Gala
photographed by Eric Schaal while
working at the "Dream of Venus"
pavilion, 1939

Salvador Dalí photographed by
Eric Schaal in front of the façade
under construction for the
"Dream of Venus" pavilion, 1939

had had to pay the bill for the
extravaganza, stayed in
New York to oversee the
construction after Dalí's
departure, and wrote to him on
22 August that the whole
installation was disastrously
changed, the Venus with fish's
head removed, "the façade
covered with unbelievable
writing explaining Surrealism
according to Gardner's ideas,
the tank filled with false Walt
Disney fish and rubber sirens."
In the May 12 issue (the last
one) of *Minotaure*, Breton's
article "Des tendances les plus
récentes de la peinture
surréaliste," traces the story of
Surrealist painting up until that
moment. Breton never cites
Dalí, a sign of their definitive
split. From 1940, when both
are in New York, Breton coins
a new name for the Catalan
artist, "Avida Dollars," an
anagram of Salvador Dalí,
and an extrinsic sign of their
separation.
Spanish Civil War ends with
a victory for Franco. In a letter
Dalí telss Luis Buñuel of the
change in his father's political
ideas. The miseries of war have
transformed Dalí senior into a
Franchist fanatic. In the
exchange of letters between
Dalí and the filmmaker, Buñuel
asks him for financial help but
Dalí refuses. This refusal means
an end to their friendship.

September: France goes to war
with Germany and Dalí and
Gala leave Paris for Arcachon,
near Bordeaux.
November 9: Premiere of the
ballet *Bacchanale* at the
Metropolitan Opera House in
New York.

1940
February: *L'Usage de la Parole*,
a small magazine published by
Christian Zervos and edited by
Georges Hugnet, publishes
Dalí's article "Les Idées
Lumineuses: 'Nous ne
mangeons pas de cette lumière-
là'," wherein the artist speaks of
his interest in science and
especially Max Planck's
quantum theory.
The Germans occupy Paris and
invade Bordeaux, and the Dalís
leave Arcachon. Gala goes to
Lisbon to prepare for the
journey to the United States.
Dalí goes to see his father and
sister in Figueres, then spends
a few days in Madrid before
joining Gala in Lisbon. They

move to the United States
where they will stay until the
end of 1948. At the beginning,
they stay at Caresse Crosby's
house in Hampton Manor,
Virginia.

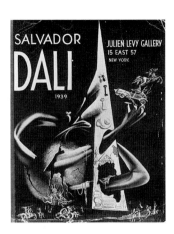

Cover of the catalogue of the exhibition held at the Julien Levy Gallery, New York, 1939

In the Summer, Dalí writes a poem in Castilian, *Sonata de la resurrección de la carne*.[46]

November: the press announces that Dalí is creating a new work aimed at surprising the world: a sofa which breathes. The artist—in *Times-Dispatch*, November 24—states, "I have always been interested in fantastic furniture. For my apartment in Paris, I created all the furniture in fantastic shapes. This chair will have life. It will breathe. There will be a mechanism which will follow the breathing of the human body. You will pour yourself into it, and rest as in a cradle. […] I try to create fantastic things, magical things, dreamlike things. The world needs more fantasy. Our civilization is too mechanical. We can make the fantastic real, and then it is more real than that which actually exists."

1941

February: An exhibition of 400 works of art for advertisements and posters opens at the Philadelphia Museum of Art. Of particular importance is the presence of five artists, Salvador Dalí, Pablo Picasso, Derain, Marie Laurencin, and Georgia O'Keeffe, whose works were used in 1940 for advertising campaigns.

March: Dalí plans a garden for Hampton Manor, Caresse Crosby's house, with a large piano in the swimming pool, gigantic crane flies with women's heads scattered all over the garden, a sleeping beauty on one side of the park and a lovers' fountain from which pours perfumed water. The artist explains that the hedges will mysteriously speak from the depths of their green foliage causing great surprise to passers-by. In September, however, they are told that the project cannot be realized because a military base is going to be installed nearby. Part of the project was published in a reportage in the April 7, 1941 issue of *Life* magazine, "Life Calls on Salvador Dalí. Surrealist artist 'enchants' Virginia manor."

April 22: The Julien Levy Gallery, New York, opens a new solo exhibition "Dalí," which will subsequently be shown at the Arts Club of Chicago (May 23-June 14) and the Dalzell Hatfield Galleries of Los Angeles (September 10-October 5). Dalí's contribution to the catalogue, *The Last Scandal of Salvador Dalí*, and the cover are a real defence of Classicism with explicit references to the Renaissance. Dalí shows paintings, drawings and jewelry made in collaboration with Duke Fulco di Verdura: Apollo and Daphne, Medusa's Head, Saint Sebastian and Angel. At the time the jewelry goes on show on July 15, *Vogue* publishes Dalí's "Dream of Jewels," an article in which he tells of his thoughts and opinions on the jewelry made with the Duke of Verdura, illustrated with photos of four of the pieces exhibited. The Dalís spend the Summer in the luxury hotel, Del Monte Lodge, in Pebble Beach, California.

Dalí finishes writing his autobiography *The Secret Life of Salvador Dalí* which is published the following year by Dial Press, New York. In the epilogue, he writes, "I am 37 years old. It is July 30, 1941, the day on which I promised my publisher that the manuscript would be ready."

September: Dalí does the decoration for the masked ball, "A Surrealist's Night in an Enchanted Forest," at the Del Monte hotel. The ball is in aid of European artists who have taken refuge in the United States. People attending the ball must come in fancy dress, the theme is "dreams" or "woodland creatures." The room is transformed into a grotto: 5,000 sacks hang from the ceiling, their purpose being to create an oppressive, depressing atmosphere for the guests. The idea emulates Marcel Duchamp's installation at the 1938 "Exposition Internationale du Surréalisme" in Paris. Dalí wears a leotard and satin jacket, a flower behind his ear, the characteristic moustache and a two-faced mask. He and Gala, who is wearing a huge horse's head, writhe around on a bed of red velvet at the head of the table. Behind the chairs of the

Salvador Dalí in Hampton Manor, 1941

Salvador Dalí and Gala at the home of Caresse Crosby in Hampton Manor, 1941

Cover of the catalogue of the exhibition "Salvador Dalí," Julien Levy Gallery, New York, 1941

"Life Calls on Salvador Dalí," published on Life magazine, March, 1941

Gala and Salvador Dalí photographed by Philippe Halsman while hanging *Piano descending by parachute*, 1941

guests, like waiters, loom life-sized snouts. The table is decorated with buffalo horns, a monkey made of ice, an amazing porcupine, various strange animals, vegetables and other foods. Amongst the guests are Gloria Vanderbilt, Bob Hope, and Mary Morse. Dalí works with Fox on a nightmare sequence for the film, *Moontide*, with the actors Jean Gabin and Ida Lupino. Fox says the sum paid to Dalí for this work is the highest amount an artist has ever been paid by a film studio. The scene is supposed to represent what happens in the human mind, according to Dalí, during the first stages of being drunk. Fox does not accept Dalí's proposal for fear that the scene will horrify the public. When the artist refuses to change it because it would mean, "undermining his integrity as a Surrealist artist," the scene is completely cut.

October 8: Premiere of the ballet *Labyrinth* at the Metropolitan Opera House in New York. John Briggs of the *New York Post* comments, "… A good many of the 'Ohs' and 'Ahs' last night were evoked by Mr. Dalí's scenery, which was imaginative and highly effective. It may be that the more conservative Surrealists in the audience, expecting an opium smoker's nightmare, were disappointed; Mr. Dalí tossed in a fruity bit of symbolism here and there, but for the most part his sets concerned themselves strictly with the business at hand."[47] In addition to *Bacchanale* and *Labyrinth*, Dalí also writes the libretto for a new opera, *Sacrifice*, with music by J.S. Bach and choreography by Léonide Massine, but it was never put on. Another project which remained unpublished was the musical *Las Nubes* (The Clouds), based on the opera of the same name by Aristophanes.[48]

Philippe Halsman, *Salvador Dalí*, 1941

Salvador Dalí at work in a photograph by Eric Schaal, 1941

The artist intent on writing *The Secret Life of Salvador Dalí* in a photograph by Eric Schaal, Hampton Manor 1941

November 18: Opening of two important retrospectives—Dalí and Miró—at the MoMA, New York. In the catalogue, James Thrall Soby goes through the artistic influences which have inspired Dalí during his career up until now, concentrating particularly on the works from his Surrealist period and his controversial stand in favor of modern architecture, Gaudí and Modernism, but he also remembers Dalí's classicist position in defence of the Renaissance. The exhibition moves from town to town, closing on May 17 and passing through Northampton, Cleveland, Indianapolis, San Francisco, Williamsburg, Utica, Detroit and Omaha.

During the year, Dalí meets the photographer, Philippe Halsman, and there begins a working relationship which will last right up until the photographer's death in 1979.

1942

The September issue of *Click* magazine commissions from Dalí a photographic report on the exploration of the subconscious through the lens. The work results in the collage *What Dalí thinks about*. The photographic report will serve to announce the publication of Dalí's autobiography, *The Secret Life of Salvador Dalí*, which will come out in October.

October: Dial Press publishes *The Secret Life of Salvador Dalí*, Dalí's autobiography translated from the French by Haakon M. Chevalier and illustrated by the author himself. The press makes all kinds of comments. *Time* defines it as "one of the most irresistible books of the year." According to the statistics of the San Francisco *Chronicle* of January 10, 1943, the book is classified as number 4 best seller in the essay category.

1943

January 27: Julien Green writes to Dalí asking him to do a *trompe-l'œil* wall decoration for him.

March 13-April 10: Dalí takes part in the exhibition "Art of this century: 15 early paintings – 15 late paintings" at the Art of this Century, the Peggy Guggenheim gallery in New York.
In the Spring, Dalí creates the decoration for Helena Rubinstein's apartment in New York. He realizes three panels representing the morning, the afternoon and the evening; an allegory of the life and mystic journey of man. The photograph of one of the three, large murals appears in *Vogue*, March 1, 1943, "In the famous Dalí room painted for Princess Gourielli." He will later paint Princess Gourielli's (Helena Rubinstein's) portrait.

April 14-May 5: Dalí exhibits at the Knoedler Gallery, New York. Amongst the most important works are the portraits of people from New York's high society and from the fashion world, two of Gala, one of Salvador and Gala together, and a study for *Galarina*. The artist writes "Dalí to the reader" for the catalogue. In it, he enumerates the many activities he has undertaken since moving to the United States two and a half years earlier, even if, as he says, "It was prophesied that, once removed from the stimulus of Paris, I would end up by immobilizing myself in a nostalgic wait for my return." A. Reynolds and Eleanor R. Morse buy their first Dalí painting, *Araña de noche…Esperanza,* known as, *Daddy Longlegs of the Evening – Hope!*, from George Keller at the Bignou Gallery. The collectors write to Dalí and the two couples meet for the first time on April 13 at the Hotel St. Regis, New York. Dalí designs the sets for a new ballet, *Café de Chinitas*, staged by Argentinita and his companion. The work is based on a true story adapted by Federico García Lorca. The ballet is put on for the Spanish Festival at the Metropolitan Opera House, New York, on May 15 and 16 and then goes to Detroit. In the Autumn, Dalí retreats to the Marquis of Cuevas's estate to write his first novel, *Hidden Faces*.
In November, Dalí's limp watches appear in the article "1933-1943 Vogue's latest ten years."

1944

February 15: *Vogue* publishes the article "Dream vs. Reality" with drawings by Salvador Dalí: a presentation of the clothes of Henri Bendel, Garfinckel's and L.S. Ayres.

Poster for the antivenereal disease campaign, 1942

Study for the panel *Evening* made for Helena Rubinstein, 1942

Illustration published in the
magazine Click, September 1942

Dalí takes part in the "First
Exhibition in America of Art of
this Century" at the Art of this
Century gallery, New York, and
in the "Religious Art Today,"
exhibition at the Dayton Art
Museum, Dayton, from April
11 to June 1.
Dial Press, New York,
publishes, *Hidden Faces*, Dalí's
first novel whose outside cover
he designs himself. The
English translation is again
done by Haakon M. Chevalier.
John Selvy writes in the *Post*
of June 9, "I doubt that
anyone can exactly explain
"Hidden Faces." It actually
is a novel in precisely the same
sense that a Dalí canvas is a
painting. All the attributes are
there, but few of them in the
expected places. He has,
apparently, tried to suggest the
decadence of prewar France
by describing certain facets
of it intimately, and yet the
product is less a strict picture
of France in the morass than it
is a picture of Dalí. Doubtless
this is according to plan,
for Dalí is a most calculating
man."
In the August 19 issue of *News*,
we read, "A novel by Dalí, not
so different in approach and
mental attitude from his
autobiography. ... The book is
a mixture of sensation and
sensuality, mysticism and

cynicism, history and fantasy—
in other words, authentic Dalí.
The latter mentions four
reasons for having written this
novel; the third is: 'If I had not
written it, another would have
done it in my place, and would
have done it badly'."
September 22: The publishing
house, Poseidón, of Buenos
Aires, publishes the first
translation in Castilian of
The Secret Life of Salvador Dalí.
October: *Vogue* publishes an
advertisement by Dalí for
Bryans Hosiery. It marks the
beginning of a working
relationship between the artist
and the company which will last
until 1947.
October 30: The International
Theater of New York stages
Sentimental Colloquy, by the
International Ballet. The ballet
was inspired by the poem of
the same name written by Paul
Verlaine, with music by Paul
Bowles and choreography by
André Eglevesky. The Marquis
of Cuevas financed the show
and asked Dalí to design the
costumes and sets—which the
press of the dance world
defines as disconcerting.
Edward Alden Jewell writes
in the *New York Times* of
November 5, "The week's
sensational backdrop was
provided by Salvador Dalí and
New York had its first glimpse
of this rare bird on Monday
night when Ballet International
opened in Columbus Circle

with all the glamor that attaches
to gala events of this kind. ...
That instantly famous backdrop
of his, with its solemn receding
planes of bicycle riders and its
grand piano into which a
fountain pours, is Dalí at his
best.
The fact becomes clear. Dalí
needs a stage with greater
urgency than he needs an art
gallery. His surrealism (which,
framed for the wall, has long
since settled into formula),
thrives in wide-open spaces.
There its sophistication, no
longer just a well-memorized
dernier cri, acquires an effect
of preciosity that is in a sense
monumental."
November: Dalí works on
seven paintings for the lounge
of the Ziegfeld Theater in New
York. Their design is inspired
by the new musical by Billy
Rose, *The Seven Lively Arts*.
Dalí takes part in an exhibition
organized by Elsa Schiapparelli
at the Wildenstein Gallery,
New York. Its aim is to raise
funds for postwar Europe.
Twenty-four works are
exhibited under the theme
health. Dalí's contribution
is a poster depicting his
interpretation of syphilis.
December 15: The show,
*Mad Tristan, the First Paranoiac
Ballet Based on the Eternal
Myth of Love in Death*,
produced by the International
Ballet, opens in New York. The
story, written by Dalí, is based
on the musical themes of
Tristan and Isolde by Wagner.
Choreography is by Léonide
Massine. One of the backdrops
represents a large brick
structure made of three horses'
heads mounted on a column;
in between the horses' heads,
a staircase leads to a terrace
covered in Böcklinian
cypresses. The program
synopsis reads, "Tristan, in
Dalí's conception, has been
driven insane with love, and in
this state he sees himself slowly
devoured by Isolde's Chimera,

a horrible and awesome
transformation of his beloved.
Thus, in the sublimity of the
human being, are reincarnated
the perverse and tragic nuptial
rites of the praying mantis,
wherein the female devours the
male as the consummation of
their union.
Dalí sees the whole romantic
philosophy of Wagner as an
uninterrupted complex of
impotence, an exasperated
procession of wheelbarrows,
heavy with the earth of
reality."[49]
The New York *Journal
American* publishes
"Crazy...like a Fox!," by Mel
Heimer, accompanied by Dalí's
drawing, *Hollywood*, which the
artist himself describes in these
words, "In the landscape of
California, the eyes and the ears
of Hollywood lure the
glamorous. The drawers
represent the diverse
departments: box office,
publicity, etc.."[50]
Eugenio D'Ors publishes a
collection of articles, *Teoria
de los estilos*, some of which go
back to the second half of the
1920's. The article, "Cúpula y
monarquía," is fundamental
to an understanding of Dalí's
devotional journey through
Renaissance styles.[51]

1945
The dropping of the first
atomic bomb on Hiroshima
marks the beginning of Dalí's
"nuclear" or "atomic" period,
as he himself states in
Unspeakable Confessions, "The
atomic explosion of August 6,
1945, gave me a seismic shiver.
From that moment, the atom
became my favorite theme.
Many of the landscapes
I painted in that period reveal
the fear I felt at the news of the
explosion."[52]
Dalí goes to Hollywood at the
invitation of Alfred Hitchcock
who has asked him to do the
dream sequences for the film,
Spellbound, with Gregory Peck

Salvador Dalí in the 1940s

Salvador Dalí nude and a swan at Port Lligat in the Forties

and Ingrid Bergman. This is one of the first American films which deal with the subject of psychoanalysis. The director turns to Dalí for help with the film because he is dissatisfied with the way in which the cinema has so far dealt with and resolved the matter of dream sequences. Hitchcock particularly chooses Dalí because of the elongated architectural forms in his paintings, something that reminds him of de Chirico with "the long shadows, the infinite distances, the lines which converge in the perspective, the formless faces…," as he explains to François Truffaut in *The Cinema According to Hitchcock*. Dalí tells his version of the story in an article in the *Dalí News* of

November 20, "Movies. *Spellbound*. I haven't yet had the occasion to see this film, but here is the story of my intervention: My movie agent and excellent friend, Fe-Fe (Felix Ferry), ordered a nightmare from me by telephone. It was for the film *Spellbound*. Its director, Hitchcock told me the story of the film with an impressive passion, after which I accepted. (Hitchcock is one of the rare personages I have met lately who has some mystery.) I got along wonderfully with Hitchcock, and set to work, but Fe-Fe telephoned me: "They adore all that you are doing at the Selznick studios, but I want to caution you, for the moment they want to use you only in small drops." Fe-Fe advised me the drops were diminishing in proportion to the advancement of the film.. In one of the scenes of my "sequence," it was necessary to create the

impression of a nightmare. Heavy weight and uneasiness are hanging over the guests in a ballroom. I said to Fe-Fe: "In order to create this impression, I will have to hang 15 of the heaviest and most lavishly sculpted pianos possible from the ceiling of the ballroom, swinging very low over the heads of the dancers. These would be in exalted dance poses, but would not move at all; they would only be diminishing silhouettes in a very accelerated perspective, losing themselves in infinite darkness." Fe-Fe communicated the idea which was accepted with enthusiasm by Hitchcock. They passed the idea along to the experts, because in Hollywood there are many, many experts to perfect everything. Some days later I went to the Selznick studios to film the scene with the pianos. And I was stupefied at seeing neither the pianos nor the cut-out silhouettes which must represent the dancers. But right then someone pointed out to me some tiny pianos in miniature hanging from the ceiling and about 40 live dwarfs who, according to the experts, would give perfectly the effect of perspective that I desired. I thought I was dreaming. Even so, they

maneuvered with the false pianos and the real dwarfs (which should be false miniatures). Result. The pianos didn't at all give the impression of real pianos suspended from ropes ready to crack, casting sinister shadows on the ground (for another expert imitated the shadows of the pianos with false shadows projected with the aid of a very complicated apparatus), and as for the dwarfs, one saw, simply that they were dwarfs. Neither Hitchcock nor I liked the result, and we decided to eliminate this scene. In truth, the imagination of the Hollywood experts will be the only thing that will ever have surpassed mine."

November: Dalí presents his prototype of an elegant woman in the year 2045. The woman is vaguely reminiscent of a scarecrow, resembling a sort of collision of electric fans. One of the models wears strips of material which flatten the bust and a kind of padding on the back like mock wings; another has gigantic eyes at chest height. Accessories include an enormous crutch with a clasp (which can be used as a bag but also for moral and spiritual support) and another, smaller, one with a cord (for lifting up the skirt).

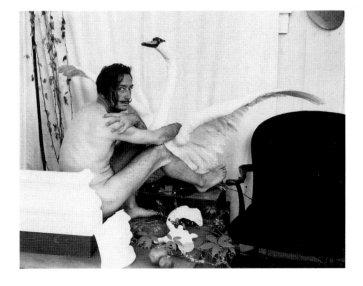

Salvador Dalí while painting the portrait of Isabel Styler-Tas, 1945

Salvador Dalí in front of one of the back drops of *Spellbound*, 1945

Town & Country publishes Gerald Kersh's research report, *Wars for Sale – An Entrepreneur of atomic destruction finds peace at last*, illustrated by Dalí. Dalí's work as illustrator for the magazine lasts several years.[53]
November 20: The exhibition, "Recent Paintings by Salvador Dalí," opens at the Bignou Gallery, New York. Dalí chooses this occasion to present the first issue of *Dalí News*, subtitled, *Monarch of the Dailies*, which he publishes himself and in which he speaks exclusively of his figures and works.
At the Bignou Gallery, he shows eleven paintings, some with neoclassical architectural themes or motifs, like *My Wife, Nude, Contemplating her own Flesh Becoming Stairs, Three*

Vertebrae of a Column, Sky and Architecture. On November 24, Henry McBride quotes Dalí on the painting, "Whenever I wish to approach purity I see the sky through the flesh."
Art News publishes the following review, "Part of the unadulterated variety of surrealism, with vast space and already academically Freudian symbols, appears among the paintings and drawings which make up Dalí's current one man show at Bignou Gallery. But two other trends are also apparent, adding much to the interest of this, as always, fashionable event. With long and intricate titles, which are so much a part of an art closely tied to literary concepts— *Napoleon's Nose, Transformed into a Pregnant Woman, Strolling His Shadow with Melancholia amongst Original Ruins*, for example—there are meticulously painted and complicated allegories of the

style by which Dalí is well known." It goes on to say, "Super-realist in its ultimate sense are the canvases *The Basket of Bread* and *Galarina*, being almost super-academic. These pass beyond trompe-l'œil into an intensity of emotional as well as tactile

values, and are very beautiful. But in the paintings, *The Broken Bridge* and *The Flight, The Temptation, etc.*, there is a new poetry, as lyric and seductive as Piero di Cosimo, as tender in mysterious green and blue tones as Fragonard, as rhythmic as Botticelli"[54].
Dalí says of *The Basket of Bread*, "I painted this picture during two consecutive months, four hours each day. It was during this period that the most staggering and sensational episodes of contemporary history took place. This painting was finished one day before the end of the war. Bread has always been one of the oldest fetishistic and obsessive subjects in my work, the one to which I have remained the most faithful. I painted the same subject nineteen years ago. In making an accurate comparison of the two pictures, one can study the entire history of painting, from the linear charm of primitivism to the stereoscopic hyper-aestheticism. This typically realistic picture is the one which has satisfied my imagination the most. Here is a painting about which there is nothing to explain: The total enigma!."[55]

Dalí News, November 25, 1945

1946

January: Twelve artists of international fame work contemporaneously, in different parts of the world, on the theme, "The temptation of Saint Anthony." A panel of judges will choose from amongst their works the one which will be used as a poster for the film, *Bel-Ami*, based on the story by Guy de Maupassant.

January 24-March 3: Dalí takes part in the exhibition "Four Spaniards: Dalí, Gris, Miró, Picasso," organized by the Institute of Modern Art, Boston. He shows nineteen works.

Walt Disney asks Dalí to work on the production, *Destino*, a short cartoon which will be part of a film made up of various shorts. *Destino* is based on the Mexican love song of the same name, by Armando Domínguez. Dalí, who works at the Disney Studios in Burbank for eight weeks, describes the short as, "a magical exposition of the problems of life in the labyrinth of time." In an interview, A. Frankenstein states that, according to Dalí, the aim of the film was to initiate the public in Surrealism, a mission better accomplished by the movies than by painting or the written word. In "Las etapas del cine," Sebastià Gasch says, "And here is some news that has just come in. The Surrealist painter, Salvador Dalí, in collaboration with Walt Disney, has made *Destino*, a short film which combines drawing and photography in a wonderful way. It is the first time that a film has managed to fully exploit this formula. From what is said, it seems that *Destino* will become a milestone in the history of cinema. The scenes are partly inspired by Gaudían architecture. The main character has the head of a child, the body of a woman and two snails in the place of feet. Pure Dalí.[56] Bob Thomas writes in the *Jersey Journal*, "The Spanish artist is creating a six-minute surrealistic sequence which will be part of a Disney feature. … The landscapes are typically Dalí, laden with cracking telephones and melting watches.

I suggested that the artist likes telephones and watches.
'Is not like', he answered.
'Is obsession'. The chase winds up in a pas de deux, or ballet duet, which takes on the semblance of a baseball game. There is even the huge figure of a catcher squatting and signaling with two fingers to the pitcher. 'Baseball it is fascinating', said Dalí. 'About the game I know nothing. But as an artist. I am obsessed'. Dalí concludes by saying, 'Here the motion is so fluid'. 'You can create effects magnifique. Surrealism will reach immense numbers of people it has not before'."[57] *Destino* was not completed and shown until 2003.

Dalí designs the cover of the May issue of *Et Cetera*. Inside, there is also a photo of Dalí taken by Philippe Halsman, entitled *Beauty and the Beast*. The photographer says of it, "An artist is a pupil of his eye, and through his work he becomes the eye of his public. The dispute about Dalí is: Does he want more to be the public's eye, or in the public eye?. Therefore, in my portrait, Dalí's head, with his hypnotic magician's eyes, forms the pupil of the giant eye —a cabalistic and Freudian symbol. The artist's link with reality is the model, Toni Hollingsworth, whose incredible body is like a violin with an exquisitely highly strung soul."

The Shulton company appoints Dalí to do three paintings for their advertising campaign for the new perfume, Desert Flower. On October 30, the paintings, *Invisible Lovers*, *Mirage* and *Oasis*, went on show at the Knoedler Gallery in New York.

An article by Tristán (the pseudonym of the Catalan author, Josep Pla), "Salvador Dalí visto desde Cadaqués," published in *Destino* magazine revives the Spanish press's interest in the painter. On November 9, 1946, *Destino* announces Dalí's imminent return to Spain, quoting from

Salvador Dalí intent on painting *White Telephone with Ruins* for the animated cartoon *Destino* by Walt Disney, 1946

one of his letters to his family. He does not return, however, until 1948. "…Due to delays in the production of *Destino*, Salvador Dalí has had to put back by a few months his longed-for return to his native Empurdà, to Cadaqués, to Port Lligat, to his obsessions…Spring therefore looks intensely Dalinian and he has announced his arrival for Easter 1947."

1947

In March, nine artists of international fame offer their works in aid of a campaign by the American Cancer Society which is aiming to collect 12 million dollars. Dalí contributes his watercolor, *The Crusader*.
Surrealist Hollywood, published in August, is the first in a series of illustrations that Dalí does

Gala and Salvador Dalí in a photo by Julian P. Graham, 1947

Salvador Dalí and Gala portrayed with *The Three Sphinxes of Bikini* (unfinished), Port Lligat 1947

for *Script*. In the illustration, Dalí presents his vision of some American cities, his impressions of the atomic era and also various fantasies on what the world would be like if it were unable to control atomic energy, and others on what the world would be like if it were controlled by atomic energy. The illustration is supplemented with an interview with Dalí.

October 8-November 9: The Cleveland Museum of Art holds a Dalí exhibition showing a large number of his works, most of which have been lent by the Morse family.

November: On several occasions, Dalí speaks about the world of strip cartoons which, according to him, represent a study of the psychology of the masses, a form of modern mythology. Dalí had done a lot of studies in this area so considered himself the most appropriate person to create strip cartoons for the American public. In the November issue of *PM,* New York, he adds, "… There would be one American character in juxtaposition to several surrealistic characters. This establishes the real contrast of the two kinds of imagination—American life in contradiction with these fantastic things. […] Imagine, for instance, a crowded cocktail party, […], everything very usual, but no one touching the ground. The crowded drinkers would just hover like helicopters without wings. …"[58]

November 25-January 3: The exhibition, "New Paintings by Salvador Dalí," opens at the Bignou Gallery in New York. In addition to his most recent works, he shows his study for *Leda Atomica*. People attending the opening receive the second and last issue of *Dalí News* in which it is announced that the artist is working on an opera

Gala and Salvador Dalí in 1947 at the Hotel St. Regis in New York; in this period, the artist was writing *Fifty Secrets of Magic Craftsmanship*

entirely created by him (and which he will never finish). Also in the magazine are the first chapter of *Fifty Secrets of Magic Craftsmanship* and *Disney-Dalí-Destiny To Be Published by Dial*. Dalí writes two essays for the catalogue: in the first, "Dalí Dalí Dalí," he says that, at 44 years old, it is his responsibility to start painting masterpieces. He has already begun the first, *Leda Atomica*, shown at the exhibition in its draft stage. The second essay is "Appendix. History of Art, Short but Clear," also reproduced in Dalí News. During the year, Dalí begins working on one of the most emblematic works of the Teatre-Museu Dalí, *Leda*

Atomica, which he finishes in 1949. In order to produce the preparatory drawings, Dalí enlists the help of the mathematician Matila Ghyka.

1948
February 18: *Destino* publishes "Carta al padre de Salvador Dalí" in which Carlos Sentis lists Dalí's latest successes and projects. It also announces Dalí's imminent return to Spain.
April: Gala writes to the actor, Errol Flynn, asking him if he has received the script of *Dalí El Cid* and what he thinks of it. The project is never carried out.[59]
July: Dalí and Gala set sail for Le Havre. They return to Spain after eight years in the United States. The couple's arrival is hailed in the August 14 issue of *Destino* in its article, "Bienvenido Salvador Dalí," written by Ignacio Agusti. As soon as they arrive in Port Lligat, they begin work on

extending the house. Dalí buys a one-storey hut nearby, situated on the highest point of the slope: it is Ca l'Arsèni, which is to become the library. The restructuring work will be finished in the Spring of the following year. In Palamós, the patron, Albert Puig Palau, has an atelier built for artists, based on plans by Dalí.
Dial Press, New York, publishes *Fifty Secrets of Magic Craftsmanship*, a book in which Dalí sings the praises of the artistic tradition represented by the painters and architects of the Renaissance (Raphael, Leonardo da Vinci, Bramante, Palladio, etc.). Dalí also publishes a short perspective section of the icosahedral study which he is planning with Gabriel Alomar, a Mallorcan-born architect (1910) who obtained a degree in Barcelona in 1934 and another one at the Massachusetts Institute of Technology in 1945. The project is to do a study of the icosahedral figure, working in Port Lligat. It is inspired by the geometric experiments of Leonardo da Vinci and Luca Pacioli but it is never carried out. Louise Bruner, journalist with the Cleveland News, after having written about some of the secrets revealed by Dalí, goes on to say, "Dalí launches his book with a vitriolic attack on modern art, which he is destined to save from chaos."
November 26: *Rosalinda* or *As You Like It*, by William Shakespeare, opens at the Teatro Elisco, Rome. It is directed by Luchino Visconti, with stage sets and costumes by Dalí. To coincide with the show, the art publishers, Carlo Bestetti, bring out the book, *As You Like It*, in which appear Dalí's piece, "Bonjour," and pictures of his stage-sets and costumes. In the same period, the Galleria

Catalogue of the exhibition "Salvador Dalí," Cleveland Museum of Art, October-November 1947

Catalogue of the exhibition "New Paintings by Salvador Dalí," Bignou Gallery, New York, November 1947-January 1948

Salvador Dalí in the gardens of Bomarzo, 1948

Salvador Dalí con "la Patum," Cadaqués 1948

Salvador Dalí photographed by Batlles Compte together with his sister Ana María and father at Port Lligat, ca. 1948

right-hand side
Salvador Dalí portrayed by Batlles Comte together with his father at Port Lligat, 1948

1949
February: The Fifth Annual March of Dimes Fashion Show presents Dalí's work, *Women in Space*, a project for clothes with moving shapes, in the ballroom of the Waldorf Astoria in New York.
April 24: The ballet by Manuel de Falla, *The Three-Cornered Hat*, opens at the Ziegfeld Theatre in New York. It is staged by theatre company Ana Maria, with stage sets and costumes by Salvador Dalí.
June: *Mad Tristan* opens at the Gran Teatre del Liceo, Barcelona.
November: Two important theatrical shows open with costumes and choreography by Dalí: *Don Juan Tenorio*, by José Zorrilla at the María Guerrero theater , Madrid (of which there will be many performances) and *Salomé* by Oscar Wilde, at Covent Garden, London, directed by Peter Brook, with music

by Richard Strauss.
The choreography for *Salomé* was problematic. The conductor writes in a telegram, "Saw Salome sets for first time today absolutely impossible for requirements of music and singers…" Brook was disappointed that Dalí did not come to London to help realize his ideas. The lighting effects of blood flooding the stage were so horrifying in the dress rehearsal they were apparently dropped. However, the production enjoyed huge press coverage partly through a policy of extreme secrecy; critics were divided, some finding it less surrealist than they feared or hoped. "Those who came for another *Mad Tristan* (New York 1944) were disappointed: the designs suggest a turning point between the extremes of surrealism and classicism." (*The Scotsman*, November 1949). "Mr Dalí's scenery was

dell'Obelisco in Rome presents "The First Exhibition of Salvador Dalí in Italy." Dalí plans another film, *The Story of a Wheelbarrow*, in which he would like Paulette Godard to star. Later, the title will be changed to *La brouette de chair*, then finally to *La carretilla de carne* with the addition of the subtitle, *Neomystic Film*. The starring role is given to Anna Magnani, the producer is Albert Puig Palau, but the film is never finished; likewise, two other film projects: the life of Goya, and the life of Dalí, which would have been based on his autobiography, *The Secret Life of Salvador Dalí*.[60] Dalí and the photographer Philippe Halsman create *Dalí Atomicus*. The photograph gives the impression that the materials which appear in the *Leda Atomica* painting are levitating.

Philippe Halsman,
Nude with popcorn, 1948

not without some weird contraptions…but created in a vague way an impression of something very old and very oriental." (*Yorkshire Post,* November 12, 1949).
November 23: Dalí has an audience with Pope Pius XII. He presents the pope with *The Madonna of Port Lligat*— a smaller version than the previous two versions of the painting. After the meeting, the artist declares to journalists that he wants to guide modern painting back into the grooves of the great medieval and Renaissance artistic traditions. At the end of the year, Dalí returns to New York. From now on, he will spend Spring and Summer in Port Lligat and Autumn and Winter between New York and Paris, always staying in the same hotels: the Saint Regis in Fifth Avenue, and the Meurice in rue Rivoli.
Ana María Dalí publishes *Salvador Dalí visto por su hermana*, a book rich in anecdotes from both their lives.

1950
Dalí writes the script for the film, *Le Sang Catalan*, but it will never be made. Notes from the beginning of the script read:
CATALAN BLOOD
In the miNeral heart of Catalonia, at the top of a strange rock in the shape of an eagle, the people run to the iNauguratioN of the symbolic monument to "Catalan blood"-
The/Some fishermen from the coast arrive by sea, the farmers on foot-
-woman playing harp
-small finger is harp-
(1) We penetrate the living reality of an unknown town, one of the most phenomenal, the most original, violent and philosophical. In order to

discover Catalonia, even if its conformity makes it easily accessible, you need all the complicated instruments of the intrepid explorer, from the empty stratosphere to the diving suit, you must constantly travel up and down in the most contradictory, the deepest and the most spectacular areas of the inhabitants lives. The life of this community bears the biological mark of blood, the authentic blood mark of blood![61]
January: In reply to his sister's book, Dalí publishes *Memorandum*, "Famous: my family accepted a reconciliation but my sister could not resist the temptation to make a show of my name, in the material and pseudo-sentimental sense of the word, selling my pictures without my permission and making public information on objective facts of my life which are absolutely untrue. It is therefore the least I can do to warn collectors and biographers."
The previous year, Dalí had bought another cottage in Port Lligat near to his but a little lower down. He built another studio on top of it, although, as always, he kept the original roof so that it came in between the two floors. The entrance to

the second floor studio was from the back whilst the entrance to the original part of the cottage was from the little square in front. On the back of a post card, Dalí sketches out what he has in mind for the cottage and adds some notes for Emilio Puignau, a builder friend. On the side of the house facing the sea, Dalí wants to keep the steps between the big windows of the new annexes. For the studio, he designs a trapezoid-shaped door and a chimney opposite. The work is completed in the Spring.[62]
It is perhaps during this period that the artist designs and builds Gala's Corral in Cadaqués. It is made from an old ship which he transforms by adding doors and chimney flues with strange bulbous or Classicist shapes. It is Gala's personal refuge and is a foretaste of their future Púbol residence.
April 9: The first version of *The Madonna of Port Lligat* is reproduced in color on the front cover of *Newsweek*. In New York, Dalí agrees to an interview with José Maria Massip. The interview is

Advertisement by Salvador Dalí and Eddie Cantor for the S.S. America, 1949

Salvador Dalí at Port Lligat
in the 1950s

Salvador Dalí photographed by
Contreras in Madrid's María
Guerrero theater for the production
of *Don Juan Tenorio* by José Zorrilla
with stage scenes by the artist, 1950

published in *Destino* on April
1. In it, Dalí talks indirectly of
his Catholic faith and his
Classicism, and when asked
if he has any other project,
he announces that the Italian
government has asked him to
illustrate the *Divine Comedy*,
"… for a monumental edition
to be published in Italy, and
I think I will be able to
complete it over the Summer,
in Cadaqués. It is a text which
attracts me to the point of
obsession because I see in it
the two souls of my own life.
I love the book and I have
already planned out the work
in my head." Later, in his
book, *Unspeakable
Confessions*, he says he has
never read the *Divine Comedy*,
"I have never read Dante.
I dream about him then Gala
adds my drawings to the
text."[63]

May: A new edition of
Anthology of Black Humor by
André Breton is published in
which the writer changes the
part about Dalí, adding a note
which clearly shows how distant
they have become, "It is
obvious that what we have said
applies only to the first Dalí,
the one who disappeared in
1935 to make way for the
person better known as Avida
Dollars, the painter of portraits
for high society, who has just
embraced the Catholic faith
and the 'artistic ideal of the
Renaissance', and who now
even receives praise from the
Pope."
June: *House and Garden*
publishes "Dalí designs his
dream studio, a geometric
fantasy on the Catalan coast
in Spain"; an article on Dalí's
project for a studio in Port
Lligat. On July 17, *Destino*
takes up the story: Luis Ripoll
writes, "It is a project for a
studio which Salvador wants
to build in Cadaqués: a giant
icosahedron whose faces of
triangular glass will be
mounted on golden supports.
The amount of light coming in
will be controlled by antique
tapestries, and Dalinian
'crutches' will play a
prominent role. The
Mediterranean olive tree that
sticks out of the big diamond is
there to show how, today, any
work has a sign of Classicism in
it. For that matter, the idea of a
regular polyhedron with twenty
faces as an ideal studio is not
new, Leonardo da Vinci had
the idea first." In October,
Gabriel Alomar publishes an
important article, "Salvador
Dalí y el juego filosofal de la
arquitectura" in *Revista
Nacional de Arquitectura.*
In the Summer, Dalí and Gala
return to Cadaqués and Dalí
paints a new version of *The
Madonna of Port Lligat*, using
a much bigger canvas. In the
Winter, the work is exhibited in
New York.

September 21: Dalí's father,
Salvador Dalí Cusí, dies.
The Museum of Modern Art,
New York, opens the itinerant
exhibition, "The Artist and the
Decorative Arts" which
highlights the growing
importance of art in industrial
production. Amongst the artists
taking part are: Salvador Dalí,
Alexander Calder, Roberto
Matta, Henry Moore, Juan
Gris, Isamu Noguchi and
Georgia O'Keefe.
October 19: Dalí gives a lecture
at the Ateneu, Barcelona,
entitled, "Why I was
sacrilegious, why I am mystic,"
where he explains some of the
episodes in his life in relation
to the Spanish mystic tradition
whose leaders are Zurbarán
and Saint John of the Cross.
The meeting ends with the
reading of a theological-type
poem, *Atòmica perfecció de la
Anunciació de la Immaculada
Concepció*, inspired by *The
Madonna of Port Lligat*.[64] The
Diario de Barcelona reports that
the lecture aroused great
interest and the Ateneu had
a full house.
Dalí enters his work, *The
Temptation of Saint Anthony*,
in the competition for the
Carnegie Institute of Pittsburgh
prize.
November 1: Zorrilla's *Tenorio*
is once again shown at the
María Guerrero theater,
Madrid, with stage sets and
costumes by Dalí.
November 27-January 10: There
is a new exhibition at the
Carstairs Gallery, New York,
in which Dalí exhibits two
versions of *The Madonna of
Port Lligat*. For the catalogue,
he writes the piece, "The Port
Lligat Madonna…."
In the handwritten *Genio y
figura de la pintura española*,
dated 1950, Dalí notes some
of his thoughts on geometry,
proportion, etc. and on Spanish
painting, "Leave it alone …
And so it was, and, at the sure
and lucid stab of Velázquez's

brush, the bull of universal esthetic dropped down dead. From this sacrifice came nothing less than Spanish realism with its physical, bleeding, viscous, cosmic and tauromachic equivalence, equivalent to the energy of the brush and to the mass of the reality of the world of vision, of genius and of the shape of Spanish painting. Beware. Zurbarán will always seem more modern to us and represent the figure of Spanish genius in a more categorical way than the 'Italianized' El Greco. Juan Gris is a mystic painter of cold structures, and Picasso is the iconoclast who invented Cubism from the polychrome geometry of Alhambra, Granada. Goya is the figure of the figure; the genius does not find room where 'mannerism' emerges, transforming itself into hierarchy. Dalí will be the Heraclitus of Spain, Ribera the darkness of the Levante and let us not forget Murillo in which, contrary to accepted opinion, Salvador Dalí sees the synthesis of genius and shape. This article gives rise to new polemic …, Spanish painting is

Salvador Dalí portrayed by Ricard Sans while pointing out his house at Port Lligat, 1951

about to be discovered and it is the best in the world." This text will be included in the book, *El alma de España*, published in 1951.

1951
April 15: Dalí finishes writing *Mystical Manifesto*, published in Paris by Michel Tapié and Robert Godet and presented to the public on June 19. The limited edition books are bound in red velvet with gold lettering. The text is set out in two columns, one in Latin and the other in French.
Mystical Manifesto represents the transcendent explanation of Dalí's admiration for the Renaissance, Classicism and religious painting.
According to *Paris Presse*, Dalí reads his manifesto to a group of friends at Arturo López's house then invites them at night to the Galerie André Weil in Paris to see his latest paintings.
In April, the publishers Juventut publish *Tot l'any a Cadaqués*, Ana María's second book on Dalí.
In May, Dalí is invited to participate in the "I Exposición Bienal Hispanoamericana de Arte" organized by the Instituto de Cultura Hispánica, which opens on October 12 in the Museo de Amigos del Arte,

Salvador Dalí with an issue of *Vogue* magazine under his arm, 1950 [Acme]

Madrid. Dalí's works will not be exhibited until the following year, from January 21 to mid-February. The newspaper *Informaciones* of January 22, 1952, tells us that Dalí presents thirty-two works: eight oils and the rest watercolors, drawings and pastels which come from the exhibition at the Lefevre Gallery in London in December.
September 3: Carlos de Beistegui organizes a masked ball at the Palazzo Labia in Venice. Dalí and Gala attend dressed in costumes designed by Dalí and made by Christian Dior.
November 11: Dalí gives a lecture, "Picasso and me," organized by the Instituto de Cultura Hispánica at the María Guerrero theater, Madrid. It evokes great expectations. Dalí begins his talk with these words, "As always, Spain boasts the honor of having the

maximum of contrasts, and this time it is in the person of the two most antagonistic painters of contemporary painting, Picasso and me, your humble servant. Picasso is Spanish, and so am I. Picasso is a genius, and so am I. Picasso is about seventy-two, I'm about forty-eight. Picasso is known throughout the world, and so am I. Picasso is a Communist, neither am I." The artist goes on to explain the reasons why Picasso supports Communism. He talks about modern art in similar terms to those he used in his mystic manifesto, and he talks about Franco. He finishes the lecture by repeating that he hopes that Picasso will abandon Communism: he again proposes sending

Salvador Dalí in a photograph by Karen Radkai, wearing the suit designed by the Maison Dior for the ball organized by Carlos de Beistegui at the Palazzo Labia, Venice, 1951

Salvador Dalí produces *Macbeth* by Willam Shakespeare in 1951 in a radio program by the BBC led by A. Montaner

watercolors, drawings and pastels. *Christ of Saint John of the Cross* is also shown. The city of Glasgow buys the work in January 1952. The *Post Dispatch* of January 25, 1952, reads, "Glasgow buys Dalí work for $22,960, and stirs protests. The city corporation of Glasgow announced yesterday the purchase of Salvador Dalí's latest work, *The Crucifixion*, for £8,200 ($22,960) for the city art galleries. The painting by the Spanish surrealist is in the traditional style, although it depicts the crucifixion from an unusual angle - from above the head of Christ. … "

1952

February: Dalí gives a series of lectures in different locations in the United States. During the lectures, he speaks to the public about his nuclear mysticism; as *The College Eye* of Cedar Fall puts it, "Dalí Lecture is unusual. Teachers College students and faculty members experienced an unconventional evening's entertainment Wednesday, when one of the most controversial figures in modern art, Salvador Dalí, appeared in the third program of the year's lecture-concert series. …
A close friend of Dalí, A. Reynolds Morse, served as an interpreter during a question and answer period. His Teachers College appearance was the first of a series of 10 lectures-demonstrations Dalí will make in the U.S. His mission during the tour is to explain the predicted "return to spiritual classicism movement" in modern art, and to clarify his own position in the movement."[65]
In response to a survey on Socialist Realism carried out by *Arts*, Dalí writes the article, "Authenticité et mensonge" in which he takes a firm stand against the movement in

him a telegram to this end and invites the Spanish intellectuals to sign it.
December 4: A Dalí exhibition opens at the Lefevre Gallery, London. Included in the works are *The Madonna of Port Lligat*, the second version of the work shown to the Pope, *Raphaelesque Head Exploding*, *Wheat Ear* and *Me aged six, when I thought I was a girl, whilst I very cautiously lifted the skin off the sea to see the dog sleeping in the shadow of the water*, plus some

question. The text, written on April 23, is published on May 1, "As the philosopher Eugenio Montes said, 'History should not be useful to itself, but it should be to artists'. This maxim is particularly apt in the most vile of all eras, that in which we have the honor of living. The artist should not serve anyone but God. (And, in the case of authenticity and genius, he never does, even through the expression of the grimmest atheism. The noble, sincere, ingenious atheism of the great Nietzsche is today even closer to God than a spirit).
The artist does not depend on History, but painting a 'historic painting' is absolutely permissible as long as the

Salvador Dalí portrayed by Ricard Sans while painting *Christ of Saint John of the Cross* in the studio at Port Lligat, 1951

Salvador Dalí photographed by C. Portillo in 1951 at Madrid's María Guerrero theater for the lecture "Picasso and me"

Salvador Dalí in front of *Christ of Saint John of the Cross*, 1951

creative act is not born of any political motive. Velázquez painted *The Surrender of Breda*. It is one of his most beautiful paintings. It is about a historical event but in the painting, the political indifference is absolute and the genius manifests itself in complete freedom. To create an immortal masterpiece without a subject is possible, just as it is using all the subjects in the world, including that terribly ungrateful one of 'Komsomol in good health'. If Vermeer had painted it, he would have made it a great work. So would Dalí if he had presented it in his 'nuclear' mode, making it explode and reducing it to an infinite number of super-gelatinous corpuscles. The ignominious shame, without precedent, of

'Socialist Realism' rests in the fact that it is a total lie. It has nothing to do with 'spiritual creation' through which man can achieve new conquests of knowledge or feeling. Actually, it is the exact opposite, or rather it limits itself to serving in the most bureaucratically adulatory way a certain political system or a form of State to the total detriment of any other State and anything else. Hello, Picasso!"
June 9: The University of Texas publishes "Le mythe de Guillaume Tell. Toute la vérité sur mon expulsion du groupe surréaliste" in which Dalí reveals the facts that led to his expulsion from the Surrealist group.
June: Dalí publishes the text, "Reconstitution du corps glorieux dans le ciel" in the Catholic magazine, *Études Carmelitains*. The article is part of a special edition entitled "Magie des extremes."

One of the people working on it is the magazine's editor, the French Carmelite, J.M.Bruno. In his piece, Dalí announces that the *Assumption of the Virgin Mary* will be made possible by the constitution of Dalinian mysticism, "… Wanting to paint a great theme of our era, as the Russians do, I found the recent proclamation by the Pope of the dogma of the Assumption of the Virgin Mary to be more important than anything else. I would not have been able to realize this work had it been before the 'constitution' of my 'nuclear mysticism', the only thing, at the moment, that allows my imagination to access a new cosmogony that incorporates the metaphysical into the general principles of the extraordinary progress of the sciences peculiar to our time. … It is in this way that I managed to imagine visually the principal constitutional elements of modern physics, revealing their shapes and structural peculiarities with a degree of precision that has so far never been seen in my realist works. … Dalí, for the very first time, has just drawn an electron, a proton, a meson, a pion and even the soft structure par excellence (of this very new 'cosmic snare',

of which I frequently talk in a near obsessive way), a lot earlier than Professor Fermi made use of it in the stricter scientific sense." In the same issue, Dalí, together with Francis Picabia, Georges Mathieu and Henri Michaux, sign the announcement, "Attitudes paroxistiques de quatre artistes contemporains."
August 20-October 5: Dalí shows twenty-two works in the exhibition, "Phantastische Kunst des XX Jahrhunderts" organized by the Kunsthalle, Basle.
November: Paul Éluard dies.
December 8: A new exhibition opens at the Carstairs Gallery in New York. Dalí presents "The first nuclear-mysticism paintings and the *Assumpta Corpuscularia Lapislazulina.*" The works shown are: *Assumpta Corpuscularia Lapislazulina, Evangelical Still Life, Nuclear Cross, Placid Gala, The Angel of Port Lligat* and *The Persistence of Corpuscular Memory*. Dalí's writing summing up his philosophy of this period is as follows, "LONG LIVE MODERN ART AS LONG AS

Salvador Dalí portrayed by Carlos Pérez de Rozas at the Port Lligat studio, during the elaboration of *Galatea of the Spheres*, ca. 1952

Gala posing for *Corpus Hypercubicus (Crucifixion)*, ca. 1952

Gala and Salvador Dalí pose in front of *Raphaelesque Head Exploding* during the Madrid Biennale of 1952

THE PAINTING BEGINS FROM RAPHAEL S.D. My *Assumption* is the opposite of the atomic bomb. Instead of the disintegration of matter, we have the integration, the reconstitution of the real and glorious body of the Virgin in the heavens.
This painting alone justifies in itself every experimental effort in modern art, since I have succeeded in bringing these experiments to a classical end; experiments which would otherwise have remained sterile, since the majority of the great and courageous innovators are today returning to archaeological inspiration; and only a few impetuous young abstract painters continue with 'interesting plastic experiments' which, unfortunately, are destined to remain decorative art because of their means of purely graphical expression. There was Seurat with his Divisionism, who, without knowing it, introduced nuclear physics; also Cubism; and especially the great Futurist genius, Boccioni, but he expresses himself in terms of speed, motor-cars and aviation. This is childish, and it is because of this lack of theological and philosophical meaning that all these efforts perished so soon.
But all of them had foreseen a thing that was to be the *great, immeasurable and categorical innovation of our time – a new conception of matter*, that of NUCLEAR PHYSICS."
The *New Yorker* writes of the exhibition, "New paintings still pursue his attempt (uneasy but fairly glittering) to effect a wedding between nuclear physics and the arts."

1953
March 28: In the article, "Notes à propos de *l'Assumpta Corpuscularia Lapislazulina*," written for the magazine *Connaissance des Arts*, Dalí explains his painting to the readers.
April: Enrico Baj lodges a complaint with the court in Milan claiming that Dalí was not the inventor of "nuclear painting."
The August issue of *Festa d'Elig* publishes the translation of the text, "Vive l'art moderne à condition de peindre à partir de Raphael. S.D.," used in the catalogue for the Carstairs Gallery exhibition of the previous year.
During his stay in Cadaqués, Dalí is inspired to create a ballet by his reading of the Prince de Rothschild's poem, *Le Sacre d'Automne*. He designs the stage sets and costumes; music is by Henri Sauguet and choreography by Serge Lifar. The project is never realized.
September: The Marquis de Cuevas organizes a masked ball in Biarritz with over two thousand guests. Dalí designs the setting.

1954
February: *La Parisienne* magazine publishes Dalí's article, "Mes secrets cinematographiques" in which, in addition to speaking about his forays into the world of cinema and giving his opinion on contemporary cinema, Dalí also describes the story of what should have been his next film, *La brouette de chair* (later renamed *La carretilla de carne*), but which will never be realized. The May issue of the same magazine publishes "Les morts et moi," an article about

the death of Dalí's two friends, Federico García Lorca and René Crével. The complete text will be included in *Diary of a Genius* (1964).

May 13: At the Casino dell'Aurora in the Pallavicini Rospigliosi Palace, Rome, the first Italian retrospective on Salvador Dalí opens with twenty-eight paintings, seventeen watercolors, some drawings, the illustrations for the *Divine Comedy* and the jewels from the Catherwood Collection (previously the Owen Cheatham Collection). The exhibition is an enormous success and is widely discussed in the press, especially with regard to the painter's planned presentation. Before opening the exhibition, Dalí symbolically dies before journalists and is then reborn inside a metaphysical cube which, as he says, "represents the maximum spiritual strength that the human mind has ever been able to invent. This cube is Ramón Llull *Ars Magna*."

An interview with Manuel del Arco for *Revista*, published on May 27, gives the translation of Dalí's speech which was given in Latin, "The day Goethe arrived in Rome, he wrote 'I feel as though I have been reborn'. We Spanish do not think, we act. And for this reason, Salvador Dalí, before reaching the age of fifty, has the shrewdness to be reborn

under the geometric center of Guido Reni's *Aurora* where he is lucky enough to meet immediately the one who inspires all his work: his wife, Gala, the Beatrice of his life. This metaphysical cube is the work of my rebirth.

This metaphysical cube is the exact opposite of the Hydrogen Bomb. This nuclear cube contains all its inscriptions, all the possible and imaginable combinations of all the spiritual explosive forces, and the maximum of corpuscular energy of the most creative amongst the moral and esthetic faculties of the human soul. This atomic cube contains in its orders all the virtues of originality, the only ones that can save art itself from the lack of technique, from chaos and from nothingness.

The ultimate consequences of modern art are the same as those of materialism. 'When painters do not believe in anything, they end up not

painting anything.' I invite young painters to follow my example: be reborn or die. To counter any skepticism there is faith. To counter any revolution or reaction there is rebirth.

This allegorical cube has been created in line with *El discurso sobre la figura cúbica* by Juan de Herrera, builder of the Escorial and architect to Philip II, and according to the doctrine of the archangelic Raimondo Lullo. And, as Luca Pacioli dedicated his *De Divina Proportione* to the Duke of Urbino, Salvador Dalí dedicates this Spanish cube, this new cubic egg of Colombus, to Princess Pallavicini and Count Rossi di Montellera, thanks to whom *The Aurora* is reborn today. God be praised."

The exhibition is also held in Venice and Milan.

In this period, Dalí begins a new film project inspired by Vermeer's *The Lace-maker* and by his obsession with

Salvador Dalí with Eugenio D'Ors, Mercedes de Prat and Luis Romero at Port Lligat, 1953

Salvador Dalí in Port Lligat, 1954

left-hand side
Cover of the catalogue of the exhibition "Salvador Dalí," Carstairs Gallery, New York, December 1952-January 1953

rhinoceros horns made to follow a perfect logarithmic spiral. The film, which is never finished, is entitled *Histoire prodigieuse de la Dentellière et du Rhinocéros*. Various scenes are filmed between 1954 and 1961, some at the zoo of Vincennes and others at the Louvre in Paris.

October: *Dalí's Mustache* appears in the bookshops, the work of Dalí and the photographer Philippe Halsman. Dalí writes the prologue in which, naturally, he speaks of his mustache, "Many marvelous and inspirational uses of this mustache are shown in this book. But every day I find new ones. This very morning, and just at the moment of not shaving myself, I discovered that my mustache can serve as an ultra-personal brush. With the point of its hair, I can paint a fly with all the details of his hair."

December 7-January 31: The Carstairs Gallery, New York, opens a new exhibition. In the catalogue, Dalí describes the success of the previous retrospective, in Rome, Venice and Milan, and comments on the works shown, "... While awaiting my retrospective exhibition across America, my new campaign in New York starts with this exhibition of my work of the last six months, on the most creative theme of all: DISCONTINUED MATTER." Amongst the works shown are the illustrations for the Divine Comedy and the *Corpus Hypercubicus* (*Crucifixion*).

Salvador Dalí in a photo by Ean at Port Lligat, 1954

Philippe Halsman, *Portrait of Salvador Dalí*, 1954

Philippe Halsman, *Dalí's Mustache*, 1954

December: José Janés publishes *La verdadera historia de Lídia de Cadaqués*, by Eugenio D'Ors, with illustrations by Dalí. According to Dalí's *Diary of a Genius*, during this year, he works on two literary projects: *Las 120 jornadas de Sodoma del Divino Marqués y a la inversa*, a project for which no documentation remains, and *Mártir*, an unfinished tragedy written in French, in Alexandrines.

1955
January: The press announces that the North American magnate, Chester Dale, has bought Dalí's *Corpus Hypercubicus* and then donated it to the Metropolitan Museum of Art, in New York. *Time* publishes a letter from Dalí to the Director, "... I consider the [Met's] acquisition now of my *Crucifixion* as being timely. My pictorial conception of *Corpus Hypercubicus* is a completely new creative idea which is in direct contrast to the current abstract academism."[66]

March 6: *This Week* magazine publishes Dalí's response to a question put to the magazine by readers: "Who is the most beautiful woman in the world?" Dalí cites various icons such as the *Venus de Milo*, da Vinci's *Mona Lisa*, and the Egyptian queen, Nefertiti, but concludes by saying that in his opinion the current most beautiful woman is the Iberian sculpture, "... La Dama de Elche is the Most Beautiful for our times because she can become the symbol of a youth that has faith in virtue and that sees through the dangers and frustrations of our time, to glimpse the vision of a new Golden Age." During the Summer, whilst in Port Lligat, Dalí paints *The Last Supper*.

December 16: Dalí gives a lecture at the Sorbonne University, in Paris, entitled,

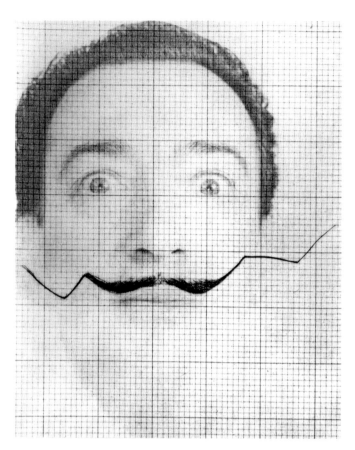

"The phenomenological aspects of the paranoid-critical method." He arrives for the lecture in Georges Mathieu's white Rolls Royce which he has filled with cauliflowers. Beforehand, Dalí had told *L'Express*, "The lecture is a pseudoscientific exsperiment. I will dance for just one minute to demonstrate something. To demonstrate other things, in my right hand I will hold a baton made of rhinoceros horn and in my left, the very rare lantern—lent to me by Jean Cocteau—which was used by Vermeer's baker in Delft. I will address the men of science. … It is only when you do things that are very well defined that you can be successful." The following year, the lecture is published in *La vie médicale* and *Nombre d'Or: revue du centre international d'études esthétiques*.

1956
March 31: Chester Dale gives Dalí's *Last Supper* to the National Gallery of Washington.
In April, to celebrate its 30th anniversary, the magazine *Amazing Stories* asks various world-famous people, including Salvador Dalí, "What will the world be like in 2001?." Dalí replies, "I believe that art and science will have merged by 2001. Art is the reflection of the complete discontinuity of

Philippe Halsman, *Salvador Dalí*, 1954

right-hand side
Gala and Salvador Dalí pose for Robert Lantos in front of *The Temptation of Saint Anthony*, 1950s

Salvador Dalí painting the portrait of Laurence Olivier playing Richard III, 1955

Salvador Dalí in London in 1955 for the exhibition of "Everething is so sad, so melanchole," sponsored by Daily Express

matter; science is its proof. By 2001, the artists, sculptors, and painters of that day will be able to portray this discontinuity in a new kind of explosive harmony.
The secret of this harmony is to be seen today in cosmic radiation. All beauty is terrible; and that radiation is at once both beautiful and terrible is to be seen in the natural portrayal of atomics in the cauliflower and the rhinoceros horn. Beauty is mathematical too— I refer you to the works of Bach—and the beauty of the logarithmic curve of the rhinoceros horn, with its repetition in the internal cedillas of the cauliflower can be seen by the aware eye of today, and *will* be seen, and acted upon, by the awakened artists of 2001.
Nor is this all: cosmic radiation, it is now evident, is causing the downfall of the rigidity which for so long has afflicted Man and his works. All things—from architecture, to politics, to gastronomy—in which Man has immersed himself are becoming soft, fluid, non-geological. By 2001, such things will have lost their final rigidity, and have gained, instead, the unity which is to be found in cosmic radiation, the cauliflower, the rhinoceros horn. They will have realized that the secret of life, of art, and of power is viscosity."
June 16: Dalí has an audience with General Franco.
September 29: Dalí pays homage to Gaudí with a lecture in Güell Park, Barcelona, during which he creates a piece of art in the presence of the audience. The money collected during the lecture goes towards the conservation of Gaudí's works and to a fund for the completion of the *Sagrada Familia* in Barcelona.
December 4-January 5: Dalí again exhibits his work at the Carstairs Gallery in New York.

The Last Supper at the studio
of the house at Port Lligat, 1955

Salvador Dalí with Joan Figueras in
a photo by Charles H. Hewitt, 1955

right-hand side
Salvador Dalí doing the illustrations
for *Don Quixotte*, 1956

The *Daily News* of December
16 comments, "It's the best
show in town. In a stunning
canvas called 'Fast-Moving
Still-Life', a table with wine and
running soda siphon rocks to
atomic blast, yet holds its own
realist-symbolist elements in
such painting perfection that
even the masters must be
moved …"
December: at the end of an
event in which Don Quijote
and Sancho Panza—
interpreted by Paul Préboist—
attack the Moulin de la Galette
in Montmartre, Dalí creates a

lithograph, in public, for
Don Quichotte, published
in Paris by Joseph Foret. The
critic, Michel Tapié, and the
lithographer, Charles Porlier,
help him.

1957
Over the year, Dalí works on
a project for a Surrealist night
club, El Presidiente, and for
the famous luxury hotel,
César Balsa, in Acapulco. Dalí
designs a sort of Dalinian Güell
Park: a sea urchin which can
hold up to five hundred
people, held up by four
enormous flies' legs. The sea
urchin is pulled by twenty-five
giraffes which are eighteen
meters high and made of
rubble. The night club is never
built but in November 1961,
eight sketches for the project
are shown in the hotel bar.
February: Dalí moves closer
to the world of hairdressing
because, according to him,
it represents a new form of
creativity. Dalí convinces the
famous Hollywood hairstylist,
Peter Leonardi, to go to New
York to create new hair styles
under his supervision.
May 20-July 31: The exhibition,
"Bosch, Goya et le fantastique"
is held as part of the Festival of
Bordeaux. *Aurore* reports,
"From Hieronymus Bosch to
Salvador Dalí, passing through
Goya on the way, the public
may admire the canvases of
the masters that have marked

the history
of painting." Dalí takes part
in the exhibition with three
works.
Nugget magazine publishes a
series of articles accompanied
by illustrations dealing with
twelve predictions for the
future, a few of which were
published the previous year
in other periodicals. In Dalí's
opinion, in the future,
buildings will be soft and
flexible, they will change
depending on the temperature
and atmospheric pressure and
will be built of materials which
derive from atomic chemistry.
In the same magazine, Dalí
presents designs for clothes
with the front at the back,
gelatinous spoons for long life,
and sofas that breathe.[67]
October: Walt Disney visits
Dalí in Port Lligat and together
they study the idea of making a
film about Don Quixote. The
project is never realized.
November: The publisher,

Joseph Foret, issues *Histoire
d'un grand livre, Don
Quichotte*, illustrated with
fifteen lithographs by Dalí.
This is accompanied by a
booklet which describes the
process of producing the book,
with photographs illustrating
the various phases. The text is
by Salvador Dalí and Michel
Deon. On December 12, the
Musée Jacquemart-André of
Paris exhibits the illustrations
that go with the book.
On Christmas day, the
Bordeaux newspaper, *Sud
Ouest*, publishes an article
in which Dalí remembers the
Christmas of 1921, when he
was seventeen and the mayor
of Figueres entrusted him with
the job of making a carriage for
the Magi, for the traditional
cavalcade, "… It was the first
public showing of my art, or
rather the beginning of my
career. I will never forget
that Christmas day in
Catalonia."

Walt Disney, his wife and Salvador Dalí at Port Lligat in 1957

right-hand side
Salvador Dalí photographed by André Micheau while presenting *Histoire d'un grand livre Don Quichotte illustrated*, published by Joseph Foret in 1957

Chrysalid, exhibition prototype to promote the contraceptive pill, Miltown, 1958

1958

The Hoechst Ibérica company gives Dalí the job of making a Christmas card with a greeting for the new year to send to Spanish doctors and chemists. Dalí's collaboration with the company will last nineteen years. At the end of January, the

shows the degree of irresponsibility that some well-known critics have reached today.

2. I do not protest, on the other hand, against the 'Gaudí Exhibition'. Quite the opposite, I enthusiastically applaud the initiative. This exhibition, ladies and gentlemen, the first on this Catalan genius to be held outside Spain, is an honor to the Museum of Modern Art, to the city of New York and to the people of the United States. The exhibition also marks a transcendental moment in the history of art. Gaudí converts himself into the prophet of an imminent Classicism; the start of this pure and simple Classicism which is quite alien to the 'universality' which is typical of Gaudí. I know exactly, however, where I will put two sculptures by the divine Boccioni and I also know how to integrate into the portentous whole of the work some microscopic realizations of heroic and neglected abstract painters such as Klein, Mathieu, Tobey, Serpent and others. I am sure [intervenes

Museum of Modern Art, New York, holds a Symposium in honor of Gaudí. Speakers include the architects Josep Lluís Sert and Henry Russell Hitchcock, and the critic James Johnson Sweeney. Dalí participates by sending a tape recording of his comments on the Catalan architect. The same comments appear in an article written by his childhood friend, Jaume Miravitlles, published in *Tele Estel* on November 4, 1966:
"1. I protest violently against certain New York critics who, in commenting on his mystic and cosmic power, have compared Gaudí to Walt Disney. I am a good friend of Disney but that comparison

the author of the article], that Dalí would have included some 'microscopic realizations' in the Sagrada Familia of Tàpies, an artist for whom he feels, as far as I can tell, great esteem and admiration."
[Dalí's declaration continues]
"Every one of the painters mentioned has found living microstructures which alone are almost nothing but which represent the symbols of the future living Classicism.

5. I applaud, right from the start, the publication of the book by Sweeney Antoni Gaudí, because I consider it a very important contribution to the history of art. All modern artists who have created something are in some sense 'Gaudian' because one of the tragedies of modern art is the requirement to deform everything violently in order to capture the life that has nearly been lost.

6. I proclaim that Francesc Pujols, Gaudí's best and dearest friend, whom no-one or nearly no-one in the world knows, is the greatest genius of philosophy of our time. Pujols has demonstrated that Gaudí was a fanatic of Greek art, of the Classicism of Praxiteles, Phidias and Apelles. According to Gaudí, their period was the only perfect one in the whole history of art.

7. Finally, my wife, Gala, who has never made a mistake when evaluating esthetics, maintains that Gaudí's most marvelous creation is the two columns which have recently been raised in the Sagrada Familia, which arise from two opposing helicoid movements. Dalí is of the same opinion as Gala and in these two columns he sees the symbol and the heralding of classic art which will still be alive tomorrow…"
From February 18, Dalí exhibits in the gallery M. Knoedler & Co. in New York where, in addition to drawings,

Chrysalid, promotion campaign for the contraceptive pill, Miltown, 1958

Salvador Dalí portrayed by J. A. Sáenz Guerrero while painting the image of Saint Narcissus on glass, Port Lligat, 1958

right-hand side
Salvador Dalí presents a a twelve-meter long loaf of bread to illustrate his lecture on the Heisenberg theories, Paris, 1958
[Agence Intercontinentale]

and watercolors which he calls "Anti-matter archangels and Celestial Visions," he also presents *Saint James, the Great*. In the catalogue, he writes a piece with the same title. The invitation to the opening of the exhibition announces that the painting will be shown in the Spanish pavilion of the Universal Exhibition, in Brussels.
May: In Paris, Dalí orders a twelve-meter-long baguette which he will use to illustrate

a lecture on the theories of Heisenberg, held at the Théâtre de l'Étoile.
August 1: *Cinemages* publishes a résumé of the script Dalí wrote for the film *Babaouo*, in 1932. The issue in which the text appears (translated into English by Jaume Miravitlles) is all about scripts for films which have never been made.
August 8: Dalí and Gala get married in the sanctuary of Els Àngels in Sant Martí Vell, near Girona.
September 29-November 1: Dalí takes part in an exhibition organized to celebrate the tenth anniversary of the Sidney Janis Gallery in New York.
November 21: During an "atomic-paranoiac" cocktail in the Eiffel Tower, in Paris, the Cuban Ambassador in Paris confers a decoration upon Dalí. On the first floor of the tower, decorated especially for the occasion, there is an enormous ear that sticks out. Dalí writes in *Libération*,
"I have had enough of rhinoceros horns, of bread crusts and cauliflowers. My goal is the papal ear, which has allowed me to begin a period of monarchic unity born of the idea that its only purpose is to weigh upon the

scientific world."[68]
November: Dalí takes part in the exhibition, "The Artist Looks at People," at the Art Institute of Chicago, with *Mae West's Face which May be Used as a Surrealist Apartment*. The exhibition is completely dedicated to portraits by painters from all ages.
December 6: Dalí exhibits at the Carstairs Gallery in New York and dedicates the exhibition to his wife, "This, my best exhibition, I dedicate in homage to Gala, my Sistine Madonna." The catalogue includes Dalí's new "Antimatter Manifesto."

1959
March: Dalí meets Robert McCloskey in the St. Regis Hotel in New York. He is the art director of Hallmark, the

biggest greetings card producer in the world. Dalí agrees to design ten postcards for them. He tells David Lyle of *The Herald Tribune Magazine*, "As a Renaissance man, I do not feel distant, as an artist, from the masses. I am prepared to draw anything people ask me to draw."
May: Pope John XXIII receives Salvador Dalí who tells him he would like to design a church to be built in the Arizona desert and dedicate it to the success of the Ecumenical Council.
May 5: Dalí gives a lecture during the Bal des Petits Lits Blancs, in Paris. He later explains in an article in *Arts*, "I agreed to participate in the Bals des Petits Lits Blancs as a guest star because I wanted to read out a message which can

Salvador Dalí immortalized by Joan Vehí while painting *The Discovery of America by Christopher Columbus*, 1958

right-hand side
Salvador Dalí presents the "ovocipete" at the Palais de Glace in Paris, 1959 [Photo Chance (Jours de France)]

be summed up in a single sentence by St. Augustine. But the dreadful way the event was organized meant that the spectators were more Dalinian than Dalí and their delirium was greater than mine. It was one of the great moments of my life."[69]
May 7: Salvador Dalí goes to London to take part in the presentation of the book, *The*

Case of Salvador Dalí, by Fleur Cowles.
December 21: Dalí disembarks from the liner which has brought him to New York inside a transparent plastic sphere, the "ovocipede," a prototype which he had already presented at the Palais de Glace, in Paris, on **December 7**: As a revolutionary means of transport. He is wearing gold leatherwork overalls. *News-Press* the following day reports, "Salvador Dalí arrived in New York today from Europe wearing his usual sweeping mustache and a gold leather suit and carrying his latest work of art—a clear Plexiglas bubble entitled 'ovocipede'.

The egg-shaped bubble, standing four feet high and big enough for him to get into, took three months to build. He described it as: 'One little part of my personality', 'an echo of the discovery of America by Columbus', and 'a metaphysical dream of Columbus'."

1960
February: The French & Co. Gallery of New York presents Dalí's work, *The Discovery of America by Christopher Columbus* (*The Dream of Christopher Columbus*), which is an enormous success. The painting was commissioned by Huntington Hartford for The Gallery of Modern Art.
April: As part of the "5th Annual Convention on Visual Communication" at the Waldorf Hotel, New York, Dalí presents the documentary, *Chaos and Creation*, made at Videotape Productions' Manhattan Studios. Working with Philippe Halsman and the musician Lleonard Balada, Dalí filmed a 15-minute performance during which he painted a picture which was later bought by an American museum.
May: Joseph Foret publishes Dante's *Divine Comedy* illustrated with Dalí's one hundred watercolors that had been commissioned by the

Italian Government in 1950 for the Dante commemoration. On the occasion of the publication of the book, the Musée Galliera, in Paris, exhibits the original pictures painted by Dalí.
July: *Esquire* magazine publishes Dalí's article, "The Contraction of New York Museums." "The title of this article should give the reader a very thorough and immediate idea of my purpose. I do not think that a museum is a storehouse or a cemetery, in which the great works of art are there only to satisfy the curiosity of the Sunday strollers. On the contrary, a museum is a living organism that grows and breathes and acts; a living organism that can die, too, if its vital purpose is not fulfilled."
July 22: Dalí receives the Gold Medal from the Province of Girona in recognition of his artistic talent. When the official ceremony is over, Dalí returns to his studio and paints St. Narcissus, patron saint of Girona, on glass, which he then donates to the town.
August 5: The *TV Times* publishes an article by Dalí on the occasion of the great retrospective on Picasso at London's Tate Gallery. "Although we have come to the end of the old Picasso period in modern art, I am

Salvador Dalí with Paulette
Goddard in a photograph
by Arnold Eagle, 1960

A reporter from *Tass* and Salvador
Dalí in a photograph by Arnold
Eagle, 1960

Salvador Dalí, in a photograph
by Gérard Thomas d'Hoste, intent
on painting *Goddess Leaning on
Her Elbow…*, Port Lligat, 1960s

right-hand side
Salvador Dalí portrayed by Antoine
Rulmolt during an interview with
Armand Bochelier, Port Lligat, 1960

sure that he has not finished
astonishing the world. I am
hoping and waiting for his next
step that will disconcert his
present admirers."
In an interview published in
Gaceta ilustrada on August 20,
Dalí announces that the
Vatican has asked him to do
a painting which represents the
mystery of the Holy Trinity, a
work which will be shown at
the next Ecumenical Council.
October: *Canigó* magazine
publishes, "La influencia de la
onomástica sobre la pintura"
in which Dalí maintains,
"Raphael's pictures, which are
the most futurist that have ever
been painted, so much so that
even now no-one understands
them and they are still a great
enigma, are the opposite of
abstract paintings which, in
order to be understood, only
need a quick glance. And the
abstract painters, seeing as
they hide any reference to
figuration, shape, from this
moment, the ABC of plastic
evocation and often, without
realizing it, represent their own
names. Valles paints the
abstract light of the Empurdà
Valley. Molons does big wheels
[mole], thanks to which he can
subject the light. In Sibecas
there is Sibecas, in Maneros
the 'maniorist' manners,
Masuts gives dashes of 'masots'
[black thrush or fish in
Catalan], and in Masanet, as

his name indicates, we find the
'masa' [person who is 'so nice'
in Catalan] following the
Tramontana. Let us not forget
that Terrats paints terrats
(terraces). Tàpies, as in
Vermeer, paints a yellow tapia
[wall panel in Catalan] which
measures a centimeter but lasts
an eternity."
November-December: As part
of the commemoration of the
tri-centenary of Velázquez's
death, the Sala Gaspar of
Barcelona holds the exhibition,
"O figura. Homenaje informal
a Velázquez." A book is issued
for the occasion, in which
writers and artists from all
kinds are invited to express
their opinion of Velázquez and
his work. Salvador Dalí's
opinion is included.
November 28-January 14: The
D'Arcy Galleries of New York
hold an international

exhibition on Surrealism,
"Surrealists' Intrusion in the
Enchanters' Domain,"
organized by Marcel
Duchamp, André Breton,
Edouard Jaguer and José
Pierre. Dalí's work causes a
stir; the Surrealists publish,
We don't EAR it that way, a
booklet in which they express
their disapproval of Dalí's
participation in the exhibition.
December-January: The
Carstairs Gallery, New York,
holds a Dalí exhibition with
watercolors, drawings and
fourteen paintings, including:
Ecumenical Council, *Portrait of
Juan de Pareja Adjusting a
String on his Mandolin*, and
The Battle of Tetuán. Contrary
to his usual habits, Dalí
includes a very important work
but one which dates back to
1933, *The Enigma of William
Tell*. Dalí writes in the

catalogue, "In this exhibition I am showing two unique pictures: The one corresponding to the Surrealist Period, 'The Enigma of William Tell', which the exegeticals only now, after twenty years, begin to decipher; the other, my latest work, representing the Ecumenical Council, which I consider the greatest historical event of our time and which, prudently, I have painted before it has met. … The ability to accomplish two works both as universal and as contradictory is the proof of DALÍ."

1961

January: To coincide with the exhibition at the Carstairs Gallery, New York, *Art News* publishes an article by Dalí, "The Secret Number of Velázquez Revealed": "I have just given a quick glance at the Dalí exhibition because, despite the fact that I have, myself, painted the works exhibited there, during the past two years, I have not yet had the leisure to look at them. These pictures are so ambitious that there is nothing more that can be said about them.

But I was overcome by the

tribute to Velázquez, because Dalí was the first to recognize in him the genius of the future; Picasso the second; and now, today, the artists of Action-Painting."

February 1-25: The Museum of Modern Art, New York, organizes an exhibition of the works in the James Thrall Soby Collection, held at the museum. Amongst the works are two of Dalí's: *Nude* and *Remains of a Car Which Give Life to a Blind Horse Biting a Telephone* (1938) about which Soby writes in the catalogue, "Whenever possible Dalí has made living organism usurp, jeopardize or obviate the function of machinery and machine products ; whenever possible he has forced the inanimate to take part in action for which the essential requisite is animation itself.." [70] In the March issue of *Town & Country*, Igor Cassini reveals that Dalí and Alemany & Company are creating a new objet d'art, "This is an electronic jeweled objet d'art representing the Chalice of Santa Teresa de Avila. When it is finished, at the end of this year, it will have cost $80,000. The gold leaves around the Chalice will open and turn into butterflies bearing precious

stones, upon command. … The 25-inch affair, which will play out the legend of Santa Teresa as the dead leaves turn to live butterflies, will be used as a display piece." Immediately after his nomination to mayor of Figueres, in October 1960, Ramón Guardiola begins the administrative process of dedicating a room of the Museu de l'Empordà to Dalí. The mayor himself recounts, "… Dalí lived between New York and Paris. When, as every year, he arrived in Port Lligat at the beginning of May, I showed him the request to dedicate a room to his paintings in the Museu de l'Empordà. In fact, I considered it a reciprocal duty of both the city of Figueres and Dalí. Some time later, Melitó Casals

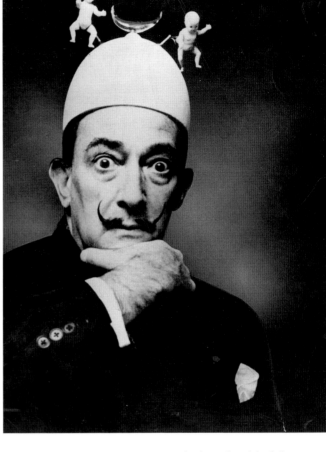

Salvador Dalí with his helmet topped by Castor and Pollux, which he wore during the lecture "Galacıdalacıdesoxyrıbonucleıcacı" given by the artist at the École Polytecnique in Paris in 1961

left-hand side
Gala, Marjorie Hartford, Huntington Hartford and Salvador Dalí immortalized by Arnold Eagle in front of *The Discovery of America by Christopher Columbus,* 1960

Casas, the photographer known as "Meli," came to see me on his way back from Cadaqués and Port Lligat. He brought me an invitation from Dalí to go and see him because it was his intention to donate to Figueres not a room but a whole museum. …" [71] It was decided to house the museum in the municipal theater, a neo-classical building built by Josep Roca i Bros in 1849,

which had been destroyed by fire at the end of the Spanish civil war.

August 12: Dalí's birthplace pays him homage through a series of public acts, the most important being a bullfight. For the event, Dalí asks Niki de Saint Phalle and Jean Tinguely to make him an enormous, gold-colored, plaster bull. The animal disintegrates whilst the horns spurt out fire, the body explodes firing off rockets and flares, and a red liquid simulates a gush of blood. But at the end, a white dove will fly out from what remains of the bull's body.

August 22: The comedy *La dama spagnola e il cavaliere romano* opens at the Fenice theater in Venice, with music

by Scarlatti and five backdrops by Dalí. The ballet, *Gala*, is also showing there, with choreography by Maurice Béjart and stage sets and costumes by Dalí. On September 1, *Time* reviews the show, "...Presumably, the select group of invited critics and music lovers came with expectation of hearing *The Spanish Lady and The Roman Cavalier*, a re-title for Alessandro Scarlatti's long-forgotten comic opera, *Scipio in Spain*, composed in 1714. What they got was Scarlatti heavily laced with Salvador Dalí, theatrical effects, erotic dancers and leering *double-entendres*. ... Commissioned two years ago to stage *The Spanish Lady*, Dalí dived into the project with his usual

manic genius. ... As the gauze tableau faded out, the heroine came on, her two-yard-long tresses supported by a red crutch. ... *The Spanish Lady* was followed by a surrealistic ballet titled *Gala* (Greek for milk), set to Scarlatti music and also richly endowed with Dalinian props. The announced theme was Woman, the supreme nourisher of mankind."

September: Janot, the Managing Director of French television, suspends Pierre Cardinall's *Gros Plan* program on Salvador Dalí because of Dalí's statement on masturbation. On October 4, the Barcelona newspaper, *La Vanguardia*, reports this news and publishes a letter from Dalí to Janot, "Dear Sir, Whilst I am convinced of the fact that freedom can only exist within order, I am nevertheless in favor of preventative censure, and accept with the greatest respect the decision to prevent the showing of the *Gros Plan* program dedicated to me. If it was considered by the competent authorities that the program could have been interpreted in the wrong way by the general public, then there was nothing more legitimate. However, any qualification or partial description of the transmission, which cannot be judged by the

La dama spagnola e il cavaliere romano, Teatro della Fenice, Venice, 1961

Salvador Dalí coming out of an enormous egg in a photograp by Gérard Thomas d'Hoste, Port Lligat, 1960s

public—because it was not aired—would constitute a pre-judgment of my morality and could harm me. As there is no specific law which foresees the existence of such a danger, the case is being studied in depth by my lawyer. For my part, it was my intention in said program to exalt faithfulness in marriage and the virtue of chastity as a prototype for achieving the strongest spirituality, and I used psycho-analytic and Freudian terminology, the same that has enabled me to see the truth of the Catholic, Apostolic and Roman Religion which I profess. Yours sincerely, Salvador Dalí"

November 9: On the occasion of the anniversary to commemorate Max Planck's report on black bodies, Dalí gives a public address at the École Polytechnique in Paris, "I have found the gold of time and space." He gives another lecture in the same place on December 12, "Gala acidalacidesoxyribonucleicaci" For this occasion, Dalí gets

Salvador Dalí in a photograph
by Gérard Thomas d'Hoste,
Port Lligat, 1960s

right-hand side
Salvador Dalí and Gala in Brussels
in 1962

himself a hat made in the
shape of an egg cut in half
and crowned with a couple
resembling Castor and Pollux.

1962
January-June: The Choate
Art School of Wallingford,
Connecticut, exhibits the
Georges Farkas Collection
which includes works of
masters, ancient and modern,
seven of which are by Dalí.
Four of these belong to the
Seven Lively Arts
commissioned by Billy Rose
and exhibited at the Ziegfeld
Theater, New York, in 1944.

Following a fire there in 1957,
Dalí had to paint a new series
and it is these that are shown in
this exhibition, except that the
artist has substituted the *Jive*
painting with one dedicated to
television.
March: The *La dama spagnola
e il cavaliere romano* and the
ballet, *Gala*, are staged in Paris
and Brussels. The *Paris-
Normandie* of April 16 reports,
"Dalí scandal in Brussels. The
painter, Salvador Dalí, added
some life to his latest sparkling
event, last Saturday evening,
at the Théâtre Royal de la
Monnaie in Brussels, by noisily
leaving the auditorium right in
the middle of the show… he
declared that he refused to
recognize the show as a work
of his genius because essential
elements were missing which
he wanted included …"
Dalí writes a new article for *Art

News* entitled, "Tàpies, Tàpies,
classic, classic!" which is
published in May. This time,
Dalí compares Velázquez's
*Portrait of the Infanta Maria
Teresa* with Antoni Tàpies's
Two Reliefs in Space 8, to
demonstrate that the chromatic
quality of the two works is
similar. "Tàpies, in Catalonian,
means 'wall panel' and Dalí
gives the following advice to all
who attack the work of Antoni
Tàpies on the grounds of its
resemblance to wall panels:
Read the greatest pages of
Marcel Proust which, precisely,
are dedicated to the little
yellow panel of wall that
Vermeer put in his immortal
work, *The View of Delft* (a city
which I, Dalí, am about to
visit). The cardinal virtues of
Tàpies, which no one has
discovered, are:
By a process of methodical
sensibility, Tàpies paints the
accidents of desoxyribonucleic
acid, which is nothing but the
central factor of Life and the
Persistence of Memory (the soft
watches of Dalí in the Museum
of Modern Art, etc. etc.).
All biological fragments which
we discover in the electron
microscope are Tàpies.
The success and the secret of
Tàpies reside in the fact that
elements in his art are
distributed chromosomatically.
Tàpies is a Catalonian, a friend
of Dalí's and is named Antoni,
like Gaudí. …."

October 15: The Saló del
Tinell, Barcelona, holds a Dalí
exhibition through which Dalí
pays homage to Mariano
Fortuny; amongst the works
are two versions of *The Battle
of Tetuán*, one by Fortuny and
one by Dalí. The pieces Dalí
shows are: *The Battle of Tetuán
(Homage to Mariano Fortuny)*,
Arabi acidodesossiribonucleici,
*Fifty abstract paintings which,
when seen from two yards
away, transform into three
Lenins disguised as Chinese
and, when seen from six yards

away, look like the head of
a royal tiger, Iparxiologic Sky
(signed by Gala and Lorca),
Arabs–Death of Raimondo
Lullo, Twist in Velázquez's
studio, Self portrait,* 1921,
and other drawings and
watercolors. By Fortuny, there
are: the above-mentioned
*Battle of Tetuán, The Alhambra
Tribunal,* from the Gala
Salvador Dalí Collection, and
Academias dibujos lent by the
Real Acadèmia de Belles Arts
de Sant Jordi, Barcelona. Dalí
contributes a piece to the
catalogue entitled, "Fortuny,
Dalí y sus batallas de Tetuán,"
"Antoni Gaudí, who
considered Fortuny the
greatest painter of modern
times, said repeatedly to
Francisco Pujols, our immortal
philosopher, that the whole
great drama of modern
painting derived from the fact
that, from laziness, artists have
followed the incapable and
clumsy ways of Cézanne rather
than following the virtuosity—
which I define as delirious—
of Mariano Fortuny … My
homage to Fortuny is a
spiritual battle and this battle
could only be the Battle of
Tetuán because it was the most
metaphyscial and transcendent
of all the battles which have
ever taken place, the most
universal and the most local."
Dalí donates his *Christ of Vallès*
to the exhibition-sale of works
offered by different artists to

collect funds for the inhabitants of the Vallès region hit by floods on September 25. The exhibition is open to the public from December 1 to 16, in the Gothic room of the Antic Hospital, Santa Creu, Barcelona. Reynolds Morse publishes a fragment of Dalí's diaries written when he was young, entitled, *Impressions and Private Memoirs of Salvador Dalí January 1920*. The collector had discovered the note book quite by chance in a Paris bookshop.

1963
January: The Doubleday bookstore in New York presents "The World of Salvador Dalí." During the presentation, the artist is in the shop window, lying on a bed and wearing a gold robe; he is connected to a machine— electromyogram— which, every time he signs a copy of his book, registers the brain waves and pressure on a sheet of paper which is then offered to the book purchaser as a gift. To complete the window display there is also a doctor, a nurse, an ambulance and Gala.
June: When the Gallery of Modern Art, New York, buys

Salvador Dalí and Gala during an audience with Pope John XXIII in 1963

Dalí's *The Battle of Tetuán*, he publishes a two part article in *Show*: in one part, he gives his esthetic interpretation of painting, "A Manifesto," and in the other, his historical interpretation in "Dalí's notes on the Battle of Tetuán." Dalí declares that after an era characterized by a profusion of "isms," he has chosen the exact moment to explain one of the most transcendental and unknown episodes in the history of Europe, the battle of Tetuán (Moroccan war, 1859-1860). According to Dalí, it was one of the most complex works he had ever done in his artistic career, a painting on which he worked for two years. In order to paint it, he used various techniques, 600 sketches, hallucinations provoked by newspaper typography,… involuntary incidents and, above all, dynamic spirals which form the basis of the whole canvas and which derive from the molecular structure of desoxyribonucleic acid.
October 25: Jean Jacques Pauvert publishes *Le mythe tragique de l'Angélus de Millet. Interprétation paranoïaque-critique*, the manuscript for which dates back to 1933. It is not clear why the manuscript remained unpublished for so long. Dalí

maintains that he had lost the original.
November 26-December 26: The Knoedler Gallery in New York presents the exhibition, "Hommage à Crick et Watson." The cover of the catalogue is dedicated to the researchers, Watson and Crick, who in 1962 won the Nobel prize for their discovery of the molecular structure of nucleic acids. In addition to the two newspaper clippings with the photographs of the scientists, there is also a picture of part of a DNA molecule in which Dalí, making use of the small circles that represent the nuclei, has drawn Arabs armed with guns which is a motif found in The Battle of Tetuán. Dalí shows various watercolors and drawings at the exhibition plus ten oil paintings, including *Galacidalacidesoxyri bonucleicacid (Homage to Crick and Watson)* which the painter explains thus, "At a time when the titles of pictures are rather short (i.e. 'Picture no. 1' or 'White on White') I call my Hommage to Crick and Watson: GALACIDALACIDESOXYRIBONUCL EICACID. It is my longest title in one word. But the theme is even longer: as long as the genetical persistence of human memory."

1964
Huntington Hartford, the owner of The Gallery of Modern Art, in New York, exhibits some of the works in his personal collection, including Dalí's *The Battle of Tetuán* and *The Discovery of America by Christopher Columbus*.
April 21-October 21: "The Universal Exhibition of New York." Dalí is there in both the Spanish and French pavilions. In the former, he shows the jewel collection he has created, the painting *The Apotheosis of the Dollar* (one of his most recent works) and the

sculpture, *Bust of Dante*. In the French pavilion, he presents his book, *The Apocalypse*.
September 8-October 18: An important retrospective of Dalí is held in the Tokyo Prince Hotel, with 103 works, including paintings, drawings, watercolors and objects. The president of the exhibition's organizing committee writes in the catalogue, "… with the Salvador Dalí Exhibition this Autumn, we shall have finished our tremendous task of introducing to the people in Japan the whole aspect of the art of the modern world. In view of the fact that although Surrealism was introduced into Japan from Europe some years ago and developed into 'Fantastic Art', it has not flourished as much in Japan as in Europe for various reasons. I feel sure that the present display of Mr. Dalí's works will give an inestimable significance to the Japanese art world. …."
November 3: Dalí wins the Gran Cruz de Isabel la Católica.
The Moderne Museet, Stockholm, buys *The Enigma of William Tell* thanks to Marcel Duchamp's intervention.

1965
Andy Warhol begins his two screen tests with Dalí.
February: Twentieth Century Fox asks Dalí to be in charge of the artistic part of the science-fiction film, "Fantastic Voyage." To promote the film, Dalí makes a portrait of Raquel Welch which is completely "hallucinatory," inspired by computer techniques.
May 10: The publisher Joseph Foret invites the public to a double presentation: the essays of Dalí on *Op-Art Microphysique* and a three-dimensional illustration made for the book *The Apocalypse*. The presentation is held in the Hotel Meurice, in Paris.

Pope John XXIII and Joseph Foret at the exhibition of *The Apocalypse* in the throne room at the Vatican, 1963

Gala and Salvador Dalí with a friend, 1964

Gala and Salvador Dalí decorated with the Gran Cruz de Isabel la Católica, Madrid, 1964

In the Autumn, Dalí meets Amanda Lear who will become one of his dearest friends for over fifteen years. They spend long periods together in Paris, New York, and his house in Port Lligat, where she poses for him on various occasions.

November 10-December 18: The Richard Feigen Gallery in Chicago organizes the exhibition, "Poetry in Painting 1931-1949," with works from the collection of the Julien Levy Gallery, New York, including some Dalís.

November 18-February 20: The Gallery of Modern Art in New York presents the most important Dalí retrospective yet held, "Salvador Dalí 1910-1965," which includes works from the private collections of Huntington Hartford and Reynolds Morse. The exhibition shows paintings, drawings, gouaches, watercolors and other objets d'art. Various parallel events are organized for the occasion, including "An Evening with Dalí," during which the guitarist Manitas de Plata plays and José Reyes sings, two dancers dance the flamenco, they show the film *Un Chien andalou* and there are various conversations between Dalí and Reynolds Morse. For the catalogue, Dalí writes "Resumé of history and the history of painting." The December 18 issue of *Journal American* reports some impressions of the retrospective, "All four exhibition floors of the Gallery of Modern Art have been given over to more than 250 works by Salvador Dalí, including 170 oils. ... The familiar Dalinian fantasy is here, some of the important religious paintings, the superb draftsmanship. One large gallery is devoted to a chronological review of his development, from a landscape of 1910 (when he was six years old) to today.

A smaller gallery covers his precocious teenage years, long before he turned to the surrealism with which he is most readily indentified. It is pre-Dalí Dalí. These paintings are among some 70 oils and 35 other works from the Dalí collection of A. Reynolds Morse of Cleveland.."

December: On the occasion of the publication in English of *Diary of a Genius*, Dalí walks down Fifth Avenue in New York, dressed as Father Christmas, to go and sign copies of his book at the Doubleday bookstore. Also in December, the Knoedler Gallery in New York presents, "Exhibition of Dalí's best painting to-date at the Knoedler gallery."

1966

Over this year and the next, Dalí paints *Tuna Fishing*, a work in which, as he himself explains, "are united op-art, pop-art, pointillisme, psychedelic action-painting, geometric abstraction, and the pompier style in the manner of Meissonier."
It is announced that *Autoportrait mou de Salvador Dalí*, a 52-minute film, in color, directed by Jean-Christophe Averty and Dalí himself, narrated by Orson Welles and produced by Seven Arts Television and Coty Television Company, will be shown in cinemas and on television at the same time. The sale of the film will be prohibited in the United States due to the excessive violence in some sequences.
Seven Arts Television completes the making of the film, *The World of Salvador Dalí*, an hour-long film.
Dalí designs a crib scene inside an enormous ear for the Paris airport, Orly.
The work is part of the exhibition, "Christmases of the world."

Poster and catalogue of the exhibition "Salvador Dalí," Prince Hotel Gallery, Tokyo, September-October 1964

1967

January: Dalí makes eight dry–point plates to illustrate the poems of Mao Tse-tung and publishes them through the Parisian publishers, Argillet. The book is presented to the public on April 26 at the Galerie Falvart in Paris.

March: Twenty-four of Dalí's watercolors are presented as part of the series, "Aliyah, the re-birth of Israel." *News*

The photomontage "Salvador Dalí in Moscow," signed J. R. M., 1965

writes, "The watercolors, now completed, are only a prelude to the main theme. The paintings are being reproduced by Mourlot's of Paris, one of the world's finest lithographers. A limited edition portfolio will be produced for private sale by the end of this year. Each portfolio will be numbered and signed by Dalí. … The original 24 watercolors will be exhibited throughout the world. …"[72] The first exhibition is held at The Gallery of Modern Art, in New York, from April 1 to 22 of the following year.

March-April: The Louisiana Museum inHumlebaek, in Denmark, organizes the exhibition, "Zes surrealistische schilders" (Six Surrealist Painters). The six are: Salvador Dalí, Paul Delvaux, Max Ernst, René Magritte, Joan Miró and Yves Tanguy. Dalí contributes sixteen works. The exhibition then moves to the Palais des Beaux-Arts in Brussels, from May 9 to June 18.

April: *Arts Magazine* publishes Dalí's article, "How an Elvis Presley becomes a Roy Lichtenstein," "… Today at the most dramatic moment of the latest pre-minimal consequences of the contemporary avant-garde, the works that have the greatest amount of *bits* of information, as much on the person of the artist himself as on the esthetic and moral reality of today, are certainly the paintings of Roy Lichtenstein, America's foremost Pop artist. And this is because, looking as he does toward the past, Lichtenstein only makes more biologically gripping all the experiences of

his memories that come from the bands of design of *Hokusai* as far as the pre-Raphaelites, passing ineluctably by way of Aubrey Beardsley. …"[73]

April 20: *La vie tragique de Sigmund Freud*, by Raymond de Becker, goes to press. On the cover is a portrait of Freud made by Dalí in 1937.

September: Dalí designs an ashtray for Air India. As a thank-you, the airline gives him an elephant which he in turn donates to the Barcelona zoo.

November 1-30: The Hotel Meurice in Paris hosts Dalí's exhibition, "Hommage à Meissonier" which includes his painting, *Tuna Fishing*. His *Manifeste en hommage à Meissonier* is published at the end of the year in *The Academy (Art News Annual XXXIII)* under the title, "The Incendiary Fireman."

December: The Sidney Janis Gallery in New York presents, "Homage to Marilyn Monroe" with works from forty-one artists, sculptors and photographers, including Willem De Kooning, Andy Warhol, Peter Blake, Richard Avedon, Henri Cartier-Bresson, Philippe Halsman, Claes Oldenburg and Salvador Dalí with his piece which mingles the actress's features with those of the Chinese leader, Mao Tse-tung.

1968

March 27-June 9: The Museum of Modern Art in New York organizes the exhibition, "Dada, Surrealism and Their Heritage." Dalí, who also makes the posters, contributes eleven works. The exhibition travels to the Los Angeles County Museum of Art and at to the Art Institute of Chicago. The March 31 issue of Philadelphia reports, "Consisting of more than 300 works, 'Dada, Surrealism and Their Heritage', as the name

implies not only gathers three shows under one roof, but far more significantly constitutes a brilliant survey of the profoundly interrelated movements of Dada and Surrealism which still contain the source for most vanguard art and experimentation. …."

May 14: Dalí's book-object, "Dalí de Draeger," is presented in Montrouge. According to the publishers, it represents the most complete study of the whole of the painter's artistic activity. It is examined under nine broad themes: war, landscape, Gala, still life, eroticism, mysticism, space-time, oneirism and imperial classicism. To finish off, there is an index of Dalí's works followed by an illustrated bibliography with snapshots of his pieces. Following the events of May, in France, Dalí publishes *Ma révolution culturelle*, which is distributed to students at the Sorbonne, "I, Salvador Dalí, catholic, apostolic and Roman, apolitic par excellence and spiritually monarchic, notice, modestly and jubilantly, that all the offensives of contemporary creative youth point in one direction: in opposition to the bourgeois culture. The most beautiful and profound cultural revolutions have been carried out without barricades, the violence of insurrection only firing the spirit, the master of time and space. It was because of the excavations, true antibarricades which offered the past a means of circulating in the future, and because of the finding of ancient fragments of sculptures, that the cultural revolution, rightly called the Renaissance, came about in the 16th-century. In order to be authentic, every cultural revolution should bring with it a new style. The style of Louis XIV, the apotheosis of the Renaissance, which would have given the bourgeoisie a degrading power, was annihilated by the French Revolution. The spherical constructions of Ledroux, destined for the workers, within a lyric, oneiric and playful vision of the city, would have been abandoned by the sceptical, rationalist and functional bourgeoisie.

I contribute to the new cultural revolution with what I have at my disposal: my paranoiac-critical method, singularly adapted, I feel, to the happily irrational nature of current events. In the light of this method, I will take the liberty of making the following suggestions…, on color, structures, quantified institutions and justice.

And I will finish by saying: There, where there is a cultural revolution going on, must bloom something of the fantastic."

Salvador Dalí, *Tuna Fishing*, 1966-67

June 26: The Fondation Paul Ricard invites the public to the salons of the Casino de Vittel for a presentation of its latest acquisition, Salvador Dalí's painting, *Tuna Fishing*. For the occasion, the interview with the painter, "Dalí donne le 'thon" is published, "This painting is one of the first dreams of my childhood," Dalí says. "In reality, I have never seen the fishing of tuna but my father, although a notary in Figueres, possessed a wonderful narrative gift. I was touched by his tale; he explained how the sea was red with blood. In his office, there was an engraving depicting tuna fishing, which I also used in working out this oil. The painting was born of these memories and images. It is the enigma of life, the collective birth, as human beings are generated from the liquid element. It is the mysterious side of the subconscious in the sense that we come from the unknown abysses of the sea. In this sort of apotheosis which is the struggle between man and beast, there is also an apocalyptic aspect. The universe is limited, as the latest scientific discoveries confirm; it converges to a point and this point, in my work, is the space that contains the maximum amount of esthetic energy and it is called Tuna Fishing."

Dalí designs the cover for the magazine, *TV Guide*, called "Today, this evening and tomorrow" and writes an article "Salvador Dalí's view of television." In the article, he says that television is for the masses. He does not like the masses. They are not cultured, they have no taste. Television should exert pressure on them to make them think. He adds that he would like to create a soft television set.[74]

December: Dalí is immortalized in wax in the Musée Grevin, Paris, next to the figures of Brigitte Bardot and Françoise Sagan.

1969
Dalí buys Púbol castle and furnishes it for Gala.
February: The airline Braniff launches an advertising campaign with a series of announcements, some of 30 seconds, in which appear various couples of famous people like Andy Warhol and Sonny Liston, and Salvador Dalí and the baseball player, Witney Ford. The magazine, *Art News*, publishes Dalí's article, "De Kooning's 300,000,000 birthday." After explaining why the microscope could not have been invented in America, Africa, Asia or Oceania, he writes, "And now be assured that we are finally reaching the conclusion, for my readers might begin to grow impatient and rightly wonder what this geological preamble is leading up to, a most justifiable expectation which, far from displeasing me delights me since it allows me at once and in the most dazzlingly veracious way to shout from the housetops that Willem De Kooning is the greatest, the most gifted and the most authentic finial point of modern painting, and the initial point of the *pompier* art of the future."
July 26: *Paris Match* publishes a report by Dalí on "his Surrealism across Barcelona and Paris."
August: The singer, Tony Bennet, says he has long been discussing making a film with John Cassavetes. The film would be a musical adaptation of the film, *Crime and Punishment*. Ivanovic's dream sequences would be done by Dalí and the music by Duke Ellington. However, the film is never made.
The Larousse bookstore re-opens on Fifth Avenue, New York. Two of Dalí's works are on show there: the bust of President John Fitzgerald Kennedy and the sculpture, *Christ Carrying the Cross*.

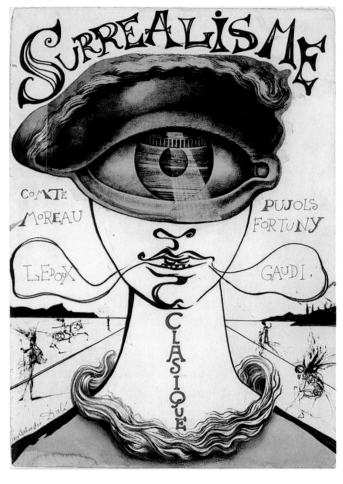

Original of the poster *Surréalisme*, 1969

The Púbol castle

and *Three Divine Personages* (1969).

April 1: During a press conference in the Musée Gustave Moreau, in Paris, Dalí announces the creation of the Teatre-Museu Dalí in Figueres. At the end of May, the work at Púbol castle is completed. On the inside, which has been restored, some of the contents have been designed by Dalí, e.g. the chimneys and some of the furniture. Dalí has also painted the trompe-l'œil vault with castle crenellations and a cupola with classic moulding. Over the months that follow, the garden is also put into order with the addition of sculptures of elephants with long, thin feet, a swimming pool whose main feature is a sculpted ceramic group from an old garden in Figueres, and a seat with irises and various busts of Wagner. Work is finally finished in the Spring of 1974.

November 21-January 10: The Museum Boijmans Van Beuningen, in Rotterdam, holds the first big Dalí

retrospective in Europe. In accordance with Dalí's wishes, his article on Willem De Kooning which first appeared in *Art News* in April 1969, is reprinted. "Port Lligat, Monday August 31, 1970. The recent earthquake in Peru, with pictures showing its effects reaching right up into the Perpignan region, and the latest discoveries about continental drift, prove once again that Vermeer was only able to exist thanks to the atavistic opening of the Bay of Biscay.

Without the opening of the Bay of Biscay, instead of enjoying the birth of Vermeer, Holland would probably have been invaded by herds of the most animal species of all, the rhinoceros. Having said this, for the opening of my exhibition at the Museum Boijmans Van Beuningen, in Rotterdam, I must pass the floor to the famous Salvador Dalí who gave a definitive view on painting on the occasion of a Willem De Kooning anniversary, the most

1970
March 10-April 4: The Knoedler Gallery, in New York, holds the exhibition, "Dalí: Paintings and Drawings 1965-70." Twenty-two works are on show, including the oils: *Salvador Dalí in the Act of Painting Gala in the Apotheosis of the Dollar, in Which One May Also Perceive to the Left Marcel Duchamp Disguised as Louis XIV, Behind a Curtain in the Style of Vermeer, Which is But the Invisible Though Monumental Face of the Hermes of Praxiteles*, known as *The Apotheosis of the Dollar* (1965), *Tuna Fishing* (1966-67), *The Hallucinogenic Toreador* (1969-70) (*work in progress*),

typical representative of Holland's triumph throughout the European and American continents. Dalí." The exhibition shows two hundred works: oils, drawings, objects and sculptures, including the works of the Edward James Foundation. In addition, there are also thirty-six pieces of jewelry from the Owen Cheatham Foundation.

A short paragraph by Dalí appears in issue no.5 of *Art Now*, the University Galleries of New York magazine, "I have used accumulations of an obsessive single image such as the venus de milo to obtain an hallucinogenic structure able to provoke for the spectator any kind of concrete image. this work is the first optical application of my paranoiac-critical method."

A picture of *The Hallucinogenic Toreador* (1969-70) appears next to the text.

1971
In solemn memory of his friendship with Marcel Duchamp, Dalí designs a chess set in silver for the American Chess Foundation. It is presented to them during a press conference in February. The figures reproduce the fingers of the artist's hands, except for the rooks which are modelled on the salt cellars from the Hotel Saint Regis in New York. He based the king and queen on his thumb, crowned with a tooth.

March 7: Inauguration of the Dalí Museum of Cleveland, Ohio, which houses the collection of A. Reynolds and Eleanor Morse.

November: Dalí's book, *Procès en diffamation plaidé devant la Conférence du Stage*, is published with the title-page designed by Dalí himself. The book is about an imaginary court case in which young lawyers debate a theme suggested by Dalí: the trial of a journalist accused of slander for saying that his "paranoia" is simulated.[75]

1972
March 9-April 1 Dalí takes part in the exhibition, "Exhibition of Works of Art of Colossal Scale by Twentieth Century Artists," at the Sidney Janis Gallery, New York, where he presents *The Hand* (*The Regrets of the Conscience*) from 1930.

March 11-May 7: Dalí takes part in the exhibition, "Der Surrealismus 1922-1942" at the Haus der Kunst, in Munich. In June, the exhibition moves to the Musée des Arts Décoratifs, in Paris, closing on September 24.

April-May: The Knoedler Gallery, New York, presents the world's first exhibition of holograms, created by Dalí with the help of Dennis Gabor (Nobel prize winner in physics for his experiments with laser beams). It was a new form of art based on the most

Salvador Dalí photographed by Gérard Thomas d'Hoste, Port Lligat, 1960s

advanced optical technology. There were three holograms in the exhibition: 1. *Polyhedron*: "Holographic view of a room in the Museum of Dalí in Figueres, containing the double portrait of Gala, basketball players in the process of becoming angels painted in the facets of a giant polyhedron, and a terrestrial globe on which are pinned Figueres in Spain and Cleveland in America, places where the two Dalí Museums are located."
2. *Submarine Fishermen*: "Analytical study homage to *Les Demoiselles d'Avignon* of Picasso, from the center of which emerges holographically a Catalan girl of the rue d'Avignon in Barcelona, who has a nose emerging from the painting constituted from the arm of a submarine fisherman grasping a knife." 3. *Holas! Holas! Velázquez! Gabor!*:

Salvador Dalí intently painting *Self-portrait* in a photograph by Enrique Sabater, 1972

"Card-players, beer-drinkers, transfigured into *Les Meninas* of Velázquez, where, for the first time, thanks to holography, one can see on a plane surface the back of the canvas and also that which is represented on the face."
The April issue of *Art News* publishes two articles to go with the exhibition: "Dalí Holos! Holos! Velázquez! Gabor!," the text which goes with the catalogue of the exhibition, and "Sonnet to the Pupils of Velazquez Eyes Gala of My Eyes" which, according to the author, "explains the holographic metaphysics in the painting, *Las Meninas*."
June: *Bollaffiarte* magazine dedicates a long, richly illustrated article on the artistic works of Dalí, the future Teatre-Museu, the house in Port Lligat and Púbol castle. Dalí designs the front cover and writes two pieces for the magazine: "Oto portrait [sic.] Holografique" and "Holograma de Gala i Dalí."

November 9: Dalí is presented with the gold medal in Fine Arts, in the Salón Goya of the Ministry of Education and Science, in Madrid.
December: Presentation of the film, *L'autoportrait mou de Salvador Dalí*, produced by Jean Christophe Averty in 1966. Through the press, Dalí expresses his disapproval of the film: "The portrait painted by Averty cannot possibly be considered an autoportrait, and it gives an imprecise and limited view of

cat. 269 Salvador Dalí, *Chessboard*, 1964-71
32 silver and vermeil pieces realized by F.J. Cooper Inc. Jewelers, Philadelphia
St. Petersburg (FL), The Salvador Dalí Museum

the imaginary and real world of Salvador Dalí."
Dalí begins work on an opera-poem entitled *Être-Dieu*. The author, Manuel Vázquez Montalbán, does the libretto and the composer, Igor Wakhévitch, writes the music. Two years later, the record is made in Paris, and ten years later, it is made available for sale.

1973
April 2: Dalí is appointed member of the Real Academia de Bellas Artes di San Fernando, Madrid.
April 23: Dalí is the author of the introduction to the catalogue for an exhibition of the grand masters of American Hyper-realism presented at the Gallerie des 4 Mouvements in Paris, May 23 to June 15. Here he writes: "SHARP REALISM. 'PAINTING: COLOR PHOTOGRAPHY, HAND-CREATED TO PRODUCE REFIGURINGS OF HYPER-DETAILED, EXTRA-PICTORIAL IMAGES OF CONCRETE IRRATIONALITY;' SALVADOR DALÍ (1930)."
The most depressing, darkest moment for modern art is

clearly the period of the painter/artist suicides, beginning with Nicolas de Stael (who committed suicide) and going up to Mark Rothko, who also took his own life. And the happiest, sybaritic, and anti-suiciDal(í) period is without a shadow of doubt that inaugurated by Malcolm Morley's famous liner *Amsterdam in front of Rotterdam*, perfected with the help of Richard Estes in the most diverse and sumptuous tones, which was one day to lead to the apotheosis of Meissonnier, and a few years later to the imperial domination of the triumphal route of the geniuses of Seville, Trajan and Velázquez!."

April: The Knoedler Gallery in New York dedicates an entire room to Dalí's holographic output. During this, his first cylindrical hologram dedicated to the singer, Alice Cooper, is exhibited, *Alice Cooper's Brain* The presentation takes place on May 21 at the Hotel Meurice, Paris.

On Picasso's death, April 8, hundreds of journalists besiege Dalí on his return to Paris until he makes a statement on the artist's death. This came in the form of the article "Picasso and the horse hairs," published May 5 in *Paris Match*.

May 15: In Paris, Dalí's book-object "Dix recettes d'immortalité" goes to press. In the ten chapters, the artist discusses the problem of life and death, the finite and the infinite. The work opens with the following maxim: "The best recipe for immortality is a grace from God: Faith."

May 29: In the Sala Velázquez in the Prado Museum in Madrid, Dalí gives a talk "Velasquez and me." After the talk, in reply to the question "Should museum exhibition rooms be used for things other than showing paintings?" he says: "Indubitably, unless we want them to become the dead barrack rooms. And I am going to put this into practice in my museum in Figueres, where certain galleries will be reserved for performance art and cultural events. An essential element in my museum will be the conversation between the artist and the public."

June 16: *Paris Match* publishes the article entitled "Les six jours de Dalí" in which the painter recounts a week in his life, "The inventory of a week of Dalinian cosmic-fluid creation should be seen as an immense Michelin map which records, centimeter by centimeter, all the details without missing one, not even the bird singing on a branch. I have prepared a Eucharistic plan for this work. The great golden chain which links Dalí to beings and things. In the morning, there is the metaphysical explosion of creative continuity. The irresistible forces of my genius drive me to act. Every morning; along with the rising sun, I consign my work to its dimension of flaming apotheosis. The voices of Velasquez and Praxiteles command me to paint, to engrave, to think. As for the rest, I work only on commission."

Dalí visits the city of Elche and is present at the performance of the sacred play, *El misterio de Elche*. Greatly struck by the work and, speaking with journalists, he declares that the *Misterio* is untouchable, even though, if it were left to him, he would add a new element every year so as to transform it into a rock opera.

Dalí announces that he is to inaugurate his Teatre-Museo with the Misterio di Figueres, using a project by the Catalan architect, Oriol Buigas, for a vertical fountain on the platea of the ancient theatre. The jet of water was to be cut at three hundred meters high. The Project was never built.

December 9: Dalí writes an article for the daily newspaper *La Vanguardia* entitled "Hiper-realismo y monarquia" which begins with the following words, "The greatest praise which could have been offered, and which was indeed offered, to my paintings is that contained in the frequent exclamation 'It looks like a photograph but it's better than a photograph.' This is an exclamation always made by immutable beings, those not corrupted intellectually. Art critics, on the other hand, whose mission is always to get it wrong, used to consider the use of photography as an authentic fraud, forgetting that the geniuses of immutable art have always used it, each one in his own way: the Greeks with their models of the human body, Vermeer with his camera-obscuras and systems of mirrors, and Velasquez with his miraculously hyper-photographic eye."

December 26-February 24: Moderna Museet in Stockholm hosts the Salvador Dalí exhibition previously held at the Louisiana Museum in Humlebaek in Denmark, from October 6 to December 2. In celebration of their thirty years collecting Dalí, the Morses publish a photo album entitled *The Dalí Adventure*. Over the course of the year, the publishing house Draeger publishes Dalí's book *Les*

Salvador Dalí, *The Prince of Sleep,* 1973-79

Salvador Dalí in the Palacio
del Viento at the Teatre-Museu
di Figueres, ca. 1975

diners de Gala, comprising
twelve chapters, some
entitled "Les caprices prinés
princier," "Les cannibalismes
d'automne," "Les suprêmes
de malaises lilliputiens,"
"Les entre-plats sodomisés."
The volume includes twelve
specially produced illustrations
and fifty-five illustrated
recipes, twenty-one of which
are offered by the grand
maestros of French
gastronomy: the chefs from
Lasserre, La Tour d'Argent,
Maxim's, and Le buffet de la
Gare de Lyon.
The film director Bruce
Gowers makes the film
Hello Dalí produced by
Aquarius London Weekend
Television.
In 1975, the Salvador Dalí
Museum and the Teatre
Museu Dalí publish
jointly Dalí's comments
on the film.

1974
March 10: René Crevel's book,
La mort difficile, is published
with an introduction by Dalí.
July 22: Pujols' volume
containing the *La Vanguardia*
text of December 9, 1973,
"Hiper-realismo y monarquia,"
is published. The book was also
to have special printing
including two-dry point
etchings by Dalí entitled
1) "Francesc Pujols' divinatory
physiognomy as if he had lived
in the time of the Emperor
Trajan," 2) "First
physiognomical study for my
imminent painting entitled
Horace's chimaera."
August 19: In the Catalan town
of Granollers, Dalí is the
protagonist at a Happening,
an event organized by the Valles
region Centre d'Iniciatives i
Turisme and produced by a
German television company,
at that time also working on the
film *Impressions de la Haute
Mongolie*.
September 27: Dalí is awarded
the gold medal of the town of

Figueres. On the following day
he inaugurates the Teatre-
Museu Dalí which, in addition
to works by the artist, has
paintings and sculptures by
Ernst Fuchs, Mariano Fortuny,
El Greco, Gerard Dou, Antoni
Pitxot, etc. Dalí makes the
poster advertising the event.
September 30: During his stay
in Port Lligat, Dalí writes the
presentation for a monograph
dedicated to the artist Antoni
Pitxot, director of the Teatre-
Museu Dalí.
In the same year he writes the
preface and draws the
illustrations for Sigmund
Freud's book *Moses and
Monotheism*. Denoël publishes
Cinquante secrets magiques,
the first French edition of the
volume published in English in
1948.

1975
January: During the
International Science Fiction
Film Festival in Avoriaz in
France, the film *Dalí
Impressions de la Haute

Mongolie, directed by José
Montes Baquer, is screened.
The film is about the hunt for
a hallucinogenic mushroom.
June: The Galeria de la Cúpula
in Figueres presents an
exhibition on Pablo Picasso.
For the catalogue, Dalí writes
the introduction entitled "El
pequeño libro Lila-Dalí-Gala-
Maorylin."
Dalí draws the poster *Dalí
Museum (Monument to Francesc
Pujols)*.
The Teatre-Museu Dalí in
Figueres and the Cleveland
Salvador Dalí Museum bring
out the previously un-published
work *Eroticism in clothing*,
dreamed up by the artist
between May 21 and 26, 1963,
in the Del Monte Lodge in
Pebble Beach, California,
written under dictation by
A. Reynolds Morse.

1976
May: Dalí in Port Lligat
writes *T*, not to be published
until 1979, in which he uses
the technique of automatic
writing driven by alliteration.
June: The artist draws the
poster for the Comité Français
pour la Sauvegarde de Venise in
which people are invited to
donate 260 Francs in order to
help save Venice from falling
into the sea.
August: Dalí, assisted by
Antoni Pitxot, gives drawing
lessons at the Teatre-Museu
Dalí in Figueres. Hundreds
of students and artists take
part in the lessons.
September 2-5: Dalí draws the
cover for the program for the
2nd International Stereoscopy
Conference held in Paris.
Dalí gives to the Paris
Bibliothèque Nationale a copy
of the book *L'Alchimie des
philosophes* illustrated by
himself.

1977
During the Summer, the Castres
museum presents an exhibition
entitled "Hommage à Goya."

In it are exhibited 81 etchings by Dalí done from engravings by Goya.

October: In order to help the football team of Sant Andreu of Barcelona overcome its financial crisis, Dalí creates the work *Goal*.

The same month saw the publication of *Les vins de Gala*, a volume in which the artist describes both his ten and Gala's ten favorite wines. In December, the book receives the Montesquieu prize awarded by the Sommellerie de France. November/December, the Galérie André-François Petit, Paris, presents a Dalí exhibition entitled "La gare de Perpignan accompagnée d'une petite retrospective." For several days in December two works by the artist, *Portrait of Gala*, in copper, and *Stereoscopic Painting*, were exhibited for

Salvador Dalí and Antoni Pitxot during drawing lessons at the Teatre-Museu in Figueres in a photograph by Melitó Casals, 1976

the first time in public.
On the occasion of the 50th anniversary of the death of Antonio Gaudí, a small book is published showing Gaudí's autograph project for the crypt of the Colonia Güell in Santa Coloma de Cervelló. The cover was done by Dalí.

1978

August: The Spanish royal family visits the Teatre-Museu Dalí in Figueres guided by Dalí and Gala.

November 8-December 30: The Salvador Dalí Museum, Beachwood (Ohio), presents an exhibition entitled "Dalí & Halsman."

December 18-20: André-François Petit presents in one of the salons of the Hôtel Meurice, Paris, Dalí's hyper-stereoscopic picture *Dalí's hand pulls back the golden fleece in the form of a cloud to show to Gala naked dawn, very far in the distance behind the sun. Homage to Claude Lorrain.*

December-January: In the Teatre-Museu Dalí in Figueres the hyper-stereoscopic work *Dalí lifts the skin of the Mediterranean to show Gala the birth of Venus* is put on show.

1979

May 9: Dalí is nominated foreign associate member of the Académie des Beaux-Arts de l'Institut de France.
The composer Tony Aubin, president of the Académie introduces him with the following words: "You are a genius. You, just as we do, know that. No-one can doubt this reality. If it were not so, you would not be here with us, and most of all you would not be yourself." Dalí for his part gave a talk entitled, "Gala, Velasquez and the golden fleece."
On the occasion of his 75th birthday and his admission to the Institut de France, Radiotelevisión Española broadcasts a three-part

The cover realized by Dalí for the Gaudí's project for the crypt of the Colonia Güell in Santa Coloma de Cervelló, 1977

documentary on Dalí's life and works, presented by Paloma Chamorro. The program was made from a two-day interview given by Dalí at the Hotel St. Regis in New York.
Dalí writes for the weekly newspaper *Destino* (October 17-23) a text entitled, "Últimes conclusions del meu llibre titulat 'Dimensions I color de Déu'." It opens in the following way, "At the end of these last five years, in which I have read so many books on science which, not only have I not understood, but also, almost always, so as not to say always, I have understood the exact opposite, I return to the very earliest intentions of my youngest years."

November: Dalí delivers to King Juan Carlos the painting entitled *The Prince of Sleep*, a large-format portrait upon which he had worked for several years.
Again in November, the French postal services bring out six million copies of an edition of a stamp designed by Salvador Dalí in 1978. It forms part of the series entitled "Création philatélique."

December 17: The day planned for the inauguration at the Centre Georges Pompidou of the most ambitious

Salvador Dalí is nominated associate member of the Académie des Beaux-Arts, Paris, 1979 [Studio Nath]

right-hand side
Salvador Dalí photographed by Melitó Casals while painting *Searching for the Fourth Dimension,* 1979

retrospective exhibition of the artist's work to that date. However, because of a strike by Museum staff the opening night is postponed until the next day. The first night coincides with the presentation of an environment specifically designed for the Centre Georges Pompidou. The exhibition is arranged around eleven themes: early works, *Un chien andalou,* the Surrealist works, the soft

works, William Tell, double images, Angelus and Maldoror, the Surrealist object, dreams and nightmares of the years 1936-1938, mysticism and science, and stereoscopy.

1980
Dalí spends the whole year at Port Llegat convalescing from an illness which he contracted during his stay in New York in the early months of the year.
May 14-June 29: Dalí retrospective at the Tate Gallery, London, a continuation of the Centre Georges Pompidou exhibition in Paris. Two hundred and fifty-one works, both oil paintings and drawings, are put on show.
October 21: At the Teatre-Museu Dalí in Figueres Dalí announces that he is to give a

press conference on 24th of that month regarding the stage of the old Teatre Municipal. During this meeting, the artist presents his most recent painting, *The Happy Horse,* and answers journalists' questions on health, economics and politics.

1981
April: The painting *Dream* (1937), from the Edward James collection, is sold for the sum of £ 360,000, the highest price ever paid for a work by a living painter, even Dalí.
August: The King and Queen of Spain, Juan Carlos and Sofía, visit Dalí at Port Lligat.
September 29: Dalí returns to his Teatre-Museu Dalí in Figueres to perform the symbolic act of placing a colored circle called *Horas Lulianas* (in memory of Ramón Llull) on the painting of the Lotería Nacional. He is accompanied by the painter, Antoni Pitxot, the writer, Ignacio Gómez de Liaño, and Gala.
October 12: The Centre d'Iniciatives i Turisme for the Vallès region celebrates the tenth anniversary of its foundation with a homage to Dalí at the Teatre-Museu Dalí in Figueres. The event opens

with a projection of the documentary, *Granollers Happening,* made in 1974, in which Dalí himself had participated. After a debate with certain writers and artists, a message from Dalí to the participants at the event is read out, "Greetings to you from Salvador Dalí Domènech, Felipe i Jacinto, and here is the most important part of my biography: firstly, they expelled me from the Academia de San Fernando (for the second time and definitively). Then, they expelled me from my family. I went to prison three times: once in Figueres, once in Girona, and a third time in New York. They expelled me from the surrealist group. After that, they bestowed upon me the Cross of Isabella the Catholic, they made me member of the Academia de San Fernando and member of the Academy of Fine Arts in Paris. I am all this. My life with Gala began with the purchase, for 500 pesetas, of the small house where we lived with René Crevel and Lidia. We later lived in the Púbol Castle. We bought the Teatre-Museu Dalí, in Figueres, and now the Gorgot

tower. This is what I am.
Port Lligat, October 9, 1981."

1982
At the beginning of January, Salvador Dalí is awarded the Grand Cross of the Order of Charles III, the most important honor awarded by the Spanish state. The actual conferral took place on June 16, when the General Delegate of the Catalonian government, Juan Rovira Tarazona, visited him in Púbol castle.
January 28: Inauguration of the exhibition dedicated to Dalí's work as an illustrator, "Obra gráfica: Ciclos literarios," held in the Galería Tiépolo of the Palacio Arbós, the head office of the Madrid Monte de Piedad, and organized by the Ministry of Culture and the Caja de Ahorros y Monte de Piedad de Madrid.
February 28-April 6: The Isetan Museum of Art in Tokyo presents a Salvador Dalí retrospective. The exhibition includes seventy-five works and a collection of nine soft clocks with their respective designs, done in 1975. After the stay in Tokyo (where the exhibition receives on average 10,000 visitors a day), the works are exhibited in Osaka at the Daimuru Art Museum, then at the Kitakyushu Municipal Museum of Art (May 8-June 6) and finally the Hiroshima Prefectoral Museum of Art.
March 7: Inauguration of the Salvador Dalí Museum in Saint Petersburg (Florida), founded by A. Reynolds Morse and Eleanor R. Morse. The museum contains the large collection which the Morses had exhibited in Cleveland in the Seventies.
March 20: During a ceremony at the Teatre-Museu Dalí in Figueres, Jordi Pujol; president of the Generalitat de Catalunya, the autonomous Catalan government, awards

Dalí the gold medal of the Generalitat de Catalunya. At the end of the ceremony, the artist turns to those present and declares, "If every word which I spoke were not an enigma, my speech would be that of a genius."
On this occasion, Dalí gave to his Teatre-Museu the painting *The Progress of the Enigma*, and the recent works, *Othello Dreaming Venice* and *Pietà*.
At the end of May, Dalí notes the seriousness of Gala's state of health and starts construction of a crypt in the cellars at Púbol.
Gala dies on June 10 in Port Lligat, and on the same day the coffin is transferred to Púbol. Dalí follows it and moves into the castle, but as time passes, he gives up and eventually returns to Port Lligat.
June 15: Inauguration of the exhibition, "Dalí i els llibres," in the Capella Reial de Santa Àgata in Barcelona.
July 26: By royal decree and recorded in the official state register, the King of Spain confers upon the artist the noble title of Marquis of Dalí de Púbol.
September: Salvador Dalí gives the painting, *Three Glorious Enigmas of Gala*, to the Spanish State. It was finished a month before the death of his wife. With this donation, the Spanish state now possesses three of Dalí's works, since it had acquired *Harlequin* (1926) and *Cenicitas* (1927-28), in July, for a hundred million pesetas.
October 8: The ballet, *Don Quixote*, is performed at the Teatro de la Zarzuela in Madrid, for which Dalí has designed the stage curtain.
November: Dalí sends a telegram to Luis Buñuel proposing a project to the film director, at that time living in Mexico, "DEAR BUÑUEL, EVERY TEN YEARS I SEND YOU A LETTER WITH WHICH YOU DISAGREE, BUT I DO NOT GIVE UP. LAST

NIGHT I HAD AN IDEA FOR A FILM WHICH WE COULD MAKE IN TEN DAYS, NOT ON THE PHILOSOPHICAL DEMON BUT ON OUR BELOVED LITTLE DEVIL. IF YOU FANCY IT, COME AND SEE ME AT PÚBOL CASTLE. LOVE, DALÍ." Buñuel replies to him that he abandoned films five years earlier and no longer leaves the house.
In the course of the year, Ediciones Scriba publishes *Atlas de microcirugia de la córnea*. A Dalí original is reproduced on the book jacket.

1983
During the year, Dalí completes what will be his last oil painting, *The Swallow's Tail (Series on Catastrophes)*, inspired by the theories of the mathematician René Thom. The first, big Dalí retrospective in Spain is organized by the Department of Culture of the Generalitat of Catalonia and by the Ministry of Culture. The exhibition is held in the Museo Español de Arte Contemporaneo in Madrid from April 15 to May 29, then in the Palau de Pedralbes, Barcelona from June 10 to July 31, and finally in the Teatre-Museu Dalí in Figueres from August 16. Dalí writes an introduction for the catalogue, dedicated to Gala.
September 3: As part of the 3rd Empordà International Music Festival, a photographic exhibition, "Dalí vist per Meli" is organized by the photographer Melitó Casals, known as "Meli." In later years, the exhibition will also be held in various other locations.
September: The Municipality of Figueres nominates Dalí freeman of the city. In October, the mayor visits him in Púbol castle and gives him the commemorative plaque.
October: Dalí does the first drafts for the restructuring of the façade of the so-called "torre

Gorgot" in Figueres (a building annexed to the Teatre-Museu Dalí). Dalí renames it the "torre Galatea" in honor of Gala. It will be Dalí's final home. The Fundació Gala-Salvador Dalí is created on December 23.

1984
May 25-June 28: The Husets Galleri di Aalborg, in Denmark, presents the "Salvador Dalí–Pitxot–Evarist Vallès" exhibition.
July 1-September 20: The Civic Gallery of Modern Art in the Palazzo dei Diamanti, Ferrara, organizes the "I Dalí di Salvador Dalí" exhibition which includes 248 works: paintings, drawings and objects, especially from his last period.
August 31: A fire breaks out in Púbol castle. Dalí moves to the Torre Galatea, in Figueres, which will become his permanent residence from October of the following year until his death.

1985
March 25: The publishing house, Mediterrània, publishes *Être Dieu: opéra-poème, audiovisuel et catharre en six parties*.

1986
September 5-25: The Galería Sant Lluc de Olot presents the works of Antoni Pitxot which refer to the frescoes of the Hall of Constantine in the Raphael Rooms. The book, *Pitxot*, by Cesáreo Rodríguez-Aguilera, also contains the text "La guerre de Troie aura lieu" written especially for this occasion by Salvador Dalí. Tusquets publishes *Procés a l'atzar* which is a collection of reports on the role of destiny in science, given by the experts P.T. Landsberg, G. Ludwig, R. Thom, E. Schatzman, R. Margalef and I. Prigogine during the seminar, "Culture and science: determinism and

freedom" held at the Teatre-Museu Dalí in the previous November. Dalí wrote the prologue and followed the seminar via closed circuit television from his home in Torre Galatea, in Figueres

1987

El Paseante magazine publishes, "Martír," the tragedy written by Dalí in 1976 but never published.[76]

1988

The Fundació Gala-Salvador Dalí publishes the poems written by Dalí during the time he has spent in the Torre Galatea: *Laureada* (Laureate) (June 17, 1985), *Oda a la monarquía* (Ode to Monarchy) (December 29, 1987), *La Alquimia de mi amor* (The Alchemy of My Love) (March 15, 1986) and *Elegías a Gala* (Eulogy to Gala) (June 8, 1988).

1989

Salvador Dalí dies in the Torre Galatea on January 23. He is buried two days later under the cupola of the Teatre-Museu Dalí, in Figueres.

[1] *The Masterpieces of Boucher: 1703-1770* (London-Glasgow: Gowans, Gray, 1911). *The Masterpieces of De Hooch and Vermeer* (London-Glasgow: Gowans, Gray, 1911). *The Masterpieces of Ingres* (London-Glasgow: Gowans & Gray, 1913).
[2] *En Patufet* (January 1918).
[3] Puvis, "L'Exposició de la Societat de Concerts" (*Empordà Federal*: January 11, 1919).
[4] *Studium* (Figueres: Edicions Federals, 1989).
[5] Salvador Dalí, *Un diari, 1919-1920: les meves impressions i records íntims,* in *Obras completas,* (Barcelona: Destino, Fundació Gala-Salvador Dalí, Sociedad Estatal de Conmemoraciones Culturales, 2003)
[6] Salvador Dalí, *Impressions and private memoirs of Salvador Dalí: January 1920* (Cleveland: The Reynolds Morse Foundation, 1962), p. 27.
[7] Salvador Dalí, *Tardes d'estiu,* ed. Víctor Fernández (Barcelona: Cave Canis, 1996), p. 21.
[8] Salvador Dalí, *Un Diari, 1919-1920,* cit., pp. 117-118.
[9] *Ibid.*, p. 168.
[10] *Exposició d'obres d'art organitzada per l'Associació Catalana d'Estudiants, Catalunya Gràfica* (February 10, 1922).
[11] Salvador Dalí, *Salvador Dalí, lletres i ninots: fons Dalí del Museu Abelló* (Mollet del Vallès: Museu Abelló, Fundació Municipal d'Art, 2001).
[12] *Dalí joven, 1918-1930* (Madrid: Museo Nacional Centro de Arte Reina Sofía, 1994), pp. 22-23.
[13] Salvador Dalí, *Vida Secreta de Salvador Dalí,* in *Obras Completas,* cit., p. 586.
[14] Carles Fages i de Climent, *Les Bruixes de Llers,* (Barcelona: Políglota, 1924).
[15] Various works were identified from the catalogue written by the Fundació Gala-Salvador Dalí: *Young Woman Seen from the Back, Portrait of Luis Buñuel, Nude and Still Life* (a work which belonged to Federico García Lorca), now kept in the Museo Nacional Centro de Arte Reina Sofía in Madrid; *Portrait of Joan Xirau* (private collection), *Still Life (Water melon)* (currently held in the Salvador Dalí Museum of St. Petersburg, FL), and *Still Life and Syphon with Bottle of Rum* (Cubist painting), which can be seen in the Teatre-Museu Dalí in Figueres.
[16] Rafael Santos Torroella (ed.), *Salvador Dalí escribe a Federico García Lorca,* "Poesía," nº 27-28, (Madrid: 1987), p. 15
[17] Centro de Estudios Dalinianos, Fundació Gala-Salvador Dalí, Figueres.
[18] Rafael Santos Torroella (ed.), *Salvador Dalí escribe a Federico García Lorca,* cit. p. 42
[19] *Ibid.*, p. 38-40.
[20] Centro de Estudios Dalinianos, Fundació Gala-Salvador Dalí, Figueres.
[21] *Ibid.*
[22] *Ibid.*
[23] *Ibid.*
[24] Salvador Dalí, Lluís Montanyà, Sebastià Gasch, *Manifest Groc,* (Barcelona: Impremta Fills de F. Sabater, March 1928), *Gallo,* no. 2 (April 1928).
[25] Rafael Santos Torroella (ed.), *Salvador Dalí escribe a Federico García Lorca,* cit., pp. 88-94
[26] *Dalí joven, 1918-1930* (Madrid: Museo Nacional Centro de Arte Reina Sofía, 1994), pp. 35-36.
[27] Centro de Estudios Dalinianos, Fundación Gala-Salvador Dalí, Figueres.
[28] *Ibid.*
[29] *Ibid.*
[30] Salvador Dalí, "Documental-Paris-1929," in *La Publicitat* (April 26, 1929; second part: April 28, 1929; third part: May 7, 1929; fourth part: May 23, 1929; fifth part: June 7, 1929; sixth part: June 28, 1929; seventh part: July 7, 1929).
[31] Jean Vigo, *Vers un cinéma social* (Paris 1930).
[32] *La Vie publique de Salvador Dalí* (Paris: Centre Georges Pompidou, Musée national d'Art moderne, 1980), p. 23.
[33] Antoni Pitxot, Montse Aguer, *Casa-Museu Salvador Dalí Port Lligat: una vida amb la llum de l'eternitat* (Figueres-Barcelona: Fundació Gala-Salvador Dalí, Escudo de Oro, 1998), p. 10.
[34] Centro de Estudios Dalinianos, Fundació Gala-Salvador Dalí, Figueres.
[35] Salvador Dalí, *Un diari, 1919-1920: les meves impressions i records íntims,* cit.

36 Centro de Estudios Dalinianos, Fundació Gala-Salvador Dalí, Figueres.

37 Salvador Dalí, *Obras completas*, cit., vol. III

38 Centro de Estudios Dalinianos, Fundació Gala-Salvador Dalí, Figueres.

39 *Ibid.*

40 *La Vie publique de Salvador Dalí*, (Paris: Centre Georges Pompidou, Musée national d'Art moderne, 1980), p. 40.

41 Centro de Estudios Dalinianos, Fundació Gala-Salvador Dalí, Figueres.

42 *Ibid.*

43 Salvador Dalí, *Vida Secreta de Salvador Dalí*, in *Obras Completas*, cit., p. 856.

44 Centro de Estudios Dalinianos, Fundació Gala-Salvador Dalí, Figueres.

45 Salvador Dalí, "Salvador Dalí. New Yorkers Stand in Line to See His Six-in-One Surrealist Painting," *Life* (April 17, 1939), p. 45.

46 Centro de Estudios Dalinianos, Fundació Gala-Salvador Dalí, Figueres.

47 John Briggs, "Ballet Russe Opens Season," New York Post (October 9, 1941).

48 Centro Estudios Dalinianos, Fundació Gala-Salvador Dalí, Figueres

49 "World of Music," *Times* (December 15, 1944).

50 Mel Heimer, *Crazy … like a Fox!* (*New York Journal American*, December 2, 1944).

51 Eugenio D'Ors Rovira, *Teoría de los estilos y espejo de la arquitectura* (Madrid: M. Aguilar, 1944).

52 Salvador Dalí, *Confesiones inconfesables*, in *Obras completas*, cit., p. 603.

53 Gerald Kersh, *Wars for Sale-An Entrepreneur of atomic destruction finds peace at last* (*Town & Country*, November 1945), pp. 115-17, 143-44, 176, 178, 181 and 183-85.

54 "Dalí: New and Old Surrealism," *Art News* (New York: November 1-14, 1945).

55 "Recent Paintings by Salvador Dalí," exhibition catalogue (New York: Bignou Gallery, November 20-December 29, 1945).

56 Sebastià Gasch, *Las Etapas del cine* (Barcelona: Instituto Transoceánico, 1948).

57 Bob Thomas, "Cinema Mirror," *Jersey Journal* (April 8 1946).

58 Louise Levitas, "Dalí: irrational sense a terrific necessity," *PM* (November 1947).

59 Centro de Estudios Dalinianos, Fundació Gala-Salvador Dalí, Figueres.

60 *Ibid.*

61 *Ibid*

62 Fundació Gala-Salvador Dalí, Figueres.

63 Salvador Dalí, *Confesiones inconfesables,* in *Obras completas,* cit., p. 658.

64 "Conferencias. Despertó extraordinaria expectación la del pintor Dalí en el Ateneo Barcelonés," *Diario de Barcelona* (October 20, 1950).

65 "Dalí Lecture is Unusual," *The College Eye*, no. 17 (February 8, 1952).

66 Salvador Dalí, "Corpus Hipercubus," *Time* (February 7, 1955), p. 2.

67 Salvador Dalí, "*Salvador Dalí Predicts,"* *Nugget* (March 1957). Salvador Dalí, "*Salvador Dalí Predicts,"* *Nugget* (April 1957). Salvador Dalí, "*Salvador Dalí Predicts,"* *Nugget*, (May 1957).

68 Jacques Franju, "*Salvador Dalí a l'oreille du Pape,"* *Libération* (November 22, 1958).

69 "Le discours de Dalí que l'on n'a pas entendu au Bal des Petits Lits Blancs," *Arts*, (May 13, 1959).

70 *The James Thrall Soby collection of works of art pledged or given to the Museum of Modern Art* (New York: The Museum of Modern Art, 1961).

71 Ramon Guadiola, *Dalí y su museo* (Figueres: Empordanesa, 1984).

72 Lester, Abelman, "*Aliyah! Israel Reborn, by Dalí,"* *News* (March 10, 1967).

73 Salvador Dalí, "*De cómo Elvis Presley se convierte en Roy Lichtenstein,"* *Arte y Parte*, no. 23 (October-November 1999), pp. 50-57.

74 Edith Efron, "Salvador Dalí's view of television," *TV guide* (June 8, 1968), cover and pp. 6-10.

75 Salvador Dalí, *Procès en diffamation plaidé devant la conférence du stage* (Paris: Pierre Belfond, 1971).

76 *El Paseante*, no. 5, Winter 1987.

Selected Writings by Salvador Dalí

POEM OF THE SMALL THINGS
To Sebastià Gasch, with all antiartistic delight

There is a very small thing placed on high in some spot.
I am pleased, I am pleased, I am pleased, I am pleased.
The sewing needles plunge into small nickels soft and sweet.
My girlfriend has a hand of cork full of Parisian fine lace.
One of my girlfriend's breasts is a calm sea urchin, the other a swarming
wasp's nest.
My friend has a knee of smoke.
The small charms, the small charms, the small charms, the small
charms, the small charms, the small charms, the small charms, the small
charms ... THE SMALL CHARMS PRICK
The partridge's eye is red.
Small things, small things, small things, small things, small things, small
things, small things, small things, small things, small things, small things,
small things…
THERE ARE SMALL THINGS, STOCK-STILL LIKE A LOAF OF BREAD

"Poema de les cosetes," *L'Amic de les Arts* (Sitges) 3(27) (August 31, 1928),
p. 211

THE NEW LIMITS OF PAINTING
to Sebastià Gasch

PART I

With Rafael Benet one runs precisely the so common risk of pronouncing nearly the same words he does, but with the absolute impossibility of establishing
an understanding.

Rafael Benet recently wrote, alluding to the extravagances of the new painting:
"They will end up by placing birds in aquariums." With these words Rafael
Benet amply demonstrates his own timidity; not too long ago André Breton
wrote, in the catalogue for an exhibition of Arp (inventor of the endless
mustache), that birds had never sung so well as they do at the bottom of
aquariums.

This has nothing to do, in spite of the coincidence, with placing birds in an
aquarium. The point is that they sing there, and that they sing there best.

If for Rafael Benet all these things are still absurd and lacking in logic, it is
quite some time now that they have not been so for us, or, rather, that they
have but in an entirely different mode, so as to become quite clear and normal. Painting and the art of today, which, as we shall see, come nearer to being a great direct art, similarly to the best examples of popular art, are beyond
common sense.

For us, the place of a nose, far from being necessarily on the face, seems to be
more adequately located on the armrest of a sofa. Nor will it be inconvenient
to find this same nose perched on top of a small trace of smoke. It isn't in vain
that Yves Tanguy has sent forth his delicate *messages*.

We can well assure Rafael Benet that decapitated figures live their organic and
perfect lives, that they rest in the shadow of the bloodiest vegetation *without
soiling themselves with blood*, and, furthermore, that they lie naked on the
most cutting and bristling surfaces of specialized marbles without risking
death.

Should Rafael Benet be reminded yet again that the lives of the creatures that
populate the surfaces of canvases and the world of poetry obey conditions
quite unlike those of the creatures populating the surface of the earth? That
the plastic and poetic physiology is not the physiology of living beings? That
the plastic or poetic life of a painting or of poetry obeys laws other than those
regulating the circulation of blood? That a monster ceases being one the moment certain relations have been established between the lines and colors
shaping it? That a decapitated figure, in the world of the plastic arts or of poetry, is not a figure without a head?

Beyond that, we might add that a figure without a head is more apt to intertwine with putrefied donkeys, and that flowers are intensely poetic precisely
because they resemble putrefied donkeys.

It is superfluous to say all these things that are so evident since the day (this
day is properly speaking that of Surrealism) which saw the beginning of the poetic autonomy of things and of words that (as noted by André Breton) cease
being *paroles mendiantes*.

For us, an eye no longer owes anything to the face, nor to immutability, nor
to a fixed idea; nor does it demand anything from the idea of being contained in the face. Quite the contrary, we have known for some time now
that eyes, similarly to a bunch of grapes, have a propensity for crazy speeds
and are well suited for launching themselves on the most contradictory of
pursuits.

That Rafael Benet could be unaware of all this is quite understandable, because these are the things that first became possible the day painters rejected
the testimony of their senses; and, recognizing the fundamental error of Paul
Cézanne and the sensory origin of his intentions (redoing Poussin *d'aprés nature,* that is to say, becoming classical by means of sensations), the painters, following a period of more or less complete cerebralization, came to rediscover
the purest and highest of abstractions.

In relation to this period, Gino Severini wrote: "I believe I may assert today
that the road to pursue is precisely the road opposite to that of Cézanne."

One does not become classical by way of sensation, but through the spirit; the
work of art should begin not by analyzing effect, but by analyzing the cause.
However removed we are today from Severini's "aesthetics of compass and
number," one should, nevertheless, note his passion for all that which should
bring about a return to spiritual creation, to abstraction, to the elimination of
the last sensory elements still persisting at the birth of Cubism; his passion for
all that which should bring a reign of category (in the sense of Eugenio d'Ors)
over matter, instead of the latter dominating the category.

Today, when the distance in time, says Severini, allows us to judge calmly the
Age of Humanism, we can see how the Humanists, far from being openly and
absolutely Doric, descended much too close to man, thus approaching too
closely the Ionians. The idea of linking up the individual to the universe, starting up in painting with Giotto, has itself been a marvelous idea, although,
probably, the Humanists regarded chiefly the individual and less so the universe. It was thus also that they became too human.

Instead of extolling Homer, Virgil, Cicero, etc., it would have been much
preferable, according to Severini, to follow closely Orpheus, Pythagoras, Aris-
totle, and Plato. Thus, instead of arriving at a mode of neopaganism, the whole
movement could have attained, perhaps, the level of the Pythagorean orders.

If we wish in painting to follow the general outline of a parallel naturalistic
process, we should establish that the specifically human principle of the
Ionic infinite divisibility fatally leads to the so-called art of perception,
which is the antidote of the abstract so-called art of conception. We shall see
that the art of perception, with its sensory root and sensuous finality, was
born under a Venetian sky, and became far more concretely defined in the
Netherlands and in Spain, acquiring, in the end, its highest expression and
exhausting and expressing its latest consequences and possibilities in
French Impressionism.

At this moment, painting is reduced to pure musical value. The art of perception, having its sweet and exciting moment in the painting of Vermeer of
Delft—that, in my opinion, represents, in the history of the proper way of
looking, a case of the highest, most humble and most dramatic probity—has
attained in Impressionism, as accurately noted by Sebastià Gasch, the moment
of its greatest discredit.

* Unless otherwise specified, the translations are by Haim Finkelstein

That which is absolute has been completely devoured by what is accidental: reality has been reduced to the unstable appearance of what are its most fugitive and confused aspects; nothing is grasped from objective reality other than the slightest resonances, which are yet deformed by the most subjective sentimentalism.

Do we need to mark once more that Monet's paintings of the Rouen Cathedral form a musical way (music that is indistinguishable from perfume) of expressing a series of emotional states?

I know by heart all the criticism that Rafael Benet might bring forth in favor of Impressionism and, in general, the art of perception; surely it is the same, more or less, as that which carries weight and is made use of in the Madrid Academy of Fine Arts, where I had the opportunity for a long time to verify the significant paradox that it is precisely at the Academy that the art of perception, so dear to Rafael Benet, is defended nowadays against the abstract, spiritualist, and antinaturalist art that we ourselves are defending.

In accordance with the gap commonly existing between creators on the one hand, and, on the other, the inept imitators who take refuge in the officialdom of the Academies and adopt the formulas that the creators themselves had since abandoned for being of no use, it is only natural, therefore, that when the Academy, with its prestige, forcefully protects the so-called art of perception, we ourselves are already so far removed from it that none of the real problems this art posed in its own day has the least interest for us.

The art of perception presents us with the highest formal and coloristic polyphony, what one never would have imagined as coming into being by way of abstraction; this fact alone powerfully enriches the resources of which the artist may avail himself.

In the least fragment of nature soaked in light … etc., etc., or so goes the pretty and rather annoying song.

We don't wish to further persist in these anachronistic questions; however easy this should prove to be, it would please us rather more to repeat what Ozenfant says gracefully and so logically:

Very well, but there is the piano.

The piano is an admirable discipline; the constant control of the medium over the work has made music homogeneous; without the control of a restricted medium, the work cannot but be translated at random, between the two rests of perceptible noises, on the one hand, and, on the other, the existence of an infinite number of different possible sounds, just as there is an infinite number of colors and forms, and just as there is an enormous quantity of words.

"What is the piano? A selection of sounds that are necessary and sufficient. Actually, isn't it possible to play Bach, Puccini, Beethoven, and Satie on the Piano? A schematic medium, no doubt, but having the power of a system.

It makes us laugh, cry or dance; happy are the musicians on whom the Pleyels have bestowed such admirable and so accomplished a means of expression, so perfectly economical and generous. What progress over the Chinese scale!

Poor painters! Chemists think only of multiplying the tones! Poor writers, served by makers of dictionaries concerned, above all, with multiplying words without ever getting rid of any!

Imagine a piano that produces 73,000 different sounds; painters are in that fix. If we speak again of the linear or the picturesque, the tactile element or the visual element, we would never be done; all these same arguments for or against would come out again… But do I still have to say that all this is about nothing of the sort?

The leaf spotted by the sun, to which Leonardo alludes, seems to us neither more nor less indistinct than this same leaf without the spots, simply on account of its having ceased to be itself in order to become a supposition. I sense the discouragement of the reader, but we won't proceed, as some might think, toward other, more confused and intricate, ways of playing with words and thoughts until reaching places that are inaccessible and labyrinthine. Nothing of the kind, and quite the contrary. By these routes we'll encounter exactly the essence of art which is the simplest, the freshest, the most direct and the least complicated: popular art.

Speaking of Picasso, Christian Zervos says that the soul of the people, when it genuinely creates, makes an abstraction of all that it wishes to express.

We already know that popular art is a movement of the spirit that does not signify anything in accordance with practical reason, but that creates countless suppositions. We should add that these suppositions become more varied and are enriched each time that a new limit is gained in the liberating measure or disequilibrium found at the heart of abstraction.

We should also say that these suppositions are never absent from reality; on the contrary, it is only possible for reality to acquire a more objective poetic emotion the moment a new and suitable mode of expression is found.

Far from the preconceived calculation and the mechanical elaboration of the Severinian results, present-day artists put their trust, rather than on chance, on probability. The find—to employ the expression of Maurice Raynal which seems to us more appropriate than that of creation, coined undoubtedly under Bergson's influence—the find of such suppositions depends more and more each day on a probability completely remote from common sense, and where truth and the absurd play a primary role.

Maurice Raynal then again wrote: "If there exists in art an Angel of Truth, it would be pointless to deny that he is often accompanied by the genius of the absurd. The absurd, I'm told, is that which has no common sense. What a beautiful praise! But we should not say that. On the contrary, let's declare loudly: Is there anything more hopelessly common than common sense? If the absurd is taken, indeed, for the contrary of common sense, it is because the assertion of individual life has always been in opposition to the assertion of social life. It seems, undoubtedly, difficult to separate the first from the second; this is so because the one, sensibly led, has been absorbed by the other. But if in politics this precaution is perhaps reasonable, art, which cannot be compared in such fashion to the conduct of state affairs, should not take this into account; its generalizations in this domain exhibit its overall poverty and uselessness.

"It is always dangerous to make definitions; dictionaries too take a risk in designating as absurd *that which lacks common sense*. The absurd will thus be something that seems like the sum of individual notions turned down outright by common sense, and which the absurd never presumes to control. Some psychologists have uncovered the action of the absurd, but only in order to embellish it, as always, with golden names and submit it, almost always, to common understanding.

"Differently stated, if this last expedient holds on to its facility and its best intentions, it remains absolutely unconnected to experience. And since truth, in philosophy, is not truth in itself, but because it is generally accepted as such, the absurd may be considered as a kind of foundation of truths on a completely personal level."

One of the new limits created by Cubism is statics, the other is the limiting of the absurd, or, in other words, the timidity and the reserve in the usage of this basis of personal truths of which Raynal speaks.

In the most austere and scientific moments of Cubism, we can already find clear signs of the cancellation of the new limits that the Cubists themselves have created while totally breaking, for their part, with those of the older painting. There will come a moment that will be critical for modern painting in which the painters will insistently utter the word lyricism; it would be close to Picasso and Chirico foremost, where, with a veritable fervor, the new and disturbing sense of the word will be sought; but, before this, one must count on the sterilized geometry and the cold draftsmanship of the aseptic marquetry and insipid volumes of Giorgio Morandi, with his still lifes from which the air has been extracted, and with their unforgettable fixity of recollection. This cold blood of Giorgio Morandi does not mean absolute harmony, absolute repose; this cold blood of Giorgio Morandi was the same that helped Max Ernst discover a new language made of the most common and conventional signs, a technique based on cold dictionary drawings or those found in instruction books, but with associations and relationships of things that form frightening ensembles, unusual and obsessive. In that period, Max Ernst already prepared himself for the most painful experiences, but the mutilations were still more imprecise a manner than the phenomena of rooms. It is possible to foresee there the epidermal horror with which he was always able to exhibit for us a complete and utter despair.

Comforting, nonetheless, was the spectacle of his spirit, which revealed to us all that remained concealed in ourselves, and something was always gained at the moment when, having discovered a new horror, it became impossible to go on hiding it.

Giorgio de Chirico, for his part, uncovered for us with a terrible calmness figurative suppositions that are born of the disparate linking of multiple objects of harmless appearance. Whereas the expressive and formal characteristics of Chirico could prompt Franz Roh to associate him with the New Objectivity, we would like to mark as a new symptom the hallucinating distribution of his volumetric relations and his bloodied perspectives.

All this calmness, all this stillness, all these statics of Giorgio Morandi, Max Ernst and Giorgio de Chirico were dramatic statics and stillness, because they were threatened at each moment.

All this geometric anesthesia held excitement in its abandoning of Futurism and in vaguely intuiting Surrealism.

Later, Man Ray will lead us away from the organization that we might call Purist, and things will become linked together in a different love, one different from that associated with rhythm or architecture.

A sponge by now will not be a movement by aiming to be a personage; this moment would be the point of departure toward achieving the very latest limits of painting.

"Nous limits de la pintura," Part I, *L'Amic de les Arts,* no. 22, (Sitges: February 29, 1928), vol. 3, pp. 167-169

PART II

A simple formal examination of the latest Surrealist plastic creation, and even of present-day poetic Cubism, will lead us to the formation of a table of signs and suppositions that are significant enough to deduce from them all but the most recent of the new limits to appear to us in the present-day world of painting. It would be best to go searching for these new limits in the opposite pole to that consolidated by the Purism of Ozenfant and Jeanneret, which is the latest consequence of Cubist plastic art.

The state-of-mind change that this involves is another proof of the continuous gymnastic training that is essential in following up the evolution of art in our time.

DINAMICS Before anything else, one should note the almost complete disappearance of the geometric stability already prefigured by the most dramatically static lyricisms and patiently outlined contents. In the annulment of the octagonal spirit is implied the appearance of a disequilibrium, a dynamic. This dynamic, however, has nothing to do with the sensory illusion of cinematographic movement par excellence that is the last refuge of Impressionism attempted by the Italian Futurists. The dynamism in question is constituted in such a manner that, to our senses, it remains specifically plastic and static while psychologically it acts like speed.

DINAMICS Speed, dynamic element that in Kandinsky had a musical value; that in the history of German Expressionism attained an expressive value; that in Futurism acquired an optical value, and that in the fundamental. questions posed by Baroque art ended up in decorativism; in recent painting, this dynamism seems to have acquired a very complex value, half decorative, half surrealistic, half plastic, half expressive of… .

This value perhaps is least explored, yet it seems, nevertheless, to be that which absolutely assures us of its very precise reality. This word again!!

Whereas Yves Tanguy attains a new ascensional ecstasy in which a rabid expurgation scrapes off all the feebleness of an exceptionally delicate spirit, Picasso whacks us with the purest and most savage sense of flight. The friezes on cornices and the wallpapers on ceilings have taken on in his latest paintings a new, swift, and voluntary direction. The curves of his contours, of his poetic torsos (monstrous in every way), risk the most audacious forms of death and volition.

From this fury of Picasso's will be born straight away, as if for each of his new states of the spirit, enthusiastic and devoted disciples.

DINAMICS De la Serna will inaugurate, between Picasso and the latest works of Braque, a change of diaphragm: he will employ the highest luminosity; Kiriato Ghika will go far toward attaining an unfocused vision, bringing to life with new youthfulness the early feelings of the fauves. Besides a curious dynamic tendency toward depth, his luminous foreground planes place him within a strange naturalist tradition.

De la Serna, on the contrary, remains freely in agreement with the canvas's dimensions, benefiting from the solutions that the canvas offers to the meaning of the surface. De la Serna achieves a very characteristic decorative poetry that is not inattentive to reality, but wholly closed to Surrealist infiltration.

LIGHTNESS One should recognize in the paintings of the Granadian and the Greek a true autonomy at work, and, in addition, purposes other than those of simple blending of Cubism and Fauvism. But Picasso indubitably wanted to say, did say, other things. Far from insisting on the arabesque, Picasso forced the straight line by means of its absence more than by pondering its generation. Preoccupied more by its invisibility than by its visualization, he proceeded with its cancellation even before generating it.

SURREALISM Let's leave Picasso aside. We should come to a better understanding with Arp, who provides for us a huge range of realizations with an almost imperceptible naturalness. If with Masson painting is still free in a way as to physically elude weight, Arp's bits of fabric retain our attention for other reasons than those of nonexistence. Being apart from any painful convictions to which Max Ernst may still aspire, Arp's reliefs, as Breton says, share the qualities of the swallow's heaviness and lightness.

ONEIRISM If man can work out a stable relation between the sawdust that falls off a bird-cage to be caught on cold skin and on hot skin, and, further, if these sawings are vestiges of cold skin and hot skin, why should we be allowed to criticize Max Ernst for having made possible a relationship and amity between words (love on earth and the vegetal lip) once we have agreed as to their extremely varied and occasional meaning?

NATURA Wax-museum figures exhibited in a fair's side-shows are as much a reality as a wisp of smoke or a nose. Minute-hands are truer when they cease being subject to their special function, the moment they are given to a rhythm other than that of following the circumference, acquiring the slightly mad choking caused by their articulation with bread crumbs.

AUTOMATIC NOTATION

If there is no willingness to accord these new despairs and joys all the importance they are due, what then will be offered to us under the name of nature? Has at least anything created until today without this impediment been at once lighter and denser, more real and more poetically physical, than a figuration of a nude by Joan Miró? Thus, it is quite terrifying that through this sense of inspiration physical reality would regain a normal appearance insofar as its having been freed of conformist application which conventional logic has endowed with insurmountable antireal attributions that are only controlled by habit, and which are of an origin that is meticulously symbolic and stereotypical.

NATURE

If nature is rediscovered in Miró through inspiration, this is no less perceptible in his works than in those of Max Ernst. Besides, the moment when the inspiration and even the most pure subconscious have taken effect through the revelation of our individual truths, an organic world full of significative attributions invades the figurations of the painters. In these moments, the most stirring and disturbing facts, dormant at the deepest layers of our most intimate horrors and joys, acquire the highest taste of light. With Cubism the intelligence had served not merely to make visible the spirit but to sensualize it and reduce it to the signification of a cipher, a sign, which, through mathematical abstraction, might move us aesthetically, by a measure and rhythm that harmonize with architecture, but that never harmonize with the most violent deprivations associated with lack of cohesion.

NATURE

ARP

SIGNIFICANCE

If finally it had become possible to believe in the necessity of agreeing, quite quickly and readily and not without irony, regarding that which might signify the words chair, shirt collar, bobbin, etc., beyond their tonal temperature—in the same manner that the Cubists one day had to come finally to an agreement with respect to small size, large size, striped thing, pointed thing, etc., concepts that have been wholly deprived today of the possibility of being put to use in the dissection of objects and of their purely lyrical and picturesque value, with a thousand sharp significative attributions having been attained—why should we evade this value of signification which is so emotionally charged and only accessible in states of mind that are particularly distracted and distraught? At any rate, once we know that, but truly know that, and in the name of a desire for the absolute—one would have to be very subtle indeed to evade this signification as being just another proof of lightness.

LE CADAVRE EXQUIS

At a time when things have been isolated from their conventional values and can freely exercise their specific and individual qualities, we have noticed (and not always by means of processes of pure automatism), at the end of a very short life that often dissolves in the red circles inside the night of our eyes, this life's hidden expirations, its particular modes of being absent and present outside of corporeality in an extremely complex and disturbing process that begins the moment these things, deprived of visuality, begin to walk or deem it convenient to modify the course of the projection of their shadow.

Quite separate already from what the new limit of present-day dynamics has formally imposed on us, and from that organic and physiological sense that has ended up supplanting the most inescapable architectonic vertebra, the word reality, placed under a conventional value in Cubism, returns to the forefront, far removed, yet, from Rembrandt's putrefied ox and quite close, nevertheless, to the most useless consumption of the epidermis.

IN REALITY

One is disposed, in cerebralizing ideas concerning surreality, to lean toward the most unexpected inclines that might bring us—in accord with a voluntary romanticism, be it superficial or profound—to regions where, having lost any magnetic indication, in order to orient ourselves we unavoidably must avail ourselves of the most aggravatingly paradoxical procedures. But perhaps the guidance was certain before such declination had begun. A good measure, which in no way could be called an agreement, but simply a different stratification layer, might give us a comfortable idea, unrelated to any personal genius, of what this multifarious ensemble of uncustomary and completely new dimensions could be.

Says Breton: "Everything I love, everything that I think and feel, inclines me toward a special philosophy of immanence according to which surreality would be embodied in the very reality and would not be superior or exterior to it. And reciprocally, for the container would also be the contents. My concern is with what is close to a communicating vessel between the container and the contained."

IN REALITY

"It goes to show that I firmly reject all attempts which, in the field of painting, as in that of literature, would precisely result in shielding thought from life as well as place life under the aegis of thought. What one hides is worth neither more nor less than what one finds. And what one hides from oneself is worth neither more nor less than what one allows others to find. One rupture, duly noticed and suffered, one single rupture testifies all at once to our beginning and our end."

NATURE

NATURE

POETRY

Nature! Should we invoke the name of this madman Heraclitus? Today's young people know something of this word and know how to rejoice in it. The slight wrinkle, a fine orbit for the eyelash hair, that cleaves, that ripens the small breast of the Virgins of the Flemish painters; the wrinkle, inevitably a painful direction, is necessarily set at variance with the contrary rhythm of the breast that tends toward sonority, toward the numerical and geometric perfection of the pure spherical theorem, denuded of the thousands of veined rivulets of red blood as in a red picture of a breast by Raphael.

POETRY

Today we all know the slightest accidents with which Nature speaks to us and could give us a very acute pain, but the conjunctivitis and the muscular fibers delicately intertwine with the cast plaster musculature, the cock's legs suffer horribly when they try getting out of the gorge of the beast that is already putrefied and dry, and the sky appearing clear behind the hollow left behind by the empty eyes of pigeons constantly reminds us of our total lack of chemical cohesion, the lack of chemical cohesion of which Max Ernst speaks to us in one of his poems.

"Nous limits de la pintura", Part II, *L'Amic de les Arts* (Sitges), vol. 3, no. 24, April 30, 1928, pp. 185-186

PART III

We have come to learn that the new modes of poetry were born beyond the limits imposed by the mechanism of the verse. Beyond the limits of literature there are a thousand ways to escape these artistic proceedings that are too slow and hardly fit for the almost always sterile rejuvenating processes. Poetry occupies an unexpected location that is entirely inaccessible and uncontrollable for those who make use of guides that have lapsed and lost their usefulness over the years. This new guide has not yet been produced. It consists of the magic of discovering poetry without the fatigue nor the crush to which one often gives oneself up. All the voluptuousness and all the

MAN RAY

COLLAGES

POETIC OBJECTS

falterings of voluptuousness become unified and come together in one attitude, an attitude unsustainable now by any system of transcendental skepticism. He who cannot satisfy himself with the quantity (dose of Léger) contained in Arp probably still feels the need to carry all the weight of tradition in order to conserve a seriousness that the news-in-brief in daily newspapers is inclined to cancel.

Forces that are of necessity confused fight it out today in the most lively domains of painting. It is the most stirring age, since psychologically it begins to excite everybody the moment one realizes what its most complete assassination consists of. It seems that nothing remains of ancient painting; not one of the concerns of ancient painters moves the hand of our contemporary artists. I believe that it is not even a question of boldness to encourage and place all our good will on this complete assassination of painting, and even of art in general. Were it not like that, we would have found, beyond art, suggestions and facts that would have moved us with greater efficacy than the ancient artistic mechanisms.

ASSASSINATION OF PAINTING

The assassination of art, what a beautiful tribute!! The Surrealists are people who honestly devote themselves to this. My thought is quite far from identifying with theirs, but can you still doubt that only those who risk all for everything in this endeavor will know all the joy of the imminent intelligence.

Surrealism risks its neck, while others continue to flirt, and, while many put something aside for a rainy day.

If truly the latest of the new limits of painting appear to be of such an order, momentarily denying the formidable conquests still closer to us; if, in the least contact with what used to be German Expressionism, the most recent painting appears to take on an expressive physiognomy, it is also quite clear to everybody's eyes that the aim of this expression is truly new in the History of Art, and that this art, expressive par excellence, stirs us still in the very marrow of our plastic art; so much so that perhaps we might be bold enough to assert, precisely because of this, that rather than being in the time of a great reaction, we find ourselves at the heart of a violent syncopated prolongation.

Does it matter that today's artist neglects the concerns that, for a brief moment, appeared fundamental, for the sake of physically miniaturized concerns? And that very far from things cold and hot, he finds the true fire and ice in trying only to let the embers freeze in the pupil of the rotting donkey, and lets the feather duster, its feathers stained with blood, become by a skillful transformation a ball of fire slowly agitating the night of our amorous simplifications?

"Nous limits de la pintura", Part III, *L'Amic de les Arts* (Sitges), vol. 3, no. 25, May 31, 1928, pp. 195-196

PLASTIC EXPRESSION

YELLOW MANIFESTO
(CATALAN ANTIARTISTIC MANIFESTO)

All courtesy in our attitude has been eliminated from this manifesto. There is no point in any discussion with the representatives of present day Catalan culture, which is artistically negative, even though efficient in other regards. Compromise or correctness lead to deliquescent and lamentable confusing of all values, to the most unbreathable spiritual atmospheres, and to the most pernicious of influences. An example: *La Nova Revista*. Violent hostility, on the other hand, sets neatly all values and attitudes and creates a hygienic state of mind.

WE HAVE ELIMINATED	all argumentation	
WE HAVE ELIMINATED	all literature	There exists an enormous bibliography and there is all the
WE HAVE ELIMINATED	all poetry	effort of today's artists to supplant all this
WE HAVE ELIMINATED	all philosophy in favor of our own ideas	

WE CONFINE OURSELVES	to the most objective enumeration of facts
WE CONFINE OURSELVES	to indicate the grotesque and utterly sad spectacle of the Catalan intellectuals of today, locked up in a confined and putrefied atmosphere
WE WARN	those still not contaminated by the infection. It's a matter of strict spiritual asepsis
WE KNOW	that we are not going to say anything new. We are certain, however, that this is the basis of everything new that now exists and of everything new that could possibly be createdin
WE LIVE	in a new age of unforeseen poetic intensity
MECHANIZATION	has revolutionized the world
MECHANIZATION	the antithesis of the circumstantially-indispensable Futurism—has brought forth the most profound change humanity has ever known
A MOLTITUDE	anonymous—and antiartistic—collaborates, with its daily efforts, on the affirmation of the new age, while still living wholly in accord with its own period

A POST-MACHINIST STATE OF MIND HAS BEEN FORMED

THE ARTISTS	of today have created a new art in accord with this state of mind. In accord with their age

HERE, HOWEVER, PEOPLE
GO ON VEGETATING IDYLLICALLY

THE CULTURE — of present-day Catalonia is of no use for the joy of our age. Nothing is more dangerous, falser or more corrupting

WE ASK THE CATALAN INTELLECTUALS

"Of what use has the Bernat Metge Foundation been to you, if afterwards you end up confounding ancient Greece with pseudo-classical dancers?"

WE DECLARE — that sportsmen are closer to the spirit of Greece than our intellectuals

WE SHALL ADD — that a sportsman, unsullied by artistic notions and all erudition, is closer and better suited to feel the art of today and the poetry of today than short-sighted intellectuals who are weighed down by negative training

FOR US — Greece is perpetuated in the numerical perfection of an airplane engine, in the antiartistic fabric, of anonymous English manufacture, meant for golf; in the naked girls of the American music-hall

WE NOTE — that the theater has ceased to exist for some people and nearly for each and every-body

WE NOTE — that concerts, lectures and shows taking place nowadays among us show the tendency of becoming synonymous with unbreathable and extremely boring scenes

IN CONTRAST — new events of intense joy and cheerfulness claim the attention of the youth of today

THERE IS — the cinema

THERE ARE — the stadium, boxing, rugby, tennis, and a thousand sports

THERE IS — the popular music of today: jazz and today's dances

THERE ARE — automobile and aeronautics trade shows

THERE ARE — games on the beach

THERE ARE — beauty contests in the open air

THERE IS — the fashion show

THERE IS — the naked performer under electric lights in the music-hall

THERE IS — modern music

THERE IS — the racetrack

THERE ARE — art exhibitions of modern artists

THERE ARE — still great engineering and magnificent ocean liners

THERE IS — today's architecture

THERE ARE — instruments, objects and furniture of the present age

THERE IS — modern literature

THERE ARE — modern poets

THERE IS — modern theater

THERE IS — the phonograph, which is a little machine

THERE IS — the camera, which is another little machine

THERE ARE — newspapers providing extremely fast and vast information

THERE ARE — encyclopedias of extraordinary erudition

THERE IS — great activity in science

THERE IS — criticism that is well-documented and well informed

THERE IS — etc., etc., etc.

THERE IS — finally, an immobile ear over a small up-right smoke

WE DENOUNCE — the sentimental influence of the racial commonplaces of Guimerà

WE DENOUNCE — the unhealthy sentimentality served by the Orfeó Català with its worn-out repertoire of popular songs adapted and adulterated by people who are absolutely hopeless in what concerns music, or, even, original composition (we think optimistically of the choir of the American "Revelers")

WE DENOUNCE	the absolute lack of youth in our young
WE DENOUNCE	the absolute lack of decision and audacity
WE DENOUNCE	the fear of new realities, of words, of the risk of ridicule
WE DENOUNCE	the lethargy of the putrefied atmosphere of the circles and egos having to do with art
WE DENOUNCE	the total lack of preparation on the part of critics with regard to the art of today and yesterday's art
WE DENOUNCE	the young people who seek to repeat ancient painting
WE DENOUNCE	the young who seek to imitate ancient literature
WE DENOUNCE	architecture that follows a style
WE DENOUNCE	decorative art which is not in line with standardization
WE DENOUNCE	painters of twisted trees
WE DENOUNCE	present-day Catalan poetry, made with hackneyed Maragallian clichés
WE DENOUNCE	artistic poisons for the use of children, of the "Jordi" type (for the joy and comprehension of children, nothing is more adequate than Rousseau, Picasso, Chagall …)
WE DENOUNCE	the psychology of little girls who sing: "Rosó, Rosó. …"
WE DENOUNCE	the psychology of little boys who sing: "Rosó, Rosó. …"

Finally we claim to ourselves the great artists of today representing the most diverse tendencies and categories:
PICASSO, GRIS, OZENFANT, CHIRICO, JOAN MIRÓ, LIPCHITZ, BRANCUSI, ARP, LE CORBUSIER, REVERDY, TRISTAN TZARA, PAUL ÉLUARD, LOUIS ARAGON, ROBERT DESNOS, JEAN COCTEAU, GARCÍA LORCA, STRAVINSKY, MARITAIN, RAYNAL, ZERVOS, ANDRÉ BRETON, ETC., ETC.

SALVADOR DALÍ LLUÍS MONTANYÀ

SEBASTIÀ GASCH

Manifest groc (Manifest antiartística català", published in collaboration with Lluís Montanyà and Sebastià Gasch (Barcelona: Fills de F. Sabater, March 1928)

WITH THE SUN

With the sun a small cornet is born to me out of a handful of more than a thousand photographs of little dry asses.

With the sun, near an empty, damp place, sing 6 blobs of spittle and a small snoring sardine.

With the sun, there is a small milk, upright above the anus of a mollusk.

With the sun, two small toothless sharks are born to me under my arms.

With the sun, there is a mucus standing up at the edge of a curbstone.

And another mucus, standing up on my fingertip, ready to fly away,

And another mucus, upright 20 meters away, on a stone that looks like a monument to parrots,

And another mucus, calm on a moth 40 meters away, that is a happy song,

And another dry mucus that is a curve,

And another flying mucus that is a tailor costume,

And another cramped mucus that is the history of a walnut,

And another mucus, given to drink, that is the sounds of the European war.

When it's sunny, when it's sunny, when it's sunny, when it's sunny, when it's sunny, when it's sunny!

When it's sunny, I make pretty castles

With cork painted red,

With colored feathers,

With saliva

With the hairs of my family's ears,

With the vomiting of happy animalcules,

With the lovely frames of artistic pictures,

With the excrements of singers, of dancers, of goats, of lovers of chrysanthemums, of dry beasts.

I make this castle expressly for it to be inhabited by a strange couple consisting of an old grasshopper and a small cinder from a cigar. The grasshopper is made up of more than 100,000,000 tiny swordfish; if it is blown on, the tiny sword fish scatter away in the air, and there remains from them only an ancient and extremely slender hairy fountain pen. As for the cinder, do I still have to hint that this has to do with an ordinary MUCUS?

"Con el sol," *La Gaceta Literaria,* no. 54 (Madrid, March 15, 1929), p. 1

AT THE MOMENT …

At the moment when it is easy, for those who are less expert, to foresee the furious and total aversion with which we all struggle against the artistic fact, and in which all the most recent SIGNS lead us to consider the achievements of what is the purest and the most demanding of the current creations of the spirit as the UMBILICAL CORD that should definitely separate us—still troubled by painful traumas—from the CANCEROUS ARTISTIC PROCESS, and lead us on the living paths of our convulsions (of which we demand no consolation, nor expect the birth of a new faith) TOWARD A SENSE OF LIBERTY;

At this moment, then, in which irony will become the most inefficacious drug, and in which the pleasure in humanitarian cruelty or morality and other sublimities, the same as any philosophy inclined toward general SOLUTIONS, will turn out to be as unacceptable or more so than this very irony;

Facing that which, having been FOUND by this one simple fact, it would already be useless for us to continue hiding, and having scraped off the motive power of our anxiety, namely that ALL VOLITION would consist merely of **LEAVING the skin exposed to the unusual violence, with which all trivialities had been endowed;**

At this moment, I repeat, SURREALISM, IN TERMS OF REALITY, as living ANTIARTISTIC fact, as MORAL SUNVERSION, is the only suitable **ANTI-IMAGINATIVE**

means, because of its unlimited mechanical faculties of accommodation and the swiftness of the simultaneities that are most fruitfully and vertiginously possible in the field of knowledge, already due to ... and to the particular constitution of the psychic apparatus which—as in dreams, thanks to the very agile and skillful superpositions of the most heterogeneous and contradictory contents (and with the aid of other mirror plays)—obtains the reality of a simple and organic figuration (such as in dream images), making possible for our spirit—on account of the saving in time and the accumulation of new intensity—to arrive before these same FACTS, being able to subject them **TO THEIR OWN FREEDOM** and make a record in addition—in the absence of any system and with the automatic aid of the NEW TRISEXUAL DRIBBLING FLOWERS—of the ONLY possibilities beyond any combination, beyond any skillful and exquisite vaudeville of LYRICISM. As for the PUTREFIEDS who FUSSYLI TAKE CARE OF THEIR CONDITION … we are very sorry … **BUT IN FACT**…

"En el moment...," *L'Amic de les Arts,* vol. 4, no. 31 (Sitges: March 31, 1929), p. 1

THE ROTTING DONKEY

An activity having a moral tendency could be provoked by the violently paranoiac will to systematize confusion.

The very fact of paranoia, and, in particular, consideration of its mechanism as a force and power, lead us to the possibility of a mental crisis, perhaps of an equivalent nature, but in any case at the opposite pole from the crisis to which we are also subjected by the fact of hallucination.

I believe the moment is drawing near when, by a thought process of a paranoiac and active character, it would be possible (simultaneously with automatism and other passive states) to systematize confusion and thereby contribute to a total discrediting of the world of reality.

*

The new simulacra which the paranoiac thought may suddenly let loose will not merely have their origin in the unconscious, but, in addition, the force of the paranoiac power will itself be at the service of the unconscious.

These new and menacing simulacra will act skillfully and corrosively with the clarity of physical and diurnal appearances; a clarity which, with its special quality of self-reserve or modesty, will make us dream of the old metaphysical mechanism which has something about it that may readily be confused with the very essence of nature, which, according to Heraclitus, delights in hiding itself.

*

Standing wholly apart from the influence of the sensory phenomena with which hallucination is more or less taken to be associated, the paranoiac activity always makes use of materials that are controllable and recognizable. Suffice it that the delirium of interpretation should have linked together the sense of the images of heterogeneous pictures covering a wall for the real existence of this link to be no longer deniable. Paranoia makes use of the external world in order to set off its obsessive idea, with the disturbing characteristic of verifying the reality of this idea for others. The reality of the external world serves as an illustration and proof, and is placed thus at the service of the reality of our mind.

All physicians are of one mind in recognizing the swiftness and inconceivable subtlety commonly found in paranoiacs, who, taking advantage of associations and facts so refined as to escape normal people, reach conclusions that often cannot be contradicted or rejected and that in any case nearly always defy psychological analysis.

*

It is by a distinctly paranoiac process that it has been possible to obtain a double image: in other words, a representation of an object that is also, without the slightest pictorial or anatomical modification, the representation of another entirely different object, this one being equally devoid of any deformation or abnormality disclosing some adjustment.

The attainment of such a double image has been made possible thanks to the violence of the paranoiac thought which has made use, with cunning and skill, of the required quantity of pretexts, coincidences, and so on, taking advantage of them so as to reveal the second image, which, in this case, supersedes the obsessive idea.

The double image (an example of which might be the image of a horse that is at the same time the image of a woman) may be extended, continuing the paranoiac process, with the existence of another obsessive idea being sufficient for the emergence of a third image (the image of a lion, for example) and thus in succession until the concurrence of a number of images which would be limited only by the extent of the mind's paranoiac capacity.

I submit to a materialist analysis the type of mental crisis that might be provoked by such an image; I submit to it the far more complex problem, of determining which of these images has the highest potential for existence, once the intervention of desire is accepted; and also the more serious and general question whether a series of such representations accepts a limit, or, whether, as we have every reason to believe, such a limit does not exist, or exists merely as a function of each individual's paranoiac capacity.

All this (assuming that no other general causes intervene) allows me, to say the least, to contend that our images of reality themselves depend on the degree of our paranoiac faculty, and that yet, theoretically, an individual endowed with a sufficient degree of this faculty, might as he wishes see the successive changes of form of an object perceived in reality, just as in the case of voluntary hallucination; this, however, with the still more devastatingly important characteristic that the various forms assumed by the object in question will be controllable and recognizable by all, as soon as the paranoiac will simply indicate them.

*

The paranoiac mechanism giving birth to the image of multiple figuration endows our understanding with a key to the birth and origin of the essence of the simulacra, whose furor dominates the aspect under which are hidden the multiple appearances of the concrete. It is precisely the violence and the traumatic essence of the simulacra with regard to reality, and the absence of the slightest osmosis between reality and the simulacra, which lead us to infer the (poetic) impossibility of any kind of *comparison*. There would be no possibility of comparing two things, unless it would be possible for them to exist with no links whatsoever, conscious or unconscious, between them. Such a comparison made tangible would clearly serve as illustration of our notion of the gratuitous.

It is by their lack of congruity with reality, and for what may be seen as gratuitous in their existence, that the simulacra so easily assume the form of reality while the latter, in its turn, may adapt itself to the violence of the simulacra, which materialist thought idiotically confounds with the violence of reality.

Nothing can prevent me from recognizing the multiple presence of simulacra in the example of the multiple image, even if one of its states adopts the appearance of a rotting donkey and even if such a donkey is actually and horribly putrefied, covered with thousands of flies and ants; and, since in this case one cannot infer the meaning of these distinct states of the image beyond the notion of time, nothing can convince me that this merciless putrefaction of the donkey is anything other than the hard and blinding glint of new precious stones.

Nor do we know if the three great simulacra, excrement, blood, and putrefaction, do not expressly conceal the coveted "treasure land."

Connoisseurs of images, we have long ago learned to recognize the image of desire hidden behind the simulacra of terror, and even the awakening of "Golden Ages" in the ignominious scatological simulacra.

*

The acceptance of simulacra, whose appearances reality strives with great difficulty to imitate, leads us to *desire ideal* things.

Perhaps no simulacrum has created ensembles to which the word *ideal* could apply so well as the great simulacrum constituted by the astounding Art Nouveau ornamental architecture. No collective effort has managed to create a dream world so pure and so disturbing as the Art Nouveau buildings, which, existing on the fringes of architecture, constitute in themselves a true realization of solidified desires, and where the most violent and cruel automatism terribly betrays a hatred of reality and the need to find refuge in an ideal world, in a manner akin to the way this happens in infantile neurosis.

Here is what we can still like, this imposing mass of frenzied and cold buildings spread over all of Europe, despised and neglected by anthologies and scholarly surveys. This is enough to put up against our porcine contemporary aestheticians, defenders of the detestable "modern art," and enough even to put up against the whole history of art.

*

It would be appropriate to say, once and for all, to all art critics, artists, and so on, that they need not expect from the new Surrealist images anything other than disappointment, foul sensation and feeling of repulsion. Being quite on the fringes of plastic investigations and other kinds of "bullshit," the new images of Surrealism will more and more take on the forms and colors of demoralization and confusion. The day is not far off when a picture would attain the value and only the value of a simple moral act, which would yet be a simple gratuitous act. The new images, as a functional form of thought, will adopt the free disposition of desire while being violently repressed. The lethal activity of these new images, simultaneously with other Surrealist activities, may also contribute to the collapse of reality, to the benefit of everything which, through and beyond the base and abominable ideals of any kind, aesthetic, humanitarian, philosophical, and so on, brings us back to the clear sources of masturbation, of exhibitionism, of crime, and of love.

The Surrealists are Idealists partaking of no ideal. The ideal images of Surrealism are at the service of an imminent crisis of consciousness, at the service of the Revolution.

"L'Âne pourri," in *La Femme visible* (Paris: Éditions surréalistes, 1930), pp. 11-20; Le Surrealisme au service de la révolution no. 1,(Paris: July 1930), pp. 9-12

LOVE

The pleasure principle acting against the reality principle, the paranoiac delirium of interpretation, the disorders of affective knowledge, overestimation, the transparent confusion of simulacra, all the things that constitute in short the most violent categories of thought, culminate in love through its continuous and lethal intensity.

According to Wittels, it seems that "one loves without intermission," as one dreams in a continuous manner, with the dream, as we know, persevering through all the states of waking life.

The relationships between dream, love, and the sense of annihilation that is peculiar to each of these, have always been obvious. Sleeping is a form of dying, or, at least, dying to reality; better still, this is the death of reality. But reality dies in love as it does in the dream. The gory osmoses of dream and love occupy man's life in its entirety. During the day we unconsciously look for the lost images of dreams, and this is why, when we find an image resembling some dream image, it seems to us that we have known it before and thus we maintain that merely seeing it has already made us dream.

The vague contours of an oneiric representation, often erased by censorship, will become in love hard and dangerous contours which are liable to injure us, and, consequently the haemorrhage resulting from such wounds might be considered the one and only genuine blood of dreams.

All this should make us think that love is nothing but a kind of incarnation of dreams that corroborates the common expression according to which the beloved woman would be the flesh and blood embodiment of dream.

If love embodies dreams, let us not forget that one often dreams of one's own annihilation and that this, to judge by our oneiric life, would be one of

man's most violent and most turbulent unconscious desires. The intrauterine signification occupies each day a more important place in the study of dreams. Its symbols, manifested in attitudes that characterize some states of mental depression, often come up again in the case of lovers who take refuge in sleep. Nothing could be more surprising than the punctilious documentary of the postures of sleep, especially in the case of love, these postures being always those of annihilation or the intrauterine curvature, and even more so when they are those adopted by the happy ones who fall asleep in the passionate and cosmic 69 position or in that of the female praying mantis devouring the male.

We have heard from Freud about the limpidity of literal interpretation, in other words, the non-interpretation of commonplace and everyday expressions. However, I dare say that, in some particular cases and above all when the death principle is latent or manifest to varying degrees, we can find in those expressions a certain lack of precision and a distraction that demand an interpretation. In view of all the above, I am beginning to suspect that, when we have described someone under the power of love as having his face "lit up and transformed like the face of a child," it is not quite childhood or the child's face that we have in mind, but, more cruelly, the more remote face of the foetus.

Analytically, I would have preferred seeing Stendhal as being equally impartial faced with the measurements of the Vatican and in the presence of the much talked about and no less measurable "crystallizations." As for myself, in my turn I would enjoy repeating, this time facing the large rock crystal of love, what Stendhal said in front of St. Peter's in Rome: "Here are exact details." One loves completely when one is ready to eat the beloved woman's shit.

All that psychophysiology has taught us about the phenomenology of repugnance leads us to believe that desire could easily overcome unconscious symbolic representations. Repugnance would be a symbolic defense against the intoxication of the death wish. One experiences repugnance and disgust for what deep inside one wishes to get closer to, and from this comes the irresistible "morbid" attraction, conveyed often by incomprehensible curiosity, of what appears to us repugnant. In love we reign over the floods of images of self-annihilation. The scatological simulacra, the simulacra of desire, and the simulacra of terror acquire a confusion of the clearest and most dazzling kind. I would like to make clear that, in love, I attach a special value to all the things generally labeled perversion and vice. I consider perversion and vice to be the most revolutionary forms of thought and activity, the way that I consider love as the only attitude worthy of man's life.

Thanks to love, the images of the external world will increasingly come to illustrate my own thought, things will finally be obediently commensurate with my tastes and will become the clever vocabulary of my own paranoiac will. A postcard I have received might illustrate and even clarify an idea that has begun to haunt me, that is to say, that has begun to take on a form of unreality in may mind and become, with every instant that passes, clearer and more enigmatic. All I think about lives and renews itself in the image of the beloved. This person is also all I could think and all I will not ever think.

Everything achieving purity in our eyes bears the unmistakable mark of the vigorous, anti-natural, and depraved aspirations of the amorous imagination. The ancient human sacrifices of the Aztecs have just taken on all the taste and all the light of love. We cherish Sade, the masochism of Thomas Hardy; the metaphysical, artificial, unnatural, and troubling character of de Chirico's mannequins; the backward-looking artifices of Gustave Moreau, of Huysmans; the anti-natural splendor of all the deviations from the Greco-Roman culture culminating in Art Nouveau.

*

… I am thinking of the abominable and squalid native land where I passed my adolescence …

Far away from love.

At home, the parents' bedroom, unventilated in the morning and exuding the hideous stench of uric acid, of bad tobacco, of fine sentiments and of shit …

Far away from love, far away from you, violent and sterilized woman.

Paris, 1930

"L'Amour," in *La Femme visible* (Paris: Éditions surréalistes, 1930), pp. 65-69

SURREALIST OBJECTS

GENERAL CATALOGUE	Suspended Ball
I. Objects Functioning Symbolically (automatic origin)	Saddle, Sphere and Leaves Shoe and Glass of Milk Sponges and Bowl of Flour Gloved Hand and Red Hand
II. Transubstantiated objects (affective origin)	Soft Watch Watch Made of Straw
III. Objects To Be Thrown (oneiric origin)	Figuratively Physically
IV. Wrapped Objects (diurnal fantasies)	Handicap Sirenion
V. Machine Objects (experimental fantasies)	Rocking Chair for Thinking Association Board
VI. Mould objects (hypnagogic origins)	Automobile-Table-Chair-Lampshade Forest

1. OBJECTS FUNCTIONING SYMBOLICALLY:

These objects, lending themselves to a minimum of mechanical functioning, are based on phantasms and representations likely to be provoked by the realization of unconscious acts.

These are acts of the kind that you cannot understand the pleasure derived from their realization, or which are accounted for by erroneous theories devised by censorship and repression. In all analyzed cases, these acts correspond to distinctly characterized erotic desires and fantasies.

The embodiment of these desires, their way of being objectified by substitution and metaphor, their symbolic realization, all these constitute a typical process of sexual perversion, which resembles in every respect the process involved in the poetic act.

Even in the case where the erotic desires and fantasies in which the objects in question have their origins would be included in the common classifications of the "normal," the object itself and the phantasms its functioning could set off always constitute a new and absolutely unknown series of perversions and, as a result, of poetic acts.

The Objects Functioning Symbolically were envisaged following the mobile and silent object, Giacometti's suspended ball, an object that already put forward and brought together all the essential assumptions of our definition, but which still stuck to the means peculiar to sculpture. The Objects Functioning Symbolically allow no leeway to formal concerns. They depend solely on everyone's loving imagination and are extra-sculptural.

The Surrealist Objects are still almost in their embryonic stage, but their analysis, which we keep for our coming issues, enables us to predict all the violent fantasy of their coming prenatal life.

The notion of man's true spiritual culture will increasingly appear to be in accordance with his capacity for perverting his thought, for to become perverted always posits being driven by one's desire, and it is conditioned by the mind's degrading capacity to modify and change to their contrary the unconscious thoughts appearing under the rudimentary simulacrum of phenomena.

Large automobiles, thrice their natural size, will be reproduced (with meticulous care for details surpassing that of the most precise moldings) in plaster or in onyx, to be enclosed, wrapped in women's linen, in sepulchers whose site would not be recognized but for the presence of a thin clock made of straw.

Museums will be quickly filled up with objects whose uselessness, large size, and clutter will make it necessary to build special towers in the deserts to hold them. The gates of these towers will be cleverly covered up from view to be replaced by a fountain with an uninterrupted flow of real milk which will be absorbed greedily in the hot sand.

In this age of knowledge, bread crusts will be crushed by men's metal shoes, to be then soiled and spattered with ink.

The culture of the mind will become identified with the culture of desire.

OBJECT BY GIACOMETTI

A wooden ball marked with a feminine groove is suspended, by a very fine violin string, above a crescent whose wedge merely grazes the cavity. The beholder feels instinctively compelled to slide the ball over the wedge, but the length of the string does not allow full contact between the two.

OBJECT BY VALENTINE HUGO

On top of a green roulette cloth from which the last four numbers have been removed, two hands are placed, one in a white glove, the other red and adorned with ermine cuff. The gloved hand, its palm open upward, holds a die between thumb and forefinger, its only movable fingers. The red hand, all its fingers supple, grips the gloved hand, introducing the forefinger into the opening of the glove and lightly raising it. The two hands are tangled in a mesh of white threads that are as tenuous as gossamer and are fastened to the roulette cloth by diversely arrayed tacks with red and white heads.

OBJECT BY ANDRÉ BRETON

The most complex and difficult to analyze. Placed on a small bicycle saddle, a fired earthenware receptacle is filled with tobacco on whose surface lie two long pink sugared almonds. A polished wooden sphere that can revolve around the axis of the saddle makes the tip of the saddle come into contact, in the course of this movement, with two antennas made of orange-colored celluloid. The sphere is linked up by two arms of the same material to an hourglass lying horizontally (so as to impede the flow of the sand), as well as to a bicycle bell that should ring when a green sugared almond is flung across the axis by means of a catapult placed behind the saddle. The whole thing is mounted on a board covered with sylvan vegetation, exposed here and there to reveal a surface made of percussion caps; on one corner of the board, which is more densely covered than the others, stands a small sculptured book made of alabaster whose board is adorned with a glass-covered photograph of the Tower of Pisa, and near it one finds, on clearing the leaves, a cap, the only one to have gone off, under a doe's hoof.

OBJECT BY GALA ÉLUARD

Two metal antennas oscillating and curved.

Two sponges at their ends, one made of metal, the other real, both trimmed into a breast shape, with the nipples represented by small bones done in red. When the antennas are given a push, the sponges come lightly in touch, one with flour in a bowl, the other with the spiked tips of a metal brush.

The bowl itself is placed in a box held at an angle that contains other objects corresponding to additional representations. A red elastic membrane, wobbling for a long time on being moved in the most imperceptible manner, a small and flexible black spiral looking like a dowel hangs in a little red cage. A whitewood brush and a pharmaceutical glass tube divide the box into compartments.

OBJECT BY SALVADOR DALÍ

A woman's shoe, inside of which a glass of warm milk has been placed, in the center of a soft paste in the color of excrement.

The mechanism consists of the dipping in the milk of a sugar lump, on which there is a drawing of a shoe, so that the dissolving of the sugar, and consequently of the image of the shoe, may be observed. Several accessories (pubic hairs glued to a sugar lump, an erotic little photograph) complete the object, which is accompanied by a box of spare sugar lumps and a special spoon used for stirring leas pellets inside the shoe.

"Objets surréalistes," *Le Surréalisme au service de la révolution,* no. 3 (Paris: December 1931), pp. 16-17

DAYDREAM

Port-Lligat, 17 October 1931

3 o'clock in the afternoon

I have just finished eating and I am going to stretch out on the couch, as I must do every day for an hour and a half, following which, for the rest of the afternoon, I intend to write a section of a very long study of Böcklin, a study which has preoccupied me greatly for some time now.

Therefore, I would like to make the most of this repose in order to reflect upon some points that appear to be particularly contradictory; for instance, and most prominently, the antagonism between the sense of death and the complete lack of perturbation with regard to spatial conceptions that is so strikingly apparent in this painter. I convince myself of the necessity to take some notes while resting. Therefore I look for something to write upon, a task that appears to me extremely difficult at this moment, not only as a result of several *actes manqués* and memory lapses, etc., but also because I refuse to write—for reasons that are none too clear to me—in a notebook in which some previous notes of mine are to be found. Thus I will need a new notebook (*especially*) for imitations of the kind of notes consisting of simple and inelaborate suggestions, otherwise the latter might tangle the earlier ones. Finally I decide that I could remember it all very precisely without taking notes, because I intend to begin writing immediately after I have rested.

I take in advance all necessary measures to remain undisturbed during the time I'll be lying down. I forbid bringing the mail over to me I am going to urinate, and yet I feel impatient to sprawl on the couch. I get then a very specific notion of the pleasure awaiting me in my bedroom, a sense that appears to me to be in contrast to the rather painful awareness of the contradictions I shall have to overcome. Thus I hasten to my bedroom, and while I'm on my way there I experience a very hard erection accompanied by great pleasure and hilarity. Having arrived in my bedroom, I lie down on the couch. The erection gives way immediately to a very light urge to urinate, and this, despite its being almost imperceptible, is enough to render useless any attempt of mine to think about the *frontality* in *Isle of the Dead.* Hence my reflections on the following absurdity: such a weak urge to urinate getting to be so annoying, the more so, given my ability to retain urine for long hours, either because of my reluctance to get up or for the pleasure of copiously urinating. I am disturbed by the prospect of having to get up, but, sensing that I have no choice, I give in and rush to urinate again. It all comes to four or five drops. Then, having hardly lain down on the couch I immediately get up again to close the curtain in order to leave the room in semi-darkness I lie down again and then I feel quite disenchanted, as if something very important were missing. I haven't the slightest idea what it might be, and this brings on a feeling of uneasiness that, as I anticipate, will disappear as soon as I know the reason for its existence. Suddenly, and with no associations at all involved, I recall that, during lunch, l set

my mind (as I have formerly been in the habit of doing) on the crusted end of the loaf of bread that seemed burned enough, which I had decided to bring over to the couch to be hollowed out with meticulous care so as to be turned into a sort of vase Then, with even greater care, I would have chewed it with my front teeth, pierced and squashed it into tiny well-ground pieces until the whole thing became a fine paste Before swallowing it, I would have kept that paste parsimoniously in my mouth, on each side, under the tongue, kneading it again and testing thus its ability to adopt several consistencies in relation to the proportion of saliva. All this in order to make the crust last longer.

As soon as I hit upon the mental image of the piece of bread, the uneasiness disappears and I hasten to seek the said crust, which has already been cleared out of the dining room, coming across it again in the kitchen.

Meanwhile, I slice off yet another piece of crust that is quite small and not burned, and thus different from the ones that I prefer, but I take it all the same, mainly because its form is that of a very sweet small horn. I am once again on the couch, but with the two crusts, and for once without apparently anything to disturb my reflections. I try to envision as distinctly as possible the famous painting of *Isle of the Dead.*.

I find myself to have been thoughtless in my belief in the total lack of spatial perturbation in this painter and, in particular, in *Isle of the Dead.*

My mistake had been due to the limitation resulting from crudely reducing the idea of spatial perturbation to merely one of perspective.

The same feeling of frontality that had struck me at first in this painting evinces a well- characterized "dominant" spatial feature. It seems now indispensable for my study to establish a system of relativity that would enable me to nullify (at least temporarily) for instance the perturbations of perspective whose meaning in Vermeer of Delft and G. de Chirico has been explored by me over a long period of time. I am thinking of the analytical shortcoming of the passage where I claim to prove the existence of unconscious funereal feeling in these two painters, which is due to the perturbation of perspective associated with the illumination. I am thinking concretely, in this respect, of Vermeer's painting entitled *The Letter.* It becomes impossible for me to represent it fully and with all the clarity I wish for. This is because of the emotional significance flowing, arising from the curtain in the foreground (on the left) of the painting in question. I pull out then automatically my smallish penis, leaving on the couch the small crust I had been emptying out. I stroke with one hand the hairs on my testicles, and, with the other, I roll up part of the bread removed from the crust. In spite of some fruitless efforts to follow up my train of thought, a wholly involuntary daydream begins to take hold of me. I have located now the curtain found in Vermeer's painting in a dream I had just a few days ago. In fact, this curtain may be identified in terms of its form, its place, and, above all, its emotional and moral significance, with the curtain that, in the dream, served to conceal several small cows, in the far end of a very dark stable, where, very excited by the stench of the place, I sodomize the woman I love, in the midst of the excrement and rotting straw.

HERE THE DAYDREAM BEGINS

I see myself the way I am now but appreciably older. In addition, I have let my beard grow, modeled on an old memory I have of a lithograph of Monte-Cristo. Friends have lent me for about ten days a large manor-farmhouse, where I intend to finish writing my study of Böcklin, which will constitute one chapter in a huge work that I name, for the time being, *Surrealist Painting Throughout the Ages.*

Following these ten days, I should return to Port-Lligat, where I will meet again the woman I love, who has been, during that time, in Berlin, engaged in amorous adventures, as it was the case in a previous daydream.

The manor I have been given the use of is the one named "The Tower Mill," in which, when I was ten years old, I spent two months together with a couple of intimate friends of my parents.

But the manor in the daydream has been changed. It appears to have become amazingly time-worn, even, here and there, to the point of having a look of ruins. The garden pond has become twenty times bigger. I am none too satisfied with its real site in the garden, surrounded by huge oaks that conceal the sky. I have now transported the pond to the back of the house, so that it might be seen from the dining room, at the same time as the skies with Böcklinian clouds and storms, that I recall having seen from this site that is overlooking a vast and unobstructed horizon. The placement of the pond has also been changed, because I had been accustomed to seeing it always lengthwise in perspective, and, in my fantasy, it appears to me situated transversely. I see myself from the back in the dining room, finishing my snack consisting of the crusty end of a loaf of bread and chocolate. I am wearing a suit in black velvet, similar to the one worn by the family friend, the owner of the manor, during my stay there as a child, merely with the difference of having a small cape in white linen, exceptionally neat, hooked to my shoulders with three small safety pins. With what is left of the crust in my hand, I very slowly walk down the central staircase of the manor leading down to the courtyard. The staircase is in semi-darkness, because of the before-twilight hour that is abetted by the heavy clouds. While coming down I hear the almost imperceptible sound of the very light rain. I think: "Why come down, as it is raining," but I go down just the same. Here I am at the entrance full of dry leaves giving off a strong odor of rot that, combined with the odor of animal excrement coming from the courtyard, brings on for me a sense of very sweet confusion tending toward dream.

All of a sudden, I am pulled out of this state of ecstasy by a very live erotic emotion. It is due to my drowsy eyes falling on the half-opened door of the stable, which I recognize, without a shadow of doubt, to be the one in my dream. But this emotion becomes amazingly more pronounced the moment I notice the well-known presence of the swaying tips of the cypresses, a cluster of which, in reality, right away beyond the stable, separates the courtyard from the meadow, where, in my daydream, my fantasy has placed the huge pond.

The emotion related to the tips of the cypresses derives from the instantaneous association with another cluster of cypresses found in a public place near Figueres called "Fountain of the Log." This cluster of very old thick cypresses surrounded a flagstone circle at the center of which, in the midst of extremely worn stone benches, flowed a ferruginous fountain. A little aluminum cup was attached to a small chain. The foliage of the cypresses starting off almost on ground level, and their tops brought close together by iron rings, formed a dome, with the fountain being enclosed within the cypresses. Hence the absolute shadow and the great coolness of this place that earned the liking of my family. After the Sunday walk, on warm spring evenings, once we were rested, after having sat down on the cool and worn benches, I would be taken there for a drink of water. I was not allowed to get near the water until I had eaten the bread and chocolate. Access to the fountain out of the warm season was even more rigorously denied me, and when autumn came, we would pass it by without stopping, because of the hazardous humidity of the place. For the continuation of my daydream, I have found it necessary to substitute the cypresses beyond the courtyard wall with those of the "Log Fountain."

In the almost complete darkness of the night falling very rapidly, I see the tops of the cypresses beyond the courtyard wall coming close together and forming a single thick black flame. From the moment I sensed the odor of the courtyard until the present moment, I gave myself over to the following automatic acts: I inserted several times the bread from within the crust, already rolled up into a ball, into my nostrils. I pulled it out slowly using my fingers, feigning some difficulty, as if it were dirt in the nose. A few times, on the contrary, I contented myself with breathing out in order to hurl the bread. It was particularly pleasant for me when I was under the illusion that this had to do with dirt in the nose, an illusion that, almost always, was directly related to the greater length of time elapsed between the insertion of the ball of bread in the nose and its expulsion.

The process of expulsion with my breath was not without some inconvenience. The ball of bread would drop anywhere, and looking for it in the creases and folds of my clothes or on the couch ended up at times in disturbing and almost interrupting my daydream, especially when (and this happened frequently) the ball of bread rolled under my body, in such a way as to force me, in order to retrieve it, to arch up my back. Thus I separated myself from the couch. I held myself up by the head and legs only, and this enabled me to grope on the couch, ending up by retrieving the ball of bread. The closer it had rolled to the legs, the more painful it became to catch it through the convulsive process, which, several times after painful efforts, I had to relinquish in order to sit up on the couch, while searching around me and raising my buttocks in the event that the ball would be found precisely where I have been sitting. But then, I would raise the buttocks in quite unaccountable fashion, with sudden leaps that only rarely gave me time enough to catch the ball.

I was forced to repeat these leaps several times, fearing at each leap that the ball might end up by bouncing to the ground, hurled by the couch's springs. I was shaken each time with fear of this eventuality, a very perceptible fear localized in the heart. Sometimes, when the ball had got out of the nose, I would secure it between my nose and the upper lip. All this while puffing warm air through my nostrils, with the ball of bread getting warmer, lightly oozing moisture and growing softer. I carry out all these operations preferring to use only one hand (the left hand) with the other releasing my penis that has grown considerably heavier, without, however, reaching a state of erection. At the exact moment in which I had summoned up the representation (which was, besides, of exceptional visual clarity) of the aluminum cup attached to the chain, I hurriedly forced out the ball that had been in my left nostril, inserting it carefully, as deeply as possible, under my foreskin that is held by my fingers, for I experience a light erection that ceases right away.

CONTINUATION OF THE DAYDREAM

On the very day on which I had encountered the stable of my dream in the manor's courtyard, after the evening meal, while I am having my coffee and a shot of cognac, I conceive, in the form of a daydream, a plan to be carried out in my general daydream. I outline very quickly this part of the daydream. It is extremely long and complicated, and I consider it more deserving of a detailed exposition. I note down here therefore only those general details that are indispensable for the continuation of the general daydream which, without them, would be far more difficult to follow. This, in brief, has to do with carrying out the act of sodomy of my dream, this in the stable that I have now identified with the one of the dream. But this time I am substituting the woman I love with an eleven-year-old girl called Dullita whom I had known five years ago. This girl had a very pale anaemic face, light eyes that were very sad and veiled. which contrasted violently with a figure that was exceptionally well developed for her age and nicely shaped, and lazy walk and movements that appeared highly voluptuous to me. In order to carry out the fantasy of sodomizing Dullita in the stable, I had to invent a few stories that would create conditions propitious for the dream, such a similitude being essential to the development of my daydream. Here is the one which I have adopted. Dullita's mother, quite a beautiful woman in her forties, a widow who is always dressed in black, falls madly in love with me and goes along, out of masochism, with my fantasy of sodomizing her daughter; she is even ready, with great eagerness and dedication, to help me accomplish this act. For this purpose, I send Matilde, Dullita's mother, to Figueres, where she should get in touch with Gallo, an old prostitute whom I have known in my time. She is extraordinarily sly and experienced, and I consider it essential to put her in touch with Dullita for the latter's forthcoming initiation.

Once Matilde, Dullita, and Gallo are settled down in the manor, they are expressly forbidden to speak to me and even to communicate with me whether by gesture or writing. Dullita should think that I am deaf-mute and a great scholar whom the slightest unwelcome gesture might seriously disturb. In the evenings, following the meal, the table is cleared and coffee and cognac are brought in. This is the only meal, the only time of day, that I spend in the company of Dullita and the two women, because, at all other times I keep to my study where I am writing my work on Böcklin and where I have all other meals. It is at this time of the evening that, in complete and reverential silence, I pass on in writing all my decisions concerning the realization of my fantasies, with the minutest details and nuances.

Gallo is the first to receive my communications, and it is on her that the whole responsibility falls regarding the (fanatically precise) fulfillment of all my orders, which, in her turn, she sometimes communicates to Matilde. Depending on the circumstances, she may also be satisfied with giving her some instructions that she considers to be essential. Here is how things should go in the course of five days. Dullita should not suspect anything, and, indeed, on the contrary, she should be made ready by edifying and extremely virtuous readings, enfolded with much sweetness and affection as if in preparation for her first Communion, which, moreover, she should receive in a short while. On the fifth day, two hours before the sun sets, Dullita will be led to the fountain of the cypresses. There she will taste some bread and chocolate, and then Gallo, with Matilde's help, will initiate Dullita in the most brutal and coarse manner. She will make use of a lavish supply of movingly pathetic pornographic postcards, which I myself should choose with great precision well beforehand.

On the same evening, Dullita should learn everything from Gallo and her mother, finding out that I am not a deaf-mute, and that in three days I am going to sodomize her among the droppings in the cowshed. For three days she should make believe as if she knows nothing about all this. She is strictly forbidden to make the slightest allusion to anything that has just been disclosed to her (in other words, she, Dullita, would know that I knew that she knew). Up to that specific moment in the cowshed, everything should go on in conformity with the daily silence and appearances.

In order to carry out the program of fantasies that I have just gone through, within the general daydream, one of the essential requirements consisted of the quite inevitable necessity, for myself, to observe Dullita's initiation in the fountain of the cypresses through the dining room's window. This in reality appeared unworkable because of various conflicts of perfectly physical nature, in relation, for instance, to the fact that the fountain was completely surrounded by the cypresses. Thus I was impeded from observing Dullita's initiation that should have taken place precisely, within the fountain area. The quite small entrance gate, that forced one to bend the head in order to enter, would not have sufficed. But a new fantasy, that appeared to me all the more exciting, has just suggested a solution to this major conflict. A fire that broke out in a badly extinguished pile of dry leaves had partially burned down the cypresses in front of the fountain, leaving the latter open to view, but with one branch having escaped the worst of the fire and creating a very slight, almost nonexistent, obstruction to the contemplation of the scene with Dullita.

Moreover, the same fire burned down the surrounding thick jumble of shrubs and trees.

This is how Dullita will get dirty, her white apron and legs blackened with soot, the day her mother and Gallo will force her to cross this area on her way to have the snack at the fountain. The idea that Dullita would have to get dirty appears to me from then on to be essential, and it culminates and achieves perfection in the next fantasy. I see Dullita arriving at the fountain and getting her feet dirty in that kind of pestilential mud mixed with rotting moss that, in reality, covers up the paving of the fountain whenever the pipe gets clogged up with leaves and thus causes one of these floods that are so frequent, especially in the fall. Although the area would be closed in, the dead leaves, thrust by the gusts of wind on these stormy days, would no less penetrate into it. But the fountain of the cypresses, whose interior should have been exposed to my sight because of the fire, still remains invisible from

the dining room. It is hidden by a section of the wall leading off the cowshed. To move the fountain right down to where it would be brought into my field of vision seems to me an inadequate solution which would destroy the whole sense of my daydream. On the contrary, I see very clearly the purpose of the fire that burned down the cypresses, and thus destroyed the separating wall, which, what's more, allows "a very direct communication between the stable and the fountain of the cypresses." The desolate and ruined appearance of the surroundings of the fountain, aggravated by the heap of scorched stones of the wall, procures for me an ambiance that suits my designs perfectly. I am thinking, all of a sudden, with a strange emotion, combining anxiety and pleasure, that the disappearance of the wall would allow the shadows of the cypresses, toward the late afternoon, to spread slowly all along the length of the courtyard, that was always lying in shadow before. The sun will reach the first steps of the entrance stairway, covered with dry leaves at this time of the year. And so the sun, a moment before setting, will penetrate in one cadmium line into the first-floor room, with its shutters half closed, its furniture without slipcovers, its parquet floor covered with drying corn, illuminating with its full dazzle for half-a-minute the fingertip in a statue in greenish marble—a figure with raised arm, its hair falling over the eyes—that was removed, together with the pond, from the fountain group. In spite of the disappearance of the wall that hid the fountain of the cypresses, it is impossible to see the fountain from the dining room, because it is still hidden too far to the left to be seen from the window.

After several inadequate fantasies, that lead me step by step to the solution, I envision the scene of Dullita's imitation to be reflected in the large mirror in Dullita's room which is adjacent to the dining room. Thus I would be able to see it all from my own chair, with the benefit of some complications and of some absolutely desirable blur of images, already felt on account of the slightly incomplete burning of the cypresses. And also, because of the great distance separating me from the site of the scene, the images reaching me would be quite vague, and this appears to be particularly disconcerting to me. I see with a very distinctive clarity and precision this new phase of the daydream that follows.

It is the evening of Dullita's initiation, the eve of the Day of the Dead; the meal is over, the table has been cleared and nothing is left on it but for three cups of coffee, three liqueur glasses and a bottle of cognac. Dullita sits on my left, in front of the half-open door of her room. She occupies the place that I myself occupied during my stay at the manor as a child. Like myself at that time, she is arranging her school homework. She has her exercise books in front of her, and an open pencil box in which I see an eraser with a lion design. The atmosphere is identical to that of my first stay at the manor. Gallo, occupying the owner's seat, smokes in silence while reading her journal. Matilde is doing her knitting, occupying the wife's place. The silence on this evening is greater and unbreathably more disturbing than ever. Finally, I perform my usual daily act, faithfully following the owner's gesture as it had been toward me: I soak a sugar cube in what is left of my cognac and extend my hand toward Dullita. Her head inclined over her notebook, Dullita senses my movement and takes the sugar with her teeth. This is the signal to go to bed. Sipping very slowly, I finish the cognac in the glass. Behind Dullita's head, through the half-open door of her room, seen in the mirror, the dark cypresses of the fountain should be moving.

It is a solemn afternoon on the insipid Day of the Dead. I get ready to observe the scene of Dullita's initiation.

I place on the dining room table the shoes worn by Dullita at all times. I pull my penis out of my pants, wrapping it with soiled linen. Eyes staring at the fountain and its surroundings reflected in the mirror, I see Dullita, dressed in white, with a very short and tight skirt and wearing new espadrilles, being led between the two women. Gallo is wearing a very bright and luminous jersey and Matilde is in black. I run to the window in Dullita's room in order to see better in all its details their route to the fountain, across the burned shrubbery.

They more forward very slowly and with difficulty, trying to avoid the large burned branches, but with Gallo and Matilde pressing Dullita, as if for fun, into the most soiling spots. With every step Dullita makes, the often thorny and unyielding shrubs cling to her legs and buttocks, leaving on her long black streaks. They sometimes stop to see where they would be better off going through. Gallo spanks Dullita pretending to dust off the stains, but with such violence and savagery that she must pretend to be playing.

Dullita attempts to get away from Gallo, after having been thrown against a wall covered with burned ivy. She hurries now all the way to the right, without heeding the bushes that scratch her till they draw blood. She rushes toward the fountain, and, arriving there she slips on the frothy mud covering the paving and falls down. She gets up on her feet quite soiled and spattered all over. She smiles as if asking to be pardoned, wipes herself with a handkerchief, straightens her hair, pulls up her stockings, while biting the hem of her skirt with her teeth and showing her dirty thighs.

Gallo and Matilde arrive later; Gallo, gentle again, kisses Dullita's forehead, and Matilde cuts pieces of bread, keeping the crusty part for Dullita who sits down between the two women. From one moment to the next, the group seems to me to have attained growing transcendence and solemnity.

Dullita now combs her hair with a very red celluloid comb that burns blindingly in the light of the setting sun. The shadow of the manor advances toward the fountain, leaving in a shade the first level of burned bushes through which the three figures have come just now.

And Dullita is eating with great slowness (a mouthful of chocolate, a mouthful of crust), swinging her right leg which is closer to Gallo.

I am thinking that the sun at this point is illuminating the fingertip in the statue found in the room on the first floor, and the corn, on the floor, for a short while attains the color of a flame. I see a dazzling image of myself sodomizing Dullita as she is lying on the corn in this room. This vision will lead to a new element of my main daydream, to which I am returning with the image of Dullita getting up in order to brush the breadcrumbs off her skirt and then bending down in order to get a drink of water.

From this moment on, Dullita's movements, as she cleans the aluminum beaker attached by a chain, pouring out the water three times across the exact and relative position of Gallo and Matilde the illumination; the buttocks fully revealed under the transparency of Dullita's clothes, as she bends forward on her knees, etc., all this, I say, takes on a lucidity and an enhanced visual concreteness that is almost hallucinatory. The duration time of the three consecutive acts of *emptying the glass* gives rise to a very clear and precise illusion of *déjà vu* that coincides with a very powerful erection. The moment Dullita rinses the glass, before drinking, is by far the most moving. In all of the daydream until the very end, it also has the greatest visual power. Afterwards, I see very vaguely Dullita, whom I was unable to see drinking, wipe her mouth with her hand. Gallo, very gently, makes Dullita sit again between herself and Matilde. I anticipate the beginning of the initiation. The shadow made by the manor reaches as far as Dullita's knees. With great trepidation, I await Gallo's signal announcing the beginning. Gallo places on her knees the album with the pornographic pictures. Matilde caresses Dullita's head and Dullita, bending her head over the album, tries to open it; but Gallo holds back her hand, and, having done so, peers into her face and raises her finger to her mouth in a sign of silence and reverence.

Gallo then raises her face, and I see in it traces of great beauty. I am highly roused when Gallo begins slowly to open the album, and, unable to take it any longer, I turn round and go to the dining room table, my eyes closed and filled with this last image.

Seated on the chair I occupy every evening at supper time, I go on observing the scene at the fountain reflected in the mirror, while masturbating pleasantly with the linen wrapped around my penis. The fountain group looks now smaller and further away. The faces and their expressions are very softly vague, and this endows my fantasy with almost unlimited scope.

I don't see anything unusual about the group. Dullita does not disclose any sign of reacting. She looks down, her head unmoving, her face revealing both shame and attention. From time to time, Gallo turns a page and murmurs things close to Dullita's bent face hidden by her hair. I see the group very vaguely now coming down the courtyard, because it gets quickly dark after the sun has set. I rush to put on Dullita's seat an ear of corn on which she would sit without noticing it, during the three days to follow. On the third evening, on the eve of the "manifest" act of my daydream, the table has just been thoroughly cleared.

Three coffees are brought in and a cognac. The same deep silence as in all other evenings. I am seized by a powerful emotion that must surely prevent me from speaking. Dullita imperceptibly shifts on the ear of corn. I give my instructions for the next day, short, necessary, and fully detailed. Finally, as in all other nights, I hold out my hand with the sugar soaked in cognac. Dullita remains motionless for a moment and then takes it with her teeth. I see her gaze through the tears, while a large drop forms on my meatus.

The following day is a Sunday. I should quickly make the most of the fact that, close to four o'clock, everybody goes to the village. I await a sign from Matilde in the meadow and I hurry, wrapped up in my only burnous, first into the room where the ear of corn is found, and then to the first floor. I find Dullita, Gallo and Matilde there, all three completely naked. In no time, Dullita masturbates me, but very clumsily, and this greatly arouses me. The three women go across the courtyard and into the cowshed. During that time I rush to the fountain of the cypresses and sit down on the wet stones of the bench. I hold up my penis with all my strength with my two hands, and then head for the cowshed where Dullita and the two women are lying down naked among the droppings and the rotten straw. I take off my burnous and throw myself on Dullita, but Matilde and Gallo have disappeared all of a sudden and Dullita is transformed into the woman I love, and my daydream ends with the same images as those I remember from my dream. The daydream then comes to an end, for I have just realized that I have, for some time now, been analyzing objectively the daydream I have just gone through, noting it down immediately and with the greatest scrupulousness.

"Rêverie," *Le Surréalisme au service de la Révolution*, no. 4 (Paris: 1931), pp. 31-36

NEW GENERAL CONSIDERATIONS REGARDING THE MECHANISM OF THE PARANOIAC PHENOMENON FROM THE SURREALIST POINT OF VIEW

Antagonism between passive states (dream, psychic automatism) and systematized active state. – Experimental relevance of automatism. – From irrationality as a general aspiration born of the critical experience of automatism to the preparanoiac concrete irrationality. – Affirmation of the productive principle of action-intervention of dreams in real life against the contemplative attitude of poetic escape. – Reminder of the "Principle of Verification" formulated by Breton at the time of the major invention of "dream objects." – The Paranoiac mechanism bears out the dialectical value of Surrealist activity in the domains of automatism and dream. – It illustrates and fulfills in a tangible and material way the Principle of Verification of delirious contents (far from the coercive regressions that the "systematic" presence might detect in keeping with the notion of "reasoning madness." – The paranoiac phenomenon, contrary to the general ideas of constitutionalist theories, would be in itself already a systematized delirium. – The paranoiac phenomenon, by virtue of its strength and authority, and its characteristics of productivity, permanence, and growth, all inherent in the systematic fact, would prominently objectify the integration of all the basic dynamic notions of "process" in the "dialectical delirium" of Surrealism.

From the still uncertain beginnings in 1929 of *La Femme visibile*. I predicted that "the moment is drawing near when, by a thought process of a paranoiac and active character, it would be possible (simultaneously with automatism and other passive states) to systematize confusion and thereby contribute to a total discrediting of the world of reality."

The "poetic drama" of Surrealism had lain for me at that moment in the antagonism (calling for a dialectical conciliation) of two types of confusion that had been implicitly predicted in that declaration: on the one hand, the passive confusion of automatism; on the other hand, the active and systematic confusion illustrated by the paranoiac phenomenon.

One could not insist too much on the extreme revolutionary value of automatism and the major importance of automatic and Surrealist texts. The hour of such experiments, far from having passed, may seem more current than ever at this moment when parallel possibilities are presented to us, resulting from the awareness we might have of the most highly developed manifestations of passive states and of the necessity for a vital communication between the two experimental principles that appeared to us above as being contradictory.

Following the joint intellectual actions to which Dada, under a great charge of sthenic emotion, laid claim under the mechanical form of a program of a reactional attitude (comprising, in truth, an intuition of almost all of the principal things to come), the assimilation of automatism by the Surrealists does away with any possibility of adopting an "attitude," what would necessarily be incompatible with their passivity, with their unreserved capitulation in the face of the very fact of the real and involuntary functioning of thought; this capitulation to automatism, this total submission to thought outside any coercive control, cannot fail to appear, more so every day, as the most sensational attempt of all time with a view to attaining freedom of the mind.

In a more coherent, and, consequently, more serious way than by the simple intuition of things to come that has just been mentioned, automatism exceeds and liberates, within the strict limits of the psychic phenomenon, the latent aspirations on which Dada imposed as a constraint the mechanical reactions of the latest "intellectual" positions and attitudes.

It is in the very flow, the most involuntary flow of thought, and outside of any poetic "obligation," that the faith in demoralization is going to blend as a matter of fact with the neutral, voracious and authoritarian hierarchies of scientific documents. Authority will not fail to be officially known by the piss-colored trepanning of the mean principle of contradiction; by the bell-shaped fine erosion of a withered and legless electrical old Breton hag suffering from a cold, spouting the shitty over-and-done-with nostalgias of spatial and temporal localizing; by the general drip-nunnery; by the light snot of shit-molded soft and pitiful "causality," similar to a miserable watch made of ashes mixed with food that is hurled, together with the said snot, out of one of the nostrils of a mean, smug, and meditative bureaucrat, following the clipped and asphyxiating cough and the noisy convulsions of the accidental and mechanical breathlessness provoked by bad swallowing, occurring at the mediocre ending of a solitary meal finished without conviction under the well-advanced light of a summer evening fillering iridescently through the timid and convalescent colored windows—with their motif of storks dressed like nurses—of the empty room of a grandiose, modest, and perpendicular restaurant.

Considering the pathetic state in which we find the basic notions of logical thought, we should expect the remains of the mechanical defense bases of the decrepit categories of reasoning to equally suffer from that high and sovereign, involuntary and generous depreciation that, with an irrevocable look, floods fruitfully the reassuring and comfortable grounds of aesthetics and morality. After the complete submergence of abstract–censorship by the very inactivity of liberation, how could one still take into consideration the obvious bad faith of mechanistic generations claiming the unavoidable limitation of productivity, as well as of the unchanging internal coherence inherent in the automatic results? How could one agree to weighing the alleged shortcomings of an automatic process and its minor disadvantages against the real havoc it creates in thought—a phenomenon that manifests itself against all the coercive hierarchies of the practical-rational world, all the rotten clandestine and transferen-

tial "combinings" of desire in the villainous domain of aesthetics, all the *agents provocateurs*, in short, of realist thought? How can one hesitate, I ask you, in choosing between, on the one hand, all that complicity in intellectual blackmail, all that police of the mind, which is discounted, actually and from the materialistic point of view, by the experience of Surrealist writing, and, on the other, the disadvantage (that seems to us to be of a rather artistic nature!), constituted, in the first place, by the presence in the setting up of this phenomenon of a measure of sthenic feeling that automatism will summon up, in the pathological functioning of thought, in order to make up for the poverty and deficiency of the latter, and, secondly, by the presence of the wretched (but still striking when considered from the angle of disillusion) seeds of stereotypy? These are, nevertheless, as we have already suggested, the kind of objections still aimed at placing Surrealism in the sphere of obscurantism and the death of the artistic phenomenon. They themselves are a clear proof of this analytical shortsightedness, which leads to viewing automatism as an end in itself, fixed, considered to be an abstract entity, feeding on its own ashes, without communication with the real, instead of conferring on it its true meaning, which requires the integration in its own life of a set of phenomena that are connected and in communication with their relative and conditioned becoming, which constitutes the concrete dialectical essence of their powers of cognitive possession.

The general irrationality that emerges from the delirious aspect of dreams and automatic productions, joined with the growing coherence that these show as their symbolic interpretation tends to become more perfectly synchronous with critical activity, leads us, for lyrical needs, to the exacerbated reduction to the concrete of what had been clarified enough to us, in order for us to release from these alleged deliriums of obsessive exactness the notion of *concrete irrationality*.

On the specifically poetic plane, concrete irrationality, yet more than a serious, and even breathtaking, predisposition of the human mind, appears to us as one of these "incurable lyrical contagions" that, in their catastrophic spread, reveal all the striking stigmas of a true vice of the intelligence. Once it is rendered virulent by the inexperienced complacency that it finds in the "general," delirious, and irrational aspect of the automatic productions and dreams, whose speed of reduction to the concrete cannot but disappoint us and instantly provoke spontaneous aggravations and complications (in which we cannot fail to recognize the larval presence of the systematic fact), the "concrete irrationality" will emerge in the imagination, and this, as might be expected, with the same frequency in which the various phantasmas organize themselves from all sides as soon as there is the awareness of a new erotic desire.

Again, in this connection, I will point out, to prevent any futile alarm regarding an alleged claim of alpine notions of "directed thought," that the presence identified above of the systematic fact involves no coercion whatsoever of thought exerted by any *a posteriori* intervention of a system or reasoning. On the contrary, as this takes place for the paranoiac phenomenon, which is consubstantial with the systematic fact, one should regard the system as a consequence of the very development of the delirious ideas, with these ideas, delirious at the moment in which they occur, appearing as being *already* systematized.

In contrast to the new coercive and reasoned interventions, which are likely to presuppose another intervention altogether of the idea of systematization in the delirious contents, consideration of the paranoiac mechanism as a force and power acting at the very foundation of the phenomenon of personality, of its "homogeneous," "total," "unexpected" character, of its characteristics of "permanence," "growth," and "productivity," which are inherent in the systematic fact, all these are only corroborated in a rigorous manner on reading Jacques Lacan's admirable thesis: "On Paranoiac Psychosis and Its Relations with the Personality."

It is due to this thesis that we have, for the first time, a homogeneous and complete idea of the phenomenon, outside the mechanistic wretchedness with which current psychiatry is bogged down. Its author protests especially against the general ideas of constitutionalist theories touching on abstraction, according to which the systematization is put together after the fact, due to the development of very vague constitutional fact, due to the development of very vague constitutional factors, and this contributes to the creation of the crude ambiguities of the "reasoning madness." This last notion, in doing away with the concrete and truly phenomenological essence of the problem, again, by its static essence, puts into high relief all the dazzling dialectical signification of the paranoiac process, which cannot fail on this occasion to appear to us as eminently exemplary. Lacan's work perfectly accounts for the objective and "communicable" hyperacuteness of the phenomenon, thanks to which de delirium assumes a tangible character that cannot be contradicted, and that situates it at the very antipodes of the stereotypy of automatism and dream. Far from constituting a passive element, as are the latter, propitious for interpretation and suitable for intervention, the paranoiac delirium already constitutes in itself a form of interpretation, the paranoiac delirium already constitutes in itself a form of interpretation. It is precisely this active element born of the "systematic presence" that, beyond general considerations that precede, intervenes as a principle of that contradiction in which resides for me the poetic drama of Surrealism. This contradiction cannot find its dialectical conciliation any better than in the new ideas about paranoia that come to light, according to which the delirium would suddenly appear *fully systematized.*

No immediate example seems to me as persuasive, as capable of illustrating the "abrupt" and "reactional" character of the phenomenon, the "profound change of the object," the simultaneous presence of the systematic, associative fact, the implicit interpretation, the objective communicability, etc., than the delirious image of the "Paranoiac Face" reproduced in the fourth issue of *Le Surréalisme au service de la révolution.* The *"real persistence of the paranoiac delirious image,"* its *"intervening and interpretative cohesion,"* also strikingly exhibit their flagrant opposition to the *"deletion during waking of the oneiric image,"* its *"dissociative condensation,"* its *"symbolic passivity that lends itself precisely to interpretative intervention."* But the Surrealist critical activity had lucidly transcended the traumatism created by that antagonism through the voluntary aspiration for categorial and intuitive principles felt to be a necessity and exhibiting a character of progressive urgency. In spite of the mechanical difficulties of apparent inconsistency or contradiction, resulting from the very inertia of compensatory disequilibrium, the whole critical concern of the Surrealists is intended, outside any easy paradox, precisely to *make the most* of dream, as well as all passive states and automatism, on the very plane of "action," and have them intervene, "interpretatively" in particular, in reality, in life. This critical concern has never striven to apply itself other than effectively: in a material, recognizable, and most physically tangible way, for want of which dream and automatism could not take on any meaning other than that of smug idealist escapes, an entertaining and harmless resource for the comfortable care of the skeptical gaiety of select poets.

Surrealist doctrine and its subversion

Surrealism, which, from its beginnings, had overcome the mechanistic materialism and stuck to a relativistic and wholly provisional idealism, has never disregarded the urgency of systematic principles of action, which are more or less the product of the "principle of verification" stated by Breton in the most lucid and prophetic moment of Surrealism. Coinciding, one recalls, with the major invention of dream objects, this is the proposal of constructing—for the purpose of faithful verification, in the most "approximate" manner possible—delirious objects meant to be put into circulation, in other words, to intervene, to get into extensive and daily clashes with life's other objects, in the broad daylight of reality.

*

The paranoiac mechanism cannot but appear to us, from the specifically Sur-

realist point of view adopted by us, as proof of the dialectical value of this principle of verification, through which the very element of delirium goes in actual fact into the tangible domain of action, as the guarantor of the sensational victory of Surrealist activity in the domain of automatism and dream.

The precious stones that disappear upon waking, and that had been cunningly "kept" and "arranged" in dream as evidence for the existence of the "desired land of treasures" to which there had been access, retain in the paranoiac delirium— and, after its extinction under everybody's stupefied look—the exact weight corresponding to their volume and the delirious concretion of their most physical luminous contours. They are "'in reality."

"Interprétation paranoïaque-critique de l'image obsédante 'L'Angélus' de Millet: Prologue: Nouvelles considérations générale sur le mécanisme du phénomène paranoïaque du point de vue surréaliste," *Minotaure* no. 1 (Paris: June 1933), pp. 65-67

CONQUEST OF THE IRRATIONAL

The waters in which we swim

It is known that the brilliant and sensational progress of the particular sciences, glory and honour of the "space" and time in which we live, entails, on the one hand, the crisis and overwhelming discredit of "logical intuition," and, on the other hand, the consideration of irrational factors and hierarchies as new positive and specifically productive values. Everyone will recall that logical and pure intuition, that pure intuition, I repeat, pure maid-of-all-work, good-for- everything, in the particular houses of the particular sciences, carried for a long time in her belly an illegitimate son who was none other than physics itself, and that this son, at the time of Maxwell and Faraday, was already perceptibly heavy with a non-equivocal persuasion and a personal force of gravity that no longer left any doubt as to the Newtonian paternity of the child. It is on account of this downward tendency and the force of gravity of these circumstances that pure intuition, continually being shown to the doors of the particular sciences' houses, ends up by becoming in our time pure prostitution, for we see her surrendering her last charms and her last turbulences in the *maison publique* of the artistic and literary world.

It is under such cultural circumstances that our contemporaries, systematically cretinised by the mechanicism and the architecture of autopunition, by psychological bureaucratic congratulations, by idealogical disorder and imaginative fasting, by affective paternal hungers of all kinds, seek in vain to bite into the doting and triumphal sweetness of the plump, atavistic, tender, militarist and territorial back of some Hitlerian nurse, in order at last to be able, no matter how, to communicate with the totemic consecrated host that has just been elevated in front of their own noses and which, as is known and understood, was nothing else than the spiritual and symbolic nourishment that Catholicism offered during the centuries to appease the cannibal frenzy of moral and irrational hungers. For in effect the irrational hunger of our contemporaries is confronted by a cultural dining-table upon which there are only, on the one hand, the cold and unsubstantial remains of art and literature, and, on the other, the burning analytical precisions of the particular sciences, inaccessible, for the moment, to a nutritious synthesis because of their inordinate extension and specialization and, in any case, totally unassimilable, except in cases of speculative cannibalism.

From all that is born the colossal, nutritive and cultural responsibility of surrealism, a responsibility which becomes more and more objective, consuming and exclusivist with each new cataclysm of collective hunger, with each new gluttonous, glutinous, ignominious and sublime bite of the terrible jaw of the masses into the congested, bleeding and par excellence biological cutlet which constitutes the political system.

It is in such circumstances that Salvador Dalí, the precise apparatus of hand-done paranoiac-critical activity, less ready than ever to desert his uncompromising cultural post, has for a long while been proposing that it might also be desirable to eat the surrealists, for we, surrealists, we are the kind of good-quality, decadent, stimulating, extravagant and ambivalent food which, in the most tactful and intelligent fashion in the world, belongs to the *faisandé*, paradoxical and succulently truculent state which is proper to and characteristic of the atmosphere of idealogical and moral confusion in which we have the honour and the pleasure to live at this moment. For we, surrealists, as you may be convinced by paying a little attention to us, we are not exactly artists and we are not exactly men of science; we are caviar, and caviar, believe me, is true extravagance and intelligence of taste, above all in concrete moments like the present moment, in which the irrational hunger that I am speaking to you about, though incommensurable, impatient and imperialist, finds itself so exasperated by the salivary anticipations of waiting that, in order to reach progressively its next glorious conquests, it is necessary for it to swallow, to begin with, the fine, intoxicating and dialectical grape of the caviar, without which the thick and stifling food of the next ideologies would threaten to paralyze as soon as it began the vital and philosophic rage of the historic belly. For, if caviar is the vital experience of the sturgeon, it is also that of the surrealists, for, like it, we are carnivorous fish who, as I have already insinuated, are swimming between two kinds of water, the cold water of art and the warm water of science, and it is precisely in this temperature and swimming against the current that the experience of our life and of our fecundation attains that agitated profundity, that irrational and moral hyper-lucidity which is only produced in this climate of Neronian osmosis brought about by the living and continual fusion of sole's thickness and crowned heat, of the satisfaction of sole's circumcision and sheet-iron, of territorial ambivalence and agricultural patience, of acute collectionism and propped-up cap-peaks, of white's letters on the old billiard-table cushions and white's letters on the old pirate bands, of all sorts of tepid and dermatological elements which preside over the notion of the "imponderable," simulacrum-notion unanimously recognized as existing simply to serve as epithet to the unrestrainable taste for caviar, and also simulacrum-notion which already conceals the timid and gustatory germs of the concrete irrationality which, being only the apotheosis and paroxysm of this imponderable objective, brought about by the exactitude and the divisionist precision of the caviar of the imagination, will constitute in an exclusivist and moreover philosophic fashion the terribly demoralizing and terribly complicated result of my experiences and discoveries in the pictorial domain.

For one thing is certain: I hate simplicity in all its forms.

MY PICTORIAL STRUGGLE

It seems to me perfectly obvious when my enemies, my friends and the public in general pretend not to understand the meaning of the images that arise and that I transcribe in my pictures. How can you expect them to understand them when I myself, who am their "maker," understand them as little? The fact that I myself, at the moment of painting, do not understand my own pictures, does not mean that these pictures have no meaning; on the contrary, their meaning is so profound, complex, coherent and involuntary that it escapes the most simple analysis of logical intuition. To describe my pictures in everyday language, to explain them, it is necessary to submit them to special analyses and preferably with the most ambitiously objective scientific rigor possible. Then all explanation arises *a posteriori*, once the picture already exists as phenomenon.

My whole ambition in the pictorial domain is to materialize the images of concrete irrationality with the most imperialist fury of precision. – In order that the world of imagination and of concrete irrationality may be as objectively evident, of the same consistency, of the same durability, of the same persuasive, cognoscitive and communicable thickness as that of the exterior world of phenomenal reality. – The important thing is what one wishes to communicate: the concrete irrational subject. – The means of pictorial expression are placed at the service of this subject. – The illusionism of the most abjectly arriviste and

irresistible imitative art, the usual paralyzing tricks of *trompe- l'œil*, the most analytically narrative and discredited academicism, can all become sublime hierarchies of thought and the means of approach to new exactitudes of concrete irrationality. – In the degree that the images of concrete irrationality approach phenomenal reality the corresponding means of expression approach those of the great realist painters Velázquez and Vermeer of Delft—to paint realistically according to irrational thought, according to the unknown imagination. Instantaneous and hand-done color photography of the superfine, extravagant, extra-plastic, extrapictorial, unexplored, super-pictorial, super-plastic, deceptive, hyper-normal and sickly images of concrete irrationality: images which provisionally are neither explicable nor reducible by the systems of logical intuition or by the rational mechanisms. The images of concrete irrationality are thus authentically unknown images. – Surrealism in its first period offered specific methods for approaching the images of concrete irrationality. – These methods, based on the exclusively passive and receptive rôle of the surrealist subject, are now in liquidation and giving place to new surrealist methods of systematic exploration of the irrational. Pure psychic automatism, dreams, experimental dreaming, surrealist objects functioning symbolically, instinctive ideographism, phosphenomenal and hypnagogic irritation, do not seem to us to-day to be evolutionary processes. – Moreover, the images obtained by these processes offer two grave inconveniences. (1) They cease to be unknown images, for in falling into the domain of psycho-analysis they are easily reduced to ordinary logical language, though they still continue to offer an uninterpretable residue and an authentic and very vast margin of enigma, especially to the great public. (2) Their essentially virtual and chimeric character no longer satisfies our "principles of verification," announced for the first time by André Breton in the *Discourse on the Dearth of Reality.* Since then the delirious images of surrealism have been tending desperately towards their own tangible possibility, towards their objective and physical existence in reality. Only those who ignore this fact can still swim in the gross equivocation of "poetic evasion" and continue to believe us to be mystics of fantasy and fanatics of the marvellous. Personally, I believe that the period of inaccessible mutilations, of unrealizable sanguinary osmoses, of loose visceral torn holes, of rocks'-hair and catastrophic emigrations, is experimentally closed, although it may very probably continue to constitute the exclusive iconography of a large period of painting provoked by surrealism. The new delirious images of concrete irrationality tend towards their physical and actual "possibility"; they surpass the domain of phantasms and "virtual," psycho-analyzable representations.

They present the evolutionary and productive appearance characteristic of systematic fact. The essays in simulation of Éluard and Breton, Breton's recent poem-objects, the latest images of René Magritte, the "method" of the latest sculpture of Picasso and the theoretic and pictorial activity of Salvador Dalí prove this need of concrete materialization in current reality, of giving objective value on the real plane to the delirious unknown world of our irrational experiences. Against the remembrance of dreams and the virtual and impossible images of purely receptive states, "that can only be recounted," there are the physical facts of "objective" irrationality, with which one can already actually wound oneself. It was in 1929 that Salvador Dalí brought his attention to bear upon the internal mechanism of paranoiac phenomena and envisaged the possibility of an experimental method based on the sudden power of the systematic associations proper to paranoia; this method afterwards became the delirio-critical synthesis which bears the name of "paranoiac- critical activity."
Paranoia: delirium of interpretive association bearing a systematic structure. *Paranoiac-critical activity: spontaneous method of irrational knowledge based upon the interpretive-critical association of delirious phenomena.* The presence of active and systematic elements does not suppose the idea of voluntarily directed thought, nor of any intellectual compromise, for, as we know, in paranoia the active and systematic structure is consubstantial with the delirious phenomenon itself;—all delirious phenomena of paranoiac character, even

when sudden and instantaneous, bears already "in entirety" the systematic structure and only becomes objective *a posteriori* by critical intervention. Critical activity intervenes solely as liquid revealer of images, associations and systematic coherences and *finesses* already existing at the moment when delirious instantaneousness is produced and that alone, for the moment to this degree of tangible reality, are given an objective light by paranoiac-critical activity. Paranoiac-critical activity is an organizing and productive force of objective chance. Paranoiac-critical activity no longer considers surrealist phenomena and images by themselves but, on the contrary, as a coherent whole of systematic and significant relations. Against the passive, disinterested, contemplative and aesthetic attitude of irrational phenomena there is the active, systematic, organizing and cognoscitive attitude of irrational phenomena considered as associative, partial and significant events in the authentic domain of our immediate and practical experience of life.

It is a question of the systematic and interpretive organization of the sensational, scattered and narcissist surrealist experimental material,—that is to say, of everyday surrealist events: nocturnal pollution, false recollection, dream, diurnal fantasy, the concrete transformation of nocturnal phosphene into a hypnagogic image or of "waking phosphene" into an objective image, – the nutritive caprice, – inter-uterine claims, – anamorphic hysteria, – the voluntary retention of the urine, the involuntary retention of insomnia, – the fortuitous image of exclusively exhibitionist tendency, – the incomplete action, – the frantic manner, – the regional sneeze, the anal wheelbarrow, the minimal mistake, the Lilliputian malaise, the super-normal physiological state, – the picture one leaves off painting, that which one paints, the territorial ringing of the telephone, "the deranging image," etc., etc., all these things, I say, and a thousand other instantaneous or successive solicitations, revealing a minimum of irrational intentionality or, on the contrary, a minimum of suspect phenomenal nullity, are associated, by the mechanisms of paranoiac-critical activity, in an indestructible delirious- interpretive system of political problems, paralytic images, more or less mammiferous questions, playing the role of the obsessing idea.

Paranoiac-critical activity organizes and objectivizes in an exclusivist manner the limitless and unknown possibilities of the systematic association of subjective and objective phenomena, which appear to us as irrational solicitations, exclusively in favor of the obsessing idea. By this method paranoiac-critical activity discovers new and objective "significances" in the irrational; it makes the world of delirium pass tangibly on to the plane of reality.

Paranoiac phenomena: common images having a double figuration; – the figuration can theoretically and practically be multiplied; – everything depends upon the paranoiac capacity of the author. The basis of associative mechanisms and the renewing of obsessing ideas allows, as is the case in a recent picture by Salvador Dalí now being elaborated, six simultaneous images to be represented without any one of them undergoing the least figurative deformation: – athlete's torso, lion's head, general's head, horse, shepherdess's bust, death's head. – Different spectators see in this picture different images; needless to say that it is carried out with scrupulous realism. – Example of paranoiac-critical activity: Salvador Dalí's next book, *The Tragic Myth of Millet's Angelus*, in which the method known as paranoiac-critical activity is applied to the delirious fact which constitutes the obsessional character of Millet's *Angelus*. Thus the history of art in particular is to be rewritten according to the method of "paranoiac-critical activity"; according to this method pictures as apparently different as the *Gioconda*, Millet's *Angelus* and the *Embarkment for Cythera* by Watteau would represent exactly the same subject, would mean exactly the same thing.

THE ABJECT MISERY OF ABSTRACTION-CREATION

The disgraceful lack of philosophic and general culture of the gay propellors of this model mental debility called abstract art, abstraction- creation, non-figurative art, etc., is one of the things which are authentically sweetest from the point of view of the intellectual and "modern" desolation of our epoch.

Sticky and retarded Kantians of scatalogical sections d'or, they continue to want to offer us upon the fresh optimism of their shiny paper the soup of the abstract aesthetic, which really and truly is even worse than the cold and colossally sordid vermicelli soups of neo-thomism, which even the most convulsively hungry cats would not go near. If, according to them, forms and colors have an aesthetic value in themselves, apart from their representative value and their anecdotal significance, how can they resolve and explain the classic paranoiac image with double and simultaneous figuration, which can offer without any difficulty an image that is, from their point of view, strictly imitative and inefficacious, and at the same time, without anything being changed, a plastically rich and valuable image? Such is the case with the minute ultra-anecdotal little figure of a vivid prone negro-boy in the style of Meissonier, which at the same time, if one looks at it vertically, is nothing less than the rich and even plastically succulent shadow of a Pompeian nose, very respectable on account of its degree of abstraction-creation! Moreover, the experience of Picasso's genius only goes to prove to them the conditional, material, ineluctable and apotheosic (in relation to the physical and geometrical precisions of aesthetic systems) character of the biological and feverish systems of the concrete object. For (and, since I am feeling inspired, allow me to speak to you in verse):

the biological and dramatic
phenomenon
which constitutes the cubism
of
Picasso
was
the first great imaginative cannibalism surpassing the experimental ambition
of modern mathematical physics

the life of Picasso
will form the polemic basis
as yet misunderstood
according to which
physical psychology
will open up anew
a niche of living flesh
and of darkness
for philosophy

For because
of the materialist
anarchist
and systematic thought
of
Picasso
we shall be able to know physically
experimentally
and without need
of new psychological "problematics"
of Kantian savor
of the gestaltists
all the misery
of
localized and comfortable
objects of consciousness
with their lazy atoms
sensations infinite
and diplomatic

For the hyper-materilist thought
of
Picasso
proves
that the cannibalism of the race
devours
'the intellectual species'
that the regional wine
already moistens
the family trouser-flap
of the phenomenologist
mathematics
of
the future
that there exist extra-psychological
'strict appearances'
intermediary
between
imaginative grease
and
monetary idealisms
between
passed-over arithmetics
and sanguinary mathematics
between the "structural entity"
of an "obsessing sole"
and the conduct of living beings
in contact with "the obsessing sole"
or the sole in question
remains
totally exterior
to the comprehension
of
the
gestalt-theory
since

this theory of the strict
appearance
and of the structure
does not possess
physical means
permitting
analysis
nor even
the registration
of human behaviour
vis-à-vis
with structures
and appearances
presenting themselves
objectively
as
Physically delitions
for
there does not exist
in our time
as far as I know
a physics
of psycho-pathology
a physics of paranoia
which can only be considered
as
the experimental basis
of the coming philosophy
of
psycho-pathology
of the coming
philosophy of "Paranoiac-critical"
activity
which one day
I shall try to envisage polemically
if I have the time
and the inclination

THE TEARS OF HERACLITUS

There exists a perpetual and synchronic physical materialization of the great simulacrums of thought, in the sense in which Heraclitus already understood it when he wept intelligently and with warm tears for the auto-pudency of nature. The Greeks realized it when they transformed the obscure and turbulent passions of man into clear, analytical and carnal anatomy in their statuary, when sculpting their psychological gods. – Today the new geometry of thought is physics, and if space, as Euclid understood it, was nothing more to the Greeks than a very distant abstraction, inaccessible still to the timid three-dimensional continuum that Descartes was to announce later, in our time space has become, as you know, that terribly material, terribly personal and significant physical thing which weighs us all down like authentic *comedones*. If the Greeks, as I have already said above, materialized their psychology and their Euclidian sentiments in the muscular, nostalgic and divine clarity of their sculpture, Salvador Dalí, in 1935, is no longer content to make auto-amorphism for you out of the agonizing and colossal question which is that of Einsteinian space-time, he is no longer content to make libidinous arithmetic out of it for you, no longer content, I repeat, to make flesh of it for you, he is making you cheese of it, for be persuaded that Salvador Dalí's famous soft watches are nothing else than the

tender extravagant and solitary paranoiac- critical camembert of time and space. To finish with, I should excuse myself, before the authentic hunger which, I suppose, is honoring my readers, for having commenced this theoretic meal, which one might have expected to be savage and cannibal, with the civilized imponderability of caviar, and for having finished it with this other and still more intoxicating and deliquescent imponderableness of camembert. Believe nothing of it, behind these two superfine simulacrums of imponderability is hiding, in better and better condition, the very well-known, sanguinary and irrational grilled cutlet which shall eat us all.

The conquest on the irrational, translation by David Gascogne (New York: Julien Levy 1935),

DECLARATION OF THE INDEPENDENCE OF THE IMAGINATION AND THE RIGHTS OF MAN TO HIS OWN MADNESS

WHEN, IN THE COURSE OF HUMAN CULTURE IT BECOMES NECESSARY FOR A PEOPLE TO DESTROY THE INTELLECTUAL BONDS THAT UNITE THEM WITH THE LOGICAL SYSTEMS OF THE PAST, IN ORDER TO CREATE FOR THEMSELVES AN ORIGINAL MYTHOLOGY WHICH, CORRESPONDING TO THE VERY ESSENCE AND TOTAL EXPRESSION OF THEIR BIOLOGICAL REALITY, WILL BE RECOGNIZED BY THE CHOICE SPIRITIS OF OTHER PEOPLE—THEN THE RESPECT THAT IS DUE PUBLIC OPINION MAKES IT NECESSARY TO LAY BARE THE CAUSES THAT HAVE FORCED THE BREAK WITH THE OUTWORN AND CONVENTIONAL FORMULAS OF A PRAGMATIC SOCIETY.

At the beginning of the Surrealist Revolution, it was declared: "We live in the era of wireless telegraphy; we announce also the era of the wireless imagination." But it is not wires that confine us now—it is chains of oppression that we must break! In confirmation of the above, we announce these truths: that all men are equal in their madness, and that madness (visceral cosmos of the subconscious) constitutes the common base of the human spirit. This oneness of the spirit was proclaimed by Count Lautréamont when he wrote: "Poetry must be made by all and not by one." Among the essential rights of man's madness is that which defines the surrealist movement itself, in these words: "*Surrealism – Pure psychic automatism by means of which it is proposed to transcribe, either in writing, or in speech, or in any other manner, the true working of thought, dictated by thought without any rational, aesthetic or moral control*" (André Breton: *First Surrealist Manifesto*).

Man is entitled to the enigma and the simulacrums that are found on these great vital constants: the sexual instinct, the consciousness of death, the physical melancholy caused by "time-space."

The rights of man to his own madness are constantly threatened, and treated in a manner that one may without exaggeration call provincial" by false "practical-rational" hierarchies. The history of the true creative artist is filled with the abuses and encroachments by means of which an absolute tyranny is imposed by the industrial mind over the new creative ideas of the poetic mind. Here are a few recent facts drawn from my own experience that I fell it my duty to expose to public opinion.

Probably most of you recall the incident provoked by the heads of a certain New York department store, when they dared alter a number of my concepts without having the consideration to inform me in advance of their decision. At that time I received hundreds of letters from American artists assuring me that in acting as I did, I had helped to defend the independence of their own art. Now an even more astounding battle has taken place. The committee responsible for the Amusement Area of the World's Fair has forbidden me to erect on the exterior of the "Dream of Venus" the image of a woman with the head of a fish. These are their exact words: "A Woman with the tail of a fish is possible; a woman with a head of a fish is impossible." This decision on the part of the committee seems to me an extremely grave one, deserving all the light possible cast upon it. Because we are concerned here with the negation of a right that is of a purely poetic and imaginative order, attacking no moral or political consideration. I have always believed that the first man who had the idea of terminating a woman's body with a tail of a fish must have been a pretty fair poet; but I am equally certain that the second man who repeated the idea was nothing but a bureaucrat. In any case, the inventor of the first siren's tail would have had by difficulties with the committee of the Amusement Area. Had there been similar committees in Immortal Greece, fantasy would have been banned and, what is worse, the Greeks would never have created and therefore never would have handed down to us their sensational and truculently surrealist mythology, in which, if it is true that there exists no woman with the head of a fish (as far as I know), there figures indisputably a Minotaur bearing the terribly realistic head of a bull.

Any authentically original idea, presenting itself without "know antecedents," is systematically rejected, toned down, mauled, chewed, rechewed, spewed forth, destroyed, yes, and even worse—reduced to the most monstrous of mediocrities. The excuse offered is always the vulgarity of the vast majority of the public. I insist that this is absolutely false. The public is infinitely superior to the rubbish that is fed to it daily. The masses have always known where to find true poetry. The misunderstanding has come about entirely through those "middle-men of culture" who, with their lofty airs and superior quackings, come between the creator and the public.

ARTISTS AND POETS OF AMERICA! IF YOU WISH TO RECOVER THE SACRED SOURCE OF YOUR OWN MYTHOLOGY AND YOUR OWN INSPIRATION, THE TIME HAS COME TO REUNITE YOURSELVES WITHIN THE HISTORIC BOWELS OF YOUR PHILADELPHIA, TO RING ONCE MORE THE SYMBOLIC BELL OF YOUR IMAGINATIVE INDEPENDENCE, AND, HOLDING ALOFT IN ONE HAND FRANKLIN'S LIGHTNING ROD, AND IN THE OTHER LAUTREAMONT'S UMBRELLA, TO DEFY THE STORM OF OBSCURANTISM THAT IS THREATENING YOUR COUNTRY! LOOSE THE BLINDING LIGHTNING OF YOUR ANGER AND THE AVENGING THUNDER OF YOUR PARANOIAC INSPIRATION!

Only the violence and duration of your hardened dream can resist the hideous mechanical civilization that is your enemy, as it is also the enemy of the "pleasure-principle" of all men. It is man's right to love women with ecstatic heads of fish. It is man's right to decide that lukewarm telephones are disgusting, and to demand telephones that are cold, green, and aphrodisiac as the augur-troubled sleep of the cantharides. Telephones as barbarous as bottles will free themselves of the lukewarm ornamentation of Louis XV spoons and will slowly cover with glacial shame the hybrid decors of our suavely degraded decadence. Man has the right to demand the trappings of a queen for the "objects off his desire": costumes for this furniture! for his teeth! and even for gardenias! Hand embroidered slipcovers will protect the extreme sensibility of "calf's lung railway track," colored glass with Persian patterns will be introduced into automobile design to keep out the ugly raw light of diurnal landscapes. The color of old absinthe will dominate the year 1941. Everything will be greenish. "Green I want you green"—green water, green wind, green ermine, green lizards swollen with sleep and gliding along the green skin and the dazzling décolletés of insomnia, green silver plate, green chocolate, green the agonizing electricity that sears the live flesh of civil wars, green the light of my own Gala!

In the nightmare of the American Venus, out of the darkness (bristling with dry umbrellas) the celebrated taxi of Christopher Columbus. Within, Christopher Columbus in person is proudly sitting. He is soaked in a persistent and dripping rain. Three hundred live Burgundy snails crawl up and down his motionless body and in the hollows of this livid face. On the breast of Christopher Columbus one may read this enigmatic sign: "Am I back already?" Why, with his index finger, does he point towards Europe? Why is the accompanied by

the invisible ghosts of the Duke and Duchess of Windsor? Why is a somnambulistic Spanish girl attached to the steering wheel of his deluxe Cadillac with golden chains? HERE ARE STILL MORE IMPENETRABLE DALINIAN MYSTERIES, HEAVY WITH OBSCURE AND FAR REACHING SIGNIFICANCE, BUT ONE THING IS CERTAIN: A CATALAN, CHRISTOPHER COLUMBUS, DISCOVERED AMERICA, AND ANOTHER CATALAN, SALVADOR DALÍ, HAS JUST REDISCOVERED CHRISTOPHER COLUMBUS, NEW YORK! YOU WHO ARE LIKE THE VERY STALK OF THE AIR, THE HALF CUT FLOWER OF HEAVEN! YOU, MAD AS THE MOON, NEW YORK! I SEE YOU WON BY THE SURREALIST "PARANOIA-KINESIS," YOU MAY WELL BE PROUD. I GO AND I ARRIVE, I LOVE YOU WITH ALL MY HEART.
DALÍ.

Declaration of the Independence of the Imagination and the Rights of Man to His Own Madness, New York, July 1939

TOTAL CAMOUFLAGE FOR TOTAL WAR
To be or not to be (Shakespeare). To see or not to see (Dalí). That is the question, or more precisely, the problem. At the beginning of the last war it was Picasso, inventor of Cubism, who found the solution. This is the authentic story. Seated in the spring sunshine on the terrace of the famous Rotonde in Montparnasse, Picasso and a group of his ardent admirers were sipping their absinthe, with the familiar ritual of the sugar spoon. The talk was naturally of war. But with this group of youthful innovators in the arts, the conversation was given to imaginative flights, rather than weighty considerations. Somebody threw out the strategic suggestion of making an army invisible.
"That's perfectly possible!" cried Picasso. Everybody kept still, waiting for the great painter to launch one of those ideas with which he always managed to eclipse other contributions to the conversation, no matter how original. And Picasso went on:
"If you want to make an army invisible, all you have to do is dress the soldiers like harlequins. At a distance the diamond patterns will merge into the landscape, and nobody will be able to see them."
Thus out of the casual and offhand talk bandied about among a handful of still little-known artists, was born the principle of camouflage so effectively used in the last war. It was not long indeed till one saw heavy guns, cuirassiers, cruisers, tanks, all covered with the same fancifully colored arabesques that figured simultaneously in the perturbing canvases of the new painters. At first people did not realize that this very same Cubism which created such a scandal in the art galleries, as being too trivial for days occupied with matters of such grave moment, was already operating with high efficiency on the fields of battle.
The profound lessons of history repeat themselves, but never in quite the same way. Outwardly they change, often beyond recognition. And just as the camouflage of 1914 was Cubist and Picassian, so the camouflage of 1942 should be Surrealist and Dalistic. For this time, the discovery is mine—namely the secret of total invisibility and the psychological camouflage. More of this later.
The discovery of "invisible images" was certainly part of my destiny. When I was six years old, I had astounded my parents and their friends by my almost mediumistic faculty of "seeing things differently." Always I saw what others did not see; and what they saw, I did not.
Among countless examples, there is a striking one which dates from that period of my life. Every Saturday I received a juvenile publication to which my father had subscribed for me. Its final page was always devoted to a puzzle picture. This would present, for instance, a forest and a hunter. In the tangled underbrush of the forest the artist had cleverly concealed a rabbit; the problem was to find it. Or, again, a doll must be discovered, lost by a child in an apparently empty room. My father would bring me the puzzle, and what was his astonishment to see me find, not one but two, three or four rabbits; not a single doll but several—and never the one which the artist had meant to conceal. Still more astonishing was the fact that my rabbits and my dolls were much clearer and better drawn than the ones which

had been intentionally hidden. As soon as I outlined them with my pencil, everybody could see them as clearly as I could, and exclaimed over them in surprise. But my seeing several rabbits—where others could find only one after long study and turning the page this way and that—was not all. The really phenomenal part of it was that in the same image I could see a mosquito, an elephant, a bathtub, or anything else, as well as a rabbit.

It was in psycho-pathology that I later found the explanation of this mysterious ability to see whatever I chose, wherever I chose. I had the paranoiac mind. Paranoia is defined as systematic delusion of interpretation. It is this systematic delusion which, in a more or less morbid state, constitutes the basis of the artistic phenomenon in general, and of my magic gift for transforming reality, in particular.

Watching fanciful images taking on more and more definite form, while gazing at the damp spots on an old wall, was one of the favorite and fascinating games of my childhood. I could see almost anything, too, in the ever-changing shape of the clouds—so prolific a source of paranoiac visions. What was my amazement, in the course of later studies, to find that back in the days before Christ, Aristophanes in *The Clouds* had declared them "the masters of delusion"—melting from the form of a leopard into the graceful contours of a nude woman, and evolving thence into the shape of a nose. In the same way, I was to read the advice of Leonardo da Vinci, who counseled his pupils to seek inspiration for painting an equestrian battle by gazing in a certain mental state at the spots of dampness on an old wall, in order to see the desired images arise out of chaos. The very same clouds and damp old walls which had evoked the hallucinations of my childhood.

Long before Aristophanes, indeed, the cave man, whose animal engravings of magic import simply followed certain lines of relief on the walls of the cave in which he saw the forms which obsessed him, was obeying the same paranoiac principle—the systematic delusion of interpretation.

And well before the cave man, even before man appeared at all on the surface of the earth, the same principle reigned in nature, taking the form of that most mysterious and least known of all phenomena—mimetism. In the beginning … was camouflage, the invisible!

The leaf-type insects represent one of the most subtle forms of mimetic camouflage in nature. Some of them not only take on the exact form and color of leaves, but even imitate their slightest surface conformations—tiny holes corresponding to drops of water pierced by a ray of sunlight, gossamer traces of mildew, the notched edges made by the gnawing of certain insects. Others imitate rotting twigs or thorny stems so closely as to be indistinguishable from the original. Thus we might say that reality playing at illusion becomes illusion; and being illusion—and therefore invisible—can serve equally well as a mechanism of defense or offense.

The leopard's spots and the tiger's stripes, imitating the effects of light and shade in the jungle, the markings of all animals in fact, obey this same obscure principle, whose least developed and most elementary manifestation is among the mammals. On the other hand, there is a variety of African sole which can identify itself so completely with its environment as to permit the amazing experiment which follows.

A checkerboard pattern of black and white squares is designed on the bottom of the aquarium. Here the fish is allowed to live, and by the end of a month, the checkerboard design appears identically reproduced on its back. The sole becomes invisible to the most knowing eye.

But the great problem of camouflage lies in the fact that cannons and tanks are not stationary. It is not enough therefore to devise a camouflage which makes them invisible by merging them with their surroundings. Some general type of camouflage must be found to serve more or less for all occasions. It is a question of looking for "constants of invisibility"; the results of which never have been and never will be satisfactory. The Germans have invented "parasitic" images—imitation flying fields, fake motorized columns. But these devices too are elementary in the extreme.

For ten years I have made a systematic study of the problems of vision, and I have come to the conclusion that we have had but the merest glimpse of the psychological significance of such phenomena. We see what we have some reason for seeing, above all what we believe we are going to sec. If the reason or the belief is upset—we see something else. In this connection, visual reactions can be controlled. To borrow the radio terms, they can be beamed, or even jammed, by purely psychological effects. My long investigation leads me to believe therefore that psychological camouflage is no idle dream. It is a question of research and of laboratory experiment. The latter I shall not elaborate here, for reasons that will be readily understood, in view of my conviction that these are matters of utilitarian importance in the field of warfare.

The examples which illustrate this article do not represent my individual research in psychological camouflage, being more in the nature of diversions. They may serve, however, to orient the reader with reference to the fact that an image can be rendered invisible—without transformation—simply by surrounding it with other images which make the spectator assume he is looking at something else.

The double images of the Romantic period were not as highly developed as these. In the former, both images were visible at the same time; whereas in mine, one of the images may remain long unnoticed. In my double images, at first, I made a diplomatic compromise between the two, transforming them and making one coincide with the other. This is true of the Invisible Bust of Voltaire. On the other hand, in the two Crusaders, the photo of a woman's face is intact, not retouched in any way. It is only the magic exercised by the surrounding images which makes you think you are seeing, not a woman's face, but a warrior on horseback. The same method of isolation and analogy makes the head of the open mouthed dog disappear.

I have carried out similar experiments with real objects. My latest success in this line has been with the statuette of a horse placed inside a miniature theatre. The lighting, and the objects I have placed around the statuette, render the horse completely invisible. Instead of a horse, the spectator thinks he is looking at the sky in a landscape.

I am a believer in magic, which in the last analysis is simply the power of materializing imagination into reality. Our over-mechanized age underestimates the properties of the irrational imagination, which seems impractical, and is in reality at the basis of all discoveries. When Laporte, in the 15th-century, announced that he had found a way to cut glass so that everything seen through it was outlined by a rainbow—he himself thought it was magic.

Leonardo was often suspected by the Inquisition of being a magician. He was just that in reality—for in the long run the Inquisition made few mistakes. He was the advance inventor of all the machines in modern warfare.

'War of Production' sounds the note of reality for today, and tomorrow. But in our world, there is still a role to be played by magic.

"Total Camouflage for Total War," *Esquire*, vol. 18, no. 2, (New York: August 1942) pp. 64-66, 129-130

MYSTICAL MANIFESTO

The two most subversive things that can happen to an ex-Surrealist in 1951 are, first, to become a mystic; and second, to know how to draw. These two forms of vigor have just happened to me together and at the same time. Catalonia can boast of three great geniuses: namely, Raymond de Sebonde, author of *Natural Theology*; Gaudí, the father of Mediterranean Gothic; and Salvador Dalí, inventor of the new Paranoiac- Critical mysticism and savior, as his very name indicates, of modern painting. The paroxysmal crisis of Dalinian mysticism mainly relies on the progress of the particular sciences of our times, especially on the metaphysical spirituality of the substantiality of quantum physics, and, at a level of less substantial simulacra, on the most ignominiously supergelatinous results—and their own coefficients of monarchic viscosity—of the whole general morphology. The Dalinian principles on which rely and rest the Bramante an bases of the aesthetic soul of his Paranoiac-Critical Activity are, in brief, the following: form is a reaction of matter under inquisitorial coercion "on all sides" of "hard" and unrelenting space. Beauty is always the ultimate spasm of a long and rigorous inquisitorial process. Liberty is formlessness. Each rose springs up in a prison. The most beautiful architectural works of the human soul are the Tempietto di San Pietro in Montorio by the divine Bramante in Rome, and the monastery of El Escorial in Spain. Both were shaped in the same "incorruptible mold: ecstasy." "Ecstasy is the incorruptible mold" in opposition to academicism which is the corruptible mold. I know something of this, I, Salvador Dalí, specialist in putrefactions and ammoniacal passions from the early and sacrilegious age of twelve!

Fear nothing, do not be afraid lest our modern pseudo-aesthetes should keep themselves busy with Bramante and Raphael's superhuman peaks! No more do they dare face perfection, beauty; they are ashamed of them, preferring to go back to the former periods of art that are more or less barbarous but are always prior to the deifications of the Renaissance at its peak, because thus only do they feel at ease being able to apply the bureaucratic formulas of their ultra-academic modern art—plagiarism that is more or less decorative, as well as simplistic and caricatural (because it is not justified by any authentic tradition) of the art of prehistoric caves, of the island of Crete, of Romanesque frescoes, et cetera, up to the aberration for the mentally feeble of African art—above all by getting out of all these the dramatically unskillful and failed aspects of their nondescript techniques. It is truly a unique drama in which we, as modern artists, are definitely superior to those of any previous era.

Only the abstract experiments, antiacademic by dint of their fierce will to ecstasy, of the kind done by Mathieu, are valid from the point of view of knowledge, although electronic photography provisionally is ready to liberate man from this type of activity in order to restore to the human eye anew its full and imperialist realist category. The purpose of mysticism is mystical ecstasy; ecstasy is achieved by St. Theresa of Avila's path of perfection, and by the successive penetration into the penitential chapels of the spiritual castle. The mystical artist must form for himself, aesthetically, through the fierce daily self-inquisition of a "mystical reverie" that is the most rigorous, architectonic, Pythagorean and exhausting of them all, a dermo- skeletal soul—bones on the outside, superfine flesh within—like that which Unamuno attributes to Castille, in which the flesh of the soul cannot help but rise up to the sky. The mystical ecstasy is "super-cheerful," explosive, disintegrated, supersonic, undulatory and corpuscular, and ultra-gelatinous, for it is the aesthetic blooming of the maximum of paradisiacal happiness that a human being can have on earth. Down on his knees, the mystical artist will see—as fruit of his inquisitorial virtue, exercised from the moment of sleep as far as the Lilliputian phosphenes brought about by the slightest digestive mishaps—he will see, singing with joy, the euphoric Malaquita Rinocerontica Explosiva, La Madonna Port-Lligata da Desintegrada Lapislazulina, La Immaculada Corpuscularia Aurea. In a state of ecstasy, a grain of wheat floating in the air at the height of one meter and a half above ground will be so firmly fixed there that a grim elephant pushing with its brow with all its might will not succeed in dislodging it. Also, in addition, an angelic child on the beach of Rosas will lift with precaution the skin of the sea to observe a libidinous dog sleeping in the shade of the water. All these subjects, however incredible they seem to you, once you will have seen them you will be able to paint them realistically.

Painter, some day to come, you will have succeeded, by your own "paranoiac-critical" disciplines of an active and inquisitorial type, in seeing that which is "immaculately corpuscular," which for me is the case at present, but for you might be an all too ineffable thing of its kind. Do not fear then anything at all and put yourself to painting daily and honestly, "from nature," that which you will have seen, and for this purpose you will use the Renaissance way of painting because it was then that the means of pictorial expression were invented once and for all and with the maximum of perfection and visual effectiveness.

The decadence of modern painting comes from skepticism and lack of belief, which are the consequence of rationalism, positivism, progressivism, as well as of mechanistic or dialectical materialism, both being equally anachronistic, and all of this having its origin in the distressing and sentimental simplemindedness, of the "Ridi Pagliaccio" type, of very repressed encyclopedists. Here are the good guys for your good government: Pythagoras, the "obscure Heraclitus." This is true today, with the unity of the universe having been confirmed, clear as the aesthetic of Luca Pacioli or Vitruvius, or that of St. John of the Cross—the highest form of poetic revelation of militant Spanish mysticism which Dalí is updating—it being observed that, every quarter of an hour and of a second, matter is in a constant and accelerated process of dematerialization, of disintegration, slipping out of the hands of scientists and thus proving to us the spirituality of all substance, for the physical light of Dalí's Paranoiac-Critical Activity, this too, is "wave and corpuscle" at one and the same time. Ever since die theory of relativity substituted the substratum of the universe for the ether, thus dethroning and reducing time to its relative role, which Heraclitus already assigned it when he said that "time is a child," and Dalí too when he painted his famous "soft watches"; ever since that unknown and delirious substance seemed to fill the whole universe; since the explosive equivalence of mass- energy—all those who think, apart from the Marxist inertia, know that it is up to the metaphysicians to work precisely on the question of matter.

And in aesthetics it is up to the mystics and only they to resolve the new "golden sections" of the soul of our time; if a powerful Renaissance of mystical painting has not yet begun, it is due to the fact that the artists, this time very late in relation to today's scientific progress, still vegetate in the abominable pastures of the last consequences of the most sordid materialism, it is because they have nothing to paint, that today's artists paint nothing, in other words, what is non-figurative, non-objective, non-expressive, non-non-no no no no no no.

NO!

Finished are the denials and demotions, finished the Surrealist malaise and existentialist anxiety. Mysticism is the paroxysm of joy in the ultra-individualist affirmation of all man's heterogeneous tendencies within the absolute unity of ecstasy. I want my next Christ to be a painting containing more beauty and joy than anything that will have been painted up to the present. I want to paint a Christ that will be the absolute contrary in every respect to the materialist and savagely antimystical Christ of Grünewald!

Absolute monarchy, perfect aesthetic dome of the soul, homogeneity, unity; biological, hereditary, and supreme continuity—all this above, brought up near the dome of the sky. Below, swarming and supergelatinous anarchy, viscous heterogeneity, ornamental diversity of ignominious soft structures compressed and yielding the last juice of their ultimate forms of reactions. "Anarchic monarchy," this is the "(almost divine) harmony of opposites" proclaimed by Heraclitus, which only the incorruptible mold of ecstasy will knead one day with new stones from the Escorial.

Picasso, thank you! With your Iberian, anarchical and integral genius you have killed the ugliness of modern painting: without you, given the prudence and moderation that characterize and are the honor of French art, we were in danger of having one hundred years of painting more and more ugly, until we have progressively arrived at your sublime *esperpentos abatesios* of the Dora Maar series. You, with a single blow of your categorical sword, you have brought down the bull of ignomiy, and also and above all, the even blacker one of materialism in its entirety. Now the new era of mystic painting begins with me.

DALÍ

Neuilly, Saturday–Sunday

April 15 1951, 3 o'clock in the morning

Manifeste Mystique (Paris: Robert J. Godet, 1951).

VIVE L'ART MODERNE A CONDITION DE PEINDRE A PARTIR DE RAPHAEL

S.D.

My "Assumption" is the opposite of the atomic bomb. Instead of the disintegration of matter, we have the integration, the reconstitution of the real and glorious body of the Virgin in the heavens.

This painting alone justifies in itself every experimental effort in modern art, since I have succeeded in bringing these experiments to a classical end; experiments which would otherwise have remained sterile, since the majority of the great and courageous innovators are today returning to archaeological inspiration; and only a few impetuous young abstract painters continue with "interesting plastic experiments" which, unfortunately, are destined to remain decorative art because of their means of purely graphical expression. There was Seurat with his Divisionism, who, without knowing it, introduced nuclear physics; also Cubism; and especially the great Futurist genius, Boccioni, but he expresses himself in terms of speed, motorcars and aviation. This is childish, and it is because of this lack of theological and philosophical meaning that all these efforts perished so soon.

But all of them had foreseen a thing that was to be *the great, immeasurable and categorical innovation of our time – a new conception of matter, that of* NUCLEAR PHYSICS.

Catalog

D'après les conceptions de la physique
nucléaire, une chaise rassemblera plutôt
à un essaim tourbillonant de moucherons.
EDDINGTON

l. Assumpta Corpuscularia Lapislazulina
2. Nature Morte Evangélique
3. Croix Nucléaire
4. Gala Placida
5. L'Ange de Port Lligat
6. Persistence de la Mémoire Corpusculaire

"Vive l'art moderne à condition de peindre à partir de Raphael," in *Dalí*, exhibition catalogue, Carstairs Gallery, New York, December 1952-January 1953

ANTI-MATTER MANIFESTO

If the physicists are producing anti-matter, let it be allowed
to the painters, already specialists in angels, to paint it.
S.D.

In the surrealist period I wanted to create the iconography of the interior world—the world of the marvelous, of my father Freud. I succeeded in doing it. Today the exterior world—that of physics—has transcended the one of psychology. My father today is Dr. Heisenberg.

It is with pi-mesons and the most gelatinous and indeterminate neutrinos that I want to paint the beauty of the angels and of reality. I will very soon succeed in doing so.

My ambition, still and always, is to integrate the experiments of modern art with the greater classical tradition. The latest microphysical structures of Klein, Mathieu and Tapiés must be used anew to paint, because they are only what, in Velázquez's day, was the "brush stroke," about which the sublime poet Quevedo, already at that time, said that he painted with "stains and distant spots."

Anti-matter Manifesto, exhibition catalogue, Carstairs Gallery, New York, December 1958 – January 1959

THE KING AND THE QUEEN TRAVERSED BY SWIFT NUDES

Personally, I consider Marcel Duchamp's prophetic title alone worth miles of pseudo-decorative modern painting, and this I can affirm for the following thirteen reasons:

1. In painting *The King and the Queen Traversed by Swift Nudes*, the genius of Marcel Duchamp proclaimed nothing less than the notarial act of the new intra-atomic structure of the universe, that is, the discontinuity of matter. In fact, the king and the queen can be traversed by swift nudes because matter is discontinuous. It is easy to understand that swift nudes are indivisible bodies, the corpuscles, the charged elementary particles of quantum physics, which, with their active energy quantum, cross the finite space that, as each day passes, becomes more and more the "supreme royal space" *par excellence* and, if objections are raised, I will add "the Divine space" *par excellence*.

The speculative distance between Duchamp's princely ideas and those of my great compatriot from Tarragona, the peasant, Joan Miró, is precisely the distance separating *The King and the Queen Traversed by Swift Nudes* from *Dog Barking at the Moon*; the distance between cosmic majesty and the dog of folklore.

2. Marcel Duchamp, in painting *The King and the Queen Traversed by Swift Nudes*, became an aristocratic anarchist, as opposed to the inventors of anarchism, Prince Kropotkin and Prince Bakunin, who were the prototypes of anarchistic aristocrats.

3. Marcel Duchamp, having become an aristocrat because of his original Dadaist anarchism, categorically refuses to take part in the contemporary artistic brawl. He does not want to be identified with those who tirelessly continue "barking at the moon," he abandons painting, not as an act of artistic suicide, but because he continues to have swift nudes cross the king and the queen in his thoughts, while playing chess.

4. Like Louis XIV, Marcel Duchamp can say: "*L'Échec c'est moi.*" His moral example is worthy of Socrates, but functions more Jesuitically, without suicide, for by aristocratically proclaiming his failure Duchamp alone is saved from the imminent collective failure of modern painting.

5. Marcel Duchamp paints the king's moustaches on Leonardo's queen Gioconda, the queen being the most maneuverable and premonitory piece on the chessboard. It is well known that Leonardo's life was a continual and dramatic chess game.

6. At the feet of his king, and his queen Gioconda, Marcel Duchamp wrote the famous inscription L H O O Q, which was the concise way for an anarchist to attest the thermal and biological condition by which he declares his belief in hereditary continuity.

7. L H O O Q, a quasi-biochemical formula, is the kind of scatological shortcut which has always delighted kings and courtesans.

8. In The King and the Queen Traversed by Swift Nudes, L H O O Q can be taken quite adequately as the epitaph of modern painting.

9. Thus Duchamp did not believe it necessary to pursue modern painting to its final consequences. Only Dalí had a secret imperialist plan, but in any case I cannot be accused of practicing modern painting.

10. The Divisionism of Gaudí and Boccioni, Analytic Cubism, Duchamp's epitaph… nothing creative has been produced since in the history of art. From Braque to Miró, there is a reversion either to archeology or to folklore. Duchamp has the enormous advantage over all the rest of having only to look at their paintings to know what they are doing, while the others cannot know what he is doing, because he is doing nothing.

11. Already after modern painting a courageous group rushed at top speed toward absolute nothingness, standing for a pre-mystical state of mind, what Tapiés calls "*art autre;*" Kline, Tàpies, Millares, de Kooning, Mathieu. Is the question that we might have access to a new dynasty here a matter of H.O.O.Q.? Being here myself, I answer yes.

12. The twelfth reason why *The King and the Queen Traversed by Swift Nudes* is a sublime title is that there is no plastic, sociological, philanthropic or bureaucratic reason for such a title, whose sole and true reason is the ultra-individualistic will of a typically royal personality.

13. That is why Marcel Duchamp has spent the rest of his life filling suitcases with everything—from near or far, or rather from quite close at hand—which could concern him; with full awareness that the excrement accumulated in Louis XVI's navel should have been preserved, though not that of an anonymous elevator operator's. In the middle of the war, during a German bombardment, Duchamp and I went back and forth between Arcachon and Bordeaux filling up his famous suitcase. I remember having mentioned this possibility of bequeathing to posterity the excrement of great personalities, and that Duchamp insisted at great length on the necessity of keeping a record of the temperatures. That was failure on the historical level; the l H.O.O.Q. of history.

"The King and the Queen Traversed by Swift Nudes," *Art News*, vol. 58, (New York: April 1959), pp. 22-25

ECUMENICAL "CHAFARRINADA" OF VELÁSQUEZ

Quevedo, in his immortal *Silva*, said that Velásquez used to paint with stains and spots and contemporary critics said of him that he painted with *refregados* and *chafarrinadas* (*chafarrinada*, according to the Dictionary of the Royal Academy of the Spanish Language, means, literally: "to tarnish with stains or spots," *deslucir con manchas y borrones*), what was called by the Italians of this period *bravura di tocco*, or "brush strokes," which corresponds exactly to modern Action Painting, the Mathieu calligraphy, the spasmodic impastoes of de Kooning. Action Painting is the equivalent of the "quantum of action" of Max Planck in modern physics and will establish the style of our epoch, which will be 'Quantified Realism.'

When Velásquez arrived in Italy and was asked what he thought about Raphael, he answered, "*Non mi piace per niente*" ("I don't like him at all"). But if we study closely his two most famous paintings, *Las Meninas* and *The Surrender of Breda*, we discover that he repeats the subject matter and general structure of the *Marriage of the Virgin* by Raphael.

In the center of all three paintings, we find a "virginal space." Raphael's is made of naked sky, metaphysically infrangible. The virginal space in *Las Meninas* is intercepted by the *aposentador* (landlord) of the king, with his keys. In *The Surrender of Breda*, we discover that he repeats the subject matter and general structure of the *Marriage of the Virgin* by Raphael.

In *The Surrender of Breda*, the algid moment of painting when the imperialistic Vision of Spain defeats the analytical, technical, bourgeois, Flemish realism, Orange (from the family of the Prince) surrenders the key, which is already a microscope of the virginal space—chaste and military, space that the victor, with a noble gesture, will not violate because behind his soldiers there is the golden door of his honor.

(The key-microscope is not merely incidental since it is of the same period as the microscopic vision of Vermeer, born in the same city and almost on the same date as Leeuwenhoek, the inventor of the microscope, and the creation of infinitesimal calculus by the German mathematician Leibnitz.)

In Raphael's *Marriage of the Virgin*, St. Joseph and his companions carry verges that are the equivalent of the lances in *The Surrender at Breda*, which is also known as *El Cuadro de las Lanzas*, *The Painting of the Lances*: Spinola (chief of the Spanish army) the victor, leans the affection of his right arm on the humiliated and grateful left shoulder of the vanquished in order that the arrow of the scales of visual justice reestablishes the verticality that oscillates and marks the erect lances, as the masts in *Sunset in the Port of Ostia*, painted by Claude Lorrain; these masts playing with the verticality of the architectural structures are, again, the lances which impede the destructive invasion of the light, foreteller

of the great Impressionist disaster which had to come about after the *Sunset in Flanders* ("*En Flandes se has puesto el Sol*," signals the defeat of the Spanish Empire), prologue to the ignominious materialistic age, called, by its contemporaries "The Age of Lights."

All the theories on relativity are already symbolized in *Las Meninas* and Picasso, who has the intuition of a genius, paints one of his interpretations of the painting with a Velásquez like a Gulliver among the Lilliputians. "*Meninas*" in Spanish means small children. *The Meninas* in his painting are the little princesses, and the king and queen that Velásquez is actually painting in his canvas are microscopically reflected in the mirror in the background. My friend, the Catalonian philosopher Francesc Pujols, remarks that bigger even than Velásquez is the canvas, his work itself, a giant among kings and princesses.

When Velásquez said about Raphael "*Non mi piace per niente*," he meant that he did not like his intellectual idealization, his esthetic brilliance. (the "*fleur-de-lis*" in the painting of Velásquez's *Marriage of the Virgin* is the glacial aura which flourishes in the masts of Lorrain).

Truth doesn't need any kind of adornment of reference. Unamuno said that you must "*vencer*" and "*convencer*," that is, win and convince, and it is not again a coincidence that the word 'convince' in English can mean both things. Today, when no one is in accord with anything, especially with the present esthetic chaos, everything coincides on one unique phenomenon: Velásquez. At the tricentennial of his death Picasso, Dalí, the "*pompiers*", the abstractionists, the followers of Action Painting, all consider Velásquez the most alive and most modern of painters.

The "*chafarrinadas*" of modern abstract art have to get inspiration from the imperialistic realism of Velásquez. "*Chafarrinada*" for "*chafarrinada's*" sake is equal to zero.

In Spain, when a situation becomes impossible and you have to start anew, they say "*borrón y centa nueva*," which means "rub out and start again."

The '*borrón*' of modern abstract art is the symbol of an end and of a beginning. That is the reason why Velásquez has reached his present glory, because his "*borrones*," his "*chafarrinadas*" are ecumenical, being the "*Chafarrinadas* of Truth."

"Ecumenical 'chafarrinada' of Velásquez," *Art News*, vol. 59 (New York: February 10, 1961), pp. 30, 55

Appendix

Exhibitions

Elliott H. King

Solo Exhibitions

"Exposició S. Dalí," Galeries Dalmau, Barcelona, 14-27 November 1925.

"Exposició S. Dalí," Galeries Dalmau, Barcelona, 31 December 1926-14 January 1927.

"Dalí," Galerie Goeman, Paris, 20 November – 5 December 1929.

"Exposition Salvador Dalí," Galerie Pierre Colle, Paris, 3-15 June 1931.

"Exposition Salvador Dalí," Galerie Pierre Colle, Paris, 26 May-17 June 1932.

"Exposition Salvador Dalí," Galerie Pierre Colle, Paris, 19-29 June 1933.

"Exhibition of Paintings by Salvador Dalí," Julien Levy Gallery, New York, 21 November-8 December 1933.

"Salvador Dalí a Galerie d'Art Catalonia,"Galerie d'Art Catalonia, Barcelona, 8-21 December 1933.

"Drawings and Etchings to illustrate Lautréamont's 'Les Chants de Maldoror' by Dalí," Julien Levy Gallery, New York, 3-28 April 1934.

"42 eaux-fortes et 30 dessins pour Les Chants de Maldoror," Quatre Chemins, Paris, 13-25 June 1934.

Galerie Jacques Bonjean, Paris, 20 June-13 July 1934.

"Salvador Dalí: Catalogue of an Exhibition of Paintings, Drawings and Etchings at the Zwemmer Gallery," Zwemmer Gallery, London, 24 October-10 November 1934.

Galerie d'Art Catalonia, Barcelona, 2-4 October 1934.

Julien Levy Gallery, New York, 21 November-10 December 1934.

Avery Memorial, Wadsworth Athenaeum, Hartford (Connecticut), 18 December 1934-7 January 1935.

"Salvador Dalí," Alex Reid and Lefevre Gallery, London, 25 June-July 1936.

"Dalí," Julien Levy Gallery, New York, 10 December 1936-9 January 1937.

Galerie Renou et Colle, Paris, 6-30 July 1937.

"Salvador Dalí," Julien Levy Gallery, New York, 21 March-18 April 1939.

"Dalí's Dream of Venus," World's Fair Amusement Area, New York, June 1939.

"Salvador Dalí," Julien Levy Gallery, New York, 22 Paril -19 May 1941; Arts Club of Chicago, Chicago, 23 May-14 June 1941; Dalzell Hatfield Galleries, Los Angeles, 10 September-5 October 1941.

"Salvador Dalí: Paintings, Drawings, Prints," Museum of Modern Art, New York, 19 November 1941-11 January 1942.

"Dalí," M. Knoedler and Co., New York, 14 Paril-5 May 1943.

"The Seven Lively Arts," Ziegfeld Theater, New York, November 1944.

"Dalí (Fortis Imaginatio Generat Casum)/ Recent Paintings by Salvador Dalí," Bignou Gallery, New York, 20 November-29 December 1945.

"Trilogy of the Desert," M. Knoedler and Co., New York, 30 October-2 November 1946; Galleries of the Society of the Four Arts, Palm Beach (Florida), winter 1947.

"Salvador Dalí: An Exhibition," The Cleveland Museum of Art, Cleveland, 8 October-9 November 1947.

"New Paintings by Salvador Dalí," Bignou Gallery, New York, 25 November 1947-3 January 1948.

"Prima Mostra in Italia de Salvador Dalí," Galerie l'Obelisco, Rome, 27 November-10 December 1948.

"The Madonna of Port Lligat," Carstairs Gallery, New York, 27 November 1950-10 January 1951.

"Jewels," Alemany and Ertman, New York, April 1951.

"Manifeste Mystique," Librairie Berggruen, Paris, 19-30 June 1951.

Galerie André Weil, Paris, 20 June-15 September 1951.

Lefevre Gallery, London, December 1951.

"Dalí," Carstairs Gallery, New York, 8 December 1952-31 January 1953.

"Jewels," Alemany and Ertman, New York, December 1952.

Museum of Modern Art, Santa Barbara (California), 1953.

"Mostra di Quadri, Disegni ed Oreficerie di Salvador Dalí," Palazzo Pallavicini-Rospigliosi, Rome, March-June 1954; Palazzo delle Prigioni vecchie, Venice, 1954; Palazzo Reale, Milan, 1954.

Carstairs Gallery, New York, 7 December 1954-31 January 1955.

"Jewels," Museo de Arte Moderno, Madrid, 1954.

"Jewels," Galerie Bernheim-Jeune, Paris, 17 November-9 December 1954.

"Jewels by Dalí, 1953," Museum of Art, Philadelphia, 15 January-13 February 1955.

"A Collection of objets d'art and jewels designed by Salvador Dalí," Denver Art Museum, Denver (Colorado), 1-29 May 1955.

"Salvador Dalí. Casino Communal," Knokke-le-Zoute, 1 July-10 September 1956.

Carstairs Gallery, New York, 4 December 1956-5 January 1957.

"Exposition du livre le plus cher du monde qu'il a imagine et réalisé Don Quichotte illustré par Salvador Dalí," Musée Jacquemart-André, Paris, 13-19 December 1957.

M. Knoedler and Co., New York, 19 February-8 March 1958.

"Dalí, Second Collection of Jewels, Sacre Coeur de Jesus Paintings," The Parrish Art Museum, Southampton (New York), 1-21 August 1958.

Carstairs Gallery, New York, 6 December 1958-31 January 1959.

"Jewels from the Owen Cheatham Foundation," French and Co., New York, 5-26 May 1959.

"Columbus Discovers America," French and Co., New York, February 1960.

100 aquarelles pour la "Divine Comédie," Musée Galliera, Paris, 19-31 May 1960.

"Loan Exhibition of Selected Paintings, Drawings and Water Colors of Salvador Dalí," Finch College Art Gallery and Museum, New York, 23 May-18 June 1960.

Galerie Isy Brachot, Brussels, 11-29 June 1960.

"Art in Jewels Exhibition," Sotheby's, London, 14 September-8 October 1960.

Carstairs Gallery, New York, December 1960-14 January 1961.

Galerie Isy Brachot, Brussels, 4-16 February 1961.

"Fortuny Dalí y sus batallas de Tetuán," Salle Tinell, Barcelona, 15 October 1962.

"Die göttliche Komödie," Karl Vonderbank Graphisches Kabinett, Frankfurt, February 1963; Galerie Schöninger, Munich, April 1963.

"Salvador Dalí: Hommage à Crick et Watson," M. Knoedler and Co., New York, 26 November-26 December 1963.

"6 eaux-fortes ayant pour theme 'La Mythologie' et présentation d'un buste de Salvador Dalí aux moustaches en vipères vivantes," Galerie Falvart, Paris, 13 November-13 December 1963.

Tokyo Prince Hotel Gallery, Tokyo, 8 September-18 October 1964; Nagoya Prefectural Museum of Art, Nagoya, 23-30 October 1964; Kyoto Municipal Art Gallery, Kyoto, 3-29 November 1964.

Municipal Art Gallery, Los Angeles, 20 November-20 December 1964.

Old Print Center, Phyllis Lucas Gallery, New York, July 1965-August 1965.

M. Knoedler and Co., New York, 18-31 December 1965.

"Salvador Dalí 1910-1965 with the Reynolds Morse Collection," Gallery of Modern Art, New York, 18 December 1965-28 Febuary 1966.

"Gravures et bijoux," Galerie D., Prague, 15 June-23 July 1967.

"Salvador Dalí: Paintings and Drawings," Staempfli Gallery, New York, 10-28 October 1967.

"Manifeste en Hommage à Meissonier,"Hôtel Meurice, Paris, 1-30 November 1967.

"Oeuvres anciennes en Hommage à Meissonier," Galerie André-François Petit, Paris, 1 December 1967.

"Aquarelles," Puiforcat, Paris, December 1967.

Palais des Beaux-Arts, Charleroi, 1-31 March 1968.

"Aliyah," Gallery of Modern Art, New York, 2-22 April 1968.

Galerie Isy Brachot, Brussels, 31 May-24 June 1968.

"La pêche au thon," Fondation Paul Ricard, Paris, 26 June 1968.

"Gravures et lithographies," London Graphic Art Gallery, London, 2-27 July 1968.

Old Print Center, Phyllis Lucas Gallery, New York, December 1968.

"Les aquarelles originales du Casanova," Galerie Isy Brachot, Brussels, 31 May-24 June 1968.

"The Spanish graphics of Salvador Dalí...loaned from the Reynolds Morse Collection," Hiram College, Hiram (Ohio), 15 April-9 May 1969.

"Oeuvre graphique," Librairie de Fleuve, Bordeaux, 3-18 October 1969.

Galerie M. Knoedler et Cle, Paris, 20 November 1969-3 January 1970.

"Lithographs," Zachary Waller Gallery, Los Angeles, 1-20 December 1969.

"34 Aguafuertes originales," Galerie René Metras, Barcelona, 3 January 1969.

"Aliyah," Galerie Isy Brachot, Brussels, 20 March-21 April 1969.

"Aquarelles," Galerie Isy Brachot, Brussels, June-August 1969.

"Dalí: Paintings and drawings, 1965-1970," M. Knoedler and Co., New York, 10 March-4 April 1970.

"Dalis Graphische Folgen," Heidelberger Kunstverein, Heidelberg, 5 April-3 May 1970.

"Tristan et Iseult," Librairie Lardanchet, Paris, 17 April-6 May 1970.

"Affiches de Dalí pour la SNCF," Buffet de la Gare de Lyon, Paris, 29 April-9 May 1970.

"Affiches de Dalí pour la SNCF," Train exposition de la SNCF, exposition itinérante, May 1970-1971.

"Illustrations du Marquis de Sade et de 'Carmen,'" Galerie Marcel Bernheim, Paris, June 1970.

"Hommage à Dalí," Musée de l'Athénée, Geneva, 2 July-30 September 1970.

"Temi cavallereschi e religiosi nell'ultimo Salvador Dalí e dipinti del Surrealismo," Galleria Gissi, Turin, July 1970.

"Grafik," Karl-Ernst-Osthaus-Museum, The Hague, 7 October-8 November 1970.

"Dalí," Museum Boymans-van Beuningen, Rotterdam, 21 November 1970-10 January 1971.

"Oeuvres anciennes," Galerie André-François Petit, Paris, November-December 1970.

Staatliche Kunsthalle, Baden-Baden, 29 January-18 April 1971.

Reiss-Cohen Gallery, New York, 9 March-April 1971.

"Lithographies," Galeria Colibri, San Juan (Puerto Rico), 26 March 1971.

"Memories of Surrealism," Allan Rich Gallery, New York, March-3 April 1971.

"L'art dans les bijoux de Salvador Dalí," Wally F. Findlay Galleries, Paris, 22 April-22 May 1971.

Old Print Center, Phyllis Lucas Gallery, New York, May 1971.

"Art-in-jewels Exhibition and Paintings," Whitechapel Art Gallery, London, 8 June-10 July 1971.

"Lithographies," Arts Contacts, Paris, 16 November 1971.

"Hommage à Albrecht Dürer," Galerie Vision Nouvelle, Paris, 30 November 1971-January 1972.

Galerie Furstenberg, Paris, 1971.

"Holograms conceived by Dalí," M. Knoedler and Co., New York, 7 April-13 May 1972.

Galerie Furstenberg, Paris, 18 April 1972.

"Estampes," Fuji Television Gallery, Tokyo, 26 June-15 July 1972.

"Bruikleen uit de collectie Edward F.W. James," Museum Boymans-van Beuningen, Rotterdam, summer 1972.

"Estampes," Kunstverein, Hamburg, 22 September-22 October 1972.

"Lithographies," MacDonald Gallery, Brussels, 27 September-23 October 1972.

"Lithographies en relief," Le Bateau ivre, Brussels, 27 September-23 October 1972.

Galerie Isy Brachot, Brussels, 8 October-4 November 1972.

"Estampes. Galerie Bussola, Turin, October 1972.

"Salvador Dalí," Centre d'Art, Montreux, 15 November-20 December 1972.

"Gouaches et lithographies," Éditions Art et Valeur, Paris, 16 November-14 December 1972.

"Salvador Dalí's Graphic Work," The Mark Gallery, London, December 1972-January 1973.

"Tapisseries," Galerie Furstenberg, Paris, 1972-10 January 1973.

"Alex Maguy présente 7 tableaux de Dalí," Galerie de l'Élysée, Paris, 15 May-8 June 1973.

"150 graphische Arbeiten. Galerie Schmüking, Braunschweig, May 1973.

" 'Roi, je t'attends à Babylone…' d'André Malraux, illustrations de Salvador Dalí," Musée d'art moderne de la Ville de Paris, Paris, 22 June-2 September 1973.

Château de Vascoeuil, Vascoeuil, 1 July-15 October 1973.

"Dalí, su arte en joyas," Museo Dalí, Figueres, August 1973.

"Special Daldalí Loan," The Salvador Dalí Museum, Cleveland, summer 1973.

"8 tapisseries. Galerie Furstenberg, Paris, 10 December 1973.

"Retrospective," Louisiana Museum, Humlebaek, 6 October-2 December 1973; Moderna Museet, Stockholm, 26 December 1973-24 February 1974.

M. Knoedler and Co., New York, 6 March-6 April 1974.

"Retrospective," Städtische Galerie und Städelsches Kunstinstitut, Frankfurt, 14 March-5 May 1974.

"Les songes drôlatiques de Pantagruel," J.P. Lehmans Gallery, London, 1974.

"Dalí, méthode paranoïaque critique, hasard objectif et troisième dimension, photographies de Robert Descharnes et Marc Lacroix," Galerie Nikon, Paris, 28 April-23 July 1975.

"Painting of Gala looking at the Mediterranean sea which from a distance of 20 meters is transformed into a portrait of Abraham Lincoln: (homage to Rothko)," The Soloman R. Guggenheim Museum, New York, 25 May-11 July 1976.

Rolly-Michaux Gallery, Boston, 1 October 1976; Rolly-Michaux Gallery, New York, 22 October-9 November 1976.

22nd Salon de Montrouge, 4 May-5 June 1977.

"Hommage à Goya," Musée Goya, Castres, 9 July-31 August 1977.

Sammlung Levy, Hamburg, 1 October 1977-7 January 1978.

"La Gare de Perpignan accompagnée d'une petite retrospective," Galerie André-François Petit, Paris, November-December 1977.

"Les Caprices de Goya de Salvador Dalí," Galerie Berggruen, December 1977-January 1978.

"Dalí lifting the skin of the Mediterranean Sea to show Gala the birth of Venus," The Solomon R. Guggenheim Museum, New York, 25-30 April 1978.

"Les Caprices de Goya de Salvador Dalí," Musée de l'Athénée, Geneva, 12 July-30 September 1978.

Galeria d'art Tertre, Mataró (Barcelona), 21 November-December 1978.

"La Main de Dalí retirant une Toison d'or en forme de nuage pour montrer à Gala l'aurore toute nue très, très loin derrière le soleil (hommage à Claude Lorrain)," Hôtel Meurice, Paris, 18-20 December 1978.

"Salvador Dalí. Rétrospective, 1920-1980," Centre Georges Pompidou, Musée National d'Art Moderne, Paris, 18 December 1979-21 April 1980.

"Salvador Dalí," Tate Gallery, London, 14 May-29 June 1980.

"Obra gráfica: Ciclos literarios," Casa del Monte de Piedad, Madrid, opened 28 January 1982.

"Rétrospective Salvador Dalí 1982," Isetan Museum of Art, Tokyo, 28 February-6 April 1982; Daimuru Art Museum, Osaka, 22 April-5 May 1982; Kitakyushu Municipal Museum of Art, Kitakyushu (8 May-6 June 1982); Hiroshima Prefectural Museum of Art, Hiroshima (11 June-11 July 1982).

"Dalí i els llibres," Capilla de Santa Ágata, Barcelona, 15 June-28 June 1982; Casa de Cultura, Girona; Instituto de Estudios Ilerdenses, Lleida

"Homage to Gala," The Salvador Dalí Museum, St. Petersburg, 13 July-12 September 1982.

"Perpignan. La Collection Salvador Dalí de Musée Perrot-Moore," Musée Perrot-Moore, Cadaqués, August-September 1982.

"400 obras de Salvador Dalí de 1914 a 1983," Museo Español de Arte Contempóraneo, Madrid, 15 April-29 May 1983; Palau Reial de Pedralbes, Barcelona., 10 June-31 July 1983; Teatro-Museo Dalí, Figueres, to 16 August 1983.

"Dalí fotògraf, Dalí en els seus fotògrafs," Centre Cultural de la Caixa de Pensions, Barcelona, June-July 1983.

"I Dalí di Salvador Dalí," Galleria Civica d'Arte Moderna, Palazzo dei Diamanti, Ferrara, 1 July-20 September 1984.

"Salvador Dalí, dessins 1936-38 et 1947-48," Galeria 1900-2000, Paris, 28 September-8 October 1987.

"Salvador Dalí: 1904-1989," Staatsgalerie, Stuttgart, 13 May-23 July 1989; Kunsthaus, Zürich, 18 August-22 October 1989.

"Los Dalís de Dalí," [colección del museo nacional centro de arte reina Sofia]. Centro cultural/Arte contemporaneo, Mexico D.F., November 1990-January 1991.

"Dalí verdadero/grabado falso. La obra impresa 1930-1934," IVAM, Centre Julio González, Valencia, 3 December 1992-7 February 1993.

"Dalí en los fondos de la Fundació Gala-Salvador Dalí," Fundación Fondo de Cultura de Sevilla, Seville, 27 April-4 July 1993.

"Salvador Dalí: The Early Years," Hayward Gallery (South Bank Centre), London, 3 March-30 May 1994; The Metropolitan Museum of Art, New York, 28 June-18 September 1994; "Dalí joven (1918-1930)," Museo Nacional Centro de Arte Reina Sofia, Madrid, 18 October 1994-16 January 1995; Palau Robert, Barcelona, 15 February-9 April 1995.

"El Siglo de Dalí," Sala de exposiciones de "San Eloy," Salamanca, 30 October 1995-31 December 1995.

"Dalí Arquitectura," La Pedrera, Barcelona (19 June-25 August 1996).

"Salvador Dalí. Antòlgia sobre paper, 1916-1980," Museu de Cadaqués, Cadaqués, 1 July 1996-31 October 1996.

"Treasures from the Salvador Dalí Museum," Fort Lauderdale Museum, Fort Lauderdale (Florida), 25 January-6 April 1997.

"Salvador Dalí. La vita e sogno," Palazzo Bricherasio, Turin, November 1996-March 1997.

"Dalí Monumental," Museu Nacional de Belas Artes, Rio de Janeiro, 23 March-20 May 1998; Museu de Arte de São Paolo, São Paolo, 8 June-1 August 1998.

"Dalí," The Andy Warhol Museum, Pittsburgh, 20 June-20 September 1998.

"Salvador Dalí: A Mythology," Tate Gallery Liverpool, Liverpool, 24 October 1998-31 January 1999; Salvador Dalí Museum, St. Petersburg, 5 March-24 May 1999.

"Salvador Dalí. Àlbum de família," Teatre-Museu Dalí, Figueres, 1 December 1998-6 January 1999; Sala Tarragona Fundació "La Caixa," Tarragona, 20 January – 28 February 1999; Cultural centre of the Fundació Caixa, Lleida, 16 March-18 April 1999; Casa Lys, Salamanca, 27 April-30 May 1999; Cultural centre of the Fundación Caixa, Granollers, 8 June–4 July 1999; Sala Pescadería Vieja, Jerez, 20 October – 20 November 1999.

"The Universe of Salvador Dalí," Yamanashi Prefectural Museum, Kofu (Japan), 24 April–30 May 1999; Marugame Genichiro-Inokuma museum of Contemporary Art, Marugame, 5 June–11 July 1999; Matsuzakaya Museum of Art, Nagoya, 15 July–17 August 1999; Museum of Art, Kintetsu, Osaka, 19 August–15 September 1999; Isetan Museum of Art, Tokyo, 23 September–1 November 1999; Hiroshima Prefectural Museum of Art, Hiroshima, 6 November–12 December 1999.

"Treasures from the Dalí Museum," Mitsukoshi Museum of Art, 12 June-20 August 1999; Fukuoka Asian Art Museum, Fukuoka, 28 August-24 October 1999.

"25th Anniversary Exhibition," Fundació Gala-Salvador Dalí, Figueres, 15 November 1999-15 March 2000.

"Salvador Dalí: Dream of Venus," Teatre-Museu Dalí, Figueres, 20 December 1999-28 February 2000; Museum of Contemporary Art, North Miami, 14 March-30 June 2002.

"Dalí's Optical Illusions," Wadsworth Anthenaeum Museum of Art, Hartford (Connecticut), 21 January-26 March 2000; Hirshhorn Museum and Sculpture Garden, Washington, D.C., 20 April – 25 June 2000; Scottish National Gallery of Modern Art, Edinburgh, 23 July-1 October 2000.

"Original Works by Salvador Dalí," National Fine Arts Gallery, Beijing, 9-27 June 2000.

"Salvador Dalí: Images of a creator," Gala-Dalí Castle Museum-House, Púbol, November 2000.

"Salvador Dalí, a Genius of the XXth Century," National Palace Museum, Taipei (Taiwan), 20 January-20 April 2001; Shanghai Art Museum, Shanghai, 11 May-31 May 2001.

"Dalí il·lustrador: Salvador Dalí, 1904-1989," Govern d'Andorra, Andorra,

2 March-20 May 2001.

"The Performing Arts World and Salvador Dalí," Gala-Dalí Castle Museum-House, Púbol, 15 March-1 November 2001.

"Dalí och fantasins kraft [Dalí and the Force of Imagination]," Nordic Watercolour Museum, Skärhamn (Sweden), 12 May-2 September 2001.

"Dalí, imatges invisibles," Cadaqués Museum, Cadaqués, 30 June-1 November 2001.

"Dalí en las colecciones españolas," Museo de arte contemporáneo Esteban Vicente, Segovia, 9 October 2001-6 January 2002.

"Dalí & Gaudí. The Revolution of the Sentiment of Originality," Gala-Dalí Castle Museum-House, Púbol, 15 March-1 November 2002.

"Dalí in Focus: Gradiva," Museo Thyssen-Bornemisza, Madrid, 21 May-8 September 2002; Salvador Dalí Museum, St. Petersburg, 2 November 2002-19 January 2003.

"Dalí and Cadaqués: Light, Colour and Life," Museu de Cadaqués, Cadaqués, 22 June-4 November 2002.

"Salvador Dalí's Surrealist World," Kalamazoo Institute of Arts Museum, Kalamazoo (Michigan), 5 July-1 September 2002.

"Salvador Dalí: Singularity and Myth," N.P. Goulandris Foundation – Museum of Cycladic Art, Athens, 23 October 2002-23 January 2003.

"Dalí and Miró, circa 1928," Salvador Dalí Museum, St. Petersburg, Florida, 1 February 2003-4 May 2003.

"The Endless Enigma: Dalí and the Magicians of Multiple Meaning," Museum Kunst Palast, Düsseldorf, 22 February-9 June 2003.

"Dalí Grafista," Gala-Dalí Castle Museum-House, Púbol, 19 March–1 November 2003.

"Os Dalís de Dalí," Sala Fundación Caixa Galicia, A Coruña (Galicia), 3 April-4 May 2003; Sala de exposiciones Fundación Caixa Galica, Santiago de Compostela, 9 May-8 June 2003; Sala de exposiciones "Casa das Artes," Vigo (13 June-13 July 2003).

"Dalí: un creador ligado a su tiempo," Fundación Marcelino Botín, Santander, 26 July-14 September 2003.

"Dalí. Mass Culture," Caixa Forum, Barcelona, 5 February-23 May 2004; Museo Nacional Centro de Arte Reina Sofia, Madrid, 15 June-30 August 2004; Salvador Dalí Museum, St. Petersburg, Florida, 1 October 2004-31 January 2005; Museum Boijmans

Van Beuningen, Rotterdam, 5 March-12 June 2005.

"Dalí. Elective Affinities," Palau Moja, Barcelona, 19 February-18 April 2004.

"La Navidad Según Dalí, 1958-1976," Real Academia de Bellas Artes de San Fernando, Madrid, 15 March-15 April 2004.

"Don Quixote de la Mancha," Casa-Museu Castell Gala Dalí, Púbol, 15 March-31 December 2004.

"Dalí & Gaudí. The Revolution of the Sentiment of Originality," Barcelona: Fundació Caixa de Catalunya, 8 April-16 May 2004.

"El país de Dalí," Museu de l'Empordà, Figueres, 1 May-31 August 2004; Museu d'Història de Catalunya, Barcelona, 3 November 2004-16 January 2005.

"Dalí desconegut. Olis, aquarelles, dibuixos i apunts," Museu de Cadaqués, Cadaqués, 24 June-2 November 2004.

"Dalí i les illusions òptiques," Museu del Cinema, Girona, 14 June-12 September 2004.

Bibliography

Elliott H. King

Writings by Salvador Dalí

"Los grandes maestros de la pintura: Goya," *Studium* (Figueres) no.1, 1 January 1919, p. 1.

"Los grandes maestros de la pintura: El Greco," *Studium* (Figueres) no. 2, 1 February 1919, p. 3.

"Capvespre," *Studium* (Figueres) no. 2, 1 February 1919, p. 5.

"Los grandes maestros de la pintura: Durero," *Studium* (Figueres) no. 3, 1 March 1919.

"Los grandes maestros de la pintura: Leonardo da Vinci," *Studium* (Figueres) no. 4, 1 April 1919, p. 3.

"Los grandes maestros de la pintura: Miguel Angel," *Studium* (Figueres) no. 5, 1 May 1919, p. 3.

"Los grandes maestros de la pintura: Velázquez," *Studium* (Figueres) no. 6, 1 June 1919, p. 3.

"Divagacions. Cuan els sorolls s'adorman," *Studium* (Figueres) no. 6, 1 June 1919.

Un diari, 1919-1920: Les meves impressions i records intims. In Fèlix Fanés (ed). *Un diari: 1919-1920. Les meves impressions i records intims* (Barcelona: Fundació Gala-Salvador Dalí, Edicions 62, 1994); *A Dalí Journal. 1920.* Translation by Joaquim Cortada i Perez of Book 6 of Dalí's diary, *Impressions and Private Memoirs.* (Cleveland: Stratford Press for the Reynolds Morse Foundation, 1962).

Dalí, Salvador (under pseudonym, Jak), "De la Rússia dels Soviets. Un museu de pintura impressionista a Moscou," *Renovació Social* (Figueres) any I, no. 1, 26 December 1921.

"Tardes d'estiu" [sixteen-page fragment of novel] (c. 1921-1922). In *Cave Canis*, no. 3 (Barcelona: Victor Fernandez, 1996).

"Ninots. Ensatjos sobre pintura. Catalec dels cuadros em rotes," In *Salvador Dalí, lletres i ninots: fons Dalí del Museu Abelló* (Mollet del Vallès: Museu Abelló, Fundació Municipal d'Art, 2001).

"Skeets [sic] arbitraris. De la fira," *Empordà Federal* (Figueres) any XIII, no. 646, 26 May 1923, p. 2.

"El Poeta en la platja d'Empuries vist per...," *La*, any II, no 15, 31 June 1927, p. 45.

"Sant Sabastià, a F. García Lorca," *L'Amic de les Arts* (Sitges) any II, no 16, 31 July 1927, pp. 52-54; *Gallo* (Grenade) no. 1, February 1928, pp. 9-12.

"Reflexions. El sentit comú d'un germá de Sant Joan Baptista de la Salle,"

L'Amic de les Arts (Sitges) any II, no. 17, 31 August 1927, p. 69.

"Federico García Lorca, exposició de debuixos colorits," *Nova Revista,* vol. III, no. 9, September 1927, pp. 84-85.

"La Fotografia, pura creació de l'esperit," *L'Amic de les Arts* (Sitges) any II, no. 18, 30 September 1927, pp. 90-91.

"Els meus quadros del Saló de Tardor," *L'Amic de les Arts* (Sitges) any II, supplement to no. 19, 31 October 1927.

"Temes actuals. Dretes i esquerres," *L'Amic de les Arts* (Sitges) any II, no. 19, 31 October 1927, pp. 98-99.

"Dues proses. Le meva amiga i la platja. Nadal a Brusselles (conte antic)," *L'Amic de les Arts* (Sitges) any II, no. 20, 30 November 1927, p. 104.

"Film-arte, film-antiartístico," *Gaceta Literaria* (Madrid) any I, no. 24, 15 December 1927, p. 4.

"Poema: a la Lydia de Cadaqués," *Gaceta Literaria* (Madrid) any II, no. 28, 15 February 1928, p. 5.

"(Se necesita más...)," cited in Miguel Pérez Ferrero, "Las ciudades y las almas," *Gaceta Literaria* (Madrid) any II, no. 25, 1 February 1928, p. 3.

"Nous límits de la pintura - part I," *L'Amic de les Arts* (Sitges) any III, no. 22, 29 February 1928, pp. 167-169.

Dalí, Salvador with Lluis Montanya and Sebastia Gasch, "Cinema," *L'Amic de les Arts* (Sitges) any III, no. 23, 31 March 1928, p. 175.

"Poesia de l'útil standarditzat," *L'Amic de les Arts* (Sitges) any III, no 23, 31 March 1928, pp. 176-177.

Dalí, Salvador with Lluis Montanya and Sebastia Gasch, "Manifest Groc," *Imo Fills de F. Sabader* (Barcelona) March 1928; *La* (Barcelona) March 1928; *Gallo* (Grenade) no. 2, April 1928; "L'Anunci comercial publicat propaganda," *L'Amic de les Arts* (Sitges) any III, no. 24, 30 April 1928, p. 184; (Barcelona: *Impr. Leteradura,* 1977).

"Nous límits de la pintura - part II," *L'Amic de les Arts* (Sitges) any III, no. 24, 30 April 1928, pp. 185-186.

"Nous límits de la pintura - part III," *L'Amic de les Arts* (Sitges) any III, no. 25, 31 May 1928, pp. 195-196.

"Per al 'meeting de Sitges'," *L'Amic de les Arts* (Sitges) any III, no. 25, 31 May 1928, pp. 194-195.

"Joan Miró," *L'Amic de les Arts* (Sitges) any III, no. 26, 31 July 1928, p. 202.

"El Decàleg d'en Dalí," *La Veu de l'Empordà* (Figueres) 30 June 1928.

"Art català relacionat amb el més recent de la jove intelligència," *La Re-*

vista (Barcelona) any XIV, July-December 1928, pp. 111-117.

"Poema de les cosetes," *L'Amic de les Arts* (Sitges) any III, no. 27, 31 August 1928, p. 211.

"Peix perseguit per un raim," *L'Amic de les Arts* (Sitges) any III, no. 28, 31 September 1928, pp. 217-218.

"Realidad y sobrerealidad," *Gaceta Literaria* (Madrid) any II, no. 44, 15 October 1928, p. 7.

"M'interessa fer constar..." *La Publicitat* (Barcelona), 24 October 1928.

"Butlleti: de les conferencies al 'Salo de Tardor'," *L'Amic de les Arts* (Sitges) any III, no. 29, 31 October 1928, p. 223.

"...Què he renegat, pot-ser?...," *L'Amic de les Arts* (Sitges) any III, no. 30, 31 December 1928, p. 233; "¿Qué he blasfemado, quizá?...," *Gaceta Literaria* (Madrid) any III, no. 50, 15 January 1929, p. 3

"La dada fotogràfica', *La Gaseta de les Arts* (Barcelona) any II, no 6, February 1929, pp. 40-42

"(Carta dirigida a Sebastià Gasch', *La Veu de Catalunya* (Barcelona) 7 March 1929.

Dalí, Salvador, "Con el sol," *Gaceta Literaria* (Madrid) no. 54, 15 March 1929.

Dalí, Salvador, "En el moment...," *L'Amic de les Arts* (Sitges) any IV, no. 31, 31 March 1929, p. 1.

"...Sempre, per damunt de la música, Harry Langdon," *L'Amic de les Arts* (Sitges) any IV, no. 31, 31 March 1929, p. 3.

"¿Per què en anar...," *L'Amic de les Arts* (Sitges) any IV, no. 31, 31 March 1929, pp. 5, 12-13.

"...L'Alliberament dels dits...," *L'Amic de les Arts* (Sitges) any IV, no. 31, 31 March 1929, pp. 6-7.

Dalí, Salvador with Sebastià Gasch, Lluís Montanyà, "Oposem Benjamin Péret..." *L'Amic de les Arts* (Sitges) any IV, no. 31, 31 March 1929, p. 8.

"Revista de tendències anti-artístiques," *L'Amic de les Arts* (Sitges) any IV, no. 31, 31 March 1929, p. 10.

Dalí, Salvador, "...Un jove," *L'Amic de les Arts* (Sitges) any IV, no. 31, 31 March 1929, pp. 13-14.

Dalí, Salvador with Sebastià Gasch, Lluís Montanyà, "El cadàver insepult... arriba a la perfecte correció (educació)," *L'Amic de les Arts* (Sitges) any IV, no. 31, 31 March 1929, p. 15.

Dalí, Salvador, "Luis Buñuel (entrevista)," *L'Amic de les Arts* (Sitges) any IV, no. 31, 31 March 1929, p. 16.

Dalí, Salvador, "...UNA PLUMA,"

Gaceta Literaria (Madrid) any III, no. 56, 15 April 1929, p. 4.

"Documentaire - Paris - 1929 - part I," *La Publicitat* (Barcelona) 26 April 1929, p. 1.

"Documentaire - Paris - 1929 - part II," *La Publicitat* (Barcelona) 28 April 1929, p. 1.

"Documentaire - Paris - 1929 - part III," *La Publicitat* (Barcelona) 7 May 1929, p. 1.

"Documentaire - Paris - 1929 - part IV," *La Publicitat* (Barcelona) 23 May 1929, p. 1.

"Documentaire - Paris - 1929 - part V," *La Publicitat* (Barcelona) 7 June 1929, p. 1.

"Documentaire - Paris - 1929 - part VI," *La Publicitat* (Barcelona) 26 June 1929, p. 1.

"No veo nada, nada en torno del paisaje. Poema," *La Gaceta Literaria* (Madrid), no. 61, 1 July 1929, p. 6.

"Un Chien Andalou," *Mirador* (Barcelona) no. 39, 24 October 1929, p. 6.

Dalí, Salvador with Luis Buñuel, "Scenario de 'Un Chien Andalou'," *La Revue du Cinéma* (Paris) no. 5, 15 November 1929, pp. 2-16; *La Révolution surréaliste* (Paris) no. 12, 15 December 1929, pp. 34-37; "An Andalusian Dog," *This Quarter* (Paris) vol. V, no. 1, September 1932, pp. 149-157.

La Femme visible. (Paris: Éditions surréalistes, 1930).

"Scenario for a Documentary on Surrealism" (c. 1930). Published by Dawn Ades, "Unpublished Scenario for a Documentary on Surrealism (1930?)', *Studio International* (London), vol. 195, nos. 93-94, 1982, pp. 62-77

"Posició moral del surrealisme," *Hélix* (Villafranca del Penedès) no. 10, March 1930, pp. 4-6.

"Documental," *Butlletí de l'Agrupament Escolar de l'Acadèmia i Laboratori de Ciències Mèdiques de Catalunya,* no 7-8. July-September 1930.

"L'Ane pourri, à Gala Eluard," *Le Surréalisme au Service de la Révolution* (Paris) no. 1, July 1930, pp. 9-12; "The Stinking Ass," *This Quarter* (Paris) vol. V, no. 1, September 1932, pp. 49-54.

"Intellectuels castillans et catalans, Expositions Arrestation d'un exhibitioniste dans le métro," *Le Surréalisme au Service de la Révolution* (Paris) no. 2, October 1930, pp. 7-9.

L'Amour et la memoire. (Paris: Éditions surréalistes, 1931).

"El surrealisme al servei de la revolució," Conference given at the Sala Capcir de Barcelona, 18 September 1931. Published by Fèlix Fanés, *Salvador Dalí. La construcción de la imagen, 1925-1930* (Madrid: Electa, 1999), 253-254.

"Objets surréalistes," *Le Surréalisme au Service de la Révolution* (Paris) no. 3, December 1931, pp. 16-17.

"Communication, Visage paranoiaque," *Le Surréalisme au Service de la Révolution* (Paris) no. 3, December 1931, p. 40.

"Rêverie," *Le Surrealisme au Service de la Revolution* (Paris) no. 4, December 1931, pp. 31-36.

"…Surtout, l'art ornemental…" (Paris: Galerie Pierre Colle) 3-15 June 1931.

Dalí, Salvador with Luis Buñuel, "L'Age d'or," *Studio 28, revue-programme* (Paris: Jose Corti) 1931.

"Notes pour l'interpretation du tableau "la Persistance de la memoire'," *Documentation des collections* (New York: Museum of Modern Art) 1931.

Dalí, Salvador with René Crevel, "Per un Tribunal terrorista de responsabilitats intelectuals," *La Hora* (Barcelona) 1931.

"Vive le surréalisme! Roman surréaliste," *Nadrealizam danas o ovde* (Belgrade) any II, no. 3, June, 1932, pp. 43-52.

"Réponse" to the enquiry on desire. *Nadrealizam danas o ovde* (Belgrade) any II, no. 3, June 1932, p. 31

"Babaouo: scénario inédit précédé d'un abrégé d'une histoire critique du cinéma et suivi de Guillaume Tell, ballet portugais" (Paris: Éditions des Cahiers libres, 1932); (Barcelona: Las Ediciones liberales, 1978).

"Binding cradled - cradle bound," *This Quarter* (Paris) vol. V, no. 1, September 1932, pp. 47-48.

"Luis Buñuel & Salvador Dalí," *This Quarter* (Paris) vol. V, no. 1, September 1932, pp. 149-157.

"The object as revealed in surrealist experiment," *This Quarter* (Paris) vol. V, no. 1, September 1932, pp. 197-207.

"Una carta," *Mirador* (Barcelona) 30 March 1933.

"Reponse à l'enquete 'Recherches experimentalles, sur la connaissance irrationnelle de l'objet: Boulde de cristal des voyantes'," *Le Surréalisme au Service de la Révolution* (Paris) no. 5, 15 May 1933, pp. 10-11.

"Objets psycho-atmosphériquesana morphiques," *Le Surréalisme au Service de la Révolution* (Paris) no. 5, 15 May 1933, pp. 45-48.

"Notes, Communications: I. Les Faux météores du Museum d'histoire naturelle sont 'aussi' des phénomènes paranoiaques, II. L'Actualité surréaliste des anamorphes coniques, III. Raymond Roussel. –Nouvelles impressions d'Afrique," *Le Surréalisme au Service de la Révolution* (Paris) no. 5, 15 May 1933, pp. 40-41.

"Interprétation paranoïaque-critique de l'image obsédante 'L'Angélus' de Millet," *Minotaure* (Paris) no. 1, 1 June 1933, pp. 65-67.

"Cher Breton," (Paris: Galerie Pierre Colle) 19-29 June 1933.

"…This exhibition of my paintings…" (New York: Julien Levy) 21 November-8 December 1933.

Dalí, Salvador, "Si je dois m'exprimer brièvement sur les questions de 'modèle'…," *Minotaure* (Paris) nos. 3-4, December 1933, pp. 18-20.

"De la beauté terrifiante det comestible de l'architecture modern style," *Minotaure* (Paris) nos. 3-4, December 1933, pp. 69-76.

"Le Phénomène de l'extase," *Minotaure* (Paris) nos. 3-4, 12 December 1933, pp. 76-77.

"Les nouvelles couleurs du sex appeal spectral," *Minotaure* (Paris) no. 5, May 1934, pp. 20-22; "den spektrale sexappeals nye farver," *Linien* (Copenhague) no. 5, 15 September 1934, pp. 7-8.

"Derniers modes d'excitation intellectuelle pour l'été," *Documents 34, no. special Intervention surréaliste* (Paris) new series no. 1, June 1934, pp. 33-35.

Dalí, Salvador, " L'Angélus de Millet/ invitation de l'exposition 'Salvador Dalí, Les Chants de Maldoror'," (Paris: Quatre Chemins) 13-25 June 1934; *The New* Hope, vol. II, no. 4, August 1934, pp. 10-21.

"Misteri surrealista i fenomenal de la tauleta de nit," Presented at the Galeries d'Art Catalonia (Barcelona) 5 October 1934. Published by Félix Fanès, *Salvador Dalí: La construcción de la imagen, 1925-1930* (Madrid: Electa, 1999), 261-263.

"Surrealism," Text read at a press conference in 1934. Published by Julien Levy, *Surrealism* (New York: Black Sun Press, 1936).

"New York Salutes Me," (New York) November 1934.

"El Surrealismo," *Revista Hispanica Moderna* I, 1934-1935, pp. 233-234.

"Poema: agafat al vol, no taquigràficament," *Art: Revista internacional de les arts* (Lleida) no. 10, 1934.

"Apparitions aérodynamiques des 'Êtres-objets'," *Minotaure* (Paris) no. 6, winter 1934, pp. 33-34.

"Written by a Madman – Illustrated by a 'Super-Realist'," *American Weekly* (New York) 16 December 1934.

"New York as seen by the Super-Realist Artist M. Dalí," *American Weekly* (New York) 24 February 1935.

"How Super-Realist Dalí Saw Broadway," *American Weekly* (New York) 17 March 1935.

"The American City Night and Day by M. Dalí," *American Weekly* (New York) 31 March 1935.

"Gangsterism and Goofy Visions of New York," *American Weekly* (New York) 19 May 1935.

"Psychologie non-euclidienne d'une photographie," *Minotaure* (Paris) no.7, 10 June 1935, pp. 56-57.

"Crazy Movie Scenario by M. Dalí, the Super-Realist," *American Weekly* (New York) 7 July 1935.

La Conquête de l'Irrationnel. (Paris: Éditions surréalistes) 1935; *Conquest of the Irrational*. (New York: Julien Levy) 1935; *Die Eroberung des Irrationalen* (Franckfurt: Verlag Ullstein, 1973).

"Iportància filosòfica dels rellotge tous," Published by Félix Fanès, *Salvador Dalí. La construcción de la imagen, 1925-1930* (Madrid: Electa, 1999), 264-265.

"Les Eaux où nous nageons," *Cahiers d'art* (Paris) nos. 5-6, 1935, pp. 123.

"Les Pantoufles de Picasso," *Cahiers d'art* (Paris) nos. 7-10, 1935, pp. 208-212.

"Salvador Dalí, té el gust d'invitar…," *Cahiers d'art* (Paris) nos. 7-10, 1935, p. 244.

"Analyse de 'L'Escalier de l'Amour et Psyche' invente par Gala," *Cahiers d'art* (Paris) any XI, nos. 1-2, 1936, p. 37.

"Analyse du veston aphrodesiaque de Salvador Dalí," *Cahiers d'art* (Paris) any XI, nos. 1-2, 1936, p. 57.

"Honneur à l'objet," *Cahiers d'art* (Paris) any XI, nos. 1-2, 1936, pp. 53-57.

"Cradled Pamphlet," *Contemporary Poetry and Prose* (London) no. 2, June 1936, p. 29.

"Le Surréalisme spectral de l'eternel féminin préraphaélite," *Minotaure* (Paris) no. 8, 15 June 1936, pp. 46-49.

"Mine befoestede stillinger," *Konkretion* (Copenhague, Oslo, Stockholm) numero special, nos. 5-6, March 1936, pp. 136-141; *xxe siecle* (Paris) no. 43, December 1974, pp. 93-95.

"Picasso's Kunst," *Konkretion* (Copenhague, Oslo, Stockholm) numero special, nos. 5-6, March 1936, pp. 158-162; "The Art of Picasso," *Contemporary Poetry and Prose* [London], nos. 4-5, August-September 1936.

"Première loi morphologique sur les poils dans les structures molles," *Minotaure* (Paris) no. 9, 15 October 1936, pp. 60-61.

"Le Sommeil, 1937," Pierre Mabille, "La conscience lumineuse," *Minotaure* (Paris) any IV, no. 10, winter 1937, pp. 22-35.

"I Defy Aragon," *Art Front* (New York) vol. III, no. 2, March 1937, pp. 7-8.

"Surrealism in Hollywood," *Harper's Bazaar* (New York) June 1937, p. 68.

Métamorphose de Narcisse. (Paris: Éditions surréalistes, 1937); *Metamorphosis of Narcissus*. (New York: Julien Levy Gallery, 1937).

Dalí, Salvador with André Breton and Paul Eluard. *Dictionnaire abregé du surréalisme*. (Paris: Galerie des Beaux-Arts, 1938).

"Prophesy on Jewels," *Vogue* (New York) 1 January 1939, pp. 56-57.

Dalí, Salvador, "Reponse a une enquete sur la poesie," *Cahiers GLM* (Paris) no. 9, March 1939.

"Geological foundations of Venusburg," *Metropolitan Opera House Program* (New York:) 9 April 1939.

"Dalí! Dalí!" (New York: Julien Levy Gallery, 21 March-18 April 1939).

"Declaration of the Independence of the Imagination and the Rights of a Man to his Own Madness," *Art Digest* (New York) vol. 13, no. 19, 1 August 1939, p. 9.

"Les Idées lumineuses, 'Nous ne mangeons pas de cette lumière-là'," *L'Usage de la parole* (Paris) any I, no. 2, February 1940; *Cahiers d'art* (Paris) any 15, nos. 1-2, 1940, pp. 24-25.

"New York Salutes Me', 23 May 1941.

"Dalí's dream of jewels," *Vogue* (New York) 17 July 1941, p. 32.

Dalí, Salvador (under the pseudonym, Felipe Jacinto), "The last scandal of Salvador Dalí," (New York: Julien Levy Gallery, 22 April-20 May 1941).

The Secret Life of Salvador Dalí. (New York: Dial Press, 1942); *Vida secreta de Salvador Dalí*. (Buenos Aires: Poseidon, 1944); (London: Vision Press, 1948); *Vita segreta di Salvador Dalí* (Milan: Longanesi, 1949); *La Vie* secrete de Salvador Dalí (Paris: La Table Ronde, 1952); "The Secret Life of Salvador Dalí, new enlarged edition," (New York: Dial Press, 1961); Zelfportret (Amsterdam: De Arbeiderspers, 1970); (Paris: Gallimard, Collection Idées, 1979).

"Total camouflage for total war," Esquire (New York) vol. 18, no. 2, August 1942, pp. 64-66, 129-130.

Hidden Faces. (New York: Dial Press, 1944); (London: Nicholson and Watson, 1947); Rostros ocultos (Barcelona: L. de Caralt, colección gigante, 1952); Hidden Faces (London: Peter Owen, 1973); Visages cachés (Paris: Stock, 1973); (New York: Marrow, 1974); Rostros ocultos, (Barcelona: Planeta, 1974).

"(I cannot understand…)," Atlantic Monthly (Concord) June 1943.

"Dalí to the reader" (New York: M. Knoedler and Co., 1943), pp. 1-5.

"Nightmare journey," Life (New York) 6 March 1944.

"Dalí News, monarch of the dailies" (New York) vol. I, no. 1, 20 November 1945.

"Foreword," Recent paintings by Salvador Dalí (New York: Bignou Gallery, 20 November -29 December 1945).

"Gelantinous space time," Life (New York) 15 October 1945, p. 10.

"Painting after the tempest," Harper's Bazaar (New York) vol. 80, no. 2, February 1946, pp. 128-129.

"Dalí News, monarch of the dailies," (New York) vol. I, no. 2, 25 November 1947.

"Dalí Dalí Dalí" (New York: Bignou Gallery, 27 November 1947-3 January 1948).

"Appendix. History of Art, Short but Clear," (New York: Bignou Gallery, 27 November 1947-3 January 1948).

"Bonjour," In William Shakespeare, Como vi piace (Rome: Bestetti, Collezione dell'Obelisco, 1948).

Fifty Secrets of magic craftsmanship. (New York: Dial Press, 1948); Cincuenta secretos "magicos" para pintar. (Barcelona: L. de Caralt, 1951); Dalí: cinquante secrets magiques (Lausanne: Edita, 1974).

"Mr. Dalí's motor car," Tribune (Minneapolis), 14 August 1949.

"Memorandum" (New York) January 1950.

"To Spain guided by Dalí," Vogue (New York) 15 May 1950, pp. 54-57, 91.

"The Decadence of modern art," Washington Times Herald (Washington) 20 May 1950; The American Weekly, 20 August 1950, pp. 16-17, 19.

"The Port-Lligat Madonna…" (New York: Carstairs Gallery, 17 November 1950-10 January 1951).

"Genio y figura de la pintura española," El Alma de España, 1951.

"De l'art moderne". Beaux-Arts (Brussels) no. 538, 15 June 1951, pp. 1, 8.

"Epilogue," Opéra (Paris) any 8, no. 302, 25 April 1951.

"Picasso y Yo', lecture given in the María Guerrero Theatre, Madrid, 11 Nov. 1951," Mundo Hispanico (Madrid) no. 46, 1952, pp. 37-42; Fiera Letteraria (Rome) 24 February 1952.

"Genio y figura de la pintura española," in D. Manuel Herrara Oria, El Alma de España (Madrid) 1951, pp. 55-57.

Manifeste Mystique. (Paris: Robert J. Godet) 1951; Manifesto místico [extracts] (Port Lligat: Ediciones extraordinarias del Empordanés, 1951); Mizue (Tokyo) no. 697, March 1963.

"Salvador Dalí raconte comment il recevait Alphonse XII" [fragment from The Secret Life of Salvador Dalí]. Ce matin (Paris) 8 February 1952.

"C'est au métaphysicien…," Études Carmelitaines (Paris) 1952, p. 62.

"Reconstitution du corps glorieux dans le ciel…," Études Carmélitaines (Paris) 1952, pp. 171-172.

"Authenticité et mensonge," Arts (Paris) no. 357, 1-7 May 1952.

"Credo," Liturgical Arts (New York) vol. 20, no. 3, May 1952, p. 75.

"Je suis un pervers polymorphe," Arts (Paris) no. 361, 29 May 1952.

"Aristocratie et béquilles," Le Courrier des letters (Paris) May 1952.

"Le Mythe de Guillaume Tell, Toute la vérité sur mon expulsion du groupe surréaliste," University of Texas, 9 June 1952; La Table Ronde (Paris) no. 55, July 1952, pp. 21-38; "The Myth of William Tell (The Whole Truth about my Expulsion from the Surrealist Group)", printed in English in The Tragic Myth of Millet's Angelus (St. Petersburg: Salvador Dalí Museum, 1986).

"A Letter from Salvador Dalí," Scottish Art Review (Glasgow) vol. IV, no. 1, 1952, p. 5.

"Vivre l'art moderne à condition de peindre à partir de Raphael', (New York: Carstairs Gallery, 8 December 1952-31 January 1953); [fragment] Asunción Corpuscularina (Elche: Festa d'Elig, August 1953), pp. 44-45.

"Dalí escribe sobre Lorca" [fragment from The Secret Life of Salvador Dalí]. Visión (New York) 17 April 1953, pp. 30-31.

"Salvador Dalí explique sa propre peinture," Connaissance des Arts (Paris) 15 July 1953.

"Salvador Dalí's mimicry in nature," Flair Annual, 1953.

"Notes a propos de l'Asumpta Corpuscularia Lapislazulina," Connaissance des Arts (Paris), 1953.

Dalí, Salvador with Philippe Halsman. Dalí's Mustache. (New York: Simon and Schuster, 1954); Dalí's Schnurrbart, Antenn zum Diesseits. (Frankfurt: Barmeier und Nikel, 1962).

"La Morte di Garcia Lorca," Popolo, 2nd semester, 1954.

"Le Club Francais du Livre', 1954.

"Mes Secrets cinématographiques," La Parisienne (Paris) February 1954, pp. 165-168.

"El día en que Goethe…" Published by Manuel del Arco, "Salvador Dalí visto por Del Arco," Revista, 27 May 1954, p. 11.

"Martyr. Tragedie lyrique en III actes" (c. 1954). Published by Ignacio Gomez de Liano, El Paseante (Madrid) no 5, 1987.

"Les Morts et moi," La Parisienne (Paris) no. 17, May 1954; "I Morti i Io," Borghese, no. 44, November 1956, p. 700.

"Fragmentos de Journal d'un génie," Arts (Paris) 24 November 1954.

"(Jo soc divinament…)," epilogue to Carles Fages de Climent, Balada del Sabater d'Ordis (Barcelona: Pérgamo, 1954).

"Report on my Italian campaign" (New York: Carstairs Gallery, 1954-1955).

"Corpus Hipercubus," Time (Chicago) vol. 65, no. 6, 7 February 1955, p. 2.

"Who is the world's most beautiful woman?" This Week Magazine (New York) 6 March 1955.

"The Dalí crucifixion," Jubilee (New York) vol. 2, no. 12, April 1955.

"Comments on the making of "Un Chien Andalou" and 'L'age d'or'," Cinemages, vol. I, no. I, 1955, pp. 26, 29.

"Aspects phénoménologiques de la méthode paranoïaique critique," La Vie Médicale (Paris) special edition of Art and Psychopathology, 1956, pp. 78-83; Nombre d'Or (Paris) nos. 22, 23, 24 (1956); Nombre d'Or (Paris) nos. 25, 37 (1956); Nombre d'Or (Paris) nos. 39-43, January 1957.

"I believe that…" Amazing Stories (New York) vol. 30, no. 4, April 1956, p. 246.

Presentation on Gaudí at Park Güell (Barcelona), 29 September 1956. Published by Dalí-Gaudí: La revolución del sentimiento de velocidad (Barcelona: Fundació Caixa de Catalunya, 2004).

"Dalí dreams. Breasts in the back!" News (Harrisburg) 30 September 1956.

"A Dalí prediction," Post (Houston) 30 September 1956.

"Cadaqués. El poble més bonic del món," Canigo (Figueres) any III, no. 31, September 1956, p. 3.

"Dalí dreams. The Anthropomorphic Couch," News (Harrisburg) 4 November 1956.

"Dalí predicts the future," Tribune (Minneapolis) 11 November 1956; Tribune (Minneapolis) 18 November 1956; Tribune (Minneapolis) 25 November 1956; Tribune (Minneapolis) 2 December 1956; "Salvador Dalí predicts," Nugget (New York) vol. 2, no. 2, 27 March 1957, pp. 27-28; Nugget (New York) vol. I, no. 9, April 1957, pp. 21-25; Nugget (New York) vol. 2, no. 4, May 1957, pp. 53-57.

Les Cocus du vieil art moderne. (Paris: Fasquelle, 1956); Dalí on modern art: the Cuckolds of antiquated modern art. (New York: Dial Press, 1957); (Tokyo: Kinokuniya, 1958).

"Metamorfosis de San Narciso," Canigo (Figueres) any IV, no. 42, August 1957.

"(Mon cher des rois mages…)," Sud Ouest (Bordeaux) 25 December 1957.

"Histoire d'un grand livre "Don Quichotte" illustre par Dalí," (Paris: Joseph Foret, 1957).

"The Face of courage," This Week Magazine (New York) 20 October 1957, p. 30.

"Santiago El Grande" (New York: M. Knoedler, 19 February-8 March 1958).

"Explication paranoia-critique de l'Angélus de Millet," Imprimerie Crété (Seine-et-Oise) 13 March 1958.

"Dalí se confesse," Arts (Paris) no. 674, 11-17 June 1958.

"An excerpt from Babaouo," Cinemages (New York) 1 August 1958.

"Salvador Dalí vous parle de sa dernière découverte: l'oreille," Aux Écoutes du Monde (Paris) 26 December 1958.

"Anti-matter manifesto," (New York: Carstairs Gallery, 6 December 1958-January 1959).

"Comments on the jewels', in *Dalí, a study of his art in jewels* (New York: Owen Cheatham Foundation, 1959).

"Le Discours de Dalí que l'on n'a pas entendu au Bal des Petits Lits Blancs". *Arts* (Paris) no. 722, 13-19 May 1959, pp. 1, 5.

"The King and Queen traversed by swift nudes," *Art News* (New York) vol. 58, April 1959, pp. 22-25.

"Louis Aragon Dubreton," *La Nation Française* (Paris) 10 June 1959.

"Du point de vue phenomenologique," *Arts* (Paris) no. 753, 16-22 December, 1959.

"Cartier-Bresson moralities," *Art News* (New York) vol. 58, no. 10, February 1960, pp. 38-39.

"Consigli e misteri di Salvador Dalí," *Rinnovamento* (Milan) 1 June 1960.

"The construction of New York Museums', *Esquire* (Chicago) July 1960, pp. 98-100.

"Picasso by Dalí," *TV Times* (London) vol. 20, no. 249, 5 August 1960, pp. 6-7.

"La influencia de la onomástica sobre la pintura," *Canigó* (Figueres) any VII, no. 80, October 1960, p. 14.

"(Velázquez el genio pictórico…)," *O figura. Homenaje informal a Velázquez* (Barcelona: Sala Gaspar, October-November 1960).

"Le Divin Fromage," *100 Aquarelles pour la Divine Comedie de Dante Alighieri par Salvador Dalí* (Paris: Musee Galliera, 1960).

"Les Faits Saillants de la vie de Salvador Dalí qui ont marqué notre époch," *100 Aquarelles pour la Divine Comedie de Dante Alighieri par Salvador Dalí* (Paris: Musee Galliera, 1960).

"Foreword," (New York: Carstairs Gallery, December 1960-January 1961).

"The Secret Number of Velasquez Revealed," *Art News* (New York) vol. 59, no. 9, January 1961, p. 45.

"Ecumenical "chafarrinada" of Velasquez," *Art News* (New York) vol. 59, February 1961, pp. 30, 59.

"Carta abierta dirigida por Salvador Dalí a M. Janot, director general de la Radio-Televisión Francesca," *La Vanguardia* (Barcelona) 4 October 1961.

"The Price is Right," *Art News* (New York) vol. 61, no. 1, March 1962, pp. 44-45.

"Tàpies, Tàpies, classic, classic!," *Art News* (New York) vol. 61, no. 3, May 1962, pp. 41, 67.

"Picasso, Rusiñol y Dalí," *El Noticiero*

universal, Art* (Barcelona) 6 June 1962, p. 15.

"¿Era Rembrandt ciego? ¡Sí! Contesta Salvador Dalí," *Hablemos Magazine*, 1 July 1962, pp. 8-9.

"Fortuny Dalí y sus batallas de Tetuan" (Barcelona: Saló del Tinell, October 1962); *La Vanguardia* (Barcelona), 14 October 1962.

"Los Sabios y Dalí; Carta abierta a don Miguel Masriera," *La Vanguardia* (Barcelona), 13 December 1962.

Le Mythe tragique de l'Angélus de Millet, Interprétation "paranoiaïque-critique" (c. 1932) (Paris: Jean-Jacques Pauvert, 1963); *El Mito tragico del "Angelus de Millet* (Barcelona: Tusquets, 1978); *The Tragic Myth of Millet's Angelus* (St. Petersburg: Salvador Dalí Museum, 1986).

"¡Fortuny, sí! ¡Dalí, no!" *La Vanguardia* (Barcelona), 17 February 1963.

"Why they attack the Mona Lisa," *Art News* (New York) vol. 62, no. 1, March 1963, pp. 36, 63-64.

"A Manifesto," *Show* (New York) vol. III, no. 6, June 1963, p. 56.

"Dalí's notes on the Battle of Tetuán," *Show* (New York) vol. III, no. 6, June 1963, pp. 56, 91.

"(Commentaries on the works)" (New York: M. Knoedler & Co., Inc., 26 November-26 December 1963).

"Vive Dalí!" (Tokyo: Tokyo Prince Hotel Gallery, 8 September-10 October 1964).

"(interior of ESTACIÓN…)," published in Rafael Santos Torroella, *Evarist Vallès* (Barcelona: Ariel, 1964).

Journal d'un génie. (Paris: La Table Ronde, 1964); *Diaro de un genio.* (Barcelona: L.de Caralt, 1964); (Lisbonne: Editoria Ulisseia, 1965); (Turin: L'Alberto, 1965); *Diary of a Genius* (New York: Double-day, 1965); (London: Hutchinson, 1966); *Mijn leven als Genie* (Amsterdam: De Arbeiderspers, 1968); *Tagebuch eines Genies* (Munich: Kurt Desch, 1968); (Tokyo: Futami-Shobo, 1970); (Paris: Gallimard, Collection Idées, 1974); (London: Pan Books and Picador edition, 1976).

"Io Salvador Dalí" (Paris: La Table Ronde, 1964).

"L'Argent fait mon bonheur," *Arts* (Paris) no. 964, 27 May-2 June 1964.

"Les ordures sont toujours près du ciel," *Le Nouvel Observateur* (Paris) 18 August 1965, p. 24.

"Reponse a une enquete: Is America a dying country?" *Fact* (New York)

September-October 1965, pp. 61-62.

Lettre ouverte à Salvador Dalí. (Paris: Albin Michel, 1966); *Open Letter to Salvador Dalí.* (New York: J.H. Heineman, 1967).

"Résumé of history and of the history of painting" (New York: Gallery of Modern Art, 18 December 1965-28 Februarry 1966), pp. 13-15.

Dalí, Salvador with Alain Bosquet. *Entretiens avec Salvador Dalí* (Paris: Pierre Belfond, 1966); *Dalí desnudado* (Buenos Aires: Paidos, 1967); *Conversations with Dalí* (New York: Dutton, 1969).

"How an Elvis Presley becomes a Roy Lichtenstein," *Arts Magazine* (New York) vol. 41, no. 6, April 1967, pp. 26-31.

Manifeste en Hommage à Meissonier (Paris: Hotel Meurice, 1-30 November 1967).

"The incendiary fireman," *Arts News Annual* (New York) 1967, pp. 108-113.

Dalí, Salvador with Louis Pauwels. *Les Passions selon Dalí.* (Paris: Éditions DeNoël, 1968); *Meine Leidenshaften* (Zurich: Ferency Verlay, 1968); (Gütersloh: Betelsmann Sachbuch, 1968); *The Passions According to Dalí* (St. Petersburg: Salvador Dalí Museum, 1985); *Dalí m'a dit* (Paris: Ergo-Press/Carrere, 1989).

"Who is Surrealism?" *Vogue* (New York) 15 April 1968, p. 82; "¿Quien es el surrealismo?" Published in Max Gerard, *Dalí de Draeger* (Barcelona and Madrid: Blume, 1968).

"Ma révolution culturelle" (Paris) 18 May 1968; (Cleveland: Salvador Dalí Museum, 18 May 1975).

"Los hijos de la calle Monturiol," *Canigó* (Figueres) any XV, no. 176, October 1968, p. 4.

"La Pêche au Thon de Salvador Dalí," (Fondation Paul Ricart, 1968).

"(Quiero…)," in Max Gerard, *Dalí de Draeger* (Barcelona and Madrid: Blume, 1968).

"Contre la pornographie et l'obscenité pour le dieu Éros et l'éroticisme', in Salvador Dalí and Robert Descharnes, *Les Metamorphoses erotiques* (Lausanne: Edita, 1969).

"DeKooning's 300,000,000th birthday," *Art News* (New York) April 1969, pp. 57, 62-63; (Rotterdam: Museum Boymans-Van Beuningen, 20 November 1970-10 January 1971).

"Io sono l'utensile!," *Le Arti* (Milan) any 19, no. 4, April 1969, pp. 19-20.

"Preface', in Robert Descharnes, Clovis Prevost and Francesc Pujols: *La*

visió artística i religiosa de Gaudí* (Barcelona: Ayma S.A., 1969); *La Vision artistique et religieuse de Gaudi* (Lausanne: Edita, 1969); *Gaudí the Visionary* (London: Patrick Stephen, 1971); (New York: Viking Press, 1971).

Dalí par Dalí (Paris: Draeger, 1970); *Dalí über Dalí* (Berlin: Propylaen, 1970); *Dalí by Dalí* (New York: Harry N. Abrams, 1972).

"The cylindrical monarchy of Guimard," *Arts Magazine* (New York) vol. 44, no. 5, March 1970, pp. 42-43.

"I have used…," *Art Now* (New York) vol. II, no. 5, May 1970, p. 310.

"(Marveling…)," Published in *The Draftsmanship of Dalí, a portfolio of watervolors and drawing* (Cleveland: The Salvador Dalí Museum, 1970).

"Le recent tremblement de terre du Perou…" (Rotterdam: Museum Boymans-van Beuningen, 21 November 1970-10 January 1971).

"Postface" (21 August 1971). Included in Robert Descharnes (ed.), *Oui: méthode paranoïaque-critique et autres textes* (Paris: Denoël/Gonthier, 1971).

"L'Echec, c'est moi ('Chess, it's me')," preface to Pierre Cabanne, *Dialogues with Marcel Duchamp* (London: Thames and Hudson, 1971).

"Procès en diffamation plaidé devant la Conférence du Stage," Fontaney-aux-Roses, 1971 (Paris: Pierre Belfond, 1971).

Scarab, no. 1, 18 November 1971, pp. 1-49.

"Le Point de vue de Dalí," *Vogue* (Paris) no. 522, December 1971-72, pp. 159-209.

"Hommage à Dürer," *Hommage à Albrecht Dürer* (Paris: Galerie Vision Nouvelle, 1971-1972).

"Holos! Holos! Velasquez! Gabor!," *Art News* (New York) vol. 71, no. 2, April 1972, pp. 45, 67.

"(All artists have been…)" (New York: M. Knoedler & Co., 7 April-13 May 1972).

"Sonnet to the pupil's of Velazquez" eyes Gala of my eyes," *Art News* (New York) vol. 71, no. 2, April 1972, p. 45.

"OTO PORTRAIT HOLOGRAFIQUE," *Bollaffiarte* (Milan) June 1972.

"HOLOGRAMA DE GALA I DALÍ," *Bollaffiarte* (Milan) June 1972.

"The glorious testicles of our emperor Trajan," *Yearbox* (Davis [CA]), 1972, pp. 30-33.

Dalí, Salvador with André Parinaud. *Comment on devient Dalí* (Paris: Robert Laffont, 1973); *So wird man Dalí* (Zurich: Fritz Molden, 1974); *Como me tornei Salvador Dalí* (Lisbonne: Futura, 1975); *Confesiones inconfesables* (Barcelona: Bruguera, 1975); *Confissoes in confessaveis de Salvador Dalí* (Rio de Janeiro: Jose Olympio, 1976); *The Unspeakable Confessions of Salvador Dalí* (New York: Marrow, 1976); (London: W. H. Allen, 1976).

Les Dîners de Gala (Paris: Draeger, 1973); *Die Diners mit Gala* (Berlin: Ullstein-Propylaen, 1973); *The Diners of Gala* (New York: Felicie, 1973).

Dix recettes d'immortalité. (Paris: Audouin-Descharnes, 1973).

"Picasso et les poils du cheval," *Paris-Match* (Paris) no. 1252, 5 May 1973, p. 6; In A. Reynolds Morse, *Salvador Dalí, Pablo Picasso: a preliminary study of their similarities and contrasts* (Cleveland: The Salvador Dalí Museum, 1973).

"(Commentaries on the works)" (Paris: Galerie de l'Elysée, 15 May-8 June 1973).

"Les Six jours de Dalí," *Paris-Match* (Paris) no. 1258, 16 June 1973, p. 3.

"Sonnet à la commode de Mallarme," *Les Nouvelles Litteraires* (Paris) 18 June 1973.

"Dice Dalí," *ABC* (Madrid) 25 August 1973.

"Réalisme sybaritique aigu', preface to Linda Chase, *Les Hypérrealistes americains* (Paris: Filipacchi, 1973); "Introduction" to Josep Pla, *Obres de museu* (Figueres: Dasa Ediciones, S.A., 1981).

"Hiper-realismo y monarquía," *La Vanguardia* (Barcelona), 9 December 1973; Included in Salvador Dalí, *Pujols per Dalí* (Barcelona: Ariel, 1974).

"Ur Salvador Dalís hemilga liv" (Stockholm: Moderna Museet, 26 December 1973-24 February 1974).

"(The "paranoiac phenomenon"...)" (Cleveland: The Salvador Dalí Museum, 1973).

"Five statements and one message from Salvador Dalí," *The New York Times* (New York) 18 May 1974: .

"So erlebte ich die Kosmetik-Konigin Helena Rubinstein," *Welt am Sonntag* (Hambourg) 30 June 1974.

"Para Miguel Masriera. Holografía en el Teatro-Museo Dalí," *La Vanguardia* (Barcelona), 29 September 1974.

"Quando i surrealisti mu fecero il processo," *Bolaffiarte* (Milan) vol. V, no. 43, October 1974, pp. 80-87.

"(Pitchot nuvelle paradoxe...)," *Antoni Pitxot* (Fondazione Dalle Molle, 1974).

"Damian del lado de Perpiñon," *Hora Damian: Galaxy* (Aachen: Galerie-Sammlung Ludwig, 1974).

"Mine befoestede stillinger," *Xxe, sciecle* (Paris) December, no. 43 1974, pp. 93-95.

"Preface". René Crevel, *La mort difficile* (Paris: Jean-Jacques Pauvert, 1974), pp. 9-20.

"Preface', in Robert Descharnes and Ogura Tadao, *Salvador Dalí* (Tokyo: Shueisha, collection l'art moderne du monde, no. 25, 1974).

"Preface" to Sigmund Freud, *Moise et le monotheisme* (Paris: Art et Valeur, 1974).

Pujols per Dalí. (Barcelona: Ariel, 1974).

Eroticism in clothing. (Cleveland: Salvador Dalí Museum, 1975); (Figueres: Teatre-Museu Dalí, 1975).

"Extracts from the book, *El Pequeño libro EL PEQUEÑO LIBRO LILA-DALÍ-GALA-MAORYLIN*" (Figueres: Galeria de la Cúpola, June 1975).

"Hello Dalí" Comments of Salvador Dalí in the film, "'Hello Dalí'" (Cleveland: Salvador Dalí Museum, 1975); (Figueres: Teatre-Museu Dalí, 1975).

"The Six Days of Dalí" (Cleveland: Salvador Dalí Museum, 1975); (Figueres: Teatre-Museu Dalí, 1975).

"T" (Port Lligat, May 1976). Published in Robert Descharnes (ed.), *Oui 2: l'Archangelisme scientifique* (Paris: Éditions Denoël, 1979).

"Eureka" (Paris, Hôtel Meurice, 12 October 1976). Published in Robert Descharnes (ed.), *Oui 2: l'Archangelisme scientifique* (Paris: Éditions Denoël, 1979), pp. 198-199.

"Quoi de neuf? Velasquez," *Le Sauvage* (Paris) no. 34, October 1976, p. 96.

"Hacer el Ampurdan universal a traves del Teatro-museo Dalí," *Setmanari Artístic Mar Empordanesa* (Figueres), 1976.

"Guia Secreta del Teatro-Museo Dalí," *Setmanari Artístic Mar Empordanesa* (Figueres), 1976.

"Una página del Nueva York...," *Setmanari Artístic Mar Empordanesa* (Figueres), 1976.

"Les Caprices de Goya de Salvador Dalí" (Hambourg: Julien Levy Gallery, 1977).

"La Gare de Perpignan" (Paris: Galerie André-François Petit, 8-22 December 1977).

Les Vins de Gala (Paris: Draeger, 1977); *Los Vinos de Gala* (Paris: Galaxys, 1977); *Die Weine mit Gala* (Berlin: Ullstein-Propylaen, 1978); *The Wines of Gala* (New York: Harry N. Abrams, 1978).

"La rendición de Breda" y "Guernica," *La Vanguardia* (Barcelona), 12 February 1978.

"Dalí aime ceux de Mijanou," *Pariscope* (Paris) 17-23 January 1979.

"Gala, Velasquez et la Toison d'Or," *Vogue* (Paris) no. 597, June-July 1979, p. 147.

"Traité des guirlandes et des nids', 1979. Published in Robert Descharnes (ed.), *Oui 2: l'Archangelisme scientifique* (Paris: Éditions Denoël, 1979).

"Mensaje preliminar," *Happenings de Happenings y todo es happening* (Granollers, April 1979).

"Últimes conclusions del meu llibre titulat "Dimensions i color de Déu," *Destino* (Barcelona) no. 2193, 17-23 October 1979.

Dalí, Salvador with Josep Pla. *Obres de museu* (Figueres: Dasa, 1981).

"Essai de traité d'écriture catastrophéiforme" (1982). Published in Robert Descharnes, *Dalí, l'oeuvre et l'homme* (Lausanne: Edita, 1984), p. 423.

"(Pour pouvoir me voir...)" (Cabries-en-Provence, November 1982).

"Message de Dalí" (Tokyo: Isetan Museum of Art, 28 February-6 April 1982).

"(A la divina Gala!...)" (Barcelona: Obra Cultural de la Caixa de Pensions, 1983).

"(Among the five...)," published in *Le Parfum Dalí* (Ray International, 1983).

"La Découverte la plus importante de ma méthode paranoiaque-critique: la gare de Perpignan" (31 October 1983). Published in Robert Descharnes, *Dalí, l'oeuvre et l'homme* (Lausanne: Edita, 1984), p. 423.

"(La única cosa...)," published in Luis Romero and Josep Postius, *Aquel Dalí* (Barcelona: Argos-Vergara, 1984).

"El bruitre de Leonardo y el "Ictíneo," *El Pais*, 11 February 1985, p. 21.

"Monturiol y Bellini, los dos aún en el fondo del mar," *El Pais*, 17 February 1985, p. 33.

"Laudatorios," *ABC* (Madrid) 17 June 1985; "Laureada" (Torre Galatea, 17 June 1985) (Figueres: Fundació Gala-Salvador Dalí, 1988).

"L'Enigma estètic," published in

Procés a l'atazar (Barcelona: Tusquets, 1986).

"Sant Narcís, Dalí i les mosques" (Salt: Casa de Cultura, 1986).

"Avant-propos," in Yann le Pichon, *L'Érotisme chez les maîtres* (Paris: Denoël, 1986).

"La guerre de Troie aura lieu," published in Antoni Pitxot and Cesáreo Rodríguez-Aguilera, *La Batalla de Constantí* (Barcelona: Àmbit, 1986).

"Mártir (1976-1982)," *El Paseante* (Madrid) no. 5, 1987.

"La Alquimia de mi amor" (Torre Galatea, 15 March 1986). (Figueres: Fundació Gala-Salvador Dalí, 1988).

"Elegías a Gala" (Torre Galatea, 8 June 1988). (Figueres: Fundació Gala-Salvador Dalí, 1988).

"Oda a la monarquía" (Torre Galatea, 29 December 1987). (Figueres: Fundació Gala-Salvador Dalí, 1988). Published in Manuel Medina González, *Oda a la monarquía española. Juan Carlos I, un rey para la humanidad* (Seville: Editoriales Andaluzas Reunidas, 1988).

Principal Works Illustrated by Salvador Dalí

Alarcón, Pedro Antonio de, *Le tricorne* (Monaco: Editions du Rocher, 1959).

L'Apocalypse de saint Jean (Paris: Joseph Foret, 1960).

Apollinaire, Guillaume, *Lettres à Marie* (Paris: Argillet, 1967).

Biblia sacra (Milan: Rizzoli, 1967-1969).

Boccaccio, *Decameron* (New York and Freiburg: Transworld Art, 1972).

Breton, André, *Le Révolver à cheveux blancs* (Paris: Éditions des Cahiers Libres, 1932).

Breton, André, *Second manifested du surréalisme* (Paris: Simon Kra, 1930).

Breton, André and Paul Eluard, *Notes sur la poésie* (Paris: G.L.M., 1936).

Breton, André, René Char and Paul Eluard, *Violette Nozières* (Paris: Nicolas Flamel, 1933).

Calderón de la Barca, *La vida es sueño* (Barcelona: Editorial E. Subirana, 1975).

Carroll, Lewis, *Alice's Adventures in Wonderland* (New York: Maecenas Press, 1969).

Cassanova, *Dalí illustre Casanova* (Paris: Cercle du Livre Précieux, 1967).

Cassou, Jean, *Bonheur du jour. Cantique d'un ouvrier nègre. Sur la côte. L'Air de la séduction...* (Paris: Les Impenitents, 1969).

Cellini, Benvenuto, *The Autobiogarphy of Benvenuto Cellini* (New York: Doubleday, 1947).

Cervantes, Miguel de, *El ingenioso hidalgo Don Quixote* (New York: Random House, 1946).

Cervantes, Miguel de, *Pages choisies Don Quichotte de la Mancha* (Paris: Joseph Foret, 1957-1959).

Char, René, *Artine* (Paris: Editions Surréalistes, 1930).

Claire and Goll, Y, *Nouvelles petites fleurs de saint François d'Assise* (Paris: Emile Paul, 1958).

Corbière, Tristan, *Les Amours jaunes* (Paris: Belfond, 1974).

Dante Alighieri, *La Divine comédie* (Paris: Joseph Foret, 1960).

D'Ors, Eugeni, *La verdadera historia de Lidia de Cadaqués* (Barcelona: José Janés, 1954).

Les Douze tribus d'Israël (New York and Freiburg: Transworld Art, 1973).

Ducasse, Isidore (Comte de Lautréamont), *Les Chants de Maldoror* (Paris: Albert Skira, 1934).

Ducasse, Isidore (Comte de Lautréamont), *Oeuvres complètes* (Paris: José Corti, 1938).

Eluard, Paul, *Cours naturel* (Paris: Sagittaire, 1938).

Eluard, Paul, *Nuits partagées* (Paris: G.L.M., 1935).

Eluard, Paul, *Voir, poèmes, peintures, dessins* (Geneva and Paris: Trois Collines, 1948).

Fages de Climent, C, *Bruixes de Llers* (1924).

Fages de Climent, C, *Balada de Sabater d'Ordis* (1954).

Freud, Sigmund, *Moïse et le monothéisme* (Paris: Art et Valeur, 1974).

Goethe, Johann Wolfgang von, *Faust: La nuit de Walpurgis* (Paris: Graphik-Europa Anstalt, 1969).

Goll, Y., *La septième rose* (Paris: Emile-Paul, 1970).

Hemingway, Ernest, *Der alte Mann und das Meer* (Stuttgart: Manus Press, 1974).

Histoire d'un grand livre: "Don Quichotte" illustré par Salvador Dalí (Paris: Joseph Foret, 1957).

Malraux, André, *Roi, je t'attends ã Babylone* (Geneva: Albert Skira, 1973).

Mao Tse-Toung, *Poèmes* (Paris: Argillet, 1967).

Les Mille et une nuits (Milan: Rizzoli, 1969).

Milton, John, *Paradis perdu: quatrième chant* (Paris: Les Biblio-

philes de l'Automobile-Club de France, 1974).

Montaigne, Michel, *Essays* (New York: Doubleday, 1947).

North, S., *Speak of the Devil* (New York: Doubleday, 1945).

Ovid, *L'Art d'aimer* (Paris: Centre Culturel de Paris, 1979).

Peret, Benjamin, *De Derrière les fagots* (Paris: Editions des Cahiers Libres, 1934).

Puig Pujades, J., *L'oncle Vicents* (1946).

La Quête du graal (Paris: Michèle Broutta, 1975).

Ronsard, Pierre de, *Les Amours de Cassandre* (Paris: Argillet, 1968).

Rose, Billy, *Wine, Women and Words* (New York: Simon and Schuster, 1946).

Sacher-Masoch, Leopold von, *La Vénus aux fourrures* (Paris: Graphik-Europa Anstalt, 1968).

Sade, Marquis de, *Misfortune's Mistake; The Twins of a Difficult Choice; Tancred* (New York: Wolfensberger, Shorewood, 1969).

Sandoz, Maurice, *Fantastic Memories* (New York: Doubleday, 1944).

Sandoz, Maurice, *Das Haus ohne Fenster* (Zurich: Morgarten, 1948).

Sandoz, Maurice, *Le Labyrinthe* (Geneva: Kundig, 1949).

Sandoz, Maurice, *La Limite* (Paris: La Table Ronde, 1951).

Sandoz, Maurice, *La Maison sans fenêtre* (Paris: Pierre Seghers, 1949)

Sandoz, Maurice, *The Maze* (New York: Doubleday, 1945).

Sandoz, Maurice, *On the Verge* (New York: Doubleday, 1950).

Shakespeare, William, *As You Like It* (London: The Folio Society, 1953).

Shakespeare, William, *Macbeth* (New York: Doubleday, 1946).

Shakespeare, William, *Roméo et Juliette* (Milan: Rizzoli, 1969).

Tauromachies (Paris: Michèle Broutta, 1966-1967 and 1969).

Tristan et Iseult (Paris: Michèle Broutta, 1970).

Tzara, Tristan, *Grains et issues* (Paris: Denoël, 1935).

Walpole, Horace, *Le Château d'Otrante* (Paris: Club Français du Livre, 1964),

Yourcenar, Marguerite, *Alexis ou le traité du van combat* (Paris: Les Cent Une, 1971).

Monographs and Solo Exhibition Catalogues

Abadie, Daniel (ed.), *Salvador Dalí.*

Rétrospective, 1920-1980 (Paris: Centre Georges Pompidou, Musée National d'Art Moderne, 1979).

Ades, Dawn, *Dalí* (London: Thames and Hudson, 1982, 1995).

Ades, Dawn and Fiona Bradley, *Salvador Dalí: A Mythology* (London: Tate Gallery Publishing, 1998).

Ades, Dawn, *Dalí's Optical Illusions* (New Haven and London: Yale University Press, 2000).

Ajame, Pierre, *La double vie de Salvador Dalí* (Paris: Ramsay, 1984).

Aleksic, Branko, *Dalí: inédits de Belgrade (1932)* (Paris: Change International/Equivalences, 1987).

Alexandrian, Sarane, *Dalí: peintures* (Paris: Fernand Hazan, 1969).

Alexandrian, Sarane, *Dalí illustre, 1930-1940, Tome I* (Paris: Fillipacchi, le Monde des Grands Musées, no.6, 1974); *Dalí illustre, Tome I, Dalí et les poetes* (Paris: Fillipacchi, les yeux fertiles, 1976).

Anderson, Robert, *Salvador Dalí* (London: Franklin Watts, 2002).

Andréu, Grace Megwinoff, *Dalí: Salvador de la pintura* (San Juan: Ramallo Bros, 1998).

Arco, Manuel del, *Dalí al desnudo* (Barcelona: José Janès, 1952).

Arco, Manuel del, *Salvador Dalí, ich und die Malerei* (Zurich: Verlag der Arche, 1959).

Bokelberg, Werner, *Salvador Dalí DA DA Dalí in Bildern* (Brême: Carl Schunemann, 1966).

Bonet, Llorenc, *Antoni Gaudi/Salvador Dalí: Duets* (New York: Harper Design International, 2003).

Bosquet, Alain, *Entretiens avec Salvador Dalí* (Paris: Pierre Belfond, 1966); *Dalí desnudado* (Buenos Aires: Paidos, 1967); *Conversations with Dalí* (New York: Dutton, 1969).

Bouguenec, André, *Salvador Dalí, Philosophe et Esotériste incompris* (Nantes: Éditions Opera, 1993).

Bradbury, Kirsten, *Essential Dalí* (Bath: Dempsey Parr., 1999).

Brans, Jan, *Salvador Dalí und seine Religiöse Malerei* (Munich: Neues Abendland, 1955).

Busquets, Jordi, *Le Dernier Dalí* (Paris: Lieu commun, 1986).

Carmona, Angel, *Dalí no esta loco* (Barcelona: G.P., 1963).

Carmona, Angel, *Salvador Dalí* (Barcelona: Fontanella Testigos del Sigio XX, 1964).

Carol, Màrius, *Dalí: El final oculto de un exhibicionista* (Barcelona: Plaza y Janes, 1990).

Carol, Màrius with Juan José Navarro Arisa, Jordi Busquets, *El último Dalí* (Madrid: El Pais, 1985).

Carter, Curtis (ed.), *Dalí and the Ballet: Set and Costumes for The Three-Cornered Hat* (Milwaukee: Haggerty Museum of Art, 2000).

Catterall, Lee, *The Great Dalí Art Fraud and Other Deceptions* (New Jersey: Barricade Books, Inc., 1992).

Cevasco, George A., *Salvador Dalí, master of surrealism and modern art* (Charlotteville, New York: Sam Har Press, 1971).

Charles, Victoria, *Salvador Dalí* (Bournemouth: Parkstone Press, 1999).

Cowles, Fleur, *The Case of Salvador Dalí* (London: Heinemann, 1959); *La Vie d'un grand excentrique* (Paris: Julliard, 1961); *Der Fall Salvador Dalí* (Munich: Albert Langen-Georges Müller).

Crevel, René, *Dalí ou l'anti-obscurantisme* (Paris: Éditions Surréalistes, 1931).

Cultura de masas (Barcelona: Fundación 'la Caixa', 2004).

Dalí – A Genius of the XX Century (Taipei: China Times, 2001).

Dalí, Ana María, *Salvador Dalí visto par su hermana* (Barcelona: Juventud, 1949); *Salvador Dalí vu par sa soeur* (Paris: Arthaud, 1960).

Dalí, Ana María, *Noves imatges de Salvador Dalí* (Barcelona: Columna, 1988).

Dalí en las colecciones españoles (Segovia: Museo de arte contemporáneo Esteban Vicente, 2001).

Dalí Grafista (Figueres: Fundació Gala-Salvador Dalí, 2003).

Dalí il-lustrador: Salvador Dalí, 1904-1989 (Andorra: Govern d'Andorra; Ministeri de Turisme i Cultura, 2001).

Dalí, imatges invisibles (Cadaqués: Museu de Cadaqués; Ajuntament de Cadaqués, 2001).

Dalí och fantasins kraft – Dalí and the force of imagination (Skärhamn: Nordiska Akvarellmuseet, 2001).

Dalí: un creador ligado a su tiempo (Santander: Fundación Marcelino Botin, 2003).

Dedicatóries, Salvador Dalí (Barcelona: Mediterránia, 1990).

Descharnes, Robert, *The World of Salvador Dalí* (New York: Harper & Row, 1962); *Il Mondo di Salvador Dalí* (Milan: Garzanti, 1962); *(Japanese trans.)* (Tokyo: Bijitsu Shuppan-Sha, 1963); *The World of*

Salvador Dalí (London: Mac Millan, 1963); (London: Viking Press, 1968); (London: Easingstoke, 1972).

Descharnes, Robert, *Dalí de Gala* (Lausanne: Éditions Denoël, 1962); (Lausanne: Edita-Vilo, 1979),

Descharnes, Robert (ed), *Oui 1: la Révolution paranoïaque-critique* (Paris: Éditions Denoël, 1971); *Sí* (Barcelona: Ariel, 1977); with Yvonne Shafir (trans.), *Oui 1: The Paranoid-critical revolution, writings 1927-1933* (Boston: Exact Change, 1998).

Descharnes, Robert, *Salvador Dalí* (Paris: Nouvelles Éditions Françaises, 1973).

Descharnes, Robert, *Salvador Dalí* (Cologne: Dumont, 1974).

Descharnes, Robert with Ogura Tadao, *Salvador Dalí* (Tokyo: Shueisha collection l'Art Moderne du Monde, no. 25, 1974).

Descharnes, Robert, *Salvador Dalí* (New York: Harry N., Abrams, 1976); (South Melbourne: Mac Millan Company of Australia, 1976); (Belgrade: Yugoslavia, 1976).

Descharnes, Robert, *Salvador Dalí* (Tokyo: Bijitsu Shuppan-Sha, 1978).

Descharnes, Robert (ed), *Oui 2: l'Archangelisme scientifique* (Paris: Éditions Denoël, 1979).

Descharnes, Robert, *Dalí, l'oeuvre et l'homme* (Lausanne: Edita, 1984); *Dalí, La obra y el hombre* (Barcelona: Tusquets/Edita, 1984); *Dalí, the Work, the Man* (New York: Harry N., Abrams, 1984).

Descharnes, Robert with Nicolas Descharnes, *Dalí* (Lausanne: Edita, 1993).

Descharnes, Robert (ed), with Jean-Yves Clément and Arnaud Hofmarcher, *Dalí: Pensées et anecdotes* (Paris: Le cherche midi éditeur, 1995).

Descharnes, Robert, *Dalí: L'Héritage Infernal* (Paris: Éditions Ramsay-La Marge, 2002); Dalí, La Herencia Infernal (La Marge, 2003).

Dopagne, Jacques, *Dalí* (Paris: Fernand Hazan, 1974); (New York: Leon Amiel, 1974).

Duane, O.B., *Salvador Dalí* (London: Brockhampton Press, 1996).

Dalí Arquitectura (Figueres: Fundació Gala-Salvador Dalí y Fundación Caixa de Catalunya, 1996).

Erasmy, Roger Michel, *Le Mystère de la gare de Perpignan* (Perpignan: R.M, Erasmy, 1985).

Erasmy, Roger Michel, *Codex Dalianus: indicateur ésotérique des prévisions paranoïaques-critiques de Salvador Dalí* (Rasiguères: R.M., Erasmy, 1987, 1989); (Jurançon: Clos Bel-Air, 2001).

Etherington-Smith, Meredith., *The Persistence of Memory: A Biography of Dalí* (New York: Da Capo Press, 1993).

Fanés, Fèlix with Empar Gime_nez and Ana Coll-Vinent., *Dalí escriptor* (Barcelona: Fundació Caixa de Pensions, 1990).

Fanés, Fèlix (ed), *Un diari: 1919-1920, Les meves impressions i records intims* (Barcelona: Fundació Gala-Salvador Dalí, Edicions 62, 1994).

Fanés, Fèlix (ed), *L'alliberament dels dits, Obra catalana completa* (Barcelona: Quaderns Crema, 1995).

Fanés, Fèlix, *Salvador Dalí: la construccion de la imagen 1925-1930* (Madrid: Electa, 1999).

Fernandez Molina, Antonio, *Dalí* (Madrid: Direction General de Bellas Artes, Artistas Espanoles Contemporaneos, 1971).

Fernandez Molina, Antonio, *Dalí. testimonios y enigmas* (Zaragoza: Libros del Innombrable, 1998).

Ferreira, José, *Dalí-Lacan, la rencontre: ce que le psychanalyste doit au peintre* (Paris, Budapest and Torino: l'Harmattan, 2003).

Ferrier, Jean-Louis, *Dalí, Léda Atomica: Anatomie d'un chef-d'oeuvre* (Paris: Denoël/Gonthier, 1980).

Finkelstein, Haim, *Salvador Dalí's Art and Writing 1927-1942: The Metamorphosis of Narcissus* (Cambridge: Cambridge University Press, 1996).

Finkelstein, Haim, *The Collected Writings of Salvador Dalí* (Cambridge: Cambridge University Press, 1998).

Fornés, Eduard, *Dalí et les livres* (Barcelona: Royal Chapel, 1982 and Nimes: Musée d'art, 1984); *Dalí y los libros* (Barcelona: Mediterrania, 1985).

Fornés, Eduard, *Les contradiccions del cas Dalí* (Barcelona: Llibres de l'Avui, 1989).

400 obras de Salvador Dalí de 1914 a 1983 (Madrid: Ministry of Culture and Barcelona: Generalitat de Catalunya, 1983).

Franquinet, Robert, *Salvador Dalí, mystiche dandy* (Tielt: Lanoo, 1936).

Gaillemin. Jean-Louis. *Salvador Dalí, désirs inassouvis. du purisme au surréalisme 1925-1935* (Paris and New York: Passage, 2002).

Gallwitz, Klaus, *Metamorphose des Narziss, Die Jugend entdeckt Dalí* (Hambourg: Hoffmann und Campe, 1971).

Garcia Lorca, Federico, *Ode à Salvador Dalí* (Paul Eluard and Louis Parrot, trans.) (Paris: G.L.M., 1938).

Gaya Nuno, Juan Antonio, *Salvador Dalí* (Barcelona: Omega, 1954).

Genzmer, Herbert, *Salvador und Gala Dalí. der Maler und die Muse* (Berlin: Rowohlt, 1998).

Gérard, Max, *Dalí de Draeger* (Paris: Le soleil noir, 1968); (New York: Harry N., Abrams, 1968).

Gérard, Max, *Dalí...Dalí...Dalí...* (Paris: Draeger, 1974); (New York: Harry N. Abrams, 1974); (Galaxis, 1974); (Barcelona: Blume, 1985); (Yugoslavia: Manfred Pawlak – Atlantis, 1985).

Gibson, Ian, *The Shameful Life of Salvador Dalí* (London: Faber and Faber, 1997); (New York and London: W.W. Norton & Co., 1998).

Gifreu, Patrick, *Dalí, un manifeste ultralocal* (Narbonne: Mare nostrum, 1997); (Monaco: Éditions du Rocher, 2000).

Gizzi, Corrado, *Salvador Dalí e Dante* (Milan: Editoriale Giorgio Mondadori, 1997).

Goff, Robert, *The Essential Salvador Dalí* (New York: Harry N. Abrams, 1998).

Gómez de la Serna, Ramón, *Dalí* (Madrid: Espasa-Galpe, 1977); (Milan: Arnoldo Mondadori, 1978); (Paris: Flammarion, 1979); *Dalí* (New York: William Marrow M. Company, 1979).

Gómez de Liaño, Ignacio, *Dalí* (Barcelona: Ediciones Poligrafa, 1982).

Guardiola Rovira, Ramón, *Dalí y su museo. La obra que no quiso Bellas Artes* (Figueres: Editora Empordanesa, 1984).

Harris, Nathaniel, *La vie et l'oeuvre de Dalí* (Nimes: Livre club, 1996).

Hartmann, Richard P., *Hommage à Dalí mit dem Gesprachen zwischen Alain Bosquet und Dalí* (Munich: Nymphenburger Verlag, 1974).

Hello Dalí! Comments on Salvador Dalí and Film (St. Petersburg: Salvador Dalí Museum, 1975).

Hernándo, María Isabel, *Biografía completa de Salvador Dalí* (Madrid:

Iberico Europea de Ediciones, 1970).

Jeffett, William, *Dalí in Focus: Gradiva* (Madrid: Museo Thyssen-Bornemisza, 2002).

Jeffett, William, *Dalí and Miró, circa 1928* (St. Petersburg: Salvador Dalí Museum, 2003).

Kachur, Lewis, *Displaying the Marvelous: Marcel Duchamp, Salvador Dalí, and Surrealist Exhibition Installations* (Cambridge and London: MIT Press, 2001).

Kliczkowski Asppan, H., *Gaudí-Dalí.* (Art Books Intl Ltd, 2002).

La Vie publique de Salvador Dalí (Paris: Centre Georges Pompidou, Musée National d'Art Moderne, 1980).

LaFountain, Marc J., *Dalí and Postmodernism: This is Not an Essence* (Albany: State University of New York Press, 1997).

Lake, Carlton, *In Quest of Dalí* (New York: G.P. Putnam's Sons, 1969).

Larkin, David, *Dalí* (Paris: Chene, 1973).

Lauryssens, Stan, *Salvador Dalí: het boeiende leven van de beroemdste kunstenaar aller tijden* (Antwerp: Kunst en Kapitaal, 1983).

Lear, Amanda, *Le Dalí d'Amanda* (Paris: Favre, 1984); *My Life with Dalí* (London: Virgin Books, Ltd., 1985); *L'Amant-Dalí: Ma Vie avec Salvador Dalí* (Paris: Michel Lafon, 1994).

Longstreet, Stephen, *The drawings of Dalí* (Alhambra (CA): Borden Publishing Company, 1964).

Maddox, Conroy, *Dalí* (New York: Crown Publishers, 1979).

Mas Peinado, Ricard, *Dalí* (Paris: Hazen, 2003).

Masters, Christopher, *Dalí* (London: Phaidon Press, 1995).

Maur, Karin von, *Salvador Dalí: 1904-1989* (Stuttgart: Verlag Gerd Hatie, 1989).

Moorhouse, Alan, *Dalí* (Wigston [Leicester]: Magna Books, 1990).

Morse, A. Reynolds, *Dalí, a documentation of Dalí source material in the vicinity of Cadaqués, Spain* (Cleveland: Reynolds Morse Foundation, Fine arts publication no. 1, 1954).

Morse, A. Reynolds, *Salvador Dalí, a portfolio in full color* (Cleveland: Reynolds Morse Foundation, Fine arts publication no. 2, 1955).

Morse, A. Reynolds, *Nature morte vivante, Salvador Dalí, 1956* (Cleveland: Reynolds Morse Foundation, Fine arts publication no. 4, 1956).

Morse, A. Reynolds with introduction by Michel Tapié, *Dalí, a study of his life and work* (Greenwich: New York Graphic Society, 1958).

Morse, A. Reynolds, *A new introduction to Salvador Dalí* (Cleveland: Reynolds Morse Foundation, 1960).

Morse, A. Reynolds, *Ode à Dalí, Santatomica* (Cleveland: Chagrin, 1964).

Morse, A. Reynolds, *An evening with Dalí at the Gallery of modern art* (Cleveland: Reynolds Morse Foundation, 1966).

Morse, A. Reynolds, *A Dalí Primer* (Cleveland: Reynolds Morse Foundation, 1970).

Morse, A. Reynolds, *The draftsmanship of Dalí, a portfolio of watercolors and drawings* (Cleveland: Salvador Dalí Museum, 1970).

Morse, A. Reynolds, *The decade 1961-1971, supplement to a new introduction to Salvador Dalí* (Cleveland: Salvador Dalí Museum, 1971).

Morse, A. Reynolds, *Dalí, the masterworks* (Cleveland: Reynolds Morse Foundation, 1971).

Morse, A. Reynolds, *Souvenir catalogue supplement* (Cleveland: Salvador Dalí Museum, 1971).

Morse, A. Reynolds, *Additional text for 'Dalí by Dalí'* (Cleveland: Salvador Dalí Museum, 1972).

Morse, A. Reynolds with Eleanor Morse, *The Dalí Adventure 1943-73, a photo album* (Cleveland: Salvador Dalí Museum, 1973).

Morse, A. Reynolds, *Salvador Dalí, Pablo Picasso. A Preliminary Study in their Similarities and Contrasts* (Cleveland: Salvador Dalí Museum, 1973).

Morse, A. Reynolds, *Poetic homage to Gala Salvador Dalí 1926-1964* (Cleveland: Salvador Dalí Museum, 1973).

Morse, A. Reynolds, *Salvador Dalí A panorama of his art, ninety-three oils 1917-1970* (Cleveland: Salvador Dalí Museum, 1974).

Morse, A. Reynolds, *Dalí's Animal Crackers* (St. Petersburg: Salvador Dalí Museum, 1993).

Néret, Gilles, *Dalí* (Cologne: Benedikt Taschen, 2000).

Nicosia, Fiorella, *Dalí* (Paris: Grund, 2003).

Obra gráfica: Ciclos literarios (Madrid: Ministerio de Cultura, la Caja de Ahorros and Monte de Piedad, 1982).

Ode à Dalí, sardonic sardanas (Cleveland: Chagrin, 1967).

Olano, Antonio D., *Dalí secreto* (Barcelona: Círculo de Lectores, 1975).

Olano, Antonio D., *Adiòs Dalí* (Madrid: Maeva Ediciones, 1989).

Oriol Anguera, A., *Mentira y verdad de Salvador Dalí* (Barcelona: Cobalto, El arte y los espanoles desde 1800, 1948).

Parcerisas, Pilar (ed.), *Dalí. Elective Affinities* (Barcelona: Department de Cultura de la Generalitat de Catalunya, 2004).

Passeron, René, *Salvador Dalí* (Paris: Filipacchi, La septième face du de, 1978).

Passoni, Franco with A. Reynolds Morse and Albert Field, *Dalí nella terza dimensione* (Milan: Edizione Master Fine Art Gallery, 1987).

Playà i Maset, Josep, *Dalí de l'Empordà* (Barcelona: Editorial Labor; 'Terra Nostra', 1992).

Pollack, Rachel, *Le Tarot de Salvador Dalí* (Paris: Seghers, 1985).

Por que se ataca a La Gioconda? (Madrid: Siruela, 1999).

Puget, Henry, *Dalí. l'œil de la folie* (Paris: Jean Boully, 1989).

Puignau, Emili, *Vivencias con Salvador Dalí* (Barcelona: Editorial Juventud, 1995).

Radford, Robert, *Dalí* (London: Phaidon Press, 1997).

Raeburn, Michael (ed.), *Salvador Dalí: The Early Years* (London: South Bank Centre, 1994).

Ramírez, Juan Antonio, *Dalí: lo crudo y lo podrido* (Madrid: A. machado Libros, S.A., 2002).

Rétrospective Salvador Dalí (Edition Art Life, 1982).

Rey, Henri-François, *Dalí dans son labyrinthe* (Paris: Grasset, 1974); *Dalí en su laberinto, Ensayo comentado por Dalí* (Barcelona: Editorial Euros, 1975).

Rodrigo, Antonina, *Lorca-Dalí. Una amistad traicionada* (Barcelona: Planeta, 1981).

Rogerson, Mark, *The Dalí Scandal: An Investigation* (London: Gollancz, 1989).

Rojas, Carlos, *El mundo mitico y magico de Salvador Dalí* (Barcelona: Plaza y Janes, 1985); *Salvador Dalí, or the Art of Spitting on Your Mother's Portrait* (University Park, PA: Pennsylvania state University Press, 1993).

Romero, Luis, *Les caprices de Goya de Salvador Dalí* (Paris: Berggruen, 1977).

Romero, Luis, *Todo Dalí en un rostro* (Barcelona: Editorial Blume, 1975); *Tout Dalí en un visage* (Paris: Chene, 1975); *Dalí* (Secaucus, New Jersey: Chartwell Books, Inc., 1975).

Romero, Luis, *Aquel Dalí* (Barcelona: Argos Vergara, 1984).

Romero, Luis, *Dedálico Dalí* (Barcelona: Ediciones B, 1989).

Romero, Luis, *Torero allucinogen* (Barcelona: Editorial Mediterrània, 1990).

Romero, Luis, *Psicodálico Dalí* (Barcelona: Editorial Mediterrània, 1991).

Sabater, Enrique, *A Sabater con un abrazon en el Quin Elisabet* (Torino: Allemandi & Company, 1998).

Sabater, Enrique, *La mirada de un genio: Salvador Dalí*, book 1 of exhibition, *La mirada de un genio: Salvador Dalí* (Fundaciôn de Cultura, Ayuntamiento de Oviedo).

Sabater, Enrique, *Las arquitecturas de Dalí*, book 2 of exhibition, *La mirada de un genio: Salvador Dalí* (Fundaciôn de Cultura, Ayuntamiento de Oviedo).

Salvador Dalí: Album de familia (Figueres: Fundació Gala-Salvador Dalí y Fundación Caixa de Catalunya, 1998).

Salvador Dalí: Dream of Venus (North Miami: Museum of Contemporary Art, 2002).

Sanchez Vidal, Agustin, *Buñuel, Lorca, Dalí: el enigma sin fin* (Barcelona: Planeta, 1988).

Santos Torroella, Raphael, *Salvador Dalí* (Madrid: Afrodisio Aguado, 1952).

Santos Torroella, Raphael, *La miel es mas dulce que la sangre. Las epocas lorquiana y freudiana de Salvador Dalí* (Barcelona: Planeta, 1984).

Santos Torroella, Raphael (ed.), *Salvador Dalí corresponsal de J.V. Foix, 1932-1936* (Barcelona: Mediterrá-nia, 1986).

Santos Torroella, Raphael (ed.), *Salvador Dalí escribe a Federico García Lorca. presentación, notas y cronología* (Madrid: Ministerio de Cultura, 1987).

Santos Torroella, Raphael, *Dalí, residente* (Madrid: Publicaciones de la Residencia de Estudiantes, Consejo de Investigaciones Cientificas, 1992).

Santos Torroella, Raphael, *La tragica vida de Salvador Dalí* (Barcelona: Parsifal, 1995).

Santos Torroella, Raphael, *Los putre-factos de Dalí y Lorca. Historia y antologia de un libro que no pudo ser* (Madrid: Residencia de Estudiantes, 1995).

Schaffner, Ingrid, *Salvador Dalí's Dream of Venus, The Surrealist Funhouse from the 1939 World's Fair* (New York: Princeton Architectural Press, 2002).a

Schiebler, Ralf, *Dalí: Genius, Obsession and Lust* (Munich and New York: Prestel Verlag, 1996); *Dalis Begierden* (Munich and New York: Prestel Verlag, 1996).

Secrest, Meryle, *Salvador Dalí* (New York: E.P. Dutton, 1986).

Shanes, Eric, *Dalí* (New York: Portland House, 1990); (London: Studio Éditions, 1994).

Soby, James Thrall, *Salvador Dalí: Paintings, Drawings, Prints* (New York: Museum of Modern Art, 1941).

Swinglehurst. Edmund, *Salvador Dalí: Exploring the irrational* (New York: Todtri, 1996).

Tapié, Michel, *Dalí* (Paris: Chene, 1957).

The Endless Enigma: Dalí and the magicians of multiple meaning (Ostfildern-Ruit: Hatje Cantz, 2003).

Thurlow, Clifford with Carlos Lozano, *Sex, Surrealism, Dalí and Me* (Cornwall: Razor Books, 2000).

Utrillo, Miguel, *Salvador Dalí y sus enemigos* (Sitges-Barcelona: Maspe, 1952).

Vilaseca, David, *The Apocryphal Subject: Masochism, Identification, and Paranoia in Salvador Dalí's Autobiographical Writings* (Catalán Studies: Translations and Criticism, Vol 17) (New York: Peter Lang Publishing, 1995).

Wenzel, Angela with Rosie Jackson, *The Mad, Mad, Mad World of Salvador Dalí (Adventures in Art)* (Munich and New York: Prestel Verlag, 2003).

Weyers. Frank, *Salvador Dalí's Auseinandersetzung mit den Naturwissenschaften* (Aachen: Verlag Mainz, 1995).

Wilson, Simon, *Salvador Dalí* (London: Tate Gallery, 1980).

Articles on Dalí

A.B., "Art moderne, Dalirama à Rotterdam," *Connaissance des Arts* (Paris), no. 225, November 1970, p. 21.

A.C., "Au casino de Knokke-le-Zoute," *La Flandre Liberale* (Gand), 7 July 1956.

A.M.F., "Dalí news: disconnected telephones and magnascoesque ragamuffins," *Art News* (New York), 1 April 1939, p. 15.

A.M.F., "Salvador Dalí," *Art News* (New York), 1 May 1941.

Abadie, Daniel, "Les obsessions deguisées de Salvador Dalí," in *Salvador Dalí rétrospective 1920-1980*. (Paris: Centre Georges Pompidou, Musée National d'Art Moderne, 1979), pp. 11-15.

"A bordo dell 'ovocipede' lo stravagante pittore," *L'Adige* (Trente), 9 December 1959.

Ades, Dawn, "Unpublished scenario for a documentary on Surrealism (1930?)," *Studio International Journal of the Creative Arts and Design'* (London), vol. 195, nos. 993-4, 1982, pp. 62-77.

Ades, Dawn, "Morphologies of Desire," in *Salvador Dalí: The Early Years*. (London: South Bank Centre, 1994): 129-160.

Ades, Dawn, "Dalí and the Myth of William Tell," in Dawn Ades and Fiona Bradley (ed.), *Salvador Dalí, A Mythology*. (London: Tate Gallery Publishing, 1999), pp. 32-50.

Ades, Dawn, "Dalí's Optical Illusions', in *Dalí's Optical Illusions*. (New Haven and London: Yale University Press, 2000), pp. 10-29.

Agostinho das Neves, J, "Salvador Dalí visionario e paranoico genial," *Dialogo* (Lisbon), 25 February 1958.

Aguado, Lola, "Quien es Dalí?," *Gaceta Ilustrada*, 3 February 1962, pp. 26-35.

Agusti, Ignacio, "Bienvenida a Salvador Dalí," *Destino* (Barcelona), no. 575, 14 August 1948.

Ajame, Pierre, "Les Mystères du panier," *Le Nouvel Observateur* (Paris), 22 July 1978.

"A la Espanola," *Variety* (New York), 8 March 1972.

"Alchimie des philosophes," *Nouvelles de l'Estampe*, no. 30, November 1976.

Aldaman-Echevarria, Pedro, "Dalínizacion del Museo Dalí," *Revista de Gerona* (Gerona), no. 68, 3rd trimester 1974, pp. 42-47.

Alexandre, Alexandre, "Un Jeu de cartes de Salvador Dalí," *Gebrauschgraphik* (Munich), vol. 1, 1 January 1969, pp. 62-65.

Alexandre, Alexandre, "Antennenschnurrbart und Eisenbahn Plakate von Salvador Dalí," *Ge-*

brauschgraphik (Munich), no. 2, February 1971, p. 2.

Alexandre, Alexandre, "L'Album Scarab et Salvador Dalí," *Novum Gebrauschgraphik* (Munich), no. 2, February 1972, pp. 34-37.

"All is ready for the big parade," *The Villager* (New York), vol. 26, no. 50, 19 March 1959.

Alomar, Gabriel, "Salvador Dalí y el juego filosofal de la Arquitectura," *Revista Nacional de Arquitectura*, 1950, pp. 458-459.

Altolaguirre, Manuel, "Gala y Dalí, en Torremolinos," *Diario 16* (Madrid), 1 September 1985, p. ii.

"A l'Université Dalí, on enseigne le nu, canne à la manne," *Paris-Match* (Paris), no. 1420, 14 August 1976, p. 3.

Alvard, Julien, "Dalí and Marx," *Art News* (New York), vol. 66, no. 9, January 1968, p. 62.

Alvarez Cervela, Jose Maria, "Dalí me dedico un libro suyo," *Revista de Arte-The Art Review* (Puerto Rico), no. 9, 1 September 1969, p. 15.

"A new book by Maurice Sandoz," *The New York Times* (New York), 4 November 1950.

"Ancient and Modern," *Scottish Art Review* (Glasgow), vol. IV, no. 2, summer 1952, p. 17.

Andrews, Wayne, "The Surrealist Parade," *New Directions* (New York), 1990.

"And now to make masterpieces," *Time* (New York), vol. 50, 8 December 1947, p. 74.

"An excerpt from 'Babaouo' by Dalí," *Cinemages* (New York), vol. 9, 1 August 1958, pp. 19-28.

Antonio, Julio, "Entrevista con Salvador Dalí," *Informacion* (La Havane), 5 February 1950.

"Ants in Brentano's," *The New Yorker* (New York), 8 May 1943, p. 15.

"Apoteosico escrito en Nueva York del Cristobal Colon de Dalí," *Solidaridad Nacional*, 14 January 1960.

"À Port Lligat…," *Paris-Match* (Paris), vol. 37, 10 September 1955, p. 79.

Appel, Frans, "Sterren van Salvador Dalí stonden goed," *Parool* (Rotterdam), 21 November 1970.

Applegate, Judith, "Paris Letter," *Art International* (Lugano), vol. 15, no. 1, 20 January 1971, p. 34.

Arbos, Albert, "Aquellos amores de Dalí y Pla," *Cambio 16* (Madrid), no. 542, 19 April 1982, pp. 44-51.

Arco, Manuel del, "Ud dira… Dalí," *Diario de Barcelona* (Barcelona), 20 October 1950.

Arco, Manuel del, "Dalí un hombre de bigotes al servicio de su pintura," *Menaje*, July 1955.

Arco, Manuel del, "Visto y oido-Dalí," *Destino* (Barcelona), 7 June 1958, p. 25.

Arco, Manuel del, "Salvador Dalí, de su proxima exposicion en el Tinell," *Vanguardia* (Barcelona), 18 May 1962, p. 27.

Arco, Manuel del, "Salvador Dalí (dialogo)," *Vanguardia* (Barcelona), 14 October 1962, p. 25.

Argillet, Pierre, "Les Hippies," in Dalí catalogue (Clermont-Ferrand: Musée Bargoin, 1989-1990).

Argillet, Pierre, "Dalí-Breton," in Dalí catalogue (Clermont-Ferrand: Musée Bargoin, 1989-1990).

Arnal, J, "Dalí fenicia y enclavo," *Revista*, 19 September 1961.

Artigas, Père, "Un film d'En Dalí," *Mirador* (Barcelona), any I, no. 17, 23 May 1929.

Atirnomis, "Salvador Dalí, Carmen, Three Plays by the Marquis de Sade," *Arts Magazine* (New York), vol. 44, no. 2, November 1969.

"Artistry in Jewels," *American Artist* (New York), vol. 23, June 1959: 12.

"Au casino de Knokke-le-Zoute, Salvador Dalí," *La Nouvelle Gazette* (Brussels), 2 August 1956.

"Au musée Grévin, Dalí reçoit Dalí," *Paris-Match* (Paris), vol. 1023, 14 December 1968.

"Auguste Leroux, Hommage à Salvador Dalí (1902)," *Le Brulot* (Belgium), vol. 21, 15 November 1963.

Aumon, C, "Exposition Dalí, les angoisses d'une ame inquiete," *La Nouvelle Republique de Centre-Ouest* (Tours), 16 May 1979.

"Auto-Dalí," *L'Aurore* (Paris), 8 December 1970.

"Aux Petits Lits Blancs un orateur-clown, Dalí," *Paris-Match* (Paris), vol. 527, May 1959: 80.

"Aux U.S.A. Salvador Dalí fait du dessin anime," *Arts* (Paris), 12 April 1946, p. 3.

Bache, Renal, "Dalí og de syge blomster," *Aalborg Stifstidende* (Aalborg), 10 October 1973.

Bachelier, Armand, "Salvador Dalí n'est pas venu a l'inauguration de Salvador Dalí a Knokke-le-Zoute," *La Nation Belge*, 2 July 1956.

Baker, Elizabeth C, "Dalí: making it surreal," *Art News* (New York), vol. 67, no. 3, May 1968, pp. 45, 61-63.

"Ballet adds two works," *The New York Times* (New York), 23 October 1940.

Banier, François-Marie, "Dalí, contre les vacances… et beaucoup d'autres choses," *Men* (Paris), no. 6, 1968, p. 66.

Barbier, H, "Les dîners de Gala," *L'Éclair* (Nantes), 18 December 1973.

Baron, Jeanine, "Salvador Dalí et la recherche de la troisième dimension," *La Croix* (Paris), 12-13 December 1971.

Baron-Supervielle, Odile, "Conversation avec Salvador Dalí," *La Nation* (Buenos-Aires), 27 February 1977.

Barotte, René, "Salvador Dalí va présenter sa Vierge à New York," *Paris-Presse* (Paris), 4 November 1950.

Barotte, René, "Dalí invite ses amis à la rêverie mystique," *Paris-Presse* (Paris), 18 June 1951.

Barotte, René, "Tu seras plus grand orfèvre que Cellini," *Paris-Presse* (Paris), 16 September 1954.

Barotte, René, "Grâce aux bijoux fous de Dalí, Roger Gollet fera le tour des USA," *Paris-Presse* (Paris), 9 August 1955.

Barotte, René, "Dalí a illustré son Don Quichotte à coups d'arquebuse," *Paris-Presse* (Paris), 18 December 1957.

Barotte, René, "Salvador Dalí a invente le boulettisme," *Le Provencal* (Marseille), 22 December 1957.

Barotte, René, "Les vrais quatre grands au Musée Galliera," *Paris-Presse* (Paris), 20 May 1960.

Barotte, René, "C'est grâce au casque mou…," *Paris-Presse* (Paris), 20 November 1963.

Barotte, René, "Inauguration à son Musée-Théâtre de Figueras," *L'Aurore* (Paris), 30 September 1974.

Bastier, Malte, "Les Lithographies de Don Quichotte seront les lithophies du siècle," *Combat* (Paris), 11 December 1957.

Bataille, Georges, "Le 'Jeu Lugubre'," *Documents* (Paris), vol. 7, December 1929, pp. 368-372.

"Bathtub bests Surrealist Dalí in 5th Avenue window bout," *Daily Mirror*, 17 March 1939.

Battcock, Gregory, "Dalí," *Domus* (Milan), no. 550, September 1975, pp. 50-52.

Baumann, F.A, "Neueerwerbungen des Zürcher Kunsthauses, 1962-1968," *Werk* (Bale), no. 55, December 1968, p. 808.

Bauschinger, Sigrid, "Was Dalí sieht, wenn er Mona Lisa betrachtet,"

Frankfurter Allgemeine Zeitung (Frankfurt), vol. 20, 24 January 1979, p. 25.

Bausset, Phillippe de with Charles Courriere, "Dalí fait battre un coeur de pierre," *Paris-Match* (Paris), vol. 296, November 1954, pp. 72-73.

Bazin, Germain, "Salvador Dalí," *L'Amour de l'Art* (Paris), vol. special l'École de Paris à New York, July 1945, pp. 39, 58.

Bazin, Germain, "Dalí (Salvador)," *Encyclopedia Universalis* (Paris), vol. V, 1969, pp. 313-314.

Beaucamp, Eduard, "Apothèose und Selbtsmord," *Frankfurter Allgemeine Zeitung* (Frankfurt), no. 294, 19 December 1970.

Beaucamp, Eduard, "Der siebzigjährhrige Skandal, Salvador Dalí kunstliche Geheimnisse," *Frankfurter Allgemeine Zeitung* (Frankfurt), 13 May 1974.

Beaucamp, Eduard, "Unabhängigkeitserklärung der Phantasie," *Frankfurter Allgemeine Zeitung* (Frankfurt), 18 January 1975.

Beaucamp, Eduard, "Impression aus der Hohen Mongolei," *Frankfurter Allgemeine Zeitung* (Frankfurt), 26 May 1977.

Beckley, Paul V, "New' Dalí here; Surrealist now 'Nuclear Mystic'," *New York Herald Tribune* (New York), 3 December 1952.

Beckley, Paul V, "Dalí is using sea urchins, dried flowers, oil paper," *New York Herald Tribune* (New York), December 1957.

"Bei der Vernissage," *Das Kunstwerk* (Stuttgart), vol. 24, no. 2, March 1971, p. 82.

Beks, Maarten, "Salvador Dalí, naadloze kunstmatigheid," *Raam*, vol. 53, March 1969, pp. 35-42.

Benet, Rafel, "Els de la darrera fornada, Un neo-verista Salvador Dalí," *Gaseta de les Arts* (Barcelona), any III, no. 41, 15 January 1926, p. 4.

Berasategui, Blanca, "En Pubol, con el genio escondido," *Abc* (Madrid), 12 May 1984, pp. vi-viii.

Berger, Arthur V, "Dalí's 'Tristan' in its première," *The New York Sun* (New York), 16 December 1944.

Bernard, Anne, "Les secrets reveles de Salvador Dalí, Salvador Dalí rétrospective 1920-1980," (Paris: Centre Georges Pompidou, Musée National d'Art Moderne, 1979), pp. 403-414.

Bernard, Charles, "L'Exposition Dalí au Casino du Zoute, un retour en flamme de la litterature en peinture," *La Nation Belge*, 4 July 1956.

Berners, Lord, "Surrealist landscape, a poem dedicated to Salvador Dalí," *Horizon* (London), vol. 6, no. 31, July 1942, pp. 5-6.

Bernils i Mach, Josep Maria, "Dalí, a la preso," *El Perdris, Revista cultural de L'Emporda* (Figueres), no. 4, 12 June 1987.

Bernils, Jose Maria, "El Teatro Museo Dalí de Figueras," *Revista de Gerona* (Girona), no. 68, 3rd trimester, 1974.

Bernlef, J, "Grootste Europese overzichtstentoonstelling in Boymans," *Algemeen Dagblad*, 14 December 1970.

Bigwood, James, "Cinquante ans de cinema dalinien, Salvador Dalí rétrospective 1920-1980," (Paris: Centre Georges Pompidou, Musée National d'Art Moderne, 1979), p. 342-353.

"Bilkørsel, forbudet aender Louisiana - museets abningstid," *Holsterbro Dagblad*, 22 November 1973.

"Biographical Sketch," *Time* (New York), vol. 28, 14 December 1936, p. 62.

"Biography," *Current Biography* (New York), 1940.

"Biography," *Current Biography* (New York), April 1951.

Bird, Paul, "Dalí Orthodoxy," *The Art Digest* (New York), 15 December 1950.

Blanchard, Gilles, "Leda Atomica de Salvador Dalí," *Telerama* (Paris), 30 December 1978.

Bockriss, Victor, "A Dalírious Evening," *Exposure* (Los Angeles), October 1990, pp. 60-63.

Bondil-Poupard, Nathalie, "Such Stuff As Dreams Are Made On: Hitchcock and Dalí, Surrealism and Oneiricism', in *Hitchcock and Art: Fatal Coincidences*. (Montreal: Montreal Museum of Fine Arts, 2001), pp. 155-171.

Bor, Vane, "Correspondance à Salvador Dalí," *Le Surrealisme au Service de la Revolution* (Paris), no. 6, 15 May 1933, pp. 46-47.

"Børnene og Dalí," *Aktuelt*, 14 October 1973.

Bornes, Georges, "Au Teatro Museo Dalí à Figueras. La magie d'un monarque," *Le Figaro* (Paris), 19-20 August 1978, pp. 13-14.

Borregaard, Svend, "Salvador Dalí," *Horsens Folkeblad*, 3 November 1973.

Bosquet, Alain, "Entretien avec Salvador Dalí," *Combat* (Paris), 5 May 1955.

Bosquet, Alain, "Salvador Dalí et sa méthode," *Combat* (Paris), 19 December 1955.

Bosquet, Alain, "Dalí érotique," *Men* (Paris), no. 2, 1968, pp. 40-43.

Bosquet, Alain, "Les Peintres du rêve," *Magazine Litteraire* (Paris), no. 213, December 1984, pp. 58-60.

Bosschardt, Robert, "Exclusif gesprek met 'genie'," *Haagsche Courant*, 28 October 1970; *Amersfoortsche Courant*, 28 November 1970.

Boswell, Peyton, "Is Dalí Crazy?," *The Art Digest* (New York), vol. 15, 1 May 1941, p. 3.

Boswell, Peyton, "Mr. Dalí goes to town," *The Art Digest* (New York), 1 December 1941, p. 3.

Bounoure, Vincent, "Dalí (Salvador)," *Librairie Larousse La Grande Encyclopedie* (Paris), pp. 3614-3615.

Bouret, Jean, "Salvador Dalí mystique," *Arts* (Paris), 29 June 1951.

Bouret, Jean, "Qu'arriverait-il…," *Les Lettres Francaises* (Paris), 26 November 1969.

Bouvard, Philippe, "La Gare de Perpignan 27 fois a l'honneur sous la coupole!" *France-Soir* (Paris), 11 May 1979, pp. 1, 6.

Bouvard, Philippe, "À la recherche de Salvador Dalí inventeur des 'montres molles' et d'un lauréat port le 'Prix de neuf'," *Le Figaro* (Paris), 2 July 1956.

Bouvard, Philippe, "Dalimatias sur la tour Eiffel," *Le Figaro* (Paris), 22 November 1958.

Bouvard, Philippe, "Dalí délire à l'X," *Le Figaro* (Paris), 13 December 1961.

Bouvard, Philippe, "Le Secret de l'éloquence selon Salvador Dalí, porter des souliers vernis trop petits…," *Le Figaro* (Paris), 24 April 1968.

Bouvard, Philippe, "Pour signer au 'Nouveau Brummel'…," *Le Figaro* (Paris), 8 December 1970.

Bouvard, Philippe, "Dalí ne travaille plus qu'avant le petit déjeuner…," *Le Figaro* (Paris), 14 December 1971.

Bowles, Jerry G, "Salvador Dalí's," *Art News* (New York), vol. 70, no. 2, April 1971, p. 10.

"Boymans komt met grote Dalí-expositie," *N.R.C.*, 12 May 1970.

"Boymans Staat van Dalí," *Kontakton* (Rotterdam), 27 November 1970.

Brackert, Gisela, "Dalí," *Das Kunstwerk* (Stuttgart), nos. 9-10, June-July 70, p. 78.

Bradley, Fiona, "Dalí as Myth-Maker: The Tragic Myth of Millet's Angelus', in *Salvador Dalí, A Mythology*. (London: Tate Gallery Publishing, 1999), pp. 12-29.

Brans, J.V.L, "La pintura religiosa de Dalí," *Goya* (Madrid), 1957, pp. 156-164.

Breerette, Genevieve, "Dalí au Salon de Montrouge," *Le Monde* (Paris), 31 May 1977.

Brenson, Theodore, "To the Editor of Liturgical Arts," *Liturgical Arts* (New York), no. 4, August 1952, p. 128.

Breton, André, "Dalí est ici…" (Paris: Galerie Goemans, 1929).

Breton, André with Paul Eluard, "Prière d'insérer pour la Femme visible," *Cahiers d'Art* (Paris), no. 1, 1930, p. 60.

Breton, André, et. al, "We Don't Ear It That Way," Tract (New York), November 1960.

Breuning, Margaret, "Nuclear Mystic," *The Art Digest* (New York), 1 January 1953, p. 15.

Breuning, Margaret, "Dalí's Ambivalent Appeal," *Arts* (New York), vol. 31, 1 January 1957, p. 48.

Breuning, Margaret, "Dalí and antimatter," *Arts* (New York), vol. 33, no. 4, 1 January 1959, p. 52.

Brincourt, André, "Salvador Dalí et J.-C. Averty, une rencontre magique," *Le Figaro* (Paris), 23-24 December 1972.

Brincourt, André, "Dalí, le conquérant de l'irrationnel," *Le Figaro* (Paris), 14 December 1974, pp. 17, 20.

Brissaud, Andre, "Dalí-Pauwels," *Carrefour* (Paris), 7 August 1968.

Brown, Gordon, "The dangers of chastity, The dalinian sufferings we go through," *Arts Magazine* (New York), vol. 42, no. 1, September-October 1967, pp. 42-44.

Brown, Gordon, "Salvador Dalí after fifty years of surrealism," *Arts Magazine* (New York), vol. 49, no. 10, June 1975, p. 20.

Brown, Mick, "Weird days and wild nights with Salvador Dalí," *Crawdaddy*, September 1974.

Brulé, Claude, "Walt Disney s'associe avec Salvador Dalí," *Paris-Presse* (Paris), 5 October 1957.

Brunet, Manuel, "Despedida al notario don Salvador Dalí y Cusi," *Destino* (Barcelona), no. 491, 14 December 1946, p. 7.

Brunet, Manuel, "Salvador Dalí visto por su hermana," *Destino* (Barcelona), no. 647, 31 December 1949, pp. 3, 5-6.

Buchwald, Art, "Dalí jewels set record passing Paris customs," *New York Herald Tribune* (New York), 28 November 1954.

Buchwald, Art, "The Cauliflower, the Rhinoceros and Salvador Dalí," *New York Herald Tribune* (New York), 29 December 1955.

Buchwald, Art, "Dalí doesn't Dally any more," *New York Herald Tribune* (New York), 17 November 1956.

Burr, James, "In André Breton's words…," *Apollo* (London), no. 77, July 1968, p. 63.

Busse, Jacques, "Dalí (Salvador)," *Librairie Grund E. Bénézit: Dictionnaire des peintres, sculpteurs, dessinateurs et graveurs* (Paris), vol. III, 1976, pp. 329-331.

"By way of Dalí," *The New York Times* (New York), 30 July 1966.

C.C, "L'art, Galeries Dalmau, Exposicio Salvador Dalí," *La Publicitat* (Barcelona), 9 January 1927.

C.J, "Le Dalí de Gala," *Le Figaro* (Paris), 13 April 1968.

Cabanne, Pierre, "Le plus singulier des immortels," *Elle* (Paris), no. 1739, 7 May 1979.

Calas, Nicolas, "Anti-surrealist Dalí, I say his flies are ersatz," *View* (New York), vol. I, no. 6, June 1941, pp. 1, 3.

Calas, Nicolas, "Dalí," *Arts Magazine* (New York), vol. 43, no. 3, December 1968-January 1969, p. 10.

"Called on Salvador Dalí…," *Liturgical Arts* (New York), no. 3, May 1952, p. 93.

Calvo Serraller, Francisco, "Una paranoia no critica," *El Pais* (Madrid), 22 June 1979, p. 28.

Calvo Serraller, Francisco, "Salvador Dalí y la vanguardia artistica espanola de los ans veinte," in *400 obras de Salvador Dalí de 1914 a 1983*. (Madrid: Museo Espanol de Arte contemporaneo, 1983), pp. 9-15.

Camon Aznar, J, "Las joyas de Dalí," *Goya* (Madrid), no. 115, July 1973, pp. 30-31.

Campion, Roger, "Salvador Dalí annonce: première nouvelle: la peinture divisionniste," *Le Havre Libre* (Le Havre), 23 November 1956.

Campion, Roger, "Salvador Dalí annonce l'ère d'un art nouveau, la peinture au canon," *Le Havre Libre* (Le Havre), 4 May 1957.

Campoy, Antonio Manuel, "Dalí-Salvador," *Iberico Europea Diccionario critico del Arte espanol contemporaneo*, 1973, p. 101.

Candamo, Luis G. de, "Crisopeya surrealista, Las esculturas de oro de Salvador Dalí," *T.G.-Revista de Las Artes Decorativas* (Madrid), no. 9, 1974, pp. 38-41.

Cano, José Luis, "Salvador Dalí en Torremolinos," *Destino* (Barcelona), no. 413, 16 June 1945.

Carcasona, José Maria, "Dalí, nueva sorpresa de la Biennal," *Revista*, 8 September 1955.

Carmona, A, "El secreto de Salvador Dalí," *Diario de Barcelona* (Barcelona), 24 November 1957.

Carol, Marius, "El escenografo de Portlligat. Muere Isidoro Bea, el hombre que durante treinta anos colaboro con Dalí," *La Vanguardia* (Barcelona), 19 March 1996, p. 2.

Carpentier, Jan de, "Dalí bevecht droombeelden met een gouden bijl," *De Typhoon*, 26 November 1971.

Carrit, David, "How does Dalí cast his spell," *Evening Standard* (London), 10 November 1959.

Carter, Curtis, "Salvador Dalí: Design for the Theater, in Curtis Carter (ed.), in *Dalí and the Ballet: Set and Costumes for 'The Three-Cornered Hat*," *Milwaukee* (Haggerty Museum of Art), 2000, pp. 7-13.

Cartier, Jean-Albert, "Les bijoux de Salvador Dalí," *Mobilier et Decoration* (Paris), January-February 1955.

Cassanyes, M.A, "L'Espai en les pintures de Salvador Dalí," *L'Amic de les Arts* (Sitges), any II, no. 13, 30 April 1927, pp. 30-31.

Cassanyes, M.A, "Dalí," *D'Aci I d'alla* (Barcelona), winter 1934.

Castillo, A. del, "Dalí," *Diario de Barcelona* (Barcelona), 23 March 1952.

Castillo, A. del, "Cronica de Barcelona," *Goya* (Madrid), no. 89, March 1969, pp. 326-327.

Castillo, J. del, "Dalí cuenta sus ultimas genialidades," *Solidaridad Nacional*, 27 September 1957.

Castillo, J. del, "La verdad esta en la escuela de Velasquez," *Solidaridad Nacional*, 28 September 1967.

"Cena homenaje a Salvador Dalí en el Hotel Rocamar en Cadaques," *Vanguardia* (Barcelona), 30 August 1960.

Cerf, B, "Trade Winds," *Saturday Review of Literature* (New York), vol. 30, 22 March 1947, p. 5.

"C'est le roi David," *Parisien Libere* (Paris), 20 October 1967.

"Ceux qui peignent comme des photographes (les hyperréalistes)," *Paris-Match* (Paris), no. 1274, 6 October 1973, p. 67.

Cevasco, G.A, "Dalí no one vs. Dalí no two," *Catholic World* (New York), vol. 185, July 1957, pp. 292-295.

Chaland, Paul with Willy Rizzo, "Dalí," *Paris-Match* (Paris), no. 111, May 1951, p. 29.

Chalon, Jean, "Salvador Dalí: 'L'Angélus' de Millet est un tableau erotique," *Le Figaro Litteraire* (Paris), 21 November 1963.

Chalon, Jean, "Avida Dollars' ne nous etonne plus," *Le Figaro* (Paris), 15 December 1973.

Champigneulle, Bernard, "Salvador Dalí et la sculpture de verre," *Le Figaro* (Paris), 19 September 1968.

Chancel, Jacques, "Dalí sur la bonne voie (SNCF)," *Paris-Jour* (Paris), 4 May 1970.

Chancel, Jacques, "Flagrant Dalí," *Paris-Jour* (Paris), 7 December 1970.

Chancel, Jacques, "Salvador Dalí: 'Ma femme aussi vaut 3 milliards'," *Paris-Jour* (Paris), 9 December 1970.

Chancel, Jacques, "Dalí veut inventer la television liquide," *Paris-Jour* (Paris), 16 July 1971.

Charmet, Raymond, "Salvador Dalí ou le génie de l'equivoque," *Arts* (Paris), no. 776, 25 May 1960, p. 8.

Chastel, André, "L'imagination surréaliste trente ans après," *Le Monde* (Paris), 17 January 1964.

Chastel, André, "Flagrant Dalí," *Le Monde* (Paris), 30 May 1968.

Cheronnet, Louis, "Salvador Dalí," *Art et Decoration* (Paris), vol. 63, July 1934, p. 280.

Chevalier, Haakon M, "Salvador Dalí as Writer, surrealism takes to the typewriter," *Saturday Review of Literature* (New York), 15 April 1944, pp. 14-16.

"Choreographical Delirium," *The Art Digest* (New York), vol. 12, 15 February 1938.

"Chronotropism," *Spanish Village Art Quarterly* (San Diego), November 1941.

Christensen, Birte, "Fra graensen til Nordsjaelland for at se Salvador Dalí-det var turen vaerd," *Flensborg Avis*, 2 November 1973.

Clara, Josep, "Salvador Dalí, empresonat pe la dictadura de Primo de Rivera," *Revista de Gerona* (Gerona), no. 162, January-February 1993, pp. 52-55.

Clarajo, Noel, "El caso Dalí," *Vanguardia* (Barcelona), 19 January 1950.

Clement, Rik, "Salvador Dalí," *De Nieuwe Gids*, 2 December 1970.

Clemmesen, Erik, "Fupmageren, Salvador Dalí," *Kristelgit Dagblad*, 11 October 1973.

Clifton, Violet, "Thoughts evoked by Salvador Dalí's painting of the Crucifixion," *Scottish Art Review* (Glasgow), vol. IV, no. 2, summer, p. 15.

"Cloitre depuis dix jours au "Meurice", Dalí fabrique des poupées pour adultes," *Le Figaro* (Paris), 22 November 1968.

"Close up of the Dalí technique, or, what sitters get for their money," *Art News* (New York), 15 April 1943, p. 11.

"Club 49, actividades y noticicias," *Dau Al Set* (Barcelona), no. 1, December 1950.

Coates, R.M, "Dalí and the atomic bomb," *The New Yorker* (New York), vol. 23, 6 December 1947, pp. 89-90.

Coates, R.M, "Art galleries, exhibition at Carstairs Gallery," *The New Yorker* (New York), vol. 32, 15 December 1956, pp. 129-130.

Cogniat, Raymond, "Salvador Dalí tete a l'envers et pied sur terre," *Le Figaro* (Paris), 4 October 1956.

Cogniat, Raymond, "Chronique dalinienne," *Le Figaro* (Paris), 11 July 1968.

Cogniat, Raymond, "Une providence," *Le Figaro* (Paris), 19 September 1968.

Cogniat, Raymond, "Dalí et 'le Décaméron'," *Le Figaro* (Paris), 26 December 1972.

Cogniat, Raymond, "Les Dalí de Maguy," *Le Figaro* (Paris), 22 May 1973.

Cogniat, Raymond, "Dalí, sompteux artisan," *Le Figaro* (Paris), 23 April 1974.

Coll, Julio, "Salvador Dalí habla para Liceo propositos tremendos de un encantador de sospientes," *Liceo* (Barcelona), October 1948.

Combaz, Christian, "Dalí hyperréaliste et métaphysique," *Le Figaro* (Paris), 18-19 February 1978.

Comin, M.P, "Las medias el algodon y salia de Dalí," *Vanguardia* (Barcelona), 4 July 1967, p. 47.

"Comedian and the straight man," *Time* (New York), vol. 86, 31 December 1965, p. 74.

"Comment Dalí invite a prendre le train," *Paris-Presse* (Paris), 5 May 1970.

Connoly, Cyrill, "Dreams of Dalí," *Art News Annual*, vol. 21, 1951, pp. 148, 149, 159.

Copp, Jacques, "La dernière clownerie d'Avida Dollars," *L'Oise-Matin*, 11 December 1959.

Cortej, Juan, "Salvador Dalí," *Liceo* (Barcelona), no. 2, March 1945.

Cortes i Vidal, Joan, "Punts de vista cabotinisme," *Mirador* (Barcelona), any I, no. 6, 7 March 1929.

"Costumes de bain, tableaux, littérature, la tournée Dalí," *Tribune de Lausanne-Dimanche* (Lausanne), no. 136, 16 May 1965.

Courvoisier, Herve, "C'est tout un art," *Telerama* (Paris), 18 February 1978, pp. 14-15.

Courvoisier, Herve, "Les Mille et Une visions de Dalí," *Telerama* (Paris), 18 February 1978, p. 41.

Cowles, Fleur, "The modern proteus," *Echo* (New York), 1960.

Cowles, Fleur, "Notebook," *Playbill* (London), vol. I, no. 3, May 1966, pp. 27, 29.

Cowley, Malcom, "The Imp of the Perverse," *The New Republic*, 18 January 1943, pp. 88, 90.

Crespelle, Jean-Paul, "Dalí a illustré Don Quichotte," *France-Soir* (Paris), 7 December 1957.

Crosa, A, "Salvador Dalí," *Hoja de Lunes* (Barcelona), 1 September 1958.

Crosbie, William, "Technical rumination," *Scottish Art Review* (Glasgow), vol. IV, no. 2, summer 1952, p. 16.

"Cuatro años del Museo Dalí," *L'Emporda* (Figueres), no. 36, 27 September 1978.

"Cuisine, la gastro-esthétique de Salvador Dalí," *Mincer 2000* (Paris), 1 April 1979, pp. 14-16.

Curzy, Lucien, "Dalí dans l'autre monde?' *L'Humanite* (Paris), 10 January 1978.

Curzy, Lucien, "Rire avec sérieux," *L'Humanite* (Paris), 18 February 1978.

Daleveze, Jean, "Voici encore un homme…," *Les Nouvelles Lit-*

teraires (Paris), June 1969.

Daleveze, Jean, "Ce sont des illustrations…," *Les Nouvelles Litteraires* (Paris), February 1970.

Daleveze, Jean, "Voici Dalí…," *Les Nouvelles Litteraires* (Paris), 25 June 1970.

Daleveze, Jean, "La Quarantaine de peintures…," *Les Nouvelles Litteraires* (Paris), 19 November 1970.

"Dalí," *Art News* (New York), December 1947, p. 45.

"Dalí," *De Tijd*, 12 November 1970.

"Dalí," *Fine Arts* (Cleveland), vol. 20, no. 929, 1 December 1972.

"Dalí," *Münchner Jahrbuch der Bildenden Kunst* (Munich), vol. 24, 1973, pp. 284, 287.

"Dalí," *Phaidon dictionary of the twentieth-century Art* (Oxford: Phaidon Press, 1973).

"Dalí," *La Fran Enciclopedia Vasca, Maestros actuales de la pintura y la escultura catalanas* (Bilbao), tome I, 1975, pp. 1-4.

"Dalí," *Umbrella* (Glendale (California)), vol. I, no. 3, May 1978, p. 56.

"Dalí (Salvador)," *Espasa-Calpe, Encyclopedia Universal Illustrada Europa—Americana* (Bilbao, Madrid, Barcelona), vol. III, 1931, p. 1403.

"Dalí (Salvador)," *Biographical Encyclopedia of the world*, 1946.

"Dalí (Salvador)," *Librairie Larousse, Grand Larousse Encyclopedique* (Paris), tome III, 1960, p. 760.

"Dalí + Dalí = Dalí," *Ondas*, 1 September 1961, p. 4.

"Dalí 75," *Kunst Echo's* (Gand), no. 3, May-June 1979, p. 26.

"Dalí 79: Beaubourg et l'Academie des Beaux-Arts," *La Dernière Heure* (Brussels), 29 August 1978.

"Dalí: 'Achetez l'art pompier, c'est de l'or'," *Paris-Match* (Paris), no. 788, 16 May 1964, p. 122.

"Dalí a Fascist?' *The Art Digest* (New York), 1 December 1941, p. 6, 14.

"Dalí, an artist's an artist for a'that," *The Art Digest* (New York), vol. 13, 1 April 1939, p. 9.

"Dalí and Shorewood and de Sade project," *Publishers' Weekly*, vol. 193, 4 March 1968, p. 97.

"Dalí and the Sir James Dunn Foundation," *Connoisseur* (London), vol. 144, January 1960, p. 249.

"Dalí, a study of his art in jewels, the collection of the Owen Cheatham Foundation by L. Livingston," *Connoisseur* (London), no. 147, March 1961, p. 46.

"Dalí at Carstairs and Knoedlers,"

Apollo (London), no. 67, May 1958, p. 180.

"Dalí at Glasgow," *Museum Journal* (Glasgow), no. 58, May 1958, p. 51.

"Dalí au musée Grévin," *Combat* (Paris), 5 December 1968.

"Dalí au service de Salvador," *Points et Contrepoints* (Paris), December 1974, pp. 79-85.

"Dalí baffles again with cauliflower," *New York World Telegram and Sun* (New York), 17 December 1955.

"Dalí bathes pique in Fur-lined tub," *Journal and American* (New York), 17 March 1939, p. 36.

"Dalí: Bible illustrée et télévision liquide," *Le Figaro* (Paris), 9-10 Nov-63, p. 21.

"Dalí bows in films as poster painter for 'Don Giovani'," *Variety* (New York), 7 February 1979.

"Dalí classics," *Art News* (New York), vol. 69, no. 70, February 1971.

"Dalí collects a masterpiece," *New York Herald Tribune* (New York), 24 January 1962.

"Dalí, comment va votre moustache?' *Paris-Match* (Paris), no. 814, 14 November 1964, pp. 110-111.

"Dalí composes a photograph," *Vogue* (New York), 15 May 1948, p. 88.

"Dalí: Danmark," *Sjaellands Tidende*, 5 November 1973.

"Dalí da nombre a la futura exposicion unicersal ':a Nabucodonosor Barcelona 1982'," *Correo Catalan* (Barcelona), 5 August 1970, p. 28.

"Dalí délire, l'oreille est son nouveau dada," *L'Aurore* (Paris), 22 November 1958.

"Dalí denuncia el conformismo del vanguardismo," *Gaceta Ilustrada*, 12 September 1964.

"Dalí desconcerto a Venecia," *Correo Catalan* (Barcelona), 27 August 1961, p. 8.

"Dalí-designed night Club will 'move and breathe'," *New York Herald Tribune* (New York), 3 March 1957.

"Dalí designs his dream studio," *House and Garden*, vol. 97, June 1950, pp. 98-99.

"Dalí desponia su Museo de Figueras," *Vanguardia* (Barcelona), 3 July 1973, p. 15.

"Dalí, Divino decadente, Miró es un pases, dice!' *Correo Catalan* (Barcelona), 26 May 1973, p. 29.

"Dalí dozin…," *The Cincinnati Enquirer* (Cincinnati), 5 April 1942.

"Dalí dream comes true," *Newsweek*

(New York), vol. 13, 27 March 1939, p. 27.

"Dalí: du pompier au thon," *Aux Ecoutes* (Paris), 18 October 1967, p. 26.

"Dalí, een onbekende Schilder, Boymans gaat er iets aan doen," *De Telegraaf*, 17 April 1970.

"Dalí en el Parque Guell, una otra vista con del Arco," *Revista*, 6 April 1953.

"Dalí en habit vert," *L'Express* (Paris), 5 June 1978.

"Dalí en vacances a Port Lligat," *Paris-Match* (Paris), no. 337, 8 September 1956, p. 78.

"Dalí et la jumpologie," *Paris-Match* (Paris), no. 557, 12 December 1959, p. 113.

"Dalí et la publicite," *Le Figaro* (Paris), 10 December 1969.

"Dalí et l'alchimie," *Le Parisien Libere* (Paris), 25 October 1976.

"Dalí et Pauwels, les passions selon Dalí," *La Libre Belgique* (Brussels), 19 April 1968.

"Dalí et sa femme presentent leur Madone," *Paris-Match* (Paris), no. 269, 22 May 1954, p. 63.

"Dalí exhibit opens Monday," *New York Herald Tribune* (New York), 24 November 1950.

"Dalí exhibition," *Vogue* (New York), 1 April 1939, p. 42.

"Dalí exhibition at the Museum of Modern Art," *Design* (New York), vol. 43, December 1941, p. 27.

"Dalí exposicion, Paris," *Goya* (Madrid), no. 94, January 1970, p. 232.

"Dalí fait des pieds de la gitane, des pinceaux," *Paris-Match* (Paris), no. 495, 4 October 1958, p. 89.

"Dalí fait maintenant son fromage avec des chevres," *Le Figaro* (Paris), 18 November 1971.

"Dalí fera pleuvoir des rhinoceros dans son film 'La brouette de chair'," *Paris-Presse* (Paris), 6 February 1954.

"Dalí fiel a si mismo," *Vanguardia* (Barcelona), 13 June 1964, p. 21.

"Dalí fires a shot," *Newsweek* (New York), vol. 48, 17 December 1956, p. 101.

"Dalí, Gala and Moolah, Exhibition at Huntington Hartford's Gallery of modern art," *Newsweek* (New York), vol. 66, 27 December 1965, pp. 68-69.

"Dalí, Gaudí, Pujols…," *Tele Estel*, 4 November 1966, p. 1.

"Dalí gets 5 000 dollars award of Hartford Foundation," *The New*

York Times (New York), 21 October 1957.

"Dalí gives his theories on painting," *The Hartford Courant* (Hartford [Connecticut]), 19 December 1934.

"Dalí goes Hollywood," *The Art Digest* (New York), vol. 11, 1 March 1937, p. 17.

"Dalí goes theatrical," *New York Herald Tribune* (New York), 10 November 1950.

"Dalí ha construido un guerano publicitario," *Solidaridad Nacional*, 6 June 1958.

"Dalí hallucinogène," *Le Figaro Littéraire* (Paris), 29 December 1969.

"Dalí has exhibit at Julien Levy's," *Art News* (New York), 25 November 1933.

"Dalí i Humlebaek," *Aalborg Stiftstidende* (Aalborg), 4 October 1973.

"Dalí in California," *The Art Digest* (New York), 1 November 1941, p. 22.

"Dalí in London, Exhibition," *Time* (New York), 17 December 1951, p. 67.

"Dalí inquiète l'Académie," *Le Figaro* (Paris), 12 April 1979.

"Dalí in San Francisco," *Script Magazine*, May 1947.

"Dalí in San Francisco," *Script Magazine*, May 1947.

"Dalí, in the news and in the Studio," *Current History* (New York), vol. 50, April 1939, pp. 48-49.

"Dalí introduces new perfume," *Art News* (New York), November 1946, p. 6.

"Dalí, inspired by own paintings, designs, jewelry on exhibit here," *New York Herald Tribune* (New York), 17 January 1950.

"Dalí: 'Je dois toute ma fortune a ma méthode paranoïaque critique'," *Le Figaro* (Paris), 11 December 1969.

"Dalí, joyero," *Goya* (Madrid), no. 103, July 1971.

"Dalí-la-Drogue," *Connaissance des Arts* (Paris), no. 213, November 1969, p. 23.

"Dalí lance l'ovocipede, boule a ecureuil humain," *Paris-Match* (Paris), 26 December 1959, p. 86.

"Dalí: latest edition," *The New York Times* (New York), 27 April 1941, p. 6.

"Dalí lauds Dalí in own Daily," *The Art Digest* (New York), 1 December 1945, pp. 7, 31.

"Dalí lecture," *Bulletin of the Museum of modern art* (New York), vol.

II, no. 4, January 1935, p. 2.

"Dalí livre ses recettes," *Minute* (Paris), 9 January 1974.

"Dalí makes Met," *Times* (New York), no. 65, 24 January 1955, p. 72.

"Dalí, Maler og provo," *Berlinske Tidende*, 6 October 1973.

"Dalí mange du caviar et flatte le peuple avant de diriger Hallyday," *Le Figaro* (Paris), 10 December 1970.

"Dalí manifests," *The Art Digest* (New York), vol. 13, no. 19, 1 August 1939, p. 9.

"Dalí marie pour se liberer une dentellière et un rhinoceros," *Paris-Match* (Paris), no. 319, 7 May 1955, p. 80.

"Dalí, méthode Paranoïaque critique, hasard objectif et troisième dimension," *L'Oeil* (Paris), no. 238, 1 May 1975, p. 83.

"Dalí modeliste visionnaire," *Le Figaro* (Paris), 23 November 1971.

"Dalí monte a Paris pour illustrer Don Quichotte," *France-Soir* (Paris), 12 October 1956.

"Dalí: new and old Surrealism," *Art News* (New York), vol. 44, 1 December 1945, p. 24.

"Dalí news," *Time* (New York), vol. 73, 5 January 1959, p. 66.

"Daliniana del desanmimiento," *Diario de Barcelona* (Barcelona), 3 November 1959.

"Dalí og Louisiana," *Silkeborg Avis*, 30 October 1973.

"Dalí on the atomic age," *Script Magazine*, January 1948.

"Dalí ordered to pay for missed TV date," *The New York Times* (New York), 8 June 1966.

"Dalí otra vez, españoles," *Goya* (Madrid), no. 110, September 1972, pp. 105-106.

"Dalí: Oui, un artiste a le droit de copier une photographie," *Arts* (Paris), no. 719, 22 April 1959, pp. 1, 8.

"Dalí Out West," *The Art Digest* (New York), 1 October 1941, p. 9.

"Dalí pä Louisiana," *Fins Stiftstidende*, 4 October 1973.

"Dalí painted plates to sell for 400 dollars per," *Pittsburgh Sun Telegraph* (Pittsburgh), 2 May 1943.

"Dalí painting," *American Artist* (New York), vol. 24, March 1960, p. 48.

"Dalí paints the seven lively arts," *Life* (New York), vol. 18, 1 January 1945, pp. 4-6.

"Dalí par Dalí de Draeger," *Combat* (Paris), 30 November 1970.

"Dalí peint une fresque qui fait 'pschitt'," *Paris-Match* (Paris), no. 1074, 6 December 1969, p. 118.

"Dalí piensa en su resurreccion," *Hola* (Madrid), August 1978.

"Dalí pinta para el Concilo," *Gaceta Ilustrada*, 20 August 1960.

"Dalí pintura la cupula del pilar," *Hola* (Madrid), February 1979.

"Dalí: 'Pompidou aurait du m'écouter'," *Paris-Match* (Paris), no. 1050, 21 June 1969, p. 112.

"Dalí poses beside his 'soft self-Portrait'," *New York Herald Tribune* (New York), 22 April 1941.

"Dalí presenta su Venus," *Gaceta Ilustrada* (), vol. , no. 0, 23 May 1964, pp. 48-49.

"Dalí prints in Cleveland," *The Art Digest* (New York), 15 October 1947, p. 20.

"Dalí proclaims Surrealism a paranoiac art," *The Art Digest* (New York), 1 February 1935, p. 10.

"Dalí, professeur de dessin pour trois francs de l'heure," *Le Figaro* (Paris), 26 October 1967.

"Dalí-Radierungen, Hemingway-Grafiken fur 4200 Mark," *Wirtschaftswoche*, 17 September 1976.

"Dalí reafirma la creation del museo Dalí: interesantes declaraciones del pintor y de los arquitectos del futuro museo," *Ampurdan* (Figueres), no. 1321, 10 July 1968, pp. 1, 3.

"Dalí reapproached," *The New Yorker* (New York), 15 February 1964.

"Dalí reporter, il vous explique son surrealisme a travers Barcelone et Paris," *Paris-Match* (Paris), no. 1055, 26 July 1969, p. 31.

"Dalí "returns" to San Francisco," *The Cory Newsletter* (San Francisco), vol. II, 1970.

"Dalí, Rizzoli Bible," *Publishers' Weekly*, vol. 193, 5 February 1968, pp. 92-93.

"Dalí romancier et cuisinier," *Bulletin du Livre*, 15 December 1973.

"Dalí, Salvador," *Librairie Larousse, Le Larousse des grands peintres* (Paris), 1976, p. 80.

"Dalí, Salvador," *Les Muses-Ecyclopedie des Arts* (Paris), vol. VI, no. 90, 23 June 1971, pp. 1794-1799.

"Dalí's Answer," *This Week Magazine, New York Herald Tribune* (New York), 5 April 1953.

"Dalí's astonishing new drawings to appear in Rizzoli Bible," *Publishers' Weekly*, vol. 188, 19 July 1965, p. 130.

"Dalí's beating heart jewel," *Vogue*

(New York), 15 May 1954.

"Dalí's 'Christ of St. John of the Cross'," *Scottish Art Review* (Glasgow), vol. VI, no. 4, 1958, pp. 14-16.

"Dalí's "Credo"...," *Liturgical Arts* (New York), no. 3, May 1952, p. 74.

"Dalí's display," *Time* (New York), 27 March 1939, p. 31.

"Dalí's domain," *MD* (New York), January 1961, pp. 87-92.

"Dalí's dream of ballet," *Vogue* (New York), 15 December 1941, pp. 34-35.

"Dalí's dream of jewels," *Vogue* (New York), 15 July 1941, pp. 32-33.

"Dalí se corto el bigote (en Nueva York y sin propaganda)," *Revista*, 17 August 1961, p. 10.

"Dalí se inspira en el busto de Jane Mansfield," *Informaciones* (Madrid), 19 August 1978.

"Dalí se vend bien," *Combat* (Paris), 14 December 1970.

"Dalí's Frozen Nightmares," *The Art Digest* (New York), vol. 8, 15 December 1933, p. 12.

"Dalí's future plans," *Catholic World* (New York), vol. 170, February 1950, p. 391.

"Dalí's Heterosexual Monster Invades Chicago," *The Art Digest* (New York), vol. 18, no. 2, 15 October 1943, p. 13.

"Dalí shoots his way to a new art form," *New York Herald Tribune* (New York), 28 November 1956.

"Dalí s'inaugure au Musée Grévin," *L'Aurore* (Paris), 4 December 1968.

"Dalí's ladies," *Time* (New York), vol. 41, no. 79, 26 April 1943.

"Dalí's New York, he calls his latest paintings 'Psycho-atomic'," *Pictures on exhibit* (New York), December 1947, pp. 10-11.

"Dalí's Rätsel und Begierden," *Lady International*, May 1974.

"Dalí's return," *New York Post* (New York), 27 November 1956.

"Dalí's surrealist dream house at the World's Fair," *Vogue* (New York), 1 June 1939, pp. 56-59.

"Dalí, surrealist, has a nightmare, while wide awake," *New York World Telegram* (New York), 17 March 1939.

"Dalí, Surreal lama," *The Guardian* (London), 9 November 1973.

"Dalí, Tentoonstelling in Rotterdam," *Eindhovens Dagblad* (Eindhoven), 15 May 1970.

"Dalí, Tentoonstelling is technisch volmaakt," *Dagblad de Stem* (Breda), 3 December 1970.

"Dalí, the surrealist," *Vanity Fair* (New York), February 1935, pp. 48-49.

"Dalí, udstilling," *Morso Folkeblad*, 3 October 1973.

"Dalí, udstilling abnes pa lørdag," *Helsinger Dagblad*, 2 October 1973.

"Dalí, udstilling på Louisiana," *Morsø Folkeblad*, 4 October 1973.

"Dalí, udstilling på Louisiana," *Roskilde Tidende*, 5 October 1973.

"Dalí, udstillingen," *Logstor Avis*, 6 October 1973.

"Dalí, un bonnet pour fêter la Catalogne libre," *Paris-Match* (Paris), no. 1480, 7 October 1977, p. 48.

"Dalí's Venusberg ballet," *Vogue* (New York), 15 October 1939, pp. 48-49.

"Dalí to make U.S. grabfest tour 'For the publicity'," *Variety* (New York), 10 October 1951.

"Dalí to provide scenario for a Massine Ballet," *New York Herald Tribune* (New York), 22 January 1938.

"Dalí: 'Toutes les coupoles me plaisent'," *Le Figaro* (Paris), 9 May 1979, p. 32.

"Dalí trabaja inspirandose en Jane Mansfield," *Abc* (Madrid), 19 August 1978.

"Dalí v. Scarlatti," *Times* (New York), 1 September 1961.

"Dalí veut créer sa 'tragédie érotique' dans un salon du Meurice," *Le Figaro* (Paris), 18 November 1970.

"Dalí, visto por los artistas," *Revista de Gerona* (Gerona), no. 68, 3rd trimester, 1974, pp. 83-92.

"Dalivres exquis," *Le Sauvage* (Paris), October 1976.

"Dalí walks out on his own show," *New York Herald Tribune* (New York), 15 April 1962.

"Dalí, Waster of a great painting talent," *The Art Digest* (New York), vol. 11, 1 January 1937, p. 7.

"Dalí wins fee fight," *The New York Times* (New York), 4 February 1955.

"Dalí worthy of Dalí," *Times* (New York), vol. 71, 24 March 1958, p. 81.

"Dalí y el futbol," *Diario de Barcelona* (Barcelona), 31 May 1961, p. 2.

"Dalí y su Santiago el Mayor," *Gaceta Ilustrada*, 28 June 1958.

Dalmas, André, "Salvador Dalí, les cocus du vieil art moderne," *Tribune des Nations* (Paris), 10 August 1956.

Dalton, J, "The Case of Salvador Dalí by Fleur Cowles," *Apollo* (London), vol. 70, no. 413, July 1959, p. 8.

"(Das) Ei-Rad des Salvatore Dalí," *Offenbach-Post* (Offenbach), 11 December 1959.

Daudet, Elvira, "Magico Dalí," *Abc* (Madrid), 1 March 1970, pp. 41-47.

Daudet, Elvira, "Magico Dalí," *Abc* (Madrid), 8 March 1970, pp. 28-33.

Daunis, T, "Dalí y su otra solucion al enigma del zoo," *Solidaridad Nacional*, 29 May 1958.

Dauriac, Jacques Paul, "Dalí, les dîners de Gala," *Graphis* (Zurich), vol. 30, no. 172, 1974-1975, pp. 152-159.

Daval, Jean-Luc, "Dalí par Dalí," *Journal de Geneve* (Geneva), 30 September 1971.

Davidson, Sol. A, "Immeasurable," *The Art Digest* (New York), 1 February 1943, p. 21.

De Boo, L.-G, "Salvador Dalí a attire la foule au Zoute," *Derniere Heure*, 2 July 1956.

De Boo, L.S, "Allo, allo ici Knocke Festival," *Le Matin* (Paris), 3 July 1956.

Debreuil, Laure, "Anatomie d'un chef-d'oeuvre," *Le Matin* (Paris), 5 January 1979.

Debreuil, Laure, "Léda Atomica' l'insolite perfection de Dalí," *Le Matin* (Paris), 5 January 1979.

"Deception: pas d'orgie romaine au Lido, par Salvador Dalí," *Arts* (Paris), no. 753, 16-22 December 1959.

Decoin, Didier, "Salvador Dalí," *Les Nouvelles Litteraires* (Paris), 18 March 1974, p. 5.

Dege, Denise, "Como vien los famosos en Francia," *El Diario Montanes* (Santander), 5 February 1964.

Del Mar, Michael, "Utiliser les etoiles pour mieux connaitre les stars," *Façade* (Paris), no. 6, 1978, pp. 6-8.

Delafortrie, Lieven, "Salvador Dalí," *Kunst-en Cultuuragenda* (Brussels), no. 30, 21 October 1970.

"Demandato en USA, un editorial reclama a Dalí la entrega de 78 'gouaches'," *Diario de Barcelona* (Barcelona), 30 January 1975.

Demhel, George, "Realizing Dalí's Scenic Designs," in Curtis Carter (ed.), *Dalí and the Ballet: Set and Costumes for The Three-Cornered Hat*. (Milwaukee: Haggerty Museum of Art, 2000), pp. 27-30.

Demoriane, Helene, "Sept Dalí," *Le Point* (Paris), 28 May 1973.

Demoriane, Helene, "Le dalirama de Figueras," *Le Point* (Paris), no. 107, 7 October 1974.

"Dentro de un año Dalí expondra en el Centro Pompidou," *Diario de Barcelona* (Barcelona), 20 December 1978.

Denvir, Bernard, "London letter," *Art International* (Lugano), vol. 17, no. 2, February 1973, p. 30.

Déon, Michel, "L'Aventure dalinienne," in *Histoire d'un grand livre Don Quichotte*. (Paris: Joseph Foret, 1957).

Déon, Michel, "Un homme de la Renaissance," *L'Aurore* (Paris), 10 May 1979.

Derval, Joel, "Dalí, bijoutier du clair de lune," *Combat* (Paris), 10 May 1971.

Descargues, Pierre, "Salvador Dalí en Espagne," *Arts* (Paris), no. 284, 10 November 1950, p. 5.

Descargues, Pierre. *Les Lettres Francaises* (Paris), 2 December 1970.

Descharnes, Robert, "Du neuf sur Dalí, Dalí mis a nu," *Arts* (Paris), no. 885, 10 October 1962, p. 307.

Descharnes, Robert, "Dalí, l'image et l'espace', in *Salvador Dalí rétrospective 1920-1980* (Paris: Centre Georges Pompidou, Musée National d'Art Moderne, 1979), pp. 391-402.

Descharnes, Robert, "L'Art d'être Salvador Dalí," in *Dalí* (Rotterdam: Museum Boymans Van-Beuningen, 1970).

Descharnes, Robert, "Ce livre cathédrale est le plus cher du monde, tirage un exemplaire, prix 100 millions," *Paris-Match* (Paris), no. 623, 18 March 1961, p. 70.

Descharnes, Robert, "La solitaria de Pubol," *Abc* (Madrid), 12 June 1992, p. 64.

Descharnes, Robert, "The Three-Cornered Hat and Other Ballets," in Curtis Carter (ed.), *Dalí and the Ballet: Set and Costumes for The Three-Cornered Hat*. (Milwaukee: Haggerty Museum of Art, 2000), pp. 14-15.

"Des Dalí en or," *Connaissance des Arts* (Paris), May 1971: 120-121.

Desgraupes, Pierre, "Pierre Desgraupes fait le Point avec Salvador Dalí," *Le Point* (Paris), no. 71, 28 January 1974, p. 72.

Desgraupes, Pierre, "Conversation with Salvador Dalí," *Oui* (New York), July 1974.

Deulofeu, Alexandre, "El complex Dalinia," *Revista de Gerona* (Gerona), no. 68, 3rd trimester, 1974, pp. 23-26.

Devay, Jean-François, "Salvador Dalí se prépare à traiter Picasso de 'mari trompé'," *Paris Presse-L'Intransigeant* (Paris), 4 July 1956.

Devree, Howard, "Exhibition Julien Levy's," *Magazine of Art* (New York), vol. 30, January 1937, p. 61.

Devree, Howard, "Portraits by Dalí," *The New York Times Magazine* (New York), 11 April 1943, p. 17.

"Deze winter werk van Dalí in Rotterdam," *Arnhems Dagblad* (Arnhems), 13 May 1970.

Dieterich, Anton, "Torso vom Genie," *Stuttgart Zeitung* (Stuttgart), 3 December 1974.

"Divine Dalí, Preview of Carstairs Gallery," *The New Yorker* (New York), vol. 28, 20 December 1952, pp. 24-25.

Diwo, Jean, "Chez Dalí le Don Quichotte peintre," *Paris-Match* (Paris), no. 465, 8 March 1958, pp. 50-64.

Doherty, Rosaleen with Gerard Duncan, "Art changed, he crashes 5th Ave store window," *Daily News* (New York), 17 March 1939.

Dominguez, Oscar, "Carta de paris, conversation con Salvador Dalí," *Gaceta de Arte* (Tenerife), vol. III, no. 28, July 1934, p. 3.

"Don Quichotte de Figueras," *Die Welt* (Hambourg), 4 July 1979.

Dormolen, Ted Van, "Ik moet voortgaanmijn broer te doden," *Panorama*, no. 47, 14-20 November 1970, pp. 44-53.

Dorner, Victor, "La originalidad de Salvador Dalí," *Cultura Peruana*, May-June 1952.

Dorsey, Hebe, "The Vogué and Salvador Dalí.," *International Herald Tribune* (Paris), 10 December 1971, p. 7.

"Dream World, picture story," *Coronet* (Boulder [Colorado]), vol. 28, October 1950, pp. 46-54.

"Dreams, Paranoiac," *Time* (New York), 3 April 1939, p. 43.

"Dreifache Ruckwendung," *Suddeusch Zeitung*, 25 March 1974.

"Drei-themen-Ausstellung im Stadel eroffnet," *Frankfurter Stadt-Rundschau* (Frankfurt), 14 March 1974.

Drucker, Michel, "Salvador Dalí voit la tele a l'envers," *France-Soir* (Paris), 1 November 1976.

Duault, Nicole, "Il est reçu aujourd'hui à l'Académie des Beaux-Arts, Dalí-le-divin sous la coupole," *France-Soir* (Paris), 10 May 1979, p. 27.

Duault, Nicole, "Il siège désormais parmi les sages membres de l'Académie des Beaux-Arts et il a 75 ans demain, Phe-no-me-nal Salvador Dalí," *France-Soir* (Paris), 11 May 1979, p. 2.

Duffy, James E, "Now, Dalí has another tag for it," *New York World Telegram and Sun* (New York), 20 December 1957.

Duister, Frans, "Het Verschijnsel Dalí," *De Tijd*, 20 November 1970.

Dumur, Guy, "Ne pas toucher," *Le Nouvel Observateur* (Paris), 30 April 1968.

Dunoyer, Jean-Marie, "Salvador Dalí recu a l'Academie des Beaux-Arts," *Le Monde* (Paris), 11 May 1979.

Dupierreux, Richard, "Étrangetés artistiques, Le phénomène Salvador Dalí," *Journal de Charleroi* (Cherleroi), 20 July 1956.

Durand, L, "First class paranoiac," *Newsweek* (New York), vol. 56, 22 August 1960, p. 86.

Durand-Gasselin, Sophie, "Rencontre avec Salvador Dalí," *Paradoxes* (Paris), November 1974, pp. 101-102.

Dutourd, Jean, "Le baladin du monde occidental," *France-Soir* (Paris), 13-14 May 1979.

Dutreix, Gilles, "Salvador Dalí: Pauwels declare que je suis un genie," *Nice-Matin* (Nice), 12 May 1968.

E.G, "Salvador Dalí's Cross of Peace," *This Week Magazine, New York Herald Tribune* (New York), 5 April 1953, pp. 1, 30.

E.H.C, "The Jewels of Dalí: Foreword," *The Philadelphia Museum Bulletin* (Philadelphia), vol. I, no. 244, winter 1955, p. 19.

Eberlé, Eugène, "Dringen voor een blick op werk van Dalí," *Algemeen Dagblad* (Rotterdam), 23 November 1970.

"Éblouissant dans une combinaison de cuir doré Salvador Dalí est apparu au Palais des Glaces dans un ovocipède," *La Lanterne* (Brussels), 8 December 1959.

"Eerst maal in Nederland: Salvador Dalí exposeert in Museum Boymans," *Haarlems Dagblad* (Haarlem), 13 May 1970.

Edgar, Natalie, "Salvador Dalí compresses," *Art News* (New York), vol. 69, no. 2, April 1970.

Edvard, Hans, "Hvis bare førsteklasse vognene bliver skånet," *Information* (Stockholm), 9 October 1973.

Efron, Edith, "He prefers to watch TV upsidedown," *TV Guide* (Radnor), 8 June 1968, pp. 7-10.

"El clavo ardiendo, Salvador Dalí y sus bigotes," *Solidaridad Nacional*, 1 August 1948.

"El director Puixvert espero a Dalí de una hernia en la ingle al parecer con resultados satisfactorios," *Diario de Barcelona* (Barcelona), 7 June 1974, p. 1.

"Elegido por una immidad Dalí ademas en Francia," *Diario de Barcelona* (Barcelona), 26 March 1979.

Elgin, Roger, "The male nudes of Salvador Dalí," *Salute Magazine* (Los Angeles), no. 8, 1969, pp. 50-51, 53.

Eluard, Paul, "Salvador Dalí' (Paris: Galerie Pierre Colle, 1932).

Eluard, Paul, "Voir, poèmes, peintures, dessins," *Trois Collines* (Geneva-Paris), 1948, p. 80.

"En el centro Georges Pompidou gram antologia desdicada a Salvador Dalí," *Diario de Barcelona* (Barcelona), 26 February 1978.

Engelhard, Gunter, "Champignons als Droge," *Kolner Stadtanzeiger* (Cologne), 13 April 1976.

Engels, Gunter, "Weiche im Halbschalf," *Kolnische Rundschau* (Cologne), 14 November 1974.

"En marge... de l'exposition Salvador Dalí a Charleroi," *Beaux-Arts* (Brussels), 4 March 1968.

"Enigmatic elements in landscape," *Washington County Museum of Fine Arts Bulletin* (Washington), January 1940, p. 4.

"Enigmatic elements in landscape," *Coronet* (Boulder [Colorado]), June 1939, p. 92.

"Entre el Dalí fossil y el Dalí vivo," *Cataluna Expres*, 18 May 1962, p. 7.

Epton, Nina, "De grands artistes et leur modele: Gala l'inspiratrice d'un mystique," *Le Soir* (Brussels), 22 October 1959.

"Et, au-dela des extravagances, un intense sentiment religieux. Dalí le Fantastique," *Marie-France* (Paris), no. 154, December 1968.

Evenson, Norma, "The Phantom Cart" by Salvador Dalí," *Yale Art Gallery Bulletin* (New Haven), vol. 29, no. 2, December 1963, pp. 34-37.

"Exhibit of Dalí Jewels," *Hobbies* (Chicago), vol. 64, August 1959, p. 49.

"Exposicio Salvador Dalí," *La Publicitat* (Barcelona), 20 November 1925.

"Exposicio Salvador Dalí," *Ampurdan* (Figueres), 4 February 1976.

"Exposicion Salvador Dalí en Rotterdam," *Goya* (Madrid), no. 103, July 1971, pp. 60-61.

"Exposite van Dalí in Museum Boymans," *De Typhoon*, 12 May 1970.

"Expositie Dalí in Museum Boymans," *Friesch Dagblad*, 16 May 1970.

"Expositie van Salvador Dalí eind '70 in Museum Boymans," *Dagblad V.H. Oosten*, 12 May 1970.

"Exposition Dalí à Genève," *Le Figaro* (Paris), 2 July 1970.

"Exposition Dalí le grand de l'Alchimie," *Semaine des Spectacles*, no. 221, 15 December 1976, p. 10.

"Exposition de bijoux surealistes a New York, House of Heydenryk," *Pictures on exhibit* (New York), November 1956, pp. 18-20.

F.C, "Papillons," *La Quinzaine Litteraire* (Paris), 16 May 1970.

Fabian, Rainer, "Menu mit Libido und Paranoia," *Welt des Buches*, 16 January 1975.

Fanés, Fèlix, "Retrato del artista adolescente. El amor, los amigos, la politica y la pintura vistos con el desparpajo y la inteligencia de un estudiante de 15 anos," *Babelia* (supplement to *El Pais*) (Madrid), 30 January 1993, pp. 7-8.

Fanés, Fèlix, "Joan Miró escribe à Salvador Dalí. El breve encuentro de los artistas catalanes en Figueres y su ambivalente relacion posterior," *El Pais* (Madrid), 25-26 December 1993, pp. 6, 11.

"Fantastic Jewelry," *Art News* (New York), vol. 50, April 1951, p. 60.

"Fashionable and very disputed," *The Art Digest* (New York), 1 December 1934, p. 14.

Fatt, A, "Salvador Dalí interview," *Dance Magazine* (New York), vol. 41, March 1967, pp. 54-56.

Favalleli, Max, "Dalí extravagant," *Midi Libre* (Montpellier), 25 November 1956.

Fayard, Jean, "Salvador Dalí en représentation de Gala devant Don Quichotte," *Le Figaro* (Paris), 13 December 1957.

Faydel, Josette, "Dalí là-bas...," *Combat* (Paris), 4 February 1971.

"Felsen, die zu Fleischwerden," *Frankfurter Allgemeine Zeitung* (Frankfurt), 21 March 1974.

Fell, Martine, "Dalí: des fringues pour l'an 2000," *Gap*, February 1972.

Felton, James P, "Figments and pigments," *Script Magazine*, August 1947, pp. 11-15.

Fermigier, André, "Une exposition Wols et les "aveux" de Dalí. Il y a besace et besace," *Le Monde* (Paris), 4 January 1974, p. 13.

Fernandez Puertas, Victor, "Anna Maria Dalí vista pel seu germa," *Hora Nova* (Figueres), August 1995, pp. 8-14, 15-21, 22-28.

Fernandez Puertas, Victor, "Anselm Domenech, l'oncle de Salvador Dalí Domenech," *Revista de Catalunya* (Barcelona), no. 97, 1995, pp. 61-81.

Fernandez Puertas, Victor, "Las cartas de Salvador Dalí al seu oncle Anselm Domenech al Museu Abello," *Revista de Catalunya* (Barcelona), no. 104, February 1996, pp. 57-73.

Fernandez, Dominique, "Dalí en v.f," *L'Express* (Paris), 12 November 1973, pp. 147-148.

Ferrier, Jean-Louis, "Les 50 secrets de Dalí," *L'Express* (Paris), 9 December 1974.

Ferrier, Jean-Louis, "Dalí redécouvre Meissonier," *L'Express* (Paris), 14 July 1979.

"Figueras, Inauguration del Teatro Museo Dalí; medalla de oro de la ciutat," *Vanguardia* (Barcelona), 29 September 1974, p. 7.

"Financial," *Scottish Art Review* (Glasgow), vol. IV, no. 2, summer 1952, pp. 29-30.

Finch, Christopher, "Dalí today, dancing-girls and DNA," *Auction* (New York), vol. IV, no. 9, May 1971, pp. 24-29.

Fisher, Gerald H, "Ambiguous figure treatments in the art of Salvador Dalí," *Perceptions and Psychophysics* (Austin [TX]), vol. 2, no. 8, August 1967, pp. 328-330.

Flemming, E.D, "People who avoided the ruts of life," *Cosmopolitan* (New York), vol. 146, January 1959, p. 32.

Flemming, Hanns Theodor, "Die galerie Levy zeigt 157 Werke von Dalí in den neuen Raumen," *Die Welt* (Hambourg), 11 October 1977.

"Fleurs de Dalí," *L'Express* (Paris), 10 May 1971.

"Flowering Dalí," *New York Herald Tribune* (New York), 14 February 1954.

Fogel, Jean-François with Jean-Louis Hue, "Les Mandalas de Dalí," *Le Sauvage* (Paris), October 1976, pp. 92-103.

Foix, J.V, "Presentacio de Salvador

Dalí," *L'Amic de les Arts* (Sitges), any II, no. 10, 31 January 1927, pp. 1-3.

Folch y Torres, Joaquim, "El pintor Salvador Dalí," *Gaseta de les Arts* (Barcelona), any III, no. 60, 1 November 1926.

Folch y Torres, Joaquim," Salvador Dalí," *Gaseta de les Arts* (Barcelona), any IV, no. 66, 1 February 1927, pp. 1-2.

Fontsere, Carles, "Dalí a Nova York," *Revista de Gerona* (Gerona), no. 68, 3rd trimester, 1974, pp. 55-60.

Forestier, Nadège, "Dopé à l'eau de Vichy, Dalí entreprend le tableau le plus cher du monde," *Le Figaro* (Paris), 24 July 1968.

"40,000 har set Dalí," *Berlinske Tidende* (Berlin), 4 November 1973.

"14,000 Dalí Ties," *The Art Digest* (New York), 1 September 1944, p. 7.

"Foundation buys 28 Dalí Jewels," *The New York Times* (New York), 30 November 1958.

"Framis: un buen consejo de Dalí," *Vanguardia* (Barcelona), 17 November 1951.

Franc, Helen, "Salvador Dalí," *Louisiana Revy* (Humlebaek), no. 2, December 1978, pp. 33-34.

Francis, Henry S., "St. George and the dragon" by Salvador Dalí," *Bulletin of the Cleveland Museum of Art* (Cleveland), no. 8, October 1947, pp. 195-196.

Francisco, Esteban, "Dalí," *Norte*, 10 August 1945, pp. 33-35.

Franju, Jacques, "Salvador Dalí a l'oreille du pape," *Liberation* (Paris), 22 November 1958.

Franquinet, Robert, "De kaken van mijn geest staan niet stil in de tijd…," *Dagblad Voor Coevorden*, 20 November 1970.

Freedley, George, "Stage today: 'Mad Tristan is a poor experiment'," *Morning Telegraph*, 21 December 1944.

Freeman, Ira Henry, "Dalí gives a view of tranquillity," *The New York Times* (New York), 5 June 1958.

Freeman, Ira Henry, "Dalí dabbles in soap bubbles; U.S. technology upstages him," *The New York Times* (New York), 14 April 1961.

Frenken, Ton, "Salvador Dalí, Genie van de absurditeit," *Brabants Dagblad*, 21 November 1970.

"Freud + Minsky = Dalí," *The Art Digest* (New York), vol. 13, 1 July 1939.

Freustie, Jean, "La Chase au mystère," *Le Nouvel Observateur* (Paris), 14 January 1974.

"From J&B to Dalí," *Dun's* (New York), vol. 98, July 1971, pp. 59-60.

"Fulfilment: the art of Salvador Dalí," *Saturday Evening Post* (Indianapolis), April 1978, pp. 62-65.

"Fund Buys Jewels Designed by Dalí," *The New York Times* (New York), 22 December 1953.

"Further afield Washington," *Studio International* (London), vol. 152, September 1956, p. 95.

"Galeries Dalmau, exposicio Dalí," *Gaseta de les Arts* (Barcelona), any II, no. 38, 1 December 1925, pp. 7-8.

"Galimatias-men han laerte verden at prostere mod tyrannerne," *Aktuelt*, October 1973.

Galloti, M.M. de, "Exposicion en Tokyo," *Vanguardia* (Barcelona), 29 October 1964.

Gallwitz, Klaus, "Salvador Dalí im Stadel," *Zeitung* (Frankfurt), no. 1, 1974.

"Gallwitz Kolossal-Einstand in Frankfurts Städel," *Nürnberger Zeitung* (Nuremdourg), 15 March 1974.

Ganz, Kate, "Dalí, artful showman," *Show* (New York), 25 June 1970, pp. 21-25.

García Lorca, Federico, "Oda a Salvador Dalí," *Revista de Occidente* (Madrid), April 1926.

Garcia-Herraiz, E, "Salvador Dalí y Henry Moore, en Knoedler," *Goya* (Madrid), no. 96, May 1970, p. 370.

Gardella, Kay, "Hello, Dalí!," *Daily News* (New York), 12 March 1975.

Garfield, F.O, "Salvador Dalí in Daliland," *Saturday Review of Literature*, vol. 27, 15 April 1944, p. 15.

Garrido Pallardo, F, "Sobre un agente externo," *Revista de Gerona* (Gerona), no. 68, 3rd trimester, 1974, pp. 71-74.

Garriga Camps, Pere, "El jove Dalí de la "Pairal" (1)," *Emporda* (Figueres), 3 February 1993, p. 25.

Garriga Camps, Pere, "El jove Dalí de la "Pairal" (2)," *Emporda* (Figueres), 10 February 1993, p. 25.

Gasch, Sebastia, "Salvador Dalí," *Gaseta de les Arts* (Barcelona), any III, no. 60, 1 November 1926.

Gasch, Sebastia, "De Galeria en galeria, Salvador Dalí," *L'Amic de les Arts* (Sitges), any I, no. 8, November 1926, pp. 3-4, 6.

Gasch, Sebastia, "Salvador Dalí," *L'Amic de les Arts* (Sitges), any II, no. 11, 28 February 1927, pp. 16-17.

Gasch, Sebastia, "Salvador Dalí," *Ciutat* (Manresa), any II, no. 10, March 1927, pp. 31-34.

Gasch, Sebastia, "Un décorat de S. Dalí," *L'Amic de les Arts* (Sitges), any II, no. 16, 31 July 1927, pp. 56-57.

Gasch, Sebastia, "L'Exposició collectiva de la Sala Pares, Salvador Dalí," *L'Amic de les Arts* (Sitges), any II, no. 19, 31 October 1927, p. 1.

Gasch, Sebastia, "Salvador Dalí," *Cahiers de Belgique* (Brussels), any III, no. 4, 1930.

Gasch, Sebastia, "Hurgando en el recuerdo. El Dalí de los anos veinte," *Diario de Barcelona* (Barcelona), 21 July 1962, p. 24.

Gaunt, W, "Art's Nightmare. The Surrealist Painting of Salvador Dalí," *The Studio* (London), vol. 118, no. 558, September 1939, pp. 108-113.

Gauthier, Xavière, "Dalí rend hommage à Dürer," *La Galerie* (Paris), December 1971, p. 58.

Gay, Victor, "Dalí profeta en su tierra?," *Revista de Gerona* (Gerona), no. 68, 3rd trimester, 1974, pp. 53-55.

Gaya Nuno, Juan Antonio, "Salvador Dalí," *Das Kunstwerk* (Stuttgart), no. 5, April 1950, pp. 13-20.

Genauer, Emily, "Dalí, here again…," *New York Herald Tribune* (New York), 19 February 1950.

Genet, "Dalí's beating heart jewel, on tour for Catherwood Foundation," *Vogue* (New York), 15 May 1954, pp. 76-77.

Genet, "Dalí jewelry purchased by the Catherwood Foundation," *The New Yorker* (New York), vol. 30, 4 December 1954, p. 95.

George, Waldemar, "Avant son départ pour New York, Salvador Dalí a présenté dans son atelier un choix de ses oeuvres," *Beaux-Arts* (Paris), 10 February 1939, p. 4.

Gérard, Max, "Dalí, le livre de ma vie chez Draeger," *Jours de France* (Paris), no. 662, July 1967.

"Gespräche mit spanischen malern, Dalí," *Das Kunstwerk* (Stuttgart), 1953, pp. 66-67.

Getlein, F, "Inimitable Dalí," *Commonweal* (New York), vol. 69, 5 December 1958, pp. 251-253.

Getlein, F, "Art-Lover's bonanza," *New Republic* (Washington), vol. 141, 14 December 1959, pp. 17-18.

Getlein, F, "Art," *New Republic* (Washington), vol. 142, 8 February 1960, p. 21.

Gibson, Ian, "Con Dalí y Lorca en Figueres," *El Pais* (Madrid), 26 January 1986, pp. 10-11.

Gibson, Ian, "Un paranoico en la familia? El extrano caso del abuelo paterno de Salvador Dalí, un "infeliz demente" que "se suicido en Barcelona en 1886," *El Pais* (Madrid), 10 April 1993, pp. 2-3.

Gibson, Ian, "Salvador Dalí: The Catalan Background," in *Salvador Dalí: The Early Years* (London: Hayward Gallery (South Bank Centre), 1994), pp. 49-64.

Gich, Juan, "Dalí, ampurdanés universal," *Revista de Gerona* (Gerona), no. 68, 3rd trimester, 1974, pp. 7-9.

Gil Bonancia, Miguel, "Hombre mediterraneo," *Revista de Gerona* (Gerona), no. 68, 3rd trimester, 1974, pp. 61-64.

Gimenez Caballero, Ernesto, "El escandalo de L'Age d'or en Paris. Palabras con Salvador Dalí," *La Gaceta Literaria* (Madrid), no. 96, 15 December 1930, p. 3.

Gimenez Caballero, Ernesto, "Robinson habla de arte, teatro. Salvador Dalí. Teatro de Bali," *La Gaceta Literaria* (Madrid), no. 112, 15 August 1931, p. 10.

Gimenez Caballero, Ernesto, "Dalí! Quierdo Dalí! Gala te ha devorado ya medio craneo," *Diario 16* (Madrid), 26 February 1981, p. x.

Giro Brugues, Pedro, "Dalí y Figueras," *Revista de Gerona* (Gerona), no. 68, 3rd trimester, 1974, pp. 15-17.

Gironella, Joaquim, "4 personajes Figuerenses "tocats de la tramuntana'," *Revista de Gerona* (Gerona), no. 68, 3rd trimester, 1974, pp. 77-82.

Glaser, Horst Albert, "Die unbefleckte Empfangnis der Phantasie," *Stuttgart Zeitung* (Stuttgart), 27 September 1975.

Glicksberg, C.I, "Art and disease," *Nineteenth Century and After*, vol. 145, March 1949, pp. 184-187.

Glozer, Laszlo, "Von Dalis 'Unsterblichkeit'," *Sudd Zeitung*, no. 310, 27-28 December 1969.

Glueck, Grace, "Dalí concocts a happening of sort," *The New York Times* (New York), 24 February 1966.

Godefroy, Roland, "Une sardine cybernétique ou le retour de Salvador Dalí," *Le Quotidien de Paris* (Paris), 16 April 1975.

Goldering, Douglas, "Artists and pictures Salvador Dalí at Zwemmer's," *The Studio* (London), vol. 109, January 1935, p. 36.

Gollin, Jane, "Salvador Dalí," *Art News* (New York), vol. 70, no. 3, May 1971, p. 12.

Gomez de la Serna, Ramón, "Las manias de Dalí," *Diario de Barcelona* (Barcelona), 10 August 1960.

Gomez de Liano, Ignacio, "Le theatre Dalí de la memoire," in *La Vie Publique de Salvador Dalí* (Paris: Centre Georges Pompidou, Musée National d'Art Moderne), April 1980, pp. 182-185.

Gomez de Liano, Ignacio, "...Llegaremos mas tarde, hacia las cinco," Dalí visto por Pitxot," in *400 obras de Salvador Dalí de 1914 a 1983*. (Madrid: Museo Espanol de Arte contemporaneo, 1983), pp. 254-257.

Gomez de Liano, Ignacio, "Odisea Dalí," in *400 obras de Salvador Dalí de 1914 a 1983*. (Madrid: Museo Espanol de Arte contemporaneo, 1983), pp. 21-43.

Gomez Sicre, José, "El caso Dalí," *El Nacional*, 16 June 1946.

Gomez-Santos, "Dalí," *Solidaridad Nacional*, 27 August 1958.

Gomez-Santos, "Dalí," *Solidaridad Nacional*, 28 August 1958.

Gomez-Santos, "Dalí," *Solidaridad Nacional*, 29 August 1958.

Gomez-Santos, "Dalí," *Solidaridad Nacional*, 30 August 1958.

Gomez-Santos, "Dalí," *Solidaridad Nacional*, 31 August 1958.

Gomez-Santos, "Dalí," *Solidaridad Nacional*, 2 September 1958.

Gomez-Santos, "Dalí," *Solidaridad Nacional*, 3 September 1958.

Gomez-Santos, "Dalí," *Solidaridad Nacional*, 4 September 1958.

"Good nait Dalí," *Architectural Forum* (New York), November 1957, pp. 171-172.

Gorafola, Lynn, "Dalí, Ana Mari, and The Three-Cornered Hat," in Curtis Carter (ed.), *Dalí and the Ballet: Set and Costumes for The Three-Cornered Hat*. (Milwaukee: Haggerty Museum of Art, 2000), pp. 17-24.

"Graphiken und Zeichnungen vom Salvador Dalí," *Werk* (Bale), vol. 57, February 1970, p. 137.

Greeley, Robin A, "Dalí's Fascism; Lacan's Paranoia," *Art History, journal of the Association of Art Historians* (Oxford: Blackwell Publishers), vol. 24, no. 4, September 2001, pp. 465-492.

Green, Julien, "Dalí le Conquistador," in *Salvador Dalí rétrospective 1920-1980*. (Paris: Centre Georges Pompidou, Musée National d'Art Moderne, 1979), pp. 7-9.

Greene, Patterson, "The Secret Life of Salvador Dalí," *California arts and architecture* (Los Angeles), June 1943, pp. 8, 15.

Grigg, William, "Dalí contributes, medical library blends science art," *Dalí Evening Star*, 13 October 1965.

Grimm, Rudolf, "Dalí schwelgt in 'Gastro-Aesthetik'," *General Auzeiger*, 28 November 1974.

Gros, Bernard, "Le Paranoiaque et le babilan," *Reforme* (Paris), 29 June 1968.

Gros, Louys, "Salvador Dalí-Max presente "l'ovocipede", sa derniere loufoquerie," *Combat* (Paris), 8 December 1959.

Grosser, M, "Art; exhibit at Carstairs Gallery," *Nation* (New York), vol. 187, 27 December 1958, pp. 503-504.

"Grote Dalí, expositie in Boymans Museum," *Tubantia*, 11 May 1970.

Guardiola Rovira, R, "El museo Dalí, no fue facil," *Revista de Gerona* (Gerona), no. 68, 3rd trimester, 1974, pp. 48-52.

Gudmundsen, Ulf, "Mellen Stankelbenselefanter: Dalí-udstillingen på Louisiana er afterarets største hjemlige kunbegivenhed," *Vestkysten*, October-November 1973.

Guillamet, Juame, "Stadium", la revista del jove Dalí," introduction to the facsimile edition of *Stadium*. (Figueres: Edicions Federals, 1993), pp. 5-11.

Guilly, René, "Grâce aux moustaches qui lui servent d'antennes Salvador Dalí est devenu le Saint-Jean de la Croix de la peinture," *Opéra* (Paris), 25 April 1951.

H.B, "Done the Dalí Way," *The Art Digest* (New York), 15 April 1943, p. 7.

H.C, "Dalí," *The Art Digest* (New York), 1 January 1955, p. 23.

H.D, "Portraits by Dalí," *The New York Times* (New York), 11 April 1943.

H.F, "Salvador Dalí at the Zwemmer Galleries," *Apollo* (London), vol. 20, December 1934.

H.L.F, "Jewelry by Dalí," *Art News* (New York), vol. 51, December 1952, p. 58.

Haas, Irvin, "New art form," *Art News* (New York), vol. 56, March 1957, p. 16.

Haggqvist, Arne, "Salvador Dalí," *Konstrevy* (Stockholm), no. 2, 1942, pp. 82-88.

Hahn, Otto, "Avida dollars," *Art and Artists* (London), no. 7, October 1966, pp. 32-33.

Hahn, Otto, "Quand Dalí ne delire pas," *L'Express* (Paris), 13 May 1968.

Hahn, Otto, "Expositions, le grand cirque de Dalí," *L'Express* (Paris), 8 December 1969.

Hahn, Otto, "L'Étrange inauguration du musée Dalí," *L'Express* (Paris), 7 October 1974.

Hains, Raymond, "Flagrant Dalí," (Paris), 1955. Published in *Raymond Hains* (Paris: Centre national d'art contemporain, 1976).

Hajo, "Dalí," *Eindhovens Dagblad* (Eindhoven), 24 November 1970.

Halimi, André, "Le Pèlerinage parisien de Dalí," *Les Nouvelles Litteraires* (Paris), 18 June 1973.

Halsman, Philippe, "Hello, Dalí," *Art in America* (New York), April 1965, p. 80.

Hammacher-van den Brande, Renilde, "Ten Geleide," in *Dalí* (Rotterdam: Museum Boymans Van-Beuningen, 1970).

Hanoteau, Guillaume, "Dalí, l'homme le plus sérieux que je connais," *Paris-Match* (Paris), no. 1015, 19 October 1968.

"Happenings are happening," *Time* (New York), vol. 87, 4 March 1966, pp. 76-77.

Hardy, Françoise, "Françoise: moi j'aime Salvador Dalí," *Salut les Copains* (Paris), no. 75, November 1968, p. 68.

Harriman, Margaret Case, "A dream walking," *The New Yorker* (New York), vol. 15, 1 July 1939, pp. 22-27.

Harris, Leonard, "Philharmonic crowd suffers with Dalí," *New York World Telegram and Sun* (New York), 24 February 1966.

Hector, "Cara sin cruz de Dalí," *Solidaridad Nacional*, 17 August 1948.

Heise, Hans Jürgen, "Dalí oder das konkrete Irrationale," *Neue Deutsche Hefte* (Berlin), cahier 4, 1974.

Helm, Everett, "Surrealistischer Opern-Ulk," *Frankfurter Allgemeine Zeitung* (Frankfurt), 28 August 1961.

Helwig, Werner, "Ein Sadist sucht Kontakt," *Welt* (Hambourg), 18 October 1973.

Hendry, Fay L, "A Salvador Dalí painting in the MSU Collection," *Kresge Art Center Bulletin* (East Lansing [Michigan]), vol. III, no. 5, February 1975.

Hennion, M.G, "Dalí, a study of his art and his work by A.R. Morse," *Liturgical Arts* (New York), no. 27, February 1959, pp. 50-51.

Herald, George W, "Vor allem liebe ich Geld," *Welt am Sonntag* (Hambourg), 11 May 1975.

Heraut, Henri, "Qui est Dalí?," *Les Cahiers de la Peinture* (Paris), no. 63, February 1978, p. 6.

"Here it is! Dalí exhibit in the amusement area of the World's Fair," *The Art Digest* (New York), vol. 13, 1 May 1939.

Hernandez, Mario, "Garcia Lorca y Salvador Dalí: del ruisenor lirico a los burros podridos (Poetica y epistolario)', in Laura Dolfi (ed.), *L'impossibile/possibile di Federico Garcia Lorca*. (Naples: Edizioni Scientifiche Italiane, 1989), pp. 267-319.

Hess, Thomas B, "Art History's Debt to Dalí, an appreciation," in *Dalí* (New York: M. Knoedler and Co., 1970).

"Hexenmeister unterwegs," *Welt* (Hambourg), no. 29, 3 February 1968, p. 2.

Hilaire, Georges, "Chez les surréalistes, Salvador Dalí," *Beaux-Arts* (Paris), 30 June 1933.

"History as it never was, Christopher Columbus discovers America," *Time* (New York), vol. 75, 15 February 1960: 88-89.

Hmggquist, Arne, "Salvador Dalí," *Konstrevy* (Stockholm), no. 2, 1952, pp. 82-88.

Hodin, J.P, "A madonna motif in the work of Munch and Dalí," *Art Quarterly* (Detroit), vol. 16, no. 2, summer 1953, pp. 106-113.

Hoffman, Daphne M., "Salvador Dalí, genius or charlatan?" *Saint Joseph Magazine*, October 1960, pp. 19-23.

"Homage," *Art News* (New York), vol. 73, no. 8, October 1974, p. 69.

"Hombre del dia, Salvador Dalí en Espana," *Correo Catalan* (Barcelona), 8 August 1948.

"Homenaje a Salvador Dalí," *Ampurdan* (Figueres), 17 December 1975.

"Homenaje de Figueras a Dalí," *Hoja*

de Lunes (Barcelona), 14 August 1961, p. 10.

"Homenaje en Barcelona: Fortuny, Dalí y sus batallas de Tétuan," Vanguardia (Barcelona), 14 October 1962, p. 33.

"Hommage à Salvador Dalí," Werk (Bale), vol. 57, August 1970, p. 554.

Hommel, Friedrich, "Pilzuche in her Hohen Mongolei," Frankfurter Allgemeine Zeitung (Frankfurt), 11 November 1975.

Honan, William H, "A visit with Salvador Dalí and Joseph Brody," The Villager (New York), vol. 26, no. 50, 19 March 1959.

Honeyman, T.J, "Editorial, recent history II," Scottish Art Review (Glasgow), vol. IV, no. 2, summer 1952, pp. 3-5.

Honeyman, T.J, "Personal and Polemical," Scottish Art Review (Glasgow), vol. IV, no. 2, summer 1952, pp. 23-26.

Hopper, Hedda, "Hollywood," New York Daily News (New York), 31 January 1946, p. 44.

"How Dalí shocked gay Paree," Vue (New York), vol. 14, no. 6, 1961.

"Hoy se habla de…," Noticiero Universal (Barcelona), 21 August 1978.

Hugli, Pierre, "Inavouables aveux de Salvador Dalí," Gazette de Lausanne (Lausanne), 19 January 1974.

Hugnet, Georges, "Petite contribution à la vie secrète de Salvador Dalí," Le Figaro Litteraire (Paris), 20 November 1954.

Hugonot, Marie-Christine, "Salvador Dalí, Capitale Cleveland," Le Figaro Magazine (Paris), 25 November 1978, pp. 96-99.

Hugues, Robert, "Dalí in 3-D," Times (New York), 15 May 1972, p. 46.

Hulten, Pontus, "A propos de l'Énigme de Guillaume Tell," xxe siècle (Paris), no. 43, December 1974, p. 92.

"I laugh tremendously'," Newsweek (New York), 27 October 1975.

"Ich bin der Grosste des Surrealismus," Welt (Hambourg), 11 May 1974.

"Ich fordere Aragon heraus', Von Salvador Dalí," Frankfurter Allgemeine Zeitung (Frankfurt), 25 November 1974.

"Illuminated Pleasures, Collection of Sidney Janis, New York," Coronet (Boulder [Colorado]), September 1939, p. 63.

"Imposicion de la medalla de oro de la Diputacion de Gerona a Salvador Dalí," Diario de Barcelona (Barcelona), 28 August 1960.

"In the Dalí room," Vogue (New York), 1 March 1943, pp. 48-49.

"Inauguration 'génialle' à Figueras! Le musée Dalí a reçu le divin baptême du maître de Cadaqués," L'Independent (Perpignan), 30 September 1974.

"Informacions artistiques," L'Amic de les Arts (Sitges), any II, no. 17, 30 August 1927, p. 73.

"Interview: Salvador Dalí," The Holy Cross Purple (Worcester), vol. 86, no. 2, 1974.

Isnard, Guy, "Le complexe de l'Angélus," Jardin des Arts (Paris), no. 127, June 1965, pp. 15-18.

J.C, "Abans d'anar a Nova York: una estona amb Dalí," Mirador (Barcelona), any VIII, 18 October 1934.

J.C, "Une heure avec Salvador Dalí," Gazette de Lausanne (Lausanne), 31 August 1957.

J.F, "En attendant Dalí… a la gare de Lyon," Le Figaro (Paris), 30 April 1970.

J.-P.C, "L'Alchimie des philosophes" de Salvador Dalí," Le Quotidien de Paris (Paris), 8 February 1977.

Jacobs, J, "In quest of Dalí, by C. Lake," Art in America (New York), no. 57, November 1969, p. 58.

Janis, Harriet, "Paintings as a key to psychoanalysis," Arts and Architecture (Los Angeles), vol. 63, no. 2, February 1946, pp. 38-40, 60.

Jans, Georges, "Le nez d'un notaire," Les Lettres Francaises (Paris), 6 June 1952.

Jarvis, Rev. Dr. E.D. with Rev. père Martin C. d'Arcy and Rev. Dr. Nevile Davidson, "From the Church," Scottish Art Review (Glasgow), vol. IV, no. 2, summer 1952, pp. 14-15.

Jean Stock, Wolfgang, "Der Köning der Wirr-Köpfe," Weser-Kurier (Breme), 11 April 1970.

Jean, Marcel, "Salvador Dalí," Louisiana Revy (Humlebaek), no. 4, March 1967, pp. 4-5.

Jensen, Jens Christian, "Salvador Dalí," Neue Zurcher Zeitung, no. 448, 27 September 1970, p. 53.

Jensen, Jens Christian, "Salvador Dalí und seine Kunst," Universitas (Stuttgart), any 26, no. 5, May 1971, pp. 531-40.

Jensen, Jens Christian, "Monstern originellen Kitsches'," Neue Zurcher Zeitung, 9 December 1973.

Jespersen, Gunnar, "Dalí på Louisiana, choket som livsform," Berlinske Tidende, 6 October 1973.

Jésus-Marie, Frère P. Bruno de, "Letter," Scottish Art Review (Glasgow), vol. IV, no. 2, summer 1952, pp. 6-7.

Jewell, E.A, "Dalí, an enigma? Only his exegesis," The New York Times (New York), 21 November 1945, p. 19.

"Jewels by Dalí," Design (New York), vol. 61, March 1960, pp. 168-169.

"Jewels designed by Salvador Dalí," The New York Times (New York), 6 December 1952.

Jimenez Robon, Carlos, "La exposicion de joyas de Dalí en el palacio de Liria," Correo Catalan (Barcelona), 19 October 1960, p. 5.

Jimenez, Xavier with J. Playa I Maset, "Dalí vist des de l'Emporda, series of fifteen articles published from January to December 1984," Hora Nova (Figueres), 1984.

Jimenez, Xavier, "Dalí, el futbol I la Unio Esportiva Figueres," Revista de Gerona (Gerona), June 1986, pp. 75-82.

Joffroy, Pierre, "Dante hante Dalí," Paris-Match (Paris), no. 582, 4 June 1960, pp. 70-83.

Johnson, J, "Dalí's Christ of St. John of the Cross," Christianity Today (Washington), vol. 18, 4 January 1974, pp. 20-22.

Jones, Christopher, "Dalí y Disney: Destino," Paris-Match (Paris), 17 December 1998; "Dalí-Disney. La strana coppia," Il venerdì, supplement to La Repubblica, 25 June 1999; "Destino: el proyecto perdido de Dalí y Disney," La Reforma (Mexico City), 9 October 1999; "When Disney met Dalí," The Boston Globe (Boston), 30 January 2000; "Destino: la accidentada historia que unió a dos genios," Blanco Y Negro // Semanario de Abc, 13 February 2000.

Joop, Gerhard, "Dalí-gastronomisch," Westermanns Monatshefte (Brunswick), November 1974.

Joseph, Robert, "Dalí making movie in Spain," The New York Times (New York), 25 September 1949.

Jouffroy, Alain, "Une spectaculaire exposition de Dalí dans les 'Prisons' de Venise," Arts (Paris), no. 480, 8 September 1954.

Jouffroy, Alain, "Dalí a peur de son délire," Arts (Paris), no. 547, 21 December 1955.

Jouffroy, Alain, "Dalí va-t-il assassiner l'Art Moderne," Arts (Paris), no. 584, 12 September 1956.

Juffermans, Jan, "Salvador Dalí Verleidt de Cultuur-Toerist," De Nieuwe Linie (Amsterdam), 20 November 1970.

Juffermans, Jan, "Dalí is meer dan één bezoek waard," Allgemeen Dagblad (Rotterdam), 21 November 1970.

Juillac, "Les Cocus du vieil art moderne," Telegramme de Brest et de l'Ouest (Morlaix), 2 August 1956, p. 3.

Julien, Pierre, "Pour la réception du génial Dalí le Tout-Paris a pris d'assault la Mazarine," L'Aurore (Paris), 10 May 1979.

Junca, "Salvador Dalí," Solidaridad Nacional, 11 May 1961, p. 7.

Junoy, José Maria, "Aun hay peor," La Vanguardia Espanola, 2 March 1947, p. 5.

Junoy, José Maria, "Mal dibujante de fama," Correo Catalan (Barcelona), 26 February 1948, p. 1.

Junoy, José Maria, "Retgrotesco de Dalí," Correo Catalan (Barcelona), 29 March 1951.

Junoy, José Maria, "Margenes, Picassadas y Dalinismos persisentes," Correo Catalán (Barcelona), 4 September 1951.

"Jurnalul unui geniu, fragmente," Arta (Bucarest), no. 12, 1969, p. 24.

Justema, William, "Sources of style for christian art," Liturgical Arts (New York), vol. 20, no. 1, November 1951, p. 35.

Justice, Samuel, "Salvador Dalí," International Herald Tribune (Paris), no. 30021, 21 August 1979, p. 14.

Kachur, Lewis, "Annals of Surrealism, Dalí's Folly," Art in America (New York), October 2003, pp. 70-73.

Kant, G, "Hello, Dalí!," Reader's Digest (Pleasantville (New York)), vol. 108, January 1976, pp. 182-183.

Kayser, Stephen S, "Salvador Dalí's search for heaven," Pacific Art Review, vol. II, nos. 3-4, winter 1942-1943, pp. 30-56.

Kelly, J.D, "Editorial, recent history I," Scottish Art Review (Glasgow), vol. IV, no. 2, summer 1952, pp. 1-2.

Kiehl, Roger, "L'Alchimie des philosophes illustre par Salvador Dalí," Les Dernieres Nouvelles d'Alsace, 1 March 1977.

Kietz Krebs, Betty, "Tax lan Snarl

slows Dalí Museum," *Herald News* (Passaic [New Jersey]), 17 September 1970.

Knox, Sanka, "Quiet Dalí unveils ceration in gems a 'Sacred Heart'," *The New York Times* (New York), 3 April 1950.

Komrij, Gerrit, "Over het letter kundig werk van Salvador Dalí," in *Dalí* (Rotterdam: Museum Boymans Van-Beuningen, 1970).

Koolhaas, Rem, "Dalí and Le Corbusier, the paranoid-critical method," *Architectural Design* (London), vol. 48, nos. 2-3, 1978, pp. 152-164.

Kording, Gijs, "Salvador Dalí onbegrijpelijk en ongrijpbaar genie," *Nieuwe Leidse Courant*, 20 November 1970.

Kousbroek, Rudy, "Het ei van Salvador Dalí," *Allgemeen Handelsblad NRC*, 27 November 1970.

Kramer-Badoni, Rudolf, "Der Zwirbelbart ist immer noch echt…," *Die Welt* (Hambourg), 11 May 1979.

Krolow, Karl, "Luftschlangen der Eitelkeit," *Frankfurter Allgemeine Zeitung* (Frankfurt), 29 August 1974.

Krolow, Karl, "Weiche Uhren im Halbschlaf," *Die Tat* (Zurich), 30 November 1974.

Kruis, G, "DALI DALI DALI DALI …," *Trow* (Amsterdam), 28 November 1970.

Kuh, Katarine, "Dreams as realty," *Saturday Review* (New York), 10 August 1974.

L.D, "Au Zoute avec Salvador Dalí et son univers insolite," *La Libre Belgique* (Brussels), 10 July 1956.

L.E, "Salvador Dalí at Julien Levy Gallery," *Arts News* (New York), vol. 32, 2 December 1933.

Laan, Adri, "Ik ben het Surralisme," *De Nieuwe Limburger* (Maastricht), 21 November 1970.

"L'Age d'Or," *The New York Times* (New York), 15 March 1933.

"L'Age d'Or…," *The New York Times* (New York), 17 March 1933.

"L'Alchimie des philosophes," *Côte-d'Ivoire Actualités*, no. 11, November 1976.

"L'Apocalypse en Delire," *Liberation* (Paris), 16 November 1960.

"Labyrinth, décor by Dalí, sketches for the Ballet Russe de Monte-Carlo," *Theatre Arts* (New York), December 1941, p. 859.

La Cossit, H, "Dalí is a dilly," *American Magazine*, vol. 162, July 1956, pp. 28-29.

"La Crise d'humilité de Dalí," *L'Aurore* (Paris), 24 November 1971.

La Drière, Craig, "Dickens, Dalí and others by George Orwell," *Journal of Aesthetics + art criticism*, vol. 5, March 1947, p. 231.

"La exposicion de Homenaje a Fortuny de Salvador Dalí," *Vanguardia* (Barcelona), 16 October 1962, p. 25.

"La Gente conocida cuando era desconocida, Salvador Dalí," *Paseo*, 13 October 1956.

"La grande madone de Port Lligat," *Scottish Art Review* (Glasgow), vol. IV, no. 2, summer 1952, pp. 18-22.

"La Jeune et le Rouge, Salvador Dalí à l'École Polytechnique," *Le Jeune et le Rouge* (Paris), January 1962.

Lake, Carlton, "Quest of Dalí," *Art in America* (New York), vol. 57, no. 6, November-December 1969, pp. 58-59.

LaLanne, Dorothée, "Je n'aime pas tellement l'Alchimie, mais il se trouve que l'alchimie m'adore," *Sortir*, no. 3, 27 October 1976, p. 15.

Landsford, Alonzo, "New exhibition reveals a modified Dalí," *The Art Digest* (New York), 1 December 1947, p. 13.

Lanoux, Armand, "Salvador Dalí 'monstre sacre'," *Jardin des Arts* (Paris), no. 11, September 1955, p. 685.

Laot, François, "Non Dalí: vous n'êtes pas fou…," *Point de Vue Images du Monde* (Paris), 5 September 1958.

"La Passion selon Dalí": a la gloire de l'or," *Le Republicain Lorrain* (Metz), 6 September 1968.

Laprade, Jacques de, "Salvador Dalí," *Beaux-Arts* (Paris), 19 June 1934, p. 1.

Lascault, Gilbert, "Une Scheherazade du gluant," in *Salvador Dalí rétrospective 1920-1980* (Paris: Centre Georges Pompidou, Musée National d'Art Moderne, 1979), pp. 235-243.

"Las joyas de Dalí," *Diario de Barcelona* (Barcelona), 6 June 1973, p. 27.

"Las joyas de Dalí cansan sensacion en la Feria de Nueva York," *Vanguardia* (Barcelona), 23 August 1964, p. 13.

Lasoury, Josephin, "Le Don Quichotte de Salvador Dalí," *Combat* (Paris), 22 September 1956.

"Las piruatas de Salvador Dalí en Venecia," *Destino* (Barcelona), 23 September 1961, p. 23.

Last, Martin, "Dalí," *Art News* (New York), vol. 68, no. 6, October 1969, p. 20.

Laurent, Jacques, "Chez Salvador Ier, roi de Cadaques," *Paris-Match* (Paris), no. 1268, 25 August 1973, p. 7.

Lazarus, H.P, "Dalí's autobiography," *Nation* (New York), vol. 156, 6 February 1943, p. 212.

Lebel, Robert, "Le Dalí de tout le monde ou la psychopathologie commercialisée," *L'Oeil* (Paris), no. 169, January 1969, pp. 28-35, 74-75.

Le Bolzer, Guy, "Passe de cape (et d'épée) avec Dalí," *Arts* (Paris), no. 434, 22 October 1953.

Lecesne, Christian, "Salvador Dalí a l'ombre de Michelet au chateau de Vascoeuil," *Paris-Normandie* (Rouen), 29 June 1973.

"Le chant d'amour de Salvador Dalí à sa femme," *Marie-Claire* (Paris), no. 258, February 1974, p. 13.

"Le Christ de S. Dalí," *Paris-Match* (Paris), no. 140, 24 November 1951, p. 33.

"Le Dalí secret et celui du labyrinthe," *Le Monde* (Paris), 10 December 1974.

"Le Dernier gag de Salvador Dalí 'l'ovocipede'," *L'Aurore* (Paris), no. 4742, 8 December 1959.

"Le "Divin Dalí" juge la chanson," *Télé 7 Jours* (Paris), January 1969.

"Le Don Quichotte de Dalí a l'assaut du Moulin de la Galette," *Paris-Match* (Paris), no. 400, 8 December 1956, p. 89.

Legrand, F.C, "Une Exposition Salvador Dalí," *Reflets du Tourisme* (Brussels), May-June 1956, pp. 8-15.

Le Grincheux Jovial, "Surréalisme en location," *Beaux-Arts* (Paris), no. 238, 23 July 1937, p. 2.

Le Grincheux Jovial, "Chez Salvador Dalí," *Beaux-Arts* (Paris), 10 February 1939, p. 2.

Legris, Michel, "De l'ovocipede a la "divine comedie" avec Salvador Dalí," *Le Monde* (Paris), no. 4631, 12 December 1959.

Leguebe, Eric, "Dalí l'ami de Grock," *Arts* (Paris), no. 739, 9 September 1959.

Leibel, Jochen, "Dalí-Lithos: Kapitalanlage mit Kunsgenuss als Zugabe," *Welt am Sonntag* (Hambourg), 15 February 1976.

"Le livre le plus fantastique de l'année," *Réalités* (Paris), no. 172, May 1960, pp. 64-71.

Lemoine, Randal, "Salvador Dalí definit les 'choses essentielles'," *Le Figaro* (Paris), 28 April 1956.

"Le Mythe tragique de l'Angélus de Millet par Salvador Dalí," *Arts* (Paris), no. 940, 11 December 1963, p. 271.

"Le Peintre Salvador Dalí elu associe étranger," *Le Monde* (Paris), 27 May 1978.

"Le Quotidien madrilene…," *Connaissance des Arts* (Paris), no. 248, October 1972.

"L'Énigme de Salvador Dalí," *xxe siècle* (Paris), no. 43, 1 December 1974, p. 92.

"Leonid Massine…," *The New York Times* (New York), 17 September 1939.

"L'Épée 'transcendentale' de l'Immortel Dalí," *L'Express* (Paris), 14 August 1978, p. 20.

Leroy, Jean, "Letters to the editors," *Life* (New York), 10 January 1938.

Leroy, Jean, "Letters to the editors," *Life* (New York), 8 May 1939.

Leroy, Jean, "Letters to the editors," *Life* (New York), 30 October 1944.

Leroy, Jean, "Letters to the editors," *Life* (New York), 22 January 1945.

Leroy, Jean, "Letters to the editors," *Life* (New York), 15 October 1945.

Leroy, Jean, "Entretien sur la photographie et Dalí, avec Robert Descharnes et Marc Lacroix," *Photo Revue* (Paris), June 1975, pp. 286-298.

"Les Actions de Meurice en hausse de 7 francs," *Le Figaro* (Paris), 23 November 1967.

"Les Airs du temps Dalí," *Télé 7 Jours* (Paris), 7 February 1969.

"Les bijoux de Salvador Dalí," *Art et Decoration* (Paris), no. 44, 1955, p. 40.

"Les Cocus du vieil art moderne par Salvador Dalí," *Echo d'Oran* (Oran), 1 June 1979.

"les Delires alchimiques de Dalí," *Galerie-Jardin des Arts* (Paris), no. 164, December 1976, pp. 57-59.

"Les Dernières inventions de Salvador Dalí," *Le Soir* (Brussels), 12 May 1956.

"Les Expositions: Dalí," *Beaux-Arts* (Paris), no. 238, 23 July 1937, p. 8.

"Les Feux de la rampe," *La Montagne* (Clermont-Ferrand), 30 September 1974.

"Les Lévres de rubis" et dents de perles: les bijoux de Dalí," *France-Soir* (Paris), 24 April 1971.

"Les Metamorphoses de Dalí," *Le Soir* (Brussels), 4 July 1956.

"Les Passions selon Dalí…," *Combat* (Paris), 18 April 1968.

"Les Passions selon Dalí," *Gazette de Lausanne* (Lausanne), 4-5 May 1968.

"Les Passions selon Dalí," *Paris-Normandie* (Rouen), 23 August 1968.

"Les Passions selon Dalí…," *Jardin des Modes* (Paris), December 1968.

Lévêque, Jean-Jacques, "200 gravures expliquent Dalí," *Elle* (Paris), 6 December 1971.

Lévêque, Jean-Jacques, "Pourquoi Dalí?," *Les Nouvelles Litteraires* (Paris), 23 February 1978.

Levy, Julien, "Cuckoldus cuckoldorum," *Art News* (New York), vol. 57, no. 10, February 1959, pp. 44, 66.

Levy, Mervyn, "Dalí the Quantum gun at Port Lligat," *The Studio* (London), vol. 162, no. 821, September 1961, pp. 82-85.

"L'exposition "L'Alchimie des philosophes" prolongée jusqu'au 16 Avril inclus," *Dernières Nouvelles d'Alsace*, 3 April 1977.

"L'Hommage de Dalí à Lénine: un bouquet de lys blancs," *Le Figaro* (Paris), 24 April 1970.

Liebmann, Mulle, "Uhyre og uhyrlig, Louisiana praesenter Salvador Dalis første separatudstilling i Danmark," *Fins Stiftstidende*, 19 October 1973.

"Life calls on Salvador Dalí," *Life* (New York), 7 April 1941.

"L'Interview de Playboy: Salvador Dalí, conversation à coeur ouvert avec le plus égocentrique des artistes excentriques," *Playboy*, February 1974, pp. 21-22, 114, 116-117.

Lipinsky, Angelo, "Le immagini Sacre di Salvador Dalí," *Arte Cristiana* (Milan), no. 5, May 1953, pp. 103-106.

Llopes, A, "Profeta en su tierra, Dalí Figueras," *Destino* (Barcelona), 19 August 1961, p. 18.

"Logarithmic spiral," *New Yorker* (New York), vol. 31, 21 January 1956, pp. 28-29.

Lomas, David, "The Metamorphosis of Narcissus: Dalí's Self-Analysis," in Dawn Ades and Fiona Bradley (ed.), *Salvador Dalí, A Mythology* (London: Tate Gallery Publishing, 1999), pp. 78-100.

Lopez Torres, Domingo, "Lo real y lo superreal en la pintura de Salvador Dalí," *Gaceta de Arte* (Tenerife), vol. III, no. 28, July 1934, pp. 1-2.

"L'Original Salvador Dalí se prepare a etonner la planete une nouvelle fois," *La Presse* (Brussels), 8 December 1953.

"Lorjou veut bien donner des cours de dessin a Dalí," *Le Figaro Magazine* (Paris), 23 June 1979, p. 18.

"Los encuentros: Salvador Dalí," *Destino* (Barcelona), 24 October 1970, p. 24.

"L'Ovocipede" de Salvador Dalí, le jouet du siècle," *La Gazette de Liege* (Liege), December 1959.

Lubar, Robert S, "Salvador Dalí: Modernism's Counter-Muse," *Romance Quarterly*, vol. 46, no. 4, Fall 1999, pp. 230-238.

Lubar, Robert S, "Salvador Dalí: Portrait of the Artist as (An)other," in Dawn Ades and Fiona Bradley (ed.), *Salvador Dalí, A Mythology* (London: Tate Gallery Publishing, 1999), pp. 106-116.

Lubecker, Pierre, "Den tyvagtige original-surrealismens feterede simulant i stor stjernerolle," *Politiken*, 7 October 1973.

Luz, Maria, "Un Nouvel éloge de la folie," *La Nation Francaise*, 8 August 1956.

Lyle, John, "Surrealist," *Art and Artists* (London), vol. IV, no. 8, November 1969, p. 58.

Lyle, John, "The mountebank, the pontiff and the Guru," *Art and Artists* (London), vol. IV, no. 10, January 1970, p. 10.

Lyle, John, "The world of Salvador Dalí," *Art and Artists* (London), vol. VII, no. 82, January 1973, p. 51.

Lyons, Leonard, "The Lyons Den," *New York Post* (New York), 8 April 1959.

M.B., "Salvador Dalí," *The Art Digest* (New York), 1 December 1952.

M.B., "Dalí Lithographs," *Arts Magazine* (New York), vol. 43, no. 3, December 1968-January 1969.

M.B., "Dalí: la magie de Léda," *L'Express* (Paris), 30 December 1978.

M.D., "Salvador Dalí ou les hallucinations d'un Mediterraneen," *Realités* (Paris), no. 185, June 1961, pp. 67-72.

M.E., "Autoportrait de Salvador Dalí, Averty, le mou et le bacon," *Le Monde* (Paris), 17-18 December 1972.

M.F.L., "Moment of fame," *This Week Magazine, New York Herald Tribune* (New York), 29 April 1951.

Mac Crary, Tex with Jinx Falkenburg, "New York close-up," *New York Herald Tribune* (New York), 15 February 1950.

"Madonna and child: painting," *House and Garden*, vol. 94, December 1948, p. 103.

"Madonna in mid-air, Dalí painting is tight squeeze for small gallery," *Life* (New York), vol. 20, 18 December 1950, pp. 48-50.

Madrid, Francisco, "El escandalo del 'Salon de Otono' de Barcelona. Salvador Dalí, pintor de vanguardia, dice que todos los artistas actuales estan putrefactos," *Estampa* (Madrid), no. 45, 6 November 1928, p. 9.

Malanga, Gerard, "Explosion of the Swan. Salvador Dalí on Federico García Lorca," *Sparrow 35*, (Santa Rosa [California]: Black Sparrow Press), August 1975.

"Malraux et Dalí à Babylone," *Le Figaro* (Paris), 23 June 1973.

"Mannequin by Salvador Dalí," *London Gallery Bulletin* (London), 1 April 1938.

"Mao Tsé-Toung illustré par Dalí," *Le Figaro* (Paris), February 1967.

Marc, André, "Pour gagner la bataille Raphael Salvador Dalí ecrit le journal d'un bouffon," *La Nation Belge*, 29 August 1956.

Maréchal, Marc, "Au Casino de Knokke où sont exposées plus de 90 oeuvres de Salvador Dalí," *Nord-Éclair* (Lille), 5 July 1956.

Marlier, G., "Salvador Dalí, Ausstellung in Knokke-le-Zoute," *Die Weltkund* (Munich), 1 August 1956.

Marnat, Marcel, "L'Angélus radiographique de Salvador Dalí," *Combat* (Paris), 16 December 1963.

Marnat, Marcel, "L'Obsession de 'L'Angélus'," *L'Express* (Paris), 21 January 1964.

Marquet, Louis, "Surréalisme, métrologie et métaphysique," *Revue de Métrologie* (Paris), no. 11, November 1968, pp. 651-654.

Marza, A, "El otro dalí," *Correo Catalan* (Barcelona), 14 May 1959.

"Mas de un million de pesetas por el Cristo del Valles," *Diario de Barcelona* (Barcelona), 8 March 1963, p. 2.

Massip, Jose Maria, "Dalí, hoy," *Destino* (Barcelona), no. 660, 1 April 1950, pp. 3-5.

"Mas sobre Dalí," *Vanguardia* (Barcelona), 6 May 1972, p. 49.

"Mas sobre la visita de Alfonso XI-II," *Vanguardia* (Barcelona), 5 May 1972, p. 37.

Massot, Josp with Josep Playa, "Six anys de correspondencia entre Miro i Dalí," *Revista de Gerona* (Gerona), no. 164, May -June 1994, pp. 36-41.

Mastrolonardo, Enotrio, "Dalí' sull' ago della 'bussola'," *Arterama* (Turin), any IV, no. 10, October 1972, p. 22.

Maur, Karen von, "Breton et Dalí, a la lumiére d'une correspondance inédite," in *André Breton: La beauté convulsive* (Paris: Centre Georges Pompidou, Musée National d'Art Moderne, 1991), pp. 196-202.

Maurici, Jaume, "Salvador Dalí en els meus records," *Revista de Gerona* (Gerona), no. 68, 3rd trimester, 1974, pp. 75-76.

Maxwell, Elsa, "Dalí-ing with Democracy," *New York Post* (New York), 23 April 1943, p. 12.

Mazars, Pierre, "Dalí s'amuse," *Le Figaro Litteraire* (Paris), 6 May 1968.

Mazars, Pierre, "Pour l'inauguration de son musée-théâtre tout Figueras célèbre l'apothéose de Dalí," *Le Figaro* (Paris), 30 September 1974.

Mazars, Pierre, "Dalí annonce l'hyperréalisme métaphysique," *Le Figaro* (Paris), 21 October 1976.

Mazars, Pierre, "…unseren Freuden in Deutschland gewidmet," *Die Kunst* (Munich), no. 3, March 1979, p. 169.

"Meesterwerken van Dalí in Museum 'Boymans'," *Noordhollands Dagblad*, 15 May 1970.

Melot, Michel, "Le chef-d'oeuvre d'un génie délirant "Tristan et Iseult" de Salvador Dalí," *Jardin des Arts* (Paris), no. 191, October 1970, pp. 38-43.

Melot, Michel, "Gravures Salvador Dalí," *Jardin des Arts* (Paris), no. 206, January 1972, pp. 70-71.

Melville, R, "Surrealists from the Edward James Collection shown at Worthing," *Architectural Review*, vol. 135, February 1964, pp. 137-138.

"Memories of surrealism, Dalí," *MD* (New York), vol. 16, no. 1, January 1972.

"Men who fascinate women," *Look* (New York), vol. 19, 17 May 1955, p. 114.

"Mercredi," *Les Lettres Françaises* (Paris), 9 December 1970.

"Meshes of Anamorphosis," *Time* (New York), vol. 43, no. 23, 5 June 1944, pp. 99-100.

Messadie, Gerald, ""La Saga de Salvador Dalí," *Saga* (Paris), no. 1, February 1978, pp. 102-110.

"Met Dalí in een koude wereld," *Tubantia*, 21 November 1970.

Michel, Jacques, "Dalí à la pêche au thon," *Le Monde* (Paris), 17 November 1967.

Michel, Jacques, "Dalí par Dalí," *Le Monde* (Paris), 17 March 1971, p. 17.

Michel, Jacques, "Salvador cent têtes," *Le Monde* (Paris), 17 March 1971, p. 17.

Michel, Jacques, "Rencontre a Figueras, Salvador Dalí et son Musée," *Le Monde* (Paris), 3 October 1974.

Michel, Jacques, "Gala de Dalí," *Le Monde* (Paris), 9 January 1979.

Millais, J.G, "Does History repeat itself?," *Scottish Art Review* (Glasgow), vol. IV, no. 2, summer 1952, p. 27.

Millau, Christian, "Dalí n'est pas si fou," *Paris-Presse l'Intransigeant* (Paris), 13 December 1961.

Millau, Christian, "Dalí a l'X," *Paris-Presse l'Intransigeant* (Paris), 16 December 1961.

"Mille services de caisselle…," *Le Monde* (Paris), 5 June 1978.

Millet, Catharine, "Salvador Dalí, le Mythe tragique de l'Angélus de Millet," *Art Press* (Paris), no. 21, October 1978.

Mills, Tony Allan with Christopher Jones, "When Dalí met Disney," *The Sunday Times Magazine* (London), 13 December 1998.

Miravitlles, Jaume, "Una vida con Dalí," in *400 obras de Salvador Dalí de 1914 a 1983* (Madrid: Museo Espanol de Arte contemporaneo, 1983), pp. 5-9.

Miravitlles, Jaume, "Dalí i l'aritmetica," *Revista de Gerona* (Gerona), no. 68, 3rd trimester, 1974, pp. 31-35.

Miravitlles, Jaume, "Encuentros en mi vida. Dalí y Buñuel," *Tele/eXpres* (Barcelona), 1 July 1977, pp. 2, 8.

Miravitlles, Jaume, "Encuentros en mi vida. Dalí y Buñuel," *Tele/eXpres* (Barcelona), 8 July 1977, p. 2.

"Modern Salamander," *Time* (New York), vol. 48, 26 August 1946, p. 44.

Molleda, M, "With Salvador Dalí at Port Lligat," *Arts Magazine* (New York), vol. 37, no. 5, February 1963, pp. 64-68.

Møller Hansen, Dorte, "Surrealismens fuldokmme beherskr på, Louisiana: den 70-arige spanier Salvador Dalís vaerker kan opleves på Louisiana," *Helsingoz Dagblad*, 6 October 1973.

Møller Nielsen, Johan, "En provokatør gennem tre menneske-aldre," *Akvelt*, 5 October 1973.

Montalbetti, Jean, "Louis Pauwels: Dalí est vraiment un genie," *Les Nouvelles Litteraires* (Paris), 2 May 1968.

Montiel, "Arte de Dalí en la Universitat de Marquete, 'La Madonna de Port Lligat'," *Abc*, 18 December 1959.

Montiel, I, "Dalí's art in Jewels," *Hobbies* (Chicago), vol. 65, October 1960, pp. 52-53.

Montiel, I, "Madonna of Port Lligat," *Hobbies* (Chicago), vol. 66, August 1961, p. 45.

Moreiro, Jose Maria, "Dalí, en el centro de los recuerdos," *El Pais Semanal* (Madrid), 23 October 1983, pp. 15-21.

"More joy in heaven - or is there?," *Apollo* (London), vol. 51, no. 299, January 1950, p. 3.

Morse, A. Reynolds, "The Dream World of Salvador Dalí," *Art in America* (New York), vol. 33, no. 3, July 1945, pp. 110-126.

Morse, A. Reynolds, "Salvador Dalí, catalogue de l'exposition Salvador Dalí," *The Cleveland Museum* (Cleveland), 1947.

Morse, A. Reynolds, "Salvador Dalí - my one man collection," *Art in America* (New York), vol. 46, no. 1, spring 1958, pp. 30-38.

Mouly, Raymond, "Une experience de surrealdaguerreosalvadordalitypie," *Photo* (Paris), no. 5, January 1968, p. 47.

Moura Sobral, Luis de, "Las Meninas" de Dalí," *Coloquio Artes* (Lisbon), no. 30, December 1976, pp. 14-23.

Mourauille, Jean, "Dalí a la VIIIe Biennale de Menton," *Nice-Matin* (Nice), 26 July 1970.

Moutard-Uldry, Renée, "Salvador Dalí," *Arts* (Paris), no. 316, 22 June 1951, p. 8.

Munkøe, Lars, "Møde med Salvador Dalís fantastike billedverden," *Syellands Tidende*, 22 November 1973.

Munson, Gretchen T, "Salvador Dalí," *Art News* (New York), vol. 53, no. 9, January 1955, p. 49.

Muratori-Philip, Anne, "Dalí ou le genie du symbolisme," *Le Figaro* (Paris), 4 January 1979.

Murray, Marian, "Dalí paintings exhibited here. Distortions of unreal world and subconscious mind explored," *The Hartford Times* (Hartford [Connecticut]), 1 January 1935.

"Mystic feeling," *Time* (New York), vol. 60, 17 November 1952, p. 99.

N.F., "Des bijoux de Dalí, son guepard et des oeuvres d'art pour les "Petits Lits Blancs'," *Le Figaro* (Paris), 23 April 1971.

"Napoleon's nose and other objects," *Time* (New York), vol. 46, no. 22, 26 November 1945, p. 77.

Newton, Eric, "Dalí goes to Knokke, the belgian summer festival," *Manchester Guardian* (Manchester), 12 July 1956.

"New York - Salvador Dalí - Pour peindre je mets une petite olive dans une de mes narines," *Arts* (Paris), no. 705, 14 January 1959.

Nichols, Dale, "Ah! Madness," *The Art Digest* (New York), 1 September 1939, p. 26.

"Night to forget," *Newsweek* (New York), vol. 59, 4 September 1961, p. 63.

"Nightmare Journey," *Life* (New York), vol. 16, 6 March 1944, pp. 17-18.

Norman, Géraldine, "Dalí fetches £86,900 in thin modern market," *The Times* (London), 1 July 1976.

Nosari, Jacques, "Salvador Dalí, Eurêka désespéré," *Le Figaro* (Paris), 8 December 1959.

"Not a madman! Dalí!," *The Art Digest* (New York), 1 January 1935, p. 16.

"Not so secret life," *Time* (New York), 28 December 1942, pp. 30-32.

"Notes from the underground," *Arts Magazine* (New York), vol. 40, no. 5, March 1966, p. 13.

Novais, Jose-Antonio, "Salvador Dalí fait don de toutes ses oeuvres a l'Etat espagnol," *Le Monde* (Paris), 15 August 1972.

"Nuclear Mysticism," *Scottish Art Review* (Glasgow), vol. IV, no. 2, summer 1952, pp. 28-29.

"Oeuvres graphiques de Dalí," *Combat* (Paris), 20 December 1971.

"Off guard in art gallery," *Look* (New York), 30 March 1948, p. 30.

Ohff, Heinz, "Avida Dollars!' *Tagessp*, 13 May 1977.

"Oh! Said Alice," *Antiques* (New York), no. 27, April 1935, p. 150.

Olano, Antonio D, "Dalí," *Los Españoles* (Madrid), no. 3, 19 October 1972.

Olano, Antonio D, "Dalí ataca de nuevo," *El Imparcial*, 10 November 1978.

Onnen, Frank, "Je ne considère pas André Breton comme un adversaire mais comme un ennemi, déclare Salvador Dalí," *Les Nouvelles Litteraires* (Paris), 16 December 1950.

"Open Secret," *Newsweek* (New York), vol. 21, no. 2, 11 January 1943, pp. 62, 64.

Ortega, "Con Dalí en Port Lligat," *Correo Catalán* (Barcelona), 14 December 1966, p. 2.

Orwell, George, "Benefit of Clergy: Some Notes on Salvador Dalí', in *Dickens, Dalí and Others, Studies in Popular Culture*. (New York: Reynal and Hitchcock, 1946).

Orwell, George, "Den gejstliges ret," *Louisiana Revy* (Humlebaek), no. 1, 26 May 1973, p. 26.

"Ottawa-Canadali," *L'Oeil* (Paris), no. 245, December 1975, p. 63.

"Paranoiac realist," *MD* (New York), vol. II, no. 10, October 1958, pp. 82-87.

Parinaud, André, "Dalí pense aujourd'hui avec sa mâchoire et peint comme Raphael," *Arts* (Paris), no. 338, 21 December 1951.

Parinaud, André, "Dalí en délire," *Arts* (Paris), no. 566, 2 May 1956, pp. 1, 6.

Parinaud, André, "Dalí, Draeger et la SNCF," *Galerie des Arts* (Paris), no. 91, 1 May 1970, pp. 11-18.

Parinaud, André, "Comment on devient Dalí," *Les Informations* (Paris), no. 1434, 6 November 1972, pp. 98-99, 101.

Parinaud, André, "Dalí théâtre," *Nouveau Journal* (Paris), 5 October 1974.

"Pass the Miltown, Salvador," *Architectural Forum* (New York), August 1958, p. 29.

Patience, Stephen, "Dalí's Waking Dream," *The World of Interiors*, vol. 23, no. 6, June 2003, pp. 124-128.

Pauwels, Louis, "Interview de Salvador Dalí," *La Revue de la Pensee-Francaise*, vol. IX, no. 3, March 1950, pp. 24-28.

Peillex, G, "La Divine Comédie illustrée par Dalí," *Werk* (Bale), no. 51, February 1964, pp. 36-37.

Penders, W, "Salvador Dalí de man die altijd weer aandacht weer te trekken," *Het Vanderland Den Haag* (The Hague), 28 November 1970.

Pennendreff, Anne de, "Les bijoux de Salvador Dalí," *Jardin des Arts*

(Paris), no. 77, April 1961, pp. 38-39.

Penning, R.E, "Fascinerende belevenis," *Het Rotterdamsch Woosblad* (Rotterdam), 20 November 1970.

Pereda, Rosa Maria, "No podemos juzgar el arte por la ideologia de sus autores," *El Pais* (Madrid), 22 June 1979, p. 28.

Perez, Nissan N., "Dalí, Horst and the Dream of Venus," *Israel Museum Journal 3* (spring 1984), pp. 53-57.

Perez Gomez, Wenceslao., "Dalí, genio I figura... 'me voy de Espana'," *Corboda* (Corboda), 8 December 1978.

Perez Gomez, Wenceslao, "Se presenta en Paris con una nueva obra Dalí esta pintando al Rey," *Hola* (Madrid), December 1978.

Perez Gomez, Wenceslao, "Salvador Dalí," *La Gaceta Regionale* (Salamanque), 17 December 1978.

Permanyer, Lluis, "Presenta a Salvador Dalí a traves del cuentionario Marcel Proust," *Destino* (Barcelona), 6 April 1963, p. 45.

Permanyer, Lluis, "Cuando Dalí no era divino ni arcangelico," *Vanguardia* (Barcelona), 7 April 1972.

Permanyer, Lluis, "El pincel erotico de Dalí. Reportaje por Lluis Permanyer," *Playboy* (Barcelona), no. 3, January 1979, pp. 73-74, 160-164.

Petronio, "La ultima Dalinada," *Ondas*, 1 September 1960, p. 14.

Pierre, José, "Dalí sauce suprême," *La Quinzaine Litteraire* (Paris), 15 March 1974.

Pierre, José, "Breton et Dalí," in *Salvador Dalí rétrospective 1920-1980* (Paris: Centre Georges Pompidou, Musée National d'Art Moderne, 1979), pp. 131-140.

Pieter B, "Salvador Salvator," *Gool En Eemlander* (Hilversum), 26 November 1970.

Pla, Josep (under pseudonym, 'Tristan') , "Salvador Dalí visto desde Cadaqués," *Destino* (Barcelona), no. 480, 28 September 1946, pp. 3-5.

Pla, Josep with Victor Fernandez, "Buñuel escribe a Dalí. Dos cartas ineditas del cinesta aclaran aspectos de 'Un chien andalou' y de las pugnas intelectuales de los años 20," *La Vanguardia* (Barcelona), 1 April 1966, p. 25.

"Playboy interview: Salvador Dalí, a candid conversation with the flamboyantly eccentric grand vizier of

surrealism," *Playboy* (New York), July 1964, pp. 41-42, 44-46, 48.

Pleynet, Marcelin, "Surréalistes et surréalisants, Dalí...," *Art International* (Lugano), January 1971, pp. 54-55.

Pluchart, François, "Meissonier rehabilite par Dalí," *Combat* (Paris), 6 November 1967.

Poirot-Delpech, B, "Ecrevisse à la nage, "Visages caches" de Salvador Dalí," *Le Monde* (Paris), 22 November 1973.

Ponsot-Nicols, André, "Avant de s'embarquer sûr le United States, Salvador Dalí a réalisé en Europe 15 toiles destinées à donner la chair de poule de l'esprit aux collectionneurs américains," *Paris-Normandie* (Rouen), 23 November 1956.

Porcel, B, "La boca del lobo con Salvador Dalí," *Destino* (Barcelona), 9 December 1976.

Porter, Fairfield, "Salvador Dalí," *Art News* (New York), vol. 51, January 1953, p. 45.

Porter, Fairfield, "Jewels by Salvador Dalí," *Art News* (New York), vol. 58, no. 4, June-August 1959.

"Port Lligat esta de luto," *Solidaridad Nacional*, 11 September 1956.

"Port Lligat, Salvador: 'la nuit je mets des lunettes pour rever en couleurs'," *Arts* (Paris), no. 691, 8 October 1958, p. 2.

"Portrait," *Time* (New York), vol. 28, 13 July 1936, p. 31.

"Portrait," *The New York Times Magazine* (New York), 8 December 1940, p. 11.

"Portrait," *Time* (New York), vol. 38, 29 September 1941, p. 44.

"Portrait," *House and Garden*, vol. 93, April 1948, p. 3.

"Portrait," *Art News* (New York), vol. 49, September 1950, p. 21.

"Portrait," *American Fabrics* (New York), no. 20, 1951, p. 68.

"Portrait," *Time* (New York), vol. 62, 28 December 1953, p. 26.

"Portrait," *Saturday Review* (New York), vol. 37, 16 January 1954, p. 13.

"Portrait," *Newsweek* (New York), vol. 44, 6 September 1954, p. 51.

"Portrait of his wife Gala; painting," *Fortune* (New York), vol. 18, December 1938, p. 85.

"Portrait photo by P. Halsman," *Camera* (Lucerne), vol. 43, September 1964, p. 10.

"Pour Salvador Dalí les échecs rapportent," *Paris-Jour* (Paris), 21 February 1971.

"Pour Salvador l'année 1971 ne sera pas... chouette," *Paris-Jour* (Paris), 28 December 1970.

"Premier élève de Dalí: un jeune oursin espagnol," *Paris-Match* (Paris), no. 455, 28 December 1957, p. 81.

"Preoccupation with time," *Vogue* (New York), 15 April 1941, p. 91.

Presott, Orville, "Books of the time," *New York Times* (New York), 21 December 1942.

Preston, Stuart, "Slemn canonization of the irrational," *Apollo* (London), vol. 83, February 1966, pp. 153-155.

"Proxima obra de Dalí inspirada en una actriz," *Diario de Barcelona* (Barcelona), 20 August 1978.

"Publications: Salvador Dalí, by James Thrall Soby," *Museum of Modern Art Bulletin* (New York), vol. 14, no. 1, autumn 1946.

"Publicité," *Arts* (Paris), no. 685, 27 August 1958.

Puccinelli, D, "At the California palaces of the Legion of Honneur," *California arts and architecture*, vol. 59, June 1942, p. 10.

"Quand Dalí n'est plus sûr le carreau," *Paris-Presse* (Paris), 8 May 1970.

"Quand Salvador Dalí decouvre l'italie," *Opéra* (Paris), 27 February 1952.

"Quand Salvador Dalí embrasse ses giraffes sûr le Rhône," *L'Aurore* (Paris), 20 June 1975.

"Quand Salvador Dalí illustré 'la Divine Comedie'," *Midi Libre* (Montpellier), 12 January 1966.

"Que pensez-vous de la musique?' *Journal Musical Francais*, July 1969.

"Quelques idées de génie," *Les Beaux-Arts* (Brussels), 2 March 1968.

"Qui a brulé le "Musée Dalí"?' *Le Monde* (Paris), 23 March 1971.

Quirt, Walter, "Wake over surrealism," *The Art Digest* (New York), vol. 16, no. 5, 1941, p. 14.

R.C, "Un peintre de talent moyen a acquis la celebrite en se faisant passer pour fou," *Samedi*, 28 July 1956.

R.F, "The American cult for Surrealism: Dalí," *Art News* (New York), 2 January 1937, pp. 17-18.

R.L, "Innombrable Dalí," *Tageblatt* (Luxembourg), 15 February 1978.

R.R, "De Dalí au disco...," *L'Aurore* (Paris), September 1978.

Rafols, Josep F, "Salvador Dalí," *D'Aci I d'alla* (Barcelona), January 1926, p. 399.

Ramo Masoliver, Juan, "Conversaiciones con Dalí," *Vanguardia* (Barcelona), 14 December 1948.

"Rapport of Fatality," *Newsweek* (New York), 26 April 1943, p. 82.

Ratcliff, Carter, "Swallowing Dalí," *Artforum* (New York), September 1982, pp. 33-39.

Ratcliff, Carter, "Dalí's Dreadful Relevance," *Artforum* (New York), October 1982, pp. 57-65.

Raynor, Vivien, "Salvador Dalí," *Arts* (New York), vol. 38, no. 4, January 1964, pp. 35-36.

Raynor, Vivien, "Dalí and the bathtub on the ceiling," *Art News* (New York), vol. 72, no. 5, May 1973, pp. 50-53.

Read, Herbert, "Bosch and Dalí," *The Listener* (London), 14 December 1934.

"Reality of Salvador Dalí," *Newsweek* (New York), vol. 26, 3 December 1945, pp. 114-115.

Reichardt, J, "An ecstatic blossoming," *Studio International* (London), no. 172, September 1966, pp. 110-111.

"Remember the colour photograph...," *Vogue* (New York), 1 May 1943, p. 80.

"Rencontre avec Dalí," *Arts* (Paris), no. 584, 12 September 1956.

Restany, Pierre, "Un Museo per Dalí," *Domus* (Milan), no. 535, June 1974, p. 55.

"Rétrospective à Baden-Baden," *Le Monde* (Paris), 17 March 1971, p. 17.

Revenga, Luis, "Imagenes de un enigma: Dalí," in *400 obras de Salvador Dalí de 1914 a 1983.* (Madrid: Museo Español de Arte contemporaneo, 1983), pp. 50-61.

Rey, Henri-François, "Salvador Dalí l'oursin et le Marxisme," *France Observateur* (Paris), December 1957.

Rey, Henri-François, "L'Eléphant'boy," *France Observateur* (Paris), 27 November 1958.

Rey, Henri-François, "Dalí à Beaubourg l'an prochain," *V.S.D.* (Paris), 7 April 1978.

Rey, Henri-François, "Le cinéma d'été de Salvador Dalí," *V.S.D.* (Paris), no. 50, 17 August 1978, p. 17.

Rey, Henri-François, "Jane Mansfield inspira la proxima obra de Dalí," *Arriba* (Madrid), 27 August 1978.

Rey, Henri-François, "Dalí a l'Académie des Beaux-Arts: "N'ayez plus peur du Chien Andalou'," *Le Matin* (Paris), 20 May 1979.

Rey, Pierre, "A l'Hôtel Meurice Dalí et Renoir jouent une piece en un acte 'L'Ours et le Rhinocéros'," *Arts* (Paris), no. 698, 26 November 1958.

Rhode, Werner, "Dalí auf Knoblauch zehen," *Frankfurter Rundschau* (Frankfurt), 7 January 1975.

Rhode, Werner, "Der möblierte Dalí," *Berliner Kunstblatt* (Berlin), no. 16, October 1977.

Ribiere, Micheline, "Espagne, Salvador Dalí deux fois chez lui a Figueras," *L'Aurore* (Paris), 19 April 1974.

Rieux, André, "Salvador Dalí, peintre de l'âge atomique," *Germinal*, 19 August 1956.

Ripper, R.C. von, "The jewels of Dalí," *The Philadelphia Museum Bulletin* (Philadelphia), vol. 50, no. 244, winter 1955, pp. 22, 26.

Rivas Cherif, Cipriano, "El caso de Salvador Dalí," *España* (Madrid), no. 413, 14 March 1924, pp. 6-7.

Robin, Pierre, "Les Conferences litteraires, Dalí," *Inquisitions* (Paris), vol. 1, June 1936, pp. 51-52.

Rodrigo, Antonina, "Le poete García Lorca et le peintre Dalí," in *Salvador Dalí rétrospective 1920-1980.* (Paris: Centre Georges Pompidou, Musée National d'Art Moderne, 1979), pp. 23-32.

Roger-Marx, Claude, "Au Casino du Zoute Salvador Dalí," *Arts* (Paris), no. 576, 10 July 1956, p. 132.

"Roi, Je t'attends a Babylone' André Malraux illustre par Salvador Dalí," *Courrier de l'Ouest* (Angers), 23 June 1973.

Rolls, John, "Blast it! It's the Dalí way," *Daily Mirror*, 7 May 1959, p. 2.

Romain, Lothar, "Salvador Dalí," *Das Kunstwerk* (Stuttgart), vol. 24, no. 2, March 1971, p. 114.

Ronfani, Ugo, "Dalí contro Picasso," *Gazetta del Popolo*, 27 November 1966, p. 1-2.

Ronner, Markus M, "Die Kunst, nicht im Rasierwasser zu planschen," *Weltwoche*, 19 November 1975.

"Rotterdam krijgt Dalí-tentoonstelling," *Haagsde Courant* (The Hague), 14 May 1970.

Roumeguère, Pierre, "Les Origines de Dalí," *La Galerie* (Paris), December 1971, p. 58.

Roumeguère, Pierre, "The Cosmic Dalí: The "Royal Way" of Access to

the Dalínian Universe," preface to *Dalí by Dalí.* (New York: Harry N. Abrams, 1972), pp. iii-ix.

Roumeguère, Pierre, "Cannibalisme et esthétique. Du cannibalisme paranoïaque de l'Gastro-Esthétique vers un esthétique biologique. Oralité, manière impériale de l'accès à l'univers Dalínienne', preface to Max Gérard, *Dalí... Dalí... Dalí....* (Paris: Draeger, 1974); 'Cannibalism and Aesthetic. From the Paranoiac Cannibalism of Gastro-Aesthetics toward a Biological Aesthetic. Orality, imperial way of access to the Dalínian universe' (New York: Harry N. Abrams, 1974); 'Canibalismo y estética. Del canibalismo paranoico de la gastro-estetica hacia una Estética Biológica. La oralidad, vía imperial de acceso al universo dalíniano' (Barcelona: Blume, 1985).

Roumeguère, Pierre, "La mística dalíniana ante la historia de las religiones," in Salvador Dalí, *Diario de un genio.* (Barcelona: Tusquets, 1983), pp. 275-278.

Rousseau, Robert, "Qui est Salvador Dalí?' *Beaux-Arts* (Paris), 24 February 1968.

Rousseau, Théodore, "Today a painting by Dalí," in *Salvador Dalí, 1910-1965* (New York: Gallery of Modern Art, 1965).

Royer, Jean-Michel, "Dalimaçon," *L'Actualité*, no. 8, December 1969.

Rubio, Enrique, "La Calle, Garcia Sanchia antidaliniano," *Solidaridad Nacional*, 28 October 1950.

Rubio, Enrique, "En contacto con el genio," *Solidaridad Nacional*, 21 July 1955.

Rubio, Enrique, "Un doble de Salvador Dalí en Barcelona, Esteban Guislert mecanico," *La Prensa*, 6 October 1958.

Rubio, Enrique, "Yo nunca me he podido digerir a mi mismo," *Diario de Barcelona* (Barcelona), 19 October 1962.

"Ruedo mundial," *El Diario Vasco* (Saint-Sebastian), 22 January 1977.

"Ruim 100,000 bezoekers verwacht Expositie van Dalí in Museum Boymans," *Nieuwe Leidse Courant*, 21 November 1970.

S., J, "Salvador Dalí, Julien Levy Gallery," *Art News* (New York), vol. 33, 1 December 1934, p. 8.

Sabbath, L, "The Case of Salvador Dalí by F. Cowles," *Canadian Art* (Ottawa), no. 17, July 1960, p. 250.

"Sacrament of the last supper lent to

the National Gallery of Art, Washington," *Studio International* (London), vol. 152, September 1956, p. 95.

"Sacrilege à Rome, Dalí invente un nouvel Enfer de Dante," *Arts* (Paris), no. 488, 3 November 1954.

Sacs, Joan, "El cas Salvador Dalí," *Mirador* (Barcelona), 16 March 1933.

Saint-Jean, Robert de, "Salvador Dalí a New York," *Formes et Couleurs* (Lausanne), no. 5, 1945-1946, p. 6.

"Salvador Dalí," *Art News* (New York), 2 December 1933.

"Salvador Dalí," *Vanity Fair* (New York), June 1934, p. 39.

"Salvador Dalí," *Art News* (New York), 1 December 1934.

"Salvador Dalí," *The Studio* (London), vol. 112, September 1936, p. 156.

"Salvador Dalí," *Life* (New York), 17 April 1939.

"Salvador Dalí...," *Fortune* (New York), vol. 14, no. 6, December 1941.

"Salvador Dalí," *Bulletin des Lettres* (Lyon), 15 January 1957.

"Salvador Dalí," *De Pook*, any I, no. 12, December 1970.

"Salvador Dalí," *Revista de arte - Art Review* (Puerto-Rico), no. 7, 1970.

"Salvador Dalí," *Le Monde* (Paris), 22 December 1971.

"Salvador Dalí," *Eisma's Schildersblad*, 1972.

"Salvador Dalí," *Fine Arts* (Cleveland), vol. 20, no. 929, 1 December 1972.

"Salvador Dalí," *Arts Magazine* (New York), vol. 48, no. 8, May 1974, p. 65.

"Salvador Dalí," *Art at Auction 1975-1976* (London), 1976, p. 161.

"Salvador Dalí," *Munzinger Archiv, International Biograph. Archiv.*, 18 November 1978.

"Salvador Dalí," *El Pais* (Madrid), 18 February 1979.

"Salvador Dalí," *Playboy* (Hambourg), April 1979.

"Salvador Dalí," *Der Spiegel* (Hambourg), 23 April 1979.

"Salvador Dalí," *Le Point* (Paris), 14 May 1979.

"Salvador Dalí, 10 millions pour 15 dessins," *Radar*, no. 448, 8 September 1957.

Salvador Dalí a Avignon, "Je prepare une etude pour Polytechnique sur la 3e dimension de la peinture a l'huile," *Midi Libre* (Montpellier), 20 October 1966.

"Salvador Dalí a Can Dalmau," *Gaseta de les Arts* (Barcelona), any IV, no. 65, 15 January 1927, p. 7.

"Salvador Dalí accuse de plagiat," *Paris-Presse* (Paris), 24 April 1952.

"Salvador Dalí a dedicacé...," *Nord-Matin* (Lille), 11 December 1970.

"Salvador Dalí adore la SNCF mais n'observe pas ses horaires," *Paris-Presse* (Paris), 5 May 1970.

"Salvador Dalí a inauguré le festival d'été de Knokke," *Journal d'Anvers* (Anvers), 6 July 1956.

"Salvador Dalí à la Sorbonne," *Paris-Presse* (Paris), 18 December 1955.

"Salvador Dalí: à la veille de ses 75 ans le peintre surréaliste entre à l'Académie des Beaux-Arts," *Nord-Éclair* (Roubaix), 9 May 1979; *Nord-Matin* (Lille), 9 May 1979.

"Salvador Dalí attaque le Moulin de la Galette avec ses cornes de rhinocéros," *Liberation* (Paris), 20 November 1956.

"Salvador Dalí a un nouveau dada: Rocinante," *Franc Tireur*, 20 November 1956.

"Salvador Dalí (avec le concours des Ponts et Chaussees) crée la machine a coudre en tartine," *Paris-Presse l'Intransigeant* (Paris), 23 October 1959.

"Salvador Dalí a Venezia," *Il Tempo* (Milan), 5 October 1948.

"Salvador Dalí chez Caudillo," *Le Monde* (Paris), 15 October 1968.

"Salvador Dalí-Daum," *Combat* (Paris), 25 September 1968.

"Salvador Dalí demontre avec de la mie de pain et des cornes de rhinocéros la realité de la transcendance paranoïaque," *Journal du Soir* (Lyon), 20 November 1956.

"Salvador Dalí due here," *The New York Times* (New York), 14 December 1953.

"Salvador Dalí en Barcelona, El genial sorprendente pintor hace entrega de un dibujo," *Vanguardia* (Barcelona), 29 June 1967.

"Salvador Dalí en France," *Arts* (Paris), no. 176, 23 July 1948.

"Salvador Dalí en la exposicion de arte Romanico," *Diario de Barcelona* (Barcelona), 24 September 1961, p. 2.

"Salvador Dalí en piste pour le prix Goncourt," *France Soir* (Paris), 19 October 1973.

"Salvador Dalí, Erbamen mit den Frauen," *Quick*, 22 December 1977.

"Salvador Dalí et la recherche de la troisième dimension," *La Croix*

(Paris), 12-13 December 1971.

"Salvador Dalí et le festival de la bonne humeur," *Le Matin* (Paris), 2 July 1956.

"Salvador Dalí et Louis Pauwels," *Le Republicain Lorrain* (Metz), 11 May 1968.

"Salvador Dalí explique sa propre peinture," *Connaissance des Arts* (Paris), vol. II, no. 17, July 1953, pp. 7-9.

"Salvador Dalí goes to Hollywood," *Theatre Arts* (New York), vol. 29, no. 3, March 1945, pp. 176-177.

"Salvador Dalí, Gradiva," *Frankfurter Allgemeine Zeitung* (Frankfurt), 17 April 1978.

"Salvador Dalí has entitled…," *New York World Telegram* (New York), 24 November 1946.

"Salvador Dalí, his most recent major work," *Apollo* (London), vol. 63, no. 375, May 1956, p. 143.

"Salvador Dalí, Ich bin ein Genie," *Stern* (Hambourg), no. 35, 29 August 1965, p. 21.

"Salvador Dalí i les lletres," *L'Amic de les Arts* (Sitges), any II, no. 16, 31 July 1927, p. 57.

"Salvador Dalí illustré Andre Malraux," *Le Monde* (Paris), 24-25 June 1973.

"Salvador Dalí illustré le livre le plus cher du monde," *Franc Tireur*, 21 September 1956.

"Salvador Dalí in," *New York Herald Tribune* (New York), 29 December 1955.

"Salvador Dalí in Museum Boymans," *Provinciale Zeeuwse Courant* (Middelburg), 12 May 1970.

"Salvador Dalí in the Atomic Age," *Script Magazine*, January 1948.

"Salvador Dalí in the studio of Jerome Ducrot," *Camera* (Lucerne), vol. 43, August 1964, pp. 10-11.

"Salvador Dalí: 'Je suis un pervers polymorphe'," *Arts* (Paris), no. 361, 29 May 1952.

"Salvador Dalí kwam zelf naar zijn expositie," *Haarlems Dagblad* (Haarlem), 21 November 1970.

"Salvador Dalí: La Conquête de l'Irrationnel (Éditions Surrealistes)," *Cahiers d'Art* (Paris), 1936, p. 68.

"Salvador Dalí, La Dama española y el caballero romano," *Gaceta Ilustrada*, 28 April 1962.

"Salvador Dalí, los Sabios y Dalí," *Vanguardia* (Barcelona), 13 December 1962, p 73.

"Salvador Dalí malt fur den Kohle-Bergbau," *W.u.V.*, 29 July 1977.

"Salvador Dalí Museum," *Design* (New York), vol. 75, Spring 1974, pp. 32-35.

"Salvador Dalí mystique," *Le Monde* (Paris), 4 July 1959.

"Salvador Dalí, narcisse obsède," *La Flandre Liberale* (Gand), 5 July 1956.

"Salvador Dalí papillon paranoïaque de l'esprit," *Civitta Cattolica* (Rome), January 1955.

"Salvador Dalí, Pe urmele lui Trajan," *Secolul 20* (Bucarest), 7 August 1977, pp. 82-100.

"Salvador Dalí: 'Picasso est chretien'," *Paris-Presse* (Paris), 14 December 1951.

"Salvador Dalí remodela el pecho de Jane Mansfield," *424* (Barcelona), 23 August 1979.

"Salvador Dalí, Richard Wagners Tannhauser-bacchanal," *Sudd Zeitung*, 28 June 1973.

"Salvador Dalí's dinner hosts," *New York Herald Tribune* (New York), 27 April 1950.

"Salvador Dalis dritter Film," *Frankfurt Rundschau* (Frankfurt), 12 September 1975.

"Salvador Dalí se propose d'organiser à Barcelone une corrida surréaliste," *Le Monde* (Paris), 2 May 1953.

"Salvador Dalí: 'Si vous voulez m'inviter, payez-moi'," *Paris-Presse* (Paris), 3 April 1970.

"Salvador Dalí… sous le Second Empire," *Le Figaro* (Paris), 30 April 1968.

"Salvador Dalí's new commission," *Soul* (Washington), March-April 1961, pp. 3-4.

"Salvador Dalí's painting…," *Art News* (New York), August 1943, p. 24.

"Salvador Dalí's Schiaparelli design…," *Art News* (New York), 1 September 1944, p. 11.

"Salvador Dalí stops traffic on New York's Fifth Avenue," *Publisher's Weekly*, vol. 183, 28 January 1963, pp. 252-254.

"Salvador Dalí, sub-conscious for two pages," *Click*, September 1942.

"Salvador Dalí's view of television," *TV Guide* (Radnor), 8 June 1968, p. 6.

"Salvador Dalí's world in Decay," *Script Magazine*, February 1948.

"Salvador Dalí turns the dove into functional new compact," *New York Herald Tribune* (New York), 24 April 1951.

"Salvador Dalí, un Catalán de l'Ampordia," *Correo Catalán* (Barcelona), 1 July 1976, p. 19.

"Salvador Dalí und der Stein der Weisen," *Frau*, no. 6, 16 March 1977.

"Salvador Dalí unveils his new madrap museum," *People Magazine* (New York), 11 November 1974.

"Salvador Dalí va plus loin avec l'Express," *L'Express* (Paris), 1 March 1971, p. 114.

"Salvador Dalí y Gala se han casado," *Solidaridad Nacional*, 3 August 1958.

San Lazzaro, Gualtieri di, "Dieci milion per la prima copia d'un libro illustrato da Salvador Dalí," *Il Campo* (Rome), 24 December 1957.

Sanchez Vidal, Agustin, "The Andalusian beasts," in *Salvador Dalí: The Early Years* (London: South Bank Centre, 1994), pp. 193-207.

Sanguisto, "Salvador Dalí nell' ex Palazzo reale di Milano," *Arte Figurativa Antica e Moderna* (Milan), no. 19, September-October 1954.

Santos Torroella, Raphael, "Arte y no arte de Salvador Dalí en su homenaje a Fortuny," *Noticiero Universal* (Barcelona), 17 October 1962.

Santos Torroella, Raphael, with Salvador Dalí, "Dalí no digiere a Dalí," *Noticiero Universal* (Barcelona), 24 October 1962.

Santos Torroella, Raphael, "La otra verdad de Salvador Dalí," *Revista de Gerona* (Gerona), no. 68, 3rd trimester, 1974, pp. 18-22.

Santos Torroella, Raphael, "Carta abierta a monsieur Robert Descharnes. La exposicion de Salvador Dalí en Gerrara," *La Vanguardia* (Barcelona), 2 September 1984, p. 30.

Santos Torroella, Raphael, "Descharnes y el estilo 'carcel de papel'," *La Vanguardia* (Barcelona), 27 September 1984, p. 38.

Santos Torroella, Raphael, "Nuevas puntualizaciones al libro de Robert Descharnes. Dalí fue un modelico alumno de instituto," *La Vanguardia* (Barcelona), 25 October 1984.

Santos Torroella, Raphael, "La ceremonia dalíniana de la confusion," *La Vanguardia* (Barcelona), 6 June 1985, p. 33.

Santos Torroella, Raphael, "Salvador Dalí i el salo de Tardor. Un episode de la vida artistica barcelonina el 1928," *Reial Academia Catalana de Belles Arts de Sant Jordi* (Barcelona), 1985.

Santos Torroella, Raphael, "Las cartas de Salvador Dalí a Jose Bello Lasierra," *Abc* (Madrid), 14 November 1987, pp. ix-xv.

Santos Torroella, Raphael, "Las rosas sangrantes" y la imposible descendencia de Dalí," *Abc* (Madrid), 26 November 1987.

Santos Torroella, Raphael, "Gimenez Caballero y Dalí: influencias reciprocas y un tema compartido," *Anthropos. Revista de documentacion cientifica de la cultura* (Barcelona), no. 84, 1988, pp. 53-56.

Santos Torroella, Raphael, "El Reina Sofia se equivoca con Dalí," *Abc de las artes* (Madrid), 2 October 1992, pp. 36-38.

Santos Torroella, Raphael, "La tragica vida de Dalí," *Diario 16* (Madrid), 25 September 1993, pp. 2-4.

Santos Torroella, Raphael, "The Madrid Years," in *Salvador Dalí: The Early Years* (London: South Bank Centre, 1994), pp. 81-89.

Sargeant, Winthrop, "Dalí, an exitable Spanish artist, now scorned by his fellow surrealists, has succeeded in making deliberate a paving proposition," *Life* (New York), 24 September 1945.

Sassone, Felipe, "Apologio del plagio," *Vanguardia* (Barcelona), 30 April 1952.

Saucet, Jean, "Dalí, je suis le pompier de la peinture," *Paris-Match* (Paris), no. 1489, 9 December 1977, p. 66.

Saulnier, Adam, "Tous cocus… sauf Dalí," *Democratie 60* (Paris), 26 May 1960.

Saulnier, Tony, "Le dernier Dalí: 'Les Vénusiens débarquent'," *Paris-Match* (Paris), no. 856, 4 September 1965, p. 66.

Sauvage, Leo, "Première oeuvre de Salvador Dalí reçue au Metropolitan Museum," *Le Figaro* (Paris), 15 January 1955.

Scavenuis, Bente, "I noerheden af geniklassen," *Frederiksborg Amisavis*, 17 October 1973.

Schaarwachter, Hans, "Dalí oder 'Die Botschaft des Schnurrbarts'," *Der Mittag* (Dusseldorf), 5 July 1956.

Schade, Virtus, "Dalí på Louisiana," *Berlingske Aftenavis*, 12 October 1973.

Schiff, G, "Dalí," *Du* (Zurich), no. 236, October 1960, p. 19.

Schippers, K, "Dalí's kracht is verwaring als stijl," *Haagse Post* (The Hague), 2 December 1970.

Schlumberger, Éveline, "Dalí, bientôt les trois coups pour l'ouverture de son musée à Figueras," *Connaissance des Arts* (Paris), no. 270, August 1974, p. 26.

Schmidt-Muhlisch, Lothar, "Das Ich gegen die Zeit gesetzt," *Die Welt* (Hambourg), 9 October 1976.

Schmitt, Patrice, "De la psychose paranoiaque dans ses rapports avec Salvador Dalí," in *Salvador Dalí rétrospective 1920-1980* (Paris: Centre Georges Pompidou, Musée National d'Art Moderne, 1979), pp. 262-266.

"Schnaps-Idee von Dalí," *Welt am Sonntag* (Hambourg), 7 August 1977.

Schreiber, Mathias, "Surreale Operette," *Kolner-Stadt-Anzeiger* (Cologne), no. 303, 31 December 1970.

Schroevers, Marinus, "Salvador Dalí zit dat wel snor?," *Vara Gids*, 21 November 1970.

"Schwäne spiegeln Elefanten," *Die Welt* (Hambourg), 4 April 1974.

Schwartz, Marvin D, "Dalí at the Carstairs Gallery," *Apollo* (London), vol. 69, February 1959, p. 50.

Seaux, Jean, "L'Exposition Dalí a Knokke," *Le Peuple* (Brussels), 16 July 1956.

"Selbstingszenierung für die Kamera," *Frankfurter Allgemeine* (Frankfurt), 8 June 1977.

Sell, H.J, "Case of Salvador Dalí by F. Cowles," *Kunstwerk* (Stuttgart), no. 14, November 1960, p. 78.

Sempronia, "Dalí, gallero," *Diario de Barcelona* (Barcelona), 14 November 1953.

Sempronia, "Dalí descubre America," *Ondas*, 15 December 1959.

Sempronia, "Dalí en plena epoca cucurista," *Destino* (Barcelona), 20 August 1960.

Sempronia, "Lo que Dalí trae entre manos," *Revista*, 20 August 1960.

Sempronia, "Pintar la Batalla de Tétuan estuva a punto de contarle la vida a dalí, quien se ha resarcido con una glore del turist," *Destino* (Barcelona), 13 October 1962, p. 37.

Sempronia, "Show" Dalí en el Tinell," *Diario de Barcelona* (Barcelona), 17 October 1962, p. 7.

Serval, P, "Les Passions selon Dalí," *Marie-Claire* (Paris), July-August 1968.

Seton, Marie, "Salvador Dalí + 3 Marxes," *Theatre Arts* (New York), vol. 23, no. 10, October 1939, pp. 734-740.

"Sets for ballets 'Sentimental Colloquy' and 'Mad Tristan'," *Vogue* (New York), 15 December 1944, p. 33.

"Seul le canapé est transparent chez le Recamier du Meurice," *Le Figaro* (Paris), 15 November 1967, p. 19.

Seuphor, Michel, "Dalí in nuclear theft charge," *The Art Digest* (New York), vol. 27, no. 19, August 1953, pp. 10-11.

Shannon, Leonard, "When Disney met Dalí," *Modern Maturity* (Long Beach), December 1978-January 1979, pp. 50-52.

Sidoine, "Pour et contre, la dernière de Salvador Dalí," *Arts* (Paris), no. 239, 2 December 1949, p. 4.

"Sidste søntag i bilen," *Berlinske Tidende*, 19 November 1973.

Siebeck, Wolfram, "Elan der Eigeweide," *Der Spiegel* (Hambourg), 11 November 1974.

"Silueta de un traidor, Salvador Dalí el excentrico," *Manana* (Barcelona), 6 September 1938.

Sinding, Ib, "Den forargelige Dalí," *Jyllands Posten-Morgenavisen*, 17 October 1973.

"Si vous ne me voyez pas, c'est que je ne suis pas la," *La Lanterne* (Brussels), 3 July 1956.

"Si vous savez parler vous savez dessiner…," *Le Figaro* (Paris), 7 November 1967.

Slocum, Bill, "Dalí a dilly in a "Nice" new sewer," *New York Journal-American* (New York), 9 February 1966.

Smits, J.W, "Salvador Dalí," *Philatelie Heemstade*, October 1970.

Soby, James Thrall, "The light fantastic show," *Town and Country* (New York), December 1936, pp. 68-69.

Soby, James Thrall, "Salvador Dalí," *Architectural Forum*, vol. 76, February 1942, p. 56.

Soby, James Thrall, "Freud and Modern Art," *Saturday Review* (New York), no. 39, 5 May 1956, pp. 11-12.

"Soixante oeuvres de Salvador Dalí exposees a Niort," *Le Courrier de l'Ouest* (Angers), 17 May 1979.

Solier, René de, "Dalí le fetichiste," *xxe siècle* (Paris), no. 36, June 1971.

"Something borrowed?' *Time* (New York), vol. 59, 26 May 1952, p. 70.

Sosset, L.L, "Salvador Dalí vedette surréaliste de la saison picturale," *Courrier du Zuyn*, 30 June 1956.

Soyer, Raphael, "Salvador Dalí," *New Masses*, vol. 58, no. 1, 1 January 1946, pp. 26-27.

"Spain decorates Dalí," *New York Times* (New York), 3 April 1964.

"Spain: Casa Dalí," *Ladies Home Journal* (Philadelphia), vol. 82, February 1965, pp. 121-125.

"Spain: Dalí's villa on the Costa Brava," *Harper's Bazaar* (New York), February 1956, pp. 118-121.

"Speaking of Pictures… Dalí paints the seven lively arts," *Life* (New York), vol. 18, no. 1, 1 January 1945, pp. 1-4.

"Speaking of Pictures," *Life* (New York), 9 August 1948, pp. 4-6.

"Special Feature: Salvador Dalí," *Mizue* (Tokyo), no. 875, February 1978, pp. 1-59.

Spector, Stephen, "Salvador Dalí at Knoedler's," *Arts Magazine* (New York), no. 6, April 1970, p. 59.

Speicher, Gunter, "Dalí, Dalí 'Ich bin das grösste Mal-Genie'," *Welt am Sonntag* (Hambourg), 10 December 1978.

Spengler, David, "Dalí offers incredible holograms," *Sunday Record*, 9 April 1972.

Spiteri, Gerard, "Dalí, un show sous la coupole," *Les Nouvelles Litteraires* (Paris), 17 May 1979.

Squirru, R, "Dalí in New York," *Americas* (Washington), vol. 18, February 1966, pp. 34-36.

Stead-Ellis, Stead H, "St. John of the Cross," *Scottish Art Review* (Glasgow), vol. IV, no. 2, summer 1952, pp. 7-8.

Steehouwer, Hein, "Dalí's verken," *Oprechte Haarlemsche Courant* (Haarlem), 28 November 1970.

Steen, Alex, "Hvad med en nogen pige til frokost," *Ekstra-Bladet*, 22 September 1973.

Sten Møller, Henrik, "kaere borgere hvor-for optraeder I dog med en så kollektiv tristhed," *B.T.*, 9 October 1973.

Stouvenot, Michèle, "Soirée de Gala, Dalí se marie…," *L'Aurore* (Paris), 21 August 1979.

"Strictly paranoïac," *Time* (New York), vol. 60, 21 July 1952, p. 67.

"Sur des voies insolites," *Presse-Française*, 3 December 1976.

"Surrealism: Dalí," *Time* (New York), 13 December 1936.

"Surrealist artist enchants Hampton manor near Fredericksburg, Va.," *Life* (New York), vol. 10, 7 April 1941, pp. 98-101.

"Surrealist Madonna," *Newsweek* (New York), vol. 34, 12 December 1942: 74.

"Surrealisten Dalí," *Morsø Folkeblad*, 4 October 1973.

Sutherland, Donald, "The Ecumenical playboy," *Arts Magazine* (New York), February 1963, pp. 69-73.

Sutra, Joan, "Records de le nostra joventut," *Revista de Gerona* (Gerona), no. 68, 3rd trimester, 1974, pp. 27-30.

Sutton, H, "Dalí and the wild coast," *Saturday Review* (New York), vol. 44, 14 October 1961, p. 56.

Sutton, Peter, "Artificial Magic," in *Dalí's Optical Illusions* (New Haven and London: Yale University Press, 2000), pp. 30-37.

"Swashbuckling cut of a cape, photographs," *Esquire*, vol. 76, July 1971: 106-109.

Swenson, G.R, "Is Dalí disgusting?," *Art News* (New York), vol. 64, December 1965: 50.

Szpiro, Maurice Alain, "Dalí est meilleur que Cellini, crie le perroquet de Salvador Dalí," *Combat* (Paris), 20 November 1954.

Tallmer, Jerry, "Dalí holds up the mirror to his art," *Post* (New York), 24 April 1978.

Tanfield, Paul, "At sea with Dalí," *Daily Mails*, 7 May 1959.

Tasset, Jean-Marie, "Devant ses pairs meduses, genie desormais immortel, Dalí fait entrer sous la Coupole la gare de Perpignan," *Le Figaro* (Paris), 10 May 1979, p. 12.

Taylor, Angela, "Even the ocelot wears jewels to Dalí exhibition," *New York Times* (New York), 18 March 1965.

Tegenbosch, Lambert, ""Poging tot benadering van het fenomeen Dalí," *Volkskrant A'Dam* (Amsterdam), 25 November 1970.

"Teihard de Chardin aux Jeux Olympiques," *Paris-Presse* (Paris), 25 August 1968.

Teriade, E, "Les Expositions, Dalí," *L'Intransigeant* (Perpignan), 25 November 1929, p. 6.

"Tête-à-tête Franco-Dalí à Madrid," *Le Figaro* (Paris), 12 October 1968.

"The Ballet Russe de Monte Carlo…," *The New York Times* (New York), 13 August 1939.

"The Critics and Dalí: Glubbel! Glubbel! Who's a Mental Cripple?' *The Art Digest* (New York), 1 May 1941: 7.

"The double Dalí cover…," *Vogue* (New York), 1 December 1946.

"The double-horned Dalí," *New York Post* (New York), 9 April 1959.

"The Madonna of Port Lligat," *Litur-*

gical Arts (New York), no. 1, November 1950, pp. 12-13.

"The moving jewel, Dalí's pliant dazzle," Vogue (New York), vol. , no. 0, 1 October 1962, pp. 154-155.

"The temptation," Art News (New York), September 1946, p. 40.

"The Weird Dream World of Surrealism," Newsweek (New York), vol. 13, 3 April 1939, p. 28.

Thomas, Robert-Marie, "Dalí tel qu'en lui-même…," La Dernière Heure (Brussels), 7 July 1956.

Tillim, Sidney, "Salvador Dalí," Arts (New York), vol. 35, no. 4, January 1961, p. 53.

Todd, Ruthven, "Salvador Dalí, 50 Secrets of Magic Craftsmanship," Magazine of Art (New York), January 1949, p. 36.

Toussaint, Philippe, "En Catalogne, chez Salvador Dalí," Pourquoi Pas? (Brussels), 29 June 1956.

"Toward Raphael," Time (New York), vol. 55, 17 April 1950, pp. 65-66.

"Traeki snoren og lokummet springer i luften," Ekstra-Bladet, 5 October 1973.

"Turbulente stuntman en geniaal kunstenarr," Nieuwe Apeldoornse Courant, 21 November 1970.

"TV goes heavy on the color in portraits of Salvador Dalí," Newsday (New York), 5 December 1966.

"Two liners in late after stormy trip," The New York Times (New York), 25 December 1951.

Tyler, Parker, "Salvador Dalí," Art News (New York), vol. 55, January 1957, p. 22.

Tyler, Parker, "Salvador Dalí," Art News (New York), vol. 57, no. 2, April 1958, pp. 13-14.

Tyler, Parker, "Salvador Dalí," Art News (New York), vol. 57, no. 10, February 1959, p. 12.

"Ubrigens, Dalí is kein Waschmittel und kein Quiz," Bild, 14 March 1974.

Ultra Violet, "Dallying with Dalí," Exposure (Los Angeles), 1990, pp. 56-59.

"Un derapage signe Dalí," L'Express (Paris), 8-14 April 1968.

"Un grand 'Dalí'," La Quinzaine Litteraire (Paris), 1 May 1968.

"Un imitador de Dalí," Destino (Barcelona), no. 749, 15 December 1951, p. 14.

"Un lienzo de Dalí, enviado al Japon," Vanguardia (Barcelona), 30 August 1964, p. 23.

"Un musée pour Dalí," L'Aurore (Paris), 14 August 1972.

"Un porc decore," Le Nouvel Observateur, no. 68, 2 March 1966.

"Un telegrafista acusa a Dalí," Solidaridad Nacional, 19 January 1957.

"Una idea de Dalí se realiza en Colombia: en una Corrida de toros, sustenia el arrastre de toros por su "raptos" a cargo de un helicoptero," Diario de Barcelona (Barcelona), 15 September 1961, p. 2.

"Una joya bibliografica que firma Dalí," La Gaceta Regionale (Salamanque), 6 February 1977.

"Une interview exceptionnelle, Dalí se confesse," Arts (Paris), no. 674, 11 June 1958.

"Une nouvelle lithographie de Salvador Dalí," L'Amateur d'Art (Paris), no. 485, 18 November 1971.

"Une visite de Salvador Dalí," Bulletin de la Bibliotheque Nationale (Paris), any I, no. 3, December 1976.

"Unieke Dalí naar R'dam," Het Uaderland, 30 May 1970.

"Unusual ideas voiced by Dalí, subconscous rules own work, says Painter," The Hartford Times (Hartford [Connecticut]), 18 December 1934.

Utrillo, Miguel, "Nuevo encuentro con Dalí en Port Lligat," Vanguardia (Barcelona), 21 August 1963, p. 32.

Vadrot, C.M, "Salvador Dalí," L'Aurore (Paris), 23 December 1972.

Valensi, Raphael, "L'Alchimie illustrée par Salvador Dalí," L'Arche, no. 233, August 1976.

Valogne, Catherine, "64 ans de folie dalinienne," Tribune de Lausanne (Lausanne), 19 May 1968.

Varia, Radu, "Dalí intelept," Secolul 20 (Bucarest), no. 198-199, 7 August 1977, pp. 101-103.

Varia, Radu, "Dalí à l'Academie," Vogue (Paris), no. 597, June-July 1979, p. 146.

Vayreda i Trullol, Montserrat, "El binomi Salvador Dalil Carles Fages de Climent," Revista de Gerona (Gerona), no. 68, 3rd trimester, 1974, pp. 65-70.

Vayreda, Maria dels Angels, "Com es Salvador Dalí?," Revista de Gerona (Gerona), no. 68, 3rd trimester, 1974, pp. 10-14.

"Velasquez and Le Nain," Scottish Art Review (Glasgow), vol. IV, no. 2, summer 1952, pp. 8-9.

Vibe, Rasmus, "Louisiana giver millionunderskud: Et bornholmsk Louisiana kraever mere end velvilje," Bornholmeren, 22 November 1973.

Vigia, "He aqui el personaje, Salvador Dalí," Revista, 14 June 1956.

Vila Juan, Juan Felipe, "Salvador Dalí, el gran pintor surrealista, ha llegado a Espana," Vanguardia (Barcelona), 1 August 1948.

Villa, Juan B, "Salvador Dalí," Hoja de Lunes (Barcelona), 14 August 1961, p. 10.

Villet, J.L, "Dalí a peint sa "Gare de Perpignan" pour se venger de l'Angelus de Millet!," Midi Libre (Montpellier), 1965.

Vincent Larsen, Ole, "Salvador Dalí pa Louisiana," Nestveo Tidende, 10 October 1973.

"Vis-à-vis, Salvador Dalí," Correo Catalan (Barcelona), 5 December 1948.

Vogel, Jean-François, "Les Mandalas de Dalí," Le Sauvage (Paris), no. 34, October 1976, pp. 92-103.

"Vogue's eye view, the double Dalí cover," Vogue (New York), 1 December 1946, pp. 161, 224.

"Voiçi six lithographies de Dalí pour le livre le plus cher du monde," Arts (Paris), no. 648, 11 December 1957.

W.B, "Salvador Dalí," Arts Magazine (New York), vol. 40, no. 5, March 1966, p. 50.

Wade, Martha, "Genius is as genius does, Conversation with Salvador Dalí," Mainliner (Los Angeles), July 1974, pp. 27-29.

Waldberg, Patrick, "Salvador Dalí' in Dalí (Rotterdam: Museum Boymans Van-Beuningen, 1970-1971).

Wallach, Arnei. "Salvador Dalí: 'Yes, I am the best'," Newsdays (Long Island), 23 June 1974.

Walter, Richard, "Not the Artist but his Art," The Connoisseur, vol. 144, January 1960, pp. 252-253.

Warnod, Jeanine, "Salvador Dalí: 'Installer un Musée surrealiste a la Villette'," Le Figaro (Paris), 2 April 1970.

Warnod, Jeanine, "Eroticisme de Dalí et de Bellmer," Le Figaro (Paris), 6 December 1971.

Warnod, Jeanine, "Dalí fait construire un temple à sa gloire," Le Figaro (Paris), 2 April 1974.

Wassenaar, Iris, "Van nagel tot nagel, reisschema voor schilderijen van Dalí," Het Vrije Volk (Amsterdam), 12 November 1970.

Watt, Alexander, "Dalí à Londres," Beaux-Arts (Paris), 30 November 1934, p. 1.

Weber, Gerhard, "Malkurs, Museumsbesuch mit Dalí," Die Welt (Hamburg), 28 December 1967.

Weiss, Evelyn, "Salvador Dalí," Bulletin-Muséen der Stadt Köln (Cologne), November 1978, pp. 1667, 1670.

Weiss, Evelyn, "Salvador Dalí: Der Bahnhof von Perpignan in: 'Sechs Neuerwerbungen," Museum Ludwig (Cologne), 1978.

Welling, Dolf, "De grote glibber is onder ons," Hangosche Courant, 27 November 1970.

Werner, A, "Avida Dollars," The Reporter (New York), vol. 34, 13 January 1966, pp. 45-47.

Wernick, R, "Dalí's dollars," Life (New York), vol. 69, 24 July 1970, p. 48.

"We take off our hat to Salvador Dalí," The Sketch, 20 May 1942, p. 280.

Widmer, Urs, "Keine Chance fur die Unendlichkeit," Frankfurter Allgemeine Zeitung (Frankfurt), 6 November 1973.

Wigcheren, D.P. Van, "Salvador Dalí in Rotterdam," Enknuizer Courant, 20 November 1970.

Wilson, Earl, "Dalí confides in me," New York Post (New York), 20 November 1944.

Wilson, Edmund, "Salvador Dalí as a novelist," New Yorker (New York), 1 July 1944.

Wingen, Ed, "Dalí houdt de spanning er in," Telegraaf (Amsterdam), 19 November 1970.

Wingen, Ed, "Dalí, Trek maar aan het touwtje…," Telegraaf (Amsterdam), 21 November 1970.

Winter, Peter, "Die Weg vom Delirium zur Dekoration," F.A.Z., 13 December 1977.

Wissig, Heinz, "Ist Dalí aktuell?," Oberbernische Presse (Bern), 2 May 1974.

Woolf, S.J, "Dalí's doodles come to town," New York Times Magazine (New York), 12 March 1939, p. 11.

Wykes-Joyce, Max, "Dalí lithographs," Arts Review (London), vol. 26, no. 8, April 1974, p. 208.

"Yan accuse Dalí: votre tableau copie ma photo," Paris-Match (Paris), no. 506, 20 December 1958, p. 109.

Zafran, Eric M, "I am not a madman": Salvador Dalí in Hartford', in Dalí's Optical Illusions (New Haven and London: Yale University Press, 2000), pp. 38-61.

"Zelfportret van Salvador Dalí," *Algemeen Dagblad*, 17 October 1970.

Zerbib, Monica, "Salvador Dalí: 'Soy demasiado inteligente para dedicarme solo a la pintura'," *El Pais* (Madrid), 30 July 1978, pp. I, IV.

Zette, M., "L'Exposition Salvador Dalí," *Journal des Petites Affiches* (Louvain), 19 August 1956.

Films

With the participation of Salvador Dalí:

Un Chien Andalou, 1929. Directed by Luis Buñuel; Script by Luis Buñuel and Salvador Dalí; Produced by Luis Buñuel.

L'Âge d'or, 1930. Directed by Luis Buñuel; Script by Luis Buñuel and Salvador Dalí; Produced by the Vicomte de Noailles.

Babaou, 1932. Unrealised script by Salvador Dalí. Completed 1997; Directed by Manuel Cussó-Ferrer.

Giraffes on Horseback Salad. 1937. Scenario for the Marx Brothers, Hollywood (unpublished).

Moontide. 1941. Scenario for a film for Jean Gabin, (unpublished).

Spellbound, The House of Dr. Edwards, 1944. Directed by Alfred Hitchcock; Produced by David O'Selznick.

Destino, 1947. Unfinished script and animation by Salvador Dalí; Produced by Walt Disney. Completed 2003; Directed by Dominic Manfrey; Produced by Baker Bloodworth and Roy Disney.

Father of the Bride, 1950. Directed by Vincente Minnelli; Produced by Loew's international corporation, New York.

L'Adventure prodigieuse de la Dentellière et du Rhinocéros, 1954-61. Script by Salvador Dalí in collaboration with Robert Descharnes. Completion by Robert Descharnes with the collaboration of Nicholas Descharnes and Christopher Jones, anticipated 2004.

Impressions de la Haute Mongolie – hommage à Raymond Roussel, 1975. Script by Salvador Dalí; Directed by José Montes-Bacquier.

Films about Salvador Dalí

Dalí. Directed by Tullio Bruschi; Produced by Este Film, 1954.

In Between 1964-1966. Directed by Jonas Mekas.

Qui est Dalí? Directed by Henri Champetier; Produced by Société

Nouvelle Pathé Cinéma, 1965.

Salvador Dalí in Museum Boymans. Produced by Polygoon, 1970.

L'autoportrait mou de Salvador Dalí avec du bacon. Directed by Jean-Christophe Averty, M.H.F. Production, 1972.

Dalí, toiles inédites. Produced by Ministère des Affaires Étrangers, Magazine France Panorama, 1973.

Hello Dalí! Directed by Bruce Gowers; Produced by Aquarius, London Weekend Television, South Bank Television, 1973.

Theatre Productions

Mariana Pineda. Première: 24 June 1927 (Barcelona: Théâtre Goya). Play by Federico García Lorca; Directed by Margarita Xirgu; Costumes and decoration by Salvador Dalí.

Rosalinda o Come vi Piace de William Shakespeare. Première: 26 November 1948 (Rome: Théâtre Eliseo). Play by William Shakespeare; Directed by Luchino Visconti; Costumes and decoration by Salvador Dalí.

Don Juan Tenorio. Première: 1 November 1949 (Madrid: Teatro Nacional María Guerrero). Play by José Zorilla; sets and figurines by Salvador Dalí.

Opera

Salome. Première: 1949 (London: Covent Garden Opera House). Libretto by Oscar Wilde; Directed by Peter Brook; Costumes and decoration by Salvador Dalí; music by Richard Strauss.

Être Dieu. (1974). Opera-poem by Salvador Dalí; Libretto by Manuel Vázquez Montalbán; music by Igor Wakhévich

Ballets

Bacchanale. Première: 9 November 1939 (New York: Metropolitan Opera). After the scene of Venusburg by Tannhäuser; Libretto, sets and costumes by Salvador Dalí; choreography by Léonide Massine; music by Richard Wagner.

Labyrinth. Première: 8 October 1941 (New York: Metropolitan Opera). Libretto, sets and costumes by Salvador Dalí; choreography by Léonide Massine; music by Franz Schubert.

El Café de Chinitas. A Quadro Flamenco. Première: 1944 (Detroit). Libretto and choreography by Argentina; curtain, sets and costumes by Salvador Dalí; music: Spanish folkloric music arranged by Federico García Lorca.

Mad Tristan. The first paranoiac ballet based on the eternal myth of love in death. Première: 1944 (New York). Libretto, curtain, sets and costumes by Salvador Dalí; choreography by Léonide Massine; music by Richard Wagner.

Sentimental Colloquy. Première: 15 December 1944 (New York: International Theatre). After a poem by Paul Verlaine; sets and costumes by Salvador Dalí; music by Paul Bowles.

Spectacles

Le Ballet de Gala. Le Dame espagnole et le Cavalier romain. Première: 22 August 1961 (Venice: Théâtre de la Fenice); 16 April 1962 (Brussels: Opéra Royal de la Monnaie); 1962 (Paris: Théâtre des Champs-Élysées); choreography by Maurice Béjart; sets by Salvador Dalí; music by Alessandro Scarlatti.

Spectacle pyrotechnique. 21 June 1975 (Avignon). Conception and narration by Salvador Dalí; Directed by Ruggieri; music by Georges Bizet.

Radio Programmes

Salvador Dalí (19 October 1947), WTAM (Cleveland). Programme by A. Reynolds Morse.

Make up your mind (10 January 1955). CBS (New York). Programme by Jack Sterling.

L'Accent grave (19-20 April 1969). France-Culture. Programme by Jacques Chancel.

Clefs pour un theatre musée (6-17 November 1978). France-Culture. Programme by Daniel le Comte.

Television Programmes

Dalí interviewed by Malcolm Muggeridge. 4 May 1955. Produced by the BBC.

Interview de Salvador Dalí, 1956. Produced by O.R.T.F.

A Paris avec un éléphant, Interview, 1958. Produced by O.R.T.F.

Premier ballet folklorique soviétique, 1958. Produced by O.R.T.F.

Bal des Petits Lits Blancs, 1959. Produced by O.R.T.F.

Salvador Dalí fait éclater une bombe au Vel'd'Hiv (en demolition), 1959. Produced by O.R.T.F.

Salvador Dalí présente l'ovocipède, 1959. Produced by O.R.T.F.

Exposition de bijoux à Londres, 1960. Produced by O.R.T.F.

Remise d'une médaille d'or à Salvador Dalí, 1960. Produced by O.R.T.F.

Salvador Dalí présente son "Christophe Colomb", 1960. Produced by O.R.T.F.

Couverture Apocalypse, 1961. Produced by O.R.T.F.

Conférence Dalí ã Polytechnique, 1961. Produced by O.R.T.F.

Salvador Dalí interviewé ã propos du livre que lui a consacré Descharnes, 1962. Produced by O.R.T.F.

Salvador Dalí inaugure la residence Élysée, 1962. Produced by O.R.T.F.

Salvador Dalí ã l'X, 1962. Produced by O.R.T.F.

Exposition Dalí en Espagne, 1963. Produced by O.R.T.F.

Salvador Dalí interviewé ã propos de la soirée Tchérina, 1962. Produced by O.R.T.F.

Exposition, 1963. Produced by O.R.T.F.

Concours de peinture sur le theme de la Joconde, 1963. Produced by O.R.T.F.

Dalí ã New York, 1964. Produced by O.R.T.F.

Première au Lido, 1964. Produced by O.R.T.F.

Salvador Dalí dédicace Salvador Dalí, 1964. Produced by O.R.T.F.

Interview Salvador Dalí, 1964. Produced by O.R.T.F.

Salvador, 1964. Produced by O.R.T.F.

Édition spéciale Salvador Dalí, 1964. Produced by O.R.T.F.

Gala de l'École de l'Air, 1964. Produced by O.R.T.F.

Salvador Dalí, 1964. Produced by O.R.T.F.

Inauguration exposition Dalí ã Fontainebleau, 1964. Produced by O.R.T.F.

Panorama: un genie par lui-même, 1965. Produced by O.R.T.F.

Salvador Dalí, 1965. Produced by O.R.T.F.

Interview Dalí, 1965. Produced by O.R.T.F.

Les voeux (avec sa femme), 1965. Produced by O.R.T.F.

Viva Dalí (avec Gala), 1965. Produced by O.R.T.F.

Exposition de peinture ã Saint-Denis, 1965. Produced by O.R.T.F.

Dalí à New York (Galerie Lucas), 1966. Produced by O.R.T.F.

Dalí à New York, 1966. Produced by O.R.T.F.

Dalí in New York, 1966. Produced and directed by Jack Bond (BBC). Presented by Jane Arden.

Salvador Dalí, exposition Jules Verne, 1966. Produced by O.R.T.F.

Vitrine du libraire, 1966. Produced by O.R.T.F.

Dernier fiacre parisien, 1966. Produced by O.R.T.F.

Picasso et son temps, 1966. Produced by O.R.T.F.

Paris brûle-t-il?, 1966. Produced by O.R.T.F.

Conférence Dalí, 1966. Produced by O.R.T.F.

Salvador Dalí devant le bronze de John Kennedy, 1966. Produced by O.R.T.F.

Dalí, 1967. Directed by Adam Saulnier. Produced by O.R.T.F.

Soirée Touthankamon. 1967. Produced by O.R.T.F.

Dalí à Paris, 1967. Produced by O.R.T.F.

Dalí dans les Pyrénées, 1967. Produced by O.R.T.F.

Salvador Dalí (interview), 1967. Produced by O.R.T.F.

Salvador Dalí au Salon de l'Enfance (il dessine une feuille), 1967. Produced by O.R.T.F.

La première d'Hugues Auffray à Bobino, 1967. Produced by O.R.T.F

Salvador Dalí, 1967. Produced by O.R.T.F.

Vol de tableaux à Grenoble, 1968. Produced by O.R.T.F.

Interview, 1968. Produced by O.R.T.F.

Musée des Arts Décoratifs, 1968. Produced by O.R.T.F.

Illustration de livre, 1969. Produced by O.R.T.F.

Les Airs du temps Dalí. 7 February 1969. Produced by O.R.T.F.

Brève apparition au Prix de Cinéma, 1969. Produced by O.R.T.F.

Exposition, 1969. Produced by O.R.T.F.

Page spectacle, 1969. Produced by O.R.T.F.

Salvador Dalí a Gala, 1969. Produced by O.R.T.F.

Interview de Joseph Foret (Apocalypse), 1969. Produced by O.R.T.F.

Exposition Dalí, 1969. Produced by O.R.T.F.

Conférence de presse Dalí, 1970. Produced by O.R.T.F.

Conférence de presse Dalí, 1970. Produced by O.R.T.F.

Dalí à Lyon (S.N.C.F.), 1970. Produced by O.R.T.F.

Affiches S.N.C.F, 1970. Produced by O.R.T.F.

Perspectives Surréalistes I et II, 1971. Directed by Daniel Le Comte. Produced by O.R.T.F., series *Ombres et Lumières*

Interview de Salvador Dalí, 1971. Produced by O.R.T.F.

Exposition (34") aux USA, 1971. Produced by O.R.T.F.

Dalí à New York (jeu d'echecs), 1971. Produced by O.R.T.F.

Salvador Dalí chez lui, 1972. Produced by O.R.T.F.

Les peintres surrealists, 1972. Produced by O.R.T.F.

Exposition de tableaux surrealists, 1972. Produced by O.R.T.F.

Les livres de la semaine, 1973. Produced by O.R.T.F.

Hello Dalí! 1973. Weekend Television, direcated by Bruce Gowers; edited with introduction by Humphrey Burton.

Salvador Dalí parle de ses livres, 1973. Produced by O.R.T.F.

Salvador Dalí, 1973. Directed by N. Risi; Produced by O.R.T.F.

Interview à propos du mauvais temps et de la tempête, 1974. Produced by O.R.T.F.

Personnage en cire au Musée Grevin, 1974. Produced by O.R.T.F.

Salvador Dalí à Figueres, 1974. Produced by O.R.T.F.

Salvador Dalí, Moïse et le monothéisme, 1975. Produced by O.R.T.F.

Salvador Dalí, gravure: la Conquête du cosmos, 1975. Produced by O.R.T.F.

Un jour futur: Message pour l'an 2000, 1975. Produced by A2

Dalí. June 1975. Produced by TF1.

Dalí, October 1975. Produced by TF1.

Salvador Dalí, 1975. Produced by TF1.

Livre Dalí, 1975. Produced by TF1.

Salvador Dalí, 1977. Produced by A2.

Un sur cinq. Qui étiez vous à dix huit ans, Salvador Dalí, 1978. Produced by A2.

Voir, Le Magazine de l'image. Dalí hors cadre, 1978. Produced by FR3.

Mille et une visions. 9 February 1978. Directed by Alain Ferrari. Produced by A2.

Dalí, 30 May 1979. *Imagênes*. Written, direcated and presented by Paloma Chamorro. Produced by Jesús González (RTE).

Dalí, 6 June 1979. *Imagênes*. Written, direcated and presented by Paloma Chamorro. Produced by Jesús González (RTE).

Dalí, 13 June 1979. *Imagênes*. Written, direcated and presented by Paloma Chamorro. Produced by Jesús González (RTE).

"Leda Atomica" de Salvador Dalí, 5 January 1979. Directed by Charles Paolini. Produced by TF1.

La mascara se transluce, 30 June 1984. Produced by TVE.

Todos los hombres de Dalí. 16 September 1984. Produced by TVE.

Dalí, 1986. Produced by Adam Low (BBC) in association with Demart.

Pintar depués de morir, 25 September 1989. Produced by TVE.

El Enigma Dalí, 7 August 1994. Scripted by Juan Manuel Sáenz; directed by Jordi Lladó; produced by TVE.

Surrealissimo, 2002. Script by Matthew Broughton; produced and directed by Richard Curson Smith (BBC).

List of Works

Index of Names

Photographic Credits

Barcelona, Dolors Junyent Galeria d'Art, p. 29

Barcelona, Gasull Fotografia, pp. 32, 68, 93, 144, 207, 332, 353, 408, 427

Barcelona, Generalitat de Catalunya, Departament de Cultura, p. 395

Barcelona, Museu Nacional d'Art de Catalunya, Photo Calveras, Mérida, Sagristà, p. 66

Basel, Kunstmuseum Basel, Martin Bühler, p. 164

Berlin, © Kupferstichkabinett, Staatliche Museen zu Berlin-Preussischer Kulturbesitz, Photo Jörg P. Anders, 1993, pp. 54, 210, 212, 248, 252, 340-341

Bern, Kunstmuseum Bern, pp. 41, 168, 195

Birmingham (Alabama), Birmingham Museum of Art, p. 361

Boston, Museum of Fine Arts, p. 382

Bruxelles, Musées Royaux des Beaux Arts, p. 343

Buffalo, Albright Knox Art Gallery, pp. 181, 303

Cambridge Fogg Art Museum, The Harvard University Rick Stafford © 2004 President and Fellows of Harvard College, p. 269

© Melitó Casals "Meli"/Fundació Gala-Salvador Dalí, Figueres, 2004, pp. 537, 538

Chicago, Alan Koppel Gallery, p. 141

Chicago, The Art Institute of Chicago, © The Art Institute of Chicago, pp. 176, 275, 279, 284

Chichester, Edward James Fund, pp. 285-287

Città del Vaticano, Musei Vaticani, Foto L. Giordano, p. 399

Cleveland, The Cleveland Museum of Art, p. 153

Corbis
Acme, p. 511
Cecil Beaton, p. 495
Charles H. Hewitt, p. 520
Henri Manuel, p. 486
Carl Van Vechten, pp. 489-490

Düsseldorf, Kunstsammlung Nordrhein-Westfalen, p. 259

East Lansing (MI), Kresge Museum of Art, Michigan State University, p. 155

Edinburgh, Scottish National Gallery of Modern Art, pp. 203, 256, 359

Essen, Folkwang Museum, p. 247

Figueres, Fundació Gala-Salvador Dalì, pp. 30, 32, 36, 38, 39, 46, 48, 50, 51, 54, 63, 64, 76, 77, 85, 89,

134, 174, 176, 186, 204, 227, 253, 295, 299, 310, 319, 328, 331, 336, 339, 344-345, 357, 409, 411, 412, 415, 419, 420, 436, 438, 452, 457

Figueres, Museu del Joguet de Catalunya, p. 54

Jacques Faujour, p. 166

Firenze, Foto Archivio Scala, pp. 80, 356

Fukuoka-shi, Fukuoka Art Museum Kempachi Fujimoto, p. 351

Genève, Financial Trustees Limited Studio Patrick Goetelen, p. XX

Glasgow, The Glasgow Art Gallery, p. 356

Grenoble, Musée de Grenoble, © Photo RMN / Christian Jean, p. 86

Hamburg, Kunsthalle, p. 165

Hannover, Sprengel Museum, p. 173

Hartford (CT), Wadsworth Atheneum Museum of Art, pp. 231, 301

Hiroshima, Prefectural Art Museum, pp. 314-315

Houston, The Menil Collection, Photo Hickey-Robertson, p. 241

Köln, Museum Ludwig, p. 405

London, Freud Museum © Freud Museum, p. 436

London, Tate, pp. 267, 271

London, The Mayor Gallery, pp. 182, 438

Madrid, Fundación Federico García Lorca, pp. 56, 78, 79, 92, 445

Madrid, Joaquin Cortés Noriega, pp. 327, 365, 393

Madrid, Museo Nacional Centro de Arte Reina Sofía, pp. 46, 52, 56, 68, 101, 106, 107, 117, 178, 193, 223, 298, 305

Madrid, Museo Thyssen Bornemisza, pp. 58, 335

Magnum / Philippe Halsman, pp. 466, 466, 500, 509, 516, 517, 518

© Man Ray Trust / ADAGP-Olaf / telimage - 2004, backcover, pp. 52, 483, 487, 495

Mie (Japan), Mie Prefectural Art Museum, p. 277

Milano, Archivio Electa, su concessione del Ministero per i Beni e le Attività culturali, pp. 132, 276

Milano, Archivio RCS, pp. 52, 62, 70, 90, 115-116, 132, 154, 266, 270, 318, 334, 346

Milano, Soprintendenza per il patrimonio storico e artistico e demoetnoantropologico per le province di Milano, Bergamo,

Como, Lecco, Lodi, Pavia, Sondrio e Varese / Pinacoteca di Brera, pp. 54, 56, 133, 278, 318, 349

Milwaukee (WI), The Patrick and Beatrice Haggerty Museum of Art, p. 347

Minneapolis, The Minneapolis Institute of Arts, p. 397

Montréal, Musée des Beaux Arts de Montreal, Richard-Max Tremblay, pp. 54, 73, 81

Montserrat, Museu de Montserrat, pp. 72, 81, 833

München, Bayerische Staatsgemäldesammlungen, Pinakothek der Moderne, Artothek, Joachim Blauel, p. 121

München, © Engelbert Seehuber / Graphische Sammlung, pp. 179, 427

New Haven (CT), Yale University Art Gallery, p. 201

New York, The Metropolitan Museum of Art, Photo by Malcolm Varon, N.Y.C. © 1988, p. 123

New York, The Metropolitan Museum of Art, Photograph © 1987 The Metropolitan Museum of Art, pp. 368, 374, 387

New York, The Museum of Modern Art, © 2004, Digital Image, The Museum of Modern Art, New York/ Scala, Firenze, pp. 82, 93, 96, 125, 140, 149, 239, 338, 375

New York, The Solomon Guggenheim Museum, p. 377

Ottawa, National Gallery of Canada, p. 199

Paris, Béatrice Hatala, p. 127

Paris, Bibliothèque Littéraire "Jacques Doucet", Suzanne Nagy, p. 184

Paris, Musée d'Orsay, Photo RMN-Hervé Lewandowski, p. 194

Paris, Musée du Louvre, Photo RMN-R.G. Ojeda, p. 374

Paris, Musée national d'Art moderne, Centre Georges Pompidou, Photo CNAC/MNAM Dist. RMN, pp. 88, 105, 109, 111, 131, 137

Paris, Musée Picasso: Photo Béatrice Hatala, pp. 452-453; Photo RMN-Hervé Lewandowski, pp. 187, 194; Photo RMN-R.G. Ojeda, p. 139; Photo RMN-Thierry Le Mage, p. 186

Paris, Serge Veignant, pp. 119, 144-145

Philadelphia, The Philadelphia Museum of Art, pp. 169, 263, 281; Photo Lynn Rosenthal, p. 457

Rio de Janeiro, Museu da Chácara do Céu, Fundaçao Raymundo Ottoni de Castro Maya, p. 126

Roma, Giuseppe Schiavinotto, p. 342

Rotterdam, Boijmans Van Beuningen Museum, pp. 256, 291-293, 296-297

© Enrique Sabater /Fundació Gala-Salvador Dalí, Figueres, 2004, p. 534

San Diego, San Diego Museum of Art, p. 388

San Francisco, San Francisco Museum of Modern Art, Photo Ben Blackwell, pp. 95, 337

Shizuoka, Ikeda Museum of 20th Century Art, p. 61

Stockolm, Moderna Museet, pp. 138, 177

St. Petersburg, The Salvador Dali Museum © 2004 Gala-Salvador Dalí Foundation, Figueres (Artist Rights Society, New York / © 2004 Salvador Dalí Museum, Inc.), pp. 27, 41, 43, 68, 87, 90, 96, 98, 113, 116, 142, 157, 163, 177, 188, 190, 213-219, 225, 233, 323, 325, 355, 358, 366, 381, 384, 398, 403, 410, 534

Stuttgart, Staatsgalerie, pp. 209, 309

Tel Aviv, Tel Aviv Museum of Art, p. 103

Utica (New York), Munson-Williams Proctor Art Institute, Photo G. R. Farley, p. 235

Valladolid, Museo de Arte Contemporáneo Español Patio Herreriano, p. 265

Venezia, Collezione Peggy Guggenheim, p. 167

Washington DC, The Hirshhorn Museum, Photography by Lee Stalsworth, p. 383

Wuppertal, Von der Heydt Museum, Antje Zeis-Loi, pp. 171, 244

Yokohama, Yokohama Museum of Art, p. 255

Zürich, Kunsthaus, pp. 205, 274

If not otherwise specified, the photographs come from the museums where the corresponding works are conserved or by the proprietors. The publisher apologizes for omissions and will include any further information in the reprint.

This volume has been published with the support
of Cartiere Burgo and it is printed
on R 400 Matt Satin 150g/m paper manufactered
by cartiere Burgo.

Grande forEdit – Monza

Printed in August 2004
by Arti Grafiche A. Pizzi
Cinisello Balsamo (Mi)